SALAD OF THE DAY

GEORGEANNE BRENNAN

PHOTOGRAPHY BY ERIN KUNKEL

weldon**owen**

CONTENTS

JANUARY   10

FEBRUARY   34

MARCH   56

APRIL   80

MAY   104

JUNE   128

JULY   152

AUGUST   176

SEPTEMBER   200

OCTOBER   224

NOVEMBER   248

DECEMBER   272

A SALAD FOR EVERY DAY

Tossed, chopped, shredded, composed—salads are versatile in both form and flavor. They're also an enticing and healthy way to showcase favorite seasonal produce. From light starters to protein-rich main-course salads to palate-cleansing accompaniments, these much-loved and adaptable dishes can play a delicious role in virtually every lunch or dinner, every day of the year.

This calendar-style cookbook offers 365 enticing salads suited for any meal, occasion, or mood. Guided by the seasons, and drawing on fresh ingredients in their prime, you'll find plenty of inspiration in the pages that follow. In the cool months of the year, hearty salads fit the bill: bowls brimming with sturdy seared greens, grains, and roasted meats. In warm weather, light fare is apropos: try refreshing fruit salads or just-picked lettuces tossed with herbs and grilled seafood. Or, choose from a wealth of modern and tantalizing recipes suitable for a full meal, such as skirt steak salad with citrus and arugula, crisp chicken and cabbage salad with peanut dressing, lemony Mediterranean-inspired octopus salad, garlicky pasta salad with crab and shrimp, and more. All the classics, like iceberg wedges with blue cheese dressing and classic Cobb, are here, as well as contemporary riffs on old standards—such as a Niçoise-style salad with seared wild salmon—to bring new life to your old favorites.

Each recipe includes a complementary dressing or vinaigrette, and helpful notes offer serving and substitution ideas. You'll learn how easy it is to vary salads by swapping in ingredients that you have on hand; varying herbs and spices; alternating dressings; and adding a protein element like seafood, poultry, or beans—even a scattering of crumbled cheese or a handful of nuts.

With this abundance of recipes as your guide, and the garden's yield as your inspiration, you're sure to find an appealing salad that fits the occasion, no matter what the day brings.

Start the new year right with healthy, hearty salads. Sturdy greens such as kale and escarole provide a perfect canvas for proteins—creamy cheeses, eggs, meats, or lentils. Warming main-course salads help to take the chill off. Wilted winter greens with poached eggs and pancetta is pure comfort food, while roasted meats shine in salads full of toothsome whole grains, from couscous and farro to quinoa.

1
FENNEL SALAD WITH BLOOD
ORANGES & ARUGULA
page 12

2
WARM ESCAROLE,
EGG & PANCETTA SALAD
page 12

3
NOODLE SALAD WITH PORK
& ASIAN LIME VINAIGRETTE
page 15

8
COUSCOUS SALAD WITH ROASTED
CHICKEN & DRIED CRANBERRIES
page 17

9
SEARED TUNA
WITH ASIAN SLAW
page 18

10
ROASTED SWEET POTATO SALAD
WITH PECANS & GREEN ONIONS
page 18

15
CAESAR-STYLE SALAD WITH POBLANO
CHILES & CORNMEAL CROUTONS
page 23

16
RADICCHIO, ENDIVE & AGED GOUDA
SALAD WITH RED-WINE VINAIGRETTE
page 23

17
ROASTED MUSHROOM SALAD
WITH BALSAMIC VINAIGRETTE
page 24

22
BABY SPINACH SALAD
WITH PARMESAN & PAPAYA
page 27

23
CRAB & SHRIMP SALAD
WITH AVOCADO & ORANGES
page 29

24
WINTER CHICORY & APPLE
SALAD WITH PECANS
page 29

29
BLACK BEAN & POBLANO
CHILE SALAD
page 32

30
WARM RUBY GRAPEFRUIT SALAD
page 32

31
CABBAGE, PEAR & GINGER SLAW
page 32

4
GRAPEFRUIT, CHICKEN & PISTACHIO SALAD
page 15

5
CLASSIC CAESAR SALAD
page 16

6
CHARRED ORANGE & ESCAROLE SALAD WITH ALMONDS
page 16

7
CRAB SALAD WITH GREEN APPLES & GRAPEFRUIT COULIS
page 17

11
QUINOA & RADICCHIO SALAD WITH DRIED CHERRIES & PISTACHIOS
page 21

12
WARM INDIAN-SPICED EGG SALAD
page 21

13
GRILLED LAMB & PINEAPPLE SALAD WITH THAI FLAVORS
page 22

14
BUTTER LETTUCE & PARMESAN SALAD
page 22

18
RIGATONI SALAD WITH CAULIFLOWER & SAFFRON
page 24

19
CANNELLINI BEAN SALAD WITH TUNA & GRILLED RADICCHIO
page 26

20
MÂCHE & ESCAROLE SALAD WITH CROSTINI
page 26

21
JERUSALEM ARTICHOKE SALAD WITH POMEGRANATE & CELERY
page 27

25
POTATO & BEET SALAD WITH DILL
page 30

26
ORANGE, ONION & OLIVE SALAD
page 30

27
MANGO, PINEAPPLE & PAPAYA SALAD
page 31

28
KIWI, APPLE & GRAPE SALAD WITH ROSEMARY SYRUP
page 31

january

1

FENNEL SALAD WITH BLOOD ORANGES & ARUGULA

serves 6–8

2 fennel bulbs, trimmed

2 Tbsp red wine vinegar

Salt and freshly ground pepper

6 Tbsp (3 fl oz/90 ml) extra-virgin olive oil

4 cups (4 oz/125 g) loosely packed arugula leaves

4 blood or navel oranges, peeled with a knife and sliced crosswise into thin slices

To make this crisp salad even more refreshing, slice the fennel just before serving rather than in advance, and keep the bulbs cold until just before slicing. Unless it is dressed, fennel will discolor if allowed to sit more than 20 minutes after slicing.

Halve the fennel bulbs lengthwise and, using a mandoline or a very sharp knife, cut the halves crosswise into paper-thin slices.

In a large bowl, whisk together the vinegar, ¼ tsp salt, and ¼ tsp pepper. Add the oil in a thin stream, whisking constantly until the dressing is smooth. Add the arugula and fennel and toss to coat evenly with the vinaigrette. Mound the mixture on a platter, distribute the orange slices over and around the salad, and serve.

2

WARM ESCAROLE, EGG & PANCETTA SALAD

serves 4

4 slices thick-cut pancetta or bacon, chopped

¼ cup (2 fl oz/60 ml) extra-virgin olive oil

1 clove garlic, bruised

1 Tbsp whole-grain mustard

2 Tbsp red wine vinegar, plus 1 tsp

4 large eggs

2 heads escarole, tough outer leaves removed, torn into bite-sized pieces

Salt and freshly ground pepper

Use the freshest eggs possible for poaching, as they have a more solid white. If the white starts to spread, use a spoon to nudge it near the yolk. Before placing the eggs on the salads, rest the base of the slotted spoon on a kitchen towel to blot away excess moisture.

If using bacon, bring a small saucepan of water to a boil. Add the bacon and simmer for 5 minutes to tame its smoky, salty flavor. Drain, transfer to paper towels, and blot dry. Wipe out the saucepan, place over medium-low heat, and add the oil, garlic, and pancetta or bacon. Cook, stirring occasionally, until the garlic is golden and the pancetta is crisp, about 3 minutes. Be careful not to let the garlic burn. Remove from the heat and discard the garlic. Stir in the mustard and the 2 Tbsp vinegar. Set aside.

Choose a large, wide pan with a tight-fitting lid. Fill with a generous amount of water, add the 1 tsp vinegar, place over high heat, and bring to a rolling boil. Reduce the heat to a very gentle simmer. Working quickly, crack the eggs one at a time into a small bowl and then slide the eggs into the simmering water. Poach the eggs until the whites are set and the yolks are still soft, 3–4 minutes.

Meanwhile, bring the vinegar mixture to a boil. Put the escarole in a large bowl. Pour the vinegar mixture over the escarole and immediately toss to wilt the leaves slightly. Season with salt and pepper. Toss again and arrange on individual plates. Remove each poached egg with a slotted spoon, blot the bottom dry, and slide onto the salads. Season the eggs with salt and pepper and serve.

3

JANUARY

NOODLE SALAD WITH PORK & ASIAN LIME VINAIGRETTE

serves 6

2 pork tenderloins, about ¾ lb (375 g) each, trimmed

1 Tbsp peanut oil

Salt and freshly ground pepper

FOR THE ASIAN LIME VINAIGRETTE

2 Tbsp peanut oil

1 Tbsp soy sauce

Juice of 1 lime

2 tsp sherry vinegar

1 tsp peeled and minced fresh ginger

⅛ tsp sugar

2 or 3 drops Sriracha or other hot sauce

1 lb (500 g) fresh Chinese egg noodles

1 red bell pepper, seeded and thinly sliced

1 small red serrano chile, seeded and thinly sliced crosswise (optional)

¼ cup (⅓ oz/10 g) *each* chopped fresh flat-leaf parsley and cilantro leaves

Chinese egg noodles are a versatile ingredient for soaking up flavor and making a salad into a heartier main-course dish. Regular vermicelli pasta may be substituted.

Prepare a charcoal or gas grill for direct-heat cooking over high heat, or preheat the broiler. Brush the pork tenderloins with the 1 Tbsp oil and season with salt and pepper. Place on the grill rack or on a broiler pan 4 inches (10 cm) from the heat source and cook, turning occasionally, until an instant-read thermometer inserted into the thickest part registers 150°F (65°C) or the pork is pale pink when cut in the thickest portion, about 12 minutes. Transfer to a cutting board and let rest for 2–3 minutes before carving. Cut crosswise into slices ¼ inch (6 mm) thick.

Meanwhile, to make the vinaigrette, in a blender, combine the 2 Tbsp oil, soy sauce, lime juice, vinegar, ginger, sugar, and Sriracha to taste. Purée until smooth.

Bring a pot three-fourths full of salted water to a boil. Add the noodles, stir, and cook until just tender, according to package directions. Drain well and transfer to a large bowl. Add the bell pepper, chile (if using), vinaigrette to taste, and half each of the parsley and cilantro, and toss to mix well.

Transfer the noodles to bowls and arrange the pork and remaining herbs over the top. Serve warm or at room temperature.

4

JANUARY

GRAPEFRUIT, CHICKEN & PISTACHIO SALAD

serves 4

2 cups (16 fl oz/500 ml) dry white wine

2 Tbsp white wine vinegar

Salt and freshly ground pepper

1 tsp whole peppercorns

2 skinless, boneless chicken breast halves

½ cup (2 oz/60 g) pistachios

2 grapefruits, peeled and segmented with a knife

¼ cup (2 fl oz/60 ml) mayonnaise

1 tsp Dijon mustard

2 Tbsp minced fresh cilantro

Juice of 1 lime

This salad takes advantage of the winter citrus season for a new twist on a classic chicken salad, spiked with lime juice and cilantro for extra zing. You can serve the salad in small butter lettuce leaves for appetizer portions, or mound on toasted peasant bread for sandwiches.

Combine the wine, 2 cups (16 fl oz/500 ml) water, the vinegar, 1 tsp salt, and the peppercorns in a shallow pan. Bring to a boil over medium-high heat. Reduce the heat to low and simmer for 5 minutes. Add the chicken, cover, and poach until just opaque, 6–8 minutes, occasionally skimming off any foam on the surface. Remove the chicken from the liquid and let cool for 5 minutes, then cut into cubes.

Meanwhile, in a dry frying pan, toast the pistachios over medium-low heat, stirring, until fragrant and starting to brown, about 5 minutes. Pour onto a plate to cool.

Cut the grapefruit segments in half crosswise and put them in a bowl with the chicken and half of the pistachios. Add the mayonnaise, mustard, cilantro, lime juice, ½ tsp salt, and ¼ tsp pepper and mix well. Garnish the salad with the remaining pistachios and serve.

15

5

Bottled Caesar dressings abound, but none will ever taste as good as the one you've whisked up fresh at home. Use a high-quality olive oil, and choose one with a character you enjoy. Oils from Greece tend to be rich, yet mellow; Tuscan and Californian oils are distinctly peppery; Sicilian oils are "big" and earthy; and those from the south coast of France are buttery.

CLASSIC CAESAR SALAD

serves 4

2 cups (4 oz/125 g) cubed sourdough or other country-style bread (1-inch/2.5-cm cubes)

3 Tbsp extra-virgin olive oil, plus ⅓ cup (3 fl oz/80 ml)

Salt and freshly ground pepper

6 cloves garlic

4 anchovy fillets, plus extra for garnish (optional)

1 tsp Worcestershire sauce

2 tsp red wine vinegar

2 hearts romaine lettuce, separated into individual leaves

1 large egg (optional; see Note)

Parmesan cheese for shaving

Preheat the oven to 350°F (180°C). Spread the bread cubes on a baking sheet and sprinkle them with the 3 Tbsp oil, ½ tsp salt, and ½ tsp pepper. Bake, turning once or twice, until golden, about 15 minutes. Remove the cubes from the sheet, let cool, and rub one or two sides of each cube with the garlic, using 3 of the cloves. Set aside.

In the bottom of a serving bowl, using a fork, crush the remaining 3 garlic cloves with ½ tsp salt to make a paste. Crush the 4 anchovy fillets into the paste. Whisk in the Worcestershire sauce, vinegar, and ½ tsp pepper. Add the ⅓ cup oil in a thin stream, whisking constantly until the dressing is smooth.

Add the lettuce leaves and three-fourths of the croutons to the bowl with the dressing and mix gently but well. Break the egg, if using, into the bowl and mix again. Top with the remaining croutons. Shave the cheese over the salad, and serve, garnished with anchovy fillets, if desired.

Note: Raw egg can carry salmonella. The risks involved in salmonella poisoning are greatest for children, the elderly, pregnant women, and anyone with a compromised immune system.

6

Citrus salads are a refreshing treat in the middle of winter. Here, the orange slices are grilled so that the outsides become slightly charred for a bittersweet taste that pairs well with escarole. Valencia oranges are ideal for this recipe because they are so sweet, but any orange variety will do.

CHARRED ORANGE & ESCAROLE SALAD WITH ALMONDS

serves 4

4 large Valencia oranges, peeled with a knife and sliced crosswise into thin slices

¼ cup (2 fl oz/60 ml) extra-virgin olive oil, plus more for drizzling

1 head escarole

¼ cup (⅓ oz/10 g) coarsely chopped fresh flat-leaf parsley

1 Tbsp sherry vinegar

Salt and freshly ground pepper

½ cup (2 oz/60 g) Marcona almonds, coarsely chopped

Prepare a charcoal or gas grill for direct-heat cooking over high heat. Alternatively, preheat a stove-top grill pan over high heat.

Drizzle the orange slices with oil. Grill, turning once, until well charred on both sides, 2–4 minutes total. Set aside.

Remove the tough outer leaves of the escarole and tear the inner leaves into bite-sized pieces. In a bowl, combine the escarole, parsley, the ¼ cup oil, and the vinegar and toss to coat. Season with salt and pepper. Add the oranges and almonds and toss well. Divide the salad among individual plates and serve.

7

Here, the apples are cut into matchsticks with a mandoline, but a sharp knife will also work well. The syruplike grapefruit coulis, slightly sweetened, is drizzled on top and around the salads for an artistic presentation.

CRAB SALAD WITH GREEN APPLES & GRAPEFRUIT COULIS

serves 8

1 grapefruit, peeled and segmented with a knife

2 tsp sugar

Juice of 1 lemon

2 Granny Smith apples

1 lb (500 g) cooked crabmeat, picked over for shell fragments

3 Tbsp extra-virgin olive oil

1½ Tbsp white wine vinegar or champagne vinegar

3 Tbsp minced fresh chives

Salt and freshly ground black pepper

Pinch of cayenne pepper

Set 2 grapefruit segments aside and coarsely chop the rest. In a saucepan, combine the chopped grapefruit with ¼ cup (2 fl oz/60 ml) water. Bring to a boil over medium-high heat, reduce the heat to low, and simmer, stirring, until soft, about 5 minutes. Transfer the mixture to a blender and purée it. Strain the purée through a fine-mesh sieve into a clean pan. Add the sugar and bring to a boil over medium-high heat, stirring. Continue to cook, stirring often, until the liquid is reduced by about half and is syrupy, 3–4 minutes. Remove from the heat and let cool.

Fill a bowl with water and add the lemon juice. Quarter and core the apples, placing them in the lemon water. Using the julienne attachment on a mandoline or a very sharp knife, julienne the apples and return them to the lemon water.

In a bowl, combine the crabmeat, oil, vinegar, 2 Tbsp of the chives, ½ tsp salt, ½ tsp black pepper, and the cayenne. Pat dry half of the apples and add them to the bowl. Squeeze 2 tsp juice from the reserved grapefruit segments into the bowl. Turn gently to mix, being careful not to shred the crab.

To serve, divide the crab salad among salad plates, mounding it on each plate. Pat dry the remaining apples and divide them among the salads. Drizzle about 2 tsp of the grapefruit coulis over and around each salad. Sprinkle the remaining 1 Tbsp chives evenly over the salads and serve.

8

Couscous, a granular pasta made with durum wheat flour, can be treated like a grain in salads. It works best when mixed with finely chopped ingredients, like the carrots and green onions used here. In this salad, the classic combination of poultry and cranberries is enhanced with fresh mint and a bracing sherry vinegar dressing.

COUSCOUS SALAD WITH ROASTED CHICKEN & DRIED CRANBERRIES

serves 4

Salt and freshly ground pepper

1 cup (6 oz/185 g) instant couscous

2 carrots, peeled and chopped

2 green onions, including green parts, chopped

⅓ cup (2 oz/60 g) dried cranberries

2 Tbsp sherry vinegar

½ cup (4 fl oz/125 ml) extra-virgin olive oil

2 cups (¾ lb/375 g) sliced roasted chicken meat

1 Tbsp thinly sliced fresh mint

In a small saucepan, combine 1½ cups (12 fl oz/375 ml) water and ⅛ tsp salt and bring to a boil. Stir in the couscous and return to a boil. Remove from the heat, cover, and let stand for 5 minutes. Transfer to a bowl and fluff with a fork to separate the grains. Add the carrots, green onions, and dried cranberries.

In a small bowl, whisk together the vinegar and salt and pepper to taste. Add the oil in a thin stream, whisking constantly until the dressing is smooth. Pour over the couscous mixture and stir to mix well.

Transfer the couscous to a serving dish and arrange the sliced chicken on top. Sprinkle with the mint and serve.

9

SEARED TUNA
WITH ASIAN SLAW

serves 4–6

FOR THE DRESSING

1 tsp peeled and grated fresh ginger

1 Tbsp mayonnaise

2 tsp honey Dijon mustard

1 Tbsp soy sauce

¼ cup (2 fl oz/60 ml) rice vinegar

5 Tbsp (3 fl oz/80 ml) peanut oil

2 Tbsp toasted sesame oil

1½ lb (750 g) sushi-grade ahi tuna steaks, patted dry

2 Tbsp peanut oil

Salt and freshly ground pepper

1 large head napa cabbage, halved, cored, and thinly sliced crosswise

6 green onions, including tender green parts, thinly sliced

2 red bell peppers, seeded and thinly sliced

Crisp in texture and mild in flavor, napa cabbage is a common ingredient in Asian cooking and works well with tropical fruits as well as vegetables: try adding a little diced mango to this slaw.

To make the dressing, in a large bowl, whisk together the ginger, mayonnaise, mustard, soy sauce, and vinegar. Add the 5 Tbsp peanut oil and the sesame oil in a thin stream, whisking constantly until the dressing is smooth.

Prepare a gas or charcoal grill for direct-heat cooking over high heat. Alternatively, preheat a stove-top grill pan over high heat. Brush both sides of the tuna steaks with the 2 Tbsp peanut oil and season generously with salt and pepper. Place the tuna on the grill rack or in the grill pan and sear without moving the steaks for 1½ minutes. Turn and sear for 1½ minutes longer, again without moving the steaks. Transfer to a cutting board and let stand for 5 minutes.

Meanwhile, whisk the dressing to recombine, then add the cabbage, green onions, and bell peppers to the bowl and toss to coat evenly. Arrange the cabbage mixture on plates. Slice the tuna steaks across the grain, arrange on top of the salads, and serve.

10

ROASTED SWEET POTATO SALAD
WITH PECANS & GREEN ONIONS

serves 4–6

3 lb (1.5 kg) sweet potatoes

2 Tbsp extra-virgin olive oil

Salt and freshly ground pepper

½ cup (2 oz/60 g) pecans

⅓ cup (3 fl oz/80 ml) fresh lime juice

3 Tbsp maple syrup

½ cup (1½ oz/45 g) minced green onions, including tender green parts

3–4 leaves kale, stemmed and leaves torn

This colorful roasted root vegetable salad is delicious alongside broiled steaks or oven-baked ribs. Use any variety of sweet potato you like, including the ones sometimes labeled "garnet yams," which have a bright orange color and moist, sweet flesh.

Preheat the oven to 400°F (200°C). Peel the sweet potatoes and cut them into 1-inch (2.5-cm) chunks. Put them in a large baking pan, drizzle with 1½ Tbsp of the oil, sprinkle with ½ tsp salt, and mix to coat. Spread the sweet potatoes in a single layer and roast, stirring occasionally, until tender when pierced with a knife, 25–30 minutes.

Meanwhile, in a dry frying pan, toast the pecans over medium-low heat, stirring, until fragrant and starting to brown, about 5 minutes. Pour onto a plate to cool.

In a large bowl, mix the lime juice, maple syrup, and remaining ½ Tbsp oil. Add the hot roasted sweet potatoes to the lime juice mixture, along with the pecans, green onions, and torn kale. Mix well and season with pepper and additional salt. Serve at once, or let cool to room temperature and mix again before serving.

11

QUINOA & RADICCHIO SALAD WITH DRIED CHERRIES & PISTACHIOS

serves 4

1 cup (6 oz/185 g) quinoa

½ head radicchio

¼ cup (2 fl oz/60 ml) balsamic vinegar

2 Tbsp extra-virgin olive oil

¼ cup (1½ oz/45 g) dried tart cherries

¼ cup (1 oz/30 g) chopped pistachios

3 Tbsp chopped fresh flat-leaf parsley, plus a few whole leaves for garnish

Salt and freshly ground pepper

Grain salads like this one will last for several days in the refrigerator, and will take on even more flavor as they sit. You can make the salad on a Sunday and pack it for lunch any day of the week.

In a saucepan, bring 2 cups (16 fl oz/500 ml) of water to a boil. Add the quinoa and reduce the heat to low. Cover and simmer until the grains are tender and the water is absorbed, about 15 minutes. Fluff with a fork and transfer to a large bowl.

Core and thinly slice the radicchio. Stir the radicchio, vinegar, oil, cherries, pistachios, and parsley into the warm quinoa. Season with salt and pepper and garnish with the whole parsley leaves. Serve warm or at room temperature.

12

WARM INDIAN-SPICED EGG SALAD

serves 6

8 large eggs

2 Tbsp unsalted butter

1 yellow onion, finely chopped

1 tsp peeled and chopped fresh ginger

1 serrano chile, thinly sliced

¼ tsp cayenne pepper

⅛ tsp ground turmeric

¼ cup (1½ oz/45 g) finely chopped tomato

Salt

¼ cup (⅓ oz/10 g) chopped fresh cilantro

6 slices bread, toasted just before serving

Think of egg salad as a canvas for your favorite flavor combinations. In this Indian-spiced version, the salad is given some heat with fresh chile and cayenne, while the ginger, cilantro, and tomato add vibrancy. Try whirling up the egg yolks with the spices and filling the whites for a delicious deviled egg hors d'oeuvre.

To hard-cook the eggs, place them in a saucepan just large enough to hold them. Add cold water to cover by 1 inch and bring just to a boil over high heat. Remove the pan from the heat and cover. Let stand for 15 minutes. Drain the eggs, then transfer to a bowl of ice water and let cool. Peel the eggs and chop into ½-inch (12-mm) pieces. Set aside.

In a nonstick frying pan, melt the butter over medium-high heat. Add the onion and cook, stirring occasionally, until golden, about 5 minutes. Stir in the ginger, chile, cayenne, turmeric, and chopped eggs. Mix well and cook, stirring gently, until the eggs are lightly fried, about 3 minutes.

Fold in the tomato and turn off the heat. Add ¼ tsp salt and stir in the cilantro. Serve alongside the hot toast.

13

To make the lemongrass-mint paste, thinly slice the tender pale green inner parts of 2 lemongrass stalks, put in a food processor, and process for 10 seconds. Add ½ cup (½ oz/15 g) mint leaves; 2 Tbsp lime juice; 2 Tbsp grapeseed oil; 1 tsp minced jalapeño; 2 minced garlic cloves; and salt and pepper to taste, and process until a paste forms, about 10 seconds.

GRILLED LAMB & PINEAPPLE SALAD WITH THAI FLAVORS

serves 6

2¼ lb (1.15 kg) boneless butterflied leg of lamb, trimmed

Lemongrass-Mint Paste *(left)*

FOR THE DRESSING

¼ cup (2 fl oz/60 ml) fresh lime juice

1 Tbsp rice vinegar

1½ tsp Asian fish sauce

½ tsp minced jalapeño chile

3 Tbsp firmly packed light brown sugar

3 Tbsp minced fresh mint

Salt and freshly ground pepper

5 Tbsp (3 fl oz/80 ml) peanut oil

1 pineapple

Peanut oil for brushing

1 cup (5 oz/155 g) unsalted dry-roasted peanuts, chopped

2 heads red-leaf lettuce, leaves torn into bite-sized pieces

8 green onions, including green parts, thinly sliced

Lay the lamb in a large baking dish and rub the lemongrass-mint paste into both sides of the meat. Cover and refrigerate for at least 6 hours or preferably overnight.

To make the dressing, in a small bowl, whisk together the lime juice, vinegar, fish sauce, chile, sugar, mint, ½ tsp salt, and several grindings of pepper until the sugar dissolves. Add the 5 Tbsp oil in a thin stream, whisking constantly until smooth. Taste and adjust the seasonings. Set aside.

About 1 hour before serving, remove the lamb from the refrigerator. Using a chef's knife, peel the pineapple and cut it crosswise into rounds about ¼ inch (6 mm) thick. Brush the pineapple on both sides with a little oil and season lightly with salt. Prepare a charcoal or gas grill for direct-heat cooking over medium-high heat. »

Grill the pineapple, turning once, until grill marked on both sides, 5–7 minutes total. Transfer to a cutting board. Scrape the paste off the lamb and lightly season both sides of the meat with salt. Grill the meat, turning once, until an instant-read thermometer inserted into the thickest part registers 130°F (54°C) for medium-rare, 10 minutes total, or until done to your liking. Transfer to the cutting board and tent with foil. Cut each pineapple round into quarters and trim away the tough core from each piece.

In a small bowl, stir together the peanuts and ½ tsp salt. In a large bowl, toss the lettuce with ¼ tsp salt and several grindings of pepper. Whisk the dressing to recombine, then drizzle about half of it over the lettuce and toss well. Taste and adjust the seasonings. Divide the dressed lettuce among individual plates.

Thinly slice the lamb. Arrange the lamb and pineapple on the salads, then drizzle each serving with the remaining dressing. Sprinkle with the peanuts and green onions and serve.

14

Inspired by the classic Italian "blacksmith salad" from the ancient city of Modena, this simple combination is designed to showcase the balsamic vinegar from the region, so use your best. It is traditionally topped with Parmesan, although any type of hard or semihard grating cheese can be used.

BUTTER LETTUCE & PARMESAN SALAD

serves 6

3 small heads butter lettuce, separated into leaves

2 Tbsp balsamic vinegar

Pinch of salt

3 Tbsp extra-virgin olive oil

1½ cups (3 oz/90 g) homemade croutons (page 285)

Parmesan, Asiago, or Gruyère cheese for shaving

Tear the large lettuce leaves in half, leaving the smaller ones whole, and place all the lettuce in a serving bowl. Sprinkle the vinegar and salt over the lettuce and toss well to mix. Drizzle with the oil, scatter the croutons over the top, and toss again.

Using a vegetable peeler, shave the cheese over the salad and serve.

15

Dry Jack is a grating cheese that originated in California. During the Second World War, Italian-made Parmesan became scarce, and Californians of Italian descent created a substitute by aging local Monterey Jack cheese. Parmesan may be substituted, of course.

CAESAR-STYLE SALAD WITH POBLANO CHILES & CORNMEAL CROUTONS

serves 4–6

2 Tbsp unsalted butter, at room temperature

2 cups (16 fl oz/500 ml) chicken broth

Salt and freshly ground pepper

1 cup (5 oz/155 g) yellow cornmeal

2 Tbsp extra-virgin olive oil

½ tsp chili powder

2 poblano chiles

½ cup (4 fl oz/125 ml) mayonnaise

1 Tbsp fresh lime juice

1 large clove garlic, minced

1½ tsp honey

½ tsp Dijon mustard

2 heads romaine lettuce, leaves torn into bite-sized pieces

4 oz (125 g) dry Jack cheese

Coat the inside of an 8-inch (20-cm) square baking dish with 1 Tbsp of the butter. In a saucepan over medium-high heat, bring the broth, ½ tsp salt, and the remaining 1 Tbsp butter to a boil. Reduce the heat to medium. Gradually add the cornmeal in a slow, steady stream while whisking constantly. Continue cooking and whisking until the mixture has thickened and pulls away from the sides of the pan, about 6 minutes. Immediately pour the mixture into the prepared baking dish, spreading it evenly. Cover and refrigerate until firm, about 1 hour.

Preheat the oven to 350°F (180°C). Cut the chilled cornmeal mixture into 1½-inch (4-cm) croutons. Transfer the croutons to a rimmed baking sheet, drizzle with the oil, sprinkle with the chili powder and ¼ tsp salt, and toss to coat. Bake until the croutons are dark gold and aromatic, about 30 minutes, shaking the pan after 10 minutes. Let cool to room temperature.

Preheat the broiler. Place the chiles on a broiler pan 4–6 inches (10–15 cm) from the heat source and broil, turning occasionally, until the skins are charred, about 10 minutes. Transfer to a bowl, cover, and let steam for 15 minutes. Remove and discard the skins, stems, and seeds and chop the flesh. ⟫

In a food processor, combine the mayonnaise, 2 Tbsp of the chopped chiles, the lime juice, garlic, honey, mustard, ½ tsp salt, and several grindings of pepper and process until smooth. Taste and adjust the seasonings.

In a large bowl, toss the lettuce with ¼ tsp salt. Drizzle with about two-thirds of the dressing and toss well. Divide the dressed lettuce among individual plates. Top each serving with cornmeal croutons and some of the remaining chopped chiles. Drizzle with additional dressing if desired (you may not need all of it). Using a vegetable peeler, shave the cheese over the salads and serve.

16

You can either cut the Gouda into small squares or use a vegetable peeler to create more delicate shavings. Serve with a rich white wine such as Chardonnay or Viognier or a medium-bodied red like Grenache or Syrah (and use the same red in making the vinaigrette).

RADICCHIO, ENDIVE & AGED GOUDA SALAD WITH RED-WINE VINAIGRETTE

serves 4–6

FOR THE VINAIGRETTE

2 Tbsp balsamic vinegar

¼ cup (2 fl oz/60 ml) dry red wine

Salt and freshly ground pepper

¼ cup (2 fl oz/60 ml) extra-virgin olive oil

4 heads red-tipped Belgian endive

½ head radicchio, torn into bite-sized pieces

½ cup (½ oz/15 g) fresh flat-leaf parsley leaves

Aged Gouda cheese for shaving

To make the vinaigrette, in a small saucepan, combine the vinegar and wine over medium-low heat and bring to a simmer. Cook until reduced by half, about 3 minutes. Set aside to cool. In a large bowl, whisk together the reduced vinegar and wine mixture and ½ tsp salt. Add the oil in a thin stream, whisking constantly until smooth. Set aside.

Cut each endive in half lengthwise and cut away the solid cone-shaped base. Coarsely chop the leaves. Add the radicchio, parsley, and endive to the bowl with the vinaigrette and toss well.

Divide the salad among individual plates. Using a vegetable peeler, shave the cheese over each, sprinkle with pepper, and serve.

17

ROASTED MUSHROOM SALAD WITH BALSAMIC VINAIGRETTE

serves 6

1 lb (500 g) mixed mushrooms such as chanterelle and shiitake

8 Tbsp (4 fl oz/125 ml) extra-virgin olive oil, plus 2 tsp

2½ tsp fresh thyme leaves

Salt and freshly ground pepper

4 large shallots

¼ cup (2 fl oz/60 ml) balsamic vinegar

1 tsp fresh lemon juice

½ tsp sugar

1 head Treviso radicchio, thinly sliced

1 small head red leaf lettuce, leaves torn into bite-sized pieces

1 cup (1½ oz/45 g) coarsely chopped fresh flat-leaf parsley

Roasting shallots and mushrooms makes this a hearty and super-flavorful salad, perfect for savoring on a chilly afternoon or evening. Serve alongside roasted salmon or chicken, with a medium-bodied red wine.

Preheat the oven to 400°F (200°C). Cut off and discard the shiitake stems, if using. Thinly slice the mushroom caps.

On a small rimmed baking sheet, toss the mushrooms with 3 Tbsp of the olive oil, 2 tsp of the thyme, ½ tsp salt, and ¼ tsp pepper. In a small baking dish, toss together the shallots, the 2 tsp olive oil, 2 pinches of salt, and several grindings of pepper. Place both pans in the oven. Roast the mushrooms until golden brown and tender, about 15 minutes, stirring once. Roast the shallots until soft and lightly browned, 25–30 minutes, stirring once. Trim off and discard the root ends of 2 of the shallots and put them in a food processor. Cover the remaining shallots and the mushrooms with foil to keep warm.

Add the remaining 5 Tbsp olive oil, the remaining ½ tsp thyme, the vinegar, lemon juice, sugar, a scant ½ tsp salt, and several grindings of pepper to the food processor and process until a smooth dressing forms. Taste and adjust the seasonings.

Trim and thinly slice the remaining shallots. In a large bowl, toss together the radicchio, lettuce, parsley, 2 pinches of salt, and several grindings of pepper. Drizzle with most of the dressing and toss again. Divide evenly among individual plates. Top each serving with an equal amount of the warm mushrooms and sliced shallots. Drizzle with some of the remaining dressing and serve.

18

RIGATONI SALAD WITH CAULIFLOWER & SAFFRON

serves 8

FOR THE SAFFRON DRESSING

¼ cup (2 fl oz/60 ml) fresh lemon juice

¼ tsp saffron threads

¼ tsp ground cumin

⅛ tsp cayenne pepper

Salt

¼ cup (2 fl oz/60 ml) extra-virgin olive oil

1 head white or green cauliflower, separated into bite-sized florets

10 oz (315 g) rigatoni pasta

2 Tbsp extra-virgin olive oil

¼ cup (¼ oz/7 g) fresh flat-leaf parsley leaves

1 tsp minced fresh thyme

2 Tbsp capers, rinsed

Replace the rigatoni with other pastas that have nooks and crannies to capture the juices, such as fusilli, rotelle, or radiatore. Choose saffron threads rather than powdered saffron, which loses its flavor with storage and is sometimes adulterated with other ingredients.

To make the dressing, in a small bowl, whisk together the lemon juice, saffron, cumin, cayenne, and ½ tsp salt. Add the ¼ cup oil in a thin stream, whisking constantly until smooth. Set aside.

Put the cauliflower in a steamer basket, sprinkle with ½ tsp salt, and place over boiling water in a saucepan. (The water should not touch the bottom of the basket.) Cover and steam until just tender, about 8 minutes. Remove the basket from the pan and run cold water over the cauliflower to halt the cooking. Let drain.

Bring a pot three-fourths full of salted water to a boil. Add the rigatoni, stir well, and cook until al dente, according to package directions. Drain and transfer to a large, deep bowl. Toss the pasta with the 2 Tbsp oil.

Add the cooled cauliflower and the dressing to the pasta and turn to coat well. Set aside a few of the parsley leaves for garnish and add the remaining parsley leaves and the thyme to the pasta, turning to distribute evenly. Cover and refrigerate for at least 1 hour and up to 6 hours before serving to allow the flavors to blend.

Before serving, let the salad return to room temperature and garnish with the remaining parsley leaves and the capers.

19

Seek out an imported Spanish or Italian canned tuna for this salad. Tuna packed in oil has a much richer, deeper flavor than water-packed, which often has a metallic tang. Tuna found off the coasts of Spain and Sicily is highly regarded for its texture and flavor.

CANNELLINI BEAN SALAD WITH TUNA & GRILLED RADICCHIO

serves 4–6

1½ cans (15 oz/470 g each) cannellini or other white beans, rinsed and drained

2 small heads radicchio

2 Tbsp olive oil, plus extra for brushing

Salt and freshly ground pepper

1 cup (5 oz/155 g) chopped celery, including some leaves

½ small red onion, chopped

Pinch of dried oregano

1–2 Tbsp fresh lemon juice

1 can (7 oz/220 g) oil-packed tuna, drained and separated into chunks

Prepare a charcoal or gas grill for direct-heat cooking over medium-high heat, or preheat the broiler.

Put the beans in a saucepan and cook gently over medium-low heat, stirring occasionally, until warm. Remove from the heat and cover to keep warm.

Meanwhile, cut each radicchio head into 4–6 wedges through the core, so that the wedges will keep their shape. Brush with oil and season with salt and pepper.

To grill, arrange the radicchio wedges over the hottest part of the fire. To broil, arrange the radicchio wedges in a single layer on a broiler pan and slide under the broiler about 6 inches (15 cm) from the heat source. Cook, turning once, until wilted and lightly browned, about 5 minutes total.

Put the beans in a bowl. Add the celery, onion, oregano, the 2 Tbsp oil, and 1 Tbsp of the lemon juice. Season with salt and pepper. Toss well. Taste and adjust the seasoning with more lemon juice, salt, and pepper.

Arrange the radicchio wedges on a platter. Spoon the beans in the center, top with the tuna, and serve.

20

To make crostini, cut a baguette into thin slices and, if possible, let sit out on a countertop overnight. Brush the slices lightly with extra-virgin olive oil, arrange in a single layer on a baking sheet, and sprinkle lightly with salt. Toast in a preheated 350°F (180°C) oven until crisp and lightly golden, about 15 minutes. Let cool.

MÂCHE & ESCAROLE SALAD WITH CROSTINI

serves 4

2 Tbsp fresh lemon juice

1 shallot, minced

Salt and freshly ground pepper

¼ cup (2 fl oz/60 ml) extra-virgin olive oil

1 head escarole

4–6 oz (125–185 g) mâche or field greens

Crostini *(left)* for serving

In a small bowl, whisk together the lemon juice, shallot, and salt and pepper to taste. Add the oil in a thin stream, whisking constantly until smooth. Set aside.

Remove the tough outer leaves of the escarole and tear the inner leaves into bite-sized pieces. In a large bowl, combine the escarole and mâche. Whisk the vinaigrette to recombine, drizzle it over the greens, and toss to coat the leaves well.

To serve, divide the salad greens among individual plates and accompany each serving with 2 crostini.

21

Bright and crunchy, this salad is ideal for a winter menu. It's also quite pretty, adding fresh color to any dinner. Serve it alongside broiled or roasted meats, especially broiled kebabs for a Mediterranean-style meal.

JERUSALEM ARTICHOKE SALAD WITH POMEGRANATE & CELERY

serves 4–6

½ lb (250 g) Jerusalem artichokes

2 Tbsp extra-virgin olive oil, plus ¼ cup (2 fl oz/60 ml)

Leaves from 2 fresh thyme sprigs

Salt and freshly ground pepper

1 pomegranate

2 celery ribs, leaves reserved

1 head radicchio, leaves separated

1 Tbsp champagne vinegar

½ cup (2 oz/60 g) crumbled ricotta salata cheese

Preheat the oven to 375°F (190°C).

Scrub the Jerusalem artichokes and cut them into slices ½ inch (12 mm) thick. Place on a roasting pan, drizzle with the 2 Tbsp oil, sprinkle with the thyme, season well with salt and pepper, and toss to combine. Spread the slices in a single layer and roast, turning once, until golden and tender, about 20 minutes. Set aside to cool.

Meanwhile, seed the pomegranate, pat the seeds dry, and set aside.

Using a mandoline or box grater, thinly slice the celery and put the slices in a large bowl along with the reserved leaves. Tear the radicchio leaves in half and add to the celery.

In a separate small bowl, combine the ¼ cup oil and the vinegar, adding the oil in a thin stream and whisking constantly until the dressing is smooth.

Add the roasted Jerusalem artichokes to the bowl with the celery and radicchio and pour the dressing over. Season with salt and pepper and toss to coat. Scatter the cheese and pomegranate seeds on top and serve.

22

Tropical papaya and white balsamic vinegar offer a sweet and unusual counterpoint to spinach. Choose papayas that are not too soft, or they will be difficult to cut into cubes. Pink peppercorns are milder than black or white, and will not compete with the exotic fruit.

BABY SPINACH SALAD WITH PARMESAN & PAPAYA

serves 6

4 oz (125 g) Parmesan cheese

½ Tbsp white balsamic vinegar

1 tsp red wine vinegar

Salt and ground pink peppercorns

2 Tbsp extra-virgin olive oil

5 cups (5 oz/155 g) baby spinach

2 ripe papayas, peeled, seeded, and cut into ½-inch (12-mm) cubes

Using a vegetable peeler, shave the cheese into thin ribbons. Set aside.

In a large serving bowl, whisk together the vinegars, ¼ tsp salt, and ¾ tsp ground pink peppercorns. Add the oil in a thin stream, whisking constantly until the dressing is smooth. Add the spinach and toss well to coat. Add the papaya and half of the cheese ribbons, and turn gently to coat. Top with the remaining cheese ribbons, garnish with more ground pink peppercorns, and serve.

23

CRAB & SHRIMP SALAD WITH AVOCADO & ORANGES

serves 4–6

12–18 large shrimp in the shell

2 large navel oranges

1 Tbsp sherry vinegar

½ Tbsp fresh lemon juice, plus more as needed

Salt and ground white pepper

6 Tbsp (3 fl oz/90 ml) extra-virgin olive oil

2 bunches watercress, tough stems removed

1 head red-leaf lettuce, leaves separated and torn into large pieces

8–12 oz (250–375 g) cooked crabmeat, picked over for shell fragments

1 large ripe avocado, pitted, peeled, and diced

Marinated Onion *(left)* for garnish

To make the marinated onion, cut 1 small red onion crosswise into slices ⅛ inch (3 mm) thick. Place the slices in a small bowl and toss with ¼ cup (2 fl oz/60 ml) red wine vinegar and a large pinch each of kosher salt and sugar. Let stand for about 30 minutes to soften and mellow the onion. Drain.

Put the shrimp in a steamer basket and place over boiling water in a saucepan over medium-high heat. (The water should not touch the bottom of the basket.) Cover, reduce the heat to medium, and steam until the shrimp are evenly pink, about 2 minutes, stirring once if needed. Remove from the heat and let cool. Peel and devein the shrimp, leaving the tail segments intact if desired.

Grate the zest of one of the oranges, then use a knife to peel and segment both oranges, catching and reserving the juices.

To make a dressing, in a small bowl, whisk together the sherry vinegar, the ½ Tbsp lemon juice, 1 Tbsp of the reserved orange juice, and salt and white pepper to taste. Add the oil in a thin stream, whisking constantly until the dressing is smooth. Taste and adjust the seasoning with a little more lemon juice if needed.

In a large bowl, combine the watercress and lettuce. Add all but 2 Tbsp of the dressing and toss to combine. Transfer the salad greens to a large, shallow bowl or platter or 4 individual bowls. Arrange the crab, shrimp, orange segments, and avocado cubes over and around the greens and drizzle the remaining dressing over them. Scatter the marinated onion over, sprinkle with the orange zest, and serve.

24

WINTER CHICORY & APPLE SALAD WITH PECANS

serves 4

¼ cup (1 oz/30 g) pecans

6 Tbsp (3 fl oz/90 ml) heavy cream

1 Tbsp cider vinegar, plus more if needed

3 oz (90 g) Roquefort or other blue cheese

Salt and freshly ground pepper

1 lb (500 g) mixed chicories such as hearts of escarole, frisée, and radicchio

1 Gala, Fuji, or Sierra Beauty apple

The creamy white dressing used here, with just a touch of vinegar, mellows out the slightly bitter winter chicories, while the apple adds a sweet-tart punch. If you have leftover dressing, use it as a dip for raw vegetables.

In a dry frying pan, toast the pecans over medium-low heat, stirring, until fragrant and starting to brown, about 5 minutes. Pour onto a plate to cool, then coarsely chop and set aside.

In a serving bowl, combine the cream and the 1 Tbsp vinegar and whisk lightly. Crumble in the cheese. Add 1 tsp salt and pepper to taste, and whisk to make a smooth dressing. Taste and adjust the seasoning with additional vinegar, salt, or pepper if needed. (The dressing should taste fairly bold to complement the bitter chicories.) Tear the chicories into bite-sized pieces and add to the bowl. Sprinkle with salt, if desired, then toss with the dressing.

Core and slice the apple. Add the slices to the salad, tossing gently. Arrange the dressed salad on individual plates, sprinkle each with the toasted pecans, and serve.

25

POTATO & BEET SALAD WITH DILL
serves 6

4 small beets (about ½ lb/250 g total weight)

1 lb (500 g) pearl potatoes

FOR THE DILL DRESSING

½ cup (4 oz/125 g) sour cream

1 Tbsp mayonnaise

1 tsp creamy-style prepared horseradish

2 Tbsp chopped fresh dill

Salt and freshly ground pepper

Chopped fresh dill for garnish

Roasted beets are easy to make and are such a welcome addition to winter salads. Beets are also appealing as a plated first course, sliced and served with crumbled goat cheese, toasted walnuts, and your favorite vinaigrette.

Preheat the oven to 400°F (200°C). Trim off the leafy beet tops and reserve for another use. Wrap the beets in foil and roast on a baking sheet until easily pierced with the tip of a knife, 45–60 minutes. Remove from the oven and let cool in the foil. Unwrap and peel, then cut each beet into small cubes.

Meanwhile, put the potatoes in a large saucepan with salted water to cover. Bring to a boil over high heat, reduce the heat to medium-low, cover, and simmer until the potatoes are tender when pierced with a knife, 12–15 minutes. Drain and set aside.

To make the dressing, in a serving bowl, stir together the sour cream, mayonnaise, horseradish, 2 Tbsp dill, and salt and pepper to taste.

Fold the beets and potatoes into the dressing. Cover and refrigerate for at least 30 minutes or up to 24 hours to blend the flavors. When ready to serve, garnish with dill.

26

ORANGE, ONION & OLIVE SALAD
serves 4

4 navel oranges

¼ small red onion, thinly sliced

½ cup (3 oz/90 g) olives, halved and pitted

Juice of ½ lemon

¼ tsp ground cinnamon

Salt and freshly ground pepper

1 Tbsp extra-virgin olive oil

1 Tbsp chopped fresh flat-leaf parsley

Sliced-orange salads are served in a variety of ways in the Mediterranean. In Italy you may find the fruit paired with fennel and parsley. This version is closer to one you may see in Morocco, where oranges are often combined with cinnamon, oil-cured black olives, chopped dates, and lemon and orange juices.

Cut a thick slice off the top and bottom of each orange. Stand each upright and, following the contour of the fruit, cut away the peel and white pith. Cut each peeled orange crosswise into slices ½ inch (12 mm) thick. Pour any orange juice from the cutting board into a small bowl.

Arrange the orange slices on a serving platter, overlapping them slightly to cover the plate nicely. Separate and scatter the onion slices over the top, then scatter the olives over.

Add the lemon juice, cinnamon, and salt and pepper to taste to the reserved orange juice. Whisk until blended. Add the oil in a thin stream, whisking constantly until the dressing is smooth.

Drizzle the salad with the dressing. Let sit at room temperature for 10–15 minutes to allow the flavors to blend. Sprinkle with parsley and serve.

27

MANGO, PINEAPPLE & PAPAYA SALAD

serves 4–6

2 papayas

1 mango

½ small pineapple, about 1 lb (500 g), peeled

Juice of 3 limes

¼ cup (⅓ oz/10 g) chopped fresh mint

Fruit salad makes a refreshing side dish for brunch or lunch, or may be served as a healthful dessert. Here, tropical fruits, which are typically in the market year-round, take center stage. When choosing mangoes and papayas, look for fruits that yield slightly to a gentle touch. A ripe pineapple will be fragrant, have deep green leaves, and give slightly when pressed.

Peel the papayas, cut them in half, and scoop out and discard the seeds. Cut the flesh into ½-inch (12-mm) cubes and place in a bowl.

Peel the mango. Stand the fruit stem end up with a narrow side toward you. Position a sharp knife about 1 inch (2.5 cm) from the stem on one side and cut down the length of the fruit, just missing the large pit. Repeat on the other side of the pit. Cut the flesh into ½-inch (12-mm) cubes. Add to the bowl.

Lay the pineapple on its side and cut shallow furrows in the flesh to remove the eyes. Cut the pineapple lengthwise into quarters, cut away the tough core, and cut the flesh into ½-inch (12-mm) cubes. Add to the bowl.

Pour the lime juice over the fruit, sprinkle with the mint, and turn gently to coat, then serve. The salad may also be covered and refrigerated for up to 4 hours before serving.

28

JANUARY

KIWI, APPLE & GRAPE SALAD WITH ROSEMARY SYRUP

serves 4

¼ cup (2 oz/60 g) sugar

Three 6-inch (15-cm) fresh rosemary sprigs

3 kiwifruits, peeled and chopped

2 tart green apples such as Granny Smith, left unpeeled, cored, and cut into ½-inch (12-mm) pieces

1 cup (6 oz/185 g) seedless green grapes

This is not your ordinary "green salad." You can use as much or as little of the rosemary syrup as you like; any remaining can be saved to drizzle over vanilla gelato or breakfast polenta, or used in a cocktail such as a rosemary gin fizz.

In a saucepan, combine the sugar and ½ cup (4 fl oz/125 ml) water and bring to a boil over medium-high heat, stirring to dissolve the sugar. Add the rosemary sprigs, reduce the heat to medium, and cook for 15 minutes. Remove the rosemary from the pan and raise the heat to high. Cook, stirring, until the liquid is reduced to about ⅓ cup (3 fl oz/ 80 ml). Let cool to room temperature.

Put the kiwifruits, apples, and grapes in a bowl. Pour the syrup over the fruit, tossing to coat, and serve.

29

BLACK BEAN & POBLANO CHILE SALAD

serves 6

2 poblano chiles

2 cans (15 oz/470 g each) black beans, drained and rinsed

FOR THE CUMIN VINAIGRETTE

2 Tbsp red wine vinegar

1 Tbsp Dijon mustard

1 tsp sugar

½ tsp ground cumin

½ tsp paprika

Salt and freshly ground pepper

¼ cup (2 fl oz/60 ml) extra-virgin olive oil

½ red onion, finely chopped

1 basket mixed pear tomatoes, halved

Crumbled queso fresco or shredded Monterey Jack cheese for garnish

Chopped fresh cilantro for garnish

This is an easy salad to assemble, but is bursting with flavor, especially from the roasted poblanos. Poblanos can vary in spiciness, so taste a piece before adding them all to the mix. For a heartier salad, add cubes of cooked chicken and serve warm tortillas alongside.

Preheat the oven to 400°F (200°C). Put the poblanos on a rimmed baking sheet and roast, turning occasionally, until softened and blistered, about 25 minutes. Remove from the oven, transfer to a bowl, cover, and let steam for 15 minutes.

Meanwhile, put the beans in a saucepan and place over medium-low heat. Stir occasionally until warm. Remove from the heat and cover to keep warm.

To make the vinaigrette, whisk together the vinegar, mustard, sugar, cumin, paprika, and salt and pepper to taste. Add the oil in a thin stream, whisking constantly until the dressing is smooth. Set aside.

When the poblanos are cool enough to handle, remove the skins, ribs, and seeds and cut the chiles into ½-inch (12-mm) pieces. In a bowl, combine the chiles, beans, onion, tomatoes, and vinaigrette. Toss to combine. Season with salt and pepper, sprinkle with the cheese and cilantro, and serve.

30

WARM RUBY GRAPEFRUIT SALAD

serves 4

1 Tbsp mild olive oil or canola oil

¼ red onion, thinly sliced

½ jalapeño chile, thinly sliced

2 ruby red grapefruits, peeled and segmented with a knife

1 avocado, pitted, peeled and sliced

¼ cup (⅓ oz/10 g) chopped fresh cilantro

Bright and lively, this salad hits the spot during the dead of winter. Serve alongside slow-roasted pork with mojo or adobo sauce for a Latin-style meal.

In a frying pan, warm the oil over medium heat. Add the onion and jalapeño and sauté until softened, about 5 minutes. Add the grapefruit segments and avocado to the pan, mix gently, and warm through. Sprinkle with cilantro and serve.

31

CABBAGE, PEAR & GINGER SLAW

serves 4

¼ cup (2 fl oz/60 ml) seasoned rice vinegar

1 Tbsp toasted sesame oil

1 tsp peeled and grated fresh ginger

1 tsp packed light brown sugar

1 tsp soy sauce

½ head napa cabbage

1 firm mango, peeled

1 Asian pear, halved and cored

1 red serrano chile

Salt and freshly ground pepper

Most of the spiciness of a chile resides in its seeds and, to a lesser extent, the white inner membranes. Seeding the serrano will cut down sharply on its heat.

In a small bowl, whisk together the vinegar, sesame oil, ginger, sugar, and soy sauce to make a dressing. Set aside.

Using a mandoline or box grater, shred the cabbage, mango, and pear. Combine in a bowl. Cut the chile into thin rings, remove the seeds, and add the rings to bowl. Add the dressing and toss to combine. Season with salt and pepper to taste and serve.

In the heart of winter, turn to cruciferous vegetables like Brussels sprouts, broccoli, and cauliflower. Shaving or shredding them and tossing with an herb vinaigrette helps keep them light and bright. Also take advantage of the seasonal citrus fruits, from juicy oranges and sweet mandarins, to ruby grapefruits, whose segments brighten green salads or are delicious on their own with a drizzle of oil.

1

SHREDDED KALE SALAD WITH
PANCETTA & HARD-COOKED EGG
page 36

2

WARM LENTIL SALAD WITH
MUSTARD VINAIGRETTE
page 36

3

SALMON & FENNEL SALAD
page 39

8

ARUGULA SALAD WITH PINE NUTS,
AVOCADO & HEARTS OF PALM
page 41

9

LENTIL SALAD WITH MOZZARELLA
& PROSCIUTTO
page 42

10

BUTTER LETTUCE WITH SHEEP'S
MILK CHEESE & HAZELNUTS
page 42

15

CRAB SALAD WITH MEYER
LEMON & FRESH MANGO
page 47

16

BROCCOLI & CAULIFLOWER
SLAW WITH RAISINS & NUTS
page 47

17

WALDORF SALAD
page 47

22

LENTIL & KALE SALAD WITH BACON
page 51

23

SHAVED FENNEL SALAD WITH
ORANGE DRESSING
page 51

24

GRILLED CHICKEN CAESAR SALAD
page 53

4

CARROT, OLIVE & ALMOND SALAD
page 39

5

WILD RICE SALAD WITH
MUSHROOMS & SAGE
page 40

6

CRAB LOUIS SALAD
page 40

7

BEET & FENNEL SALAD
WITH RICOTTA SALATA
page 41

11

MESCLUN & ROASTED PEARS WITH
GRAINY MUSTARD VINAIGRETTE
page 45

12

SALAD OF MANDARINS, ROASTED
BEETS & FARMER CHEESE
page 45

13

WINTER GREENS WITH
LEMON VINAIGRETTE
page 46

14

SPINACH SALAD WITH ORANGES
& ROASTED BEETS
page 46

18

THAI BEEF SALAD
page 48

19

CANNELLINI BEAN, FENNEL
& SHRIMP SALAD
page 48

20

JICAMA-MANGO SALAD WITH
CILANTRO DRESSING
page 50

21

GARLICKY PASTA SALAD
WITH CRAB & SHRIMP
page 50

25

BABY SPINACH WITH
GINGER-GLAZED SCALLOPS
page 53

26

COUSCOUS SALAD WITH
DRIED FRUIT & PINE NUTS
page 54

27

BRUSSELS SPROUT & ARUGULA
SALAD WITH WALNUTS
page 54

28

MOROCCAN CARROT SALAD
page 54

february

1

SHREDDED KALE SALAD WITH PANCETTA & HARD-COOKED EGG

serves 4–5

5 large eggs

2 bunches kale

Salt and freshly ground black pepper

¼ lb (125 g) thick-cut pancetta or bacon, coarsely chopped

3 Tbsp extra-virgin olive oil

1 clove garlic, minced

4 Tbsp (2 fl oz/60 ml) balsamic vinegar

2 Tbsp red wine vinegar

4 Tbsp (⅓ oz/10 g) fresh flat-leaf parsley

½ tsp cayenne pepper

Shredding and briefly blanching kale for a salad softens its sturdy texture, but keeps it crunchy enough to support hearty, heavier ingredients like hard-cooked eggs and pancetta. The kale can be left raw, too, for a crunchier effect.

To hard-cook the eggs, place them in a saucepan just large enough to hold them. Add cold water to cover by 1 inch (2.5 cm) and bring just to a boil over high heat. Remove the pan from the heat and cover. Let stand for 15 minutes. Have ready a bowl of ice water. Drain the eggs, then transfer to the ice water and let cool before peeling. Mince the eggs and set aside.

With a knife, strip the ribs from the kale, then roll the leaves up and slice them thinly crosswise. Bring a large saucepan three-fourths full of water to a boil over medium-high heat. Add 1 tsp salt and the kale and cook until the greens are just tender, about 5 minutes. Using a slotted spoon, lift out the kale and drain it well. Rinse under cold running water until cool. Drain again and gently squeeze out the excess liquid from the kale with your hands, then coarsely chop it. Gently squeeze out the liquid with your hands again. Set aside.

In a frying pan, cook the pancetta or bacon over medium heat, turning occasionally, until nearly golden, about 5 minutes. (If using bacon, pour off the rendered fat at this point.) Add 1 Tbsp of the oil and the garlic and cook just until the garlic is golden, about 1 minute. Using a slotted spoon, transfer the pancetta or bacon and garlic to paper towels to drain. ↠

Add 2 Tbsp of the balsamic vinegar to the frying pan and cook over medium heat, stirring to scrape up any browned bits on the pan bottom. Pour into a bowl and whisk in the remaining 2 Tbsp balsamic vinegar, the red wine vinegar, and the remaining 2 Tbsp oil. Add the kale, the pancetta and garlic, 3 Tbsp of the parsley, and ½ tsp black pepper. Mix well. Add the minced eggs and gently fold them in.

Garnish the mixture with the remaining 1 Tbsp parsley and the cayenne and serve.

2

WARM LENTIL SALAD WITH MUSTARD VINAIGRETTE

serves 4–6

1 cup (7 oz/220 g) green French (du Puy) lentils, picked over and rinsed

1 yellow onion, finely chopped

1 clove garlic, halved

¼ tsp dried thyme

2 fresh flat-leaf parsley sprigs, plus ½ cup (1½ oz/45 g) finely chopped

1 shallot, minced

2 tsp white wine vinegar

4½ tsp Dijon mustard

Salt and freshly ground pepper

¼ cup (2 fl oz/60 ml) extra-virgin olive oil

This is delicious as a side for herb-roasted chicken or pork tenderloin, or grilled sausages. To add more greenery, stir in a handful or two of baby spinach when you add the parsley.

In a heavy saucepan, combine the lentils with 6 cups (48 fl oz/1.5 l) water, the onion, garlic, thyme, and parsley sprigs over medium heat. Bring to a simmer, cover, and cook until the lentils are tender, about 30 minutes.

Meanwhile, transfer 2 Tbsp of the lentil-cooking liquid to a bowl and whisk in the shallot, vinegar, mustard, and salt and pepper to taste. Add the oil in a thin stream, whisking constantly until the dressing is well blended. Set the vinaigrette aside.

Drain the lentils well in a fine-mesh sieve and discard the parsley sprigs and garlic halves. Transfer the lentils to a bowl, add the vinaigrette and chopped parsley, and toss to combine. Season with salt and pepper and serve warm or at room temperature.

3

SALMON & FENNEL SALAD
serves 4

1 lb (500 g) salmon fillet,
pin bones removed

Salt and freshly ground pepper

FOR THE MUSTARD VINAIGRETTE

Grated zest and juice of 1 lemon

1 Tbsp champagne or white wine vinegar

2 tsp Dijon mustard

1 Tbsp minced fresh chives

6 Tbsp (3 fl oz/90 ml) extra-virgin olive oil

2 fennel bulbs, trimmed

6 oz (185 g) mixed baby greens

1 Tbsp minced fresh chives

If the salmon fillet still has its skin, you don't need to spend time removing it before you cook the salmon. The skin will protect the delicate flesh during steaming. After cooking, the salmon flesh will flake easily away from the skin, which can then be discarded.

Season both sides of the salmon with salt and pepper. Lightly oil a steamer rack and place in a pot. Fill the pot with water to just below the base of the steamer rack and bring to a simmer. Add the salmon, cover, and cook until opaque throughout, about 10 minutes per inch (2.5 cm) of thickness. Transfer to a plate. Let cool slightly, then flake with a fork into large chunks, discarding any skin.

To make the vinaigrette, in a large bowl, whisk together the lemon zest and juice, vinegar, mustard, ½ tsp salt, a pinch of pepper, and 1 Tbsp chives. Add the oil in a thin stream, whisking constantly until well blended.

Quarter the fennel bulbs and, using a mandoline or sharp knife, slice the quarters crosswise as thinly as possible. Add the fennel to the vinaigrette and toss to coat evenly. Add the greens and salmon and toss to combine. Arrange on plates, sprinkle with 1 Tbsp chives, and serve.

4

CARROT, OLIVE & ALMOND SALAD
serves 4

½ tsp cumin seeds

1 lb (500 g) multicolored carrots

¼ cup (1½ oz/45 g) green olives, pitted

¼ cup (⅓ oz/10 g) lightly packed
fresh flat-leaf parsley leaves

1 tsp fresh lemon juice

2 Tbsp extra-virgin olive oil

Salt and freshly ground pepper

¼ cup (1 oz/30 g) unsalted roasted
almonds, chopped

If shaving the carrots lengthwise seems too labor-intensive or difficult, you can shave or thinly slice the carrots into coins. Meaty green olives are delicious in this salad, although any olives, including oil-cured black ones, will impart a pleasant briny and salty note to the mix.

In a dry frying pan, toast the cumin seeds over medium-low heat, stirring, until fragrant and starting to brown, 2–3 minutes. Pour onto a plate and let cool.

Using a mandoline or a box grater, shave the carrots lengthwise into thin ribbons. Set aside in a bowl.

With a large knife, coarsely chop the olives and parsley. Transfer to a small bowl, add the lemon juice and cumin seeds, and stir with a fork to combine. Add the oil in a thin stream, whisking until the dressing is well blended. Season with salt and pepper to taste.

Add the olive mixture to the carrots and toss well. Divide the salad among individual plates, sprinkle with the almonds, and serve.

5

Cooking mushrooms separately and then folding them into wild rice lets them contribute their distinctive earthy flavor to this dish, but keeps their smooth and meaty texture at its best. You can use shiitakes or chanterelles in place of button mushrooms, or a mixture. This is a great dish for entertaining a crowd.

WILD RICE SALAD WITH MUSHROOMS & SAGE

serves 10–12

6 celery ribs

3 Tbsp extra-virgin olive oil

½ cup (2½ oz/75 g) finely chopped yellow onion

2 cups (12 oz/375 g) wild rice

1 Tbsp minced fresh flat-leaf parsley

1 tsp minced fresh sage

Salt and freshly ground pepper

6 cups (48 fl oz/1.5 l) chicken broth

1 Tbsp unsalted butter

½ lb (250 g) cremini mushrooms, sliced

Trim the celery ribs and cut each rib crosswise into 2-inch (5-cm) lengths, then cut the pieces on the diagonal to make long slivers about ¼ inch (6 mm) thick. Set aside.

In a large saucepan, warm the oil over medium heat. Add the onion and celery and sauté until soft, 7–8 minutes. Add the wild rice, parsley, sage, ¾ tsp salt, and ½ tsp pepper and stir until the rice glistens, 1–2 minutes. Pour in the broth, raise the heat to high, and bring to a boil. Reduce the heat to medium-low, cover, and cook until the wild rice is tender, about 50 minutes.

About 5 minutes before the rice is ready, cook the mushrooms: In a frying pan, melt the butter over medium-high heat. When it foams, add the mushrooms and sauté until lightly golden, about 5 minutes. Season with ¼ tsp each salt and pepper.

When the rice is done, drain off any excess liquid and stir in the hot mushrooms. Transfer to a warmed bowl and serve hot.

6

This retro salad is often made with shrimp instead of crab, or with a combination of the two. Use cooked, peeled, and deveined shrimp in the size you prefer (on the West Coast, tiny bay shrimp are usually the first choice). You can also top the salad with lightly cooked asparagus.

CRAB LOUIS SALAD

serves 4–6

4 large eggs

FOR THE DRESSING

1 cup (8 fl oz/250 ml) mayonnaise

¼ cup (2 fl oz/60 ml) ketchup-style chile sauce

2 Tbsp minced green bell pepper

2 green onions, including tender green parts, minced

1 Tbsp fresh lemon juice

½ head iceberg lettuce

2 hearts of romaine lettuce

1 lb (500 g) cooked crabmeat, picked over for shell fragments

½ cup (3 oz/90 g) cherry tomatoes, halved

¼ English cucumber, thinly sliced

1 lemon, cut into wedges

To hard-cook the eggs, place them in a saucepan just large enough to hold them. Add cold water to cover by 1 inch (2.5 cm) and bring just to a boil over high heat. Remove the pan from the heat and cover. Let stand for 15 minutes. Drain the eggs, then transfer to a bowl of ice water and let cool before cutting into quarters.

To make the dressing, in a small bowl, whisk together the mayonnaise, chile sauce, bell pepper, green onions, and lemon juice. Cover and refrigerate until serving.

Tear the iceberg lettuce into bite-sized pieces and coarsely chop the romaine hearts. In a large bowl, toss together the lettuces. Distribute the lettuces in a thick layer on a large platter or among individual plates. Heap the crabmeat down the center of the lettuce. Arrange the tomatoes, cucumber, and quartered eggs around the crab. Garnish with the lemon wedges, and serve, passing the dressing on the side.

BEET & FENNEL SALAD WITH RICOTTA SALATA

serves 4

4 beets, preferably golden or Chioggia (about 1¼ lb/625 g total weight)

1½ Tbsp fresh lemon juice

1 shallot, minced

Salt and freshly ground pepper

¼ cup (2 fl oz/60 ml) extra-virgin olive oil

1 small fennel bulb, trimmed

Ricotta salata or feta cheese

½ large avocado

1 Tbsp minced fresh flat-leaf parsley

Preheat the oven to 400°F (200°C). Trim off the leafy beet tops. Wrap the beets in foil and roast on a baking sheet until easily pierced with the tip of a knife, about 1 hour. Remove from the oven and let cool in the foil.

Meanwhile, in a small bowl, whisk together the lemon juice, shallot, and a generous pinch of salt. Let stand for 30 minutes to allow the shallot flavor to mellow, then add the oil in a thin stream, whisking constantly until the dressing is well blended. Season with additional salt and pepper to taste.

Unwrap and peel the cooled beets, then slice very thinly. Put them in a bowl and toss gently with about one-third of the vinaigrette, taking care not to break up the slices. Make a thin bed of the beets on a large platter or divide among individual plates.

Halve the fennel lengthwise and, using a mandoline or a very sharp knife, slice each half crosswise paper-thin. Put the fennel in a bowl, add about one-half of the remaining vinaigrette, and toss to coat. Scatter the fennel over the beets. With a vegetable peeler, shave the cheese evenly over the fennel.

Peel and pit the avocado and slice thinly crosswise. Arrange the avocado slices attractively on top of the salad. Drizzle the salad with as much of the remaining vinaigrette as desired (you may not need it all). Top with the parsley and serve.

7

FEBRUARY

Autumn through spring, beets are a highlight at farmers' markets, especially the golden and pink-and-white-striped Chioggia varieties. In this colorful composed salad, crisp fennel and creamy avocado provide textural contrast with the beets, and thin shavings of ricotta salata cheese add a salty tang.

ARUGULA SALAD WITH PINE NUTS, AVOCADO & HEARTS OF PALM

serves 4

6 cups (6 oz/185 g) baby arugula leaves

1 basket grape tomatoes, halved

⅓ cup (2 oz/60 g) pine nuts

4 stalks jarred hearts of palm, cut on a slight diagonal into ½-inch (12-mm) slices

1 avocado, pitted, peeled, and cut into thin slices

FOR THE LEMON DRESSING

2 Tbsp fresh lemon juice

Salt and freshly ground pepper

6 Tbsp (3 fl oz/90 ml) extra-virgin olive oil

Parmesan cheese for shaving

In a serving bowl, toss together the arugula, tomatoes, pine nuts, hearts of palm, and avocado.

To make the dressing, in a small bowl, whisk together the lemon juice and salt and pepper to taste. Add the oil in a thin stream, whisking constantly until the dressing is smooth. Pour over the salad and toss well. Using a vegetable peeler, shave the cheese over the salad and serve.

8

FEBRUARY

True, February is not tomato season, but tiny grape tomatoes are often quite decent even in the wintertime and can satisfy that late-winter hankering for the fresh fruit.

9

LENTIL SALAD WITH MOZZARELLA & PROSCIUTTO

serves 6

Salt and freshly ground pepper

1¼ cups (9 oz/280 ml) green French (du Puy) lentils, picked over and rinsed

¼ cup (2 fl oz/60 ml) red wine vinegar

2 Tbsp minced red onion

¼ cup (⅓ oz/10 g) julienned fresh basil leaves, plus small whole leaves for garnish

¼ lb (125 g) paper-thin prosciutto slices, cut into strips 1 inch (2.5 cm) wide

3 Tbsp extra-virgin olive oil

5 oz (155 g) fresh mozzarella cheese, torn into generous pieces

This is a great dish to bring to a potluck, as it holds up well and absorbs more flavor as it sits. If you're transporting it, tear up the mozzarella, then return it to the liquid in which it came. This will keep it fresh and moist. Just before serving, add the mozzarella and the garnishes to the platter.

In a saucepan, combine 4 cups (32 fl oz/1 l) water and ½ tsp salt and bring to a boil. Add the lentils, reduce the heat to medium-low, cover, and cook until the lentils are tender but still hold their shape, 20–25 minutes. Remove from the heat and drain well. Let cool to room temperature.

In a large bowl, using a fork, stir together the vinegar, ½ tsp pepper, the onion, the julienned basil, and all but one-fourth of the prosciutto. Add the oil in a thin stream, stirring constantly until the dressing is well blended. Add the lentils and toss to mix.

Spoon the lentils onto a platter. Tuck the cheese into the lentils. Sprinkle the basil leaves and the remaining prosciutto over the lentils and serve.

10

FEBRUARY

BUTTER LETTUCE WITH SHEEP'S MILK CHEESE & HAZELNUTS

serves 4–6

¾ cup (4 oz/125 g) hazelnuts

1 large or 2 medium heads butter lettuce

3 Tbsp extra-virgin olive oil

1 Tbsp white balsamic vinegar

1 Tbsp champagne vinegar

2 tsp honey

Salt

4 oz (125 g) aged sheep's milk cheese, crumbled

If you can find it, the creamy, tart-rinded Ossau-Iraty cheese from the Pyrenees region of France is delicious in contrast with the sweet honey and crunchy nuts in this salad. Aged pecorino or Manchego is a nice pick too. Serve with a crisp, dry rosé.

In a dry frying pan, toast the hazelnuts over medium-low heat, stirring, until fragrant and starting to brown, about 5 minutes. Wrap the hazelnuts in a towel and rub to remove the skins. Pour onto a plate to cool slightly, then chop coarsely and set aside.

Tear the larger leaves of lettuce into several pieces, but keep the medium and small leaves whole. You should have 4–5 cups (4–5 oz/125–155 g).

In a large serving bowl, whisk together the oil, the white balsamic and champagne vinegars, the honey, and ½ tsp salt. Add the lettuce leaves and toss to coat well. Add half of the cheese and half of the hazelnuts and toss well. Top with the remaining cheese and nuts and serve.

FEBRUARY

11

11

MESCLUN & ROASTED PEARS WITH GRAINY MUSTARD VINAIGRETTE

serves 6

Grainy mustard, more robust and less pungent than some other varieties, is delicious mixed with apple juice and cider vinegar in this dressing. The pears turn sweet when roasted, and toasted pumpkin seeds add an appealing crunch. Try this salad with roasted apples or Asian pears as well.

3 firm pears, preferably Anjou or Bosc

2 Tbsp extra-virgin olive oil, plus ¼ cup (2 fl oz/60 ml)

Salt and freshly ground pepper

3 Tbsp pumpkin seeds

¼ cup (2 fl oz/60 ml) cider vinegar

3 Tbsp apple juice

1 large shallot, minced

2 tsp whole-grain mustard

1½ tsp firmly packed light brown sugar

2 large Belgian endives

4 heaping cups (4 oz/125 g) mesclun

Preheat the oven to 400°F (200°C). Halve the pears lengthwise, then core and slice lengthwise about ½ inch (12 mm) thick. Put the slices on a rimmed baking sheet, drizzle with the 2 Tbsp oil, sprinkle with ¼ tsp salt, and toss to coat. Arrange in a single layer and roast for 20 minutes. Carefully turn the slices over and continue to roast until they are golden brown and tender but still hold their shape, about 20 minutes. Let cool.

Meanwhile, in a dry frying pan, toast the pumpkin seeds over medium-low heat, stirring, until starting to brown, 5 minutes. Pour into a bowl and stir in a pinch of salt.

In a small bowl, whisk together the vinegar, apple juice, shallot, mustard, sugar, ¼ tsp salt, and ⅛ tsp pepper. Add the ¼ cup oil in a thin stream, whisking constantly until the dressing is smooth. Taste and adjust the seasonings.

Slice the endives crosswise. In a large bowl, toss together the mesclun, endive, a big pinch of salt, and several grindings of pepper. Whisk the dressing to recombine, then drizzle about half of it over the greens and toss well. Taste and adjust the seasonings. Divide the dressed greens among individual plates. Arrange the roasted pear slices on top of the greens and drizzle with enough of the dressing to coat the greens lightly; you may not need all of it. Sprinkle with the pumpkin seeds and serve.

12

SALAD OF MANDARINS, ROASTED BEETS & FARMER CHEESE

serves 6

To make toasted spicy-sweet pecans, preheat the oven to 325°F (165°C). In a bowl, toss ½ cup (2 oz/60 g) pecan halves with 1 Tbsp melted unsalted butter; 2 Tbsp sugar; ½ tsp salt; and ¼ tsp cayenne pepper until evenly coated. Spread on a rimmed baking sheet and bake until lightly toasted, about 10 minutes.

4 beets (about 1¼ lb/625 g total weight)

FOR THE HONEY VINAIGRETTE

2 Tbsp wildflower honey

2 Tbsp red wine vinegar

2 Tbsp rice vinegar

Salt and freshly ground pepper

½ cup (4 fl oz/125 ml) extra-virgin olive oil

2 heads Bibb lettuce, leaves left whole

6 satsumas, clementines, or other seedless mandarin oranges, peeled and segmented

Toasted Spicy-Sweet Pecans *(left)*, chopped

7–8 oz (220–250 g) smooth-style farmer cheese or other soft cheese such as Crescenza

Preheat the oven to 400°F (200°C). Trim off the leafy beet tops. Wrap the beets in foil and roast on a baking sheet until easily pierced with the tip of a knife, about 1 hour. Remove from the oven and let cool in the foil. Unwrap, peel, and cut each beet into slices ¼ inch (6 mm) thick. Set aside.

Meanwhile, to make the vinaigrette, in a bowl, whisk together the honey and vinegars. Season with salt and pepper, whisking until dissolved. Add the oil in a thin stream, whisking constantly until the dressing is smooth. Taste and adjust the seasonings.

Divide the lettuce among individual plates. Arrange the mandarin segments and beet slices on top of the lettuce. Drizzle with the vinaigrette. Top each serving with an equal amount of the pecans and a dollop of the cheese and serve.

13

WINTER GREENS WITH LEMON VINAIGRETTE

serves 4

FOR THE LEMON VINAIGRETTE

½ Tbsp fresh lemon juice

½ small shallot, minced

Salt and freshly ground pepper

1 Tbsp extra-virgin olive oil

¼ cup (1 oz/30 g) walnut pieces

1 head yellow-tipped Belgian endive, cored and cut lengthwise into narrow strips

1 head red-tipped Belgian endive, cored and cut lengthwise into narrow strips

1 bunch watercress, tough stems removed

The bitter greens in this salad demand an emphatic dressing, and this vinaigrette—heavy on the lemon and light on the oil—rises to the challenge. Serve as a refreshing counterpoint to a rich winter braise.

To make the vinaigrette, in a small bowl, whisk together the lemon juice and shallot. Season with salt and pepper to taste. Let stand for 30 minutes to let the shallot flavor mellow. Add the oil in a thin stream, whisking constantly until the dressing is well blended.

In a small frying pan over medium heat, toast the walnuts, shaking the pan often, until fragrant, about 7 minutes. Transfer to a small dish and set aside.

In a large bowl, combine the endives and watercress. Whisk the vinaigrette to recombine, drizzle it over the greens, and toss to coat the leaves well. Divide the salad among individual plates, top with the toasted walnuts, and serve.

14

SPINACH SALAD WITH ORANGES & ROASTED BEETS

serves 6

4 small beets (about ½ lb/250 g total weight)

FOR THE SHALLOT DRESSING

1 Tbsp fresh lemon juice, plus more as needed

1 shallot, minced

Salt and freshly ground pepper

3 Tbsp extra-virgin olive oil

2 large navel oranges, peeled and segmented with a knife

6 cups (6 oz/185 g) baby spinach

Plump, sweet navel oranges turn up frequently in winter salads—and not just fruit salads. They add appealing color and zing to this mix of beets and spinach, a good prelude to a main course of pork chops or duck. Red-fleshed blood oranges, at their delicious peak during winter, can be used in place of the navel oranges.

Preheat the oven to 375°F (190°C). Trim off the leafy beet tops. Wrap the beets in foil and roast on a baking sheet until easily pierced with the tip of a knife, 45–60 minutes. Remove from the oven and let cool in the foil.

Meanwhile, in a small bowl, combine the lemon juice and shallot. Season with salt and pepper. Let stand for 30 minutes to allow the shallot flavor to mellow, then add the oil in a thin stream, whisking constantly until the dressing is well blended.

Cut a slice off the top and bottom of each orange. Stand each upright and, following the contour of the fruit, cut away all the peel and white pith. Cut along both sides of each segment to free it from the membrane.

When the beets are cool enough to handle, peel and cut them into wedges about the size of the orange segments. Put the beet wedges in a bowl and toss with just enough of the dressing to coat them lightly.

Put the spinach in a large bowl and add the orange segments. Add the remaining dressing and toss to coat. Taste and adjust the seasoning with salt, pepper, and lemon juice.

Divide the spinach and oranges among individual plates. Arrange the beets on top and serve.

15

CRAB SALAD WITH MEYER LEMON & FRESH MANGO

serves 6

Meyer lemons, sweeter and more fragrant than traditional lemons, infuse the mayonnaise dressing for this salad with their heady citrus perfume. Creamy-textured mangoes add a tropical flair, but sweet, delicate crabmeat is the star of the show.

2 Meyer lemons or regular lemons

1½ lb (750 g) cooked crabmeat, picked over for shell fragments

¾ cup (6 fl oz/185 ml) mayonnaise

Salt and freshly ground pepper

2 Tbsp extra-virgin olive oil

2 mangoes

1 large head red-leaf lettuce, leaves torn into bite-sized pieces

4 green onions, including tender green parts, thinly sliced

Finely grate the zest of 1 lemon. Halve both of the lemons and juice the halves to measure out 5 Tbsp (2½ fl oz/75 ml) juice.

In a bowl, combine the crabmeat, mayonnaise, lemon zest, 4 Tbsp (2 fl oz/60 ml) of the lemon juice, ¾ tsp salt, and ½ tsp pepper and stir gently to mix. Taste and adjust the seasonings.

In a small bowl, whisk together the remaining 1 Tbsp lemon juice, ⅛ tsp salt, and several grindings of pepper. Add the oil in a thin stream, whisking constantly until well blended. Taste and adjust the seasonings.

Peel the mangoes and stand a fruit stem end up with a narrow side toward you. Position a sharp knife about 1 inch (2.5 cm) from the stem and cut down the length of one side, just missing the large pit. Repeat on the other side of the pit. Cut the flesh into pieces about 1½ inches (4 cm) long and about ¼ inch (6 mm) thick. Repeat with the remaining mango. Don't worry if the mango pieces are uneven or irregular in shape.

In a large bowl, toss the lettuce with a pinch of salt and a few grindings of pepper. Whisk the dressing to recombine, then drizzle it over the lettuce and toss well. Taste and adjust the seasonings. Divide the dressed lettuce among individual plates, arranging it in a mound in the center. Place a spoonful of the crab mixture on each mound of lettuce. Scatter the mango pieces around the crab, sprinkle with the green onions, and serve.

16

BROCCOLI & CAULIFLOWER SLAW WITH RAISINS & NUTS

serves 4–6

An old-fashioned mayonnaise dressing made with a hint of sugar and vinegar gives this contemporary salad the feel of comfort food. Adjust the creaminess by adding more or less mayonnaise and milk. For a variation, currants, dried cherries, or dried cranberries could be used instead of raisins.

3 heads of broccoli, cut into quarters, stem end intact, tough stems peeled

½ head cauliflower

1 cup (6 oz/185 g) pine nuts

1½ cups (9 oz/280 g) raisins

½ cup (4 fl oz/125 ml) mayonnaise

¼ cup (2 fl oz/60 ml) milk

2 tsp sugar

2–3 tsp red wine vinegar

Using a mandoline or box grater, thinly slice the broccoli quarters. Cut the pieces in half. Do the same with the cauliflower.

In a small frying pan, toast the pine nuts over medium-low heat until just turning golden brown, 3–4 minutes. Pour onto a plate to let cool.

In a bowl, combine the broccoli, cauliflower, raisins, and pine nuts. In another bowl, mix together the mayonnaise, milk, sugar, and vinegar to taste. Pour the dressing over the salad, toss to coat, and serve.

17

WALDORF SALAD

serves 6–8

The traditional Waldorf salad gets a fresh twist with the addition of dried cranberries, a drizzling of sherry vinegar, and a splash of fragrant walnut oil.

½ cup (2 oz/60 g) walnuts

4 large Granny Smith apples, left unpeeled

2 Tbsp fresh lemon juice

1 cup (5 oz/155 g) chopped celery

2 green onions, including tender green parts, chopped

½ cup (3 oz/90 g) dried cranberries

⅓ cup (3 fl oz/80 ml) walnut oil

3 Tbsp sherry vinegar

In a small frying pan, toast the walnuts over medium-low heat, stirring, until fragrant and starting to brown, about 5 minutes. Pour onto a plate to cool and then chop coarsely.

Halve and core the apples, cut into ½-inch (12-mm) pieces, and add to a large bowl with the lemon juice. Add the celery, green onions, cranberries, and toasted walnuts. Add the walnut oil and vinegar, toss to mix, and serve.

18

This salad, popular on Thai-restaurant menus, is easy to prepare at home. Fish sauce, essential to creating authentic Southeast Asian flavor, is widely available at well-stocked supermarkets or Asian groceries. The low-fat vinaigrette and lean meat make this a healthful main-course salad.

THAI BEEF SALAD

serves 4

FOR THE SPICY DRESSING

3 Tbsp Asian fish sauce

3 Tbsp fresh lime juice

2 tsp sugar

1–2 tsp minced Thai chiles with seeds

1 flank steak, ¾–1 lb (375–500 g)

Salt and freshly ground pepper

2 tsp peanut oil

1 large head butter lettuce, torn into bite-sized pieces

1 cup (5 oz/155 g) thinly sliced English cucumber

½ cup (2 oz/60 g) thinly sliced sweet onion or red onion

½ cup (2½ oz/75 g) red bell pepper strips

½ cup (¾ oz/20 g) lightly packed torn fresh mint leaves

½ cup (¾ oz/20 g) lightly packed torn fresh cilantro leaves

¼ cup (⅓ oz/10 g) lightly packed torn fresh Thai or regular basil leaves

To make the dressing, in a large bowl, stir together the fish sauce, lime juice, sugar, and chiles until well blended. Set aside.

Preheat the broiler or prepare a charcoal or gas grill for direct-heat cooking over high heat. Sprinkle the steak evenly with salt and pepper and rub into the meat. Brush lightly on both sides with the oil.

To cook the steak, place it on a broiler pan and slide it under the broiler about 4 inches (10 cm) from the heat source, or place it on the grill rack. Cook, turning once, until the meat is seared on the outside and cooked rare to medium-rare in the center, about 4 minutes per side. Transfer the steak to a cutting board and let rest for 20 minutes.

Cut the steak across the grain into very thin slices, then cut each slice in half lengthwise if needed. Add the slices of meat to the dressing and toss to coat. Add the lettuce, cucumber, onion, bell pepper, mint, cilantro, and basil, toss to coat, and serve.

19

Frozen shrimp is reliably good in quality, and you can keep it on hand in the freezer for pulling together a salad like this one. Thaw the shrimp overnight in the refrigerator, and then let it come to room temperature for at least 30 minutes before adding it to the warm beans.

CANNELLINI BEAN, FENNEL & SHRIMP SALAD

serves 6

1½ cans (15 oz/470 g each) cannellini or other white beans, drained and rinsed

1 fennel bulb (about 1 lb/500 g), trimmed, fronds reserved

½ tsp fennel seeds

3 Tbsp red wine vinegar

½ tsp minced garlic

Salt and freshly ground pepper

¼ cup (2 fl oz/60 ml) extra-virgin olive oil

1 lb (500 g) cooked medium shrimp, peeled and deveined

½ cup (2 oz/60 g) thinly sliced red onion

Put the beans in a saucepan and place over medium-low heat. Stir occasionally until warm. Remove from the heat and cover to keep warm.

Have ready a bowl of ice water. Quarter the fennel bulb lengthwise. Add the fennel to the ice water and let soak for 30 minutes. Drain well and thinly slice crosswise. Finely chop ½ cup (¾ oz/20 g) of the reserved fennel fronds.

In a mortar, coarsely crush the fennel seeds with a pestle. In a large bowl, whisk together the vinegar, crushed fennel seeds, garlic, ½ tsp salt, and pepper to taste. Add the oil in a thin stream, whisking constantly until the dressing is well blended.

Put the shrimp in a bowl and add the fennel, chopped fennel fronds, beans, and onion. Fold gently until all the ingredients are evenly distributed and serve.

20

JICAMA-MANGO SALAD
WITH CILANTRO DRESSING

serves 4

½ cup (3 oz/90 g) minced red onion

FOR THE CILANTRO DRESSING

6 Tbsp (½ oz/15 g) chopped fresh cilantro

¼ cup (2 fl oz/60 ml) plus 2 tsp
extra-virgin olive oil

3 Tbsp fresh lime juice

3 Tbsp fresh orange juice

4 tsp honey

¼ tsp chili powder

Salt and freshly ground pepper

5 small mangoes (about 3½ lb/1.75 kg
total weight)

1 small jicama (about 1 lb/500 g total weight)

Chili powder for garnish

Crisp jicama and sweet, silky mango are enlivened by a honeyed, slightly tart vinaigrette in this refreshing salad with tropical Latin flavors. Pungent, lemony cilantro adds complexity, and chili powder brings subtle heat.

In a small bowl, soak the onion in cold water to cover for 15 minutes.

To make the dressing, in a food processor or blender, combine the cilantro, oil, lime juice, orange juice, honey, chili powder, a scant ½ tsp salt, and a few grindings of pepper and purée until smooth. Taste and adjust the seasonings.

Peel the mangoes. Stand a fruit stem end up with a narrow side toward you. Position a sharp knife about 1 inch (2.5 cm) from the stem and cut down the length of one side, just missing the large pit. Repeat on the other side of the pit. Cut the flesh into ½-inch (12-mm) pieces. Repeat with the remaining mangoes. Peel the jicama and cut the flesh into ½-inch pieces.

Drain the onion in a fine-mesh sieve and transfer to a bowl. Add the mango, jicama, ½ tsp salt, and ¼ tsp pepper. Drizzle with the dressing and toss well. Taste and adjust the seasonings.

Divide the salad among plates. Garnish each serving with a light dusting of chili powder and serve.

21

FEBRUARY

GARLICKY PASTA SALAD
WITH CRAB & SHRIMP

serves 4

1½ lb (750 g) asparagus,
tough ends trimmed

Salt and freshly ground pepper

¾ lb (375 g) penne, fusilli, or tubetti

1 clove garlic, minced

3 Tbsp balsamic vinegar

1 tsp Dijon mustard

2 Tbsp prepared aioli

¼ cup (2 fl oz/60 ml) extra-virgin olive oil

¼ lb (125 g) cooked crabmeat, picked over
for shell fragments

¼ lb (125 g) cooked small shrimp,
peeled and deveined

2 tsp finely chopped fresh tarragon

1 small head green- or red-leaf lettuce,
leaves torn into bite-sized pieces

The ingredients that you add to a pasta salad can be as varied as the shape of pasta you choose. Replace the crab, shrimp, and asparagus in this recipe with shredded poached chicken and shelled peas, or experiment with your own combinations of meat, poultry, or seafood and vegetables.

If the asparagus spears are thick, peel them to within about 2 inches (5 cm) of the tips. Cut the spears on the diagonal into pieces.

Bring a large pot of salted water to a boil. Add the pasta and cook, stirring occasionally to prevent sticking, until al dente, according to package directions. About 4 minutes before the pasta is finished cooking, add the asparagus to the boiling water and cook until crisp-tender, 3–4 minutes. Drain the pasta and asparagus, rinse under cold running water to halt the cooking, and drain again.

In a large bowl, whisk together the garlic, vinegar, mustard, aioli, ½ tsp salt, and a pinch of pepper. Add the oil in a thin stream, whisking constantly until smooth. Add the pasta and asparagus to the dressing and toss to coat evenly.

Add the crabmeat (breaking it up slightly), shrimp, and tarragon to the pasta and toss to combine. Arrange the lettuce on plates, top with the pasta salad, and serve.

22

FEBRUARY

Woodsy, aromatic thyme pairs beautifully with the hearty flavors of winter. Here, it enhances brown lentils topped with crisp bacon, sweet roasted carrots and sautéed onions, and earthy kale.

LENTIL & KALE SALAD WITH BACON

serves 6

6 small carrots, peeled and finely chopped

4 Tbsp (2 fl oz/60 ml) extra-virgin olive oil

Salt and freshly ground pepper

1 large red onion, thinly sliced

1 large bunch kale, stemmed and thinly sliced crosswise

4 large cloves garlic

10 fresh thyme sprigs

1 cup (7 oz/220 g) brown lentils, picked over and rinsed

4 cups (32 fl oz/1 l) chicken broth

6 slices bacon

1 tsp sherry vinegar

Preheat the oven to 400°F (200°C). Line a rimmed baking sheet with foil. Put the carrots on the prepared sheet, drizzle with 2 Tbsp of the oil, sprinkle with ¾ tsp salt and ¼ tsp pepper, and toss to coat evenly. Spread the carrots in a single layer and roast until tender, about 15 minutes, stirring once or twice. Let cool to room temperature.

Meanwhile, in a nonstick frying pan, warm the remaining 2 Tbsp oil over medium heat. Add the onion, ¼ tsp salt, and several grindings of pepper and sauté until the onion is soft and lightly caramelized, about 15 minutes. Set aside.

Bring a saucepan two-thirds full of water to a boil over high heat. Add 1 Tbsp salt and the sliced kale and cook until tender, about 6 minutes. Drain and set the saucepan aside.

Place the garlic and thyme on a square of cheesecloth, bring the corners together, and secure with kitchen string. In the same saucepan you used to cook the kale, combine the lentils, broth, ½ tsp salt, ¼ tsp pepper, and the cheesecloth sachet and bring to a boil over high heat. Reduce the heat to medium and simmer, uncovered, until the lentils are tender but not mushy, 15–20 minutes. ↠

While the lentils are cooking, in a large frying pan, cook the bacon over medium heat, turning once, until crisp and browned, about 7 minutes. Transfer to paper towels to drain. Let cool, and then coarsely chop.

Drain the lentils, discard the sachet, and return the lentils to the saucepan. Stir in the kale, vinegar, and ½ tsp salt. Taste and adjust the seasonings. Transfer the lentil mixture to a serving bowl. Top with the sautéed onion, roasted carrots, and bacon, and serve.

23

FEBRUARY

This crunchy, vibrant-tasting salad is the perfect accompaniment to hearty roast meats and stews. For an even more beautiful presentation, add a few slices of orange and layer on a platter, Caprese style.

SHAVED FENNEL SALAD WITH ORANGE DRESSING

serves 4

2 Tbsp fresh orange juice

Salt and freshly ground pepper

2 Tbsp extra-virgin olive oil

2 fennel bulbs, trimmed

Parmesan cheese for shaving

In a small bowl, whisk together the orange juice and ½ tsp each salt and pepper. Add the oil in a thin stream, whisking constantly until the dressing is smooth.

Cut the fennel bulb in half lengthwise. Using a mandoline or a very sharp knife, cut the halves crosswise into paper-thin slices.

Put the fennel slices in a bowl and drizzle with the dressing. Toss to combine and arrange on salad plates. Using a vegetable peeler, shave the cheese over each salad and serve.

24

GRILLED CHICKEN CAESAR SALAD

serves 4

Pounding the chicken breasts lightly before cooking helps them cook more evenly. Place each breast between two sheets of wax paper or plastic wrap and pound gently with a meat mallet to an even thickness. Repeat with the remaining breasts.

FOR THE CAESAR DRESSING

1 large egg (see Note) or 1 Tbsp mayonnaise

2 cloves garlic, minced

1–3 anchovy fillets, finely chopped (optional)

2 tsp Dijon mustard

Juice of 1 lemon

1 tsp Worcestershire sauce

1 tsp red wine vinegar

4 Tbsp (2 fl oz/60 ml) extra-virgin olive oil

Salt and freshly ground pepper

1¼ lb (625 g) skinless, boneless chicken breast halves, pounded lightly to an even thickness

Olive oil

3 romaine lettuce hearts

Parmesan cheese for shaving

To make the dressing, in a blender, combine the egg or mayonnaise, garlic, anchovies to taste (if using), mustard, lemon juice, Worcestershire sauce, vinegar, extra-virgin olive oil, ½ tsp salt, and a generous grinding of pepper. Purée until smooth, and set aside.

Prepare a charcoal or gas grill for direct-heat cooking over high heat. Alternatively, preheat a stove-top grill pan over high heat. Brush both sides of the chicken breasts with oil and season generously with salt and pepper. Place the chicken on the grill rack or in the grill pan and cook, turning once, until opaque throughout, 4–5 minutes per side. Transfer to a cutting board and let stand for 5–7 minutes. Cut on the diagonal into slices.

Meanwhile, in a large bowl, combine the lettuce and dressing and toss to coat evenly. Arrange the lettuce on individual plates and top with the chicken slices. Using a vegetable peeler, shave the cheese over each salad and serve.

Note: Raw egg can carry salmonella. The risks involved in salmonella poisoning are greatest for children, the elderly, pregnant women, and anyone with a compromised immune system.

25

BABY SPINACH WITH GINGER-GLAZED SCALLOPS

serves 4

Grapefruit and scallops are excellent partners. Play up this affinity by adding a few segments of carefully peeled grapefruit to each plate. For a more pronounced ginger flavor, pound the ginger in a mortar, or crush it as you would a garlic clove with the flat side of a chef's knife.

FOR THE CITRUS VINAIGRETTE

1 Tbsp minced shallot

½ cup (4 fl oz/125 ml) fresh grapefruit juice

1½ Tbsp fresh lime juice

1½ tsp fresh lemon juice

1½ tsp grapeseed oil

Salt

2½ Tbsp soy sauce

1½ Tbsp peeled and grated fresh ginger

1½ tsp honey

½ tsp Dijon mustard

¾ lb (375 g) baby spinach leaves

8 sea scallops, tough muscles removed

2½ tsp grapeseed oil

To make the vinaigrette, in a small saucepan, combine the minced shallot and the grapefruit juice and let stand for about 10 minutes. Add the lime and lemon juices and place the pan over medium-high heat. Bring to a boil and cook until the liquid is reduced slightly, to about ½ cup (4 fl oz/125 ml), 1–2 minutes. Remove and whisk in the 1½ tsp oil in a thin stream until well blended. Stir in ¼ tsp salt and set aside.

In a small bowl or cup, stir together the soy sauce, ginger, honey, and mustard and set aside.

Just before beginning to cook the scallops, put the spinach in a bowl and pour the vinaigrette over it. Toss well. Divide the dressed spinach among individual plates.

Pat the scallops dry. In a frying pan large enough to hold all the scallops in a single layer, warm the 2½ tsp oil over medium-high heat. When it is hot, add the scallops and sear, turning once, until golden, about 30 seconds on each side. Add the soy sauce mixture, reduce the heat to low, and turn the scallops in the sauce for about 45 seconds. They will become a deep mahogany brown.

Divide the scallops among the plates, placing them on the spinach. Drizzle with any sauce remaining in the pan and serve.

26

Tangy citrus, dried fruit, and toasted pine nuts flavor this savory Middle Eastern salad. It is hearty enough for a main course, and it also makes a delicious side dish to accompany simple broiled fish or roast chicken. You can substitute regular couscous, Israeli couscous, or fregola, a Sardinian pasta similar to Israeli couscous, for the whole-wheat couscous.

COUSCOUS SALAD WITH DRIED FRUIT & PINE NUTS

serves 4

½ cup (3 oz/90 g) pine nuts

⅛ tsp saffron threads

1½ Tbsp extra-virgin olive oil

1½ cups (9 oz/280 g) instant whole-wheat couscous

⅓ cup (2 oz/60 g) thinly slivered dried apricots

¼ cup (1½ oz/45 g) golden raisins

Salt and freshly ground pepper

¼ tsp ground cinnamon

½ cup (¾ oz/20 g) chopped fresh mint leaves

1 tsp grated orange zest

¼ cup (2 fl oz/60 ml) fresh orange juice

¼ cup (2 fl oz/60 ml) fresh lemon juice

In a small frying pan, toast the pine nuts over medium-low heat, stirring, until starting to brown, 3–4 minutes. Pour onto a plate to cool. In the same frying pan, shake the saffron threads over medium heat until fragrant and a shade darker, about 1 minute. Transfer to a small bowl and, when cool, crumble with your fingertips.

In a large heatproof bowl, drizzle the oil over the couscous and mix well to coat. Scatter the couscous with the apricots and raisins.

In a small saucepan, bring 2 cups (16 fl oz/ 500 ml) water to a boil. Stir in the saffron, ½ tsp salt, and the cinnamon and pour over the couscous. Cover the bowl tightly with foil and let stand until the couscous is tender and the liquid is absorbed, about 5 minutes.

Remove the foil and fluff the couscous grains well with a fork. Stir in the mint, pine nuts, orange zest, orange juice, and lemon juice. Season with pepper and additional salt and serve.

27

Walnut oil has a rather short shelf life, only about 6–8 months. To forestall spoilage, check the date of the pressing on the label to make sure it's fairly fresh, and store the oil in the refrigerator.

BRUSSELS SPROUT & ARUGULA SALAD WITH WALNUTS

serves 4

1 lb (500 g) Brussels sprouts, trimmed

½ cup (2 oz/60 g) chopped walnuts

1½ Tbsp walnut oil

1 Tbsp cider vinegar

Salt and freshly ground pepper

1 cup (1 oz/30 g) arugula leaves

Using a mandoline, thinly shave the Brussels sprouts lengthwise.

In a small frying pan, toast the walnuts over medium-low heat, stirring, until starting to brown, about 5 minutes. Let cool.

Put the shaved Brussels sprouts in a bowl and add the walnut oil, vinegar, ½ tsp pepper, and ¼ tsp salt and gently mix.

Divide the arugula among individual plates. Spoon the Brussels sprouts and their juices over the arugula, garnish with the walnuts, and serve.

28

For an interesting visual take on this classic salad, use multicolored carrots—from white to purple—from your local farmers' market. Serve with grilled lamb or beef.

MOROCCAN CARROT SALAD

serves 4–6

6 carrots, trimmed and peeled

3 Tbsp extra-virgin olive oil

Pinch ground cumin

Rosewater or lemon juice to taste

Salt and freshly ground pepper

3 Tbsp chopped pistachios

2 Tbsp chopped fresh cilantro

With a vegetable peeler, shave the carrots into a large bowl. Mix in the oil, cumin, and a splash of rosewater or lemon juice, and season to taste with salt and pepper. Toss with the pistachios and cilantro and serve.

With signs of the frost waning, ease into spring with young greens such as frisée, dandelion, mâche, fava leaves, and baby arugula and spinach. Try them in simple, fresh combinations, topped with tangy cheese, toasted nuts, or a tender salmon fillet served cold or warm. Or, lightly dress spring greens like pea shoots and watercress with lemon juice, herbs, and shallots. Seasonal favorites like peas, haricots verts, new potatoes, and asparagus make perfect toppings.

1
SHAVED ARTICHOKE
& BLUE CHEESE SALAD
page 58

2
PAN-SEARED SALMON WITH
PEA SHOOTS & WATERCRESS
page 58

3
ISRAELI COUSCOUS SALAD
WITH MINT VINAIGRETTE
page 61

8
WARM FARRO SALAD WITH HERBS
page 63

9
WILD RICE & LEEK SALAD
page 64

10
MESCLUN SALAD WITH
BALSAMIC VINAIGRETTE
page 64

15
WHEAT BERRY SALAD WITH WALNUTS
& SUN-DRIED TOMATOES
page 69

16
FINGERLING POTATO SALAD
WITH SHRIMP & DILL
page 69

17
ROASTED ASPARAGUS SALAD
page 70

22
SPRING PEAS WITH PANCETTA,
MINT & RICOTTA SALATA
page 73

23
OLD-FASHIONED MACARONI
SALAD WITH SWEET PICKLES
page 75

24
POMELO, CILANTRO
& CASHEW SALAD
page 75

29
MÂCHE, RADISH, BLUE CHEESE
& SUGARED PECAN SALAD
page 78

30
ARUGULA SALAD WITH
PECORINO & PINE NUTS
page 78

31
GREEN APPLE & CELERY SALAD
page 78

4
FAVA GREENS WITH CHICKEN, PECANS & KUMQUATS
page 61

5
SLICED FLANK STEAK, HARICOT VERT & POTATO SALAD
page 62

6
BUTTER LETTUCE WITH DIJON VINAIGRETTE
page 62

7
WARM BEEF & WATERCRESS SALAD
page 63

11
ADISH, FENNEL & PARSLEY SALAD
page 66

12
SEARED SCALLOP, ORANGE & RED ONION SALAD
page 66

13
LENTIL & PARSLEY SALAD WITH DUCK BREAST
page 67

14
FRISÉE SALAD WITH HERBED FRESH CHEESE
page 67

18
CLASSIC SALADE NIÇOISE
page 70

19
CHICKEN & ORZO SALAD
page 72

20
ASPARAGUS & SMOKED SALMON SALAD WITH TARRAGON CREAM
page 72

21
SMOKED TROUT SALAD WITH CUCUMBER & DILL
page 73

25
MARINATED EDAMAME, CUCUMBER & RED BELL PEPPER SALAD
page 76

26
CHICKPEA SALAD WITH MINT
page 76

27
SOBA NOODLE SALAD WITH SUGAR SNAP PEAS & SOY-PEANUT DRESSING
page 77

28
ROASTED POTATO SALAD WITH SPRING ONION DRESSING
page 77

march

1

SHAVED ARTICHOKE
& BLUE CHEESE SALAD

serves 4

⅓ cup (2 oz/60 g) almonds

1 or 2 lemons

8 small to medium artichokes

4 Tbsp (2 fl oz/60 ml) extra-virgin olive oil

¼ cup (½ oz/15 g) frisée

Salt and freshly ground pepper

2 Tbsp crumbled blue cheese

Plan to serve this salad as soon as you're done tossing it, as the artichokes will start turning brown fast. Artichokes are notoriously hard to pair with wine, but a light pinot noir would match nicely with the blue cheese.

In a small frying pan, toast the almonds over medium-low heat, stirring, until fragrant and starting to brown, about 5 minutes. Pour onto a plate to cool, chop coarsely, and set aside.

Squeeze the juice of 1 lemon half into a large bowl of cold water. Snap off the tough outer leaves of each artichoke until you reach the pale green inner leaves. Trim the stem flush with the base and trim away the dark green portions from the base. Cut off the top one-third of the artichokes, removing the pointed tips. Halve each artichoke lengthwise and, using a small spoon, remove the fuzzy choke. As each artichoke is trimmed, immerse it in the lemon water.

Using a mandoline or a very sharp knife, slice the artichokes thinly lengthwise. Put in a bowl, drizzle with 2 Tbsp of the olive oil, and toss well. Add the frisée, season with salt and pepper, drizzle with the remaining 2 Tbsp olive oil, and squeeze in the juice from 1 lemon half. Toss gently and season with salt and with more lemon juice, if needed. Scatter with the cheese and almonds and serve.

2

PAN-SEARED SALMON WITH
PEA SHOOTS & WATERCRESS

serves 8

FOR THE DRESSING

⅓ cup (3 fl oz/80 ml) fresh Meyer lemon or regular lemon juice

3 shallots, minced

Salt and freshly ground pepper

⅔ cup (5 fl oz/160 ml) extra-virgin olive oil

8 salmon fillets, each about ⅓ lb (155 g) and ½ inch (12 mm) thick, pin bones removed

½ cup (4 fl oz/125 ml) dry white wine

8 Tbsp (4 fl oz/125 ml) fresh lemon juice

5 cups (5 oz/155 g) watercress leaves

5 cups (5 oz/155 g) pea shoots

In this perfect spring salad, salmon and its pan juices become a topping for a tangle of sprightly greens dressed with a tangy lemon vinaigrette. Pea shoots, the clippings from young pea plants, have a mild pealike flavor. Look for them at well-stocked grocery stores, farmers' markets, or Asian markets—or substitute additional watercress.

To make the dressing, in a large bowl, combine the lemon juice, shallots, ½ tsp salt, and ½ tsp pepper. Whisk until the salt dissolves, then let stand for 30 minutes to allow the shallot flavor to mellow. Add the oil in a thin stream, whisking constantly until the dressing is well blended.

Meanwhile, to prepare the salmon, sprinkle 1½ tsp salt in a wide, heavy frying pan and place over medium-high heat until nearly smoking. Add the salmon fillets and sear for 2 minutes on one side. Turn and sear for 1 minute on the second side. Sprinkle with 1 tsp pepper. Reduce the heat to low, then pour in the white wine and 2 Tbsp of the lemon juice. Cover and cook until the juices are nearly absorbed and the fish is halfway cooked, about 3 minutes. Uncover and pour in 2 more Tbsp of the lemon juice and 3 Tbsp water. Re-cover and cook just until the fish flakes easily with a fork, about 3 minutes. Most of the pan juices will have been absorbed.

Whisk the dressing to recombine. Add the watercress and pea shoots to the dressing and toss gently to coat, then divide the greens among individual plates. Place a salmon fillet on each mound of greens.

Raise the heat under the frying pan to high, add the remaining 4 Tbsp (2 fl oz/60 ml) lemon juice and 1 Tbsp water, and stir to scrape up any browned bits on the pan bottom. Pour the pan juices evenly over the fish and serve.

3

ISRAELI COUSCOUS SALAD WITH MINT VINAIGRETTE

serves 4

1 Tbsp grapeseed oil

1 small onion, finely chopped

1½ cups (9 oz/280 g) Israeli couscous

2 cups (16 fl oz/500 ml) chicken broth

Salt and freshly ground pepper

FOR THE MINT VINAIGRETTE

3 Tbsp red wine vinegar

1 tsp Dijon mustard

¼ cup (2 fl oz/60 ml) extra-virgin olive oil

1 Tbsp finely chopped fresh mint

Serve this light Mediterranean-style salad with braised lamb shanks or grilled oregano-rubbed lamb chops or chicken breasts. For more color, you can add fresh pomegranate seeds or dried fruits to the mix.

In a saucepan, warm the grapeseed oil over medium heat. Add the onion and sauté until softened, about 5 minutes. Add the couscous and stir until the couscous begins to brown, about 6 minutes. Add the broth, ¾ tsp salt, and several grindings of pepper. Raise the heat to high and bring to a boil. Reduce the heat to medium-low, cover, and cook until the couscous is tender and all the liquid has been absorbed, about 8 minutes.

Meanwhile, to make the vinaigrette, in a small bowl, whisk together the vinegar, mustard, ¼ tsp salt, and a few grindings of pepper. Add the oil in a thin stream, whisking constantly until the dressing is smooth. Stir in the mint.

Transfer the couscous to a bowl, drizzle with ⅓–½ cup (3–4 fl oz/80–125 ml) of the vinaigrette, and fluff with a fork. Add more vinaigrette to taste (you may not need all of it) and serve.

4

FAVA GREENS WITH CHICKEN, PECANS & KUMQUATS

serves 4

30 kumquats (½–¾ lb/250–375 g)

¼ cup (2 fl oz/60 ml) blood orange–infused olive oil or extra-virgin olive oil

1 Tbsp honey

½ tsp ground ginger

2 Tbsp champagne vinegar

4 cups (4 oz/125 g) young fava leaves or baby spinach leaves, loosely packed

½ cup (2 oz/60 g) pecans

2 cups (¾ lb/375 g) chopped roasted chicken meat

In early spring, start checking your local farmers' market for fava greens, which are the leaves from the fava bean plant. They are a boon to fava bean lovers who often avoid the legume for its highly demanding prep. They taste milder than the beans and are delicious in salads, contributing a touch of sweetness and acidity.

Cut 20 of the kumquats crosswise into thin slices, removing any seeds as you go. Set aside and quarter the remaining kumquats lengthwise.

In a serving bowl, combine the oil and honey and whisk until the honey dissolves. Stir in the ginger and vinegar. Add the fava leaves, half the pecans, and the chicken and toss to combine. Divide among individual plates. Garnish with the remaining pecans and the sliced and quartered kumquats and serve.

5

Crumbled feta makes an equally delicious but lower-fat substitute for the blue cheese used here. When grilling or broiling steaks for dinner, cook an extra one and give it an encore performance at lunchtime the next day in a simple salad or sandwich.

SLICED FLANK STEAK, HARICOT VERT & POTATO SALAD

serves 6

1 flank steak, 1 lb (500 g)

Salt and freshly ground pepper

Olive oil

FOR THE DRESSING

¼ cup (2 fl oz/60 ml) red wine vinegar

¼ cup (1½ oz/45 g) minced shallots

2 tsp Dijon mustard

½ cup (4 fl oz/125 ml) extra-virgin olive oil

⅔ lb (315 g) haricots verts, stem ends trimmed, or other green beans, trimmed and cut on the diagonal into 2-inch (5-cm) lengths

2 lb (1 kg) red potatoes, left unpeeled

2½ tsp chopped fresh thyme

6 Tbsp (2 oz/60 g) crumbled blue cheese

Preheat the broiler or prepare a charcoal or gas grill for direct-heat cooking over high heat. Sprinkle the flank steak evenly with salt and pepper and rub into the meat. Brush lightly on both sides with olive oil.

To broil the steak, place it on a broiler pan and slide it under the broiler about 4 inches (10 cm) from the heat source. Broil, turning once, until the meat is seared on the outside and cooked rare to medium-rare in the center, about 4 minutes per side. To grill the steak, place it on the grill and cook, turning once, until seared on the outside and cooked rare to medium-rare in the center, about 4 minutes per side. Transfer the steak to a cutting board and let rest for 20 minutes.

To make the dressing, in a small bowl, whisk together the vinegar, shallot, mustard, 1 tsp salt, and 1 tsp pepper. Add the oil in a thin stream, whisking constantly.

Bring a large pot of lightly salted water to a boil. Add the beans and boil until just tender, 3–4 minutes for haricots verts or 5 minutes or longer for larger beans. Using a strainer, scoop out the beans and place under cold running water to halt the cooking. Pat dry with paper towels and set aside. »→

Add the potatoes to the boiling water. Boil until easily pierced with a sharp knife, 15–20 minutes. Drain.

When cool enough to handle, cut the cooked potatoes into 1-inch (2.5-cm) cubes. Place them in a large bowl along with the beans. Re-whisk the dressing and pour two-thirds of it over the potatoes and beans. Sprinkle with thyme, salt, and pepper and mix well. Taste and adjust the seasonings.

Cut the steak against the grain and on the diagonal into slices ¼ inch (6 mm) thick, then cut each slice in half lengthwise if needed.

To serve, divide the potato and bean mixture among individual plates. Mound some steak strips in the center of each portion. Drizzle the meat with the remaining dressing, sprinkle each serving with 1 Tbsp cheese, and serve.

6

At bistros in France, you'll often find a simple green salad like this one on the menu. Usually the butter lettuce leaves are served atop several spoonfuls of thick, mustard-laced vinaigrette in an individual bowl. It's the perfect simple side salad for any time of year.

BUTTER LETTUCE WITH DIJON VINAIGRETTE

serves 4–6

1 large or 2 medium heads butter lettuce

2 Tbsp red wine vinegar

2 tsp Dijon mustard

Salt

¼ cup (2 fl oz/60 ml) extra-virgin olive oil

Separate the heads of lettuce into individual leaves. Tear the larger leaves into several pieces; keep the medium and small leaves whole. You should have 4–5 cups (4–5 oz/125–155 g). Rinse the leaves, spin dry, and set aside.

In a large bowl, whisk together the vinegar, mustard, and ½ tsp salt. Add the oil in a thin stream, whisking constantly until the mixture is thick. Add the lettuce leaves and toss well to coat. Divide the salad among individual plates and serve.

7

WARM BEEF &
WATERCRESS SALAD

serves 4–6

This salad of seared beef with spicy watercress and paper-thin slices of onion is popular in both Cambodia and Vietnam. Fresh, peppery watercress and marinated raw onions are tossed with a lime vinaigrette, and the warm beef and pan juices are poured over the salad for an effect that is both cooling and crisp, savory and sweet.

FOR THE MARINADE

1 Tbsp peanut oil

3 cloves garlic, minced

1 Tbsp Asian fish sauce

½ tsp sugar

Freshly ground pepper

1 lb (500 g) beef tenderloin, cut into 1-inch (2.5-cm) cubes

FOR THE SAUCE

2 Tbsp fresh lime juice

1 Tbsp rice vinegar

1 Tbsp light soy sauce

1 Tbsp Asian fish sauce

1 tsp sugar

½ small yellow onion, sliced paper-thin

1 Tbsp peanut oil

2 green onions, including tender green parts, thinly sliced on the diagonal

3 cloves garlic, minced

2 cups (2 oz/60 g) loosely packed watercress, tough stems removed

To make the marinade, in a large bowl, combine the oil, garlic, fish sauce, sugar, and ⅛ tsp pepper and stir to mix well. Add the beef and stir to coat thoroughly. Cover and refrigerate for at least 2 hours or overnight.

To make the sauce, in a small bowl, whisk together the lime juice, vinegar, soy sauce, fish sauce, sugar, and ⅛ tsp pepper. Put the onion slices in a small bowl and drizzle with 1 Tbsp of the sauce. Set the onions and the remaining sauce aside.

In a large wok or frying pan, warm the oil over high heat. Add the beef and stir-fry until browned, 4–5 minutes. Add the green onions and garlic and stir-fry just until fragrant, a few seconds. Remove the pan from the heat, pour in the remaining sauce, and toss to mix.

To serve, toss the watercress with the marinated sliced onions and mound on a platter. Using a slotted spoon, spoon the beef over the greens, drizzle the pan juices over the beef, and serve.

8

WARM FARRO SALAD
WITH HERBS

serves 4–6

Farro is a great base for salads as the seasons change. It is both hearty and nutty, pairing nicely with spring's fresh herbs, new onions, and lemon juice. Serve the salad warm if there is still chill in the air, or at room temperature if you venture out on a picnic.

4 Tbsp (2 fl oz/60 ml) extra-virgin olive oil

1 bay leaf

1 fresh rosemary sprig

1 cup (6 oz/185 g) farro

2 cups (16 fl oz/500 ml) chicken broth

Salt and freshly ground pepper

Grated zest and juice of 1 lemon

¼ cup (½ oz/15 g) chopped fresh chives

¼ cup (⅓ oz/10 g) chopped fresh chervil

¼ cup (⅓ oz/10 g) chopped fresh flat-leaf parsley

¼ cup (¾ oz/20 g) chopped green onion, including tender green parts

1½ tsp chopped fresh tarragon

In a large saucepan, warm 2 Tbsp of the olive oil over medium heat. Add the bay leaf, rosemary, and farro and cook, stirring, for 1 minute. Add the broth, 2 cups (16 fl oz/ 500 ml) water, 1 tsp salt, and several grindings of pepper. Bring to a boil, then cover, reduce the heat, and simmer until the farro is tender and the liquid is absorbed, about 20 minutes. Remove from the heat and let cool slightly.

Discard the bay leaf and rosemary and transfer the farro to a bowl. Add the lemon zest and juice, the remaining 2 Tbsp olive oil, the chives, chervil, parsley, green onion, and tarragon and toss to combine. Season with salt and serve warm.

9

For the fullest flavors, make the salad in the morning and let it stand for several hours at room temperature before serving. Be sure that the zucchini are small and fresh; they turn bitter if stored for more than 2 or 3 days.

WILD RICE & LEEK SALAD

serves 10–12

2 large leeks, dark green leaf tops reserved, white and pale green parts thinly sliced

1½ cups (9 oz/280 g) wild rice, rinsed until water runs clear

Salt and freshly ground black pepper

1 cup (7 oz/220 g) brown rice

1 cup (6 oz/185 g) dried currants

¾ cup (3 oz/90 g) slivered blanched almonds

⅔ cup (5 fl oz/160 ml) olive oil

1 lb (500 g) slender zucchini, trimmed and cut into ½-inch (12-mm) chunks

½ cup (⅔ oz/20 g) chopped fresh flat-leaf parsley

2 tsp ground cumin

1 tsp ground allspice

1 tsp ground coriander

¼ tsp cayenne pepper

¼ cup (2 fl oz/60 ml) fresh lemon juice

In a large saucepan, combine 2 pieces of the dark green leek tops, the wild rice, 3 cups (24 fl oz/750 ml) water, and 1½ tsp salt over high heat. Bring to a boil, stir once, reduce the heat to low, cover, and simmer until the water is absorbed and the wild rice is fluffy and tender, 35–55 minutes. Remove from the heat and let stand, covered, for 10 minutes. Discard the leek tops and drain any excess water. Transfer to a large serving bowl.

While the wild rice is cooking, in another large saucepan, combine the brown rice, 2 cups (16 fl oz/500 ml) water, 2 more pieces of the leek tops, and 1 tsp salt over high heat. Bring to a boil, reduce the heat to low, cover, and simmer until the water is absorbed and the brown rice is fluffy and tender, 35–45 minutes. Remove from the heat and let stand, covered, for 10 minutes. Discard the leek tops and add the brown rice along with the currants to the bowl holding the wild rice.

In a small frying pan, toast the almonds over medium-low heat, stirring, until fragrant and starting to brown, about 5 minutes. Pour onto a plate to cool and set aside. ≫→

In a large frying pan, warm half of the oil over medium-high heat. Add the sliced leeks and ½ tsp salt and cook until tender, 4–5 minutes. Transfer to the bowl with the rices.

Heat the remaining olive oil in the same pan over high heat. Add the zucchini and cook until crisp-tender, 8–10 minutes. Stir in the parsley, cumin, allspice, coriander, cayenne, ¾ tsp salt, ½ tsp black pepper, and the lemon juice. Transfer to the bowl holding the rices, add the almonds, and mix gently. Taste and adjust the seasonings. Serve warm or at room temperature.

10

A simple salad of mesclun, a mix of tender, young lettuces and herbs, is a welcome foil to the typically rich dishes of a celebratory meal, making this salad perfect for a dinner party. The balsamic vinegar adds a pleasant touch of sweetness to the vinaigrette.

MESCLUN SALAD WITH BALSAMIC VINAIGRETTE

serves 8–10

FOR THE BALSAMIC VINAIGRETTE

2 Tbsp balsamic vinegar

2 tsp minced shallot

1 tsp Dijon mustard

Salt and freshly ground pepper

½ cup (4 fl oz/125 ml) extra-virgin olive oil

1–1¼ lb (500–625 g) mesclun

To make the vinaigrette, in a large bowl, whisk together the vinegar, shallot, mustard, and ¼ tsp salt. Let stand for 30 minutes to allow the flavor of the shallot to mellow. Add the oil in a thin stream, whisking constantly until the dressing is well blended.

Add the mesclun to the bowl with the vinaigrette and toss gently to coat evenly. Season with salt and pepper to taste and serve.

11

RADISH, FENNEL & PARSLEY SALAD

serves 6

2 fennel bulbs, trimmed

1 small bunch fresh flat-leaf parsley, stemmed and minced

12 radishes, thinly sliced

2 Tbsp fresh lemon juice

1 clove garlic, minced

Salt and freshly ground pepper

3 Tbsp extra-virgin olive oil

For a light, healthful meal, this crisp, refreshing salad with bursts of garlic and lemon is perfect served alongside panfried or poached white fish, such as sea bass, sole, or halibut.

Cut each fennel bulb in half through the stem end. Cut away any tough base portions. With a mandoline or very sharp knife, cut the bulbs crosswise into paper-thin slices. Put the slices in a bowl and mix in the parsley and radishes. Set aside.

In a small bowl, whisk together the lemon juice and garlic. Season with salt and pepper to taste. Add the oil in a thin stream, whisking constantly until the dressing is well blended.

Drizzle the dressing over the salad to coat evenly and serve.

12

SEARED SCALLOP, ORANGE & RED ONION SALAD

serves 4

½ red onion, thinly sliced

1½ Tbsp rice vinegar

3 oranges

½ cup (2½ oz/75 g) pitted mild green olives

2 Tbsp extra-virgin olive oil

1 lb (500 g) sea scallops, tough muscles removed

Salt and freshly ground pepper

2 Tbsp coarsely chopped fresh mint leaves

This salad makes a nice main-course lunch dish or a light supper, pairing nicely with a dry Riesling or a light-bodied red wine such as a pinot noir or Chianti.

Rinse the onion slices under cold running water, then drain. In a bowl, combine them with the rice vinegar and set aside.

Grate the zest of 1 orange to yield 1 tsp zest, and reserve. Cut a slice off the top and bottom of each orange. Stand each upright and, following the contour of the fruit, cut away all the peel and white pith. Slice the oranges in half lengthwise, then slice crosswise into thin half-rounds. In a bowl, combine the orange slices with the olives, reserved zest, and 1 Tbsp of the olive oil.

Pat the scallops dry and season them lightly with salt and pepper. In a large nonstick frying pan, warm the remaining 1 Tbsp oil over medium-high heat. Add the scallops and cook, turning once, until browned on both sides and opaque in the center, 4–5 minutes total. Take care not to overcook the scallops, as they go quickly from perfectly tender to overcooked and tough.

Add the onion (including the vinegar), the mint, a pinch of salt, and a few grindings of pepper to the orange mixture and mix gently. Divide the orange salad among dinner plates, top with the warm scallops, and serve.

13

LENTIL & PARSLEY SALAD WITH DUCK BREAST

serves 4

1½ cups (10½ oz/330 g) green French (du Puy) lentils, picked over and rinsed

2 fresh bay leaves, or 1 dried bay leaf

Salt and freshly ground pepper

½ tsp dried thyme

½ tsp ground juniper berries

1 duck breast, about ¾ lb (375 g)

1 Tbsp fresh lemon juice

3 Tbsp extra-virgin olive oil

¼ cup (⅓ oz/10 g) chopped fresh flat-leaf parsley, plus 1 Tbsp

2 small heads frisée, torn pale inner leaves only

A satisfying main-course salad, this dish has it all, nutritionally speaking: protein from the duck, calcium and iron from the lentils, and vitamins A and C from the frisée.

Put the lentils in a saucepan with 5 cups (40 fl oz/1.25 l) water, the bay leaves, and 1 tsp salt. Bring to a boil, reduce the heat to low, and simmer, uncovered, until tender, 20–30 minutes. Drain and let cool. Discard the bay leaves.

Preheat the oven to 450°F (230°C). Rub and press the thyme, juniper, ¼ tsp salt, and ¼ tsp of the pepper into the duck breast. Place on a baking sheet, skin side up. Roast until the skin is crisp but the meat is still pink at the center, 20–25 minutes. Let cool slightly, remove the skin, and cut the breast crosswise on the diagonal into very thin slices; set aside.

In a bowl, whisk together the lemon juice and ¼ tsp each salt and pepper. Add the oil in a thin stream, whisking constantly until the dressing is smooth. Mix in the ¼ cup parsley and the lentils; taste and adjust the seasonings.

Divide the frisée among individual plates and top with the lentils. Arrange the sliced duck over the lentils, garnish with the 1 Tbsp parsley, and serve.

14

FRISÉE SALAD WITH HERBED FRESH CHEESE

serves 4

4 small heads frisée

¾ cup (6 oz/185 g) fromage blanc, or 5 oz (155 g) fresh goat cheese, softened

1 Tbsp milk

½ Tbsp minced fresh chives

½ Tbsp minced fresh flat-leaf parsley

½ tsp minced fresh tarragon

½ small shallot, minced

½ Tbsp extra-virgin olive oil, plus 3 Tbsp

1 tsp red wine vinegar, plus 1 Tbsp

Salt and freshly ground pepper

Fresh and pretty, this salad is a perfect palate cleanser for a rich and meaty main course. If you like, serve it with warm bread or crostini for spreading the cheese on top.

Remove the outer leaves from each head of frisée until you reach the pale inner heart. Reserve the outer leaves for another use and tear the inner leaves into large bite-sized pieces; you should have about 2 cups (2 oz/60 g).

In a bowl, combine the cheese and milk and beat until smooth. Add the chives, parsley, tarragon, shallot, the ½ Tbsp olive oil, the 1 tsp vinegar, a pinch of salt, and a little pepper. Whisk together until smooth.

In a large bowl, toss the frisée with the 3 Tbsp olive oil and ¼ tsp salt until coated. Sprinkle with the 1 Tbsp vinegar and pepper to taste. Toss again.

Divide the salad among individual plates. Using 2 spoons, scoop up large dollops of cheese, place atop each salad, and serve.

15

WHEAT BERRY SALAD WITH WALNUTS & SUN-DRIED TOMATOES

serves 6

Wheat berries, wheat kernels minus the hull, have a fine crunch, a slightly sweet nutty taste, and a high nutritional value. Spelt, a type of wheat, or cracked wheat could be used instead.

1 cup (5 oz/155 g) wheat berries

Salt and freshly ground pepper

FOR THE VINAIGRETTE

1½ Tbsp finely chopped oil-packed sun-dried tomatoes

1 shallot, finely chopped

¼ cup (2 fl oz/60 ml) extra-virgin olive oil

1 Tbsp walnut oil

2 Tbsp red wine vinegar

1 tsp balsamic vinegar

3 Tbsp walnuts

3 Tbsp chopped fresh flat-leaf parsley

1 Tbsp minced fresh chervil

1 Tbsp minced fresh chives, plus several stems about 4 inches (10 cm) long

4 oz (125 g) feta cheese, crumbled

In a saucepan, combine the wheat berries and 6 cups (48 fl oz/1.5 l) water. Bring to a simmer over medium-high heat. Cook, uncovered, until the grain is tender, about 1 hour, adding more water if needed. When almost done, add 1 tsp salt. When done, drain and rinse the grain briefly under cold running water. Drain again and let cool in the sieve.

Meanwhile, to make the vinaigrette, in a small bowl, whisk together the tomatoes, shallot, olive and walnut oils, red wine and balsamic vinegars, ½ tsp salt, and ¼ tsp pepper. Set aside.

In a small frying pan, toast the walnuts over medium-low heat, stirring, until fragrant and starting to brown, about 5 minutes. Pour onto a plate to cool, then chop.

In a serving bowl, combine the cooled grain, the vinaigrette, the walnuts, parsley, chervil, and minced chives. Taste and adjust the seasonings. Gently fold in the cheese, and garnish with the reserved chive stems. If possible, let stand at room temperature for 1–2 hours before serving.

16

FINGERLING POTATO SALAD WITH SHRIMP & DILL

serves 4

Fingerling potatoes are the best choice for this salad because, when cut into pieces, their size matches the size of the baby shrimp. But any thin-skinned potato with waxy, firm flesh makes a fine choice for potato salad.

2½ lb (1.25 kg) fingerling potatoes

Salt and freshly ground pepper

½ cup (4 oz/125 g) plain yogurt

½ cup (4 oz/125 g) light sour cream

2 Tbsp mayonnaise

½ lb (250 g) cooked bay shrimp

¾ cup (2 oz/60 g) chopped green onion, including green parts

½ cup (¾ oz/20 g) chopped fresh dill, plus sprigs for garnish

In a large saucepan, combine the potatoes with water to cover by 2 inches (5 cm). Add 1 tsp salt and bring to a boil over high heat. Reduce the heat to medium and cook until the potatoes are tender when pierced with a sharp knife, 20–25 minutes.

Drain the potatoes and, as soon as they are cool enough to handle, peel, if desired, and cut crosswise into slices ¼ inch (6 mm) thick. Put the slices in a bowl and add the yogurt, sour cream, and mayonnaise. Turn gently to coat evenly. Add the shrimp, the green onion, chopped dill, 1 tsp pepper, and ½ tsp salt and turn again to mix well. Cover and refrigerate for at least 6 hours or up to 24 hours to allow the flavors to blend fully.

When ready to serve, top the salad with the sprigs of dill and serve chilled.

17

ROASTED ASPARAGUS SALAD

serves 6

2 lb (1 kg) medium-thick asparagus

4 Tbsp (2 fl oz/60 ml) extra-virgin olive oil

Salt and freshly ground pepper

Finely grated zest of 1 lemon

1 tsp fresh lemon juice

1 tsp Cognac or brandy

2 Tbsp prepared tapenade

½ small red onion, sliced paper-thin and separated into rings

3 cups (3 oz/90 g) baby arugula leaves

To snap off the tough, woody ends of asparagus spears at the correct point, grasp a spear at each end between your thumbs and index fingers. Flex the asparagus until it snaps, leaving as much of the tender stem as possible. The additional step of peeling the stalks yields beautiful, bright green spears that cook evenly from top to bottom.

Preheat the oven to 450°F (230°C).

To prepare the asparagus, trim off the tough ends and peel the bottom 2 inches (5 cm) or so of the spears. Arrange the asparagus in a baking dish, drizzle with 2 Tbsp of the olive oil, and turn gently to coat evenly. Season with salt and pepper and roast until golden, tender, and slightly wrinkled, about 15 minutes.

Meanwhile, in a large bowl, combine the lemon zest and juice, Cognac, tapenade, and remaining 2 Tbsp olive oil. Whisk with a fork, then add the red onion and arugula and toss gently to coat and distribute the ingredients.

Transfer the roasted asparagus to a platter, mound the salad mixture over the top, and serve.

18

CLASSIC SALADE NIÇOISE

serves 6

4 large eggs

1 lb (500 g) haricots verts, stem ends trimmed

1 lb (500 g) new potatoes

4 tomatoes

1 head butter lettuce, leaves separated

1 can (7 oz/220 g) tuna, preferably Italian olive oil–packed

12 anchovy fillets

⅓ cup (2 oz/60 g) Niçoise olives

¼ cup (2 fl oz/60 ml) extra-virgin olive oil

2 Tbsp red wine vinegar

Salt and freshly ground pepper

Although it has many versions, the classic salad of Nice, France, typically includes haricots verts—slender, young green beans—along with boiled potatoes, hard-cooked eggs, and lettuce. The most authentic version calls for canned olive oil–packed tuna, rather than fresh or water-packed tuna, and Niçoise olives.

To hard-cook the eggs, place them in a saucepan just large enough to hold them. Add cold water to cover by 1 inch (2.5 cm) and bring just to a boil over high heat. Remove the pan from the heat and cover. Let stand for 15 minutes. Have ready a bowl of ice water. Drain the eggs, then transfer to the ice water and let cool.

Meanwhile, bring another saucepan of water to a boil over medium-high heat. Add the haricots verts and cook until tender, 3–4 minutes. Using a strainer, scoop out the beans and transfer them to a colander. Rinse under running cold water. Add the potatoes to the boiling water and cook until tender, 5–10 minutes depending on size. Drain and rinse under running cold water until cool enough to handle. Cut the potatoes into halves or quarters.

Cut the tomatoes into quarters. Peel the hard-cooked eggs and cut in half lengthwise. Arrange the lettuce leaves on a large platter. Make small mounds of the haricots verts, potatoes, tomatoes, tuna, and egg halves on and around the lettuce. Scatter the anchovies and olives over the potatoes.

Drizzle the salad with the olive oil and vinegar. Sprinkle with ½ tsp each salt and pepper and serve.

19

In the past, if you wanted to serve pesto, you had to make it from scratch. Now it is widely available in the refrigerated section of most markets. Avoid the pesto sold in glass jars on store shelves, as the fresh basil flavor is lost.

CHICKEN & ORZO SALAD

serves 4

⅔ cup (5 fl oz/160 ml) prepared pesto sauce

2 Tbsp white wine vinegar

Salt and freshly ground pepper

3 Tbsp olive oil

¾ lb (375 g) orzo pasta

2½ cups (about 1 lb/500 g) shredded cooked chicken meat

½ lb (250 g) cherry tomatoes, halved

6 oz (185 g) baby spinach

In a large bowl, whisk together the pesto, vinegar, ¼ tsp salt, and a pinch of pepper. Add the oil in a thin stream, whisking constantly until the dressing is smooth.

Bring a large pot of salted water to a boil. Add the orzo and cook, stirring occasionally to prevent sticking, until al dente, according to package directions. Drain, rinse under cold running water, and drain again. Add the orzo to the vinaigrette and toss to coat evenly with the dressing.

Add the chicken, tomatoes, and spinach to the orzo and toss gently to combine, then serve.

20

This salad combines two iconic ingredients of spring: asparagus and tarragon. The cream-enriched dressing is kept light and bright by the acidic tang of cider vinegar as well as lemon juice.

ASPARAGUS & SMOKED SALMON SALAD WITH TARRAGON CREAM

serves 4

FOR THE TARRAGON CREAM

1 cup (8 fl oz/250 ml) heavy cream

2 Tbsp cider vinegar

1 tsp fresh lemon juice

Salt and freshly ground pepper

2 Tbsp minced fresh tarragon

1½ lb (750 g) asparagus, tough ends trimmed

⅓ lb (155 g) smoked salmon, thinly sliced

1½ tsp fresh lemon juice

Fresh tarragon sprigs for garnish

To make the tarragon cream, put the cream in a small bowl, then whisk in the cider vinegar, 1 tsp lemon juice, ¼ tsp each salt and pepper, and the 2 Tbsp tarragon. Set aside. The cream will curdle and thicken within 4–5 minutes.

If the asparagus spears are thick, peel them to within about 2 inches (5 cm) of the tips. Arrange the asparagus in a steamer basket and place over boiling water. (The water should not touch the bottom of the basket.) Cover and steam just until tender to the bite, 3–4 minutes. Transfer the asparagus to a colander and immediately place under cold running water to stop the cooking and preserve the bright green color. Slice the spears on the diagonal about ½ inch (12 mm) thick. Set aside. (At this point, the tarragon cream and asparagus may be chilled before serving, if desired.)

Arrange the salmon in a bed on a platter or individual plates. Drizzle evenly with the 1½ tsp lemon juice. Top with the asparagus, and drizzle the tarragon cream over all. Garnish with the tarragon sprigs and serve.

21

SMOKED TROUT SALAD
WITH CUCUMBER & DILL

serves 4–6

1 lb (500 g) smoked trout fillets

1 English cucumber, cut into 4 equal pieces

½ cup (4 oz/125 g) nonpareil capers, rinsed

2 Tbsp coarsely chopped fresh dill

½ cup (⅔ oz/20 g) torn fresh flat-leaf parsley leaves

½ cup (4 oz/125 g) plain Greek yogurt

1 small red onion, minced

1 Tbsp fresh lemon juice

¼ cup (2 fl oz/60 ml) extra-virgin olive oil

Salt and freshly ground pepper

Easy yet delicious, this salad is a smoky, salty, and crunchy blend of smoked trout, cucumber, and capers. Tossed with a light yogurt dressing, this is a great salad to use as a topping for toasted bagels.

With a fork, flake the trout into 1-inch (2.5-cm) pieces.

Using a mandoline or box grater, cut the cucumber pieces lengthwise into paper-thin slices and place in a large bowl. Add the trout, capers, dill, and parsley to the bowl and toss to mix.

In a small bowl, combine the yogurt, onion, and lemon juice. Add the oil in a thin stream, whisking constantly until the dressing is smooth. Pour the mixture over the salad, season to taste with salt and pepper, and toss to combine. Serve.

22

SPRING PEAS WITH PANCETTA,
MINT & RICOTTA SALATA

serves 4–6

Salt and freshly ground pepper

5 lb (2.5 kg) English peas in the pod, shelled

2 thin slices pancetta, chopped

1 tsp raspberry vinegar

1 Tbsp extra-virgin olive oil

2 Tbsp minced fresh mint, plus sprigs for garnish

4 oz (125 g) ricotta salata cheese, crumbled

Fresh English peas, full of natural sugars, are a hallmark of spring. Look for young, tender pods that are plump with whole peas that will need only brief cooking. This simple salad showcases them with complementary flavors of fried pancetta, aromatic mint, and ricotta salata cheese.

Bring a large pot three-fourths full of salted water to a boil over high heat. Add the peas and cook until barely tender, about 2 minutes. Drain, place under cold running water until cool, and drain again. Set aside.

In a frying pan, sauté the pancetta over medium heat until lightly crisped, 4–5 minutes. Using a slotted spoon, transfer to paper towels to drain.

In a large bowl, whisk together the vinegar and ½ tsp each salt and pepper. Add the oil in a thin stream, whisking constantly until the dressing is smooth. Add the peas, pancetta, and chopped mint and turn to coat. Stir in half of the cheese. Garnish with the remaining cheese and the mint sprigs, then serve.

23

OLD-FASHIONED MACARONI SALAD WITH SWEET PICKLES

serves 6

3 cups (10½ oz/330 g) elbow macaroni

Salt and freshly ground pepper

FOR THE DRESSING

⅓ cup (3 fl oz/80 ml) mayonnaise

¼ cup (2 oz/60 g) sour cream

1 tsp Dijon mustard

1–2 tsp sweet pickle juice

½ white onion, finely chopped

3 celery ribs, finely chopped, leaves reserved and finely chopped

3 sweet pickles, finely chopped

2 hard-cooked eggs, chopped

½ cup (2½ oz/75 g) pimiento-stuffed green olives, chopped

½ bunch fresh chives, snipped

The secret to the old-fashioned flavor of this salad is the addition of a little sweet pickle juice and sliced pimiento-stuffed olives, along with the more traditional ingredients like mayonnaise, onions, and hard-cooked eggs. Make this in abundance for a springtime family gathering.

Bring a pot of salted water to a boil over high heat. Reduce the heat to medium, add the macaroni, and cook until tender, according to package directions. Drain and rinse under cold running water and set aside to drain.

To make the dressing, in a serving bowl, combine the mayonnaise, sour cream, mustard, pickle juice, ½ tsp pepper and ½ tsp salt. Stir to mix well.

Add the onion, celery, and pickles and stir to mix again. Add the macaroni and turn to coat. Add the hard-cooked eggs, green olives, and celery leaves and turn once again. Taste and adjust the seasoning with salt, if needed. Transfer to a serving bowl, garnish with the snipped chives, and serve.

24

POMELO, CILANTRO & CASHEW SALAD

serves 6

½ cup (2½ oz/75 g) cashews

2 pomelos, peeled and segmented with a knife

1 red jalapeño chile, minced

¼ cup (⅓ oz/10 g) chopped fresh cilantro

1 Tbsp Asian fish sauce

1 tsp packed light brown sugar

Grated zest of 1 lime

An ancestor of the grapefruit, the pomelo is thought to have originated in Malaysia. Ranging in color from yellow to light pink, they are larger than a grapefruit and have a sweet-tart flavor. Choose pomelos that are heavy for their size, free of blemishes, and fragrant. Use them as you would grapefruits.

In a dry frying pan, toast the cashews over medium-low heat, stirring, until fragrant and starting to brown, about 5 minutes. Pour onto a plate to cool, then chop coarsely and set aside.

Put the pomelo segments in a bowl and add the chile and cilantro and toss. In a small bowl, stir together the fish sauce, brown sugar, and lime zest. Pour over the pomelo and toss gently. Stir in the chopped cashews and serve.

25

A sweet-sour-salty dressing inspired by Asian pickled vegetables melds with the mild flavor of edamame, the coolness of cucumbers, and the satisfying crunch of red bell peppers in this superbly refreshing and healthful salad. Toasted sesame oil and sesame seeds add an appealing nuttiness.

MARINATED EDAMAME, CUCUMBER & RED BELL PEPPER SALAD

serves 6

½ cup (4 fl oz/125 ml) rice vinegar

4 tsp tamari sauce

5 Tbsp (2½ oz/75 g) sugar

Salt and freshly ground pepper

⅓ cup (3 fl oz/80 ml) canola oil

2 tsp toasted sesame oil

1 bag (1 lb/500 g) frozen shelled edamame, thawed

1½ English cucumbers

2 red bell peppers

3 Tbsp sesame seeds

In a bowl, whisk together the vinegar, tamari, sugar, 1½ tsp salt, and a few grindings of pepper until the sugar dissolves. Add the canola and sesame oils in a thin stream, whisking constantly until the dressing is well blended. Taste and adjust the seasonings.

Pat the edamame dry with paper towels and place in a large bowl. Halve and cut the cucumbers into ½-inch (12-mm) pieces and add to the bowl with the edamame. Seed the bell peppers, trim away the ribs, cut the flesh into ½-inch pieces, and add to the bowl.

In a small frying pan, toast the sesame seeds over medium-low heat, stirring, until fragrant and starting to brown, about 2 minutes. Pour onto a plate and let cool.

Whisk the dressing to recombine, then drizzle it over the vegetable mixture, sprinkle with the sesame seeds, and toss well. Cover and refrigerate for at least 1 hour or up to 1 day to blend the flavors.

When ready to serve, drain the salad and discard the dressing.

26

For superior texture and flavor in this salad, use cooked dried beans: Place 2 cups (14 oz/440 g) dried chickpeas in a large pot and fill with water to cover. Turn the heat to high and bring to a boil, then turn down the heat and simmer, loosely covered. Cook, stirring occasionally, until the beans are tender 1½–2 hours. Drain and use.

CHICKPEA SALAD WITH MINT

serves 6–8

5 Tbsp (2½ fl oz/75 ml) red wine vinegar, plus extra to taste

3 or 4 cloves garlic, minced

1 tsp ground cumin

Salt and freshly ground pepper

5 Tbsp (2½ fl oz/75 ml) extra-virgin olive oil

2 cans (15 oz/470 g each) chickpeas, drained and rinsed

1 small red onion, chopped

¼ cup (⅓ oz/10 g) chopped fresh mint, plus shredded mint for garnish

In a small bowl, whisk together the vinegar, garlic, cumin, and salt and pepper to taste. Add the oil in a thin stream, whisking constantly until the dressing is smooth. Add the chickpeas and toss together to coat evenly. Add the red onion and toss gently. Let stand for 20 minutes at room temperature.

Taste the salad and adjust the seasoning with more salt, pepper, and vinegar, if needed. Add the chopped mint and toss to mix well. Transfer the salad to a platter or individual plates. Garnish with the shredded mint and serve.

27

SOBA NOODLE SALAD WITH SUGAR SNAP PEAS & SOY-PEANUT DRESSING

serves 4

Pairing soba, the Japanese buckwheat noodle, with delicate spring vegetables and crisp herbs counterbalances the dense, rich texture of the noodles. The peanut dressing binds the whole together to create a hearty main dish.

1 lb (500 g) dried soba noodles
or whole-wheat spaghetti

1 cup (⅓ lb/155 g) sugar snap peas, trimmed
and cut in half on the diagonal

3 or 4 small carrots, peeled and julienned

½ cup (⅔ oz/20 g) chopped fresh
cilantro leaves

½ cup (⅔ oz/20 g) chopped fresh mint leaves

FOR THE SOY-PEANUT DRESSING

1 tsp canola or peanut oil

1-inch (2.5-cm) piece fresh ginger,
peeled and minced

2 cloves garlic, minced

1 Tbsp soy sauce

4 tsp rice vinegar

½ tsp red pepper flakes

⅓ cup (3 oz/90 g) chunky peanut butter

½ cup (4 fl oz/125 ml) chicken
or vegetable broth

Salt

In a large pot of boiling water, cook the noodles until tender, according to package directions. Two minutes before the noodles are ready, add the snap peas and carrots. After 2 minutes, drain the noodles and vegetables and place in a large bowl along with the cilantro and mint.

To make the dressing, in a saucepan, heat the oil over medium-high heat. Add the ginger and garlic and stir. Add the soy sauce, vinegar, red pepper flakes, peanut butter, broth, and salt to taste. Stir until the mixture is smooth, then reduce the heat to low and simmer until thick, 5–7 minutes.

Pour the dressing over the noodles, vegetables, and herbs and gently turn to coat well. Let cool to room temperature before serving.

28

ROASTED POTATO SALAD WITH SPRING ONION DRESSING

serves 10–12

With no peeling or cutting needed, this potato salad is fast to prepare and feeds a crowd. High-heat roasting produces potatoes with crisp skin and a soft interior. Tossing the potatoes with the creamy dressing while they are still warm loosens and melts the dressing as it coats the warm potatoes, and helps the potatoes absorb the dressing's rich flavors.

3 lb (1.5 kg) baby Yukon Gold potatoes,
each about 1 inch (2.5 cm) in diameter

3 Tbsp olive oil

Salt and freshly ground pepper

FOR THE DRESSING

½ cup (¾ oz/20 g) fresh cilantro leaves,
plus sprigs for garnish

3 green onions, including tender
green parts, chopped

1 clove garlic, chopped

½ cup (4 oz/125 g) sour cream

¼ cup (2 fl oz/60 ml) mayonnaise

4 tsp red wine vinegar

4 tsp Dijon mustard

Preheat the oven to 400°F (200°C). Put the potatoes on a rimmed baking sheet, drizzle with the olive oil, sprinkle with ½ Tbsp salt, and toss to coat evenly. Roast, tossing every 15 minutes, until the skins are crisp and golden brown, about 45 minutes. Set aside to let cool slightly.

Meanwhile, to make the dressing, in a food processor or blender, combine the cilantro leaves, green onions, garlic, sour cream, mayonnaise, vinegar, and mustard and process until smooth. Season to taste with salt and pepper, cover, and refrigerate until ready to use.

To serve, put the slightly cooled potatoes in a serving bowl, add the dressing, and toss to coat. Garnish with the cilantro sprigs. Serve at once, or cover and refrigerate for up to 4 hours. Let the salad return to room temperature before serving.

29

MARCH

MÂCHE, RADISH, BLUE CHEESE & SUGARED PECAN SALAD

serves 4

Mâche is a tender, nutty-flavored salad leaf that is sold in ready-to-use bags in the produce section of many supermarkets. For a substitute, use field greens or a mixture of baby or wild arugula and baby spinach leaves. You can make the sugared pecans up to 1 week in advance and store them in an airtight container at room temperature.

FOR THE VINAIGRETTE

1 shallot, minced

2 Tbsp red wine vinegar

1 tsp Dijon mustard

Salt and freshly ground black pepper

⅓ cup (3 fl oz/80 ml) olive oil

½ cup (2 oz/60 g) pecan halves

1 tsp sugar

¼ tsp dry mustard

Pinch of cayenne pepper

4 oz (125 g) mâche or field greens

8 radishes, thinly sliced

4 oz (125 g) blue cheese, crumbled

Preheat the oven to 350°F (180°C).

To make the vinaigrette, in a small bowl, whisk together the shallot, vinegar, and Dijon mustard. Season to taste with salt and black pepper. Let stand at room temperature for 30 minutes to allow the shallot flavor to mellow, then add the oil in a thin stream, whisking constantly until the dressing is smooth and thick.

Rinse the pecans in a sieve and set aside to drain. In a small bowl, combine the sugar, dry mustard, and cayenne and mix well. Add the pecans and toss until evenly coated. Spread the pecans on a nonstick rimmed baking sheet and toast in the oven until dark brown, about 10 minutes. Transfer the pecans to a plate to let cool, and set aside.

To serve, combine the mâche leaves and radish slices in a serving bowl. Whisk the vinaigrette to recombine, if needed. Drizzle the mâche with the vinaigrette and toss until evenly coated. Top with the cheese and the pecans and serve.

30

MARCH

ARUGULA SALAD WITH PECORINO & PINE NUTS

serves 4–6

If pecorino, a sheep's milk cheese, is unavailable, use Parmesan instead. Young, tender baby arugula leaves are best for this salad. If you can find only larger leaves, trim off the stems.

3 Tbsp pine nuts

1 Tbsp balsamic vinegar

1 tsp red wine vinegar

Salt and freshly ground pepper

3 Tbsp extra-virgin olive oil

4–5 cups (4–5 oz/125–155 g) baby arugula

Pecorino cheese for shaving

In a small frying pan, toast the pine nuts over medium heat, shaking the pan gently, until lightly golden, 2–3 minutes. Transfer to a plate and set aside.

In a large serving bowl, whisk together the vinegars and ½ tsp each salt and pepper. Add the oil in a thin stream, whisking constantly until the dressing is smooth. Add the arugula and toss to coat evenly.

Divide the arugula among plates. Using a vegetable peeler, shave the cheese over the salads. Sprinkle with the pine nuts and serve.

31

MARCH

GREEN APPLE & CELERY SALAD

serves 4

This is a crisp, refreshing salad to serve as a starter, side salad, or palate cleanser between courses. Try adding thinly sliced fennel, fresh cilantro, or tarragon to the mix.

1 tsp coriander seeds

4 tart green apples

Juice of 1 lemon

1 tsp walnut oil

2 celery ribs, thinly sliced

Salt and freshly ground pepper

In a small frying pan, toast the coriander over medium heat, shaking the pan occasionally, until aromatic, 2–3 minutes. Pour into a mortar, crush with a pestle, and set aside.

Without peeling the apples, core them and cut into matchsticks. In a bowl, combine the apples, lemon juice, walnut oil, celery, crushed coriander, and salt and pepper to taste. Toss to mix well and serve.

As the sun shines brighter and the days grow longer this month, artichokes, asparagus, peas, and fava beans proliferate at the market. These hardly need more than a light simmer before scattering them into countless fresh combinations, with olive oil and shaved of Parmesan as simple but flavorful adornments. Enliven classic salads with verdant spring herbs: think chives for egg salad, tarragon for chicken, and dill for tender new potatoes.

1
BABY BEET SALAD WITH SUGARED WALNUTS
page 82

2
SHAVED RHUBARB SALAD WITH ALMONDS & CHEESE
page 82

3
WARM SPINACH SALAD WITH ARTICHOKES & GRUYÈRE
page 84

8
LOBSTER SALAD WITH CUCUMBER & DILL
page 87

9
WATERCRESS & RADISH SALAD WITH GRAPEFRUIT
page 88

10
CALAMARI & WHITE BEAN SALAD
page 88

15
GLASS-NOODLE SALAD WITH SHRIMP, CHICKEN & MINT
page 93

16
LEMON CHICKEN SALAD WITH TARRAGON
page 93

17
SEASONED BEAN SPROUT SALAD
page 94

22
BITTER GREENS WITH DUCK BREAST & CHERRIES
page 96

23
ISRAELI COUSCOUS SALAD WITH FAVA BEANS & OLIVES
page 99

24
CLASSIC EGG SALAD
page 99

29
MÂCHE, PURSLANE & GREEN ONION SALAD
page 102

30
GRILLED HALLOUMI & LITTLE GEM SALAD WITH PRESERVED-LEMON DRESSING
page 102

4
ARFALLE SALAD WITH TOMATOES & SMOKED MOZZARELLA
page 84

5
NEW POTATO & RADISH SALAD WITH MUSTARD-DILL VINAIGRETTE
page 85

6
CHOPPED SALAD OF CHICKEN, WATERCRESS & RICOTTA SALATA
page 85

7
WHEAT BERRY SALAD WITH SNOW PEAS & CARROTS
page 87

11
SALAD OF GRILLED LAMB, POTATOES & AIOLI
page 90

12
FAVA BEAN SALAD WITH PECORINO
page 90

13
PASTA SALAD WITH SPRING ASPARAGUS & SNAP PEAS
page 91

14
SHRIMP, CRAB & MÂCHE SALAD
page 91

18
INSALATA DI CAMPO
page 94

19
BULGUR SALAD WITH LEMON, PEAS & MINT
page 95

20
CRAB SUNOMONO
page 95

21
ASPARAGUS SALAD WITH LEMON & SHAVED PARMESAN
page 96

25
RTICHOKE & WHITE BEAN SALAD
page 100

26
DANDELION GREENS SALAD
page 100

27
POTATO SALAD WITH FAVA BEANS, GREEN GARLIC & CRÈME FRAÎCHE
page 101

28
SNOW PEA & RADISH SALAD
page 101

april

1

BABY BEET SALAD WITH SUGARED WALNUTS

serves 6

Seek out baby beets in an array of colors, such as golden yellow, pale pink, and magenta red, for an eye-catching presentation. If you can find them, blood oranges contrast nicely with the earthy beets.

3 bunches mixed baby beets (3–4 lb/1.5–2 kg total weight), trimmed

FOR THE SUGARED WALNUTS

½ cup (2 oz/60 g) walnut pieces

1 tsp grapeseed oil

2 tsp confectioners' sugar

1 tsp Dijon mustard

3 Tbsp balsamic vinegar

⅓ cup (3 fl oz/80 ml) plus 2 Tbsp extra-virgin olive oil

5 oranges, preferably blood oranges

Salt and freshly ground pepper

3 cups (3 oz/90 g) arugula leaves, stemmed

1 red onion, thinly sliced

2 Tbsp chopped fresh flat-leaf parsley

Preheat the oven to 375°F (190°C). Wrap the beets in squares of foil and roast on a baking sheet until easily pierced with the tip of a knife, 30–40 minutes. Let cool in the foil, then unwrap and peel. Cut each beet in half or into wedges and set aside.

To make the sugared walnuts, in a bowl, toss the walnuts with the grapeseed oil. Add the sugar and toss to coat evenly. Heat a small frying pan over medium heat. Add the walnuts and sauté just until they start to brown and the sugar begins to caramelize, about 3 minutes. Transfer to a small plate and let cool.

In a bowl, whisk together the mustard and vinegar. Add the olive oil in a thin stream, whisking constantly until the vinaigrette is smooth. Grate the zest from 1 of the oranges and add to the dressing, then season to taste with salt and pepper. Add the beets, toss to coat, and let stand at room temperature for 2–4 hours.

Using a small, sharp knife, cut a slice off both ends of each of the remaining 4 oranges to reveal the flesh. Stand an orange upright on a cutting board and thickly slice off the peel and pith in strips, following the contour of the fruit. Holding the orange in one hand over a bowl, cut along either side of each section to release it from the membrane, »»

letting the sections drop into the bowl. Repeat with the remaining oranges. Pour any juice in the bowl over the beets.

Scatter the arugula over a platter. Using a slotted spoon, remove the beets from the vinaigrette and arrange over the greens along with the orange sections, onion slices, and walnuts. Drizzle a little of the vinaigrette over the top and toss to combine. Add more vinaigrette if needed to lightly coat the greens (you may not need it all). Garnish with parsley and serve.

2

SHAVED RHUBARB SALAD WITH ALMONDS & CHEESE

serves 6

Tangy raw rhubarb is a bright, refreshing match to the creamy cheese and earthy nuts in this salad. To prepare rhubarb, first trim away any leaves—they should not be eaten. Since you're slicing the rhubarb paper-thin, it's not necessary to remove the fibrous strings as is done for other preparations.

⅓ cup (1½ oz/45 g) slivered almonds

Grated zest of 1 orange

1 Tbsp fresh orange juice

1 Tbsp white wine vinegar

Pinch of sugar

Salt and freshly ground pepper

½ cup (4 fl oz/125 ml) extra-virgin olive oil

1 rib rhubarb, trimmed (left)

6 cups (6 oz/185 g) mesclun

4 oz (125 g) fresh goat cheese

In a small frying pan, toast the almonds over medium-low heat, stirring, until fragrant and lightly golden, 3–4 minutes. Pour onto a plate to cool.

In a small bowl, stir together the orange zest and juice, vinegar, sugar, and a pinch each of salt and pepper. Add the olive oil in a thin stream, whisking constantly until the vinaigrette is well combined.

Using a mandoline or a very sharp knife, shave the rhubarb into paper-thin slices. Put it in a bowl with the mesclun and almonds. Add half the vinaigrette and toss to combine. Add more vinaigrette as needed to lightly coat the lettuces (you may not need it all). Crumble the cheese over the top and serve.

3

WARM SPINACH SALAD WITH ARTICHOKES & GRUYÈRE

serves 6

2 lemons

12 baby artichokes

6 fresh thyme sprigs

6 fresh flat-leaf parsley sprigs

2 bay leaves

10 cloves garlic

½ cup (4 fl oz/125 ml) olive oil

Salt and freshly ground pepper

¾ lb (375 g) baby spinach leaves

FOR THE DRESSING

1 Tbsp red wine vinegar

1 Tbsp balsamic vinegar

5 Tbsp (2½ fl oz/75 ml) extra-virgin olive oil

3 hard-cooked eggs *(left)*, coarsely chopped

Gruyère cheese for shaving

To hard-cook the eggs, place them in a saucepan just large enough to hold them. Add cold water to cover by 1 inch (2.5 cm) and bring just to a boil over high heat. Remove the pan from the heat and cover. Let stand for 15 minutes. Have ready a bowl of ice water. Drain the eggs, then transfer to the ice water and let cool before peeling.

Peel the zest from both lemons and combine it in a large saucepan with the juice from the lemons. Peel off the tough outer leaves of an artichoke until you reach the tender, pale green leaves. Cut ½ inch (12 mm) off the top and trim the stem flush with the base. Add the artichoke to the saucepan, tossing gently to coat with the lemon juice. Repeat with the remaining artichokes.

Add the thyme and parsley sprigs, bay leaves, garlic, olive oil, and salt and pepper to taste to the saucepan. Add water to just cover the artichokes. Place a round piece of parchment paper the diameter of the pan directly on top of the artichokes to prevent browning. Bring the water to a boil over high heat, reduce the heat to medium-low, and simmer the artichokes until they begin to soften, about 5 minutes. Remove from the heat and let cool in the pan.

Meanwhile, put the spinach in a large bowl.

To make the dressing, in a bowl, whisk together the vinegars and salt and pepper to taste. Add the extra-virgin olive oil in a thin stream, whisking constantly until the dressing is smooth. ⟫

When the artichokes have cooled, drain and cut lengthwise into quarters. In a frying pan, combine the artichokes and dressing over medium heat and cook, stirring occasionally, until the artichokes are warm, about 2 minutes. Remove from the heat and season with salt and pepper to taste.

Add the artichokes and dressing to the spinach and toss to mix. Transfer to individual plates, if desired, and garnish with the chopped egg. Using a vegetable peeler, shave the cheese over the salad(s) and serve.

4

FARFALLE SALAD WITH TOMATOES & SMOKED MOZZARELLA

serves 6

Salt and freshly ground pepper

¾ lb (375 g) farfalle or other shaped pasta

5 Tbsp (2½ fl oz/75 ml) extra-virgin olive oil

2 Tbsp balsamic vinegar

1¼ cups (5 oz/155 g) coarsely shredded smoked mozzarella cheese

1 cup (6 oz/185 g) cherry tomatoes, halved

1 cup (1 oz/30 g) packed fresh basil leaves

The classic combination of mozzarella, tomatoes, and basil can be enjoyed any time of the year if you use cherry or grape tomatoes. Smoked mozzarella adds depth and a little more punch than its fresh counterpart.

Bring a large pot three-fourths full of salted water to a boil. Add the farfalle and cook until al dente, according to package directions. Drain the farfalle and toss it immediately with 1 Tbsp of the olive oil. Cover and let cool completely in the refrigerator, 1–24 hours.

In a large bowl, whisk together the vinegar and salt and pepper to taste. Add the remaining 4 Tbsp (2 fl oz/60 ml) olive oil in a thin stream, whisking constantly until the dressing is smooth. Add the farfalle, cheese, tomatoes, and basil, tearing the larger leaves. Toss to mix well and serve at room temperature.

5

NEW POTATO & RADISH SALAD WITH MUSTARD-DILL VINAIGRETTE

serves 6

Cornichons are tart, salty, and full of pickled flavor. Along with the mustard, they add zip to the tender waxy potatoes and crunchy radishes and celery in this salad. A spoonful of crème fraîche on individual servings tempers the salad's tanginess and adds a luxurious touch.

FOR THE VINAIGRETTE

6 Tbsp (3 fl oz/90 ml) cider vinegar

7 cornichons, minced

¼ cup minced fresh dill

1 shallot, minced

3 Tbsp Dijon mustard

1 Tbsp sugar

Salt

½ cup (4 fl oz/125 ml) plus 1 Tbsp extra-virgin olive oil

2 lb (1 kg) red new potatoes

4 celery ribs, finely chopped

8 large radishes, trimmed and finely chopped

2 Tbsp coarsely chopped fresh dill

⅓ cup (3 oz/80 g) crème fraîche or sour cream

To make the vinaigrette, in a large bowl, whisk together the vinegar, cornichons, minced dill, shallot, mustard, sugar, and ½ tsp salt until the salt and sugar dissolve. Add the oil in a thin stream, whisking constantly until the dressing is well blended. Taste and adjust the seasonings.

Have ready a bowl of ice water. In a large saucepan, combine the potatoes, 1 Tbsp salt, and water to cover by 1 inch (2.5 cm) and bring to a boil over high heat. Reduce the heat to medium, cover partially, and simmer until the potatoes are just tender when pierced with the tip of a paring knife, about 10 minutes.

Drain the potatoes in a colander and then plunge them into the ice water. Let cool, then drain again and pat dry. Cut each potato into halves or quarters.

Whisk the vinaigrette to recombine, then add the potatoes to the bowl. Add the celery and radishes and toss gently. Taste and adjust the seasonings. Sprinkle the salad with the chopped dill. Serve, passing the crème fraîche at the table.

6

CHOPPED SALAD OF CHICKEN, WATERCRESS & RICOTTA SALATA

serves 4–6

A chopped salad is a good way to use up leftover salad vegetables and small pieces of cheese. Create new combinations with your favorite ingredients. Try chopped chicken, crumbled blue cheese, chopped apples, and toasted walnuts with a cider vinegar–walnut oil vinaigrette.

2 cups (¾ lb/375 g) bite-sized pieces roasted chicken meat

2 cups (¾ lb/375 g) cherry tomatoes, cut in half lengthwise

1 large cucumber, peeled, seeded, and cut into ½-inch (12-mm) pieces

1 bunch watercress, tough stems removed and leaves coarsely chopped

4 oz (125 g) ricotta salata or feta cheese, crumbled

2 green onions, including tender green parts, chopped

¼ cup (1½ oz/45 g) chopped pitted black Mediterranean olives

2 Tbsp fresh lemon juice

1 clove garlic, crushed through a press

Salt and freshly ground pepper

½ cup (4 fl oz/125 ml) extra-virgin olive oil

In a serving bowl, combine the chicken, tomatoes, cucumber, watercress, cheese, green onions, and olives.

In a small bowl, whisk together the lemon juice, garlic, and salt and pepper to taste. Add the oil in a thin stream, whisking constantly until the dressing is well blended.

Pour the dressing over the salad, mix gently, and serve.

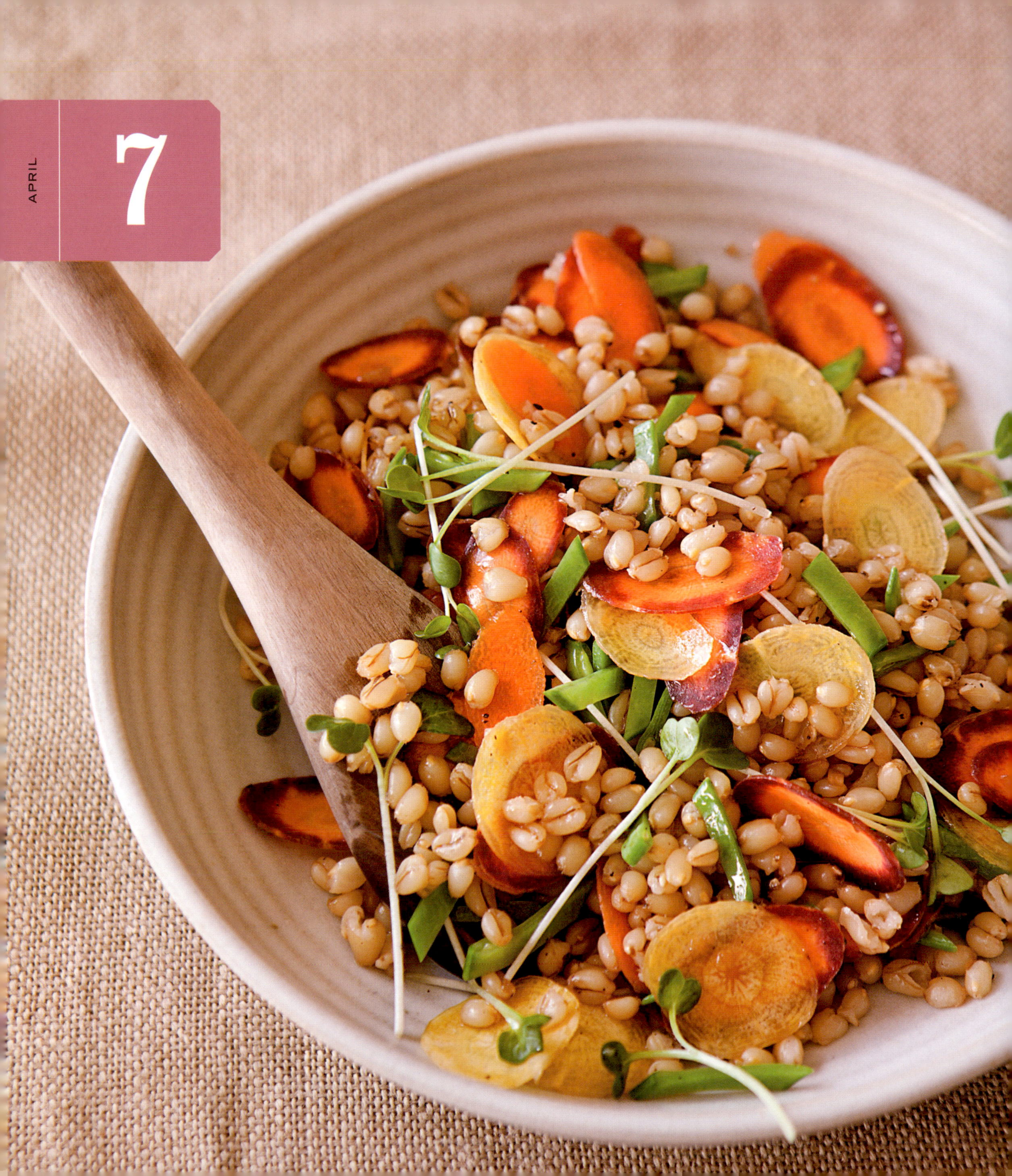

7

This simple salad is very healthful and high in fiber. Wheat berries are whole kernels of wheat, and their mild flavor lets this savory Asian-inspired dressing shine. Carrots and snow peas mark this as a springtime dish. Look for interesting varieties of carrots in different colors, and use a mandoline to slice them paper-thin.

WHEAT BERRY SALAD WITH SNOW PEAS & CARROTS

serves 6

1 cup (5 oz/155 g) wheat berries
Salt

FOR THE VINAIGRETTE
¼ cup (2 fl oz/60 ml) peanut oil
1 tsp toasted sesame oil
2 Tbsp rice vinegar
1 Tbsp honey or sugar
1–2 tsp soy sauce

4 carrots, peeled and very thinly sliced
½ lb (250 g) snow peas, trimmed and cut on the diagonal into thin slices
Handful of radish sprouts or other sprouts

In a saucepan, combine the wheat berries and 6 cups (48 fl oz/1.5 l) water. Bring to a simmer over medium-high heat. Cook, uncovered, until the grain is tender, about 1 hour, adding more water if needed. When almost done, add 1 tsp salt. When tender, drain and rinse briefly under cold running water. Drain again and allow to cool in the colander.

Meanwhile, to make the vinaigrette, in a small bowl, whisk together the peanut and sesame oils, vinegar, honey, and 1 tsp soy sauce. Taste and add more soy sauce if desired. Put the drained wheat berries in a bowl and add the vinaigrette, gently mixing. Let stand at room temperature for 1–2 hours, if possible, before adding the vegetables.

For the carrots and peas, bring a saucepan of water to a boil over medium-high heat. Have ready a bowl of ice water. Add the carrots and blanch until just tender but still slightly crunchy, 2–3 minutes. Add the peas during the last 30 seconds. Drain and plunge the vegetables into the ice water, then remove and pat dry.

Add the vegetables to the wheat berries and toss gently. Garnish with the radish sprouts and serve.

8

Fresh lobster is available year-round, but if you aren't sure about its quality, choose frozen lobster tails. Serve this elegant salad with toasted brioche slices and a chilled chardonnay.

LOBSTER SALAD WITH CUCUMBER & DILL

serves 4

1 lb (500 g) fresh-cooked lobster meat (from about 2 lb/1 kg lobster in the shell)
1 cucumber, peeled, seeded, and chopped
1 tsp grated lemon zest
2½ Tbsp fresh lemon juice
1 small shallot, minced
Salt and freshly ground pepper
½ cup (4 fl oz/125 ml) extra-virgin olive oil
2 Tbsp minced fresh dill
4 cups (4 oz/125 g) loosely packed watercress, tough stems removed

Pick the lobster over for shell fragments and cut the meat into bite-sized chunks. In a bowl, combine the lobster and chopped cucumber. Set aside.

In a small bowl, whisk together the lemon zest and juice, shallot, and salt and pepper to taste. Add the olive oil in a thin stream, whisking constantly until the dressing is well blended. Stir in the dill, then taste and adjust the seasonings.

Pour the dressing over the lobster and toss to coat evenly. Cover the salad and refrigerate to chill and marinate for at least 30 minutes or up to several hours.

Divide the watercress among individual plates, top with the lobster salad, and serve.

9

WATERCRESS & RADISH SALAD WITH GRAPEFRUIT

serves 10–12

Here, pink grapefruits, which deliver a tart-sweet flavor, are paired with peppery green watercress and piquant radishes in a colorful salad fit for a dinner party.

3 Tbsp red wine vinegar

1 Tbsp whole-grain mustard

Salt and freshly ground pepper

6 Tbsp (3 fl oz/90 ml) olive oil

3 pink grapefruits, peeled and segmented with a knife

4 bunches watercress, tough stems removed

6 large radishes, trimmed and thinly sliced lengthwise

In a large, shallow serving bowl, whisk together the vinegar, mustard, and ½ tsp each salt and pepper. Add the oil in a thin stream, whisking constantly until the dressing is smooth.

Just before serving, add the grapefruit sections, watercress, and radishes to a large bowl. Drizzle in the dressing and toss gently to coat. Serve right away.

10

CALAMARI & WHITE BEAN SALAD

serves 4

Enjoying this salad, it won't be hard to imagine you are in coastal Italy, sipping a glass of crisp vino bianco while enjoying a mix of fresh calamari, velvety white beans, and sweet roasted peppers tossed in a citrus-and-garlic dressing.

Salt and freshly ground pepper

¼ cup (2 fl oz/60 ml) white wine vinegar, or as needed

3 Tbsp fresh lemon juice

1 Tbsp minced garlic

½ cup (4 fl oz/125 ml) extra-virgin olive oil

1 lb (500 g) cleaned squid, cut into bite-sized rings and tentacles

1 can (15 oz/470 g) cannellini beans or other white beans, rinsed and drained

2 jarred roasted red bell peppers, cut into strips

1 cup (4 oz/125 g) thinly sliced red onion

2 Tbsp capers, rinsed

⅓ cup (2 oz/60 g) green olives, pitted and chopped

Fresh flat-leaf parsley leaves for garnish

In a large pot, bring 4 qt (4 l) salted water to a boil over medium-high heat. Have ready a bowl of ice water.

In a large bowl, combine the vinegar, lemon juice, garlic, 1 tsp salt, and ¼ tsp pepper and let stand for 5 minutes. Add the olive oil in a thin stream, whisking constantly until the dressing is well blended.

Add the squid to the boiling water and cook until just tender, about 1 minute. Drain the squid and plunge into the ice water to stop the cooking. Drain well and pat dry.

Add the cooked squid, beans, peppers, onion, capers, and olives to the dressing and mix well. Cover and refrigerate for 2–4 hours to blend the flavors.

Just before serving, taste the salad and adjust the vinegar and seasonings. Divide among individual plates, garnish with parsley leaves, and serve.

11

SALAD OF GRILLED LAMB, POTATOES & AIOLI

serves 6

This is a delicious Provençal-style main-course salad. Roast the meat just for the salad, or keep the recipe in your repertoire when looking for ways to use up leftover beef, lamb, or chicken roasts.

2 lb (1 kg) small red potatoes, left unpeeled

2 Tbsp olive oil

Salt and freshly ground pepper

FOR THE AIOLI

1 egg yolk

1 tsp Dijon mustard

5 Tbsp (3 fl oz/80 ml) olive oil

⅓ cup (3 fl oz/80 ml) grapeseed oil

Juice of ½ lemon

2 or 3 cloves garlic, minced

3–3¼ lb (1.5–1.65 kg) leg of lamb, trimmed, boned, and butterflied

2 Tbsp olive oil

3 jarred roasted red bell peppers, cut lengthwise into thick strips (optional)

Preheat the oven to 375°F (190°C). Prepare a charcoal or gas grill for direct-heat cooking over high heat, or preheat the broiler.

Arrange the potatoes in a single layer in a baking dish. Add the oil and salt and pepper to taste, and turn the potatoes to coat evenly. Cover with foil and bake until tender, 40–50 minutes. Remove from the oven and uncover.

Meanwhile, to make the aioli, in a bowl, whisk together the egg yolk, mustard, and 1 Tbsp of the olive oil until thoroughly blended. In a cup, combine the remaining 4 Tbsp olive oil and the grapeseed oil. Gradually add the oils to the egg yolk mixture in a thin, steady stream, whisking constantly until the mixture thickens. Add the lemon juice, garlic, and salt and pepper to taste. Whisk in 2 Tbsp warm water to make the aioli barely fluid. Cover and refrigerate.

Rub the lamb with the 2 Tbsp olive oil and salt and pepper to taste. About 10 minutes after placing the potatoes in the oven, place the lamb on the grill rack or a broiler pan. Grill or broil 4–6 inches (10–15 cm) from the heat source until an instant-read thermometer inserted into the thickest portion registers 130–135°F (54–57°C) for medium-rare, »»

about 15 minutes on each side. Transfer to a cutting board and cover loosely with foil. Let rest for 10 minutes before carving.

Meanwhile, place the potatoes on the grill rack or broiler pan and grill or broil, turning occasionally, until hot and well marked, about 10 minutes.

Cut the lamb across the grain into thin slices and arrange on a platter with the potatoes and roasted bell peppers, if using. Serve the aioli on the side.

12

FAVA BEAN SALAD WITH PECORINO

serves 4

This classic Tuscan salad is made as soon as fava beans ripen in the spring garden. Use a slightly aged pecorino, which will hold its shape better when cut.

Salt and freshly ground pepper

3 lb (1.5 kg) fava beans in the pod, shelled

6 oz (185 g) pecorino cheese

¼ cup (2 fl oz/60 ml) extra-virgin olive oil

Bring a pot three-fourths full of lightly salted water to a boil. Add the shelled beans and blanch for 1–2 minutes. Drain, rinse under cold running water, and drain again. Pinch each bean to pop it from its skin. Transfer the beans to a serving bowl.

Cut the cheese into ½-inch (12-mm) cubes and add the cubes to the bowl of favas. Add the olive oil, a light sprinkling of salt, and pepper to taste. Toss all the ingredients together and serve.

13

PASTA SALAD WITH SPRING ASPARAGUS & SNAP PEAS

serves 6

For a more substantial dish, add fresh fava beans to this bright-tasting salad. Shell them and blanch in a pot of boiling water for 1–2 minutes. Drain, and when cool enough to handle, pinch each bean to pop it out of its skin.

Salt and freshly ground pepper

8 oz (250 g) asparagus

8 oz (250 g) sugar snap peas, trimmed

¾ lb (375 g) penne or other shaped pasta

5 Tbsp (3 fl oz/80 ml) extra-virgin olive oil

1 orange

2 Tbsp red wine vinegar

3 Tbsp finely chopped fresh chives

In a large pot over high heat, bring 5 qt (5 l) salted water to a boil. Trim the tough ends from the asparagus and, if the spears are thick, peel them to within 2 inches (5 cm) of the tips. Cut on the diagonal into 1½-inch (4-cm) pieces. Boil the asparagus until tender, 4–5 minutes. Using a strainer, remove the asparagus, drain, and let cool completely in the refrigerator.

Add the sugar snap peas to the boiling water and cook until tender, 1–2 minutes. Drain and let cool completely in the refrigerator.

Add the penne to the boiling water and cook until al dente, according to package directions. Drain the penne and toss immediately with 1 Tbsp of the oil. Cover and let cool completely in the refrigerator, 1–24 hours.

Grate the zest of the uncut orange, then juice the orange. In a large bowl, whisk together the orange zest, orange juice, vinegar, and salt and pepper to taste. Add the remaining 4 Tbsp (2 fl oz/60 ml) oil in a thin stream, whisking constantly until the dressing is well blended. Add the penne, asparagus, sugar snap peas, and chives. Toss to mix well and serve at room temperature.

14

SHRIMP, CRAB & MÂCHE SALAD

serves 4–6

This salad is simple but elegant, perfect served as a first course at a brunch or luncheon. You can mix up the type of seafood: try bay shrimp, lobster, or even smoked fish.

1 watermelon radish or daikon radish

¼ cup (2 oz/60 g) plain yogurt

3 Tbsp mayonnaise

4½ tsp Dijon mustard

Grated zest and juice of 1 lemon

2 Tbsp minced fresh chives

6 oz (185 g) mâche or field greens

½ lb (250 g) cooked shrimp, peeled with tail segments left intact and deveined

½ lb (250 g) cooked crabmeat, picked over for shell fragments

Using a mandoline or a very sharp knife, thinly slice the radish. Set aside.

In a small bowl, whisk together the yogurt, mayonnaise, mustard, lemon zest and juice, and chives to make a dressing.

Divide the mâche among individual plates and top with the shrimp, crabmeat, and radish slices. Drizzle with the dressing and serve.

15

GLASS-NOODLE SALAD WITH SHRIMP, CHICKEN & MINT

serves 4

½ cup (4 fl oz/125 ml) chicken broth

6 oz (185 g) ground chicken

Salt and freshly ground pepper

6 oz (185 g) shrimp, peeled with tail segments left intact and deveined

¼ lb (125 g) bean thread noodles, soaked in warm water for 15 minutes and drained

FOR THE DRESSING

Juice of 2 limes

3 Tbsp Asian fish sauce

2 tsp sugar

1 Tbsp roasted chile paste

2 large red Fresno or serrano chiles, seeded and finely chopped

1 green onion, including tender green parts, chopped

3 Tbsp coarsely chopped fresh cilantro

1 Tbsp finely shredded fresh mint

4 large red-leaf lettuce leaves, torn into pieces

2 Tbsp fried shallot garnish *(left)*

To make the fried shallot garnish, slice 4 shallots into very thin slices, then separate the slices. Pour canola oil to a depth of about 1 inch (2.5 cm) in a small frying pan, place over medium heat, and heat to 325°F (165°C) on a deep-frying thermometer. Add the slices and fry until they turn light golden brown, about 5 minutes. Drain and let cool on paper towels.

In a saucepan, bring the broth to a gentle boil over medium heat. Add the chicken and cook, stirring to break up the meat, until the meat turns opaque and has a crumbled texture, about 3 minutes. Using a wire skimmer, transfer the chicken to a bowl. Season with salt and pepper and let cool.

Raise the heat under the boiling broth to medium-high, add the shrimp, and boil until they turn bright orange-pink, about 30 seconds. Drain well and let cool, then add to the bowl with the chicken.

Bring a saucepan three-fourths full of salted water to a boil over high heat. Add the noodles and cook until they are translucent, about 1 minute. Pour into a colander and rinse under cold running water. Drain well and transfer to a bowl. ⟫

To make the dressing, in a large bowl, combine the lime juice, fish sauce, sugar, roasted chile paste, and chiles. Stir together until the sugar dissolves. Add the chicken-shrimp mixture and the noodles to the dressing and toss to mix. Mix in the green onion, cilantro, and mint.

Divide the lettuce among individual salad bowls and mound the noodle salad on top. Garnish with the fried shallots. Serve at room temperature.

16

LEMON CHICKEN SALAD WITH TARRAGON

serves 4

1 lemon

2 skinless, boneless chicken breast halves (about 1 lb/500 g total weight)

Salt and freshly ground pepper

1 Tbsp grapeseed oil

½ fennel bulb, trimmed, quartered lengthwise, and finely chopped

1 green onion, including tender green parts, finely chopped

¾ tsp chopped fresh tarragon

⅓ cup (3 oz/80 g) mayonnaise

Tarragon and fennel are classic and delicious additions to chicken salad, but feel free to try other herb-and-vegetable combinations. One idea: chopped dill and diced Belgian endive for a Scandinavian-inspired version.

Grate ½ tsp zest from the lemon, then halve and squeeze 1 tsp juice. Set the zest and juice aside.

Place the chicken breast halves between 2 sheets of wax paper and pound them with a meat mallet to an even thickness. Pat dry.

Season both sides of the chicken breast halves with salt and pepper. In a large frying pan, warm the oil over medium heat. Add the chicken and cook until golden brown and opaque throughout, 4–5 minutes per side. Transfer to a cutting board and let stand for 5 minutes.

In a bowl, combine the lemon zest and juice, the fennel, green onion, tarragon, mayonnaise, ¾ tsp salt, and pepper to taste and mix until smooth. Chop the chicken finely and add to the fennel mixture. Toss until thoroughly blended and serve.

17

SEASONED BEAN SPROUT SALAD

serves 4–6

1 Tbsp sesame seeds

1½ lb (750 g) mung bean sprouts

2 Tbsp rice vinegar

1 Tbsp peanut oil

2 tsp toasted sesame oil

2 green onions, including tender green parts, minced

3 cloves garlic, minced

½ tsp chili powder

Salt

This salad, Korean in origin, is often served as one of many side dishes offered along with the usual steamed short-grain rice and soup. The salad may be made a day in advance. Mung bean sprouts release water as they marinate, so be sure to drain any excess liquid before serving the salad.

In a small frying pan, toast the sesame seeds over medium-low heat, stirring, until fragrant and starting to brown, about 2 minutes. Pour onto a plate and let cool.

Put the bean sprouts in a saucepan and add water to just cover. Bring to a boil over high heat and cook for 1 minute. Remove the pan from the heat, cover, and let stand for 2 minutes. Drain the sprouts and rinse under cold running water. Drain again, then gently squeeze the excess water from the sprouts. Transfer the sprouts to a clean kitchen towel, wring gently, and pat dry. Put the dry sprouts in a large bowl.

Put the vinegar in a bowl and add the peanut and sesame oils in a thin stream, whisking constantly until well blended. Add the green onions, garlic, sesame seeds, chili powder, and 1½ tsp salt and stir to mix well. Taste and adjust the seasonings. Pour the dressing over the bean sprouts and toss to coat thoroughly. Let stand at room temperature for 30 minutes before serving, or cover and refrigerate for at least 1 hour or up to overnight. Serve at room temperature or chilled.

18

INSALATA DI CAMPO

serves 4

1 bunch dandelion greens, or 12 large arugula leaves

1 head escarole, pale inner leaves only

½ small head radicchio

1 head frisée, pale yellow inner leaves only

¼ cup (1 oz/30 g) walnuts, coarsely chopped

4 Tbsp (2 fl oz/60 ml) extra-virgin olive oil

1 Tbsp red wine vinegar

1–2 Tbsp balsamic vinegar, depending upon age and intensity

Salt and freshly ground pepper

4 oz (125 g) thick slices pancetta, finely chopped

Parmesan cheese for shaving

An Italian favorite, this salad is full of the sharp, bitter flavors of chicories and dandelion greens. The more varied the greens, the better. Use the commonly available greens in this recipe, or look for specialty Italian chicories at farmers' markets and Italian produce markets. You should have about 6 cups (6 oz/185 g) of greens to make 4 salads.

Stem about 12 dandelion leaves, coarsely chop, and set aside. Tear the large leaves of escarole, radicchio, and frisée into bite-sized pieces, but leave small ones whole.

In a small frying pan, toast the walnuts over medium-low heat, stirring, until fragrant and starting to brown, about 5 minutes. Pour onto a plate to cool.

In a serving bowl, combine the oil and the vinegars and whisk well to make a vinaigrette. Stir in ½ tsp each salt and pepper. Taste and adjust the seasonings if needed. Set aside.

In a frying pan, cook the pancetta over medium-high heat until lightly browned, 3–4 minutes. Remove and set aside.

Just before serving, add the greens to the vinaigrette and toss. Divide among individual plates, topping each with pancetta and walnuts. Using a vegetable peeler, shave the cheese over the salad and serve.

19

BULGUR SALAD WITH LEMON, PEAS & MINT

serves 4

1 cup (6 oz/185 g) bulgur wheat

Salt and freshly ground pepper

2 tsp extra-virgin olive oil, plus 1 Tbsp

2/3 lb (315 g) sugar snap peas, trimmed and sliced on diagonal (about 2 cups)

1/3 cup (1/2 oz/15 g) minced fresh mint, plus sprigs for garnish

1 Tbsp fresh lemon juice

1 Tbsp capers, rinsed and chopped

2 oil-packed sun-dried tomatoes, chopped

In a saucepan, bring 2 cups (16 fl oz/500 ml) water to a boil. Add the bulgur and 1/2 tsp salt. Return to a boil, then reduce the heat to low. Cover and cook until the bulgur is tender and the water is absorbed, about 20 minutes.

Combine the bulgur and the 2 tsp oil in a bowl, turning gently to coat and fluff the grains. Let cool to room temperature.

Add the sugar snap peas, minced mint, lemon juice, capers, sun-dried tomatoes, 1/2 tsp salt, 1/2 tsp pepper, and the 1 Tbsp oil to the bulgur. Stir well to blend. Garnish with the mint sprigs and serve at room temperature.

Bulgur, the featured grain in the classic Mediterranean salad tabbouleh, is sometimes confused with cracked wheat. Bulgur comes in a variety of grinds, from fine to coarse, and is the better choice for salads. (Cracked wheat is crushed, and is better used as an addition to breads or in cereals.)

20

CRAB SUNOMONO

serves 4

1 large English cucumber, or 2 or 3 Japanese cucumbers

Salt

1 tsp sesame seeds

1/2 lb (250 g) cooked crabmeat, picked over for shell fragments

1/4 cup (2 fl oz/60 ml) seasoned rice vinegar

1 Tbsp sake

1 tsp sugar

1 tsp soy sauce

1/4 tsp toasted sesame oil

Using a mandoline or box grater, slice the cucumber into very thin slices. Sprinkle with 1 tsp salt and toss to combine. Place in a fine-mesh sieve and let stand at room temperature until most of the liquid has drained out, about 10 minutes. Discard the liquid and squeeze the cucumbers to remove any remaining moisture.

Meanwhile, in a small frying pan, toast the sesame seeds over medium-low heat, stirring, until they are fragrant and starting to brown, about 2 minutes. Pour onto a plate and let cool.

In a bowl, combine the crabmeat and cucumber slices. In a separate small bowl, combine the vinegar, sake, sugar, soy sauce, and sesame oil and whisk until well combined. Pour the vinegar mixture over the cucumber and crab mixture and toss to combine.

Divide the crab mixture among individual plates and sprinkle with the sesame seeds before serving.

In Japanese, su means "vinegar," and mono means "thing." So this delicious dish literally translates to "vinegared thing." Pickled crab and cucumber salad is a healthful, simple salad that is the perfect start to a meal of sushi or other fish entrée. You can try thinly sliced daikon or raw asparagus in place of the cucumber.

21

In this simple first course, salty, nutty-tasting Parmesan provides a suitably bold contrast to the natural acidity of lemon and the grassiness of asparagus. Extra-virgin olive oil, preferably a fruity one, binds together all of the elements nicely.

ASPARAGUS SALAD WITH LEMON & SHAVED PARMESAN
serves 6

3½ lb (1.75 kg) pencil-thin asparagus

Salt and freshly ground pepper

1 large lemon

2 Tbsp extra-virgin olive oil

Parmesan cheese for shaving

Bring a large saucepan two-thirds full of water to a boil over high heat. Have ready a bowl of ice water.

Trim off the tough end of each asparagus spear and cut the spears on the diagonal into 1½-inch (4-cm) lengths.

Add 1 Tbsp salt and the asparagus pieces to the boiling water and cook until the asparagus is crisp-tender and bright green, about 2½ minutes. Drain and then immediately plunge the asparagus into the ice water. Let stand until cool, about 2 minutes, then drain again and pat dry. Transfer to a serving platter.

Finely grate 1 Tbsp zest from the lemon, then halve and squeeze 1 Tbsp juice. In a small bowl, whisk together the lemon zest and juice, ¼ tsp salt, and ¼ tsp pepper. Add the oil in a thin stream, whisking constantly until the dressing is well blended. Taste and adjust the seasonings. Drizzle the dressing evenly over the asparagus. Using a vegetable peeler, shave the cheese over the asparagus and serve.

22

For the bitter greens in this recipe, try red Asian mustard greens, watercress, or dandelion leaves torn into bite-sized pieces, or a blend. You can also use additional whole baby arugula leaves.

BITTER GREENS WITH DUCK BREAST & CHERRIES
serves 4

FOR THE CHAMPAGNE VINAIGRETTE

3 Tbsp fresh lemon juice

1 tsp champagne vinegar

Salt and freshly ground pepper

2 Tbsp extra-virgin olive oil

2 small heads radicchio

1 cup (1 oz/30 g) baby arugula leaves

½ cup (½ oz/15 g) torn bitter greens *(left)*

2 Tbsp chopped fresh flat-leaf parsley

1 whole boneless duck breast

1 cup (¼ lb/125 g) fresh cherries, pitted and halved, or ¼ cup (1½ oz/45 g) dried tart cherries

To make the vinaigrette, in a large bowl, whisk together the lemon juice, vinegar, ½ tsp salt, and ¼ tsp pepper. Add the oil in a thin stream, whisking constantly until the dressing is well blended. Set aside.

Using a sharp knife, cut away the hard white core from the base of the radicchio. Cut the head lengthwise into slices ¼ inch (6 mm) thick, then separate the layers and remove the hard *V*-shaped core. Put the cut radicchio into the bowl holding the vinaigrette. Add the arugula, bitter greens, and parsley and gently mix. Set aside.

Pat the duck breast dry. In a frying pan, warm ½ tsp salt over high heat. When it is hot, add the duck breast, skin side down. Reduce the heat to medium-high and cook until crisp and golden brown on the first side, 6–7 minutes. Turn and cook the other side until lightly browned, about 4 minutes. Cover the pan and cook until the duck breast is medium-rare, another 3–4 minutes. Transfer to paper towels to drain briefly.

Place the duck breast on a cutting board and separate the breast halves. Cut each half crosswise into slices ¼ inch (6 mm) thick.

Heap the dressed radicchio mixture onto a platter and arrange the duck slices and cherries on top of it. Serve warm.

ISRAELI COUSCOUS SALAD WITH FAVA BEANS & OLIVES

serves 6

3 cups (24 fl oz/750 ml) chicken broth

½ cup (4 fl oz/125 ml) fresh lemon juice

Salt

4 Tbsp (2 fl oz/60 ml) extra-virgin olive oil

2⅓ cups (¾ lb/375 g) Israeli couscous

2½ lb (1.25 kg) fava beans in the pod, shelled

4 carrots, peeled and finely chopped

¾ cup (1 oz/30 g) coarsely chopped fresh flat-leaf parsley

24 oil-cured black olives, pitted and coarsely chopped

5 oz (155 g) feta cheese, crumbled

If you prefer mild olives, try a large, meaty bright green Italian variety— Castelvetrano or Cerignola. They can be found jarred in most well-stocked supermarkets.

In a small saucepan, combine the broth, lemon juice, and ½ tsp salt and bring to a boil over high heat. Meanwhile, in a saucepan, warm 2 Tbsp of the olive oil over medium heat. Add the couscous and cook, stirring occasionally, until light golden brown, about 4 minutes.

Pour the hot broth mixture over the couscous, raise the heat to high, and bring to a boil. Cover immediately, reduce the heat to medium-low, and simmer until all of the liquid has been absorbed, about 15 minutes. Drizzle the remaining 2 Tbsp olive oil over the couscous, stir to mix, and transfer to a large bowl. Let cool to room temperature.

While the couscous cools, fill a saucepan three-fourths full with salted water and bring to a boil over high heat. Have ready a bowl of ice water. Add the fava beans to the boiling water and blanch just until tender, about 2 minutes. Use a slotted spoon to remove the beans and immediately transfer them to the ice water. Let stand until cool, then lift out the beans with the slotted spoon. Add the carrots to the boiling salted water and cook until crisp-tender, about 2 minutes. Transfer the carrots to the ice water. Let stand until cool, then drain again.

Pinch each fava bean to pop it from its skin. You should have about 1¼ cups skinned beans. Add the fava beans, carrots, parsley, olives, and cheese to the bowl with the couscous, toss well, and serve.

CLASSIC EGG SALAD

serves 4

8 eggs

¼ cup (2 fl oz/60 ml) mayonnaise

1 Tbsp Dijon mustard

1 Tbsp chopped fresh tarragon

1 Tbsp chopped fresh chives

2 tsp chopped fresh dill

¼ cup (1 oz/30 g) thinly sliced celery

Salt and freshly ground pepper

What's more comforting than a classic, creamy egg salad sandwiched between two slices of toasted bread? Or a few spoonfuls accompanied with slices of fresh tomato and some crisp lettuce? If you ever have a carton of eggs that is about to expire, this salad is a most delicious way to use them up.

To hard-cook the eggs, place them in a saucepan just large enough to hold them. Add cold water to cover by 1 inch (2.5 cm) and bring just to a boil over high heat. Remove the pan from the heat and cover. Let stand for 15 minutes. Have ready a bowl of ice water. Drain the eggs, then transfer to the ice water and let cool.

Peel the eggs and slice them into a bowl. Then, using 2 table knives, scissor-cut them into smaller pieces. Add the mayonnaise, mustard, herbs, celery, salt to taste, and a few grindings of pepper, and mix to combine evenly. Serve.

25

ARTICHOKE & WHITE BEAN SALAD

serves 8

This salad makes enough for a crowd and is great for festive spring gatherings, alongside a pork roast or grilled chicken. You can make the salad in advance and keep it covered in the refrigerator for up to 24 hours. Remove from the refrigerator 30 minutes before serving.

FOR THE DRESSING

¼ cup (2 fl oz/60 ml) fresh lemon juice

1 clove garlic, thinly sliced

1 tsp Dijon mustard

¼ tsp red pepper flakes

1 tsp ground fennel seeds

Salt and freshly ground pepper

½ cup (4 fl oz/125 ml) extra-virgin olive oil

½ lemon (if using fresh artichokes)

6 baby artichokes, or 1 package (8 oz/250 g) frozen quartered artichoke hearts, thawed and brought to room temperature

2 cans (15 oz/470 g each) white beans, rinsed and drained

1 small red onion, chopped

2 celery ribs, thinly sliced

2 Tbsp chopped fresh oregano

To make the dressing, in a large bowl, whisk together the lemon juice, garlic, mustard, red pepper flakes, and fennel seeds. Season with salt and pepper to taste. Add the oil in a thin stream, whisking constantly until the dressing is well blended.

If using fresh artichokes, squeeze the lemon half into a large bowl of cold water. Trim the artichoke stems, leaving about ½ inch (12 mm). Cut ½ inch off the tops. Peel off the tough outer leaves until you reach the tender, pale green leaves. Cut each artichoke lengthwise into 6 wedges and immerse in the lemon water. Bring a pot three-fourths full of salted water to a boil. Add the artichokes and cook until tender, about 15 minutes. Drain and let cool to room temperature.

In a large bowl, combine the artichokes, beans, onion, celery, and oregano and toss well. Let stand for at least 30 minutes or refrigerate for up to 4 hours to allow the flavors to blend before serving.

26

DANDELION GREENS SALAD

serves 6

6 oz (185 g) young dandelion leaves, tough stems removed

2 Tbsp blanched hazelnuts, coarsely chopped (optional)

3 oz (90 g) thick-cut bacon, cut crosswise into pieces ½ inch (12 mm) wide

1½ Tbsp sherry vinegar or red wine vinegar

2–3 Tbsp olive oil

Salt and freshly ground pepper

If dandelion greens are unavailable, use other sturdy leaves so the greens do not wilt excessively when the hot dressing is poured over the salad. The outer dark green leaves of curly endive work well, as does mature spinach.

Pick over the dandelion leaves, tearing the larger ones in half. Place in a serving bowl. Add the hazelnuts, if using.

In a small frying pan, fry the bacon over high heat until the fat has been rendered and the bacon is crisp, about 1 minute. Using a slotted spoon, transfer the bacon to the bowl holding the dandelion leaves, leaving the fat in the pan.

Return the pan to high heat, add the vinegar, and swirl the pan or stir with a wooden spoon to pick up the sediment on the bottom.

Depending on the amount of fat in the pan, pour in enough oil to make 3 Tbsp fat, swirl once to heat a little, and then pour the contents of the pan over the salad. Season with salt and pepper to taste, toss, and serve.

27

Strictly seasonal, green garlic and spring onions are the season's gems. Green garlic is milder than its mature relative and looks like a slightly larger green onion. True spring onions resemble green onions but have an oversized white bulb close to the size of a conventional white onion.

POTATO SALAD WITH FAVA BEANS, GREEN GARLIC & CRÈME FRAÎCHE

serves 4–6

1 lb (500 g) young fava beans in the pod, shelled (about 1 cup)

6 stems green garlic

4 spring onions

2½ lb (1.25 kg) small waxy potatoes such as Yukon Gold, Yellow Finn, or Red Rose

Salt and freshly ground pepper

½ cup (4 fl oz/125 ml) mayonnaise

½ cup (4 oz/125 g) crème fraîche

2 tsp Dijon mustard

2 tsp fresh lemon juice

1 Tbsp minced fresh tarragon, plus ½ tsp

1 Tbsp minced fresh flat-leaf parsley, plus ½ tsp

Bring a saucepan of water to a boil over medium-high heat. Blanch the shelled favas just until the skin plumps, about 20 seconds. Drain and pinch each bean to pop it from its skin. Set the beans aside.

Remove the tough outer skin from each green garlic stem. Finely chop the bulbs and set aside.

Trim the spring onions, leaving about 2 inches (5 cm) of light green, and finely chop. Set aside.

In a saucepan, combine the potatoes with water to cover by 2 inches (5 cm) and add 1 tsp salt. Bring to a boil over medium-high heat, then reduce the heat to medium and cook, uncovered, until tender and easily pierced with a fork, 20–25 minutes. Drain, and when just cool enough to handle, peel and cut into ½-inch (12-mm) cubes. Place the still-warm potatoes in a large bowl.

In a bowl, combine the mayonnaise, crème fraîche, mustard, lemon juice, ½ tsp salt, and ½ tsp pepper. Mix well. Taste and adjust the seasoning. Spoon this dressing over the warm potatoes, turning gently. Add the green garlic, spring onions, the 1 Tbsp each tarragon and parsley, and the fava beans, reserving a few for garnish. Turn well.

Garnish with the remaining tarragon, parsley, and fava beans before serving.

28

Cutting the radishes into thin slivers tempers their peppery bite and spreads it evenly throughout the dish. The sweet-tart dressing contrasts nicely with the radishes and complements the snow peas.

SNOW PEA & RADISH SALAD

serves 4

Salt and freshly ground pepper

½ lb (250 g) snow peas, trimmed

5 radishes

1½ Tbsp rice vinegar

½ tsp honey

¼ cup (2 fl oz/60 ml) grapeseed oil

Fresh mint leaves from 2 sprigs, cut into thin ribbons

Bring a large pot of salted water to a boil over high heat. Have ready a large bowl of ice water. Add the snow peas to the boiling water and cook until tender, 1–2 minutes. Drain the peas and then plunge them into the ice water. Let stand until cool, then drain and pat dry.

Cut the snow peas on the diagonal into 1-inch (2.5-cm) pieces and place in a bowl. Thinly slice the radishes, then cut the slices into thin strips. Add the radishes to the bowl with the snow peas.

In a small bowl, whisk together the vinegar, honey, and a pinch each of salt and pepper. Add the oil in a thin stream, whisking constantly until the dressing is well blended. Taste and adjust the seasonings.

Add enough dressing to coat the snow peas and radishes and toss well to coat (you may not need all of the dressing). Add the mint to the salad, toss gently to mix, and serve.

29

MÂCHE, PURSLANE & GREEN ONION SALAD

serves 4–6

Purslane, a succulent with a slightly sour taste, is a bright and flavorful green to use in salads. Here, a mix of purslane and the milder mâche strikes just the right flavor balance, and is delicious with a citrusy vinaigrette.

FOR THE LEMON-THYME VINAIGRETTE

Grated zest and juice of ½ lemon

¼ cup (2 fl oz/60 ml) white wine vinegar

1½ tsp fresh thyme leaves

Salt and freshly ground pepper

½ cup (4 fl oz/125 ml) extra-virgin olive oil

4 cups (4 oz/125 g) mâche or field greens

4 cups (4 oz/125 g) purslane, thick stems removed, or baby arugula

4 green onions, including tender green parts, cut into 1-inch (2.5-cm) pieces (on the diagonal if thick)

To make the vinaigrette, in a large bowl, whisk together the lemon zest and juice, vinegar, thyme, and salt and pepper to taste. Add the oil in a thin stream, whisking constantly until the dressing is well blended.

Add the mâche, purslane, and green onions to the bowl and toss with the vinaigrette. Season with salt and pepper to taste and serve.

30

GRILLED HALLOUMI & LITTLE GEM SALAD WITH PRESERVED-LEMON DRESSING

serves 4–6

Halloumi is a firm cheese that originated in Cypress, but is increasingly made domestically. Its claim to fame is that it holds its shape when grilled or fried. Preserved lemon, more intense in flavor than fresh lemon, is available in specialty food shops or can be made at home.

8 oz (250 g) halloumi cheese, cut into slices

6 Tbsp (3 fl oz/90 ml) extra-virgin olive oil

Salt and freshly ground pepper

3 Tbsp (¼ oz/7 g) fresh oregano leaves, chopped

2 Tbsp sherry vinegar

1 preserved lemon, cut into slices

2 romaine hearts, or 2 or 3 heads Little Gem lettuce, halved lengthwise

Arrange the cheese slices in a shallow baking dish and drizzle with 1½ Tbsp of the oil, ¼ tsp salt, ¾ tsp pepper, and 1½ Tbsp of the oregano. Let marinate for 1 hour.

Meanwhile, in a large bowl, combine 3½ Tbsp oil, the vinegar, ¼ tsp salt, and ¾ tsp pepper. Whisk well to make a vinaigrette. Reserve a few of the lemon slices and finely chop the remaining slices. Add them to the vinaigrette, mix well, and set aside.

Prepare a charcoal or gas grill for direct-heat cooking over medium-high heat. When ready, remove the cheese slices from the marinade, place them on the grill rack, and cook until the edges soften, the interior is warm, and grill marks appear on the bottom side, about 2 minutes. Turn and grill on the second side until lightly golden, 1–2 minutes. Transfer to a plate.

Brush the lettuce halves with the remaining tablespoon of oil and place, cut sides down, on the grill rack. Cook until grill marks appear, about 2 minutes, then transfer to a serving platter. Top with the warm cheese and drizzle the lettuce and cheese with the vinaigrette. Garnish with the reserved lemon slices and serve.

Now is the right time of year to enjoy alfresco lunches of crisp young greens, shoots, and edible flowers drizzled with herb vinaigrette or just a squeeze of lemon juice. For main-course salads, marinate tuna or spring lamb in garlic, or pair goat cheese with chicken for a satisfying meal. Garnet-colored cherries and the first berries of the season add sweet, jammy accents to salads, or they can be puréed into tangy, vibrant dressings.

1
PEA & ASPARAGUS SALAD WITH MEYER LEMON DRESSING
page 106

2
CHEF'S SALAD WITH SOPRESSATA, FONTINA & PICKLED PEPPERS
page 106

3
SALAD OF SPRING BEANS, PEAS & ZUCCHINI RIBBONS
page 108

8
SPRING GREENS & FLOWERS SALAD
page 111

9
WARM GOAT CHEESE & CHICKEN SALAD
page 112

10
POTATO SALAD WITH ARTICHOKES, FETA CHEESE & OLIVE RELISH
page 112

15
GREEN BEAN SALAD WITH MUSTARD SEEDS, HERBS & BABY CHARD
page 117

16
LITTLE GEM WEDGES WITH RADISHES & GREEN GODDESS DRESSING
page 117

17
GRILLED SALMON, POTATO & ASPARAGUS SALAD
page 118

22
GREEN MANGO & GRILLED SHRIMP SALAD
page 121

23
WATERCRESS & DUCK SALAD WITH GINGERED STRAWBERRY DRESSING
page 123

24
TABBOULEH WITH FETA CHEESE
page 123

29
ARUGULA SALAD WITH BERRIES & GORGONZOLA
page 125

30
GRILLED TUNA WITH POTATO, AVOCADO & TOMATO CONFIT
page 126

31
CHOPPED CHICKEN SALAD WITH LEMON-TARRAGON DRESSING
page 126

4
**MELON SALAD WITH
YOGURT-HONEY DRESSING**
page 108

5
**BULGUR SALAD WITH ZUCCHINI,
ASPARAGUS & GREEN ONIONS**
page 109

6
**FAVA BEAN & CORN SALAD
WITH FRESH MINT**
page 109

7
**CARROT & JICAMA SALAD
WITH LIME VINAIGRETTE**
page 111

11
**SPRING HERB SALAD WITH
WALNUT-CRUSTED GOAT CHEESE**
page 114

12
**GRILLED LAMB &
COUSCOUS SALAD**
page 114

13
**PASTA SALAD WITH BABY
ARTICHOKES & GRILLED TUNA**
page 115

14
**LOBSTER & AVOCADO SALAD
WITH SHAVED MEYER LEMONS**
page 115

18
**BABY ARTICHOKE, PARMESAN
& ARUGULA SALAD**
page 118

19
**FENNEL, CHICKPEA & SUN-DRIED
TOMATO SALAD WITH MOZZARELLA**
page 120

20
**SPRING RICE SALAD WITH
DILL-LEMON DRESSING**
page 120

21
**LEMONY QUINOA SALAD WITH
RADISHES, AVOCADO & BASIL**
page 121

25
**ORZO SALAD WITH ARTICHOKES,
PINE NUTS & GOLDEN RAISINS**
page 124

26
**ROAST BEEF SALAD WITH LEEKS &
CREAMY MUSTARD VINAIGRETTE**
page 124

27
**GRILLED ASPARAGUS
& PROSCIUTTO SALAD**
page 125

28
STRAWBERRY & CHERRY SALAD
page 125

may

1

PEA & ASPARAGUS SALAD WITH MEYER LEMON DRESSING

serves 6–8

Salt and freshly ground pepper

2 cups (10 oz/315 g) fresh shelled English peas (about 2 lb/1 kg unshelled)

2 lb (1 kg) thin asparagus tips

2 cups (2 oz/60 g) pea shoots

Shredded zest and juice of 1 Meyer lemon or regular lemon

¼ cup (2 fl oz/60 ml) extra-virgin olive oil

¼ tsp sugar, if needed

An all-green salad makes a bold statement that spring has arrived, but you can also use a mix of asparagus colors— green, white, and purple—for a very pretty combination. Shaved Parmesan or pecorino can be added for a rich, nutty note, and any leftover salad can be stirred into risotto, pasta, or omelettes.

Bring a saucepan three-fourths full of salted water to a boil. Meanwhile, prepare a large bowl of ice water. Add the peas to the boiling water and blanch for 1 minute. Using a strainer, scoop out the peas and refresh them in the ice water. Scoop them out of the ice water with the strainer, and set aside.

Using the same boiling water, cook the asparagus until tender, 3 minutes. Add more ice to the bowl of ice water, if needed. Drain the asparagus and refresh in the same bowl of ice water. Drain again, slice in half lengthwise, and set aside.

In a bowl, combine the peas, asparagus, pea shoots, lemon zest and juice, and oil, and toss to combine. Add the sugar if not using Meyer lemon juice. Season with salt and pepper to taste. Transfer to a platter or divide among individual plates and serve.

2

CHEF'S SALAD WITH SOPRESSATA, FONTINA & PICKLED PEPPERS

serves 6

5 thick slices day-old country-style bread

2 Tbsp extra-virgin olive oil

Salt and freshly ground pepper

FOR THE OREGANO VINAIGRETTE

¼ cup (2 fl oz/60 ml) extra-virgin olive oil

1 Tbsp minced shallot

2 Tbsp red wine vinegar

2 Tbsp chopped fresh oregano

12–15 cherry tomatoes, halved

1½ heads romaine lettuce, torn into bite-sized pieces (about 6 cups/6 oz/185 g)

18 slices sopressata or salami, cut into triangles

6 oz (185 g) fontina cheese, thinly sliced and cut into strips ½ inch (12 mm) wide

8 oz (250 g) peperoncini, coarsely chopped

1 Tbsp chopped fresh oregano

Think of this as an antipasto platter transformed into a chef's salad with the addition of lettuce and a dressing, and this will help you to create your own variations. Different cured meats, such as salami or bresaola, could be used, or cheeses such as pecorino or mozzarella.

Preheat the oven to 400°F (200°C).

Cut the bread into 1-inch (2.5-cm) cubes. Put them on a baking sheet just large enough to hold the cubes in a single layer, drizzle with the 2 Tbsp oil, and toss several times to coat. Sprinkle with ½ tsp salt. Bake, turning several times, until golden, 10–15 minutes. Set the croutons aside.

To make the vinaigrette, in the bottom of a large bowl, combine the ¼ cup oil, shallot, vinegar, 2 Tbsp oregano, ¼ tsp salt, and ¼ tsp pepper. Mix well with a fork or whisk.

Add the tomatoes to the vinaigrette and press them slightly with the back of a fork to release their juices. Just before serving, add the lettuce and half the croutons and toss.

Divide the dressed salad evenly among individual bowls. Divide and arrange the sopressata, cheese, peperoncini, and remaining croutons on each salad. Sprinkle with the 1 Tbsp oregano and serve.

3

SALAD OF SPRING BEANS, PEAS & ZUCCHINI RIBBONS

serves 4

To make this dish into a pasta salad, simply toss about ¾ lb (375 g) cooked and drained fettuccine with the prepared salad. As a pasta salad, the recipe will yield 8 to 10 servings.

Salt and freshly ground pepper

1 cup (5 oz/155 g) fresh shelled English peas (about 1 lb/500 g unshelled)

2 lb (1 kg) fava beans in the pod, shelled

½ lb (250 g) haricots verts or other young, tender green beans, stem ends trimmed

4 zucchini (about 1 lb/500 g total weight)

FOR THE BASIL MARINADE

2 cloves garlic

⅓ cup (3 fl oz/80 ml) extra-virgin olive oil

3 Tbsp fresh lemon juice

⅓ cup (½ oz/15 g) julienned fresh basil leaves

15 anchovy fillets

½ cup (2 oz/60 g) Parmesan cheese shavings

Bring a saucepan three-fourths full of salted water to a boil over medium-high heat and add the peas. Boil until just tender, 3–5 minutes. Do not overcook. Using a strainer, scoop out the peas and place them under cold running water to stop the cooking. Drain again and set aside.

Add the fava beans to the same boiling water. Blanch until just tender, about 2 minutes. Drain and let cool, then pinch each bean to pop it from its skin. Set aside.

Arrange the green beans in a steamer basket, pour out most of the water from the saucepan, return it to the heat, and place the basket over the boiling water. (The water should not touch the bottom of the basket.) Cover and steam just until the beans are tender, 3–4 minutes for haricots verts and 5–7 minutes for larger beans. Lift out the basket and place under cold running water to stop the cooking. Drain and set aside.

Using a vegetable peeler, peel the zucchini. Then, still using the vegetable peeler, cut the flesh of the zucchini into long, thin, fettuccinelike ribbons. Set aside. ⟫

To make the marinade, in a bowl or mortar, combine the garlic and ½ tsp salt. Using a fork or a pestle, crush them into a paste. Using a fork, stir vigorously as you add the oil in a thin stream, and then stir in the lemon juice and ½ tsp pepper. Pour this mixture into a large bowl and add the peas, favas, green beans, zucchini ribbons, and the basil. Turn until well coated, cover, and refrigerate for at least 1½ hours or up to 5 hours.

To serve, gently mix all but 4 or 5 of the anchovy fillets into the vegetables. Transfer the mixture to a serving bowl or a platter and top with the remaining anchovies. Scatter the cheese shavings over the vegetables and anchovies and serve.

4

MELON SALAD WITH YOGURT-HONEY DRESSING

serves 4

If serving this salad as a dessert, try pairing it with a dessert wine to enhance its flavors. Sauternes or ice wine pair beautifully with the ripe melon flavors and the honey as well as the splash of orange muscat wine in the dressing.

FOR THE YOGURT-HONEY DRESSING

1 cup (8 oz/250 g) plain Greek yogurt

¼ cup (3 oz/90 g) honey

2 Tbsp orange muscat dessert wine or other sweet, fruity wine

¼ small ripe honeydew melon, seeded

½ small ripe cantaloupe melon, seeded

¾ cup (4 oz/125 g) seedless green grapes, halved

½ cup (2 oz/60 g) coarsely chopped pistachios

To make the dressing, in a small bowl, whisk the yogurt, honey, and wine together. Set aside.

Using a large spoon, scoop out the honeydew and cantaloupe melon flesh and cut into ¾-inch (2-cm) pieces, or scoop out with a melon baller. In a serving bowl, combine the melon pieces and the grapes and toss together gently. If desired, transfer to individual serving bowls.

Drizzle the dressing back and forth across the fruit. Scatter with the pistachios and serve.

5

BULGUR SALAD WITH ZUCCHINI, ASPARAGUS & GREEN ONIONS

serves 6

For a spring twist on tabbouleh, this salad gives you the chance to fire up the grill and embrace the warmer weather. Bursting with green vegetables and herbs of spring— asparagus, zucchini, green onions, and mint and parsley— the salad is fresh and bright-tasting. Serve alongside grilled lamb chops for a quick and healthful dinner.

8–10 spears asparagus, tough ends trimmed

2 zucchini, cut on diagonal into slices ¼ inch (6 mm) thick

1 tsp olive oil

1½ cups (9 oz/280 g) bulgur wheat

FOR THE LEMON-CARDAMOM DRESSING

2 tsp grated lemon zest

2 Tbsp fresh lemon juice

2 tsp ground cumin

½ tsp ground turmeric

½ tsp cardamom seeds, crushed

3 Tbsp extra-virgin olive oil

1 cup (7 oz/220 g) canned chickpeas, drained and rinsed

2 green onions, including tender green parts, thinly sliced

1 bunch fresh mint leaves, minced

2 Tbsp minced fresh flat-leaf parsley

Prepare a charcoal or gas grill for direct-heat cooking over medium heat.

If the asparagus spears are thick, peel them to within about 2 inches (5 cm) of the tips. Put the asparagus and zucchini in a heatproof bowl, pour boiling water over to cover, and let stand for 2 minutes to soften slightly. Drain, let cool, and toss with the 1 tsp oil. If desired, put them in a grill basket.

When the grill is ready, put the bulgur in a heatproof bowl and add boiling water to cover by 2 inches (5 cm). Let stand for 10 minutes. Meanwhile, grill the asparagus and zucchini, turning often, until lightly browned and crisp-tender, 4–5 minutes. Remove to a platter and let cool slightly. Cut the asparagus spears on the diagonal into thirds.

To make the dressing, in a bowl, whisk together the lemon zest and juice, cumin, turmeric, cardamom, 1 tsp salt, and several grindings of pepper. Add the 3 Tbsp oil in a thin stream, whisking constantly until the dressing is smooth. »→

Pour the dressing into a saucepan, add the chickpeas, and warm over medium heat for a couple of minutes, stirring occasionally.

Drain the bulgur. Combine the bulgur, grilled vegetables, green onions, mint, parsley, and chickpeas with the dressing in a serving bowl and toss to coat evenly. Serve warm or at room temperature.

6

FAVA BEAN & CORN SALAD WITH FRESH MINT

serves 4

Sweet young corn and buttery fresh fava beans make an irresistible pair in this simple salad. Even after shelling, fava beans have a second skin that needs to be peeled away in all but the youngest, most tender beans. Serve with warm sourdough bread and sweet butter.

Salt and freshly ground pepper

2 cups (12 oz/375 g) fresh or thawed frozen corn kernels (from about 2 ears of corn)

1½ lb (750 g) fava beans in the pod, shelled

2 Tbsp extra-virgin olive oil

1½ Tbsp cider vinegar

8 radishes, trimmed and thinly sliced

2 Tbsp coarsely chopped fresh mint leaves

Bring a large pot of salted water to a boil. Add the corn and cook for 1 minute. Using a strainer, scoop out the corn and set aside.

Add the fava beans to the boiling water and cook until just tender, about 2 minutes. Drain and rinse under cold running water. Pinch each fava bean to pop it from its skin.

In a bowl, whisk together the oil and vinegar until well blended. Stir in the corn, favas, radishes, and mint. Season with ½ tsp salt and a few grindings of pepper. Serve at once, or cover and refrigerate for up to 4 hours and serve chilled.

7

Carrots and jicama, both of them crunchy and sweet, are a winning combination in this tangy, low-calorie salad. Serve as an accompaniment to a smoked turkey sandwich, or grilled chicken, shrimp, or fish.

CARROT & JICAMA SALAD WITH LIME VINAIGRETTE

serves 4–6

2 tsp ground cumin

3 Tbsp fresh lime juice

1 Tbsp seeded and minced jalapeño chile

1 tsp minced garlic

Salt

2 Tbsp grapeseed oil

1 large or 2 medium jicamas, about ¾ lb (375 g)

3 carrots (about 10 oz/315 g total weight), peeled

¼ cup (⅓ oz/10 g) minced fresh cilantro

In a small frying pan over medium-low heat, warm the cumin just until fragrant, about 20 seconds. Transfer to a small bowl. Add the lime juice, jalapeño, garlic, and ½ tsp salt and whisk. Add the oil in a thin stream, whisking constantly until the vinaigrette is smooth. Set aside.

Using a sharp knife, trim the stem and root ends from the jicama(s), then cut into 4 or 6 manageable wedges. Cut and lift up a small piece of the brown skin near the stem end and pull down to remove. Use a vegetable peeler to remove any stubborn remnants of skin and the tough layer underneath.

Using a food processor fitted with the shredding disk or the largest holes of a box grater, shred the carrots and jicama(s). In a large bowl, combine the carrots, jicama(s), and cilantro. Pour the vinaigrette over the vegetables and toss gently to mix. Divide the salad among individual plates and serve.

8

Celebrate spring with this colorful, simple-to-make salad. You can buy edible, pesticide-free flowers at many greengrocers and farmers' markets, or grow some in your garden at home. Other pretty, edible flowers include pansies, violets, hibiscuses, and scented geraniums.

SPRING GREENS & FLOWERS SALAD

serves 6

4 cups (4 oz/125 g) baby spinach leaves

4 cups (4 oz/125 g) oakleaf lettuce leaves

1 cup (1 oz/30 g) mâche or field greens

½ cup (¾ oz/20 g) garlic chive flowers, or 2 Tbsp minced fresh chives

¼ cup (2 fl oz/60 ml) rice vinegar

2 Tbsp peeled and minced fresh young ginger or 1 Tbsp mature fresh ginger

1 clove garlic, minced

½ cup (4 fl oz/125 ml) safflower oil

Salt and freshly ground pepper

12 nasturtiums or other edible flowers

In a large bowl, combine the spinach, oakleaf lettuce, mâche, and chive flowers. Toss gently to mix and set aside.

In a small bowl, combine the rice vinegar, ginger, and garlic. Add the oil in a thin stream, whisking constantly until the vinaigrette is well blended. Season with salt and pepper to taste.

Drizzle the vinaigrette over the greens and toss to mix well. Transfer to a serving bowl, garnish with the nasturtiums, and serve.

9

WARM GOAT CHEESE & CHICKEN SALAD

serves 4

½ cup (2 oz/60 g) fine dried bread crumbs or panko

Salt and freshly ground pepper

1 large egg

8 oz (250 g) fresh goat cheese, cut into 8 thick rounds

Grated zest and juice of 1 lemon

1 tsp tarragon mustard or Dijon mustard

5 Tbsp (2½ fl oz/75 ml) olive oil

2 tsp finely chopped fresh tarragon

6 oz (185 g) mixed baby salad greens

3 cups (18 oz/560 g) shredded roasted chicken

2 Tbsp grapeseed oil

This salad is also delicious without the chicken, as a classic goat cheese side salad. Serve with a crisp white wine like sauvignon blanc or pinot gris.

In a shallow bowl, combine the bread crumbs and a pinch each of salt and pepper. Lightly beat the egg in another shallow bowl. Dip 1 flat surface of each cheese round into the egg, letting the excess egg drip back into the bowl. Then dip the egg-coated surface of each in the bread crumbs, patting the crumbs in place. Leave the second side and the rims of the cheese rounds uncoated. Set aside.

In a large bowl, whisk together the lemon zest and juice, mustard, ¼ tsp salt, and a pinch of pepper. Add the olive oil in a thin stream, whisking constantly until the dressing is smooth. Stir in the tarragon.

Add the mixed greens and the chicken to the dressing and toss to coat evenly. Arrange on individual plates. In a large nonstick frying pan, warm the grapeseed oil over medium-high heat until it shimmers. Working in batches if needed, add the cheese rounds and cook on the crumbed side until just beginning to soften but not melt, about 45 seconds. Carefully flip the rounds and cook for about 30 seconds on the other side. Top the salads with the cheeses and serve.

10

POTATO SALAD WITH ARTICHOKES, FETA CHEESE & OLIVE RELISH

serves 4–6

FOR THE OLIVE RELISH

5 Tbsp (2½ fl oz/75 ml) olive oil

2½ Tbsp white wine vinegar

1 large clove garlic, minced

1½ tsp dried oregano

Salt and freshly ground pepper

6 large Greek or Sicilian green olives, pitted and chopped

6–8 brine-cured black Mediterranean olives, pitted and chopped

½ cup (2½ oz/75 g) chopped fennel

3 large green onions, including green parts, chopped

12 small multicolored potatoes (about 2½ lb/1.25 kg total weight)

1 can (14 oz/440 g) quartered artichoke hearts in water

5 oz (155 g) feta cheese, coarsely crumbled

Although feta originated in Greece, French feta, milder and less salty, is better for this salad because of the saltiness of the olive relish. You can make the olive relish up to a day in advance. Cover and refrigerate, stirring occasionally, until ready to use.

To make the olive relish, combine the oil, vinegar, garlic, oregano, and ¼ tsp pepper in a bowl. Whisk to blend. Stir in the olives, fennel, and two-thirds of the green onions.

Bring a large pot of salted water to a boil. Add the potatoes and cook until tender when pierced with a small knife, about 25 minutes. Drain and let stand until cool to the touch, about 20 minutes. Cut the potatoes in half, then transfer to a large bowl. Sprinkle with salt and pepper to taste. Add the artichokes and olive relish. Toss to blend. Stir in most of the cheese, reserving some for sprinkling on top.

Sprinkle the remaining green onions and the remaining cheese over the salad and serve.

11

Goat cheese crusted with nuts and baked until warm is a delicious topping for a fresh herb salad with a slightly sweet, acidic dressing. If you like, serve with a basket of garlic-rubbed crostini and spread the goat cheese on top.

SPRING HERB SALAD WITH WALNUT-CRUSTED GOAT CHEESE

serves 6

6 Tbsp (3 fl oz/90 ml) champagne vinegar

2 shallots, minced

1 Tbsp honey

Salt and freshly ground pepper

½ cup (4 fl oz/125 ml) plus 2 Tbsp walnut oil

3 cups (12 oz/375 g) walnuts

2 logs (9 oz/280 g each) fresh goat cheese

¼ cup (2 fl oz/60 ml) extra-virgin olive oil

7 cups (7 oz/220 g) mâche, field greens, baby arugula, baby spinach, or a combination

½ cup (¾ oz/20 g) coarsely chopped fresh dill

1 cup (1½ oz/45 g) coarsely chopped fresh flat-leaf parsley

½ cup (¾ oz/20 g) minced fresh chives

Preheat the oven to 350°F (180°C).

In a small bowl, whisk together the vinegar, shallots, honey, 2 pinches of salt, and several grindings of pepper. Add the walnut oil in a thin stream, whisking constantly until the vinaigrette is well blended. Taste and adjust the seasonings. Set aside.

In a small frying pan, toast the walnuts over medium-low heat, stirring, until fragrant and starting to brown, about 5 minutes. Pour onto a plate to cool, then finely chop. In a bowl, stir together the chopped walnuts and ¼ tsp salt.

Season each cheese log with salt and pepper. Using a thin-bladed knife, cut each log crosswise into 6 equal slices. Coat the slices on all sides with the walnuts, pressing gently so that the nuts adhere. Transfer to a rimmed baking sheet and drizzle lightly with the olive oil. Bake until warm, about 5 minutes.

Meanwhile, in a large bowl, toss together the mâche, dill, parsley, chives, 2 pinches of salt, and several grindings of pepper. Whisk the vinaigrette to recombine, then drizzle one-third of it over the greens and toss well. Taste and adjust the seasonings. Divide the dressed greens among individual plates. Top each serving with 2 warm cheese rounds. Pass the remaining dressing at the table for drizzling.

12

If you can't find Israeli couscous, substitute 1½ cups (9 oz/280 g) instant couscous: place in a heatproof bowl; bring 2¾ cups (22 fl oz/680 ml) chicken broth to a boil with the onion, salt, and pepper; pour over the couscous and stir to combine; cover and let stand for 15 minutes. Or, boil 10 oz (315 g) orzo pasta until al dente, drain, and toss with the cooked onion, salt, pepper, oil, mint, and lemon juice.

GRILLED LAMB & COUSCOUS SALAD

serves 4

1¼ lb (625 g) boneless leg of lamb, cut into thick slices

2 Tbsp extra-virgin olive oil, plus ¼ cup (2 fl oz/60 ml)

Salt and freshly ground pepper

¼ tsp dried thyme

1 Tbsp grapeseed oil

1 small yellow onion, finely chopped

1½ cups (9 oz/280 g) Israeli couscous

2 cups (16 fl oz/500 ml) chicken broth

¼ cup (⅓ oz/10 g) minced fresh mint

Juice of 1 lemon

2 cups (2 oz/60 g) mixed baby greens

Place the lamb in a large baking dish and brush both sides with the 2 Tbsp olive oil. Season generously with salt and pepper and the thyme. Let stand for up to 1 hour at room temperature or up to 2 hours in the refrigerator (and let return to room temperature before cooking).

In a saucepan over medium heat, warm the grapeseed oil. Add the onion and cook, stirring occasionally, until softened, about 5 minutes. Add the couscous and cook, stirring, until just beginning to brown, about 6 minutes. Add the broth, 1 tsp salt, and a pinch of pepper. Bring to a boil, reduce the heat to low, cover, and simmer until the couscous is tender and all the liquid is absorbed, about 8 minutes. Remove from the heat and stir in the ¼ cup olive oil and the mint.

Prepare a gas or charcoal grill for direct-heat cooking over high heat. Alternatively, preheat a stove-top grill pan over high heat. Place the lamb slices on the grill rack or in the grill pan and cook, turning once, until rare or medium-rare, 2–3 minutes per side. Transfer to a cutting board and let rest for 5 minutes before cutting into thin strips. Add most of the lemon juice to the couscous. Taste and adjust the seasoning with salt, pepper, and lemon juice, then fluff again. Spoon the couscous onto plates and surround with the salad greens. Top with the lamb and serve.

13

PASTA SALAD WITH BABY ARTICHOKES & GRILLED TUNA

serves 4–6

Baby artichokes grow lower down on the stalk than the larger variety. They do not have chokes, which saves on prep time. Drop them into a bowl of water mixed with the juice of a lemon to slow discoloration after cutting them.

Salt and freshly ground pepper

1 lb (500 g) cavatappi, penne, or fusilli pasta

9 Tbsp (5 fl oz/160 ml) extra-virgin olive oil, plus more for coating

1 lemon

About 20 baby artichokes

3 cloves garlic, very thinly sliced

½ cup (4 fl oz/125 ml) dry white wine

3 ripe tomatoes, peeled, seeded, and finely chopped

1 lb (500 g) tuna steak, about 1½ inches (4 cm) thick

½ red onion, very thinly sliced

Grated zest and juice of 1 large orange

Leaves from 5–6 large sprigs fresh mint

Leaves from 5–6 large sprigs fresh marjoram, coarsely chopped

Bring a large pot of salted water to a boil. Add the pasta and cook until al dente, according to package directions. Drain and rinse under cold water to stop the cooking. Drain well, transfer to a large bowl, and toss with 3 Tbsp of the oil. Set aside.

Halve and squeeze the lemon into a large bowl of cold water. Trim the artichoke stems, leaving about ½ inch (12 mm). Cut ½ inch off the tops. Peel off the tough outer leaves until you reach the tender, pale green leaves. Halve each artichoke lengthwise and immerse in the lemon water.

In a frying pan, warm 3 Tbsp of the oil over medium heat. Drain the artichokes well, pat dry, and add them, along with the garlic, to the pan. Season with salt and pepper to taste. Sauté until they are just turning golden at the edges, about 5 minutes. Add the white wine and let it boil away. Add ½ cup (4 fl oz/125 ml) warm water and simmer, uncovered, on medium-low heat until the artichokes are tender, about 5 minutes (if the liquid evaporates before the artichokes are tender, add a little extra warm water). Turn off the heat and add the tomatoes, tossing gently.

Prepare a charcoal or gas grill for direct-heat cooking over high heat. Alternatively, heat a stove-top grill pan over high heat. ⟫

Coat the tuna lightly with oil and season with salt and pepper to taste. Place the tuna on the grill or in the grill pan and sear on one side without moving it until you can see the edges are nicely browned, about 4–5 minutes. Turn and sear the other side, about 4 minutes, or until it just starts to flake when prodded with a fork; the center should be slightly pink. Let cool and cut into small chunks.

Add the artichoke mixture, onion, orange zest and juice, and herbs to the pasta. Add the tuna, the remaining 3 Tbsp oil, and salt and pepper to taste. Toss gently and serve, or let sit at room temperature for up to 2 hours.

14

LOBSTER & AVOCADO SALAD WITH SHAVED MEYER LEMONS

serves 4

Sweeter than regular Lisbon or Eureka lemons, Meyer lemons add an intriguing taste to this California-style lobster salad.

1 very firm Meyer lemon or Valencia orange

¼ cup (2 fl oz/60 ml) extra-virgin olive oil

1 Tbsp minced shallot

2 Tbsp champagne vinegar

Salt and freshly ground pepper

3 cooked, shelled lobster tails, cut into 1-inch (2.5-cm) chunks

1 head butter lettuce, torn into pieces

1 cup (1½ oz/45 g) fresh flat-leaf parsley leaves

½ cup (¾ oz/20 g) fresh cilantro leaves

½ cup (¾ oz/20 g) fresh chives, cut into ½-inch (12-mm) lengths

2 avocados, pitted, peeled, and diced

Using a mandoline or a very sharp knife, slice the lemon as thinly as possible. Set aside.

In a large bowl, combine the oil, shallot, vinegar, and ¼ tsp each salt and pepper. Mix well with a fork.

Add the lobster chunks to the vinaigrette, then remove and set aside. Just before serving, add the lettuce and parsley to the vinaigrette. Also add the cilantro and chives, reserving a little of each for garnish. Toss the salad and divide among individual plates. Top each salad with an equal portion of the lobster chunks, Meyer lemon slices, and diced avocado. Garnish with a sprinkling of the reserved cilantro and chives and serve.

15

Even if you're not a fan of the sturdier greens like chard and kale, look for baby chard in spring. The leaves are picked when they are small and tender, but they still offer the array of benefits found in this nutritional powerhouse.

GREEN BEAN SALAD WITH MUSTARD SEEDS, HERBS & BABY CHARD

serves 4

Salt

⅔ lb (315 g) young, tender green beans, preferably haricots verts

1 cup (5 oz/155 g) fresh shelled English peas

3 Tbsp olive oil

1 tsp black mustard seeds

½ small red onion, finely chopped

1 jalapeño or serrano chile, seeded and minced

1 clove garlic, minced

Grated zest of 1 lemon

1 Tbsp chopped fresh tarragon

1 Tbsp chopped fresh flat-leaf parsley

1 cup (1 oz/30 g) baby chard or spinach leaves

Bring a large saucepan three-fourths full of salted water to a boil over high heat. Meanwhile, prepare a large bowl of ice water. Add the green beans to the boiling water and cook until crisp-tender, about 4 minutes. Using a strainer, scoop out and immerse them in the ice water, then drain and pat dry. Put the green beans in a large bowl.

Return the water in the saucepan to a boil, add the peas, and cook for 1 minute. Using the strainer, scoop out and immerse them in the ice water, then drain and pat dry and add to the bowl with the green beans.

In a small saucepan over low heat, warm the oil with the mustard seeds until the seeds begin to pop. Add the mixture to the bowl with the vegetables. Add the red onion, chile, garlic, lemon zest, tarragon, and parsley to the bowl and stir to mix well. Season to taste with salt. Just before serving, gently fold in the chard leaves.

16

Little Gem is a small, compact lettuce, upright like romaine, but with ruffled leaves like a butter lettuce head, that hold up well when cut into wedges. Green Goddess dressing, full of the herbs that give the dressing its name, is exceptionally flavorful.

LITTLE GEM WEDGES WITH RADISHES & GREEN GODDESS DRESSING

serves 4

FOR THE DRESSING

1 cup (8 fl oz/250 ml) mayonnaise

½ cup (4 oz/125 g) sour cream

1 clove garlic, minced

5 anchovy fillets, minced

½ cup (¾ oz/20 g) minced fresh chives

⅓ cup (½ oz/15 g) minced fresh flat-leaf parsley

3 Tbsp minced fresh tarragon

1 Tbsp fresh lemon juice

1 Tbsp champagne vinegar

Salt and freshly ground pepper

4–6 heads Little Gem lettuce, or more if very small

8 radishes, red or white tipped, trimmed

To make the dressing, combine the mayonnaise, sour cream, garlic, anchovies, chives, parsley, tarragon, lemon juice, vinegar, ½ tsp salt, and ¼ tsp pepper and mix well. Set aside.

Halve the Little Gems lengthwise and thinly slice the radishes crosswise.

Arrange the Little Gems on a serving platter or distribute among salad plates. Sprinkle with the radish slices, drizzle with the dressing, and serve.

17

Perfect for a light supper or a special lunch, this salad can be prepared quickly just before serving, or the salmon, potatoes, and asparagus can be prepared up to a day ahead, then combined with the dressing at the last minute.

GRILLED SALMON, POTATO & ASPARAGUS SALAD

serves 4

1 lb (500 g) salmon fillet, pin bones removed

Olive oil

Salt and freshly ground pepper

1 lb (500 g) small, multicolored potatoes

¾ lb (375 g) asparagus, tough ends trimmed

FOR THE VINAIGRETTE

4 dry-packed sun-dried tomato halves

3 Tbsp fresh lemon juice

1 Tbsp minced fresh flat-leaf parsley

1 Tbsp minced fresh dill

1 tsp grated orange zest

½ tsp minced garlic

¼ cup (2 fl oz/60 ml) extra-virgin olive oil

10 oz (315 g) mixed baby greens

3 green onions, including tender green tops, thinly sliced

Prepare a charcoal or gas grill for direct-heat cooking over high heat. Alternatively, preheat a stove-top grill pan over high heat. Brush the salmon with oil and season with salt and pepper. Place the fillet on the grill rack or in the pan and grill, turning once, until opaque throughout, about 4 minutes per side.

Transfer the salmon to a plate and let cool to room temperature. Meanwhile, put the potatoes in a large saucepan with water to cover. Bring to a boil over high heat, reduce the heat to medium-low, cover, and simmer until the potatoes are tender when pierced with a knife, about 15 minutes. Drain, cut in half, and set aside to cool completely.

Place the asparagus in a steamer basket over boiling water in a saucepan, cover the pan, and cook until crisp-tender, about 3 minutes. Rinse the asparagus under cold running water until cool. Pat dry and set aside.

To make the vinaigrette, put the sun-dried tomatoes in a heatproof bowl, pour in boiling water to cover, and let stand for 5 minutes. Drain and cut into ¼-inch (6-mm) pieces. In a small bowl, whisk together the chopped tomatoes, lemon juice, parsley, dill, orange zest, garlic, 2 Tbsp water, ½ tsp salt, and ⟫⟫

a grinding of pepper. Add the oil in a thin stream, whisking constantly until the dressing is well blended.

In a large bowl, toss the salad greens with 2 Tbsp of the vinaigrette. Peel off the salmon skin. Cut the flesh into 4 pieces. Divide the salmon, asparagus, potatoes, and greens evenly among 4 plates and drizzle with the remaining vinaigrette. Sprinkle with the green onions and serve.

18

This classic salad appears on Italian menus in early spring when baby artichokes are in season. If you wish to make the salad with larger artichokes, trim and quarter the artichokes, cut out the chokes, and blanch in boiling water for about 5 minutes. Let cool, then toss with the greens and serve.

BABY ARTICHOKE, PARMESAN & ARUGULA SALAD

serves 4

½ lemon

6 baby artichokes

FOR THE LEMON VINAIGRETTE

2 Tbsp fresh lemon juice

Salt

¼ cup (2 fl oz/60 ml) extra-virgin olive oil

1 bunch arugula, stemmed and shredded

Parmesan cheese for shaving

Freshly ground pepper

Squeeze the lemon into a large bowl of cold water. Trim the artichoke stems, leaving about ½ inch (12 mm). Cut ½ inch off the tops. Peel off the tough outer leaves until you reach the tender, pale green leaves. Halve each artichoke lengthwise and then thinly slice. Immerse in the lemon water.

To make the vinaigrette, in a small bowl, combine the lemon juice and salt to taste. Add the oil in a thin stream, whisking constantly until the dressing is smooth. Taste and adjust the seasoning with salt.

Put the arugula in a serving bowl. Drain the artichoke slices and pat dry. Add to the greens and toss gently. Drizzle the dressing over the salad and, using a vegetable peeler, shave the cheese over the salad. Season generously with pepper and serve.

19

FENNEL, CHICKPEA & SUN-DRIED TOMATO SALAD WITH MOZZARELLA

serves 6

Sun-dried tomatoes offer the concentrated essence of ripe tomatoes and have a chewy, meaty texture. In this salad, their intensity is kept in check by nutty chickpeas and mild-tasting fresh mozzarella. Slices of fennel add crunch and a licorice flavor, while fresh dill and oregano bring fragrant, herbal hints.

1 can (15 oz/470 g) chickpeas, drained and rinsed

1 cup (5 oz/155 g) drained olive oil–packed sun-dried tomatoes, coarsely chopped

7 Tbsp (3½ fl oz/105 ml) extra-virgin olive oil

⅔ cup (1 oz/30 g) minced fresh dill

1 tsp minced fresh oregano

1 tsp fresh lemon juice, plus ¼ cup (2 fl oz/60 ml)

Salt and freshly ground pepper

1 tsp sugar

2 small fennel bulbs, trimmed and thinly sliced

1 head romaine lettuce, leaves torn into bite-sized pieces

6 oz (185 g) bocconcini (small fresh mozzarella balls), cut into quarters

In a bowl, toss together the chickpeas, sun-dried tomatoes, 1 Tbsp of the olive oil, 2 Tbsp of the dill, the oregano, the 1 tsp lemon juice, ¼ tsp salt, and several grindings of pepper. Let stand at room temperature for 15 minutes.

In a small bowl, whisk together the ¼ cup lemon juice, the sugar, ¼ tsp salt, and several grindings of pepper until the sugar dissolves. Add the remaining 6 Tbsp (3 fl oz/90 ml) olive oil in a thin stream, whisking constantly until the dressing is well blended. Taste and adjust the seasonings.

In a large bowl, toss together the fennel, lettuce, the remaining dill, ¼ tsp salt, and several grindings of pepper. Whisk the dressing to recombine, then drizzle it over the fennel-lettuce mixture and toss well. Taste and adjust the seasonings. Divide the dressed mixture among individual plates. Top with the chickpea mixture and the cheese and serve.

20

SPRING RICE SALAD WITH DILL-LEMON DRESSING

serves 6–8

This light and colorful salad makes a terrific first course. If any of the vegetables are unavailable in the market, you can substitute green beans, zucchini, broccoli, or even fresh peas with equally delicious results.

1 cup (7 oz/220 g) long-grain white rice or basmati rice

2½ cups (20 fl oz/625 ml) vegetable broth or water

Salt and freshly ground pepper

1 large fennel bulb, trimmed and cut lengthwise into slices ¼ inch (6 mm) thick

½ lb (250 g) sugar snap peas or snow peas, trimmed

½ lb (250 g) thin asparagus, tough ends trimmed and spears cut into 1-inch (2.5-cm) lengths

FOR THE DILL-LEMON DRESSING

4 Tbsp (2 fl oz/60 ml) fresh lemon juice

4 Tbsp (⅓ oz/10 g) chopped fresh dill

1 clove garlic, minced

½ cup (4 fl oz/125 ml) extra-virgin olive oil

Lemon wedges for garnish

Fresh dill sprigs for garnish

If using basmati rice, rinse well and drain.

In a heavy saucepan, combine the broth and ½ tsp salt and bring to a boil. Slowly add the rice, reduce the heat to low, cover, and cook for 20 minutes. After 20 minutes, uncover and check to see if the rice is tender and the water is absorbed. If not, re-cover and cook for a few minutes until the rice is done. Remove from the heat, fluff the grains with a fork, and transfer to a bowl to cool.

Bring a saucepan three-fourths full of salted water to a boil. Add the fennel and the peas and blanch for 2 minutes. Using a slotted spoon, transfer the vegetables to a bowl and let cool. Add the asparagus to the same water and cook just until tender, 3–4 minutes. Drain and let cool with the other vegetables.

To make the dressing, in a large bowl, whisk together the lemon juice, dill, garlic, and salt and pepper to taste. Add the oil in a thin stream, whisking constantly until the dressing is smooth. Add the cooled rice and vegetables and toss together. Garnish with lemon wedges and dill sprigs and serve.

21

LEMONY QUINOA SALAD WITH RADISHES, AVOCADO & BASIL

serves 6

Crisp, peppery radishes are one of the hallmarks of springtime. Their texture and flavor are highlighted here, contrasted against creamy avocado, bright-tasting citrus segments, and nutty, mild quinoa.

1 cup (6 oz/185 g) quinoa, well rinsed

2 lemons

2 small avocados, peeled, pitted, and cut into thin slices

2 cloves garlic, minced

2 bunches radishes, trimmed and halved lengthwise

½ cup (2½ oz/75 g) crumbled feta cheese

Leaves from 1 bunch fresh basil, torn into pieces

1 Tbsp ground coriander

¼ tsp red pepper flakes

⅓ cup (3 fl oz/80 ml) extra-virgin olive oil

Salt and freshly ground black pepper

Drain the quinoa and combine it in a pot with 3 cups (24 fl oz/750 ml) water. Bring to a boil, then reduce the heat to low, cover, and simmer until the grains are tender and the water is absorbed, about 15 minutes. Remove from the heat, fluff the quinoa, and let cool completely.

Peel the lemons with a knife. Working over a bowl, cut between the membranes to release the segments into the bowl. Squeeze the juice from the membranes into the bowl. Add the avocado slices and toss to coat with the lemon juice. Transfer the quinoa to the bowl and add the garlic, radishes, cheese, and torn basil and toss gently to mix well without breaking up the avocado.

In a small bowl, whisk together the coriander, red pepper flakes, oil, ½ tsp salt, and ¼ tsp pepper. Pour the dressing over the salad, toss gently, and serve.

22

GREEN MANGO & GRILLED SHRIMP SALAD

serves 4–6

A slawlike salad composed of green mangoes, carrots, and chopped chile is the base of this Vietnamese salad. Grilled shrimp sit atop, and the savory, citrusy, slightly sweet dressing draws everything together. Serve on a hot day with light beer.

½ lb (250 g) large shrimp, peeled and deveined

1 Tbsp peanut oil

Salt and freshly ground pepper

FOR THE DRESSING

1 large clove garlic

1 fresh red chile, seeded

¼ cup (2 fl oz/60 ml) fresh lime juice

5 Tbsp (2½ fl oz/75 ml) Asian fish sauce

3 Tbsp sugar

2 Tbsp grated carrot

2 green mangoes, peeled and grated

1 carrot, peeled and finely grated

1 Tbsp chopped fresh Thai basil or cilantro leaves

1 red Fresno or serrano chile, seeded and chopped

Prepare a charcoal or gas grill for direct-heat cooking over high heat. In a bowl, toss the shrimp with the oil, ½ tsp salt, and pepper to taste. If desired, put them in a grill basket.

To make the dressing, in a mortar, pound together the garlic and red chile with a pestle until puréed. Mix in the lime juice, fish sauce, sugar, and 6 Tbsp (3 fl oz/90 ml) water. Pour into a bowl and add the 2 Tbsp carrot.

Place the shrimp over the hottest part of the fire and grill, turning as needed, until they turn bright orange-pink and feel firm to the touch, about 2 minutes. Transfer to a plate and set aside to cool.

In a large bowl, combine the mangoes, carrot, basil, chile, and ¼ cup (2 fl oz/60 ml) of the dressing and toss well.

Arrange the salad on a platter and top with the shrimp. Drizzle with more dressing (you may not need all of it) and serve.

23

This springtime salad features the classic pairing of fruit with crisp-skinned duck. Crystallized ginger lends sweetness and a spiced flavor to a strawberry dressing that balances the duck's richness.

WATERCRESS & DUCK SALAD WITH GINGERED STRAWBERRY DRESSING
serves 4

2 baskets (1 lb/500 g) large strawberries, stemmed and hulled

1½ tsp minced crystallized ginger

1½ tsp fresh lemon juice

1 tsp sugar

Salt and freshly ground pepper

4 Tbsp (2 fl oz/60 ml) walnut oil

2 boneless duck breast halves (about ¾ lb/375 g each)

¾ cup (3 oz/90 g) pecans

2 small bunches watercress, tough stems removed

Preheat the oven to 400°F (200°C). Put 4 or 5 of the berries in a blender. Add the ginger, lemon juice, sugar, and a pinch each of salt and pepper and process until smooth. Pour through a fine-mesh sieve into a small bowl. Add 1 Tbsp of the walnut oil in a thin stream, whisking constantly until the dressing is well blended. Taste and adjust the seasonings and set aside. Quarter the remaining berries lengthwise and set aside.

Using a sharp, thin-bladed knife, score the skin of each duck breast half in a ½-inch (12-mm) crosshatch pattern, being careful not to cut into the meat. Season each duck breast on both sides with salt and pepper.

Warm a large, heavy, ovenproof frying pan over medium-low heat for 2 minutes. Add the duck breasts, skin side down, and cook without disturbing until the skin is crisp and medium brown, about 5 minutes. Remove the duck from the pan, pour off and discard all but 2 Tbsp of the fat, and return the duck, skin side up, to the pan. Place the pan in the oven and cook until an instant-read thermometer inserted into the center of each breast registers 130°F (54°C) for medium-rare, 10–12 minutes, or until cooked to your liking. Transfer the duck to a cutting board, tent with foil, and let rest for 5 minutes.

In a small frying pan, toast the pecans over medium-low heat, stirring, until fragrant and starting to brown, about 5 minutes. Pour onto a plate to cool, then coarsely chop. ⤷

In a small bowl, stir together the toasted pecans and a pinch of salt.

In a large bowl, combine the watercress and the quartered strawberries, drizzle with the remaining 3 Tbsp walnut oil, and season with a scant ¼ tsp each of salt and pepper. Toss well. Divide the greens and berries among individual plates.

Thinly slice the duck breasts on the diagonal. Fan an equal amount of duck on top of the greens on each plate. Drizzle each serving with the dressing, sprinkle with the pecans, and serve.

24

For this recipe, look for bulgur labeled fine, which will marry best with the other ingredients in this intensely green salad. Letting the salad stand to soak up the lemon dressing is also important. Traditional tabbouleh is made with more parsley than bulgur, so don't skimp on the amount called for here.

TABBOULEH WITH FETA CHEESE
serves 4

1 cup (8 fl oz/250 ml) boiling water

½ cup (3 oz/90 g) fine bulgur

Leaves of 1 large bunch fresh flat-leaf parsley, most minced, a few left whole and reserved for garnish

Leaves of 1 bunch fresh spearmint, minced

½ cup (2½ oz/75 g) finely chopped red onion

2 cups (¾ lb/375 g) cherry tomatoes, quartered

1 cup (5 oz/155 g) crumbled feta cheese

Juice of 1 large lemon

2 Tbsp extra-virgin olive oil

Salt and freshly ground pepper

In a large bowl, pour the boiling water over the bulgur. Let stand for 30 minutes, uncovered, until the bulgur has absorbed all of the liquid and has softened.

Add the chopped parsley, mint, and onion to the bulgur and mix with a fork to combine.

Put the tomatoes in a colander and work them with your fingers to drain off some of their liquid and eliminate some of the seeds. Add the drained tomatoes and crumbled cheese to the salad.

Pour the lemon juice and oil over the tabbouleh and mix well. Season with salt and pepper to taste. Cover and refrigerate for at least 2 hours or up to 24 hours before serving to let the flavors blend. Let the salad return to room temperature, garnish with the whole parsley leaves, and serve.

25

ORZO SALAD WITH ARTICHOKES, PINE NUTS & GOLDEN RAISINS

serves 8

Sturdy and easily transportable, this is a great salad to make for potlucks, picnics, or cookouts. The orzo and dressing will pair well with almost any combination of ingredients, so try other options with veggies you have on hand.

FOR THE DRESSING

¼ cup (2 fl oz/60 ml) fresh lemon juice

1 Tbsp Dijon mustard

2 cloves garlic

½ cup (½ oz/15 g) fresh basil leaves

½ cup (4 fl oz/125 ml) extra-virgin olive oil

Salt and freshly ground pepper

1 lb (500 g) orzo pasta

Extra-virgin olive oil

½ lemon (if using fresh artichokes)

12 baby artichokes or 1 package (1 lb/500 g) frozen quartered artichoke hearts, thawed and brought to room temperature

⅓ cup (2 oz/60 g) pine nuts

¾ cup (4½ oz/140 g) golden raisins

½ cup (½ oz/15 g) fresh basil leaves, julienned

3 green onions, including tender green tops, thinly sliced on the diagonal

To make the dressing, in a food processor or blender, combine the lemon juice, mustard, garlic, basil leaves, and oil and purée until smooth. Season with salt and pepper to taste. Transfer to a small bowl and set aside.

Bring a large pot three-fourths full of salted water to a boil over high heat. Add the orzo and cook until al dente, according to package directions. Rinse well in cold water to remove any excess starch and drain in a colander. Transfer to a large bowl and toss lightly with a little oil to prevent the pasta from sticking together.

If using fresh artichokes, squeeze the lemon half into a large bowl of cold water. Trim the artichoke stems, leaving about ½ inch (12 mm). Cut ½ inch off the tops. Peel off the tough outer leaves until you reach the tender, pale green leaves. Cut each artichoke lengthwise into 6 wedges and immerse in the lemon water. Bring a pot three-fourths full of salted water to a boil. Add the artichokes and cook until tender, about 14 minutes. Drain and let cool to room temperature. »→

In a small frying pan, toast the pine nuts over medium-low heat, stirring, until fragrant and starting to brown, 3–4 minutes. Pour onto a plate to cool.

Add the artichokes, pine nuts, raisins, basil, and green onions to the bowl containing the orzo. Whisk the dressing to recombine and drizzle it over the orzo. Toss to coat evenly. Taste and adjust the seasonings and serve.

26

ROAST BEEF SALAD WITH LEEKS & CREAMY MUSTARD VINAIGRETTE

serves 4–6

This is an excellent way to use leftover grilled or roast beef—or purchased roast beef from the deli. The spicy vinaigrette brings together the mild flavor of the leeks and the robust flavor of the meat.

16 small leeks

¼ cup (2 fl oz/60 ml) extra-virgin olive oil

2–3 Tbsp Dijon mustard

1½ Tbsp sherry vinegar

2 tsp minced shallot

Salt and freshly ground pepper

1½ lb (750 g) lean roast beef, such as flank steak or tri-tip roast, cut against the grain into slices at least ¼ inch (6 mm) thick

Trim the leeks, leaving the root end intact and keeping about half of the dark greens. Prepare a bowl of ice water. Place the leeks in a large frying pan with about 1 inch (2.5 cm) of water. Bring to a boil over medium heat, cover, reduce the heat to low, and cook, adding more water if needed, until just fork-tender, about 10 minutes. Transfer to the ice water, and let cool. Remove and pat dry.

In a small bowl, whisk together the oil and mustard. Whisk in the vinegar, shallot, and salt and pepper to taste.

Lay the leeks together on a cutting board, side by side. Cut into 2-inch (5-cm) lengths and place them on a platter, still arranged together. Drizzle with half the vinaigrette. Top with the sliced beef, drizzle with the remaining dressing, and serve.

27

GRILLED ASPARAGUS & PROSCIUTTO SALAD

serves 4

1¼ lb (625 g) asparagus, tough ends trimmed

7 Tbsp (3½ fl oz/105 ml) olive oil

Salt and freshly ground pepper

1 clove garlic, minced

2 Tbsp red wine vinegar

1 tsp tarragon mustard or Dijon mustard

1 Tbsp minced fresh chives

6 oz (185 g) mixed baby greens

3 oz (90 g) thinly sliced prosciutto, cut into strips

Parmesan cheese for shaving

For a pretty presentation, after grilling the asparagus, try making bundles by wrapping spears with the prosciutto strips. Plate the greens and then nestle a bundle of asparagus on top of each serving.

Prepare a gas or charcoal grill for direct-heat cooking over medium-high heat. Alternatively, preheat a stove-top grill pan over medium-high heat. If the asparagus spears are thick, use a vegetable peeler to pare away the tough skins to within about 2 inches (5 cm) of the tips. Brush the asparagus with 1 Tbsp of the oil and season with salt and pepper. Place the spears on the grill rack, in a grill basket, or in the pan and grill, turning occasionally with tongs, until slightly charred and tender, about 8 minutes.

In a large bowl, whisk together the garlic, vinegar, mustard, ¼ tsp salt, and a pinch of pepper. Add the remaining 6 Tbsp (3 fl oz/ 90 ml) oil in a thin stream, whisking constantly until smooth. Stir in the chives.

Add the greens and prosciutto to the vinaigrette and toss to coat evenly. Arrange the asparagus on individual plates and top with the greens. Using a vegetable peeler, shave the cheese over the salads and serve.

28

STRAWBERRY & CHERRY SALAD

serves 4

Hazelnuts or walnuts for garnish

2 cups (8 oz/250 g) strawberries, hulled and halved

2 cups (8 oz/250 g) cherries, pitted and halved

Juice of 1 lemon

5–10 fresh tarragon or mint leaves, chopped

If serving this salad as a starter, use tarragon and, if you like, serve the fruit over spinach with a lemony dressing. Or, use mint for a refreshing dessert salad.

In a small frying pan, toast the hazelnuts over medium-low heat, stirring, until fragrant and starting to brown, about 5 minutes. Wrap the hazelnuts in a towel and rub to remove the skins. Pour onto a plate to cool. Chop coarsely, and set aside.

In a bowl, toss the strawberries and cherries with the lemon juice. Add the tarragon and toss gently. Garnish with the chopped nuts and serve.

29

ARUGULA SALAD WITH BERRIES & GORGONZOLA

serves 4–6

2 Tbsp balsamic vinegar

Salt and freshly ground pepper

3 Tbsp extra-virgin olive oil

6 cups (6 oz/185 g) baby arugula

8 oz (250 g) Gorgonzola or other blue cheese, crumbled

1 cup (4 oz/125 g) fresh blackberries or blueberries

Dark, jammy berries are a delicious match with creamy, rich Gorgonzola and peppery arugula. If you can't find nice-looking berries, substitute fresh or dried cherries, currants, or cranberries.

In a large bowl, whisk together the vinegar and salt and pepper to taste. Add the oil in a thin stream, whisking constantly until the dressing is smooth.

Add the arugula to the dressing and toss to coat. Add the cheese and toss gently. Divide among plates, top with the berries, and serve.

30

GRILLED TUNA WITH POTATO, AVOCADO & TOMATO CONFIT

serves 4

12 small fingerling potatoes, about 1½ lb (750 g)

3 Tbsp extra-virgin olive oil, plus ¼ cup (2 fl oz/60 ml)

2 red onions, cut crosswise into slices ⅓ inch (9 mm) thick

4 ahi tuna steaks, each about 4 oz (125 g) and ½–¾ inch (12 mm–2 cm) thick

12 butter lettuce leaves

Tomato Confit *(left)*

2 avocados, pitted, peeled, and cut lengthwise into ½-inch (12-mm) slices

½ cup (2½ oz/75 g) pitted olives

2 Tbsp red wine vinegar

To make the tomato confit, preheat the oven to 350°F (270°C). Cut 12 Roma tomatoes in half and toss with 2 Tbsp olive oil, and sprinkle with salt and pepper. Arrange the tomatoes, cut sides down on a baking sheet, and roast until they have collapsed and most of the moisture is gone, 1½–2 hours.

Raise the oven temperature to 400°F (200°C). Arrange the potatoes in a baking dish just large enough to hold them in a single layer, and drizzle with 1 Tbsp of the oil. Turn to coat. Sprinkle with ½ tsp salt. Roast until easily pierced with a fork, about 30 minutes. Remove from the oven and set aside.

Prepare a charcoal or gas grill for direct-heat cooking over high heat. Brush the onion slices with 1 Tbsp of the oil and place on the grill or in a grill basket. Grill, turning once, until golden on both sides, about 8 minutes. Set aside.

Brush the tuna steaks with 1 Tbsp of the oil and sprinkle lightly with salt and pepper. Grill until the first ⅛ inch (3 mm) is opaque, about 1 minute. Turn and sear the other side. The steaks should be pink in the middle. Set aside and let rest briefly.

Divide the butter lettuce leaves among plates. Top each with an ahi steak, 2 potatoes, a few slices of onion, 3 tomato confit halves, and a few slices of avocado. Garnish with the olives.

In a bowl, whisk together the ¼ cup oil and the vinegar and season to taste with salt and pepper. Drizzle a little of this dressing over each serving and serve.

31

CHOPPED CHICKEN SALAD WITH LEMON-TARRAGON DRESSING

serves 2

1 skinless, boneless chicken breast half, about ½ lb (250 g)

1½ cups (12 fl oz/375 ml) chicken broth, or as needed

FOR THE LEMON-TARRAGON DRESSING

1½ Tbsp fresh lemon juice, plus more if needed

2 tsp minced fresh tarragon

1 tsp Dijon mustard

1 small clove garlic, minced

2½ Tbsp olive oil

Salt and freshly ground pepper

¼ lb (125 g) romaine lettuce heart, chopped

¼ small fennel bulb, trimmed and chopped

6 small fresh mushrooms, chopped

5 radishes, chopped

1 small carrot, peeled and chopped

¼ small head radicchio, chopped

¼ small red onion, chopped

This versatile salad can accommodate the odds and ends of raw vegetables that tend to accumulate in the refrigerator bin. Instead of fennel, mushrooms, or radishes, try cucumber, zucchini, celery, or cauliflower. Or, eliminate the chicken to make a vegetarian version.

In a small saucepan over medium heat, combine the chicken breast half and the 1½ cups (12 fl oz/375 ml) broth, or as needed to cover. Bring to a simmer, adjust the heat to keep the broth just below a simmer, and cook, uncovered, until the chicken is just cooked through, about 10 minutes. Using a slotted spoon, transfer the chicken breast to a cutting board. When the chicken is cool, cut it into small, neat pieces.

To make the dressing, in a bowl, whisk together the 1½ Tbsp lemon juice, tarragon, mustard, and garlic. Add the olive oil in a thin stream, whisking constantly until the dressing is well blended. Season with salt and pepper to taste. Set aside to allow the flavors to blend.

In a large bowl, combine the romaine, fennel, mushrooms, radishes, carrot, radicchio, and red onion.

Add the chicken to the dressing and stir to coat. Add the chicken and all the dressing to the vegetables and toss well. Taste and adjust the seasoning with lemon juice and serve.

This month, spring's greenery makes way for the colorful bounty of summer fruits—melons, figs, stone fruits, and berries—all delicious when simply tossed with basil or mint. Or, try peaches paired with goat cheese, strawberries matched with spinach, or watermelon mixed with feta cheese. For vegetables, turn to cool cucumbers and crisp, refreshing lettuces, which are the perfect canvas for creamy, herb-flecked yogurt dressings.

1
CHICKEN, ROASTED RED PEPPER & GREEN BEAN SALAD
page 130

2
CHERRY TOMATO SALAD WITH BURRATA & PESTO
page 130

3
GRILLED SUMMER SQUASH SALAD
page 133

8
CHOPPED SALAD WITH LEMON & OLIVE OIL
page 135

9
CHIPOTLE BEEF & CORN SALAD
page 136

10
GRILLED LAMB SALAD
page 136

15
FRESH STRAWBERRY & SPINACH SALAD
page 141

16
POACHED SALMON SALAD WITH PRESERVED LEMON & GARLIC
page 141

17
CHICKEN TOSTADA SALAD
page 142

22
POTATO SALAD WITH GREEN BEANS & CUCUMBER-YOGURT DRESSING
page 145

23
FARRO SALAD WITH CREAMY ARTICHOKE DRESSING
page 147

24
STONE FRUIT SALAD WITH HAZELNUTS & BLUE CHEESE
page 147

29
BLACK BEAN & WHITE CORN SALAD
page 150

30
GRILLED SQUASH & ORZO SALAD WITH PINE NUTS & MINT
page 150

4
MELON & FIG SALAD
WITH BASIL CREAM
page 133

5
FARRO SALAD WITH GRAPE
TOMATOES & RICOTTA SALATA
page 134

6
LOBSTER, POTATO & GREEN BEAN
SALAD WITH PESTO VINAIGRETTE
page 134

7
ORZO SALAD WITH PEAS,
PEPPERS & TOMATOES
page 135

11
GOLDEN BEET & YELLOW
TOMATO SALAD
page 138

12
CHICKEN & MANGO SALAD WITH
CHUTNEY VINAIGRETTE
page 138

13
CAESAR SALAD WITH CHIPOTLE
CHILE DRESSING
page 139

14
ARUGULA, OAKLEAF LETTUCE
& BASIL SALAD
page 139

18
PEACH, ARUGULA &
GOAT CHEESE SALAD
page 142

19
LENTIL SALAD WITH FETA
page 144

20
ROASTED BELL PEPPER
& QUINOA SALAD
page 144

21
SALADE VERTE
page 145

25
SALADE NIÇOISE WITH
SEARED WILD SALMON
page 148

26
CUCUMBER SALAD WITH
YOGURT-DILL SAUCE
page 148

27
FRIED CHICKEN SALAD
page 149

28
GREEN PAPAYA SALAD
page 149

june

1

CHICKEN, ROASTED RED PEPPER & GREEN BEAN SALAD

serves 4

Beans and lean poultry make this high in protein and low in saturated fat, for a main-course salad that is as satisfying as it is healthful. Sweet, slightly floral sherry vinegar creates a vibrant salad dressing, which doubles as a glaze for the tender strips of chicken.

2 large red bell peppers
(about 1 lb/500 g total weight)

Salt and freshly ground pepper

½ lb (250 g) green beans, trimmed

FOR THE SHERRY-THYME VINAIGRETTE

3 Tbsp sherry vinegar

1 Tbsp chopped fresh thyme

½ tsp minced garlic

¼ cup (2 fl oz/60 ml) extra-virgin olive oil

1 tsp olive oil

¾ lb (375 g) skinless, boneless chicken breast halves, cut lengthwise into strips 1 inch (2.5 cm) wide

1 small red onion

2 celery ribs

10 oz (315 g) mixed baby salad greens

Preheat the broiler. Place the peppers on a baking sheet and slide under the broiler about 6 inches (15 cm) from the heat source. Broil, turning often, until the skins are blackened on all sides, 10–15 minutes. Transfer to a covered bowl or seal in a paper bag. Let the peppers steam until cool, about 10 minutes. Rub and peel off the charred skins. Cut the peppers in half lengthwise, remove the seeds and membranes, and cut lengthwise into strips 1 inch (2.5 cm) wide. Set aside.

Bring a saucepan three-fourths full of salted water to a boil, add the green beans, and boil until tender, 4–7 minutes; the timing will depend on their size. Drain and immerse in a bowl of ice water. Drain and set aside.

To make the vinaigrette, in a small bowl, whisk together the vinegar, thyme, garlic, ½ tsp salt, and a grinding of pepper. Add the extra-virgin olive oil in a thin stream, whisking constantly until well blended.

Brush a large, nonstick frying pan with the 1 tsp olive oil. Place over medium heat and heat until hot enough for a drop of water to sizzle and then immediately evaporate. Add the chicken, a few pieces at a time, and cook for 2 minutes. ⟫

Turn the chicken pieces, whisk the vinaigrette to recombine, and drizzle 2 Tbsp of the vinaigrette on the chicken. Continue to cook for 2 minutes; the chicken should be opaque throughout. Turn the chicken to coat it well with the vinaigrette and remove the pan from the heat. Let the chicken stand in the pan.

Cut the onion in half through the stem end. Place cut side down and thinly slice lengthwise until you have about ½ cup (2 oz/60 g). Reserve the remainder for another use. Cut the celery ribs on the diagonal into ¼-inch (6-mm) slices.

In a large bowl, combine the salad greens and 1 Tbsp of the vinaigrette. Toss to coat the greens. Spread the greens in a layer on a large platter. In the same bowl, combine the roasted bell peppers, green beans, cooked chicken and any pan juices, onion, celery, and remaining vinaigrette. Toss to mix. Spoon on top of the greens and serve.

2

CHERRY TOMATO SALAD WITH BURRATA & PESTO

serves 4–6

Burrata is a moist, fresh ball of mozzarella filled with curds and cream, which slowly ooze out with each forkful.

3 Tbsp prepared basil pesto

1½ Tbsp red wine vinegar

¼ cup (2 fl oz/60 ml) extra-virgin olive oil

Salt and freshly ground pepper

About 4 cups (1½ lb/750 g) mixed red, yellow, and orange cherry tomatoes

1 burrata cheese

Small fresh basil leaves for garnish

In a bowl, whisk together the pesto and vinegar. Add the oil in a thin stream, whisking constantly until the dressing is well blended. Season with salt and pepper to taste.

Slice the tomatoes in half, add to the bowl, and toss gently. Season with salt and pepper and use a slotted spoon to mound them on a serving platter. Nestle the cheese in the center and drizzle with some pesto dressing from the bowl. Garnish with the basil leaves and serve.

3

GRILLED SUMMER SQUASH SALAD

serves 6

Zucchini, crookneck, and pattypan squashes are all terrific grilled and lightly dressed with a tomato-basil vinaigrette. When shopping for squashes, choose an eye-catching variety of shapes, colors, and sizes.

FOR THE TOMATO-BASIL VINAIGRETTE

5–6 fresh basil leaves

2 oil-packed sun-dried tomatoes, drained

1 Tbsp balsamic vinegar

1 Tbsp red wine vinegar

1 Tbsp maple syrup

1 Tbsp Dijon mustard

½ cup (4 fl oz/125 ml) grapeseed oil

¼ cup (2 fl oz/60 ml) extra-virgin olive oil

Salt and freshly ground pepper

¼ cup (1½ oz/45 g) pine nuts

5–6 small to medium zucchini (about 2 lb/1 kg total weight)

5–6 yellow crookneck squashes (about 2 lb/1 kg total weight)

10 pattypan squashes (about 2 lb/1 kg total weight)

2 plum tomatoes, cored, quartered, and seeded

½ cup (4 fl oz/125 ml) extra-virgin olive oil

1 Tbsp minced fresh marjoram

2 Tbsp minced fresh flat-leaf parsley

5 cups (5 oz/155 g) field greens or baby lettuce leaves

To make the vinaigrette, roll the basil leaves together lengthwise and slice crosswise into thin ribbons. In a blender or food processor, combine the sun-dried tomatoes, balsamic and red wine vinegars, maple syrup, and mustard. Pulse several times to chop the sun-dried tomatoes and incorporate ingredients into a thick, red paste. With the motor running, add the oils in a thin, steady stream. Add the basil, 1 tsp salt, and pepper to taste; pulse once to incorporate.

In a dry frying pan, toast the pine nuts over medium-low heat, stirring, until fragrant and starting to brown, 3–4 minutes. Pour onto a plate to cool.

Prepare a charcoal or gas grill for indirect-heat cooking over medium-high heat. Cut the zucchini and squashes in half lengthwise, and then cut each half into wedges about ¾ inch (2 cm) thick. In a large bowl, combine the squash wedges, tomatoes, ½ cup olive oil, and marjoram and toss to coat. ↦

Season with 2 tsp salt and 1 tsp pepper. If desired, put them in a grill basket. Grill the squashes and tomatoes, turning as needed, until lightly charred on all sides, 8–10 minutes. Move the vegetables to the side of the grill where the heat is less intense, cover, and grill until cooked through, 5–6 minutes.

Transfer the grilled vegetables back to the bowl. Stir in the pine nuts and parsley. Taste and adjust the seasonings.

In a separate medium bowl, season the field greens with salt and pepper and dress with 2 Tbsp of the vinaigrette. Divide the greens among individual plates, arrange the grilled vegetables on top, and serve. Pass the remaining vinaigrette at the table.

4

MELON & FIG SALAD WITH BASIL CREAM

serves 4

The best way to serve fruits is at the height of their season and as simply as possible, allowing the natural flavors to have full impact. Very ripe, intensely sweet figs and melons are delicious when drizzled with a sauce of cream and basil.

½ cup (4 fl oz/125 ml) heavy cream

2½ Tbsp fresh lemon juice

¼ cup (⅓ oz/10 g) minced fresh basil, plus small leaves for garnish

1½ tsp sugar

3 cups (18 oz/560 g) thinly sliced cantaloupe, honeydew, or other sweet melon

1–1½ lb (500–750 g) very ripe figs, halved or quartered lengthwise

In a bowl, stir together the cream, lemon juice, minced basil, and sugar. Cover and refrigerate for at least 1 hour or for up to 6 hours.

When ready to serve, divide the melon and figs among individual plates. Pour a little of the cream mixture over each plate of fruit, garnish with basil leaves, and serve.

5

FARRO SALAD WITH GRAPE TOMATOES & RICOTTA SALATA

serves 4

1 cup (6 oz/185 g) farro

Salt and freshly ground pepper

2 Tbsp extra-virgin olive oil

1 Tbsp fresh lemon juice

1 cup (6 oz/185 g) grape or cherry tomatoes, stemmed and halved

½ cup (2 oz/60 g) crumbled ricotta salata cheese

2 green onions, including tender green tops, thinly sliced

¼ cup (⅓ oz/10 g) shredded fresh basil

Farro, an ancient form of wheat, is cultivated primarily in the regions of Tuscany and Umbria. The light brown grains have a full, nutty flavor that is delicious in soups and salads. Salty ricotta, juicy tomatoes, and a handful of fresh basil unite in this rustic Italian salad.

In a large saucepan, combine the farro and 2 qt (2 l) water. Place the pan over medium-high heat, bring to a boil, and add 1 tsp salt. Reduce the heat to medium or medium-low, so the farro simmers steadily, and cook, uncovered, until tender yet still slightly firm and chewy, about 30 minutes. Remove from the heat and drain well in a fine-mesh sieve.

In a serving bowl, whisk together the olive oil and lemon juice until well blended. Whisk in salt and pepper to taste. Add the farro and toss well. Gently stir in the tomatoes, cheese, green onions, and basil until all the ingredients are evenly distributed. Serve at room temperature.

6

LOBSTER, POTATO & GREEN BEAN SALAD WITH PESTO VINAIGRETTE

serves 6

12–18 small red potatoes or Yellow Finn potatoes (about 2 lb/1 kg total weight)

Salt and freshly ground pepper

2 Tbsp pine nuts or chopped walnuts

1½ lb (750 g) green beans, trimmed and cut into 2-inch (5-cm) lengths

1 cup (1½ oz/45 g) tightly packed fresh basil leaves

1 tsp minced garlic

About ¾ cup (6 fl oz/180 ml) olive oil

¼ cup (2 fl oz/60 ml) red wine vinegar

Butter lettuce for lining plates

4 cooked, shelled lobster tails, cut into 1-inch (2.5-cm) chunks

Cherry tomatoes for garnish

Summer means seafood, and tender hunks of lobster make this salad special enough for an outdoor party. Accompany with crusty bread and Champagne or prosecco. The pesto vinaigrette can be made a day ahead and stored in the refrigerator. Bring to room temperature before using.

Put the potatoes in a saucepan with salted water to cover and bring to a boil over high heat. Reduce the heat to medium and simmer, uncovered, until the potatoes are cooked through but still firm, 10–20 minutes. Drain and rinse under cold water.

In a dry frying pan, toast the pine nuts over medium-low heat, stirring, until fragrant, 3–4 minutes. Pour onto a plate to cool.

Bring a large pot three-fourths full of salted water to a boil. Drop in the green beans and cook until crisp-tender, 2–4 minutes. Drain the beans and plunge them into ice water to stop the cooking. Drain again and set aside.

In a food processor, combine the basil leaves, garlic, and nuts. Pulse to combine. Add about ½ cup (4 fl oz/125 ml) of the olive oil and process to form a coarse purée. Transfer to a bowl and stir in the vinegar and enough of the remaining oil to make a spoonable vinaigrette. Season with salt and pepper.

To serve, cut the potatoes into slices ¼ inch (6 mm) thick. In a large bowl, combine the potatoes and green beans with half of the vinaigrette. Toss to coat. Line individual plates with lettuce leaves. Divide the potato mixture among the plates, top with the lobster meat, and drizzle with the remaining vinaigrette. Garnish with cherry tomatoes and serve.

7

Barley-shaped orzo pasta is the perfect size for tossing with petite peas and bites of sweet peppers. This is an easy side for summer gatherings: the sturdy vegetables hold up well, the flavors will blend together even better if you make it a day ahead, and it's substantial enough to feed a crowd.

ORZO SALAD WITH PEAS, PEPPERS & TOMATOES

serves 6–8

Salt and freshly ground pepper

1 lb (500 g) orzo pasta

1 cup (5 oz/155 g) fresh shelled English peas (about 1 lb/500 g in the shells)

1–2 Tbsp extra-virgin olive oil

FOR THE DIJON VINAIGRETTE

2 Tbsp red wine vinegar

1 Tbsp Dijon mustard

¼ cup (2 fl oz/60 ml) extra-virgin olive oil

½ cup (4 fl oz/125 ml) grapeseed oil

1 red onion, sliced ½ inch (12 mm) thick

1 white onion, sliced ½ inch (12 mm) thick

3 bell peppers, mixed colors (red, orange, yellow)

Olive oil

1 cup (1½ oz/45 g) minced fresh flat-leaf parsley

12 small heirloom tomatoes (about 3 lb/1.5 kg total weight) cored and quartered

Bring a large pot three-fourths full of salted water to a boil. Add the orzo to the pot, stirring with a large spoon to prevent sticking. Bring to a boil and cook the orzo until al dente, according to package directions. Meanwhile, prepare a bowl of ice water. During the last minute of cooking the orzo, add the peas to the pot. Drain into a colander. Pour the orzo and peas into the ice water and drain again. Transfer to a serving bowl. Drizzle with the 1–2 Tbsp extra-virgin olive oil and stir to coat. Cover and refrigerate.

To make the vinaigrette, in a bowl, whisk together the vinegar and mustard. Add the oils in a thin stream, whisking constantly until the dressing is smooth. Taste and adjust the seasoning with salt and pepper. Set the vinaigrette aside.

Prepare a charcoal or gas grill for direct-heat cooking over high heat. Brush the onions and bell peppers with oil. Arrange the onions in a grilling basket. Grill the bell peppers, turning occasionally, until nicely charred on all sides. Transfer the grilled peppers to a bowl, cover, and let steam for 10 minutes. ⟩⟩

Meanwhile, grill the onions, turning once, until nicely charred on both sides, 8–10 minutes per side. Transfer the grilled onions to a plate.

Peel the bell peppers and discard the skins. Seed and chop the peppers and chop the onions. Add the peppers, onions, parsley, and vinaigrette to the bowl with the orzo and peas and toss to coat. Taste and adjust the seasoning with salt and pepper. Garnish with tomatoes and serve.

8

This Mediterranean-inspired chopped salad combines summery tomatoes, cucumbers, onion, and parsley, and is tossed simply with lemon juice and olive oil. Sumac, a ground dark red berry with a lemony flavor, makes a vibrant garnish.

CHOPPED SALAD WITH LEMON & OLIVE OIL

serves 4

3 tomatoes, seeded and chopped

2 Persian cucumbers or 1 small English cucumber, seeded and cut into ½-inch (12-mm) pieces

½ sweet onion such as Vidalia or Walla Walla, finely chopped

1 fresh green chile, seeded and chopped (optional)

2 Tbsp fresh lemon juice

¼ cup (2 fl oz/60 ml) extra-virgin olive oil

Salt and freshly ground pepper

¼ cup (⅓ oz/10 g) chopped fresh flat-leaf parsley

4 cups (4 oz/125 g) torn romaine lettuce

½ tsp ground sumac (optional)

In a serving bowl, combine the tomatoes, cucumbers, onion, and chile, if using.

In a small bowl, whisk together the lemon juice and olive oil until well blended. Season with salt and pepper to taste.

Pour the dressing over the vegetables and toss until well combined. Add the parsley and toss again until the ingredients are well combined.

Line individual plates or a large platter with the lettuce. Top with the tomato mixture. Sprinkle the sumac on the salad, if using, and serve.

9

CHIPOTLE BEEF & CORN SALAD

serves 4

1¼ lb (625 g) boneless sirloin or rib-eye steak, about 1½ inches (4 cm) thick

2 Tbsp olive oil, plus ¼ cup (2 fl oz/60 ml)

Salt and freshly ground pepper

¼ cup (1½ oz/45 g) canned chipotle chiles in adobo, with sauce

Juice of 2 limes

1 Tbsp white wine vinegar

1 large clove garlic, sliced

2 cups (12 oz/375 g) corn kernels (from about 2 ears of corn)

6 radishes, chopped

4 plum tomatoes, chopped

¼ cup (⅓ oz/10 g) minced fresh cilantro

2 heads romaine lettuce, pale inner leaves only, torn into bite-sized pieces

Grilled steak, corn, and romaine get a smoky infusion from dried chiles in this dressing. Chipotle chiles, which are dried and smoked jalapeños, are commonly sold in cans, preserved in a spicy, vinegary tomato sauce called adobo. Transfer unused chiles and sauce to a glass jar with a tight cap and refrigerate for up to 6 months.

Place the steak on a plate, brush both sides with the 2 Tbsp oil, and season both sides generously with salt and pepper. Let stand for 30 minutes.

Meanwhile, in a blender, combine the chipotle chiles with their sauce, the ¼ cup oil, half of the lime juice, the vinegar, garlic, 1 Tbsp water, ¼ tsp salt, and a pinch of pepper. Process until smooth.

In a bowl, toss together the corn, radishes, tomatoes, cilantro, the remaining lime juice, and ¼ tsp salt.

Prepare a gas or charcoal grill for direct-heat cooking over medium-high heat. Alternatively, preheat a stove-top grill pan over medium-high heat. Place the steak on the grill rack or in the grill pan and cook, turning every 4 minutes, about 16 minutes total for medium-rare. Transfer to a cutting board and let stand for 5–10 minutes. Cut the steak on the diagonal across the grain into thin slices. Arrange the lettuce on plates and top with the beef and corn mixture. Drizzle with the dressing and serve.

10

GRILLED LAMB SALAD

serves 4

FOR THE SPICY YOGURT DRESSING

1 cup (8 oz/250 g) plain yogurt

Salt and freshly ground black pepper

¼ tsp paprika

¼ tsp ground cumin

⅛ tsp cayenne pepper

1 tsp fresh lemon juice

1 cucumber, peeled, seeded, and chopped

6 oil-packed sun-dried tomatoes, chopped

1½ lb (750 g) boneless leg of lamb, trimmed and cut into 1-inch (2.5-cm) cubes

2 Tbsp extra-virgin olive oil

1 tsp paprika

½ cup (½ oz/15 g) fresh mint leaves

½ cup (½ oz/15 g) fresh flat-leaf parsley leaves

1 heart of romaine lettuce, torn into bite-sized pieces

2 cucumbers, peeled and cut into slices ¼ inch (6 mm) thick

2 cups (12 oz/375 g) cherry tomatoes, halved

This recipe draws inspiration from gyros, the popular Middle-Eastern street food. Instead of wrapping the lamb and greens in a flatbread, here it is served as a plated salad. Serve with lightly grilled pita triangles alongside.

To make the dressing, combine the yogurt, ¼ tsp salt, ½ tsp pepper, the ¼ tsp paprika, the cumin, cayenne, lemon juice, cucumber, and sun-dried tomatoes in a blender or food processor and purée. Taste and adjust the seasonings. Refrigerate, covered, until ready to use.

Put the lamb cubes in a bowl and add the oil, 1 tsp salt, ½ tsp pepper, and the 1 tsp paprika. Turn and let marinate for at least 30 minutes or up to several hours.

Prepare a charcoal or gas grill for direct-heat cooking over high heat. Thread the lamb onto 8 skewers. When the grill is hot, place the skewers on the grill rack and cook, turning several times, until lightly charred, 6–8 minutes for medium-rare. For medium, cook for 2–3 minutes more. Remove from the heat and let rest briefly.

In a bowl, combine the mint and parsley and the romaine. Divide among individual plates, and add slices of cucumber and the cherry tomatoes. Drizzle with the dressing, top each salad with 2 skewers of lamb, and serve.

15

FRESH STRAWBERRY & SPINACH SALAD

serves 6

¼ cup (1 oz/30 g) pecans

FOR THE POPPY-SEED VINAIGRETTE

¼ cup (2 fl oz/60 ml) rice vinegar

2 Tbsp sugar

2 tsp poppy seeds

½ tsp dry mustard

Salt and freshly ground pepper

¾ cup (6 fl oz/180 ml) grapeseed oil

6 cups (6 oz/185 g) baby spinach leaves

2 cups (8 oz/250 g) strawberries, hulled and halved

It is easy to love this popular combination. Light, healthful, and delicious, it is best prepared when strawberries are at their early-summer peak. The dressing is slightly sweet, and the poppy seeds and chopped pecans add nice texture. Goat cheese, ricotta salata, or feta cheese would make a great addition.

In a dry frying pan, toast the pecans over medium-low heat, stirring, until fragrant and starting to brown, about 5 minutes. Pour onto a plate to cool, then coarsely chop and set aside.

To make the vinaigrette, in a small bowl, whisk together the vinegar, sugar, poppy seeds, dry mustard, and a pinch each of salt and pepper. Add the oil in a thin stream, whisking constantly until the dressing is well blended.

In a large bowl, toss together the spinach, strawberries, and pecans. Add half of the vinaigrette and toss gently to coat. Add more vinaigrette as needed (you may not need all of it), and serve.

16

POACHED SALMON SALAD WITH PRESERVED LEMON & GARLIC

serves 4–6

1 lb (500 g) salmon fillet, pin bones removed

Salt and freshly ground pepper

1 garlic clove, mashed to a paste

2 green onions, minced

Rind of 1 small preserved lemon, minced

¼ cup (2 fl oz/60 ml) extra-virgin olive oil, plus 1 Tbsp

Juice of 1 lemon

1 head butter lettuce, leaves torn

Use a mortar to crush the garlic for this boldly flavored salad. Preserved lemons, which are salted and then pickled in their own juices, can be found jarred in specialty food shops, Middle Eastern markets, or online.

Cut the salmon into pieces as needed to fit into a large saucepan. Cover the fish with water, add 1 tsp salt, and bring to a boil over medium heat, then reduce the heat to a simmer and poach the salmon gently until just opaque throughout, about 20 minutes.

Peel off and discard the salmon skin, put the flesh in a bowl, and break up into pieces with a fork. Add the mashed garlic, green onions, preserved lemon rind, and the ¼ cup oil to the bowl and toss to mix. Season to taste with pepper and set aside.

In a small bowl, whisk together the lemon juice and the 1 Tbsp oil and season to taste with salt and pepper. Put the lettuce leaves in a large bowl, drizzle with the lemon dressing, and toss to mix. Distribute the greens among individual plates and top with some of the salmon salad. Season to taste with salt and pepper and serve.

17

JUNE

CHICKEN TOSTADA SALAD
serves 4

FOR THE LIME VINAIGRETTE

Grated zest and juice of 2 limes

1 clove garlic, minced

Salt and freshly ground pepper

⅔ cup (5 fl oz/160 ml) olive oil

1 can (15 oz/470 g) black beans, drained and rinsed

2 cups (12 oz/375 g) fresh corn kernels (from about 2 ears of corn, grilled if desired)

2 cups (12 oz/375 g) cherry tomatoes, halved

4 canned green chiles, chopped

1 cup (8 fl oz/250 ml) corn oil

4 corn tortillas, each 6 inches (15 cm) in diameter, halved

1 small head romaine lettuce, cut into bite-sized pieces

2 cups (¾ lb/375 g) shredded cooked chicken meat

1 avocado, peeled, pitted and sliced

Fresh cilantro leaves and sliced green onion for garnish (optional)

This is a refreshed version of the ubiquitous taco salad, with lean chicken and chopped vegetables piled high on a crispy tortilla. For a shortcut, omit frying the tortillas and serve the chicken salad over large handfuls of good-quality corn tortilla chips.

To make the vinaigrette, in a bowl, whisk together the lime zest and juice, garlic, ¼ tsp salt, and ⅛ tsp pepper. Add the oil in a thin stream, whisking constantly until the vinaigrette is smooth.

Transfer 3 Tbsp of the vinaigrette to a large bowl and add the beans, corn, tomatoes, and chiles; mix gently. Reserve the remaining vinaigrette. Let the salsa stand for at least 10 minutes to blend the flavors.

Meanwhile, in a frying pan, warm the corn oil over medium-high heat. When it is hot, slip 3 tortilla halves into the oil and cook until golden and almost crisp, 1–2 minutes. Using tongs, transfer to paper towels to drain. Repeat with the remaining tortilla halves.

Add the lettuce to the reserved vinaigrette and toss to coat. Place 2 fried tortilla halves on each of 4 plates and divide the lettuce among them. Spoon the salsa over the lettuce, top with the chicken and avocado, garnish with the cilantro and green onion, if desired, and serve.

18

JUNE

PEACH, ARUGULA & GOAT CHEESE SALAD
serves 4

½ cup (4 fl oz/125 ml) balsamic vinegar, plus 2 Tbsp

2 peaches

2 Tbsp firmly packed light brown sugar

2 cups (2 oz/60 g) arugula leaves, stemmed

2 Tbsp grapeseed oil

Salt and freshly ground pepper

4 oz (125 g) fresh goat cheese, crumbled

This salad showcases ripe peaches in season. Sample local varieties at the farmers' market, including white or yellow peaches, or smaller, flatter, donut peaches. Balsamic vinegar reduces to a syrupy consistency to make a simply delicious condiment for grilled fruit and salads.

In a small, heavy saucepan, bring the ½ cup vinegar to a boil over medium-high heat. Reduce the heat to a simmer and cook the vinegar down until it is thick enough to coat the back of a spoon. Let cool.

Cut the peaches in half lengthwise; remove and discard the pits. Cut each half into 6 wedges. Place the wedges in a shallow dish, sprinkle with the brown sugar, and drizzle with the 2 Tbsp vinegar.

Prepare a charcoal or gas grill for direct-heat cooking over medium-high heat. Oil the grill rack or a grill basket. Grill the peaches, turning once, until grill marks appear, about 1 minute per side.

In a large bowl, combine the arugula and the oil and toss to coat. Season with salt and pepper to taste. Put the arugula in a large serving bowl or divide among individual plates. Arrange the grilled peaches on top of the arugula. Drizzle with the balsamic reduction and sprinkle with the cheese. Top with a few grindings of pepper and serve.

142

19
JUNE

LENTIL SALAD WITH FETA
serves 4

1 lb (500 g) green French (du Puy) lentils, picked over and rinsed

1 carrot, peeled and halved

1 celery rib, cut into 3 pieces

1 yellow onion, peeled and halved

5 fresh flat-leaf parsley sprigs, plus ⅔ cup (1 oz/30 g) chopped parsley

1 red onion, chopped

1 jarred roasted red bell pepper, chopped

2 Tbsp red wine vinegar

1 Tbsp olive oil

½ cup (2½ oz/75 g) crumbled feta cheese

Salt and freshly ground pepper

A big pot of lentils inspires a week of textured salads, legume-flecked soups, or spicy vegetarian curries. France's du Puy lentils are among the prettiest for salads, as they keep their shape and jade color during cooking. Store any leftover lentils in an airtight container in the refrigerator for up to 3 days.

In a large saucepan, combine the lentils, carrot, celery, yellow onion, parsley sprigs, and 8 cups (64 fl oz/2 l) water. Bring to a boil over medium-high heat, reduce the heat to medium-low, cover, and simmer until the lentils are tender and the liquid has been absorbed, 30–35 minutes. Remove and discard the vegetables, leaving 2½ cups (17½ oz/545 g) of the lentils for the salad. Set aside the remaining lentils to cool before storing for another use.

In a bowl, stir together the red onion, bell pepper, chopped parsley, and the reserved lentils. Mix in the vinegar and oil. Add the cheese and toss to combine. Season with salt and pepper to taste and serve.

20
JUNE

ROASTED BELL PEPPER & QUINOA SALAD
serves 4–6

1 cup (6 oz/185 g) quinoa

2 red bell peppers

2 yellow bell peppers

Grated zest of 1 lemon

2 Tbsp fresh lemon juice

1 medium tomato, coarsely chopped

1 clove garlic, chopped

½ cup (½ oz/15 g) loosely packed fresh basil leaves, plus small leaves for garnish

1 tsp sherry vinegar or white wine vinegar

1 Tbsp extra-virgin olive oil

Salt and freshly ground pepper

Quinoa, a mild grain that originated in Peru, can provide a backdrop for many different flavors. This salad combines it with bold Mediterranean ingredients: garlic, basil, vinegar, and blistered peppers.

In a dry frying pan, toast the quinoa over medium heat, stirring, until fragrant with a nutty aroma, 2–3 minutes. Transfer to a fine-mesh sieve and rinse under cold running water until the water runs clear. Drain thoroughly and put in a pot with 3 cups (24 fl oz/750 ml) water. Bring to a boil, then reduce the heat to low, cover, and simmer until the water is absorbed and the grains are translucent, about 15 minutes. Remove from the heat, fluff the quinoa, and let cool completely.

Preheat the broiler. Place the peppers on a baking sheet and slide under the broiler 4–6 inches (10–15 cm) from the heat source. Broil, turning often, until the skins are blackened on all sides, 10–15 minutes. Remove to a covered bowl or seal in a paper bag. Let the peppers steam until cool, about 10 minutes. Rub and peel off the charred skins. Cut the peppers in half lengthwise, reserving their juices, remove the seeds and membranes, and chop finely.

In a blender or food processor, combine the reserved juice from the peppers, lemon zest, lemon juice, tomato, garlic, the ½ cup basil, vinegar, olive oil, 2 Tbsp water, 1 tsp salt, and several grindings of pepper and process until smooth. Add to the cooled quinoa along with the bell peppers and toss until evenly combined. Season with salt and pepper to taste.

Mound on a platter or divide among plates. Garnish with basil leaves and serve.

21

SALADE VERTE

serves 4–6

A traditional salade verte is a tangle of greens coated in a mustardy vinaigrette. In France, it is typically served after the main course, frequently alongside a cheese plate. The best versions include seasonal greens and a smattering of fragrant herbs.

FOR THE VINAIGRETTE

2 tsp white wine vinegar

3 or 4 drops balsamic vinegar

Salt and freshly ground pepper

½ tsp Dijon, champagne, tarragon, or other mustard, or to taste

3 Tbsp extra-virgin olive oil or equal parts extra-virgin olive oil and walnut or hazelnut oil

5 or 6 large handfuls mixed torn greens, such as frisée, mâche, arugula, dandelion greens, butter lettuce, Belgian endive, and/or baby romaine

1 shallot, thinly sliced or chopped

1 Tbsp chopped fresh chives

1 tsp chopped fresh chervil

1 tsp chopped fresh tarragon

Thin slices of country-style bread for serving (optional)

To make the vinaigrette, in a large serving bowl, whisk together the vinegars and a pinch of salt until the salt dissolves, then stir in the mustard. Add the oil in a thin stream, whisking constantly until the vinaigrette is smooth. Season with pepper, then taste and adjust the seasonings.

Add the mixed greens and shallot to the vinaigrette and toss until the leaves are well coated. Add the chives, chervil, and tarragon and toss again to distribute the herbs evenly. Divide the salad among individual plates and serve with the bread alongside, if desired.

22

POTATO SALAD WITH GREEN BEANS & CUCUMBER-YOGURT DRESSING

serves 6

This salad provides two sides in one by combining a fresh green vegetable with filling potatoes. Serve as an accompaniment to grilled or roasted meat. The summery cucumber-yogurt dressing may be prepared a day in advance, covered, and refrigerated.

FOR THE CUCUMBER-YOGURT DRESSING

⅔ cup (5 oz/155 g) plain whole-milk yogurt

⅓ cup (3 fl oz/80 ml) mayonnaise

¼ cup (⅓ oz/10 g) minced fresh dill

½ tsp dried oregano

Salt and freshly ground pepper

¾ cup (4 oz/125 g) peeled, seeded, and finely chopped cucumber (from about one 3½-inch/9-cm piece)

5 Yukon Gold potatoes (about 1¾ lb/875 g total weight), peeled, halved lengthwise, and cut crosswise into slices ⅓ inch (9 mm) thick

½ lb (250 g) green beans, trimmed and cut into 2-inch (5-cm) pieces

½ Tbsp white wine vinegar

To make the dressing, in a bowl, whisk together the yogurt, mayonnaise, dill, oregano, ½ tsp salt, and ½ tsp pepper. Stir in the cucumber. Set aside.

To steam the potatoes, pour water to a depth of 1 inch (2.5 cm) into a large pot and bring to a boil. Put the potatoes in a steamer basket and set the basket over the boiling water. (The water should not touch the bottom of the steamer basket.) Cover and steam until the potatoes are tender when pierced with a knife, about 14 minutes. Transfer the potatoes to a large bowl. Let cool for 5 minutes, then sprinkle lightly with salt and pepper.

In the same steamer, cook the green beans until just crisp-tender, about 5 minutes. Transfer the green beans to the bowl with the potatoes. Sprinkle with salt and pepper and let cool to lukewarm, about 20 minutes.

Using a slotted spoon, transfer the cucumbers from the yogurt mixture to the bowl with the potatoes and beans. Mix the vinegar into the yogurt mixture. Stir enough of the dressing into the salad to coat generously and serve.

23

FARRO SALAD WITH CREAMY ARTICHOKE DRESSING

serves 4

1½ cups (9 oz/280 g) farro

Salt and freshly ground pepper

FOR THE ARTICHOKE DRESSING

1 jar (6 oz/185 g) water-packed artichoke hearts

1 cup (4 oz/125 g) freshly grated Parmesan cheese

1 Tbsp finely grated lemon zest

2 tsp fresh lemon juice

½ cup (½ oz/15 g) chopped fresh flat-leaf parsley

½ cup (2½ oz/75 g) Kalamata olives, pitted

2 Tbsp small capers, rinsed

Italy's favorite grain has a mild, nutty flavor and crunchy texture. It is an excellent base for salads, and hearty enough for vegetarian mains. Treat it to a thick dressing of artichoke hearts, lemon, and Parmesan in this toothsome salad.

Rinse and drain the farro, then transfer to a large saucepan and add 3 cups (24 fl oz/750 ml) cold water. Stir in 1 teaspoon salt and bring to a boil over high heat. Reduce the heat to medium-low, cover partially, and simmer until the farro is tender but still chewy, about 20 minutes. Drain thoroughly and set aside.

Drain and rinse the artichoke hearts, then pat them dry and coarsely chop them.

In a food processor, combine half of the artichoke hearts, the cheese, ¼ tsp pepper, and the lemon zest and juice and process until a paste forms. Taste and adjust the seasoning with salt and pepper.

In a serving bowl, combine the dressing and the farro and turn to coat. Add the parsley, olives, and the reserved artichoke hearts and turn again. Sprinkle with the capers and serve.

24

STONE FRUIT SALAD WITH HAZELNUTS & BLUE CHEESE

serves 6

¼ cup (1½ oz/45 g) hazelnuts

2 Tbsp rice vinegar

1 tsp honey

Salt and freshly ground pepper

½ cup (4 fl oz/125 ml) extra-virgin olive oil

6 cups (6 oz/185 g) baby arugula leaves

2 small plums, halved, pitted, and cut into ¼-inch (6-mm) slices

2 small apricots, halved, pitted, and cut into ¼-inch (6-mm) slices

1 firm peach, halved, pitted, and cut into ¼-inch (6-mm) slices

¼ cup (1½ oz/45 g) crumbled blue cheese

Stone fruits—peaches, plums, apricots—have a special affinity for nuts, as their pits themselves carry a bitter almond flavor. A sprinkling of savory blue cheese balances the sweetness of the fruit and the bitter edge of the hazelnuts, making this a sophisticated summertime salad.

In a dry frying pan, toast the hazelnuts over medium-low heat, stirring, until fragrant and starting to brown, about 5 minutes. Wrap the hazelnuts in a towel and rub to remove the skins. Pour onto a plate to cool, then chop coarsely and set aside.

In a small bowl, whisk together the vinegar, honey, and a pinch each of salt and pepper. Add the olive oil in a thin stream, whisking constantly until the vinaigrette is smooth.

In a large bowl, gently toss together the arugula, plums, apricots, peach, and hazelnuts. Add half of the vinaigrette and toss gently, adding more as needed to lightly coat the arugula. Sprinkle with the cheese and serve.

25

SALADE NIÇOISE WITH SEARED WILD SALMON

serves 6

To hard-cook the eggs, place them in a saucepan just large enough to hold them. Add cold water to cover by 1 inch (2.5 cm) and bring just to a boil over high heat. Remove the pan from the heat and cover. Let stand for 15 minutes. Have ready a bowl of ice water. Drain the eggs, then transfer to the ice water and let cool before peeling.

FOR THE OLIVE-ANCHOVY DRESSING

2 Tbsp chopped pitted niçoise olives

2 or 3 olive oil–packed anchovy fillets

5 Tbsp (2½ fl oz/75 ml) extra-virgin olive oil

3 Tbsp white wine vinegar

2 Tbsp minced fresh chives

¾ tsp sugar

¼ tsp Dijon mustard

2 lb (1 kg) small red potatoes, quartered

Salt and freshly ground pepper

¾ lb (375 g) haricots verts or other young, tender green beans, stem ends trimmed

6 wild salmon fillets (6 oz/185 g each), pin bones removed

1 Tbsp grapeseed oil

1 head romaine lettuce, thinly sliced

3½ cups (21 oz/655 g) cherry tomatoes, halved

6 eggs, hard-cooked *(left)* and cut into quarters

2 Tbsp minced fresh chives

To make the dressing, in a food processor, combine the olives and anchovies and process until smooth, about 10 seconds. Add the olive oil, vinegar, chives, sugar, and mustard and process until the dressing is smooth. Set aside.

Have ready a bowl of ice water. In a large saucepan, combine the potatoes, 1 Tbsp salt, and water to cover by 1 inch (2.5 cm) and bring to a boil over high heat. Reduce the heat to medium, cover partially, and simmer until the potatoes are just tender when pierced with the tip of a paring knife, 5–7 minutes. Drain and immediately transfer the potatoes to the ice water. Let stand until cool, then transfer the potatoes to a large bowl.

Fill a saucepan two-thirds full of water and bring to a boil over high heat. Have ready another bowl of ice water. Add 1 Tbsp salt and the haricots verts to the boiling water and cook until crisp-tender, about 3 minutes. Drain and transfer to the ice water. Let stand until cool and drain. Add the beans to the bowl with the potatoes. ⟫

Season the salmon fillets on both sides with salt and pepper. In a large nonstick frying pan, warm the oil over medium-high heat until shimmering. Working in batches, add the salmon to the pan, skin side up, and cook until golden brown, about 2 minutes. Turn the salmon over and cook until just opaque at the center, 2–3 minutes. Transfer to a large plate, remove the skin, and tent with foil.

Add the lettuce, ¾ tsp salt, and several grindings of pepper to the potatoes and beans and toss to mix. Drizzle with half of the vinaigrette and toss again. In a bowl, toss the tomatoes with ¼ tsp salt.

Divide the mixture among individual plates. Top each serving with some of the tomatoes, and then with a piece of salmon. Arrange 4 egg quarters on each serving and sprinkle them lightly with salt. Sprinkle each salad with chives and serve, passing the remaining vinaigrette at the table.

26

CUCUMBER SALAD WITH YOGURT-DILL SAUCE

serves 4

Cool cucumbers shine through in this quintessential summer salad. It comes together quickly for an outdoor supper, but would be equally charming with toasted bagels and slices of smoked salmon for brunch. For a touch of heat, add a pinch of cayenne pepper.

4 English cucumbers, peeled and thinly sliced

Salt and ground white pepper

⅔ cup (5 oz/155 g) plain yogurt

1 Tbsp fresh lemon juice

2 Tbsp minced fresh dill

3 cloves garlic, minced

3 Tbsp extra-virgin olive oil

Place the cucumber slices in a single layer on a plate. Salt lightly and let stand for about 1 hour. Drain off the excess liquid.

In a large bowl, combine the yogurt, lemon juice, dill, and garlic. Season with salt and white pepper to taste and whisk to combine. Add the oil in a thin stream, whisking constantly until the dressing is well blended.

Add the drained cucumber slices to the bowl and toss with the dressing. Refrigerate for 1 hour, then serve chilled.

27

Crispy-tangy buttermilk fried chicken meets its match with a plate of fresh lettuce, tomatoes, and a mustard dressing. Add any other vegetables you like—avocado, radishes, or cucumbers would be tasty. Don't bother with side dishes; this salad completely satisfies on its own.

FRIED CHICKEN SALAD
serves 4

FOR THE DIJON DRESSING

1 Tbsp honey Dijon mustard

1 Tbsp red wine vinegar

Salt and freshly ground pepper

½ cup (4 fl oz/125 ml) extra-virgin olive oil

Peanut or grapeseed oil for frying

1 cup (5 oz/155 g) all-purpose flour

1½ tsp garlic powder (optional)

1 cup (8 fl oz/250 ml) buttermilk

1 lb (500 g) skinless, boneless chicken breast halves, cut into large bite-sized pieces

1 heart of romaine lettuce, torn into bite-sized pieces

1 large tomato, cut into bite-sized chunks

1 small red onion, halved and cut into thin slivers

1 cup (4 oz/125 g) pecan halves, coarsely chopped

To make the dressing, in a large bowl, whisk together the mustard, vinegar, and 1 tsp salt. Add the olive oil in a thin stream, whisking constantly until smooth.

Preheat the oven to 200°F (95°C). Pour ½ inch (12 mm) peanut oil into a deep, heavy pot and set over high heat. Line a large baking sheet with a double layer of paper towels and place it in the oven. In a large, resealable bag, combine the flour and 1½ tsp each salt and pepper, and the garlic powder, if using. Pour the buttermilk into a shallow bowl. When the oil reaches 360°F (185°C) on a deep-frying thermometer, dip the chicken pieces in the buttermilk. Remove, letting any excess drip back into the bowl, and place in the bag of flour. Seal the bag and toss until the chicken is evenly coated. Using tongs, add half of the chicken to the hot oil and fry, turning occasionally, until opaque throughout and golden, 2–4 minutes. Using the tongs, transfer to the lined baking sheet to drain and keep warm. Let the oil return to 360°F between batches.

Add the lettuce, tomato, onion, and pecans to the vinaigrette and toss to coat evenly. Arrange on plates, top with the chicken, and serve.

28

Sriracha sauce is a tantalizing combination of sun-ripened chiles ground up with garlic into a paste. Along with fish sauce and rice vinegar, it adds spice and piquancy to shreds of crunchy papaya in this classic Southeast Asian salad.

GREEN PAPAYA SALAD
serves 4–6

1 large green papaya, about 1½ lb (750 g)

1 carrot

4 shallots, thinly sliced, plus 1 Tbsp chopped

1 red Fresno chile, cut into thin rings and seeded

2 Tbsp chopped fresh cilantro

2 cloves garlic, chopped

1 tsp sugar

¼ cup (2 fl oz/60 ml) rice vinegar

¼ cup (2 fl oz/60 ml) Asian fish sauce

2 Tbsp fresh lime juice

2 Tbsp Sriracha chile sauce

3 Tbsp canola oil

Using a vegetable peeler, peel the papaya. Cut the papaya in half lengthwise and then scoop out and discard the seeds. Using the largest holes on a box grater or a mandoline, and holding each papaya half lengthwise, shred the flesh into long, thin strips. Peel the carrot and shred into long, thin strips.

In a large bowl, combine the papaya, carrot, sliced shallots, chile, and cilantro and toss gently to mix well.

In a mini food processor or mortar, combine the chopped shallot, garlic, and sugar and process or grind with a pestle until a smooth paste forms. Add 1–2 tsp water if needed to facilitate the grinding. Transfer the garlic paste to a bowl and whisk in the vinegar, fish sauce, lime juice, and Sriracha sauce. Add the oil in a thin stream, whisking constantly until the dressing is well combined.

Pour the dressing over the papaya mixture and toss to coat thoroughly. Refrigerate for at least 2 hours or up to overnight before serving. Serve chilled.

29

BLACK BEAN & WHITE CORN SALAD

serves 4

2 tsp canola oil

⅔ cup (4 oz/125 g) chopped red bell pepper

⅔ cup (3 oz/90 g) chopped red onion

½ can (8 oz/250 g) black beans, rinsed and drained

1 cup (6 oz/185 g) fresh or frozen white corn kernels (from about 1 ear of corn)

1 tsp chili powder

2 Tbsp fresh lime juice

Salt and freshly ground pepper

Romaine lettuce leaves for serving (optional)

⅓ cup (½ oz/15 g) chopped fresh cilantro

Beans and corn are so easy to toss together, and they taste fresh and filling alongside Latin dinners of grilled fish tacos, chicken quesadillas, or skirt steak with chimichurri sauce. This sturdy salad can be made ahead and stored in the refrigerator for up to 2 days.

Heat the oil in a frying pan over medium-high heat. Add the bell pepper and onion and sauté until the juices from the bell pepper moisten the bottom of the pan, about 3 minutes.

Stir in the beans, corn, and chili powder. Cook until the beans and corn are heated through, about 3 minutes. The beans and corn will be just crisp-tender. Remove the pan from the heat and stir in the lime juice. Toss well and season with salt and pepper to taste.

Line a platter with lettuce leaves, if using, and spoon the beans and corn on top. Garnish with the cilantro and serve.

30

GRILLED SQUASH & ORZO SALAD WITH PINE NUTS & MINT

serves 4

2 lb (1 kg) mixed yellow squash and zucchini

1½ Tbsp olive oil

Salt and freshly ground pepper

½ lb (250 g) orzo pasta

½ cup (2½ oz/75 g) pine nuts

3 Tbsp fresh lemon juice

1 Tbsp champagne vinegar or white wine vinegar

3 Tbsp chopped fresh mint leaves

Parmesan cheese for shaving (optional)

Early in the summer, seek out baby squashes in a variety of shapes. Combining these with halved larger squash makes a beautiful presentation on a bed of pasta. Use a grill basket so you don't lose any cherry tomatoes and baby squash, if using.

Trim and cut the squash lengthwise into slices ¼ inch (6 mm) thick. Put in a bowl and add ½ Tbsp of the oil, ½ tsp salt, and a few grindings of pepper. Mix to coat.

Prepare a charcoal or gas grill for direct-heat cooking over medium-high heat. Grill the squash, turning once, until tender, 5–8 minutes total. Let cool and cut into 1½-inch (4-cm) pieces, and put in a large bowl.

Bring a pot of salted water to a boil. Add the orzo and cook until al dente, according to package directions. Drain and rinse under cold running water.

Meanwhile, in a dry frying pan, toast the pine nuts over medium-low heat, stirring, until fragrant and starting to brown, 3–4 minutes. Pour onto a plate to cool.

Add the orzo to the squash along with the remaining 1 Tbsp oil, lemon juice, vinegar, and pine nuts and toss to combine. Season with salt and pepper to taste. Garnish with the mint. Just before serving, use a vegetable peeler to shave the cheese over the salad, if using, and serve.

High summer means high season for sun-loving corn and tomatoes. Toss a handful of corn kernels into salads to add a sweet, fresh bite. Slice tomatoes thinly for caprese; toss diced ones with bread cubes and arugula for a panzanella; or enjoy cheerful bursts of cherry and grape varieties in nearly anything. Make good use of the outdoor grill this season, too: salmon and steak love a bed of leafy greens. Or, create innovative chopped salads of charred eggplant, yellow squash, and zucchini.

1
HEIRLOOM TOMATO SALAD WITH BLUE CHEESE DRESSING
page 154

2
QUICK GRILLED SQUID SALAD
page 154

3
PASTA SALAD WITH SUMMER BEANS & HERBS
page 157

8
OLD-FASHIONED POTATO SALAD
page 159

9
PASTA SALAD WITH GRILLED VEGETABLES
page 160

10
GRILLED PLUOT SALAD WITH GOAT CHEESE & WILD ARUGULA
page 160

15
GRILLED SALMON, YELLOW POTATO & CORN SALAD
page 165

16
MINTED FRUIT SALAD
page 165

17
SHAVED ZUCCHINI SALAD WITH PECORINO & ALMONDS
page 166

22
GRILLED CORN SALAD
page 169

23
GRILLED SHRIMP SALAD WITH AVOCADO & CHIPOTLE DRESSING
page 171

24
WATERMELON RADISH SALAD WITH ROMAINE & AVOCADO
page 171

29
WHITE NECTARINE & MINT SALAD
page 173

30
ASIAN CHICKEN SALAD WITH LIME DRESSING
page 174

31
GRILLED FLANK STEAK SALAD WITH TOMATOES
page 174

4 ARUGULA SALAD WITH BREADED GOAT CHEESE *page 157*	**5** GREEN BEAN & YELLOW TOMATO SALAD WITH MINT *page 158*	**6** CLASSIC GREEK SALAD *page 158*	**7** SPINACH, TOMATO & CORN SALAD *page 159*
11 BLT & POACHED EGG SALAD *page 163*	**12** SWEET-AND-SOUR CUCUMBER SALAD *page 163*	**13** INSALATA ROSSA *page 164*	**14** CHICKEN & ROASTED TOMATO SALAD *page 164*
18 CHICKEN, AVOCADO & SPINACH SALAD *page 166*	**19** CREAMY COLESLAW *page 168*	**20** YELLOW SQUASH & FARRO SALAD *page 168*	**21** GRILLED ROMAINE & HALLOUMI WITH MINT VINAIGRETTE *page 169*
25 GRILLED STEAK, PEPPER & ONION SALAD WITH ROMESCO DRESSING *page 172*	**26** FRESH FIG & GOAT CHEESE SALAD *page 172*	**27** LOBSTER SALAD WITH TARRAGON & CHAMPAGNE VINAIGRETTE *page 173*	**28** CELERY SALAD WITH BLUE CHEESE & LEMON *page 173*

july

1

Ripe summer tomatoes need no more than a sprinkle of sea salt or a classic vinaigrette, but a creamy dressing enriched with crumbled blue cheese only improves on a good thing. Serve with a light white wine such as sauvignon blanc or pinot grigio.

HEIRLOOM TOMATO SALAD WITH BLUE CHEESE DRESSING

serves 4

1½ lb (750 g) heirloom tomatoes, in a variety of sizes and colors

FOR THE BLUE CHEESE DRESSING

¼ cup (2 fl oz/60 ml) mayonnaise

¼ cup (2 fl oz/60 ml) buttermilk

1 clove garlic, thinly sliced

2 tsp champagne vinegar, or more to taste

2 oz (60 g) blue cheese, plus extra for crumbling

Salt and freshly ground pepper

2 Tbsp minced green onion, including tender green parts

1 Tbsp minced fresh flat-leaf parsley

Core large tomatoes and cut them into wedges or slices. Cut cherry tomatoes in half. Arrange all the tomatoes attractively on a serving platter.

To make the dressing, in a food processor or a blender, combine the mayonnaise, buttermilk, garlic, the 2 tsp vinegar, and the cheese and process until smooth. Transfer to a bowl and stir in salt to taste and more vinegar if desired.

In a small bowl, combine the green onion and parsley, mixing well.

Drizzle the dressing over the tomatoes, using as much as you like (you may not need it all), then garnish with the green onion–parsley mixture and several grindings of pepper. If desired, crumble extra cheese over the salad and serve.

2

If you can't find squid readily at your grocer, this fresh seafood salad would be equally appealing with shrimp. Purchase 1 lb (16 oz/500 g) medium-sized shrimp; peel and devein them, then thread 4–6 on a skewer and grill or broil them until they turn pink and curl slightly.

QUICK GRILLED SQUID SALAD

serves 4–6

Juice of 2 limes

¼ cup (⅓ oz/10 g) lightly packed fresh mint leaves

¼ cup (⅓ oz/10 g) coarsely chopped fresh cilantro

2 red Thai chiles, seeded and minced

4 Tbsp (2 fl oz/60 ml) olive oil

1 lb (500 g) cleaned squid, cut into bite-sized rings and tentacles

Salt and freshly ground pepper

Lemon wedges for squeezing

Prepare a charcoal or gas grill for direct-heat cooking over medium-high heat.

In a bowl, whisk together the lime juice, mint, cilantro, and chiles. Add 2 Tbsp of the olive oil in a thin stream, whisking constantly until the dressing is smooth. Set aside.

In a bowl, toss the squid with the remaining 2 Tbsp olive oil and season lightly with salt and pepper.

Put the squid in a grill basket and grill, turning once, until opaque and lightly charred on the edges, about 1 minute per side.

Toss the squid with the dressing, and serve hot or at room temperature, with the lemon wedges alongside.

3

Fresh shelling beans thrive in the late summer months, before the pods begin to show signs of drying. Because most varieties, such as kidney, cannellini, scarlet runner, lima, cranberry and black-eyed peas, are used dried, few cooks realize the distinctive qualities they add when included fresh in summer dishes. Select any type you like for this recipe.

PASTA SALAD WITH SUMMER BEANS & HERBS

serves 6

Salt and freshly ground pepper

¾ lb (375 g) fusilli pasta

6 Tbsp (3 fl oz/90 ml) extra-virgin olive oil

1 lb (500 g) assorted snap beans, such as green beans, yellow wax beans, and haricots verts, stem ends trimmed

2 lb (1 kg) fresh shelling beans of choice *(left)*, shelled

5 Tbsp (2½ fl oz/75 ml) red wine vinegar

2 cloves garlic, minced

2 Tbsp chopped fresh flat-leaf parsley

1 Tbsp chopped fresh mint

2 tsp chopped fresh oregano

Bring a large pot three-fourths full of salted water to a boil over high heat. Add the fusilli, stir well, and boil until al dente, according to package directions. Using a strainer, scoop out the pasta and transfer to a large bowl. Immediately add 1 Tbsp of the olive oil and toss well. Cover and refrigerate to cool.

Return the water to a boil. Add the snap beans and boil until tender, 5–6 minutes (3–4 minutes for haricots verts). Scoop out with the strainer and rinse under cold water to halt the cooking. Add the beans to the pasta in the refrigerator.

Return the water to a boil. Add the shelling beans and boil until tender, 4–6 minutes. Scoop out, rinse, and add to the pasta and snap beans; let cool completely in the refrigerator for at least 1 hour or up to 24 hours.

In a large bowl, whisk together the remaining 5 Tbsp olive oil, the vinegar, and the garlic. Pour over the pasta and beans and add the chopped parsley, mint, and oregano. Toss together well. Season with salt and pepper to taste and serve.

4

This version of the classic French bistro dish uses a fresh goat cheese that is shaped into disks, covered lightly with bread crumbs, and panfried. Crisp on the outside and melting at the center, the cheese is the perfect match for a bed of peppery arugula. You can use seasoned or herbed goat cheese, if you like.

ARUGULA SALAD WITH BREADED GOAT CHEESE

serves 4

4 oz (125 g) fresh goat cheese

½ cup (2 oz/60 g) dried bread crumbs

Salt and freshly ground pepper

½ tsp fresh thyme leaves

1 Tbsp vinegar

¼ cup (2 fl oz/60 ml) extra-virgin olive oil, plus 1 Tbsp

4 cups (4 oz/125 g) arugula leaves, stemmed

Shape the cheese into 4 equal rounds, each 3 inches (7.5 cm) in diameter and ½ inch (12 mm) thick. If using a log-shaped cheese, cut 4 equal slices, each about ¾ inch (2 cm) thick.

In a shallow bowl, stir together the bread crumbs, ¼ tsp salt, ½ tsp pepper, and the thyme. Working with 1 round of cheese at a time, press both sides into the bread crumb mixture to coat it. Set aside.

In a large bowl, whisk together the vinegar, ¼ tsp salt, and ⅛ tsp pepper. Add the ¼ cup oil in a thin stream, whisking constantly to make a smooth vinaigrette.

Add the arugula to the bowl with the vinaigrette and toss to coat. Divide the salad among individual plates and set aside.

In a small frying pan over medium heat, warm the 1 Tbsp oil. Add the cheese rounds and cook until lightly golden on the first side, 1–2 minutes. Turn the rounds and cook until the cheese begins to melt and spread slightly, about 1 minute. Remove the pan from the heat and set aside.

Using a spatula, quickly transfer each browned cheese round to a salad, gently sliding it on top, and serve.

5

GREEN BEAN & YELLOW TOMATO SALAD WITH MINT

serves 4

Salt and freshly ground pepper

1 lb (500 g) long, slender green beans, stem ends trimmed

½ cup (¾ oz/20 g) chopped fresh mint

2 Tbsp extra-virgin olive oil

1 or 2 yellow tomatoes

½ cup (2 oz/60 g) thin red onion wedges

2 tsp red wine vinegar, or to taste

You can't go wrong with simple salad pairings of sun-loving vegetables, like fresh beans and tomatoes. Yellow tomatoes have a sweeter, less acidic flavor than red, but use any color or combination you like. Just reduce the amount of red wine vinegar to taste if you use tart varieties.

Bring a large pot three-fourths full of salted water to a boil. Add the beans to the boiling water and cook until tender, 5–7 minutes. Drain.

In a large serving bowl, combine the hot beans, mint, oil, and ½ tsp salt and toss to mix. Set aside to cool to room temperature, about 20 minutes.

Cut the tomatoes into wedges about ½ inch (12 mm) thick. Just before serving, add the tomatoes, onion, 2 tsp vinegar, and a grinding of pepper to the bean mixture and toss to mix. Taste and add more vinegar, if needed. Serve at room temperature.

6

CLASSIC GREEK SALAD

serves 4

Juice of 1 lemon

1 clove garlic, minced

Freshly ground pepper

¼ cup (2 fl oz/60 ml) extra-virgin olive oil, plus 2 Tbsp

4 rounds pita bread

½ tsp dried oregano

2 hearts of romaine lettuce, coarsely chopped

1 English cucumber, halved crosswise and thickly sliced

2 tomatoes, cut into wedges

1 cup (5 oz/155 g) assorted brine-cured olives

8 oz (250 g) feta cheese, crumbled

8 green onions, including tender green parts, thinly sliced

In Greece you'll find this salad both with and without the lettuce, but what is crucial is using the freshest ingredients and ripest tomatoes you can find. Seek out authentic Greek feta cheese, which is creamy and salty. Kalamata olives are the favorite choice.

In a large bowl, whisk together the lemon juice, garlic, and a generous amount of pepper. Add the ¼ cup olive oil in a thin stream, whisking constantly until the dressing is smooth.

Preheat the oven to 300°F (150°C). Cut each pita round into 4 wedges. Arrange on a baking sheet and brush both sides with the 2 Tbsp oil. Sprinkle with the oregano and place in the oven to warm for about 10 minutes.

Meanwhile, add the lettuce, cucumber, and tomatoes to the dressing and toss to coat evenly. Arrange on plates and top with the olives, cheese, and green onions. Place the warm pita wedges alongside the salads and serve.

7

*Baby spinach gains
even more fresh
flavor with chopped
basil, mint, parsley,
and dill, and a pinch
of toasted cumin
enlivens ordinairy
vinaigrette. Fresh
sweet corn does
not require cooking;
look for the freshest
young ears you can
find, at a farmers'
market or roadside
farm stand.*

SPINACH, TOMATO & CORN SALAD

serves 4

2 ears corn, husks and silk removed

1 large tomato, chopped

½ cup (2½ oz/75 g) chopped English cucumber

½ cup (2 oz/60 g) chopped sweet onion such as Vidalia

2 Tbsp *each* chopped fresh basil, mint, flat-leaf parsley, and dill

1 tsp chopped garlic

1 tsp ground cumin

¼ cup (2 fl oz/60 ml) extra-virgin olive oil

2 Tbsp red wine vinegar

Salt and freshly ground pepper

5 oz (155 g) baby spinach leaves

Hold each ear of corn upright, stem end down, in the center of a wide, shallow bowl and cut off the kernels.

Add the tomato, cucumber, and onion to the corn. Add the basil, mint, parsley, dill, and garlic.

In a small, dry frying pan over medium-low heat, warm the cumin just until fragrant, about 20 seconds. Transfer to a small bowl. Add the olive oil, vinegar, ½ tsp salt, and a grinding of pepper and whisk until a smooth dressing forms.

Add the dressing to the corn-tomato mixture and toss to coat. Add the spinach, toss again, and serve.

8

*Easy-to-handle
red potatoes and
common pantry
staples define this
creamy classic,
essential at backyard
barbecues. Every
family has their own
favorite recipe, so
don't hesitate to add
coarsely chopped
olives, sliced hard-
boiled eggs, chopped
pickles, or flaked
tuna, according to
your tradition.*

OLD-FASHIONED POTATO SALAD

serves 8

3 lb (1.5 kg) red-skinned potatoes

Salt and freshly ground pepper

3 Tbsp white wine vinegar

1 cup (8 fl oz/250 ml) mayonnaise

2 Tbsp whole-grain mustard

4 celery ribs, finely chopped

4 green onions, including green parts, chopped

2 Tbsp minced fresh flat-leaf parsley

Place the unpeeled potatoes in a large saucepan, add salted water to cover by 1 inch (2.5 cm), cover the pan, and bring to a boil over high heat. Set the lid askew, reduce the heat to medium-low, and cook at a brisk simmer until the potatoes are tender, about 25 minutes. Drain, then rinse the potatoes under cold running water until they are cool enough to handle.

Cut the potatoes into chunks about ½ inch (12 mm) thick and place in a large bowl. Sprinkle with the vinegar. Let cool completely.

In a small bowl, mix together the mayonnaise and mustard. Add to the potatoes along with the celery, green onions, and parsley and mix gently. Season with salt and pepper to taste. Cover and refrigerate until chilled, at least 2 hours. Serve chilled.

9

PASTA SALAD WITH GRILLED VEGETABLES

serves 10

FOR THE TOMATO DRESSING

½ cup (4 fl oz/125 ml) prepared marinara sauce

½ cup (4 fl oz/125 ml) olive oil

⅓ cup (3 fl oz/80 ml) red wine vinegar

Salt and freshly ground pepper

1 lb (500 g) penne or other tube-shaped pasta

2 Tbsp olive oil

1 lb (500 g) assorted grilled vegetables, coarsely chopped

1 Tbsp capers, rinsed

¼ cup (⅓ oz/10 g) torn fresh basil leaves

A great dish for summer barbecues and picnics, this salad can consist of any pasta shape and vegetables you have on hand—think bowties or corkscrews, summer squash and eggplant. You can make the salad ahead, up to the point of adding the dressing, and then cover and refrigerate for up to 12 hours. Dress and garnish the salad just before serving.

To make the dressing, in a small bowl, whisk together the marinara sauce, ½ cup oil, and vinegar. Season with salt and pepper to taste. Set aside.

Bring a large pot three-fourths full of salted water to a boil over high heat. Add the penne, stir well, and cook until al dente, according to package directions. Drain the pasta, refresh under cold water, and then drain again thoroughly. Toss the pasta with the 2 Tbsp olive oil to keep it from sticking.

Combine the pasta and grilled vegetables in a large bowl. Just before serving, add the dressing and toss to coat evenly. Garnish with the capers and basil and serve.

10

GRILLED PLUOT SALAD WITH GOAT CHEESE & WILD ARUGULA

serves 6

9 or 10 pluots, about 1½ lb (750 g), halved and pitted

5 Tbsp (2½ fl oz/75 ml) extra-virgin olive oil

2 Tbsp sugar

2 Tbsp champagne vinegar

Salt and freshly ground pepper

2–3 cups (2–3 oz/60–90 g) arugula leaves, stemmed

½ head butter lettuce, torn into bite-sized pieces (about 2 cups/2 oz/60 g)

4 oz (125 g) fresh goat cheese, crumbled

1 tsp minced fresh thyme blossoms or leaves

Like all stone fruits, the pluot, a cross between a plum and an apricot, grills well. The heat caramelizes the surface, intensifying the sweet-tart flavor. A mix of peppery arugula, tender butter lettuce, and tangy goat cheese complements the beautiful grilled fruit halves.

Place the pluot halves in a baking dish, drizzle with 2 Tbsp of the oil, and turn to coat. Sprinkle with the sugar and turn again. Set aside.

In a serving bowl, combine the remaining 3 Tbsp oil, the vinegar, ½ tsp salt, and ¼ tsp pepper and mix well. Add the arugula and butter lettuce and set aside without tossing. (This can be done up 30 minutes in advance of serving.)

Prepare a charcoal or gas grill for direct-heat cooking over medium-high heat, or preheat a stove-top grill pan over medium-high heat. When ready, place the pluots directly on the grill or in the grill pan, cut side down. Cook until lightly golden and grill marked, about 2 minutes. Turn and cook on the other side until the skin shrinks slightly, about 1 minute. Do not overcook.

Toss the salad and divide among individual plates. Top each salad with a few grilled pluot halves, crumbles of cheese, and a sprinkling of thyme, and serve.

11

The classic French salad of frisée, chewy bacon, and a runny poached egg has been updated here with sweet cherry tomatoes and crisp Little Gem lettuces. Don't cook the bacon too long; you want it to be a bit chewy rather than crunchy.

BLT & POACHED EGG SALAD

serves 4–6

1 Tbsp Dijon mustard

1 tsp minced shallot

¼ tsp sugar

Salt and freshly ground pepper

4 Tbsp (2 fl oz/60 ml) white wine vinegar

3 Tbsp extra-virgin olive oil

6 slices thick-cut bacon, coarsely chopped

6 heads Little Gem lettuce, or 4 romaine lettuce hearts, halved

2 cups (¾ lb/375 g) halved cherry tomatoes or 3 large tomatoes, chopped

4–6 large eggs

To make the vinaigrette, in a bowl, whisk together the mustard, shallot, sugar, ½ tsp salt, pepper to taste, and 2 Tbsp of the vinegar. Let stand for 10 minutes to allow the flavor of the shallot to mellow, then add the oil in a thin stream, whisking constantly until the dressing is smooth. Set aside.

In a frying pan, sauté the bacon over medium heat until most of the fat is rendered and the bacon is crisp on the edges but still chewy at the center, about 5 minutes. Remove with a slotted spoon and let drain on paper towels.

Half-fill a wide sauté pan with water and bring to a boil. Reduce the heat to a gentle simmer, and stir in the remaining 2 Tbsp of the vinegar and 2 tsp salt.

Divide the lettuce among individual plates and distribute the tomatoes and bacon pieces evenly among the servings. Drizzle each serving with vinaigrette to taste and season with salt and pepper.

Working quickly, crack the eggs one at a time into a small bowl and slide them into the simmering water. Poach until the whites are set and the yolks are still soft, 3–4 minutes. Remove each egg with a slotted spoon, blot the underside with a paper towel, and slide onto a salad. Season the eggs with salt and pepper and serve.

12

Slender, dark green English cucumbers, also called hothouse cucumbers, are a good choice for this classic Asian salad. They have thin peels and fewer and softer seeds than other varieties.

SWEET-AND-SOUR CUCUMBER SALAD

serves 4–6

2 lb (1 kg) cucumbers

Salt

½ cup (4 fl oz/125 ml) rice vinegar

2 Tbsp sugar

4 shallots, thinly sliced

1 red Fresno chile, cut into thin rings and seeded

2 Tbsp chopped fresh cilantro

Peel the cucumbers and cut each in half lengthwise. Using the tip of a spoon, remove the seeds. Cut each half crosswise into slices ¼ inch (6 mm) thick. Put the cucumbers in a colander, sprinkle with 1 tsp salt, and toss to mix well. Set aside at room temperature and let drain for 1 hour.

In a small saucepan, combine the vinegar, sugar, and 1 tsp salt. Bring to a simmer over medium heat and cook, stirring to dissolve the sugar, for 2 minutes. Set aside and let cool to room temperature.

Pat the cucumbers dry with paper towels. In a large bowl, combine the cucumbers, shallots, chile, and cilantro and toss to mix well. Pour the dressing over the cucumber mixture and toss to coat thoroughly. Cover and refrigerate for at least 2 hours or up to overnight. Serve chilled.

13

INSALATA ROSSA

serves 4

2 large or 3 medium tomatoes, preferably an heirloom variety, or about 16 cherry or grape tomatoes

4 young, tender carrots

1 small red onion or 3 green onions, white parts only, thinly sliced

Salt and freshly ground pepper

Balsamic or red wine vinegar (optional)

1 Tbsp extra-virgin olive oil

A few fresh basil leaves, torn into pieces

This "red salad" plays with the rosy hues of tomatoes, carrots, and red onions. Taste the salad for acidity before adding the vinegar; you may not need it. You can prep the vegetables an hour or so ahead, but dress and toss the salad just before serving.

If using large tomatoes, core them, then cut them in half crosswise and into wedges. If using medium tomatoes, core and cut them into wedges through the stem end. If using cherry or grape tomatoes, cut them into halves or quarters. Set the tomatoes aside.

Using a mandoline, the slicing blade of a food processor, or a box grater, cut the carrots into very thin rounds and put them in a serving bowl.

Add the onion to the carrots, then season with salt and pepper to taste. Mix in vinegar to taste, if using, and then the oil. Add the tomato pieces and the torn basil leaves and stir to mix. Divide the salad among individual plates and serve.

14

CHICKEN & ROASTED TOMATO SALAD

serves 4

1½ lb (750 g) plum tomatoes, halved lengthwise and seeded

6 Tbsp (3 fl oz/90 ml) olive oil

1 Tbsp fresh thyme leaves

Salt and freshly ground pepper

1¼ lb (625 g) skinless, boneless chicken breast halves, pounded lightly to an even thickness

2 Tbsp unsalted butter

1 Tbsp safflower oil

6 oz (185 g) arugula leaves, stemmed

1½ Tbsp balsamic vinegar

Parmesan cheese for shaving

In the dry heat of the oven, tomatoes shrink into sweet, juicy concentrations of themselves, becoming the perfect partners for chicken and arugula. But for ease, you can substitute sun-dried tomatoes. Oil-packed tomatoes can be taken straight from the jar and chopped. Dry-packed tomatoes should be soaked in hot water for about 20 minutes, then drained and chopped.

Preheat the oven to 350°F (180°C). Oil a large rimmed baking sheet. Arrange the tomatoes, cut side up, on the prepared sheet in a single layer. Brush with 2 Tbsp of the olive oil, sprinkle with thyme, and season with salt and pepper. Roast the tomatoes until shriveled on top but still juicy underneath, about 50 minutes. Let cool on the baking sheet. Cut the tomatoes in half again.

Season both sides of each chicken breast with salt and pepper. In a large frying pan over medium heat, melt the butter with the safflower oil. Add the chicken and cook, turning once, until golden brown and firm, 4–5 minutes per side. Transfer to a cutting board and let stand for 5 minutes.

Place the arugula in a large bowl, drizzle with the remaining 4 Tbsp (2 fl oz/60 ml) olive oil, and toss to coat evenly. Sprinkle with the vinegar, ¼ tsp salt, and a pinch of pepper, and toss again. Arrange the arugula on plates. Cut the chicken on the diagonal into slices and place on the arugula. Top with the roasted tomatoes. Use a vegetable peeler to shave cheese over the salads and serve.

15

Feast on summer seafood with big flakes of salmon and charred corn straight off the grill. To boil potatoes, put them in a large pot and cover with plenty of salted water. Bring to a boil, reduce the heat to medium-high, and cook the potatoes until tender when pierced with a small, sharp knife, about 20 minutes. Drain and let cool to the touch, about 15 minutes.

GRILLED SALMON, YELLOW POTATO & CORN SALAD

serves 4

4 salmon fillets, about 5 oz (155 g) each, skin on and pin bones removed

1 cup (2 oz/60 g) tightly packed fresh basil leaves

½ cup (4 fl oz/125 ml) olive oil, plus more for brushing

Salt and freshly ground pepper

4 ears corn, husks and silk removed

½ lemon

½ lb (250 g) yellow all-purpose potatoes such as Yukon Gold or Yellow Finn, boiled until tender and chopped *(left)*

2 Tbsp finely chopped sweet onion such as Vidalia or Maui

1 cup (6 oz/185 g) yellow cherry tomatoes, halved

Put the salmon fillets, skin side down, in a shallow dish. Combine the basil, ½ cup oil, ¼ cup (2 fl oz/60 ml) water, ½ tsp salt, and several grindings of pepper in a blender or food processor and process until smooth. Set aside half of the basil mixture for the dressing. Brush the other half over the flesh sides of the salmon. Cover and refrigerate for 30 minutes or up to 6 hours. Remove from the refrigerator 15 minutes before grilling.

Prepare a charcoal or gas grill for direct-heat cooking over medium-high heat. Brush the corn with olive oil. Grill, turning often, until the corn is lightly browned and crisp-tender, about 15 minutes. Transfer to a platter and let cool.

If using a charcoal grill, let the coals burn down to medium-low. If using a gas grill, reduce the heat. Arrange the fish in an oiled grill basket or place on a sheet of oiled heavy-duty foil, skin side down. Place the basket or slide the foil onto the grill. Cover the grill and cook until white droplets start to appear on the surface of the fish, about 8 minutes. Turn carefully and grill just until nicely seared, about 2 minutes. Transfer the fish to a platter, squeeze the lemon half over, tent with foil, and let stand for 5 minutes. ↠

Cut the kernels from the corn cobs and put them in a large bowl. Add the potatoes, onion, tomatoes, and reserved basil mixture. Toss gently to distribute and coat evenly. Remove and discard the skin from the salmon and flake the flesh into large chunks and add to the bowl. Toss again gently, taking care not to break up the salmon further. Taste and adjust the seasoning and serve.

16

Ripe seasonal fruit comes alive with a sprinkle of mint and a drizzle of syrup. To make simple syrup, combine equal parts sugar and water in a saucepan and place over low heat. Stir until the sugar is completely dissolved. Remove from the heat and let cool to room temperature. Pour into a clean jar or other airtight container, and refrigerate for up to 2 months.

MINTED FRUIT SALAD

serves 8–10

1¼ cups (10 fl oz/310 ml) simple syrup *(left)*

3 Tbsp fresh lime juice

1 large papaya, about 2 lb (1 kg)

1 mango

6 cups (1½ lb/750 g) mixed raspberries, strawberries, and blackberries

2 cups (¾ lb/375 g) chopped pineapple

½ cup (½ oz/15 g) fresh mint leaves

1 Tbsp dark rum (optional)

Put the syrup in a saucepan over low heat, cover, and bring just to a simmer. Pour into a heatproof bowl, stir in the lime juice, and set aside to cool to room temperature. Cover and refrigerate until well chilled, at least 2 hours.

Prepare the fruits for the salad: Peel and seed the papaya and cut it into 1-inch (2.5-cm) chunks. Peel and pit the mango, and cut it into 1-inch chunks as well. Hull and halve the strawberries and quickly rinse all of the berries. In a large glass or ceramic bowl, combine the papaya, mango, berries, and pineapple and toss to mix. Coarsely chop the mint, setting aside a few nice small leaves for garnish. Drizzle with the syrup, scatter with the chopped mint, and toss very gently. If desired, drizzle with the rum. Garnish with the reserved mint leaves and serve.

17

SHAVED ZUCCHINI SALAD WITH PECORINO & ALMONDS

serves 4–6

½ cup (2½ oz/75 g) raw almonds

1 Tbsp balsamic vinegar

1 tsp red wine vinegar

Salt and freshly ground pepper

3 Tbsp extra-virgin olive oil

2 small zucchini and/or summer squash, about 4 inches (10 cm) long and 1 inch (2.5 cm) in diameter, trimmed

Pecorino cheese for shaving

Zucchini can be overly abundant at this time of year. If you feel like you've cooked it in every way imaginable, try thinly shaving it for this fresh raw salad. An aged pecorino cheese, nutty but still light, is delicious in this salad, but any cheese hard enough to be shaved may be used, such as Parmesan, grana padano, or aged goat cheese.

In a dry frying pan, toast the almonds over medium-low heat, stirring, until fragrant and lightly golden, 5 minutes. Pour onto a plate to cool, coarsely chop, and set aside.

In a large bowl, whisk together the vinegars and ½ tsp each salt and pepper. Add the oil in a thin stream, whisking constantly until the vinaigrette is smooth. Set aside.

Using a mandoline or very sharp chef's knife, slice the zucchini lengthwise into thin ribbons. Pat the zucchini dry on paper towels.

Add the zucchini to the bowl with the vinaigrette and toss to coat well. Divide the salad among individual plates. Using a vegetable peeler, shave the cheese over the salads in thin curls. Scatter the toasted almonds over the top and serve.

18

CHICKEN, AVOCADO & SPINACH SALAD

serves 4

1 Tbsp cumin seeds

1 tsp fennel seeds

1 cup (8 oz/250 g) plain low-fat yogurt

4 Tbsp (2 fl oz/60 ml) olive oil, plus more for brushing

3 cloves garlic, crushed

2 tsp paprika

Salt and freshly ground pepper

4 skinless, boneless chicken breast halves

¼ cup (1 oz/30 g) sliced almonds

5 cups (5 oz/155 g) baby spinach leaves

2 avocados, pitted, peeled, and cut into thin wedges

1 jarred roasted red bell pepper, thinly sliced

Juice of 1 lemon

Marinating chicken breasts in spiced yogurt tenderizes the meat and keeps it moist under the broiler. Toss slices of the succulent meat with spinach leaves and buttery avocado for a quick and nutritious dinner. Any nuts could replace the sliced almonds; try chopped hazelnuts.

In a small, dry frying pan over medium heat, toast the cumin and fennel seeds, stirring often, until fragrant, about 1 minute. Grind the seeds coarsely in a mortar with a pestle or in a spice grinder. Combine the ground seeds, yogurt, 2 Tbsp of the oil, the garlic, paprika, and ½ tsp salt in a large bowl and stir to mix. Set aside one-third of the yogurt mixture. Add the chicken to the bowl and stir to coat evenly. Cover and refrigerate for at least 30 minutes or up to 12 hours.

In the same dry frying pan, toast the almonds over medium-low heat, stirring, until fragrant and lightly golden, 3–4 minutes. Pour onto a plate to cool.

Preheat the broiler. Cut the chicken crosswise into thick slices (4 or 5 per breast). Spread the slices in a single layer on a foil-lined baking sheet. Sprinkle with salt and pepper and brush with oil. Slide under the broiler about 4 inches (10 cm) from the heat source and broil, turning once, until browned and cooked through, 10–12 minutes. Transfer to a large bowl, add the reserved yogurt mixture, stir to coat, and let rest for 5–10 minutes.

Add the spinach, avocados, roasted pepper, and almonds to the chicken. Drizzle with the remaining 2 Tbsp oil and the lemon juice and toss gently. Drizzle any dressing remaining in the bowl over the salad and serve.

19

CREAMY COLESLAW
serves 6–8

1 head green cabbage (about 2 lb/1 kg)

2 celery ribs

1 Granny Smith apple

1 small yellow or red onion

2 small carrots, peeled

2 Tbsp cider vinegar, or as needed

2 Tbsp minced fresh flat-leaf parsley

1¼ cups (10 fl oz/310 ml) mayonnaise

Salt and freshly ground pepper

This crunchy-creamy classic is essential for barbecues, alongside burgers and dogs, or piled on top of a pulled pork sandwich. If you don't have a food processor, prep the vegetables by hand with a chef's knife and the large holes of a box grater. Thinly sliced red bell pepper and cucumber would be nice additions.

Cut the cabbage through the stem end into wedges, and cut out the core. Using a food processor fitted with the thin slicing attachment, slice the cabbage into thin slivers. Transfer to a large bowl. Slice the celery crosswise in the same way and add it to the cabbage.

Replace the slicing attachment with the shredding attachment. Halve and core the apple but do not peel. Cut the apple and the onion into wedges. Shred the apple, onion, and carrots, and add to the cabbage and celery.

Sprinkle the vegetables with the vinegar and toss to coat evenly. Add the parsley and mayonnaise and mix well. Season with salt and pepper to taste. Cover and refrigerate until chilled, at least 2 hours. Taste and adjust the seasoning with more vinegar, salt, and pepper before serving. Serve chilled.

20

YELLOW SQUASH & FARRO SALAD
serves 6

1½ cups (9 oz/280 g) farro

Salt

2 Tbsp extra-virgin olive oil, plus ½ cup (4 fl oz/125 ml)

1 lb (500 g) yellow squash, cut into ½-inch (12-mm) chunks

1 clove garlic

¼ cup (2 fl oz/60 ml) fresh lemon juice

1 small cucumber, about ½ lb (250 g), peeled and cut into ½-inch (12-mm) chunks

5 green onions, including tender green parts, cut on the diagonal into ¼-inch (6-mm) pieces

¼ cup (⅓ oz/10 g) chopped fresh basil

¼ cup (⅓ oz/10 g) chopped fresh mint

5 oz (155 g) feta cheese, crumbled

Nutty farro quickly soaks up liquids and flavors, in this case lemon and garlic. Because of this, just be sure to add the dressing when you're ready to serve, to prevent the grain from becoming dry. Crumbled feta, goat cheese, or ricotta salata would all be delicious alongside the crisp cucumber and sweet squash.

Rinse and drain the farro, then transfer to a large saucepan and add 3 cups (24 fl oz/750 ml) cold water. Stir in 1 teaspoon salt and bring to a boil over high heat. Reduce the heat to medium-low, cover partially, and simmer until the farro is tender but still chewy, about 20 minutes. Drain thoroughly and set aside.

In a large frying pan over medium-high heat, warm the 2 Tbsp oil. Add the squash, season with salt, and sauté until crisp-tender, 3–4 minutes. Transfer to a plate and let cool.

To make the dressing, mash the garlic into a paste with a pinch of salt. In a small bowl, stir together the garlic and lemon juice and let stand for 10 minutes. Add the remaining ½ cup oil in a thin stream, whisking constantly until the dressing is smooth.

Put the farro, squash, cucumber, green onions, basil, mint, and feta in a large bowl. Drizzle with the dressing and toss. Season to taste with salt and serve.

21

Romaine is hearty enough to withstand a stint on a grill, which renders it slightly smoky. It pairs nicely with halloumi, a Middle Eastern cheese that is sturdy enough to be grilled or fried while retaining its firm structure. You can try different cheeses, such as fresh mozzarella, pecorino, or feta.

GRILLED ROMAINE & HALLOUMI WITH MINT VINAIGRETTE

serves 6–8

FOR THE MINT VINAIGRETTE

2 Tbsp red wine vinegar

Salt and freshly ground black pepper

3 Tbsp extra-virgin olive oil

¼ cup (⅓ oz/10 g) minced fresh mint

¼ tsp red pepper flakes

2 heads romaine lettuce, quartered lengthwise

½ lb (250 g) halloumi cheese, cut into slices ⅓ inch (9 mm) thick

2 Tbsp extra-virgin olive oil

Prepare a charcoal or gas grill for direct-heat cooking over medium-high heat.

To make the vinaigrette, in a bowl, whisk together the vinegar and ¼ tsp salt. Add the 3 Tbsp oil in a thin stream, whisking constantly until well blended. Stir in the mint, ¼ tsp black pepper, and the red pepper flakes. Taste and adjust the seasoning with salt. Set aside.

Place the romaine quarters and cheese slices on a baking sheet and brush them with the 2 Tbsp olive oil. Place the romaine, cut side down, on the grill rack and cook until the edges of the leaves are golden, about 5 minutes. Turn and grill the other side until almost limp, 3–4 minutes. Transfer to a platter, cut side up. Place the cheese slices on the grill and grill until the edges soften, the interior is warm, and golden grill marks appear, about 2 minutes. Turn and grill on the second side for 1–2 minutes, until lightly golden. Add the cheese to the platter with the grilled romaine.

Pour the vinaigrette over the warm salad and serve.

22

Fresh corn is best between the months of July and September, making it a popular vegetable for summer barbecue. Try it grilled and folded into this salad with bright cherry tomatoes and tangy feta cheese.

GRILLED CORN SALAD

serves 8

Juice of 3 limes

2 tsp ground cumin

1 tsp mild chili powder

¾ cup (6 fl oz/180 ml) olive oil, plus more for brushing

Salt and freshly ground pepper

2 tsp cumin seeds, toasted and lightly crushed

6 ears corn, husks and silk removed

3 cups (18 oz/560 g) cherry tomatoes, stems removed and halved

½ cup (2 oz/60 g) chopped red onion

½ cup (¾ oz/20 g) chopped fresh cilantro

4 oz (125 g) feta cheese, diced

In a bowl, whisk together the lime juice, ground cumin, and chili powder. Add the ¾ cup oil in a thin stream, whisking constantly until the vinaigrette is smooth. Season with salt and pepper to taste.

In a small dry frying pan, toast the cumin seeds over medium-low heat, stirring, until fragrant, about 2 minutes. Pour onto a plate and let cool.

Prepare a gas or charcoal grill for direct-heat cooking over medium-high heat. Brush a little olive oil on each ear of corn. Grill the corn, turning the ears often so that they cook evenly, until lightly charred, about 10 minutes.

Cut the kernels off the corn cobs and put them in a large bowl. Add the tomatoes, onion, cilantro, feta, and the vinaigrette and toss to coat evenly. Transfer the salad to a platter, sprinkle with the toasted cumin seeds, and serve.

23

Charred shrimp acquire a smoky flavor on the grill, accentuated by dried chiles. Chipotle chiles, dried and canned, add heat to a creamy cilantro dressing. Avocados and black beans balance the heat with their mellow richness.

GRILLED SHRIMP SALAD WITH AVOCADO & CHIPOTLE DRESSING

serves 6–8

⅓ cup (3 fl oz/80 ml) plus 1 Tbsp mayonnaise

¾ cup (1 oz/30 g) coarsely chopped fresh cilantro

2½ Tbsp fresh lime juice

1½ Tbsp fresh orange juice

1 small shallot, minced

1 Tbsp seeded and minced chipotle chile in adobo, plus 1½ Tbsp adobo sauce

Salt and freshly ground pepper

1½ lb (750 g) large shrimp, peeled and deveined

1 can (15 oz/470 g) black beans, drained and rinsed

2 avocados, pitted and peeled

1 large head romaine lettuce, leaves torn into bite-sized pieces

To make the dressing, in a food processor, combine the mayonnaise, half of the cilantro, 2 tsp of the lime juice, the orange juice, shallot, chile, ¼ tsp salt, and several grindings of pepper and process until a creamy, smooth dressing forms. Taste and adjust the seasonings. Cover and refrigerate until needed.

Soak 12 bamboo skewers in water to cover for 30 minutes. Prepare a charcoal or gas grill for direct-heat cooking over high heat.

In a bowl, combine the shrimp, 1 Tbsp of the lime juice, and 1 Tbsp of the adobo sauce and toss to coat evenly. Let stand at room temperature for 15 minutes to blend the flavors.

In a small bowl, combine the beans, the remaining ½ Tbsp adobo sauce, ½ tsp of the lime juice, ¼ tsp salt, and a few grindings of pepper. Let stand at room temperature for 15 minutes to blend the flavors.

Drain the skewers and thread 3 or 4 prawns onto each skewer. Sprinkle lightly with salt and pepper and grill, turning once, until the shrimp are pink and opaque throughout, 3–5 minutes total. Transfer to a plate and sprinkle the shrimp with the remaining 2 tsp lime juice. Slide the shrimp off the skewers and set aside. ⟫

Cut the avocados lengthwise into wedges about ⅜ inch (1 cm) thick.

In a large bowl, toss the lettuce with ¼ tsp salt and several grindings of pepper. Divide the lettuce among individual plates. Top each serving with black beans, shrimp, and avocado wedges. Drizzle each salad with the dressing, sprinkle with the remaining cilantro, and serve.

24

Cousins of the daikon radish, watermelon radishes are a humble greenish-white on the outside, but contain a burst of bright pink at their centers. Here, they are gorgeous thinly sliced and drizzled with a creamy, citrusy avocado dressing.

WATERMELON RADISH SALAD WITH ROMAINE & AVOCADO

serves 4

1 shallot, minced

1½ Tbsp fresh lemon juice, plus more if needed

1½ Tbsp white wine vinegar

Salt

¼ cup (2 fl oz/60 ml) extra-virgin olive oil

1 avocado, pitted, peeled, and cubed

2 heads romaine lettuce, leaves cut crosswise into ½-inch (12-mm) strips

1 watermelon radish or daikon radish, thinly sliced

In a small bowl, stir together the shallot, 1½ Tbsp lemon juice, vinegar, and a pinch of salt. Add the oil in a thin stream, whisking constantly until the vinaigrette is smooth. Gently stir in the avocado, season with salt, and let stand for 10 minutes.

In a large bowl, combine the romaine and radish. Spoon the vinaigrette and avocado over the salad, toss gently, taste, and adjust the seasoning with salt and additional lemon juice. Serve.

25

Spanish smoked paprika is rich with earthy nuances of chiles and cocoa. In this recipe, it lends a robust smokiness and gorgeous red color to a steak marinade and romesco-style dressing. It's an apt seasoning for a dish brimming with charred flavors from the grill.

GRILLED STEAK, PEPPER & ONION SALAD WITH ROMESCO DRESSING

serves 6

½ cup (4 fl oz/125 ml) extra-virgin olive oil, plus 2 Tbsp

⅓ cup (3 fl oz/80 ml) sherry vinegar

2 Tbsp fresh orange juice

1 Tbsp Spanish sweet smoked paprika

5 cloves garlic, minced

1½ Tbsp fresh oregano leaves

2¾ lb (1.4 kg) flank steak

2 small red onions

3 bell peppers, in assorted colors

Salt and freshly ground pepper

FOR THE ROMESCO DRESSING

2 Tbsp extra-virgin olive oil

1 Tbsp fresh orange juice

2 Tbsp sherry vinegar

¼ tsp Spanish sweet smoked paprika

2 cloves garlic, minced

3 jarred piquillo peppers or roasted red peppers

1½ Tbsp chopped blanched almonds

½ large head green-leaf lettuce, leaves torn into bite-sized pieces

2 Tbsp chopped fresh flat-leaf parsley

In a large baking dish, combine the ½ cup oil, the vinegar, orange juice, paprika, garlic, and oregano. Lay the steak in the baking dish and turn a few times to coat it with the marinade. Cover and refrigerate for at least 2 hours or preferably overnight, turning once or twice.

About 1 hour before cooking, remove the flank steak from the refrigerator. Cut the onions crosswise into rounds ½ inch (12 mm) thick (do not separate the layers). Stem, seed, and derib the bell peppers, then cut into wide strips. Brush the vegetables with the 2 Tbsp oil and season lightly with salt and pepper.

Prepare a charcoal or gas grill for direct-heat cooking over medium-high heat.

Meanwhile, to make the dressing, in a food processor or blender, combine the oil, orange juice, vinegar, paprika, garlic, piquillo peppers, almonds, a scant ½ tsp salt, and a few ⟩⟩→

grindings of pepper. Process until relatively smooth. Taste and adjust the seasonings. Set aside.

Grill the onions and peppers, turning once, until softened and lightly charred on both sides, 7–10 minutes for the onions and about 15 minutes for the peppers. Transfer to a plate. Remove the steak from the marinade and season both sides with salt and pepper. Grill, turning once, until the steak is browned on both sides and an instant-read thermometer inserted into the thickest part registers 130°F (54°C) for medium-rare, 10–15 minutes total, or until cooked to your liking. Transfer to a board and tent with foil. Cut the peppers into ½-inch (12-mm) strips and separate the onion slices into rings.

In a bowl, toss the lettuce with ⅛ tsp salt. Divide the lettuce among individual plates. Thinly slice the steak on the diagonal. Top each mound of lettuce with a portion of the steak, onions, and peppers. Spoon the dressing over each salad, sprinkle with a little parsley, and serve.

26

Fresh figs only appear in markets briefly, so pair them with your best ingredients: a lush goat cheese and a high-quality balsamic vinegar—a thick, aged one that's so good, you reserve it for drizzling on salads like this one.

FRESH FIG & GOAT CHEESE SALAD

serves 4

8 purple figs, stemmed

2 tsp extra-virgin olive oil, plus 3 Tbsp

1 Tbsp red wine vinegar

Salt and freshly ground pepper

2 cups (2 oz/60 g) mixed baby greens

3 oz (90 g) soft goat cheese, cut into 4 pieces

½ tsp balsamic vinegar

Coat the figs with the 2 tsp oil, then cut them lengthwise into quarters.

In a serving bowl, combine all but a few drops of the 3 Tbsp oil with the red wine vinegar. Add ¼ tsp salt, ¼ tsp pepper, and the greens and toss well to coat.

Divide the dressed greens among individual plates. Arrange 8 fig quarters on each and top with a piece of cheese. Drizzle the cheese with the remaining oil and a few drops of balsamic vinegar and serve.

27

You can use either whole lobsters or lobster tails to make this elegant salad, worthy of a special occasion. Serve it on a bed of fresh herbs for maximum flavor, or if you prefer, substitute equal portions of field greens and baby arugula leaves.

LOBSTER SALAD WITH TARRAGON & CHAMPAGNE VINAIGRETTE

serves 8–10

Salt and freshly ground pepper

1½ lb (750 g) cooked lobster meat, or 5 frozen lobster tails, thawed and halved lengthwise

2½ Tbsp champagne vinegar

2 tsp fresh lemon juice

2 tsp minced fresh tarragon

3½ Tbsp olive oil

2–2½ cups (2–2½ oz/60–75 g) mixed delicate fresh herbs and greens such as whole tarragon leaves, baby arugula, flat-leaf parsley leaves, watercress leaves, and small chervil sprigs

If using frozen lobster tails, bring a large pot three-fourths full of salted water to a boil over high heat. Add the lobster tails and boil them until the shells are bright red and the meat is almost opaque throughout, about 8 minutes.

Meanwhile, ready a large bowl full of ice. When the lobster tails are done, transfer them immediately to the bowl and cover with ice. (This quick cooling causes the flesh to pull away from the shell, making it easier to remove the meat.) Leave in the ice for 30 minutes. Remove the meat from the tails.

Cut the cooked lobster meat into generous bite-sized pieces. Set aside.

In a large bowl, whisk together 2 Tbsp of the vinegar, the lemon juice, ½ tsp salt, ½ tsp pepper, and the minced tarragon. Add 2 Tbsp of the oil in a thin stream, whisking constantly until the vinaigrette is smooth. Add the lobster meat and gently turn the pieces in the vinaigrette until well coated.

Divide the mixed herbs and greens among individual plates. Mound the lobster salad on each bed of herbs. Stir together the remaining 1½ Tbsp olive oil and ½ Tbsp vinegar, drizzle a little over each serving, and serve.

28

JULY

Celery stars in this super simple, crunchy salad with hits of flavor from the blue cheese and lemon. If you have leftover roasted poultry, dice it and stir it into this salad for a heartier dish.

CELERY SALAD WITH BLUE CHEESE & LEMON

serves 4

3 celery hearts, including some of the leafy tops, thinly sliced crosswise

7 green onions, including tender green parts, thinly sliced

Grated zest of 1 lemon

1½ Tbsp fresh lemon juice

3 Tbsp extra-virgin olive oil

Salt and freshly ground pepper

⅔ cup (3½ oz/105 g) crumbled blue cheese

In a bowl, combine the celery hearts and leaves, green onions, lemon zest and juice, and oil. Season to taste with salt and pepper and toss well. Fold in the cheese and serve.

29

JULY

You can just as easily use peaches or yellow nectarines in this fruit salad. For color, add cherries, raspberries, or blackberries to the mix.

WHITE NECTARINE & MINT SALAD

serves 4

Grated zest and juice of 1 lemon

1 tsp honey

4 nectarines, pitted and cut into wedges

2 Tbsp minced fresh mint

In a small saucepan, heat the lemon zest and juice with the honey until the honey melts. Set aside to cool to room temperature.

Put the nectarines in a bowl, pour the lemon-honey mixture over the fruit, and toss to coat evenly. Sprinkle with the mint, toss to mix, and serve.

30

This salad is bursting with flavor and packed with fresh vegetables. If making the salad for a family dinner, you may have to leave out the chile for the younger set; otherwise, it adds delicious kick.

ASIAN CHICKEN SALAD WITH LIME DRESSING

serves 4–6

FOR THE LIME DRESSING

¼ cup (2 fl oz/60 ml) fresh lime juice

3 Tbsp Asian fish sauce

1 Tbsp rice vinegar

2 Tbsp packed brown sugar

1–2 tsp thinly sliced serrano chile (optional)

1 clove garlic, pressed

7 oz (220 g) rice stick noodles

2½ cups (15 oz/470 g) shredded cooked chicken breast

3 cups (9 oz/280 g) shredded napa cabbage

1 cup (3½ oz/105 g) shredded carrot

2 cups (10 oz/315 g) thinly sliced cucumber

¼ cup (¾ oz/20 g) thinly sliced green onion, including tender green parts

½ cup (¾ oz/20 g) chopped fresh cilantro

¼ cup (⅓ oz/10 g) torn fresh basil leaves

¼ cup (⅓ oz/10 g) fresh mint leaves

Salted dry-roasted peanuts

Lime wedges for serving

To make the dressing, in a small bowl, whisk together the lime juice, fish sauce, vinegar, sugar, chile, if using, and garlic until the sugar dissolves. Let stand for at least 10 minutes to let the flavors blend.

Bring a saucepan three-fourths full of water to a boil, add the noodles, and remove from the heat. Let soak until tender, 8–10 minutes. Drain into a large sieve, rinse under cold running water, and then drain well again.

In a large bowl, combine the noodles, chicken, cabbage, carrot, cucumber, green onion, cilantro, basil, and mint. Pour about ¼ cup (2 fl oz/60 ml) dressing over the top and toss well. Taste and adjust with more dressing, if needed. Let stand for 5 minutes and then toss again. Garnish with a small handful of peanuts and serve. Pass the lime wedges at the table.

31

Flank steak is a great choice for salads, as it is full flavored but must be tenderized by thin slicing across the grain—letting you toss it easily with other ingredients. Look for cherry tomatoes in mixed sizes and colors for visual interest.

GRILLED FLANK STEAK SALAD WITH TOMATOES

serves 6

FOR THE MUSTARD-HERB VINAIGRETTE

⅓ cup (3 fl oz/80 ml) balsamic vinegar

1½ Tbsp chopped fresh thyme

1½ Tbsp chopped fresh marjoram

1½ Tbsp Dijon mustard

2 large cloves garlic, minced

Salt and freshly ground pepper

¾ cup (6 fl oz/180 ml) extra-virgin olive oil

1 flank steak, about 1½ lb (750 g) and 1–1½ inches (2.5–4 cm) thick

1 red onion, cut into wedges

1 large head romaine lettuce, leaves torn into bite-sized pieces

2–3 tomatoes, preferably heirloom, cut into wedges, plus a handful of mixed cherry tomatoes, halved

To make the vinaigrette, in a small bowl, whisk together the vinegar, thyme, marjoram, mustard, garlic, and ¾ tsp each salt and pepper. Add the oil in a thin stream, whisking constantly until the vinaigrette is well blended. Place the steak in a shallow dish. Pour half of the vinaigrette over the steak and turn to coat both sides. Cover and refrigerate for at least 4 hours or for up to 24 hours, turning occasionally. Cover and refrigerate the remaining vinaigrette. Remove the steak from the refrigerator 30 minutes before grilling.

Prepare a charcoal or gas grill for direct-heat cooking over high heat. Remove the steak from the marinade, reserving the marinade, and grill the steak, turning once or twice and brushing with the reserved marinade for up to 5 minutes before the steak is done, until nicely charred and cooked to your liking, 10–12 minutes total for medium-rare. Let the steak rest for 5–10 minutes.

While the steak is resting, place the onion wedges on the grill and cook until softened and nicely grill-marked, about 5 minutes. Thinly slice the steak across the grain, reserving any juices that accumulate. Toss the lettuce with the reserved vinaigrette, and divide among individual plates. Top with the steak, onion wedges, and tomatoes. Drizzle the steak with the meat juices and serve.

Scorching days inspire light suppers of seafood and fresh vegetables. Whether or not you can make it to the shore this time of year, indulge in shrimp or scallops tossed with avocado; halibut tangled with arugula; or classic lobster cloaked in a creamy dressing. Or, escape the kitchen with sturdy, easy-to-pack salads: potato and pasta combinations and buttermilk-dressed coleslaw are always favorites—all perfect for transporting to picnics and barbecues.

1
WATERMELON, FETA & MINT SALAD
page 178

2
GREEK-STYLE BEEF SALAD
page 178

3
EDAMAME, CORN & TOMATO SALAD
page 180

8
HEIRLOOM TOMATO SALAD WITH TWO VINEGARS
page 183

9
GRILLED EGGPLANT, CORN & BREAD SALAD WITH TOMATO-BASIL VINAIGRETTE
page 184

10
ORZO SALAD WITH CHERRY TOMATOES, FETA & OLIVES
page 184

15
ARUGULA & ZUCCHINI SALAD WITH HALIBUT SKEWERS
page 189

16
SESAME-CUCUMBER SALAD
page 189

17
WHITE BEAN & CHERRY TOMATO SALAD
page 190

22
GERMAN POTATO SALAD
page 193

23
CURRIED CHICKEN SALAD
page 195

24
SHAVED ZUCCHINI WITH LEMON, MINT & FETA
page 195

29
TOMATO & CORN SALAD WITH BLUE CHEESE
page 198

30
NECTARINE, MELON & BLACKBERRY SALAD
page 198

31
BUTTER LETTUCE SALAD WITH BLUEBERRIES, FETA & ALMONDS
page 198

4
PEACH SALAD WITH
MINT & INDIAN SPICES
page 180

5
BUTTERMILK COLESLAW
page 181

6
GRILLED FRUIT SALAD
page 181

7
CHICKEN SALAD WITH TOMATOES,
BLACK BEANS & CILANTRO
page 183

11
GRILLED POTATO SALAD
page 186

12
CREAMY PASTA SALAD
WITH LOBSTER
page 186

13
SCALLOP, MANGO
& AVOCADO SALAD
page 187

14
CORN, ARUGULA &
CHERRY TOMATO SALAD
page 187

18
MIXED GARDEN BEAN
SALAD WITH SHALLOTS
page 190

19
CORN & BLACK-EYED
PEA SALAD
page 192

20
BLACK BEAN, AVOCADO
& SHRIMP SALAD
page 192

21
CHICKEN, EGGPLANT & TOMATO
SALAD WITH PESTO DRESSING
page 193

25
QUINOA SALAD WITH TOMATOES,
CUCUMBERS & FRESH HERBS
page 196

26
INSALATA CAPRESE
page 196

27
BREAD SALAD WITH
CHICKEN BITES
page 197

28
ORZO SALAD WITH BASIL
& HEIRLOOM TOMATOES
page 197

august

1

WATERMELON, FETA & MINT SALAD

serves 6

¾ cup (¾ oz/20 g) fresh mint leaves

1 Tbsp sugar

1 serrano chile, seeded and chopped (optional)

2 Tbsp rice vinegar

1 Tbsp fresh lime juice

3 Tbsp extra-virgin olive oil

Salt and freshly ground pepper

1 small seedless watermelon, about 3 lb (1.5 kg), peeled, seeded, and cut into wedges or cubes

6 oz (185 g) feta cheese, crumbled into pieces

Salty and tangy, feta cheese is a delicious match with sweet, luscious watermelon in this salad. The chile adds an interesting hit of heat, but you can leave it out with equally good results. A refreshing dressing with just enough acid from the vinegar and lime juice completes this ultimate summer side dish.

Process ½ cup (½ oz/15 g) of the mint leaves and the sugar in a food processor until well blended. Add the chile (if using), vinegar, and lime juice and process again. With the motor running, drizzle in the olive oil. Transfer the vinaigrette to a bowl and season with a pinch each of salt and pepper.

Arrange the watermelon and cheese on individual plates and drizzle with the vinaigrette. Garnish with the remaining mint and serve.

2

GREEK-STYLE BEEF SALAD

serves 4–6

FOR THE MINT VINAIGRETTE

Juice of 2 lemons

3 Tbsp chopped fresh mint

1 large clove garlic, minced

Salt and freshly ground pepper

½ cup (4 fl oz/125 ml) extra-virgin olive oil

1 tri-tip roast (about 1 lb/500 g)

1 large bunch watercress, tough stems removed

1 red onion, halved lengthwise and thinly sliced

1 cucumber, halved lengthwise, seeded, and thinly sliced crosswise

1 cup (6 oz/185 g) grape or cherry tomatoes, halved

¾ cup (3 oz/90 g) Kalamata or other Mediterranean black olives, pitted

4 oz (125 g) feta cheese, crumbled

This versatile Mediterranean mix of cucumber and tomato is joined with grilled steak for summer. Rotisserie chicken could easily take its place on a weeknight, or lamb would pair beautifully with the minty vinaigrette. Serve with warm pita bread.

To make the vinaigrette, in a small bowl, whisk together the lemon juice, 2 Tbsp of the mint, and the garlic. Season with about ½ tsp each salt and pepper. Add the oil in a thin stream, whisking constantly until the dressing is smooth.

Prepare a gas or charcoal grill for direct-heat cooking over medium-high heat. Season the tri-tip generously with salt and pepper. Let stand at room temperature for 10 minutes.

Place the tri-tip over the hottest part of the fire. Cover the grill and cook, turning once or twice with tongs, for about 30 minutes total for medium-rare, or until cooked to your liking. Transfer to a carving board and let rest 5–10 minutes before slicing.

While the tri-tip is resting, in a bowl, toss the watercress with about half of the vinaigrette. Thinly slice the tri-tip across the grain. Arrange the beef, onion, cucumber, tomatoes, olives, and cheese on top of the watercress and gently toss. Divide the salad among individual plates. Drizzle with the remaining vinaigrette, sprinkle with the remaining mint, and serve.

3

EDAMAME, CORN & TOMATO SALAD

serves 4

Edamame is the Japanese word for fresh soybeans. Simply steamed or boiled and sprinkled with salt, they make a delicious snack. Here, they pair with classic summer produce for a fresh-tasting salad that can accompany anything hot off the grill.

¾ cup (5 oz/155 g) fresh or frozen corn kernels (from about 1 ear)

1½ cups (9 oz/280 g) frozen shelled edamame

12 cherry tomatoes, halved

1 large avocado, pitted, peeled, and cubed

2 Tbsp fresh lime juice

Salt and freshly ground pepper

1 Tbsp canola oil

8 dark outer leaves romaine lettuce

2 Tbsp chopped fresh cilantro

Bring a saucepan of water to a boil and have ready a bowl of ice water. Add the corn and the edamame and cook for 3 minutes. Using a slotted spoon, transfer to the bowl of ice water. Drain the corn and edamame, place in a large bowl, and add the tomatoes and avocado to the bowl.

In a small bowl, whisk together the lime juice, 1 tsp salt, and ⅛ tsp pepper. Add the oil in a thin stream, whisking constantly until the dressing is smooth. Pour the dressing over the salad and gently toss to combine. Arrange the lettuce leaves on a serving platter and spoon the salad onto the leaves. Garnish with the cilantro and serve.

4

PEACH SALAD WITH MINT & INDIAN SPICES

serves 6

In India, the word chaat is used both for snacks in general and for this fruit salad designed to pique the appetite. Its primary seasoning is chaat masala, a spice blend that includes roasted cumin, asafetida, black salt, mango powder, cayenne pepper, and black pepper. Look for it in Indian markets, or substitute toasted cumin seeds.

6 medium-ripe peaches

2 tsp fresh lemon juice

½ tsp cumin seeds

Lettuce leaves for serving

1½ tsp chaat masala *(left)*, or 1 tsp cumin seeds

½ tsp salt

½ tsp finely grated lemon zest

¼ cup (⅓ oz/10 g) loosely packed fresh mint leaves

8 blackberries or 16 raspberries (optional)

Bring a large saucepan three-fourths full of water to a boil and fill a large bowl with ice water. Using a sharp knife, cut an X in the bottom of each peach and immerse the peaches in the boiling water for 30 seconds. Using a slotted spoon, transfer to the bowl of ice water to cool, then peel off the skin. Pit and thinly slice the peaches. Immediately place the peach slices and lemon juice in a bowl and toss to coat the slices with the juice to prevent them from discoloring.

In a small dry frying pan over high heat, toast the cumin seeds, tossing and shaking the pan, until they turn very dark brown, almost black, about 5 minutes. Remove from the heat and let cool for a few minutes, then lightly bruise them. (You can do this with a mortar and pestle or by putting the seeds in a paper or plastic bag on a work surface and running a rolling pin over them.)

Line a platter with lettuce leaves. Sprinkle the chaat masala, salt, lemon zest, and half of the mint over the peaches, toss well, and transfer to the platter. Scatter the cumin seeds, berries (if using), and the remaining mint leaves over the top. Serve.

5

August is the perfect time of year for an all-out barbecue, where coleslaw is mandatory. This version lightens up the old-fashioned recipe with tangy buttermilk, enlivened with fresh herbs and sweet golden raisins.

BUTTERMILK COLESLAW

serves 4

½ cup (3 oz/90 g) golden raisins

FOR THE BUTTERMILK DRESSING

¾ cup (6 fl oz/180 ml) mayonnaise

½ cup (4 fl oz/125 ml) buttermilk

¼ cup (2 oz/60 g) sour cream

½ bunch fresh flat-leaf parsley, stemmed and minced

½ bunch fresh chives, minced

Salt and ground white pepper

1 large carrot, peeled

½ red onion

2 shallots

3 Tbsp white vinegar

½ head *each* green and red cabbages

Chopped fresh flat-leaf parsley for garnish

Chopped fresh chives for garnish

Put the raisins in a small bowl. Add warm water to cover and soak until plump, about 30 minutes.

To make the dressing, in a bowl, stir together the mayonnaise, buttermilk, and sour cream. Stir in the minced parsley and chives. Season with salt and pepper. Set aside until ready to use.

Using a mandoline or a very sharp knife, cut the carrot into matchsticks. Very thinly slice the red onion and shallots. In a small bowl, combine the carrot, onion, shallots, and vinegar, and toss to coat.

Core and thinly shred the cabbages. In a large serving bowl, toss together the green and red cabbage. Drain the raisins and add them to the cabbage along with the carrot-vinegar mixture and buttermilk dressing, and toss to coat. Taste and adjust the seasoning with salt and pepper. Garnish with the chopped parsley and chives and refrigerate until ready to serve.

6

Grilled fruits combine in this warm salad drizzled with a creamy tart-sweet dressing. Almost any kind of firm seasonal fruit can be cubed, sliced, halved, or quartered, then tossed on the grill. If you can't find lemon-infused olive oil, add a few drops of fresh lemon juice to 2 Tbsp extra-virgin olive oil.

GRILLED FRUIT SALAD

serves 6

2 mangoes

2 nectarines

2 cups (¾ lb/375 g) chopped pineapple

2 Tbsp lemon-infused olive oil *(left)*

¼ cup (2 fl oz/60 ml) heavy cream

1 tsp red wine vinegar

1 Tbsp sugar

Canola oil for grilling

Prepare a charcoal or gas grill for direct-heat cooking over medium-high heat.

Peel the mangoes and, avoiding the pit, cut the flesh into slices 1 inch (2.5 cm) thick. Place in a bowl.

Cut each nectarine in half, remove the pit, and cut each half in half again. Add the nectarine and pineapple to the bowl. Drizzle the fruit with the lemon-infused olive oil and turn gently to coat evenly.

In a small bowl, whisk together the cream, vinegar, and sugar. Set aside.

Oil a grill basket. Arrange the fruit in a single layer in the basket and grill, turning once or twice, until the surface of the fruit begins to caramelize, about 5 minutes total.

Arrange the fruit on a platter, drizzle with the cream mixture, and serve.

CHICKEN SALAD WITH TOMATOES, BLACK BEANS & CILANTRO

serves 4–6

Cilantro appears twice in this recipe: the stems season the poaching liquid for the chicken breasts, while the leaves join the greenery of the salad. The mild flavors of the chicken and black beans are sharpened by ripe heirloom tomatoes and tart lime juice, for a bright, tasty summertime dish.

1 white onion

2 skin-on, bone-in chicken breast halves (about ¾ lb/375 g each)

¼ bunch fresh cilantro, leaves coarsely chopped, stems reserved

2 cloves garlic, crushed, plus 1 clove, minced

Salt and freshly ground pepper

2 Tbsp fresh lime juice

1 jalapeño chile, seeded and minced

⅓ cup (3 fl oz/80 ml) extra-virgin olive oil

2 heirloom tomatoes, preferably 1 red and 1 yellow or green, seeded and cut into ½-inch (12-mm) pieces

½ can (8 oz/250 g) black beans, drained and rinsed

1 head butter lettuce, separated into leaves

Cut the onion in half lengthwise. Cut one half into thin slices and finely chop the other.

Put the chicken breasts in a large saucepan and add the cilantro stems, sliced onion, crushed garlic, and 1 tsp salt. Add water to barely cover the chicken. Bring to a boil over high heat, skimming off any foam on the surface. Reduce the heat to low and simmer, partially covered, for 20 minutes. Remove from the heat, cover, and let stand until a breast shows no sign of pink when pierced with the tip of a sharp knife near the bone, about 15 minutes. Transfer to a plate and let cool, then remove the skin and bones and shred the meat into bite-sized pieces.

Combine the lime juice, half of the minced jalapeño, the minced garlic, ½ tsp salt, and ¼ tsp pepper in a large bowl. Gradually whisk in the olive oil. Add the chicken, tomatoes, chopped onion, chopped cilantro, and black beans. Mix gently to combine. Taste and adjust the seasoning with additional salt, pepper, and chile. Cover and refrigerate to chill, at least 20 minutes or up to 2 hours.

Arrange a couple of lettuce leaves on each salad plate. Spoon some of the salad on top and serve.

HEIRLOOM TOMATO SALAD WITH TWO VINEGARS

serves 4

Available in a wealth of sizes and colors— yellow, orange, zebra striped—heirloom tomatoes are one of the glories of summer. Splash them with a double dose of bright vinegars, and they'll really shine. Other fresh herbs can replace the oregano: try 1 tsp chopped thyme or rosemary, 1 Tbsp chopped flat-leaf parsley, or 2–3 Tbsp chopped basil.

6–8 very ripe heirloom tomatoes, in a variety of sizes, shapes, and colors

¼–½ tsp sugar

Salt

2 green onions, including tender green parts, chopped

2 cloves garlic, minced (optional)

2 tsp minced fresh oregano, or to taste

Balsamic vinegar

Sherry vinegar or white wine vinegar

3–5 Tbsp (1½–2½ fl oz/45–75 ml) extra-virgin olive oil

Country-style bread for serving

Slice the tomatoes, capturing their juices. Layer the tomatoes on a platter, sprinkling them with the sugar, salt to taste, green onions, garlic (if using), oregano, and the captured juices as you arrange them.

Drizzle lightly with balsamic vinegar and sherry vinegar and then drizzle generously with olive oil. Let stand at room temperature until ready to serve, up to 2 hours. Serve accompanied with the bread for sopping up the juices.

9

Italian bread salad gets a non-traditional spin with the addition of smoky grilled eggplant and toasty charred corn. The classic flavors shine through in the form of a tomato-basil vinaigrette, full of the herb's sweet anise-like taste.

GRILLED EGGPLANT, CORN & BREAD SALAD WITH TOMATO-BASIL VINAIGRETTE

serves 6–8

2 large, ripe tomatoes (about 1 lb/500 g total weight)

⅓ cup (⅓ oz/10 g) fresh basil leaves, cut into thin ribbons

2 Tbsp balsamic vinegar

8 Tbsp (4 fl oz/125 ml) olive oil, plus more for grill

2 large cloves garlic, minced

Salt and freshly ground pepper

3 ears corn, husks and silk removed

2 large eggplants (about 2½ lb/1.25 kg total weight), cut crosswise into slices ½ inch (12 mm) thick

1 loaf day-old country-style bread, cut into 1-inch (2.5-cm) cubes

To make the vinaigrette, bring a saucepan two-thirds full of water to a boil over high heat. Have ready a bowl of ice water. Using a paring knife, score an X on the bottom of each tomato. Drop the tomatoes into the boiling water and heat until the skins loosen, 15–30 seconds. Using a slotted spoon, transfer the tomatoes to the ice water and let stand until cool. Remove the tomatoes from the ice water and pull off the skins. Core the tomatoes and halve them crosswise. Gently squeeze each half to ease out the seeds, then coarsely chop the tomato flesh.

Transfer the chopped tomatoes to a food processor or blender. Add about one-third of the basil, the vinegar, 1 Tbsp of the olive oil, the garlic, ½ tsp salt, and several grindings of pepper. Process until a chunky vinaigrette forms. Taste and adjust the seasonings. Set aside.

Prepare a charcoal or gas grill for direct-heat cooking over medium-high heat. Brush the corn on all sides with 1 Tbsp of the olive oil and season with salt and pepper. Brush the eggplant slices on both sides with the remaining 6 Tbsp olive oil and season both sides with salt and pepper. ⟫

Grill the eggplant slices, turning once, until softened and grill-marked on both sides, about 12 minutes total. Transfer to a cutting board. Grill the corn, turning frequently, until charred in spots, 10–12 minutes. Transfer to the cutting board. Cut the eggplant slices into ¾-inch (2-cm) pieces. Using a chef's knife, cut the ears of corn in half crosswise. Stand each half flat end down on a cutting board and cut the kernels from the cob.

In a large bowl, combine the eggplant, corn, the remaining basil, and the bread cubes. Pour in the tomato vinaigrette, toss well, and serve.

10

For a salad that includes pasta but is not dominated by it, orzo is a great choice. It is small—the size of a grain of rice—so it blends into the salad easily while adding some substance. A general rule when making pasta salads is to cut the vegetables about the size of the pasta, for the best balance of ingredients with every bite.

ORZO SALAD WITH CHERRY TOMATOES, FETA & OLIVES

serves 6

Salt and freshly ground pepper

1½ cups (9 oz/280 g) orzo pasta

8 cherry tomatoes, quartered

1 cucumber, peeled, seeded, and finely chopped

1 red onion, finely chopped

1 cup (5 oz/155 g) crumbled feta cheese

½ cup (3 oz/90 g) chopped black olives, drained

¼ cup (⅓ oz/10 g) chopped fresh flat-leaf parsley

1 Tbsp fresh lemon juice, or as needed

½ tsp dried oregano

¼ cup (2 fl oz/60 ml) extra-virgin olive oil

Bring a large pot of lightly salted water to a boil. Add the orzo and cook until just tender, according to package directions. Drain well.

In large bowl, combine the orzo, tomatoes, cucumber, onion, cheese, olives, parsley, 1 Tbsp lemon juice, oregano, oil, and ½ tsp pepper. Toss, then cover and refrigerate to chill for at least 20 minutes or up to 2 hours. Taste and adjust the seasoning as needed with salt, pepper, and lemon juice before serving.

11

GRILLED POTATO SALAD

serves 8

2 cups (2 oz/60 g) fresh flat-leaf
parsley leaves

¼ cup (2 oz/60 g) capers, rinsed

2 cloves garlic, chopped

1 Tbsp Dijon mustard

2 Tbsp red wine vinegar

¼ cup (2 fl oz/60 ml) olive oil, plus 2 Tbsp

Salt and freshly ground pepper

2 lb (1 kg) fingerling potatoes, each about
1 inch (2.5 cm) in diameter, boiled until
almost tender

*Fingerling potatoes,
named for their long,
slender profile, are
relatively small and
irregularly shaped
and have a dense,
creamy yellow
interior. Their size
and texture make
them a good choice
for grilling. Tossed
with mustard,
olive oil, and briny
capers, this is not
your grandmother's
potato salad.*

In a food processor, combine the parsley,
capers, garlic, mustard, and vinegar and
pulse until coarsely chopped. Slowly stream
in the ¼ cup olive oil, pulsing just until the
parsley mixture is well blended but still has
a coarse texture. Season with 1 tsp salt and
pepper to taste. Transfer to a large bowl.

Prepare a charcoal or gas grill for direct-heat
cooking over medium-high heat. Toss the
potatoes with the 2 Tbsp olive oil and thread
them onto metal skewers. Grill the potatoes,
turning occasionally, until tender, about
10 minutes.

Slide the potatoes off the skewers onto
a cutting board and cut into slices ¼ inch
(6 mm) thick. Transfer the potato slices to
the bowl holding the parsley mixture and
toss well. Season with salt and pepper to
taste, toss again, and serve.

12

CREAMY PASTA SALAD WITH LOBSTER

serves 6

Salt and freshly ground black pepper

¾ lb (375 g) pasta shells

2 Tbsp extra-virgin olive oil

¾ lb (375 g) cooked lobster meat or
2–3 frozen lobster tails, thawed and
halved lengthwise

½ cup (4 fl oz/125 ml) heavy cream

2 Tbsp tomato paste

3 Tbsp red wine vinegar

Cayenne pepper

8 cherry tomatoes, halved

Chopped fresh flat-leaf parsley
for garnish

*Luxurious lobster
is coated with a
rose-colored dressing
in this elegant pasta
salad fit for an
upscale lunch. Pasta
shells pool the sauce
in their indents
(and seem to fit the
crustacean theme).
Fresh crab can
replace the lobster,
if desired. Serve
with an aromatic
white wine, such
as a dry riesling.*

In a large pot over high heat, bring 5 qt (5 l)
salted water to a boil. Add the pasta shells
and cook until al dente, according to package
directions. Drain the pasta and toss it
immediately with 1 Tbsp of the olive oil.
Cover and let cool completely in the
refrigerator, at least 1 hour or overnight.

If using frozen lobster tails, bring a large
pot three-fourths full of salted water to
a boil over high heat. Add the lobster tails
and boil them until the shells are bright
red and the meat is almost opaque throughout,
about 8 minutes.

Meanwhile, ready a large bowl full of ice.
When the lobster tails are done, transfer them
immediately to the bowl and cover with ice.
Leave in the ice for 30 minutes. Remove
the meat from the tails.

Whether using fresh or frozen, cut
the cooked lobster meat into generous
bite-sized pieces. Set aside.

In a large bowl, whisk the cream just until
it begins to thicken, about 1 minute. Add the
remaining 1 Tbsp olive oil, the tomato paste,
vinegar, and cayenne to taste. Whisk until
mixed thoroughly. Add the pasta shells,
lobster, tomatoes, and salt and black pepper
to taste. Toss to mix well.

Place in a serving bowl or divide among
individual plates, garnish with the parsley,
and serve.

13

Look for uniformly sized sea scallops about 1½ inches (4 cm) in diameter. They should be pale ivory or have the slightest hint of pink, with a mild, sweet scent. The combination of rich scallops and tropical mango and avocado results in a light but satisfying salad.

SCALLOP, MANGO & AVOCADO SALAD

serves 4

FOR THE CHILE-LIME VINAIGRETTE

½ jalapeño chile, seeded and minced

Juice of 2 limes

¼ cup (2 fl oz/60 ml) **extra-virgin olive oil**

Salt and freshly ground pepper

1 mango, peeled and cut into ½-inch (12-mm) cubes

1 avocado, pitted, peeled, and cut into ½-inch (12-mm) cubes

Juice of ½ lime

2 Tbsp unsalted butter, melted

12 sea scallops, tough muscles removed

6 cups (6 oz/185 g) mixed salad greens

2 green onions, including tender green tops, sliced on the diagonal

To make the vinaigrette, in a small bowl, combine the jalapeño and lime juice. Add the olive oil in a thin stream, whisking constantly until the dressing is smooth. Season with ½ tsp salt and pepper to taste. Set aside.

Put the mango and avocado in a bowl, add the lime juice, and toss together. Set aside.

Preheat the broiler and line a rimmed baking sheet with foil. Put the melted butter in a shallow bowl. Add the scallops and turn to coat lightly. Arrange the scallops on the baking sheet, spacing them evenly. Season with salt and pepper to taste. Slide the scallops under the broiler about 6 inches (15 cm) from the heat source and broil until golden on top, about 1½ minutes. Turn the scallops over and broil until the tops are golden and the centers are still slightly translucent, about 1 minute.

In a bowl, toss the salad greens with half of the vinaigrette and divide them among individual plates. Divide the mango and avocado cubes among the plates of greens, scattering them on top. Place 3 scallops on each salad. Add any pan juices from the scallops to the remaining vinaigrette, whisk to recombine, and then drizzle the vinaigrette on and around the scallops. Garnish the salads with the green onions, and serve.

14

Sweet corn, petite tomatoes, and bold greens—what more could you want? Try crumbled salty bacon. Corn can be grilled in two ways: in the husks, which essentially steams the kernels; or out of the husks and directly on the grill, which chars the kernels and heightens their natural sweetness. Choose either method you prefer.

CORN, ARUGULA & CHERRY TOMATO SALAD

serves 6

5 slices lean bacon, chopped

6–8 large ears corn, husks and silk removed if desired (*left*)

2 cups (¾ lb/375 g) cherry tomatoes, halved

2 cups (2 oz/60 g) arugula leaves, stemmed

¼ cup (⅓ oz/10 g) minced fresh cilantro

2 cloves garlic, minced

¼ cup (2 fl oz/60 ml) fresh lime juice

Salt and freshly ground pepper

Prepare a charcoal or gas grill for direct-heat cooking over medium-high heat. Place the bacon in a cast-iron frying pan over the hottest part of the fire. Cook the bacon until crisp, 7–9 minutes. Transfer to paper towels to drain. Grill the corn over the hottest part of the fire, turning occasionally, until just tender, 10–12 minutes total.

Let the corn cool just until it can be handled, then remove the husks and silk if not already done. Cut the kernels off the cob. In a bowl, combine the corn kernels, bacon, tomatoes, arugula, cilantro, garlic, and lime juice and toss well. Season to taste with salt and pepper and serve warm.

15

Toast pine nuts in a dry nonstick frying pan over medium-low heat, shaking the pan frequently, until fragrant and golden, about 5 minutes. Or, spread them evenly on a baking sheet and place in a preheated 350°F (180°C) oven for about 10 minutes. Remove the nuts just when they are starting to turn golden, and pour them onto a plate to stop the cooking.

ARUGULA & ZUCCHINI SALAD WITH HALIBUT SKEWERS

serves 4

Juice of 1 lemon

2 tsp Dijon mustard

1 tsp minced fresh tarragon

Salt and freshly ground pepper

6 Tbsp (3 fl oz/90 ml) olive oil, plus 1 Tbsp

1¼ lb (625 g) halibut fillet, cut into large cubes

4 small zucchini, halved lengthwise and thinly sliced crosswise

4 small plum tomatoes, cut into thin wedges

¼ red onion, cut into slivers

½ lb (250 g) arugula leaves, stemmed

⅓ cup (2 oz/60 g) pine nuts, toasted *(left)*

Prepare a gas or charcoal grill for direct-heat cooking over high heat or preheat the broiler. Soak 4 bamboo skewers in water for at least 30 minutes.

In a large bowl, whisk together the lemon juice, mustard, tarragon, ½ tsp salt, and a pinch of pepper. Add the 6 Tbsp oil in a thin stream, whisking constantly until the vinaigrette is smooth.

Thread the halibut on the soaked skewers. Season all sides with salt and pepper and brush the skewers with the 1 Tbsp oil. Grill the skewers, turning occasionally, until the halibut is opaque throughout, about 5 minutes. Or, arrange the skewers on a rimmed baking sheet and slide under the broiler 4–6 inches (10–15 cm) from the heat source. Cook, turning occasionally, until lightly golden and opaque throughout, 5–6 minutes total.

Add the zucchini, tomatoes, onion, arugula, and pine nuts to the dressing and toss to coat evenly. Arrange on plates, top with the halibut skewers, and serve.

16

Don't skimp on the chilling time for this pretty green salad: part of its charm comes from the cool, juicy texture of the marinated cucumbers. Let the sweet-tart interplay of the vinegar and sugar really sink in.

SESAME-CUCUMBER SALAD

serves 4–6

4 English cucumbers

Salt

1 Tbsp sugar

½ cup (4 fl oz/125 ml) rice vinegar

3 cloves garlic, minced

Scant 1 tsp red chile flakes

1 Tbsp sesame seeds

6 green onions

Thinly slice the cucumbers crosswise. Combine the cucumbers, ¾ tsp salt, and the sugar in a large bowl and toss to coat the cucumbers evenly with the salt and sugar. Let stand for 30 minutes. Transfer to a colander, rinse, and drain well, then press out the excess moisture with your hands.

In a serving bowl, stir together the vinegar, garlic, chile flakes, and sesame seeds. Add the cucumbers and toss to coat. Thinly slice the green onions, including the tender green parts, and sprinkle them over the top. Cover and refrigerate until well chilled, at least 2 hours or overnight. Serve the salad cold.

17

WHITE BEAN & CHERRY TOMATO SALAD

serves 6

Serve this well-balanced side dish any time sweet, ripe cherry tomatoes are in the market. It is an ideal companion to grilled chicken and zucchini for a warm-weather supper, and with the filling beans, you won't need to worry about other sides.

FOR THE PARSLEY VINAIGRETTE

1 tsp Dijon mustard

2 cloves garlic, pressed

3 Tbsp red wine vinegar

Salt and freshly ground pepper

¼ cup (2 fl oz/60 ml) extra-virgin olive oil, or as needed

1 Tbsp minced fresh flat-leaf parsley

2 cans (15 oz/470 g each) white beans, drained and rinsed

2 cups (¾ lb/375 g) cherry tomatoes, halved or quartered

2 Tbsp chopped fresh flat-leaf parsley

Pecorino romano cheese for shaving

To make the vinaigrette, in a small bowl, whisk together the mustard, garlic, vinegar, ¼ tsp salt, and a few grindings of pepper. Add the oil in a thin stream, whisking constantly until the dressing is smooth. Stir in the minced parsley and set aside.

Put the beans in a serving bowl. Stir in the vinaigrette and tomatoes. Season the beans with salt and pepper to taste. Add a little more oil if needed to moisten the beans. Let stand at room temperature for at least 15 minutes to let the flavors blend.

To serve, sprinkle the beans with the chopped parsley. Using a vegetable peeler, shave cheese over the top, then serve.

18

MIXED GARDEN BEAN SALAD WITH SHALLOTS

serves 6–8

We tend to take beans for granted in their frozen, canned, and dried forms, but don't underestimate fresh favas and haricots verts in their peak season. Toast the coriander to coax out its flavorful oils, and if you like, add a little minced cilantro as a garnish: the spice and the herb are different parts of the same plant.

Salt and freshly ground pepper

½ lb (250 g) fresh shelling beans such as favas or cranberry beans, shelled

1 lb (500 g) wax beans, trimmed and cut into 2-inch (5-cm) lengths

½ lb (250 g) romano beans (optional)

1 lb (500 g) haricots verts, stem ends trimmed

1 tsp ground coriander

¼ cup (2 fl oz/60 ml) fresh lemon juice

2 Tbsp white wine vinegar

2 shallots, minced

¾ cup (6 fl oz/180 ml) grapeseed oil

1 tsp grated lemon zest

Bring a large saucepan of salted water to a boil. Have ready a bowl of ice water. Add the shelling beans and boil until tender, 2–3 minutes. Remove with a slotted spoon, plunge into the bowl of ice water, then drain. (If using favas, pinch the end of each one to pop it out of its skin.) Repeat with the wax beans, romano beans, if using, and haricots verts, cooking the wax beans and romano beans for 7–8 minutes and the haricots verts for 3–4 minutes. Drain and set aside.

In a dry frying pan, toast the coriander over medium-low heat, stirring, until fragrant, 20 seconds. Pour onto a plate and let cool.

In a small bowl, whisk together the lemon juice, vinegar, and shallots. Add the oil in a thin stream, whisking constantly until the dressing is smooth. Stir in the lemon zest and toasted coriander, and season with salt and pepper to taste.

Combine all the beans in a large bowl. Add the vinaigrette and toss. Let stand for at least 1 hour, or refrigerate for up to 3 hours. Serve at room temperature or chilled.

19

A pantry staple for many, black-eyed peas may be better known for thick soul-food soups. But they can be found fresh, too, and are a delight in summer salads. If fresh peas are unavailable, use 2 cups (14 oz/440 g) frozen shelled black-eyed peas in this salad.

CORN & BLACK-EYED PEA SALAD

serves 6–8

2 lb (1 kg) fresh black-eyed peas in the pod, shelled

Salt and freshly ground pepper

6 slices bacon, coarsely chopped

1 small red onion, chopped

2 cloves garlic, chopped

Kernels cut from 1 ear corn

⅔ cup (5 fl oz/160 ml) cider vinegar

1 Tbsp sugar

2 tomatoes, seeded and coarsely chopped

1 cucumber, peeled, halved, seeded, and finely chopped

2 Tbsp fresh lime juice

⅓ cup (3 fl oz/80 ml) extra-virgin olive oil

¼ cup (⅓ oz/10 g) chopped fresh cilantro

2 tsp ground coriander

2–3 bunches watercress, tough stems removed

2 green onions, including tender green tops, finely chopped

In a saucepan, combine the black-eyed peas, 4 cups (32 fl oz/1 l) water, and ½ tsp salt over high heat. Bring to a boil, then reduce the heat to medium. Cover and cook until the peas are tender, about 30 minutes. Drain and cool under running cold water. Drain again, place in a large bowl, and set aside.

In a frying pan, cook the bacon over medium heat, stirring often, until crispy and golden brown, about 6 minutes. Using a slotted spoon, transfer to paper towels to drain.

Add the red onion, garlic, and corn kernels to the hot drippings in the pan and cook over medium heat until tender, about 5 minutes. Stir in the vinegar and the sugar. Continue cooking until the liquid has reduced by one-third, 3–5 minutes. Using a slotted spoon, transfer the contents of the frying pan to the bowl with the peas. Reserve the pan. Add the tomatoes and cucumber to the bowl and season with salt and pepper to taste. Toss to mix well. ⪢

Add the lime juice and the oil to the reserved pan and swirl over medium heat until heated through, about 1 minute. Stir in the cilantro and ground coriander. Pour over the pea mixture and toss to coat.

Divide the watercress among individual plates. Divide the pea mixture among the plates. Garnish with the green onions and bacon and serve.

20

Favorite Latin ingredients combine in this protein-packed bean salad. If you plan to eat them right away, choose avocados that yield to gentle pressure. If you're buying them for later in the week, chose slightly underripe avocados; they will ripen at room temperature in a few days.

BLACK BEAN, AVOCADO & SHRIMP SALAD

serves 4–6

½ cup (2 oz/60 g) finely chopped red onion

2 cans (15 oz/470 g each) black beans, drained and rinsed

¼ cup (2 fl oz/60 ml) fresh lime juice

1½ Tbsp olive oil

1 jalapeño chile, seeded and minced

¾ tsp crumbled dried oregano, preferably Mexican

¾ tsp ground cumin

Salt

2 avocados

1 lb (500 g) cooked medium shrimp, peeled and deveined if needed

½ cup (¾ oz/20 g) chopped fresh cilantro leaves

Put the onion in a fine-mesh strainer and rinse under cold running water. Drain well.

In a large bowl, stir together the onion, beans, lime juice, olive oil, jalapeño, oregano, cumin, and ½ tsp salt. Let stand at room temperature for at least 15 minutes to let the flavors blend.

Just before serving, pit the avocados. Scoop the flesh from the peel and cut into 1-inch (2.5-cm) chunks. Gently fold the avocado, shrimp, and cilantro into the beans. Taste and adjust the seasonings and serve.

21

With fresh basil, late-August eggplant and tomatoes, and smoky grilled chicken, this salad screams summer. A dollop of fresh pesto is an easy trick for quick and bold dressings. Purchase it or make a big batch a few days ahead of time, and toss the salad together on a busy weeknight.

CHICKEN, EGGPLANT & TOMATO SALAD WITH PESTO DRESSING

serves 4

⅓ cup (3 fl oz/80 ml) extra-virgin olive oil, plus more for brushing

3 Tbsp prepared pesto

Grated zest of 1 lemon

⅓ cup (3 fl oz/80 ml) fresh lemon juice

4 skinless, boneless chicken breast halves (about 2 lb/1 kg total weight), sliced on the diagonal

1 globe eggplant

Salt and freshly ground pepper

2 cups (¾ lb/375 g) cherry tomatoes, halved

1 cup (5 oz/155 g) pitted Kalamata or other brine-cured black olives

9 cups (9 oz/280 g) mixed baby salad greens

In a glass measuring pitcher, whisk together the ⅓ cup oil, the pesto, lemon zest, and lemon juice. Pour two-thirds of the mixture into a bowl to use as a marinade; set aside the remainder to use as a dressing. Add the sliced chicken to the bowl and turn it to coat with marinade. Cover and refrigerate for at least 30 minutes and up to 6 hours.

Prepare a charcoal or gas grill for direct-heat cooking over medium-high heat. Halve the eggplant lengthwise, then cut each half crosswise into slices ½ inch (12 mm) thick. Brush the eggplant slices on both sides with olive oil and sprinkle with salt and pepper. Remove the chicken from the marinade, discarding the marinade. Grill the chicken and eggplant, turning once, until the eggplant is golden and the chicken is opaque throughout, 3–4 minutes per side. Transfer to a serving bowl and let cool completely.

Add the reserved pesto mixture, tomatoes, olives, and salad greens to the bowl. Toss gently to combine the ingredients and serve at room temperature.

22

This is a bacon-lover's potato salad, full of crispy, salty, smoky bits and bites. For a classic German potato salad, look for bacon that has been smoked over applewood, which gives it a sweet flavor. Still-warm potatoes soak up the mustard vinaigrette. Serve with meaty grilled pork chops or bratwursts.

GERMAN POTATO SALAD

serves 4

12–14 very small red-skinned potatoes (about 1½ lb/750 g total weight)

Salt and freshly ground pepper

4 slices thick-cut bacon, coarsely chopped

Olive oil as needed

½ yellow onion, halved lengthwise and thinly sliced crosswise

1 large celery rib, thinly sliced

2 Tbsp white wine vinegar

2 tsp minced fresh marjoram

½ tsp dry mustard

½ cup (4 fl oz/125 ml) beef broth

Put the potatoes in a large pot and cover with salted water. Bring to a boil, reduce the heat to medium-high, and cook the potatoes until tender when pierced with a small knife, about 20 minutes. Drain well and return to the pot. Let cool for 10 minutes, then halve.

In a large, heavy frying pan, cook the bacon over medium-high heat until brown and crisp, about 6 minutes. Using a slotted spoon, transfer to paper towels to drain. Pour the drippings from the pan into a small dish.

Return 3 Tbsp of the drippings to the frying pan (if needed, add enough olive oil to yield 3 Tbsp). Add the onion and celery and sauté over medium heat until just beginning to soften, about 3 minutes. Whisk in the vinegar, minced marjoram, ½ tsp salt, ¼ tsp pepper, and the dry mustard. Add the broth, potatoes, and bacon. Cook, tossing gently, until the dressing thickens and coats the potatoes, about 1 minute. Transfer the salad to a serving bowl and serve warm.

23

CURRIED CHICKEN SALAD
serves 4–6

3 skin-on, bone-in chicken breast halves
(about 1½ lb/750 g total weight)

Salt and freshly ground pepper

2 tsp olive oil

3 fresh rosemary sprigs,
each 2 inches (5 cm) long

½ cup (4 fl oz/125 ml) dry white wine

¼ cup (2 fl oz/60 ml) mayonnaise

¼ cup (2 oz/60 g) plain nonfat yogurt

3 Tbsp crème fraîche or sour cream

1 tsp ground cumin

¼ tsp cayenne pepper

½ tsp ground turmeric

5 celery ribs, finely chopped

½ small white onion, finely chopped

¼ cup (⅓ oz/10 g) chopped fresh
flat-leaf parsley

¼ cup (1½ oz/45 g) coarsely chopped
cashews (optional)

Red leaf lettuce leaves for serving

Turmeric tints this familiar Anglo-Indian chicken salad a marigold-yellow color. For a spicier dish, add a touch more fiery cayenne. The salad can be served mounded on lettuce leaves, stuffed into avocado halves, or even between slices of bread for sandwiches.

Season the chicken breasts with ½ tsp salt and ½ tsp pepper. In a frying pan over medium-high heat, warm the olive oil. Add the chicken breasts, skin sides down, and cook until lightly browned, about 5 minutes. Add the rosemary, turn the chicken breasts over, and cook until browned on the second side, 4–5 minutes.

Pour the wine into the pan with the chicken and stir to scrape up any browned bits on the pan bottom. Add ¼ cup (2 fl oz/60 ml) water, cover, reduce the heat to low, and cook, adding more water if needed, until the chicken is opaque throughout, about 35 minutes. Set aside and let cool. The chicken can be cooked ahead, covered, and refrigerated overnight. Remove the skin from the chicken breasts and discard. Remove the meat from the bones and tear into bite-sized pieces. Set aside.

In a bowl, whisk together the mayonnaise, yogurt, crème fraîche, cumin, cayenne, turmeric, ½ tsp salt, and ½ tsp pepper. Add the chicken, celery, onion, chopped parsley, and nuts (if using). Turn to coat with the mayonnaise mixture. To serve, line individual plates with red leaf lettuce leaves and top with a portion of chicken salad.

24

SHAVED ZUCCHINI WITH LEMON, MINT & FETA
serves 4–6

4 zucchini (about 2 lb/1 kg total weight)

¼ cup (2 fl oz/60 ml) extra-virgin olive oil

1 tsp finely grated lemon zest

Salt and freshly ground pepper

¼ cup (⅓ oz/10 g) torn fresh mint leaves

5 oz (155 g) feta cheese, coarsely chopped

Cool, refreshing mint brightens this simple salad, in which shaved raw zucchini resembles wide ribbons of pasta. Leaving the zucchini unpeeled adds color and texture. The gentle squash flavor is punctuated by the salty tang of feta cheese. Olive oil infuses the dish with richness, and lemon zest adds bright citrusy notes.

Trim the zucchini but do not peel it. Using a sharp vegetable peeler, shave the zucchini lengthwise into long, thin strips, letting the strips fall into a bowl.

In a small bowl, whisk together the olive oil and lemon zest. Drizzle this mixture over the zucchini and season with ¼ tsp each salt and pepper. Add the mint and cheese to the bowl and toss gently. Taste and adjust the seasonings and serve.

25

QUINOA SALAD WITH TOMATOES, CUCUMBERS & FRESH HERBS

serves 4–6

A trio of green onion, parsley, and mint brings an abundance of verdant flavor to this salad inspired by traditional Middle Eastern tabbouleh. Quinoa makes an earthy backdrop for summery vegetables and a dressing made with fruity olive oil and tangy-sweet pomegranate.

1½ cups (9 oz/280 g) quinoa, well rinsed

3 cups (24 fl oz/750 ml) chicken or vegetable broth

Salt and freshly ground pepper

2 large lemons

2 cloves garlic, minced

1 Tbsp pomegranate molasses

1 tsp sugar

½ cup (4 fl oz/125 ml) extra-virgin olive oil

2 large tomatoes

½ large English cucumber

4 green onions, including tender green parts, thinly sliced

¼ cup (⅓ oz/10 g) coarsely chopped fresh flat-leaf parsley

¼ cup (⅓ oz/10 g) coarsely chopped fresh mint

In a saucepan, combine the quinoa, broth, and ¼ tsp salt and bring to a boil over high heat. Cover, reduce the heat to medium-low, and simmer until all of the liquid has been absorbed and the quinoa is tender, about 15 minutes. Immediately transfer the quinoa to a fine-mesh sieve and rinse with cold running water until cooled, 1–2 minutes. Drain well, then transfer to a bowl.

Finely grate the zest from 1 lemon, then halve both lemons and juice the halves to measure 5 Tbsp (2½ fl oz/75 ml) juice. In a small bowl, whisk together the lemon juice and zest, garlic, pomegranate molasses, sugar, ½ tsp salt, and several grindings of pepper until the sugar dissolves. Add the olive oil in a thin stream, whisking constantly until the dressing is well blended. Taste and adjust the seasonings. Add about three-fourths of the dressing to the quinoa and stir well.

Core the tomatoes and halve them crosswise. Gently squeeze each half to ease out the seeds, then cut the tomato flesh into ½-inch (12-mm) pieces. In a small bowl, toss the tomatoes with ¼ tsp salt and let stand until they release their juices, about 5 minutes. Pour into a sieve set over a second bowl. Cut the cucumber into ½-inch (12-mm) ⇒

pieces and add it to the bowl you used to season the tomatoes. Add the green onions and the remaining dressing to the cucumber, toss well, then pour the cucumber mixture over the tomatoes in the sieve to drain. Add the drained tomato-cucumber mixture to the quinoa and stir in the parsley and mint. Taste and adjust the seasonings and serve.

26

INSALATA CAPRESE

serves 4

As one of the simplest and prettiest salads around, there's good reason why caprese has a devoted following. Slice and plate this any way you like—stuff whole tomatoes with mozzarella and basil leaves; layer big rounds; or toss grape tomatoes with bocconcini.

4 large tomatoes, preferably heirlooms

2 balls fresh mozzarella cheese (about 5 oz/155 g total weight)

16 fresh basil leaves

Extra-virgin olive oil for drizzling

Salt and freshly ground pepper

Place the tomatoes on a cutting board, stem sides down. Using a sharp knife, make 4 evenly spaced slits crosswise in each tomato, stopping about ½ inch (12 mm) from the bottom.

Cut the cheese into 16 thin, uniform slices. Working with 1 tomato at a time, insert 1 cheese slice and 1 basil leaf into each slit.

When ready to serve, place the prepared tomatoes on a platter. Drizzle with the olive oil, season generously with salt and pepper, and serve.

27

BREAD SALAD WITH CHICKEN BITES

serves 4–5

4 cups (10 oz/315 g) dried bread cubes *(left)*

5 Tbsp (3 fl oz/80 ml) extra-virgin olive oil

1 clove garlic, minced

3 Tbsp red wine vinegar

Salt and freshly ground pepper

6 large, ripe tomatoes, coarsely chopped

FOR THE CHICKEN BITES

1 cup (4 oz/125 g) dried bread crumbs *(left)*

3 skinless, boneless chicken breast halves, cut into 1-inch (2.5-cm) cubes

Peanut or grapeseed oil for deep-frying

½ cup (½ oz/15 g) fresh basil leaves, coarsely chopped

You can purchase the bread cubes for this tasty chicken salad, but making your own is a great way to repurpose day-old bread: Cut a country-style loaf into 1-inch (2.5-cm) cubes, and let them sit out for a day or two. For dried bread crumbs, let day-old bread dry in a 200°F (95°C) oven for about 1 hour. Break into bite-sized pieces and pulse in a food processor to form fine crumbs.

Preheat the oven to 400°F (200°C). Spread the bread cubes on a baking sheet and drizzle them with 2 Tbsp of the olive oil. Bake, turning once, until lightly golden, about 15 minutes. Remove from the oven and set aside.

In a large bowl, whisk together the minced garlic, the vinegar, ½ tsp salt, and ½ tsp pepper. Add the remaining 3 Tbsp olive oil in a thin stream, whisking constantly until the dressing is well blended. Add the tomatoes and toss well. Set aside.

To make the chicken bites, spread the bread crumbs on waxed paper or a plate. Roll the chicken cubes, a few at a time, in the bread crumbs to coat evenly, then set aside. Pour peanut oil into a deep frying pan to a depth of 2 inches (5 cm) and heat it until it registers 375°F (190°C) on a deep-frying thermometer. Add the breaded chicken pieces and fry, turning them as needed, until golden and opaque throughout, about 4 minutes total. Using a slotted spoon, transfer to paper towels to drain briefly. Add the hot chicken bites, bread cubes, and basil to the tomatoes and mix to distribute all the ingredients evenly, then serve.

28

ORZO SALAD WITH BASIL & HEIRLOOM TOMATOES

serves 6–8

1 lb (500 g) mixed heirloom tomatoes of various sizes, including cherry tomatoes

Salt and freshly ground pepper

1 lb (500 g) orzo pasta

2 Tbsp extra-virgin olive oil

1 tsp red wine vinegar

½ cup (½ oz/15 g) fresh basil leaves, minced, plus 4–6 whole leaves for garnish

Different colors and shapes of heirloom tomatoes will add interest to this simple pasta salad, which favors fresh, bright basil over a heavier pesto. Use any small pasta you like; rice-shaped orzo is always a favorite. For extra flavor, add crumbles of feta and 1 cup (5 oz/155 g) pitted Mediterranean-style black olives.

Cut large or medium tomatoes into ½-inch (12-mm) cubes. Halve the cherry tomatoes. Set aside.

Bring a large pot of salted water to a boil. Add the orzo. When the water returns to a boil, reduce the heat to medium and cook until the pasta is al dente, according to package directions. Drain and place in a large bowl. (The orzo can be prepared up to 6 hours in advance, tossed with a small amount of olive oil to keep it from sticking, and refrigerated. Return to room temperature before serving.)

Add the tomatoes, ½ tsp salt, oil, vinegar, and 1 tsp pepper and turn gently until all the ingredients are well mixed. Add half of the minced basil and turn again until well mixed. Garnish with the remaining minced basil and the whole leaves. Serve at room temperature.

29

TOMATO & CORN SALAD WITH BLUE CHEESE

serves 4

2 Tbsp cider vinegar

Salt and freshly ground pepper

½ cup (4 fl oz/125 ml) safflower or canola oil

4 large tomatoes (about 1¾ lb/875 g total weight), seeded and cut into 1-inch (2.5-cm) cubes

3 ears corn, husks and silk removed, kernels cut from the cobs

2 green onions, including tender green tops, finely chopped

1 large celery rib, finely chopped

4 oz (125 g) blue cheese, crumbled

4 large leaves red-leaf lettuce

This raw salad of corn and tomatoes calls for uncooked corn kernels, so be sure to use the freshest, ripest corn in its peak summer season. Creamy but crumbly, with a pleasantly sharp flavor, blue cheese brightens and enriches salads. If you prefer less potent cheeses, you can use a soft fresh goat cheese or even mozzarella.

In a small bowl, whisk together the vinegar, ⅛ tsp salt, and ⅛ tsp pepper. Add the oil in a thin stream, whisking constantly until the dressing is smooth. Set aside.

Place the tomatoes in a colander and sprinkle with ¼ tsp salt. Let drain for 30 minutes.

In a bowl, combine the tomatoes, corn, green onions, and celery. Add the dressing and half of the blue cheese and mix gently.

Place a lettuce leaf on each of 4 salad plates. Using a slotted spoon, arrange a portion of salad on top of the leaves. Sprinkle each portion with some of the remaining blue cheese. Drizzle some of the vinaigrette left in the bowl over the lettuce leaves and serve.

30

NECTARINE, MELON & BLACKBERRY SALAD

serves 4

3 white or yellow nectarines, pitted and thinly sliced

1 small cantaloupe, peeled, seeded, and cut into 1-inch (2.5-cm) cubes

1 Tbsp fresh lemon juice

1 cup (4 oz/125 g) blackberries

2 Tbsp julienned fresh mint leaves

Heat waves are good news for juicy stonefruits, melons, and berries. Handle delicate berries with care, washing them just before you use them, to keep them dry and mold-free.

In a bowl, combine the nectarine slices and melon cubes. Add the lemon juice and gently mix the fruits with a large spoon. Add all but 4 or 5 of the berries and all but about 1 tsp of the mint, and again mix gently. Garnish with the reserved berries and mint and serve.

31

BUTTER LETTUCE SALAD WITH BLUEBERRIES, FETA & ALMONDS

serves 4

¼ cup (1½ oz/45 g) chopped raw or blanched almonds

3 Tbsp extra-virgin olive oil

4 tsp raspberry vinegar

Salt and freshly ground pepper

2 tsp minced shallot

1½ cups (6 oz/185 g) blueberries

1 Tbsp minced fresh chives

1 head butter lettuce, torn into bite-sized pieces

3 oz (90 g) feta cheese, crumbled

Here, a simple savory salad of butter lettuce, feta cheese, chives, and almonds is given a summery spin with fresh blueberries and a tart-sweet raspberry vinaigrette.

Preheat the oven to 300°F (150°C). Put the almonds on a baking sheet and bake until lightly golden, about 7 minutes. Remove from the oven and set aside.

In a serving bowl, combine the oil, vinegar, ¼ tsp salt, and ¼ tsp pepper and mix well. Add the shallot, blueberries, and half of the chives. Let stand for 10–15 minutes.

Add the lettuce and feta and toss well. Garnish with the almonds and remaining chives and serve.

September welcomes fall's first apples and pears, exceptional partners for piquant blue cheese and fragrant toasted nuts. Back-to-school season inspires quick and easily packed lunches such as cold noodles in sesame dressing, tomatoes tossed with orzo, and big chopped salads full of delicious tidbits from the vegetable drawer. For easy-to-assemble weeknight suppers, a classic Cobb or a kid-friendly tostada salad satisfies with plenty of filling protein.

1
BITTER GREENS WITH PECANS & BALSAMIC VINAIGRETTE
page 202

2
FIGS & PURPLE ENDIVE SALAD WITH CURRANT DRESSING
page 202

3
COBB SALAD
page 205

8
GRILLED PORTOBELLO SALAD
page 207

9
CUCUMBER, CILANTRO & JALAPEÑO SALAD
page 208

10
FIELD SALAD WITH PANCETTA & WALNUTS
page 208

15
SOBA NOODLE SALAD WITH TOFU & MARINATED EGGPLANT
page 213

16
LETTUCE & HERB SALAD WITH DIJON VINAIGRETTE
page 213

17
FRISÉE SALAD WITH LARDONS
page 214

22
CELERY, PEAR & TOASTED HAZELNUT SALAD
page 217

23
BEET & WATERCRESS SALAD WITH FRESH MOZZARELLA
page 219

24
RICE SALAD WITH TUNA & CAPERS
page 219

29
SMOKED CHICKEN SALAD WITH ROASTED CHERRY TOMATOES
page 222

30
PANZANELLA
page 222

4 FALL SALAD OF APPLES & WALNUTS WITH STILTON CHEESE *page 205*	**5** ARUGULA, FENNEL & PROSCIUTTO SALAD WITH PEAR VINAIGRETTE *page 206*	**6** ORZO SALAD WITH TOMATOES, CAPERS & ROASTED GARLIC *page 206*	**7** MARINATED CALAMARI & RICE SALAD *page 207*
11 QUINOA SALAD WITH BELL PEPPER, TOMATO & EGGPLANT *page 210*	**12** ARUGULA, BLUE CHEESE & GRAPE SALAD *page 210*	**13** POTATO & RED PEPPER SALAD WITH SAFFRON DRESSING *page 211*	**14** COUSCOUS SALAD WITH CHICKPEAS, PEPPERS & BLACK OLIVES *page 211*
18 ANTIPASTO SALAD WITH PEPERONCINI VINAIGRETTE *page 214*	**19** BLACK BEAN, CORN & QUINOA SALAD *page 216*	**20** CHOPPED SALAD OF PEPPERS, TOMATOES, OLIVES & MANCHEGO *page 216*	**21** SPICY CASHEW CHICKEN SALAD *page 217*
25 SUCCOTASH SALAD *page 220*	**26** ASIAN SEARED-SALMON SALAD *page 220*	**27** SALAD OF GRILLED PORK, PEARS & TOASTED PECANS *page 221*	**28** TOSTADA SALAD WITH TOMATILLO SALSA *page 221*

september

1

BITTER GREENS WITH PECANS & BALSAMIC VINAIGRETTE

serves 4

½ cup (2 oz/60 g) pecans

3 Tbsp balsamic vinegar

Salt and freshly ground pepper

2 Tbsp olive oil

5 cups (5 oz/155 g) mixed torn greens and chicories, such as watercress, radicchio, and/or escarole

Parmesan cheese for shaving

With the return of cold weather comes the pleasantly bitter chicories and dark greens of fall. A sweet balsamic dressing and nutty shavings of Parmesan balance the salad's bold flavors nicely.

In a dry frying pan, toast the pecans over medium-low heat, stirring, until fragrant, about 5 minutes. Pour onto a plate to cool, and set aside.

In a small bowl, whisk together the vinegar and salt and pepper to taste. Add the olive oil in a thin stream, whisking constantly until the vinaigrette is smooth.

Put the greens in a large bowl, drizzle with some of the vinaigrette, and toss to lightly coat. Add the toasted pecans and toss well, adding more vinaigrette if needed to coat the leaves (you may not need it all). Using a vegetable peeler, shave Parmesan over the salad, and serve.

2

FIGS & PURPLE ENDIVE SALAD WITH CURRANT DRESSING

serves 4–6

FOR THE CURRANT DRESSING

2 Tbsp dried currants

2 Tbsp fresh orange juice

3 Tbsp extra-virgin olive oil

1 Tbsp balsamic vinegar

1 tsp sugar

1 tsp Dijon mustard

Salt and freshly ground pepper

2 Tbsp pine nuts (optional)

1 fennel bulb, trimmed and thinly sliced lengthwise

6 ripe but firm purple figs, halved

2 large heads purple-tipped Belgian endive, cores intact, halved or quartered lengthwise

1 Tbsp extra-virgin olive oil

1 Tbsp fresh lemon juice

2 Tbsp crumbled blue cheese

Grilling endive caramelizes the leaves and takes away some of its bitter edge. Sweet figs, bold blue cheese, and tart currant-orange dressing complete this salad, which is delicious served with a pinot noir or other earthy red wine.

Prepare a charcoal or gas grill for direct-heat cooking over medium heat.

Combine the currants and orange juice in a microwave-safe bowl, cover, and microwave on "high" for 1 minute.

In a large bowl, whisk together the 3 Tbsp olive oil, vinegar, sugar, mustard, ½ tsp salt, and a few grindings of pepper. Stir in the currant mixture. Let the dressing stand for 15 minutes.

In a dry small frying pan, toast the pine nuts (if using) over medium-low heat, stirring, until fragrant, 2–3 minutes. Pour onto a plate.

In a bowl, combine the fennel, figs, endive, the 1 Tbsp olive oil, and lemon juice and toss to coat evenly. Put the figs, endive, and fennel in a grill basket and grill, turning often, until the vegetables are wilted and the figs are softened, about 5 minutes. Transfer to the bowl with the dressing and toss gently to mix. Taste and adjust the seasonings, then serve garnished with the crumbled blue cheese and pine nuts.

3

COBB SALAD

serves 4–6

3 eggs, hard-cooked (page 70)

8 slices bacon

1 head romaine lettuce, leaves separated and torn into bite-sized pieces

4 cups (1½ lb/750 g) chopped cooked turkey or chicken meat

2 avocados, pitted, peeled, and cubed

2 tomatoes, chopped

4 oz (125 g) Roquefort or other blue cheese, crumbled, plus 1 oz (30 g)

2 cups (4 oz/125 g) chopped stemmed watercress

2 Tbsp minced fresh flat-leaf parsley

2 Tbsp minced fresh chives

¼ cup (2 fl oz/60 ml) red wine vinegar

1 tsp Worcestershire sauce

½ tsp Dijon mustard

1 clove garlic, minced

Salt and freshly ground pepper

⅓ cup (3 fl oz/80 ml) extra-virgin olive oil

Cobb salad is a classic favorite that has stuck around for good reason. With eggs, turkey, bacon, and blue cheese, there's plenty to love. For the poultry in this recipe, use leftover roasted turkey or a purchased rotisserie chicken. Use any blue cheese you prefer, from mild Danish or Maytag to creamy, pungent Gorgonzola.

Cut the hard-cooked eggs into bite-sized pieces and set aside.

In a frying pan, fry the bacon over medium heat until crisp, about 10 minutes. Transfer to paper towels to drain. When cool, crumble and set aside.

On a platter or individual plates, arrange the romaine, eggs, turkey, avocados, tomatoes, and the 4 oz crumbled cheese. Top with the bacon and watercress. Mix together the parsley and chives and sprinkle over the salad.

In a small bowl, whisk together the vinegar, Worcestershire sauce, mustard, garlic, ¼ tsp salt, and ½ tsp pepper. Using a fork, mash in the 1 oz cheese. Add the oil in a thin stream, whisking until smooth.

Pour some of the dressing over the salad and serve, passing the remaining dressing at the table.

4

FALL SALAD OF APPLES & WALNUTS WITH STILTON CHEESE

serves 6

½ cup (2 oz/60 g) coarsely chopped walnuts

6 oz (185 g) Stilton cheese

1 Tbsp extra-virgin olive oil

1 Tbsp red wine vinegar

2 Tbsp heavy cream

Freshly ground pepper

6 sweet eating apples such as Braeburn, Gala, or Red Delicious, cored and cut into ½-inch (12-mm) pieces

4 celery ribs, thinly sliced, plus several whole celery leaves for garnish

2 Tbsp dried currants or raisins

1 Tbsp fresh lemon juice

Apples and blue cheese have a magical affinity, especially when you throw in some toasted nuts. If you prefer, you can toast nuts in the oven: Preheat to 325°F (165°C). Spread the nuts in a single layer on a baking sheet, place in the oven, and toast, stirring occasionally, until the nuts are fragrant and lightly browned, 10–20 minutes.

In a small frying pan, toast the chopped walnuts over medium-low heat, stirring, until fragrant and starting to brown, about 5 minutes. Pour onto a plate to cool and set aside.

Put one-third of the cheese in the bottom of a large bowl. Add the oil and, using a fork, mash together the cheese and oil. Add the vinegar and continue to mash. Add the cream and 1 tsp pepper and mix well to make a thick, chunky dressing.

Add the apples, sliced celery, currants, and lemon juice to the dressing and toss well. Crumble the remaining cheese and sprinkle it over the salad along with half of the walnuts. Mix them into the salad gently and evenly.

Garnish the salad with the remaining walnuts and the celery leaves and serve.

5

ARUGULA, FENNEL & PROSCIUTTO SALAD WITH PEAR VINAIGRETTE

serves 4

Thick, sweet pear nectar, available at most supermarkets, is a boon to salad dressings. It adds a delicious autumnal flavor to this seasonal salad featuring thinly shaved fennel and plump figs.

FOR THE PEAR VINAIGRETTE

⅔ cup (5 fl oz/160 ml) pear nectar

¼ cup (2 fl oz/60 ml) seasoned rice vinegar

Salt and freshly ground pepper

1 fennel bulb, trimmed

5 oz (155 g) mesclun

1 cup (1 oz/30 g) torn arugula leaves

2 oz (60 g) thinly sliced prosciutto, julienned

4 figs, quartered through the stem end

Parmesan cheese for shaving

To make the vinaigrette, in a small bowl, stir together the pear nectar and vinegar. Season with salt and pepper to taste. Set aside.

Using a mandoline or a very sharp knife, cut the fennel bulb crosswise into paper-thin slices and set aside.

In a bowl, combine the mesclun and arugula. Add half of the dressing and toss well. Arrange the greens on individual plates. Top the greens with the fennel, prosciutto, and figs, and drizzle with the remaining dressing. Using a vegetable peeler, shave Parmesan over the salads. Season with pepper and serve.

6

ORZO SALAD WITH TOMATOES, CAPERS & ROASTED GARLIC

serves 4–6

Capers are small in size, but they're mighty in flavor. They dot this salad of rice-like orzo pasta, offering a welcome piquant contrast to sweet grape tomatoes, licorice-like basil, and nutty roasted garlic.

1 head garlic

1½ Tbsp plus ½ cup (4 fl oz/125 ml) extra-virgin olive oil

¼ cup (2 fl oz/60 ml) red wine vinegar

1 tsp sugar

Salt and freshly ground pepper

2 cups (¾ lb/375 g) orzo pasta

4 cups (1½ lb/750 g) grape tomatoes, preferably a mixture of red and yellow, halved lengthwise

¼ cup (2 oz/60 g) capers, rinsed

1 Tbsp finely grated lemon zest

½ cup (½ oz/15 g) fresh basil leaves, torn

Preheat the oven to 400°F (200°C). Slice off the top ½ inch (12 mm) of the garlic head. Set the garlic head cut side up on a square of foil, drizzle it with ½ Tbsp of the olive oil, and wrap tightly in the foil. Bake until soft when gently squeezed, about 1 hour. Unwrap and let cool.

When the garlic is cool enough to handle, squeeze the roasted garlic cloves from the skins; discard the skins. Measure out 2 Tbsp roasted garlic (reserving the remainder for another use) and put it in a small bowl. Add the vinegar, sugar, ½ tsp salt, and several grindings of pepper and whisk until the sugar dissolves. Add the remaining ½ cup plus 1 Tbsp olive oil in a thin stream, whisking constantly until the dressing is well blended. Taste and adjust the seasonings.

Bring a large saucepan two-thirds full of water to a boil over high heat. Add 1 Tbsp salt and the orzo, stir well, and cook until al dente, according to package instructions. Drain in a colander and rinse with cold running water. Drain well again and transfer to a large bowl.

In a bowl, toss the tomatoes with ½ tsp salt and let stand until they release their juices, about 5 minutes, then drain in a sieve. Add the drained tomatoes to the pasta along with about two-thirds of the dressing, ¾ tsp salt, the capers, lemon zest, and basil. Taste and add more dressing, if needed (you may not use it all), and serve.

7

MARINATED CALAMARI & RICE SALAD

serves 4–6

Salt and freshly ground pepper

1 lb (500 g) cleaned squid, cut into bite-sized rings and tentacles

⅓ cup (3 fl oz/80 ml) extra-virgin olive oil

⅓ cup (3 fl oz/80 ml) red wine vinegar

2 Tbsp fresh lemon juice

1 small red onion, finely chopped

1 clove garlic, minced

½ cup (¾ oz/20 g) coarsely chopped fresh flat-leaf parsley

1½ cups (10½ oz/330 g) long-grain rice

¼ cup (1½ oz/45 g) pine nuts

¼ cup (1½ oz/45 g) dried currants

1⅓ cups (½ lb/250 g) cherry tomatoes, halved

¼ cup (⅓ oz/10 g) coarsely chopped fresh mint

Rice salads are popular throughout the Mediterranean, inspiring this tender mixture of calamari, fluffy rice, dried fruit, and toasted pine nuts. Serve this grain salad as a simple meal with pita bread.

Bring a saucepan three-fourths full of salted water to a boil over medium-high heat. Have ready a bowl of ice water. Add the squid to the boiling water and cook until just tender, about 1 minute. Drain the squid and plunge it into the ice water to stop the cooking. Drain well and pat dry. Transfer to a large bowl. Add the olive oil, vinegar, lemon juice, onion, garlic, parsley, ¼ tsp salt, and pepper to taste and stir to mix well. Cover and refrigerate for at least 30 minutes or overnight.

In a saucepan, bring 2¼ cups (18 fl oz/560 ml) water to a boil. Add the rice, reduce the heat to low, cover, and cook until the rice is tender and the water is absorbed, about 20 minutes. Remove from the heat and let stand, covered, for 10 minutes. Fluff the rice with a fork and let cool to room temperature.

In a dry small frying pan, toast the pine nuts over medium-low heat, stirring, until fragrant, 3–4 minutes. Pour onto a plate.

Add the rice to the squid mixture along with the currants, toasted pine nuts, tomatoes, and mint. Toss to distribute the ingredients evenly, then taste and adjust the seasoning with salt and pepper. Serve.

8

GRILLED PORTOBELLO SALAD

serves 4

4 large portobello mushrooms, stems removed

3 Tbsp olive oil, plus ¼ cup (2 fl oz/60 ml)

Salt and freshly ground pepper

2 cloves garlic, minced

2 tsp balsamic vinegar

Juice of 1 lemon

½ tsp minced fresh thyme

3 pears

3 romaine lettuce hearts, torn into bite-sized pieces

Manchego cheese for shaving

Rich and hearty, portobellos have become a mainstay of vegetarian grilling because of their meaty texture and the smoky flavor they take on from the fire. Here they are sliced and arrayed on a bed of romaine, and topped with shavings of sheep's milk cheese.

Prepare a gas or charcoal grill for direct-heat cooking over medium-high heat. Alternatively, preheat the broiler.

Brush both sides of the mushrooms with the 3 Tbsp oil and season generously with salt and pepper. Place the mushrooms, gill side down, on the grill rack and cook without turning for about 8 minutes. Transfer to a plate, rounded sides down, and sprinkle with the garlic and vinegar. Return the mushrooms to the grill, rounded side down, and cook until grill-marked on the outside and softened on the inside, about 10 minutes.

Alternatively, arrange the mushrooms on a rimmed baking sheet and slide under the broiler 4–6 inches (10–15 cm) from the heat source. Cook, using the same timing and seasoning as for grilling.

Meanwhile, in a large bowl, whisk together the lemon juice, thyme, ¼ tsp salt, and a pinch of pepper. Add the ¼ cup oil in a thin stream, whisking constantly until the dressing is smooth.

Cut the warm mushrooms into thin slices. Peel, halve, and core the pears, then cut them into thin wedges. Add the lettuce and pears to the vinaigrette, toss to coat evenly, and arrange on plates. Top with the mushroom slices, use a vegetable peeler to shave the cheese over the salad and serve.

9

CUCUMBER, CILANTRO & JALAPEÑO SALAD

serves 4

2 medium cucumbers or 1 large cucumber

1 cup (1½ oz/45 g) coarsely chopped fresh cilantro

1 red or green jalapeño chile, seeded and very thinly sliced

Salt

¼ cup (2 fl oz/60 ml) fresh lime juice

2 Tbsp canola oil

4–6 oz (125–185 g) soft goat cheese

Here, cool cucumbers are interspersed with assertive jalapeño chiles. Slicing them very thinly moderates the spice of the chiles, as do crumbles of creamy, mouth-coating goat cheese. Serve alongside grilled or roasted fish or chicken.

Peel the cucumbers and cut them in half lengthwise. Use a teaspoon to scrape out the seeds. Cut the cucumbers crosswise into half-moons about ¼ inch (6 mm) thick.

In a bowl, combine the cucumbers, cilantro, and chile. Sprinkle with ½ tsp salt and add the lime juice and oil. Stir to mix well, then let stand to allow the flavors to blend, about 30 minutes.

When ready to serve, divide the salad among individual plates, crumble the goat cheese on top, and serve.

10

FIELD SALAD WITH PANCETTA & WALNUTS

serves 4

½ cup (2 oz/60 g) walnuts

3 oz (90 g) thinly sliced pancetta or bacon, cut into 1-inch (2.5-cm) pieces

FOR THE BALSAMIC VINAIGRETTE

2–3 Tbsp balsamic vinegar

Salt and freshly ground pepper

¼ cup (2 fl oz/60 ml) extra-virgin olive oil

6–8 cups (6–8 oz/185–250 g) torn salad greens, including some bitter varieties *(left)*

Parmesan cheese for shaving

In Italy, this salad is known as insalata del campo, or "field salad." Choose whatever combination of greens looks the best at the market, but include at least one or two bold or bitter varieties, such as dandelion, frisée, escarole, arugula, or radicchio, that will stand up to the big flavors of the walnuts, cheese, and crisp pancetta.

In a dry frying pan, toast the walnuts over medium-low heat, stirring, until fragrant and starting to brown, about 5 minutes. Pour onto a plate to cool, then coarsely chop and set aside.

In a frying pan, fry the pancetta over medium heat, stirring frequently, until browned and crisp, about 10 minutes. Using a slotted spoon, transfer the pancetta to paper towels to drain.

To make the vinaigrette, in a small bowl, whisk together the vinegar and salt and pepper to taste. Add the oil in a thin stream, whisking constantly until well blended.

Put the greens in a large serving bowl, drizzle with the vinaigrette, and toss to coat evenly. Add the pancetta and nuts and toss well. Using a vegetable peeler, shave Parmesan over the salad, and serve.

11

Snap up the last hot-weather eggplants and heirloom tomatoes at the market, and indulge in this late-summer feast. Quinoa cooks up faster than rice, making it perfect for weeknight suppers, and leftovers hold up well in packed lunches to bring to school or work.

QUINOA SALAD WITH BELL PEPPER, TOMATO & EGGPLANT

serves 6

1 globe eggplant, stemmed

2 large red bell peppers

2 Tbsp balsamic vinegar

¼ cup (2 fl oz/60 ml) extra-virgin olive oil, plus 1 Tbsp

Salt

½ cup (½ oz/15 g) fresh basil leaves, torn

1 cup (6 oz/185 g) quinoa, well rinsed

2 cloves garlic, minced

2 large heirloom tomatoes

Trim the eggplant, then cut it lengthwise into slices ½ inch (12 mm) thick. Halve the peppers lengthwise and remove the seeds, ribs, and stems. In a large bowl or shallow baking dish, combine the vinegar, the ¼ cup oil, and ½ tsp salt. Add the eggplant, peppers, and half of the basil. Turn several times to coat, then let marinate for 30 minutes, turning several times.

In a saucepan, warm the 1 Tbsp oil over medium heat. Add the quinoa and garlic and sauté until the quinoa is opaque, about 2 minutes. Slowly add 1½ cups (12 fl oz/375 ml) water and ½ tsp salt and bring to a simmer. Cover, reduce the heat to low, and continue to simmer until the water has been absorbed and the quinoa is tender to the bite, about 15 minutes. Remove from the heat and let stand, covered, until ready to use.

Prepare a charcoal or gas grill for direct-heat cooking over high heat. Remove the vegetables from the marinade, reserving the marinade, and lay them directly on the grill or in a single layer in a grilling basket. Cook on one side until lightly charred, 6–7 minutes for the eggplant and 4 minutes for the peppers. Turn and cook until lightly charred on the other side. Transfer the peppers to a bowl, cover, and let steam for 10 minutes. Transfer the eggplant to a platter and cut each slice in half. When the peppers are cool enough to handle, peel and cut into ½-inch (12-mm) pieces. ⇥

Cut the tomatoes into slices a scant ½ inch (12 mm) thick, reserving the trimmings, and lay a slice on each of 6 salad plates. Finely chop the trimmings and add them to the reserved marinade. Add the quinoa to the marinade and turn several times to coat. Taste and adjust the seasonings.

Top each tomato with a scoop of quinoa, a slice of eggplant, and a sprinkling of grilled peppers. Garnish with the remaining basil and serve.

12

The purple grapes in this recipe have enough piquancy that no vinegar is needed in the dressing. If you wish, a squeeze of lemon can add a nice vibrancy, but taste your grapes first to gauge the flavor.

ARUGULA, BLUE CHEESE & GRAPE SALAD

serves 4–6

6 cups (6 oz/185 g) arugula leaves, stemmed

2 Tbsp extra-virgin olive oil

Salt and freshly ground pepper

1½ cups (9 oz/280 g) seedless purple grapes

5 oz (155 g) blue cheese, crumbled

Put the arugula in a large bowl. In a small bowl, whisk together the oil and salt and pepper to taste to make a dressing. Drizzle the dressing over the arugula and toss well. Add the grapes and cheese and toss again.

Divide the salad among individual plates and serve.

13

POTATO & RED PEPPER SALAD WITH SAFFRON DRESSING

serves 6

This salad is tinted a warm yellow color from the saffron dressing that coats the tender red potatoes. A handful of slivered peppers and onions lend crisp texture. To reduce the heat from the chile, cut out the membranes, or veins, and discard the seeds, where most of the heat is concentrated.

FOR THE SAFFRON DRESSING

1½ large red jalapeño chiles, seeded and deveined, then minced

1½ Tbsp brine-cured capers, plus ½ Tbsp caper brine

2 Tbsp white wine vinegar

Salt and freshly ground pepper

¼ tsp saffron threads

¼ cup (2 fl oz/60 ml) olive oil

1 large red onion, halved lengthwise and cut crosswise into paper-thin slices

1 large red bell pepper, seeded, deribbed, and cut into matchsticks

12 small red-skinned potatoes (about 2 lb/1 kg total weight)

Salt and freshly ground pepper

To make the dressing, in a large bowl, combine the chiles, capers and caper brine, vinegar, ½ tsp salt, ¼ tsp pepper, and saffron. Add the oil in a slow stream, whisking constantly until the dressing is smooth. Add the red onion and toss to blend well. Let stand for 15 minutes, stirring occasionally, to let the flavors blend. Stir the bell pepper into the dressing.

Meanwhile, put the potatoes in a large pot and cover with salted water. Bring to a boil, reduce the heat to medium-high, and cook the potatoes until tender when pierced with a small knife, about 20 minutes. Drain and let cool to the touch, about 10 minutes.

Cut the potatoes lengthwise into quarters and add to the bowl with the dressing. Toss to coat, season with salt and pepper to taste, and serve.

14

SEPTEMBER

COUSCOUS SALAD WITH CHICKPEAS, PEPPERS & BLACK OLIVES

serves 4

Couscous, which is sometimes mistakenly called a grain, is actually a pasta, made from wheat dough rolled into tiny pearls. Widely available "instant" couscous has been presteamed and fluffs up in only a few minutes. Fold in hearty chickpeas, meaty olives, and citrus and parsley for this easy but satisfying salad.

2 Tbsp plus ¼ cup (2 fl oz/60 ml) extra-virgin olive oil

1 yellow onion, finely chopped

2 cloves garlic, minced

2¾ cups (22 fl oz/680 ml) chicken broth

Salt and freshly ground pepper

1½ cups (9 oz/280 g) instant couscous

¾ cup (3 oz/90 g) slivered almonds

1 can (15 oz/470 g) chickpeas, drained and rinsed

1 red bell pepper, seeded and chopped

¾ cup (3½ oz/105 g) brine-cured black olives, pitted and chopped

Juice of 1 lemon

¼ cup (⅓ oz/10 g) minced fresh flat-leaf parsley

In a large saucepan over medium-low heat, warm 1 Tbsp of the oil. Add the onion and cook, stirring occasionally, until softened, about 4 minutes. Add the garlic and cook for 1 minute. Add the broth, ½ tsp salt, and several grindings of pepper and bring to a boil. Place the couscous in a large heatproof bowl and pour the hot liquid over it. Blend well with a fork, cover with a plate, and let stand for 5 minutes.

Meanwhile, in a large frying pan over medium heat, warm 1 Tbsp of the oil. Add the almonds and toast, stirring, until crisp and golden, 5–7 minutes. Transfer to a plate and let cool.

Fluff the couscous with a fork. Add the toasted almonds, chickpeas, bell pepper, olives, lemon juice, parsley, and the ¼ cup oil to the couscous. Toss gently to combine. Taste, adjust the seasoning with salt and pepper, and serve.

15

Soba means "buckwheat" in Japanese, and not surprisingly, soba noodles are made with flour milled from buckwheat groats. Both the noodles and tofu make satisfying background flavors for the slightly caramelized eggplant and ginger-soy dressing.

SOBA NOODLE SALAD WITH TOFU & MARINATED EGGPLANT

serves 4

FOR THE MARINADE

1 Tbsp toasted sesame oil

2 Tbsp sherry vinegar

2 Tbsp soy sauce

½ tsp sugar

1 clove garlic, chopped

FOR THE DRESSING

½ tsp toasted sesame oil

1 Tbsp sherry vinegar

1 tsp soy sauce

2 tsp peanut oil

1 Tbsp grated fresh ginger

3 Japanese eggplants, trimmed

Salt

8 oz (250 g) soba noodles

½ tsp peanut oil, plus 2 Tbsp, or as needed

12 oz (375 g) firm tofu, cut into ½-inch (12-mm) cubes

5 green onions, including tender green parts, thinly sliced

To make the marinade, in a large bowl, combine the 1 Tbsp sesame oil, 2 Tbsp vinegar, 2 Tbsp soy sauce, sugar, and garlic and stir well. Set aside.

To make the dressing, in a large bowl, combine the ½ tsp sesame oil, 1 Tbsp vinegar, 1 tsp soy sauce, 2 tsp peanut oil, and ginger and stir to mix well. Set aside.

Halve the eggplants lengthwise and cut into ½-inch (12-mm) pieces. Add to the bowl with the marinade, toss, and let stand for at least 1 hour.

In a large saucepan over medium-high heat, bring 4 cups (32 fl oz/1 l) water to a boil. Reduce the heat to medium, add 1 tsp salt and the soba noodles and cook until tender but not mushy, about 6 minutes. Drain and rinse with cold water until cool. Drain again, transfer to a bowl, and toss with the ½ tsp peanut oil. Set aside. ⟫→

In a wok over medium-high heat, warm the 2 Tbsp peanut oil, tilting the wok to coat the pan. When the oil is hot, add the eggplant cubes and cook, turning until they are golden and tender, 3–5 minutes. Remove with a slotted spoon and set aside. Put the tofu cubes in the wok, adding more oil if needed, and cook until they are just golden, 3–4 minutes. Remove and set aside along with the eggplant.

Put the soba noodles in the bowl with the dressing and turn to coat. Add the eggplant and tofu and mix and coat. Sprinkle with the green onions and serve.

- - - - - - - - - - - - - - - - - - - -

16

The French have perfected the art of gilding tender lettuces with a handful of fresh green herbs, as shown in this classic recipe. Sweet and mild butter lettuce is hard to surpass, but use any greens you like. To keep herbs fresh, wrap them loosely in a damp paper towel and store in a zippered plastic bag in the vegetable drawer of the refrigerator.

LETTUCE & HERB SALAD WITH DIJON VINAIGRETTE

serves 4

FOR THE DIJON VINAIGRETTE

1½ Tbsp red wine vinegar

½ clove garlic, pressed

½ tsp Dijon mustard

3 Tbsp walnut oil

Salt and freshly ground pepper

1 head butter lettuce, leaves separated and torn into bite-sized pieces

½ bunch fresh chervil, tough stems removed

½ bunch fresh tarragon, tough stems removed

½ cup (½ oz/15 g) fresh flat-leaf parsley leaves

To make the vinaigrette, in a small bowl, whisk together the vinegar, garlic, and mustard and let stand for 5 minutes. Add the oil in a thin stream, whisking constantly until the dressing is smooth. Season to taste with salt and pepper.

In a large serving bowl, combine the lettuce, chervil, tarragon, and parsley. Drizzle the vinaigrette over the greens and toss to coat the leaves well. Serve.

17

SEPTEMBER

FRISÉE SALAD WITH LARDONS

serves 4

You'll find this curly tangle of frisée on many a continental bistro menu, with or without the poached egg. Ask for lardons, small strips of salt pork or unsmoked bacon, at your butcher shop. If they are not available, thick-cut bacon cut crosswise into ½-inch (12-mm) pieces is a fine substitute.

1 cup (2 oz/60 g) cubed country-style bread (1-inch/2.5-cm cubes)

1½ Tbsp extra-virgin olive oil

Salt and freshly ground pepper

¾ lb (375 g) lardons *(left)*, or thick-cut bacon cut into ½-inch (12-mm) pieces

2 shallots, minced

5 Tbsp (2½ fl oz/75 ml) red wine vinegar

1 tsp white wine vinegar

4 large eggs

2 heads frisée, cored and leaves torn into 3-inch (7.5-cm) pieces

Preheat the oven to 350°F (180°C). Spread the bread cubes on a baking sheet, sprinkle them with the oil, and season to taste with salt and pepper. Bake, turning once or twice, until golden, about 15 minutes. Set aside.

In a frying pan over medium-high heat, sauté the lardons, stirring occasionally, until crisp, 4–5 minutes. Add the shallots and sauté until softened, about 1 minute. Add the red wine vinegar, reduce the heat to medium, and simmer until slightly thickened, about 1 minute. Season to taste with salt and pepper. Set aside and keep warm.

Pour 6 cups (48 fl oz/1.5 l) water into a large, deep frying pan or wide saucepan and add 1 tsp salt and the white wine vinegar. Bring to a simmer over high heat. Reduce the heat to maintain a gentle simmer. Working quickly, break 1 egg at a time into a small bowl and slide each carefully into the simmering water. Carefully spoon the simmering water over the eggs until the whites are just opaque and firm and the yolks are still soft, about 3 minutes. Using a slotted spoon, lift the eggs from the water, blot the bottoms with paper towels, transfer to a plate and set aside.

In a large serving bowl, combine the toasted bread cubes and frisée. Pour the warm dressing with the lardons over the salad and toss to coat evenly. Divide the greens among shallow individual bowls, distributing the lardons evenly.

Place a poached egg on top of each salad and serve.

18

SEPTEMBER

ANTIPASTO SALAD WITH PEPERONCINI VINAIGRETTE

serves 6

An array of Italian cured meats and cheese inspired this lively chopped salad, topped with zesty peperoncini. The plate becomes especially pretty if you use a mixture of red and yellow cherry tomatoes. Accompany with toasted slices of garlicky sourdough bread for texture.

FOR THE CROSTINI

¼ cup (2 fl oz/60 ml) extra-virgin olive oil

4 cloves garlic, minced

1 sourdough baguette

Salt

FOR THE PEPERONCINI VINAIGRETTE

¼ cup (2 fl oz/60 ml) red wine vinegar

5 peperoncini, stemmed, seeded, and minced

1 Tbsp minced fresh oregano

2 tsp sugar

6 Tbsp (3 fl oz/90 ml) extra-virgin olive oil

4 cups (1½ lb/750 g) cherry or grape tomatoes, halved lengthwise

3 avocados

8 oz (250 g) provolone cheese, cut into ½-inch (12-mm) cubes

1–2 cups (1–2 oz/30–60 g) arugula leaves, stemmed

10 oz (315 g) thinly sliced prosciutto

To make the crostini, preheat the oven to 350°F (180°C). In a bowl, mix together the ¼ cup oil and the garlic. Cut the baguette into 18 slices, each about ½ inch (12 mm) thick, and arrange in a single layer on a baking sheet. Brush both sides of the baguette slices with the garlic oil and sprinkle lightly with salt. Toast in the oven until crisp and lightly golden, about 10 minutes. Let cool.

In a small bowl, whisk together the vinegar, peperoncini, oregano, sugar, and ¼ tsp salt. Add the 6 Tbsp oil in a thin stream, whisking until the dressing is well blended.

In a bowl, toss the tomatoes with ¼ tsp salt and let stand until they release their juices, about 5 minutes, then drain. Pit and peel the avocados and cut them crosswise into slices about ⅜ inch (1 cm) thick. Sprinkle with a large pinch of salt.

Arrange the tomatoes, avocados, cheese, and arugula on a large platter. Whisk the vinaigrette to recombine, then drizzle it over the arranged salad. Arrange the prosciutto and crostini on the platter and serve.

19

BLACK BEAN, CORN & QUINOA SALAD

serves 6

FOR THE LIME DRESSING

2 Tbsp fresh lime juice

3 Tbsp distilled white vinegar

2 Tbsp minced fresh cilantro

1 serrano chile, seeded and minced

¼ tsp dried oregano

Salt and freshly ground pepper

½ cup (4 fl oz/125 ml) olive oil

½ cup (3 oz/90 g) quinoa, well rinsed

½ can (8 oz/250 g) black beans, drained and rinsed

⅔ cup (4 oz/125 g) fresh or thawed frozen corn kernels (from about 1 ear corn)

1 tomato, seeded and finely chopped

1 small red bell pepper, seeded and finely chopped

Quinoa, a South American staple crop, is prized for its earthy yet delicate flavor, as well as its nutritional value: it is the only grain that boasts a complete protein. A medley of corn with glossy black beans, pale gold quinoa, and red tomatoes and bell pepper makes this a colorful, eye-catching salad.

To make the dressing, in a bowl, whisk together the lime juice, vinegar, cilantro, chile, oregano, ½ tsp salt, and ½ tsp pepper. Add the oil in a thin stream, whisking constantly until the dressing is smooth. Set aside.

In a saucepan over medium-high heat, combine the quinoa and 1½ cups (12 fl oz/375 ml) water. Stir in ¼ tsp salt. Cover and bring to a boil, then reduce the heat to low and simmer until the quinoa is tender and all the water has been absorbed, about 15 minutes. Transfer the quinoa to a colander and rinse under cold running water. Drain thoroughly.

Meanwhile, put the beans in a saucepan and place over medium-low heat. Stir occasionally until warm. Remove from the heat and cover to keep warm.

Combine the quinoa and the black beans in a bowl. Pat the corn dry with paper towels and add to the bowl along with the tomato and bell pepper. Pour in the dressing and toss to coat all the ingredients well. Let stand at room temperature for at least 15 minutes to let the flavors blend before serving.

20

CHOPPED SALAD OF PEPPERS, TOMATOES, OLIVES & MANCHEGO

serves 6

FOR THE SHERRY VINAIGRETTE

3 Tbsp sherry vinegar

1 tsp Dijon mustard

1 clove garlic, minced

Salt and freshly ground pepper

¼ cup (2 fl oz/60 ml) olive oil

1 small yellow bell pepper, seeded and chopped

1 small orange bell pepper, seeded and chopped

2 cups (¾ lb/375 g) cherry or grape tomatoes, halved

4 celery ribs, thinly sliced

¾ cup (3½ oz/105 g) pitted large green olives, quartered

¼ cup (1½ oz/45 g) finely chopped red onion

1 Tbsp chopped fresh flat-leaf parsley

1 tsp chopped fresh thyme

8 oz (250 g) Manchego cheese, cut into ¼-inch (6-mm) cubes

Chopped vegetable salads improve when made a couple of hours before serving, so that the flavors have time to mingle. Use vegetables that have some crunch, like the peppers listed here, or try cucumbers, fennel, and carrots. For a more substantial salad, add 6 oz (185 g) diced ham or dry salami.

To make the vinaigrette, in a large bowl, whisk together the vinegar, mustard, garlic, ¼ tsp salt, and ½ tsp pepper. Add the oil in a thin stream, whisking constantly until the dressing is smooth.

Add the bell peppers, tomatoes, celery, olives, onion, parsley, thyme, and cheese to the vinaigrette in the bowl. Toss until all the ingredients are coated with the vinaigrette and serve.

21

SPICY CASHEW CHICKEN SALAD

serves 6

2 Tbsp light sesame oil

½ yellow onion, finely chopped

1½-inch (4-cm) piece fresh ginger, peeled and minced

7 large cloves garlic, minced

1½ lb (750 g) ground chicken

1 cup (5 oz/155 g) cashews

¾ cup (6 fl oz/180 ml) hoisin sauce

6 Tbsp (3 fl oz/90 ml) tamari sauce

1¼ tsp Sriracha chile sauce

2 tsp firmly packed light brown sugar

1 large head butter lettuce, separated into leaves

Salt and freshly ground pepper

3 green onions, including pale green parts, thinly sliced

Salty-sweet hoisin sauce has a deep, spicy, molasses-like flavor. It defines this easy-to-make ground chicken salad, which also includes generous doses of ginger and garlic. Toasted cashews add both a delicious nuttiness and welcome crunch. To serve, mound the salad on a pile of greens, or pass little lettuce cups at a party.

In a large frying pan over medium heat, warm the sesame oil. Add the onion, ginger, and garlic and sauté until aromatic and the onion has softened slightly, about 2 minutes. Add the ground chicken and raise the heat to medium-high. Cook, stirring and breaking up the meat with a wooden spoon, until the chicken is evenly crumbled, cooked through, and no longer pink, about 8 minutes.

Meanwhile, in a dry frying pan, toast the cashews over medium-low heat, stirring, until fragrant, about 5 minutes. Pour onto a plate to cool, then chop and set aside.

In a small bowl, whisk together the hoisin, tamari, Sriracha sauce, and brown sugar. When the chicken is ready, add the hoisin mixture and half of the cashews to the pan and cook, stirring occasionally, until aromatic, about 3 minutes. Remove from the heat and cover to keep warm.

In a large bowl, toss the lettuce with 2 pinches of salt and several grindings of pepper. Divide the lettuce leaves among individual plates or arrange on a platter, and spoon the warm chicken mixture into the lettuce leaves. Garnish with the remaining cashews and the green onions and serve.

22

CELERY, PEAR & TOASTED HAZELNUT SALAD

serves 6–8

8–10 celery ribs, strings removed

½ cup (2½ oz/75 g) hazelnuts

2½ Tbsp hazelnut oil

1 Tbsp white balsamic vinegar or pear vinegar

Salt and ground white pepper

4 ripe pears such as Bosc or Bartlett

Crisp autumn apples and pears are good partners for crunchy celery. Remove the strings from the celery to make slicing easier and ensure a tender bite. Nut oils are more costly than staple varieties, but they are supremely rich and delicious. If you like, walnuts and walnut oil can be substituted for the hazelnuts and hazelnut oil.

Preheat the oven to 350°F (180°C). Using a mandoline or a very sharp knife, cut the celery into slices ⅛ inch (3 mm) thick. Cut the tops into small pieces. Put all the celery in a bowl of ice water and set aside.

Spread the hazelnuts in a single layer on a baking sheet. Place in the oven and toast, stirring once or twice, until the skins start to darken and wrinkle, 12–15 minutes. Remove from the oven and rub in a kitchen towel to remove the skins. Pour onto a plate to cool, then chop coarsely and set aside.

In a large bowl, combine the hazelnut oil, vinegar, and ¼ tsp each salt and pepper and whisk well. Drain the celery and pat dry with a paper towel. Add to the bowl and turn to coat with the vinaigrette.

Peel, halve, and core the pears then cut them lengthwise into slices ½ inch (12 mm) thick. Set aside.

Using a slotted spoon, remove the celery from the vinaigrette and divide among chilled salad plates. Arrange the pear slices on top and drizzle with the vinaigrette. Sprinkle with the toasted hazelnuts and serve.

SEPTEMBER

23

23

BEET & WATERCRESS SALAD WITH FRESH MOZZARELLA

serves 4

1½–1¾ lb (750–875 g) baby red and/or golden beets, or striped Chioggia beets, trimmed

2 Tbsp champagne vinegar

1 tsp grated orange zest

2 Tbsp fresh orange juice

Salt and freshly ground pepper

3 Tbsp extra-virgin olive oil

¼ lb (125 g) watercress, tough stems removed

1 lb (500 g) fresh mozzarella cheese, cut into thin wedges

For a delicious variation on this salad, check your local cheese shop or specialty-foods market for burrata, a fresh mozzarella cheese filled with cream and curds. Its melting texture makes it a delicious counterpoint to the earthiness of beets and the bite of watercress in this salad.

Preheat the oven to 400°F (200°C). Wrap the beets in foil, making a separate packet for each color, and roast until the beets can be pierced easily with a knife, 45 minutes–1 hour. Unwrap and let cool. Gently peel the beets, cut into quarters, and put in a small bowl.

In a large bowl, whisk together the vinegar, orange zest and juice, and ½ tsp salt. Add the oil in a thin stream, whisking constantly until the dressing is smooth. Pour half of the dressing over the beets and stir to coat. Add the watercress to the remaining dressing and toss to coat.

Arrange the watercress on individual plates or on one large platter, and top with beets. Arrange the cheese around the beets and drizzle with any remaining vinaigrette. Season with a few grindings of pepper and serve.

24

RICE SALAD WITH TUNA & CAPERS

serves 8

Salt and freshly ground pepper

2 cups (14 oz/440 g) long-grain white rice

2 cans (6 oz/185 g each) tuna, preferably Italian olive oil–packed

¼ cup (2 fl oz/60 ml) fresh lemon juice or white wine vinegar

¼ cup (2 fl oz/60 ml) extra-virgin olive oil

1½ Tbsp capers, rinsed

½ cup (¾ oz/20 g) chopped fresh flat-leaf parsley

½ cup (¾ oz/20 g) chopped fresh basil, plus whole leaves for garnish

½ cup (¾ oz/20 g) chopped fresh cilantro

This is a tempting fish-and-grain salad, packed with fresh herbs. To make individual servings, cut large tomatoes in half and scoop them out, leaving a shell. Fill the halves with heaping portions of the salad and garnish each with a basil sprig.

In a saucepan over high heat, combine 4 cups (32 fl oz/1 l) water and ½ tsp salt and bring to a boil. Add the rice, return to a boil, reduce the heat to low, cover, and cook until the rice is tender and the liquid is absorbed, about 20 minutes. Remove from the heat and let stand, covered, until completely cool, at least 1 hour. Fluff the rice with a fork.

Drain the tuna of its oil, transfer to a bowl, and flake with a fork.

In a large bowl, stir together the lemon juice, olive oil, 1 tsp salt, and 1 tsp pepper. Add the rice, flaked tuna, capers, parsley, chopped basil, and cilantro and mix gently. Garnish with the whole basil leaves and serve.

25

SUCCOTASH SALAD

serves 6–8

Kernels cut from 6 ears of corn

6 Tbsp (3 fl oz/90 ml) olive oil

Salt and freshly ground pepper

2 lb (1 kg) fava beans in the pod, shelled

1 lb (500 g) small potatoes such as fingerling, Yukon Gold, or red-skinned, quartered

FOR THE HONEY VINAIGRETTE

3 Tbsp red wine vinegar

½ tsp Dijon mustard

1 tsp honey

⅓ cup (3 fl oz/80 ml) extra-virgin olive oil

1 can (15 oz/470 g) lima beans, drained and rinsed

¼ red onion, cut into paper-thin slices

2 Tbsp minced fresh flat-leaf parsley

2 tsp chopped fresh thyme

This dish will help you savor those few weeks of the year in late summer when shelling beans are still in abundance, juicy corn is piled high at farm stands, and potatoes are thin-skinned and tender. Roasting the corn makes it slightly chewy and enhances its natural sweetness.

Preheat the oven to 400°F (200°C). Put the corn kernels on a baking sheet. Drizzle with 2 Tbsp of the olive oil and season with salt and pepper. Toss and spread out in an even layer. Roast until the corn is light brown and slightly shriveled, about 15 minutes.

Bring a saucepan three-fourths full of salted water to a boil. Add the fava beans and blanch for 2 minutes. Drain and rinse under cold running water. Pinch each bean to pop it from its skin, and set aside.

In a large frying pan, combine the remaining 4 Tbsp (2 fl oz/60 ml) olive oil and ½ cup (4 fl oz/125 ml) water over medium heat. Add the potatoes, season with salt and pepper, cover, bring to a simmer, and cook until the potatoes are tender and begin to sizzle, 10–20 minutes. Toss the potatoes with the oil remaining in the pan, and sauté until light golden, about 5 minutes.

To make the vinaigrette, in a small bowl, stir together the vinegar, mustard, and honey. Add the olive oil in a thin stream, whisking constantly until the dressing is smooth. Season to taste with salt and pepper.

In a large bowl, combine the roasted corn, fava and lima beans, potatoes, onion, parsley, and thyme. Drizzle with the vinaigrette, toss to coat, and serve.

26

ASIAN SEARED-SALMON SALAD

serves 4

FOR THE GINGER MARINADE

¼ cup (2 fl oz/60 ml) soy sauce

3 Tbsp honey

1 Tbsp peeled and finely grated fresh ginger

Finely grated zest of 2 limes

Juice of 1 lime

1 Tbsp toasted sesame oil

1 cucumber, peeled and finely sliced

Salt

1 Tbsp sugar

1 Tbsp white wine vinegar

2 heads butter lettuce, leaves separated

2 cups (2 oz/60 g) arugula leaves, stemmed

6 green onions, white parts only, thinly sliced

3 Tbsp olive oil

4 salmon fillets, about 6 oz (185 g) each, skin on and pin bones removed

Cucumbers and salmon are a classic combination, but the duo feels fresh when paired with a gingery marinade and some added shoots and greens. If you can find it, try to use wild salmon, as it is leaner than farmed salmon and deeper in flavor. Serve with a dry Japanese beer.

To make the marinade, in a small saucepan, combine the soy sauce, honey, and ginger. Set over low heat and cook, stirring, until the honey is dissolved. Simmer for 1 minute and remove from the heat. Add the lime zest and let stand to cool to room temperature, about 30 minutes. Whisk in the lime juice and sesame oil. Set aside.

In a bowl, combine the cucumber and ¼ tsp salt and let stand for 10 minutes. Stir in the sugar and vinegar. In a large bowl, combine the lettuce leaves, arugula, and green onions. Set aside.

In a nonstick frying pan over high heat, warm the olive oil. Add the salmon fillets, skin side down, and cook until crisp, about 5 minutes. Turn and cook until the flesh is golden, about 5 minutes. Transfer to a dish and generously spoon half of the marinade over the fillets. Let stand until cool.

Before serving, remove and discard the skin from each fillet. Add the remaining marinade and the cucumber and any liquid to the salad and toss to combine. Divide the salad among individual plates. Top each salad with a salmon fillet and serve.

27

SALAD OF GRILLED PORK, PEARS & TOASTED PECANS

serves 6

½ cup (2 oz/60 g) pecans

1 Tbsp peanut oil

Salt and freshly ground pepper

Pinch of sugar

2 pork tenderloins, about ¾ lb (375 g) each, trimmed

1 Tbsp olive oil

FOR THE HAZELNUT VINAIGRETTE

6 Tbsp (3 fl oz/90 ml) olive oil

2½ Tbsp sherry vinegar

1 Tbsp hazelnut oil

2 firm but ripe pears, preferably Bosc

6 handfuls (about 6 oz/185 g) mixed salad greens

Pork matches well to the sweetness of cider, but instead of braising, sear tenderloins for a quick weeknight salad with slices of fresh green pear. If the weather is too chilly to fire up the grill, the broiler works just as well.

Preheat the oven to 350°F (180°C). In a bowl, combine the pecans, peanut oil, salt and pepper to taste, and sugar and toss well to coat the nuts. Spread the pecans evenly on a baking sheet and bake until lightly golden, 5–7 minutes. Let cool.

Prepare a charcoal or gas grill for direct-heat cooking over high heat, or preheat the broiler.

Brush the pork tenderloins with the 1 Tbsp olive oil and season with salt and pepper. Place on the grill rack or on a broiler pan 4 inches (10 cm) from the heat source and cook, turning occasionally to brown evenly, until an instant-read thermometer inserted into the thickest part registers 150°F (66°C) or the pork is pale pink when cut in the thickest portion, about 12 minutes. Transfer to a cutting board, cover loosely with foil, and let rest for 2–3 minutes before carving. Cut crosswise into slices ¼ inch (6 mm) thick.

To make the vinaigrette, in a small bowl, whisk together the 6 Tbsp olive oil, vinegar, and salt and pepper to taste. Add the hazelnut oil in a thin stream, whisking constantly until the dressing is smooth.

Halve, core, and cut the pears lengthwise into very thin slices. In a large bowl, combine the greens, pecans, and vinaigrette and toss to mix well. Arrange the dressed greens on a platter or individual plates, top with the pork and pear slices, and serve.

28

TOSTADA SALAD WITH TOMATILLO SALSA

serves 6

FOR THE TOMATILLO SALSA

2 cans (12 oz/375 g each) tomatillos, drained and chopped

⅓ cup (½ oz/15 g) chopped fresh cilantro

¼ cup (1½ oz/45 g) minced red onion

2 Tbsp fresh lime juice

½ fresh jalapeño or serrano chile, seeded and minced

Salt and freshly ground pepper

½ can (8 oz/250 g) black beans, rinsed and drained

1 cup (8 fl oz/250 ml) corn oil

6 corn tortillas, each 6 inches (15 cm) in diameter

2 cups (8 oz/250 g) coarsely shredded Monterey jack cheese

1 small head romaine lettuce, thinly sliced crosswise

This Mexican-style salad has plenty of flavor and texture for a satisfying meatless meal. Garnish it with sour cream, chopped green onions, sliced avocados, lime wedges, and cilantro sprigs. Other cheeses, such as Cheddar or mozzarella, can be used in place of the jack cheese.

To make the salsa, in a bowl, stir together the tomatillos, cilantro, onion, lime juice, jalapeño, and salt and pepper to taste. Set aside until ready to use.

Put the beans in a saucepan and place over medium-low heat. Stir occasionally until warm. Remove from the heat and cover to keep warm.

Meanwhile, in a frying pan over medium-high heat, warm the corn oil. When it is hot, slip a tortilla into the oil and cook until golden and almost crisp, 1–2 minutes. Using tongs, transfer to paper towels to drain. Repeat with the remaining tortillas.

Place each tortilla on a plate. Distribute the beans, cheese, lettuce, and salsa over the tortillas, and serve.

29

This simple chicken and tomato salad gains extra flavor from a basil dressing, but the croutons really steal the show. Savory Parmesan polenta cubes become crispy, panfried delicacies, adding crunch and a hint of sweet cornmeal.

SMOKED CHICKEN SALAD WITH ROASTED CHERRY TOMATOES

serves 4

FOR THE POLENTA CROUTONS

2 cups (14 oz/440 g) instant polenta

4 Tbsp (2 oz/60 g) unsalted butter

2/3 cup (3 oz/90 g) grated Parmesan cheese

2 Tbsp olive oil

FOR THE PESTO DRESSING

2 Tbsp extra-virgin olive oil

1 tsp grated lemon zest

2 Tbsp fresh lemon juice

1 Tbsp prepared pesto

2 cups (3/4 lb/375 g) cherry tomatoes

3 Tbsp extra-virgin olive oil

Salt and freshly ground pepper

1/2 tsp fresh thyme, chopped

1 smoked or roasted whole chicken breast

To make the polenta croutons, in a large, heavy saucepan, cook the polenta according to package instructions. Remove from the heat and vigorously stir in the butter and cheese until evenly distributed. Quickly rinse a 12-by-17-inch (30-by-43-cm) rimmed baking sheet with cold water and shake it dry. Immediately mound the polenta in the pan and, working quickly and using a spatula repeatedly dipped in hot water, spread the polenta in an even layer about 1/2 inch (12 mm) thick. Cover with a kitchen towel and let stand for at least 1 hour at room temperature, or refrigerate for up to 24 hours. Remove the chilled polenta from the refrigerator about 1 hour before using. Cut the polenta into 1/2-inch cubes.

In a frying pan over medium-high heat, warm the 2 Tbsp olive oil. When hot, add the polenta cubes, in batches as needed to avoid crowding, and sauté until lightly browned on all sides. Transfer to paper towels to drain.

To make the dressing, in a glass measuring pitcher, whisk together the 2 Tbsp extra-virgin olive oil, lemon zest and juice, and pesto. Set aside. »→

Preheat the oven to 400°F (200°C). Put the cherry tomatoes in a bowl and drizzle with the 3 Tbsp olive oil and sprinkle with 1/4 tsp each salt and pepper and the thyme. Toss to coat. Place on a baking sheet and roast in the oven until their skins are wrinkled but not yet collapsed, about 15 minutes. Remove from the oven and set aside.

Reset the oven to 350°F (180°C). Wrap the chicken breast in foil and place it in the oven to warm, about 15 minutes. Remove it and slice it very thinly.

Arrange the chicken slices on a serving platter. Top with the cherry tomatoes and drizzle with some of the pesto dressing. Sprinkle with the polenta croutons, add another drizzle of the pesto dressing, and serve.

30

This hearty Italian salad originated as a way to use up stale bread. Traditionally, it evolved from the bland, salt-free bread of Tuscany, but you can use any day-old country-style bread. The drier the bread, the more absorbent it is, which means it will soak up more of the delicious juices and dressing. As the salad sits, the bread will soften and the flavors will blend together.

PANZANELLA

serves 6

2 large tomatoes, cut into bite-sized pieces

1 small English cucumber, peeled, halved lengthwise, and sliced

1 small red onion, halved and very thinly sliced

1 cup (1 1/2 oz/45 g) fresh basil leaves, torn, plus whole small leaves for garnish

1/2 cup (4 fl oz/125 ml) extra-virgin olive oil, or to taste

3 Tbsp red wine vinegar, or to taste

Salt and freshly ground pepper

6–8 day-old slices country-style bread

In a large mixing bowl, combine the tomatoes, cucumber, onion, and torn basil. Drizzle with the 1/2 cup olive oil and the 3 Tbsp vinegar and season with salt and pepper. Toss well to coat evenly.

Cut or tear the bread into bite-sized pieces. Place half of the bread in a wide, shallow serving bowl. Spoon half of the tomato mixture over. Layer the remaining bread on top and then the remaining tomato mixture. Cover and let stand for 1 hour.

Toss the salad, then taste and adjust the seasoning with salt, pepper, and vinegar. If the bread seems dry, add a little more olive oil. Garnish with the whole basil leaves and serve.

Fall is the time of year when thick-skinned squashes appear in markets. Sugar pie pumpkins and butternut, acorn, and Delicata squash all boast tender, sweet orange flesh, worth roasting and tossing with greens. Toast leftover pumpkin seeds, and use them for a crunchy topping. The damp fall weather also bodes well for mushrooms. Seek out wild and local varieties, and enjoy them raw and thinly sliced, or sautéed and tossed with a bold vinaigrette while still warm.

1
SMOKED TROUT & APPLE SALAD WITH POLENTA CROUTONS
page 226

2
WATERCRESS & ORANGE SALAD WITH TOASTED PUMPKIN SEEDS
page 226

3
THREE-BEAN SALAD WITH CORIANDER VINAIGRETTE
page 228

8
GREEK POTATO SALAD
page 231

9
TROUT & GREEN PEAR SALAD
page 232

10
WARM WILD MUSHROOM SALAD WITH BACON VINAIGRETTE
page 232

15
FARRO SALAD WITH ARTICHOKE HEARTS
page 237

16
ROASTED BEET & CURLY ENDIVE SALAD WITH BALSAMIC VINAIGRETTE
page 237

17
CHICKEN–BROWN RICE SALAD WITH DATES & CASHEWS
page 238

22
BULGUR SALAD WITH ROASTED PEPPERS, CHICKPEAS & PISTACHIOS
page 240

23
ARUGULA & FENNEL SALAD WITH BLACK PEPPER–CRUSTED TUNA
page 243

24
MIXED GREENS WITH BACON-WRAPPED FIGS
page 243

29
CUCUMBER SALAD WITH POMEGRANATE, FETA & MINT
page 245

30
SPICY CRAB SALAD
page 246

31
CRANBERRY BEAN, BROCCOLI RABE & BACON SALAD
page 246

4	5	6	7
GREEN GRAPE, PEAR & DUCK SALAD *page 228*	**CHICKEN SALAD WITH APPLES & WALNUTS** *page 229*	**MEDITERRANEAN OCTOPUS SALAD** *page 229*	**VIETNAMESE FLANK STEAK SALAD** *page 231*
11	**12**	**13**	**14**
SHREDDED KALE SALAD WITH ANCHOVIES & PECORINO *page 234*	**HEARTS OF ROMAINE WITH GARLIC CROUTONS** *page 234*	**ROASTED PEPPER SALAD WITH GARLIC BREAD** *page 235*	**CUCUMBER & FENNEL SALAD** *page 235*
18	**19**	**20**	**21**
ROASTED PORK TENDERLOIN & CORNICHON SALAD *page 238*	**ARUGULA, BUTTERNUT SQUASH & SALAMI SALAD** *page 239*	**GARLICKY PENNE & CHICKEN SALAD** *page 239*	**CELERY SLAW WITH SHRIMP & CREAMY CIDER VINAIGRETTE** *page 240*
25	**26**	**27**	**28**
CHICKPEA, TOMATO & CHORIZO SALAD *page 244*	**LENTIL, BACON & FRISÉE SALAD** *page 244*	**GRILLED RADICCHIO SALAD** *page 245*	**APPLE-FENNEL SLAW** *page 245*

october

1

SMOKED TROUT & APPLE SALAD WITH POLENTA CROUTONS

serves 10–12

Golden polenta croutons flavored with Parmesan add sweet crunch to this elegant salad of delicate flaked trout and crisp sliced apples. You can try other smoked fish in place of the trout, such as sturgeon or whitefish. Serve as a first course at your next dinner party.

FOR THE POLENTA CROUTONS

2 cups (14 oz/440 g) instant polenta

4 Tbsp (2 oz/60 g) unsalted butter

²/₃ cup (3 oz/90 g) grated Parmesan cheese

2 Tbsp grapeseed oil

2 small Gala or Fuji apples, cored and thinly sliced

½ lb (250 g) smoked trout, skin and bones removed, flaked with a fork

4 cups (4 oz/125 g) loosely packed mâche

¾ cup (3 oz/90 g) coarsely chopped walnuts

¼ cup (2 fl oz/60 ml) mayonnaise

1 Tbsp fresh lemon juice

Salt and freshly ground pepper

2 Tbsp minced fresh chives

To make the polenta croutons, in a large, heavy saucepan, cook the polenta according to package instructions. Remove from the heat and vigorously stir in the butter and cheese until evenly distributed. Quickly rinse a 12-by-17-inch (30-by-43-cm) rimmed baking sheet with cold water and shake it dry. Immediately mound the polenta in the pan and, working quickly and using a spatula repeatedly dipped in hot water, spread the polenta in an even layer about ½ inch (12 mm) thick. Cover with a kitchen towel and let stand for at least 1 hour at room temperature, or refrigerate for up to 24 hours. Bring the chilled polenta to room temperature for about 1 hour before serving. Cut the polenta into ½-inch cubes.

In a frying pan over medium-high heat, warm the 2 Tbsp oil. When hot, add the polenta cubes, in batches as needed to avoid crowding, and sauté until lightly browned on all sides. Transfer to paper towels to drain.

Arrange the apples on a platter. Scatter with the trout, greens, walnuts, and polenta croutons. In a small bowl, stir together the mayonnaise, lemon juice, ¼ tsp salt, and pepper to taste. Drizzle this dressing over the salad, scatter with chives and a grinding of pepper, and serve.

2

WATERCRESS & ORANGE SALAD WITH TOASTED PUMPKIN SEEDS

serves 6

The peppery bite of watercress pairs well with the bright, sweet taste of oranges in this salad. Pumpkin seeds are known as pepitas in Spanish, and they are a favorite ingredient in Mexican cooking. They are delicious when toasted and sprinkled over salads.

¼ cup (2 oz/60 g) pumpkin seeds

1 tsp extra-virgin olive oil

1 tsp ground cumin

FOR THE SPICY CITRUS DRESSING

¼ cup (2 fl oz/60 ml) fresh lime juice

1 jalapeño chile, thinly sliced and seeded

Salt and freshly ground pepper

⅓ cup (3 fl oz/80 ml) extra-virgin olive oil

3 navel oranges

2 bunches watercress, tough stems removed

In a small bowl, toss the pumpkin seeds with the 1 tsp oil and the cumin. Spread the pumpkin seeds in a dry frying pan over medium heat and cook, stirring constantly, just until they begin to darken, about 5 minutes. Pour onto a plate to cool.

To make the dressing, in a small bowl, whisk together the lime juice, chile, 1 tsp salt, and ¼ tsp pepper. Add the ⅓ cup oil in a thin stream, whisking constantly until the dressing is smooth.

Use a knife to peel the oranges. Cut each in half vertically, then cut each half crosswise into half-moon slices about ¼ inch (6 mm) thick. Put the orange slices in a bowl, add the watercress, and toss to mix.

Just before serving, drizzle the dressing over the watercress and oranges. Taste and adjust the seasoning with salt. Divide the salad among serving plates, sprinkle each serving with the toasted pumpkin seeds, and serve.

3

Three-bean salad is a venerable favorite. Here is an updated version that calls for fresh shelling beans, slender French green beans, and pale wax beans. You can substitute other green beans for the haricots verts. The flavor intensifies if the salad is allowed to marinate for at least 1 hour.

THREE-BEAN SALAD WITH CORIANDER VINAIGRETTE

serves 6–8

Salt and freshly ground pepper

½ lb (250 g) fresh flageolet beans or other fresh shelling beans, shelled

1 lb (500 g) yellow wax beans, stem ends trimmed and beans cut into 2-inch (5-cm) lengths

1 lb (500 g) haricots verts, stem ends trimmed

FOR THE CORIANDER VINAIGRETTE

1 tsp ground coriander

¼ cup (2 fl oz/60 ml) fresh lemon juice

2 Tbsp white wine vinegar

2 shallots, minced

¾ cup (6 fl oz/180 ml) safflower oil

1 tsp grated lemon zest

Bring a large saucepan three-fourths full of salted water to a boil. Add the shelling beans and boil just until tender, 10–15 minutes. Have ready a bowl of ice water. Scoop out the beans and immediately immerse in ice water to stop the cooking. Scoop the beans out of the ice water and set aside to drain. Repeat with the yellow wax beans and haricots verts, cooking the wax beans for 7–8 minutes and the haricots verts for 3–4 minutes.

To make the vinaigrette, in a small, dry frying pan, toast the coriander over medium heat, shaking the pan occasionally, until aromatic, 2–3 minutes. Pour onto a plate to cool and set aside. In a small bowl, combine the lemon juice, vinegar, and shallots. Add the safflower oil in a thin stream, whisking constantly until the dressing is smooth. Stir in the lemon zest and coriander and season with salt and pepper.

Combine all the beans in a large mixing bowl. Add the vinaigrette and toss to mix well. Let stand for at least 1 hour, or refrigerate for up to 3 hours. Serve at room temperature or chilled.

4

Dark, gamy duck meat classically pairs with fruit flavors—just think of a cherry compote, or an orange glaze. Salads are a fantastic way to feature these same flavors, except with fresh fruit. In this case, rich breast meat joins fall grapes and pears in an elegant dish fit for company.

GREEN GRAPE, PEAR & DUCK SALAD

serves 4

1 duck breast half, about 1 lb (500 g)

Salt and freshly ground pepper

½ tsp ground coriander

2 Tbsp minced shallot

2 Tbsp balsamic vinegar

2 cups (¾ lb/375 g) seedless green grapes, some halved for garnish

2 bunches watercress, tough stems removed

2 green pears, such as Comice or Seckel, cored and thinly sliced

Remove the skin and fat from the duck by pulling the fatty layer back and cutting it from the meat with a small knife. Set the breast aside. Place the fatty layer, skin side down, in a frying pan over medium heat. Cook, turning occasionally, until about ¼ cup (2 fl oz/60 ml) fat is rendered, 10 minutes. Discard the skin. Measure out 2 Tbsp fat and set aside. (Save the rest for another use.)

Raise the heat to high. Season the duck breast on both sides with 1 tsp salt, ½ tsp pepper, and the coriander. Sear until browned, about 3 minutes. Add the shallot, turn the duck, and cook on the other side for 3 minutes. Reduce the heat to medium and cook until the duck is rosy only in the center, 1–2 minutes. Transfer to a cutting board and let rest.

Add the reserved duck fat to the pan and place over high heat. When the fat is hot and glistening, add ½ cup (4 fl oz/125 ml) water, the vinegar, and the whole grapes to the pan, and stir to scrape up any browned bits on the pan bottom. Simmer until the liquid is reduced by half, about 2 minutes. Slice the duck on the diagonal into thin slices, and pour any collected juices into the pan.

Arrange the watercress on a platter and top with alternating slices of pear and duck. Pour the grape sauce over, scatter with the grape halves, and serve.

5

This contemporary chicken salad forgoes mayo in favor of a lighter, lemony vinaigrette, deliciously drizzled over strips of freshly sautéed breast meat. It also appropriates some of the fresh touches of the famous Waldorf salad—apples, celery, and walnuts.

CHICKEN SALAD WITH APPLES & WALNUTS

serves 4

½ cup (2 oz/60 g) coarsely chopped walnuts

1 large or 2 small bunches watercress, tough stems removed

1 large tart apple such as Granny Smith

½ lemon, plus 1 Tbsp fresh lemon juice

Salt and freshly ground pepper

¼ cup (2 fl oz/60 ml) walnut oil

4 skinless, boneless chicken breast halves (about 2 lb/1 kg total weight)

2 Tbsp unsalted butter

2 Tbsp extra-virgin olive oil

2 or 3 celery ribs with leaves, preferably the tender inner ribs, thinly sliced crosswise

In a dry frying pan over medium-low heat, toast the walnuts, stirring until fragrant and starting to brown, about 5 minutes. Pour onto a plate to cool.

Put the watercress in a serving bowl, cover with a damp kitchen towel, and refrigerate for 20–30 minutes.

Peel, quarter, and core the apple. Cut the quarters in half crosswise and then thinly slice lengthwise. Put them in a bowl. Squeeze the juice from the lemon half over the apple to slow the discoloration. Toss to coat well and set aside.

In a small bowl, stir together the 1 Tbsp lemon juice, ⅛ tsp salt, and pepper to taste until the salt dissolves. Add the walnut oil in a thin stream, whisking constantly until the dressing is well blended. Set aside.

Remove any excess fat from the chicken breasts. Rinse and pat dry with paper towels. Place each breast between 2 sheets of plastic wrap and, using a meat mallet, pound to an even thickness. Season with salt and pepper. In a large frying pan (preferably nonstick), melt the butter with the olive oil over medium-high heat. When hot, add the chicken breasts and sauté, turning once, until lightly browned and opaque throughout, 3½–4 minutes per side. Transfer to a plate and keep warm. ⟩⟩

Add the celery, apple, and half of the walnuts to the watercress. Whisk the dressing to recombine, pour it over the salad, and toss well. Divide among individual plates. Slice the warm chicken breasts crosswise into strips ½ inch (12 mm) thick and arrange them over the salads. Sprinkle with the remaining toasted walnuts and serve.

6

This salad, served throughout the Mediterranean, is best with just-caught octopus. If fresh is not available, frozen octopus is the next best thing. Octopus has a wonderfully meaty texture, and when chilled and thinly sliced, it almost takes on the flavor of lobster.

MEDITERRANEAN OCTOPUS SALAD

serves 4

1½ lb (750 g) octopus, cleaned

Salt and freshly ground pepper

1 clove garlic, crushed

½ cup (4 fl oz/125 ml) extra-virgin olive oil

Juice of 1 lemon

2 green onions, including tender green tops, sliced crosswise

1 red bell pepper, seeded and finely chopped

2 inner celery ribs, thinly sliced

Rinse the octopus well under running cold water. If the octopus has not previously been frozen, place it in a large lock-top freezer bag and freeze it overnight, then thaw in the refrigerator to tenderize the flesh.

In a saucepan, combine the octopus with water to cover and bring to a boil over high heat. Add 2 Tbsp salt and the garlic, cover, reduce the heat to low, and simmer without lifting the lid for about 45 minutes. The octopus should turn white.

Drain the octopus and let cool until it can be handled. Cut into bite-sized pieces and place in a serving bowl. Add the oil and lemon juice, cover, and let marinate for at least 1 hour at room temperature or for up to 4 hours in the refrigerator.

Just before serving, add the green onions, bell pepper, and celery and toss well. Season with salt and pepper and toss again, then serve at room temperature or slightly chilled.

7

Scoring the meat before marinating it allows the flavors to penetrate fully, and helps prevent the steak from curling on the grill. Tender rice noodles and a trio of green herbs define this fresh, Asian main. If you can find Thai basil, use it here for authentic flavor.

VIETNAMESE FLANK STEAK SALAD

serves 4

FOR THE SPICY MARINADE

2 Tbsp peeled and grated fresh ginger

½ cup (4 fl oz/125 ml) soy sauce

2 Tbsp Asian fish sauce

2 Tbsp toasted sesame oil

3 cloves garlic, minced

2 green onions, including tender green parts, thinly sliced

1 shallot, minced

1 Thai chile, seeded and thinly sliced

Grated zest and juice of 1 lime

1 flank steak, 1½–1¾ lb (750–875 g), trimmed

Salt and freshly ground pepper

1 head Bibb lettuce, torn into small pieces

1 heart of romaine lettuce, chopped into 1-inch (2.5-cm) chunks

1 carrot, peeled and shredded

1 cucumber, peeled, seeded, and shredded

1 small red onion, thinly sliced

2 Tbsp minced fresh basil, plus small leaves for garnish

2 Tbsp minced fresh mint, plus small leaves for garnish

2 Tbsp minced fresh cilantro, plus small leaves for garnish

1 lb (500 g) Asian cellophane noodles, soaked in water until soft, then drained

To make the marinade, in a bowl, whisk together the ginger, soy sauce, fish sauce, sesame oil, garlic, green onions, shallot, chile, and lime zest and juice. Spoon one-half of the marinade into a small serving bowl and set aside.

Using a sharp knife, score the meat on both sides in a crosshatch pattern, cutting no more than ½ inch (12 mm) deep. Place the steak in a shallow dish, pour the remaining marinade over the top, and turn to coat well. Cover and refrigerate for at least 1 hour or up to overnight.

Prepare a charcoal or gas grill for direct-heat cooking over medium-high heat. »→

Remove the steak from the marinade, letting the excess drip back into the pan; discard the marinade. Pat the steak dry with paper towels and season generously with salt and pepper. Grill the steak directly over medium-high heat, turning once and brushing with some of the remaining marinade, until cooked to your liking. Transfer to a carving board, tent with foil, and let rest for 5 minutes.

Assemble the salad in individual bowls by dividing equal portions of the lettuces, carrot, cucumber, red onion, herbs, and noodles among them. Pour 1 Tbsp of the marinade over each bowl.

Slice the steak across the grain into thin strips and place on top of the noodles and salad greens. Garnish with the herb leaves and serve, passing the remaining marinade at the table.

8

The variety of potato salads found across Greece proves the popularity of the dish. In this version, the potatoes soak up a red wine vinaigrette, and are served warm. The addition of capers, coriander, parsley, and lemon zest gives the salad a pleasantly citrusy, salty flavor.

GREEK POTATO SALAD

serves 4–6

1½ lb (750 g) small red potatoes

2 Tbsp red wine vinegar

1 tsp ground coriander

2 Tbsp extra-virgin olive oil

Salt and freshly ground pepper

1 Tbsp capers, preferably salt-packed, rinsed

¼ cup (⅓ oz/10 g) coarsely chopped fresh flat-leaf parsley

1 tsp grated lemon zest

Put the potatoes in a large saucepan with cold water to cover by 2 inches (5 cm) and bring to a boil over medium-high heat. Reduce the heat to medium and cook until tender when pierced with the tip of a knife, 20–25 minutes. Drain the potatoes, let cool until they can be handled, and cut in half. Transfer to a serving bowl, and set aside.

In a small bowl, whisk together the vinegar and coriander. Add the oil in a thin stream, whisking constantly until smooth. Season to taste with salt and pepper. Pour the dressing over the warm potatoes. Scatter the capers, parsley, and lemon zest over the top. Using a fork, toss until the potatoes are evenly coated with the dressing. Set aside for 20 minutes to let the flavors blend, then serve.

9

Fresh pink trout fillets and soft autumn pears make a good match of delicate flavors. Sprinkle with a mild herb such as chervil, valued for its subtle anise flavor. A member of the classic French fines herbes combination, chervil is far less well known than its sister herbs parsley, tarragon, and chives.

TROUT & GREEN PEAR SALAD

serves 4

2 Tbsp sliced almonds

4 skinless steelhead trout or salmon fillets, each about ⅓ lb (155 g) and 1 inch (2.5 cm) thick

Olive oil

Salt and freshly ground pepper

2 Tbsp minced fresh chervil or flat-leaf parsley

2 just-ripe crisp green pears, halved, cored, and cut into thin wedges

2 Tbsp fresh lime juice

1 Tbsp fresh lemon juice

1 bunch watercress, tough stems removed

In a dry frying pan, toast the almonds over medium-low heat, stirring, until fragrant, 2–3 minutes. Pour onto a plate to cool.

Prepare a charcoal or gas grill for direct-heat cooking over medium-high heat. Brush the fish with a little oil, season with salt and pepper, and sprinkle with the chervil.

Combine the pears with the lime and lemon juices in a mixing bowl and toss to coat. Set aside. Arrange the fish in a single layer in an oiled grill basket or on oiled heavy-duty foil. Place the basket on or slide the foil onto the grill. Cover the grill and cook, turning once, until the flesh just flakes when prodded with a fork and is barely opaque in the center, about 3 minutes per side. Transfer to a plate, tent with foil, and let rest for 5 minutes.

Add the watercress to the pears and toss gently to combine. Break the trout into bite-sized pieces and toss into the salad. Add the almonds, season to taste with salt and pepper, and toss again gently. Divide among individual plates and serve.

10

Fry bacon until crisp and brown, and then warm sherry vinegar in the same pan to form a salty-smoky vinaigrette for autumn mushrooms. Bitter radicchio and peppery arugula are layered with the warm mushroom mixture for extra flavor, color, and crunch.

WARM WILD MUSHROOM SALAD WITH BACON VINAIGRETTE

serves 4

1 lb (500 g) mixed wild and cultivated mushrooms

1 Tbsp unsalted butter

3 shallots, minced

2 slices applewood-smoked bacon, cut crosswise into ¼-inch (6-mm) pieces

2 Tbsp extra-virgin olive oil

2 Tbsp sherry vinegar

1 Tbsp whole-grain mustard

Salt and freshly ground pepper

1 head radicchio, cored and separated into leaves

1 cup (1 oz/30 g) arugula leaves, stemmed (optional)

Remove any tough stems from the mushrooms. Trim the bases of the remaining stems. If desired, thickly slice the mushrooms.

In a large frying pan, melt the butter over medium heat. Add about two-thirds of the shallots and sauté until translucent, about 5 minutes. Add the mushrooms and sauté until they are tender and the moisture they release evaporates, 6–8 minutes.

Meanwhile, in another large frying pan over medium-high heat, cook the bacon, stirring occasionally, until browned and crisp, about 6 minutes. Remove from the heat and stir in the remaining shallots, the oil, vinegar, and mustard. Keep warm.

Transfer the mushrooms to a large bowl, add the bacon mixture, and toss to mix. Season to taste with salt and pepper. Add the radicchio and arugula, if using, and toss to coat the leaves well with the dressing. Serve warm.

OCTOBER

16

15

FARRO SALAD WITH ARTICHOKE HEARTS

serves 4–6

1¼ cups (7½ oz/235 g) farro

½ cup (3 oz/90 g) pine nuts

¼ cup (2 oz/60 g) oil-packed sun-dried tomatoes

1 package (14 oz/440 g) frozen artichoke hearts, thawed and brought to room temperature

6 Tbsp (3 fl oz/90 ml) red wine vinegar

3 Tbsp extra-virgin olive oil

½ cup (2½ oz/75 g) finely chopped red onion, rinsed

½ cup (¾ oz/20 g) chopped fresh flat-leaf parsley leaves

Salt and freshly ground pepper

Artichokes thrive in the cool spring, but they have a second, smaller harvest in fall. Their nutty flavor makes them a delicious addition to hearty grain salads. If you can still find good-looking specimens in the market, use fresh hearts in this salad. Quarter the hearts and simmer in salted water until tender, about 8 minutes.

Rinse the farro and put it in a saucepan with 2½ cups (20 fl oz/625 ml) water; bring to a boil. Reduce the heat, cover, and simmer until the grains are tender and the water is absorbed, about 25 minutes.

In a small frying pan, toast the pine nuts over medium-low heat, stirring, until fragrant and starting to brown, 3–4 minutes. Pour onto a plate to cool.

Cut the tomatoes into thin strips, reserving the oil to use in place of some of the olive oil, if you like. Quarter the artichoke hearts.

In a large bowl, whisk together the vinegar and olive oil. Add the cooked farro, sun-dried tomatoes, artichoke hearts, onion, parsley, and toasted pine nuts and mix well. Season generously with salt and pepper and serve.

16

ROASTED BEET & CURLY ENDIVE SALAD WITH BALSAMIC VINAIGRETTE

serves 4

6 small beets, trimmed

¾ cup (3 oz/90 g) coarsely chopped pecans

FOR THE BALSAMIC VINAIGRETTE

¼ cup (2 fl oz/60 ml) balsamic vinegar

Salt and freshly ground pepper

2 Tbsp extra-virgin olive oil

4 cups (4 oz/125 g) torn curly endive leaves, pale inner leaves only

1 cup (1 oz/30 g) arugula leaves

¼ cup (1 oz/30 g) grated orange zest

As the frost sets in, sturdy root vegetables grow even sweeter. Golden beets, or a mixture of golden and red beets, make an especially attractive presentation in this autumnal salad, combined with pleasantly bitter greens and toasted nuts.

Preheat the oven to 350°F (180°C). Wrap the beets in foil, place in a baking pan, and roast, turning occasionally, until tender when pierced with a fork, 40–45 minutes. Remove and let cool until they can be handled, then peel and cut into rounds ¼ inch (6 mm) thick. Place in a bowl, cover to keep warm, and set aside.

In a small frying pan, toast the chopped pecans over medium-low heat, stirring, until fragrant and starting to brown, about 5 minutes. Pour onto a plate to cool, and set aside.

To make the vinaigrette, stir together the vinegar, ¼ tsp salt, and ½ tsp pepper. Add the extra-virgin olive oil in a thin stream, whisking constantly until the dressing is smooth.

Divide the curly endive and arugula among individual plates. Top with the beet rounds and drizzle with the dressing. Garnish with the orange zest and the toasted pecans and serve.

21

CELERY SLAW WITH SHRIMP & CREAMY CIDER VINAIGRETTE

serves 8

Old-fashioned coleslaw is updated here with generous additions of celery, radishes, shrimp, and smoked paprika. A sprinkle of crispy bacon pieces and crumbled blue cheese gives it even more impact. We often think of slaws as side dishes, but this is one that deserves to take center place.

FOR THE CREAMY CIDER VINAIGRETTE

½ cup (4 fl oz/125 ml) mayonnaise

¼ cup (2 oz/60 g) sour cream, or ¼ cup (2 fl oz/60 ml) buttermilk

¼ cup (2 fl oz/60 ml) olive oil

¼ cup (2 fl oz/60 ml) unfiltered cider vinegar

1 tsp dry mustard

1 clove garlic, chopped

2 lb (1 kg) shrimp, peeled and deveined

3 Tbsp extra-virgin olive oil

1 tsp mild Spanish smoked paprika

Salt and freshly ground pepper

¼ lb (125 g) applewood-smoked bacon

½ head green cabbage, cored and thinly sliced crosswise

5 celery ribs, thinly sliced

6 green onions, including tender green tops, chopped

1 bunch red radishes, trimmed and thinly sliced

½ cup (¾ oz/20 g) chopped fresh flat-leaf parsley

2 oz (60 g) blue cheese, crumbled (optional)

To make the vinaigrette, combine the mayonnaise, sour cream, oil, vinegar, mustard, and garlic in a food processor or blender and process until smooth. Set aside.

In a large bowl, toss together the shrimp, 3 Tbsp olive oil, paprika, and a little salt and pepper. Preheat a large nonstick frying pan over medium-high heat. Add half of the shrimp and sauté until they turn pink and are opaque throughout, about 3 minutes. Transfer to a large bowl and repeat with the remaining shrimp. Set aside to cool.

Rinse and wipe dry the frying pan and return to medium heat. Add the bacon and fry, turning as needed, until crisp, about 6 minutes. Transfer to paper towels to drain. Let cool, then crumble and set aside.

Add the cabbage, celery, green onions, radishes, parsley, and vinaigrette to the shrimp and toss. Season to taste with salt and pepper and toss again. Sprinkle the crumbled bacon and the cheese, if using, over the top, and serve.

22

BULGUR SALAD WITH ROASTED PEPPERS, CHICKPEAS & PISTACHIOS

serves 6

Pomegranate molasses, a Middle Eastern specialty, has hints of fruitiness and a concentrated sweet-sour taste. Here, its intensity combines with lemon juice and olive oil to create a dressing with full-ranging flavor. If you have a choice of bulgur styles, choose a medium grind to stand up to the hearty beans, nuts, and dried fruits.

1½ cups (9 oz/280 g) medium-grind bulgur wheat

2¼ cups (18 fl oz/560 ml) chicken broth

¼ cup (2 fl oz/60 ml) fresh lemon juice

¼ cup (2 fl oz/60 ml) pomegranate molasses

2 tsp sugar

Salt and freshly ground pepper

6 Tbsp (3 fl oz/90 ml) extra-virgin olive oil

1 can (15 oz/470 g) chickpeas, drained and rinsed

¾ cup (3 oz/90 g) pistachios

2 large jarred roasted red bell peppers, chopped

½ cup (¾ oz/20 g) chopped fresh flat-leaf parsley, cilantro, and/or mint, plus small whole leaves for garnish

1 cup (6 oz/185 g) sweetened dried cranberries or dried sweet cherries

2 cups (16 oz/500 g) plain yogurt (optional)

Put the bulgur in a heatproof bowl. In a small saucepan over high heat, bring the broth to a boil. Pour the broth over the bulgur, cover, and let stand until the liquid has been absorbed, about 30 minutes.

Meanwhile, in a small bowl, whisk together the lemon juice, pomegranate molasses, sugar, 1½ tsp salt, and several grindings of pepper until the sugar dissolves. Add the oil in a thin stream, whisking constantly until the dressing is well blended.

In a small bowl, stir together the chickpeas and ½ tsp salt. Whisk the dressing to recombine, then add it, along with the chickpeas, to the bowl with the bulgur and stir to mix well. Cover and refrigerate for 2 hours.

When ready to serve, in a small bowl, stir together the pistachios and a pinch of salt. Add the pistachios, chopped peppers, chopped herbs, and cranberries to the bulgur and toss well. Taste and adjust the seasonings. Divide the salad among individual plates, garnish with whole herb leaves, top each with a dollop of yogurt, if using, and serve.

23

Meaty tuna steaks with a cracked peppercorn crust add dimension to this salad. Bitter arugula, crunchy fennel, sweet caramelized onions, and an assertively flavored vinaigrette add to the contrasting tastes and textures.

ARUGULA & FENNEL SALAD WITH BLACK PEPPER–CRUSTED TUNA

serves 6

¼ cup (2 fl oz/60 ml) balsamic vinegar

1 large shallot, minced

2 tsp Dijon mustard

½ tsp sugar

Salt

10 Tbsp (5 fl oz/160 ml) extra-virgin olive oil

2 small sweet onions such as Vidalia, thinly sliced

2 Tbsp black peppercorns

6 tuna steaks (2 lb/1 kg total weight), each about 1 inch (2.5 cm) thick

8 cups (8 oz/250 g) arugula leaves, stemmed

1 large fennel bulb, trimmed and thinly sliced

In a small bowl, whisk together the vinegar, shallot, mustard, sugar, and ¼ tsp salt until the sugar dissolves. Add 7 Tbsp (3½ fl oz/ 105 ml) of the olive oil in a thin stream, whisking constantly until the vinaigrette is smooth and thick. Taste and adjust the seasonings and set aside.

In a large nonstick frying pan over medium heat, warm 2 Tbsp of the olive oil. Add the sliced onions and 1 tsp salt and sauté until the onions are softened and browned, 10–12 minutes. Transfer to a plate and set aside. Wipe the pan clean.

Place the peppercorns in a resealable plastic bag and seal. Using a mallet or the bottom of a small, heavy pan, coarsely crack the peppercorns. Season each tuna steak on both sides with a little salt. Then, dividing them evenly, press the cracked peppercorns into one side of each tuna steak.

Return the frying pan to medium-high heat and add the remaining 1 Tbsp olive oil. When the oil is hot but not smoking, add the tuna steaks, peppered side down. Sear, turning once, until lightly golden on the outside and still dark pink and rare in the center, about 2 minutes per side, or until cooked to your liking. Transfer to a platter, tent with foil, and let rest for 5 minutes. »→

In a large bowl, toss together the arugula, fennel, and ¼ tsp salt. Whisk the vinaigrette to recombine, then drizzle about half of it over the arugula mixture and toss well. Taste and adjust the seasonings. Divide the dressed arugula mixture among individual plates. Spoon the sautéed onions over the top. Thinly slice each tuna steak and arrange on top of the onions. Drizzle each salad with some of the remaining vinaigrette and serve.

24

Crispy bacon-wrapped figs are delightful party fare, especially when paired with a decadent Stilton. The figs should be browned just before serving, but you can wrap them with the bacon several hours in advance. Loosely cover them with plastic and refrigerate, letting them return to room temperature before proceeding.

MIXED GREENS WITH BACON-WRAPPED FIGS

serves 8

16 large, plump figs, preferably Black Mission, fresh or dried

8 strips thin-cut smoked bacon, halved crosswise

1 lb plus 2 oz (560 g) mixed baby salad greens

⅓ cup (3 fl oz/80 ml) extra-virgin olive oil

Salt and freshly ground pepper

3½ Tbsp sherry vinegar

8 oz (250 g) Stilton or other blue cheese, crumbled

Wrap each fig in a half-strip of bacon, overlapping it as needed and securing it with a toothpick.

Heat a large nonstick frying pan over medium heat. Add the figs and cook, turning occasionally, until the bacon is browned and crisp on most sides. Remove the toothpicks and turn the figs to finish browning the bacon on all sides. Transfer to a plate and keep warm.

In a very large bowl, toss the greens with the oil. Add ½ tsp salt and toss again. Add the vinegar and toss. Add the cheese, season generously with pepper, and toss again.

Divide the salad among serving plates. Place 2 figs on each plate. Season the figs with pepper and serve.

25

OCTOBER

CHICKPEA, TOMATO & CHORIZO SALAD

serves 4

This bean salad gets a kick from Spanish chorizo and a pinch of cayenne pepper. Serve with a spicy, medium-bodied Spanish red wine such as Rioja crianza. The salad can be prepared up to 4 hours in advance and stored in the refrigerator. Bring to room temperature and garnish with parsley before serving.

FOR THE RED WINE VINAIGRETTE

2 Tbsp red wine vinegar

1 clove garlic, minced

6 Tbsp (3 fl oz/90 ml) extra-virgin olive oil

Salt and freshly ground black pepper

2 jarred roasted red bell peppers, coarsely chopped

1 lb (500 g) cherry tomatoes, halved

1 small red onion, chopped

2 cans (15 oz/470 g each) chickpeas, drained and rinsed

1 cup (1 oz/30 g) fresh flat-leaf parsley leaves, coarsely chopped, plus wholes leaves for garnish

Cayenne pepper

1 Tbsp olive oil

½ lb (250 g) Spanish chorizo sausage, cut into half moons

To make the vinaigrette, in a large bowl, whisk together the vinegar and garlic. Add the oil in a thin stream, whisking constantly until the dressing is smooth. Season to taste with salt and black pepper.

Add the chopped peppers to the vinaigrette along with the tomatoes, onion, chickpeas, and parsley. Season to taste with cayenne, salt, and black pepper. Set aside.

In a large frying pan over medium heat, warm the olive oil. Add the chorizo and fry until crisp, 2–3 minutes on each side. Transfer to paper towels to drain.

Add the chorizo to the salad and toss to combine. Taste and adjust the seasonings. Serve, garnished with parsley leaves.

26

OCTOBER

LENTIL, BACON & FRISÉE SALAD

serves 4

This classic French preparation of earthy green lentils, curling leaves, and savory bacon relies on a quintessential mustard vinaigrette. Make a big batch of this versatile dressing and use it to drizzle over sliced tomatoes, avocado, or your favorite baby greens. Store the vinaigrette in an airtight container in the refrigerator for up to 1 week.

FOR THE MUSTARD VINAIGRETTE

2 cloves garlic, sliced

1 shallot, sliced

¼ cup (2 fl oz/60 ml) sherry vinegar

1 Tbsp Dijon mustard

¾ cup (6 fl oz/180 ml) extra-virgin olive oil

Salt and freshly ground pepper

4 slices thick-cut bacon, chopped

2 shallots, minced

1 celery rib, finely chopped

1 carrot, peeled and finely chopped

2 cups (14 oz/440 g) green French (de Puy) lentils

2 cups (16 fl oz/500 ml) chicken broth

1 head frisée, tough stems removed

To make the vinaigrette, in a blender, combine the garlic, sliced shallot, vinegar, mustard, oil, ¾ tsp salt, and ¼ tsp pepper. Process until smooth. Set aside.

In a large, heavy saucepan over low heat, cook the bacon, stirring occasionally, until crisp, about 8 minutes. Using a slotted spoon, transfer to paper towels to drain.

Return the saucepan to low heat, add the minced shallots to the bacon fat, and cook, stirring occasionally, until softened, about 4 minutes. Add the celery and carrot and cook, stirring occasionally, until wilted, 3–4 minutes. Add the lentils, broth, and enough water to just cover the lentils. Bring to a boil, reduce the heat to low, cover, and simmer gently until just tender but not yet mushy, about 20 minutes. Add a little more water if the lentils become too dry. Remove from the heat and let stand, covered, for 5 minutes. Immediately add half of the vinaigrette and toss to combine.

Scatter the frisée on plates and spoon the lentils over the top. Drizzle a little more vinaigrette over the salads. (You will have more vinaigrette than you will need for the lentil salad; store the remainder in the refrigerator for up to 1 week, and whisk to recombine before using.) Sprinkle with the bacon and serve.

27

GRILLED RADICCHIO SALAD

serves 4–6

2 Tbsp balsamic vinegar

1 Tbsp honey

2–3 heads radicchio

Juice of 1 lemon

2 Tbsp extra-virgin olive oil, plus 1–2 Tbsp

Salt and freshly ground pepper

Grana padano or pecorino romano cheese for shaving

2 Tbsp minced fresh flat-leaf parsley

Radicchio adds gorgeous red color to fall salads, but it does have quite an assertive flavor when raw. When the weather permits, fire up the grill, which will help to mellow that bitter chicory edge. Look for elongated Treviso radicchio, which is more mild than other varieties.

In a small, heavy saucepan over medium-high heat, combine the vinegar and honey and bring to a boil. Reduce the heat to low and simmer until slightly thickened, about 2 minutes. Remove from the heat and let cool.

Peel away the outer leaves from the radicchio heads and discard. Cut the heads in half lengthwise, and then cut each half into wedges 1½ inches (4 cm) thick. Trim away some of the core from each wedge, leaving the leaves attached at the base.

In a large bowl, combine the radicchio, lemon juice, the 2 Tbsp oil, and one-half of the balsamic syrup mixture. Toss to coat and season with salt and pepper. Let stand for 10 minutes.

Prepare a charcoal or gas grill for direct-heat cooking over medium-high heat. Grill the radicchio, turning often, until nicely charred on all sides, about 3–5 minutes.

Transfer the grilled radicchio to a shallow dish and drizzle with the remaining balsamic syrup and the 1–2 Tbsp oil. Using a vegetable peeler, shave the cheese over the top. Sprinkle with the parsley and serve hot off the grill or at room temperature.

28

APPLE-FENNEL SLAW

serves 4

¼ cup (2 fl oz/60 ml) fresh lime juice

¼ cup (2 oz/60 g) sour cream

¼ cup (2 fl oz/60 ml) mayonnaise

½ tsp paprika

¼ tsp sugar

Salt

¾ cup (1 oz/30 g) fresh cilantro leaves, minced

2 large fennel bulbs, trimmed, quartered, and thinly sliced

2 small tart red or green apples, peeled, cored, and thinly sliced

This is a pretty and modern slaw, full of refreshing sweet-tart flavors. If you prefer a light vinaigrette to a creamy dressing, omit the sour cream and mayonnaise and whisk about ½ cup (4 fl oz/125 ml) olive oil into the lime juice mixture.

In a large bowl, whisk together the lime juice, sour cream, mayonnaise, paprika, sugar, ½ tsp salt, and the cilantro. Add the fennel and apples and toss to mix well. Cover and refrigerate for 1 hour to allow the flavors to blend before serving.

29

CUCUMBER SALAD WITH POMEGRANATE, FETA & MINT

serves 4

2 Tbsp olive oil

¼ cup (2 fl oz/60 ml) fresh lemon juice

2 English cucumbers

1 cup (4 oz/125 g) pomegranate seeds

⅓ cup (⅓ oz/10 g) coarsely torn fresh mint leaves

Salt and freshly ground pepper

1 cup (5 oz/155 g) crumbled feta cheese

Whole pomegranate fruits usually appear in late November, but you may be able to find seeds in the refrigerator case of the produce department. Tart and textured, they give a new direction to this minty cucumber salad.

In a large bowl, add the oil to the lemon juice in a thin stream, whisking constantly until the dressing is smooth.

Slice the cucumbers into rounds ⅛ inch (3 mm) thick. Add the cucumbers, pomegranate seeds, and mint to the bowl with the dressing. Mix gently to coat and season to taste with salt and pepper. Just before serving, gently fold in the cheese and serve.

30

SPICY CRAB SALAD

serves 6

3 cups (18 oz/560 g) cooked crabmeat, picked over for shell fragments

1 or 2 red or green chiles such as Thai or serrano, minced

Finely grated zest of 2 limes

Juice of 1 lime

2 Tbsp coarsely chopped fresh mint

2 Tbsp mayonnaise

Salt and freshly ground pepper

FOR THE LIME DRESSING

6 Tbsp (3 fl oz/90 ml) extra-virgin olive oil

2 Tbsp fresh lime juice

1 small red onion

2 hearts of romaine lettuce, leaves separated and torn into pieces

2 bunches watercress, tough stems removed

3 avocados

This lighter, spicier version of traditional crab salad is dressed in a modest amount of mayonnaise and spiked with fresh lime juice, mint, and chiles. Rather than cook whole crabs, you can purchase freshly cooked lump crabmeat.

Put the crabmeat in a bowl and, using a paper towel, gently pat dry. Add the chiles, lime zest and juice, mint, and mayonnaise to the crabmeat. Stir gently to combine. Season to taste with salt, cover, and refrigerate until serving.

To make the dressing, in a small bowl, add the oil to the lime juice in a thin stream, whisking constantly until the dressing is smooth. Season to taste with salt and pepper.

Slice the onion thinly and soak in hot water for 15 minutes. Reserve one-fourth of the onion to use as a garnish. In a large bowl, combine the remaining onion slices, lettuce, and watercress. Drizzle with the dressing and toss gently to combine.

Halve and pit the avocados. Using a large metal spoon, carefully scoop the flesh of each avocado half from the peel in one piece.

Divide the greens and onion among individual plates. Top each with an avocado half. Spoon some of the crabmeat mixture onto each avocado half. Garnish with the reserved onion slices and serve.

31

CRANBERRY BEAN, BROCCOLI RABE & BACON SALAD

serves 4

4 cups (2 lb/1 kg) fresh cranberry beans, shelled

Salt and freshly ground pepper

1 bay leaf

2 fresh thyme sprigs

1 lb (500 g) broccoli rabe, stemmed

1/3 cup (3 fl oz/80 ml) extra-virgin olive oil

2 cloves garlic, minced

1/4 lb (125 g) thin-sliced bacon, cut into 1-inch (2.5-cm) pieces

3–4 Tbsp (1½–2 fl oz/45–60 ml) red wine vinegar

Look for fresh cranberry beans in the pod at farmers' markets this time of year. The creamy-textured, nutty-flavored beans pair beautifully with autumn greens. Broccoli rabe has nicely jagged leaves for sautéed salads, but you could easily substitute kale or chard.

Put the beans in a saucepan with water to cover by 2 inches (5 cm). Add ½ tsp salt, the bay leaf, and the thyme sprigs and bring to a boil. Reduce the heat to a simmer and cook until the beans are tender, 15–25 minutes.

Chop the tender portions of the broccoli rabe. In a large frying pan, warm the oil over medium-high heat, then sauté the garlic until fragrant, 2–3 minutes. Add the broccoli rabe, ¼ tsp salt, and ½ tsp pepper. Cook, stirring often, until the greens are tender, 4–5 minutes. Remove from the heat and cover to keep warm.

In a small frying pan, cook the bacon until crisp, 3–4 minutes. Drain the beans and place in a serving bowl. Add the broccoli rabe and the bacon along with its rendered fat. Add vinegar to taste, toss to mix, and serve.

Deep autumn promises an abundance of root vegetables. Shredded carrots and celery root yield great texture to salads, while roasted beets and parsnips offer appealing earthy and sweet flavors. Approaching the holidays, salads can also serve as a vehicle for leftover roasts: tuck chopped turkey breast meat into nutty grains such as brown rice, farro, or bulgur, and garnish with a sprinkling of pomegranate seeds or dried cranberries.

1
WARM SPINACH SALAD WITH DELICATA SQUASH & RICOTTA SALATA
page 250

2
ENDIVE SALAD WITH PERSIMMONS & POMEGRANATE
page 250

3
FARRO SALAD WITH TURKEY & ROASTED SQUASH
page 253

8
SHAVED FENNEL, PARMESAN & ARUGULA SALAD
page 255

9
MUSHROOM, RADICCHIO & BULGUR SALAD
page 256

10
SAVORY BREAD SALAD WITH PANCETTA & PINE NUTS
page 256

15
MOROCCAN-SPICED CARROT & PARSNIP SALAD
page 261

16
CELERY ROOT RÉMOULADE
page 261

17
BROCCOLI & CAULIFLOWER SALAD WITH PICKLED ONIONS & BACON
page 262

22
FRISÉE, ENDIVE & WATERCRESS SALAD WITH ROQUEFORT & PEAR
page 265

23
SPICED APPLE, CRANBERRY & PECAN SALAD
page 267

24
FATTOUSH SALAD WITH TURKEY & PITA CROUTONS
page 267

29
CRAB CAKE & BUTTER LETTUCE SALAD
page 270

30
BELGIAN ENDIVE, PEAR, FETA & WALNUT SALAD
page 270

4
SALT COD SALAD WITH POTATOES & BLACK OLIVES
page 253

5
CELERY ROOT & CARROT SALAD WITH DIJON-TARRAGON DRESSING
page 254

6
RADICCHIO SALAD WITH PEARS, WALNUTS & GOAT CHEESE
page 254

7
WILTED BEET GREENS WITH ROASTED BEETS & ORANGE VINAIGRETTE
page 255

11
SHAVED MUSHROOM & FENNEL SALAD WITH PARMESAN CRISPS
page 259

12
WILD RICE SALAD WITH ROASTED RED PEPPERS & ANCHOVIES
page 259

13
SPICY CUCUMBER SALAD WITH ROASTED PEANUTS
page 260

14
MIXED GREENS WITH HEARTS OF PALM, RED ONION & AVOCADO
page 260

18
TROUT, WATERCRESS & APPLE SALAD
page 262

19
FENNEL SALAD WITH APPLE, WALNUTS & MANCHEGO
page 264

20
VIETNAMESE SHRIMP & NOODLE SALAD
page 264

21
WATERCRESS & ENDIVE SALAD WITH WARM BACON VINAIGRETTE
page 265

25
PERSIMMON & YELLOW APPLE SALAD
page 268

26
GREEN LENTIL SALAD WITH RED PEPPERS & SHALLOTS
page 268

27
CROTTIN SALAD WITH PEARS, FENNEL & CURRANTS
page 269

28
TURKEY & CELERY SALAD WITH DRIED CHERRIES
page 269

november

1

WARM SPINACH SALAD WITH DELICATA SQUASH & RICOTTA SALATA

serves 4

Delicata squash, which has sweet, pale-orange flesh, is a good source of vitamins A and C, potassium, and iron. When roasted, the pretty scalloped peel of this winter squash becomes tender enough to eat. If you can't find Delicata, use cubes of butternut squash or sweet potato.

1½ lb (750 g) Delicata squash

4 Tbsp (2 fl oz/60 ml) olive oil

Salt and freshly ground pepper

½ cup (2½ oz/75 g) chopped almonds

3 Tbsp sherry or red wine vinegar

8 oz (250 g) baby spinach leaves

4 oz (125 g) ricotta salata or feta cheese, crumbled

Preheat the oven to 400°F (200°C). Rinse and dry the squash. Halve the squash lengthwise and remove the seeds, then cut crosswise into half-moons ½ inch (12 mm) thick. In a 12-by-17-inch (30-by-43-cm) baking pan, toss the squash with 1 Tbsp of the oil, ¼ tsp salt, and a few grindings of pepper. Roast until the squash is tender, about 20 minutes.

In a dry heavy frying pan over medium heat, toast the almonds until browned, about 30 seconds. Transfer to a plate to cool.

In a large bowl, mix the vinegar and ¼ tsp salt. Add the squash, spinach, cheese, and toasted almonds. Heat the remaining 3 Tbsp oil in a small frying pan over medium-high heat. Pour the oil over the salad (carefully, as the oil may spatter), toss to coat and wilt the spinach evenly, and serve.

2

ENDIVE SALAD WITH PERSIMMONS & POMEGRANATE

serves 4

Serve this crisp and refreshing salad when persimmons and pomegranates are in season. Look for the Fuyu variety of persimmons, which are sweet and firm, and easy to cut very thin. Any salty or tangy cheese will do; try using fresh goat cheese or ricotta salata in place of the feta.

¾ cup (3 oz/90 g) pistachios

4 heads red or white Belgian endive

1 large pomegranate

2 Fuyu persimmons

8 oz (250 g) feta cheese, crumbled

Grated zest and juice of 1 lemon

1 tsp champagne vinegar

Salt and freshly ground pepper

½ cup (4 fl oz/125 ml) extra-virgin olive oil

In a small frying pan, toast the pistachios over medium-low heat, stirring, until fragrant and starting to brown, about 5 minutes. Pour onto a plate to cool, then chop coarsely and set aside.

Trim the ends from the endive, separate the leaves, and place in a large bowl. Seed the pomegranate and pat the seeds dry. Using a mandoline or a very sharp knife, slice the persimmons into thin slices.

Add the pomegranate seeds, persimmons, cheese, and pistachios to the endive leaves.

To make the vinaigrette, in a small bowl, whisk together the lemon zest and juice, and vinegar. Season to taste with salt and pepper. Add the oil in a thin stream, whisking constantly until the dressing is smooth.

Drizzle the vinaigrette over the salad and gently toss. Season with additional salt and pepper and serve.

3

FARRO SALAD WITH TURKEY & ROASTED SQUASH

serves 6

1⅓ cups (about 8 oz/250 g) farro

4 cups (32 fl oz/1 l) chicken broth

Salt and freshly ground pepper

1 butternut squash (about 3 lb/1.5 kg), halved, seeded, peeled, and cut into ½-inch (12-mm) cubes

8 Tbsp (4 fl oz/125 ml) extra-virgin olive oil

¼ cup (2 fl oz/60 ml) fresh lemon juice

1 tsp honey

1 Tbsp minced fresh flat-leaf parsley

6 oz (185 g) boneless smoked turkey or chicken, cut into ½-inch (12-mm) cubes

⅔ cup (3 oz/90 g) sweetened dried cranberries

3 green onions, including tender green parts, thinly sliced

In this grain-based salad, sweet-and-sour dried cranberries contrast with smoked turkey and earthy butternut squash. Lemon juice and green onions add freshness, while the nutty taste of farro serves as a neutral flavor backdrop. The result is a dish with an inviting fall spirit and a wonderful layering of tastes and textures.

Put the farro in a saucepan, add the broth and 1 tsp salt, and bring to a boil over high heat. Reduce the heat to medium-low and simmer, uncovered, until the farro is tender and all of the liquid is absorbed, about 30 minutes. Transfer to a large bowl and let cool to room temperature.

Meanwhile, preheat the oven to 400°F (200°C). On a rimmed baking sheet, toss the squash cubes with 2 Tbsp of the oil, 1 tsp salt, and ¼ tsp pepper. Spread the cubes in an even layer on the baking sheet and roast until tender but still slightly firm to the bite, about 12 minutes. Let cool to room temperature.

In a small bowl, whisk together the lemon juice, honey, parsley, ¼ tsp salt, and several grindings of pepper. Add the remaining 6 Tbsp (3 fl oz/90 ml) oil in a thin stream, whisking constantly until the dressing is well blended. Taste and adjust the seasonings.

Add the dressing, squash, turkey, cranberries, and green onions to the cooled farro and toss well. Serve.

4

SALT COD SALAD WITH POTATOES & BLACK OLIVES

serves 4

1 lb (500 g) salt cod

1 lb (500 g) Yukon gold or other boiling potatoes

Salt

1 small red onion, halved and thinly sliced crosswise

½ cup (3 oz/90 g) pitted brine-cured black olives, coarsely chopped

¼ cup (2 fl oz/60 ml) extra-virgin olive oil

3 Tbsp fresh lemon juice, plus lemon wedges for serving

1 tsp minced garlic

¼ tsp red pepper flakes, or as needed

¼ cup (⅓ oz/10 g) coarsely chopped fresh flat-leaf parsley leaves

Salt cod is a favorite Mediterranean ingredient. Italians enjoy salt cod in many preparations, including this antipasto salad. Slices of potato and slivers of red onion join the salty, flavorful flakes of fish.

Rinse the salt cod under cool running water, then cut it into 4 pieces. Place in a bowl, add cold water to cover, then cover and refrigerate for 24 hours, changing the water 4 or 5 times.

In a saucepan, combine the potatoes with salted cold water to cover generously and bring to a boil over high heat. Reduce the heat to medium and cook until tender, about 20 minutes. Drain the potatoes, let cool slightly, then peel and slice.

Meanwhile, drain the salt cod. Pour water into a large frying pan to a depth of 2 inches (5 cm) and bring to a boil over high heat. Reduce the heat to low, add the salt cod, and simmer until tender when tested with a fork, 5–7 minutes. Using a slotted spoon, remove the salt cod and blot dry with paper towels.

Remove any bits of skin and bones from the salt cod and arrange the pieces on a serving platter, breaking it up into large chunks. Scatter the potato and onion slices and the olives over the fish.

In a small bowl, whisk together the oil, lemon juice, garlic, and ¼ tsp red pepper flakes, and drizzle the dressing over the salad. Taste and adjust the seasoning with salt and red pepper flakes. Garnish with the parsley, and serve with the lemon wedges.

9

Meaty roasted mushrooms are a perfect match for nutty grains and bittersweet radicchio. In place of the cremini, feel free to play with a medley of wild and cultivated mushrooms, such as chanterelle, shiitake, morel, and/or porcini.

MUSHROOM, RADICCHIO & BULGUR SALAD

serves 4

2 lb (1 kg) cremini mushrooms, halved

⅓ cup (3 fl oz/80 ml) olive oil, plus 2 Tbsp

3 cloves garlic, coarsely chopped

Salt and freshly ground pepper

3 oz (90 g) thick-cut pancetta or bacon, chopped

1 cup (2½ oz/75 g) bulgur wheat

Boiling water as needed

1 head radicchio, cored and thinly sliced

1 Tbsp sherry vinegar

Parmesan cheese for shaving

Preheat the oven to 475°F (245°C). In a large roasting pan, combine the mushrooms, the ⅓ cup oil, and the garlic. Season generously with salt and pepper and toss to coat evenly. Spread the mushrooms in a single layer. Roast for 5 minutes, turn the mushrooms, and continue roasting until the edges are crisp, 2–3 minutes. Set aside.

In a frying pan over medium heat, cook the pancetta, stirring occasionally, until crisp, about 10 minutes. Using a slotted spoon, transfer to paper towels to drain.

In another frying pan over medium-high heat, toast the bulgur until its nutty aroma is released, 3–4 minutes. Add 2 cups (16 fl oz/ 500 ml) boiling water and 1 tsp salt to the bulgur, cover, and simmer over low heat until tender, about 20 minutes; or, cook according to the package directions. Transfer to a large bowl. Add the radicchio and the 2 Tbsp oil and toss to combine.

Add the roasted mushrooms, pancetta, vinegar, ½ tsp salt, and a pinch of pepper to the radicchio. Toss to combine and spoon onto individual plates. Using a vegetable peeler, shave the cheese over the salads and serve.

10

Although this salad has plenty of peppery arugula, what makes it memorable is the interplay of the warm toasted bread, crunchy pine nuts, and slightly chewy pancetta. The vinaigrette is made special by sautéing the shallots, which helps distribute their flavor throughout the salad.

SAVORY BREAD SALAD WITH PANCETTA & PINE NUTS

serves 4

2 cups (4 oz/125 g) cubed country-style sourdough bread or pain au levain (1-inch/2.5-cm cubes)

3 Tbsp extra-virgin olive oil, plus ½ cup (4 fl oz/125 ml)

⅓ cup (2 oz/60 g) pine nuts

¼ lb (125 g) sliced pancetta, chopped

2 Tbsp minced shallots

2 Tbsp red wine vinegar

Salt and freshly ground pepper

6 oz (185 g) baby arugula leaves

Preheat the oven to 350°F (180°C). Spread the bread cubes on a rimmed baking sheet and drizzle with 2 Tbsp of the oil. Bake until the bread is toasted but still slightly chewy, about 8 minutes. Let cool.

In a dry frying pan, toast the pine nuts over medium-low heat until golden, stirring constantly, 3–4 minutes. Remove from the pan and set aside. In the same frying pan, combine the pancetta and 1 Tbsp of the oil over medium heat and cook, stirring occasionally, until the pancetta is browned and crisp, about 8 minutes. Using a slotted spoon, transfer to paper towels to drain. Pour off all but 1 Tbsp of the fat from the pan. Let the pan cool slightly.

Return the pan to medium heat, add the shallots, and cook, stirring frequently, until softened, about 2 minutes. Transfer to small bowl and let cool. Add the vinegar to the cooled shallots, then slowly add the ½ cup oil in a thin stream, whisking constantly until well blended to make a vinaigrette. Season with salt and pepper.

In a large serving bowl, toss together the toasted bread cubes, arugula, toasted pine nuts, and pancetta. Add the vinaigrette and toss to coat evenly. Season with salt and pepper and serve.

11

SHAVED MUSHROOM & FENNEL SALAD WITH PARMESAN CRISPS

serves 4

2 oz (60 g) **Parmesan cheese**

1½ **small to medium fennel bulbs, trimmed**

½ lb (250 g) **firm white button or cremini mushrooms**

3 Tbsp **fresh lemon juice**

3 Tbsp **extra-virgin olive oil**

Salt and freshly ground pepper

4 Tbsp (⅓ oz/10 g) **chopped fresh flat-leaf parsley**

4 cups (4 oz/125 g) **field greens**

When vegetables are sliced very thinly, their texture becomes delicate yet still crisp, and they readily absorb dressings. Use a very sharp knife, or better yet, a mandoline, a sturdy, freestanding tool with an adjustable blade that can be set to render paper-thin slices.

Preheat the broiler. Line a baking sheet with parchment paper.

Using a mandoline or a sharp knife, slice the cheese into very thin slices. Lay the cheese slices in a single layer on the prepared baking sheet. Slide under the broiler about 6 inches (15 cm) from the heat source. Broil until the cheese slices become crisp and lightly golden, like a potato chip, 6–8 minutes. They should no longer be pliable and should lift easily from the baking sheet. Set aside.

Using a mandoline or a very sharp knife, cut the fennel bulbs lengthwise into very thin slices. Each slice will look like a delicate fan. Set aside. Still using the mandoline or a sharp knife, cut the mushrooms lengthwise into very thin slices.

Put the mushrooms and the fennel in a bowl. Add the lemon juice, oil, ½ tsp salt, 1 tsp pepper, and 3 Tbsp of the parsley and turn to coat well.

Line a serving platter with the greens. Spoon the fennel-mushroom mixture on top of the lettuce leaves. Sprinkle with the remaining 1 Tbsp parsley, surround with the Parmesan crisps, and serve.

12

WILD RICE SALAD WITH ROASTED RED PEPPERS & ANCHOVIES

serves 4

Salt and freshly ground black pepper

1 cup (6 oz/185 g) **wild rice**

1 Tbsp **sherry vinegar**

1 tsp **red wine vinegar**

¼ cup (¾ oz/20 g) **chopped green onion, including tender green part**

6 **olive oil–packed anchovy fillets, minced**

2 **jarred roasted red bell peppers, chopped**

¼ cup (½ oz/15 g) **chopped fresh flat-leaf parsley, plus 2 or 3 sprigs**

3–4 Tbsp (1½–2 fl oz/45–60 ml) **extra-virgin olive oil**

Wild rice is not a true rice, but rather the grains of a marsh grass. It is, however, prepared like rice, usually steamed or boiled and then sometimes combined with white or brown rice to create a variety of textures. This anchovy-laced salad makes a delicious starter, accompanied with a crusty baguette and a bowl of olives. You can substitute any rice or grain, varying the cooking time accordingly.

In a saucepan over medium-high heat, combine 3 cups (24 fl oz/750 ml) water and 1 tsp salt and bring to a boil. Add the wild rice, return to a boil, then reduce the heat to low, cover, and cook until the rice has absorbed the water and many of the kernels have split, 20–25 minutes. Remove from the heat and let stand, covered, to steam for about 15 minutes.

Transfer the rice to a bowl. Add the sherry and red wine vinegars, green onion, anchovies, all but 1 Tbsp or so of the bell peppers, ½ tsp black pepper, and the parsley. Add 3 Tbsp olive oil and gently mix. If it seems a little dry, add 1 Tbsp olive oil. Cover and let stand for 1 hour to let the flavors blend.

Garnish with the reserved bell pepper and the parsley sprigs and serve.

17

These pickled red onions are briskly tart and sweet and redolent of black pepper and cloves. They contrast beautifully in flavor and color with smoky, salty bacon and cabbage-like steamed broccoli and cauliflower for this simple and hearty cool-weather salad.

BROCCOLI & CAULIFLOWER SALAD WITH PICKLED ONIONS & BACON

serves 6–8

2 cups (16 fl oz/500 ml) cider vinegar

3 Tbsp sugar

16 black peppercorns

10 whole cloves

Salt and freshly ground pepper

1 large red onion, thinly sliced

5 slices bacon

1 head cauliflower, cut into 1-inch (2.5-cm) florets

1 large head broccoli, cut into 1-inch (2.5-cm) florets

¼ cup (2 fl oz/60 ml) extra-virgin olive oil

In a small saucepan, combine the vinegar, sugar, peppercorns, cloves, and ¼ tsp salt and bring to a boil over high heat. Reduce the heat to medium-low and simmer for 10 minutes. Pour the mixture into a heatproof bowl, add the onion, and let stand at room temperature for 1 hour to pickle.

Meanwhile, in a large frying pan, cook the bacon over medium heat, turning once, until crisp and browned, about 7 minutes. Transfer to paper towels to drain. Let cool to room temperature, then coarsely chop.

Fill a large bowl two-thirds full with ice water and stir in 1 Tbsp salt until the salt dissolves. Arrange the cauliflower florets in a single layer in a steamer basket set over boiling water in a saucepan (the water should not touch the bottom of the basket), cover, reduce the heat to medium, and steam until crisp-tender, about 8 minutes. Immediately transfer the cauliflower to the ice water. Let stand until cool, then use a slotted spoon to transfer the cauliflower florets to a large bowl, reserving the ice water bath. Steam the broccoli florets in the same manner until crisp-tender, about 4 minutes, then transfer to the ice water until cool. Drain well and add to the bowl with the cauliflower. »→

Drizzle the oil over the cauliflower and broccoli, season with ¼ tsp salt and several grindings of pepper, and toss well. Taste and adjust the seasonings. Transfer to a serving bowl and top with some of the pickled onion slices, lifting them out with a fork and removing any whole spices (reserve the remaining pickled onions for another use). Sprinkle with the bacon and serve.

18

As the holidays approach, smoked fish appears often as a special-occasion ingredient to share with family and friends. In this instance, flakes of pink-fleshed trout make an elegant and light starter, pairing perfectly with crisp apples and sprigs of watercress.

TROUT, WATERCRESS & APPLE SALAD

serves 4–6

¾ lb (375 g) smoked trout fillets

2 bunches watercress, tough stems removed

2 Fuji or Gala apples, halved, cored, and sliced ¼ inch (6 mm) thick

¼ cup (2 fl oz/60 ml) canola oil

2 Tbsp fresh lemon juice

2 tsp grated lemon zest

With a fork, flake the trout into 1-inch (2.5-cm) pieces.

In a bowl, toss together the trout, watercress, and apples. Drizzle with the oil and lemon juice and sprinkle with the lemon zest. Toss well and serve.

NOVEMBER 24

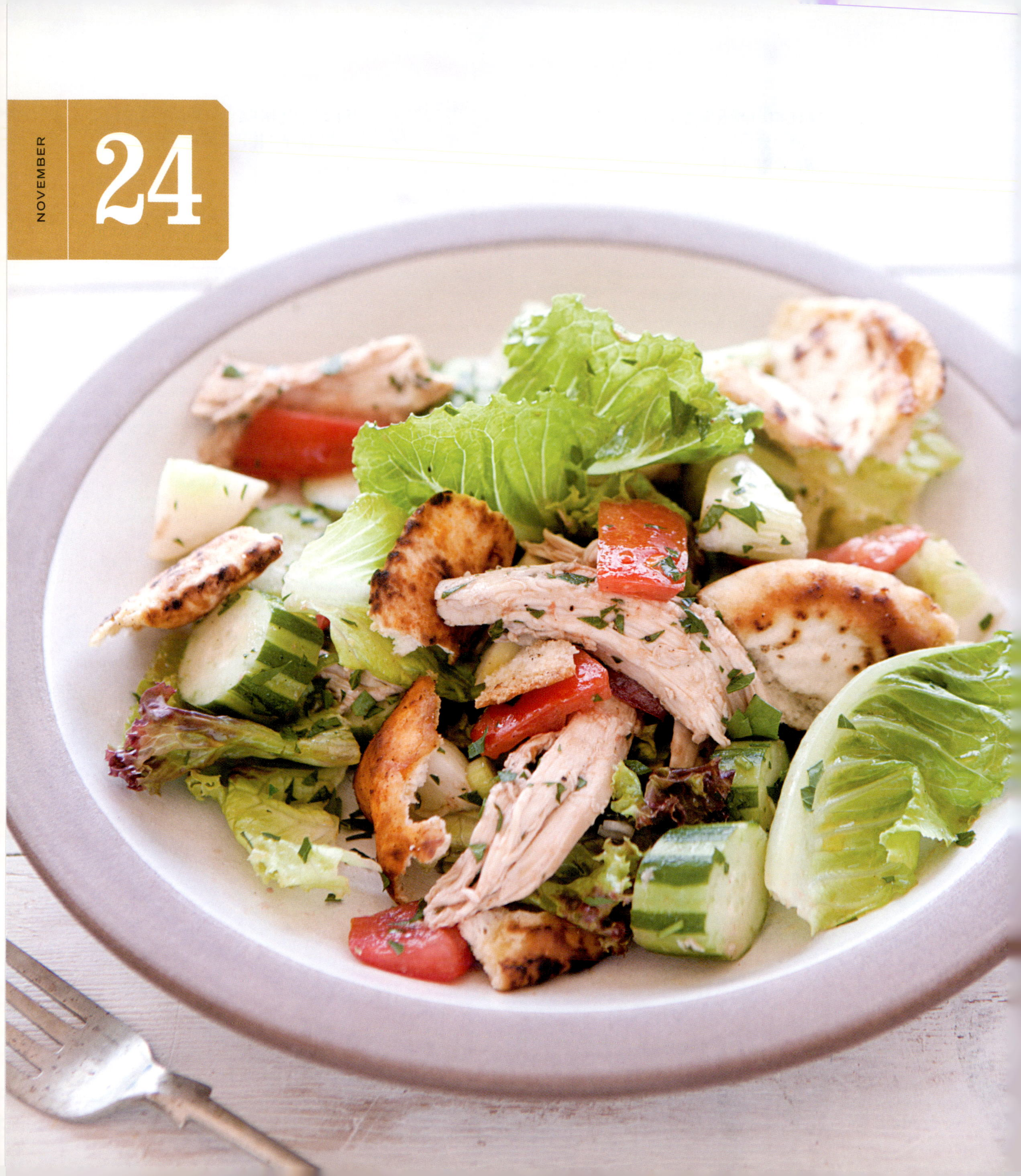

23

SPICED APPLE, CRANBERRY & PECAN SALAD

serves 4

¾ tsp ground cumin

⅛ tsp cayenne pepper

½ Tbsp olive oil

½ cup (2 oz/60 g) pecan halves

1½ Tbsp sugar

¼ cup (2 oz/60 g) plain yogurt

¼ cup (2 fl oz/60 ml) mayonnaise

1 Tbsp honey

½ tsp sherry vinegar or balsamic vinegar

2–3 large sweet apples such as Gala, Golden Delicious, or Fuji

2 large celery ribs, thinly sliced

¼ cup (1 oz/30 g) dried cranberries

4 red-leaf lettuce leaves

Apples and celery are a tried-and-true combination, but this salad spices it up for the holiday season with a crunch of candied pecans. The dressing is cut with a little yogurt, so it's not too rich.

In a bowl, combine half of the cumin and half of the cayenne. In a small saucepan, warm the oil over medium heat. Add the pecans and stir until the nuts are lightly browned, about 5 minutes. Sprinkle with the sugar and cook, stirring constantly, until the sugar melts and begins to brown, 2–3 minutes. Add the hot nut mixture to the bowl containing the spices and stir to coat. Let cool completely. Chop the nuts coarsely. Set aside.

In a small bowl, stir together the yogurt, mayonnaise, honey, and vinegar. Add the remaining cumin and cayenne.

Quarter and core each apple. Cut each quarter in half crosswise, then slice lengthwise. In a large bowl, combine the apples, celery, and dried cranberries. Add the yogurt dressing and toss to coat.

Line individual plates with lettuce leaves. Mound an equal amount of the salad in the center of each plate. Sprinkle with the spiced nuts and serve.

24

FATTOUSH SALAD WITH TURKEY & PITA CROUTONS

serves 4

4 pita bread rounds

¼ cup (2 fl oz/60 ml) extra-virgin olive oil, plus more for brushing

¼ tsp paprika

Salt and freshly ground pepper

¼ cup (2 fl oz/60 ml) fresh lemon juice

½ head red-leaf lettuce, torn into bite-sized pieces

1 lb (500 g) cooked turkey or chicken meat, shredded or cut into pieces

1 cup (5 oz/155 g) peeled, seeded, and chopped English or Persian cucumbers

1 cup (6 oz/185 g) seeded and chopped tomatoes

3 Tbsp chopped fresh flat-leaf parsley leaves

An Eastern Mediterranean salad, fattoush is traditionally made with coarsely chopped garden vegetables, a tart lemon dressing, and large croutons made of toasted or fried pita bread. This main dish salad is a fantastic way to use up leftover roast turkey or chicken.

Preheat the oven to 375°F (190°C). Separate each pita into 2 rounds. Brush the top side of each round lightly with oil and sprinkle lightly with paprika and salt. Arrange in a single layer on 2 large baking sheets and bake until crisp, 10–12 minutes. When cool enough to handle, break each round into 4 or 5 pieces.

In a large bowl, whisk together the lemon juice, ¼ tsp salt, and ⅛ tsp pepper. Add the ¼ cup oil in a thin stream, whisking constantly until the dressing is smooth. Add the lettuce, turkey, cucumbers, tomatoes, parsley, and pita pieces to the bowl, toss to coat, and serve.

25

PERSIMMON & YELLOW APPLE SALAD

serves 4

2 Fuyu persimmons

2 yellow apples, such as Golden Delicious

2 tsp fresh lemon juice

2 Tbsp finely ground walnuts

1½ Tbsp sherry vinegar

Salt and freshly ground pepper

¼ tsp sugar

2 Tbsp walnut oil or extra-virgin olive oil

Snap up Fuyu persimmons when they make their brief appearance in late autumn. The jewel-like orange fruits are delicious eaten out of hand. Sliced and tossed with apples and a light vinaigrette, they become the basis for this distinctive seasonal salad.

Cut the persimmons in half lengthwise, scoop out any seeds with a spoon, and cut the halves into ½-inch (12-mm) cubes. Core the apples and cut into slices ¼ inch (6 mm) thick.

Combine the persimmon cubes and apple slices in a large bowl and drizzle with the lemon juice. Toss well, then set aside.

In another bowl, combine the ground walnuts, vinegar, ½ tsp salt, ¼ tsp pepper, and the sugar. Add the oil in a thin stream, whisking constantly until the dressing is well blended. Pour the dressing over the persimmons and apples, toss, and serve.

26

GREEN LENTIL SALAD WITH RED PEPPERS & SHALLOTS

serves 4

1 cup (7 oz/220 g) small green French (du Puy) lentils, picked over and rinsed

3 Tbsp extra-virgin olive oil

1½ cups (6 oz/185 g) thinly sliced shallots

½ cup (2½ oz/75 g) jarred roasted red peppers, cut into strips

3½ Tbsp sherry vinegar

3 Tbsp coarsely chopped fresh flat-leaf parsley leaves

Salt

Green French lentils have a nutty, peppery flavor and a firm texture that holds up well to cooking and marinating. This flavorful legume salad makes a wonderful accompaniment to a broiled salmon fillet or steak.

Bring a pot of water to a boil. Add the lentils, reduce the heat, and simmer until they are tender to the bite, 18–25 minutes.

While the lentils cook, heat 2 Tbsp of the oil in a large nonstick frying pan over medium-high heat. Add the shallots and cook until softened, 2–3 minutes. Reduce the heat and cook, stirring frequently, until the shallots are browned, 5–8 minutes. Set aside.

Drain the lentils and put them in a large bowl. Stir in the peppers, vinegar, parsley, ½ tsp salt, the shallots, and the remaining 1 Tbsp oil.

Serve warm or at room temperature, stirring well before serving.

27

CROTTIN SALAD WITH PEARS, FENNEL & CURRANTS

serves 4–6

2 fennel bulbs, trimmed, any fronds reserved

1 Tbsp sherry vinegar

1 aged Crottin de Chavignol or other small, round aged goat cheese, about 2 oz (60 g), grated

Salt and ground white pepper

3 Tbsp extra-virgin olive oil

1½ cups (1½ oz/45 g) mâche, field greens, or baby arugula

3 pears, halved, cored, and thinly sliced

⅓ cup (2 oz/60 g) dried currants

Using a mandoline or a very sharp knife, cut each fennel bulb lengthwise into paper-thin slices. Then, using a knife, cut each slice lengthwise into strips ¼ inch (6 mm) wide.

In a large bowl, using a fork, mix together the vinegar, 1 Tbsp of the cheese, ½ tsp salt, and ¼ tsp white pepper. Add the oil in a thin stream, whisking constantly until the dressing is well combined. Add the fennel and toss to coat well.

Divide the mâche among individual plates. Top with some of the dressed fennel, then add the sliced pears and a sprinkle of currants. Sprinkle with the remaining cheese and garnish with a few fennel fronds, if available, and serve.

Try different cheeses in place of the crottin: any aged goat's milk cheese will be delicious. Serve with a crisp, minerally white wine, such as Sancerre, Pouilly-fumé, or Sauvignon Blanc.

28

TURKEY & CELERY SALAD WITH DRIED CHERRIES

serves 4

1 small celery root, about ¾ lb (375 g)

4 celery ribs, finely chopped

2 cups (¾ lb/375 g) chopped cooked turkey or chicken, chilled

¼ cup (1½ oz/45 g) pine nuts

¼ cup (1½ oz/45 g) dried tart cherries, halved, or other dried fruits

2 Tbsp light sour cream

2 Tbsp mayonnaise

1 tsp Dijon mustard

1½ Tbsp champagne vinegar

Salt and freshly ground pepper

8–10 lettuce leaves

Peel the celery root and shred it on the large holes of a box grater. Place in a large bowl.

Add the celery, turkey, pine nuts, dried cherries, sour cream, mayonnaise, mustard, vinegar, and ½ tsp each salt and pepper to the celery root and mix well. Cover and refrigerate for at least 1 hour or up to 24 hours before serving.

Line a platter or individual plates with the lettuce leaves, mound the turkey mixture on top, and serve.

This salad presents an ideal opportunity to use up leftover roasted turkey. Dried cranberries could easily replace the cherries, if you'd like to savor the holiday flavors a little longer. This is an excellent choice for packed lunches, and equally appealing mounded on lettuce greens or tucked between toasted slices of wheat bread.

29

CRAB CAKE & BUTTER LETTUCE SALAD

serves 4

2 large eggs

1 Tbsp mayonnaise, plus ⅓ cup (3 fl oz/80 ml)

1 lb (500 g) cooked crabmeat, picked over for shell fragments and squeezed to remove excess water

½ cup (1 oz/30 g) fresh fine white bread crumbs

Salt and freshly ground pepper

4 green onions, including tender green parts, finely chopped

2 tsp Dijon mustard

Juice of 1 lemon

2 Tbsp unsalted butter

2 heads butter lettuce, torn into bite-sized pieces

In a bowl, whisk the eggs lightly. Add the 1 Tbsp mayonnaise, the crab, bread crumbs, 2 tsp salt, ½ tsp pepper, and green onions. Stir with a fork until well mixed. Divide the mixture into 8 equal portions and gently form each portion into a small patty.

In a small bowl, whisk together the ⅓ cup mayonnaise, the mustard, lemon juice, and ¼ tsp pepper until smooth.

In a large frying pan, melt the butter over medium-low heat. Working in batches if needed, add the crab cakes and cook without moving them until golden brown on the first side, about 4 minutes. Turn and cook until golden brown on the second side, 3–4 minutes. Arrange the lettuce on plates and place the crab cakes on top. Drizzle with the dressing and serve.

In many areas, crab season kicks off in late November. The milky-sweet meat is a treat when formed into little cakes and panfried. If you can resist eating them immediately on their own, a bed of tender butter lettuce and a drizzle of creamy lemon dressing are a match made in heaven.

30

BELGIAN ENDIVE, PEAR, FETA & WALNUT SALAD

serves 4

FOR THE VINAIGRETTE

2 Tbsp white wine vinegar or champagne vinegar

Salt and freshly ground pepper

6 Tbsp (3 fl oz/90 ml) walnut oil

4 heads Belgian endive

¼ cup (⅓ oz/10 g) chopped fresh chives

1 cup (4 oz/125 g) walnut halves

8 oz (250 g) feta cheese, crumbled

4 small pears such as Comice or Concorde

To make the vinaigrette, in a small bowl, whisk together the vinegar and salt and pepper to taste. Add the oil in a thin stream, whisking constantly until the dressing is smooth. Set aside.

Separate the leaves of the endive. In a large bowl, combine the endive leaves, chives, walnuts, and cheese.

Quarter the pears lengthwise and core. Cut each quarter lengthwise into thin slices.

Add the pear slices to the salad, drizzle with the vinaigrette, and toss gently to combine. Taste and adjust the seasonings. Divide the salad among individual plates and serve.

To ensure that this simple salad tastes superb, seek out barrel-cured Greek feta cheese and fresh walnuts from specialty shops, and try the farmers' market for the ripest local organic pears, such as Comice or Concorde. Serve with a buttery white Burgundy such as Meursault or an apple-scented Bourgogne blanc.

Fresh salads are a welcome addition to the holiday table, balancing out rich roasts and creamy gratins. Brisk winter days yield crisp greens, from unassuming iceberg and pleasantly bitter frisée to refreshing endive and vibrant radicchio. Add a touch of decadence here and there with special-occasion ingredients such as silky prosciutto, potent Stilton cheese, or elegant seafood, such as smoked trout, crab, oysters, and even lobster.

1
WARM SPINACH & BACON SALAD
page 274

2
WINTER PEAR SALAD WITH BLUE CHEESE, WALNUTS & POMEGRANATE
page 274

3
SMOKED CHICKEN SALAD WITH TARRAGON DRESSING
page 276

8
ARUGULA WITH ORANGES, MARCONA ALMONDS & PECORINO
page 279

9
SALAD OF WINTER GREENS & FRIED OYSTERS
page 280

10
CURRIED CELERY ROOT & APPLE SALAD WITH GOLDEN RAISINS
page 280

15
SALMON & FRISÉE SALAD WITH POACHED EGG
page 285

16
CHOPPED CELERY, PARSLEY & PROSCIUTTO SALAD
page 285

17
ICEBERG WEDGES WITH BLUE CHEESE DRESSING
page 286

22
SKIRT STEAK SALAD WITH CITRUS & ARUGULA
page 288

23
RADICCHIO, SPINACH & RED SORREL SALAD
page 291

24
CRAB, FENNEL & RADICCHIO SALAD WITH TRUFFLE OIL
page 291

29
LOBSTER SALAD WITH GRAPEFRUIT & AVOCADO
page 294

30
WARM PURPLE POTATO SALAD
page 294

31
ARUGULA SALAD WITH QUINCE PASTE & SERRANO HAM
page 294

4
ESCAROLE SALAD WITH SALT COD, ANCHOVIES & OLIVES
page 276

5
CRISPY CHICKEN & CABBAGE SALAD WITH PEANUT DRESSING
page 277

6
INSALATA VERDE
page 277

7
DAIKON RADISH SLAW WITH CRAB & BLACK SESAME SEEDS
page 279

11
RED CABBAGE SALAD WITH APPLES & DRIED FRUIT
page 282

12
WARM BORLOTTI BEAN & RADICCHIO SALAD
page 282

13
TUNA & WHITE BEAN SALAD
page 283

14
RED OAKLEAF LETTUCE & FRISÉE SALAD WITH PERSIMMON
page 283

18
EDAMAME & ORANGE SALAD
page 286

19
MIXED GREENS & FENNEL WITH RICOTTA SALATA
page 287

20
JICAMA, GRAPEFRUIT & AVOCADO SALAD
page 287

21
ASIAN NOODLE SALAD WITH SALMON & SNOW PEAS
page 288

25
BEET & STILTON SALAD WITH ORANGE VINAIGRETTE
page 292

26
GRAPEFRUIT, ENDIVE & POMEGRANATE SALAD
page 292

27
TACO SALAD IN TORTILLA BOWLS
page 293

28
SMOKED TROUT & CURLY ENDIVE SALAD
page 293

december

1

WARM SPINACH & BACON SALAD

serves 6–8

8 Tbsp (4 fl oz/125 ml) extra-virgin olive oil

1 lb (500 g) button mushrooms, halved

1½ Tbsp fresh lemon juice

2 cloves garlic, thinly sliced

1 tsp minced fresh thyme

¼ tsp red pepper flakes

Salt and freshly ground black pepper

3 large eggs

10 oz (315 g) baby spinach

8 slices thick-cut applewood-smoked bacon, chopped

3 Tbsp balsamic vinegar

1 Tbsp whole-grain mustard

1 small red onion, thinly sliced

1½ cups (9 oz/280 g) cherry tomatoes, halved

Smoky, salty bacon makes almost everything taste better, and this hearty salad is no exception. It may even make kids happily eat their greens. Bacon has lots of presence here, so look for good-quality, thick-cut bacon for the tastiest results. And try not to eat all the crisp bits while you assemble the salads. Chopped hard-cooked egg is the classic topping, but you can top each serving with a poached egg if you prefer.

In a frying pan over medium-high heat, warm 2 Tbsp of the oil. Add the mushrooms and sauté until they release their juices and brown lightly, 5–6 minutes. Transfer to a bowl. Add 4 Tbsp (2 fl oz/60 ml) of the oil, the lemon juice, garlic, thyme, red pepper flakes, and salt and pepper to taste, and toss to coat. Let marinate for at least 1 hour.

To hard-cook the eggs, place them in a saucepan just large enough to hold them. Add cold water to cover by 1 inch (2.5 cm) and bring just to a boil over high heat. Remove the pan from the heat and cover. Let stand for 15 minutes. Have ready a bowl of ice water. Drain the eggs, then transfer to the ice water and let cool. Peel and coarsely chop the eggs.

Put the spinach in a large bowl. In a large frying pan over medium heat, fry the bacon, stirring occasionally, until crisp and browned, about 7 minutes. Transfer to paper towels to drain. Pour off all but 2 Tbsp of the fat in the pan. Off the heat, whisk the vinegar and mustard into the fat in the pan, then whisk in the remaining 2 Tbsp oil. Season with salt and pepper, drizzle over the spinach, and toss to coat well.

Divide among individual plates, top with the onion, tomatoes, marinated mushrooms, chopped eggs, and bacon, and serve.

2

WINTER PEAR SALAD WITH BLUE CHEESE, WALNUTS & POMEGRANATE

serves 4

⅓ cup (1½ oz/45 g) walnut pieces

FOR THE CIDER DRESSING

3 Tbsp cider vinegar

1 Tbsp honey

1 tsp Dijon mustard

Salt and freshly ground pepper

2 Tbsp extra-virgin olive oil

8 oz (250 g) mixed baby greens

2 pears such as Bartlett, cored and sliced

½ cup (2 oz/60 g) pomegranate seeds

1 oz (30 g) blue cheese, crumbled

Combining mixed baby greens with some favorite elements of a winter cheese plate, this succulent salad makes a stunning starter. The juicy pomegranate seeds and slightly tart cider dressing brighten toasted walnuts, thin slices of grainy pear, and a potent blue cheese. Any variety of blue works here, from mild Gorgonzola to more powerful Stilton and Roquefort, all perfect matches for pear.

In a dry frying pan, toast the walnut pieces over medium-low heat, stirring, until fragrant and starting to brown, about 5 minutes. Pour onto a plate to cool, then coarsely chop and set aside.

To make the dressing, in a large bowl, whisk together the vinegar, honey, mustard, ¼ tsp salt, and ⅛ tsp pepper. Add the oil in a thin stream, whisking constantly until the dressing is smooth.

Add the greens, pears, pomegranate seeds, and walnuts to the bowl of dressing and mix gently to coat. Divide the salad among individual plates, garnish each with some cheese crumbles, and serve.

7

DAIKON RADISH SLAW WITH CRAB & BLACK SESAME SEEDS

serves 4

1 daikon radish, about 2 lb (1 kg), peeled and trimmed

2 Tbsp rice vinegar

1 tsp toasted sesame oil

½ lb (250 g) cooked crabmeat, picked over for shell fragments

2 tsp black sesame seeds

½ cup (½ oz/15 g) radish sprouts

This beautiful salad is full of delicate Asian flavors. Daikon radish and sprouts are refreshing and mild, a cool foil to the rich crabmeat. Serve as a starter to accompany grilled fish or meat or as a light main course.

Using a mandoline, slice the radish into threads using the finest teeth. Alternatively, cut the radish into 3-inch (7.5-cm) pieces and julienne the pieces.

In a bowl, whisk together the vinegar and oil. Add the radish pieces and turn to coat well. Add the crabmeat and turn again. Divide the slaw among bowls or plates, sprinkle with the sesame seeds, garnish with the radish sprouts, and serve.

8

ARUGULA WITH ORANGES, MARCONA ALMONDS & PECORINO

serves 4–6

4 oranges, peeled and segmented with a knife, juices caught and reserved

½ tsp honey

Salt and freshly ground pepper

2 Tbsp extra-virgin olive oil

¾ cup (3 oz/90 g) Marcona almonds, coarsely chopped

6 cups (6 oz/185 g) baby arugula leaves

Pecorino romano cheese for shaving

Delectable Spanish Marcona almonds are lighter in color and richer in taste than other types of almonds. They add elegance and depth to this exquisite salad of sweet oranges and salty-tangy cheese. Grassy extra-virgin olive oil contributes a lusciousness that rounds out the contrasting tastes.

After segmenting the oranges, measure out 3 Tbsp of the juice. In a small bowl, whisk the orange juice with the honey, ⅛ tsp salt, and a few grindings of pepper. Add the oil in a thin stream, whisking constantly until the dressing is smooth. Taste and adjust the seasonings.

In a small bowl, stir together the almonds and ¼ tsp salt. Put the arugula in a large bowl. Whisk the dressing to recombine, then drizzle it over the arugula and toss well. Taste and adjust the seasonings. Divide the dressed arugula among individual plates, mounding it in the center. Top each mound with the orange segments, and sprinkle the oranges very lightly with salt. Scatter the almonds over the salads. Using a vegetable peeler, shave the cheese over the salads and serve.

9

SALAD OF WINTER GREENS & FRIED OYSTERS

serves 6

Here, snipped chives suffuse a tangy sour cream dressing with their sublte, onionlike essence. The dressing's creamy coolness is the perfect balance to the spicy cornmeal that coats the briny fried oysters. A bed of romaine and radicchio offers crunch and color.

1 cup (5 oz/155 g) all-purpose flour

2 large eggs

1½ cups (7½ oz/235 g) yellow cornmeal

¼ tsp cayenne pepper

Salt and freshly ground black pepper

24 shucked oysters, drained and picked over for shell pieces

FOR THE SOUR CREAM–CHIVE DRESSING

½ cup (4 oz/125 g) sour cream

¼ cup (2 fl oz/60 ml) buttermilk

¼ cup (⅓ oz/10 g) minced fresh chives

1½ tsp fresh lemon juice

½ tsp Dijon mustard

½ tsp sugar

¼ cup (2 fl oz/60 ml) grapeseed oil

1 small head romaine lettuce, thinly sliced

1 small head radicchio, thinly sliced

Put the flour in a shallow bowl. In a second shallow bowl, whisk the eggs until blended. In a third shallow bowl, stir together the cornmeal, cayenne, ½ tsp salt, and ¼ tsp pepper. One at a time, dip the oysters first in the flour, coating evenly and shaking off the excess, then in the eggs, allowing the excess to drip off, and finally in the seasoned cornmeal, coating evenly and shaking off the excess. Place the coated oysters on a large plate and refrigerate for 30 minutes.

Meanwhile, to make the dressing, in a food processor or blender, combine the sour cream, buttermilk, chives, lemon juice, mustard, sugar, a scant ½ tsp salt, and several grindings of pepper. Process until well blended. Taste and adjust the seasonings, and set aside.

Remove the coated oysters from the refrigerator and let stand at room temperature for 20 minutes. In a large frying pan, preferably nonstick, warm the oil over medium-high heat until hot but not smoking. Working in batches to avoid crowding, add the oysters to the pan and cook, turning once, until golden brown and slightly crisp, about 2 minutes on each side. Using a slotted spoon, transfer ⇥

to paper towels to drain. When all of the oysters are cooked, sprinkle them lightly with salt and tent loosely with foil to keep warm.

In a large bowl, toss together the romaine, radicchio, ¼ tsp salt, and several grindings of pepper. Divide the greens among individual plates. Divide the fried oysters among the salads, drizzle each serving with about 2 Tbsp dressing, and serve.

10

CURRIED CELERY ROOT & APPLE SALAD WITH GOLDEN RAISINS

serves 6

The spiciness and golden hue of curry powder enlivens this simple slaw-like salad while adding depth of flavor. Curry both accentuates the earthy taste of the celery root and complements the sweetness of the apples and raisins.

6 Tbsp (2 oz/60 g) slivered blanched almonds

1 celery root (about ¾ lb/375 g)

2 Granny Smith apples

2 tsp fresh lemon juice

Salt and freshly ground pepper

½ cup (4 fl oz/125 ml) plus 1½ Tbsp mayonnaise

1½ tsp honey

1⅛ tsp curry powder

6 Tbsp (2 oz/60 g) golden raisins

2 Tbsp coarsely chopped fresh flat-leaf parsley

In a dry frying pan, toast the almonds over medium-low heat, stirring, until fragrant and lightly golden, 3–4 minutes. Pour onto a plate and let cool.

Peel the celery root and shred on the large holes of a box grater.

Halve and core the apples, then cut them into thin strips. Sprinkle with ½ tsp of the lemon juice to prevent them from discoloring.

Sprinkle the almonds with a pinch of salt and stir. In a large bowl, whisk together the mayonnaise, the remaining 1½ tsp lemon juice, the honey, the curry powder, a scant ½ tsp salt, and ¼ tsp pepper. Stir in the almonds, celery root, apples, raisins, and parsley until combined. Taste and adjust the seasonings and serve.

9

DECEMBER

15

SALMON & FRISÉE SALAD WITH POACHED EGG

serves 4

To make croutons, preheat the oven to 350°F (180°C). Cut country-style bread into 1-inch (2.5-cm) cubes. Put them on a baking sheet just large enough to hold the cubes in a single layer, drizzle with 2 Tbsp oil, and toss several times to coat. Sprinkle with ½ tsp salt. Bake, turning several times, until golden, 10–15 minutes.

FOR THE WHITE WINE VINAIGRETTE

1 Tbsp white wine vinegar

1 Tbsp whole-grain mustard

¼ cup (2 fl oz/60 ml) extra-virgin olive oil

Salt and freshly ground pepper

1 Tbsp distilled white vinegar

1 head frisée

Croutons (left)

8 oz (250 g) thinly sliced smoked salmon, torn into 1-inch (2.5-cm) strips

4 large eggs

¼ cup (⅓ oz/10 g) fresh chervil leaves

1 Tbsp minced fresh chives

To make the vinaigrette, in a large bowl, combine the white wine vinegar and the mustard. Add the oil in a thin stream, whisking constantly until the dressing is smooth. Season with salt and pepper to taste, then set aside.

Bring a sauté pan halfway full of water to a simmer, and add the distilled vinegar.

Meanwhile, tear the frisée leaves into bite-sized pieces and toss with the vinaigrette. Add the croutons and smoked salmon. Divide the salad among individual plates.

Working quickly, crack the eggs one at a time into a small bowl and slide them into the simmering water. Poach until the whites are just set and the yolks still soft, 3–4 minutes. Remove each with a slotted spoon, blot the underside with a paper towel, and slide onto a salad. Garnish with the chervil and chives, season with salt and pepper, and serve.

16

CHOPPED CELERY, PARSLEY & PROSCIUTTO SALAD

serves 6

1 fennel bulb, trimmed and halved lengthwise

6 celery ribs, thinly sliced on the diagonal

4 green onions, including tender green parts, thinly sliced on the diagonal

1 cup (1 oz/30 g) fresh flat-leaf parsley leaves

¼ cup (⅓ oz/10 g) small fresh mint leaves

Salt and freshly ground pepper

3 Tbsp extra-virgin olive oil

2 Tbsp fresh lemon juice, or as needed

6 thin slices prosciutto

Pecorino romano cheese for shaving

Groceries stock celery year-round, but its natural peak season is in fact winter. The humble vegetable stars in this salad, which takes advantage of both the stalks and tender green leaves. Salty prosciutto and pecorino add protein and punch, but you can substitute any ham or hard grating cheese you like.

Using a mandoline or a very sharp knife, cut the fennel bulb halves crosswise into thin slices.

Put the celery, fennel, green onions, parsley, and mint in a bowl and season with salt and pepper. Drizzle with the oil and the 2 Tbsp lemon juice and toss gently. Taste and season with salt and more lemon juice, if desired. Arrange the prosciutto on a serving platter and top with the fennel mixture. Using a vegetable peeler, shave the cheese over the salad and serve.

17

ICEBERG WEDGES WITH BLUE CHEESE DRESSING

serves 6

½ cup (4 fl oz/125 ml) mayonnaise

½ cup (4 oz/125 g) sour cream

Juice of 1 lemon

Dash of Tabasco sauce

Salt and freshly ground pepper

6 oz (185 g) blue cheese, crumbled (about 1½ cups)

3 Tbsp minced fresh chives, plus slivers of chive for garnish

1 head iceberg lettuce, chilled

A wedge of iceberg lettuce topped with a thick, luscious blue cheese dressing is an all-time classic. If available, add a sprinkling of halved cherry or grape tomatoes. This favorite makes a fitting first course for a New York–style steak dinner.

In a small bowl, whisk together the mayonnaise, sour cream, lemon juice, Tabasco, ¼ tsp salt, and ¼ tsp pepper. Stir in the cheese and 3 Tbsp chives. Taste and adjust the seasonings.

Using a small, sharp knife, core the iceberg lettuce. Remove and discard the outer leaves if they are limp or blemished. Cut the head into 6 uniform wedges.

Place each wedge on an individual plate. Spoon a generous amount of the dressing over each wedge. (You may not need all of the dressing.) Garnish with the chive slivers and serve.

18

EDAMAME & ORANGE SALAD

serves 4

Salt

1 package (10–12 oz/315–375 g) frozen shelled edamame

2 navel oranges, peeled and segmented with a knife, juices caught and reserved

½ cup (2½ oz/75 g) finely chopped red onion

¼ cup (2½ oz/75 g) finely chopped red bell pepper

FOR THE DRESSING

3 Tbsp rice vinegar

1 tsp soy sauce

½ tsp grated orange zest

½ tsp peeled and grated fresh ginger

2 Tbsp peanut oil

You can purchase edamame or soybeans, in their fuzzy pods, fresh or frozen, cooked or uncooked. They are also available shelled, most convenient for this salad. In addition to being tasty, the beans are an excellent source of protein, calcium, iron, and many B vitamins.

Bring a saucepan three-fourths full of salted water to a boil. Add the edamame and cook according to the package directions. Drain well and set aside.

Cut each orange segment crosswise into 3 or 4 pieces. In a serving bowl, combine the orange slices, edamame, onion, and bell pepper.

To make the dressing, in a small bowl, whisk together the reserved orange juice, rice vinegar, soy sauce, orange zest, and ginger. Add the oil in a thin stream, whisking constantly until the dressing is smooth.

Pour the dressing over the salad, stir gently to mix, and serve.

19

MIXED GREENS & FENNEL WITH RICOTTA SALATA

serves 8

1 Tbsp fresh lemon juice

Salt and freshly ground pepper

3 Tbsp extra-virgin olive oil

1 head escarole

1 head green or red oakleaf lettuce

1 fennel bulb, trimmed

4 oz (125 g) ricotta salata cheese

The addition of fennel gives this easy salad an accent of anise, while the light and lemony dressing highlights the individual ingredients. You can substitute feta, goat cheese, or pecorino for the ricotta salata.

In a large serving bowl, whisk together the lemon juice and ½ tsp each salt and pepper. Add the oil in a thin stream, whisking constantly until the dressing is smooth.

Separate the escarole leaves and select the yellow innermost leaves, tearing them into bite-sized pieces; you should have about 3 cups (4½ oz/140 g). Separate the oakleaf lettuce leaves, choosing as many of the small leaves as possible to make 3 cups (3 oz/90 g). If using some of the larger leaves, tear them into bite-sized pieces. Reserve the remaining escarole and lettuce leaves for another use.

Cut the fennel bulb in half lengthwise and core. Using a mandoline or a very sharp knife, cut the bulb halves crosswise into slices about ⅛ inch (3 mm) thick. Cut the slices lengthwise into pieces ½ inch (12 mm) wide.

Add the fennel slices, escarole, and oakleaf lettuce to the bowl holding the dressing and toss to coat evenly. Crumble the cheese on top, toss again, and serve.

20

JICAMA, GRAPEFRUIT & AVOCADO SALAD

serves 4–6

2 small jicamas (about 1 lb/500 g total weight)

1 Ruby grapefruit, peeled and segmented with a knife, juices caught and reserved

1 large avocado, pitted, peeled, and cubed

FOR THE CITRUSY DRESSING

2 Tbsp fresh lime juice

1 Tbsp fresh orange juice

2 tsp honey

Pinch cayenne pepper

Salt

¼ cup (⅓ oz/10 g) fresh cilantro leaves

In this refreshing salad, the mix of jicama and grapefruit is thirst-quenching and light, while the avocado adds a silky creaminess. The simple dressing of citrus juice and a pinch of cayenne elevates the flavors. Party perfect, this salad is excellent served with fish or pork shoulder.

Cut each jicama in half and peel it. Place the jicama halves cut side down on a cutting board and cut lengthwise into ¼-inch (6-mm) slices. Stack the slices in piles of 3 or 4 and cut each stack in half crosswise at ¼-inch intervals to create matchsticks. If some of the matchsticks seem too long, cut them in half. Put the jicama in a serving bowl. Add the grapefruit and avocado.

To make the dressing, in a small bowl, stir together 2 Tbsp of the reserved grapefruit juice, the lime juice, orange juice, honey, cayenne, and salt to taste. Mix well to dissolve the honey completely. Pour about half of the dressing over the salad and toss gently. Taste and add more dressing or adjust the seasoning with more salt, if needed. Garnish with the cilantro and serve.

21

ASIAN NOODLE SALAD WITH SALMON & SNOW PEAS

serves 4–6

Here, the cooling mint and citrus enchance the noodles and salmon. If Chinese egg noodles are unavailable, you can substitute linguine. This salad can be made a day ahead, covered, and refrigerated until ready to serve.

2 carrots, peeled and julienned

½ lb (250 g) snow peas, trimmed and julienned

¾ lb (375 g) salmon fillet, pin bones removed

1 lb (500 g) Chinese egg noodles

1 Tbsp peanut oil

FOR THE DRESSING

¼ cup (2 fl oz/60 ml) rice vinegar

1 Tbsp fresh lime juice

1 Tbsp honey

2 cloves garlic, minced

1½ tsp peeled and grated fresh ginger

2 Tbsp minced fresh basil, plus sprigs for garnish

2 Tbsp minced fresh mint, plus sprigs for garnish

Salt and freshly ground pepper

¼ cup (2 fl oz/60 ml) peanut oil

2 tsp toasted sesame oil

Preheat the oven to 400°F (200°C). Bring a saucepan two-thirds full of water to a boil and have ready a bowl of ice water. Add the carrots and cook for 30 seconds. Scoop out and immerse them in the ice water. Repeat with the snow peas, cooking them for 1 minute. Set aside.

Put the salmon in a small roasting pan and bake until opaque throughout, 12 minutes. Let cool, then flake into bite-sized pieces.

Bring a large pot of water to a boil. Add the noodles, stir, and cook until barely tender and still firm, about 7 minutes or according to package directions. Drain and rinse under cold running water until cooled. Drain well, put in a large bowl, and toss with the 1 Tbsp peanut oil.

To make the dressing, in a small bowl, whisk together the vinegar, lime juice, honey, garlic, ginger, minced basil and mint, and salt and pepper to taste. Add the ¼ cup peanut oil and the sesame oil in a thin stream, whisking constantly until the dressing is smooth. ⤐

Pour the dressing over the noodles and toss to coat. Add the carrots and snow peas and toss again. Carefully fold in the salmon, keeping the pieces intact. Taste and adjust the seasonings. Garnish with the herb sprigs. Cover and refrigerate until ready to serve.

22

SKIRT STEAK SALAD WITH CITRUS & ARUGULA

serves 4

Marinated skirt steak is a delicious partner for winter citrus. If it's too cold to grill outside, cook the steak in a grill pan over high heat for 3–4 minutes per side, or in a frying pan for the same amount of time. For a spicier dressing, add some minced jalapeño chile to the lime juice and oil mixture before tossing with the arugula, orange, and radishes.

¼ cup (2 fl oz/60 ml) soy sauce

¼ cup (2 fl oz/60 ml) fresh orange juice

4 Tbsp (2 fl oz/60 ml) fresh lime juice

1 Tbsp peeled and minced fresh ginger

2 cloves garlic, minced

½ tsp Asian red chile paste

1½ lb (750 g) skirt steak, about ½ inch (12 mm) thick, cut into 2 or 3 pieces for ease of handling

1½ Tbsp extra-virgin olive oil

8 oz (250 g) wild or baby arugula leaves

1 navel orange, peeled with a knife and sliced crosswise

5 radishes, trimmed and sliced if desired

5 kumquats, sliced

Combine the soy sauce, orange juice, 1 Tbsp of the lime juice, the ginger, garlic, and chile paste in a zippered plastic bag. Add the steak, shake to mix the marinade, and refrigerate for 8–24 hours.

Prepare a charcoal or gas grill for direct-heat cooking over high heat. Oil the grill rack. Remove the steak from the bag and discard the marinade. Grill the steak, turning once, for 4–6 minutes total for medium-rare. Transfer to a platter and let stand for 10 minutes.

In a large bowl, whisk together the remaining 3 Tbsp lime juice and the oil. Add the arugula, orange, radishes, and kumquats and mix well. Mound on a platter. Cut the steak across the grain into slices ¼ inch (6 mm) thick, arrange over the salad, and serve.

23

This red-and-green medley is a feast for the eyes as well as the palate. Blood oranges impart their deep color to the vinaigrette, and small bites of the orange segments tucked among the leaves are both gorgeous and delicious.

RADICCHIO, SPINACH & RED SORREL SALAD

serves 4–6

FOR THE BLOOD-ORANGE VINAIGRETTE

1 blood orange, peeled and segmented with a knife

¼ cup (2 fl oz/60 ml) red wine vinegar

½ cup (4 fl oz/125 ml) extra-virgin olive oil

Salt and freshly ground pepper

1 head radicchio, leaves torn

4 cups (4 oz/125 g) baby spinach leaves

1 cup (1 oz/30 g) red sorrel leaves or additional baby spinach leaves

To make the vinaigrette, using a fork, break up the blood orange segments into bite-sized pieces. Add the vinegar and then the oil in a thin stream, whisking constantly until the vinaigrette is smooth. Season to taste with salt and pepper and set aside.

Combine the radicchio, spinach, and sorrel in a serving bowl and toss with the vinaigrette. Season to taste with salt and pepper and serve.

24

This show-stopping salad is worthy of a celebratory eve. Fresh Dungeness crab needs no embellishment, but decadent truffle oil sends it over the top. Mound the crab salad on individual radicchio leaves, which are perfect to pass with cocktails.

CRAB, FENNEL & RADICCHIO SALAD WITH TRUFFLE OIL

serves 10–12

1 fennel bulb, trimmed and coarsely chopped

1 lb (500 g) cooked Dungeness or other crabmeat, picked over for shell fragments

2 shallots, minced

2 celery ribs, finely chopped

2 Tbsp minced fresh chives

2 Tbsp minced fresh flat-leaf parsley

3 Tbsp white or black truffle oil

1½ Tbsp fresh lemon juice

1 Tbsp mayonnaise

Salt and freshly ground pepper

3 large or 4 medium heads radicchio

In a bowl, combine the fennel, crabmeat, shallots, celery, chives, and parsley. Add the truffle oil, lemon juice, mayonnaise, ½ tsp salt, and a few grindings of pepper. Gently mix with a fork until evenly blended; do not break up the lumps of crabmeat. Taste and adjust the seasonings.

Remove and discard any blemished leaves from each head of radicchio. Separate the largest outer leaves, keeping them as intact as possible. You should have about 40 cupped leaves (reserve the inner leaves for another use). Arrange on serving platters.

Mound about 2 Tbsp of the crab salad in each radicchio cup. Serve at once, or refrigerate for up to 1 hour and then let stand at room temperature for 10 minutes before serving.

25

BEET & STILTON SALAD WITH ORANGE VINAIGRETTE

serves 4

4 beets (about 1¼ lb/625 g total weight), trimmed

FOR THE ORANGE VINAIGRETTE

3 Tbsp fresh orange juice

1 Tbsp red wine vinegar

1 Tbsp minced fresh dill

1 tsp grated orange zest

¼ tsp minced garlic

Salt and freshly ground pepper

2 Tbsp extra-virgin olive oil

3 green onions, including tender green parts, thinly sliced on the diagonal

1 Tbsp finely slivered orange zest

10 oz (315 g) mixed salad greens

½ cup (2½ oz/75 g) thinly sliced English cucumber

3 oz (90 g) Stilton cheese, crumbled

Fresh dill sprigs for garnish

Roasted beets have a deep, rich, and comforting taste. Select a mix of red, orange and golden beets for a festive, jewel-toned salad. You can cook them a day or two ahead and refrigerate, still wrapped in foil, until you are ready to peel and slice them for this salad. Stilton, a sharply flavored English blue cheese, balances the natural sweetness of the beets, but other blue-veined cheeses, such as Gorgonzola, Roquefort, or Danish blue, can be substituted.

Preheat the oven to 400°F (200°C). Wrap the beets in foil and roast on a baking sheet until easily pierced with the tip of a knife, about 1 hour. Remove from the oven and let cool in the foil. Unwrap and peel. Cut each beet crosswise into 4 or 5 slices and put in a bowl.

To make the orange vinaigrette, in a small bowl, whisk together the orange juice, vinegar, minced dill, grated orange zest, garlic, ½ tsp salt, and a grinding of pepper. Add the oil in a thin stream, whisking constantly until the dressing is smooth.

Pour all but 2 Tbsp of the vinaigrette over the beets. Add half of the green onions and half of the slivered orange zest; stir gently just to blend. In a separate bowl, combine the salad greens and the reserved 2 Tbsp vinaigrette and toss to coat the greens.

Divide the salad greens among individual plates. Top with the beets and tuck the cucumber slices in among the beets. Drizzle any vinaigrette remaining in the bowl over the beets. Sprinkle the salad with the remaining green onions and slivered orange zest. Top with the cheese, garnish with the dill sprigs, and serve.

26

GRAPEFRUIT, ENDIVE & POMEGRANATE SALAD

serves 10–12

3 heads butter or Bibb lettuce, leaves separated and torn into large pieces

2 bunches watercress, tough stems removed

3 heads Belgian endive, cored and separated into leaves

3 pink grapefruits, peeled and segmented with a knife, juices caught and reserved

1 Tbsp fresh orange juice

⅛ tsp lemon or orange oil

2 Tbsp balsamic vinegar

3 Tbsp minced shallots

6 Tbsp (3 fl oz/90 ml) extra-virgin olive oil

Salt and freshly ground pepper

½ cup (2 oz/60 g) pomegranate seeds

Grapefruit and pomegranate rise to the occasion for festive winter gatherings. This recipe aims to serve a crowd, and your guests may be grateful for a light starter, free of cheese or nuts, to balance out the often decadently rich holiday table.

In a large serving bowl, toss together the lettuce, watercress, and endive. Add the grapefruit segments to the bowl, scattering them over the greens.

To make the dressing, in a food processor or blender, combine 2 Tbsp of the reserved grapefruit juice, the orange juice, citrus oil, vinegar, shallots, olive oil, and ¼ tsp each salt and pepper. Process until smooth, then taste and adjust the seasonings.

Pour the dressing over the salad. Add the pomegranate seeds, toss, and serve.

27
DECEMBER

There's nothing too mysterious about taco seasoning mix—make some at home, store it in an airtight container, and you can make this fun and pleasing salad anytime. Blend 2 Tbsp chili powder, 1½ tsp ground cumin, 1 tsp salt, 1 tsp black pepper, ½ tsp paprika, and ¼ tsp each onion powder, garlic powder, dried oregano, and red pepper flakes. Adjust the quantities to taste and desired spiciness.

TACO SALAD IN TORTILLA BOWLS
serves 4

FOR THE TORTILLA BOWLS
Four 8-inch (20-cm) flour tortillas

Corn oil

Salt

FOR THE DRESSING
1 Tbsp mild tomato salsa

1 Tbsp red wine vinegar

2 tsp fresh lime juice

4–6 Tbsp (2–3 fl oz/60–90 ml) extra-virgin olive oil

1 lb (500 g) ground beef

¼ cup (1 oz/30 g) taco seasoning mix (about ½ package; see note)

1 cup (7 oz/220 g) canned black or pinto beans, drained and rinsed

½ head iceberg lettuce

3 plum tomatoes, chopped

1 avocado, pitted, peeled, and chopped

1½ cups (6 oz/185 g) shredded Cheddar cheese

Tortilla chips for serving (optional)

To make the tortilla bowls, preheat the oven to 350°F (180°C). Choose 4 shallow ovenproof bowls 4–6 inches (10–15 cm) in diameter. Using a pastry brush, brush corn oil over both sides of each tortilla and sprinkle with salt. Line the bowls with the tortillas to make bowl shapes. Bake the tortillas in the bowls until browned and crisp, about 12 minutes. Remove the tortillas from the oven, let cool, then remove them from the bowls and place each on a plate.

To make the dressing, in a small jar with a tight-fitting lid, mix the salsa, vinegar, and lime juice. Add 4 Tbsp (2 fl oz/60 ml) of the oil, cover, and shake until mixed. Taste and add more oil if needed. Set the dressing aside.

Place a large frying pan over medium heat. Add the ground beef and cook, using a wooden spoon to break it up into small pieces, until evenly cooked, 8–10 minutes. Add the seasoning mix and ⅔ cup (5 fl oz/160 ml) water to the pan. Bring to a boil over high heat. Reduce the heat to low and simmer, stirring often, until the liquid is absorbed, about 12 minutes. »

While the meat is cooking, put the beans in a saucepan and place over medium-low heat. Stir occasionally until warm. Remove from the heat and cover to keep warm.

Cut the lettuce into slices and separate the pieces. Divide the lettuce among the tortilla bowls, then top each with equal portions of the tomatoes, beans, and avocado.

When the meat is done, use a slotted spoon to divide it among the salads, then sprinkle the cheese on top. Spoon some of the dressing over each salad, and serve, topped with tortilla chips if desired.

28
DECEMBER

Smoked trout, readily available in most supermarkets, needs only a little endive and a light dressing to bring out its subtle flavor. Serve this salad as a starter, or pair with fresh bread and a chocolate dessert for a light meal. For a crunchier salad, substitute 6 heads Belgian endive, torn into bite-sized pieces, for the curly endive.

SMOKED TROUT & CURLY ENDIVE SALAD
serves 8

FOR THE DRESSING
1 Tbsp champagne vinegar

2 tsp grated lemon zest

Salt and freshly ground pepper

3 Tbsp extra-virgin olive oil

2 heads curly endive

1 cup (1 oz/30 g) fresh flat-leaf parsley leaves

1 lb (500 g) smoked trout fillets

8 lemon slices for garnish

To make the dressing, in a large bowl, whisk together the vinegar, zest, ½ tsp salt, and ½ tsp pepper. Add the oil in a thin stream, whisking constantly until the dressing is smooth.

Separate the curly endive leaves and select the yellow and pale green inner leaves. Tear the leaves into bite-sized pieces. Put the endive and the parsley leaves in the bowl with the vinaigrette and toss to coat.

Using two forks, flake the trout into bite-sized pieces and add to the bowl. Toss gently once or twice to mix. Mound the salad onto individual plates, garnish each with a lemon slice, and serve.

29

LOBSTER SALAD WITH GRAPEFRUIT & AVOCADO

serves 6–8

1 grapefruit, peeled and segmented with a knife, juices caught and reserved

2½ Tbsp champagne vinegar

Salt and freshly ground pepper

2 tsp minced shallot

5 tsp minced fresh chives

3½ Tbsp extra-virgin olive oil

1½ lb (750 g) cooked lobster meat, picked over for shell fragments

2–2½ cups (2–3 oz/60–90 g) mixed baby salad greens

1 avocado, pitted, peeled, and sliced

The grapefruit juice in this vinaigrette, along with the grapefruit sections in the salad, accentuate the sweetness of succulent lobster. Smooth, creamy avocado adds a hint of richness. If using frozen lobster tails, allow enough time to thaw them overnight in the refrigerator.

In a large bowl, whisk together 2 tsp of the reserved grapefruit juice, 2 Tbsp of the vinegar, ½ tsp each salt and pepper, the shallot, and 3 tsp of the chives. Add 2 Tbsp of the oil in a thin stream, whisking constantly until the dressing is smooth. Add the lobster meat and turn gently until well coated.

Divide the greens among individual plates or shallow bowls. Arrange the grapefruit segments on the greens. Top with the lobster mixture and then with the avocado. Add the remaining 1½ Tbsp oil and remaining ½ Tbsp vinegar to the bowl, mix well, and drizzle over the salads. Garnish with the remaining 2 tsp chives and serve.

30

WARM PURPLE POTATO SALAD

serves 4

2½ lb (1.25 kg) small purple potatoes

Salt and freshly ground pepper

3 Tbsp extra-virgin olive oil

2 tsp red wine vinegar

¼ cup (1 oz/30 g) finely chopped celery

¼ cup (1 oz/30 g) finely chopped red onion

¼ cup (⅓ oz/10 g) minced fresh flat-leaf parsley

Freshly boiled potatoes, still warm and steaming, soak up vinaigrettes. It's an easy method for imparting flavor to this favorite comfort salad. Purple potatoes are eye-catching, but you could just as easily use other types of small potatoes.

Put the potatoes in a large pot and add cold water to cover by 3 inches (7.5 cm) and 1 tsp salt. Bring to a boil, then reduce the heat to medium-low and cover. Simmer until tender, about 15 minutes. Drain and let cool to the touch. Peel and carefully cut into slices ¼ inch (6 mm) thick.

Combine the potato slices, oil, and vinegar in a shallow bowl and turn gently to coat. Add the celery, red onion, parsley, ½ tsp salt, and ½ tsp pepper. Gently stir until well mixed. Cover and let stand at room temperature for 20 minutes before serving.

31

ARUGULA SALAD WITH QUINCE PASTE & SERRANO HAM

serves 6

1 cup (8 oz/250 g) quince paste

1 tsp fresh lemon juice

Salt and freshly ground pepper

1½ Tbsp extra-virgin olive oil

5 oz (155 g) arugula leaves, stemmed

9 oz (280 g) thinly sliced serrano ham or prosciutto

Often called by its Spanish name, membrillo, quince paste is a delicious accompaniment for nuts and cheeses. In this salad, it balances the salty ham and peppery arugula.

Dip a sharp knife into very hot water and cut the quince paste into slices ¼ inch (6 mm) thick. Trim the slices into triangles or diamonds, if desired. Set the slices aside.

In a large bowl, whisk together the lemon juice and salt and pepper to taste. Add the oil in a thin stream, whisking constantly until the dressing is smooth. Add the arugula and toss thoroughly. Arrange the prosciutto on 6 individual plates. Divide the arugula salad among the plates, scatter with the quince paste triangles, and serve.

A

Apples
   Apple-Fennel Slaw, 245
   Fall Salad of Apples & Walnuts with Stilton Cheese, 205
   Green Apple & Celery Salad, 78
   Persimmon & Yellow Apple Salad, 268
   Smoked Trout & Apple Salad with Polenta Croutons, 226
   Spiced Apple, Cranberry & Pecan Salad, 267
   Waldorf Salad, 47
   Winter Chicory & Apple Salad with Pecans, 29
Artichokes
   Artichoke & White Bean Salad, 100
   Baby Artichoke, Parmesan & Arugula Salad, 118
   Farro Salad with Artichoke Hearts, 237
   Orzo Salad with Artichokes, Pine Nuts & Golden Raisins, 124
   Potato Salad with Artichokes, Feta Cheese & Olive Relish, 112
   Shaved Artichoke & Blue Cheese Salad, 58
   Warm Spinach Salad with Artichokes & Gruyère, 84
Asparagus
   Asparagus Salad with Lemon & Shaved Parmesan, 96
   Asparagus & Smoked Salmon Salad with Tarragon Cream, 72
   Grilled Asparagus & Prosciutto Salad, 125
   Pasta Salad with Spring Asparagus & Snap Peas, 91
   Pea & Asparagus Salad with Meyer Lemon Dressing, 106
   Roasted Asparagus Salad, 70
Avocados
   Chicken, Avocado & Spinach Salad, 166
   Grilled Shrimp Salad with Avocado & Chipotle Dressing, 171
   Lobster & Avocado Salad with Shaved Meyer Lemons, 115
   Spicy Crab Salad, 246

B

Bacon
   BLT & Poached Egg Salad, 163
   Frisée Salad with Lardons, 214
   Lentil, Bacon & Frisée Salad, 244
   Warm Spinach & Bacon Salad, 274
Beans. See also Green beans; Lentils
   Artichoke & White Bean Salad, 100
   Black Bean, Avocado & Shrimp Salad, 192
   Black Bean, Corn & Quinoa Salad, 216
   Black Bean & Poblano Chile Salad, 32
   Black Bean & White Corn Salad, 150
   Calamari & White Bean Salad, 88
   Cannellini Bean, Fennel & Shrimp Salad, 48
   Cannellini Bean Salad with Tuna & Grilled Radicchio, 26
   Chickpea Salad with Mint, 76
   Chickpea, Tomato & Chorizo Salad, 244
   Corn & Black-Eyed Pea Salad, 192
   Cranberry Bean, Broccoli Rabe & Bacon Salad, 246
   Edamame, Corn & Tomato Salad, 180
   Edamame & Orange Salad, 286
   Fava Bean & Corn Salad with Fresh Mint, 109
   Fava Bean Salad with Pecorino, 90
   Israeli Couscous Salad with Fava Beans & Olives, 99
   Marinated Edamame, Cucumber & Red Bell Pepper Salad, 76
   Mixed Garden Bean Salad with Shallots, 190
   Pasta Salad with Summer Beans & Herbs, 157
   Potato Salad with Fava Beans, Green Garlic & Crème Fraîche, 101
   Salad of Spring Beans, Peas & Zucchini Ribbons, 108
   Succotash Salad, 220
   Three-Bean Salad with Coriander Vinaigrette, 228
   Tuna & White Bean Salad, 283
   Warm Borlotti Bean & Radicchio Salad, 282
   White Bean & Cherry Tomato Salad, 190
Bean Sprout Salad, Seasoned, 94
Beef
   Chipotle Beef & Corn Salad, 136
   Greek-Style Beef Salad, 178
   Grilled Flank Steak Salad with Tomatoes, 174
   Grilled Steak, Pepper & Onion Salad with Romesco Dressing, 172
   Roast Beef Salad with Leeks & Creamy Mustard Vinaigrette, 124
   Skirt Steak Salad with Citrus & Arugula, 288
   Sliced Flank Steak, Haricot Vert & Potato Salad, 62
   Taco Salad in Tortilla Bowls, 293
   Thai Beef Salad, 48
   Vietnamese Flank Steak Salad, 231
   Warm Beef & Watercress Salad, 63
Beets
   Baby Beet Salad with Sugared Walnuts, 82
   Beet & Fennel Salad with Ricotta Salata, 41
   Beet & Stilton Salad with Orange Vinaigrette, 292
   Beet & Watercress Salad with Fresh Mozzarella, 219
   Golden Beet & Yellow Tomato Salad, 138
   Potato & Beet Salad with Dill, 30
   Roasted Beet & Curly Endive Salad with Balsamic Vinaigrette, 237
   Salad of Mandarins, Roasted Beets & Farmer Cheese, 45
   Wilted Beet Greens with Roasted Beets & Orange Vinaigrette, 255
Berries. See also Strawberries
   Arugula Salad with Berries & Gorgonzola, 125
   Butter Lettuce Salad with Blueberries, Feta & Almonds, 198
Bread-based salads
   Bread Salad with Chicken Bites, 197
   Fattoush Salad with Turkey & Pita Croutons, 267
   Grilled Eggplant, Corn & Bread Salad with Tomato-Basil Vinaigrette, 184
   Panzanella, 222
   Savory Bread Salad with Pancetta & Pine Nuts, 256
Broccoli & Cauliflower Salad with Pickled Onions & Bacon, 262
Broccoli & Cauliflower Slaw with Raisins & Nuts, 47
Broccoli Rabe, Cranberry Bean & Bacon Salad, 246
Brussels Sprouts & Arugula Salad with Walnuts, 54
Bulgur
   Bulgur Salad with Lemon, Peas & Mint, 95
   Bulgur Salad with Roasted Peppers, Chickpeas & Pistachios, 240
   Bulgur Salad with Zucchini, Asparagus & Green Onions, 109
   Mushroom, Radicchio & Bulgur Salad, 256
   Tabbouleh with Feta Cheese, 123

C

Cabbage
   Buttermilk Coleslaw, 181
   Cabbage, Pear & Ginger Slaw, 32
   Creamy Coleslaw, 168
   Red Cabbage Salad with Apples & Dried Fruit, 282
Carrots
   Carrot & Jicama Salad with Lime Vinaigrette, 111
   Carrot, Olive & Almond Salad, 39
   Celery Root & Carrot Salad with Dijon-Tarragon Dressing, 254
   Insalata Rossa, 164
   Moroccan Carrot Salad, 54
   Moroccan-Spiced Carrot & Parsnip Salad, 261
Cauliflower
   Broccoli & Cauliflower Salad with Pickled Onions & Bacon, 262
   Broccoli & Cauliflower Slaw with Raisins & Nuts, 47
   Rigatoni Salad with Cauliflower & Saffron, 24
Celery
   Celery, Pear & Toasted Hazelnut Salad, 217
   Celery Salad with Blue Cheese & Lemon, 173
   Celery Slaw with Shrimp & Creamy Cider Vinaigrette, 240
   Chopped Celery, Parsley & Prosciutto Salad, 285
Celery root
   Celery Root & Carrot Salad with Dijon-Tarragon Dressing, 254
   Celery Root Rémoulade, 261
   Curried Celery Root & Apple Salad with Golden Raisins, 280
   Turkey & Celery Salad with Dried Cherries, 269

Cheese
    Arugula Salad with Breaded Goat Cheese, 157
    Arugula Salad with Pecorino & Pine Nuts, 78
    Asparagus Salad with Lemon & Shaved Parmesan, 96
    Beet & Stilton Salad with Orange Vinaigrette, 292
    Butter Lettuce with Sheep's Milk Cheese & Hazelnuts, 42
    Celery Salad with Blue Cheese & Lemon, 173
    Cherry Tomato Salad with Burrata & Pesto, 130
    Crottin Salad with Pears, Fennel & Currants, 269
    Fava Bean Salad with Pecorino, 90
    Fresh Fig & Goat Cheese Salad, 172
    Frisée Salad with Herbed Fresh Cheese, 67
    Grilled Halloumi & Little Gem Salad with Preserved-Lemon Dressing, 102
    Grilled Romaine & Halloumi with Mint Vinaigrette, 169
    Heirloom Tomato Salad with Blue Cheese Dressing, 154
    Iceberg Wedges with Blue Cheese Dressing, 286
    Insalata Caprese, 196
    Lentil Salad with Feta, 144
    Lentil Salad with Mozzarella & Prosciutto, 42
    Shaved Artichoke & Blue Cheese Salad, 58
    Shaved Zucchini Salad with Pecorino & Almonds, 166
    Spring Herb Salad with Walnut-Crusted Goat Cheese, 114
    Warm Goat Cheese & Chicken Salad, 112
Cherries
    Bitter Greens with Duck Breast & Cherries, 96
    Strawberry & Cherry Salad, 125
Chicken
    Asian Chicken Salad with Lime Dressing, 174
    Bread Salad with Chicken Bites, 197
    Chicken, Avocado & Spinach Salad, 166
    Chicken–Brown Rice Salad with Dates & Cashews, 238
    Chicken, Eggplant & Tomato Salad with Pesto Dressing, 193
    Chicken & Mango Salad with Chutney Vinaigrette, 138
    Chicken & Orzo Salad, 72
    Chicken, Roasted Red Pepper & Green Bean Salad, 130
    Chicken & Roasted Tomato Salad, 164
    Chicken Salad with Apples & Walnuts, 229
    Chicken Salad with Tomatoes, Black Beans & Cilantro, 183
    Chicken Tostada Salad, 142
    Chopped Chicken Salad with Lemon-Tarragon Dressing, 126
    Chopped Salad of Chicken, Watercress & Ricotta Salata, 85
    Couscous Salad with Roasted Chicken & Dried Cranberries, 17

Crispy Chicken & Cabbage Salad with Peanut Dressing, 277
Curried Chicken Salad, 195
Fava Greens with Chicken, Pecans & Kumquats, 61
Fried Chicken Salad, 149
Garlicky Penne & Chicken Salad, 239
Glass-Noodle Salad with Shrimp, Chicken & Mint, 93
Grapefruit, Chicken & Pistachio Salad, 15
Grilled Chicken Caesar Salad, 53
Lemon Chicken Salad with Tarragon, 93
Smoked Chicken Salad with Roasted Cherry Tomatoes, 222
Smoked Chicken Salad with Tarragon Dressing, 276
Spicy Cashew Chicken Salad, 217
Warm Goat Cheese & Chicken Salad, 112
Chile peppers
    Black Bean & Poblano Chile Salad, 32
    Caesar-Style Salad with Poblano Chiles & Cornmeal Croutons, 23
    Cucumber, Cilantro & Jalapeño Salad, 208
Corn
    Black Bean & White Corn Salad, 150
    Chipotle Beef & Corn Salad, 136
    Corn, Arugula & Cherry Tomato Salad, 187
    Corn & Black-Eyed Pea Salad, 192
    Edamame, Corn & Tomato Salad, 180
    Fava Bean & Corn Salad with Fresh Mint, 109
    Grilled Corn Salad, 169
    Grilled Eggplant, Corn & Bread Salad with Tomato-Basil Vinaigrette, 184
    Succotash Salad, 220
    Tomato & Corn Salad with Blue Cheese, 198
Couscous
    Couscous Salad with Chickpeas, Peppers & Black Olives, 211
    Couscous Salad with Dried Fruit & Pine Nuts, 54
    Couscous Salad with Roasted Chicken & Dried Cranberries, 17
    Grilled Lamb & Couscous Salad, 114
    Israeli Couscous Salad with Fava Beans & Olives, 99
    Israeli Couscous Salad with Mint Vinaigrette, 61
Crabmeat
    Crab Cake & Butter Lettuce Salad, 270
    Crab, Fennel & Radicchio Salad with Truffle Oil, 291
    Crab Louis Salad, 40
    Crab Salad with Green Apples & Grapefruit Coulis, 17
    Crab Salad with Meyer Lemon & Fresh Mango, 47
    Crab & Shrimp Salad with Avocado & Oranges, 29
    Crab Sunomono, 95
    Daikon Radish Slaw with Crab & Black Sesame Seeds, 279
    Garlicky Pasta Salad with Crab & Shrimp, 50

Shrimp, Crab & Mâche Salad, 91
Spicy Crab Salad, 246
Cucumbers
    Cucumber, Cilantro & Jalapeño Salad, 208
    Cucumber & Fennel Salad, 235
    Cucumber Salad with Pomegranate, Feta & Mint, 245
    Cucumber Salad with Yogurt-Dill Sauce, 148
    Sesame-Cucumber Salad, 189
    Spicy Cucumber Salad with Roasted Peanuts, 260
    Sweet-and-Sour Cucumber Salad, 163

D, E

Daikon Radish Slaw with Crab & Black Sesame Seeds, 279
Duck
    Bitter Greens with Duck Breast & Cherries, 96
    Green Grape, Pear & Duck Salad, 228
    Lentil & Parsley Salad with Duck Breast, 67
    Watercress & Duck Salad with Gingered Strawberry Dressing, 123
Eggplant
    Chicken, Eggplant & Tomato Salad with Pesto Dressing, 193
    Grilled Eggplant, Corn & Bread Salad with Tomato-Basil Vinaigrette, 184
    Quinoa Salad with Bell Pepper, Tomato & Eggplant, 210
    Soba Noodle Salad with Tofu & Marinated Eggplant, 213
Eggs
    BLT & Poached Egg Salad, 163
    Classic Egg Salad, 99
    Frisée Salad with Lardons, 214
    Salmon & Frisée Salad with Poached Egg, 285
    Shredded Kale Salad with Pancetta & Hard-Cooked Egg, 36
    Warm Escarole, Egg & Pancetta Salad, 12
    Warm Indian-Spiced Egg Salad, 21

F

Farro
    Farro Salad with Artichoke Hearts, 237
    Farro Salad with Creamy Artichoke Dressing, 147
    Farro Salad with Grape Tomatoes & Ricotta Salata, 134
    Farro Salad with Turkey & Roasted Squash, 253
    Warm Farro Salad with Herbs, 63
    Yellow Squash & Farro Salad, 168
Fennel
    Apple-Fennel Slaw, 245
    Beet & Fennel Salad with Ricotta Salata, 41
    Cucumber & Fennel Salad, 235
    Fennel, Chickpea & Sun-Dried Tomato Salad with Mozzarella, 120

Fennel Salad with Apple, Walnuts & Manchego, 264

Fennel Salad with Blood Oranges & Arugula, 12

Mixed Greens & Fennel with Ricotta Salata, 287

Radish, Fennel & Parsley Salad, 66

Salmon & Fennel Salad, 39

Shaved Fennel, Parmesan & Arugula Salad, 255

Shaved Fennel Salad with Orange Dressing, 51

Shaved Mushroom & Fennel Salad with Parmesan Crisps, 259

Figs

Figs & Purple Endive Salad with Currant Dressing, 202

Fresh Fig & Goat Cheese Salad, 172

Melon & Fig Salad with Basil Cream, 133

Mixed Greens with Bacon-Wrapped Figs, 243

Fruit. See also specific fruits

Minted Fruit Salad, 165

Stone Fruit Salad with Hazelnuts & Blue Cheese, 147

G

Grapefruit

Grapefruit, Chicken & Pistachio Salad, 15

Grapefruit, Endive & Pomegranate Salad, 292

Jicama, Grapefruit & Avocado Salad, 287

Lobster Salad with Grapefruit & Avocado, 294

Warm Ruby Grapefruit Salad, 32

Watercress & Radish Salad with Grapefruit, 88

Green beans

Green Bean Salad with Mustard Seeds, Herbs & Baby Chard, 117

Green Bean & Yellow Tomato Salad with Mint, 158

Mixed Garden Bean Salad with Shallots, 190

Pasta Salad with Summer Beans & Herbs, 157

Potato Salad with Green Beans & Cucumber-Yogurt Dressing, 145

Three-Bean Salad with Coriander Vinaigrette, 228

H

Halibut Skewers, Arugula & Zucchini Salad with, 189

Ham. See also Prosciutto

Arugula Salad with Quince Paste & Serrano Ham, 294

Hearts of palm

Arugula Salad with Pine Nuts, Avocado & Hearts of Palm, 41

Mixed Greens with Hearts of Palm, Red Onion & Avocado, 260

Herbs. See also specific herbs

Lettuce & Herb Salad with Dijon Vinaigrette, 213

Spring Herb Salad with Walnut-Crusted Goat Cheese, 114

J, K

Jerusalem Artichoke Salad with Pomegranate & Celery, 27

Jicama

Carrot & Jicama Salad with Lime Vinaigrette, 111

Jicama, Grapefruit & Avocado Salad, 287

Jicama-Mango Salad with Cilantro Dressing, 50

Kale

Lentil & Kale Salad with Bacon, 51

Shredded Kale Salad with Anchovies & Pecorino, 234

Shredded Kale Salad with Pancetta & Hard-Cooked Egg, 36

Kiwi, Apple & Grape Salad with Rosemary Syrup, 31

L

Lamb

Grilled Lamb & Couscous Salad, 114

Grilled Lamb & Pineapple Salad with Thai Flavors, 22

Grilled Lamb Salad, 136

Salad of Grilled Lamb, Potatoes & Aioli, 90

Lentils

Green Lentil Salad with Red Peppers & Shallots, 268

Lentil, Bacon & Frisée Salad, 244

Lentil & Kale Salad with Bacon, 51

Lentil & Parsley Salad with Duck Breast, 67

Lentil Salad with Feta, 144

Lentil Salad with Mozzarella & Prosciutto, 42

Warm Lentil Salad with Mustard Vinaigrette, 36

Lobster

Creamy Pasta Salad with Lobster, 186

Lobster & Avocado Salad with Shaved Meyer Lemons, 115

Lobster, Potato & Green Bean Salad with Pesto Vinaigrette, 134

Lobster Salad with Cucumber & Dill, 87

Lobster Salad with Grapefruit & Avocado, 294

Lobster Salad with Tarragon & Champagne Vinaigrette, 173

M

Mangoes

Chicken & Mango Salad with Chutney Vinaigrette, 138

Crab Salad with Meyer Lemon & Fresh Mango, 47

Green Mango & Grilled Shrimp Salad, 121

Jicama-Mango Salad with Cilantro Dressing, 50

Mango, Pineapple & Papaya Salad, 31

Scallop, Mango & Avocado Salad, 187

Meat. See Beef; Lamb; Pork

Melon

Melon & Fig Salad with Basil Cream, 133

Melon Salad with Yogurt-Honey Dressing, 108

Nectarine, Melon & Blackberry Salad, 198

Watermelon, Feta & Mint Salad, 178

Mushrooms

Grilled Portobello Salad, 207

Mushroom, Radicchio & Bulgur Salad, 256

Roasted Mushroom Salad with Balsamic Vinaigrette, 24

Shaved Mushroom & Fennel Salad with Parmesan Crisps, 259

Warm Wild Mushroom Salad with Bacon Vinaigrette, 232

Wild Rice Salad with Mushrooms & Sage, 40

N

Nectarines

Nectarine, Melon & Blackberry Salad, 198

White Nectarine & Mint Salad, 173

Noodles

Asian Noodle Salad with Salmon & Snow Peas, 288

Glass-Noodle Salad with Shrimp, Chicken & Mint, 93

Noodle Salad with Pork & Asian Lime Vinaigrette, 15

Soba Noodle Salad with Sugar Snap Peas & Soy-Peanut Dressing, 77

Soba Noodle Salad with Tofu & Marinated Eggplant, 213

Vietnamese Shrimp & Noodle Salad, 264

O

Octopus Salad, Mediterranean, 229

Oranges

Arugula with Oranges, Marcona Almonds & Pecorino, 279

Charred Orange & Escarole Salad with Almonds, 16

Edamame & Orange Salad, 286

Fennel Salad with Blood Oranges & Arugula, 12

Orange, Onion & Olive Salad, 30

Salad of Mandarins, Roasted Beets & Farmer Cheese, 45

Watercress & Orange Salad with Toasted Pumpkin Seeds, 226

Oysters, Fried, & Winter Greens, Salad of, 280

P

Papaya

Baby Spinach Salad with Parmesan & Papaya, 27

Green Papaya Salad, 149

Mango, Pineapple & Papaya Salad, 31

Parsnip & Carrot Salad, Moroccan-Spiced, 261

Pasta. See also Couscous; Noodles

Chicken & Orzo Salad, 72

Creamy Pasta Salad with Lobster, 186

Farfalle Salad with Tomatoes & Smoked Mozzarella, 84

Garlicky Pasta Salad with Crab & Shrimp, 50

Garlicky Penne & Chicken Salad, 239

Grilled Squash & Orzo Salad with Pine Nuts & Mint, 150

Old-Fashioned Macaroni Salad with Sweet Pickles, 75

Orzo Salad with Artichokes, Pine Nuts & Golden Raisins, 124

Orzo Salad with Basil & Heirloom Tomatoes, 197

Orzo Salad with Cherry Tomatoes, Feta & Olives, 184

Orzo Salad with Peas, Peppers & Tomatoes, 135

Orzo Salad with Tomatoes, Capers & Roasted Garlic, 206

Pasta Salad with Baby Artichokes & Grilled Tuna, 115

Pasta Salad with Grilled Vegetables, 160

Pasta Salad with Spring Asparagus & Snap Peas, 91

Pasta Salad with Summer Beans & Herbs, 157

Rigatoni Salad with Cauliflower & Saffron, 24

Peach, Arugula & Goat Cheese Salad, 142

Peach Salad with Mint & Indian Spices, 180

Pears

Belgian Endive, Pear, Feta & Walnut Salad, 270

Cabbage, Pear & Ginger Slaw, 32

Celery, Pear & Toasted Hazelnut Salad, 217

Crottin Salad with Pears, Fennel & Currants, 269

Green Grape, Pear & Duck Salad, 228

Mesclun & Roasted Pears with Grainy Mustard Vinaigrette, 45

Radicchio Salad with Pears, Walnuts & Goat Cheese, 254

Salad of Grilled Pork, Pears & Toasted Pecans, 221

Trout & Green Pear Salad, 232

Winter Pear Salad with Blue Cheese, Walnuts & Pomegranate, 274

Peas & pea shoots

Pan-Seared Salmon with Pea Shoots & Watercress, 58

Pea & Asparagus Salad with Meyer Lemon Dressing, 106

Snow Pea & Radish Salad, 101

Soba Noodle Salad with Sugar Snap Peas & Soy-Peanut Dressing, 77

Spring Peas with Pancetta, Mint & Ricotta Salata, 73

Pecans & Balsamic Vinaigrette, Bitter Greens with, 202

Peppers. See also Chile peppers

Chopped Salad of Peppers, Tomatoes, Olives & Manchego, 216

Green Lentil Salad with Red Peppers & Shallots, 268

Grilled Steak, Pepper & Onion Salad with Romesco Dressing, 172

Potato & Red Pepper Salad with Saffron Dressing, 211

Roasted Bell Pepper & Quinoa Salad, 144

Roasted Pepper Salad with Garlic Bread, 235

Wild Rice Salad with Roasted Red Peppers & Anchovies, 259

Persimmons

Endive Salad with Persimmons & Pomegranate, 250

Persimmon & Yellow Apple Salad, 268

Red Oakleaf Lettuce & Frisée Salad with Persimmon, 283

Pineapple

Grilled Fruit Salad, 181

Grilled Lamb & Pineapple Salad with Thai Flavors, 22

Mango, Pineapple & Papaya Salad, 31

Pluot, Grilled, Salad with Goat Cheese & Wild Arugula, 160

Pomegranate

Cucumber Salad with Pomegranate, Feta & Mint, 245

Endive Salad with Persimmons & Pomegranate, 250

Grapefruit, Endive & Pomegranate Salad, 292

Winter Pear Salad with Blue Cheese, Walnuts & Pomegranate, 274

Pomelo, Cilantro & Cashew Salad, 75

Pork. See also Bacon; Ham

Noodle Salad with Pork & Asian Lime Vinaigrette, 15

Roasted Pork Tenderloin & Cornichon Salad, 238

Salad of Grilled Pork, Pears & Toasted Pecans, 221

Potatoes

Fingerling Potato Salad with Shrimp & Dill, 69

German Potato Salad, 193

Greek Potato Salad, 231

Grilled Potato Salad, 186

Grilled Salmon, Potato & Asparagus Salad, 118

Grilled Salmon, Yellow Potato & Corn Salad, 165

Grilled Tuna with Potato, Avocado & Tomato Confit, 126

New Potato & Radish Salad with Mustard-Dill Vinaigrette, 85

Old-Fashioned Potato Salad, 159

Potato & Beet Salad with Dill, 30

Potato & Red Pepper Salad with Saffron Dressing, 211

Potato Salad with Artichokes, Feta Cheese & Olive Relish, 112

Potato Salad with Fava Beans, Green Garlic & Crème Fraîche, 101

Potato Salad with Green Beans & Cucumber-Yogurt Dressing, 145

Roasted Potato Salad with Spring Onion Dressing, 77

Roasted Sweet Potato Salad with Pecans & Green Onions, 18

Salad of Grilled Lamb, Potatoes & Aioli, 90

Salt Cod Salad with Potatoes & Black Olives, 253

Warm Purple Potato Salad, 294

Poultry. See Chicken; Duck; Turkey

Prosciutto

Antipasto Salad with Peperoncini Vinaigrette, 214

Chopped Celery, Parsley & Prosciutto Salad, 285

Grilled Asparagus & Prosciutto Salad, 125

Lentil Salad with Mozzarella & Prosciutto, 42

Q, R

Quince Paste & Serrano Ham, Arugula Salad with, 294

Quinoa

Black Bean, Corn & Quinoa Salad, 216

Lemony Quinoa Salad with Radishes, Avocado & Basil, 121

Quinoa & Radicchio Salad with Dried Cherries & Pistachios, 21

Quinoa Salad with Bell Pepper, Tomato & Eggplant, 210

Quinoa Salad with Tomatoes, Cucumbers & Fresh Herbs, 196

Roasted Bell Pepper & Quinoa Salad, 144

Radicchio

Bitter Greens with Duck Breast & Cherries, 96

Grilled Radicchio Salad, 245

Mushroom, Radicchio & Bulgur Salad, 256

Quinoa & Radicchio Salad with Dried Cherries & Pistachios, 21

Radicchio, Endive & Aged Gouda Salad with Red-Wine Vinaigrette, 23

Radicchio Salad with Pears, Walnuts & Goat Cheese, 254

Radicchio, Spinach & Red Sorrel Salad, 291

Salad of Winter Greens & Fried Oysters, 280

Warm Borlotti Bean & Radicchio Salad, 282

Radishes

Little Gem Wedges with Radishes & Green Goddess Dressing, 117

Mâche, Radish, Blue Cheese & Sugared Pecan Salad, 78

New Potato & Radish Salad with Mustard-Dill Vinaigrette, 85

Radish, Fennel & Parsley Salad, 66

Snow Pea & Radish Salad, 101

Watercress & Radish Salad with Grapefruit, 88

Rhubarb, Shaved, Salad with Almonds & Cheese, 82

Rice. See also Wild Rice

Chicken–Brown Rice Salad with Dates & Cashews, 238

Marinated Calamari & Rice Salad, 207

Rice Salad with Tuna & Capers, 219

Spring Rice Salad with Dill-Lemon Dressing, 120

Wild Rice & Leek Salad, 64

S

Salmon
- Asian Noodle Salad with Salmon & Snow Peas, 288
- Asian Seared-Salmon Salad, 220
- Asparagus & Smoked Salmon Salad with Tarragon Cream, 72
- Grilled Salmon, Potato & Asparagus Salad, 118
- Grilled Salmon, Yellow Potato & Corn Salad, 165
- Pan-Seared Salmon with Pea Shoots & Watercress, 58
- Poached Salmon Salad with Preserved Lemon & Garlic, 141
- Salade Niçoise with Seared Wild Salmon, 148
- Salmon & Fennel Salad, 39
- Salmon & Frisée Salad with Poached Egg, 285

Salt cod
- Escarole Salad with Salt Cod, Anchovies & Olives, 276
- Salt Cod Salad with Potatoes & Black Olives, 253

Scallops
- Baby Spinach with Ginger-Glazed Scallops, 53
- Scallop, Mango & Avocado Salad, 187
- Seared Scallop, Orange & Red Onion Salad, 66

Shrimp
- Black Bean, Avocado & Shrimp Salad, 192
- Cannellini Bean, Fennel & Shrimp Salad, 48
- Celery Slaw with Shrimp & Creamy Cider Vinaigrette, 240
- Crab & Shrimp Salad with Avocado & Oranges, 29
- Fingerling Potato Salad with Shrimp & Dill, 69
- Garlicky Pasta Salad with Crab & Shrimp, 50
- Glass-Noodle Salad with Shrimp, Chicken & Mint, 93
- Green Mango & Grilled Shrimp Salad, 121
- Grilled Shrimp Salad with Avocado & Chipotle Dressing, 171
- Shrimp, Crab & Mâche Salad, 91
- Vietnamese Shrimp & Noodle Salad, 264

Spinach
- Baby Spinach Salad with Parmesan & Papaya, 27
- Baby Spinach with Ginger-Glazed Scallops, 53
- Fresh Strawberry & Spinach Salad, 141
- Radicchio, Spinach & Red Sorrel Salad, 291
- Spinach Salad with Oranges & Roasted Beets, 46
- Spinach, Tomato & Corn Salad, 159
- Spring Greens & Flowers Salad, 111
- Warm Spinach & Bacon Salad, 274
- Warm Spinach Salad with Artichokes & Gruyère, 84
- Warm Spinach Salad with Delicata Squash & Ricotta Salata, 250

Squash. See also Zucchini
- Arugula, Butternut Squash & Salami Salad, 239
- Farro Salad with Turkey & Roasted Squash, 253
- Grilled Squash & Orzo Salad with Pine Nuts & Mint, 150
- Grilled Summer Squash Salad, 133
- Warm Spinach Salad with Delicata Squash & Ricotta Salata, 250
- Yellow Squash & Farro Salad, 168

Squid
- Calamari & White Bean Salad, 88
- Marinated Calamari & Rice Salad, 207
- Quick Grilled Squid Salad, 154

Strawberries
- Fresh Strawberry & Spinach Salad, 141
- Strawberry & Cherry Salad, 125
- Watercress & Duck Salad with Gingered Strawberry Dressing, 123

Sweet Potato, Roasted, Salad with Pecans & Green Onions, 18

T

Tofu & Marinated Eggplant, Soba Noodle Salad with, 213

Tomatillo Salsa, Tostada Salad with, 221

Tomatoes
- Cherry Tomato Salad with Burrata & Pesto, 130
- Chickpea, Tomato & Chorizo Salad, 244
- Chopped Salad with Lemon & Olive Oil, 135
- Farfalle Salad with Tomatoes & Smoked Mozzarella, 84
- Farro Salad with Grape Tomatoes & Ricotta Salata, 134
- Golden Beet & Yellow Tomato Salad, 138
- Green Bean & Yellow Tomato Salad with Mint, 158
- Heirloom Tomato Salad with Blue Cheese Dressing, 154
- Heirloom Tomato Salad with Two Vinegars, 183
- Insalata Caprese, 196
- Insalata Rossa, 164
- Orzo Salad with Basil & Heirloom Tomatoes, 197
- Orzo Salad with Cherry Tomatoes, Feta & Olives, 184
- Orzo Salad with Tomatoes, Capers & Roasted Garlic, 206
- Panzanella, 222
- Quinoa Salad with Tomatoes, Cucumbers & Fresh Herbs, 196
- Spinach, Tomato & Corn Salad, 159
- Tomato & Corn Salad with Blue Cheese, 198
- White Bean & Cherry Tomato Salad, 190

Trout
- Smoked Trout & Apple Salad with Polenta Croutons, 226
- Smoked Trout & Curly Endive Salad, 293
- Smoked Trout Salad with Cucumber & Dill, 73
- Trout & Green Pear Salad, 232
- Trout, Watercress & Apple Salad, 262

Tuna
- Arugula & Fennel Salad with Black Pepper–Crusted Tuna, 243
- Cannellini Bean Salad with Tuna & Grilled Radicchio, 26
- Classic Salade Niçoise, 70
- Grilled Tuna with Potato, Avocado & Tomato Confit, 126
- Pasta Salad with Baby Artichokes & Grilled Tuna, 115
- Rice Salad with Tuna & Capers, 219
- Seared Tuna with Asian Slaw, 18
- Tuna & White Bean Salad, 283

Turkey
- Cobb Salad, 205
- Farro Salad with Turkey & Roasted Squash, 253
- Fattoush Salad with Turkey & Pita Croutons, 267
- Turkey & Celery Salad with Dried Cherries, 269

V, W, Z

Vegetables. See also specific vegetables
- Pasta Salad with Grilled Vegetables, 160

Walnuts
- Baby Beet Salad with Sugared Walnuts, 82
- Fall Salad of Apples & Walnuts with Stilton Cheese, 205
- Spring Herb Salad with Walnut-Crusted Goat Cheese, 114
- Waldorf Salad, 47

Watercress
- Beet & Watercress Salad with Fresh Mozzarella, 219
- Chopped Salad of Chicken, Watercress & Ricotta Salata, 85
- Trout, Watercress & Apple Salad, 262
- Warm Beef & Watercress Salad, 63
- Watercress & Duck Salad with Gingered Strawberry Dressing, 123
- Watercress & Endive Salad with Warm Bacon Vinaigrette, 265
- Watercress & Orange Salad with Toasted Pumpkin Seeds, 226
- Watercress & Radish Salad with Grapefruit, 88

Watermelon, Feta & Mint Salad, 178

Watermelon Radish Salad with Romaine & Avocado, 171

Wheat Berry Salad with Snow Peas & Carrots, 87

Wheat Berry Salad with Walnuts & Sun-Dried Tomatoes, 69

Wild Rice & Leek Salad, 64

Wild Rice Salad with Mushrooms & Sage, 40

Wild Rice Salad with Roasted Red Peppers & Anchovies, 259

Zucchini
- Bulgur Salad with Zucchini, Asparagus & Green Onions, 109
- Grilled Summer Squash Salad, 133
- Shaved Zucchini Salad with Pecorino & Almonds, 166
- Shaved Zucchini with Lemon, Mint & Feta, 195

SALADS BY TYPE

BEAN & GRAIN SALADS

Artichoke & White Bean Salad, 100
Black Bean, Avocado & Shrimp Salad, 192
Black Bean, Corn & Quinoa Salad, 216
Black Bean & Poblano Chile Salad, 32
Black Bean & White Corn Salad, 150
Bulgur Salad with Lemon, Peas & Mint, 95
Bulgur Salad with Roasted Peppers, Chickpeas
    & Pistachios, 240
Bulgur Salad with Zucchini, Asparagus & Green
    Onions, 109
Chickpea Salad with Mint, 76
Chickpea, Tomato & Chorizo Salad, 244
Corn & Black-Eyed Pea Salad, 192
Cranberry Bean, Broccoli Rabe & Bacon Salad, 246
Edamame, Corn & Tomato Salad, 180
Edamame & Orange Salad, 286
Farro Salad with Artichoke Hearts, 237
Farro Salad with Creamy Artichoke Dressing, 147
Farro Salad with Grape Tomatoes & Ricotta
    Salata, 134
Farro Salad with Turkey & Roasted Squash, 253
Fava Bean & Corn Salad with Fresh Mint, 109
Fava Bean Salad with Pecorino, 90
Green Lentil Salad with Red Peppers
    & Shallots, 268
Lemony Quinoa Salad with Radishes, Avocado
    & Basil, 121
Lentil, Bacon & Frisée Salad, 244
Lentil & Kale Salad with Bacon, 51
Lentil & Parsley Salad with Duck Breast, 67
Lentil Salad with Feta, 144
Lentil Salad with Mozzarella & Prosciutto, 42
Marinated Edamame, Cucumber & Red Bell
    Pepper Salad, 76
Mushroom, Radicchio & Bulgur Salad, 256
Quinoa & Radicchio Salad with Dried Cherries
    & Pistachios, 21
Quinoa Salad with Bell Pepper, Tomato
    & Eggplant, 210
Quinoa Salad with Tomatoes, Cucumbers & Fresh
    Herbs, 196
Rice Salad with Tuna & Capers, 219
Roasted Bell Pepper & Quinoa Salad, 144
Savory Bread Salad with Pancetta & Pine Nuts, 256
Spring Rice Salad with Dill-Lemon Dressing, 120
Tabbouleh with Feta Cheese, 123
Three-Bean Salad with Coriander Vinaigrette, 228
Tostada Salad with Tomatillo Salsa, 221
Warm Borlotti Bean & Radicchio Salad, 282
Warm Farro Salad with Herbs, 63
Warm Lentil Salad with Mustard Vinaigrette, 36
Wheat Berry Salad with Snow Peas & Carrots, 87
Wheat Berry Salad with Walnuts & Sun-Dried
    Tomatoes, 69
White Bean & Cherry Tomato Salad, 190

Wild Rice & Leek Salad, 64
Wild Rice Salad with Mushrooms & Sage, 40
Wild Rice Salad with Roasted Red Peppers
    & Anchovies, 259
Yellow Squash & Farro Salad, 168

EGG SALADS

BLT & Poached Egg Salad, 163
Classic Egg Salad, 99
Warm Escarole, Egg & Pancetta Salad, 12
Warm Indian-Spiced Egg Salad, 21

FRUIT SALADS

Apple-Fennel Slaw, 245
Arugula Salad with Quince Paste & Serrano
    Ham, 294
Arugula with Oranges, Marcona Almonds
    & Pecorino, 279
Belgian Endive, Pear, Feta & Walnut Salad, 270
Charred Orange & Escarole Salad with Almonds, 16
Crottin Salad with Pears, Fennel & Currants, 269
Fall Salad of Apples & Walnuts with Stilton
    Cheese, 205
Fennel Salad with Blood Oranges & Arugula, 12
Figs & Purple Endive Salad with Currant
    Dressing, 202
Fresh Fig & Goat Cheese Salad, 172
Fresh Strawberry & Spinach Salad, 141
Grapefruit, Endive & Pomegranate Salad, 292
Green Apple & Celery Salad, 78
Green Papaya Salad, 149
Grilled Fruit Salad, 181
Grilled Pluot Salad with Goat Cheese & Wild
    Arugula, 160
Jicama-Mango Salad with Cilantro Dressing, 50
Kiwi, Apple & Grape Salad with Rosemary
    Syrup, 31
Mango, Pineapple & Papaya Salad, 31
Melon & Fig Salad with Basil Cream, 133
Melon Salad with Yogurt-Honey Dressing, 108
Mesclun & Roasted Pears with Grainy Mustard
    Vinaigrette, 45
Minted Fruit Salad, 165
Nectarine, Melon & Blackberry Salad, 198
Orange, Onion & Olive Salad, 30
Peach, Arugula & Goat Cheese Salad, 142
Peach Salad with Mint & Indian Spices, 180
Persimmon & Yellow Apple Salad, 268
Pomelo, Cilantro & Cashew Salad, 75
Salad of Mandarins, Roasted Beets & Farmer
    Cheese, 45
Shaved Rhubarb Salad with Almonds & Cheese, 82
Spiced Apple, Cranberry & Pecan Salad, 267
Stone Fruit Salad with Hazelnuts & Blue
    Cheese, 147

Strawberry & Cherry Salad, 125
Waldorf Salad, 47
Warm Ruby Grapefruit Salad, 32
Watercress & Orange Salad with Toasted Pumpkin
    Seeds, 226
Watermelon, Feta & Mint Salad, 178
White Nectarine & Mint Salad, 173
Winter Pear Salad with Blue Cheese, Walnuts
    & Pomegranate, 274

GREENS & VEGETABLE-BASED SALADS

Arugula, Blue Cheese & Grape Salad, 210
Arugula, Butternut Squash & Salami Salad, 239
Arugula, Fennel & Prosciutto Salad with Pear
    Vinaigrette, 206
Arugula, Oakleaf Lettuce & Basil Salad, 139
Arugula Salad with Berries & Gorgonzola, 125
Arugula Salad with Breaded Goat Cheese, 157
Arugula Salad with Pecorino & Pine Nuts, 78
Arugula Salad with Pine Nuts, Avocado & Hearts
    of Palm, 41
Asparagus Salad with Lemon & Shaved
    Parmesan, 96
Asparagus & Smoked Salmon Salad with Tarragon
    Cream, 72
Baby Artichoke, Parmesan & Arugula Salad, 118
Baby Beet Salad with Sugared Walnuts, 82
Baby Spinach Salad with Parmesan & Papaya, 27
Beet & Fennel Salad with Ricotta Salata, 41
Beet & Stilton Salad with Orange Vinaigrette, 292
Beet & Watercress Salad with Fresh
    Mozzarella, 219
Bitter Greens with Pecans & Balsamic
    Vinaigrette, 202
Broccoli & Cauliflower Salad with Pickled Onions
    & Bacon, 262
Broccoli & Cauliflower Slaw with Raisins & Nuts, 47
Brussels Sprouts & Arugula Salad with Walnuts, 54
Butter Lettuce & Parmesan Salad, 22
Butter Lettuce Salad with Blueberries, Feta
    & Almonds, 198
Butter Lettuce with Dijon Vinaigrette, 62
Butter Lettuce with Sheep's Milk Cheese
    & Hazelnuts, 42
Buttermilk Coleslaw, 181
Cabbage, Pear & Ginger Slaw, 32
Caesar Salad with Chipotle Chile Dressing, 139
Caesar-Style Salad with Poblano Chiles & Cornmeal
    Croutons, 23
Carrot & Jicama Salad with Lime Vinaigrette, 111
Carrot, Olive & Almond Salad, 39
Celery, Pear & Toasted Hazelnut Salad, 217
Celery Root & Carrot Salad with Dijon-Tarragon
    Dressing, 254
Celery Root Rémoulade, 261
Celery Salad with Blue Cheese & Lemon, 173

Celery Slaw with Shrimp & Creamy Cider Vinaigrette, 240

Cherry Tomato Salad with Burrata & Pesto, 130

Chopped Celery, Parsley & Prosciutto Salad, 285

Chopped Salad of Peppers, Tomatoes, Olives & Manchego, 216

Chopped Salad with Lemon & Olive Oil, 135

Classic Caesar Salad, 16

Classic Greek Salad, 158

Corn, Arugula & Cherry Tomato Salad, 187

Creamy Coleslaw, 168

Cucumber, Cilantro & Jalapeño Salad, 208

Cucumber & Fennel Salad, 235

Cucumber Salad with Pomegranate, Feta & Mint, 245

Cucumber Salad with Yogurt-Dill Sauce, 148

Curried Celery Root & Apple Salad with Golden Raisins, 280

Daikon Radish Slaw with Crab & Black Sesame Seeds, 279

Dandelion Greens Salad, 100

Endive Salad with Persimmons & Pomegranate, 250

Fennel, Chickpea & Sun-Dried Tomato Salad with Mozzarella, 120

Fennel Salad with Apple, Walnuts & Manchego, 264

Field Salad with Pancetta & Walnuts, 208

Fingerling Potato Salad with Shrimp & Dill, 69

Frisée, Endive & Watercress Salad with Roquefort & Pear, 265

Frisée Salad with Herbed Fresh Cheese, 67

Frisée Salad with Lardons, 214

German Potato Salad, 193

Golden Beet & Yellow Tomato Salad, 138

Greek Potato Salad, 231

Green Bean Salad with Mustard Seeds, Herbs & Baby Chard, 117

Green Bean & Yellow Tomato Salad with Mint, 158

Grilled Asparagus & Prosciutto Salad, 125

Grilled Corn Salad, 169

Grilled Eggplant, Corn & Bread Salad with Tomato-Basil Vinaigrette, 184

Grilled Halloumi & Little Gem Salad with Preserved-Lemon Dressing, 102

Grilled Portobello Salad, 207

Grilled Potato Salad, 186

Grilled Radicchio Salad, 245

Grilled Romaine & Halloumi with Mint Vinaigrette, 169

Grilled Squash & Orzo Salad with Pine Nuts & Mint, 150

Grilled Summer Squash Salad, 133

Hearts of Romaine with Garlic Croutons, 234

Heirloom Tomato Salad with Blue Cheese Dressing, 154

Heirloom Tomato Salad with Two Vinegars, 183

Iceberg Wedges with Blue Cheese Dressing, 286

Insalata Caprese, 196

Insalata di Campo, 94

Insalata Rossa, 164

Insalata Verde, 277

Jerusalem Artichoke Salad with Pomegranate & Celery, 27

Jicama, Grapefruit & Avocado Salad, 287

Lettuce & Herb Salad with Dijon Vinaigrette, 213

Little Gem Wedges with Radishes & Green Goddess Dressing, 117

Mâche & Escarole Salad with Crostini, 26

Mâche, Purslane & Green Onion Salad, 102

Mâche, Radish, Blue Cheese & Sugared Pecan Salad, 78

Mesclun Salad with Balsamic Vinaigrette, 64

Mixed Garden Bean Salad with Shallots, 190

Mixed Greens & Fennel with Ricotta Salata, 287

Mixed Greens with Bacon-Wrapped Figs, 243

Mixed Greens with Hearts of Palm, Red Onion & Avocado, 260

Moroccan Carrot Salad, 54

Moroccan-Spiced Carrot & Parsnip Salad, 261

New Potato & Radish Salad with Mustard-Dill Vinaigrette, 85

Old-Fashioned Potato Salad, 159

Panzanella, 222

Pea & Asparagus Salad with Meyer Lemon Dressing, 106

Potato & Beet Salad with Dill, 30

Potato & Red Pepper Salad with Saffron Dressing, 211

Potato Salad with Artichokes, Feta Cheese & Olive Relish, 112

Potato Salad with Fava Beans, Green Garlic & Crème Fraîche, 101

Potato Salad with Green Beans & Cucumber-Yogurt Dressing, 145

Radicchio, Endive & Aged Gouda Salad with Red-Wine Vinaigrette, 23

Radicchio Salad with Pears, Walnuts & Goat Cheese, 254

Radicchio, Spinach & Red Sorrel Salad, 291

Radish, Fennel & Parsley Salad, 66

Red Cabbage Salad with Apples & Dried Fruit, 282

Red Oakleaf Lettuce & Frisée Salad with Persimmon, 283

Roasted Asparagus Salad, 70

Roasted Beet & Curly Endive Salad with Balsamic Vinaigrette, 237

Roasted Mushroom Salad with Balsamic Vinaigrette, 24

Roasted Pepper Salad with Garlic Bread, 235

Roasted Potato Salad with Spring Onion Dressing, 77

Roasted Sweet Potato Salad with Pecans & Green Onions, 18

Salad of Spring Beans, Peas & Zucchini Ribbons, 108

Salade Verte, 145

Seasoned Bean Sprout Salad, 94

Sesame-Cucumber Salad, 189

Shaved Artichoke & Blue Cheese Salad, 58

Shaved Fennel, Parmesan & Arugula Salad, 255

Shaved Fennel Salad with Orange Dressing, 51

Shaved Mushroom & Fennel Salad with Parmesan Crisps, 259

Shaved Zucchini Salad with Pecorino & Almonds, 166

Shaved Zucchini with Lemon, Mint & Feta, 195

Shredded Kale Salad with Anchovies & Pecorino, 234

Shredded Kale Salad with Pancetta & Hard-Cooked Egg, 36

Snow Pea & Radish Salad, 101

Spicy Cucumber Salad with Roasted Peanuts, 260

Spinach Salad with Oranges & Roasted Beets, 46

Spinach, Tomato & Corn Salad, 159

Spring Greens & Flowers Salad, 111

Spring Herb Salad with Walnut-Crusted Goat Cheese, 114

Spring Peas with Pancetta, Mint & Ricotta Salata, 73

Succotash Salad, 220

Sweet-and-Sour Cucumber Salad, 163

Tomato & Corn Salad with Blue Cheese, 198

Warm Purple Potato Salad, 294

Warm Spinach & Bacon Salad, 274

Warm Spinach Salad with Artichokes & Gruyère, 84

Warm Spinach Salad with Delicata Squash & Ricotta Salata, 250

Warm Wild Mushroom Salad with Bacon Vinaigrette, 232

Watercress & Endive Salad with Warm Bacon Vinaigrette, 265

Watercress & Radish Salad with Grapefruit, 88

Watermelon Radish Salad with Romaine & Avocado, 171

Wilted Beet Greens with Roasted Beets & Orange Vinaigrette, 255

Winter Chicory & Apple Salad with Pecans, 29

Winter Greens with Lemon Vinaigrette, 46

MEAT & POULTRY SALADS

Antipasto Salad with Peperoncini Vinaigrette, 214

Asian Chicken Salad with Lime Dressing, 174

Bitter Greens with Duck Breast & Cherries, 96

Bread Salad with Chicken Bites, 197

Chef's Salad with Sopressata, Fontina & Pickled Peppers, 106

Chicken, Avocado & Spinach Salad, 166

Chicken–Brown Rice Salad with Dates & Cashews, 238

Chicken, Eggplant & Tomato Salad with Pesto Dressing, 193

Chicken & Mango Salad with Chutney
Vinaigrette, 138

Chicken & Orzo Salad, 72

Chicken, Roasted Red Pepper & Green Bean
Salad, 130

Chicken & Roasted Tomato Salad, 164

Chicken Salad with Apples & Walnuts, 229

Chicken Salad with Tomatoes, Black Beans
& Cilantro, 183

Chicken Tostada Salad, 142

Chipotle Beef & Corn Salad, 136

Chopped Chicken Salad with Lemon-Tarragon
Dressing, 126

Chopped Salad of Chicken, Watercress & Ricotta
Salata, 85

Cobb Salad, 205

Crispy Chicken & Cabbage Salad with Peanut
Dressing, 277

Curried Chicken Salad, 195

Fattoush Salad with Turkey & Pita Croutons, 267

Fava Greens with Chicken, Pecans & Kumquats, 61

Fried Chicken Salad, 149

Grapefruit, Chicken & Pistachio Salad, 15

Greek-Style Beef Salad, 178

Green Grape, Pear & Duck Salad, 228

Grilled Chicken Caesar Salad, 53

Grilled Flank Steak Salad with Tomatoes, 174

Grilled Lamb & Couscous Salad, 114

Grilled Lamb & Pineapple Salad with Thai
Flavors, 22

Grilled Lamb Salad, 136

Grilled Steak, Pepper & Onion Salad with
Romesco Dressing, 172

Lemon Chicken Salad with Tarragon, 93

Noodle Salad with Pork & Asian Lime Vinaigrette, 15

Roast Beef Salad with Leeks & Creamy Mustard
Vinaigrette, 124

Roasted Pork Tenderloin & Cornichon Salad, 238

Salad of Grilled Lamb, Potatoes & Aioli, 90

Salad of Grilled Pork, Pears & Toasted
Pecans, 221

Skirt Steak Salad with Citrus & Arugula, 288

Sliced Flank Steak, Haricot Vert & Potato
Salad, 62

Smoked Chicken Salad with Roasted Cherry
Tomatoes, 222

Smoked Chicken Salad with Tarragon
Dressing, 276

Spicy Cashew Chicken Salad, 217

Taco Salad in Tortilla Bowls, 293

Thai Beef Salad, 48

Turkey & Celery Salad with Dried Cherries, 269

Vietnamese Flank Steak Salad, 231

Warm Beef & Watercress Salad, 63

Warm Goat Cheese & Chicken Salad, 112

Watercress & Duck Salad with Gingered
Strawberry Dressing, 123

PASTA & NOODLE SALADS

Couscous Salad with Chickpeas, Peppers & Black
Olives, 211

Couscous Salad with Dried Fruit & Pine Nuts, 54

Couscous Salad with Roasted Chicken & Dried
Cranberries, 17

Creamy Pasta Salad with Lobster, 186

Farfalle Salad with Tomatoes & Smoked
Mozzarella, 84

Garlicky Pasta Salad with Crab & Shrimp, 50

Garlicky Penne & Chicken Salad, 239

Glass-Noodle Salad with Shrimp, Chicken
& Mint, 93

Israeli Couscous Salad with Fava Beans
& Olives, 99

Israeli Couscous Salad with Mint Vinaigrette, 61

Old-Fashioned Macaroni Salad with Sweet
Pickles, 75

Orzo Salad with Artichokes, Pine Nuts & Golden
Raisins, 124

Orzo Salad with Basil & Heirloom Tomatoes, 197

Orzo Salad with Cherry Tomatoes, Feta
& Olives, 184

Orzo Salad with Peas, Peppers & Tomatoes, 135

Orzo Salad with Tomatoes, Capers & Roasted
Garlic, 206

Pasta Salad with Baby Artichokes & Grilled
Tuna, 115

Pasta Salad with Grilled Vegetables, 160

Pasta Salad with Spring Asparagus & Snap Peas, 91

Pasta Salad with Summer Beans & Herbs, 157

Rigatoni Salad with Cauliflower & Saffron, 24

Soba Noodle Salad with Sugar Snap Peas
& Soy-Peanut Dressing, 77

Soba Noodle Salad with Tofu & Marinated
Eggplant, 213

SEAFOOD SALADS

Arugula & Fennel Salad with Black Pepper–Crusted
Tuna, 243

Arugula & Zucchini Salad with Halibut Skewers, 189

Asian Noodle Salad with Salmon & Snow Peas, 288

Asian Seared-Salmon Salad, 220

Baby Spinach with Ginger-Glazed Scallops, 53

Calamari & White Bean Salad, 88

Cannellini Bean, Fennel & Shrimp Salad, 48

Cannellini Bean Salad with Tuna & Grilled
Radicchio, 26

Classic Salade Niçoise, 70

Crab Cake & Butter Lettuce Salad, 270

Crab, Fennel & Radicchio Salad with Truffle Oil, 291

Crab Louis Salad, 40

Crab Salad with Green Apples & Grapefruit
Coulis, 17

Crab Salad with Meyer Lemon & Fresh Mango, 47

Crab & Shrimp Salad with Avocado & Oranges, 29

Crab Sunomono, 95

Escarole Salad with Salt Cod, Anchovies
& Olives, 276

Green Mango & Grilled Shrimp Salad, 121

Grilled Salmon, Potato & Asparagus Salad, 118

Grilled Salmon, Yellow Potato & Corn Salad, 165

Grilled Shrimp Salad with Avocado & Chipotle
Dressing, 171

Grilled Tuna with Potato, Avocado & Tomato
Confit, 126

Lobster & Avocado Salad with Shaved Meyer
Lemons, 115

Lobster, Potato & Green Bean Salad with Pesto
Vinaigrette, 134

Lobster Salad with Cucumber & Dill, 87

Lobster Salad with Grapefruit & Avocado, 294

Lobster Salad with Tarragon & Champagne
Vinaigrette, 173

Marinated Calamari & Rice Salad, 207

Mediterranean Octopus Salad, 229

Pan-Seared Salmon with Pea Shoots
& Watercress, 58

Poached Salmon Salad with Preserved Lemon
& Garlic, 141

Quick Grilled Squid Salad, 154

Salad of Winter Greens & Fried Oysters, 280

Salade Niçoise with Seared Wild Salmon, 148

Salmon & Fennel Salad, 39

Salmon & Frisée Salad with Poached Egg, 285

Salt Cod Salad with Potatoes & Black Olives, 253

Scallop, Mango & Avocado Salad, 187

Seared Scallop, Orange & Red Onion Salad, 66

Seared Tuna with Asian Slaw, 18

Shrimp, Crab & Mâche Salad, 91

Smoked Trout & Apple Salad with Polenta
Croutons, 226

Smoked Trout & Curly Endive Salad, 293

Smoked Trout Salad with Cucumber & Dill, 73

Spicy Crab Salad, 246

Trout, Watercress & Apple Salad, 262

Trout & Green Pear Salad, 232

Tuna & White Bean Salad, 283

Vietnamese Shrimp & Noodle Salad, 264

weldonowen

415 Jackson Street, Suite 200, San Francisco, CA 94111
www.weldonowen.com

SALAD OF THE DAY
Conceived and produced by Weldon Owen, Inc.
In collaboration with Williams-Sonoma, Inc.
3250 Van Ness Avenue, San Francisco, CA 94109

A WELDON OWEN PRODUCTION
Copyright © 2012 Weldon Owen, Inc. and Williams-Sonoma, Inc.
All rights reserved, including the right of reproduction
in whole or in part in any form.

Printed and bound in China by Toppan-Leefung Printing Limited

First printed in 2012
20 19 18 17 16 15 14 13 12

Library of Congress Control Number: 2011939909

ISBN 13: 978-1-61628-212-7
ISBN 10: 1-61628-212-6

Weldon Owen is a division of
BONNIER

WILLIAMS-SONOMA, INC.
Founder and Vice-Chairman Chuck Williams

WELDON OWEN, INC.
CEO and President Terry Newell
VP, Sales and Marketing Amy Kaneko
Director of Finance Mark Perrigo

VP and Publisher Hannah Rahill
Associate Publisher Amy Marr
Editor Julia Humes
Associate Editor Julie Nelson
Assistant Editor Becky Duffett

Creative Director Emma Boys
Senior Art Director Kara Church
Senior Designer Lauren Charles

Production Director Chris Hemesath
Production Manager Michelle Duggan

Photographer Erin Kunkel
Food Stylist Robyn Valarik
Prop Stylist Leigh Noe

ACKNOWLEDGMENTS
Weldon Owen wishes to thank the following people for their generous support
in producing this book: David Bornfriend, Sarah Putman Clegg, Carolyn Miller,
Elizabeth Parson, and Jason Wheeler.

The Complete Chinese Cookbook

The Complete Chinese Cookbook

Over 500 Authentic Recipes from China

Jacki Passmore and Daniel P. Reid
Photographs in China taken by Nik Wheeler

Exeter Books

NEW YORK

Editorial and production co-ordinator: Allan Amsel

Editors: Betsy Gurlatz and Lesley Hargreaves

Recipes edited and tested by Jacki Passmore

Photography in China: Nik Wheeler

Food preparation for photography: Annie Wong

Food photography: John Leung Studio

Art Direction: Hon Bing-wah

Acknowledgements: The reproduction from 'Going Down the River at the Ch'ing Ming Festival', p.10-11, is by kind permission of Nigel Cameron.
Settings for photography kindly loaned by Amazing Grace Elephant Company; Nic Nac; and Cynthia Ambrose.

Editor's Note:
The recently introduced Pin Yin system of romanisation of Chinese characters is shown, where appropriate, in parentheses after the Wade Giles romanisation, which is still more commonly used in reference to regions and food.

Lansdowne Press
Published by Lansdowne Press
176 South Creek Road, Dee Why West,
NSW, Australia 2099
© RPLA Pty Ltd 1982

The Complete Chinese Cookbook
was created, edited and produced by
CFW Publications Limited
130 Connaught Road Central, Hong Kong
Printed in Hong Kong

First published in USA 1982 by Exeter Books
Exeter is a trademark of Simon & Schuster
Distributed by Bookthrift
New York, New York

ISBN 0 89673 150 2

Contents

	Introduction	6
I	Historical Perspectives on Chinese Food	10
II	Chinese Cooking Utensils, Condiments, and Methods	26
III	Northern Style Cuisine	38
IV	Eastern/Coastal Style Cuisine	92
V	Western/Central Style Cuisine	172
VI	Southern Style Cuisine	242
VII	Dishes for Special Occasions	322
VIII	Noodles and Rice — Accompaniments	342
IX	Dim Sum, Bread, and Cold Platters — Appetisers	358
X	Sauces, Spices, and Seasonings	382
XI	Preparation and Cooking Techniques	390
XII	A Word on Wines and Spirits	400
	Glossary	406
	Guide to Recipes	413
	Index	418
	Measurement Charts	423

MONGOLIA

SINKIANG
(XINJIANG)

KANSU
(GANSU)

TSINGHAI
(QINGHAI)

TIBET
(XIZANG)

SZECHUAN
(SICHUAN)

Chengtu ●
(Chengdu)

YUNNAN

Introduction

HEILUNGKIANG
(HEILONGJIANG)

KIRIN
(JILIN)

INNER MONGOLIA
(NEI MONGGOL)

LIAONING

Hwang Ho (Yellow River)

Peking
(Beijing)

Tientsin
(Tianjin)

SHANSI
(SHANXI)

HOPEH
(HEBEI)

SHANTUNG
(SHANDONG)

YELLOW SEA

INGSIA
(INGXIA)

NORTHERN REGION

KIANGSU
(JIANGSU)

SHENSI
(SHAANXI)

HONAN
(HENAN)

Nanking
(Nanjing)

Soochow
(Suzhou)

Shanghai

ANHWEI
(ANHUI)

Hangchow
(Hongzhou)

HUPEH
(HUBEI)

Ningpo
(Ningbo)

EAST CHINA SEA

Yangtze River

Wuhan

Chungking
(Chongqing)

KIANGSI
(JIANGXI)

CHEKIANG
(ZHEJIANG)

WESTERN REGION

EASTERN REGION

HUNAN

Foochow
(Fuzhou)

KWEICHOW
(GUIZHOU)

FUKIEN
(FUJIAN)

Taipei
(Taibei)

KWANGSI
(GUANGXI)

KWANGTUNG
(GUANGDONG)

TAIWAN

SOUTHERN REGION

Canton
(Guangzhou)

Namning

Si Kiang (Xijiang) (West River)

Hong Kong

SOUTH CHINA SEA

HAINAN

'Have you eaten yet?'

This common Chinese greeting is roughly equivalent to the English, 'Hi, how are you?' It carries the implicit cultural assumption that if you've eaten recently, you must be feeling fine. And if you haven't, whoever asked you is obliged to offer you something to eat before proceeding with the business at hand. First things first.

Food is the most central concern of the Chinese people in their day-to-day

lives, and both its quality and quantity are the most direct measures by which the Chinese judge their standard. So important is food in Chinese culture that even the spirits of the dead must be regularly offered the tastiest delica-

The pictures here and opposite correspond to those introducing Chapters III, IV, V and VI (Northern, Eastern, Western and Southern cuisine). The Chinese character in the box on each chapter introduction represents North, East, West and South.

cies which the living family can afford. After the spirits have devoured the 'essence' of the tempting offerings set before them on the alter, the family consumes the 'gross' remains. In this world or the next, the Chinese eat better and more often than any other people in the world.

The reason the Chinese eat so well lies in the past: food has periodically been very scarce in China, and the people know the gnawing pangs of hunger all too well. To the Chinese, it is no mere cliché that food is 'the staff of life.' Over the centuries they have hewn and fashioned that staff from a wider range of materials than anyone else. In times of famine, the discovery of a new food, or a new way to preserve food, or a better way to utilise food was literally a matter of life and death. The Chinese have been so inventive in their cuisine simply because they had to be in order to survive.

The infinite variety of Chinese cuisine is based upon this broad foundation of necessity. But the sophisticated refinement and high aesthetic standards associated with Chinese culinary culture go far beyond mere necessity. Chinese cuisine is a direct reflection of Chinese civilization as a whole. To the style-conscious Chinese, *how* one does something is at least as important as *what* one does. Historically, the average Chinese could not afford to be fussy about *what* was available or how *much* he could purchase, but he could be particular about

how it was prepared, *how* it tasted, and *how* it looked on the table. The key to Chinese cooking is not in the materials, but in the methods.

Chinese cuisine evolved from the distinctive regional styles of the far-flung provinces. In ancient times, when means of preserving and transporting foods were still insufficient for regional exchange of ingredients, regional styles of cooking were relatively restricted to their places of origin. Each unique style was based on the prevailing geographic conditions, climate, available ingredients, and local customs.

Chinese regional cooking styles began to coalesce and form a national cuisine during the Sung Dynasty (960 1279 A.D.), when methods of growing, preserving, storing and distributing food progressed rapidly. Many foreign culinary influences were also absorbed, for so important was good food to the Chinese that they readily dropped their usual air of cultural superiority in order to absorb and adapt foods and cooking methods from barbarians. During the Sung era, Chinese writers also began to expound the principles and practices of Chinese cuisine, which established it as one of the most respected and well-defined arts of traditional China. Food and eating became an extension of Chinese philosophy and was intimately connected with other aspects of Chinese civilization such as art and medicine.

Like *Yin* and *Yang*, complementary opposing forces, food and culture were distinct yet inseparable elements of life in ancient China.

This book is written to serve the general reader as a comprehensive guide to Chinese culinary culture. Food, cooking and culture are inseparable in Chinese cuisine; ingredients, methods of preparation, and eating customs are all equally important. Chapter I describes Chinese culinary history — the various historical, geographical, and social factors which have contributed to Chinese cuisine — and delineates the most important principles which underlie and govern it. Chapter II introduces the basic utensils, condiments, and methods commonly used and offers some advice regarding the best ways to successfully put this information into practice.

The next four chapters are brief introductions to Chinese regional cuisine. Debate continues to rage among Chinese gourmets and scholars over the classification of regional styles of Chinese food. Many factors are involved, so these divisions are somewhat arbitrary. Nine major regional styles are officially recognised by chefs in China today: Peking (Beijing), Anhui, Shantung (Shandong), Chekiang (Zhejiang), Fukien (Fujian), Kiangsu (Jiangsu), Hunan, Szechuan (Sichuan), and Canton (Guangdong).

Our regional classification of Chinese cuisine is based on commonly shared historical, geographical, and cultural factors; and have divided China into four broad culinary regions. They are Northern Style, Eastern/Coastal Style, Western/Central Style, and Southern Style. These divisions are based upon real geographic, historical, and hence culinary boundaries. The nine styles recognised in contemporary China fall into our culinary categories as follows: Northern — Peking (Beijing), Shantung (Shandong), Anhui; Eastern/Coastal — Chekiang (Zhejiang), Fukien (Fujian), Kiangsu (Jiangsu); Western/Central — Hunan, Szechuan (Sichuan); Southern — Canton (Guangdong). Each regional chapter describes the food of the area in terms of prevailing geographic conditions, climate, major ingredients and condiments used, favoured cooking methods, and overall cultural style.

Chapter VII, 'A Word on Wines and Spirits', offers an overview of the roles of liquor and drinking in Chinese culinary culture. The various types of Chinese and Western beverages suitable for consumption with Chinese food are discussed, as well as various Chinese drinking customs.

The recipe section, which follows the text, presents 518 Chinese recipes garnered from original sources. To collect recipes and other vital information, we interviewed renowned chefs in Peking (Beijing), Nanking (Nanjing), Soochow (Suzhou), Hangchow (Hang-

zhou), Chengtu (Chengdu), Canton (Guangzhou), Taipei (Taibei), and Hong Kong. Other recipes were translated from such authoritative sources as the *Peking Hotel Cookbook*, a collection of 1,000 recipes written by top-ranked chefs from all over China. Original recipes, or new versions of old favourites, were also developed by the author, editors, and other cooks of gourmet Chinese food. The recipes are presented in the clear-cut format used

in most Chinese-language cookbooks.

The text will have served its purpose if it kindles in the reader a strong enough interest in Chinese cuisine to try a few of the recipes. From there, the food will take over and speak for itself.

The reproduction on the following page, part of an early 17th century handscroll more than eight metres (27 feet) long, shows country folk going to town for special food and other things for the Ch'ing Ming festival.

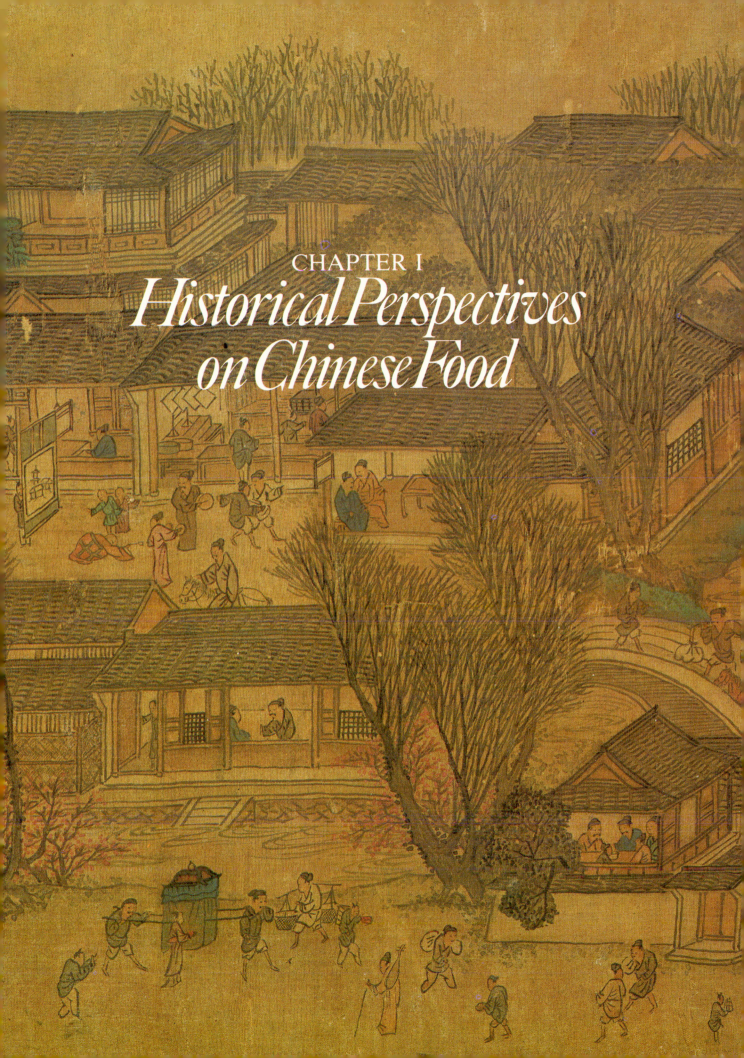

CHAPTER I
Historical Perspectives on Chinese Food

Food has never been regarded as a mere necessity in China. Since earliest antiquity, Chinese eating habits have been intimately bound to and reflective of other aspects of Chinese culture. What and how the Chinese eat is highly symbolic of their general view of the world and their overall philosophy of life. Chinese food and eating habits have always been, and still remain, dominated by two major considerations: the pleasure principle, reflected in China's sophisticated gourmet traditions, and — equally important — the health principle, based on traditional Chinese medical theories. Nowhere else in the world has food been so exhaustively researched and categorised and the culinary arts so highly developed as in China. And no people in the world maintain such a high degree of culinary consciousness as the Chinese. They are, quite literally, a nation of gourmets.

The principles and practices which define Chinese cuisine as we know it today evolved gradually over a period of 5,000 years. To fully understand why the Chinese cook and eat as they do, and to appreciate the subtle sophistications of their cuisine, it is necessary first to review China's long culinary history, tracing those developments and conditions which have had a decisive influence on its evolution. Our historical review begins with the earliest recorded dynasty, the Shang, and takes us down through 3,500 years to the present-day People's Republic of China.

Early Antiquity: Shang (1766-1123 B.C.) — Han (206 B.C.-220 A.D.)

The earliest archeological artifacts discovered in China are ornate bronze eating and drinking vessels dating from the Shang dynasty, which flourished 3,500 years ago in the region of the Yellow River. This fact alone proves that eating and drinking had already become formalised activities in Chinese culture as early as the 18th century B.C. Eating and drinking were ritualised affairs governed by a codified etiquette. Indeed, it seems that the ruling house of Shang did little else but eat and drink, for gluttony and drunkenness are usually cited as major reasons for its downfall. In 1123 B.C., the house of Shang fell in an orgy of wretched excess and was replaced by the virtuous house of Chou, thus beginning China's longest historical era (1122-249 B.C.) and its classical age of philosophy.

It was during the Chou era that food

first became associated with native Chinese philosophy, cosmic theories, and medical practices. The theories of Yin and Yang and the Five Elements, China's oldest cosmological concepts, were broadly applied to food and drink. For example, drinking was viewed as a Yang activity (hot, stimulating, depleting) and eating as Yin (cool, calming, nourishing). Grain was associated with the element Earth and therefore always served in earthenware clay vessels. Meat, on the other hand, was identified with the element Fire and served in bronze vessels because the elements Fire and Metal were considered to be harmonious rather than antagonistic. These early associations with cosmic theory were very basic compared to the colourful elaborations which would appear in succeeding eras, but they laid the philosophical foundations of Chinese food culture for all time to come. The many rules and regulations stipulated by the Chou classics to govern ritualistic and ceremonial uses of food, for example, continued to be followed in the imperial palaces and private homes of China right through to the 20th century.

Two words sum up all the intricate principles and cosmic premises of Chinese cuisine: balance and harmony. The cosmic significance of food lay in the effects it had on the body after ingestion: if the food is balanced and harmoniously blended, then the body and spirit will naturally become so too after eating it. The *Tso Chuan*, a classical text about Chou life and philosophy dating from 521 B.C., contains an excellent statement of this concept:

Harmony may be illustrated by soup. You have water and fire, vinegar, pickle, salt, and plums with which to cook fish and meat. It is made to boil by firewood, and then the cook mixes the ingredients, harmoniously equalising the several flavours, so as to supply whatever is deficient and carry off whatever is in excess. Then the master eats it, and his mind is made equable.

Another important aspect of traditional China's eating habits which dates back to the Chou and earlier times is the sensual appreciation of food. Kaotze, a 5th century B.C. philosopher, summed it all up with his famous equation, 'Food plus sex equals nature.' Throughout China's long epicurean history, gourmet food has been intimately associated with gourmet sex, and both pleasures were commonly en-

joyed together in the restaurants, wine-houses, and tea-shops of ancient China.

The oldest, most fundamental principle of Chinese cuisine was formulated so long ago that it had already marked

Chinese eating habits long before the dawn of recorded history. The *tsai/fan* principle is the universally recognised mark of Chinese cuisine the world over. *Tsai* means any cooked dish of meat, fish, vegetables, and so forth, and *fan* literally means 'cooked rice,' although it refers to any staple grain food such as rice, noodles, buns, cakes, bread-rolls, gruel, etc. The idea is quite simple: no meal is complete unless it is built around a basic staple food derived from rice, wheat, millet, barley, sorghum, or other grain. So ingrained is this habit that the average Chinese misses the rice or noodles at a meal much more than any *tsai*. Regardless of how costly and tasty the *tsai*, without *fan* it does not qualify as a Chinese meal. In fact, many Chinese refuse to eat at all without some form of *fan* before them. The central role of grains in the Chinese diet and the indispensability of grain-derived staples at any Chinese meal is the oldest definitive aspect of Chinese cuisine and stems from pre-historic times.

By the time Confucious appeared on the scene towards the end of the Chou era, cultured Chinese gentlemen were already quite fussy about what and how they ate. This passage from the *Analects* describes the eating habits of the Sage himself and is quite revealing:

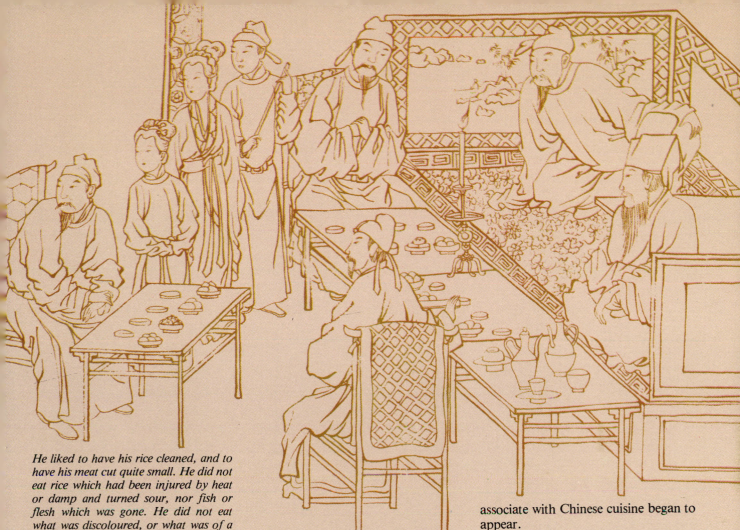

He liked to have his rice cleaned, and to have his meat cut quite small. He did not eat rice which had been injured by heat or damp and turned sour, nor fish or flesh which was gone. He did not eat what was discoloured, or what was of a bad flavour, nor anything which was ill-cooked, or was not in season. He did not eat meat which was not cut properly, nor what was served without its proper sauce...He did not partake of wine and dried meat bought in the market. He was never without ginger when he ate. He did not eat much.

The importance of fresh foods, foods in season, proper preparation, appropriate condiments, correct proportions, Chinese medicine (ginger), home cooking, and general avoidance of excess are all reflected in this 2,300-year-old passage.

After a prolonged period of disunity and political turmoil, the Han dynasty finally established itself in the wake of the Chou and the short-lived Chin. The Han dynasty (220 B.C. — 206 A.D.) was so decisive in the development of Chinese culture and society that ever since ethnic Chinese have called themselves 'People of Han.' From the Han come the first written recipes and detailed descriptions of food, and fully prepared, recognisable *tsai* have been unearthed recently in China in tombs dating from the Han era.

The most common form of Han food was *keng*, a rich, slow-cooked stew consisting of grains, vegetables, fish, and meats. The latter two were generally omitted among poorer families. *Keng* is cooked in large cauldrons over slow fires and usually contains a wide variety of ingredients. Roasted and broiled wild game comprised the other major element in the Han diet.

The expansion of China's borders to the west and south by the Han emperors was an important factor in the development of Chinese cuisine. Formerly restricted to the relatively arid, cold regions of the north, the Chinese empire now embraced the lush, temperate zones of the south and the rugged, mountainous regions to the west. The southern regions, in those days called Ling-nan (present-day Kuangchou, or Guangzhou province), produced litchis, longans, and many other Oriental fruits which we today identify with the Chinese diet, as well as a whole new range of vegetables and wild game. From the western regions came grapes, both for eating and as wine, sesame, walnuts, peas, coriander, and much more. Prior to the Han, the range of ingredients used in the Chinese diet was relatively narrow, but after China's expansion to the west and south, the endless variety and infinite combinations of foods which we today associate with Chinese cuisine began to appear.

So delicious and renowned had Chinese food become by the dawn of the Han era that food was an effective strategic weapon in China's perennial confrontations with barbaric tribes on its borders. Chia I, a Han strategist of the 2nd century B.C., left this advice regarding the best way to deal with the Hsiung-nu, a fierce and troublesome tribe that had plagued civilised China for centuries:

When the Hsiung-nu have developed a craving for our cooked rice, keng stew, roasted meats, and wine, this will have become their fatal weakness.

He suggested to the emperor that a string of Chinese restaurants be established along the frontiers to entice the fierce barbarians to eat and drink with rather than fight the Chinese. Chinese food and wine have always ranked high among the items demanded as tribute from China by victorious barbaric tribes. This and a similar strategy involving the betrothal of beautiful Chinese princesses to powerful tribal chiefs have been remarkably successful in taming the ferocious barbarians who have troubled China throughout its history.

The two most important culinary innovations of the Han era were the creation of a fermented bean paste condiment and the development of various wheat-based foods. Fermented bean paste rapidly became the primary condiment in the kitchens and on the tables of rich and poor alike, and today it still plays a vital role in Chinese cooking. Even more significant was the appearance of various wheat-derived foods, such as noodles, breads, buns, baked cakes, fried pancakes, dumplings, and others. This development made a whole new range of nutritious yet inexpensive foods available to the common people of China. Rice was still considered a southern luxury product in those days, and the only other choice of grain was millet or sorghum, which are not nearly as versatile or nourishing as wheat. The writer Shu Hsi (ca. 300 A.D.) makes this significant observation about the origins of wheat foods in China:

The various kinds of noodles and cakes were mainly the invention of the common people, while some of the cooking methods came from foreign lands.

Both the technique of grinding wheat to flour for cooking and the art of baking breads came to China from its western frontiers, perhaps originating in Persia. But the infinite variety of dishes based on these techniques which appeared in China after their introduction grew directly from the culinary inventiveness of the Chinese people.

T'ang (618-906 A.D.)
The T'ang dynasty is known as China's 'Golden Age,' when the 'good life' as the Chinese define it flourished in the fabulous T'ang capital of Chang-an (contemporary Sian). In its heyday, Chang-an was the world's greatest, most civilised city.

Chinese cuisine developed by leaps and bounds during the T'ang, and the variety of form and content in food continued to multiply. Many new foreign foods were borrowed and adopted by the Chinese during this open-minded, adventurous period of Chinese history. However, it would not be until the studious Sung dynasty which followed that the many disparate styles of cooking in use throughout the empire would coalesce into a consciously cultivated national style which could be distinctively defined as 'Chinese.'

The most important culinary development of T'ang lies in the intimate association which grew between the principles and practices of food and medicine. During the T'ang, Chinese herbal pharmacologists rather than cooks or gourmets determined what foods could and could not be eaten, when, how, in what quantities and which combinations. This close identification of food and medicine became, and still remains, one of the most distinctive features of Chinese cuisine.

Many renowned Chinese herbal physicians flourished during the T'ang era, the most famous of whom were Meng Shen and Sun Ssu-mo. Both lived during the 7th century A.D. and wrote important treatises on food. Sun Ssu-mo, who lived to the ripe old age of 101 and attended to emperors and peasants alike, is well remembered in China for his famous statement about food's role as medicine:

A truly good physician first finds out the cause of the illness, and having found out that, he tries first to cure it by food. Only when food fails does he prescribe medication.

T'ang physicians and pharmacologists had much to say about food, most of which made a lot of sense, and their advice was seriously heeded by the people of China. A few examples will suffice to illustrate the subtlety of their insights. T'ang doctors recommended eating whole rather than milled barley in order to provide balance between the heating (Yang) effects of the meal and the cooling (Yin) effects of the bran. Some 1,200 years later, modern Western nutritional science has come to the same conclusion about the nutritional value of whole grains, though the specific terminology differs. Sun Ssu-mo prescribed a diet rich in seaweed for persons suffering from goiter, an iodine-deficiency disease of the thyroid glands common in land-locked areas far from the sea. This is probably the earliest recorded case of nutritional therapy in the world. He also prescribed a rich porridge of wheat-germ for similar vitamin-deficiency diseases such as scurvy and beri-beri. Though the medical terminology and concepts of ancient China differ from those of the modern West, the conclusions reached have much in common.

The culinary advice offered by the doctors of T'ang is endless. Meng Shen warned sternly against eating leeks in combination with honey or beef. Peo-

ple with sluggish digestion were advised to include plenty of *ta-huang* (rhubarb) in their diets. Onions, leeks, and garlic were all highly recommended in winter for their warming properties but generally avoided on hot summer days.

Interestingly, T'ang doctors were unanimous in their condemnation of the flesh of domestic animals as food for man: pork, beef, and mutton were considered highly deleterious to health, unless consumed very sparingly. The only exception to this rule was dog, the flesh of which was regarded by all pharmacologists as highly beneficial to man's health, dog's liver being especially recommended for weak kidneys. Such advice runs throughout traditional Chinese treatises on both food and medicine.

The T'ang emperors also significantly expanded China's borders, opening up vast new sources of food. The lush southern regions provided new fruits such as limes, oranges, tangerines, and pomelos, in addition to the beloved litchis and longans. History claims that the emperor T'ang Ming-huang's favourite concubine Yang kui-fei ('Precious Concubine') was so enamoured of litchis that she established a special pony express between their source in the far southeast corner of China and the T'ang capital of Chang-an in the northwest in order to provide fresh litchis for her table. Crab-apples were discovered in the south and appealed greatly to the Chinese palate: one common method of eating them was to steep them in honey and cinnabar and take them as a stimulating

elixir after dinner. The cinnabar and its aphrodisiac properties reflect both the influence of Chinese medicine and the connection of food to sex.

The sugar palm (Arenga saccharifera) provided sago meal, jaggery sugar, and a fermented beverage called toddy. This useful plant probably came to China from India as a result of the proliferous cultural exchanges between the two countries during the T'ang era. Wheat and millet remained the primary staple grains of China, although consumption of rice increased steadily as agricultural technology improved. When available, rice was always preferred. Grains were often supplemented in the north with 'Job's Tears' (Coix lacryma-job), a wild grain. Three new fruits were considered by the medical community to have 'magical' curative properties: they were emblic (Phyllanthus emblica), belleric (Terminalia bellerica), and chebullic (Terminalia chebula).

Since the flesh of domestic animals other than dog was considered bad for health, the people of T'ang relied on wild game for their meats. In the north, venison had always been an important part of the Chinese diet, and it continued to be so throughout the T'ang. The 'racoon-dog' or li (Nyctereutes procyonoides) was a popular food all over China, as it still is today, and was listed by Sun Ssu-mo as an excellent tonic food. The marmot or to-pa (Marmota himalyana robusta) was highly prized as food among both Han Chinese and minorities along the western frontier regions. In addition,

the T'ang diet included all sorts of deer, wild boar, bear, otter, bamboo rat, and many other varieties of wild game.

Naturally the natives of Ling-nan (forebears of the Cantonese) led the culinary field in exotica when it came to game. A favourite dish was stewed elephant's trunk, preferably from a black variety with pink ivory. Dog was consumed all over China, but in Ling-nan cats of all kinds comprised a favourite source of meat as well. Another banquet specialty was newborn baby rats stuffed with honey and placed live on the table, where they crawled blindly around waiting to be picked up at will by a diner's roving chopsticks, popped into his mouth, and eaten alive. Yet another artfully contrived dish was produced by dumping live frogs into a boiling urn of soup with bamboo shoots in it: when they hit the scalding water, the poor creatures clutch at the bamboo shoots so that when picked up with chopsticks they 'carry' a bamboo shoot along into the diner's mouth. The variety of culinary exotica in this region of China is endless, and some of the reasons for this will be discussed in the chapter on Southern Style Cuisine.

For fowl, T'ang Chinese used both domestic and wild varieties. Of the latter, chicken (especially black chickens), duck (especially white ducks), and goose were most common. All sorts of songbirds were eaten in China all year round, including sparrows, swallows, thrushes, and, in the south, parrots and parakeets as well. Songbirds were considered especially beneficial to male sexual potency during winter. Wild birds such as pheasant, quail, partridge, dove, and others were hunted with birds of prey such as falcons, peregrines, and goshawks, each of which was used for a specific type of prey.

All sorts of wild and cultivated fish appeared on the T'ang menu. Carp was, and still remains, the great favourite. Many varieties of carp have been cultivated in China for millenia, the most popular being Black Carp. Pomfret, mullet, bass, trout, perch, white-bait, yellowfish, and all sorts of shrimps and shellfish also comprised important parts of the T'ang diet. Strangely, the favourite T'ang method of preparing and eating fish seems to have all but disappeared from China. There are many references in T'ang literature to fresh fish finely sliced into extremely delicate, paper-thin leaves,

variously described as 'snow flakes,' 'silver threads,' 'butterfly wings,' and other poetic metaphors. Chefs skilled in this dainty art of flaking fish were in great demand at the court and in the kitchens of wealthy families.

Contrary to the popular misconception that the Chinese have never used or liked dairy products, milk and milk products formed important and well-liked elements of the Chinese diet during T'ang times. The Chinese and most other Asian peoples stop producing the enzyme required to break down the lactose in raw milk soon after the age of six. After boiling, fermenting, and otherwise processing the raw milk, however, it becomes a perfectly acceptable part of Asian diets, as attested to by its central role in the diet of India. The Chinese probably learned the use of dairy products from the northern nomads with whom they mingled on the frontiers. Though many Chinese writers have claimed that the Chinese deliberately refrained from using dairy products in order not to be identified too closely with milk-consuming barbarians, this theory hardly seems plausible in light of the facts. For example, the famous T'ang poet Pai Chu-yi records in his journal that he preferred Rehmannia (a Chinese herbal medicine) mixed with milk first thing in the morning. Milk was modified in three stages and valued as food accordingly. Lo or kumiss was prepared by heating milk and letting it ferment naturally. Su or kaymak was skimmed from the top of the kumiss and is the equivalent of 'Devonshire' cream. Ti-hu or clarified butter was made by reducing kaymak over heat and is the same as the ghee of India. Clarified butter was highly valued as food: Sun Ssu-mo wrote that it tones the bones and marrow and promotes longevity. Clarified butter also played an important ceremonial role as a food offering in Buddhist religious rituals.

Sweets became more popular than ever during the T'ang and led to the invention of many new dishes. Ever since antiquity honey had been the most common sweetener in China and was highly valued as food, both wild and cultivated varieties being used. Even more precious than honey was the so-called 'thorn honey,' the sweet exudate of a leafless desert plant called Camel Thorn (Alhagi camelorum). During the T'ang, however, the technique of refining sugar from cane was introduced to China from the western regions, and gradually it replaced honey as the primary sweetener. Sugar was a less expensive and far more versatile ingredient than honey and was used in a wide variety of pastries and beverages. More significantly, sugar also became a common seasoning in the kitchen and was used along with salt, soy, sesame, vinegar, and other condiments to balance the flavours of foods while cooking them.

The spices used in T'ang China were drawn mostly from Chinese herbal pharmocopeias. Their purpose was as much to balance the physiological effects of various ingredients in a dish as it was to balance the flavours for the palate. An excessively 'hot' food could be somewhat neutralised by adding some 'cool' spices, and vice versa. Peppers of the fagara family, indigenous to China, had been used since antiquity to spice up dishes, but during the T'ang the more pungent black peppers were introduced from Indonesia and quickly became the favourite type. Salt was used generously, for it too was highly recommended by T'ang physicians. Nutmeg, cinnamon, ginger, and ginseng were other commonly used spices. Perhaps the most popular spice was licorice, which pharmacologists said could counteract any and all toxins which might appear in other ingredients used in a dish.

Pickling and preserving, common food processing methods since antiquity, remained important during the T'ang as well. Vegetables, meats, fish, and fowl of every type were pickled with vinegar, salt, or wine or preserved by wind-drying and smoking. This type of food became especially important during times of scarcity and during the long cold winters in the north.

The relatively new technique of baking, first introduced during the Han, became even more widespread in T'ang times, and many new varieties of baked cakes and breads, both sweet and salty, appeared on the culinary scene. Wheatcakes were baked in the north and ricecakes in the south.

There were important new developments in the realm of beverages as well. Grape wine imported from the western frontiers became so popular at the T'ang court that it was demanded as tribute from subjugated tribes there. The technology of fermenting wine from grapes was gradually absorbed in the north, and grapes were cultivated there as well. Today in the P.R.C., the best grape

wines still come from Shensi (Shaanxi) province, where Chang-an was located, and from Chi-lin in Manchuria. Kumiss retained its popularity as a drink throughout the T'ang and following Sung eras. Most important, that quintessential Chinese beverage, tea, finally became the national drink of China. Formerly it had been available only to the wealthy and privileged, but during the T'ang it became everyman's drink. The *Cha-Ching* or *Classic of Tea*, China's bible of tea lore and etiquette, was written by Lu Yu during the late 8th century A.D.

As for eating and cooking utensils, metal became increasingly important, gradually displacing wood, stone, and clay implements. Precious metals such as gold and silver were used to fashion the chopsticks, wine goblets, and dishes of the imperial court and wealthy families of China: the type and quantity of metal used became an important indicator of one's social status.

T'ang China had taverns, inns, and wine-shops which offered drinks, girls, and entertainment, but there were still no restaurants as such, which specialised mainly in food service. Food in these T'ang establishments was provided by sending servants out to nearby open-air food stalls, which sprouted up like mushrooms in the streets of Chinese cities every evening. Permanent facilities for the preparation, sale, and enjoyment of food, i.e. restaurants as we know them, did not appear until the Sung era.

Sung: Northern (960-1126 A.D.) and Southern (1127-1279 A.D.)

The Sung era was the greatest single period of development in the history of Chinese food culture. The distinctive features which we identify with Chinese cuisine and eating habits today grew directly from the historical and cultural conditions which prevailed during the Sung. The appearance of the restaurant industry, the commercialisation of agriculture and food distribution, the move from cushions on the floor to tables and chairs, the emergence of rice as the primary staple, the codification of culinary principles, and the conscious cultivation of regional style cuisines can all be traced back to the culturally rich and active Sung period.

Three main reasons may be cited for the rapid development of culinary culture and agriculture in Sung China. The first is urbanisation: during the

Sung period there was a large-scale movement of people into the cities, which became great centres of culture and commerce. Concurrently with urbanisation came the rise of sophisticated urban culture and cosmopolitan tastes. The second watershed development was the conquest of the north by the Jurchen Mongols in 1126 A.D., a traumatic event which forced the Sung court to flee south of the Yangtze, where it established a new southern capital at Hangchou (Hangzhou). The transfer of the seat of empire to the south strongly influenced Chinese eating habits. Finally, the introduction of Champa and other high-yield, fast-growing strains of rice made China a primarily rice-eating nation for the first time and permitted a major expansion of the population. The pre-eminence of rice, a southern grain, coupled with the emperor's flight to the south shifted the overall culinary emphasis in China from northern to southern styles.

The shift to rice as the staple foundation of the Chinese diet was highly significant. Rice can support a greater number of people per acre at a lower cost than any other food in the world. It also contains the most concentrated source of nutritionally balanced calories per acre of any food. The introduction of Champa rice south of the Yangtze created for the first time a sufficient surplus of the grain to feed other regions of China as well. Gradually wheat and millet, staple grains of the Chinese diet since earliest antiquity, became less important sources of food energy. This process was completed when the Jurchens conquered the north, China's major wheat and millet producing region. So salient became the role of rice in agriculture and other aspects of the food industry that its price and availability became general barometers for the state of the entire food industry. This remains true today.

Commercialisation of agriculture and food distribution during the Sung stemmed from both increased production and rapid urbanisation. The rise of cities led the way to the emergence of vast, centralised markets where everything edible in the empire was available. Consequently, the variety and supply of food items in the cities increased significantly, permitting ever greater culinary diversification and supporting the burgeoning restaurant industry. These huge open-air urban markets still comprise the primary daily source of food for households and restaurants alike in China, Hong Kong, and Taiwan. They also gave rise to another important agricultural industry: cash crops. With the appearance of city markets where large quantities of food could be sold out in less than a day, nearby farm communities began to cultivate fast-growing, high-profit specialty items, especially vegetables and fresh-water fish. The cash crop industry contributed much to the great leap forward in food variety during the Sung. To support all these new developments, the food distribution system in China also underwent great improvement: the Grand Canal and other inland waterways formed intricate commercial networks which brought food from and supplied food to every part of the empire, not just the capital. Storage depots and wholesalers made distribution more efficient. Rice, tea, and sugar became the most important and heavily traded items in the food distribution networks.

The needs of city dwellers and their urban life-styles gave birth to the restaurant industry in China. Urbanisation produced a broad new range of gourmets with refined culinary tastes and plenty of money to indulge those tastes. Formerly, haute cuisine was enjoyed exclusively by the imperial court and by wealthy, noble families. But in the cities of Sung China entire new classes of gourmets appeared: merchants, bureaucrats, artisans, professionals of all types, and city dwellers in general all required places to eat out and to entertain their friends and associates. Restaurants of all types arose to serve them: multi-storied gourmet palaces, simple and inexpensive specialty restaurants, private catering establishments, floating restaurants on Hangchou's (Hangzhou's) West Lake and other waterways, and wine-houses and tea-shops which prepared food. During this time, the transition from sitting on cushions on the floor to using tables and chairs was completed, an important development in Chinese food service. To top it all off, a class of professional chefs appeared to operate the great commercial kitchens of Sung China. It was finally possible not only to eat out every night but also to choose from a wide variety of food styles and accompanying entertainment whenever doing so.

The restaurant industry in Sung China was intimately bound with the lives of courtesans and prostitutes, for food and sex continued to be enjoyed together as they had for millenia. Girls (or boys) of all types and ages were available to customers who wanted them. Eating also continued to be strongly associated with drinking, and famous wines from all over the empire were stocked by restaurants. The motto in a Sung restaurant seemed to be *chr, he, wan, lle,* 'eat, drink, and be merry,' and — with the sole exception of sexual services — this remains generally true today in the restaurants of modern China. In effect, food, drink, and sex were a package deal in many of the restaurants of old China.

The best restaurants and wine-houses were located in the Northern Sung capital of Kaifeng and later in the Southern Sung capital of Hangchou (Hangzhou). These were places where 'wind and rain, cold and heat do not occur, and day mingles with night.' Guests often stayed ensconced in these pleasure palaces for several days. Paintings and calligraphy by famous poets and painters decorated the walls, and utensils of sterling silver and gold were common. The apex of Sung culinary life occurred in the southern capital of Hanchou, which Marco Polo described as 'the greatest city which may be found in the world, where so many pleasures may be found that one fancies himself in Paradise.' It is a significant point that Marco Polo rarely distinguished among the pleasures of food, drink and sex in his descriptions of China, for all three were part and parcel of the good life in Hangchou (hangzhou). The 'Lou-Wai'Lou' restaurant, one of the original Chinese restaurants in Hangchou located directly on the banks of West Lake, still operates at the same location under the same name in the Peoples' Republic 800 years later.

There was progress in the realm of beverages as well. The art of distilling spirits from grains entered China during the Sung, resulting in the creation of a variety of potent new liquors. Most of these were distilled from sorghum or *kaoliang.* Fermented alcoholic beverages, such as grape wine and kumiss of mare's milk, continued to enjoy great popularity as well.

The links between food and medicine remained just as important during the Sung as they had been previously and were further elaborated. This aspect of Chinese cuisine is well illustrated by the fact that the Chinese written character used for 'prescription' (*fang*) is the same one used for 'recipe,' a semantic usage established by Sung scholars.

The Sung was the most studious, intellectually oriented period of Chinese history. Sung scholars liked to philosophise about everything and food was certainly no exception. Under the direction of Sung scholar-gourmets, the traditional principles germane to Chinese cuisine were discussed, elaborated, and explicitly analysed in writing. The importance of naturalness (*dze-ran*) in food received great emphasis: the primary ingredients in a dish must be absolutely fresh that day, in season, and locally produced to fully meet the requirements of naturalness. The intrinsic natures and pharmodynamics of foods were meticulously analysed based on both medical and philosophical considerations: the con-

clusions reached determined what one should eat, in what quantities and combinations, at what time of year, and which methods of preparation should be used. The cosmological concepts of balance and harmony, the theories of Yin/Yang, 'hot/cold', and the Five Elements were extended to cover increasing varieties of foods and other relevant culinary factors. Wretched excess, a perennial problem among the ruling classes of old China, was viewed as the ultimate infraction of the laws of balance and harmony.

An important yet subtle aspect of Chinese food philosophy, and a theme which has run throughout Chinese literature on food ever since the Sung era, is the cardinal contradiction between rustic simplicity and gourmet extravagance. This dichotomy was created by Sung scholars, who, on the one hand, preached the philosophical and pharmacological superiority of simple foods simply prepared and, on the other, regularly indulged in gourmet extravaganzas featuring the most exotic, complex culinary creations which their cooks could muster. The very scholars who praised the rustic purity of country life did so from the cosmopolitan comfort of the city. These two opposite culinary options have never been compromised in China. And since it is impossible to mix simplicity and extravagance in the same dish, they appear side by side in different dishes on the same table instead. Authentic Shark's Fin Soup, for example, which requires over a dozen chickens just for the broth alone and at least three days for proper preparation, might well appear on the same banquet menu alongside a simple but equally delicious country dish like 'Pock-marked Mama's Bean-curd,' a famous Szechuan (Sichuan) specialty. Since the Chinese have never been able to choose decisively between the rustic, earthy tendencies of their philosophy and the extravagant, highly aesthetic preferences of their senses, they have preserved both. This dichotomy appears over and over again in culinary references of the succeeding Yuan, Ming, and Ch'ing dynasties and constitutes one of the most singular aspects of Chinese cuisine.

To the Sung flight south we owe both the emergence of a Chinese cuisine *per se* and the conscious cultivation of distinctive regional styles. When the imperial court moved south across the Yangtze to Hangchou (Hangzhou), an inevitable blending of typical northern and southern cooking styles resulted in the new capital city. It was this new hybrid which finally bridged the culinary gap between north and south and gave birth to a distinctive national cuisine with universally recognised principles. At the same time, however, this new hybrid awakened a renewed awareness and appreciation of the special regional styles from which it grew. Hard-core connoisseurs of northern style food demanded places where their favourite dishes could be found, as did southern purists. Consequently, a hybrid 'all-China' cuisine developed side by side with thoroughbred regional styles in the southern cities of Sung China. Urbanisation and commercialisation accelerated this process, for thousands of

merchants and bureaucrats from all over China constantly travelled among the cities on business and pleasure, and they usually demanded food from their own native provinces wherever they went. To accommodate these influential travellers, regional specialty restaurants sprang up all over the empire.

The irony of Sung culinary literature is that all of it was written by cultured intellectuals with gourmet interests, not by professional chefs and restaurateurs, who remained by and large illiterate in those days. This fact explains the subtlety and sophistication of these writings, as well as their tendency to emphasise the subjective and theoretical while overlooking the technical details of cooking. This situation remained true down through the early decades of the 20th century, when professional chefs began for the first time to leave their own written culinary records.

By the end of the Sung era, China's population had leapt to 150 million people, a development directly attributable to food factors. Increased production, improved rice strains, better use of land, faster and more efficient food distribution, and the rise of great cities, where everything was available in abundance and sophisticated urban culture flourished, all contributed to the boom in population and the flowering of culinary culture during the Sung.

Yuan (1260-1368) and Ming (1368-1644)

The Mongol invasion and occupation of China devastated the sophisticated society and flourishing economy which had developed under the Sung. By the end of the Mongol Yuan dynasty, the population of China had dropped from 150 million back down to 100 million — a loss of 40% in only 100 years!

Genghis Khan's grandson Kublai Khan declared himself the founding emperor of the Yuan in 1260 and built the city of Peking (Beijing) as his capital. Both Chinese and foreign observers alike have recorded that drunkenness, gluttony, and riotous behaviour prevailed at the Yuan court. The Mongols never quite succeeded in absorbing the niceties of Chinese civilisation. They enjoyed Chinese food and women but rejected the cultural context which was so vital for a true appreciation of them. They remained barbarians in Mandarin clothing

throughout their occupation of China.

While the Mongol interlopers often enjoyed Chinese food as daily fare, Yuan imperial banquets and other formal occasions clove closely to traditional Mongol eating habits. Their favourite dish was lamb boiled whole in huge cauldrons and brought out whole to the dining room. There a servant hacked the carcasses into big joints and placed one before each diner, who tore into it with the small, sharp daggers carried by all Mongols and ate the meat barehanded. They washed down the mutton with copious quantities of kumiss, the Mongols' favourite drink, the best of which was made from 'the milk of young mares which have not conceived.' Imagine the consternation of refined Chinese court officials as they stood by and witnessed the emperor of China and his imperial entourage carrying on with such barbaric customs and uncivilised behaviour!

The Mongol interlude in China was brief: no barbarian power could hold the Dragon Throne for long unless it fully absorbed Chinese culture and customs and became, in effect, Chinese. After driving the Mongols back to the northern steppes and restoring Chinese rule, the founder of the Ming took strong and effective measures to revive traditional Chinese culture and promote orthodox Chinese life-styles. Traditional culture and cuisine developed rapidly under this policy. The only culinary legacy which might be attributed to the Mongols was an increased appetite for mutton in the north.

Since Chinese orthodoxy was central to Ming society, the ritualistic and ceremonial uses of food, so important in previous eras, were revived and strongly emphasised. In one year alone, the myriad shrines and altars of the Forbidden City, the fabulous home of Ming emperors in Peking (Beijing), required thousands of sheep, pigs, and oxen for slaughter and tens of thousands of chickens, ducks, and geese. Sacrificial animals slaughtered before a shrine were cooked whole in large bronze cauldrons according to the rules and regulations stipulated in the ancient Chou classics. Ritualistic use of food became an important factor in the lives of the common people as well. On the first and fifteenth days of the lunar calendar, special food offerings were made to ancestral spirits at the family altars kept in all Chinese homes. The offerings were as elaborate as the fami-

18

ly could afford. After proper ceremonial observances and a long enough interval for the spirits to descend and glean the 'essence' of the food before the shrine, the living family itself would feast on the gross remains of the offerings. This custom is still very much alive in Hong Kong, Singapore, Taiwan, and other Chinese communities around the world.

The kitchens of the Forbidden City employed a staff of over 5,000 persons to attend to the meals of the emperor, his concubines, and their entourage. To mention just one item, 250 head of sheep per day were required to provide mutton for the imperial tables of the palace. Entire ministries were occupied solely with the various functions of procuring, transporting, storing, allocating, cooking, and serving food within the confines of the Forbidden City. The sheer quantities of food prepared in the kitchens of the Forbidden City alone combined with the Ming demand for orthodox Chinese cuisine gave great impetus to the further development and subtle refinement of Chinese food.

The abundance and variety of foods available in the markets of Peking (Beijing) during the Ming era were even greater than in Chang-an during the T'ang or Hangchou (Hangzhou) under the Southern Sung. By the Ming period, refrigerated transport and storage of food was systematised and in common use, permitting fresh fruits and vegetables, fish, and other perishable delicacies from every corner of the empire to be shipped fresh to the capital all year round. Huge blocks of ice were carved from frozen rivers and lakes during the winter, wrapped in clean straw, and stored in deep mountain caves for use during the warmer seasons. These ice-blocks kept perishables fresh on the long journeys to Peking (Beijing) and were also used for cold storage underground. Strawberries, plums, fresh fish from far-away regions, and many other items formerly unavailable in the far north could now be enjoyed daily in the Forbidden City and were on sale in Peking's (Beijing's) markets.

The theoretical and practical connections between Chinese cuisine and Chinese medicine continued to grow significantly under the Ming, who were interested in anything traditionally Chinese. The identification of food as medicine was one of the most orthodox and ancient aspects of Chinese food. It

has always been a basic tenet of traditional Chinese medicine that 'many diseases can be cured by food alone.' Joseph Needham quotes a Chinese physician of the 11th century:

> Old people are generally averse to taking medicine but are fond of food. It is therefore better to treat their complaint with proper food than with drugs. Nutritional therapy should be resorted to first, and drugs only after proper feeding has failed.

This statement bears remarkable resemblance to that of Sun Ssu-mo, the great T'ang physician quoted earlier.

Two important books dealing with the pharmacology of food appeared during the Ming. The first, *Essential Knowledge for Eating and Drinking*, was presented to the Ming founder in 1368, the year he declared his new dynasty, by the author Chia Ming, who had just celebrated his 100th birthday that year. When the emperor asked him for his secret to health and longevity, Chia Ming simply replied, 'It is essential to be most cautious about what one eats and drinks.' After presenting his book to the throne, Chia Ming returned to his native home in Chekiang (Zhejiang), where he died at the ripe old age of 106.

Chia Ming's book describes hundreds of varieties of food items and their deleterious affects on health when improperly prepared or taken in combination with the wrong items. He lists their intrinsic pharmacological properties and presents other relevant medical information about food. In the foreword to his book, he states his purpose clearly:

> Drink and food are relied upon to nourish life, yet if one does not know that the natures of substances may be opposed to each other and even incompatible with each other, and one consumes them all together indiscriminately, at the least, the five viscera will be thrown out of harmony, and at the most, disastrous consequences will immediately arise. Thus it is that persons nourishing their lives have always avoided doing such damage to life. I have examined all the commentaries and subcommentaries in all the various authorities' herbals and have found that, for each substance discussed, both good and bad properties are noted, so that the reader is left not knowing what to do. I have made a point of selecting those facts relating to opposition and incompatibility in compiling the present work, as a contribution to those who in practicing reverence for life will find it convenient to investigate matters here.

In other words, those interested in living long, healthy lives must acquire a working knowledge of the pharmoadynamics of food. Otherwise, they risk 'doing such damage to life' through indiscriminate eating habits that their vital organs will not function properly and their lives will be considerably shortened.

The other great Ming treatise which discussed food pharmacology was Li Shih-chen's massive tome, *General Outlines and Divisions of Herbology* (*Pen Tsao Kang Mu*), which today still remains the bible of Chinese herbalists. Dr. Li spent 27 years of his life researching and compiling this definitive book on Chinese herbal medicine, and much of it deals with the medicinal properties and therapeutic uses of food.

Food culture permeated every aspect of life in Ming society. Appropriate foods were designated for every conceivable occasion, formal or informal. The journals and diaries left by Ming scholars are full of references to food etiquette, cooking, regional specialties, famous recipes, and other food lore. Gourmet interests comprised the great common denominator among the literati of the Ming. Educated gentlemen were expected to be gourmets.

The *Golden Lotus* (*Ching Ping Mei*), China's great novel of sensuality, captures in perfect, vivid details the central role of food in Ming social life. Not a single one of the book's 100 long chapters fails to mention and describe food and eating in colourful, elaborate details. Every visitor to the hero's household, regardless of his station in life or the occasion of his visit, is greeted with a dazzling array of delicacies provided by the host's kitchen. If a casual guest drops by unexpectedly to gossip with one of the hero's six wives, the hostess first orders her servants to set up a table and serve tea immediately. Within a few minutes a tray of food is brought out, typically consisting of such tasty treats as Flaked Ice-fish, Pickled Duck's Feet, Sweet Lotus Seeds, Fresh Walnut Meats, Goose in Aspic, Pork Knuckle in Vinegar, and fruits and pastries of all kinds. Wine is heated and served. Only after the guest has drunk a few cups of wine and tasted a few bites of food does the gossip get under way and the plot continue. As an erotic novel, *The Golden Lotus* also elaborates in great detail the link between enjoyment of food and sex, and one rarely appears

19

without the other close behind.

The restaurant industry grew rapidly during the Ming, especially those specialising in regional cuisines. One reason for this was the development and immense popularity of tourism in China at this time. City life was well established, and the number of wealthy merchants, officials, scholars, and writers grew steadily as China prospered. These cultured, wealthy urbanites loved to travel to famous scenic spots throughout the empire. Being cultured and wealthy, they were by definition also gourmets. While always open to experimentation with local cuisines, these wealthy gourmet travellers also demanded the availability of their own native provincial foods wherever they went. Thus, regional specialty restaurants catering to the tourist trade sprang up all over China, not just in the capital and other major cities. And since these travellers also required a place to sleep at night as well as someone to sleep with, the extent of sensual indulgence in the restaurants/ inns of Ming China exceeded even that of Hangchou (Hangzhou) 500 years earlier, where the restaurant industry was born. Food, drink, sex, music, and poetry all mixed together in a heady but harmonious blend of refined sensuality

in these places. And while only the wealthy could afford the more extravagant dishes and pleasures, Ming restaurants catered to every taste and budget, and people from all walks of life used them frequently. The Sung gave birth to restaurants in China, but the Ming institutionalised and popularised them.

Ch'ing (1644-1911)

The Ch'ing dynasty was a period of both continuity and change in the patterns of Chinese eating habits. The momentum of 5,000 years of steady culinary development provided the continuity. The changes were brought about by population pressures and by contacts with the West.

During the Ch'ing era, China underwent the greatest population growth in its history, from 150 million in the early 18th to 450 million by the mid-19th century, a leap of 300 percent in less than 150 years. This phenomenal growth was made possible not so much by improvements in native crops or agricultural technology as it was by the introduction of vital new crops from the New World. Maize, sweet potatoes, Irish potatoes, and peanuts came to China during the Ch'ing era and soon became the staple diets of significant

portions of the population. These new foods did not much affect eating habits in the agricultural and demographic heartland of China, but they did make life possible in corners of China which were formerly considered uninhabitable. Where rice, wheat, millet, barley, and other common crops could not

their calling, and the cuisine they enjoyed accordingly became all the more refined and elaborate. The 'Great Manchu Banquets' and 'Great Chinese Banquets' which evolved at the Ch'ing court in Peking are perfect examples of the extravagance and self-indulgence of Ch'ing gourmets.

As for the common people, their culinary disparity with the rich made them all the more appreciative of whatever food they could get and provided fuel to fire their creative imaginations. The poor in China were, and still are, heirs to the great Chinese gourmet traditions every bit as much as the rich. Thus, they excelled in inventing new dishes from simple, inexpensive ingredients, dishes which nourished the body and pleased the palate just as well as the fare of the wealthy. The poor pioneered the fuel-saving cooking methods and cost-efficient recipes for which Chinese cooking is so renowned today. The one cooking method universally identified with Chinese cuisine today is *chao*, variously translated as 'stir-fry,' 'sauté,' or 'fast-fry.' This

method was not commonly used before the Ch'ing era, but its efficiency and economy made it the most popular technique of all by the turn of the 20th century. Not only does the *chao* method save precious fuel and cooking oil, it also turns out to be the superior method from gourmet and nutritional points of view: it beautifully and quickly blends the flavours of the various main ingredients and condiments without sacrificing their texture, colour, fragrance, or nutritional potency. Flavour and nutrients are sealed in rather than cooked out. Many of China's most beloved recipes come not from the kitchens of wealthy, jaded gourmets, but rather from the in-

genious inventions and clever improvisations of the common people. Many such recipes are included in this book.

The Ch'ing dynasty produced a wealth of gourmet literature, the most famous of which is the poet Yuan Mei's cookbook, *The Menu*. *The Menu* provides both an important summary of all previous principles, practices, and lore connected with food in China as well as significant elaborations and practical explanations of gourmet cooking and eating habits. Again, the three principles most often alluded to are pristine naturalness, food pharmacology, and harmonious balance. One of Yuan Mei's most salient themes is that correct preparation is far more important than costly ingredients in food. He states his case with amusing examples:

A good cook cannot with the utmost application produce more than four successful dishes in one day, and even then it is hard for him to give proper attention to every detail; and he certainly won't get through unless everything is in its right place and he is on his feet the whole time. It is no use to give him a lot of assistants; each of them will have his own ideas, and there will be no proper discipline. The more help he gets, the worse the results will be.

I once dined with a merchant. There were three successive sets of dishes and sixteen different sweets. Altogether, more than 40 kinds of food were served. My host regarded the dinner as an enormous success. But when I got home I was so hungry that I ordered a bowl of plain rice-gruel. From this it may be imagined how little there was, despite this profusion of dishes, that was at all fit to eat.

I always say that chicken, pork, fish, and duck are the original geniuses of the board, each with a flavour of its own, each with its distinctive style; whereas sea-slug and swallows-nest (despite their costliness) are commonplace fellows, with no character — in fact, mere hangers-on. I was once asked to a party given by a certain Governor, who gave us a plain boiled swallows-nest, served in enormous vases, like flower-pots. It had no taste at all. The other guests were obsequious in their praise of it. But I said, 'We are here to eat swallows-nest, not to take delivery of it wholesale.' If our host's object was simply to impress, it would have been better to put a hundred pearls into each bowl. Then we should have known that the meal had cost him tens of thousands, without the unpleasantness of being expected to eat what was uneatable.

grow, New World crops such as maize and sweet potatoes thrived. The sweet potato became especially important as a source of vital nutrients, particularly in the north, during times of food shortages. The humble peanut provided a valuable new source of oil-seed to produce the voluminous quantities of cooking oil required for Chinese cuisine. Tobacco, incidentally, was also introduced to China at this time. The ultimate importance of these new crops cannot be underestimated.

By the time of the Ch'ing, the principles and techniques which defined Chinese cuisine were already fully developed. During the Ch'ing, they spread to every segment of China's population until they were in universal use throughout the empire. China had become, in effect, a nation of gourmet cooks and eaters. Robert Fortune, an Englishman travelling in China during the 1850's, noted in his journal that even 'the poorest classes in China seem to understand the art of preparing their food much better than the same classes at home.' Basically, the only difference in the eating habits of the rich and the poor was the cost and variety of ingredients each could afford to use.

Due to the Maltheusian pressures of a booming population and limited food supplies, wide disparities between the fares of the rich and the poor became a marked aspect of Chinese society for the first time during the Ch'ing. This very disparity, however, made wealthy gourmets all the more conscious of

Yuan Mei had strong opinions about the correct way to prepare and enjoy food, and the above passages reflect his willingness to state his views frankly. This was a common characteristic of Ch'ing gourmet writers.

The dichotomy between the rustic and the extravagant, between the requirements of frugality and the demands of refinement, became even more pronounced in Ch'ing culinary culture due to the disparities between the rich and poor. This theme runs throughout Yuan Mei's lively discussion of food in *The Menu*. He roundly criticizes many famous Ch'ing gourmets for tasteless extravagance, pompous pretension, and wretched excess. Similarly, he has nothing but praise for many . rustic, inexpensive dishes which are prepared simply and reflect perfectly the cardinal principle of balance and harmony in food. *The Menu* is both a practical cookbook containing famous recipes from throughout the empire as well as a rich storehouse of Chinese food lcre, gourmet opinion, and amusing anecdotes.

The aesthetic link between the enjoyment of food and sex continued to thrive among gourmet circles in Ch'ing China. Ch'ing literature is full of food terminology applied to sex, such as a virgin girl described as 'a sweet, ripe melon ready to cut,' hands as white and slender as 'freshly peeled Spring onions,' a mouth like a 'fresh cherry,' cheeks as white and fresh as the 'flesh of the litchi,' and many more. *The Dream of the Red Chamber*, *The Scholars*, and other Ch'ing novels offer colourful and insightful descriptions of food, food lore, and the sensual enjoyment of food and sex together.

A significant economic development of the Ch'ing era was the emergence of large, commercial corporate associations to handle the logistics of food supply, transport, distribution, and other aspects of the food industry. These associations were usually based on provincial and professional affiliations, such as the fishermen of Chekiang (Zhejiang), the wheat-millers of Shantung (Shandong), the rice-dealers of Kuangtung (Guangdong), the tea producers of Kiangsu (Jiangsu), and so forth. The associations gained enormous economic power, often monopoly, in their respective fields. These were highly organised, large-scale enterprises which greatly promoted the commercialisation of the food industry and helped spread Chinese culinary culture to every corner of the empire.

The restaurant industry continued to flourish during the Ch'ing, and courtesans, singers, and musicians continued to be associated with and provided by restaurants. The centre of the restaurant world during the Ch'ing was the famous commercial and pleasure city of Yangchou (Yangzhou), located where the Grand Canal meets the Yangtze River in Kiangsu (Jiangsu). Elaborate floating restaurant boats, with full banquet and entertainment services, became the rage of the day in Yangchou (Yangzhou), Hangchou (Hangzhou), and Canton (Guangzhou). By the mid-19th century, most gourmet restaurants offered another new diversion as well — opium-smoking.

The grand Chinese tradition of itinerant vendors of prepared foods thrived throughout the Ch'ing era, as it still does today in China, Taiwan, Hong Kong, and Singapore. Even the Son of Heaven, ensconced in the Forbidden City, occasionally tired of the fancy fare in his palace and sent a runner out to the local night market to get a bowl of 'Old Man Wang's Spicy Beef Noodles,' 'Pock-marked Mama's Bean-curd,' or other such rustically named, simply prepared, and incomparably delicious snacks. The kitchens of fancy restaurants and palaces simply could not duplicate these marvellous folk dishes.

The Ch'ing was the last imperial dynasty of China, during which time classical Chinese cuisine developed to its highest stage, traditional culinary principles were universally recognised throughout the empire, and sophisticated gourmet literature flourished. Such original, subtle gourmets as Yuan Mei cut through the fancy facades of costliness and exotica with which so many self-styled epicures surrounded themselves and got down to the real heart of the matter — correct preparation, originality, and creative improvisation. Yuan once said to his cook, 'What astonishes me is that, out of a couple of eggs, you can make a dish that no one else could have made.' His clever cook replied,

The cook who can work only on a large scale must lack daintiness, just as one who can handle common ingredients but fails with rare and costly ones can only be reckoned as a feeble practitioner. Good cooking, however, does not de-

pend on whether the dish is large or small, expensive or economical. If one has the art, then a piece of celery or salted cabbage can be made into a marvellous delicacy; whereas if one has not the art, not all the greatest delicacies and rarities of land, sea, or sky are of any avail.

20th Century China and the People's Republic

The 20th century has seen some of China's worst and best times for food. During the final decade of the Ch'ing dynasty and the early years of the Republic, political upheavals disrupted agriculture and destroyed the delicate local trade networks so vital to equitable distribution of food supplies; most Chinese lived a very marginal existence at this time. Central authority was weak and ineffectual, and all effective power fell to the hands of rapacious warlords. Dams and dikes, roads and canals, and other vital facilities for producing and distributing food were left in hopeless states of disrepair.

There was another reason for the paucity of the Chinese diet during the opening decades of this century: opium. Widely used among rich and poor alike, opium had become the bane of Chinese society by the time the Republic was established in 1912. Money normally spent on food went for opium instead. Land normally used to raise food crops was converted to cultivation of opium poppies. And one of the most basic physiological effects of opium on the body is to kill the appetite: addicts gradually waste away from malnutrition and indifference, regardless of how much food might be available to them.

In 1937, the Japanese invaded China with one of the most vicious, destructive military campaigns ever launched by one country against another. Burning, pillaging, and raping their way across the land, they deliberately ruined China's economic infrastructure. Rich and poor alike suffered from hunger and starvation in the wake of the Japanese onslaught.

No sooner had the Japanese been defeated by America than the Chinese Civil War broke out again, further prolonging the misery of the people and the stagnation of China's food production. Finally, in 1949, halfway through the 20th century, the Communist victory brought peace and stability to China again for the first time in a cen-

tury. The gradual recovery of agriculture and food distribution networks resulted in the restoration of nutritional balance and sufficiency in the Chinese diet. The early years were lean, but at least people stopped starving. Today, it is a well-known fact that as many people suffer from malnutrition and other dietary problems in certain parts of America as anywhere in China.

Looking at the Chinese diet today, we see that the traditional reliance on *fan*, grains, is more evident than ever. When rice or wheat are in short supply in contemporary China, millet, sorghum, *kaoliang*, soybeans, and even sweet potatoes are routinely substituted. An interesting survey of the dietary habits of typical rural households in central and coastal China was done during the 1920's. The households surveyed were in relatively peaceful and prosperous areas of China and representative of typical Chinese culinary habits. This survey revealed that 90 percent of food energy was derived from grains and grain products, only 1 percent from animal products, and the balance from vegetables, fruits, and sweets. The average American household of the same period derived only 39 percent of food energy from grains, a whopping 38 per cent from animal products, and the balance from other sources, mostly sugar. The successful reliance on grain foods in China is instructive, for it may well be the wave of the future as population explosions make animal products less and less viable as major sources of food energy.

It is interesting to note that the centrality of grain in the Chinese diet is built directly into the language. For example, one of the highest compliments you can give a *tsai* is that it really *hsia fan*, or 'helps the rice go down,' the implicit assumption being that the proper role of good *tsai* is to help the all-important grain staples go down pleasantly. Only at major festivals or other important occasions do the *tsai* receive major emphasis, and less *fan* is consumed. When asking someone in Chinese whether he has eaten yet or not, the correct phrase translates literally as, 'Have you eaten rice yet?' And just as children in the West were once told by their mothers to eat everything on their plates because 'there are children starving in China,' so Chinese mothers have always admonished their children to eat up every last grain of

rice in their bowls because 'each and every grain is bitter toil' in the fields.

Next to rice, the main items which comprise the daily diet of the common people in contemporary China are soy beans, cabbages, several varieties of mustard greens and turnips, and the various onions, scallions, and garlics of the Allium family. These items form the bulk of the food consumed on a daily basis, though there are regional differences in the mix, the diet being somewhat richer and more varied south of the Yangtze. In semi-arid and inclement regions, where the above won't grow, New World food staples form the basis of the diet: Maize, sweet potatoes, Irish potatoes, peanuts, tomatoes, and red chilies. Though these foods have been common in China for less than a century, they have already been fully integrated into the Chinese diet. Red chillies are an especially valuable import from the New World, for they contain among the richest and most available sources of Vitamins A and C of any food in the world.

The greatest legacy inherited by modern China from its imperial past is a diet which is naturally balanced. Due to its intrinsic diversity and its long-standing concurrent role as medicine, Chinese food needs no artificial supplements such as vitamin pills, protein powders, fiber supplements, and other nutritional boosters commonly used to bring contemporary Western diets up to nutritional par. Moreover, the nutritional balance is built into every dish and has nothing to do with the cost of ingredients. Despite the disparity in cost and content of a 12-course gourmet banquet and a simple bowl of noodles with beef, vegetables, and stock taken with a few side-orders such as dried beancurd and salt-fish, the actual nutritional balance of the two is about the same, and the supply of vital nutrients provided by the latter is perfectly sufficient for health and vitality. Indeed, the most concentrated and complete sources of proteins in the world are soy bean products and dried salt-fish, both of which comprise major portions of the Chinese diet and are among the least expensive of all foods. In China, the lack of money is no object to getting a nutritious — and delicious — meal.

Not only has modern science verified that the Chinese diet is the most nutritionally well balanced in the world, it has also proven that it is the most efficient and economical in terms of utilisation of land and other natural resources. The Chinese style of growing, preparing, cooking, and eating food can adequately support more people on less land at lower per capita cost than any other diet in the world. Coastal and southern China, with its intense agriculture and dense population, is living proof of this fact. Whether one uses the modern scientific jargon of the West (vitamins, proteins, minerals, etc.) or the more colourful terminology of traditional Chinese medicine (Yin/Yang, hot/cold, Five Elements, etc.), the singular conclusion remains the same: the Chinese have developed the world's most well balanced and economical cuisine, one that can equally satisfy the refined demands of the wealthiest gourmet and the frugal requirements of the poorest peasant. In this modern day and age, when poor nations are starving due to inadequate food supplies and rich nations are starving from serious nutritional imbalances and deficiencies, despite their gluttonous eating habits, it would seem that the entire world stands to benefit by adopting some of the ancient, time-tested principles and practices of Chinese cuisine.

Every food item that has evolved to a position of prominence in the Chinese diet turns out to be the most nutritious item of its kind. Modern nutritional science verifies this fact as well. Red chillies, for example, which are so popular in all styles of Chinese cooking, are one of the very best sources of Vitamins A and C. Pork, the favourite and most widely consumed meat in China past and present, is the most nutritious of domestic meats: it contains the highest deposits of riboflavin and other vitamins and minerals of all flesh foods, and pork liver contains double the amount of iron of any other liver. Soybeans have already been mentioned as the world's greatest source of complete proteins, especially when processed into bean-curd, a staple food almost as common as rice in China today. Sweet potatoes, the best source of carotene (from which Vitamin A is derived), have supported millions of Chinese during times of scarcity ever since their introduction. And the traditional Chinese love of fish as food goes far beyond its gourmet value: fish is the best, and in many places the only, source of certain vital amino acids such as methione, which are missing both in flesh and fowl. The point is that today, after 5,000 years of continuous culinary

and medical evolution, you can implicitly trust each Chinese recipe to be nutritionally well balanced and the Chinese diet in general to give you everything your body needs on a daily basis.

The diet in the P.R.C. today provides balanced nutrition without sacrificing the traditional Chinese demand for good taste. The gourmet inclinations of the Chinese people are very much alive and well: restaurants which fail to satisfy them are not patronised, and their managers soon find themselves called upon the carpet before some stern cadre to explain why they have failed to properly 'Serve the People,' modern China's great motto. Nor has home-cooking in China lost its traditional flair: gourmet cuisine aside, a typical meal prepared in the kitchen of a typical rural commune in China today is better balanced and better tasting than a typical meal prepared in a typical household in the West. And in China, it is prepared at a mere fraction of the cost of its Western equivalent.

Ironically, the traditional balance and nutrition of the Chinese diet is today being somewhat eroded by incursions of the three 'whites' from the West: low-extraction white flour, highly polished white rice, and refined white sugar. Western methods of milling and polishing wheat and rice are more convenient, especially for shipping and storage, and have been largely adopted in China, Taiwan, and elsewhere in the Orient. But these Western methods rob wheat and rice of virtually all of their vital nutrients, leaving nothing but 'empty calories.' As for white sugar, its evils are well known: It erodes both the teeth and the appetite for better foods. In former times, adults and children alike in China snacked on such things as dried bean-curd, pickled vegetables, preserved meats, dried salt-fish, watermelon and pumpkin seeds, and other nutritionally valuable items. Today, sugary soft-drinks, factory-made candies and cookies, cakes of white flour, white sugar, and cheap oil, chewing gum, and other banes of good nutrition are slowly but surely replacing the traditional snacks of China. The power of mass advertising and the automatic identification with the 'progressive, modern West' which these 'foods' impart are partly to blame for this unfortunate state of affairs. Perhaps only when the West begins to appreciate and adopt certain traditional Chinese eating habits

will the Chinese themselves once again realise the superiority of their own native culinary system.

It is at best difficult and arbitrary to conclude that one cuisine is 'superior' to another, especially in light of the many subjective factors involved. Yet in a comparative analysis of different cuisines, China's comes out on top in so many respects that it is equally difficult not to conclude that it is the overall superior diet from both nutritional and gourmet standpoints. On this ever more crowded planet of ours, it is certainly the most viable diet in the world. Its superiority in terms of variety, nutrition, taste, and economy have already been discussed. However, the actual style of eating food is also a crucial aspect of any cuisine, and here again the Chinese way seems to be far ahead of the rest of the field.

Eating *a la Chinoise* provides each diner with automatic portion control, something lacking in Western-style food service. Each diner may select as much or little as he wishes from the various dishes on the table without insulting his host or the chef. In Western cuisine, each person receives a set portion of one type of food on his plate: If the portion is insufficient to satisfy his appetite, it is awkward and usually socially impermissible to order a second entrée from the kitchen. If the portion is too large and he fails to finish it, he risks insulting the host or chef.

Chinese eating style also permits each diner to exercise automatic flavour control and to mix the tastes of the dishes and condiments creatively. Diners select more from the dishes that please their palates and less from those that don't, again without insulting the host or chef. Morsels may be dipped in a variety of sauces provided on the table to alter or enhance their flavours. Best of all, bites of food from various different dishes may be mixed together in the mouth to produce infinite different combinations of taste sensations. This is impossible in Western cuisine, in which you are often tantalised by the aroma and appearance of the food on your neighbour's plate but prevented from tasting it by social etiquette and the constrictions of Western food service.

Finally, in the Chinese style of eating, with a wide assortment of nutritionally and pharmacologically different dishes on the table before you, your body automatically guides your chopsticks to those dishes richest in the

24

elements your body needs most at the moment. This is a chemical response, triggered perhaps by the aromas of the foods. Again, this is impossible in Western cuisine, in which set meals are placed before each diner, and it becomes a matter of pure luck whether the food on your plate happens to be what your body needs most that day.

A discussion of food in the P.R.C. would be incomplete without mentioning the social functions of food as distinct from its nutritional and gourmet aspects. Food has always been an important form of social communication in China, and this still holds true today. With the relative abundance, availability, and equitable distribution of food in China, a far greater proportion of the populace can now afford to eat out in restaurants than at any other time in Chinese history. Everywhere you travel in the P.R.C. you notice that restaurants are jammed with people eating, drinking, and socialising. While the fare is generally simple and inexpensive, it is still highly nutritious and very delicious. Simple, rustic foods have always formed an important part of Chinese cuisine and are actually preferred on a regular basis to complex and fancy dishes, even by those who can afford the latter.

Those who can afford it, however, can still find the very best of China's traditional *haute cuisine* in the best restaurants of contemporary China. Such excellent establishments as the 'Pine Crane' in Soochou (Suzhou) — now in its fourth century of operation, the 'Lou-Wai-Lou' (800 years old) and the 'Hangchou Wine-House' in Hangchou (Hangzhou), the 'North Garden' and the 'South Garden' in Canton (Giangzhou), and many others still serve the famous gourmet dishes of China with traditional flair and original style. In the 'V.I.P. Rooms' of these restaurants, where the best dishes are available and all foreign visitors are entertained, you will invariably notice that most of the tables are occupied by important comrades and cadres entertaining or being entertained by their colleagues. Eating out is the one traditional pleasure which the new state has not eliminated from the Chinese scene, simply because its social functions are far too important and the habit too well ingrained in Chinese society.

Going out to eat in China, Hong Kong, Taiwan, Singapore, or other Chinese communities is different from going out to eat Western style. First of all, a special occasion of some kind is usually involved: should one be missing, one is invented. The criteria for selecting a restaurant are also quite different. As long as the food is famously good, Chinese will climb the highest mountains, ford the widest rivers, and endure all manner of inconvenience to get to a simple open-air food stall in some remote village just to sample a famous specialty unrivalled anywhere else. In Hong Kong and Taiwan, people sometimes drive for hours through unbearable traffic to get to a 'famous restaurant,' which, to the novice Western eye, would appear little better than a hovel, with bare walls, spartan furnishings, peeling ceilings, and no 'atmosphere' whatsoever. Yet Chinese gourmets, rich and poor alike, flock to such places to sample some unique dish produced only by the proprietor.

In the West, the measure of a meal's worth when dining out is often gauged by factors unrelated to the food itself: fancy decor, soft music, and candlelight, sterling silver tableware and crystal goblets, liveried waiters hovering in attendance, and plush furnishing are the important requirements. After all, how much can be done with a grilled steak, baked potato, boiled vegetables, and a salad? In effect, eating out in expensive gourmet restaurants in the West is often more a matter of renting sumptuous premises and elegant ambiance in which to eat a mediocre meal than it is of purchasing creatively original and unusually good food. In China, the main criterion for eating out has always been, and still remains, the quality and nature of the food itself. Chinese restaurants are notorious among sensitive Western diners for their complete indifference to ambiance and the cacophonous din which prevails in them. But the Chinese don't even notice these things: to them the quality of the food and the company with which it is enjoyed are the all-important and overriding factors. You can't eat atmosphere, and in a country where money and resources are limited but everyone has gourmet tastes, you cannot afford to waste money and materials on it either.

Hosting a banquet for one's friends and associates has always been the most quintessentially Chinese way of celebrating an important event in one's life or a major public festival. Even in spartan, egalitarian China today, this still remains true. The degree of formality and the lavishness which mark the banquet are still accurate indicators of the host's social position, his relationship to his guests, and the importance of the occasion itself. None of these factors are ever explicitly stated: They are all implicitly implied by the dishes which appear on the table under the host's directions. The dishes he selects reflect not only his economic status (how much he can afford to spend), and his social status (how much he owes his guests and the occasion), but also his culinary cultural status (whether he has gourmet or plebeian tastes). Communism has rid China of the wretched excess of the rich as well as the abject dearth of the poor, but the gourmet tastes which have always been shared by both remain intact, and the foods available now fall somewhere in between the former extremes. Numerically, more people than ever can afford to eat out in China today and indulge their native craving for good food. By 'breaking bread together,' social bonds are re-affirmed, and one of life's most natural and gratifying pleasures, one that can be renewed and enjoyed each and every day, is shared with one's chosen companions. While the camaraderie of eating together is shared to some extent all over the world, it lies at the very heart of the Chinese concept of eating. Rarely does a Chinese eat alone at home or in a restaurant.

The foregoing culinary tour of Chinese history is meant to give the reader some fundamental feelings and facts about Chinese cuisine. It is always easier to understand and accept foreign ways if you first glimpse the historical context in which they evolved and grasp the underlying principles through which they developed. For a complete, detailed account of Chinese food history, the reader is referred to *Food in Chinese Culture*, edited by K.C. Chang (Yale, 1977). Much of the information presented in this chapter is derived from this comprehensive and scholarly book, a pioneer in the field of food history.

The authors hope that this chapter whets your intellectual appetite for Chinese cuisine and encourages you to pursue the art of Chinese cooking and eating in your own home. Should you do so, you will surely derive the same nutritional, aesthetic, and economic advantages enjoyed today by one quarter of the world's population.

CHAPTER II
Chinese Cooking Utensils,
Condiments and Methods

Of all the world's great cuisines, Chinese cooking is probably the easiest to learn and practise. All the utensils and cooking methods commonly used to produce even the most complex dishes are very simple. With only four of the most ancient and rudimentary implements (cleaver, board, wok, and spatula), plus any source of intense heat, (charcoal or wood are fine), at least 75 percent of a typical Chinese menu is easily prepared. Recipes are never rigid in application, there is always plenty of room for substitution and creative improvisation.

Yet many people regard Chinese cooking as an inscrutable art, supremely difficult, if not impossible, to master. Ironically, the perceived difficulties lie precisely in its very simplicity: in Chinese cooking, one need not follow complex recipes by rote, and many of the modern technological conveniences of the Western kitchen prove of no use. Instead, one simply needs to develop the proper 'touch' or 'feel' for Chinese cooking. But since such vague, non-rational concepts are foreign to the Western mind, most Westerners view Chinese cuisine as a highly contrived and basically unapproachable Oriental art. Nothing could be further from the truth.

The utensils, methods, and most of the condiments employed today in Chinese cooking have been in continuous use in China for several thousand years. After such a long evolution, only the simplest, most flexible tools and techniques have survived. The utensils, condiments, and methods introduced below are commonly used by millions of Chinese cooks — from gourmet chefs to simple peasants — and there is absolutely no reason why the average Westerner with an interest in cooking should not be able to acquire these skills as well.

It is the concept of 'feel' or 'touch' in Chinese cooking that troubles most aspiring Western adepts of the art: they would prefer to have everything laid out in recipes, especially seasoning proportions and exact cooking times, rather than have to rely on their own senses and intuition. In Chinese cuisine, however, written recipes should only serve as guidelines, especially for pre-cooking preparations in the kitchen. As for the exact proportions of cooking condiments and the correct cooking times, these decisions are ultimately in the hands of the cook, and they usually must be made instantly, without

thought, while cooking. Many Western cooks are needlessly cowed by this requirement, but it is no different than developing a 'touch' for tennis or a 'feel' for driving sports cars. More than any other style of cooking, practice makes perfect in Chinese cuisine.

There are four basic goals in cooking Chinese food, and these are also the basic indicators which tell you how much to add when, how hot the fire should be, and how long the dish should be cooked. All these indicators are directly related to the senses.

The four cardinal conditions by which every Chinese dish must be judged are flavour, fragrance, colour, and texture. The primary purpose of all the different ways of cutting meats and vegetables, marinating various ingredients, pre-cooking some while leaving others raw, and all the elaborate preparations prior to cooking, is to ensure that these four classical requirements are properly met. Successful Chinese cooking is simply a matter of learning how to use your basic senses rather than your head while in the kitchen.

The foremost factor is flavour. The goal is to capture and preserve the innate, natural fresh flavours of the main ingredients. Seasonings are used to enhance these 'fresh-natural'(*xian*) flavours while suppressing any foul or rank (*xing*) flavours. Excessive use of strong seasonings not only masks the natural (*xian*) flavours of foods, but is also employed by unskilled chefs to mask their culinary shortcomings. Properly prepared foods should leave a pleasant aftertaste on the palate, vaguely reminiscent of the main ingredients' original flavours, rather than the flavours of the condiments.

Closely related to flavour is fragrance. It is perhaps even more vital to the full enjoyment of gourmet foods, for many subtle flavours come through only through the fragrance. Note how food tastes absolutely flavourless when you have a cold. Fragrance passes not only through the nostrils but up from the mouth and into the sinuses while chewing. Fragrance is easily diluted or lost in cooking, and proper prior preparation protects the innate fragrance of foods before they hit the fire. Treatment with appropriate seasonings, application of proper cooking methods, and, most important, proper timing for each different kind of food are the methods employed to preserve and enhance natural fragrances.

Colour is the visual indicator used in Chinese cooking. It is also important for the full appreciation of gourmet foods, for we all eat with our eyes first and then with our mouths as we sit down to a beautifully arranged banquet table. Various ingredients with contrasting colours are combined in the same dish for visual effect, such as green and red peppers, black mushrooms and yellow bamboo shoots, orange carrots and white turnips, etc. Colour also indicates when many foods are done in sauté cooking, such as string beans turning from light to dark green, meat turning from red to brown and translucent fish meat turning opaque white. Chinese food preparation and cooking methods aim at preserving beautiful colours and altering drab ones in food.

Finally, there is texture, which is perhaps the most unique requirement of classical Chinese cuisine. Nowhere

else is so much emphasis placed on texture. This opens up an entirely new realm of sensual enjoyment of food: the feel and consistency on the tongue, palate, throat, and especially between the teeth. The number of different textures distinguished by Chinese cooks and gourmets is incredible. There are crunchy, crispy, tender, slippery, melting, smooth, soft, hard, creamy, spongy, dry, juicy, rubbery, chewy, fluffy, and fibrous textures, plus infinite combinations thereof. This is by far the most sophisticated and subtle aspect of gourmet Chinese cuisine and one that is purely aesthetic in nature. Ingredients are selected for similar or contrasting textures within the same dish and in the meal as a whole. A classical example is fresh bamboo shoots (crunchy) cooked with black mushrooms (soft and chewy); this particular dish also offers a similar contrast in colours. Deep-fried foods are favoured for their crispy, dry texture outside and tender, juicy texture inside. Eel has a slippery texture, steamed pastries are creamy, squid is rubbery, and so forth.

Texture is also the most difficult aspect of foods to control while cooking. Once the texture 'sets,' it is impossible to alter it. Unlike flavour and fragrance, textures cannot be influenced by condiments. Texture is where the 'magic touch' in Chinese cooking is most vital. Certain pre-cooking methods such as parboiling, steaming, deep-frying, and light sautéing are sometimes employed to properly set the textures of certain ingredients. Some ingredients used to prepare a dish are there purely to lend textural qualities to it: 'wood ears' (tree fungus), jellyfish,

peanuts, beancurd, and other texture foods often appear in supporting rather than primary roles in a dish to provide contrasting textures. Fortunately, if the conditions of flavour, fragrance, and colour are all properly met in cooking, texture usually comes out correctly as well. The main trick to texture is to select the appropriate ingredients in the first place, making sure that they are absolutely fresh. If not, substitute something else or leave it out altogether. Different textures are enjoyed with different parts of the mouth, including lips, tongue, palate, and throat, but most of them are best appreciated between the molars.

Below, various vital aspects of Chinese cooking are briefly introduced, beginning with common cooking utensils, then proceeding to pre-cooking kitchen preparations, followed by common cooking condiments, and ending with the most common cooking methods. The chapter concludes with a brief word on creative improvisation in Chinese cooking.

CHINESE COOKING UTENSILS

Chinese cooking utensils are the simplest, most practical, and easiest to maintain cooking implements in the world. Of ancient design, they are made of basic, sturdy, and inexpensive materials, primarily iron, wood, and bamboo. The overwhelming majority of Chinese dishes can be prepared with only four basic implements: a Chinese cleaver, a sturdy cutting board, a round-bottomed pan or 'wok', and a spatula.

Chinese Cleaver: A good Chinese cleaver is the most versatile implement

in the kitchen. It can cut, chop, slice, shred, mince (grind), pound, peel, scrape, flatten, and otherwise process every type of ingredient used in Chinese cooking. When charcoal and wood are used for stoves, the cleaver is used to cut kindling. It can also be used to ward off unwanted intruders from the kitchen.

The most important skills to develop for using the cleaver are rhythm and relaxation. Start out slowly with a cutting rhythm you can handle and gradually increase the tempo. Wrist and arm should be loose and relaxed, a short burst of strength applied only at the actual moment of cutting. A properly used and cared-for cleaver will last a lifetime; indiscriminate hacking and careless cutting will ruin it in less than a year. The great taoist philosopher and humourist Zhuang-Zi (4th century B.C.) relates the words of a bullock butcher in one of his anecdotes:

A good cook changes his chopper once a year — because he cuts, an ordinary cook once a month — because he hacks. But I have had this chopper for 19 years, and although I have cut up many thousands of bullocks, its edge is as if fresh from the whetstone.

It is best to have two types of cleavers: a light one for fine cuts such as shredding and mincing (grinding) and a heavy one for chopping through meat with bones. When chopping up spareribs, whole chickens, or ducks and so forth, you should aim for the joints, ligaments, and relatively soft spots. Cleavers come in steel and iron; steel is best for heavy choppers, but iron is infinitely superior for lighter cleavers used in most cutting. Iron holds a better edge and can be easily honed on a whetstone. The stainless steel cleavers available now in many home-product stores tend to lose their edge quickly and are also less suited to the heavy tasks an iron or steel cleaver manages so capably. See also page 396 for specific techniques with the Chinese cleaver.

Chopping Board: A good hardwood board is indispensable for proper cutting and other preparations. The type most favoured by Chinese cooks is a round cross-section of a hardwood tree. Western-style standing butcher blocks are ideal for use in the Chinese kitchen. After use, cutting boards may be scraped clean with the back edge of the cleaver, rinsed with warm water, and hung to dry.

An efficient Chinese kitchen will have several chopping boards reserved for different tasks. An older board for use when chopping through bones, one reserved for preparing such strong-smelling ingredients as onions, garlic, and ginger and another for preparing fruit.

The Wok: Today the round-bottomed wok (Cantonese pronunciation; Mandarin is guo) is the most universally recognised utensil of the Chinese kitchen. It is highly versatile and may be substituted for all other Chinese cooking vessels whenever necessary.

Woks come in many sizes, shapes, and materials; there are flat-bottomed, teflon-coated woks for use on electric hotplates, and even electric woks, but these are a poor substitute for the simple, traditional Chinese iron wok, particularly if used with a gas wok cooker, see also below. The best type of wok is one with a single, sturdy wooden handle rather than the double 'ear' type of handles which can be difficult to manipulate.

Iron has the advantage of distributing heat very quickly and uniformly throughout the surface of the pan. Iron seasons well, and an iron wok improves with age. With the high heat and constant rapid stirring used in most wok cookery, nutritionally significant amounts of natural iron are also imparted to foods during the cooking process, an important consideration in restricted diets. A single, wooden handle permits you to manipulate the pan with one hand while wielding a spatula with the other, and makes pouring from the wok considerably easier as well.

Due to the round shape of this original Chinese cooking vessel, minimum amounts of cooking oil and cooking fuel are used, an important consideration for everyone in this energy-conscious age. The wok's versatility is legend; you can fry a single egg or saute a kilo of chopped cabbage, sauté a few slivers of meat or stew a whole chicken, fry, steam, stew, boil, or braise just about anything.

New woks tend to stick. A new iron wok should first be heated dry over an intense flame to burn off any surface impurities or coatings. However, this same process should not be undertaken with a stainless steel or aluminium wok as the result may be a 'burn' spot which will affect its performance later. The wok should then be well oiled and heated again, then the oil poured off and the inside of the wok rubbed vigorously with a piece of crumbled kit-chen paper. Rinse the wok well and hang to dry, or wipe out with a cloth and store upside down. After each use, clean the wok by rinsing it under hot water while scrubbing well with a bamboo or hair wok brush. Do not use detergents unless absolutely necessary. Woks should be treated like the old iron skillets common to many Western kitchens; the older and more seasoned they become, the better they cook.

When using the wok for sautéing, first heat it dry, then add the oil, swirling it around the sides just below the rim and allowing it to run to the bottom, thus coating the entire interior of the wok. Heat again until it smokes, after which the ingredients can be thrown in and stir-fried. This way the pan always remains slightly hotter than the oil, which helps prevent sticking. This is called 'hot pan/warm oil' in Chinese. When cooking fish or other delicate items that stick easily, it is helpful to rub the entire interior surface of the wok well with a piece of peeled fresh ginger before heating and adding the oil

Wok Spatula ('Charn'): The indispensable long-handled, shovel-like implement used for lifting and stirring foods in the wok. Steel is the best material, and the scraping edge should be slightly rounded to fit the wok. The spatula should have a wooden or plastic grip to insulate the heat. An egg slice (egg lifter) or wooden spatula will handle the task fairly well.

In addition to the basic four implements described above, there are a variety of other traditional Chinese cooking utensils which are useful to have on hand in the kitchen.

Wok Lid: The wok usually comes equipped with a large dome-shaped lid which fits inside the lip of the wok, giving an excellent seal. It is used when braising, slow-cooking, and poaching and sometimes also in the final stages of cooking stir-fried vegetables, and when the wok is used as a steamer or smoking pan. There is plenty of space beneath the wok lid for a rack (see below) and the ingredients to be steamed or smoked.

Wok Rack: A collapsible bamboo (see illustration, page 32) or fixed-in-place wire or aluminium stand for use inside the wok to hold dishes or ingredients above the surface of the wok when steaming or smoking. The open construction of the rack allows free and even distribution of the steam or smoke. A makeshift rack can be made using two wooden (bamboo) chopsticks. Place them across the wok, with a reasonable space between them and balance the plate or dish on top. Another makeshift rack can be produced using a wide, empty food can, such as that used to pack processed fish. Puncture the can in several places around the sides and across the bottom; the top should be removed completely. Place upside-down in the bottom of the wok and support the dish on top. This is ideal when using an old saucepan as a steamer.

Wok Stand: A metal ring which fits over a gas or electric element to provide a firm base for a round-bottomed wok.

Ladle: Ladles of various sizes and shapes are useful in preparing, tasting, and serving soups and stews. unlike the deep soup ladles used in the Western kitchen, the Chinese ladle is shallower, more saucer-shaped. An experienced cook needs only his ladle for measuring even the smallest quantities of ingredients and seasonings.

Strainer/Slotted Spoon: Two basic types of strainers are used in Chinese cooking. A flat, woven wire strainer retrives food from deep-frying oil or hot stock and is used for supporting items in a deep-fryer. The larger smooth metal strainer with round perforations and flat saucer-shape is best used for retrieving fried foods from hot oil and for draining these same foods over a basin. Many come complete with a fitted drip dish.

A slotted spoon, a metal colander, and a frying basket can replace the Chinese strainers. The wire strainers used in several recipes for shaping noodle or potato 'nests' are standard round, deep, wire mesh strainers with handles.

Frying Basket: A wire basket with one long handle, or two hooped handles, is invaluable in deep-frying, particularly for cooking smaller ingredients or shredded meats. The larger metal Chinese strainer can be used for this purpose also.

Cooking Chopsticks: These are a jumbo version of the smaller type used for eating. They are long enough to reach into a wok or stew-pot without getting the hands burned or splattered. They

are useful for plucking, arranging, stirring, turning, testing, and otherwise manipulating various types of food in the kitchen.

Steamer/Bamboo Steaming Basket: One of the most ancient of Chinese cooking vessels, the steamer (illustrated on page 33) is used to steam foods to final perfection, to pre-cook ingredients, warm up leftovers, and keep foods waiting to be served hot and moist. Steamers preserve the pristine flavours of foods, seal in nutrients, keep food moist, and require no fats or oils for cooking. Bamboo steaming baskets are used for the many kinds of steamed buns, pastries, and breads in the Chinese diet. The baskets can be placed inside the wok and a piece of clean cheesecloth or perforated greaseproof paper placed over the slats before putting in the food, to prevent

sticking. Or the slats may be well oiled with lard or vegetable oil before use. When a single steaming basket is used, it should be covered with its own lid and placed inside the wok or steamer and the pan lid set firmly in place. However, the baskets are designed to be stacked, and fit tightly one on top of the other, with a single lid on top. Stacked baskets can be set in a wok or over a saucepan of boiling water and, if well enough sealed around the lower edge, will not require a lid covering the lot. Certain recipes require that the lid be removed for a few seconds at several intervals during cooking. This is to prevent the food from bursting open due to the intense cooking heat. Snack foods such as dim sum are taken straight from straight from steamer to table in the attractive bamboo baskets. These are now readily available from Chinese products and rattanware retailers.

Aluminium multi-tiered steamers are useful for cooking the many types of steamed dishes and whole fish, poultry, or large cuts of meat. There is ample space in the Chinese steamer for cooking several dishes at once. Most have at least two tiers over a lower water dish and have a domed lid. Each tier has a series of large round holes in its base to allow the steam to circulate freely. Meats may be placed directly onto the well-oiled surface of the steamer, but usually foods are placed in a dish to prevent sticking and to collect the cooking liquids. Foods can be effectively steamed in a wok, see above, or in a saucepan with a rack, see above, Wok Rack.

Casserole/'Sand Pot': For braising, stewing, soup making, and a multitude of other cooking processes, the Chinese lightweight clay 'sand pot' has few rivals (two types are illustrated here). Its base is usually reinforced with a wire bracket making it strong enough for cooking over a gas flame or directly over high charcoal heat. They have, however, been known to stick to flat electric hot plates, and it is not advisable to use them directly on these. An asbestos mat placed underneath will protect the base. A wok or heavy metal pot may be used instead, but earthenware stew pots have certain advantages: they diffuse heat slowly and evenly: excess moisture is released through the surface while excess grease is absorbed by it; and the thick surface protects simmering foods from intense exposure to the heat. The pots come in varying sizes and shapes and each has a well-fitted heavy clay lid. Additional useful cooking vessels and implements include:

'Fire-Pot': A table-top cooking device with a tray in the base to contain char-

coal, and a funnel-shaped chimney surrounded with a moat in which stock is heated for cooking at the table. Small woven wire baskets on long handles come with the fire-pot, but wooden chopsticks may be used instead to add and retrieve food from the hot stock. A substitute fire-pot can be made with a table-top gas ring or electric hot plate and an attractive saucepan or stew pan. Or use a fondue pot with a strong spirit or gas flame underneath.

Electric Rice Cookers: These are rapidly replacing conventional saucepan cooking in Chinese households. They cook rice perfectly and keep it warm throughout a meal. They are also used for rice-pot dishes and other simple cooking. A thick aluminium saucepan

with a tight-fitting lid also produces excellent results, see more on rice cooking, Chapter VIII, Noodles and Rice-Accompaniments

Bamboo Wok Brush: This ancient implement has two uses. Immediately after use, the wok should be held under hot running water and scrubbed with the bamboo brush. The brush cleans the surface without requiring detergents and therefore without sacrificing the seasoning of the wok. They are sometimes also used instead of a spatula when stir-frying very finely shredded meats which must be cooked as quickly as possible. The bamboo brush-ends turn and stir such finely cut meats faster than a spatula. Separate brushes should be kept for each type of use. The brush is made from hair-thin slivers of bamboo and bound together at one end with strips of bamboo. They

should be well rinsed in hot water after use and hung to drip-dry.

Bamboo Tongs: A simple but useful tool to have on hand, bamboo tongs may be used to pluck unwanted items from a dish while cooking, pull out a tender morsel for tasting, transfer hot foods from oil to plate, and other similar uses. Tongs are a handy tool for those who have not yet mastered the art of using cooking chopsticks.

Dough Roller: Rollers are used to prepare dumpling skins, dough for buns and breads, and other pastry preparations. The heavy rollers common to Western kitchens are too big and unwieldy for the precision work required to make Chinese pastry wrappers. Look for a small, thin, short roller for this task.

Pastry Cleaver: A type of blunt-edged cleaver is used to make the crystal-clear pastries for such dim sum as 'shrimp dumplings.' These are sold at Chinese specialist stores, but a large metal cake spatula will perform the function just as well. It should be of the rigid-bladed type rather than one with a thin flexible blade.

Cookers: An important point to remember when cooking Chinese food, especially when using the ever-popular stir-frying method, is that the intensity of the heat must be sufficient, or else all of your careful kitchen preparations will have gone to nought. Electric ranges are unsuited to Chinese cooking; the heat being too highly concentrated at the bottom of the dish and changes in temperature too slow. The various

rings and stands sold with woks in the West to 'adapt' them to electric ranges do not overcome these drawbacks. The most ideal source of heat for Chinese cooking is an intense charcoal fire flamed by a fan, or gas heating. As charcoal is impractical in the home kitchen, we turn to gas and the gas cooker. Provided that at least one burner produces a flame big enough for stir-frying, the ordinary gas cooker will do. Unfortunately, most gas ranges manufactured in the West for household use do not produce such a flame. This problem may be overcome by having one burner in the range adjusted to produce the required flame, or by having a separate single burner for stir-frying. There are several types of portable gas wok-cookers available. All have a curved stand to accommodate the round-bottomed wok and produce the necessary high heat. The correct flame is one that is intense and large enough to lick up over the entire exterior surface of the wok when turned on full blast. A sufficient source of intense heat is one element in Chinese cooking for which there is no substitute. Single-burner gas cookers, of the kind using bottled gas are additionally practical in their portability. They can be used in the kitchen and stored away when not needed, they can be taken to the dining room for table-top cooking, and they can be used outdoors. Another type of simple portable cooker much used in traditional Chinese households is a small, clay, charcoal-and wood-burning cooker which supports just one wok or a 'sand pot.' These can be found in some specialist Chinese goods stores.

KITCHEN PREPARATIONS

The purpose of the various methods described in this section is to enhance the desirable aspects of flavour, fragrance, colour, and texture in foods, while suppressing the undesirable qualities. In Chinese cuisine, much more time and effort go into initial preparation of ingredients prior to cooking than into the actual cooking itself; the opposite is true in Western cuisine. Pre-cooking preparations are aimed at fine tuning the factors of flavour, fragrance, colour, and texture so that in the final product an optimum balance and harmony is achieved. Each ingredient must preserve its own unique identity while blending harmoniously with all the other ingredients used in the dish. To achieve this, each ingredient must be treated in specific ways prior to cooking everything together.

Cutting is the first step in preparing ingredients for Chinese cooking. All cutting is done in the kitchen, not at the table: all foods are prepared so that they can be eaten with chopsticks. Different cutting methods are used for different ingredients and purposes. When preparing meat, fish, and fowl, first scrape and cut away tendons, ligaments, and other extraneous membranes to ensure evenness of texture. When nothing but the meat is desired, skin and bones should also be removed.

The most common cut is called *si* or 'silk-cut' which involves finely shredding the meat across the grain to produce long, slender slivers. Beef, pork, and mutton are commonly cut this way for sautés. Meats are finely minced (*sui*) when they play supporting roles in dishes dominated by vegetables or for dumpling stuffings. Silk and mince cuts expose the maximum surface area to the hot oil and the condiments, permitting quick cooking and facilitating the blending of juices and condiments. Dicing into small cubes is used for boned chicken and lean meats for sautés, while large cubes are cut for simmered stews. Chopping into rough chunks complete with bone is used for spareribs, chicken, and duck, usually for 'red-stew' cooking. All of these cuts are done with cleaver and cutting board. See also page 392 for detailed instructions on preparation of ingredients and the use of the Chinese cleaver.

After cutting, marinating is the most common method used to prepare foods for cooking. Marinades are used for pre-cut meat, fish, and fowl to enhance their natural flavours, balance and impart others, and eliminate any rank tastes. Salt and wine are used to marinate kidneys: the salt extracts undesirable juices while the wine suppresses *xing* (rank) flavours. Salt is used alone to extract excess water from foods prior to cooking. Marination in water alone adds water to the ingredient; it is often used for prawns, fish, chicken, and certain vegetables. Water should never be added to cut beef or pork. The most common marinade for shredded or diced meats and chicken consists of soy sauce and wine with sugar and cornflour (cornstarch). Cornflour (Cornstarch) tenderises meats and imparts the 'slippery' texture. Wine counteracts rankness, while soy

sauce and sugar bring out the proper balance of salty and sweet flavours. An unusual marinade called *zao* consists of the fermented grain-mash dregs left over from distilling spirits. This method is used for meat, fish, and fowl and gives a very rich, aromatic flavour while tenderising at the same time.

Pre-cooking is a common preparatory technique in the Chinese kitchen, especially when various ingredients used in a dish have widely differing cooking times. Blanching is achieved by dumping the cut ingredients into boiling water: this sets the texture, tenderises, and removes any undesirable slime or scum from the tissues of meat, fish, and fowl. Hard vegetables to be used for stir-fried dishes with meat are often prepared this way.

Poaching is also a common way of preparing foods for the final cooking process. Similar to the Western method, it requires that the temperature of the water be kept below the boiling point, while the food remains in the hot water anywhere from 5 minutes to an hour or more. When preparing water for poaching fish or fowl, add sliced ginger root and spring onions (scallions) to help suppress rankness. Poultry and seafoods are the most commonly poached foods.

Steaming is often used to soften or

pre-cook such items as shark's fin, lotus root, whole chickens, and ducks. Stir-frying is also used to pre-cook certain ingredients prior to mixing with others in the final cooking process. Sometimes minced ginger, garlic, spring onions (scallions), and chillies are pre-sautéd to release their flavours into the oil before the oil is used to cook other items.

Pre-soaking in hot water softens certain ingredients prior to cooking. Dried tree fungus ('wood ears'), dried salted shrimps, and dried black mushrooms are commonly treated this way. The remaining water is often used as a seasoning during the subsequent cooking process. See also page 392 for specific preparation of dried ingredients.

Air-drying is an important preparatory process for fowl. After marination and pre-steaming, chicken and duck are hung to air-dry. This method dries out the skin thoroughly and ensures the proper crispy texture when the subsequent deep-frying method is applied.

Bone-breaking with the dull edge of a cleaver is applied to bones before boiling them for stock. This exposes the marrow, which gives the best flavour to stocks. When whole joints of chicken are marinated for deep-frying or broiling, the bones should be cracked first by hitting the joint hard with the dull edge of a cleaver, making sure not to break the flesh open. This way the cooking time is reduced because heat is more evenly distributed inside; it also releases the flavour and fragrance of the marrow into the meat during cooking.

COMMON CHINESE COOKING CONDIMENTS

The Chinese style of cooking has often been called 'a marriage of flavours.' While the oil or fat used in cooking brings the partners together, the condiments enhance and harmonise their relationship. The oil or fat used to cook a dish is often an important condiment as well.

Most Chinese cooking is done with some type of vegetable oil, usually peanut oil. This gives a slightly nutty flavour and fragrance to foods. Soybean oil, corn oil, and mixed vegetable oils are also used. For fat, the most common choice is lard: it has a rich aromatic flavour of its own and is commonly used to sauté bland ingredients or pre-fry foods prior to further cooking. Rendered chicken fat is also an excellent shortening, especially for sautéing green, leafy vegetables such as spinach. Duck fat may also be used.

Among the vast array of Chinese condiments available, the five 'S's' are the most important items: soy sauce, sherry, salt, sugar, and sesame oil. It is impossible to cook Chinese food properly without these, but other condiments may be improvised when they are unavailable. Below, a dozen common Chinese cooking condiments are briefly introduced, starting with the indispensable five 'S's':

Soy sauce (jiang-you): Fermented from soybeans, wheat, salt, and water, soy sauce is the cardinal condiment of Chinese cuisine. It is used in marinades, cooking, and table sauces. Few meat dishes are prepared without it. Soy sauce has a salty, smoky flavour, rich fragrance, and reddish-brown colour. The best, most consistently reliable brand on the market is Japan's excellent 'Kikkoman.'

Sherry or rice wine (mi-jiu): The Chinese generally use rice wine or *Shao-xing* wine in cooking. The closest Western equivalent is dry sherry, which many experienced connoisseurs of Chinese cooking deem to be superior. Japanese *sake* is also quite good for

Chinese cooking. Sherry or rice wine is used in marinades and in cooking, mostly for meat, fish, and fowl. Its foremost purpose is to eliminate rank flavours and unpleasant odours in animal foods, and secondly to tenderise the texture and facilitate the blending of flavours in the sauce.

Salt (yan): Salt is used in marinades to extract excess water or unwanted juices from fish, chicken, and vegetables. In cooking, it lends the basic salty flavour to foods, while balancing sweet flavours. Salt should be used sparingly in Chinese cooking, especially when large quantities of soy sauce, which is quite salty, are called for in the recipe.

Sugar (tang): The Chinese use sugar in the kitchen, but rarely on the dining table. White refined, raw, and rock crystal varieties are used. White refined sugar is used in most marinades and as a flavouring agent during cooking. It brings out the natural sweet flavours of all foods, including vegetables. Raw sugar is used for stews, sweet soups, and pastries. Rock crystal sugar appears in 'red-stews,' especially with pork knuckle spareribs and fish. Besides adding sweetness to the flavour, rock crystal sugar imparts a slightly viscous texture to the sauce and a bright sheen to the colour.

Sesame oil (ma-you): This is a highly aromatic condiment with a strong, smoky flavour. It should always be used sparingly. It is generally added to dishes at the last moment, and its purpose is both to add its smoky flavour and to suppress strong or rank tastes in certain foods, especially fish and fowl. It is a common ingredient in cold-plate dressings and table sauces used for dipping. A few drops dribbled onto prawns and fish while steaming eliminate the 'fishy' taste.

Garlic (suan), *ginger* (jiang), *spring onion* (cong), *and red chilli* (hong-la-jiao): In various proportions and combinations, these four items are the most common fresh seasonings in Chinese cooking. Hardly a dish in the vast repertoire of Chinese cuisine is prepared without at least one of these condiments. For sauces, dips, and sautés, they are finely minced; for stews they are roughly cut or bruised and removed after cooking. They intensify the 'fresh-natural' (xian) flavours and give pungency and piquance to the sauce. In larger quantities, they have a

tingling effect on the palate and improve the appetite. All are prominently listed in traditional Chinese herbal pharmacopeias and have important 'food-as-medicine' therapeutic uses. They also subdue rank flavours and offensive odours.

Vinegar (cu): Vinegar imparts the basic sour (*suan*) flavour to foods and sauces. It should be used sparingly at the last minute so that its piquant flavour is not lost in the heat of cooking. It is generally used with an equivalent amount of sugar, producing the renowned Chinese 'sweet-and-sour' flavour. Vinegar is used in most cold-plate dressings and table sauces, as well as in sautés and stews. The dark, smoky variety is most commonly used.

Below and right: *Prepared condiments in a Chinese grocery.*

A selection of Chinese condiments: Centre *Garlic, spring onion and red chilli.* Clockwise from top *Soy sauce; Shrimp paste; Chinese pepper-salt and brown vinegar; mustard and chilli sauce; fermented beancurd.*

Cornflour (chien-fen): Cornflour (Cornstarch) is used to control texture, not flavour. Added to marinades, it tenderises meat, fish, and fowl prior to cooking. A teaspoon or two dissolved in some cold water is added at the last minute to sautés, stews, or soups to thicken the sauce, bind the juices of meats to the condiments and oils, and lend a smooth and slippery texture to foods. Cornflour (Cornstarch) also makes the colours of foods shine. For tender, boned chicken and fish, cornflour (cornstarch) and egg white are used to marinate the diced meat before applying the bao-style sauté method: this forms a protective coating between the delicate meat and the scalding hot oil, ensuring a maximum tenderness and flavour inside and a golden-brown colour and slightly crisp texture outside.

Fermented Bean Paste (dou-ban-jiang): This is a very commonly used cooking condiment in western/central-style cuisine. It consists of fermented beans and chilli sauce, at once pungent, piquant, and slightly sour. It is used in meat, fish, and fowl sautés and is added directly to the hot oil with the ingredients and other condiments.

Fermented Salted Black Beans (doushi): This is the classical Chinese condiment developed during the Han dynasty and popular in China ever since. It is fermented black beans packed in salt. The flavour is very salty, highly piquant, but not pungent. It is used to spice up sautés, and to add flavour and remove rankness from steamed fish.

Oyster Sauce (hao-you): Oyster sauce imparts a very rich taste to sautéed meats and vegetables. It enhances the 'fresh-natural' (*xian*) flavours of foods as well. It is most commonly used with beef and green, leafy vegetables.

Sesame Paste (zhi-ma-jiang): Chinese sesame paste is made from roasted rather than raw sesame seeds; it is dark in colour and smoky in flavour. Western-style blond sesame *tahini* may be substituted but is not as good. It is most commonly employed to make dressings for cold-plates and table sauces for dipping. It has a pleasant, nutty taste and is highly aromatic. You can make your own sesame powder by roasting plain sesame seeds in a dry wok with some salt until they turn golden-brown, then grinding them up with mortar and pestle or a food processor. This makes an excellent table condiment all by itself.

All of the condiments described above are generally available in Chinese and Japanese grocery stores the world over. China, Hong Kong, and Taiwan produce all of them for export to world markets.

A few practical words on the use of Chinese condiments are in order here. First of all, have everything conveniently arranged on a shelf or counter near the stove. Most condiments must be added at just the right time, a splash here and a dash there, and there is no time to rummage through your pantry or refrigerator while cooking. Second, original Chinese recipes never indicate measures for seasonings, and it is important for the aspiring cook to develop the habit of 'free-pouring' from the very start. There are no correct or incorrect proportions for condiments in Chinese cooking, just the general goal of harmony and balance in the final product. How much of this or that seasoning you use depends entirely on the quantity of food being cooked and the type of flavour balance which appeals to you and your guests. Change the proportions and experiment with different combinations from time to time until you achieve an instinctive 'feel' for using Chinese condiments. It's easier than you think. The only prerequisites are a sufficient measure of self-confidence and the willingness to exercise one's creative culinary imagination.

Detailed information on all Chinese ingredients used in this book, their uses, how to store them and suggested substitutes can be found in the Glossary page 406.

CHINESE COOKING METHODS

Other than fresh fruits, the Chinese eat very little raw food. Almost everything in the Chinese diet is subjected to some degree of cooking, from a few seconds up to a full day. Over a dozen cooking techniques are distinguished by Chinese chefs, and many of them are used in sequence to prepare the final product for the table. The techniques chosen depend upon the nature of the foods to be cooked, the heat and time required for the cooking, considerations of flavour, fragrance, colour, and texture and the type of utensils available.

Three broad categories of cooking are used in the Chinese kitchen: cooking with oil, cooking with water, and cooking with neither oil nor water. Including the preparation of rice, stews, and soups as well as parboiling, parsteaming, and poaching techniques, cooking with water remains the single most commonly used category of cooking. Cooking with oil includes deep-frying, shallow-frying, sautéing, 'explode-frying,' and other oil-based methods. Cooking with neither oil nor water, which includes baking, roasting, and grilling/broiling, is far less common in Chinese cuisine, for applying fire directly to foods has always been considered a custom of the nomadic barbarians. Chinese chefs usually prefer to have an 'honourable in-

35

termediary' of oil or water between the food and the fire.

Chao, 'stir-fry,' 'sauté': This is the most popular method of cooking cai (food). Chao cooking is done in a wok with a very little oil over high heat with constant turning and turning. It seals in flavours and nutrients and preserves original textures. Since chao-cai (stir-fried dishes) cook quickly, they should be cooked last so they may be served fresh and piping hot.

Zheng, 'steam': Foods are placed on a rack in a closed container over boiling water and cooked by intense, concentrated, moist heat. Multi-tiered bamboo or metal steamers are the right tool. Cooking times range anywhere from 15 minutes to 5 hours or more. Steaming is often used to cook seafood and poultry as well as a wide variety of snacks and pastries.

Hong-shao, 'red-stew,' 'red-braise': This is a uniquely Chinese cooking method which derives its name from the characteristically reddish-brown colour a stew gets from soy sauce and sugar, the primary condiments. Either water or stock is used as a base and Hong-shai-cai (red-stewed foods) have a rich, sweet-and-salty flavour, reddish-brown colour, and smooth, slippery texture. Meat, fish, and fowl are the major ingredients, followed by hard vegetables such as carrots or potatoes. Cooking times range from 1 to 6 hours, depending on the type of ingredient used. Like spaghetti sauce and other Western stews, red-stews many connoisseurs claim, taste even better after a night or two in the refrigerator.

Zhu, 'boil': Other than cooking rice and soups, boiling is primarily a preparatory method applied to foods prior to the final cooking process. This parboiling (blanching) is often applied to vegetables and is followed by cold rinsing to set the colours and textures. Intense but brief boiling in a covered vessel is used to cook prawns, squid, and other types of seafood when they are to be served plain with a variety of table sauces for dipping.

Zha, 'deep-fry': Cooking in a large quantity of hot vegetable oil or sometimes lard. The zha method is often the last step in cooking, after pre-steaming or simmering. Such dishes are called ziang-su, 'fragrant-crispy.' Zha-

cai (deep-fried foods) should be crispy and dry on the outside and tender and juicy on the inside. Cooking times vary; the general indicators are a golden-brown colour and a puffy appearance.

Jian, 'shallow-fry': This method is done in a flat pan; the ordinary Western cast-iron frying pan (skillet) is best, with a thin layer of oil on the bottom. Medium heat is used and ingredients are spread evenly across the surface and turned occasionally. 'Potsticker' dumplings are also made this way, with a splash of water and a tight lid added at the last moment to produce a steam.

Men, 'simmer': This method is similar to hong-shao, but it does not necessarily use soy sauce or sugar. It is applied to foods which require long cooking times, such as tendon, ligament, pork knuckle, whole joints of meat, etc. It is important to keep the pot tightly covered with the flame very low. This ensures that the cooking liquid remains perfectly clear. 'Sand pot' casseroles are best for this kind of cooking.

Kao, 'roast,' 'bake,' 'grill/broil': In China, kao-cai (roasted foods) are usually prepared in specialty shops or restaurants since most household kitchens are not equipped with the necessary ovens and grills. Roasting and baking are done in brick and clay ovens of the Indian 'tandoor' kind over open charcoal or wood fires. Roasted meats are hung inside on metal hooks, baked breads stuck to the inside of the oven. Grilled/broiled foods are cooked on iron grills over charcoal fires. Happily, most Western kitchens are ideally equipped for cooking all sorts of roasted, baked, and grilled/broiled Chinese foods with excellent results. Besides, as the Chinese themselves admit, barbarians are best at roasting and grilling/broiling meats. Foods are usually marinated first and then basted with the remaining marinade throughout the cooking process.

Xun, 'smoke': Smoke is applied to meat, fish, and fowl. Smokehouses are ideal for large quantities of meat, but single cuts or smaller fish and fowl may be smoked in the kitchen in an old iron wok or cooking pot, or even in the oven. Tea leaves, fragrant wood shavings, sugar, and orange peel provide the smoke-fuel which imparts its fragrant

essences to the food. Smoked foods are usually submitted to additional cooking processes before or after the smoking.

Liang-ban 'cold-mix': This is the Chinese version of the mixed salad or cold-cut plate, except that Chinese liang-ban are far more complex, varied, and spicy than their Western equivalents. The main ingredients are usually blanched, poached, or steamed and then chilled prior to mixing. Rich and piquant dressings of soy sauce, sesame oil, vinegar, garlic, ginger, sugar, and other condiments are added and stirred in just before serving. Chicken, kidneys, seafoods, cold meats, and all sorts of vegetables readily lend themselves to this form of cai (dish).

Speed and a hot wok are the keys to stir-frying above. Below, left deep frying, and right a specialty shop displays its succulent roasted ducks.

Detailed information on Chinese cooking processes and techniques is included in Chapter XI, Preparation and Cooking Techniques.

CREATIVE IMPROVISATION IN CHINESE COOKING

The foregoing information on utensils, preparations, condiments, and methods should serve as a general guide to Chinese cooking techniques. Exact proportions of condiments and combinations of methods actually used, however, must ultimately be determined by the cook and may well vary each

time a dish is prepared. The possibilities are infinite. The key to learning Chinese cooking is not to memorise individual recipes but rather to master the underlying concepts and the common techniques. The opposite case is true in Western cooking, in which exact recipe proportions and cooking times must be followed, but cooking concepts and methods are relatively easy and require little attention. To acquire the 'magic touch' and precision timing, you must exercise your imagination and constantly practise your skills. Chinese cooking brings out the creative cook in all of us and is never boring.

One of the best opportunities for creativity in Chinese cooking is substitution. Many common condiments may be used as replacements: in the West, sherry is a common, if not superior, substitute for rice wine; if you run out of soy sauce, try a bit of Worcestershire sauce instead; substitute some of the many spicy vinegars available in the West for Chinese vinegar in various dishes. The wok may be used as a steamer, stewer, deep-fryer, boiler, or smoker in the absence of specialised vessels. Main ingredients are as flexible as condiments and utensils: apply your favourite recipes to a wide range of ingredients, not just the ones specified in the recipes. For example, if you try a pork recipe but really prefer the taste of beef, use beef the next time. If carp is offensive to your palate or unavailable in your town, try the same recipe with trout instead. The opportunities for exercising creative imagination in Chinese cooking are endless. One of the drawbacks of Western-style cooking is that it is too rigid and repetitive to sustain interest and thus becomes boring after a while. In Chinese-style cooking, each and every trip to the kitchen is an opportunity to try something new, to exercise your culinary imagination, and to create better and different versions of your favourite dishes.

We recommend that newcomers to Chinese cooking begin with the most basic methods and recipes and gradually work into the more complex. To aid in the selection of dishes for menus from simple through more complex to quite intricate and exotic, we have grouped these recipes into three sections of varying complexity, see page 413, Guide to Recipes. When self-confidence and familiarity with techniques develop, try a few of the more complex recipes, using costly ingredients and multiple-cooking methods.

Meanwhile, continue to experiment with, improvise, and improve the basic recipes you've already mastered.

Don't over-extend yourself when cooking a Chinese meal. As Yuan Mei stated in *The Menu*, even a great cook is hard-pressed to successfully produce more than four dishes for a single meal. Should you wish to prepare a 12-course Chinese banquet for your friends, recruit two more cooks and assign each person four specific dishes. Do not help each other, for too many cooks spoil the broth, especially when the broth is Chinese. The best way is for each cook to prepare the few dishes at which he or she excels.

Create your own original menus, always bearing in mind the basic principles of balance and harmony. You might select a chicken, a fish, a beef, and a vegetable dish. Based on cooking methods and textures, your menu might include a crispy, deep-fried dish, a fluffy steamed dish, a smooth stew, and a tender, slippery sautéed dish. Creative flavour balancing might result in a menu of pungent, sour, salty, and sweet dishes. Colour considerations could lead to a menu of green, leafy vegetables, a steamed white fish, a red-stew, and a multi-coloured sauté. Once again, the combinations are endless, the senses play vital roles, and creative improvisation is the key.

While the ingredients, condiments, utensils, and methods used in Chinese cooking are highly flexible, the basic principles are inviolate and must always be followed faithfully. Naturalness must never be sacrificed: select fresh ingredients in season as much as possible, and apply cooking methods and condiments which are naturally suited to them. One of the fundamentals of Chinese cuisine is the medical aspect, the basic principles of which have long influenced cooking in China. The ingredients and procedures which comprise each recipe have undergone centuries of evolution based on medical principles. For those interested in further pursuing this subject, a fascinating new area of creative improvisation in Chinese cooking awaits you: ingredients and dishes may be selected for their pharmacodynamics and suited to the season, the weather, and your own health. Above all, always bear in mind the key words to Chinese cuisine: balance and harmony.

CHAPTER III
Northern Style Cuisine

Northern Chinese winters are long and cold, reducing the variety of available culinary ingredients. The lake of the Summer Palace previous page *outside Peking freezes over in winter, but still provides fresh-water fish to nearby restaurants.*

The Great Wall of China above *historically separated the civilized Middle Kingdom from nomadic barbarian tribes such as the Mongols, who nevertheless taught the Chinese to eat mutton and to barbecue meats.*

Northern-style cuisine embraces the geographical areas of China which lie north of the Yangtze River and includes three of the nine distinct regional styles recognised in China today: Peking (Beijing), Shantung (Shandong), and Anhwei (Anhui). The cooking of Honan also falls into this regional category. The entire northern region is relatively dry and arid compared to the rest of China, and this has severely limited the variety of ingredients available for cooking. Dusty, biting winds from Mongolia pervade the northernmost parts of the area, especially around Peking (Beijing), and the winters are long and cold.

Peking (Beijing) has been the capital of China since the Mongols established it as such in the 13th century. Therefore, despite the paucity of food produced locally, Peking (Beijing) has generally had abundant supplies of the best food products from every province of China, and this remains true today. Excellent regional restaurants have been in operation in Peking (Beijing) for centuries. In this section, however, we deal only with the nature of the foods indigenous to the region.

Shantung (Shandong) and Anhwei (Anhui) are among China's oldest provinces. Shantung (Shandong) was the birthplace of Confucius, and Anhui gave birth to several founding emperors of Chinese dynasties. Despite their rich cultural and historical heritages, however, these two provinces have remained relatively poor in terms of agriculture. The climate and topography are not suitable for the cultivation of the wide range of food crops required to support an elaborate gourmet cuisine. Northern gourmet cuisine relies heavily on foods brought in from other provinces.

The most distinctive feature native to northern cuisine is the fan: wheat and millet, not rice, are the staple foundations of the northern diet. It is too cold and dry to grow rice, which must be brought in from the warm, lush southern regions. Millet is perhaps the oldest of all foods in China, pre-dating both rice and wheat. The most common preparation is millet-gruel, a hearty, warming dish most suitable for winter consumption. Taken with a few side-dishes such as dried beancurd, salt-fish, beans, and pickled vegetables, millet-gruel makes a complete and satisfying winter meal.

Wheat has been popular in the north ever since the Han dynasty, when the arts of milling flour and baking breads were first introduced to China. Steamed and baked buns, noodles of every type, dumplings, rolls, and other wheat-derived foods are common fare in the north, while rice has generally been regarded as a luxury there. Two wheat-based foods which are original innovations of the Peking (Beijing) kitchen are *jiao-zi* (stuffed dumplings) and *chun-juan* (spring rolls), both of which may be stuffed with a wide variety of different fillings, depending on what's available.

As for *cai*, the northern menu is the briefest, simply because locally produced ingredients are limited. The classic dish associated with the capital city is Peking (Beijing) Duck, a truly original and delicious northern innovation. This is served with three very typical northern items: wheat crepes in which to wrap the tender meat and crispy skin; sliced spring onions, a favourite northern condiment; and fermented sweet flour paste, also native to the north. The preparation of Peking (Beijing) Duck is a long, involved process and is usually handled by specialty restaurants. However, with a good oven, this dish may also be prepared at home.

Mongolian Barbecue and Mongolian Fire-Pot are two other world-famous foods of northern China, and their origins provide an excellent example of how the Chinese have managed to adapt barbarian innovations to suit their own refined culinary requirements. The Mongols were a primitive people with simple customs, but they just happened to be neighbours of the world's most cultured, civilised society. After a hard day of fighting or hunting on the steppes, Mongol horsemen would gather in camps at night to eat. Animals hunted or slaughtered that day were cleaned and the raw meat cut up. Wild onions, garlic, and other edible herbs and vegetables gathered on the steppes were also chopped up. The only remaining problem was how to cook them, and here the Mongols must be credited with an original idea: they placed their sturdy iron shields, which protected them from enemy arrows and lances by day, over hot coal fires until they became smoking hot. Then the meat and vegetables were dumped onto the hot metal surface, stirred around until cooked, and removed. Mongolian Fire-Pot has similar origins, except instead of using shields, the diners used their

From the fields to the markets, timeless traditional ways still mark China's agricultural life, and manpower remains the primary source of energy.

metal helmets. Water was brought to boil in the helmets, and each diner could cook his own meat and wild vegetables in the boiling liquid. When everyone was finished, the rich broth in the helmet was drunk as a final course.

The Chinese were familiar with this barbaric manner of eating, and after the Mongol occupation of China in the 13th century, Chinese chefs embellished it, civilised it, and renamed it Peking (Beijing) Barbecue. Custom-designed iron griddles and brass cooking pots replaced the shields and helmets of the steppes, and the variety of meats and vegetables used increased many-fold. More important, a wide range of fragrant, flavourful condiments was added to the meal, so that each diner could create his own blend of ingredients to suit his own palate. Today, Mongolian or Peking (Beijing) Barbecue and Hot-Pot are among the most popular of all Chinese specialty foods throughout the Far East. Both are quint-essentially northern contributions to the Chinese menu and are readily adaptable to Western kitchens and ingredients. Ingredients and condiments for these meals are highly flexible, and the host has ample opportunity to exercise his culinary imagination in preparing them. These meals are invariably a big hit at parties because they permit each individual guest to vary the blend of flavours and control the cooking times himself. Recipes for Mongolian Barbecue and Hot-Pot are included in the recipe section.

Other *cai* commonly consumed in the north are made from mutton, freshwater fish, and chicken. Mutton is very popular due to the influence of northern nomads as well as large Moslem minorities living there. Moslem restaurants specialising in mutton dishes are still among the most popular in Peking (Beijing) today. Various breeds of fish from rivers and lakes are highly favoured when available: Mandarin fish is particularly popular. Chicken and ducks are raised for food on farms. From the vegetable world, the selection in the north is quite limited due to climatic and geographical conditions. The most common vegetables are those of the cabbage, turnip, and onion families.

The most popular condiments in the north are garlic, spring onions, and ginger. Chillies are not so highly favoured as elsewhere in China. Northerners like their food to have *xien* ('fresh-natural') flavours but shy away from excessively pungent tastes. Soy sauce, wine, sesame oil, sesame paste, and fermented sweet flour paste are other commonly employed cooking condiments in the northern kitchen.

Steaming (*zheng*), baking (*kao*), and 'explode-frying' (*bao*) are the most popular cooking methods in the north. Steaming is applied primarily to the many varieties of wheat-derived foods, such as buns and dumplings. It has already been noted that *kao*, which includes the techniques of baking, grilling, and roasting, is the least commonly employed method in Chinese cooking because of its historical associations with the barbarians. It is more common in the north because contact with barbarian tribes has been most frequent there. These methods are used to bake breads, roast ducks and meats, and grill all sorts of meat and poultry.

Most northern *cai*, however, are cooked in the *bao* style. One reason for this is the scarcity of cooking fuel in the north: *bao* is by far the fastest cooking method in the Chinese repertoire, usually requiring only 30 — 90 seconds. Though *bao* cooking consumes more oil (5 — 6 oz.) than other sautés, the north has had sufficient supplies of oil-seed to support *bao* cooking ever since the introduction from the New World of the humble peanut, which thrives in the harsh northern environment. There are many varieties of *bao*-style cooking, including oil-*bao*, onion-*bao*, sauce-*bao*, and salt-*bao*. The main differences between them are the seasonings added and the order of preparatory and cooking processes.

Some use marinated raw ingredients, some require pre-cooking, but either way, the final cooking process involves dumping all the prepared ingredients into a bowl together with the condiments, then turning the entire contents into a wok with 5 — 6 oz of oil. The oil must be heated until it smokes over the highest possible flame before the ingredients are added. When they hit the scalding oil, it sounds like an explosion, hence the name 'explode-fry.' *Bao*-cooking locks original flavours inside of foods and keeps condiments coated on their outside surfaces, so that both fresh-natural and contrived flavours achieve a harmonious balance.

For Westerners, the most appealing features of northern-style Chinese cuisine are the relatively conventional ingredients and condiments and the relatively bland flavours. Of all Chinese

foods, northern food strikes the most familiar note on the Western palate and is usually preferred by newcomers to China. The Chinese, on the other hand, generally regard northern-style food as simple and unsophisticated compared to the fancier southern styles. While northern food may be less fancy than southern styles, it is far more filling: you are unlikely to feel hungry again an hour later. From a nutritional standpoint, northern cooking styles are perhaps superior because they rely heavily on steam and *bao* techniques, both of which seal in nutrients. However, due to the relatively narrow range of ingredients, northern dishes probably do not provide as broad a balance of vital nutrients as the more diverse southern styles.

BRAISED SHARK'S FIN WITH PORK KNUCKLE AND CHICKEN

500 g (1 lb)	prepared shark's fin (see page 393), about 125 g (4 oz) dry weight
315 g (10 oz)	pork knuckle (hock/shank)
½ 1¼ kg (2½ lb)	chicken
4	dried scallops (about 30 g / 1 oz), soaked for 1 hour
2 cups (16 fl oz)	enriched stock
45 g (1½ oz)	Chinese or cured (Smithfield) ham
1 tablespoon	rendered chicken fat (chicken grease)
1 tablespoon	softened lard
1 tablespoon	frying or sesame oil
3 tablespoons	cornflour (cornstarch)
¼ cup (2 fl oz)	cold water

Seasoning:

1½ teaspoons	salt
1¼ teaspoons	m.s.g. (optional)
2 tablespoons	rice wine or dry sherry
2	spring onions (scallions), trimmed and sliced
4 thick slices	fresh ginger

Prepare the shark's fins according to the directions on page 393, allowing at least 4 hours. Drain well.

Blanch the pork knuckle and chicken in boiling water for 5 minutes. Drain well. Add the drained scallops to the water, simmer for 10 minutes, then drain.

Place the pork knuckle and chicken in a casserole and add the shark's fin, scallops, enriched stock, the ham and seasonings. Add water to cover and bring to the boil. Reduce the heat to simmer for about 2½ hours, skimming occasionally.

Remove the pork and chicken and debone. Shred the meat and place in a serving dish. Add the drained shark's fin. Thinly slice the ham and place on top of the fin. Discard the ginger and onion.

Bring the stock to the boil and add the fat, lard, and oil, then check the seasonings and thicken the sauce with a mixture of the cornflour and water. Simmer for 2 minutes, then pour over the shark's fin and serve.

SEA CUCUMBER IN BROWN SAUCE

3	prepared dried sea cucumbers (about 375 g / 12 oz, dry weight) (see page 392)
3	spring onions (scallions), trimmed and sliced
3 thick slices	fresh ginger
2½ tablespoons	softened lard or frying oil
2 cups (16 fl oz)	chicken stock
1 tablespoon	rendered chicken fat (chicken grease), optional
½ teaspoon	sesame oil
1½ tablespoons	cornflour (cornstarch)

Seasoning/Sauce:

¼ cup (2 fl oz)	dark soy sauce
1 tablespoon	rice wine or dry sherry
1 teaspoon	m.s.g. (optional)
1 teaspoon	sugar

Prepare the sea cucumber according to the directions on page 392 Drain and cut into pieces about 5 × 2 cm (2 × ¾ in).

Fry the spring onions and ginger in the lard or oil for 45 seconds. Remove. Add the sea cucumber and stir-fry for about 2 minutes on moderate heat, then add the seasoning/sauce ingredients and stir-fry on high heat for 30 seconds. Pour in the chicken stock, return the onions and ginger and bring to the boil.

Reduce the heat and simmer for 15 minutes, then add the rendered chicken fat, if used, and the sesame oil. Thicken with a thin paste of the cornflour and cold water and simmer until the sauce thickens.

Pour into a serving dish and serve hot.

Drunken Chicken (recipe page 48).

SMOKED CHICKEN

Serve hot or cold as an appetiser or main dish.

1 1¼ kg (2½ lb)	chicken
2 tablespoons	brown peppercorns
2 teaspoons	salt
1	spring onion (scallion), trimmed and halved
3 slices	fresh ginger
2	star anise
1	cinnamon stick
1 cup (8 fl oz)	light soy sauce
1 tablespoon	sesame oil, softened rendered chicken fat or lard

For smoking:

½ cup	sugar
⅓ cup	flour
½ cup	black tea leaves

Clean the chicken, wash in cold water and wipe dry. Dry-fry the peppercorns in a wok until fragrant, remove and grind to a fine powder, then reheat with the salt, taking care not to burn. Rub the spiced salt thoroughly over the chicken and pour the remainder into the cavity.

Bring a large saucepan of water to the boil and add the spring onion, ginger, star anise, cinnamon stick, and soy sauce. Put in the chicken and simmer on low heat for 10 minutes, turning once. Remove from the heat, cover the pan with a thick towel, and leave the chicken to gently poach in the hot liquid for a further 30 minutes.

Place the smoking ingredients in a large old iron wok or saucepan and set a rack over them. Lift out the chicken and drain well. Set on the rack. Heat until the ingrèdients begin to smoke, then cover tightly and smoke on moderate heat for about 7 minutes. Turn the chicken, decrease the heat and smoke for a further 6 minutes.

Remove, brush with sesame oil and cut into bite-sized pieces. Serve hot or prepare in advance and chill thoroughly before serving.

Use also for dishes requiring smoked chicken, see following (Crisp-Fried Shredded Smoked Chicken).

JELLIED CHICKEN

Serve as an appetiser or main dish.

1 kg (2 lb)	chicken pieces
185 g (6 oz)	pork rind (skin)*
2	spring onions (scallions), trimmed and cut in halves
3 slices	fresh ginger
1	star anise
5 cups (1¼ litres)	water
1 tablespoon	chopped fresh coriander (optional)
1 tablespoon	chopped cooked ham (optional)

Seasoning:

⅓ cup	light soy sauce
1 teaspoon	dark soy sauce
1 tablespoon	rice wine or dry sherry
1 teaspoon	salt
2 teaspoons	sugar

Debone the chicken and cut into cubes. Cut the pork rind into several pieces. Place the chicken and pork rind in a saucepan and cover with boiling water. Leave for 2 minutes, then drain well. Scrape any fat from the pork skin and return to the saucepan with the chicken.

Add the spring onions, ginger, star anise, and water, then stir in the seasoning ingredients and bring to the boil. Simmer on low heat until the liquid is reduced to about 1½ cups (12 fl oz). Remove the chicken and pork skin. Cut the pork skin into very small squares and return to the saucepan. Simmer for a further 30 minutes.

Return the chicken and simmer together for about 10 minutes, then transfer the lot to a greased baking tin and add the fresh coriander and ham, if used. Stir in lightly and leave to set, then refrigerate until firm.

Slice to serve.

* If preferred, use unflavoured gelatine in place of the pork rind. Cook chicken as outlined above and reduce the liquid, then add 1 package of unflavoured gelatine, dissolved in ½ cup of boiling water. Cook for 10 minutes, then leave to cool and set.

CRISP-FRIED SHREDDED SMOKED CHICKEN

½	smoked chicken (see previous recipe, Smoked Chicken)
2½ tablespoons	sweet bean paste
1¼ teaspoons	spiced salt
1½ teaspoons	caster sugar
2 tablespoons	cornflour (cornstarch)
4 cups (1 litre)	deep-frying oil

Debone the chicken and tear the meat into slivers along the grain. Mix with the sweet bean paste, spiced salt, and sugar and leave for 20 minutes. Add the cornflour and mix well.

Heat the deep-frying oil to smoking point. Reduce the heat slightly and deep-fry the chicken in a frying basket until crisp and golden. Drain well.

Pile onto a serving plate and surround with sprigs of fresh coriander. Serve with extra spiced salt (see page 384) and light soy sauce as dips.

CHICKEN IN SWEET WINE

1 1¼ kg (2½ lb)	chicken
2/3 cup	ginger wine, see page 387
185 g (6 oz)	lean pork
20 g (¾ oz)	dried 'wood ear' fungus, soaked for 25 minutes
4 5cm (2 in) pieces	fresh ginger, peeled
3 cloves	garlic
2	spring onions (scallions), trimmed and sliced
2½ tablespoons	softened lard or frying oil

Seasoning A:

1 teaspoon	light soy sauce
1 teaspoon	rice wine or dry sherry
1 teaspoon	cornflour (cornstarch)

Seasoning B:

3 cups (24 fl oz)	sweet rice wine or Japanese mirin*
1 cup (8 fl oz)	rice wine or dry sherry
1½ teaspoons	salt
1½ teaspoons	sugar

Clean and dress the chicken. Cut into large pieces. Place in a dish and pour on the ginger wine. Leave for 30 minutes, turning occasionally. Drain, reserving the wine.

Cut the pork into thin slices and place in a dish with the seasoning A ingredients. Leave for 25 minutes. Cut the 'wood ears' into bite-sized pieces. Cut the ginger into smaller pieces and bruise with the handle of a cleaver.

Heat the wok and sauté the ginger, garlic, and spring onions in the lard or oil over moderate heat. Add the chicken pieces and sauté until lightly coloured, about 5 minutes. Pour in the pre-mixed seasoning B ingredients and the reserved ginger wine and bring to the boil. Cover, reduce heat and simmer for 15 minutes, then add the 'wood ears' and pork and simmer until tender.

Transfer to a deep serving dish and serve in the sauce.

* Or use sweet or cream sherry.

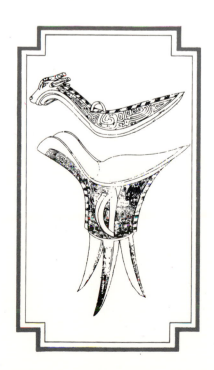

DRUNKEN CHICKEN

Serve cold as an appetiser or main dish.

½ 1¼ kg (2½ lb)	chicken
1 teaspoon	salt
2½ teaspoons	sugar
½ teaspoon	m.s.g. (optional)
1¼ cups (10 fl oz)	rice wine*
2 tablespoons	frying oil
	fresh coriander

Wash the chicken and place in a saucepan. Cover with boiling water and bring to the boil. Reduce the heat and simmer, tightly covered, for about 20 minutes.

Drain the chicken and place in a dish. Mix the remaining ingredients, except the coriander and pour over the chicken. Cover with plastic wrap and leave overnight to marinate. Garnish with fresh coriander and serve cold.

* The yellow *Shao Hsing* wine is usually used. The dish has a strong flavour of wine and therefore a good quality wine should be used. Japanese *mirin,* not unlike a sweet sherry, is ideal. If using this, use less sugar.

CHICKEN 'TEH-CHOW' STYLE

1 1¼ kg (2½ lb)	chicken
2 tablespoons	malt sugar
¼ cup (2 fl oz)	boiling water
8 cups (2 litres)	deep-frying oil
1 tablespoon	sesame oil

Seasoning/Sauce:

5 cups (1¼ litres)	chicken stock
¾ cup (6 fl oz)	light soy sauce
¾ cup (6 fl oz)	rice wine or dry sherry
1½ teaspoons	salt
¾ teaspoon	m.s.g. (optional)
½ cup	sugar
2	spice bags

Clean and dress the chicken. Rinse and dry with kitchen paper. Mix the malt sugar and boiling water and pour evenly over the chicken. Tie a string under the wings and across the back and suspend the chicken in a well-ventilated place until the skin dries, about 6 hours.

Heat the deep-frying oil to moderately hot. Fry the chicken completely immersed until golden all over. Lift out and drain well. Leave to cool slightly.

Bring the seasoning/sauce ingredients to the boil and reduce to a simmer. Add the chicken, cover and simmer until cooked through and completely tender, about 1¾ hours. Remove, drain, and brush with sesame oil.

Cut into bite-sized pieces and arrange on a serving plate. Serve with dips of spiced salt (see page 384) and light soy sauce.

FRIED DICED CHICKED WITH SWEET BEAN PASTE

500 g (1 lb)	chicken pieces
2	eggs, well beaten
	cornflour (cornstarch)
5 cups (1¼ litres)	deep-frying oil
2 tablespoons	sweet bean paste*
½ teaspoon	m.s.g. (optional)
1	large spring onion (scallion), trimmed and thinly sliced

Cut the chicken into bite-sized pieces through the bones. Dip into beaten egg, then coat thickly with cornflour.

Heat the deep-frying oil to smoking point and deep-fry the chicken pieces for about 2 minutes. Lift out and drain well. Pour off all but 2 tablespoons of the oil. Or if the wok is floury, pour off all the oil, wipe out the wok and return about 2 tablespoons of the oil.

Heat the oil and stir-fry the chicken briefly, then add the sweet bean paste, m.s.g., if used, and spring onion and stir-fry together on moderate heat until the chicken is cooked through and well glazed with the sauce and the spring onion is tender.

* Oyster sauce, hot bean paste, salted yellow beans, or hot black bean sauce can be used in place of the sweet bean paste, adding a little sugar to taste. Add diced drained water chestnuts for variety.

Three Courses of Peking Duck (recipe page 51).

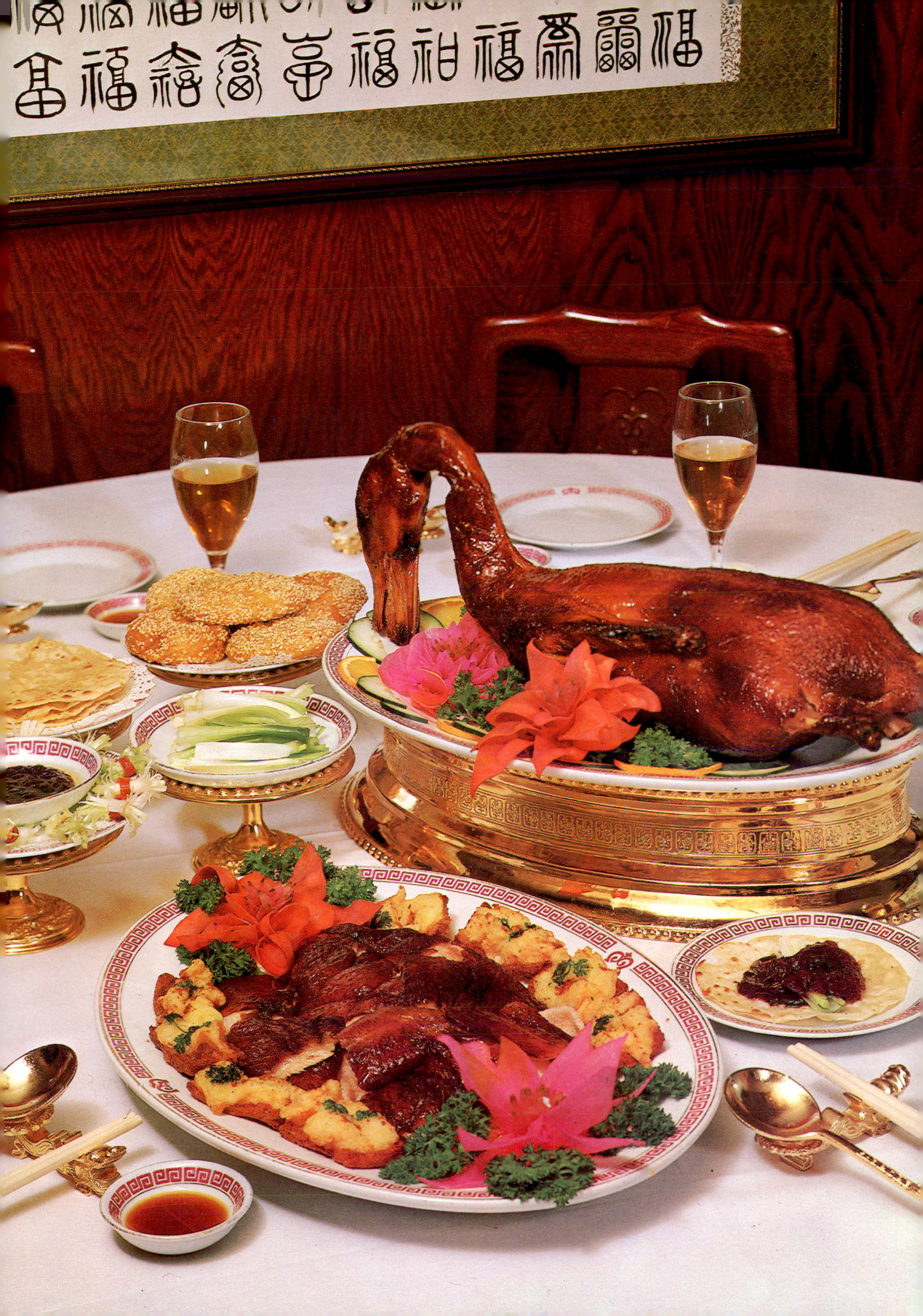

CHICKEN WITH CRISP HOT PEPPERS AND ORANGE PEEL

375 g (12 oz)	boneless chicken
2	dried red chilli peppers
3 pieces	dried orange peel
3 cups (24 fl oz)	deep-frying oil
1 slice	fresh ginger
2	spring onions (scallions), trimmed and sliced

Seasoning A:

¼ teaspoon	salt
½ teaspoon	m.s.g. (optional)
½ teaspoon	rice wine or dry sherry
2 teaspoons	cornflour (cornstarch)

Seasoning B:

¼ teaspoon	salt
½ teaspoon	m.s.g. (optional)
1½ teaspoons	sugar
1 tablespoon	light soy sauce
½ teaspoon	white vinegar
½ teaspoon	sesame oil
1 tablespoon	water
½ teaspoon	cornflour (cornstarch)

Cut the chicken into small cubes and mix with the seasoning A ingredients. Marinate for 15 minutes. Cut the chillies into 3 — 4 pieces and the orange peel into 2 — 3 pieces.

Heat the deep-frying oil to moderately hot and fry the chillies and orange peel until both are dark brown. Remove and set aside. Add the chicken and fry until white and firm, about 1½ minutes. Remove. Pour off all but 2½ tablespoons of the oil and add the ginger and spring onions. Stir-fry briefly, then return the chillies, orange peel, and chicken and stir-fry together for 1 minute. Add the pre-mixed seasoning B ingredients and simmer until the chicken is well glazed with the sauce, then serve.

CHICKEN BRAISED WITH CHESTNUTS

625 g (1¼ lb)	chicken pieces
¼ cup (2 fl oz)	light soy sauce
5 cups (1¼ litres)	deep-frying oil
90 g (3 oz)	fresh chestnuts, blanched and peeled*
1½ tablespoons	finely chopped spring onion (Scallion)
1½ teaspoons	finely chopped fresh ginger
1 tablespoon	rice wine or dry sherry
1 teaspoon	rendered chicken fat (chicken grease) optional

Seasoning/Sauce:

1¼ cups (10 fl oz)	chicken stock
⅓ teaspoon	salt
⅓ teaspoon	m.s.g. (optional)
¼ teaspoon	ground black pepper
2 teaspoons	sugar

Cut the chicken into bite-sized pieces, cutting through the bones. Place in a dish with the soy sauce and leave for 10 minutes, then drain reserving the sauce. Heat the deep-frying oil to smoking point and deep-fry the drained chicken for 2 minutes. Drain well. Add the chestnuts and deep-fry for 2 minutes and drain.

Pour off all but 2 tablespoons of the oil and sauté the spring onion and ginger. Add the chicken and chestnuts and sizzle the wine onto the sides of the pan. Add the seasoning/sauce ingredients and bring to the boil. Simmer until the chicken and chestnuts are both tender, about 15 minutes. Add the chicken fat, if used, and serve.

* Chestnuts can also be purchased in dried or canned form. Dried chestnuts need to be soaked for about 20 minutes. Canned chestnuts should be drained and rinsed before using. Deep-fry, then add to the dish.

THREE COURSES OF PEKING DUCK

Dish 1:

1	Peking duck, freshly roasted (see recipe, page 329)
12	steamed flower-shaped buns or 'Mandarin' pancakes (see recipes, page 372 and 373)
1	young leek or 6 spring onions (scallions), trimmed and sliced
½ cup	'duck' sauce (see page 385)

Dish 2:

2 tablespoons	softened lard or frying oil
1 — 2	fresh red chilli peppers, shredded
125 g (4 oz)	fresh bean sprouts*
1	spring onion (scallion), trimmed and shredded
¼ teaspoon	grated fresh ginger
½ teaspoon	finely chopped garlic
1 tablespoon	rice wine or dry sherry
½ teaspoon	salt
½ teaspoon	m.s.g. (optional)

Dish 3:

6 cups (1¼ litres)	chicken stock
2 tablespoons	evaporated milk
1	spring onion (scallion), trimmed and sliced
1 slice	fresh ginger
155 g (5 oz)	young Chinese green vegetables, trimmed
1¼ teaspoons	salt
½ teaspoon	m.s.g. (optional)
2 — 3 teaspoons	rice wine or dry sherry

First slice the crisp skin of the roasted duck into in bite-sized pieces and serve with the pancakes or buns, sauce and sliced leek or spring onion.

Slice off the meat and place the carcass in a soup pot with the dish 3 ingredients. Simmer for 15 minutes.

In the meantime, stir-fry the chilli, bean sprouts, or other vegetables, onion, ginger and garlic in the lard or oil for 1½ — 2 minutes. Add the sliced meat and stir-fry a further 1½ minutes, then sizzle the wine onto the sides of the pan and add the salt and m.s.g., if used. Serve with steamed white rice.

Check the seasoning of the soup, lift out the carcass, and scrape the meat into the soup. Pour into a tureen and serve as the last course.

DUCK FAT IN STEAMED EGG CUSTARD

185 g (6 oz)	fresh duck fat, minced (ground)
3	whole eggs, well beaten
1 cup (8 fl oz)	chicken stock
1¼ teaspoons	salt
½ teaspoon	m.s.g. (optional)
1¼ tablespoons	cornflour (cornstarch)
2 tablespoons	finely chopped spring onion (scallion)

Mix all the ingredients except the spring onion and pour into a dish. Set on a rack in a steamer and steam over rapidly boiling water for 5 minutes. Remove the lid of the steamer for a few seconds to release the steam which will cause the custard to puff up unevenly. Re-cover and steam for a further 10 minutes or until the mixture is softly set.

Lift out and garnish the dish with the spring onion. Serve at once. If preferred, pour off any fat which has accumulated on top of the dish.

Fresh chicken fat can be used, but the flavour will be much less interesting.

CRISPY HOME-STYLE DUCK

1 2 kg (4 lb)	duck
2 tablespoons	Chinese brown peppercorns
2 tablespoons	table salt
2 tablespoons	finely chopped spring onion (scallion)
1 tablespoon	finely chopped fresh ginger
1 tablespoon	rice wine or dry sherry
1 tablespoon	dark soy sauce
	flour
8 cups (2 litres)	deep-frying oil
12	steamed flower-shaped buns or 'Mandarin' pancakes (see recipes page 372 and 373)

Clean and dress the duck. Fry the peppercorns in a dry wok for 2 minutes over moderate heat, then pour into a mortar and grind to a fine powder. Return to the wok and add the salt. Dry-fry together on moderate to low heat, stirring constantly to avoid burning, for 2 minutes.

Mix the spiced salt with the spring onion, ginger and wine and rub thoroughly over the duck, pour the remainder inside and leave for 2 hours.

Place the duck breast up in a large dish and set on a rack in a steamer. Steam over high heat until the duck is completely tender, about 3 hours. Remove and leave to cool, then brush with the soy sauce and coat lightly with flour.

Heat the deep-frying oil to smoking point and then reduce the heat slightly. Deep-fry the duck, completely immersed in the oil if possible, for 3 minutes. Lift out and reheat the oil, then deep-fry a further 3 minutes until the duck is very crisp and deeply coloured on the surface.

Serve with the buns or pancakes and with additional spiced salt (see page 384) as a dip. For a sweeter flavour, serve 'duck' sauce (see recipe, page 385) or plum sauce as an additional dip.

WHOLE BAKED FISH SERVED ON A HOT PLATE

1 1 kg (2 lb)	Hilsa herring (sea bass or snapper)
75 g (2½ oz)	'five flowered' pork (belly/fresh bacon)
5 cm (2 in) piece	fresh young leek, shredded
1	fresh red chilli pepper, shredded
4 thick slices	fresh ginger, shredded
6 sprigs	fresh coriander
2 tablespoons	frying oil

Seasoning A:

¾ teaspoon	salt
½ teaspoon	m.s.g. (optional)
1 tablespoon	rice wine or dry sherry
2 teaspoons	sesame oil
1 tablespoon	frying oil
1¾ teaspoons	five spice powder

Seasoning B/Sauce:

¼ cup (2 fl oz)	chicken stock
1½ tablespoons	rice wine or dry sherry
¼ cup (2 fl oz)	light soy sauce
2 teaspoons	dark soy sauce
1 tablespoon	sugar
½ teaspoon	salt
2 tablespoons	frying oil

Cut the fish in halves lengthways, cutting right through the head, but do not sever along the top of the back, so the fish can be pressed out flat in one piece. Trim away the backbone. Leave the skin and scales intact. Place the fish in a large dish and cover with boiling water. Leave for 2 minutes, then drain well. Rub on both sides with the seasoning A ingredients and leave for 25 minutes.

Heat a baking pan or large ovenproof dish and add the frying oil. Spread the fish, scales upwards, on the tray and arrange the shredded ingredients on top. Bake in a preheated moderately hot oven at 220°C (425°F) for about 30 minutes. Put a metal serving tray, preferably one with a sturdy wooden detachable base, in the oven while the fish is cooking so it heats through thoroughly.

Drain the pan juices into a wok and return the fish to the oven. Heat the wok and add the seasoning B/sauce ingredients. Bring to the boil and check the seasoning.

Remove the fish and the heated tray from the oven. Use two large spatulas or egg lifters to transfer the fish to the hot serving tray. Pour on the piping hot sauce and carry sizzling to the table.

Whole Baked Fish Served on a Hot Plate (recipe this page).

STEAMED GOLDEN CARP

1 750 g (1½ lb)	golden carp (or fresh water trout)
30 g (1 oz)	Chinese or cured (Smithfield) ham
4	dried black mushrooms, soaked for 25 minutes
30 g (1 oz)	canned bamboo shoots, drained
1	spring onion (scallion), trimmed and shredded
3 slices	fresh ginger, shredded
90 g (3 oz)	pork omentum, or use 3 slices streaky bacon
¼ cup (2 fl oz)	chicken stock
¼ cup (2 fl oz)	frying oil

Seasoning:

1¼ teaspoons	salt
½ teaspoon	m.s.g. (optional)
½ teaspoon	sugar
2 teaspoons	rice wine or dry sherry
1 tablespoon	softened lard

Clean the carp and score diagonally on one side at 2 cm (¾ in) intervals. Cut the ham into slices. Drain the mushrooms and remove the stems. Cut the caps in halves. Thinly slice the bamboo shoots.

Place the fish on an oiled plate, score side upwards. Insert the slices of ham, mushroom halves, and bamboo shoot slices in alternate rows in the cuts. Arrange the spring onion and ginger on top of the fish and sprinkle the seasonings evenly over it.

Place the pork omentum, if used, on top or arrange the streaky bacon so that it covers as much of the fish as possible. Pour on the chicken stock, then set the plate on a rack in a steamer and steam over high heat for about 20 minutes.

Test if the fish is done by pushing a fork into the thickest part. If the meat lifts cleanly from the bones it is ready. Lift out the plate. Remove the bacon or pork fat and discard.

Strain the liquid into a wok and bring to the boil. Adjust seasoning to taste and thicken slightly, if preferred, with a thin solution of cornflour (cornstarch) and cold water. Pour over the fish.

Heat the frying oil to smoking point and pour quickly over the fish. Serve at once.

FRIED YELLOW FISH WITH GARLIC CHIVES

1 750 g (1½ lb)	yellow fish (trout or grouper)
1 teaspoon	salt
	flour
2	eggs, beaten
8 cups (2 litres)	deep-frying oil
5 cm (2 in) piece	fresh ginger, peeled
10	garlic chives, shredded (or use 4 — 5 spring onions/scallions)
1 tablespoon	sesame oil
1 teaspoon	salt
2 teaspoons	rice wine or dry sherry
	vinegar and ginger dip

Clean the fish and score diagonally on both sides, cutting almost to the bones. Rub with the salt, then coat lightly with flour and brush with beaten egg. Coat with the flour again and set aside.

Heat a large wok and rub vigorously with the piece of ginger to prevent the fish from sticking. Add the deep-frying oil and heat to smoking point. Carefully slide in the fish, holding it by its tail. Cook for 1 minute, then turn and cook the other side for 1 minute. Turn again and cook for 4 minutes on one side, then 4 minutes on the other side. Decrease the heat after the first side has cooked for about 2 minutes.

Lift out the fish on two spatulas and place it on a serving dish. Drain off the oil and wipe out the wok. Return about 3 tablespoons of the oil and fry the shredded garlic chives or spring onion until softened. Add the sesame oil, salt, and wine and stir in.

Pour over the fish and serve at once with small dishes of vinegar and ginger dip (see page 384).

'BULLFROG' SILVER CARP

1 1 kg (2 lb)	silver carp (trout, bream, or snapper)
8 cups (2 litres)	deep-frying oil
	cornflour (cornstarch)
2	spring onions (scallions), trimmed and shredded
2 thick slices	fresh ginger, shredded
	extra shredded spring onion (scallion) and ginger

Seasoning:

1	egg white, beaten
½ teaspoon	salt
¼ teaspoon	m.s.g. (optional)
1 tablespoon	rice wine or dry sherry
¼ teaspoon	white pepper
1 tablespoon	cornflour (cornstarch)

Sauce:

½ cup (4 fl oz)	chicken stock
⅓ teaspoon	salt
½ teaspoon	m.s.g. (optional)
¼ teaspoon	white pepper
1 teaspoon	rice wine or dry sherry
1 teaspoon	cornflour (cornstarch)

Clean and scale the fish and cut in halves along the backbone. Remove the backbone entirely, but keep the tail fin attached to the fillets. Cut off the head and cut open from the underside so it can be pressed out flat. Separate the fillets by cutting the tail in halves in the centre, then trim each part 'vandyke' style into two points to resemble the original tail.

Turn the fillets meat side up on a board and use a sharp paring knife to score right to the skin without piercing it, in a criss-cross pattern. Run the fingers from tail to top several times to make the points created by the scoring stand up. Mix the seasoning ingredients and pour over the fish. Leave for 10 minutes.

Heat the deep-frying oil to fairly hot. Coat the fillets with cornflour and deep-fry until cooked through and golden on the surface, about 3 minutes. Remove and drain well. Crisp-fry the head in the deep-frying oil and set on a plate to resemble a bullfrog head. Place the fillets with the points upwards on the plate so that the centre parts of the fillets curve outward giving the appearance of a jumping frog.

Pour off the oil from the wok, wipe out and return 2 tablespoons. Stir-fry the spring onion and ginger for 45 seconds, then add the pre-mixed sauce ingredients and simmer until thickened. Pour over the fish and garnish the dish with the extra shredded spring onion and ginger.

YELLOW CROAKER WITH PINE SEEDS

1 750 g (1½ lb)	yellow croaker (or fresh trout or perch)
45 g (1½ oz)	pine seeds*
3 cups (24 fl oz)	frying oil
3	dried black mushrooms, soaked for 25 minutes
30 g (1 oz)	canned bamboo shoots, drained
2	spring onions (scallions), trimmed

Seasoning A:

½ teaspoon	salt
2 teaspoons	rice wine or dry sherry
1 tablespoon	cornflour (cornstarch)

Seasoning B/Sauce:

2 tablespoons	cold water
1 tablespoon	light soy sauce
2 tablespoons	white vinegar
1 teaspoon	rice wine or dry sherry
¼ teaspoon	salt
¼ teaspoon	white pepper
1 teaspoon	cornflour (cornstarch)

Clean the fish and remove the head. Cut the fish from the underside to the back without cutting in halves. Remove the backbone by trimming the meat away all around, then press the two sides out flat. Turn the fish meat upwards on a board and score in a close criss-cross pattern, cutting down to the skin but not through it. Rub with the seasoning A ingredients and leave for 20 minutes.

Heat the frying oil and fry the pine seeds or other nuts until golden. Drain and set aside. Keep the oil warm. Squeeze the water from the mushrooms and cut the mushrooms, bamboo shoots and spring onions into small dice.

Reheat the oil to fairly hot and fry the fish, meat downwards, until crisp and golden, about 4 minutes. Remove and drain well. Place on a serving plate with the spikes facing upwards. Pour off all but 2 tablespoons of the oil and stir-fry the diced ingredients for 1 minute. Add the seasoning B/sauce ingredients, pre-mixed, and simmer until the sauce has thickened.

Pour over the fish and garnish with the fried pine seeds or nuts. Serve at once.

* Or use almonds, raw cashew nuts or walnuts, chopped.

FISH IN WINE SAUCE WITH 'WOOD EAR' FUNGUS

500 g (1 lb)	meaty white fish fillets
1	spring onion (scallion), trimmed and sliced
20 g (¾ oz)	dried 'wood ear' fungus, soaked for 25 minutes
3 cups (24 fl oz)	frying oil

Seasoning A:

1	egg white, beaten
½ teaspoon	salt
½ teaspoon	m.s.g. (optional)
2 teaspoons	ginger wine
1 tablespoon	cornflour (cornstarch

Seasoning B/Sauce:

¾ cup (6 fl oz)	fish or chicken stock
2 tablespoons	sweet rice wine, Japanese mirin or sweet sherry
½ teaspoon	salt
¼ teaspoon	m.s.g. (optional)
¾ teaspoon	sugar
2 teaspoons	cornflour (cornstarch)

Cut the fish into thin slices and place in a dish with the seasoning A ingredients. Leave for 20 minutes, turning occasionally.

Heat about 2 tablespoons of the frying oil and stir-fry the spring onion briefly. Cut the 'wood ears' into bite-sized squares and add to the pan. Stir-fry for 45 seconds. Remove and set aside.

Wipe out the wok and add the frying oil. Heat to moderate, then add the fish in a frying basket and deep-fry until white and firm, 45 seconds to 1 minute. Remove and drain off all but 2 tablespoons of the oil.

Add the pre-mixed seasoning B/sauce ingredients and return the spring onions and 'wood ears.' Simmer for 1 minute, then add the sliced fish and heat through. Serve at once.

CURLED PRAWNS STEAMED WITH FIVE SHREDS

500 g (1 lb)	large green prawns (shrimps), in the shell
1	egg, well beaten
3	dried black mushrooms, soaked for 25 minutes
45 g (1½ oz)	canned bamboo shoots, drained and shredded
30 g (1 oz)	cooked ham, shredded
2	spring onions (scallions), trimmed and shredded

Seasoning:

⅓ teaspoon	salt
1 teaspoon	rice wine or dry sherry
1 teaspoon	cornflour (cornstarch)

Sauce:

½ cup (4 fl oz)	enriched or chicken stock
2 teaspoons	rice wine or dry sherry
1 teaspoon	sesame oil
½ teaspoon	salt
¼ teaspoon	m.s.g. (optional)
1 teaspoon	cornflour (cornstarch)

Peel the prawns leaving the tail section intact. Place the prawns in a dish with the seasoning ingredients and leave for 15 minutes. Reserve the heads.

Wipe out an omelette pan with an oiled cloth and heat to moderate. Pour in the beaten egg and tilt the pan to give a thin even coating. Cook until firm but not coloured underneath, turn and cook the other side. Remove and spread on a board to cool. Roll up and cut into narrow shreds.

Squeeze the water from the mushrooms and remove the stems. Shred the caps.

Cut down the centre backs of the prawns, cutting deep enough to allow the prawns to be pressed out flat. Remove the dark veins. Make a central slit and pass the tails through this so that the prawns are curled up.

Arrange the prawns with their heads in a dish and arrange the shredded ingredients on top. Set the dish on a rack in a steamer and steam over high heat for 5 minutes.

Remove from the steamer and drain any liquid into a wok. Add the pre-mixed sauce ingredients and bring to the boil. Simmer until the sauce thickens, then pour over the prawns and serve at once.

Curled Prawns Steamed with Five Shreds (recipe this page).

FISH MASQUERADING AS CRAB

An imaginative dish employing less expensive ingredients to give the appearance and taste of stir-fried fresh crabmeat.

125 g (4 oz)	white fish fillets, coarsely minced (ground)
2	dried scallops or 1 tablespoon dried shrimps, soaked for 1½ hours
6	egg whites, well beaten
1 teaspoon	finely chopped fresh ginger
1½ teaspoons	finely chopped spring onion (scallion)
30 g (1 oz)	cooked crabmeat (optional)
2 tablespoons	softened lard or frying oil
½ teaspoon	Chinese red vinegar
1	egg yolk (optional)

Seasoning A:

½ teaspoon	salt
½ teaspoon	m.s.g. (optional)
2 teaspoons	rice wine or dry sherry
½ teaspoon	white vinegar
1¼ tablespoons	cold water
2 teaspoons	cornflour (cornstarch)

Seasoning B:

2 tablespoons	liquid from soaked scallops or shrimps
1 teaspoon	rice wine or dry sherry
1 teaspoon	light soy sauce
¼ teaspoon	salt
¼ teaspoon	sugar
¾ teaspoon	cornflour (cornstarch)

Mix the fish with the seasoning A ingredients and leave for 20 minutes. Steam the dried scallops or shrimps in 2 tablespoons of water until soft, then drain, reserving the liquid. Flake the scallops by rubbing between forefinger and thumb or finely chop the shrimps.

Mix the fish, shrimps or scallops, beaten egg, ginger, onion, and crabmeat, if used. Heat the lard or oil to warm and add the mixture. Cook, stirring slowly, until just set, then pour in the pre-mixed seasoning B ingredients and continue to cook until the mixture is firm and a small amount of liquid remains in the pan.

Transfer the mock crabmeat to a serving dish, or serve in a well-washed crab or clam shell. Make a small depression in the centre. Drizzle in the red vinegar and add the egg yolk, if used. Stir lightly into the crabmeat to give the appearance of roe. Serve at once.

BRAISED PRAWNS

500 g (1 lb)	large green prawns (shrimps) in the shell
⅓ cup	melted lard or frying oil
2 tablespoons	finely chopped spring onion (scallion)
2 teaspoons	finely chopped fresh ginger
2 teaspoons	cornflour (cornstarch)

Seasoning/Sauce:

2/3 cup	chicken stock
1 tablespoon	rice wine or dry sherry
¼ teaspoon	salt
¼ teaspoon	m.s.g. (optional)
1½ teaspoons	sugar

Wash the prawns and cut open on the underside to allow the sauce to penetrate. Remove the legs. Heat the lard or oil to moderately hot and fry the prawns until red, about 1¾ minutes. Remove and keep warm.

Add the onions and ginger and stir-fry briefly, then add the seasoning/sauce ingredients and bring to the boil. Return the prawns, cover and simmer for 5 — 6 minutes until the prawns are cooked through. Mix the cornflour with a little cold water and stir into the sauce. Simmer until thickened then transfer to a serving plate.

For extra flavour, add 2 tablespoons of tomato sauce (ketchup) or sweet bean paste, or 1 tablespoon of hot bean paste.

PRAWNS PEKING STYLE

6	green prawn cutlets* (about 280 g/9 oz)
3	egg whites
2 tablespoons	cornflour (cornstarch)
2 teaspoons	flour
¼ teaspoon	salt
1 cup	dry breadcrumbs
	extra cornflour (cornstarch)
7 cups (1¾ litres)	deep-frying oil
	Chinese pepper-salt

Seasoning:

1 tablespoon	finely chopped spring onion
1 teaspoon	grated fresh ginger
1 teaspoon	rice wine or dry sherry
¼ teaspoon	salt

Rinse the prawn cutlets and wipe dry. Rub on the seasoning ingredients and leave for 15 minutes.

Beat the eggs to soft peaks and stir in the cornflour, flour, and salt lightly. Heat the deep-frying oil to moderately hot. Coat the cutlets lightly with cornflour, shaking off excess. Dip into the batter, then into breadcrumbs.

Cook 3 at a time in the oil until golden and cooked through, about 1¾ minutes. Drain well. Arrange on a paper napkin in a serving dish or basket and serve with dips of Chinese pepper-salt (see recipe, page 384).

* Prawns with heads and shells removed, with the tail section left intact and cut deeply down the back so they can be pressed out flat, 'butterfly' style.

PRAWNS IN SWEET WINE SAUCE WITH CHILLIES AND GARLIC

500 g (1 lb)	fresh green prawns (shrimps) in the shell
5 cups (1¼ litres)	deep-frying oil
5 cloves	garlic, sliced
1 slice	fresh ginger, shredded
1 — 2	fresh red chilli peppers, shredded
2	spring onions (scallions), trimmed and shredded

Batter:

1	whole egg, well beaten
⅓ cup	cornflour (cornstarch)
1 tablespoon	flour
¼ teaspoon	salt

Sauce:

¾ cup (6 fl oz)	chicken stock
2¾ tablespoons	sweet rice wine or Japanese mirin*
¾ teaspoon	salt
1½ teaspoons	sugar
2¼ teaspoons	cornflour (cornstarch)

Peel the prawns and cut in halves lengthways, devein and rinse in cold water. Dry on kitchen paper, then coat very lightly with cornflour.

Mix the batter ingredients together adding enough water to make a creamy batter.

Heat the deep-frying oil to moderate. Dip the prawns into the batter and deep-fry about 8 pieces at a time until cooked through, crisp and golden, about 1¼ minutes. Remove and drain well, then keep warm.

Pour off the oil and wipe out the wok. Return about 2½ tablespoons of the oil and add the garlic, ginger, chillies, and spring onions. Stir-fry for 45 seconds, then pour in the premixed sauce ingredients. Bring to the boil and simmer for 1½ minutes, or until the sauce has thickened.

Arrange the drained prawns on a serving plate and pour on the sauce. Serve at once. To make the prawns crisper, fry a second time in hot oil immediately before adding the sauce.

* Or use sweet or cream sherry.

CRISP-FRIED SHRIMPS WITH GARLIC AND CHILLI

625 g (1¼ lb)	raw shrimps, in the shell
6 cups (1½ litres)	deep-frying oil
2	spring onions (scallions), trimmed and diced
5 — 6 cloves	garlic, thinly sliced
1 — 2	fresh red chilli peppers, seeded and sliced
1 tablespoon	rice wine or dry sherry

Seasoning:

1 teaspoon	salt or Chinese pepper-salt
½ teaspoon	m.s.g. (optional)
¼ teaspoon	ground black pepper (omit if using pepper-salt)

Thoroughly wash the shrimps and wipe dry. Do not peel. Heat the deep-frying oil to fairly hot and fry the whole shrimps until they turn bright pink, about 35 seconds. Remove and drain.

Pour off all but 2½ tablespoons of the oil and stir-fry the spring onions, garlic, and chilli for 1 minute on moderate heat. Return the shrimps and stir-fry briefly, then sizzle the wine onto the sides of the pan and stir in.

Add the seasoning ingredients and mix well. Transfer to a serving plate.

The shrimps should be served in their shells, the intention being to first nibble the whole thing to extract the flavour and saltiness on the shell, then to remove the shell and eat the tender shrimps. They may, however, be cooked without the shells. In this instance, do not deep-fry but quickly sauté in shallow oil with the other ingredients and serve at once.

SHRIMPS, PORK, AND VEGETABLES IN TOMATO SAUCE ON CRISP RICE

185 g (6 oz)	small peeled raw shrimps
125 g (4 oz)	pork fillet (tenderloin)
90 g (3 oz)	canned water chestnuts or bamboo shoots, drained
6	dried black mushrooms, soaked for 25 minutes
3 tablespoons	cooked green peas
2 tablespoons	finely chopped spring onion (scallion)
¾ teaspoon	finely chopped fresh ginger
½ teaspoon	finely chopped garlic (optional)
10 pieces	crisp rice cakes (see page 417)
4 cups (1 litre)	deep-frying oil

Seasoning A:

½ teaspoon	salt
2 teaspoons	ginger wine, see page 387
2 teaspoons	cornflour (cornstarch)

Seasoning B:

1 tablespoon	light soy sauce
2 teaspoons	cornflour (cornstarch)

Sauce:

3 cups (24 fl oz)	chicken stock
½ cup (4 fl oz)	tomato sauce (ketchup)
2 tablespoons	frying oil
1 tablespoon	light soy sauce
1 tablespoon	white vinegar
1 teaspoon	sesame oil (optional)
1½ teaspoons	salt
2 teaspoons	sugar
½ teaspoon	m.s.g. (optional)
3 tablespoons	cornflour (cornstarch)

Wash the shrimps and dry well. Devein with a toothpick (see page 394), and place in a dish with the seasoning A ingredients. Leave for 10 minutes. Cut the pork into narrow shreds and mix with the seasoning B ingredients.

Cut the water chestnuts or bamboo shoots and the mushrooms into small dice and stir-fry in 2½ tablespoons of the deep-frying oil for 1 minute. Push to one side of the pan and add the spring onion, ginger, and garlic, if used and stir-fry a further 30 seconds. Remove.

Add the shrimps and pork and stir-fry together in the remaining oil, adding a little more if needed. When lightly coloured, return the other fried ingredients and the sauce ingredients and bring to the boil.

In the meantime, heat the deep-frying oil to smoking hot. Place the rice cakes in a frying basket or strainer and dip into the hot oil. Fry until golden and crisp, then remove and drain well. Transfer to a deep serving dish.

When the sauce has thickened, check seasonings and pour over the rice cakes. Serve immediately, or if preferred take the rice cakes and sauce separately to the table. When the sauce is poured over the cakes, it should snap and crackle, so it is necessary to ensure that the rice cakes have been freshly fried and are still piping hot when served.

Pearls Hiding in a Crab (recipe page 63).

SAUTÉD SHRIMPS, SCALLOPS, AND ABALONE

125 g (4 oz)	raw peeled shrimps
125 g (4 oz)	fresh sea scallops, without shells
90 g (3 oz)	canned abalone, drained
1	small carrot, thinly sliced
30 g (1 oz)	canned bamboo shoots, drained and sliced
15 g (½ oz)	dried 'wood ear' fungus, soaked for 25 minutes*
2½ tablespoons	softened lard or frying oil

Seasoning A:

1	large egg white, beaten
¾ teaspoon	salt
2 teaspoons	rice wine or dry sherry
2 teaspoons	cornflour (cornstarch)

Seasoning B/Sauce:

2½ tablespoons	chicken stock
⅓ teaspoon	salt
¼ teaspoon	m.s.g. (optional)
2 teaspoons	rice wine or dry sherry
¼ teaspoon	sesame oil (optional)
⅓ teaspoon	cornflour (cornstarch)

Rinse the shrimps, devein with a toothpick (see page 394), and place in a dish with the scallops and the seasoning A ingredients. Leave for 15 minutes to marinate.

Thinly slice the abalone and soak in cold water.

Heat the frying oil in a wok and sauté the carrot, bamboo shoots, and 'wood ears' for 1½ minutes. Push to one side of the pan and add the shrimps and scallops. Sauté until the scallops turn white and firm and the shrimps pink, about 1¾ minutes. Add the seasoning B/sauce ingredients, pre-mixed, and the sliced abalone and stir in the vegetables.

Sauté together for a further 30 seconds, then serve.

* Or use canned straw mushrooms, sliced.

SALTED JELLYFISH AND SHRIMP SALAD

Serve cold as an appetiser or main dish.

310 g (10 oz)	prepared salted jellyfish
90 g (3 oz)	raw peeled shrimps*
1	small cucumber
4	garlic chives or 1 spring onion (scallion)

Seasoning:

1 cup (8 fl oz)	chicken stock
½ teaspoon	salt
¾ teaspoon	rice wine or dry sherry

Sauce:

2 tablespoons	sesame oil
2¼ tablespoons	white vinegar
2 teaspoons	rice wine or dry sherry
1½ teaspoons	salt
½ teaspoon	m.s.g. (optional)
1¼ teaspoons	sugar

Prepare the jellyfish according to the directions on page 392 and pile on a serving plate. Devein the shrimps with a toothpick (see page 394) and poach with the seasoning ingredients until pink and firm. Drain well. Peel the cucumber and cut into matchstick pieces, discarding the seeds. Shred the garlic chives or spring onion.

Mix the sauce ingredients together, beating until thoroughly amalgamated. Pile the shrimps, cucumber, and chives or onion onto the jellyfish and pour on the sauce. Stir in lightly with chopsticks and serve.

* Or substitute fresh squid cut into matchstick strips, or cooked chicken.

SHRIMP TOAST

Serve as an appetiser. Makes 12.

250 g (8 oz)	shrimp meat, finely minced (ground)
60 g (2 oz)	pork fat, finely minced (ground)
6 slices	fresh white bread
2	beaten eggs
1 teaspoon	black or white sesame seeds
1 tablespoon	finely chopped cooked ham (optional)
3 cups (24 fl oz)	deep-frying oil

Seasoning:

1	egg white, beaten
1 teaspoon	ginger wine, (see page 387)
¾ teaspoon	salt
1 tablespoon	cornflour (cornstarch)

Mince the shrimp and pork with a cleaver or food processor (see page 395). Mix with the seasoning ingredients and work until smooth and sticky, then cover with plastic wrap and refrigerate for 1 hour.

Remove crusts from the bread and cut each slice in halves. Brush one side with beaten egg and cover with a thick layer of the shrimp paste, smoothing around the edges. Brush with more beaten egg and decorate with sesame seeds and ham, if used.

Heat the deep-frying oil to moderately hot and fry the toasts, topping downwards, until golden and crisp. Drain well and serve with dips of Chinese pepper-salt or spiced salt (see page 384) and light soy sauce, or with sweet and sour sauce (see page 385).

PEARLS HIDING IN A CRAB

1 625 g (1¼ lb)	fresh crab
6	canned quail or pigeon eggs, drained
½ cup (4 fl oz)	chicken stock
1	egg white

Seasoning:

¾ teaspoon	salt
¼ teaspoon	m.s.g. (optional)
¼ teaspoon	white pepper
1 teaspoon	rice wine or dry sherry
2 teaspoons	cold water
2 teaspoons	cornflour (cornstarch)

Place the crab in a dish and steam over rapidly boiling water for 12 — 15 minutes. Lift out and leave until cool enough to handle, then remove the top shell and discard the inedible parts. Lift out the meat and flake finely. Clean the shell thoroughly, rubbing with salt. Rinse well.

Break open the legs and extract the meat, or leave intact to decorate the dish.

Place the quail eggs in a small saucepan with the stock and bring to the boil. Add the seasoning ingredients and simmer briefly, then add the flaked crabmeat and heat until the sauce thickens.

Place the lower part of the crab shell on a bed of shredded lettuce on a serving plate and arrange the legs in place around it. Pile the crab and egg mixture into the shell and set the top shell in place.

Beat the egg white until it forms soft peaks. Heat a small saucepan of slightly salted water to a rolling boil and add the beaten egg. Cook until set and firm, then place in front of the crab to resemble bubbles exuding from its mouth. Serve at once.

CLAMS IN EGG CUSTARD

500 g (1 lb)	fresh clams, in the shell
2	spring onions (scallions), trimmed and sliced
2 slices	fresh ginger, shredded
2 tablespoons	frying oil
6	egg whites, well beaten
3	whole eggs, beaten
1¾ cups (14 fl oz)	chicken stock
2 tablespoons	cornflour (cornstarch)

Seasoning:

1¾ teaspoons	salt
½ teaspoon	m.s.g. (optional)
1 tablespoon	rice wine or dry sherry
¼ teaspoon	ground black pepper

Thoroughly wash the clams, brushing the shells with a soft brush. Rinse well in cold water and place in a wok with the spring onions, ginger, and frying oil. Cover and cook on moderate heat, shaking the pan occasionally to encourage the shells to open. When most of the shells have opened, discard those which are still closed. Transfer to a large dish.

Mix the egg whites, whole eggs, and chicken stock with the cornflour and seasoning ingredients and pour into the dish. Set the dish on a rack in a steamer and steam over rapidly boiling water for about 20 minutes.

Serve hot in the same dish.

SQUID STIR-FRIED WITH GARLIC AND PICKLED CUCUMBER

625 g (1¼ lb)	fresh squid
2	spring onions (scallions), trimmed and chopped
2 teaspoons	finely chopped garlic
2 tablespoons	finely chopped sweet pickled cucumber or Chinese mixed pickles
⅓ cup	frying oil

Seasoning/Sauce:

¼ cup (2 fl oz)	chicken stock
½ teaspoon	salt
¼ teaspoon	m.s.g. (optional)
¾ teaspoon	rice wine or dry sherry
½ teaspoon	white vinegar
1 tablespoon	liquid from pickled cucumbers
½ teaspoon	cornflour (cornstarch)

Clean the squid by removing the heads and stomach, pulling away the pink skin with fins attached and washing thoroughly. Cut along the length and press open. Scrape away any remaining gelatinous tissue and score on the inside in a close criss-cross pattern, cutting at a slight angle (see page 397). Cut the squid into 4 cm (1 2/3 in) squares, then drop into a saucepan of boiling water to blanch for 30 seconds. Remove and drain well.

Stir-fry the spring onions and garlic in the frying oil for 1 minute, then add the chopped cucumber or pickles and stir-fry briefly. Add the squid and stir-fry for 30 seconds, then add the pre-mixed seasoning/sauce ingredients and simmer until heated through and the sauce slightly thickened. Transfer to a serving plate and serve at once.

ABALONE SOUP WITH CHICKEN AND EGG

½ 315 g (10 oz) can	abalone, drained
2 tablespoons	softened lard
1	spring onion (scallion), shredded
4 cups (1 litre)	enriched stock *
1½ teaspoons	salt
2 teaspoons	rice wine or dry sherry
90 g (3 oz)	boneless chicken, coarsely minced (ground)
3	egg whites, well beaten
1 tablespoon	finely shredded cooked ham
1 tablespoon	rendered chicken fat (chicken grease)

Thinly slice the abalone and set aside. Heat the lard and briefly fry the spring onion, then add the abalone and fry lightly. Remove.

Bring the stock to the boil, add the salt (to taste), wine, and the chicken and simmer until the chicken turns white. Remove from the heat, slowly drizzle in the beaten egg whites and do not stir for at least 45 seconds while the egg sets into white strands in the soup. Return the abalone and onion and heat through.

Transfer to a soup tureen and garnish with the shredded ham. Stir in the chicken fat and serve at once.

* Or use chicken stock with ½ stock cube crumbled into it. Adjust salt to taste.

Shredded Pork in Sesame Pouches (recipe page 67).

HOT POT OF FISH, SHRIMPS, PORK, AND CHICKEN

155 g (5 oz)	white fish fillets
90 g (3 oz)	boneless chicken breast
90 g (3 oz)	pork fillet (tenderloin)
125 g (4 oz)	raw peeled shrimps
1 teaspoon	salt
2 teaspoons	cornflour (cornstarch)
155 g (5 oz)	fresh young Chinese green vegetables or spinach (collard greens)
45 g (1½ oz)	bean thread vermicelli
4	dried black mushrooms, soaked for 25 minutes
6 cups (1½ litres)	chicken stock
1¼ teaspoons	salt
½ teaspoon	m.s.g. (optional)
45 g (1½ oz)	canned bamboo shoots, drained and sliced

Special Equipment: A table-top chafing dish, fondue pot, or table-top gas or electric ring and a large saucepan.

Very thinly slice the fish, chicken, and pork and arrange on separate plates. Devein the shrimps with a toothpick (see page 394) and rub with the salt and cornflour. Rinse well with cold water and dry on kitchen paper. Place on another plate.

Thoroughly wash the vegetables and arrange on a plate. Soak the vermicelli in warm water until softened, cut into 10 cm (4 in) lengths, drain well and place in a dish. Squeeze the water from the mushrooms and remove the stems. Cut the caps into quarters.

Bring the chicken stock to the boil in the chafing dish, fondue pot or saucepan and add the mushrooms, salt, m.s.g., and bamboo shoots.

Add the remaining ingredients at the table all together, or separately, and simmer until just done. The meat and seafood should be rare, the vegetables still crisp.

Serve some vegetables and the noodles in the stock as a soup after the meat and most of the vegetables have been eaten.

Soft beancurd, fish balls, and water chestnuts can be added to the hot pot, or substituted for any of the above ingredients.

COLD SPICY PEKING-STYLE PORK

Serve cold as an appetiser.

700 g (1⅓ lb)	pork leg (fresh ham)*
6 cups (1½ litres)	chicken stock

Seasoning:

2 teaspoons	salt
1 tablespoon	sugar
1 teaspoon	Chinese brown peppercorns
2	star anise
2 tablespoons	light soy sauce
1 tablespoon	rice wine or dry sherry
3	spring onions (scallions), trimmed and diced
3 slices	fresh ginger, shredded

Remove the rind and boil for about 8 minutes in lightly salted water. Remove and scrape off any fat. Cut the rind into small pieces. Dice the pork and place rind and pork in a saucepan with the chicken stock and seasoning ingredients.

Cover and bring to the boil, then reduce to a simmer and cook for 2 hours on very low heat. Skim once or twice during cooking. Discard the spices, onion, and ginger, transfer the meat to a dish and pack tightly.

Reduce the liquid, if necessary, until just enough to cover the meat. Pour over and leave to set, then refrigerate until firm. Slice and serve cold as an appetiser or use with other cold meat cuts.
* Select a cut with a large covering of rind (skin).

SAUTÉD PORK WITH PINE SEEDS

375 g (12 oz)	pork fillet (tenderloin)
1 cup	pine seeds*
2 cups (16 fl oz)	frying oil
½ teaspoon	salt
1¼ teaspoons	sugar
3	spring onions (scallions), trimmed and sliced

Seasoning:

1 tablespoon	light soy sauce
2 tablespoons	rice wine or dry sherry
2 teaspoons	cornflour (cornstarch)

Cut the pork into thin slices across the grain and mix with the seasoning ingredients. Leave for 20 minutes, turning several times.

Heat the deep-frying oil to moderate and fry the pine seeds in a basket until golden, about 30 seconds. Drain and pour off all but 3 tablespoons of the oil. Add the salt, sugar, and spring onions and sauté briefly, then push to one side of the pan and add the pork slices. Sauté until cooked through, stirring continually.

Add the fried pine seeds and serve at once.
* Sometimes called 'olive seeds' in Chinese stores. Use cashews or walnuts, if unobtainable. Often stocked by Middle Eastern food suppliers.

'MU HSU' PORK

250 g (8 oz)	pork fillet (tenderloin)
15 g (½ oz)	dried 'wood ear' fungus, soaked for 25 minutes
30 g (1 oz)	canned champignons or straw mushrooms, drained
4	dried black mushrooms, soaked for 25 minutes
3	eggs, well beaten
½ teaspoon	salt
2	spring onions (scallions), trimmed and sliced
2 slices	fresh ginger, shredded
45 g (1½ oz)	canned bamboo shoots, drained and sliced
½ cup (4 fl oz)	frying oil

Seasoning A:

¼ teaspoon	sugar
¼ teaspoon	m.s.g. (optional)
2 teaspoons	light soy sauce
1 teaspoon	rice wine or dry sherry
2 teaspoons	cornflour (cornstarch)

Seasoning B/Sauce:

⅓ cup	chicken stock
1½ tablespoons	light soy sauce
1 teaspoon	rice wine or dry sherry
½ teaspoon	salt
¼ teaspoon	m.s.g. (optional)
½ teaspoon	sesame oil (optional)
¾ teaspoon	cornflour (cornstarch)

Cut the pork into thin slices, then cut each in halves. Place in a dish with the seasoning A ingredients, mix well and leave for 20 minutes.

Drain the 'wood ears' and chop into small pieces. Slice the champignons or straw mushrooms into two or three pieces each. Squeeze the water from the mushrooms, remove stems and cut the caps into quarters.

Mix the egg with salt. Add about 1 tablespoon of the oil to the wok and heat to moderate. Pour in the beaten egg and cook until firm underneath. Lift a corner to allow the uncooked egg to run underneath. Continue cooking until firm enough to turn, then carefully turn and cook the underside until lightly coloured. Remove and break into several large pieces with a fork. Leave to cool.

Add the remaining oil and stir-fry the pork on fairly high heat until lightly coloured. Add the ginger and fry briefly, then add the spring onion and stir-fry until beginning to soften. Add the 'wood ear', mushrooms, and bamboo shoots and fry on moderate heat for about 2 minutes.

Pour off any excess oil, then add the pre-mixed seasoning B/sauce ingredients and bring to the boil. Return the egg and simmer in the sauce until thickened.

This dish is often served with *Mandarin* pancakes or sesame pocket bread in the West (see recipes, page 373 and 372), though this custom is not necessarily one adopted directly from China where this dish is usually served with plain rice.

SHREDDED PORK IN SESAME POUCHES

375 g (12 oz)	pork leg (fresh ham)
1 tablespoon	dark soy sauce
60 g (2 oz)	Szechuan preserved vegetable or salted mustard root*
¼ cup (2 fl oz)	frying oil
6 pieces	sesame pocket bread (see recipes, page 372)

Seasoning:

2 teaspoons	sugar (or to taste)
½ teaspoon	m.s.g. (optional)
1 tablespoon	rice wine or dry sherry

Thinly slice the pork across the grain, then cut into very fine short shreds. Place in a dish and add the soy sauce. Mix well and leave for 20 minutes. Soak the preserved vegetables in cold water for 20 minutes, then drain and squeeze out as much water as possible. Cut into fine shreds.

Heat the frying oil and stir-fry the pork until it changes colour, about 1 minute. Add the preserved vegetables and fry for 1 minute, then stir in the seasoning ingredients and mix well. Cook for about 4 minutes on fairly high heat, stirring continually.

Warm the breads in the oven if cooked in advance. Cut in halves and arrange on a plate. Serve with the shredded pork. To eat, a portion of the meat is stuffed into the 'pocket' of the bread and eaten like a sandwich.

* Finely shredded dry beancurd is often added to this dish and may be substituted for the preserved or salted vegetable.

67

FIVE SPICE AND GARLIC SPARE RIBS

18	American-style spare ribs (about 700 g / 1⅓ lb)
8 cups (2 litres)	deep-frying oil
	Chinese pepper-salt

Seasoning A:

½ teaspoon	salt
2 teaspoons	sugar
¾ teaspoon	five spice powder
2 teaspoons	light soy sauce
1 teaspoon	white vinegar
2 teaspoons	rice wine or dry sherry
3 tablespoons	cornflour (cornstarch)

Seasoning B:

1 tablespoon	chopped garlic
2 tablespoons	light soy sauce
1 tablespoon	white vinegar
1 tablespoon	sugar

Cut the ribs into 7.5 cm (3 in) pieces or leave whole as preferred. Place in a dish and add the pre-mixed seasoning A ingredients, rubbing thoroughly over each piece. Leave for 1 hour.

Heat the deep-frying oil to fairly hot and deep-fry the ribs until crisped on the surface and cooked through, about 3 minutes. Remove and retain the oil.

Transfer about 2 tablespoons of the oil to another wok and add the seasoning B ingredients. Cook, stirring on high heat for 1 minute, then remove from the heat. Reheat the deep-frying oil and fry the ribs again briefly, until very crisp. Remove and drain, then add to the sauce and simmer briefly.

Transfer to a serving plate and serve with a Chinese pepper-salt (see page 384).

PORK LIVERS IN SWEET FERMENTED RICE SAUCE

315 g (10 oz)	pork liver
2 slices	fresh ginger
2 tablespoons	frying oil
1 cup	sweet fermented rice (see page 387)*
2	spring onions (scallions), trimmed and chopped
½ teaspoon	salt
½ teaspoon	m.s.g. (optional)

Seasoning:

1 tablespoon	light soy sauce
½ teaspoon	sugar
2 teaspoons	cornflour (cornstarch)

Remove the skin from the liver and slice thinly. Soak in cold water for 10 minutes, drain and place in a dish with the seasoning ingredients. Leave for 10 minutes.

Heat the frying oil in a wok and sauté the ginger briefly, then add the sliced liver and sauté until lightly coloured. Add the fermented rice or substitute ingredients and the spring onions. Bring just to the boil and reduce heat to a simmer. Cook until the liver is cooked through but is still slightly pink inside, then add the salt and m.s.g., if used, and serve.

* Or mix 1¾ tablespoons Japanese light miso paste with 1 tablespoon sugar, 2 tablespoons rice wine or dry sherry, and ½ cup (4 fl oz) water.

SAUTÉD PORK KIDNEYS WITH BAMBOO SHOOTS, CARROTS AND 'WOOD EARS'

310 g (10 oz)	pork kidneys
60 g (2 oz)	canned bamboo shoots, drained
20 g (2/3 oz)	dried 'wood ear' fungus, soaked for 25 minutes
1	small carrot, thinly sliced
4	garlic chives, sliced
1 cup (8 fl oz)	frying oil
1 teaspoon	rice wine or dry sherry
2 teaspoons	light soy sauce

Seasoning/Sauce:

2½ tablespoons	water
½ teaspoon	white vinegar
½ teaspoon	sesame oil
1 teaspoon	salt
½ teaspoon	m.s.g. (optional)
½ teaspoon	sugar
¼ teaspoon	ground black pepper
1 teaspoon	cornflour (cornstarch)

Cut the kidneys in halves diagonally and trim away the white fatty tissue. Remove the skin and soak in cold water for 10 minutes. Drain well. Score on the skin side in a close criss-cross pattern (see page 397), then cut into thin slices. This gives slices with one fluted edge. Blanch in boiling water for 1 minute and drain well.

Thinly slice the bamboo shoots. Drain the fungus and cut into small squares. Heat the frying oil and sauté the kidneys until lightly coloured, then add the prepared vegetables and chives and sauté for 30 seconds. Sizzle the wine and soy sauce onto the sides of the wok and stir in, then add the pre-mixed seasoning/sauce ingredients.

Simmer until the kidneys are cooked through and the sauce thickened, about 1¼ minutes. Do not overcook or the kidneys will toughen.

PORK FILLET SAUTÉD WITH BAMBOO SHOOTS AND MUSHROOMS

280 g (9 oz)	pork fillet (tenderloin)
60 g (2 oz)	canned champignons or straw mushrooms, drained
1 cup (8 fl oz)	frying oil
2	spring onions (scallions), trimmed and sliced
2 slices	fresh ginger, shredded
30 g (1 oz)	canned bamboo shoots, drained and sliced
1 teaspoon	sesame oil (optional)

Seasoning A:

1	egg white, beaten
½ teaspoon	salt
½ teaspoon	m.s.g. (optional)
2 teaspoons	cornflour (cornstarch)

Seasoning B/Sauce:

¼ cup (2 fl oz)	chicken stock
1 tablespoon	light soy sauce
2 teaspoons	rice wine or dry sherry
½ teaspoon	salt
½ teaspoon	cornflour (cornstarch)

Cut the pork into thin slices across the grain and place in a dish with the seasoning A ingredients. Leave for 20 minutes, turning several times.

Thinly slice the mushrooms. Heat a frying pan and sauté the onion and ginger briefly, then add the sliced pork and sauté on moderate heat until it changes colour. Remove and add the mushrooms and bamboo shoots. Sauté briefly, then pour off as much oil as possible and add the pre-mixed seasoning B/sauce ingredients. Return the pork and bring to the boil. Simmer until the sauce thickens, stir in the sesame oil, if used, and serve.

RED-BRAISED FIVE SPICE BEEF

Serve hot or cold as an appetiser or main dish.

1 kg (2 lb)	braising beef (shank, round, topside)
3	spring onions (scallions), trimmed and sliced
5 thick slices	fresh ginger, bruised
2	spice bags
3 pieces	dried orange peel

Seasonings:

¼ cup (2 fl oz)	rice wine or dry sherry
¾ cup (6 fl oz)	light soy sauce
2 tablespoons	dark soy sauce (optional)
⅓ cup	sugar

Cut the beef into three large pieces and blanch in boiling water for 2 minutes. Drain and place in a stew pan with the onions, ginger, spice bags, and orange peel. Add the seasoning ingredients with water to just cover. Place a plate on top of the meat and weight with a heavy heatproof and waterproof object. Cover the pan and bring to the boil. Cook for about 8 minutes on high heat, then turn the heat to the lowest point and simmer until the meat is completely tender, about 1 hour. Remove the weight when the heat is decreased.

Place the beef in a dish and weight again. When cool, chill thoroughly before cutting very thinly to serve as an appetiser by itself or with other cold cuts.

The sliced cooked meat may also be crisp-fried (see the following recipe).

CRISP-FRIED BEEF WITH SESAME SEEDS

280 g (9 oz)	Red-Braised Five Spice Beef (see previous recipe)
1¼ tablespoons	white sesame seeds
4 cups (1 litre)	deep-frying oil

Seasoning:

¼ teaspoon	salt
½ teaspoon	m.s.g. (optional)
1¼ tablespoons	sugar
1 teaspoon	light soy sauce
1 tablespoon	sweet rice wine, Japanese mirin or sweet sherry
1½ tablespoons	chicken stock or cold water

Very thinly slice the beef and cut into 4 cm (1 2/3 in) squares. Place in a frying basket. Wipe out a wok with an oiled cloth and dry-fry the sesame seeds until lightly toasted. Set aside.

Wipe out the wok again and add the deep-frying oil. Heat to smoking point. Deep-fry the beef for 1 minute, then remove and reheat the oil. Fry the meat again and remove. Continue frying and reheating the oil until the meat is very dark and crisp, then remove and drain well. Pour off the oil.

Return the meat to the wok and add the pre-mixed seasoning ingredients. Stir on moderate heat until the liquid has been completely absorbed. Add the sesame seeds, stir well, and transfer to a warmed serving plate.

STEWED BEEF NORTHERN STYLE

750 g (1½ lb)	silverside or shin (brisket or shank)
3	spring onions (scallions), trimmed and halved
5 thick slices	fresh ginger, bruised
¼ cup (2 fl oz)	softened lard or frying oil

Seasoning:

3	star anise
2 tablespoons	sugar
2/3 cup	light soy sauce
2 tablespoons	dark soy sauce
¼ cup (2 fl oz)	rice wine or dry sherry

Cut the beef into cubes and blanch in boiling water to cover for 2 minutes. Remove the beef and drain well. Skim the stock and add the seasonings, return to the boil.

Stir-fry the cubed beef, spring onions, and ginger in the lard or oil until lightly coloured. Transfer to the stock and cover the pan. Simmer on low heat for at least 2 hours until the meat is completely tender and the sauce well reduced. Thicken the remaining sauce if necessary with a thin solution of cornflour (cornstarch) and cold water.

SLICED BEEF WITH ORANGE PEEL AND CHILLI PEPPERS

315 g (10 oz)	lean beef steak (rump or fillet/tenderloin)
2	dried red chilli peppers, cut into quarters
3 pieces	dried orange peel
1 teaspoon	Chinese brown peppercorns (optional)
¼ cup (2 fl oz)	frying oil

Seasoning A:

¼ teaspoon	salt
¼ teaspoon	m.s.g. (optional)
1 tablespoon	dark soy sauce
1 tablespoon	finely chopped spring onion (scallion)
1 teaspoon	grated fresh ginger
2 teaspoons	cornflour (cornstarch)
1 tablespoon	frying oil

Seasoning B:

1 tablespoon	light soy sauce
2 teaspoons	dark soy sauce
2 teaspoons	sesame oil

Partially freeze the beef to cut into paper-thin slices across the grain, then cut into strips about 4 × 2.5 cm (1 2/3 × 1 in). Place in a dish and rub on the seasoning A ingredients. Leave for 20 minutes.

Heat the frying oil and fry the peppers, orange peel, and peppercorns for about 3 minutes, until dark brown. Remove and set aside. Reheat the wok and add the beef. Stir-fry on high heat until the meat is crisp on the edges, then return the fried ingredients and add the seasoning B ingredients. Stir briefly on high heat, then transfer to a warmed serving plate.

If preferred, the beef may be deep-fried in fairly hot oil until quite crisp, then stir-fried with the seasoning B and other fried ingredients.

BEEF BRAISED WITH DRY BEANCURD AND VEGETABLES

625 g (1¼ lb)	braising beef (round, topside/chuck)
2 squares	dry beancurd
2 cups (16 fl oz)	frying oil
3	small sweet white turnips
5	small carrots
60 g (2 oz)	fresh or frozen peas
3	spring onions (scallions), trimmed and sliced
3 thick slices	fresh ginger, braised
5 cloves	garlic, sliced
1 — 2	fresh red chilli peppers, sliced (optional)

Seasoning A:

1 tablespoon	finely chopped spring onion (scallion)
½ teaspoon	grated fresh ginger
1 tablespoon	light soy sauce
2 teaspoons	rice wine or dry sherry
2 teaspoons	cornflour (cornstarch)

Seasoning B:

¼ cup (2 fl oz)	light soy sauce
2 teaspoons	rice wine or dry sherry
1½ teaspoons	sugar
½ teaspoon	m.s.g. (optional)

Cut the beef into cubes and place in a dish with the seasoning A ingredients, mix well and leave for 20 minutes.

Cut the beancurd into small cubes. Heat the frying oil and fry the beancurd until crisp on the surface, about 2 minutes. Remove and drain well.

Peel and cube the turnips and carrots. Pour off all but 2½ tablespoons of the oil and sauté the vegetables, spring onions, ginger, garlic, and chillies, if used, for 2 minutes. Add the meat and sauté until evenly coloured.

Transfer meat and vegetables to a casserole and add the beancurd. Add boiling water or beef stock to cover and the seasoning B ingredients. Simmer until the beef is tender, about 1 hour. Add salt to taste and a dash of sesame oil. Serve hot in the casserole.

Sliced Beef with Orange Peel and Chilli Peppers (recipe this page).

BEEF IN BUDDHIST ROBES

Serve as an appetiser.

This is a classic Northern dish, named after the bright yellow coloured egg pancake pastry which resembles a Buddhist monk's saffron robes.

Batter:

5	eggs, well beaten
1 tablespoon	cornflour (cornstarch)
1 tablespoon	water
1 teaspoon	vegetable oil
¾ teaspoon	salt
¼ teaspoon	m.s.g. (optional)
	few drops of orange-red food colouring

Filling:

375 g (12 oz)	lean beef, finely minced (ground)
1½ tablespoons	finely chopped spring onion (scallion)
1 teaspoon	grated fresh ginger

Seasoning:

1 tablespoon	Chinese pepper-salt*
1 tablespoon	light soy sauce
2 tablespoons	water
1 tablespoon	cornflour (cornstarch)

Sealing Paste:

1	egg, well beaten
1 tablespoon	cornflour (cornstarch)
2 teaspoons	water

Beat the batter ingredients together thoroughly, then set aside for 25 minutes. Mix the beef, spring onion, and ginger with the seasoning ingredients and leave for 20 minutes, then refrigerate for 1 hour.

Wipe out an omelette pan with a 22 cm (9 in) diameter and rub with an oiled cloth. Pour in one-sixth of the batter and cook on moderate heat until small bubbles appear on the surface and the underside is specked with brown. Lift one corner and carefully turn. Cook the other side until firm and very lightly coloured. Cook the remaining batter in this way, giving 6 pancakes.

Mix the sealing paste ingredients together and spread on one side of each pancake when cool. Cover half of the pancakes with a thick layer of the beef mixture and press the remaining pancakes on top, pasted sides down.

Cut each into wide slices, then into diamond shaped pieces by cutting diagonally to the first cuts.

Heat shallow oil to moderately hot and fry the pancake slices until golden brown, turning once. Lift out and drain well. Arrange on a bed of shredded lettuce or a paper napkin on a serving plate and serve with dips of Chinese pepper-salt (see page 384) and light soy sauce.

* Made with 1 tablespoon of Chinese brown peppercorns and 1¼ teaspoons of salt (see directions on page 384).

MONGOLIAN BEEF FIRE-POT

Serve as a complete main course.

1 kg (2 lb)	beef sirloin steak (loin, striploin)
2 squares	soft beancurd
500 g (1 lb)	young Chinese green vegetables
90 g (3 oz)	bean thread vermicelli, soaked to soften
8	large spring onions (scallions), trimmed and sliced
6	whole eggs
8 cups (2 litres)	water
1½ teaspoons	salt
½ teaspoon	m.s.g. (optional)
2 teaspoons	rice wine or dry sherry

Sauce Dips:

1 small jar	sha chia jiang or commercial satay sauce
½ cup	Hoisin sauce
	light soy sauce
	chillies sauce
	hot mustard

Special Equipment: A charcoal heated 'fire-pot' or table-top chafing dish.

Partially freeze the beef so that it can be cut into wafer-thin slices across the grain. Arrange on several plates. Cut the beancurd into small cubes. Soak in cold water for 10 minutes, then drain and place on a serving plate. Thoroughly wash the vegetables, cut into pieces and place in a dish. Drain the vermicelli and transfer to a serving dish. Serve the spring onions on another plate and place one egg in each of six rice bowls. Place one in front of each diner.

Serve the various sauce dips in small plates so they are all within reach of each diner.

Take the plates of meat and other ingredients to the table. Heat the fire-pot and add the water, salt, m.s.g., if used, and wine. Bring to the boil, then reduce to a simmer.

Use wooden chopsticks to place slices of meat and vegetables in the simmering stock. Retrieve when the meat is still quite rare and the vegetables crisp and lightly cooked. Dip into one or several of the sauces before eating.

The eggs should be broken into the rice bowls, beaten lightly and used as an additional tasty dip. Omit, if preferred.

The noodles may be eaten with the soup when the meat, vegetables, and beancurd are finished.

SAUTÉD LAMB WITH GARLIC

280 g (9 oz)	lean lamb
2	spring onions (scallions), trimmed and sliced
10 cloves	garlic, sliced
¼ cup (2 fl oz)	frying oil

Seasoning A:

¼ teaspoon	salt
1½ teaspoons	ground Chinese brown peppercorns
2 tablespoons	light soy sauce
2 teaspoons	rice wine or dry sherry
1 tablespoon	frying oil
1 teaspoon	sesame oil
1 teaspoon	cornflour (cornstarch)

Seasoning B:

1 tablespoon	light soy sauce
1 teaspoon	rice wine or dry sherry
2 teaspoons	sesame oil

Slice the lamb thinly across the grain, then cut into fine shreds. Place in a dish with the seasoning A ingredients, mix well and leave for 20 minutes.

Heat the oil in a wok and fry the spring onions for 30 seconds. Remove, add the garlic and fry until lightly coloured. Remove.

Reheat the pan to fairly hot and fry the shredded lamb until lightly coloured, about 2 minutes. Return the onions and garlic and add the seasoning B ingredients, sizzling them separately onto the sides of the pan. Stir in and cook for a few seconds more until the lamb is just done.

Transfer to a warmed serving plate.

MONGOLIAN LAMB

280 g (9 oz)	lean lamb*
¼ cup (2 fl oz)	frying oil
1	small leek, shredded
1	small carrot, parboiled and thinly sliced
2 teaspoons	toasted white sesame seeds

Seasoning A:

½ teaspoon	m.s.g. (optional)
2 teaspoons	sugar
1 teaspoon	crushed garlic
2 tablespoons	dark soy sauce
2 tablespoons	rice wine or dry sherry
1 tablespoon	sesame oil
2 teaspoons	cornflour (cornstarch)

Seasoning B/Sauce:

¼ cup (2 fl oz)	cold water
1 tablespoon	light soy sauce
1 tablespoon	rice wine or dry sherry
1 tablespoon	sesame oil
¼ teaspoon	salt
½ teaspoon	m.s.g. (optional)
1 teaspoon	sugar
1¼ teaspoons	cornflour (cornstarch)

Special Equipment: An iron frying pan or steak pan with a wooden stand.

Partially freeze the meat, cut into wafer-thin slices across the grain, then into pieces about 5 cm (2 in) square. Mix with the seasoning A ingredients and leave for about 45 minutes.

Heat the oil in a wok and stir-fry the shredded leek until lightly coloured. Push to one side of the pan and add the sliced carrot. Stir-fry briefly, then push aside. Heat the pan to very high and stir-fry the lamb (or beef) until lightly coloured.

Place the frying pan or steak pan on another heat source to thoroughly heat through. Pour the pre-mixed seasoning B/sauce ingredients onto the meat and stir in the vegetables. Heat to boiling point, then pour into the prepared hot pan and garnish with the sesame seeds. Carry sizzling to the table.

* Or use fillet (tenderloin) of beef.

VENISON SAUTÉD WITH LEEKS

315 g (10 oz)	fresh venison fillet (tenderloin), or rump
2	fresh young leeks
¼ cup (2 fl oz)	frying oil
1 teaspoon	sesame oil
½ teaspoon	white vinegar

Seasoning A:

¼ teaspoon	salt
1 teaspoon	sugar
2 tablespoons	light soy sauce
1 tablespoon	rice wine or dry sherry
2 teaspoons	sesame oil
1 tablespoon	finely chopped spring onion (scallion)
1½ teaspoons	grated fresh ginger
1½ teaspoons	cornflour (cornstarch)
1 tablespoon	frying oil

Seasoning B:

½ teaspoon	salt
¾ teaspoon	sugar
2 tablespoons	light soy sauce
1 tablespoon	rice wine or dry sherry

Cut the meat across the grain into thin slices, then into shreds, and place in a dish with the seasoning A ingredients. Mix well and leave for 1 hour.

Thoroughly wash the leeks and cut into 5 cm (2 in) pieces, then shred finely lengthwise. Heat the oil in a wok and fry the leeks until softened. Push to one side of the pan and add the meat. Sauté until it changes colour, then cook for a further 1 minute. Stir in the sesame oil and add the seasoning B ingredients, sizzling the soy and wine separately onto the sides of the pan.

Mix in the leeks and cook, stirring, until the meat is just done. Transfer to a warmed serving plate. Sprinkle on the vinegar and stir in lightly.

SLOW-SIMMERED PIGEONS

3	young pigeons (about 700 g / 1⅓ lb dressed weight)
2	spice bags
1½ cups (12 fl oz)	light soy sauce
¼ cup (2 fl oz)	dark soy sauce
¼ cup (2 fl oz)	rice wine or dry sherry
1 cup	sugar
2 teaspoons	sesame oil

Blanch the pigeons in boiling water for 1 minute. Remove and drain well. Pour out the water and return the pigeons to the saucepan. Add the remaining ingredients, except the sesame oil and add water to cover. Bring just to the boil, then reduce heat and simmer until the pigeons are completely tender, about 1¼ hours. Remove and drain well. Brush with sesame oil, cut in halves or quarters and serve on a bed of shredded or fresh whole lettuce leaves.

Beef in Buddhist Robes (recipe page 74).

SAUTÉD PIGEON MEAT WITH LIVERS AND EGGS IN NOODLE NEST

250 g (8 oz)	sliced pigeon meat
60 g (2 oz)	pigeons' livers
6	pigeon eggs
6 cups (1½ litres)	deep-frying oil
45 g (1½ oz)	rice vermicelli or bean thread vermicelli
1	spring onion (scallion), trimmed and diced
2 slices	fresh ginger, shredded
45 g (1½ oz)	canned straw mushrooms, drained and thinly sliced
45 g (1½ oz)	canned bamboo shoots, drained and thinly sliced
2 teaspoons	rice wine or dry sherry
1 teaspoon	sesame oil

Seasoning A:

1 teaspoon	dark soy sauce
1 teaspoon	ginger wine
1½ teaspoons	cornflour (cornstarch)

Seasoning B/Sauce:

⅓ cup	chicken stock
1 teaspoon	light soy sauce
½ teaspoon	salt
¼ teaspoon	m.s.g. (optional)
½ teaspon	sugar
¼ teaspoon	ground black pepper
1 teaspoon	cornflour (cornstarch)

Special Equipment: Two wire strainers, one slightly larger than the other.

Blanch the pigeon meat in biling water for a few seconds, then drain well and place in a dish with the diced livers and the seasoning A ingredients. Leave for 20 minutes.

Hard boil (hard cook) the eggs and drain, then cool under running cold water and remove the shells. Heat the deep-frying oil to smoking point and decrease the heat slightly. Break the rice vermicelli (or cut the bean threads) into short lengths and use to line the inside of the larger strainer. Press the smaller strainer inside to compress the noodles into a nest shape. Lower into the hot oil, holding the two handles firmly together. Deep-fry until the nest is crisp and a light golden colour. Remove and upturn onto absorbent paper.

Place the pigeon meat and livers in one of the strainers and deep-fry for about 45 seconds. Remove and drain well. Deep-fry the eggs until golden and drain well.

Pour off all but 2 tablespoons of the oil and stir-fry the spring onion, ginger, mushrooms, and bamboo shoots for 1½ minutes. Push to one side of the pan and add the pigeon meat and livers and stir-fry briefly, then mix in with the vegetables and sizzle the wine onto the sides of the pan and add the sesame oil. Add the seasoning B/sauce ingredients, pre-mixed. Simmer for about 1 minute, then add the eggs and heat through thoroughly.

Place the nest on a bed of shredded lettuce or fresh coriander and spoon the cooked dish into the centre. Serve at once.

SPICED PIGEON EGGS

Serve hot or cold as an appetiser.

12	fresh pigeon eggs, or use canned quail eggs, drained

Seasoning:

½ teaspoon	salt
¼ teaspoon	m.s.g. (optional)
1 teaspoon	Chinese brown peppercorns
2 tablespoons	light soy sauce
1 cup (8 fl oz)	chicken stock
1	spring onion (scallion), trimmed and sliced
2 slices	fresh ginger

Boil the eggs in gently bubbling water until firm, about 4 minutes. Lift out and cool under running cold water. Remove the shells and set aside.

Bring the seasoning ingredients to the boil in another saucepan and add the eggs. Simmer for 8 minutes, then remove and leave to cool. Cut in halves and arrange on a bed of shredded lettuce. Serve hot or cold.

EGG DUMPLINGS

Makes 18

Batter:

4	eggs
2 teaspoons	cornflour (cornstarch)
1 teaspoon	water
⅓ teaspoon	salt

Filling:

90 g (3 oz)	lean pork, finely minced (ground)
3 — 4	water chestnuts, finely chopped
1½ teaspoons	finely chopped spring onion (scallion)
½ teaspoon	grated fresh ginger

Seasoning:

½ teaspoon	salt
¼ teaspoon	m.s.g. (optional)
½ teaspoon	sugar
	pinch of white pepper
¼ teaspoon	sesame oil
1 teaspoon	cornflour (cornstarch)

Sauce:

¾ cup (6 fl oz)	chicken stock
1 tablespoon	light soy sauce
½ teaspoon	rice wine or dry sherry
¼ teaspoon	salt
½ teaspoon	sugar
¼ teaspoon	m.s.g. (optional)
¼ teaspoon	ground black pepper

Beat the batter ingredients together thoroughly, then leave for 25 minutes.

Mix the filling ingredients with the seasoning ingredients and knead until smooth and evenly mixed, then cover with plastic wrap and refrigerate.

Wipe out a small omelette pan with an oiled cloth and heat to moderate. Pour in about 1 tablespoon of the mixture and tilt the pan to spread the batter as evenly as possible in a round shape about 6.5 cm (2½ in) in diameter. Cook until very lightly coloured underneath and still soft and sticky on top. Do not overcook.

Place a small spoonful of the filling in the centre of the pancake and fold in halves. Gently press the edges together with the back of a spoon to stick down firmly. Proceed with the remaining dumplings.

Bring the sauce ingredients to a slow simmer in a larger frying pan or wok and add the dumplings. Simmer for about 5 minutes, then invert the pan onto a serving plate and serve the dumplings with any remaining sauce while piping hot.

FRIED FRESH MILK WITH CRABMEAT ON RICE NOODLES

1½ tablespoons	chopped cooked ham or bacon
1 tablespoon	frying oil
1 cup (8 fl oz)	fresh milk
6	egg whites
½ cup (4 fl oz)	softened lard
90 g (3 oz)	cooked crabmeat, flaked
1 tablespoon	finely chopped canned champignons (optional)
1½ tablespoons	canned sweet corn kernels, well drained (optional)
45 g (1½ oz)	rice vermicelli, broken
4 cups (1 litre)	deep-frying oil

Seasoning:

1½ teaspoons	salt
½ teaspoon	m.s.g. (optional)
2 tablespoons	cornflour (cornstarch)

Fry the chopped ham or bacon in the oil until crisp. Remove and set aside. Wipe out the wok. Pour the milk into a basin and add the seasoning ingredients. Beat the egg whites to soft peaks and mix with the milk. Add the flaked crabmeat and stir in lightly, adding the chopped champignons and sweet corn, if used.

Heat the lard in the wok until warm, pour in the mixture and cook, stirring slowly until the mixture begins to set.

In another pan, heat the deep-frying oil to smoking point. Place the broken rice vermicelli in a frying basket and lower into the hot oil to fry until it expands into a cloud of crisp white noodles. Remove, drain well and place on a serving dish. Pour the softly cooked milk and crabmeat mixture on top and garnish with the cooked ham. Serve at once.

OMELETTE IN SPICY SAUCE

6	whole eggs, well beaten
½ teaspoon	salt
2½ tablespoons	softened lard
30 g (1 oz)	lean pork, minced (ground)
4	canned water chestnuts, drained and finely chopped
15 g (½ oz)	dried 'wood ear' fungus, soaked for 25 minutes, then finely chopped
1 tablespoon	finely chopped spring onion (scallion)
1 teaspoon	finely chopped fresh ginger
¾ teaspoon	finely chopped garlic (or to taste)

Sauce:

½ cup (4 fl oz)	chicken stock
1 tablespoon	hot bean paste
1 tablespoon	light soy sauce
½ teaspoon	white vinegar
2 teaspoons	sugar
½ teaspoon	sesame oil (optional)
1½ teaspoons	cornflour (cornstarch)

Mix the eggs with the salt. Heat a wok and add 1 tablespoon of the lard. Pour in the egg mixture when the oil is quite warm and cook on moderate heat until firm underneath, then turn and cook the underside until firm. Lift onto a serving plate and cut into 6 pieces. Keep warm.

Wipe out the wok and add the remaining lard. Heat to moderate and add the remaining prepared ingredients. Stir-fry for 2 minutes, then add the sauce ingredients and simmer until the sauce is thickened. Check the seasoning and simmer a further 1 minute.

Pour over the omelette and serve at once.

PEKING STYLE FRIED DUMPLINGS

Makes 24

Pastry:

1½ cups	flour
½ cup	warm water

Filling:

125 g (4 oz)	lean pork, finely minced (ground)
1	medium white onion, finely chopped
1 tablespoon	finely chopped spring onion (scallion)
½ teaspoon	finely chopped fresh ginger

Seasoning:

1	egg, beaten
½ teaspoon	salt
½ teaspoon	m.s.g. (optional)
2 teaspoons	light soy sauce
2 teaspoons	sesame oil
2 teaspoons	cornflour (cornstarch)

Sift the flour into a bowl and make a well in the centre. Pour in the warm water and work until well mixed, then knead to a smooth soft dough, about 5 minutes. Cover with a damp cloth and leave for 30 minutes.

Mix the pork, onion, spring onion, and ginger with the seasoning ingredients. Knead to produce a smooth paste, then chill until needed.

Roll the dough into a long sausage shape and cut into 24 pieces. Roll each out on a lightly oiled board with a dry rolling pin, making sure that the upper side remains free of oil. Place a spoonful of the mixture in the centre of each wrapper and fold in halves. Press the edges firmly together. Slightly flatten the dumplings at the fold so they can be stood up, with the joined edges upwards.

Wipe out a large flat frying pan, preferably a heavy iron type, with an oiled cloth and add about 1½ tablespoons of clean vegetable or frying oil. Heat to moderate, then arrange the dumplings in a circle in the pan. Cook over moderate heat until the dumplings are golden underneath, then pour in ⅓ cup of chicken stock or water and cover the pan tightly. Cook on moderate heat until the liquid has been absorbed, about 6 minutes.

Invert the pan onto a serving plate and serve at once with accompanying sauce dips of hot mustard, chilli sauce, and light soy sauce.

Venison Sautéd with Leeks (recipe page 76).

SMOKED VEGETARIAN 'DUCK'

Serve as an appetiser or main dish.

10 sheets	dried beancurd skin
1	medium carrot
4	dried black mushrooms, soaked for 25 minutes
¼ cup (2 fl oz)	frying oil
1 cup	sugar

Seasoning:

1 cup (8 fl oz)	light soy sauce
1 tablespoon	dark soy sauce
1 tablespoon	sesame oil
1½ tablespoons	sugar
¼ teaspoon	salt
½ teaspoon	m.s.g. (optional)

Wipe the beancurd skins with a damp cloth to clean and soften. Set two aside and roll the others up. Shred coarsely. Peel and dice the carrot and parboil. Drain well. Squeeze the water from the mushrooms, remove the stems and dice the caps.

Heat the frying oil and stir-fry the carrot and mushrooms for 1 minute. Add the shredded beancurd skins and stir-fry for 2 minutes on moderate heat. Add half the pre-mixed seasoning ingredients and cook a further 1 minute.

Place the two remaining sheets of beancurd skin on a board and brush with some of the remaining seasoning ingredients. Divide the stir-fried vegetables and beancurd skin between the two sheets, arranging in a 5 cm (2 in) strip across the centre of each piece. Pour on some of the remaining sauce, then fold in the sides and then the two larger flaps to produce two long flat sausage shapes. Press in the sides to form into square-sided, rectangular shape. Place the two rolls in a dish and pour on the remaining sauce.

Leave for 1 hour to absorb the sauce, then set the dish on a rack in a steamer and steam for 10 minutes. Drain any water or sauce from the dish and discard. Wipe out the wok and add the sugar. Heat until the sugar begins to smoke, then place the dish on a rack over the sugar, cover the pan tightly and smoke for 5 minutes.

Remove and cut diagonally into thick slices. Serve hot or cold.

The rolls, smoked or unsmoked, can be used in vegetarian dishes as a meat substitute, or can be thinly sliced to serve with other cold cuts.

BEANCURD SKIN 'NOODLES' WITH YOUNG SOYBEANS

2 sheets	dried beancurd skin, about 30 cm (12 in) square
250 g (8 oz)	fresh or frozen young soy or lima beans
⅓ cup	frying oil or softened lard

Seasoning:

¾ teaspoon	salt
½ teaspoon	sugar
1 tablespoon	light soy sauce
1 teaspoon	rice wine or dry sherry

Cover the beancurd skins with a wet cloth until softened, then cut into noodle-like shreds. Boil the soy or lima beans in lightly salted water until beginning to soften, about 5 minutes. Drain. Rub off the outer skin of lima beans, if used.

Heat the oil in a wok and stir-fry the beans for 2½ minutes on moderate heat. Add the noodles and stir-fry for 1½ minutes, then add the seasoning ingredients, sizzling the soy sauce and wine separately onto the sides of the pan. Stir in and transfer to a warmed serving plate.

SWEET AND SOUR CABBAGE

1 kg (2 lb)	Chinese (celery) cabbage
1 tablespoon	salt
3	fresh red chilli peppers, shredded
2.5 cm (1 in) piece	fresh ginger, shredded

Seasoning:

½ cup (4 fl oz)	sesame oil
2 teaspoons	Chinese brown peppercorns
½ cup	sugar
½ cup (4 fl oz)	white vinegar
½ teaspoon	m.s.g. (optional)

Thoroughly wash the cabbage and cut into bite-sized pieces. Drain very well and place in a large glass dish. Add the salt and toss lightly. Cover with plastic wrap and leave for 4 hours. Add the chilli and ginger and toss again lightly.

Heat the sesame oil to smoking point and add the peppercorns. Remove immediately from the heat and leave to cool, then add the remaining seasoning ingredients, stirring until the sugar dissolves.

Pour over the salad and toss lightly. Re-cover and leave for a further 4 hours, tossing occasionally. Serve as a side dish with appetisers and main courses.

To store the cabbage, first blanch in boiling water until softened, then proceed as above. Keeps for up to a week in the refrigerator.

SOUR AND HOT CUCUMBER

Serve as an appetiser or side dish.

3	small cucumbers
2.5 cm (1 in) piece	fresh ginger
2	fresh red chilli peppers
¼ cup (2 fl oz)	white vinegar
⅓ cup	sugar

Slice the cucumbers thickly lengthways, scrape out the seeds, then cut into sticks about 6 cm (2½ in) long. Shred the ginger and chilli, removing the chilli seeds for a milder taste.

Mix the cucumber, ginger, and chilli in a dish. Pour on the pre-mixed vinegar and sugar and leave for about 5 hours, turning occasionally. Serve cold.

COLD MARINATED CORIANDER

500 g (1 lb)	fresh coriander
½ cup	shelled roasted peanuts

Dressing:

½ teaspoon	salt
1 tablespoon	sugar
1¼ tablespoons	white vinegar
¼ cup (2 fl oz)	light soy sauce
1 tablespoon	sesame oil
1 tablespoon	frying or vegetable oil
1 teaspoon	crushed garlic

Thoroughly wash the coriander and remove the stalks. Drop into a saucepan of boiling water and poach for 1¼ minutes. Remove and drain well. When cool, squeeze out as much water as possible. Chop coarsely and place in a salad bowl.

Coarsely chop the peanuts or leave whole as preferred. Add to the coriander. Mix the dressing ingredients, stirring until the sugar dissolves. Pour over the salad, stir and toss lightly, and chill before serving. Serve as a side dish to appetisers or main courses.

CELERY WITH DRIED SHRIMPS

250 g (8 oz)	fresh young celery
45 g (1½ oz)	dried shrimps
2 tablespoons	Shao Hsing or other yellow wine*

Seasoning:

1½ tablespoons	sesame oil
1½ teaspoons	Chinese brown peppercorns
¾ teaspoon	salt
¼ teaspoon	m.s.g. (optional)

Cut the celery into 5 cm (2 in) pieces, then cut each piece into two or three strips, lengthways. Blanch in boiling water until just softened, about 2½ minutes. Drain thoroughly and leave to cool.

Soak the dried shrimps in the wine until softened. Drain, reserving the wine. Heat the sesame oil to smoking point, add the peppercorns and remove from the heat. Let stand until cool, then strain off the oil and discard the peppercorns. Add the salt, m.s.g., and a little of the wine and pour over the celery, add the shrimps and toss lightly.

Serve cold as a vegetable or side dish.

* Or use brandy or Japanese sake.

STIR-FRIED BEAN SPROUTS WITH CHICKEN

280 g (9 oz)	fresh bean sprouts
185 g (6 oz)	boneless chicken
2 tablespoons	frying oil

Seasoning A:

1	egg white, beaten
½ teaspoon	salt
1 teaspoon	rice wine or dry sherry
2 teaspoons	cornflour (cornstarch)

Seasoning B:

½ teaspoon	salt
¼ teaspoon	m.s.g. (optional)
½ teaspoon	sugar
¼ teaspoon	ground black pepper
½ teaspoon	rice wine or dry sherry
½ teaspoon	sesame oil
1 tablespoon	cold water
½ teaspoon	cornflour (cornstarch)

Remove the roots and pods from the sprouts and wash well. Dry thoroughly in a kitchen towel.

Thinly slice the chicken, then cut into fine shreds. Place in a dish with the seasoning A ingredients, mix well and leave for 15 minutes.

Heat the oil in a wok and stir-fry the bean sprouts for 1 minute. Push to one side of the pan and add the chicken shreds. Stir-fry until white, about 1½ minutes, then mix in the bean sprouts and add the pre-mixed seasoning B ingredients.

Stir on high heat until thoroughly mixed, then serve.

Beancurd Skin 'Noodles' with Young Soybeans (recipe page 82) and Mandarin Fish with Vinegar and Pepper in Rich Soup (recipe page 88).

'FOUR JEWELS' IN CHICKEN OIL SAUCE

½ 315 g (10 oz) can	asparagus spears, drained
¾ 280g (9 oz) can	quail eggs, drained
½ 315 g (10 oz) can	straw mushrooms or champignons
250 g (8 oz)	Chinese green vegetable hearts (young bok choy, kale, or mustard)
2 tablespoons	softened lard or frying oil
2½ tablespoons	rendered chicken fat (chicken grease)

Seasoning:

1 tablespoon	finely chopped spring onion (scallion)
¾ teaspoon	grated fresh ginger
1 cup (8 fl oz)	chicken stock
1½ teaspoons	salt
½ teaspoon	m.s.g. (optional)
¾ teaspoon	sugar
2 teaspoons	rice wine or dry sherry

Cut the asparagus in halves. Simmer the quail eggs in chicken stock or water for 5 minutes, then remove with a slotted spoon. Add the mushrooms and simmer for 5 minutes, then remove. Thoroughly wash the vegetables and cut in halves lengthways. Simmer in slightly salted water until softened. Drain well.

Heat the lard or frying oil in a wok and fry the spring onion and ginger briefly. Add the stock and remaining seasoning ingredients and then add the vegetables, asparagus, mushrooms, and quail eggs keeping them in separate groups. Cover and simmer for 5 minutes.

Drain off and reserve the liquid, then slide the contents of the wok carefully onto a serving plate without disturbing the arrangement of the ingredients. Return the stock and bring to the boil. Thicken with a solution of cornflour (cornstarch) and cold water and stir in the chicken fat. Heat to boiling and pour over the vegetables. Serve at once.

'EIGHT TREASURE' WINTER MELON POND

Serves 8 — 10.

1 3½ — 4 kg (7 — 8 lb)	winter melon
60 g (2 oz)	dried lotus seeds, soaked for 1 hour
2	dried scallops, soaked for 1 hour
4	dried black mushrooms, soaked for 25 minutes
150 g (5 oz)	duck gizzards
30 g (1 oz)	canned champignons, drained and sliced
60 g (2 oz)	canned bamboo shoots, drained and diced
90 g (3 oz)	lean pork, diced
30 g (1 oz)	Chinese or cured (Smithfield) ham, diced
6 — 8 cups (1½ — 2 litres)	chicken stock, boiling
2 teaspoons	salt, or to taste
1 teaspoon	m.s.g. (optional)
6 slices	fresh ginger, bruised
1 tablespoon	rendered chicken fat (chicken grease), optional or use lard
½ teaspoon	white pepper (optional)

Wash the melon and cut a large slice from the top. Scoop out the seeds and decorate the rim in a zig-zag or scalloped design. Carve a pattern in the skin around the sides, if desired. Fill the melon with boiling, lightly salted water, stand in a bowl and steam for 10 minutes.

Drain the lotus seeds, cover with cold water and bring to the boil. Simmer for 25 minutes. Simmer the scallops in water or chicken stock until tender, about 25 minutes, then shred between forefinger and thumb. Squeeze the water from the black mushrooms, remove stems and dice. Cut open the gizzards, clean well and trim away the thick inner skin. Cut into dice and blanch in boiling water for 2 minutes. Drain well.

Drain the winter melon and return to the bowl. Add all the ingredients except chicken fat and white pepper and return to the steamer. Cover and steam over rapidly boiling water for 35 — 40 minutes until the ingredients are cooked through and the melon tender but retaining its shape.

Stir in the chicken fat and white pepper, if used, and serve the melon still in its bowl or transfer to a decorative bowl or rack before taking to the table.

CRISP-FRIED BAMBOO SHOOTS AND SCALLOPS

1 500 g (1 lb) can	bamboo shoots, drained
4	dried scallops (about 30 g / 1 oz), soaked for 1 hour
1 large bunch	fresh coriander or parsley
5 cups (1¼ litres)	deep-frying oil

Seasoning:

¼ cup (2 fl oz)	light soy sauce
1½ tablespoons	sugar
1 tablespoon	sesame oil

Cut the bamboo shoots into 4 cm (1 2/3 in) cubes. Place in a plastic bag and add the seasoning ingredients. Leave for 40 minutes, shaking the bag occasionally.

Drain the scallops, cover with water or chicken stock and simmer until softened, about 35 minutes. Drain and shred by rubbing between forefinger and thumb.

Heat the deep-frying oil to smoking point, then decrease the heat slightly. Drain the bamboo shoots and place in a frying basket. Deep-fry until crisp on the surface and thoroughly cooked, about 4 minutes. Remove and drain well.

Reheat the oil. Remove the stems from the coriander or parsley. Place in the frying basket and deep-fry for about 30 seconds. Drain well and arrange around the rim of a serving plate. Return the bamboo shoots to the oil to briefly fry for a second time. Drain and place on the serving plate. Add the shredded scallops to the oil, in a wire strainer, and fry until crisp. Scatter over the bamboo shoots and serve at once.

ASSORTED MEAT AND SHARK'S FIN SOUP

90 g (3 oz)	prepared shark's fin (see page 393)
90 g (3 oz)	prepared shark's skin (see page 393)*
2 tablespoons	softened lard
2	spring onions (scallions), trimmed and finely shredded
2 thick slices	fresh ginger, finely shredded
3 cups (24 fl oz)	chicken stock
60 g (2 oz)	lean pork, shredded
60 g (2 oz)	boneless chicken, shredded
45 g (1½ oz)	canned bamboo shoots, drained and shredded
3	large dried black mushrooms, soaked and shredded
2 tablespoons	finely shredded cooked ham
2 tablespoons	chopped fresh coriander
1 tablespoon	white vinegar
1 teaspoon	ground black pepper

Seasoning:

¾ teaspoon	salt
½ teaspoon	m.s.g. (optional)
2 tablespoons	light soy sauce
½ teaspoon	dark soy sauce
2 teaspoons	rice wine or dry sherry
2 tablespoons	cold water
2 tablespoons	cornflour (cornstarch)

Prepare the shark's fin and shark's skin according to the directions on page 393. Shred the shark's skin finely. Drain well.

Lightly fry the onion and ginger in the lard then add the shark's fin and shark's skin and fry briefly.

Bring the chicken stock to the boil in a large saucepan. Add the shark's fin and skin, the onions, ginger, pork, chicken, bamboo shoots, and ginger.

Return to the boil and skim, then add the pre-mixed seasoning ingredients. Simmer for 20 minutes, then transfer to a soup tureen and add the ham coriander, vinegar, and pepper. Stir well and serve.

* Or use fish maw or fish lips.

HOT AND SOUR SOUP

60 g (2 oz)	lean pork, finely shredded
30 g (1 oz)	Chinese or cured (Smithfield) ham, shredded
45 g (1½ oz)	cleaned fresh squid or prepared sea cucumber, finely shredded*
30 g (1 oz)	dried 'wood ear' fungus, soaked and shredded
2	dried black mushrooms, soaked and shredded
30 g (1 oz)	bean thread vermicelli, soaked
1 square	dry beancurd, finely shredded
30 g (1 oz)	canned bamboo shoots, drained and shredded
1	small carrot, peeled and shredded
2	spring onions (scallions), trimmed and shredded
2	eggs, well beaten
4 cups (1 litre)	chicken stock
2 tablespoons	cornflour (cornstarch)

Seasoning:

1½ teaspoons	salt
1 teaspoon	m.s.g. (optional)
½ teaspoon	sugar
1½ tablespoons	light soy sauce
2 tablespoons	white vinegar
1½ teaspoons	sesame oil (optional)
½ teaspoon	ground black pepper

Blanch the pork and ham in boiling water and drain. Bring the stock to the boil and add the salt, m.s.g., if used, and sugar. Add the shredded meat and vegetables and the noodles and return to the boil. Reduce to a simmer and cook for 2 minutes. Slowly drizzle in the beaten eggs and do not stir for at least 45 seconds while the egg sets into fine strands in the soup. Add the remaining seasoning and stir in.

Thicken with a thin paste of the cornflour and cold water and simmer until the soup thickens. Transfer to a soup tureen and garnish with generous amounts of chopped fresh coriander or flat leaf parsley, shredded fresh ginger, and shredded spring onions (scallions).

* Or use shredded congealed chicken blood.

MANDARIN FISH WITH VINEGAR AND PEPPER IN RICH SOUP

1 750 g (1½ lb)	Mandarin fish (perch, trout, or grouper)
5 cm (2 in) piece	fresh ginger
4 cups (1 litre)	deep-frying oil
4 slices	fresh ginger, shredded
4 cups (1 litre)	enriched stock*

Seasoning A:

1¼ teaspoons	salt
¾ teaspoon	m.s.g. (optional)
¼ teaspoon	white pepper
1 tablespoon	rice wine or dry sherry

Seasoning B:

10	garlic chives, shredded
8 — 10 sprigs	fresh coriander
⅓ cup	white vinegar
1½ teaspoons	sesame oil
¾ teaspoon	ground black pepper

Clean the fish, remove fins and gills and place in boiling water for 20 seconds. Lift out and carefully scrape off the skin. Heat a large wok and rub vigorously with the ginger to prevent the fish sticking.

Add the deep-frying oil and heat to smoking point, then reduce the heat slightly. Slide in the fish and deep-fry for 3 minutes on each side. Remove and reheat the oil to smoking point. Fry the fish for a further 2 minutes on each side.

Carefully lift out the fish and set aside. Pour off all but 2½ tablespoons of the oil and fry the shredded ginger briefly on moderate heat. Add the stock and seasoning A ingredients and bring to the boil. Add the fish, reduce the heat and simmer for 20 minutes.

Use two spatulas to lift the fish carefully into a soup tureen and strain the stock onto it. Add the seasoning B ingredients, stir in lightly and serve at once.

*See recipe page 388, or use chicken stock and additional stock powder or crumbled stock cube. Adjust salt to taste.

Candied Apples (recipe page 90) and *Lotus Seeds in Sugar Syrup (recipe page 91).*

CANDIED APPLES

3	cooking apples
6 cups (1½ litres)	clean deep-frying oil
1 cup	sesame oil
½ cup	sugar
	flour
2 teaspoons	toasted white sesame seeds
	iced water

Batter:

2	eggs, beaten
⅓ cup	flour
⅓ cup	cornflour (cornstarch)
	cold water

Peel and core the apples and cut into thick slices. Heat the deep-frying oil to moderate. Brush a serving plate with sesame oil, then add the remainder to the frying oil.

Beat the batter ingredients, adding enough water to make a smooth, fairly thick batter. Lightly coat the apple slices with flour and dip into the batter. Deep-fry the slices, several at a time, until golden on the surface and softening inside, about 1 minute. Drain and set aside.

Reheat the oil to hot and fry the apple pieces for a second time until crisp, about 45 seconds. Drain and set aside. Pour off all but 2 tablespoons of the oil and add the sugar. Stir constantly on high heat until the sugar caramelises and turns golden. Quickly return the apple pieces and add the sesame seeds. Turn the apple slices to coat evenly with the sugar syrup. Transfer to the oiled plate and serve at once with a dish of iced water.

Dip the apple into the water before eating to set the hot syrup into crisp toffee.

Sliced firm bananas, pineapple, sweet potato, or taro may all be used for this recipe, varying the deep-frying times accordingly.

ALMOND CREAM

1½ cups	blanched sweet almonds*
½ cup	sugar
5 cups (1¼ litres)	water
½ cup (4 fl oz)	evaporated milk or cream
2 tablespoons	cornflour (cornstarch)
2 tablespoons	cold water

Place the almonds in a low oven to cook until completely dried out, but without taking on any colour. Grind in a food processor, coffee grinder, or heavy duty blender (adding a little water to prevent the machine clogging).

Bring the water to the boil and add the sugar and powdered almonds. Stir until boiling again, then add the evaporated milk, if used, and the cornflour mixed to a paste with the cold water. Boil, stirring for 4 minutes. If using cream, add at this point.

Pour into a deep dish and serve hot or cold.

* Most Chinese food suppliers have both sweet and bitter almonds, the latter being smaller and more rounded in shape.

SWEET FERMENTED RICE WITH DICED FRESH FRUIT

1 cup	sweet fermented rice (see page 387)
½ cup	sugar
6 cups (1½ litres)	water
1 tablespoon	cornflour (cornstarch)
1	small red apple
6	maraschino cherries
½	orange
2 slices	canned or fresh pineapple
1	canned or fresh pear

Pour the rice and its liquid into a saucepan and add the sugar, water, and cornflour. Stir until the cornflour is well mixed, then bring to the boil and simmer for 2 minutes.

Peel and finely dice the apple, cut the cherries in halves, discarding the stones, if any, peel and dice the orange and dice the pineapple and pear. Stir the fruit into the rice liquid and simmer briefly.

Serve hot or allow to cool, then chill thoroughly and serve cold. Use additional fresh fruit to garnish.

EGG PUFFS WITH RED BEAN FILLING

5	egg whites
2 tablespoons	cornflour (cornstarch)
250 g (8 oz)	red bean paste (see page 386)
3 cups (24 fl oz)	vegetable oil
1 cup (8 fl oz)	sesame oil
2 tablespoons	castor sugar

Beat the egg whites to stiff peaks, then carefully fold in the cornflour.

Heat the vegetable oil and sesame oil together until warm. Dip each ball of red bean paste into the egg whites, coating thickly. Place in the oil, about 6 at a time and cook gently until golden, turning once.

Arrange on a warmed serving plate and sprinkle on the sugar to garnish. As the egg puffs deflate quickly after cooking, for best results serve as soon as they leave the pan.

In place of red bean filling, sweet lotus seed paste, a mixture of crunchy peanut paste (butter) and sugar or sweetened mashed taro or sweet potato could be substituted. Or use thoroughly drained canned fruit coated lightly with cornflour (cornstarch) so the batter will adhere.

'SNOW' FUNGUS IN SWEET SOUP

60 g (2 oz)	dried lotus seeds, soaked for 2 hours
6	dried lung an fruit, soaked for 1 hour (optional)*
15 g (½ oz)	'snow' fungus (white wood ears), soaked for 1 hour
60 g (2 oz)	Chinese red dates
¾ cup	sugar
12	canned quail eggs, drained

Drain the lotus seeds and place in a small saucepan with plenty of hot water. Bring to the boil and simmer gently until softened, about 30 minutes. Drain well. Separately simmer the lung an and 'snow' fungus for 10 minutes and drain well.

Place the dates and sugar in a saucepan and add 7 cups (1¾ litres) cold water. Bring to the boil and simmer for 10 minutes, then add the 'lung an' and snow fungus and simmer for a further 30 minutes.

Add the drained lotus seeds and the quail eggs and simmer gently for about 3 minutes. Serve hot.

* A dried fruit similar to loquat. Use sliced pear, papaya or apple as a substitute, or omit.

LOTUS SEEDS IN SUGAR SYRUP

250 g (8 oz) dried lotus seeds	
6 cups (1½ litres) boiling water	
2/3 cup sugar, or to taste	

Soak the lotus seeds in cold water for 20 minutes, then drain. Cover with cold water and simmer briefly, then drain again. Use a needle to pick out the bitter central core and then place the lotus seeds in a dish with half of the boiling water and set in a rack in a steamer.

Steam until tender, about 30 minutes over rapidly boiling water. Dissolve the sugar in the remaining water and pour into a serving bowl. Add the cooked lotus seeds and the liquid. Serve hot, or refrigerate until well chilled and serve as a refreshing cold dessert.

CHAPTER IV
Eastern Coastal Style Cuisine

東

Previous page: *Grain ripens along canal in scenic Soochow (Suzhou), one of China's great culinary centres.*

Ancient sailing sampans above *still ply the canals of Soochow (Suzhou) as they have for over 2,000 years.*

The eastern/coastal culinary region centres around the lower Yangtze River basin and extends south along the coast as far as the borders of Kuangtung (Guangdong) province. It includes the provinces and culinary styles of Kiangsu (Jiangsu), Chekiang (Zhejiang), and Fukien (Fujian). The native cuisine of Taiwan is an offshoot of Fukien (Fujian) style and is included in that category. The main gastronomic centres of this region are Nanking (Nanjing), Shanghai, Hangchow (Hangzhou), Soochow (Suzhou), and Taipei (Taibei).

The climate of the eastern/coastal region is the mildest in China, rainfall is abundant, and the soil is fertile. The four seasons are distinct and well balanced in this area, and major gastronomic festivals mark the changing of the seasons. The region is dominated by the lower Yangtze River and its intricate network of mini-rivers and lakes, which are further interconnected by countless man-made canals. These multi-purpose waterways provide water for irrigation, produce fresh-water fish and molluscs, and form extensive transportation networks for harvested foods. Gentle rolling hills and verdant foliage mark this pleasant, temperate region.

Historically, this part of China has been the favourite destination of Chinese tourists and gastronomes ever since the T'ang dynasty. Hangchow (Hangzhou) was the city which Marco Polo praised with such rapture as a 'Heavenly Paradise.' Soochow (Suzhou) has been renowned since ancient times as the city which produces the most beautiful women in China, and many writers have attributed this to the benefits of the excellent food, for which the city is equally famous. An ancient Chinese adage says, 'Above there is heaven; below there are Soochow (Suzhou) and Hangchow (Hangzhou).' Food is one of the main reasons that these cities acquired their 'celestial' reputation. Poets have praised the culinary arts of this region for centuries, as illustrated by this ode to the kitchens of Soochow (Suzhou), written by the Shing dynasty poet Gu Die-Jing:

Soochow (Suzhou), the good place.
At dawn
The bamboo is cut as smooth as jade,
Fresh and tender on a crockery plate.

Soochow (Suzhou), the good place.
Fresh arbutus,
Sweet as heavenly dew,
Fills my cheeks with juice.

Soochow (Suzhou), the good place.
Big beans
Picked when the flowers bend low
And munched at tea-time.

Soochow (Suzhou), the good place.
Where the shad
Are found, and globefish from the river
Are cooked in spring with ginger and chives.

Soochow (Suzhou), the good place.
In summer
Plump fish dart about the river
Avoiding the fisherman's boat.

Purple crabs in red-wine dregs
Make the autumn pass,
And when at last the sturgeon appear,
Carp and bream leap into the pot.

Seafood and fresh-water fish form the mainstays of the eastern/coastal menu. China's favourite fish are found here in abundance: carp, river eel, shad, Mandarin fish, whitebait, mullet, bream, perch, and many varieties of molluscs. Crab, prawn, and other seafoods are caught off the eastern seaboard. The fish recipes from this area are among the best in China. Abundant supplies of every type of vegetable are available as well, adding much colour and variety to the menu. Meat and poultry are also popular, the favourite choices being pork and chicken.

Eastern/coastal cooking involves

Manual labour still prevails on China's farms. Here and opposite page, greening fields of grain are carefully tended by hand for maximum output. Harvested and winnowed with ancient implements, the grain then travels by canal to town for distribution.

heavy use of vegetable oils, and the dishes appear somewhat oily as a result. This does not detract from the taste, however, since most of the oil remains on the platter. Sugar is used in cooking more than elsewhere, while soy sauce is employed sparingly: consequently, sauces are slightly on the sweet side and light in colour. Spring onions and ginger are the favoured fresh seasonings. For flavour, the people of this region prefer distinct, fresh tastes in the main ingredients and sweet, rich flavours in the sauces. For fragrance, the *xian* (fresh-natural) aromas are emphasized, especially in fish and seafoods. For colour, chefs aim for bright colours with a shiny sheen, the latter effect produced with cornflour (cornstarch). The region is famous for its cold hors-d'oeuvre plates contrived

in elaborate floral and animal designs with multi-coloured, multi-textured ingredients. In texture, the dishes tend towards the soft and tender, smooth and slippery types, though crispy textures are also provided in deep-fried foods.

The eastern/coastal region is home of the *hong-shao* or 'red-stew,' and this technique is applied to a wide range of ingredients. The other three most commonly employed cooking methods in Soochow (Suzhou), Hangchow (Hangzhou), and other culinary centres of the region are *bao, zhao*, and *zha*.

The eastern/coastal region is one of the most diverse culinary areas of China, and each of the three provincial cuisines which comprise it has its own distinct features. Fukien (Fujian) is most famous for its rich stews, soups,

and stocks, as well as *congee* or rice-gruel. Coagulated pig's and chicken's blood are also used extensively in Fukien (Fujian) cuisine. The most distinctive aspect of this cooking is the rich stock which is always kept on hand in the kitchen for use in practically every dish. To produce this stock, the bones and leftover meat of beef, pork, ham, and mutton are thrown together and boiled for a long time, after which the stock is filtered. Then, splintered chicken bones (to expose the marrow) are added, and the stock is boiled again, reduced, and filtered once more. The rich broth which remains is used as a general, multi-purpose cooking condiment and lends rich flavour to all dishes. Fukien (Fujian) is also home of the *zao* method of marination: meat, fish, and fowl are marinated in the fermented dregs of grain-mash left over from distilling spirits.

Kiangsu's (Jiangsu's) culinary capital is the charming city of Soochow (Suzhou), where the 'red-stew' was developed to perfection. Soochow's (Suzhou's) red-stews employ rock crystal sugar to achieve the light sweetness, the shiny colours, and the smooth textures which characterize this type of dish. This city boasts China's best river eel, Mandarin fish, and fresh-water crab, which are supplied by beautiful Lake Tai and other waterways in the vicinity. Even today, Chinese gourmets from Shanghai flock to Soochow (Suzhou) in droves several times a year to participate in seasonal food festivals and sample the famous specialties. The great Ching emperor Chian-lung was converted to eastern/coastal cuisine when he paid a visit to Soochow (Suzhou) during one of his pleasure excursions to the south. He ate at the Pine-Crane restaurant, which still operates at the same address and serves some of the best food in all China.

Hangchow (Hangzhou), provincial capital of Chekiang (Zhejiang), has been one of China's greatest culinary centres since its heyday as the capital of the Southern Sung. The restaurant industry was born there, and today the city still boasts some of China's top eating establishments. Elaborate kitchen preparations, especially very fine, even cutting into slender slivers, are involved in Hangchow's (Hangzhou's) style of cooking. To protect the fresh-natural flavours and produce the light colours favoured in Hangzhou, soy sauce is used sparingly. West Lake, China's most famous scenic spot, provides much of the fish favoured in Hangzhou cuisine, especially the much-loved and highly prized Silver Carp. Silver Carp is used to make the city's most renowned dish, 'West Lake Sour Fish,' an unforgettable taste treat in which the whole fish is split in half lengthwise, lightly poached, covered with minced fresh ginger, and smothered with a rich, viscous sweet/sour sauce. The recipe, which is included in the recipe section, may be applied to other types of fresh-water fish as well. West Lake also provides *shun-chai*, a highly nutritious aquatic weed used to make soup. *Shun-chai* is as rich in flavour as it is in nutrition and has a unique slippery texture.

Other famous dishes of Hangchow (Hangzhou) are Onion-and-Oil Fish,

Typical open-air noodle stand in Shanghai, serving China's traditional version of fast-food. Menus in such stalls haven't changed for millennia.

Eel Fried in Batter, Boned Chicken with Green Chillies, Fried Beancurd Skin, Beggar's Chicken, and One Fish/Two Flavours, in which a fresh carp is split in half lengthwise, one half poached and the other half braised.

Taiwanese cuisine is an elaboration of Fukien (Fujian) style, with strong emphasis on fresh seafoods and rich, piquant sauces. The island produces an incredible variety of fresh garden vegetables, most of which are available year round and comprise important elements of the diet. *Geng* stew, one of the most ancient of Chinese dishes, is still very popular in Taiwan and is sold everywhere from little itinerant food stalls. Taipei's (Taibei's) restaurants offer not only the best of Taiwanese (Fukien (Fujian)) cuisine, but also excellent versions of all the other great regional cuisines of China.

Eastern/coastal China is one of the most pleasant regions in the country, and the food there reflects its natural blessings. Textures tend towards the soft and tender, smooth and slippery, while flavours and fragrances lean towards the sweet and the *xian* (fresh-natural). The heavy reliance on fresh fish and fresh vegetables makes the eastern/coastal diet one of the healthiest and best balanced in the world, as attested to by the dense population it supports. Connoisseurs of fresh-water fish and seafood will prefer the recipes from this region.

While southern-style cuisine, specifically Cantonese, has generally been, and still is, regarded as China's most highly developed, elaborate gourmet style, many experienced connoisseurs of Chinese food still prefer the eastern/coastal style above all else. If northern food is viewed as relatively austere and rustic while southern food is seen as highly exotic and complex, then eastern/coastal cuisine strikes a harmonious balance somewhere in between.

Hungry youngsters above *wait for woman vendor to finish frying 'Chinese doughnuts' in Shanghai alley. Bucolic West Lake* left *is the source of Hangchow's (Hangzhou's) Silver Carp, main ingredient of the city's famous 'West Lake Vinegar Fish.'* Right: *Foreign guests tuck into big bountiful winter banquet, including traditional 'hot-pot,' in Nanking (Nanjing) restaurant.*

CHICKEN STUFFED WITH SHARK'S FIN

750 g (1½ lb)	prepared shark's fin (see page 393) (about 185 g/6 oz dry weight)
1 — 1¾ kg (3½ lb)	chicken, deboned *
3	spring onions (scallions) cut in halves
4 thick slices	fresh ginger, bruised
1 tablespoon	rice wine or dry sherry
6 cups (1½ litres)	enriched stock
125 g (4 oz)	lean pork, thinly sliced (optional), or use 3 slices cooked ham or 1 ham bone
1½ teaspoons	salt
	m.s.g. (optional)

Drain the shark's fin and stuff into the chicken. Secure the opening with poultry pins and place in a casserole on the onions and ginger. Add the wine and stock and spread the pork or ham (or place the ham bone) on top. Add the salt and cover tightly.

Bring to the boil, then reduce heat to the very lowest point and simmer for about 4 hours. Discard the ham bone, if used, or serve the ham or pork separately (or reserve for another use). Remove the onion and ginger. Check the seasoning, adding a dash of m.s.g., if used. Serve in the pot.

* A deboned duck may be used instead of the chicken. If so, use ham or a ham bone in preference to pork.

STEAMED CHICKEN STUFFED WITH EIGHT PRECIOUS INGREDIENTS

1 — 1¾ (3½ lb)	chicken
1 teaspoon	salt
1 tablespoon	rice wine or dry sherry
60 g (2 oz)	glutinous rice, soaked for 1 hour
45 g (1½ oz)	dried lotus seeds, soaked for 1 hour
6	dried black mushrooms, soaked for 25 minutes
2 sets	chicken gizzards, blanched and drained
15 g (½ oz)	dried shrimps, soaked for 1 hour
30 g (1 oz)	frozen or fresh peas, parboiled
30 g (1 oz)	canned bamboo shoots, drained and diced
30 g (1 oz)	Chinese or cured (Smithfield) ham, finely diced
¼ cup (2 fl oz)	frying oil or softened lard
7 cups (1¾ litres)	chicken stock
1 tablespoon	dark soy sauce
8 cups (2 litres)	deep frying oil
	Chinese pepper-salt or spiced salt

Seasoning A:

½ teaspoon	salt
½ teaspoon	m.s.g. (optional)
1 teaspoon	rice wine or dry sherry
¼ cup (2 fl oz)	chicken stock

Seasoning B:

1 tablespoon	rice wine or dry sherry
1 teaspoon	Chinese brown peppercorns
2	spring onions (scallions), trimmed and diced
2 slices	fresh ginger
1½ teaspoons	salt

Debone the chicken, leaving the leg and wing bones intact. Rub inside with the salt and wine.

Place the rice and lotus seeds in a dish with ¾ cup (6 fl oz) water and steam until tender. Remove mushroom stems, squeeze out water and cut into small dice. Trim off the thick inner skin from the gizzards and cut into small dice. Drain the shrimp and peas.

Heat the frying oil in wok and stir-fry the diced gizzards for 3 minutes, then add the mushrooms, bamboo shoots, ham, and shrimps and stir-fry for 2 minutes. Add the seasoning A ingredients, the peas, rice, and lotus seeds and mix thoroughly.

Stuff the 'eight precious' ingredients mixture into the chicken, taking care not to tear the skin. Sew up the opening or secure with poultry pins.

Place the chicken bones in a casserole and set the chicken, breast upwards, on top. Cover with chicken stock and add the seasoning B ingredients. Cover and place on a rack in a steamer over rapidly boiling water. Steam for 1¾ hours until tender. Lift out carefully and wipe dry. Brush with the dark soy sauce while still hot and leave to dry for ½ hour.

Heat the deep-frying oil to smoking point, then reduce the heat slightly. Fry the chicken, completely immersed if possible, until brown. Drain well. Make several cuts across the body to expose the filling and serve whole, with Chinese pepper-salt or spiced salt dips.

STEWED SHARK'S FIN WITH CHICKEN, DUCK, AND PORK

Serves 6 as the main course.

250 g (8 oz)	prepared shark's fin, see page 393 (about 60 g/2 oz dry weight)
1 kg (2 lb)	chicken
500 g (1 lb)	duck meat
500 g (1 lb)	boneless pork (leg or shoulder)
2	spring onions (scallions), trimmed
4 thick slices	fresh ginger, bruised
2 tablespoons	rice wine or dry sherry
8 cups (2 litres)	enriched stock
6 pieces	dried scallops (about 45 g/1½ oz), soaked for 2 hours
125 g (4 oz)	Chinese cabbage or bok choy (celery cabbage)
¼ cup (2 fl oz)	frying oil
30 g (1 oz)	Chinese or cured (Smithfield) ham, shredded
60 g (2 oz)	canned bamboo shoots, drained and sliced
	white pepper
	extra frying oil
2 tablespoons	rendered chicken fat (chicken grease), optional

Seasoning:

	salt to taste
1 teaspoon	m.s.g. (optional)
1 teaspoon	sugar
1 tablespoon	rice wine or dry sherry
¼ cup (2 fl oz)	light soy sauce
3 tablespoons	cornflour (cornstarch)
¼ cup (2 fl oz)	chicken stock or cold water

Prepare dried shark's fin according to the instructions on page 393, allowing at least 3 hours advance preparation.

Cut the chicken, duck, and pork into 2.5 cm (1 in) cubes and blanch in boiling water.

Arrange the drained shark's fin in a bamboo basket which fits into a casserole or slow cooker and place the cubed meats on top with the onions and ginger slices. Add the wine and enriched stock and bring to the boil. Cover tightly and simmer on low heat for 3 hours, until the meat and fins are tender.

In the meantime, steam the drained scallops in ¾ cup (6 fl oz) water with a dash of rice wine or dry sherry and salt added, until tender

Wash the vegetables and cut into 5 cm (2 in) pieces. Shake out excess water. Heat the wok, add the oil and fry the vegetables on moderately high heat for 2 minutes. Add the ham and fry for 1 minute, then add the sliced bamboo shoots and the drained scallops and fry together a further 1 minute. Add a dash of rice wine or dry sherry, salt and sugar to taste. Set aside.

Remove the meat from the casserole and cut into small dice, discarding all bones. Wipe out the wok and heat about 3 tablespoons frying oil to very hot. Add the meat and fry for 2 minutes.

Remove the shark's fin to a serving dish. Strain the juices into the wok and bring to the boil. Add the pre-mixed seasoning ingredients and bring to the boil. Return the vegetables, ham, and scallops and simmer for about 3 minutes. Adjust seasoning as necessary, adding plenty of white pepper. Stir in the chicken fat, if used, and pour over the shark's fin. Serve.

STEAMED SHARK'S FIN WITH CRABMEAT

250 g (8 oz)	prepared shark's fin (see page 393), about 60 g/2 oz dry weight
4 cups (1 litre)	enriched stock
2	spring onions (scallions), trimmed
4 thick slices	fresh ginger
315 g (10 oz)	Chinese cabbage hearts or young bok choy
⅓ cup	frying oil or softened lard
1 tablespoon	rice wine or dry sherry
250 g (8 oz)	fresh, frozen, or canned crabmeat, flaked
60 g (2 oz)	crab roe (optional)

Seasoning:

	salt to taste
1 teaspoon	m.s.g.(optional)
2 tablespoons	cornflour (cornstarch)
¼ cup (2 fl oz)	cold water

Prepare dried shark's fins according to the instructions on page 393, allowing at least 3 hours advance preparation. Arrange the drained fins in a covered dish and add the enriched stock, spring onions and ginger. Cover and set on a rack in a steamer or large saucepan of rapidly boiling water. Cover the steamer tightly and steam in high heat for 2½ hours.

Wash the vegetables and cut any larger pieces in halves. Shake out the excess water. Heat the wok and add the oil or lard. Fry the vegetables on moderately high heat for 3 minutes. Remove. Splash in the wine and add the crabmeat and roe, if used. Saute for 1 minute and add the pre-mixed seasoning ingredients with the liquid from the shark's fins. Bring to the boil. Simmer until thickened. Arrange the drained fins in a serving dish and pour on the sauce.

Arrange the vegetables around the edge of the dish and serve.

SLICED ABALONE WITH MINCED CHICKEN

1 310 g (10 oz) can	abalone
185 g (6 oz)	boneless chicken, finely minced (ground)
90 g (3 oz)	pork fat, finely minced (ground)
2 tablespoons	finely chopped spring onion (scallion)
½ teaspoon	grated fresh ginger
2 tablespoons	frying oil or softened lard
2 teaspoons	rendered chicken fat, (chicken grease), optional
2 tablespoons	finely chopped cooked ham

Seasoning:

2	large egg whites, beaten
½ teaspoon	salt
¾ teaspoon	m.s.g. (optional)
½ teaspoon	white pepper
⅓ cup	cold water or chicken stock

Drain the abalone and place on a cutting board. Trim the ruffled edges, then ·slice thinly, following directions on page 392

Mix the chicken, pork fat, onion, and ginger with the seasoning ingredients, stirring thoroughly.

Heat the wok and add lard. Fry the creamed chicken on moderate heat until white, about 2 minutes, then add the sliced abalone and stir gently on low heat until well warmed through. Add a little chicken stock or water if the mixture begins to stick. Stir in chicken fat, if used.

Transfer to a warmed serving plate and garnish with the ham.

STEAMED SEA CUCUMBER AND HAM

700 g (1⅓ lb)	prepared sea cucumber (see page 392), about 4 large dried sea cucumbers
90 g (3 oz)	Chinese or cured (Smithfield) ham, sliced
6	spring onions (scallions), cut in halves
6 thick slices	fresh ginger, bruised
1 tablespoon	rice wine or dry sherry cornflour (cornstarch) white pepper
1 tablespoon	rendered chicken fat (chicken grease), optional
3 cups (24 fl oz)	hot chicken stock

Drain the sea cucumbers, cut open and score in a criss-cross pattern on the inside. Cut into 4 cm (l 2/3 in) squares. Place the cucumber and sliced ham in separate dishes and divide the spring onions, ginger, and wine between them. Add the salt to the sea cucumbers and cover each with the chicken stock. Place on a rack in a steaming pot, cover tightly and steam over rapidly boiling water for 25 minutes.

Strain the liquid from the ham over the sea cucumbers and thicken the sauce with a thin solution of cornflour mixed with cold water. Add white pepper to taste and the rendered chicken fat, if used, and arrange the sliced ham on top. Serve in the same dish.

Stewed Shark's Fin with Chicken, Duck and Pork (recipe page 99).

FISH MAW SALAD WITH SESAME SAUCE

Serve hot as a main dish, or cold as an appetiser.

125 g (4 oz)	dried fish maw
3 cups (24 fl oz)	chicken stock
2	spring onions (scallions), trimmed and sliced
3 slices	fresh ginger
	fresh coriander

Seasoning:

1½ teaspoons	salt
¾ teaspoon	m.s.g. (optional)
1 tablespoon	rice wine or dry sherry

Sauce:

½ cup (4 fl oz)	chicken stock
2 tablespoons	sesame paste
1 tablespoon	sesame oil
½ teaspoon	salt
½ teaspoon	m.s.g. (optional)
	chilli oil (optional)

Prepare the fish maw according to the directions on page 392, cutting it into bite-sized pieces.

Place in a saucepan with the spring onions and ginger and add the chicken stock. Bring to the boil and simmer for 15 minutes, then add the seasoning ingredients and simmer until the liquid has been completely absorbed and the fish maw is tender. Increase the heat to high to evaporate any remaining liquid, if necessary.

If serving cold, remove from the heat and transfer to a serving plate. Leave to cool. Mix the sauce ingredients and pour over the dish. Stir in lightly and garnish with fresh coriander. Serve.

To serve hot, add the sauce to the fish maw immediately after it is removed from the heat. Stir in and transfer to a serving plate. Serve at once.

BRAISED FISH MAW WITH ASSORTED MEATS

90 g (3 oz)	dried fish maw
2 cups (16 fl oz)	chicken stock
1	spring onion (scallion), trimmed and sliced
2 slices	fresh ginger, shredded
90 g (3 oz)	raw peeled shrimps
90 g (3 oz)	boneless chicken breast
45 g (1½ oz)	cooked ham
90 g (3 oz)	Chinese cabbage or bok choy (celery cabbage)
1½ cups (12 fl oz)	softened lard or frying oil
	cornflour (cornstarch)
1 tablespoon	rendered chicken fat (chicken grease), optional

Seasoning A and B: (Prepare two)

1	egg white
⅓ teaspoon	salt
2 teaspoons	cornflour (cornstarch)

Seasoning C:

2 tablespoons	chicken stock
2 teaspoons	rice wine or dry sherry
¾ teaspoon	salt
½ teaspoon	m.s.g. (optional)

Prepare the fish maw according to the directions on page 392, cutting into short strips. Drain well and place in a saucepan with the chicken stock, spring onion, and ginger. Bring to the boil and simmer on low heat until most of the liquid has been absorbed and the fish maw is tender.

Devein the shrimps with a toothpick (see page 394). Wash and pat dry, then place in a dish with the seasoning A ingredients. Cut the chicken into narrow strips, mix with the seasoning B ingredients and leave for 10 minutes. Shred the ham and cut the cabbage into bite-sized pieces.

Heat the lard and quickly fry the shrimps and chicken until almost cooked, about 45 seconds. Remove and drain off most of the oil. Thicken the remaining fish maw sauce with a thin solution of cornflour and cold water and transfer to a serving dish.

Reheat the wok and add the ham and cabbage. Briefly stir-fry, then return the shrimps and chicken and add the seasoning C ingredients. Stir-fry briefly, then pour over the fish maw and serve at once.

STEWED STUFFED CHICKEN

1 1¾ kg (3½ lb)	chicken
250 g (8 oz)	slightly fat pork, finely minced (ground)
75 g (8 oz)	pine seeds or walnuts, blanched and drained
4 cups (1 litre)	deep frying oil
155 g (5 oz)	Chinese cabbage hearts, young bok choy or kale
¼ cup (2 fl oz)	frying oil or softened lard
2 teaspoons	rendered chicken fat (chicken grease), optional

Batter:

1	egg white, beaten
¼ teaspoon	salt
	pinch of white pepper
2 tablespoons	cornflour (cornstarch)

Seasoning:

1 tablespoon	finely chopped spring onion (scallion)
½ teaspoon	grated fresh ginger
½ teaspoon	m.s.g. (optional)
½ teaspoon	sugar
½ teaspoon	rice wine or dry sherry
1½ tablespoons	light soy sauce

Sauce:

¾ cup (6 fl oz)	chicken stock
½ cup (4 fl oz)	sugar colouring (see page 388)
2 teaspoons	rice wine
1 tablespoon	light soy sauce

Remove legs and wings from the chicken and set aside. Cut the body into four even-sized pieces and place, skin downwards, on a cutting board. Use a sharp paring knife to score the meat closely in a criss-cross pattern, cutting almost through but taking care not to pierce the skin. Sprinkle on a little salt. Mix the batter ingredients and add a little water to make a creamy paste. Spread over the chicken where scored.

Mix the pork with the seasoning ingredients and divide between the chicken pieces, moulding it on smoothly. Lightly toast the nuts and chop coarsely. Spread thickly over the pork filling, pressing on lightly with the fingertips. Heat the deep oil to fairly hot and fry the stuffed chicken pieces, stuffing downwards, until brown, Drain well.

Arrange the legs and wings in a saucepan and place the stuffed chicken pieces on top, filling upwards. Carefully pour in the sauce ingredients, cover tightly and braise on moderate to low heat for 45 minutes.

Wash the vegetables, cutting any larger ones in halves. Shake out excess water and sauté in the frying oil or lard on moderate heat for 4 minutes. Season with a splash of wine and a dash of sugar, salt, and white pepper. Arrange in a ring around the edge of a serving plate.

Drain the chicken pieces, discarding legs and wings or serving these separately. Cut the stuffed chicken into thin slices and arrange on the plate. Strain the cooking liquid into the wok and bring to the boil. Adjust seasoning and thicken with a thin solution of cornflour (cornstarch) mixed with cold water. Stir in the chicken fat, if used, and pour over the chicken.

CHICKEN SHREDS SAUTÉD WITH TUBERROSE PETALS

250 g (8 oz)	boneless chicken breasts
50	tuberrose petals (or use white chrysanthemum petals)
2 tablespoons	frying oil or softened lard
1 teaspoon	rendered chicken fat (chicken grease), optional

Seasoning:

1	egg white, beaten
¼ teaspoon	salt
½ teaspoon	m.s.g. (optional)
1 teaspoon	cornflour (cornstarch)

Sauce:

½ cup (4 fl oz)	chicken stock
½ teaspoon	rice wine or dry sherry
¼ teaspoon	salt
½ teaspoon	m.s.g. (optional)
1 teaspoon	cornflour (cornstarch)

Skin the chicken breasts and slice thinly, then cut into shreds and mix with the seasoning ingredients. Leave to marinate for 15 minutes.

Rinse the rose (or chrysanthemim) petals in warn water and drain well.

Heat the wok and add the oil or lard. Sauté the chicken shreds on moderate heat until white, about 1½ minutes. Remove to a serving plate. Sauté the petals with a little more oil, if needed, for 30 seconds then pour in the pre-mixed sauce ingredients and bring to the boil.

Stir in the chicken fat, if used, just before serving.

CHICKEN WALNUT ROLLS

250 g (8 oz)	boneless chicken breast
45 g (1½ oz)	walnuts, blanched and drained
4 cups (1 litre)	deep frying oil
155 g (5 oz)	young bok choy or broccoli broken into florets
½ teaspoon	white vinegar
1 teaspoon	sesame oil (optional)

Seasoning A:

1	egg white, beaten
¼ teaspoon	salt
½ teaspoon	m.s.g. (optional)
1 tablespoon	cornflour (cornstarch)
1 tablespoon	water

Seasoning B:

2 tablespoons	softened lard
¼ teaspoon	grated fresh ginger
1 tablespoon	finely chopped spring onion (scallion)
¼ teaspoon	crushed garlic

Sauce:

½ cup (4 fl oz)	chicken stock
1 tablespoon	light soy sauce
¼ teaspoon	salt
¼ teaspoon	m.s.g. (optional)
½ teaspoon	sugar
¼ teaspoon	white pepper
½ teaspoon	cornflour (cornstarch)

Skin the chicken breasts and cut the meat across the grain into reasonably thin slices. Bat gently with the side of a cleaver to flatten a little more. Mix with the seasoning A ingredients and set aside to marinate for 15 minutes. Dry the walnuts and deep-fry in fairly hot oil until lightly coloured. Lift out and drain well. Leave to cool. Place a walnut in the centre of each chicken slice, roll up and squeeze gently to hold. Toothpicks may be necessary to secure some of the rolls, but most should stay in place unaided.

Reheat the deep-frying oil to moderate and fry the chicken walnut rolls until the meat whitens, about 1 minute. Lift out and drain well. Pour off all but 2 tablespoons of the oil and sauté the vegetables for 4 minutes. Add a dash of wine, salt and sugar and 2 tablespoons of cold water or chicken stock and cook, covered, for a further 1 minute.

Fry the seasoning B ingredients together in another pan, then add the pre-mixed sauce ingredients and bring to the boil. Add the chicken rolls and warm through in the sauce. Season with vinegar and sesame oil, if used. Transfer to a warmed serving dish.

OYSTER SAUCE CHICKEN IN PARCELS

Serve as an appetiser or main course.

250 g (8 oz)	boneless chicken breast
	several sheets of edible rice paper, cellophane or greaseproof paper
	sesame oil
3 cups (24 fl oz)	deep-frying oil
	small bunch of fresh coriander, broken into sprigs with stems removed

Seasoning:

½ teaspoon	m.s.g. (optional)
1¼ teaspoons	sugar
	pinch of white pepper
1 tablespoon	oyster sauce
2 teaspoons	sesame oil
¼ teaspoon	grated fresh ginger
1 tablespoon	finely chopped spring onion (scallion)

Skin the chicken breasts and cut across the grain into thin slices, about 5 × 2.5 cm (2 × 1 in). Mix with the seasoning ingredients and leave to marinate for 20 minutes.

Cut the paper into 12 cm (5 in) squares and brush one side with sesame oil. Place a slice of chicken on each paper, towards one corner. Add a sprig of coriander and top with another chicken slice. Fold the closest corner over the chicken, then fold in the two sides and lastly the end flap, tucking it securely inside the other folds.

Heat the deep oil to moderate and fry the chicken parcels, turning once or twice, until they float to the surface, about 3 minutes.

Drain well, arrange on a serving plate and surround with fresh coriander. Serve piping hot. If using cellophane or greaseproof paper, use scissors to cut an opening in the tops to facilitate removal of the chicken.

Chicken Walnut Rolls (recipe this page).

DEEP-FRIED MOCK-CHICKEN DRUMSTICKS

Serve as an appetiser or main course.

12	small chicken feet, about 375 g (12 oz), optional, or use short wooden sticks or bamboo skewers
185 g (6 oz)	boneless chicken, minced (ground)
60 g (2 oz)	canned water chestnuts, drained and finely chopped
2	large eggs, beaten
	cornflour (cornstarch)
4 cups (1 litre)	deep-frying oil

Seasoning A:

1 teaspoon	salt
1 teaspoon	m.s.g. (optional)
2	spring onions (scallions), trimmed
3 thick slices	fresh ginger

Seasoning B:

1	egg white, beaten
¼ teaspoon	salt
½ teaspoon	m.s.g. (optional)
	pinch of white pepper
½ teaspoon	sugar
1 tablespoon	onion and ginger infusion (see page 386)
1 tablespoon	cornflour (cornstarch)

Place the chicken feet in a saucepan with water to cover. Add the seasoning A ingredients and bring to the boil. Simmer for 1 hour or until tender, then drain well and remove the claws. If the chicken feet have the skin on, remove by blanching in boiling water for 2 minutes, draining and pulling the skin away before cooking.

Mix the chicken, pork, and water chestnuts with the seasoning B ingredients, kneading to a smooth sticky paste. Divide into 12 portions and form each into a ball shape around the leg-end of each foot to resemble drumsticks. Dip into beaten egg and coat thickly with cornflour.

Heat deep-frying oil to moderately hot and fry the drumsticks until golden brown and cooked through, about 4 minutes. Lift out and drain well. Arrange on a bed of shredded lettuce and serve with a chilli pepper and soy sauce dip (see page 407)

CHICKEN WINGS SIMMERED IN WINE

('Wings of the Magnificent Concubine')

12	chicken wings
6	large dried black mushrooms, soaked for 25 minutes
½ cup (4 fl oz)	frying oil or softened lard
2 tablespoons	finely chopped spring onion (scallion)
1 teaspoon	grated fresh ginger
1	large brown onion, thinly sliced
2 tablespoons	red grape wine

Seasoning A:

2 tablespoons	light soy sauce
½ teaspoon	m.s.g. (optional)
1 teaspoon	sugar

Seasoning B/Sauce:

2¼ cups (18 fl oz)	chicken stock
1 tablespoon	light soy sauce
2 teaspoons	dark soy sauce
1¼ teaspoons	sugar
¼ teaspoon	salt
2 tablespoons	red grape wine

Cut off the wing tips and divide each wing into two at the joints. Drain the mushrooms and remove the stems.

Heat half the oil or lard and fry the spring onions and ginger on moderately high heat for 1 minute. Add the wings with the seasoning A ingredients and stir-fry on high heat until the seasoning is absorbed into the wings and they turn a red-brown colour.

Transfer to a casserole or slow cooker and add the seasoning B/sauce ingredients. Cover and braise for 20 minutes, or the equivalent in a slow cooker.

Fry the sliced onion in the remaining oil or lard until well browned. Add the mushrooms and fry briefly, then add to the casserole. Re-cover and braise a further 15 minutes. Stir in the remaining red wine just before serving.

SPRING CHICKEN SHOWERED WITH HOT OIL

1 1¼ kg (2 lb)	spring chicken
8 cups (2 litres)	deep frying oil

Seasoning:

¼ teaspoon	salt
½ teaspoon	m.s.g. (optional)
2 teaspoons	sugar
¼ teaspoon	white pepper
¼ teaspoon	ground Chinese brown pepper
2 tablespoons	light soy sauce
1 tablespoon	rice wine or dry sherry
1 teaspoon	white vinegar (optional)
1 tablespoon	spring onion (scallion), finely chopped
1¼ teaspoon	grated fresh ginger

Sauce:

2 tablespoons	enriched or chicken stock
¼ cup	light soy sauce
1½ tablespoons	white vinegar
¼ cup	sesame oil
1½ tablespoons	sugar
1½ tablespoons	spring onion (scallion), finely chopped
1½ tablespoons	grated fresh ginger

Cut the chicken in halves through back and breast bones, rub with the pre-mixed seasoning ingredients and set aside for 1 hour.

Bring the sauce ingredients to a rolling boil. Remove from the heat and leave to cool, then pour into several small dishes.

Heat the deep oil to moderate. Place the chicken, skin upwards, in a large frying basket and suspend over the oil. Ladle the hot oil over the chicken continually until cooked through, about 45 minutes.

As this process is somewhat tedious, acceptable results can be obtained by gently poaching the chicken in warm oil until cooked through. To avoid greasiness, remove the chicken every 6-7 minutes and reheat the oil to moderate. Cooking time is approximately 25 minutes.

Drain well and slice. Serve with the prepared sauce dips.

PRESERVED CUCUMBER, AND GINGER STEWED CHICKEN WITH BEANS

750 g (1½ lb)	chicken pieces
125 g (4 oz)	fresh or frozen lima (fava) beans (or fresh soybeans, shelled, if available)
30 g (1 oz)	soy-preserved cucumber (see page 389)
30 g (1 oz)	soy-preserved ginger (see page 389)
¼ cup (2 fl oz)	frying oil or softened lard
2	spring onions (scallions), trimmed and diced salt to taste sesame oil (optional)

Seasoning A:

¼ teaspoon	salt
½ teaspoon	sugar
1 tablespoon	light soy sauce
1 tablespoon	rice wine or dry sherry

Seasoning B/Sauce:

⅓ cup	chicken stock or cold water
1 tablespoon	light soy sauce
½ teaspoon	rice wine or dry sherry
2 teaspoons	sugar

Wash the chicken and cut into bite-sized pieces through the bones. Mix with the seasoning A ingredients and set aside for 20 minutes. Boil the lima or soybeans until just tender in slightly salted water. Drain, refresh in cold water and drain again. Wash the cucumber and ginger in warm water, drain well and cut into small shreds.

Heat the lard in a wok and stir-fry the chicken until almost cooked through, about 6 minutes on moderate heat. Add the cucumber, ginger, and onion and stir-fry a further 1 minute. Stir in the seasoning B/sauce ingredients, pre-mixed, and cover. Reduce heat when boiling and simmer for 4 minutes. Add the beans and heat through. Adjust seasoning with salt and stir in sesame oil, if used.

Transfer to a serving dish.

CREAMED CHICKEN WITH MUSHROOMS, HAM AND PEA SPROUTS

185 g (6 oz)	boneless chicken, finely minced (ground)
60 g (2 oz)	sweet pea sprouts, snow peas, bean sprouts, or fresh spinach (collard greens)
60 g (2 oz)	canned straw mushrooms or champignons, drained and sliced
30 g (1 oz)	fresh ham, sliced the size of the champignons
1½ cups (12 fl oz)	frying oil
1½ teaspoons	rendered chicken fat (chicken grease), optional

Seasoning A:

2	egg whites, beaten
¼ teaspoon	salt
½ teaspoon	m.s.g. (optional)
¼ teaspoon	sugar
½ teaspoon	rice wine or dry sherry
1 tablespoon	onion and ginger infusion (see page 386)
1 tablespoon	cornflour (cornstarch)
2 tablespoons	cold water

Seasoning B/Sauce:

⅓ cup	chicken stock
¼ teaspoon	salt
½ teaspoon	m.s.g. (optional)
¼ teaspoon	sugar
½ teaspoon	rice wine or dry sherry
½ teaspoon	cornflour (cornstarch)

Mix the minced chicken with the seasoning A ingredients, stirring in one direction for about 5 minutes to make a smooth creamy paste. Wash the vegetables and chop the spinach finely, if used. Heat the oil to moderate in a wok and pour in the chicken paste. Stir gently in the oil until it turns white, about 1¾ minutes. Transfer to a plastic strainer to drain.

Pour off all but 2 tablespoons of the oil and sauté the vegetables, mushrooms, and ham on moderate to high heat for 2 minutes. Add the seasoning B/sauce ingredients, pre-mixed, and bring to the boil.

Reduce heat and simmer for about 2 minutes, then return the chicken paste and heat through, stirring continually. Add the chicken fat, if used, and transfer to a warmed serving plate.

STEAMED CHICKEN AND MUSHROOM POT

750 g (1½ lb)	chicken pieces
8 — 10	dried black mushrooms, soaked for 25 minutes
3	spring onions (scallions), trimmed and sliced
1 thick slice	fresh ginger, shredded finely
1 teaspoon	cornflour (cornstarch)
1 tablespoon	cold water

Seasoning:

1 tablespoon	light soy sauce
2 teaspoons	rice wine or dry sherry
½ teaspoon	salt
¼ teaspoon	m.s.g. (optional)
	pinch of white pepper
½ teaspoon	sugar
½ cup (4 fl oz)	chicken stock or cold water

Wash the chicken and cut through the bones into bite-sized pieces. Drain the mushrooms and remove the stems.

Arrange the chicken, mushrooms, onion, and ginger in a covered dish and add the pre-mixed seasoning ingredients. Set on a rack in a steamer over gently boiling water. Cover the pan and steam for 1¼ hours on moderate heat. Thicken the sauce with the mixed cornflour and cold water and serve the chicken and mushrooms in the dish in which they were cooked.

Chicken Wings Simmered in Wine (recipe page 106).

DEEP-FRIED CHICKEN LIVERS WITH SPICY DRESSING

375 g (12 oz)	fresh chicken livers
6 cups (1½ litres)	deep-frying oil
1 tablespoon	sesame oil
3 tablespoons	finely chopped spring onion scallion)
2 teaspoons	finely chopped fresh ginger
1½-2 teaspoons	Chinese pepper-salt

Seasoning:

1½ teaspoons	rice wine or dry sherry
¼ teaspoon	white pepper
½ teaspoon	m.s.g. (optional)
2 teaspoons	sugar
2 teaspoons	grated fresh ginger

Batter:

2	eggs, well beaten
3 tablespoons	cornflour (cornstarch)
3 tablespoons	flour

Wash the livers and cut into bite-sized pieces. Mix with the seasoning ingredients, and leave to marinate for 20 minutes. Make a thick batter with the eggs, cornflour, and flour, adding a little water. Beat well.

Heat the deep-frying oil to smoking. Drain the chicken and dip into the batter, coating thickly. Deep-fry until well browned. Drain well.

Pour off the oil and wipe out the pan. Add the sesame oil and heat through, then return the chicken livers and add the spring onion, ginger, and pepper-salt. Stir on moderate heat until the chicken livers are cooked through, about 3 minutes. Serve.

SLICED ROAST DUCK WITH BROCCOLI

½	cold roast duck (see recipe page 111, Charcoal Roast Duck)
500 g (1 lb)	fresh broccoli, broken into florets
2	spring onions (scallions), trimmed and sliced
⅓ cup	frying oil or softened lard
2 slices	fresh ginger, shredded
½ teaspoon	white vinegar (optional)
½ teaspoon	sesame oil (optional)

Seasoning:

½ teaspoon	salt
¾ teaspoon	m.s.g. (optional)
¾ teaspoon	sugar
1 tablespoon	light soy sauce
2 teaspoons	rice wine or dry sherry
⅓ cup	chicken stock
¾ teaspoon	cornflour (cornstarch)

Debone the duck and cut into bite-sized pieces. Fry in a wok with the oil or lard until lightly browned, then add the broccoli and spring onions and fry a further 3 minutes, stirring constantly.

Add the ginger and seasoning ingredients and bring to the boil. Stir until thickened. Add sesame oil and vinegar, if used, and transfer to a serving plate.

CHARCOAL-ROASTED DUCK STUFFED WITH LOTUS LEAVES

1 2½ kg (5 lb)	fairly fat duck
1 teaspoon	salt
1 tablespoon	rice wine or dry sherry
6	dried or fresh lotus leaves
12	large spring onions (scallions), trimmed
	sweet bean paste or hoisin sauce
	sesame oil (optional)
	sugar
24	mandarin pancakes (see recipe, page 373)

Glaze:

3 tablespoons	malt sugar (or golden syrup, clear honey, or light corn syrup)
½ cup (4 fl oz)	boiling water

If possible, have the duck drawn through an incision beneath one wing. Rub the salt and wine inside the cavity and prop the body open with a short stick placed inside the breast cavity between the shoulders.

soak dried lotus leaves, if used, in boiling water until softened. If using fresh leaves, blanch in boiling water for 10 seconds. Drain and roll the leaves up together, then shred coarsely. Place the lotus leaves and two spring onions into the cavity and tie a string around the neck, then under the wings. Hang in a well-ventilated area over a drip tray. Pour on several lots of boiling water to tighten the skin, then mix the malt sugar, or substitute, with the ½ cup boiling water and pour slowly and evenly over the duck. Leave for at least 6 hours until the skin is dry to the touch

Charcoal roast the duck, turning frequently until cooked through, with skin crisp and dark, about 1½ hours, oven roast on a rotisserie at 200°C (400°F).

Using a sharp carving knife, pare off the crisp skin in pieces about 4 cm (1 2/3 in) square and arrange on a plate. Cut the meat into bite-sized pieces and serve on another plate. Save the carcass for soup or stock. Discard the lotus leaves.

Have the pancakes warm and ready. (They keep well if wrapped in aluminium foil.) Heat the sweet bean paste with sugar and sesame oil to taste, or use pre-made duck sauce (hoisin or plum). Cut the trimmed spring onions into 5 cm (2 in) lengths and cut in halves lengthwise.

To eat the duck, place a slice of spring onion in the centre of a pancake. Dip a piece of crisp skin into the sauce, followed by a piece of meat. Place on the pancake, add more onion if desired and roll up, tucking in the ends.

ROAST DUCK WITH SPICY SAUCE

1	hot roast duck (see recipe, on this page) Charcoal-Roasted Duck)

Sauce:

⅓ cup	chicken stock
1 tablespoon	light soy sauce
1 teaspoon	white vinegar
1½ tablespoons	soybean paste or dark soy sauce
1 tablespoon	sesame oil
¼ teaspoon	m.s.g. (optional)
1 tablespoon	sugar
½ teaspoon	ground black pepper
1 tablespoon	finely chopped spring onion (scallion)
¾ teaspoon	grated fresh ginger
1 teaspoon	crushed garlic
½ teaspoon	cornflour (cornstarch)

Slice the duck, debone if preferred, and arrange on a plate. Mix the sauce ingredients in a saucepan and bring to the boil, pour over the duck and serve.

DEEP-FRIED AND SIMMERED DUCK STUFFED WITH EIGHT PRECIOUS INGREDIENTS

1 2¼ kg (4½ lb)	duck with giblets
1½ teaspoons	salt
1 tablespoon	rice wine or dry sherry
30 g (1 oz)	pearl barley, washed
45 g (1½ oz)	dried lotus seeds, soaked for 1 hour
60 g (2 oz)	glutinous rice, soaked for 1 hour
5	dried black mushrooms, soaked for 25 minutes
45 g (1½ oz)	Chinese or cured (Smithfield) ham, diced
60 g (2 oz	canned bamboo shoots, drained and diced
30 g (1 oz)	dried shrimps, soaked for 1 hour
2	spring onions (scallions), trimmed and diced
2 slices	fresh ginger finely chopped
1 tablespoon	dark soy sauce
8 cups (2 litres)	deep-frying oil
¼ cup (2 fl oz)	frying oil

Seasoning A:

¾ teaspoon	salt
1 teaspoon	m.s.g. (optional)
1½ teaspoon	sugar
½ teaspoon	ground black pepper
1 tablespoon	light soy sauce
1 teaspoon	rice wine or dry sherry
¼ cup (2 fl oz)	chicken stock

Seasoning B/Sauce:

2½ cups (20 fl oz)	chicken stock or water
¾ cup (6 fl oz)	sugar colouring (see page 388)
2 tablespoons	light soy sauce
1 tablespoon	rice wine or dry sherry
1 teaspoon	sugar
2	spring onions (scallions), trimmed and sliced
4 slices	fresh ginger

Debone the duck, leaving the legs and wings intact. Turn inside out and scald with boiling water. Pat dry and rub with the salt and wine, then turn right side out again.

Drain the barley, lotus seeds, and rice and steam together with 1 cup (8 fl oz) chicken stock or water until tender. Drain the mushrooms, remove stems and dice. Blanch the duck giblets in boiling water. Skin the gizzard, trim the heart, and cut all into small dice.

Fry the giblets in the frying oil for 3 minutes on moderate heat. Add the onions, ginger, mushrooms, and ham and stir-fry for 1 minute, then add the bamboo shoots, drained shrimp, rice, barley, and lotus seeds. Fry together, mixing well, for 2 minutes, then add the seasoning A ingredients, mix well and remove from the heat. Leave to cool for 10 minutes, then stuff into the duck and sew up the opening or secure carefully with poultry pins.

Rub the skin wth the dark soy sauce. Heat the deep-frying oil to smoking point and deep-fry the duck on high heat until the skin is a rich red-brown. Drain and place, breast downwards, in a casserole. Add the seasoning B/sauce ingredients and cover the pot. Bring to the boil, then reduce heat and simmer for about 2 hours until completely tender.

Carefully lift the duck onto a serving plate and make several cuts across the breast to expose the filling. Strain the cooking liquid into a wok, bring to the boil and simmer until wellreduced. Thicken if necessary with a thin solution of cornflour (cornstarch) and cold water and check the seasoning. Pour over the duck.

Deep-Fried and Simmered Duck Stuffed with Eight Precious Ingredients (recipe this page).

STEAMED STUFFED DUCK WITH PINE SEED CRUST

1 2 kg (4 lb)	duck
1 teaspoon	salt
1 tablespoon	rice wine or dry sherry
315 g (10 oz)	slightly fat pork, finely minced (ground)
2	small egg whites, beaten
2 tablespoons	cornflour (cornstarch)
75 g (2½ oz)	pine seed or walnuts, blanched and drained
6 cups (1½ litres)	deep frying oil

Seasoning:

1½ tablespoons	finely chopped spring onion (scallion)
¾ teaspoon	grated fresh ginger
1	egg, beaten
¾ teaspoon	salt
½ teaspoon	m.s.g. (optional)
½ teaspoon	sugar
1 teaspoon	rice wine or dry sherry

Sauce:

1 cup (8 fl oz)	chicken stock or water
½ cup (4 fl oz)	sugar colouring (see page 388)
2 tablespoons	light soy sauce
1 tablespoon	rice wine or dry sherry
¼ teaspoon	salt
1 teaspoon	m.s.g. (optional)
3	spring onions (scallions), trimmed and sliced
4 slices	fresh ginger

Wash the duck and cut open along the backbone. Debone, leaving the drumsticks in place but removing the wings. Keep the bones.

Slice off any thick parts of the meat and chop finely. Use a sharp knife to score quite deeply in a criss-cross pattern across the meat, taking care not to pierce the skin. Season with the salt and wine or sherry.

Mix the chopped duck meat with the pork and seasoning ingredients. Make a paste of the egg whites and cornflour, adding a little water. Brush over the duck where scored, and cover with a thick layer of the pork paste, smoothing the edges. Brush with any remaining batter. Toast the pine seeds or walnuts and chop coarsley. Press onto the pork stuffing, coating thickly. Place the duck in a large frying basket.

Heat the deep oil to smoking hot and fry the duck until browned. Lift out and drain well. Arrange the wings and reserve bones in a casserole and set the duck, stuffing upwards, on top. Add the sauce ingredients, cover and set on a rack in a steamer. Steam over rapidly boiling water until tender, about 1½ hours.

Strain the juices into a pan, bring to the boil and adjust the seasoning. Thicken if necessary with a thin solution of cornflour and water. Pour over the duck and serve.

STEAMED DUCK IN LOTUS LEAF PACKAGES

1½ 2 kg (4 lb)	duck
4	dried or fresh lotus leaves
1 cup	spiced rice powder (see page 386)

Seasoning:

2 tablespoons	finely chopped spring onion (scallion)
1 tablespoon	finely chopped fresh ginger
1 teaspoon	finely chopped fresh red chilli pepper (optional)
2 tablespoons	light soy sauce
1 tablespoon	dark soy sauce or soybean paste
1 tablespoon	vegetable oil
2 teaspoons	sesame oil
1 tablespoon	rice wine or dry sherry
1 tablespoon	sugar

Cut the duck into bite-sized pieces, deboning if preferred. Place in a dish with the pre-mixed seasoning ingredients. Mix thoroughly, then leave for 1 hour.

Soak dried lotus leaves in warm water to soften, then cut into squares. Blanch fresh leaves, if used, in boiling water until softened.

Brush off most of the onion, ginger, and chilli pepper and dip the duck pieces into the rice powder, coating generously. Divide between the lotus leaf squares and fold each into a parcel shape.

Place the parcels in a dish with the open side upwards. Put a plate over them to hold in place and set the dish on a rack in a steamer. Steam over rapidly boiling water for about 1 hour.

Invert the dish onto a serving plate so the smooth sides of the parcels are upmost. Serve at once. Remove the leaves before eating.

*The lotus leaves should be large enough to cut each into 3 pieces, about 15 cm (6 in) square. If lotus leaves are unobtainable, use pieces of greased aluminium foil and remove before serving.

RED-SIMMERED DUCK

1 2¼ kg (4½ lb)	duck
1½ teaspons	salt
4 tablespoons	red fermented rice (or use 2½ tablespoons Japanese dark miso paste)

Seasoning:

3 pieces	rock candy (or 1½ tablespoons sugar)
1 teaspoon	salt
2	spice bags (see page 386)
1 tablespoon	rice wine or dry sherry

Wash the duck and dry well. Rub inside and out with the salt and leave for 1 hour, then rinse and drain again.

Mix the miso, if used, with enough water to make a smooth paste and rub this or the red rice over the duck. Place, breast downwards, on a bamboo rack in a casserole and add the seasoning. Pour in water to just cover the duck, adding it slowly down the side of the pan. Cover and bring to the boil, then reduce the heat and simmer until the duck is completely tender, about 2½ hours. In the last 20 minutes of cooking, uncover the pan to reduce the sauce.

Lift out the duck and cut into bite-sized pieces. Serve with the sauce.

GARLIC CATFISH

An excellent dish which is at its best if a live catfish is used, in which case the method involves 'drowning' the fish in rice wine before cooking.

1 1½ kg (3 lb)	live catfish (jewfish, monkfish, halibut)
3 cups (24 fl oz)	rice wine or dry sherry
5 cm (2 in) piece	fresh ginger
6 cups (1½ litres)	deep frying oil

Seasoning A:

½ cup (4 fl oz)	light soy sauce
½ cup (4 fl oz)	rice wine or dry sherry
1 tablespoon	soybean paste or dark soy sauce
1 tablespoon	grated fresh ginger
3 tablespoons	crushed garlic
1	fresh red chilli pepper, seeds removed and chopped
1 teaspoon	salt
2 teaspoons	sugar
½ ccp (4 fl oz)	fish stock or water

Seasoning B/Sauce:

¼ cup (2 fl oz)	cold water
2 teaspoons	white vinegar
1 teaspoon	sesame oil
2 teaspoons	cornflour (cornstarch)

Place the fish in a pot with a tight-fitting lid, add the wine or sherry, cover and leave for at least 20 minutes. Drain.

Rub the peeled ginger over the wok vigorously. This prevents the fish from sticking during cooking. The ginger may be trimmed and used again. Pour in the oil and heat to smoking point, then reduce heat slightly. Deep-fry the fish for 6 minutes on each side. Carefully lift out and pour off all but 3 tablespoons oil. Set the fish aside, keeping warm.

Add the pre-mixed seasoning A ingredients to the pan and bring to the boil. Return the fish, cover and cook on moderately high heat for 2 minutes, then add the pre-mixed seasoning B/sauce ingredients, and bring to the boil again. Stir carefully around the fish until the sauce thickens.

Serve with a garnish of shredded spring onions and fresh chilli pepper or coriander.

FISH IN BROWN SAUCE

1 1 kg (2 lb)	fresh carp (or 2 mackerel or red snapper)
1 tablespoon	cornflour (cornstarch)
1 tablespoon	flour
2 cups (16 fl oz)	frying oil
5 cm (2 in) piece	fresh ginger, peeled
6 cloves	garlic, thinly sliced
3 thick slices	fresh ginger, shredded
2 — 3	fresh red chilli peppers, seeds removed and shredded
1	star anise (optional)
¾ teaspoon	salt
1¼ cups (10 fl oz)	fish stock or water
2	spring onions (scallions), trimmed and shredded
½ teaspoon	sesame oil (optional)
½ teaspoon	white vinegar

Seasoning A:

½ teaspoon	salt
2 tablespoons	light soy sauce
1½ tablespoons	rice wine or dry sherry
1 teaspoon	grated fresh ginger

Seasoning B:

½ teaspoon	sugar
2 tablespoons	dark soy sauce
2 teaspoons	rice wine and dry sherry
½ cup (4 fl oz)	sugar colouring (see page 388) (optional)

Clean, scale and thoroughly wash the fish. Score several times diagonally acorss each side, cutting almost through to the bone. Rub with the seasoning A ingredients and leave for 10 minutes, then coat lightly with a mixture of the cornflour and flour.

Heat a large wok and rub vigorously with the peeled ginger to prevent the fish from sticking during cooking. Heat the oil to hot and fry the fish for about 5 minutes on each side. Remove and keep warm. Drain the oil.

Rinse out the wok and return ⅓ cup of the drained oil. Heat to moderate and fry the garlic, chillies and the star anise, if used, for 2 minutes. Add the seasoning B ingredients, salt, and fish stock and bring to the boil. Return the fish and simmer, covered, for 10 minutes. Remove the lid and cook a further 5 minutes or until the fish is completely tender, with the meat easily lifting from the bones.

Transfer the fish carefully to a serving plate and place the garlic, ginger, and chilli pepper on top with the shredded spring onions over them. Keep warm. Bring the sauce to the boil, add the sesame oil, if used, and the vinegar. Check the seasonings and thicken if preferred with a thin solution of cornflour mixed with cold water. Pour over the fish and serve at once.

RED-BRAISED MACKEREL TAILS

2 kg (4 lb)	mackerel (fresh trout or grass carp), use the tail halves only
½ teaspoon	salt
2 teaspoons	rice wine or dry sherry
⅓ cup	frying oil or softened lard
2	spring onions (scallions), trimmed and sliced
2 teaspoons	grated fresh ginger
60 g (2 oz)	canned bamboo shoots, drained and diced
30 g (1 oz)	canned straw mushrooms or champignons drained and diced
½ teaspoon	m.s.g. (optional)
1 teaspoon	white vinegar
½ teaspoon	sesame oil (optional)

Seasoning/Sauce:

¼ cup (2 fl oz)	light soy sauce
1½ cups (12 fl oz)	chicken stock or cold water
1 tablespoon	rice wine or dry sherry
1 tablespoon	sugar

Scale and wash the fish tails. The heads may be reserved for other dishes (see Index). Rub with the salt and wine and leave for 20 minutes.

Heat the oil or lard in a wok and fry the tails on moderate heat until beginning to colour, about 3 minutes. Add the onion and ginger and cook a further 2 minutes, then add the diced vegetables and the seasoning/sauce ingredients and bring to the boil.

Cover, reduce heat and braise for 10 minutes. Increase the heat and stir in 1 tablespoon vegetable oil, the m.s.g. and sesame oil, if used, and the vinegar. The sauce may be thickened, if preferred, with a thin solution of cornflour and cold water.

116

'Squirrel' Fish (recipe page 120).

'WESTLAKE STYLE' BRAISED CARP

1 1½ kg (3 lb)	fresh silver or grass carp (or fresh water trout)
5 cm (2 in) piece	fresh ginger, peeled
8 cups (2 litres)	deep-frying oil
	cornflour (cornstarch)
	flour

Seasoning:

½ teaspoon	salt
½ teaspoon	m.s.g. (optional)
1 tablespoon	rice wine or dry sherry

Sauce A:

1½ teaspoons	grated fresh ginger
2 teaspoons	crushed garlic
1½ cups (12 fl oz)	fish stock or water
½ cup (4 fl oz)	light soy sauce
1 tablespoon	rice wine or dry sherry
½ teaspoon	salt
2 tablespoons	sugar
1 teaspoon	m.s.g. (optional)
½ teaspoon	ground black pepper

Sauce B:

½ cup (4 fl oz)	fish stock or cold water
1 — 2	fresh red chilli peppers, seeds removed and shredded
3 slices	fresh ginger, shredded
2	spring onions (scallions), trimmed and shredded
1½ tablespoons	sesame oil
2 teaspoons	white vinegar
¾ teaspoon	cornflour (cornstarch)

Clean, scale, and thoroughly wash the fish. Trim the fins and remove gills. Slit open from the underside without cutting right through, open flat and rub with the seasoning ingredients.

Heat a large wok, rub vigorously with the peeled ginger to prevent the fish from sticking during cooking, and heat the deep-frying oil to smoking point. Reduce heat slightly with a mixture of cornflour and flour and deep-fry for 6 minutes on one side, turn and fry the other side for 3 minutes. Lift out and drain well.

Pour off the oil, rinse the pan and return only ¼ cup (2 fl oz) of the oil. Fry the ginger and garlic for 30 seconds and add the remaining sauce A ingredients. Bring to the boil, return the fish skin side upwards, and when the sauce boils again, cover and braise over lowered heat for 4 minutes. Turn the fish and cook, covered, for a further 10 minutes. Lift onto a serving plate, skin upwards, and keep warm.

Add the sauce B ingredients to the pan. Bring to the boil and simmer until reduced to about 1½ cups (12 fl oz). Pour over the fish and serve.

BRAISED GOLDEN CARP WITH ONIONS

2 375 g (12 oz)	golden carp (snapper or perch)
¾ teaspoon	salt
2 teaspoons	rice wine or dry sherry
2	large brown onions
75 g (2½ oz)	slightly fat pork, diced
3 cups (24 fl oz)	frying oil
1 tablespoon	light soy sauce
1 teaspoon	dark soy sauce
	m.s.g. (optional)
	white vinegar (optional)

Seasoning:

2 teaspoons	rice wine or dry sherry
⅓ teaspoon	salt
¾ teaspoon	sugar
2 teaspoons	softened lard
3 slices	fresh ginger, shredded

Clean and scale the fish and score diagonally across each side. Rub with the salt and wine and leave for 20 minutes. Peel the onions and slice narrowly from stem to root.

Heat the frying oil to moderately hot and fry the diced pork until lightly coloured. Remove and fry the onions for 30 seconds. Remove and set aside with the pork. Wipe the fish, rub with the light and dark soy sauce and deep-fry until half-cooked, about 7 minutes cooking, turning once. Lift out and drain well.

Pour off the oil, wipe out the wok and return about 2 tablespoons of the oil. Return the onions and pork and fry briefly, then add the fish and the seasoning ingredients with water to cover. Bring to the boil, cover the wok and reduce the heat. Simmer until the fish are cooked through and the sauce well reduced, about 40 minutes. Add a dash of m.s.g. and white vinegar, if used, and transfer to a serving plate. Serve at once.

GOLDEN CARP STUFFED WITH PORK AND BAMBOO SHOOTS

1 1 kg (2 lb)	golden carp (or red snapper)
155 g (5 oz)	slightly fat pork
45 g (1½ oz)	canned bamboo shoots, drain-ed
3	dried black mushrooms, soak-ed for 25 minutes
1 tablespoon	finely chopped spring onion (scallion)
1 teaspoon	finely chopped fresh ginger
5 cups (1¼ litres)	deep-frying oil
5	spring onions (scallions), trim-med and sliced
5 thick slices	fresh ginger, shredded
2 teaspoons	softened lard
⅓ teaspoon	m.s.g. (optional)

Seasoning A:

1 tablespoon	rice wine or dry sherry
1½ teaspoons	salt
1 tablespoon	light soy sauce

Seasoning B:

½ teaspoon	salt
¼ teaspoon	m.s.g. (optional)
¼ teaspoon	white pepper
1 teaspoon	sugar
2 teaspoons	light soy sauce
2 teaspoons	rice wine or dry sherry
1 tablespoon	cornflour (cornstarch)

Seasoning C/Sauce:

2 cups (16 fl oz)	chicken stock
1½ tablespoons	light soy sauce
1 tablespoon	rice wine or dry sherry
1 teaspoon	salt
½ teaspoon	sugar

Clean the fish through an opening made near the gills. Scale and wash thoroughly. Make several diagonal scores across each side, cutting almost to the bone. Rub on both sides with the seasoning A ingredients and pour the remainder inside. Set the fish aside.

Finely dice the pork, bamboo shoots, and mushroom caps, and mix with the chopped spring onion and ginger and the seasoning B ingredients. Stuff into the fish and secure the opening with toothpicks or a poultry pin.

Heat the deep-frying oil in a wok and deep-fry the fish until lightly coloured, about 1½ minutes on each side. Remove and drain off the oil.

Arrange the shredded spring onions and ginger in the wok and place the fish on top. Pour in the seasoning C/sauce ingredients and bring to the boil. Cover and simmer until the fish is tender and the filling cooked through, about 45 minutes. Stir in the lard and m.s.g., if used.

Thicken the sauce, if preferred, with a thin solution of corn-flour and cold water. Transfer the fish to a serving plate and pour on the sauce.

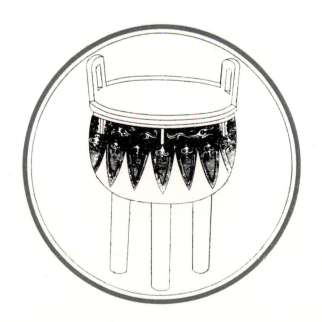

'SQUIRREL' FISH

So named by the imaginative chef who created it centuries ago. The fish is turned inside out and the meat scored so that it stands in spikes when cooked, thereby resembling the furry creature after which it was named.

1 1 kg (2 lb)	yellow fish or sea bass
1 teaspoon	salt
1 tablespoon	rice wine or dry sherry
	cornflour (cornstarch)
8 cups (2 litres)	deep-frying oil
155 g (5 oz)	canned straw mushrooms or champignon, drained and diced
30 g (1 oz)	canned bamboo shoots, drained and diced
1	small carrot, diced and parboiled
2 tablespoons	frozen or fresh peas, parboiled
1 tablespoon	finely chopped spring onion (scallion)
1½ teaspoons	grated fresh ginger
¾ teaspoon	crushed garlic
¼ cup (2 fl oz)	frying oil

Sauce:

¼ cup (2 fl oz)	chicken stock
1 tablespoon	light soy sauce
¼ cup (2 fl oz)	white vinegar
½ cup (2 fl oz)	tomato sauce (ketchup)
2 teaspoons	rice wine or dry sherry
⅓ teaspoon	salt
½ cup	sugar
1 teaspoon	cornflour (cornstarch)

Clean the fish, scale and trim the fins. Cut open from the underside and remove the backbone and gills. Lay the fish flat, meat upwards and use a sharp paring knife to score the meat closely in a criss-cross pattern, taking care not to pierce through the skin. Sprinkle on the salt and wine and leave for 15 minutes, then coat thickly with cornflour and rub with fingers from tail to head until the meat stands up in spikes.

Heat the deep oil to moderate and deep-fry the fish until crisp and golden on the surface with the meat tender inside, about 7 minutes, turning once. Drain and keep warm.

In another pan, stir-fry the diced vegetables and ham with the onion, ginger, and garlic for 3 minutes, add the sauce ingredients and bring to the boil. Stir unitl thickened and pour over the fish.

SLICED FISH IN WALNUT CRUMB BATTER

Serve as an appetiser or main course.

315 g (10 oz)	meaty white fish fillets
155 g (5 oz)	walnuts, blanched, skinned and dried
3	egg whites, beaten
2 tablespoons	flour
3 tablespoons	cornflour (cornstarch)
6 cups (1½ litres)	deep-frying oil

Seasoning:

½ teaspoon	salt
½ teaspoon	m.s.g. (optional)
	pinch of white pepper
½ teaspoon	rice wine or dry sherry
1 tablespoon	finely chopped spring onion (scallion)
1½ teaspoons	grated fresh ginger

Cut the fish into pieces about 4 × 2 cm (1 2/3 × ¾ in) and mix with the seasoning ingredients. Leave for 15 minutes.

Toast the walnuts and chop finely. Make a thick batter with the egg whites, flour, and cornflour, adding just a little water.

Heat the deep oil to moderate. Dip the fish into the batter, coat thickly with the chopped walnuts and deep-fry until golden brown, about 2½ minutes. Drain well.

STEAMED GRASS CARP DRESSED WITH SHREDDED VEGETABLES

1 1¼ kg (2½ lb)	grass carp (fresh water trout or sea bass)
1 tablespoon	rice wine or dry sherry
¾ teaspoon	salt
3	spring onions (scallions), trimmed and shredded
3 slices	fresh ginger, shredded
2 tablespoons	frying oil or softened lard
30 g (1 oz)	canned bamboo shoots, drained and shredded
15 g (½ oz)	canned champignons, drained and shredded
1	small green capsicum (bell pepper), trimmed and shredded

Seasoning A:

1½ tablespoons	rendered chicken fat (chicken grease), warmed
1 teaspoon	m.s.g. (optional)
	pinch of white pepper
¼ cup (2 fl oz)	chicken stock

Seasoning B:

1 teaspoon	rice wine or dry sherry
½ teaspoon	m.s.g. (optional)
1 teaspoon	sugar
2 tablespoons	light soy sauce
½ teaspoon	white vinegar

Clean, scale, and thoroughly wash the fish and trim the fins. Remove the gills, cut open on the underside and remove the backbone entirely. Blanch the fish in boiling water for 1 minute and drain well. Rub with the wine and salt and place in an oiled large oval dish with the shredded spring onions and ginger arranged op top. Add the seasoning A ingredients and set on a rack in a steamer. Steam over high heat, tightly covered, for 20 to 25 minutes.

Heat the oil or lard in a wok and sauté the shredded vegetables for 2 minutes. Add the seasoning B ingredients and cook a further 1 minute. Lift the fish onto a serving plate and strain any liquid from the oval dish into the wok. Bring to the boil and thicken, if preferred, with a thin solution of cornflour and cold water. Pour the sauce and vegetables over the fish and garnish with shredded spring onion or fresh coriander. Serve at once.

MANDARIN FISH IN POT-STICKER STYLE

Serve as an appetiser or main dish.

250 g (8 oz)	mandarin fish (pearl perch, sea bass, or grouper)
185 g (6 oz)	pork fat
5 pieces	preserved mustard green leaves (omit if unavailable)
2	egg whites, beaten
2 tablespoons	cornflour (cornstarch)
2 tablespoons	onion-pepper-salt (see page 384)
2 tablespoons	frying oil or softened lard
1 tablespoon	rice wine or dry sherry
2 tablespoons	chicken stock

Seasoning:

¼ teaspoon	salt
½ teaspoon	m.s.g. (optional)
	pinch of white pepper
½ teaspoon	rice wine or dry sherry
½ teaspoon	sugar
1	egg white, beaten
1 tablespoon	onion and ginger infusion (see page 386)

Cut the fish into thin slices about 5 × 2.5 cm (2 × 1 in) and mix with the seasoning ingredients. Leave for 15 minutes.

Cut the pork fat into very thin slices the same size as the fish. Wash the mustard leaves, dry and cut to fit the pork fat and fish. Make a smooth, creamy batter with the egg whites and cornflour and brush over the pork fat. Sprinkle on a generous amount of the onion-pepper-salt and top each piece with a slice of fish and a portion of the mustard leaf. Brush on the remaining batter after thinning with a dash of water.

Heat a shallow flat pan to moderate and add the oil or lard. Arrange the pot-stickers in the pan, fat downwards, and cook on moderate to low heat for 3 minutes. Cover the pan and cook gently until the fish is tender and the fat crisp and almost transparent. Remove the lid, increase the heat and splash in the wine, followed by the chicken stock a few seconds later. Cook briefly and serve.

DEEP-FRIED CARP WITH SWEET AND SOUR SAUCE

1 1¼ kg (2½ lb)	grass carp (sea bass or fresh water trout)
¾ teaspoon	salt
2 teaspoon	rice wine or dry sherry
5 cm (2 in) piece	fresh ginger, peeled
8 cups (2 litres)	deep-frying oil

Batter:

2	egg whites, well beaten
2 tablespoons	cornflour (cornstarch)
	extra cornflour (cornstarch)

Sauce:

¼ cup (2 fl oz)	frying oil
2 tablespoons	finely chopped spring onion
1 tablespoon	finely shredded fresh ginger
1½—2 teaspoons	chopped garlic
⅓ cup	chicken stock
1 tablespoon	light soy sauce
2 teaspoons	rice wine or dry sherry
¼ cup (2 fl oz)	white vinegar
⅓ cup	sugar
2 teaspoons	sesame oil (optional)
	pinch of salt
	pinch of ground black pepper
1½ teaspoons	cornflour (cornstarch)

Clean and scale the fish and trim the fins. Remove the gills, wash well and wipe dry. Score diagonally on both sides and rub with the salt and wine. Leave for 10 minutes.

Mix the egg whites and cornflour with a very little cold water to make a thick batter. Brush over the fish, then coat lightly with extra cornflour. Shake off excess. Heat the wok and rub vigorously with the peeled ginger to prevent the fish from sticking during cooking. Add the oil and heat to smoking. Fry the fish until golden and crisp on both sides, about 12 minutes total cooking time, reducing the heat after the first 3 minutes. The fish should be cooked through. Test by inserting a fork into the thickest part. It should lift easily from the bones. Remove the fish and place in a strainer or on absorbent paper to drain.

In another pan, heat the frying oil and fry the onions, ginger, and garlic for 2 minutes on moderate heat. Increase the heat and add the remaining sauce ingredients, pre-mixed, and boil until thickened. Keep hot.

Reheat the deep oil and fry the fish a further 2 minutes, then lift out and drain well. Place on a heated metal serving tray. Transfer the hot sauce to a jug, and pour over the fish at the table.

CUBED MANDARIN FISH AND PINEAPPLE IN TOMATO SAUCE

315 g (10 oz)	mandarin fish fillets (or pearl perch)
¼ teaspoon	salt
1½ teaspoons	rice wine or dry sherry
1 cup	cornflour (cornstarch)
4 cups (1 litre)	deep-frying oil
2	spring onions (scallions), trimmed and diced
3 slices	fresh ginger, shredded
1 teaspoon	crushed garlic (or to taste)
90 g (3 oz)	fresh or canned pineapple, drained and diced
45 g (1½ oz)	cooked green peas

Sauce:

2½ tablespoons	white vinegar
¼ cup (2 fl oz)	tomato sauce (ketchup)
2 teaspoons	rice wine or dry sherry
¼ cup (2 oz)	sugar
½ teaspoon	salt
¼ teaspoon	m.s.g. (optional)
1 teaspoon	cornflour (cornstarch)
1 tablespoon	cold water

Cut the fish into bite-sized pieces and season with the salt and wine. Pour the cornflour into a plastic or paper bag and add the fish. Close the bag and shake vigorously to thickly coat the fish. Empty into a collandar and shake well to remove excess flour.

Heat the deep oil to fairly hot and deep fry the fish, 10 pieces at a time, until golden and crisp. Drain well and keep the oil warm.

In another wok or pan, add about ½ cup (4 fl oz) of the fish frying oil and heat to smoking. Sauté the onion, ginger, and garlic for 1 minute, then add the sauce ingredients and bring to the boil. Stir in the pineapple and peas and keep warm.

Reheat the deep-frying oil and re-fry the fish for a further 1 minute, drain and transfer to the sauce. Heat through, turning with a wok spatula until evenly coated with the sauce. Arrange on a warmed serving plate.

MANDARIN FISH BALLS WITH VEGETABLES IN CHICKEN STOCK

500 g (1 lb)	mandarin fish fillets (or pearl perch)
6 cups (1½ litres)	deep-frying oil
¼ cup (2 fl oz)	frying oil or softened lard
30 g (1 oz)	canned champignons, sliced
30 g (1 oz)	cooked ham, shredded
155 g (5 oz)	fresh sweet pea sprouts, snow peas, or chopped spinach
1 tablespoon	finely chopped spring onion (scallion)
1 teaspoon	grated fresh ginger

Seasoning:

2	egg whites, beaten
2 tablespoons	onion and ginger infusion (see page 386)
½ teaspoon	salt
1 teaspoon	m.s.g. (optional)
¼ teaspoon	white pepper
1 tablespoon	cornflour (cornstarch)

Sauce:

2 cups (16 fl oz)	chicken stock
¾ teaspoon	salt
½ teaspoon	m.s.g. (optional)
¾ teaspoon	rice wine or dry sherry
2 teaspoons	cornflour (cornstarch)

Pulverise the fish in a food processor or by using two cleavers simultaneously (see page 396). Mix thoroughly with the seasoning ingredients, working in one direction only until the mixture is smooth, thick and creamy.

Heat the deep oil to moderate. Squeeze the fish mixture through the right hand to form small balls (see page 395), and scoop into the oil with a spoon. Cook until they rise to he surface and colour lightly, then remove and drain well.

In another pan, heat the frying oil and sauté the mushrooms, ham, and washed vegetables, adding the onion and ginger. When softened, pour in the pre-mixed sauce ingredients and bring to the boil. Add the fish balls and heat through before transferring to a serving dish.

FRIED FISH SLICES WITH GINGER AND SWEET PICKLES

375 g (12 oz)	meaty white fish fillets
1½ cups (12 fl oz)	frying oil
2	spring onions (scallions), trimmed and shredded
6-8 thin slices	fresh young ginger, shredded
60 g (2 oz)	canned bamboo shoots, drained and shredded
30 g (1 oz)	sweet Chinese pickles, shredded
1 tablespoon	Chinese pickle liquid
1 teaspoon	sesame oil (optional)

Seasoning:

1	egg white, beaten
½ teaspoon	salt
½ teaspoon	sugar
2 teaspoons	cornflour (cornstarch)

Sauce:

⅓ cup	chicken stock
½ teaspoon	salt
½ teaspoon	sugar
½ teaspoon	rice wine or dry sherry
½ teaspoon	cornflour (cornstarch)

Cut the fish into 1 cm (⅓ in) slices, cutting across the fillets at an angle. Mix with the seasoning ingredients and leave to marinate for 20 minutes.

Heat the oil in a wok and fry the fish for 2 minutes, until cooked through. Remove and drain. Pour off all but 2 tablespoons of the oil and sauté the spring onions briefly, then add the ginger, bamboo shoots, and pickles and sauté for 1 minute. Add the pickle liquid and the pre-mixed sauce ingredients and bring to the boil. Simmer until thickened, then return the fish and heat through.

ONE FISH SERVED IN TWO WAYS

1 1 kg (2 lb)	sea bass or fresh trout
2½ tablespoons	softened lard or rendered chicken fat (chicken grease)
1	large white onion, thickly sliced
2 slices	fresh ginger, chopped
60 g (2 oz)	canned bamboo shoots, drained and shredded
20 g (¾ oz)	dried 'wood ear' fungus, soaked for 25 minutes and shredded
2	spring onions (scallions), trimmed and shredded
2 slices	fresh ginger, shredded
¼ cup (2 fl oz)	frying oil

Seasoning A:

2	egg whites, well beaten
¾ teaspoon	salt
1 tablespoon	cornflour (cornstarch)

Seasoning B:

1 tablespoon	rice wine or dry sherry
1¼ teaspoons	salt
¼ teaspoon	m.s.g. (optional)
	pinch of white pepper

Seasoning C/Sauce:

½ cup (4 fl oz)	reserved fish stock*
2 teaspoons	rice wine or dry sherry
½ teaspoon	salt
¼ teaspoon	m.s.g. (optional)
¾ teaspoon	sugar
¾ teaspoon	cornflour (cornstarch)

Clean and scale the fish and remove the two fillets. Skin the fillets and cut across them into thin slices. Place in a dish and add the seasoning A ingredients, rub in lightly and leave for 20 minutes.

Wash the head and backbone and cut into several pieces. Heat half the lard in a wok and sauté the onion and chopped ginger for 1 minute. Add the head and bone pieces and sauté until lightly coloured. Sizzle in the wine, then add the remaining seasoning B ingredients and pour in about 3 cups (24 fl oz) cold water. Bring to the boil, cover tightly and simmer for 25 minutes.

Bring a saucepan of water to a rolling boil and add the sliced fish. Poach for about 1½ minutes, until the fish is firm and white, then drain, reserving ½ cup of the stock for the sauce.

Heat another wok, and stir-fry the bamboo shoots and shredded 'wood ears,' spring onions, and ginger in the frying oil until softened and lightly colored. Add the pre-mixed seasoning C/sauce ingredients and bring to the boil. Add the fish and simmer until cooked through. Transfer to a serving plate.

Stir the remaining lard into the fish soup and adjust the seasoning to taste. Transfer to a soup tureen and serve at the same time as the stir-fried fish. Serve with small dishes of Vinegar and Ginger Dip (see page 384).

* Reserved from poaching the sliced fish.

SILVER CARP'S HEAD SIMMERED IN AN EARTHEN CROCK

1	1¼ kg (2½ lb)	silver carp's head, or several fish heads of the same weight
2 cups (16 fl oz)		frying oil
2 tablespoons		dark soy sauce
2		bean sheets, or 30 g bean thread vermicelli, soaked
8		garlic chives, sliced
15 cm (½ oz)		dried 'wood ear' fungus, soaked for 25 minutes and diced
30 g (1 oz)		canned bamboo shoots, drained and diced
60 g (2 oz)		lean pork
6 cups (1½ litres)		water or fish stock
1½		pickled or fresh red chilli peppers, sliced

Seasoning:

¼ cup (2 fl oz)	light soy sauce
1 tablespoon	rice wine or dry sherry
1½ teaspoons	salt
½ teaspoon	white pepper
1 teaspoon	sugar

Thoroughly wash the fish head(s) and cut in halves. Rub with the dark soy sauce. Heat the deep-frying oil to smoking point and add the fish heads. Fry until lightly coloured, then remove and drain well.

Place the fish heads in a casserole and add the shredded bean sheets or soaked vermicelli, the garlic chives and diced 'wood ears.' Fry the bamboo shoots briefly and add to the casserole, then fry the pork until lightly coloured. Drain and add to the casserole with the water or fish stock. Add pickled or fresh red chilli peppers.

Add the seasoning ingredients and bring to the boil. Simmer until the fish heads are completely cooked, then scrape the meat from the bones. Discard as many bones as possible before serving.

JUMBO PRAWNS SERVED IN TWO STYLES

Serves 8

16	large raw prawns (shrimps), in the shell, about 1¼ kg (2½ lb)
¾ teaspoon	salt
2 teaspoons	rice wine or dry sherry
1 tablespoon	onion and ginger infusion (see page 386)
4 slices	white bread
2	egg whites, beaten cornflour (cornstarch)
4	spring onions (scallions), trimmed and shredded
3 slices	fresh ginger, shredded
¼ cup (2 fl oz)	frying oil or softened lard
4 cups (1 litre)	deep-frying oil

Sauce:

⅓ cup	chicken stock
2 teaspoons	rice wine or dry sherry
2 teaspoons	white vinegar
¼ cup (2 fl oz)	tomato sauce (ketchup)
1½ tablespoons	sugar
½ teaspoon	salt
¼ teaspoon	m.s.g. (optional)
1½ teaspoons	cornflour (cornstarch)

Cut the prawns in halves across the widest part of the body. Shell the lower half and cut deeply down the back, removing the dark vein. Spread flat and season with ½ teaspoon salt and the rice wine. Leave for 10 minutes. Wash the heads and season with the remaining ¼ teaspoon salt and the onion and ginger infusion. Leave for 15 minutes.

Remove crusts from the bread and cut each slice into quarters. Dip the prawn tails into beaten egg, coat lightly with cornflour, then dip into the beaten egg again. Press one onto each piece of bread and coat lightly all over with cornflour. Heat the deep-frying oil.

Heat the oil or lard and fry the onion and ginger for 1 minute on moderate heat. Increase the heat slightly and fry the heads, stirring frequently until red, about 2½ minutes. Pour in the pre-mixed sauce ingredients and bring to the boil. Reduce the heat slightly and simmer until the prawns are cooked through.

At the same time, fry the prawn and bread slices, prawn-side downwards, in the moderately hot oil to a rich golden brown. Turn once during cooking. Drain well.

Arrange the prawn toast on one serving plate and the sautéd prawns on another and serve together.

PHOENIX TAIL PRAWNS

500 g (1 lb)	fresh green prawns (shrimps), in the shell
1	large brown onion, sliced
4 cups (1 litre)	deep-frying oil
60 g (2 oz)	canned bamboo shoots, drained and sliced
3	dried black mushrooms, soaked for 25 minutes
¼ teaspoon	white vinegar (optional)
½ teaspoon	sesame oil

Seasoning:

1	egg white, beaten
½ teaspoon	salt
2 teaspoons	cornflour (cornstarch)

Sauce:

¼ cup (2 fl oz)	chicken stock
2 teaspoons	light soy sauce
1 teaspoon	rice wine or dry sherry
½ teaspoon	salt
¼ teaspoon	m.s.g. (optional)
½ teaspoon	sugar

Shell the prawns leaving the tail sections intact. Remove the dark veins with a toothpick (see page 394), and mix with the seasoning ingredients. Leave for 15 minutes.

Heat the deep-frying oil to moderate and fry the prawns until they turn white with the tails bright red, about 1½ minutes. Lift out and drain well.

Squeeze the water from the mushrooms, remove the stems and slice thinly. Pour off all but 1½ tablespoons of the oil and fry the sliced onion until beginning to colour, then add the bamboo shoots and sliced mushrooms and stir-fry on high heat for ½ minute. Return the prawns and pour in the pre-mixed sauce ingredients. Bring to the boil, season with white vinegar, if used, and the sesame oil. Serve.

DEEP-FRIED PRAWN PUFFS

Serve as an appetiser or main dish.

375 g (12 oz)	fresh green prawns, in the shell (shrimps)
6	egg whites
1¼ tablespoons	flour
2 tablespoons	cornflour (cornstarch)
1 tablespoon	finely chopped cooked ham
1 tablespoon	finely chopped spring onion (scallion)

cornflour (cornstarch)

4 cups (1 litre)	deep-frying oil

Chinese pepper-salt

Seasoning:

2 tablespoons	onion and ginger infusion (see page 386)
½ teaspoon	salt
¼ teaspoon	m.s.g. (optional)
	pinch of white pepper
½ teaspoon	rice wine or dry sherry

Shell the prawns and cut in halves lengthwise, discarding the dark veins. Cut any larger prawns in halves again. Mix with the seasoning ingredients and leave for 10 minutes.

Beat the egg whites to stiff peaks and carefully fold in the flour, cornflour, chopped ham, and onion.

Heat the deep-frying oil to moderate. Drain the prawns, pat dry, and coat lightly with cornflour, shaking off excess. Dip into the egg white batter, coating thickly. Deep-fry several pieces at a time until golden, about 1¼ minutes. Remove from oil, drain for a minute and lower prawn puffs into hot oil again. Deep-fry for 30 seconds. Drain and arrange on a serving plate. Sprinkle on pepper-salt or serve in separate dishes for dipping. Serve at once.

CRYSTAL SHRIMP BALLS GLAZED WITH SWEET AND SOUR SAUCE

Serve as an appetiser or main course.

375 g (12 oz)	shrimp meat
45 g (1½ oz)	pork fat
45 g (1½ oz)	canned water chestnuts, drained
6 cups (1½ litres)	deep-frying oil

Seasoning:

1	egg white, beaten
¼ teaspoon	salt
½ teaspoon	m.s.g. (optional)
½ teaspoon	sugar
1 teaspoon	ginger wine
2 tablespoons	cornflour (cornstarch)

Sauce:

⅓ cup	chicken stock
2 tablespoons	white vinegar
2 tablespoons	sugar
2 teaspoons	finely chopped spring onion (scallion)
½ teaspoon	grated fresh ginger
¼ teaspoon	crushed garlic
½ teaspoon	cornflour (cornstarch)

Pulverise the shrimp meat and pork fat in a food processor or by using two cleavers (see page 396). Add finely chopped water chestnuts and the seasoning ingredients and beat in one direction until the paste is smooth.

Heat deep-frying oil to moderately hot. Form the mixture into balls in the left hand as explained on page 395 and scoop into the oil with a spoon. Cook gently until they rise to the surface. Lift out in a perforated spoon and drain.

In a wok, heat about 2 tablespoons of the deep-frying oil and add the sauce ingredients. Bring to the boil, stirring. Add the shrimp balls and gently move the pan to keep the balls slowly turning in the sauce until evenly glazed. Transfer to a serving plate.

DRUNKEN CRABS

6	small fresh Shanghai hairy crabs*
2 pieces	dried orange peel, chopped
1 tablespoon	finely chopped fresh ginger
2 teaspoons	finely chopped spring onion (scallion)
2 teaspoons	sugar
2 tablespoons	salt
3 cups (24 fl oz)	yellow rice wine
½ teaspoon	m.s.g. (optional)

* Available from specialist food suppliers in late November. They are distinguishable by their small hair-covered pincers and coveted by Chinese gourmets around the world.

Thoroughly wash the crabs, cleaning with a soft brush to ensure all muddy particles are removed. Rinse in cold water and place, live in a large preserving jar. Add the remaining ingredients, place a piece of greaseproof paper over the top of the jar and press the lid firmly into place over it. Leave for 1 week in a cool place, though do not refrigerate unless the weather is particularly hot.

To serve, lift off the top shell and discard the inedible parts. Cut the crabs, with legs attached, into quarters and rearrange in their original shapes on a serving plate. Return the top shells.

Serve with ginger tea made by infusing fresh sliced ginger in boiling water. This counteracts the excessive richness of the crab. The yellow creamy roe is eaten along with the tender white meat.

Silver Carp's Head Simmered in an Earthen Crock (recipe page 126).

SAUTÉD CRABMEAT ON CRISP NOODLES

60 g (2 oz)	rice vermicelli, broken
4 cups (1 litre)	deep-frying oil
2	spring onions (scallions), trimmed and shredded
2 slices	fresh ginger, shredded
3 tablespoons	softened lard or vegetable oil
1 tablespoon	rice wine or dry sherry
185 g (6 oz)	fresh, frozen, or canned crabmeat, flaked
1½ cups (12 fl oz)	chicken stock
3	egg whites, well beaten

Seasoning:

¾ teaspoon	salt
¾ teaspoon	sugar
½ teaspoon	m.s.g. (optional)
1 tablespoon	light soy sauce
2 teaspoons	cornflour (cornstarch)
1 tablespoon	cold water

Heat the deep oil and fry the broken rice vermicelli in a frying basket until it expands into a mass of crisp white noodles, about 15 seconds. Drain and transfer to a serving plate.

Fry the shredded spring onions and ginger in the lard or vegetable oil in another pan for 1 minute. Add the wine and stir for a few seconds, then add the crabmeat and sauté briefly. Pour in the chicken stock, add the seasoning ingredients and bring to the boil. Slowly drizzle in the beaten egg and cook without stirring for 1 minute, then stir into the sauce and pour over the noodles. Serve at once.

DEEP-FRIED CRABMEAT BALLS

Serve as an appetiser or main dish.

315 g (10 oz)	fresh crabmeat
60 g (2 oz)	prawn meat (shrimp meat)
45 g (1½ oz)	pork fat
2	egg whites, beaten
1 tablespoon	finely chopped spring onion (scallion)
1½ teaspoons	grated fresh ginger
6 cups (1½ litres)	deep-frying oil
	Chinese pepper-salt
	sweet soy sauce (see page 385)

Seasoning:

½ teaspoon	salt
½ teaspoon	sugar
1 teaspoon	rice wine or dry sherry
1 tablespoon	cornflour (cornstarch)

Pulverise the crabmeat, prawn meat, and pork fat in the food processor or by using two cleavers (see page 396). Add the egg whites, onion, ginger, and seasonings and mix in one direction only, adding ½ — 1 tablespoon of water to make a smooth paste.

Heat the deep-frying oil to moderate. Form the mixture into balls in the left hand as explained on page 395 and scoop the balls into the oil with a spoon. Cook gently until they rise to the surface and colour lightly. Lift out with a perforated spoon and drain well.

Serve on a bed of shredded lettuce with accompaniments of pepper-salt and sweet soy sauce.

CLAMS IN YELLOW BEAN SAUCE

1 kg (2 lb)	fresh clams, in the shell
2	spring onions (scallions), trimmed and sliced
2 teaspoons	chopped garlic
¼ cup (2 fl oz)	frying oil

Seasoning/Sauce:

½ cup (4 fl oz)	chicken stock
1½ tablespoons	salted yellow bean sauce
2 teaspoons	rice wine or dry sherry
¼ teaspoon	m.s.g. (optional)
2 teaspoons	sugar
1 teaspoon	cornflour (cornstarch)
1 — 2 teaspoons	finely chopped fresh red chilli pepper (optional)

Thoroughly wash the clams, brushing the shells with a soft brush. Rinse well in cold water and place in a large wok. Add the spring onions, garlic, and oil and cover the pan. Cook on moderate heat, shaking the pan occasionally to encourage the shells to open.

When the shells are open, add the seasoning/sauce ingredients and bring to the boil. Simmer for about 1½ minutes. Discard those shells which have not opened, then transfer the clams and sauce to a serving dish.

OYSTERS WITH BARBECUED PORK AND VEGETABLES IN SAUCE

155 g (5 oz)	dried oysters, soaked overnight (or use 250 g / 8 oz fresh oysters)
125 g (4 oz)	Chinese barbecue or roast pork, diced
30 g (1 oz)	canned bamboo shoots, drained and diced
30 g (1 oz)	canned champignons, drained and diced
30 g (1 oz)	canned water chestnuts, drained and diced
2 tablespoons	finely chopped salted mustard greens, rinsed
3	spring onions (scallions), trimmed and diced
2 slices	fresh ginger, finely chopped
2 tablespoons	frying oil
1 tablespoon	vegetable oil, smoking hot

Seasoning A:

½ teaspoon	rice wine or dry sherry
1 tablespoon	frying oil
1	spring onion (scallion), trimmed and cut in halves
2 slices	fresh ginger
¼ cup (2 fl oz)	chicken stock

Seasoning B/Sauce:

2/3 teaspoon	salt
½ teaspoon	sugar
1 teaspoon	rice wine or dry sherry
2 teaspoons	oyster sauce, or dark soy sauce
2 teaspoons	light soy sauce
¼ teaspoon	white pepper
½ teaspoon	sesame oil
¼ cup (2 fl oz)	chicken stock or cold water
1 teaspoon	cornflour (cornstarch)

Drain the oysters and place in a dish with the seasoning A ingredients. Set on a rack in a steamer and steam for 1 hour, then discard the onion and ginger and dice the oysters. Set aside.*

Heat the 2 tablespoons oil and sauté the onion and ginger for 1 minute. Add the diced ingredients (except oysters) and sauté for 2 minutes, then add the pre-mixed seasoning B/sauce ingredients and bring to the boil. Reduce heat, add the oysters and simmer on moderate heat for 3 minutes. Transfer to a serving plate and pour on the piping hot oil just before serving.

*If using fresh oysters, omit the steaming and use whole.

SQUID IN SOUR AND HOT SAUCE ON CRISP RICE CAKES

2 cups	cooked white rice
750 g (1½ lb)	fresh squid
45 g (1½ oz)	canned bamboo shoots, drained and sliced
15 g (½ oz)	canned champignons, drained and thinly sliced
90 g (3 oz)	boneless chicken, shredded
2	spring onions (scallions), trimmed and diced
1 teaspoon	grated fresh ginger
1½ teaspoons	crushed garlic (or to taste)
6 cups (1½ litres)	deep-frying oil

Sauce:

4 cups (1 litre)	chicken stock
2 teaspoons	rice wine or dry sherry
1 tablespoon	white vinegar
½ cup (4 fl oz)	tomato sauce (ketchup)
½ teaspoon	chilli oil
1 teaspoon	sesame oil (optional)
¾ teaspoon	salt
¼ teaspoon	m.s.g. (optional)
½ teaspoon	white pepper
1 teaspoon	sugar
1 tablespoon	cornflour (cornstarch)

To make the rice cakes, press the cooked rice into a greased baking tray and bake in a low oven for 1 hour, then increase the heat to hot and roast until golden. Break into pieces about 5 cm (2 in) square.

Clean the squid, removing the heads, stomachs, skin, tentacles, and fins. Wash well and cut open. Score the inside in a close crisscross pattern then cut into 5 cm (2 in) squares.

Bring the sauce ingredients to the boil and add the bamboo shoots, champignons, chicken, onions, ginger, and garlic and simmer for 2 minutes. Add the squid and cook for just 2 minutes.

In the meantime, heat the deep-frying oil to fairly hot and fry the rice cakes until deep gold and crisp. Drain and place in a deep serving dish. Transfer the squid and sauce to a large jug and pour over the rice cakes at the table.

It is important to prepare both elements of this dish simultaneously. The rice cakes will lose their crispness if done in advance, and the squid becomes tough and chewy with overcooking.

POACHED SQUID WITH SESAME SAUCE

Serve warm or cold.

500 g (1 lb)	large fresh squid
2	spring onions (scallions), trimmed
3 thick slices	fresh ginger, bruised

Sauce:

⅓ cup	chicken stock or water
1 tablespoon	light soy sauce
½ teaspoon	white vinegar
2 tablespoons	sesame paste
1 teaspoon	sesame oil
¾ teaspoon	chilli oil (or to taste)
1 teaspoon	sugar
1 tablespoon	finely chopped spring onion (scallion)
1 teaspoon	grated fresh ginger

Clean the squid, removing skin, head and tentacles, stomach, and fins. Cut the tubular bodies open and wash well. Pat dry and score on the inside with a closely worked criss-cross pattern, taking care not to pierce the skin (see page 397) Cut into pieces of 5 × 2.5 cm (2 × 1 in).

Bring a saucepan of water to the boil, add the spring onions and ginger and boil for 2 minutes, then add the squid and poach for 1½ minutes. Drain and set aside. Discard the onion and ginger.

Mix the sauce ingredients together. Pour into a small bowl and place in the centre of a large serving plate. Arrange the poached squid around the bowl of sauce, garnish with shredded spring onion, ginger, or fresh coriander and serve. Dip the squid into the sauce before eating.

Clams in Yellow Bean Sauce (recipe page 131).

STEAMED FRESH-WATER EEL WITH SPICY AND HOT SAUCE

750 g (1½ lb)	small fresh-water eels
2	spring onions (scallions), trimmed and shredded
3 thick slices	fresh ginger, finely shredded
1 tablespoon	sesame oil, heated to smoking point
¼ — ½ teaspoon	white pepper
	fresh coriander or shredded spring onion (scallion)

Seasoning:

¼ teaspoon	salt
1 teaspoon	Chinese brown peppercorns
1½ tablespoons	rice wine or dry sherry
1 cup (8 fl oz)	chicken stock

Sauce:

¼ cup (2 fl oz)	light soy sauce
2 teaspoons	white vinegar
1 teaspoon	sesame oil
1½ teaspoons	sugar
1 tablespoon	finely chopped garlic, or to taste
1 — 2 teaspoons	finely chopped fresh red chilli pepper
1 tablespoon	finely chopped spring onion

Remove the heads and the lower tail sections of the eels, split open, remove stomachs and wash well. Drop into boiling water for 1 minute, lift out, and rub with salt, then rinse well with cold water. They may be skinned, if preferred, by securing the heads firmly to a work top and cutting through the skin around the heads. Take a firm grip with a pair of pincers and strip off the entire skin in one clean action. The meat, however, will become much drier after skinning.

Cut the eels into 5 cm (2 in) pieces and place in a dish with the onion, ginger, and seasoning ingredients. Set on a rack in a steaming pot, cover and steam over rapidly boiling water until tender, about 15 minutes. Remove the onion and ginger and strain off the cooking liquid.

Mix the sauce ingredients together. Pour the piping hot sesame oil over the eel and then pour on the sauce. Add the white pepper, if used, and garnish with fresh coriander or spring onion. Serve at once.

FRESH WATER EEL AND HAM STEAMED IN A POT

750 g (1½ lb)	large fresh-water eel
1 tablespoon	rice wine or dry sherry
1 tablespoon	salt
125 g (4 oz)	Chinese or cured (Smithfield) ham, cubed
2	spring onions (scallions), trimmed and sliced
3 slices	fresh ginger
1 cup (8 fl oz)	chicken stock

Seasoning:

1½ teaspoons	salt
1 teaspoon	sugar
½ teaspoon	m.s.g. (optional)
½ teaspoon	white pepper

Remove the eel head, slit open the stomach, clean and wash well. Cut into 2.5 cm (1 in) pieces and rub with the salt and wine. Leave for 10 minutes, then rinse again and place in a greased casserole with the cubed ham and the onions and ginger. Add the chicken stock and seasonings and place a piece of wet greaseproof paper across the top of the casserole. Press the lid firmly in place over the paper and stand the pot on a rack in a steamer. Steam over gently boiling water for 1½ — 1¾ hours until the eel is tender. Remove the onion and ginger and taste for seasoning before serving in the casserole.

Garnish, if desired, with white pepper and chopped fresh coriander.

134

STIR-FRIED FRESH-WATER EEL

500 g (1 lb)	small fresh-water eels
2 teaspoons	salt
¼ cup (2 fl oz)	softened lard or frying oil
2 teaspoons	rice wine or dry sherry
2 tablespoons	light soy sauce
6	spring onions (scallions), trimmed and shredded
2 tablespoons	finely shredded fresh ginger
2 tablespoons	chopped garlic, or to taste

Seasoning/Sauce:

¼ teaspoon	salt
½ teaspoon	m.s.g. (optional)
2 teaspoons	sugar
½ teaspoon	ground black pepper
¾ cup (6 fl oz)	chicken stock
2 teaspoons	cornflour (cornstarch)

Cut off the heads, slit the eels open, remove the stomachs and rinse well. Drop into boiling water to blanch for 1 minute, drain and rub with salt, then rinse again. Cut into three lengthwise strips, and cut these into 5 cm (2 in) pieces.

Heat the lard or frying oil in a wok and fry the eels on high heat until almost cooked through, about 3 minutes. Drizzle the wine into the sides of the wok, then do the same with the soy sauce. Pour in the pre-mixed seasoning/sauce ingredients and bring to the boil. Reduce the heat slightly and simmer for 5 minutes.

Transfer to a serving plate and make a hollow in the centre. Add the spring onions, ginger and garlic. Reheat the wok and add 2½ — 3 tablespoons frying oil. Heat to smoking and quickly pour over the onion, ginger, and garlic. Stir lightly into the eels and serve.

RED-BRAISED TURTLE

1 1 kg (2 lb)	turtle, preferably alive
1 tablespoon	rice wine or dry sherry
2 tablespoons	dark soy sauce
⅓ cup	frying oil
8 — 10 cloves	garlic, bruised
4	spring onions (scallions), trimmed and cut into 5 cm (2 in) pieces
4 thick slices	fresh ginger, bruised
125 g (4 oz)	'five flowered' pork (belly/fresh bacon)
1½ cups (12 fl oz)	chicken stock or water
75 g (2½ oz)	canned bamboo shoots, drained and cubed (or use fresh chestnuts and omit the garlic)
2 teaspoons	cornflour (cornstarch)
1 tablespoon	cold water
½ teaspoon	white vinegar

Seasoning:

¼ cup (2 fl oz)	light soy sauce
1 tablespoon	rice wine or dry sherry
1 tablespoon	sugar
½ teaspoon	m.s.g. (optional)
¼ teaspoon	ground black pepper

See page 395 for the preparation of live turtle. Cut the meat into 4 cm (1 2/3 in) cubes and rub with the wine and soy sauce. Heat the wok, add oil and when smoking, fry the turtle until evenly coloured. Remove and keep warm. Add the garlic and fry until lightly browned, and set aside.

If using chestnuts, they should be blanched to loosen the skin, the skin removed, and the nuts dried before frying to a light golden colour. Remove and set aside.

Add the onion, ginger, and pork and sauté until the pork is lightly coloured. Pour in the chicken stock or water. Add the bamboo shoots (or chestnuts) and garlic, the turtle meat and seasoning ingredients and mix well. Bring to the boil, then transfer to a casserole and cover tightly. Simmer or steam until the turtle is tender, about 20 minutes if simmered, 45 minutes if steamed.

Transfer the turtle meat, bamboo shoots and garlic, or the chestnuts, to a serving dish. Discard the pork, onion, and ginger and return the cooking liquid to the boil.

Thicken with the cornflour mixed with the cold water and check the seasoning. Pour over the turtle and garnish with shredded spring onion or ham.

SLOW-COOKED CORNED PORK

Serve hot or cold, as an appetiser or main dish.

1¼ kg (2½ lb)	pork shoulder (butt)
1 tablespoon	saltpetre

Seasoning:

1 tablespoon	rice wine or dry sherry
3	spring onions (scallions), trimmed
1½ teaspoons	grated fresh ginger
1½ teaspoons	salt
2	star anise
2 teaspoons	Chinese brown peppercorns
5 cm (2 in) piece	cinnamon stick

Blanch the pork in boiling water, then place in a pan with water to cover and add the saltpetre. Leave, covered, for 2 hours. Blanch again in boiling water and rinse in cold water. Drain well. This process gives a rosy colour to the meat and helps to preserve and tenderise.

Place the pork with seasoning ingredients in a heavy saucepan and add water to cover. Bring to the boil, reduce heat to low and simmer for 2½ hours, turning often. Remove from the heat and leave to cool in the pot.

Remove the meat when cool, slice thinly and arrange on a serving plate. Pour a little of the sauce on top. Serve with a dip of shredded ginger and garlic in vinegar (see page 384).

Pork leg (fresh ham) can also be prepared in this way. The skin may be left on and pricked thoroughly all over to allow the seasonings to penetrate. The resultant cooking liquid will have a gelatinous quality which will keep the sliced meat moist if brushed over before serving.

PORK AND CRABMEAT 'LION'S HEAD' MEATBALLS

750 g (1½ lb)	lean pork, minced (ground)
185 g (6 oz)	crabmeat
2 tablespoons	finely chopped spring onion (scallion)
1 teaspoon	grated fresh ginger
750 g (1½ lb)	Chinese cabbage, bok choy (celery cabbage)
¼ cup (2 fl oz)	frying oil
1 teaspoon	salt
	hot chicken stock

Seasoning:

1½ teaspoons	salt
½ teaspoon	m.s.g. (optional)
¼ teaspoon	white pepper
1 tablespoon	rice wine or dry sherry
2 tablespoons	cornflour (cornstarch)

Mix the pork with half the crabmeat, the onion and ginger, and the seasoning ingredients. Knead to a smooth paste and form into five large meatballs. Press a thumb into the centre of each to form a cavity and fill with the remaining crabmeat. Re-form the balls.

Wash the cabbage and cut into 7.5 cm (3 in) pieces. Sauté in the oil for 2-3 minutes until beginning to change colour, add the salt, stir well and transfer half to a casserole. Place the meatballs on the vegetables and arrange the remaining vegetables on top. Pour hot chicken stock into the casserole until the meatballs are just covered. Cover the pan and simmer on low heat for 1½ hours, adding more stock during cooking if needed, though this is usually unnecessary as the vegetables provide substantial extra liquid.

Remove the vegetables and place around the edge of a serving dish. Place the meatballs in the centre and pour on some of the sauce, which may be thickened slightly with a cornflour (cornstarch) solution if preferred. Or remove the top layer of vegetables to a separate plate and serve the meatballs in the casserole.

SLOW-COOKED LEG OF PORK WITH FERMENTED BEANCURD AND GARLIC

750 g (1½ lb)	pork leg (fresh ham)
4 cubes	fermented beancurd, with the liquid
8 — 10 cloves	garlic, bruised
¼ cup (2 fl oz)	frying oil or softened lard
3	spring onions (scallions), trimmed and cut in halves
3 thick slices	fresh ginger, bruised
1 teaspoon	m.s.g. (optional)

Seasoning:

⅓ cup	light soy sauce
2 tablespoons	rice wine or dry sherry
1 cup (8 fl oz)	sugar colouring (see page 388)
	chicken stock
1 tablespoon	sugar

Cut the pork into 4 cm (1 2/3 in) cubes and blanch in boiling water. Drain. Mash the beancurd with a fork, adding the liquid and sauté with the garlic cloves in the oil or lard for 2 minutes. Add the pork and fry until well coloured.

Add the onions and ginger, fry briefly, then pour in the pre-mixed seasoning ingredients with enough chicken stock to barely cover the meat. Bring to the boil and transfer to a casserole.

Simmer for 1½ — 1¾ hours until the pork is completely tender, add the m.s.g., if used, and serve.

SHREDDED BEEF AND BEAN SPROUTS ON CRISP NOODLES

250 g (8 oz)	frying steak (rump, fillet/tenderloin)
30 g (1 oz)	bean thread vermicelli
3 cups (24 fl oz)	deep-frying oil
185 g (6 oz)	fresh bean sprouts
1	large spring onion (scallion), shredded

Seasoning A:

1	egg white, beaten
¼ teaspoon	salt
½ teaspoon	sugar
2 teaspoons	light soy sauce
2 teaspoons	sesame oil
2 teaspoons	cornflour (cornstarch)
2 tablespoons	cold water

Seasoning B/Sauce:

½ cup (4 fl oz)	beef or chicken stock
¾ teaspoon	light soy sauce
½ teaspoon	rice wine or dry sherry
¼ teaspoon	salt
½ teaspoon	m.s.g. (optional)
	pinch of white pepper
½ teaspoon	cornflour (cornstarch)

Partially freeze the beef to facilitate slicing and cut across the grain into very thin slices, then cut these into shreds. Place in a dish and add the seasoning A ingredients. Mix well and leave to marinate for 15 minutes.

Break the vermicelli into short pieces and place in a frying basket. Heat the deep-frying oil in a wok until smoking and fry the noodles for a few seconds until they expand into a cloud of crisp white noodles. Do not allow to colour. Remove quickly, drain well, and pile on a serving plate.

Transfer the beef to the frying basket and lower into the hot oil for 10 seconds only. Lift out and shake the basket to remove excess oil. Set aside.

Drain off all but 2 tablespoons oil and fry the bean sprouts with the shredded onion until softened. Return the beef to fry briefly, stirring continually, then pour in the pre-mixed seasoning B/sauce ingredients and bring to the boil. Cook, stirring, for 1 minute then pour over the noodles and serve at once.

'SU TUNG PO' PORK

825 g (1¾ lb)	'five flowered' pork (belly/fresh bacon)
1 tablespoon	salt
8 pieces	rock candy (or ½ cup crystal sugar)
⅓ cup	light soy sauce
¼ cup (2 fl oz)	rice wine or dry sherry
2	spring onions (scallions), trimmed and cut in halves
4 thick slices	fresh ginger, bruised
90 g (3 oz)	canned champignons, drained and sliced
8	dried black mushrooms, soaked for 25 minutes

Rub the salt over the pork and leave for 1 hour, then blanch in boiling water for 2 minutes and rinse thoroughly in cold water. Drain well. Sear in a very hot dry pan until the surface is coloured and beginning to crisp. Cut into slices about 1 cm (⅓ in) thick, then into strips 5 cm (2 in) wide. Arrange in a covered pot and add the remaining ingredients. (First squeeze excess water from the black mushrooms and remove the stems.) Simmer for 2½ — 3 hours until the pork is completely tender.

Transfer the meat and mushrooms to a serving dish and discard the onion and ginger. Bring the sauce to the boil, check the seasoning and strain over the meat. Serve at once.

SIMMERED BELL PEPPERS STUFFED WITH PORK

Serve as an appetiser or main dish.

6	small green capsicums (bell peppers)
125 g (4 oz)	lean pork, finely minced (ground)
45 g (1½ oz)	fresh shrimp meat, minced (ground)
30 g (1 oz)	canned water chestnuts, drained and finely chopped
1 tablespoon	finely chopped spring onion (scallion)
½ teaspoon	grated fresh ginger
1 cup (8 fl oz)	frying oil
	cornflour (cornstarch)

Seasoning A:

1	egg white, beaten
¼ teaspoon	salt
½ teaspoon	m.s.g. (optional)
1 tablespoon	onion and ginger infusion (see page 386)
1 teaspoon	rice wine or dry sherry
1 tablespoon	cornflour (cornstarch)

Seasoning B/Sauce:

¾ cup (6 fl oz)	chicken stock
1 tablespoon	light soy sauce
1 teaspoon	rice wine or dry sherry
½ teaspoon	salt
½ teaspoon	m.s.g. (optional)
¼ teaspoon	sugar
1	spring onion (scallion), trimmed and shredded
1 slice	fresh ginger, shredded

Wash the peppers, cut in halves and remove the stem and seed core and the inner white ribs. Mix the minced pork, shrimp, water chestnuts, onion, and ginger with the seasoning A ingredients, stirring thoroughly.

Heat the shallow oil to moderate. Dust the inside of the peppers lightly with cornflour and fill each with a portion of the stuffing mixture, smoothing the edges. Squeeze each gently and coat lightly with cornflour.

Fry for about 8 minutes, turning occasionally. Remove and drain well. Bring the seasoning B/sauce ingredients to the boil in another pan and add the stuffed peppers. Simmer, uncovered, for a further 5 minutes. Serve with the sauce which may be thickened slightly with a thin solution of cornflour (cornstarch) and cold water, if preferred.

ROASTED PORK 'COINS'

Serve as an appetiser or main dish.

500 g (1 lb)	pork fillet (tenderloin)
500 g (1 lb)	pork fat
125 g (4 oz)	Chinese or cured (Smithfield) ham
2 tablespoons	softened lard or frying oil

Seasoning:

1 tablespoon	oyster sauce
1 tablespoon	soy bean paste (or dark soy sauce)
1 tablespoon	rice wine or dry sherry
1 tablespoon	sugar
¼ teaspoon	white pepper
1 teaspoon	m.s.g. (optional)
2 teaspoons	finely chopped spring onion (scallion)
¾ teaspoon	grated fresh ginger

Cut the pork into slices across the grain and bat lightly with the side of a cleaver to produce thin escalopes. Thinly slice the pork fat and ham and cut into pieces the same size as the pork. Mix the three meats with the seasoning ingredients and leave to marinate for 25 minutes.

Thread pork, pork fat, and ham pieces alternately onto small bamboo skewers previously soaked in oil, and arrange on an oiled baking sheet (cookie tray).

Roast in a preheated hot oven at 230°C(450°F) for about 25 minutes, turning frequently.

Remove from the skewers and arrange on a warmed plate to serve.

MINCED PORK IN CLAMS SERVED IN A CROCK

24	fresh clams (about 750 1½ g lb)
185 g (6 oz)	fatty pork, finely minced (ground)
45 g (1½ oz)	canned water chestnuts, drained and chopped
1 tablespoon	finely chopped spring onion (scallion)
1 teaspoon	grated fresh ginger
	cornflour (cornstarch)
5 cups (1¼ litres)	deep-frying oil

Seasoning A:

½ teaspoon	salt
½ teaspoon	m.s.g. (optional)
2 teaspoons	rice wine or dry sherry
½ teaspoon	sesame oil
1 tablespoon	cornflour (cornstarch)

Seasoning B/Sauce:

2 tablespoons	finely chopped spring onion (scallion)
1 tablespoon	finely chopped fresh ginger
½ cup (4 fl oz)	sugar colouring (see page 388)
1½ tablespoons	rice wine or dry sherry
2 teaspoons	dark soy sauce
1 teaspoon	salt
½ teaspoon	m.s.g. (optional)
½ teaspoon	sugar
¼ teaspoon	ground black pepper
1 teaspoon	sesame oil (optional)

Mix the pork with the seasoning A ingredients and set aside. Thoroughly wash the clams and place in a saucepan with water to cover. Bring to the boil and simmer until the clams open. Shake the pan occasionally as this helps them open. Drain, reserving the liquid.

Remove the clams and chop finely. Wipe out the shells, separating the two pieces. Mix the chopped clam with the pork, water chestnuts, spring onion, and ginger. Stuff into the clam shells, smooth the edges and coat lightly with cornflour.

Heat the deep-frying oil to smoking point and deep-fry the clams in several lots until well coloured. Remove to an earthenware crock. Bring the reserved stock to the boil and pour over the clams. Add the seasoning B/sauce ingredients and simmer for 12 minutes.

Thicken the sauce with a thin solution of cornflour and cold water and serve in the pot.

139

PORK KIDNEYS, TURNIP, AND DRIED SCALLOPS STEAMED IN A BOWL

Serve as an appetiser or main dish.

280 g (9 oz)	pork kidneys
5	dried scallops (about 40 g (1⅓ oz)), soaked for 25 minutes
280 g (9 oz)	sweet white turnips or giant white (icicle) radish, peeled
2 cups (16 fl oz)	deep-frying oil
2	spring onions (scallions), trimmed and shredded
2 slices	fresh ginger, shredded
125 g (4 oz)	ham skin (or use 2 streaky bacon rashers)

Seasoning A:

⅓ cup	chicken stock
1½ teaspoons	rice wine or dry sherry

Seasoning B:

½ teaspoon	salt
1 tablespoon	finely diced fresh chicken fat (chicken grease)

Sauce:

⅓ cup	reserved stock*
½ teaspoon	m.s.g. (optional)
¾ teaspoon	cornflour (cornstarch)
	pinch of white pepper
1 tablespoon	vegetable oil

Cut the pork kidneys in halves and remove the white fatty tissue. Peel off the skin. Place cut sides down on a cutting board and score to the depth of ⅓ cm (1/8 in) in a criss-cross pattern across each piece of kidney. Cut into thin slices, to give pieces with one fluted edge. Soak in boiling water for 30 seconds, then drain and place in a dish of cold water.

Drain the scallops and place in a dish with the seasoning A ingredients. Steam for 30 minutes, then drain, reserving the stock for the sauce. Shred the scallops by rubbing between forefinger and thumb. Arrange in the bottom of a bowl.

Cut the turnip or radish into small cubes and deep-fry until lightly coloured on the surface, or cook in shallow oil. Drain and transfer to a small saucepan of boiling water. Simmer until tender. Drain and arrange over the shredded scallops. Place the sliced kidneys on top and add the seasoning B ingredients and the shredded spring onions and ginger.

Cover the lot with the ham skin or bacon and set the bowl in a steamer to steam over rapidly boiling water for 20 minutes. Remove and discard the ham skin or bacon and chicken fat residue.

Heat a wok and strain in the liquid from the bowl, then add the sauce ingredients and bring to the boil. Simmer until thickened, then pour into the bowl and serve.

* Liquid from steamed scallops.

SAUTÉD LIVER AND ONIONS IN HOT SAUCE

280 g (9 oz)	fresh pork or calves liver
1	large white onion
1 cup (8 fl oz)	frying oil

Seasoning A:

2	egg whites, well beaten
½ teaspoon	salt
½ teaspoon	m.s.g. (optional)
¼ teaspoon	white pepper
2 teaspoons	rice wine or dry sherry
2 slices	fresh ginger, shredded
1 tablespoon	cornflour (cornstarch)

Seasoning B/Sauce:

1 tablespoon	hot bean paste
1½ tablespoons	light soy sauce
1 tablespoon	rice wine or dry sherry
1½ teaspoons	sugar
¼ teaspoon	m.s.g. (optional)
¼ teaspoon	white pepper

Very thinly slice the liver and place in a dish with the seasoning A ingredients, except the cornflour. Mix well and leave for 15 minutes, then add the cornflour and stir in lightly.

Peel the onion and cut from stem to root into thin slices. Heat the frying oil to smoking point and add the liver. Separate with chopsticks and fry until it changes colour, then remove the liver and drain off all but 2 tablespoons of the oil. Return the liver and fry on both sides until lightly coloured. Remove. Add the onions and fry until softened. Add the seasoning B/sauce ingredients and sauté briefly, then return the liver and splash in a very little water. Sauté together until the liver is just cooked through, about 45 seconds. Serve.

140

Red-Braised Turtle (recipe page 135).

BONELESS RACK OF LAMB FLAVOURED WITH WHITE RICE WINE

Serve as an appetiser or main dish.

1½ kg (3 lb)	boned rack of lamb
185 g (6 oz)	giant white (icicle) radish, small red radishes or sweet white turnips
	sesame oil

Seasoning A:

½ teaspoon	salt
¼ teaspoon	white pepper
1 tablespoon	sugar
1 tablespoon	light soy sauce
2 tablespoons	white rice wine (Mao Tai or similar, or use malt whisky or brandy)
1½ tablespoons	finely chopped spring onion
1 teaspoon	grated fresh ginger

Seasoning B:

1 teaspoon	salt
1 tablespoon	sugar
¼ cup (2 fl oz)	white vinegar

Trim away excess fat from the rack, score the skin side with a criss-cross pattern and rub the pre-mixed seasoning A ingredients on both sides of the rack. Leave covered for 2 hours, preferably in a sealed plastic bag.

Preheat the oven to moderate, 200°C (375°F). Place the rack on an oiled baking tray, brush with sesame oil and roast for 30 minutes, then turn and roast for a further 25 — 30 minutes until cooked through, but remaining tender and slightly pink inside.

In the meantime, peel and thinly slice the radish or turnip, and marinate with the seasoning B ingredients with water to cover.

To serve, cut the lamb into pieces about 5 × 2 cm (2 × ¾ in) and arrange on a plate surrounded with the drained pickled radish or turnip.

SAUTÉD SHREDDED LAMB AND SPRING ONIONS

375 g (12 oz)	boneless lamb (leg or loin)
10	large spring onions (scallions), (or use 2 brown onions),* thinly sliced
¼ cup (2 fl oz)	frying oil
2 teaspoons	sesame oil (optional)

Seasoning A:

½ teaspoon	sugar
½ teaspoon	m.s.g. (optional)
1 tablespoon	light soy sauce
½ teaspoon	rice wine or dry sherry

Seasoning B:

½ teaspoon	sugar
¼ teaspoon	white pepper
¼ teaspoon	m.s.g. (optional)
1 tablespoon	light soy sauce
½ teaspoon	rice wine or dry sherry
2 teaspoons	sesame oil

Partially freeze the lamb, cut into very thin slices across the grain, then cut into shreds. Mix with the seasoning A ingredients and leave to marinate for 20 minutes.

Trim away most of the green parts of the spring onions, cut into 4 cm (1 2/3 in) pieces and shred finely.

Heat the oil with sesame oil, if used, in a wok and when smoking sauté the shredded lamb on fairly high heat until the colour changes, about 1½ minutes. Add the spring onions and fry a further ½ minute, then stir in the pre-mixed seasoning B ingredients and cook on high heat until well mixed and bubbling. Transfer to a serving plate.
* If using sliced brown onions, brown in the oil before cooking the meat.

BRAISED LAMB AND HOT SPICES

750 g (1½ lb)	boneless lamb (leg or shoulder)
125 g (4 oz)	canned bamboo shoots or water chestnuts, drained
90 g (3 oz)	small carrots
¼ cup (2 fl oz)	frying oil or softened lard
2	spring onions (scallions), trimmed and shredded
2 thick slices	fresh ginger, shredded
2 tablespoons	hot bean paste, hot black bean sauce (or 2 teaspoons chilli sauce and 2 tablespoons soy sauce)
1 small bunch	garlic chives or 1 fresh young leek, shredded
2 teaspoons	sesame oil (optional)

Seasoning:

¾ teaspoon	salt
1 teaspoon	sugar
1 tablespoon	light soy sauce
1 teaspoon	rice wine or dry sherry

Trim the lamb and cut into 2.5 cm (1 in) cubes. Cut bamboo shoots into 2 cm (¾ in) cubes, or cut water chestnuts in halves horizontally, if used. Peel and cube the carrots.

Heat the oil or lard in a wok and sauté the lamb on moderately high heat for 1½ — 2 minutes, until lightly coloured. Add the spring onion and ginger, fry briefly, then add the hot bean paste, the bean sauce or chilli and soy sauce mixed together and fry for 1 minute.

Add the seasoning ingredients and water to just cover the meat. Stir well and bring to the boil. Cover the pan, reduce heat to low and simmer for 1½ hours until the lamb is tender. Remove the cover for the last stages of cooking to reduce the sauce. Thicken if needed with a thin solution of cornflour (cornstarch) and cold water.

Stir in the shredded garlic chives or leek and the sesame oil, if used, and transfer to a warmed plate to serve.

BRAISED AND STEAMED WILD DUCK

Serves 10

2 1 kg (2 lb)	wild ducks (or use domestic ducks)
15 large	spring onions (scallions)
155 g (5 oz)	lean pork
125 g (4 oz)	canned bambo shoots, drained
4 thick slices	fresh ginger, bruised
1 cup (8 fl oz)	frying oil
	cornflour (cornstarch)

Seasoning/Sauce:

4 cups (1 litre)	chicken stock
1 cup (8 fl oz)	sugar colouring (see page 388)
⅓ cup	light soy sauce
1½ tablespoons	rice wine or dry sherry
1½ teaspoons	sugar

Clean and dress the ducks. Prick the thighs with a skewer to release any blood and blanch in boiling water for 2 minutes. Drain well, then rinse in cold water and set aside.

Trim the green ends from the onions. Cut each in halves lengthwise, then into 4 cm (1 2/3 in) pieces.

Slice the pork and cut into short strips. Cube the bamboo shoots.

Arrange half the pork with several pieces of onion in a casserole or heavy-based cooking pot and place the ducks, breasts down, on top. Cover with the remaining pork and add several more pieces of onion and the ginger slices. Pour the pre-mixed seasoning/sauce ingredients into the pan and cover. Bring to the boil over high heat, then reduce to low and simmer for 1¾ hours.

Remove the ducks, leave to cool and cut into bite-sized pieces, discarding the bones if preferred.

Fry the remaining onions in the oil until lightly browned. Remove and fry the bamboo shoots until lightly coloured. Place the onions and bamboo shoots in a large dish and arrange the duck meat and pork on top. Pour in ¾ cup (6 fl oz) of the braising liquid and set the dish on a rack in a steaming pot. Cover tightly and steam over high heat for 20 minutes.

Strain the liquid into a wok and bring to the boil. Check seasoning and thicken with a thin solution of cornflour and cold water. Pour over the dish and serve.

WILD DUCK WITH MASHED TARO STUFFING AND OYSTER SAUCE

½ 2 kg (4 lb)	wild duck (or use domestic duck)
2 tablespoons	dark soy sauce
8 cups (2 litres)	deep-frying oil
2	spring onions (scallions), trimmed and shredded
4 slices	fresh ginger, shredded
1½	star anise, broken
1½ teaspoons	Chinese brown peppercorns cornflour (cornstarch)

Stuffing:

500 g (1 lb)	taro, sweet potato or potato, peeled
¾ cup	taro flour (potato flour or cornflour)
½ cup	boiling water
¼ cup (2 fl oz)	softened lard or pastry shortening
1½ teaspoons	salt
½ teaspoon	ground black pepper
2	dried black mushrooms, soaked and finely diced
2 tablespoons	cooked ham, finely diced

Sauce:

1½ tablespoons	oyster sauce
1½ tablespoons	light soy sauce
½ cup (4 fl oz)	chicken stock
1 teaspoon	sugar
	pinch of salt
	pinch of ground black pepper
2 teaspoons	cornflour (cornstarch)
2 tablespoons	finely chopped spring onion (scallion)

Wash the duck and blanch in boiling water. Drain well. Rub with the soy sauce and leave for 15 minutes, then deep-fry in smoking hot deep-frying oil until well coloured, about 3 minutes. Remove and drain well.

Place the duck on a plate, cut side upwards, and sprinkle on the shredded spring onion, ginger, the star anise, and the peppercorns. Set the plate on a rack in a steamer and steam over rapidly boiling water for 1¾ hours.

Boil the taro or potato until soft enough to mash smoothly. Mix the taro flour with the boiling water and add to the mashed taro. Work in the lard, salt pepper, and the diced ingredients and knead to a smooth paste.

Remove the duck and wipe dry. Carefully debone, keeping it in its original shape. Discard the spices, onion, and ginger, and sprinkle with cornflour. Spread the stuffing over the inside of the duck in a thick layer, smoothing the top and edges. Coat lightly with cornflour.

Reheat the deep-frying oil and slide the stuffed duck carefully into the oil. Deep-fry until golden brown and the stuffings crisp. Carefully lift onto a cutting board and cut into bite-sized pieces. Arrange on a plate of shredded lettuce.

Bring the sauce ingredients, except the spring onions, to the boil and simmer until thickened, then add the onions. Pour over the duck or serve as a dip.

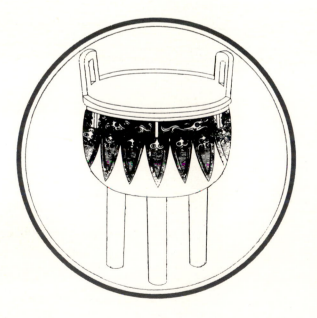

144

Pork and Crabmeat 'Lion's Head' Meatballs (recipe page 136)

WILD DUCK, VEGETABLES, AND ASSORTED MEATS SIMMERED WITH RICE

Serves 6 as a main course

½ — 1½ kg (3 lb)	wild duck (or use domestic duck)
2	spring onions (scallions), trimmed and diced
3 thick slices	fresh ginger, bruised
125 g (4 oz)	lean pork, diced
125 g (4 oz)	boneless chicken, diced
6	dried black mushrooms, soaked for 25 minutes
60 g (2 oz)	Chinese or cured (Smithfield) ham, diced
2 cups (13 oz)	short grain white rice, soaked for 10 minutes
250 g (½ lb)	fresh green vegetables (Chinese cabbage, mustard, broccoli)
1 thin slice	fresh ginger, shredded
1½ tablespoons	frying oil or softened lard

Seasoning A:

½ teaspoon	salt
2 teaspoons	rice wine or dry sherry
	pinch of white pepper

Seasoning B:

2 tablespoons	dried shrimps, soaked (optional)
2 teaspoons	salt
1 teaspoon	m.s.g. (optional)
½ teaspoon	ground black pepper
2 teaspoons	rice wine or dry sherry
1 tablespoon	lard or rendered chicken fat (chicken grease), warmed

Clean and dress the wild duck and place in a saucepan with the diced onions and ginger slices. Cover with water, bring to the boil and simmer, covered, until tender. Remove, drain well and reserve the stock. Debone the duck and cut into small dice.

In another saucepan, simmer the pork and chicken with just enough water to cover, and the seasoning A ingredients. When tender, drain and reserve this stock also.

Squeeze the water from the mushrooms, trim off stems and shred the caps finely.

Mix the duck, pork, chicken, mushrooms, ham, and drained rice thoroughly in a heavy-based saucepan. Stir in the seasoning B ingredients and add equal amounts of the two reserved stocks. The liquid should be 2 cm (¾ in) above the level of the rice and meats. Cover the pan tightly, bring to the boil, then reduce the heat to very low and simmer for 15 minutes.

In the meantime, wash and dry the vegetables, cutting larger stems into pieces about 7.5 cm (3 in) long.

Sauté in the oil or lard for 3 minutes, adding a dash of rice wine, the shredded ginger and seasoning with salt, sugar, and white pepper to taste.

Arrange the vegetables on the rice, re-cover and continue to simmer for a further 6 — 8 minutes until the rice is tender and fluffy.

Transfer the vegetables to a serving plate, making a border around the edge. Stir the rice lightly with a chopstick or the handle of a wooden spoon, pile onto the serving plate.

FROGS' LEGS BRAISED WITH GARLIC

625 g (1¼ lb)	skinned frogs' legs
2 teaspoons	light soy sauce
1 teaspoon	rice wine or dry sherry
12 cloves	garlic, peeled and bruised
¼ cup (2 fl oz)	frying oil or softened lard
2	spring onions (scallions), trimmed and cut into 2.5 cm (1 in) pieces
1 thin slice	fresh ginger, shredded
	sesame oil

Seasoning/Sauce:

½ cup (4 fl oz)	chicken stock or water
2 teaspoons	light soy sauce
¼ teaspoon	salt
½ teaspoon	sugar
	pinch of ground black pepper
½ teaspoon	cornflour (cornstarch)

Divide the frogs' legs at the central joint, rinse in cold water, pat dry and rub with the soy sauce and wine. Set aside for 15 minutes.

Heat the oil or lard in a wok and fry the garlic until lightly coloured. Remove. Increase the heat to high and stir-fry the frogs' legs for 2 minutes and add the onion and ginger. Fry briefly, then pour in the pre-mixed seasoning/sauce ingredients and bring to the boil. Return the garlic, reduce heat and braise for 10 — 12 minutes, covered. Stir in sesame oil to taste and transfer to a serving plate.

Add shredded fresh chilli pepper for extra piquancy, or stir in 1 — 2 teaspoons hot black bean sauce or hot bean paste, adding a little more sugar to taste.

SLICED PHEASANT SAUTÉD WITH BAMBOO SHOOTS AND MUSTARD GREENS

250 g (8 oz)	boneless breast of pheasant (or use wild duck, domestic duck or pigeon)
90 g (3 oz)	canned winter bamboo shoots, drained
45 g (1½ oz)	salted mustard root, soaked for 20 minutes
¼ cup (2 fl oz)	frying oil or softened lard
2	spring onions (scallions), trimmed and diced
2 slices	fresh ginger, shredded
1 teaspoon	sesame oil (optional)
½ teaspoon	white vinegar (optional)

Seasoning A:

1	egg white, beaten
¼ teaspoon	salt
1½ teaspoons	sesame oil (optional)
½ teaspoon	cornflour (cornstarch)

Seasoning B/Sauce:

½ cup (4 fl oz)	chicken stock
1 tablespoon	light soy sauce
½ teaspoon	rice wine or dry sherry
¼ teaspoon	salt
½ teaspoon	m.s.g. (optional)
	pinch of white pepper
¼ teaspoon	sugar
½ teaspoon	cornflour (cornstarch)

Blanch the pheasant breasts in boiling water for 1 minute, drain and slice thinly, then cut into narrow shreds. Mix the meat with the seasoning A ingredients and leave to marinate for 20 minutes. Shred the bamboo shoots and the drained mustard root.

Heat the oil or lard in a wok until smoking and sauté the pheasant on high heat for 1½ minutes. Remove and sauté the bamboo shoots for 1 minute, then add the onions and ginger and sauté briefly before returning the meat.

Add the shredded mustard root and fry for a few seconds, then pour in the pre-mixed seasoning B/sauce ingredients and cook, stirring, until the sauce thickens.

Season with vinegar and sesame oil, if used, and transfer to a warmed serving plate.

DEEP-FRIED BEANCURD, SHRIMP, AND CHICKEN FRITTERS

Serve as an appetiser or main dish.

4 squares	soft beancurd (or 16 pieces canned beancurd, drained)
75 g (2½ oz)	shrimp meat, minced (ground)
60 g (2 oz)	boneless chicken, minced (ground)
60 g (2 oz)	pork fat, minced (ground)
60 g (2 oz)	pine seeds or toasted peanuts
	cornflour (cornstarch)
4 cups (1 litre)	deep-frying oil

Seasoning:

2	egg whites, beaten
1 teaspoon	salt
1 tablespoon	onion and ginger infusion (see page 386)
1½ tablespoons	cornflour (cornstarch)

Mash the beancurd with a fork and mix with the shrimp, chicken, and pork fat. Add the seasoning ingredients and mix thoroughly. Blanch the pine seeds, if used, in boiling water for 1 minute. Drain then dry and deep-fry until golden. Drain and chop finely. Stir half into the beancurd mixture.

Press the mixture into an oiled square baking tin and decorate with the remaining chopped nuts, pressing on lightly. Set the tin on a rack in a steaming pot and steam over rapidly boiling water for 15 — 20 minutes until firm.

Remove the tin from the steamer and invert onto a board. Cut the beancurd into pieces about 4 × 2 cm (1 2/3 × ¾ in) and coat lightly with cornflour.

Heat the deep-frying oil to moderately hot and fry the fritters until golden brown. Drain and season generously with pepper-salt. Serve hot.

RED-BRAISED PIGEONS WITH FIVE SPICES

6	small pigeons, about 825 g / 1¾ lb dressed weight
125 g (4 oz)	lean pork, thinly sliced (optional)
2	spring onions (scallions), cut into 2.5 cm (1 in) pieces
3 thick slices	fresh ginger, bruised
2	spice bags (see page 386)
	sesame oil

Seasoning/Sauce:

1 cup (8 fl oz)	sugar colouring (see page 388)
1 cup (8 fl oz)	light soy sauce
¼ cup (2 fl oz)	rice wine or dry sherry
1 teaspoon	salt
1 teaspoon	m.s.g. (optional)
2/3 cup (5 oz)	sugar

Blanch the pigeons in boiling water for 1 minute, then rinse well in cold water. Place a bamboo rack in a casserole and arrange the pigeons, breasts up, on the rack with the sliced pork on top, if used.

Push the onions, ginger slices, and the two spice bags down the inside of the casserole, taking care not to disturb the pigeons or pork slices. Add the pre-mixed seasoning/sauce ingredients with water to cover.

Bring to the boil, tightly cover the casserole and reduce the heat to low. Simmer for 40 minutes until the pigeons are completely tender. Lift out, brush lightly with sesame oil and arrange the whole birds on a serving plate, breasts up. Keep warm.

Strain the cooking liquid into a wok, bring to the boil and reduce to about 1 cup (8 fl oz). Thicken with a thin solution of cornflour mixed with cold water, if desired, and pour over the pigeons. Serve.

SAUTÉD MINCED PIGEON WITH VEGETABLES AND HOT PEPPERS

185 g (6 oz)	boneless breast of pigeon (or use duck)
¼ cup (2 fl oz)	frying oil or softened lard
125 g (4 oz)	canned water chestnuts, drained and diced
2	spring onions (scallions), trimmed and diced
¾ teaspoon	grated fresh ginger
¾ teaspoon	crushed garlic (or to taste)
1 stalk	fresh celery, diced
1 — 2	fresh red chilli peppers, seeds removed and chopped
1 piece	dried orange peel (see page 416)
	sesame oil
	white vinegar
	toasted white sesame seeds
	prawn crackers (see page 416), optional deep-frying oil, optional

Seasoning A:

1	egg white, beaten
½ teaspoon	salt
2 teaspoons	sesame oil
¾ teaspoon	cornflour (cornstarch)

Seasoning B:

¼ teaspoon	salt
¼ teaspoon	m.s.g. (optional)
1 teaspoon	sugar
¼ teaspoon	ground black pepper
1 tablespoon	light soy sauce
½ teaspoon	rice wine or dry sherry

Blanch the pigeon breasts in boiling water, rinse in cold water and wipe dry. Cut into small dice and mix with the seasoning A ingredients, leaving to marinate for 20 minutes.

Heat the oil or lard in a wok until smoking and sauté the diced pigeon over high heat for 2 minutes. Add the water chestnuts, onion, ginger, and garlic and fry briefly, then add the celery, chilli pepper, and orange peel and continue to sauté on slightly reduced heat for a further 2 minutes.

Increase the heat, add the seasoning B ingredients and fry for 30 seconds. Season with a dash each of sesame oil and vinegar and transfer to a serving plate. Garnish with toasted sesame seeds.

If the prawn crackers are used, they should be quickly fried in very hot deep-frying oil until they expand and become crisp. Drain well and arrange around the dish.

'Su Tung Po' Pork (recipe page 138).

WINTER BAMBOO SHOOTS IN CHICKEN OIL SAUCE

1 315 (10 g oz) can	winter bamboo shoots, drained
1 cup (8 fl oz)	frying oil
60 g (2 oz)	fresh spinach, mustard or watercress, finely chopped
2 tablespoons	rendered chicken fat (chicken grease)
30 g (1 oz)	Chinese or cured (Smithfield) ham, finely shredded

Seasoning/Sauce:

¾ cup (6 fl oz)	chicken stock
½ teaspoon	rice wine
½ teaspoon	salt
¼ teaspoon	m.s.g. (optional)
½ teaspoon	sugar
¾ teaspoon	cornflour (cornstarch)

Thinly slice the bamboo shoots. Warm the frying oil in a wok and gently cook the bamboo shoots for 2 minutes. Remove and drain.

Thoroughly wash the green vegetables and squeeze out as much water as possible. Drain off all but 2 tablespoons oil from the wok, reheat to moderate and fry the chopped vegetables for 1 minute. Return the bamboo shoots and add the pre-mixed seasoning/sauce ingredients. Bring to the boil and cook, stirring, until the sauce thickens.

Stir in the chicken fat and heat through. Transfer to a serving plate and garnish with the shredded ham.

STEAMED BLACK MUSHROOMS WITH SHRIMP STUFFING

Serve as an appetiser or main dish.

12	large black mushrooms, soaked for 25 minutes
155 g (5 oz)	fresh prawn meat (shrimp meat) minced (ground)
60 g (2 oz)	fatty pork, finely minced (ground) cornflour (cornstarch)
1	hard-boiled (hardcooked) egg yolk large bunch of fresh coriander leaves (optional)

Seasoning A:

2 cups (16 fl oz)	chicken stock
¾ teaspoon	salt
½ teaspoon	m.s.g. (optional)
1	spring onion (scallion), trimmed and sliced
2 slices	fresh ginger, bruised

Seasoning B:

1	egg white, beaten
½ teaspoon	ginger wine (see page 387)
⅓ teaspoon	salt
½ teaspoon	m.s.g. (optional) pinch of white pepper
2 teaspoons	cornflour (cornstarch)

Sauce:

1 tablespoon	frying oil
½ cup (4 fl oz)	chicken stock
¼ teaspoon	salt
¾ teaspoon	cornflour (cornstarch)

Drain the mushrooms and squeeze out excess water. Remove the stems and simmer the caps in a saucepan with the seasoning A ingredients for 40 minutes.

Mix the minced prawn and pork meat with the seasoning B ingredients, kneading to a smooth paste.

Drain the mushrooms and squeeze dry again. Coat the undersides lightly with cornflour and press in a generous amount of the filling, smoothing the edges.

Garnish with the egg yolk, finely chopped, and set on an oiled plate to steam.

Bring the stock used to simmer the mushrooms (or use water) to boil in a steaming pot and add the washed coriander. Set a rack on top and place the mushrooms on their plate on this. Cover tightly and steam over high heat for 10 minutes.

Heat the wok and add the frying oil. When it is smoking, pour in the remaining pre-mixed sauce ingredients and bring to the boil, stirring. Drain any liquid from the mushroom plate into the wok and mix well, then pour the sauce over the mushrooms and serve.

CAULIFLOWER WITH CREAMED CHICKEN SAUCE

625 g (1¼ lb)	fresh cauliflower, divided into florets
2 teaspoons	salt
125 g (4 oz)	boneless chicken, finely minced (ground)
30 g (1 oz)	pork fat, finely minced (ground)
⅓ cup	frying oil
1 tablespoon	finely chopped cooked ham or spring onion

Seasoning:

½ teaspoon	salt
½ teaspoon	m.s.g. (optional)
1 teaspoon	ginger wine (see page 387)
1	egg white, beaten
1½ tablespoons	cornflour (cornstarch)
½ cup (4 fl oz)	chicken stock

Sauce:

1 cup (8 fl oz)	chicken stock
¾ teaspoon	salt
½ teaspoon	m.s.g. (optional)
	pinch of white pepper

Wash the cauliflower, drain, then boil in water to cover with the salt added for 2 minutes. Drain well and leave to cool.

Mix the minced chicken and pork fat with the seasoning ingredients, stirring to a smooth creamy paste.

Heat half the oil to warm and fry the chicken cream until it turns white, about 2 minutes. Remove and rinse the pan. Add the remaining oil and stir-fry the cauliflower on fairly high heat for 2 minutes, then add the pre-mixed sauce ingredients and bring to the boil.

Cook on moderately high heat until the liquid has evaporated and the cauliflower is tender but retaining crispness.

Pour in the creamed chicken and mix in carefully. Warm through, then transfer to a warmed serving plate and garnish with the ham or onion.

LIMA BEANS SAUTÉD WITH MUSHROOMS, HAM, AND SHRIMPS

250 g (8 oz)	shelled fresh or frozen lima (fava)beans
60 g (2 oz)	raw shrimps, peeled
2 tablespoons	frying oil or softened lard
30 g (1 oz)	canned champignons, thinly sliced
2 — 3 teaspoons	rendered chicken fat (chicken grease)
1 tablespoon	finely diced cooked ham

Seasoning A:

½	egg white, beaten
¼ teaspoon	salt
¼ teaspoon	cornflour (cornstarch)

Seasoning B/Sauce:

½ cup (4 fl oz)	chicken stock
¼ teaspoon	salt
½ teaspoon	m.s.g. (optional)
½ teaspoon	sugar
½ teaspoon	rice wine or dry sherry
½ teaspoon	cornflour (cornstarch)

Rinse or thaw the beans and dry thoroughly. Mix the shrimps with the seasoning A ingredients and leave to marinate for 15 minutes. Heat the wok and add the oil or lard. Fry the lima beans on moderate heat until they turn bright green, about 2 minutes, then add the shrimps and sliced mushrooms and fry together, stirring frequently, for 1 minute.

Pour in the pre-mixed seasoning B/sauce ingredients and bring to the boil. Reduce the heat and simmer for 2 minutes, then stir in the diced ham and chicken fat and warm through.

CRISP-FRIED SALTED MUSTARD GREENS WITH BAMBOO SHOOTS

1 500g (1 lb) can	bamboo shoots, drained
75 g (2½ oz)	dried salted mustard leaves, soaked for 20 minutes
4 cups (1 litre)	deep-frying oil
2	spring onions (scallions), shredded
2 teaspoons	sesame oil (optional)

Seasoning/Sauce:

½ cup (4 fl oz)	chicken stock
1 tablespoon	light soy sauce
½ teaspoon	rice wine or dry sherry
½ teaspoon	m.s.g. (optional)
½ teaspoon	sugar

Cut the bamboo shoots into 2.5 cm (1 in) cubes. Drain the mustard leaves and squeeze out the excess water, cut into pieces about 5 cm (2 in) square.

Heat the deep-frying oil to smoking point and deep-fry the mustard greens until crisp. Remove and drain well. Add the bamboo shoots and fry until crisped on the surface and well coloured. Remove.

Drain off all but 1 tablespoon oil and pour in the pre-mixed seasoning/sauce ingredients and bring to the boil. Return the bamboo shoots and cook on high heat until the sauce is well reduced. Stir occasionally. Add the onions, cook briefly and transfer with the bamboo shoots and sauce to a warmed serving plate. Surround with the crisp mustard leaves and sprinkle on sesame oil, if used.

FRESH MUSTARD GREENS WITH SCALLOPS IN CREAM SAUCE

750 g (1½ lb)	fresh mustard greens or Chinese spinach
6 pieces	dried scallops (about 1½ oz), soaked for 2 hours

Seasoning A:

1 tablespoon	rice wine or dry sherry
1	spring onion (scallion), trimmed
1 slice	fresh ginger, bruised
1 cup (8 fl oz)	chicken stock

Seasoning B:

¾ teaspoon	salt
½ teaspoon	m.s.g. (optional)
¾ teaspoon	sugar
1 teaspoon	rice wine or dry sherry
¼ cup (2 fl oz)	chicken stock

Sauce:

¾ cup (6 fl oz)	chicken stock
2 teaspoons	rendered chicken fat (chicken grease)
2 tablespoons	evaporated or fresh milk
1 teaspoon	cornflour (cornstarch)

Thoroughly wash the vegetables and cut into 10 cm (4 in) pieces. Steam the dried scallops with the seasoning A ingredients for 1 hour, then drain and shred, using fingers.

Simmer the vegetables with the seasoning B ingredients, tightly covered, for 10 minutes. Add the shredded scallops and simmer a further 5 minutes. Drain and remove to a serving plate. Bring the sauce to the boil and simmer until thickened. Pour over the vegetables and scallops and serve.

Wild Duck, Vegetables, and Assorted Meats Simmered with Rice (recipe page 146).

CHOPPED PEA SPROUTS WITH CREAMED CHICKEN

500 g (1 lb)	sweet pea sprouts (spinach or watercress)
155 g (5 oz)	boneless chicken, minced (ground)
60 g (2 oz)	pork fat, minced (ground)
1/3 cup	frying oil or softened lard

Seasoning A:

1	egg white, beaten
1/2 teaspoon	salt
1/2 teaspoon	m.s.g. (optional)
1 tablespoon	onion and ginger infusion (see page 386)
2 teaspoons	rice wine or dry sherry
1 tablespoon	cornflour (cornstarch)
3/4 cup (6 fl oz)	chicken stock

Seasoning B:

3/4 teaspoon	salt
1/4 teaspoon	m.s.g. (optional)
1/2 teaspoon	sugar
1/3 cup	chicken stock
3/4 teaspoon	cornflour (cornstarch)

Wash the pea sprouts or other vegetables and chop finely. Mix the chicken and pork fat with the seasoning A ingredients and stir until smooth and creamy.

Heat half the oil or lard in a wok and gently fry the chicken mixture until it turns white. Remove to one side of a warmed serving plate. Keep warm. Add the remaining oil and gently fry the vegetables for 5 minutes, adding the seasoning B ingredients after the first 2 minutes. Pour onto the other side of the plate and serve.

ASSORTED SAUTÉD VEGETABLES IN CREAM SAUCE

2	small cucumbers
6	dried black mushrooms, soaked for 25 minutes
2	medium carrots, sliced
60 g (2 oz)	sweet white turnips, peeled and cubed
4 cups (1 litre)	chicken stock
1/3 cup	frying oil
45 g (1 1/2 oz)	canned bamboo shoots, drained and sliced
6 cubes	deep-fried beancurd, soaked for 10 minutes (optional)
1 tablespoon	rendered chicken fat (chicken grease), optional

Seasoning/Sauce:

3/4 cup (6 fl oz)	chicken stock
1 tablespoon	light soy sauce
3/4 teaspoon	salt
1/2 teaspoon	m.s.g. (optional)
1/2 teaspoon	sugar
1 teaspoon	cornflour (cornstarch)

Cut the cucumber into sticks about 5 cm (2 in) long and discard the seeds but do not peel. Drain the mushrooms and remove stems. Parboil the cucumbers, mushrooms, carrots, and turnips in the chicken stock for 5 minutes and drain well.

Heat the oil in a wok and sauté all the vegetables together for 2 minutes. Add the beancurd, if used, after squeezing out excess water. Fry for 2 minutes, then pour in the pre-mixed seasoning/sauce ingredients and bring to the boil. Simmer for 1 minute, stir in the chicken fat, if used, and transfer to a serving plate.

CHINESE CABBAGE WITH CRABMEAT AND CRAB ROE SAUCE

625 g (1¼ lb)	Chinese cabbage (celery cabbage)
1½ teaspoons	salt
½ cup (4 fl oz)	frying oil or softened lard
1 tablespoon	finely chopped spring onion (scallion)
¼ teaspoon	grated fresh ginger
75 g (2½ oz)	fresh frozen or canned crabmeat
15 g (½ oz)	crab roe (optional)

Seasoning A:

¾ cup (6 fl oz)	chicken stock
1 teaspoon	salt
¾ teaspoon	sugar
¼ teaspoon	white pepper

Seasoning B/Sauce:

1¼ cups (10 fl oz)	chicken stock
¾ teaspoon	salt
½ teaspoon	rice wine or dry sherry
1 tablespoon	cornflour (cornstarch)
2	egg whites, well beaten

Thoroughly wash the cabbage and cut into 10 cm (4 in) pieces. Parboil in water to cover with the salt added, or in chicken stock, for 2 minutes. Drain well. Heat half the oil in a wok and sauté the cabbage for 3 minutes. Add the seasoning A ingredients and bring to the boil. Simmer for 2 minutes. Drain and arrange on a serving plate.

Heat the remaining oil and fry onion and ginger for 45 seconds. Add the crabmeat and sauté for 2 minutes, then add the pre-mixed seasoning B/sauce ingredients and bring to the boil. Stir in the crab roe and slowly drizzle in the beaten eggs which will set into white strings in the sauce. Heat for 1 minute, then pour over the cabbage and serve.

Florets of broccoli or cauliflower are also excellent with this sauce.

BAMBOO SHOOTS WITH CHICKEN, HAM, AND SPINACH BALLS IN SOUP

90 g (3 oz)	boneless chicken, minced (ground)
1½ tablespoons	finely chopped cooked ham
90 g (3 oz)	fresh young spinach leaves (collard greens), washed
125 g (3 oz)	canned bamboo shoots, drained and thinly sliced
6 cups (1½ litres)	chicken stock
2	spring onions (scallions), cut in halves
3 thick slices	fresh ginger, bruised
1 tablespoon	rice wine or dry sherry (optional)
1½ teaspoons	salt, or to taste

Seasoning:

1	egg white, beaten
1 teaspoon	ginger wine (see page 387)
¼ teaspoon	salt
¼ teaspoon	m.s.g. (optional)
2 teaspoons	cornflour (cornstarch)

Mix the chicken and ham with the seasoning ingredients, knead well, then form into small balls. Wrap a spinach leaf around each ball, squeezing to hold in shape.

Bring the chicken stock to the boil, then reduce heat to a gentle simmer. Add the bamboo shoots, spring onions, and ginger, the rice wine, if used, and salt. Simmer for 2 — 3 minutes, then add the chicken balls and simmer in the soup until cooked through, about 5 minutes. Transfer to a soup tureen and serve.

RADISH BALLS WITH SCALLOPS IN CREAM SAUCE

375 g (12 oz)	peeled giant white (icicle) radishes, sweet white turnips or about 24 small red radishes, peeled
1½ teaspoons	salt
4 pieces (30 g / 1 oz)	dried scallops, soaked for 2 hours
2 cups (16 fl oz)	chicken stock
1 thick slice	fresh ginger, bruised
2 slices	fresh ginger, shredded
⅓ cup	frying oil or softened lard
1 tablespoon	rendered chicken fat (chicken grease)

Seasoning/Sauce:

¾ teaspoon	salt
½ teaspoon	m.s.g. (optional)
½ teaspoon	sugar
1 teaspoon	rice wine or dry sherry

Wash the radishes or turnips and use a melon scoop to form into balls. Boil for 10 minutes in water to cover with the salt added. Drain well. Simmer the drained scallops in the chicken stock with the slice of ginger for 1 hour, until completely tender. Drain and reserve the liquid. Shred the scallops by rubbing gently between forefinger and thumb.

Heat the frying oil or lard in a wok and fry the vegetable balls with shredded ginger for 1½ minutes. Add the shredded scallop and fry briefly, then pour in the reserved stock mixed with the seasoning/sauce ingredients and bring to the boil.

Thicken with a paste of 1 tablespoon cornflour mixed with 1 tablespoon cold water and stir in the chicken fat. Transfer to a serving dish.

TOMATOES IN CREAM SAUCE

500 g (1 lb)	firm ripe tomatoes
1 tablespoon	cornflour (cornstarch)
¼ cup (2 fl oz)	fresh milk
2 teaspoons	rendered chicken fat (chicken grease) (optional)

Seasoning:

¾ teaspoon	salt
½ teaspoon	m.s.g. (optional)
2 teaspoons	rice wine or dry sherry
¾ teaspoon	sugar
½ cup (4 fl oz)	chicken stock

Scald the tomatoes in boiling water for 8 seconds, drain and peel. Cut into quarters. Simmer in a wok with the seasoning ingredients until softened, about 4 minutes, then thicken the sauce with the cornflour mixed with milk. Add the chicken fat, if used, and serve.

SPINACH EGG PUFFS

Serve as an appetiser or accompanying a main course.

500 g (1 lb)	fresh spinach (collard greens)
8	egg whites
½ teaspoon	salt
2 tablespoons	flour
1 tablespoon	cornflour (cornstarch)
6 cups (1½ litres)	deep-frying oil
	Chinese pepper-salt

Thoroughly wash the spinach and squeeze out as much water as possible. Spread on kitchen towels and leave to dry, then cut into pieces about 5 cm (2 in) long.

Beat the egg whites to stiff peaks and gently fold in the salt, flour, and cornflour. Heat the deep-frying oil to moderate. Dip small bundles of the spinach into the egg batter, coating thickly. Deep-fry until golden and cooked through, about 2½ minutes.

Drain well and sprinkle generously with pepper-salt before serving.

Radish Balls with Scallops in Cream Sauce (recipe this page).

STEAMED ASPARAGUS ON EGG CUSTARD

1 315 g (10 oz) can	asparagus spears, drained
8	eggs
1 tablespoon	shredded cooked ham

Seasoning:

¾ teaspoon	salt
½ teaspoon	m.s.g. (optional)
2 tablespoons	chicken stock

Sauce:

¾ cup (6 fl oz)	chicken stock
½ teaspoon	rice wine or dry sherry
¼ teaspoon	salt
¼ teaspoon	m.s.g. (optional)
½ teaspoon	cornflour (cornstarch)

Soak the asparagus in cold water for 10 minutes. Drain well. Discard three egg yolks and beat the remaining eggs and whites together, adding the seasoning ingredients.

Pour into an oiled dish and set on a rack in a steamer. Steam over rapidly boiling water for 10 minutes. Arrange the well-drained asparagus on top and steam for a few more minutes until set.

In a wok or saucepan, boil the sauce ingredients together until thickened. Pour over the egg and garnish with the ham.

EGGPLANT BRAISED WITH SOYBEAN PASTE

375 g (¾ lb)	eggplant (aubergine)
2 teaspoons	salt
2 cups (16 fl oz)	deep-frying oil
2 tablespoons	finely chopped spring onion (scallion)
1¼ teaspoons	grated fresh ginger
1½ teaspoons	crushed garlic
1¼ tablespoons	soybean paste (or hot bean paste, if preferred)
	sesame oil

Seasoning/Sauce:

½ cup (4 fl oz)	chicken stock
1 tablespoon	light soy sauce
1 teaspoon	rice wine or dry sherry
½ teaspoon	m.s.g. (optional)
1 tablespoon	sugar

Wash the eggplants, remove skin if preferred, and cut into 2.5 cm (1 in) cubes. Sprinkle on the salt, cover with a plate and leave, weighted lightly, for 45 minutes. Rinse in cold water and pat dry.

Deep-fry the eggplant in moderately hot oil until brown. Drain and pour off all but 2 tablespoons oil.

Sauté the onion, ginger, and garlic for 1 minute, add the bean paste and cook a further 1 minute, stirring constantly.

Pour in the pre-mixed seasoning/sauce ingredients and bring to the boil. Return the eggplant, reduce heat and cook, covered, until the eggplant is tender and the sauce absorbed. Stir in a dash of sesame oil.

SLICED CUCUMBER STUFFED WITH SHRIMP AND PORK

2	large cucumbers
60 g (2 oz)	fresh shrimp meat, minced (ground)
185 g (6 oz)	fatty pork, finely minced (ground)
1 tablespoon	finely chopped spring onion (scallion)
1 teaspoon	grated fresh ginger
	cornflour (cornstarch)
2 cups (16 fl oz)	frying oil

Seasoning A:

1	egg white, beaten
2 teaspoons	light soy sauce
1 teaspoon	rice wine or dry sherry
¼ teaspoon	salt
¼ teaspoon	m.s.g. (optional)
¾ teaspoon	sugar

Seasoning B/Sauce:

¾ cup (6 fl oz)	chicken stock
1 tablespoon	light soy sauce
½ teaspoon	rice wine or dry sherry
1 teaspoon	salt
¾ teaspoon	sugar

Cut the cucumbers into 4 cm (1 2/3 in) pieces without peeling and use a sharp paring knife to trim away the seed cores. Mix the shrimp, pork, onion, and ginger with the seasoning A ingredients, kneading to a smooth paste. Dust the cucumber rings with cornflour and fill with the prepared stuffing. Smooth the edges and coat lightly all over with cornflour.

Heat the shallow oil to moderate and fry the cucumbers on both sides until golden brown, about 3 minutes. Drain well.

Bring the seasoning B/sauce ingredients to the boil in another pan. Add the stuffed cucumbers and simmer, covered, for 20 minutes. Remove the lid and continue to cook until the cucumber is tender and the sauce well reduced.

Transfer cucumbers to a serving plate. Reheat the sauce and adjust seasonings. Thicken, if preferred, with a thin solution of cornflour (cornstarch) and cold water. Pour over the cucumbers and serve.

PORK AND CABBAGE DUMPLINGS

Makes 24

Pastry:

2 cups	flour
1	whole egg, well beaten
¾ cup	water
1 teaspoon	baking powder
¾ teaspoon	salt

Filling:

185 g (6 oz)	lean pork, finely minced (ground)
3	cabbage leaves, finely chopped
1 tablespoon	finely chopped spring onion (scallion)
½ teaspoon	crushed garlic
1½ tablespoons	frying oil

Seasoning:

1 tablespoon	light soy sauce
2 teaspoons	rice wine or dry sherry
2 teaspoons	sesame oil
2 teaspoons	sugar
¼ teaspoon	ground black pepper
2 tablespoons	water
2½ teaspoons	cornflour (cornstarch)
3 — 4	fresh cabbage leaves, blanched

Sift the flour into a mixing bowl and make a well in the centre. Add the beaten egg and half the water. Mix lightly into the flour, then add the baking powder and salt and slowly add the remaining water to make a soft batter. Knead for 4 — 5 minutes, then cover with a damp cloth and set aside.

Mix the filling ingredients together and fry in the oil for 2 minutes. Add the seasoning ingredients (excluding the whole cabbage leaves) and sauté until the mixture thickens. Transfer to a plate to cool.

Roll the dough into a long sausage shape and divide into 24 parts.

Roll each into a ball and roll out flat on a lightly greased board, using a dry rolling pin and ensuring the top side does not become greasy. Place a spoonful of the filling in the centre of each wrapper and pull up the edges to meet at the top. Pleat into a central point and twist the point to seal in the filling. Hold by the points and press the dumplings, one by one, to flatten the bases.

Use the cabbage leaves to line large bamboo steaming baskets and set the dumplings on top. Steam over high heat for about 15 minutes, then serve hot in the baskets.

DUCK IN ORANGE-FLAVOURED SOUP

1½ — 2 kg (4 lb)	duck
1½ teaspoons	salt
2 tablespoons	rice wine or dry sherry
6 cups (1½ litres)	deep-frying oil
5 cups (1¼ litres)	water
6 pieces	dried orange peel
3 pieces	fresh ginger
15 g (1 oz)	dried 'wood ear' or 'snow' fungus, soaked for 25 minutes
	white pepper

Wash the duck and rub with the salt and wine. Leave for 30 minutes, then wipe the skin. Heat the deep-frying oil to smoking point and deep-fry the duck until lightly coloured. Remove and drain well, then wipe off excess oil.

Bring the water to the boil and add the orange peel and ginger. Transfer to a casserole, place the duck in the stock, cover and simmer on very low heat until the duck is completely tender, about 1½ hours.

Drain the fungus and cut into bite-sized pieces. Add to the pot in the last 25 minutes of cooking. Check the seasonings and add a dash of white pepper. Serve in the casserole.

ASPARAGUS AND PIGEON EGG SOUP

½ 315 g (10 oz) can	asparagus spears or cuts
1 280 g (9 oz) can	quail or pigeon eggs
5 cups (1¼ litres)	chicken stock
1½ teaspoons	salt
½ teaspoon	m.s.g. (optional)
¼ teaspoon	ground black pepper
2 teaspoons	rice wine or dry sherry
2 teaspoons	softened lard

Drain the asparagus and eggs. If using asparagus spears, cut in halves. Divide among individual soup bowls.

Bring the chicken stock to the boil and add the remaining ingredients. Simmer for 2 minutes, then pour over the asparagus and eggs and serve at once.

WHITE FUNGUS, PIGEON EGGS, AND DICED HAM SOUP

45 g (1½ oz)	dried white (snow) fungus, soaked for 1 hour
12	pigeon eggs*
2 teaspoons	finely chopped cooked ham
2 teaspoons	finely chopped fresh coriander
5 cups (1¼ litres)	chicken stock
2 teaspoons	rice wine or dry sherry
1½ teaspoons	salt
½ teaspoon	m.s.g. (optional)
¼ teaspoon	ground black pepper

Prepare the white fungus according to the directions on page 393 Lightly grease 12 small soy sauce dishes and break an egg into each. Garnish with the ham and coriander and set on a rack in a steamer to steam until set, about 5 minutes. Remove the eggs from the dishes and soak in cold water for 10 minutes.

Bring the chicken stock to the boil and add the wine, salt, m.s.g., if used, and pepper. Simmer for 1 minute, then add the white fungus and simmer for 2 — 3 minutes. Drain the eggs and pour on a cupful of the boiling stock to heat through, then drain, returning the stock to the saucepan to reheat and divide the eggs among 6 individual soup bowls.

Pour the stock and the fungus over the eggs and serve.
* If fresh pigeon eggs are unobtainable, used canned quail or pigeon eggs. As these are hard boiled (hard cooked), the diced ham and coriander may be omitted or added to the soup as a garnish.

YOUNG PIGEONS AND HAM STEAMED IN SOUP

3	young pigeons, plucked and cleaned (about 625 g (1¼ lb)
60 g (2 oz)	Chinese or cured (Smithfield) ham, sliced
6 cups (1½ litres)	hot chicken stock
1 tablepoon	rice wine or dry sherry
¾ teaspoon	salt
¼ teaspoon	ground black pepper
1	spring onion (scallion), trimmed and sliced
3 slices	fresh ginger
½ teaspoon	m.s.g. (optional)

Cut the pigeons in halves and boil gently in just enough water to cover for 20 minutes. Drain and rinse in cold water. Arrange the pigeons in a casserole with the sliced ham on top. Add the hot chicken stock, wine, salt and pepper, the spring onion and ginger. Cover and set on a rack in a steamer to steam over gently boiling water for 2½ — 3 hours until the pigeons are completely tender.

Remove from the heat, adjust the seasonings, and add m.s.g., if used. Discard the ginger and onion and serve in the casserole.

Avoid stirring the dish during cooking to maintain optimum clarity of the stock.

CHICKEN SLIVERS AND JASMINE IN CLEAR BROTH

90 g (3 oz)	boneless chicken breast
12	jasmine flowers
6 cups (1½ litres)	chicken stock
2	spring onions (scallions), trimmed and diced
3 slices	fresh ginger, shredded
	cornflour (cornstarch)

Seasoning A:

1	egg white, beaten
¼ teaspoon	salt
½ teaspoon	m.s.g. (optional)
½ teaspoon	sugar
	pinch of white pepper
2 teaspoons	cornflour (cornstarch)

Seasoning B:

1 tablespoon	rice wine or dry sherry
1¼ teaspoons	salt
¼ teaspoon	m.s.g. (optional)
¼ teaspoon	ground black pepper

Cut the chicken into small cubes. Mix with the seasoning A ingredients and leave for 5 minutes. Trim the stems from the jasmine flowers and rinse in cold water. Bring the chicken stock to the boil, add the onions, ginger, and the seasoning B ingredients and simmer on low heat.

Spread cornflour thickly over a board. Roll the chicken cubes in the cornflour, then bat with the side of a cleaver, alternating with a further coating of cornflour, until the chicken is reduced to thin, near transparent slivers.

Bring a saucepan of water to the boil, then turn heat to the lowest point and leave until it stops bubbling. Add the chicken and cook until white, about 1½ minutes. Drain and rinse in cold water.

Place two jasmine flowers into each of six individual soup bowls.

Add the chicken slivers to the simmering soup, cook briefly, then pour over the jasmine. Serve immediately. The jasmine flavour may be enhanced by simmering them in hot stock for 1 — 2 minutes before adding the chicken, if preferred.

CREAMY FISH SOUP WITH SOUR AND HOT FLAVOURS

1 750 g (1½ lb)	yellow fish (herring, sea bass, or flounder)
90 g (3 oz)	prepared sea cucumber (optional), or use 2 squares soft beancurd, diced, or 90 g (3 oz) diced fresh squid
30 g (1 oz)	canned bamboo shoot, drained and diced
2	spring onions (scallions), trimmed and diced
2 slices	fresh ginger, shredded
⅓ cup	frying oil or softened lard
1½ cups (12 fl oz)	chicken stock
2	egg whites, well beaten
2 tablespoons	white vinegar
1	spring onion (scallion), trimmed and finely shredded
2 slices	fresh ginger, finely shredded

Seasoning:

2 teaspoons	salt
¼ teaspoon	sugar
¼ teaspoon	ground white pepper
2 teaspoons	rice wine or dry sherry
1 tablespoon	cornflour (cornstarch)
1 tablespoon	cold water

Clean and scale the fish and wash well. Place in a saucepan with water to cover and bring to the boil. Simmer until the meat is tender enough to flake from the bones. Strain the liquid into a jug and set aside. Flake the meat and discard the head and bones.

Fry the spring onions and ginger in the oil or lard for about 1 minute until lightly coloured and beginning to soften. Add the sea cucumber and the bamboo shoots and fry lightly. Pour in the strained stock and bring to the boil, adding the chicken stock and seasoning ingredients. Simmer for 3 minutes, then add the flaked fish.

If beancurd or squid are being used instead of sea cucumber, add at this point. Simmer for 2 minutes, then slowly drizzle in the beaten egg and add the vinegar. Cook without stirring for 1 minute, then transfer to a soup tureen and garnish with the shredded spring onion and ginger.

SILVER CARP'S HEAD IN RICH SOUP

1 1 kg (2 lb)	silver carp's head or several fish heads of the same weight
2 slices	fresh ginger
45 g (1½ oz)	straw mushrooms, or 3 dried black mushrooms soaked to soften
45 g (1½ oz)	Chinese or cured (Smithfield) ham
30 g (1 oz)	chicken breast or leg meat
6	young Chinese green vegetables
6 cups (1½ litres)	chicken or enriched stock
2 tablespoons	softened lard
2	spring onions (scallions), trimmed and shredded
4 slices	fresh ginger, shredded
1 tablespoon	rendered chicken fat (chicken grease)
	salt
	m.s.g. (optional)

Wash the fish head(s) and cut in halves. Place in a saucepan with water to cover and bring to the boil. Add the sliced ginger and simmer the fish heads until completely tender. Drain and scrape all the meat from the bones, then discard the bones and ginger.

Finely shred the mushrooms, ham, and chicken and thoroughly wash the vegetables. Bring the chicken or enriched stock to the boil and add the fish meat. Simmer gently. Heat the lard and sauté the spring onions and ginger briefly, then add the mushrooms, ham, and chicken and sauté for 1 minute. Transfer to the soup and simmer for 2 minutes, then add the vegetables and simmer until tender. Add the chicken fat, salt to taste, and the m.s.g., if used, and transfer to a soup tureen.

ASSORTED MEAT AND CHRYSANTHEMUM FIRE-POT

Serves 6 — 8 as the main course.

125 g (4 oz)	boneless fish fillet
125 g (4 oz)	fillet of beef (tenderloin)
125 g (4 oz)	boneless chicken breast
125 g (4 oz)	lean pork
125 g (4 oz)	pork kidney, trimmed and blanched
125 g (4 oz)	peeled raw prawns (shrimps)
60 g (2 oz)	frozen wonton wrappers, thawed and sliced
30 g (1 oz)	bean thread vermicelli, broken into short pieces and deep-fried until crisp (about 15 seconds)
90 g (3 oz)	fresh spinach leaves (collard greens), well washed
30 g (1 oz)	white chrysanthemum petals, well washed (or use sliced champignons or bamboo shoots)
90 g (3 oz)	young bok choy or other green vegetable leaves
60 g (2 oz)	young cabbage hearts, halved and well washed small bunch of fresh coriander
8 cups (2 litres)	chicken stock

Seasoning:

2	spring onions (scallions), cut in halves
3 thick slices	fresh ginger, bruised
1 tablespoon	rice wine or dry sherry

Sauce Dip:

3 tablespoons	finely chopped spring onion (scallion)
3 tablespoons	finely shredded fresh ginger
3 tablespoons	finely chopped fresh coriander
2 tablespoons	sesame paste (mixed with 2 tablespoons cold water)
¼ cup (2 fl oz)	rice wine or dry sherry
¾ cup (6 fl oz)	light soy sauce
¼ cup (2 fl oz)	peanut or vegetable oil
2 tablespoons	sesame oil (optional)
¼ cup (2 fl oz)	white vinegar
1 tablespoon	chilli oil, or to taste
	salt
	m.s.g. (optional)
	ground black pepper

Special Equipment: A charcoal 'fire-pot,' or a table-top gas or electric cooker, wooden chopsticks.

To prepare the sauce dip, place the spring onion, ginger, and coriander on small individual plates. Mix the remaining ingredients, adding more or less of each according to taste. Divide among 6 — 8 small bowls and place on the table with a pair of wooden chopsticks for each diner.

Partially freeze the meat to make it easier to cut into wafer-thin slices. Arrange on individual plates. Cut the prawns in halves, lengthwise, or slice any large ones. Serve all the remaining ingredients except the chicken stock and seasonings, on separate plates.

Heat the fire-pot or a large stewpan and bring the chicken stock to the boil. Add the seasoning ingredients.

Cook the meats first, holding them in the bubbling stock with the wooden chopsticks. When the stock has been enriched by the meats, add the vegetables and other ingredients. Both meat and vegetables should be cooked rare to retain maximum flavour and texture.

Mix chopped spring onion, ginger, and coriander into the sauce dip to taste and dunk each mouthful before eating.

The soup may be served at the end of the meal, with a splash of the sauce dip for extra flavour.

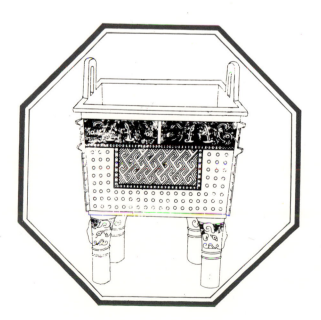

SALTED AND FRESH PORK IN SOUP

250 g (8 oz)	salt-cooked pork (see page 136. Slow Cooked Corned Pork)
250 g (8 oz)	'five flowered' pork (belly/fresh bacon)
5 cups (1¼ litres)	chicken stock
60 g (2 oz)	canned bamboo shoots, drained and diced
1 tablespoon	finely chopped spring onion (scallion)
¾ teaspoon	finely shredded fresh ginger
1 tablespoon	rice wine or dry sherry
½ teaspoon	m.s.g. (optional)
	salt to taste

Cut the salt-cooked pork and the fresh pork into small cubes. Parboil the fresh pork only in water to cover for 3 minutes. Drain and rinse with cold water.

Bring the chicken stock to the boil and add the meats, bamboo shoots, onion, ginger, and the wine. Bring to the boil. Skim, then reduce heat to very low, cover tightly and simmer until the meat is completely tender. Skim once or twice during cooking, if necessary. Very slow cooking will ensure that the soup remains clear, with flavours well blended and the meat tender rather than stringy.

Add the m.s.g., if used, and salt to taste just before serving.

ASSORTED MEAT AND VEGETABLES IN WINTER MELON

8 pieces	dry scallops, soaked for 1 hour (about 60 g (2 oz))
1 3½ — 4 kg (7 — 8 lb)	winter melon
1 set	duck gizzards, trimmed and diced
4	dried black mushrooms, soaked for 25 minutes
125 g (4 oz)	cooked duck meat, diced
20 g (1 oz)	Chinese or cured (Smithfield) ham, diced
60 g (2 oz)	peeled raw shrimps, well washed
60 g (2 oz)	canned champignons, drained and sliced
6 slices	fresh ginger, bruised
5 — 6 cups (1¼ — 1½ litres)	chicken stock, heated
1 tablespoon	rice wine or dry sherry (optional)
1½ teaspoons	salt, or to taste
1 teaspoon	m.s.g. (optional)
1 tablespoon	rendered chicken fat (chicken grease) (optional)

Cover the dry scallops with ½ cup chicken stock and steam for 1 hour until tender, then drain and flake between forefinger and thumb. Wash the winter melon and remove the top section with a sharp knife. Carve a scalloped or zig-zag pattern around the rim. Scoop out the seeds and discard. Rinse with plenty of cold water, then fill with lightly salted boiling water and set in a close-fitting bowl or in a heatproof stand and place in a steamer. Cover and steam over high heat for 25 minutes. Pour off the stock and set the melon back into the bowl or stand.

Blanch the diced gizzards in boiling water and drain well. Squeeze water from the soaked mushrooms, remove the stems and dice.

Place all the ingredients, except the m.s.g. and chicken fat, in the melon and return to the steamer. Steam for 35 minutes or until the ingredients are tender and the flesh of the melon can be easily scraped from the skin. Add the m.s.g. and chicken fat, if used, and serve the melon in the bowl or stand, or transfer to an ornamental stand to take to the table.

To serve, scoop out the mixed ingredients with a portion of the stock, then carefully remove the soft melon with the ladle.

Sliced Cucumber Stuffed with Shrimp and Pork (recipe page 159).

'EMBROIDERED' SOUP

Serves 12

60 g (2 oz)	prepared fish maws (see page 392), diced
60 g (2 oz)	prepared sea cucumber (see page 393), diced
60 g (2 oz)	boneless fish fillet, sliced
125 g (4 oz)	lean pork, finely minced (ground)
60 g (2 oz)	pork kidney, trimmed, blanched and sliced
45 g (1½ oz)	peeled raw shrimps
375 g (12 oz)	bok choy, spinach or kale leaves
90 g (3 oz)	rice vermicelli, soaked in cold water
60 g (2 oz)	cooked chicken, diced
60 g (2 oz)	cooked beef tongue, diced
45 g (1½ oz)	cooked ham, shredded
45 g (1½ oz)	canned bamboo shoots, drained and sliced
3	spring onions (scallions), cut in halves
4 thick slices	fresh ginger, bruised
8 cups (2 litres)	chicken stock

Seasoning A:

¼ teaspoon	salt
½ teaspoon	m.s.g. (optional)

Seasoning B:

1 tablespoon	rice wine or dry sherry
2 teaspoons	salt (or to taste)
½ teaspoon	ground black pepper
¾ teaspoon	m.s.g. (optional)
1 tablespoon	rendered chicken fat (chicken grease), or use lard

Rinse the prepared fish maw and sea cucumber with cold water, then leave to soak until needed. Rub a dash of salt and rice wine into the fish. Mix the pork with the seasoning A ingredients, kneading until smooth, then form into small meatballs and soak in cold water until needed. Rinse the kidney and shrimps in cold water and drain well.

Line a large earthenware pot or heavy-based saucepan with the washed *bok choy* or other green vegetables and arrange the drained rice vermicelli on top. Layer the other ingredients into the pot, beginning with the fish maw and sea cucumber.

Mix the seasoning B ingredients with the stock in a separate saucepan. Bring to the boil and pour into the pot. Simmer on low heat until all the ingredients are cooked through and the flavours well blended, about 30 minutes. Serve in the pot using a table-top hot plate or a portable gas or electric cooker to keep it piping hot.

DRIED OYSTERS AND CHICKEN IN SOUP

500 g (1 lb)	chicken pieces
125 g (4 oz)	dried oysters, soaked overnight*
1 tablespoon	salt
1 slice	Chinese or cured (Smithfield) ham, shredded
2	spring onions (scallions), trimmed and sliced
3 slices	fresh ginger
6 cups (1½ litres)	chicken stock
1 tablespoon	rice wine or dry sherry
1¼ teaspoons	salt
1 teaspoon	m.s.g. (optional)

Cut the chicken into 2.5 cm (1 in) pieces through the bones and blanch in boiling water for 2 minutes. Drain and rinse in cold water. Drain the soaked oysters, rub with 1 tablespoon of salt, then rinse thoroughly in cold water. Steam until tender about 40 minutes, then dice.

Arrange the chicken, ham, ginger, and onions in a saucepan and add the chicken stock, wine, and salt. Bring to the boil and simmer on very low heat for 3 hours. Add the oysters and season with the m.s.g., if used. Remove the onion and ginger before serving.

* Fresh oysters may be used instead of dried. Use about 250 g (8 oz) whole fresh oysters, removed from the shell and rinsed thoroughly in salted water, then in cold water.

SLICED KIDNEYS AND BEANCURD SKIN IN SOUP

2	pork kidneys (about 315 g / 10 oz)
3 strips	dried beancurd skin, soaked for 25 minutes
12	dried black mushrooms, soaked for 25 minutes
30 g (1 oz)	canned bamboo shoots, drained and thinly sliced
5 cups (1¼ litres)	chicken stock
1 teaspoon	salt
½ teaspoon	m.s.g. (optional)
¼ teaspoon	ground black pepper
2 teaspoons	light soy sauce
2	spring onions (scallions), trimmed and sliced
2 slices	fresh ginger

Skin the kidneys and cut in halves. Remove the white fatty membrane and turn over. Score in a close criss-cross pattern, cutting to about ½ cm (1/6 in) deep. Cut into thin slices and blanch in boiling water, then drain and soak in cold water for 10 minutes. Drain the beancurd skin and cut into 5 cm (2 in) squares. Drain mushrooms and remove stems, then slice thinly.

Bring the chicken stock to the boil. Add the salt, m.s.g., if used, pepper, soy sauce, the spring onions, and ginger and boil for 2 minutes. Add the sliced kidney and simmer for 1 minute, then remove to individual soup bowls with enough soup to cover. Return the soup to the boil, skim if necessary and add the beancurd skin, mushrooms, and bamboo shoots. Simmer for 5 minutes, then pour over the kidneys and serve.

BEANCURD, MUSHROOMS AND VEGETABLES SIMMERED IN AN EARTHENWARE CROCK

3 squares	soft beancurd
45 g (1½ oz)	golden mushrooms*
6	dried black mushrooms, soaked for 25 minutes
30 g (1 oz)	canned bamboo shoots, drained and shredded
½ cup (4 fl oz)	frying oil or softened lard
30 g (1 oz)	cooked chicken breast, shredded
30 g (1 oz)	cooked ham, shredded
7 cups (1¾ litres)	chicken stock
6	Chinese cabbage hearts, young bok choy or kale
1 tablespoon	rendered chicken fat (chicken grease) (optional)

Seasoning:

1 tablespoon	rice wine
1¾ teaspoons	salt
¼ teaspoon	m.s.g. (optional)
½ teaspoon	ground black pepper

Cut the beancurd into small diamond-shaped pieces and soak in hot water for 10 minutes. Drain the golden mushrooms and rinse in cold water. Squeeze the water from soaked mushrooms, remove the stems and slice finely.

Heat half the lard or frying oil in a wok and fry the golden mushrooms, black mushrooms, and bamboo shoots for 1 minute. Add the ham and chicken and fry briefly, then add the chicken stock and the seasoning ingredients and bring to the boil. Simmer for 1 minute and transfer to an earthenware casserole. Add the beancurd and cover tightly. Simmer for 15 minutes on very low heat.

Fry the washed vegetable hearts in the remaining oil or lard for 2 minutes, then add to the crock and simmer a few more minutes. Check the seasoning, adding the chicken fat, if used. Serve in the crock.

* Golden mushrooms have minute golden caps on long, thin golden stems. They are sold in cans or jars where Chinese or Japanese foods are available. If unobtainable, substitute thinly sliced champignons.

SWALLOWS' NESTS IN CLEAR BROTH

30 g (1 oz)	dried birds' nests
6 cups (1½ litres)	chicken or enriched stock
2 teaspoons	rice wine or dry sherry
2 teaspoons	salt
1 teaspoon	m.s.g. (optional)
¼ teaspoon	white pepper

Soak the birds' nests in boiling water, covered, until the water cools. Drain, cover again with boiling water and leave until this lot of water cools also, then add 1 tablespoon clean vegetable oil. This will collect any fragments of feather or grit trapped in the nests. Drain off and rinse with cold water.

Place the drained birds' nests in a casserole and add the remaining ingredients. Set on a rack in a steamer and steam, tightly covered, over rapidly boiling water for 30 minutes. Serve.

APPLE FRITTERS STUFFED WITH RED BEAN PASTE

3	large cooking apples
155 g (5 oz)	sweet red bean paste (see page 00)
5	egg whites
1½ tablespoons	flour
1½ tablespoons	cornflour (cornstarch)
6 cups (1½ litres)	deep-frying oil
2 tablespoons	sesame oil (optional)

Glaze:

1 cup	sugar
¾ cup (6 fl oz)	water
	few drops of red food colouring

Peel the apples and cut out the cores. Cut each apple into 6 even-sized wedges. Make a slit on the rounded side of each apple wedge and fill with red bean paste. Sprinkle lightly with cornflour.

Beat the egg whites until they form soft peaks, then carefully fold in the flour and cornflour. Heat the deep-frying oil to moderate and add the sesame oil, if used.

Bring the sugar and water to a slow boil and colour a bright red. Reduce heat and simmer slowly while the apple is cooking.

Coat the apple pieces with the batter and deep-fry several at a time until the batter is golden and crisp and the apple beginning to soften, about 2½ minutes. Drain and set aside while the remainder is cooked.

Reheat the oil and quickly deep-fry the apple pieces a second time until deep golden in colour. Drain and arrange on an oiled serving plate. Drizzle the hot toffee over the fritters and serve at once.

TARO CUBES WITH CINNAMON FLAVOUR

1 kg (2 lb)	fresh taro or yam
¾ teaspoon	bicarbonate of soda
210 g (7 oz)	rock candy (sugar)
¼ cup	sugar
1 stick	cinnamon
	cornflour (cornstarch)

Peel the taro, wash thoroughly and cut into 4 cm (1 2/3 in) cubes, then trim the edges to give oval shapes. Place in a saucepan of boiling water, add the soda and return to the boil. Cook for 5 minutes, then drain and rinse with cold water. Spread on a plate to cool. The taro will turn a reddish colour.

Dissolve the lightly crushed rock candy and the sugar in several cups of boiling water. Transfer the taro to a large dish and pour on the sugar syrup, adding enough water to just cover the taro. Break the cinnamon stick into several pieces and place on the taro.

Set the dish on a rack in a steamer and steam over rapidly boiling water until the taro is completely tender. Strain the syrup into a saucepan and bring to the boil. Thicken with a paste of cornflour and cold water and continue to simmer until the sauce is thick and clear.

Transfer the taro to a serving dish and discard the cinnamon. Pour on the hot syrup and serve at once.

Beancurd, Mushrooms and Vegetables Simmered in an Earthenware Crock (recipe page 167)

SWEET WALNUT AND RED DATE SOUP

210 g (7 oz)	fresh walnuts, shelled
45 g (1½ oz)	Chinese dried red dates
½ cup	glutinous rice, soaked for 2 hours
1 cup	sugar

Soak the walnuts in boiling water until the skins loosen. Drain and cool slightly, then peel away the skins and chop the walnuts coarsely.

Steam the red dates with water to cover until tender. Drain and mash to a smooth paste, discarding the skin and stones.

Drain the rice and place it and walnuts in a blender with enough water to blend to a smooth paste.

Bring about 3½ cups (28 fl oz) water to the boil and add the sugar. Stir until dissolved, then add the walnut and rice paste and bring to the boil. Reduce to a simmer and add the mashed red dates. Stir in thoroughly and cook until the soup is sweet and thick. Serve hot.

STEAMED LOTUS SEED AND RED BEAN PASTE PUDDING

250 g (8 oz)	dried lotus seeds, soaked for 15 minutes
155 g (5 oz)	long grain glutinous rice
90 g (3 oz)	sweet red bean paste (see page 389)
155 g (5 oz)	rock candy (sugar)
⅓ cup	softened lard
2 tablespoons	sugar
¾ teaspoon	powdered cinnamon

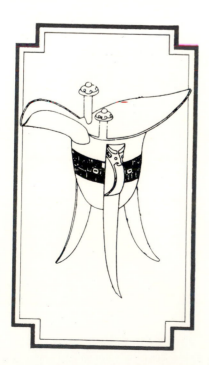

Drain the lotus seeds, place in a saucepan with water to cover and a pinch of bicarbonate of soda and bring to the boil. Remove and rinse well in cold water. Use a needle to pick out the bitter tasting central core. Place the seeds in a dish, crumble on a little rock sugar and cover with water. Set the dish in a steamer and steam until the seeds are beginning to soften. Remove, drain and leave to cool.

Wash the rice well and pour into a saucepan of boiling water. Cook for 10 minutes, then drain and pour into a dish lined with a piece of clean cheesecloth. Steam over rapidly boiling water until cooked.

Thickly grease a pudding basin with the lard, and arrange the lotus seeds in a formation in the bottom and as far up the sides as they will go. Crush the remaining rock sugar and sprinkle over the lotus seeds.

Add the remaining lard and sugar to the rice and add the cinnamon. Work in evenly, then spread a thick layer of rice over the lotus seeds, reserving about one-third. Leave a depression in the centre of the bowl. Put the sweet red bean paste in the depression and cover with the remaining rice. Smooth the top and cover with a piece of perforated and greased greaseproof paper.

Set the dish in a steamer and steam over rapidly boiling water for 1 hour. Turn out the pudding onto a serving plate. The rock sugar will have melted into a sweet clear syrup. Serve hot.

BIRDS' NEST DESSERT

30 g (1 oz)	dried birds' nests, soaked for 1 hour
210 g (7 oz)	rock candy (sugar)
¾ teaspoon	bicarbonate of soda

Drain and thoroughly wash the birds' nests, picking out any bits of feather or grit with tweezers. Pour on boiling water and soak until tender, then drain.

Sprinkle on the bicarbonate of soda and cover again with boiling water. Leave for 5 minutes to soften and expand, then drain and cover with more boiling water. Drain and rinse thoroughly.

Crumble the rock sugar and place in a saucepan with about 5 cups (1½ litres) of cold water. Bring to the boil and simmer very slowly until the sugar has completely dissolved. Strain into a bowl. Add the prepared birds' nests and steam for 10 minutes over rapidly boiling water.

Serve hot, or chill thoroughly and serve cold.

FRIED THREE-TREASURE PURÉE

700 g (1⅓ lb)	yam or sweet potato
75 g (2½ oz)	Chinese dried red dates
280 g (9 oz)	fresh or frozen peas
1 stick	cinnamon
2/3 cup	softened lard
1¼ cups	sugar

Thoroughly wash the yam and place in a saucepan of boiling water. Simmer until completely softened, then drain and leave to cool. Peel off the skin and mash the yam to a smooth paste.

Steam the dates until softened, then mash to a smooth paste, discarding the skin and stones. Boil the peas until softened, mash and remove as much skin as possible.

Steam the cinnamon stick in ½ cup water until softened and the water well flavoured. Discard the stick.

Heat one-third of the lard in a wok and add the yam paste, one-third of the sugar and half the cinnamon water. Stir on moderate heat until the mixture is dry and smooth. Remove to one end of an oval serving plate.

Wash the wok, reheat with half the remaining lard, add the dates and one-third of the sugar and stir on moderate heat until the paste is smooth and dry. Place at the other end of the serving plate.

Wash the wok again, heat the remaining lard with the remaining sugar and cinnamon water and the pea paste. Stir on moderate heat until smooth and dry, then pour into the remaining section of the serving plate. Serve hot.

SWEET YAM SOUP

625 g (1¼ lb)	peeled fresh yams (taro or sweet potato)
5 cups (1¼ litres)	water
2/3 cup	sugar
⅓ cup	softened lard
2½ tablespoons	cornflour (cornstarch)
¼ cup (2 fl oz)	cold water

Cut the yam into cubes and place in a saucepan with the water and sugar. Bring to the boil and simmer until softened, then transfer to a blender and blend until smooth and creamy. Return to the heat and add the lard. Stir for 2 — 3 minutes, then thicken with the cornflour and cold water and serve hot.

For extra flavour, add diced candied winter melon, gourd, or peel.

西

CHAPTER V
Western Central Style Cuisine

Previous page: *Field workers pause to pose for camera on agricultual commune near Chengtu (Chengdu) in Szechuan (Sichuan). Electricity is about the only modern covenience such communes enjoy.*

Above from left to right: *Western cuisine features river fish, pork, and a variety of vegetables, as well as fresh herbs from the mountains.* Opposite from left to right: *fisherman and his faithful cormorant fishing-bird pause for rest on a sampan near Kweilin (Guilin); typical farmhouse near Chengtu (Chengdu), captial of Szechuan (Sichuan); herbal medicine shop in Chengtu (Chengdu) displays fresh-picked herbs from the mountains, commonly used in Szechuanese cooking; farmers tend their greening fields outside of Chengtu (Chengdu); farmers sell their products on the free market in Chengtu (Chengdu), which has recently seen a remarkable boom in production due to private enterprise; a pig enroute to market by bicycle in suburb of Chengtu (Chengdu).*

The western/central culinary region of China includes the provinces and cuisines of Szechuan (Sichuan) and Hunan, two of China's most ancient provinces. Sichuan, today the largest and most populous province of China, thrived for many centuries as the Kingdom of Shu prior to the unification of China in 221 B.C. Hunan is centrally located, grographically as well as historically, and today is best known as the birthplace of Mao Tse-tung (Mao Zedong), who continued to demand the fiery flavours of his native province throughout his life. The cuisine of the western/central region is the most distinctive in all of China in terms of flavour.

While the climates of Szechuan (Sichuan) and Hunan are quite similar, their geographical conditions differ significantly, and these differences are reflected in the food. Both provinces are dominated by hot, humid weather. Hunan is a verdant province of fertile soil, abundant rainfall, and gentle topography, where most ingredients for the Chinese kitchen thrive. Meat, fish, and fowl play prominent roles on the Hunan menu, and the entire spectrum of the vegetable kingdom is represented as well. Sichuan, however, is a land of craggy mountains, abrupt, deep valleys, and steep, jagged cliffs. The bulk of the province's crops are grown in the broad plains surrounding the capital city of Chengtu (Chengdu): this entire area is supplied by a vast, highly efficient irrigation system first built to harness the Min River over 2,000 years ago. Szechuan (Sichuan) cuisine offers less variety of cultivated ingredients than Hunan, but the mountain recesses

provide a wide range of medicinal cooking herbs as well as wild game.

Red chillies of the *capsicum* family are the king of condiments in the western/central style of cooking. Due to their pharmacological effects — they tend to dry out the body and thus balance excess dampness — chillies have been extremely popular in this intensely humid region ever since their introduction from the New World. The native *fagara* pepper is also extensively used, as well as garlic, ginger, and spring onions. Fermented bean paste and chilli sauce play prominent roles too. The flavours of western/central style dishes tend toward the pungent.

Lush Hunan province produces plenty of meat, fish, and fowl for its tables, and these rich items are central in the Hunan diet. However, they are rarely, if ever, cooked in the raw state: instead, they are usually cured, marinated, pickled, or otherwise processed prior to use in cooking. A classic Hunan specialty is Honey-glazed Ham, served with thinly sliced bread to form dainty, fragrant, little 'Chinese sandwiches.' Vagabond Ham, Beggar's Chicken, and Squirrel Fish are other rich, flavourful specials of Hunan made with meat, fish, or fowl.

Szechuan (Sichuan) has a more limited selection of ingredients for cooking. Most prominent in the Szechuan (Sichuan) kitchen are pork, poultry, legumes, soybean products, nuts of various sorts, and wild mountain products, including medicinal herbs and wild game. Szechuan (Sichuan) produces the world's most potent Chinese medicinal herbs in its deep valleys and high mountains. Many are used to prepare potent, highly nourishing dishes: Chinese Wolfberry (*Lycium chinensis*), medlar, ginseng, aconite, Shepherd's Purse, jujubes, licorice root, and many others appear in Szechuan (Sichuan) dishes. Medicinal herbs are usually applied to wild game, which, according to tradi-

174

tional Chinese medical theories, is the most potent source of energy. For more conventional dishes, pork and poultry are utilised in an incredible variety of ways. Some popular dishes from the Szechuan (Sichuan) menu include Pine-and-Tea-Smoked Duck, Exotic Flavoured Chicken, Chicken and Chillies, Fragrant Spicy Shredded Pork, Pock-marked Mama's Bean-curd, Braised Eggplant, Braised String Beans, and Hot-and-Sour Soup.

A few brief remarks about red chillies and their uses are in order here. Used extensively throughout the western/central region, red chillies serve a variety of functions. They provide the pungent flavour in cooking, but such dishes need not be so 'hot' that they scorch the palate and throat. Since most dishes in which chillies appear are *chao* or *bao* cooked, their pungent flavour enters the oil and sauces but has no time to cook deeply into the main ingredients, such as in the slowly simmered curries of India and Southeast Asia. The pungency of red chillies is all contained in the seeds and white fibres which cling to the interior. The red, fleshy exterior has a very fragrant, fresh, delectable flavour. Therefore, in order to tame chillies for more tender palates, all you need to do is cut them open lengthwise and scrape away some, or all, of the seeds and fibres.

The primary reason for the prominence of chillies in this region, however, is medical, not culinary: they stave off excess dampness by providing a pharmacological drying factor to balance it. The evils of excessive external humidity are thus negated by the introduction of an internal 'dehumidifier': chillies induce perspiration and literally 'squeeze' the excess moisture out of your system like a sponge. This is also why chillies are not so popular in the excessively dry climates of the north. In addition, chillies are antiseptic (kill germs) and anthelmintic (kill worms), important

considerations in hot, humid climates with no refrigeration facilities to keep foods absolutely fresh. The concentrated pungency of the seeds and fibres stimulates the palate and greatly facilitates *xia-fan* ('getting the rice down'), also important in a region such as Szechuan (Sichuan), where the selection and quantity of *cai* are often severely limited. Red chillies also serve the function of 'opening up' the palate with a strong, frontal assault so that the many other flavours which follow in the aftertastes can be more fully appreciated.

The most distinctive features of this region's cuisine reside in the flavour: flavour and freshness are emphasised far more than colour and appearance. This feature reflects the earthy, practical, 'no-nonsense' nature of the region's inhabitants. The distinctive flavours of the region go far beyond the pungent frontal assault referred to above. After chillies have opened up the palate and paved the way for subtle appreciation of other flavours experienced during chewing, swallowing, and aftertasting, the true uniqueness of western/central flavours comes out. As soon as the palate cools down, the other flavours suddenly burst upon the taste buds in a harmonious medley. This second wave of sensations on the palate and olfactory buds reveals the 'manifold' flavour and fragrance of the region's food, which comprise its most unique feature. The 'five flavours' of traditional Chinese medical theory — sweet, sour, salty, pungent, bitter — all appear together in subtle combinations and harmonious balance. Manifold flavour is no doubt the

source of this cuisine's enduring popularity.

As noted above, colour and appearance are not strongly emphasised, and therefore western/central-style dishes are not as pretty to look at as those of the eastern/coastal and southern regions. In texture, the dishes tend towards the dry (another medical balance to excess humidity) and the chewy. Many of the dishes are highly potent and stimulating to the system and are not recommended for people with weak digestive systems or gastrointestinal ailments. They are best suited for energetic, naturally active people, and for consumption in damp climates.

Another distinctive feature of Szechuan (Sichuan) cuisine is its rustic, 'down-home' style. *Jia-chang-cai*, literally 'dishes often eaten at home,' appear prominently on the Szechuan (Sichuan) menu, even in the fanciest restaurants. This is another reflection of the earthy, informal personality of Suzchuan's (Sichuan's) people, who want their guests to 'make themselves at home' even in the most formal settings. While *jia-chang-cai* are neither fancy in appearance nor expensive to make, they are among the tastiest and most nourishing dishes in China, which accounts for their everlasting popularity. The classic example of this type of dish is 'Pock-marked Mama's Beancurd,' which was invented by, and carries the name of, an old pock-marked woman who operated a small beancurd stall on some obscure street corner in Chengdu countless centuries ago. Employing only a few cakes of beancurd, a little ground pork, and some spices, this is one of the least expensive and easiest to produce of all Chinese dishes. Yet it is also one of the most nourishing and well balanced (beancurd and pork provide complete protein), medically potent (ginger, garlic, chillies, and spring onions are all used), and delicious dishes in the entire Chinese culinary repertoire.

Opposite: *'To market, to market to sell a fat pig;'* pork is popular in Szechuan (Sichuan) cuisine and every morning farmers can be seen driving their prize pigs to market strapped snugly on bicycles.

Left: *Vendor preparing a bowl of spicy Szechuan (Sichuan) beef-noodles in open-air market at Kuansian near Chengtu (Chengdu). Note the big bamboo steamers and the pack-clay stove fired by charcoal, still a common sight throughout China.*

Today, Szechuan (Sichuan) cuisine is the overall most popular Chinese (regional) style in the world, and Hunan is not far behind. One of the reasons for the contemporary popularity of Szechuan (Sichuan) food among Chinese and foreigners alike lies in recent history, for prior to World War II Szechuan (Sichuan) food was virtually unknown outside its provincial borders. However, to escape the Japanese onslaught in 1937, the Nationalist government of China moved its headquarters to the city of Chungking (Chongqing), deep within the rugged recesses of Szechuan (Sichuan) province. Here, for eight long years, everyone from top government ministers and military officers down to simple clerks and foot-soldiers ate Szechuan (Sichuan)-style food exclusively. For one thing, nothing else was available; for another, the newcomers quickly discovered that the chillies, garlic, ginger, and onions used so extensively in Szechuan (Sichuan) dishes effectively helped to ward off the oppressive dampness of summer and the penetrating damp chills of winter. When the government and army returned to Shanghai and Nanking (Nanjing) after the Japanese surrender, they brought along thousands of skilled Szechuan (Sichuan) chefs, to whose culinary style their palates and systems had become addicted. In the subsequent Nationalist move to Taiwan, most of these chefs followed, and there

they set up their own Szechuan (Sichuan) restaurants. Many soon moved on to the west to ply their trade. In Taipei (Taibei), an affluent city of sophisticated, highly fussy gourmets who have thousands of the best regional Chinese restaurants to choose from, Szechuan (Sichuan) cuisine remains the most popular, frequent choice for eating out. The same is increasingly true in San Francisco, New York, Paris, and London.

The other reason for the immense contemporary popularity of Szechuan (Sichuan) food has already been mentioned: manifold flavour. Both the initial pungency and the subsequent aftertastes are highly stimulating to the senses and make eating more exciting and interesting. In this crowded, busy, sensation-oriented world, the fiery flavours and stimulating sensations of Szechuan (Sichuan) food stand out as highly appealing. The jaded palates of jet-setters and trend-makers, their threshholds of stimulation driven sky-high by their lavish life-styles, were the first to discover the sensory delights of Szechuan's (Sichuan's) manifold flavours and appreciate the physical stimulation imparted by the dishes to the system. As usual, the rest of the world has begun to follow their lead. The strong flavours and stimulating after-effects of Szechuan (Sichuan) and Hunan dishes are perhaps best suited to the fast pace and excitement of modern urban life-styles.

BRAISED SHARK'S FINS IN BROWN SAUCE

750 g (1½ lb)	prepared whole shark's fins (see page 393), (about 185 g / 6 oz dry weight)
250 g (8 oz)	fresh chicken fat
375 g (12 oz)	lean pork
2	spring onions (scallions), trimmed and sliced
3 slices	fresh ginger
1½ tablespoons	rice wine or dry sherry
4 cups (1 litre)	water
60 g (2 oz)	Chinese or cured (Smithfield) ham
30 g (1 oz)	dried scallops, soaked for 1 hour

Seasoning:

2½ tablespoons	dark soy sauce or oyster sauce
½ teaspoon	m.s.g. (optional)
2 teaspoons	sugar
¼ teaspoon	white pepper
3 tablespoons	cornflour (cornstarch)
¼ cup (2 fl oz)	cold water
1 tablespoon	finely chopped fresh coriander (optional)

Drain the prepared shark's fins and set aside. Cut the chicken fat and pork into dice and stir-fry with the spring onions and ginger on fairly high heat for 1½ minutes. Sizzle the wine onto the side of the pan and then add the water and the drained shark's fins and bring to the boil. Reduce to simmer and cook for 1½ hours.

Strain the stock into another saucepan and add the ham, cut into small cubes, and the drained scallops. Simmer for about 45 minutes, then add the seasoning ingredients and simmer, stirring, until the sauce is thick. Add the shark's fins and pork, discarding the chicken fat and simmer until thoroughly heated, then transfer to a serving dish and serve at once.

'LUNGCHING' TEA-FLAVOURED ABALONE

2/3 500 g (1 lb) can	abalone*
1½ tablespoons	Lungching tea (or use oolong tea)
¾ cup (6 fl oz)	chicken stock
90 g (3 oz)	fresh pea sprouts or young spinach

Seasoning:

½ teaspoon	salt
⅓ teaspoon	m.s.g. (optional)
2 teaspoons	rice wine or dry sherry

Drain the abalone, reserving the liquid. Trim the ruffled edges and cut the abalone into thick slices, then return to the liquid to soak until needed.

Brew the tea with 1 cup (8 fl oz) of water and leave to infuse for 30 seconds, then drain away the water and brew with a second lot of freshly boiled water.

Bring the chicken stock to the boil and add the seasoning ingredients, the sliced abalone and pea sprouts or spinach. Simmer briefly.

Strain the tea liquid (about ½ cup) into a cup and discard the remaining tea, reserving the leaves. Transfer the leaves to a small porcelain teacup and upturn in the centre of a serving dish. Leave the cup in place. Pour in the reserved half cup of tea and add the heated abalone and its suace. Stir very lightly without disturbing the teacup.

Carry to the table and remove the teacup to expose the tea leaves immediately before serving.

* Unused abalone can be frozen for later use.

BRAISED FISH MAW WITH HAM AND MUSHROOMS

250 g (8 oz)	dried fish maw, precooked (see page 392)
125 g (4 oz)	Chinese or cured (Smithfield) ham
8	dried black mushrooms, soaked for 25 minutes
2½ tablespoons	frying oil
2	spring onions (scallions), trimmed and sliced
4 slices	fresh ginger
1 tablespoon	rendered chicken fat (chicken grease), (optional)
3 cups (24 fl oz)	chicken stock
1 teaspoon	salt
¼ teaspoon	m.s.g. (optional)
1 tablespoon	rice wine or dry sherry
375 g (12 oz)	fresh spinach (collard greens)
2 tablespoons	softened lard or frying oil cornflour (cornstarch)

Seasoning:

½ teaspoon	salt
⅓ cup	chicken stock
¼ teaspoon	m.s.g. (optional)
½ teaspoon	sugar

Prepare the fish maw following the directions on page 392. Cut into bite-sized pieces and soak in cold water until needed. Cut the ham into dice. Squeeze the water from the mushrooms, remove the stems and cut the caps into quarters.

Heat the frying oil and stir-fry the spring onions and ginger briefly. Add the chicken fat, if used, and the chicken stock and bring to the boil. Add the salt, m.s.g., and wine and add the well-drained fish maw, ham, and mushrooms. Cover and simmer or steam for about 1 hour until the fish maw is completely tender.

Wash the spinach and discard any stems. Sauté in the lard or frying oil for a few seconds, then add the seasoning ingredients, cover and simmer until tender.

Thicken the sauce on the fish maw with a paste of cornflour and cold water and cook until the sauce turns clear. Transfer to a serving dish and surround with the spinach. Serve.

FISH LIPS WITH VEGETABLES ON CRISP RICE

155 g (5 oz)	dried fish lips, precooked (see page 392)
¼ cup (2 fl oz)	frying oil
2	spring onions (scallions), trimmed and diced
1½ teaspoons	finely chopped fresh ginger
60 g (2 oz)	canned bamboo shoots, drained and sliced
60 g (2 oz)	canned straw mushrooms, drained and sliced
90 g (3 oz)	bok choy or choy sum stems, parboiled
1 tablespoon	cornflour (cornstarch)
1 teaspoon	sesame oil
12 pieces	rice cakes (see page 417)
5 cups (1¼ litres)	deep-frying oil

Seasoning/Sauce:

3 cups (24 fl oz)	chicken stock
¾ teaspoon	salt
½ teaspoon	m.s.g. (optional)
1 tablespoon	dark soy sauce or oyster sauce
2 teaspoons	rice wine or dry sherry
½ teaspoon	Chinese brown vinegar

Prepare the fish lips according to the directions on page 392. Soak until needed. Stir-fry the spring onions, ginger, bamboo shoots, straw mushrooms, and sliced vegetable stems in the frying oil for 1½ minutes. Add the pre-mixed seasoning/sauce ingredients and bring to the boil.

Drain the fish lips and cut into bite-sized pieces. Add to the pan and simmer for 4 — 5 minutes. Heat the deep-frying oil to smoking point and deep-fry the rice cakes in a frying basket until crisp and golden. Drain and transfer to a serving dish.

Thicken the sauce with the cornflour mixed with an equal amount of cold water and stir in the sesame oil. Pour immediately over the rice cakes and serve.

'PRECIOUS CONCUBINE' CHICKEN

Serve as an appetiser or main dish.

1 1¼ kg (2½ lb)	chicken
2	spring onions (scallions), trimmed and halved
3 thin slices	fresh ginger
1 tablespoon	rice wine or dry sherry
1	medium carrot, peeled and shredded
1	medium cucumber, shredded
½	giant white (icicle) radish, shredded
1 tablespoon	salt

Seasoning:

1 teaspoon	salt
½ teaspoon	m.s.g. (optional)
1 tablespoon	sesame oil
¼ cup (2 fl oz)	warm chicken stock

Sauce 1:

2 tablespoons	finely chopped spring onion (scallion)
¼ cup (2 fl oz)	light soy sauce
2 tablespoons	water
2 tablespoons	sesame oil
¾ teaspoon	chilli sauce or chilli oil
2 teaspoons	dark soy sauce
2 teaspoons	sugar
½ teaspoon	m.s.g. (optional)

Sauce 2:

2 tablespoons	finely shredded fresh ginger
2 tablespoons	Chinese red vinegar
1 teaspoon	salt
¼ teaspoon	m.s.g. (optional)
1½ teaspoons	sugar
1 tablespoon	water
2 teaspoons	sesame oil

Clean and dress the chicken and place in a saucepan with the spring onions, ginger, and wine. Cover with water and bring to the boil. Simmer on very low heat until just cooked, about 50 minutes. Drain, debone (see page 394), and slice.

Sprinkle the salt onto the carrot and radish and stir in lightly. Leave for about 25 minutes, then rinse with cold water and drain thoroughly. Pile each of the shredded vegetables onto separate serving dishes, or into separate groups on a large serving platter.

Arrange the sliced chicken breast on the cucumber, the sliced thigh meat on the carrots, and the remaining meat, torn into shreds, on the radish.

Garnish the dish with parsley or fresh coriander. Mix the seasoning ingredients together and pour over the chicken.

Mix the two sauces in separate jugs and serve with the chicken, to be poured over or transferred to small dip dishes at the table.

180

Chicken Steamed in a Pumpkin (recipe page 187).

'BON BON' CHICKEN

Serve hot or cold as an appetiser or main dish.

1 1½ kg (3 lb)	chicken
1	cucumber, peeled and shredded
5 — 6	fresh lettuce leaves
1 tablespoon	toasted white sesame seeds (optional)

Sauce:

2½ tablespoons	sesame paste
2 tablespoons	chicken stock
1 tablespoon	sesame oil
2 tablespoons	light soy sauce
1 tablespoon	Chinese brown vinegar
1 tablespoon	grated fresh ginger
2 — 3 teaspoons	finely chopped garlic
½ teaspoon	salt
½ teaspoon	m.s.g. (optional)
1 tablespoon	sugar

Clean and dress the chicken, place in a saucepan with water to cover and bring to the boil. Cover tightly and cook on very low heat for 10 minutes. Remove from the heat and leave to stand in the hot stock for a further 30 minutes. Return to the boil and remove again from the heat. Leave for 5 — 6 minutes.

Remove the chicken. The meat should be white and moist with a hint of pink around the bones. Drain well and rub a little of the sesame oil over the skin. Debone and tear the meat into strips.

Line a serving plate with the lettuce and pile the cucumber and chicken on top. Sprinkle on the sesame seeds, if used.

Mix the sauce ingredients together, stirring until thoroughly amalgamated. Serve separately as a dip or pour over the chicken at the table.

ROAST STUFFED CHICKEN

1 1½ kg (3 lb)	chicken
90 g (3 oz)	fresh bean sprouts
125 g (4 oz)	fat pork
3 slices	fresh ginger
4	spring onions (scallions)
¼ cup (2 fl oz)	softened lard or frying oil
500 g (1 lb)	pork omentum (caul fat)
1 tablespoon	sesame oil

Batter:

| 3 | egg whites, well beaten |
| 3 tablespoons | cornflour (cornstarch) |

Seasoning A:

1 tablespoon	finely chopped spring onion (scallion)
1 teaspoon	grated fresh ginger
1 teaspoon	salt
2 teaspoons	light soy sauce
1 tablespoon	rice wine or dry sherry
¼ teaspoon	m.s.g. (optional)

Seasoning B:

¼ teaspoon	m.s.g. (optional)
2 teaspoons	light soy sauce
1 teaspoon	rice wine or dry sherry
1 teaspoon	chilli oil or chilli flakes

Wash the chicken and wipe dry. Rub thoroughly with the pre-mixed seasoning A ingredients and set aside. Wash and drain the bean sprouts, then chop finely. Finely dice the pork and mix with the seasoning B ingredients. Chop 1 slice of ginger and 2 spring onions into small dice and sauté in the lard or oil for 30 seconds. Add the pork and sauté until lightly coloured, then add the bean sprouts and cook very briefly.

Stuff the mixture into the chicken with the remaining ginger and spring onions. Close the opening with poultry pins. Mix the batter ingredients together and spread thickly over the chicken, then cut the pork net in halves and wrap one piece around the chicken. Brush with the remaining batter and cover with the other piece of pork net.

Roast over an open charcoal fire, securely fastened to a spit, or cook in a moderate oven 190°C (375°F), preferably on a rotisserie, until the chicken is golden brown and cooked through, about 1 hour. Increase the heat and cook for a further 6 — 7 minutes until the pork net coating is very crisp and quite dark. Brush with the sesame oil.

Remove from the oven and open the first piece of pork net. Cut into diamond-shaped pieces and place on one side of a serving plate. Discard the inner piece of net and cut the chicken into serving slices. Arrange on the plate with the stuffing on the other side. Discard the ginger and onion. Serve at once.

CHICKEN STEAMED IN A YUNNAN STEAMPOT

The Yunnan Steam-Pot is an unglazed ceramic cooking pot which has a central funnel inside. This allows a small but continuous flow of steam to enter the pot, thus gently cooking the ingredients and adding liquid to the dish by way of condensation. These pots are available at most leading suppliers of Chinese food and kitchen products. No other cooking pot can produce the same results.

1 1½ kg (3 lb)	chicken
90 g (3 oz)	Chinese or cured (Smithfield) ham
90 g (3 oz)	canned bamboo shoots, drained
1	spring onion (scallion), trimmed and sliced
2 slices	fresh ginger
	salt
	m.s.g. (optional)

Seasoning:

¾ teaspoon	salt
1 teaspoon	sugar
2½ tablespoons	rice wine or dry sherry
½ teaspoon	chilli oil (optional)

Clean the chicken and cut into 5 cm (2 in) squares. Place in a dish with the seasoning ingredients and leave for 30 minutes, turning occasionally.

Transfer to the steam-pot. Cut the ham and bamboo shoots into small cubes and add to the pot with the spring onion and ginger. Mix the ingredients together using chopsticks.

Place the pot in a steamer without using a rack and pour in water until it reaches a level half way up the sides of the steam-pot. Cover the steam-pot with its lid, then cover the steamer and bring the water to the boil. Reduce to a simmer and cook for 1 — 1¼ hours until the chicken is completely tender. Add salt and m.s.g. to taste and serve in the steam-pot.

HOT SPICED CHICKEN WITH GREEN ONIONS

625 g (1¼ lb)	chicken pieces
8	large spring onions (scallions)
⅓ cup	frying oil
1 teaspoon	Chinese brown peppercorns
1 — 2	dried red chilli peppers, cut into 3 pieces each
1 tablespoon	soybean paste
4 slices	fresh ginger
½ teaspoon	m.s.g. (optional)
¾ teaspoon	Chinese brown vinegar (optional)

Seasoning/Sauce:

¾ cup (6 fl oz)	chicken stock
2 teaspoons	light soy sauce
2 teaspoons	dark soy sauce
1 tablespoon	rice wine or dry sherry
1 tablespoon	sugar

Cut the chicken into bite-sized pieces through the bones. Cut the spring onions into 2 cm (¾ in) pieces after trimming the roots and tops.

Heat the frying oil and fry the peppercorns and sliced chilli peppers until the chillies are dark brown and crisp. Remove and set aside. Add the bean paste and stir on moderate heat for 20 seconds, then add the chicken pieces and ginger and stir-fry until almost cooked, about 3 minutes.

Add the spring onions and return the chillies and peppercorns. Stir-fry on lowered heat for 1 minute, then stir in the pre-mixed seasoning/sauce ingredients and simmer until the chicken is tender and the sauce well reduced.

Thicken the sauce lightly, if preferred, with a solution of cornflour and cold water, and add the m.s.g. and vinegar, if used.

'KUNG PAO' CHICKEN

440 g (14 oz)	boneless chicken breasts, or use slightly more chicken on the bone
5	fresh red chilli peppers
90 g (3 oz)	raw peanuts (ground nuts)
¾ cup (6 fl oz)	frying oil
3	spring onions (scallions), trimmed and sliced
5 — 6 cloves	garlic, sliced
¾ teaspoon	Chinese brown vinegar

Seasoning A:

2 tablespoons	light soy sauce
2 tablespoons	rice wine or dry sherry
1 teaspoon	sugar
1½ teaspoons	cornflour (cornstarch)
1 tablespoon	finely chopped spring onion (scallion)
1½ teaspoons	grated fresh ginger

Seasoning B/Sauce:

2/3 cup	chicken stock
2 tablespoons	light soy sauce
1 tablespoon	rice wine or dry sherry
1 teaspoon	salt
1½ teaspoons	sugar
1½ teaspoons	cornflour (cornstarch)

Cut the chicken into bite-sized pieces. Place in a dish with the seasoning A ingredients, mix well and leave for 20 minutes. Drop the peanuts into a pot of boiling water and leave for 2 minutes, then drain and remove the skins. Cut the chillies into about 4 pieces each and discard the seeds for a milder taste.

Heat the frying oil and fry the chillies until they turn dark brown. Remove and set aside. Add the peanuts and fry until golden. Remove and drain well.

Pour off all but 2½ tablespoons of the oil and stir-fry the chicken for 2 minutes. Add the sliced spring onions and garlic and stir-fry a further 30 seconds, then add the chilli peppers and the pre-mixed seasoning B/sauce ingredients. Cover and simmer until the chicken is tender, about 2 minutes. Cooking will take longer for chicken on the bone, so leave out the cornflour until the chicken is done, then mix to a paste with cold water and use to thicken the sauce.

Stir in the vinegar and the peanuts and transfer to a serving plate. Serve at once.

FRIED CHICKEN PATTIES WITH MARINATED CABBAGE

210 g (7 oz)	boneless chicken
90 g (3 oz)	pork fat
3	egg whites, well beaten
155 g (5 oz)	white cabbage
	cornflour (cornstarch)
5 cups (1¼ litres)	deep-frying oil

Seasoning A:

½ teaspoon	salt
½ teaspoon	m.s.g. (optional)
¼ teaspoon	white pepper
2 teaspoons	rice wine
1½ tablespoons	onion and ginger infusion (see page 386)
2 tablespoons	cornflour (cornstarch)

Seasoning B:

¼ cup (2 fl oz)	boiling water
¼ cup (2 fl oz)	white vinegar
1½ teaspoons	salt
1½ tablespoons	sugar
2 teaspoons	finely chopped fresh ginger

Pulverise the chicken and pork fat in a food processor or by using two cleavers (see page 396). Add egg whites and the seasoning A ingredients and mix in one direction only until the mixture is smooth and fairly thick. Wipe out a dish with an oiled cloth and pour in the chicken paste. Set on a rack in a steamer and steam over rapidly boiling water until firm, about 15 minutes.

Wash the cabbage and shred finely. Squeeze out excess water and place the cabbage in a dish. Add the seasoning B ingredients and toss lightly. Cover with plastic wrap and leave for about 30 minutes.

Remove the chicken from the steamer and turn out onto an oiled plate or board. Leave to cool, then cut into bite-sized pieces and coat lightly with cornflour. Heat the deep-frying oil to fairly hot and deep-fry the chicken patties, several at a time, until crisp and golden. Remove and drain well.

Thoroughly drain the marinated cabbage and arrange around the edge of a serving plate. Place the fried chicken patties in the centre and serve at once.

Crisp-skin Fish with Hot and Sour Sauce (recipe page 195).

SPICED CHICKEN WITH PEANUTS AND BAMBOO SHOOTS

310 g (10 oz)	boneless chicken breast
90 g (3 oz)	canned bamboo shoots or water chestnuts, drained
60 g (2 oz)	raw peanuts (groundnuts)
¼ cup (2 fl oz)	softened lard or frying oil
1 — 2	pickled red chilli peppers, shredded
4	garlic chives, sliced
2	spring onions (scallions), trimmed and diced
2 thick slices	fresh ginger, diced
1¼ tablespoons	hot bean paste

Seasoning A:

1	egg white, beaten
½ teaspoon	salt
2 teaspoons	light soy sauce
1 teaspoon	rice wine or dry sherry
½ teaspoon	cornflour (cornstarch)

Seasoning B/Sauce:

⅓ cup	chicken stock
1 tablespoon	light soy sauce
2 teaspoons	dark soy sauce
2 teaspoons	rice wine or dry sherry
1¾ teaspoons	sugar
1¼ teaspoons	cornflour (cornstarch)

Cut the chicken into 2 cm (¾ in) cubes and place in a dish with the seasoning A ingredients. Mix well and leave for 45 minutes, turning occasionally.

Cut the bamboo shoots or water chestnuts into small cubes. Drop the peanuts into a saucepan of boiling water and cook for 1 minute, then drain and remove the skins. Drain thoroughly.

Heat the lard or frying oil in a wok and stir-fry the chicken for 1 minute. Remove and keep warm. Add the bamboo shoots or water chestnuts and the peanuts and stir-fry for 1 minute, then push to one side of the pan and add the chilli peppers, garlic chives, spring onions, and ginger and stir-fry for 30 seconds. Add the hot bean paste and fry briefly, then return the chicken and stir in the vegetables and peanuts.

Add the pre-mixed seasoning B/sauce ingredients and simmer on moderate heat until the sauce thickens, then transfer to a serving plate.

For a crunchier texture, deep-fry the peanuts separately and add to the dish just before serving.

'HIBISCUS' CHICKEN

155 g (5 oz)	boneless chicken breast
2 tablespoons	onion and ginger infusion (see page 386)
¼ cup (2 fl oz)	chicken stock
3	egg whites, well beaten
1½—2 tablespoons	cornflour (cornstarch)
3 cups (24 fl oz)	deep-frying oil
60 g (2 oz)	canned bamboo shoots, drained
60 g (2 oz)	'silver' sprouts

Seasoning A:

½ teaspoon	salt
¼ teaspoon	m.s.g. (optional)
½ teaspoon	sugar
1 teaspoon	rice wine or dry sherry

Seasoning B/Sauce:

½ cup (4 fl oz)	chicken stock
¾ teaspoon	salt
¼ teaspoon	m.s.g. (optional)
1 teaspoon	rice wine or dry sherry
1 teaspoon	cornflour (cornstarch)

Pulverise the chicken in a food processor using the chopping blade, or use two cleavers (see page 396). Mix with the onion and ginger infusion, chicken stock, egg whites, cornflour, and the seasoning A ingredients and beat in one direction only until the mixture is smooth and thick.

Heat the deep-frying oil to moderate and slide in spoonfuls of the mixture to cook until white and firm, remove and drain on absorbent paper. Cut the bamboo shoots into thin slices and rinse the 'silver' sprouts.

Pour off all but 2½ tablespoons of the oil and stir-fry the bamboo shoots and 'silver' sprouts for 1½ minutes, then add the pre-mixed seasoning B/sauce ingredients and simmer for 1 minute. Return the chicken and simmer until the sauce has thickened. Adjust the seasoning if necessary and serve.

'FIRECRACKER' CHICKEN

185 g (6 oz)	boneless chicken breast
4	Chinese sausages*
6 cups (1½ litres)	deep-frying oil
60 g (2 oz)	canned bamboo shoots, drained
60 g (2 oz)	fresh young spinach leaves (collard greens)

Seasoning A:

1	egg white, beaten
½ teaspoon	salt
½ teaspoon	m.s.g. (optional)
1 teaspoon	sugar
1 teaspoon	rice wine or dry sherry
2 teaspoons	cornflour (cornstarch)

Seasoning B/Sauce:

¾ cup (6 fl oz)	chicken stock
¾ teaspoon	salt
¼ teaspoon	ground black pepper
½ teaspoon	m.s.g. (optional)
½ teaspoon	sugar
1 teaspoon	rice wine or dry sherry
1 tablespoon	finely chopped spring onion (scallion)
¾ teaspoon	grated fresh ginger
2 teaspoons	cornflour (cornstarch)

Cut the chicken into thin slices and dust lightly with cornflour. Gently bat with the end of the cleaver handle until spread into thin escalopes. Place in a dish with the seasoning A ingredients, mix well and leave for 20 minutes.

Steam the Chinese sausage for 10 minutes, then cut each piece into three. Wrap a piece of chicken around each piece of sausage and squeeze firmly to hold in place. If the sausage feels too moist, coat very lightly with cornflour before covering with the chicken.

Cut the bamboo shoots into thin slices and rinse the spinach leaves. Set aside. Heat the deep-frying oil to moderate and deep-fry the chicken and sausage rolls for about 1 minute, then drain and set aside. Pour off all but 2½ tablespoons of the oil and stir-fry the bamboo shoots for 30 seconds, then add the spinach leaves and stir-fry briefly.

Add the pre-mixed seasoning B/sauce ingredients and bring to the boil. Reduce heat and simmer briefly, then return the chicken rolls and simmer until the sauce thickens enough to glaze the rolls. Transfer to a warmed serving plate.

* Dried pork and liver sausage. If unobtainable use sticks of steamed Chinese ham.

CHICKEN STEAMED IN A PUMPKIN

1 2 kg (4 lb)	fresh pumpkin
1¼ kg (2½ lb)	chicken pieces
2	spring onions (scallions), trimmed and sliced
2 slices	fresh ginger, shredded
1 cup	spiced rice powder*

Seasoning:

½ teaspoon	salt
¼ teaspoon	m.s.g. (optional)
1 tablespoon	sugar
2 teaspoons	dark soy sauce
2 cubes	fermented beancurd, mashed with the liquid
1 tablespoon	rice wine or brandy

Wash the pumpkin and wipe with kitchen paper. Cut off the top and scrape away the seeds. Trim the stem to form a handle and scrape the inside and edges so it forms a lid for the pumpkin. Rinse the pumpkin and lid with salted water and upturn to drain.

Cut the chicken into bite-sized pieces, cutting through the bones. Place in a dish and mix with the seasoning ingredients. Leave for 20 minutes, then roll the chicken in the spiced rice and place inside the pumpkin, distributing the spring onions and ginger evenly between the chicken pieces.

Set the lid in position and place the pumpkin on a rack in a steamer to steam over rapidly boiling water for about 55 minutes, or until the chicken and pumpkin are both tender. Serve straight from the steamer and eat the pumpkin with the chicken.

* Use Chinese brown peppercorns in preference to star anise when preparing the spiced rice powder (see page 386).

COUNTRY-STYLE CHICKEN

210 g (7 oz)	boneless chicken
60 g (2 oz)	canned bamboo shoots, drained
1	small carrot, peeled
⅓ stalk	celery*
4 thin slices	fresh ginger
1 — 2	fresh red chilli peppers
6	garlic chives
1½ cups (12 fl oz)	frying oil
1 tablespoon	soybean paste

Seasoning A:

2	egg whites, well beaten
½ teaspoon	salt
½ teaspoon	m.s.g. (optional)
½ teaspoon	sugar
2 teaspoons	rice wine or dry sherry
1 tablespoon	cornflour (cornstarch)

Seasong B/Sauce

1 tablespoon	light soy sauce
1 tablespoon	rice wine or dry sherry
¼ cup (2 fl oz)	chicken stock
1 teaspoon	Chinese brown vinegar
½ teaspoon	m.s.g. (optional)
1¼ teaspoons	sugar
1½ teaspoons	cornflour (cornstarch)

Cut the chicken into thin slices, then into narrow shreds and place in a dish with the seasoning A ingredients. Mix well and leave for 15 minutes. Cut the bamboo shoots, carrot, celery, ginger, chillies, and chives into narrow shreds.

Heat the frying oil to moderate and fry the shredded chicken in a frying basket for about 45 seconds, remove and drain well. Pour off all but 2½ tablespoons of the oil and stir-fry the shredded ingredients for about 1½ minutes, then push to one side of the pan and add the soybean paste. Fry briefly, then sizzle the soy sauce and wine onto the sides of the pan and add the remaining seasoning B/sauce ingredients, pre-mixed. Bring to the boil, return the chicken and stir all ingredients together.

Simmer until the sauce thickens, then serve.

* Or use shredded green capsicum (bell pepper).

'TWICE EATEN' CHICKEN

1¼ kg (2½ lb)	chicken pieces
¼ cup (2 fl oz)	softened lard or frying oil
2	spring onions (scallions), trimmed and sliced
3 slices	fresh ginger
1 tablespoon	rice wine or dry sherry
⅓ teaspoon	ground black pepper
4 cups (1 litre)	water
20 g (¾ oz)	dried 'wood ear' fungus, soaked for 25 minutes
1 tablespoon	rendered chicken fat (chicken grease)
	salt
	m.s.g. (optional)

Wash the chicken and cut through the bones into 2.5 cm (1 in) pieces. Heat the lard and stir-fry the chicken until lightly coloured, about 2½ minutes. Push to one side of the pan and add the spring onions and ginger and stir-fry briefly.

Sizzle the wine onto the sides of the pan and add the black pepper, stir in, then pour in the water and bring to the boil. Simmer on low heat until the chicken is completely tender, about 35 minutes.

Strain the liquid into a saucepan and simmer slowly, adjusting the seasoning with salt and m.s.g., if used, to taste.

Drain the 'wood ears' well and cut into small squares. Stir-fry the well-drained chicken pieces with the 'wood ears' in the chicken fat for about 1 minute. Add a dash of salt and m.s.g., to taste.

Serve the soup in a deep dish and arrange the chicken and 'wood ears' on another dish to serve at the same time. For extra flavour, add sliced young green vegetables to the soup.

Szechuan (Sichuan) Prawns in Chilli Oil Sauce (recipe page 204).

SPICED DEEP-FRIED CHICKEN LEGS

Sever as an appetiser or main dish.

12	small chicken drumsticks
2	eggs, well beaten
	cornflour (cornstarch)
	dry breadcrumbs (optional)
7 cups (1¾ litres)	deep-frying oil
	Chinese pepper-salt

Seasoning:

½ teaspoon	salt
¾ teaspoon	five spice powder
1 tablespoon	light soy sauce
2 teaspoons	dark soy sauce
2 teaspoons	rice wine or dry sherry
½ teaspoon	sesame oil
1 tablespoon	finely chopped spring onion (scallion)
2 teaspoons	finely chopped fresh ginger

Prick the drumsticks all over with a sharp skewer and place in a dish. Add the pre-mixed seasoning ingredients and rub the drumsticks thoroughly. Leave for 1 hour to marinate, turning occasionally.

Heat the deep-frying oil to moderate. Wipe the drumsticks with kitchen paper and brush with beaten eggs, then coat with the cornflour or dry breadcrumbs. Deep-fry several at a time until well coloured and cooked through, about 3½ minutes.

Drain and arrange on a serving plate on crisp fresh lettuce. Sprinkle on a generous amount of Chinese pepper-salt (see page 384) or serve separately as a dip.

DUCK SMOKED OVER CAMPHOR WOOD AND TEA LEAVES

1 2¼ kg (4½ lb)	fat duck
2½ tablespoons	Chinese pepper-salt (see page 384)
1½ tablespoons	saltpetre (optional)
8 cups (2 litres)	deep-frying oil

For Smoking:

2 cups	camphor wood chips
½ cup	Chinese black tea leaves
2 pieces	dried orange peel

Clean and dress the duck. Wash well and dry with kitchen paper, then rub thoroughly inside and out with a mixture of the pepper-salt and saltpetre, if used. Place in a dish and leave for at least 5 hours to absorb the flavours. Wrap with plastic wrap to prevent the skin drying out while marinating.

Place the wood chips, tea leaves, and orange peel in a large old iron wok or cooking pot and set a rack over it. Place the duck, breast down, on the rack. Cover with a wok lid or another old cooking pan and smoke over moderate heat for about 10 minutes. Reduce the heat once the wood starts smoking well. Turn the duck and smoke the other side for about 6 minutes, then remove.

Transfer to a dish and set in a steamer to steam for 1¾ hours. Remove, drain well and wipe the moisture from the skin. Heat the deep-frying oil to smoking point and deep-fry the duck until the skin is dark brown and very crisp, about 2 minutes.

Cut into serving portions and arrange on a plate, or debone and tear the meat into slivers. Serve with accompaniments of sliced spring onion or leek, hoisin, plum, or 'duck' sauce (see page 385) and steamed bread or 'Mandarin' pancakes (see page 373).

Another method of preparing a smoked duck involves marinating in the same way, then steaming for about 45 minutes before smoking over a mixture of jasmine tea leaves and pine needles, then deep-frying until the skin is crisp and red-gold.

Either method produces moist meat permeated with a delicate smoky flavour.

CRISP OIL-BASTED DUCK COOKED TWICE

1 1¾ kg (3½ lb)	duck
375 g (12 oz)	salted turnip or mustard leaves*
¼ cup (2 fl oz)	rice wine or dry sherry
⅓ cup	sugar
2 tablespoons	boiling water
8 cups (2 litres)	deep-frying oil

Dish 1:

12	flower-shaped steamed buns (see recipe, page 372)
4 tablespoons	'duck', hoisin, or plum sauce (see page 385)
6	spring onions (scallions), or 1 shredded leek

Dish 2:

2 tablespoons	softened lard or frying oil
½	small leek, shredded
1	small green or red capsicum (bell pepper), shredded
1	fresh red chilli pepper, shredded
45 g (1½ oz)	'silver' or bean sprouts, blanched
2 slices	fresh ginger, shredded
2 cloves	garlic, sliced (optional)

Seasoning:

¼ teaspoon	salt
¼ teaspoon	m.s.g. (optional)
¾ teaspoon	sugar
2 teaspoons	rice wine or dry sherry
1 tablespoon	hot black bean sauce or sweet bean paste

Clean and dress the duck and rinse well. Wipe dry and stuff the salted vegetables into the cavity, or put in the pepper-salt and shake the bird to evenly distribute around the inside. Tie a string around the neck and hang in a well-ventilated place over a drip tray. Leave for 2 hours. Heat the wine, sugar, and water together until the sugar has completely dissolved, then pour slowly and evenly over the duck and leave until the skin is completely dry, about 6 hours.

Prepare the steamed buns and other accompaniments for dish 1, and the ingredients for dish 2.

Heat the deep-frying oil to smoking point. Place the duck in a large strainer or frying basket and hold over the oil. Ladle the hot oil continuously over the duck until completely cooked through, about 45 minutes. Or lower the duck into slightly cooler oil to deep-fry for 10 minutes, then remove and leave to cool. Re-fry again in warm oil until cooked through, about 25 minutes more, removing several times to cool.

To serve, take the accompaniments for dish 1 to the table. Slice off the crisp skin and arrange on a serving plate with a little of the meat, preferably the breast cuts. Return the duck to the kitchen.

The duck skin, together with a few shreds of spring onion, or leek, should be dipped into the sauce and eaten with the buns. Or the buns may be opened at the fold and the skin and onion inserted, sandwich fashion.

Slice off the remaining meat and cut any of the larger pieces into bite-sized chunks. Heat the lard or oil and stir-fry the duck until the edges are crisp and lightly coloured. Remove and keep warm. Add the shredded ingredients and the garlic, if used, and stir-fry together for about 2 minutes, then add the seasoning ingredients and stir-fry briefly. Return the duck pieces and reduce the heat slightly. Stir-fry together until evenly mixed and heated through.

Serve with any remaining steamed buns or with white rice. As an additional course, the duck carcass can be simmered in water with spring onion, ginger, and seasonings added to be served as a soup at the end of the meal.

*Or use 1 tablespoon of Chinese pepper-salt (see page 384)

SMOKED DUCK SAUTÉD WITH YOUNG GINGER

½	smoked duck (see previous page)
2½ tablespoons	softened lard or frying oil
5 cm (2 in) piece	fresh young ginger, peeled and thinly sliced*
2	fresh red chilli peppers, shred
1 tablespoon	hot bean paste**
5	garlic chives, sliced
½ teaspoon	Chinese brown vinegar

Seasoning:

2 tablespoons	light soy sauce
1 tablespoon	rice wine or dry sherry
1 tablespoon	sugar

Debone the duck and cut the meat into bite-sized pieces. Heat the lard or frying oil in a wok and sauté the duck until lightly coloured and crisp on the edges, about 2 minutes. Remove and drain.

Reheat the pan and add the ginger and chilli peppers. Sauté briefly on moderate heat and add the hot bean paste, or sweet bean paste, if used. Sauté for 20 seconds, then return the duck and add the garlic chives and stir-fry briefly.

Add the seasoning ingredients and sauté together for 1 minute, then stir in the vinegar and transfer to a serving plate.
* Choose a piece with smooth pale cream skin and pink buds.
** If preferred, omit the hot bean paste, substitute sweet bean paste and use less sugar.

ROAST DUCK STUFFED WITH PORK AND BEAN SPROUTS

1 1½ kg (3 lb)	duck
90 g (3 oz)	fresh bean sprouts
90 g (3 oz)	lean pork
2	spring onions (scallions), trimmed and shredded
3 slices	fresh ginger, shredded
2 tablespoons	frying oil
185 g (6 oz)	Chinese (celery) cabbage

Glaze:

2 tablespoons	rice wine or dry sherry
2½ tablespoons	malt sugar
¾ teaspoon	salt

Seasoning:

¾ teaspoon	salt
1 tablespoon	light soy sauce
2 teaspoons	rice wine or dry sherry

Sauce:

2 teaspoons	sugar
1 tablespoon	light soy sauce
1 tablespoon	white vinegar
1 tablespoon	sesame oil
¼ teaspoon	m.s.g. (optional)
½ teaspoon	chilli oil

Clean and dress the duck and pour several lots of boiling water over the skin. Mix the glaze ingredients in a small saucepan and heat until the sugar has completely dissolved, then pour slowly and evenly over the duck. Tie a string around the neck and hang in a well-ventilated place to dry, about 7 hours.

Wash the bean sprouts, drain well, and chop coarsely. Cut the pork into small dice. Stir-fry the spring onions and ginger in the frying oil for 30 seconds, then add the pork and stir-fry until the colour changes. Add the seasoning ingredients and stir-fry briefly, then remove from the heat and mix in the chopped bean sprouts.

Stuff into the duck and close the openings with poultry pins. Roast the duck slowly on a spit over a glowing charcoal fire or on a rotisserie in a moderate oven (190°C/375°F) for 1 hour, then increase the heat to fairly hot and continue to cook until the skin is crisp and deep gold in colour. Remove from the heat and cut into serving pieces.

Wash and shred the cabbage and mix with the sauce ingredients. Arrange around the edge of a large serving plate. Place the duck in the centre with the stuffing underneath the meat. Serve.

HUNAN CRISPY DUCK

1 2kg (4 lb)	duck
8 cups (2 litres)	deep-frying oil
	Chinese pepper-salt (see page 384)
	'duck', hoisin, or plum sauce (see page 385)
	steam flower-shaped buns (see page 372)

Seasoning:

4	star anise, crushed
1 tablespoon	Chinese brown peppercorns, crushed
1 tablespoon	fennel seeds, crushed
2 teaspoons	salt
1 tablespoon	rice wine or dry sherry
2 tablespoons	fine chopped spring onion (scallion)
2 tablespoons	fine chopped fresh ginger

Clean and dress the duck and rub inside and out with the pre-mixed seasoning ingredients. Set in a large dish and place on a rack in a steamer. Cover and steam over rapidly boiling water for 2½ hours. Remove duck and wipe off the seasonings, scraping away those that are inside.

Heat the deep-frying oil to fairly hot and place the duck in a frying basket. Lower into the oil to deep-fry until the duck is completely crisp. Serve whole to be torn into strips and served with the accompaniments of pepper-salt, sauce, and steamed buns.

The duck will be so tender after the long steaming and deep-frying that the bones can be eaten with the meat. Top up the level of the water in the steamer frequently during cooking to prevent it from boiling dry.

Honey-Glazed Ham (recipe page 210).

STEAMED DUCK MARINATED WITH PRESERVED EGG AND WINE

1 1½ kg (3 lb)	duck
2	spring onions (scallions), trimmed and sliced
5 slices	fresh ginger

Seasoning:

2	preserved duck eggs*
¼ cup (2 fl oz)	rice wine or dry sherry
2 tablespoons	sweet rice wine or Japanese mirin (optional)
1½ teaspoons	salt
2 teaspoons	sugar
¾ teaspoon	m.s.g. (optional)

Clean and dress the duck, wash well and dry with kitchen paper. Tie a string around the neck and hang the duck in a well-ventilated place for about 4 hours to dry the skin. Place the spring onions and ginger in the cavity.

Mix the seasoning ingredients together, mashing to a smooth paste. Smear thickly over the duck and leave for 30 minutes. Place the duck in a casserole, breast up, and cover with a sheet of greaseproof paper, then press the lid firmly into place over it. Set on a rack in a steamer and steam over high heat until the duck is tender, about 1½ hours.

Serve whole to be sliced at the table.

* 'Thousand Year' eggs. If unobtainable, use salted duck eggs (see page 363) or mash two hard-boiled (hard cooked) duck or chicken egg yolks with 2 cubes of fermented beancurd.

DEEP-FRIED DUCK WITH LAVER

1 1¾ kg (3½ lb)	duck
45 g (1½ oz)	dried laver or Japanese nori*
8 cups (2 litres)	deep-frying oil
¾ teaspoon	salt
2 teaspoons	rice wine or dry sherry
2 tablespoons	duck stock**
1 tablespoon	rendered chicken fat (chicken grease) (optional)

Seasoning A:

¾ teaspoon	salt
1 tablespoon	rice wine or dry sherry
2 tablespoons	finely chopped spring onion (scallion)
2 teaspoons	grated fresh ginger

Seasoning B/Sauce:

2 tablespoons	finely chopped spring onion (scallion)
2 teaspoons	finely chopped fresh ginger
1 — 2 tablespoons	finely chopped fresh red chilli peppers
2 tablespoons	light soy sauce
2 teaspoons	dark soy sauce
¼ cup (2 fl oz)	duck stock**
1½ teaspoons	rice wine or dry sherry
1 tablespoon	sugar
2 teaspoons	white vinegar
1½ teaspoons	cornflour (cornstarch)

Clean and dress the duck and place in a dish. Rub with the seasoning A ingredients and leave for 20 minutes, then set the dish on a rack in a steamer and add ½ cup water. Steam over high heat until the duck is tender, about 1¼ hours.

Remove the duck and wipe off the moisture, reserving the liquid for later use. Soak the laver or nori in cold water to soften. Heat the deep-frying oil to smoking point and deep-fry the duck until golden. Remove, drain, and place, breast up, on a serving plate.

Pour off all but 2½ tablespoons of the oil and sauté the well-drained laver for 45 seconds. Add the salt, wine, 2 tablespoons of the duck stock, and the chicken fat, if used, and sauté a further 1 minute, then arrange around the duck.

Wipe out the wok and add another 2½ tablespoons of oil. Sauté the spring onion, ginger, and chilli peppers for about 45 seconds, then add the remaining ingredients, pre-mixed. Bring to the boil and simmer until thickened, then pour over the duck.

If using broccoli or cauliflower, sauté with the same ingredients until softened.

* Use fresh broccoli or cauliflower broken into florets as a substitute.
** Reserve after steaming the duck.

'LANTERN' CHICKEN

1 1¼ kg (2½ lb)	chicken
750 g (1½ lb)	pork omentum (caul fat)
1 teaspoon	chilli oil
3	eggs, beaten
	cornflour (cornstarch)
8 cups (2 litres)	deep-frying oil
1 cup	canned sweet pickled garlic* (optional)

Seasoning:

¾ teaspoon	salt
½ teaspoon	m.s.g. (optional)
1½ tablespoons	rice wine or dry sherry
2 tablespoons	chopped spring onion (scallion)
1 tablespoon	chopped fresh ginger
1½ teaspoons	five spice powder

Clean and dress the chicken and wipe with kitchen paper. Mix the salt, m.s.g., if used, and wine and rub over the skin, then pour the remainder into the cavity. Place the remaining seasoning ingredients inside the bird and place in a dish. Cover with plastic wrap and leave for 2½ hours.

Place the chicken, breast up, in a heatproof dish and cover with a sheet of greaseproof paper. Stick the paper onto the bowl with a thick paste of flour and water, then set the dish on a rack in a steamer and steam over high heat until cooked, about 50 minutes.

Remove, drain, and cut off the leg and wing bones, leaving just the body section. Spread the caul fat on a board and wipe carefully with a wet cloth to clean. Rub the chilli oil over the chicken. Cut the caul fat into three even-sized pieces, each large enough to wrap the chicken. Wrap one piece around the chicken, then brush thickly with beaten egg and wrap another piece of fat around. Coat with more beaten egg and the final piece of fat, then coat with cornflour.

Heat the deep-frying oil to moderately hot. Place the chicken in a large strainer and lower into the hot oil to deep-fry until the surface is crisp and golden. Drain well.

Cut open the uppermost layer of crisp fat and remove. Cut into cubes and arrange on one side of a serving plate. Remove and discard the other layers of fat, unless very crisp. Cut the chicken into serving portions and arrange in the centre of the plate, then arrange the drained sweet pickled garlic on the other side.

* If sweet pickled garlic is unobtainable, substitute pickled shallots or ginger, or prepare home-made sweet pickled cucumber and carrot by marinating sliced cucumber and carrot in a mixture of white vinegar, salt, and sugar.

CRISP-SKIN FISH WITH HOT AND SOUR SAUCE

1 1 kg (2 lb)	whole fresh fish
2	egg whites, beaten
2 tablespoons	cornflour (cornstarch)
	extra cornflour (cornstarch)
8 cups (2 litres)	deep-frying oil
2	pickled red chilli peppers, shredded
2	spring onions (scallions), trimmed and shredded
5 thick slices	fresh ginger, shredded

Seasoning:

½ teaspoon	salt
1 tablespoon	light soy sauce
1 tablespoon	rice wine or dry sherry

Sauce:

⅓ cup	chicken stock
2 tablespoons	light soy sauce
1 teaspoon	dark soy sauce
¼ cup (2 fl oz)	Chinese brown vinegar
¼ cup	sugar
2 teaspoons	rice wine or dry sherry
2½ teaspoons	cornflour (cornstarch)
1½ teaspoons	chilli oil

Clean and scale the fish and score diagonally across each side. Mix the seasoning A ingredients together and rub over the fish. Leave for 20 minutes, turning once. Mix the cornflour and egg whites together and brush thickly over the fish. Coat lightly with extra cornflour.

Heat the deep-frying oil to fairly hot and slide in the fish. Fry for 3 minutes on one side, then turn and fry for about 4 minutes on the other side. Turn again and cook for about 2 minutes, then lift out, drain well and place on a serving plate. Keep warm.

Pour off the oil, wipe out the wok and return about 2 tablespoons of the oil, or use softened lard. Stir-fry the chilli peppers, spring onions, and ginger for 1 minute, then add the pre-mixed sauce ingredients and bring to the boil. Simmer for 2 minutes, then pour over the fish.

GOLDEN CARP WITH A PHOENIX TAIL

2 625 g (1¼ lb)	golden carp (sea bass or red snapper)
1 440 g (14 oz) can	asparagus spears*
45 g (1½ fl oz)	canned small champignons, drained
3 cups (24 fl oz)	frying oil
1½ tablespoons	finely chopped spring onion
2 teaspoons	finely chopped fresh ginger

Seasoning A:

1 tablespoon	ginger wine (see page 387)
1½ teaspoons	salt
1 tablespoon	cornflour (cornstarch)

Seasoning B/Sauce:

1¾ cups (14 fl oz)	chicken stock
1½ tablespoons	evaporated milk (optional)
1 tablespoon	light soy sauce
2 teaspoons	rice wine or dry sherry
¾ teaspoon	salt
¼ teaspoon	white pepper

Clean and scale the fish and score in a criss-cross pattern across each side. Place in a dish with the seasoning A ingredients and leave for 25 minutes, turning occasionally. Drain the asparagus and cut each spear in halves lengthwise. Return to the canning liquid. Cut the mushrooms in halves horizontally.

Heat the frying oil in a wok to fairly hot and fry the fish on both sides until lightly coloured. Remove and drain well. Pour off all but 3 tablespoons of the oil and add the spring onion and ginger. Sauté briefly, then return the fish, placing them head to tail. Add the seasoning B ingredients, then arrange the asparagus on one side of the fish and the mushrooms on the other side.

Cover and simmer for about 20 minutes until the fish are tender, then carefully slide the fish onto a serving plate, keeping the two heads at opposite ends of the plate. Arrange half of the asparagus over each fish tail in an elaborate phoenix-tail shape and decorate with the sliced mushrooms. Bring the sauce to the boil, check the seasoning and thicken with a paste of cornflour and cold water. Pour over the fish and serve.
* Choose the dark green type.

WHOLE STUFFED FISH DEEP-FRIED IN A CRISP PORK FAT COATING

1 750 g (1½ lb)	whole fish (sea bass, fresh trout, snapper)
90 g (3 oz)	fatty pork, coarsely minced (ground)
60 g (2 oz)	Szechuan (Sichuan) preserved vegetables, soaked
8 cups (2 litres)	deep-frying oil
625 g (1¼ lb)	pork omentum (caul fat)
3	egg whites, well beaten
¼ cup	cornflour (cornstarch)
	Chinese pepper-salt
	chilli oil

Seasoning A:

1 teaspoon	salt
½ teaspoon	m.s.g. (optional)
1 tablespoon	rice wine or dry sherry

Seasoning B:

2 tablespoons	finely chopped spring onion (scallion)
1½ teaspoons	finely chopped fresh ginger
1 tablespoon	rice wine or dry sherry
1 tablespoon	light soy sauce

Scale the fish, then remove the backbone and entrails by cutting down through the back. Score in a criss-cross pattern across each side, cutting just through the skin. Rub with the seasoning A ingredients and leave for 15 minutes.

Mix the pork with the seasoning B ingredients and stir-fry in 2 tablespoons of the deep-frying oil until the pork changes colour. Drain the preserved vegetable and squeeze out as much water as possible. Cut into fine dice and add to the pork, frying briefly. Remove and spread on a plate to cool.

Wipe the pork net with a wet cloth and cut into two pieces, each large enough to completely wrap the fish. Stuff the pork and vegetable mixture into the fish. Make a paste with the egg whites and cornflour and brush thickly over the fish. Wrap in one piece of the pork net, then brush the whole wrapped fish from one end to the other with the remaining egg batter.

Wrap with the other piece of pork net and coat thickly with cornflour. Heat the deep-frying oil to smoking point, then lower the heat slightly. Slide the fish in carefully and deep-fry, completely immersed, until the coating has turned crisp and golden and the fish is cooked through, about 7 minutes. Decrease the heat if the surface colours too quickly.

Remove the fish and carefully remove the outer layer. Cut into diamond-shaped pieces and arrange around the edge of a serving plate. Remove the second layer of net and discard, then scrape the skin off the fish and place the whole fish in the centre of the plate. Garnish and serve with dips of Chinese pepper-salt and chilli oil (see pages 384 and 385).

196

'Pearl' Balls (recipe page 216).

STEAMED FRESH FISH WITH SZECHUAN(SICHUAN) PICKLED VEGETABLES AND 'WOOD EARS'

1 825 g (1¾ lb)	whole fresh fish (snapper, sea bass, etc.)
30 g (1 oz)	fat pork
20 g (¾ oz)	Szechuan (Sichuan) preserved vegetables, soaked
10 g (⅓ oz)	dried 'wood ear' fungus, soaked for 25 minutes
2	spring onions (scallions), trimmed and shredded
4 slices	fresh ginger, shredded
1	fresh red chilli pepper, shredded
2 cloves	garlic, cut into slivers
2 tablespoons	frying oil
1 teaspoon	sesame oil
	white pepper

Seasoning:

1 teaspoon	salt
½ teaspoon	m.s.g. (optional)
¼ teaspoon	white pepper
1 tablespoon	light soy sauce
1 tablespoon	rice wine or dry sherry
1 tablespoon	vegetable oil
1 teaspoon	sesame oil
½ teaspoon	cornflour (cornstarch)

Wash the fish and scale. Make several diagonal scores across each side. Place on a large oval plate. Cut the pork, drained vegetables and 'wood ears' into fine shreds and arrange with the spring onions, ginger, chilli peppers, and garlic over the fish. Pour on the pre-mixed seasoning ingredients and set the plate on a rack in a steamer.

Steam over high heat for 17 — 20 minutes, then test by inserting a fork into the thickest part of the meat. It should easily lift away from the bones. Remove from the heat and strain the pan juices into a wok. Bring to the boil and adjust the seasoning to taste.

In a separate pan, heat the frying oil and sesame oil together to smoking point. Pour over the fish, then pour on the sauce and season generously with white pepper. Serve at once.

WHOLE FISH WITH GARLIC IN HOT SAUCE

1 1 kg (2 lb)	reef fish (sea bass, snapper, perch)
¾ teaspoon	salt
1 tablespoon	rice wine or dry sherry
2 cups (16 fl oz)	frying oil
2 whole heads	fresh garlic, peeled
1½ tablespoons	hot bean paste
2	spring onions (scallions), trimmed and sliced
2 teaspoons	finely chopped fresh ginger
½ teaspoon	m.s.g. (optional)

Seasoning/Sauce:

1¾ cups (14 fl oz)	chicken or fish stock
2 tablespoons	light soy sauce
2 teaspoons	Chinese brown vinegar
2 teaspoons	sugar
2 teaspoons	rice wine or dry sherry

Clean and scale the fish and score diagonally across both sides, cutting almost to the bone. Rub with the salt and wine and set aside.

Heat the oil to moderate and fry the garlic until softened, about 2 minutes. Remove and set aside. Add the fish to the oil and fry on both sides until golden, then carefully lift out. Pour off all but 2 tablespoons of the oil and fry the bean paste briefly, then add the spring onions and ginger and fry for a few seconds.

Pour in the pre-mixed seasoning/sauce ingredients and return the fish. Bring to the boil, add the garlic, cover the pan and simmer until the fish is tender and the sauce well reduced, about 25 minutes.

Thicken the sauce, if necessary, with a thin solution of cornflour (cornstarch) and cold water. Stir in the m.s.g., if used, and serve.

HERRING IN BLACK BEAN SAUCE

1 1 kg (2 lb)	Hilsa herring (sea bass or perch)
1	small red capsicum (bell pepper)
1	small green capsicum (bell pepper)
1½ tablespoons	fermented black beans
6 cups (1½ litres)	deep-frying oil
3	spring onions (scallions), trimmed and diced
3 slices	fresh ginger, chopped
1 teaspoon	Chinese brown vinegar

Seasoning A:

1	egg white, beaten
¾ teaspoon	salt
1 tablespoon	light soy sauce
1 tablespoon	rice wine or dry sherry
2 tablespoons	cornflour (cornstarch)

Seasoning B/Sauce:

1¼ cups (10 fl oz)	fish stock or water
2 tablespoons	light soy sauce
2 teaspoons	dark soy sauce
2 teaspoons	rice wine or dry sherry
2¼ teaspoons	sugar

Clean and scale the fish and place in a dish with the seasoning A ingredients. Leave for 20 minutes, turning once. Cut the peppers in halves and trim away the stems, seed cores, and inner white ribs and cut into narrow shreds. Wash the black beans, dry and chop finely.

Heat the deep-frying oil to smoking point, then reduce the heat slightly. Slide in the fish to fry for about 2 minutes on each side. Lift out and set aside. Pour off all but 2 tablespoons of the oil and add the peppers, black beans, spring onions, and ginger. Stir-fry together for 1½ minutes, then add the seasoning B/sauce ingredients and bring to the boil. Return the fish, cover and simmer for about 20 minutes until the fish is tender and the sauce reduced.

Transfer the fish to a serving plate with the shredded pepper on top. Bring the sauce to the boil and thicken with a thin solution of cornflour and cold water. Check the seasonings and add the vinegar. Pour over the fish and serve.

POACHED FISH IN EGG FLOWER SAUCE

1 750 g (1½ lb)	fresh-water fish
2 tablespoons	rice wine or dry sherry
2	spring onions (scallions), trimmed and halved
3 slices	fresh ginger, shredded
2/3 teaspoon	salt
¼ teaspoon	m.s.g. (optional)
1 tablespoon	frying oil
3	whole eggs, well beaten

Clean and scale the fish and place in a large oval-shaped fish kettle. Add the remaining ingredients, except the eggs, and cover with warm water. Allow the water to come almost to the boil, then reduce the heat to low and gently poach until the fish is tender, about 15 minutes.

Lift out the fish, using two large spatulas, and place in a serving dish. Bring the stock to a rapid boil and discard the onion and ginger. Remove from the heat and slowly drizzle in the beaten egg, then leave to set without stirring. Check the seasoning and pour over the fish.

If preferred, thicken the sauce slightly with a thin solution of cornflour (cornstarch) and cold water. Add finely chopped fresh coriander or spring onion for extra flavour and colour.

SZECHUAN (SICHUAN) SMOKED FISH

1 750 g (1½ lb)	fresh fish (perch, snapper, sea bass)
6 cups (1½ litres)	deep-frying oil
1½ cups	wood chips
1 cup	chopped dry straw (or use black tea leaves)
	sesame oil

Seasoning A:

2 tablespoons	finely chopped spring onion (scallion)
1 tablespoon	finely chopped fresh ginger
1 tablespoon	rice wine or dry sherry
1¼ teaspoons	salt

Seasoning B:

2 tablespoons	frying oil
1½ tablespoons	finely chopped spring onion (scallion)
2 teaspoons	finely chopped fresh ginger
1 — 2	fresh red chilli peppers, chopped
¼ cup (2 fl oz)	light soy sauce
1 tablespoon	Chinese brown vinegar
2 teaspoons	rice wine or dry sherry
1 tablespoon	sugar
¼ teaspoon	m.s.g. (optional)
1½ cups (12 fl oz)	chicken stock

Clean the fish and remove the gills and fins. Score in a criss-cross pattern over both sides. Place in a dish with the seasoning A ingredients and leave for 20 minutes, turning occasionally. Heat the deep-frying oil to fairly hot and deep-fry the fish until golden, about 2 minutes. Remove and drain well.

Heat the frying oil and stir-fry the spring onion, ginger, and chilli peppers briefly, then add the remaining seasoning B ingredients and bring to the boil. Add the fish and simmer on low heat until the fish is tender, about 15 minutes, then carefully lift out the fish and place on a wire rack. Retain the sauce.

Heat the smoking ingredients (wood chips and straw or tea) in a large old iron wok or saucepan until they begin to smoke. Place the fish on the rack in the wok or pan and cover. Smoke for about 6 minutes on one side, then carefully turn and smoke the other side for 4 — 5 minutes.

Return the fish to the sauce and simmer briefly. Add sesame oil to taste and transfer to a serving plate with the sauce. Serve hot.

SLICED FISH AND CELERY IN HOT AND SOUR SAUCE

250 g (8 oz)	white fish fillets
1 stalk	young celery
3	egg whites, well beaten
	cornflour (cornstarch)
4 cups (1 litre)	deep-frying oil
1 tablespoon	softened lard (optional)
1	spring onion (scallion), trimmed and shredded
3 thick slices	fresh ginger, shredded
1 — 2	pickled red chilli peppers, shredded
	sesame oil (optional)

Seasoning A:

½ teaspoon	salt
½ teaspoon	m.s.g. (optional)
2 teaspoons	rice wine or dry sherry

Seasoning B/Sauce:

2/3 cup	fish or chicken stock
¾ teaspoon	salt
½ teaspoon	m.s.g. (optional)
2 teaspoons	sugar
1 tablespoon	Chinese brown vinegar
1½ teaspoons	cornflour (cornstarch)

Skin the fillets and cut into thin slices, then rub with the seasoning A ingredients and leave for 15 minutes. Cut the celery into matchstick pieces. Coat the fish first in beaten egg white, then thickly with cornflour, shaking off the excess.

Heat the deep-frying oil to fairly hot and deep-fry the fish slices, about 6 at a time, until crisp and lightly coloured, about 1½ minutes. Remove and drain well.

Pour off the oil and add the lard, or retain 2 tablespoons of the oil. Stir-fry the celery and carrot until softened on moderate heat, then add the spring onions, ginger and chilli and stir-fry briefly. Pour in the pre-mixed seasoning B/sauce ingredients and bring to the boil. Reduce the heat slightly and return the fish slices. Simmer until the sauce thickens, then stir in a dash of sesame oil and serve.

200

Shredded Beef with Bamboo Shoots (recipe page 219).

SLICED FISH BRAISED IN SPICY SAUCE

375 g (12 oz)	meaty white fish fillets
3 cups (24 fl oz)	deep-frying oil
1½	spring onions (scallions), trimmed and diced
3 thick slices	fresh ginger, shredded
2	pickled red chilli peppers, shredded
¾ teaspoon	crushed garlic
2 tablespoons	soy bean paste
2 teaspoons	Chinese brown vinegar

Seasoning A:

½ teaspoon	salt
½ teaspoon	sugar
1 tablespoon	rice wine or dry sherry

Seasoning B/Sauce:

1½ cups (10 fl oz)	fish stock or water
2 tablespoons	light soysauce
2¼ teaspoons	sugar
1 tablespoon	rice wine or dry sherry

Cut the fish into thick slices across the fillets, cutting at a slight angle. Place in a dish with the seasoning A ingredients and leave for 15 minutes, turning occasionally.

Heat the deep-frying oil to moderately hot and fry the fish for about 20 seconds, then remove and drain well. Pour off all but 2½ tablespoons of the oil and stir-fry the spring onions, ginger, chillies, and garlic for 1 minute, then add the soybean paste and stir-fry a further 30 seconds. Add the pre-mixed seasoning B/sauce ingredients and simmer briefly, return the fish and cover the pan. Simmer on moderate to low heat until the fish is completely tender and the sauce well reduced. Stir in the vinegar and thicken the sauce with a thin solution of cornflour (cornstarch) and cold water. Transfer to a serving plate.

TWO-TONED STEAMED FISH CAKE

250 g (8 oz)	white fish fillets
75 g (2½ oz)	pork fat
90 g (3 oz)	young spinach leaves (collard greens)
⅓ cup	boiling chicken stock or water
¼ cup (2 fl oz)	onion and ginger infusion (see page 386)
4	egg whites, well beaten
3 tablespoons	cornflour (cornstarch)

Seasoning A:

¾ teaspoon	salt
½ teaspoon	m.s.g. (optional)
¼ teaspoon	ground black pepper
2 teaspoons	rice wine or dry sherry

Seasoning B:

½ cup (4 fl oz)	chicken stock
½ teaspoon	salt
¼ teaspoon	ground black pepper
1 teaspoon	rice wine or dry sherry
2 tablespoons	rendered chicken fat (chicken grease) (optional)
1 teaspoon	cornflour (cornstarch)

Pulverise the fish and pork fat using two cleavers (see page 396) or in a food processor with the chopping blade. Mix with the seasoning A ingredients. Blend the spinach leaves and hot stock or water until well puréed, then transfer to a dish lined with a piece of clean muslin and squeeze out as much green liquid as possible.

Divide the fish paste into two equal parts and add the spinach liquid to one and the onion and ginger infusion to the other. Add half of the beaten egg whites and cornflour to each portion and stir in one direction only until both mixtures are smooth and thick.

Grease a dish and pour in the white mixture. Place on a rack in a steamer and steam for 6 minutes, then carefully wipe the moisture from the top and pour on the green-coloured paste. Return to the steamer and steam until the fish cake is firm.

Invert onto a serving plate. Bring the seasoning B ingredients to the boil in a wok, adding 2 tablespoons of softened lard or oil if the chicken fat is not being used. Add the squeezed spinach and simmer in the sauce until thickened. Pour over the cake and serve at once.

FISH HEADS AND BEANCURD SIMMERED IN A POT

750 g (1½ lb)	*fresh fish heads**
⅓ cup	*frying oil*
1 tablespoon	*softened lard (optional)*
2 tablespoons	*finely chopped spring onion (scallion)*
1½ teaspoons	*finely chopped fresh ginger*
1 tablespoon	*rice wine or dry sherry*
6	*dried black mushrooms, soaked for 25 minutes*
30 g (1 oz)	*dried shrimps, soaked for 1 hour (optional)*
60 g (2 oz)	*canned bamboo shoots, drained*
3 squares	*soft beancurd*
¾ teaspoon	*m.s.g. (optional)*
4	*garlic chives, shredded*

Seasoning/Sauce:

5 cups (1¼ litres)	*fish stock*
1¼ teaspoons	*salt*
¼ teaspoon	*white pepper*
1 tablespoon	*rice wine or dry sherry*

Wash the fish heads and cut in halves. Heat the oil and fry the heads until lightly coloured, then transfer to a casserole. Pour off the oil and add the lard, if used, or retain 1½ tablespoons of the oil. Stir-fry the spring onion and ginger for 30 seconds, then sizzle in the rice wine and stir in. Add to the casserole.

Drain the mushrooms and squeeze out the water, remove the stems and cut the caps into dice. Drain the shrimps, if used. Cube the bamboo shoots. Stir-fry for 1 minute, then add to the casserole. Pour in the seasoning/sauce ingredients and bring to the boil. Reduce heat to low and simmer for 35 minutes.

Soak the beancurd in cold water after cutting into small cubes. When the fish heads are done, remove the smaller bones and add the beancurd. Simmer for 3 minutes, add the m.s.g., if used, and garlic chives and simmer briefly, then serve in the casserole.

* Choose large meaty heads of oily fish such as reef fish, mullet, or herring.

SLICED PRAWNS IN SOUR SAUCE

6	*large raw prawns (shrimps), in the shell (about 500 g / 1 lb)*
	cornflour (cornstarch)
15 g (½ oz)	*dried 'snow' fungus, soaked for 25 minutes*
45 g (1½ oz)	*fresh or frozen green peas, parboiled*
1	*small carrot, thinly sliced and parboiled*
4 cups (1 litre)	*deep-frying oil*
⅓ teaspoon	*sesame oil*

Seasoning A:

2	*egg whites, well beaten*
½ teaspoon	*salt*
1 teaspoon	*ginger wine*
1 tablespoon	*cornflour (cornstarch)*

Seasoning B/Sauce:

⅓ cup	*chicken stock*
⅓ cup	*sugar*
¼ cup (2 fl oz)	*Chinese brown vinegar*
½ teaspoon	*salt*
½ teaspoon	*m.s.g. (optional)*
1 teaspoon	*cornflour (cornstarch)*

Shell the prawns leaving the tail sections intact. Slit in halves down the centre back and remove the dark vein. Cut the prawn halves crosswise to give 24 pieces. Place in a dish with the seasoning A ingredients, mix well and leave for 10 minutes, then coat lightly with cornflour. Squeeze the water from the fungus and trim off the hard root sections, then cut into small squares. Prepare the peas and carrot and set aside.

Heat the frying oil to moderate and deep-fry the prawns for 45 seconds, then remove and drain well. Leave to cool for 10 minutes, then reheat the oil and deep-fry the prawns for a second time until the surface is crisp and golden. Drain and transfer to a plate. Keep warm.

Pour off all but 2½ tablespoons of the oil and stir-fry the fungus, peas, and carrot for 45 seconds, then add the pre-mixed seasoning B/sauce ingredients and simmer until thickened. Return the prawns and turn carefully in the sauce until thoroughly glazed, then transfer to a warmed serving plate and pour on the sauce. In another pan, heat 1 tablespoon of frying oil to smoking point and add the sesame oil. Pour over the dish and serve at once.

SZECHUAN (SICHUAN) PRAWNS IN CHILLI OIL SAUCE

500 g (1 lb)	medium-sized raw peeled prawns (shrimps)
4 cups (1 litre)	deep-frying oil
2 tablespoons	chopped leeks
1 tablespoon	finely chopped ginger
1 teaspoon	sesame oil
1 tablespoon	chilli oil

Seasoning A:

1	egg white, beaten
1 teaspoon	salt
¼ teaspoon	m.s.g. (optional)
1½ teaspoons	ginger wine
1½ tablespoons	cornflour (cornstarch)

Seasoning B/Sauce:

2 tablespoons	tomato sauce (ketchup)
½ teaspoon	salt
1 teaspoon	sugar
¼ cup (2 fl oz)	chicken stock
1 teaspoon	cornflour (cornstarch)

Wash the prawns and cut in halves lengthwise. Place in a dish with the seasoning A ingredients, mix well and leave for 20 minutes. Heat the deep-frying oil to moderately hot and deep-fry the prawns in a basket for about 45 seconds. Remove and drain well.

Pour off all but 2 tablespoons of the oil and fry the leeks and ginger for 30 seconds. Add the sesame and chilli oil and stir-fry for 1 — 2 seconds, then add the pre-mixed seasoning B/sauce ingredients and bring to the boil. Return the prawns and stir in the sauce until warmed through.

Transfer to a serving plate and garnish with chopped fresh coriander or spring onions.

SHRIMP ROLLS SERVED ON MARINATED CARROT AND RADISH

Serve as an appetiser or main dish.

Makes 12.

2	medium carrots, peeled
½	giant white (icicle) radish, peeled
185 g (6 oz)	raw peeled shrimps
90 g (3 oz)	pork fat
6	canned water chestnuts, drained
1	large round beancurd skin*
1	egg white, beaten
1 tablespoon	cornflour (cornstarch)
2 teaspoons	flour
5 cups (1¼ litres)	deep-frying oil

Seasoning A:

⅓ cup	white vinegar
¼ cup (2 fl oz)	cold water
2½ teaspoons	salt
1 tablespoon	sugar
¼ cup (2 fl oz)	sesame oil

Seasoning B:

¼ teaspoon	salt
½ teaspoon	m.s.g. (optional)
¼ teaspoon	white pepper
1 teaspoon	sugar
1 teaspoon	light soy sauce
1 teaspoon	finely chopped spring onion (scallion)
¼ teaspoon	grated fresh ginger
1	egg white, beaten
2 teaspoons	cornflour (cornstarch)

Cut the vegetables into short sticks or thin slices and place in a dish with the seasoning A ingredients. Leave for at least 1 hour.

Pulverise the shrimps and pork fat in a food processor with the chopping blade, or use two cleavers (see page 396). Finely chop the water chestnuts and stir into the pork, adding the seasoning B ingredients. Mix thoroughly, then chill.

Wipe the beancurd skin with a damp cloth and cut into 12 squares of even size. Mix the egg white, cornflour, and flour into a paste. Brush over the beancurd skins, reserving a little. Place a portion of the filling in one corner of each beancurd wrapper and fold over the closest corner, then fold in the two sides, sticking down with the egg paste, and roll up. Use more egg paste to stick down the final flaps.

Heat the deep-frying oil to moderate and deep-fry the shrimp rolls, about 4 at a time, until crisp and cooked through, 3 — 4 minutes. Drain well. Drain the vegetables thoroughly and arrange on a serving plate. Place the shrimp rolls on top. Serve with Chinese pepper-salt (see page 384) and red or brown Chinese vinegar as dips.
* Or use dried beancurd skin pieces soaked until soft.

Szechuan Beef Stew (recipe page 220).

SHRIMPS IN HOT SAUCE ON CRISP RICE CAKES

375 g (12 oz)	raw peeled shrimps
1 stalk	celery
3 cups (24 fl oz)	chicken stock
2 teaspoons	salt
2 teaspoons	sesame oil
10 pieces	rice cakes (see page 386)
4 cups (1 litre)	deep-frying oil

Seasoning A:

½ teaspoon	salt
½ teaspoon	sugar
1½ teaspoons	cornflour (cornstarch)
2 teaspoons	rice wine or dry sherry

Seasoning B:

1 tablespoon	finely chopped fresh ginger
1 teaspoon	finely chopped garlic
⅓ cup	tomato sauce (ketchup)
1 tablespoon	chilli oil
1 tablespoon	light soy sauce
1 tablespoon	Chinese brown vinegar
1 tablespoon	sugar
3 tablespoons	cornflour (cornstarch)
¼ cup (2 fl oz)	cold water

Wash and devein the shrimps and place in a dish with the seasoning A ingredients. Cut the celery into fine dice and set aside. Use a little of the deep-frying oil to stir-fry the shrimps until pink. Remove and set aside. Add the celery and stir-fry until softened, about 1½ minutes. Remove and set aside.

Stir-fry the ginger and garlic, then add the stock and remaining seasoning B ingredients. Bring to the boil and simmer until thickened. Add the salt and sesame oil and the shrimps and celery. Simmer briefly.

Heat the deep-frying oil to smoking point and deep-fry the rice cakes in a frying basket until golden and crisp. Drain and place in a large, well-warmed serving dish. Heat the shrimp sauce to boiling and pour over the rice cakes. Serve at once.

SEA CUCUMBER WITH VEGETABLES AND CRISP PRETZELS

700 g (1⅓ lb)	prepared sea cucumbers (about 4 pieces) (see page 392)
2	spring onions (scallions), trimmed and sliced
6 slices	fresh ginger
45 g (1½ oz)	canned bamboo shoots, drained and sliced
45 g (1½ oz)	canned straw mushrooms or champignons, drained and sliced
60 g (2 oz)	fresh bok choy, cut into 2.5 cm (1 in) pieces
⅓ cup	frying oil
12	wonton wrappers (see page 376)
3 cups (24 fl oz)	deep-frying oil

Seasoning/Sauce:

2 tablespoons	light soy sauce
2 teaspoons	rice wine or dry sherry
¼ teaspoon	m.s.g. (optional)
½ teaspoon	sugar
½ teaspoon	sesame oil
¾ cup (6 fl oz)	chicken stock
1 tablespoon	cornflour (cornstarch)

Soak the prepared sea cucumbers in cold water until needed. Sauté the spring onions, ginger, bamboo shoots, mushrooms, and vegetables in the frying oil for 2 minutes. Drain the sea cucumber and cut into bite-sized pieces. Add to the oil and stir-fry for 1 minute. Add the seasoning/sauce ingredients and bring to the boil.

Simmer until the sauce thickens and the ingredients are cooked. In the meantime, heat the deep-frying oil to smoking point. Cut the wonton wrappers into strips and deep-fry in a frying basket until crisp and golden. Remove and drain well.

Place the fried wonton strips in a serving dish and pour on the sea cucumber mixture. Serve at once.

BRAISED FRESH-WATER EELS

1 625 g (1¼ lb)	fresh-water eel
2	young leeks, trimmed and shredded
4 cloves	garlic, slivered
5 slices	fresh ginger, shredded
⅓ cup	frying oil
1 tablespoon	rice wine or dry sherry
2 teaspoons	soybean paste
1½ tablespoons	cornflour (cornstarch)
2 tablespoons	cold water
	sesame oil
	Chinese brown vinegar

Seasoning:

¼ cup (2 fl oz)	light soy sauce
1 tablespoon	sugar
¼ teaspoon	ground black pepper

Clean and gut the eel and remove the head. Drop into a large pot of boiling water and blanch for 1 minute, then remove and rub with salt to remove the slimy residue on the skin. Rinse thoroughly in cold water. Cut into 4 cm (1 2/3 in) pieces.

Stir-fry the leeks, garlic, and ginger in the frying oil for 30 seconds. Push to one side of the pan and add the eel. Stir-fry on high heat for about 2 minutes, then sizzle the wine onto the sides of the pan and add the soybean paste. Stir in thoroughly.

Add the pre-mixed seasoning ingredients and water to cover and simmer, stirring occasionally, until the eel is tender, about 10 minutes. Add the cornflour mixed with cold water and cook until the sauce thickens. Season with a dash of sesame oil and brown vinegar and serve.

STIR-FRIED SEA SCALLOPS WITH PORK KIDNEYS

280 g (9 oz)	fresh or frozen sea scallops with coral removed
250 g (8 oz)	pork kidneys
¼ cup (2 fl oz)	softened lard or frying oil
1½ tablespoons	finely chopped spring onion (scallion)
1½ teaspoon	finely chopped fresh ginger
45 g (1½ oz)	canned champignons, drained
2 teaspoons	rice wine or dry sherry

Seasoning A:

¼ teaspoon	salt
¼ teaspoon	m.s.g. (optional)
2 teaspoons	ginger wine

Seasoning B:

⅓ teaspoon	salt
½ teaspoon	m.s.g. (optional)
1 teaspoon	rice wine or dry sherry
1 teaspoon	cornflour (cornstarch)

Seasoning C/Sauce:

⅓ cup	chicken stock
⅓ teaspoon	salt
¼ teaspoon	m.s.g. (optional)
½ teaspoon	sugar
1 tablespoon	light soy sauce
¼ teaspoon	sesame oil (optional)
1 teaspoon	cornflour (cornstarch)

Defrost the frozen scallops, if used, and drain thoroughly. Rinse in cold water and dry on kitchen paper, then place in a dish with the seasoning A ingredients and leave for 10 minutes. Cut the kidneys in halves, horizontally and trim away the white fatty tissue. Pull off the skin and then score the outside in a close criss-cross design (see page 397), cutting about 0.5 cm (1/5 in) deep. Cut across into thin slices and place in a saucepan of boiling water to blanch for 30 seconds, then drain and transfer to a dish of cold water. Leave for 5 minutes, then drain again and add the seasoning B ingredients.

Heat the lard or oil and stir-fry the scallops until white and beginning to firm up, about 45 seconds. Remove and set aside. Add the spring onion and ginger and stir-fry for 30 seconds, then add the champignons and stir-fry for a further 30 seconds. Remove and drain well.

Add a very little more oil or lard if needed and reheat the wok to fairly hot. Stir-fry the kidney for 2 minutes until cooked, then return the scallops and stir-fry briefly. Sizzle the wine onto the sides of the pan and stir in. Add the other cooked ingredients and the pre-mixed seasoning C/sauce ingredients and simmer until the sauce thickens. Serve.

SQUID WITH GARLIC AND GINGER SAUCE

Serve as an appetiser or main dish.

625 g (1¼ lb)	fresh large squid
5 cm (2 in) piece	fresh ginger

Sauce:

2 teaspoons	finely chopped garlic
¼ cup (2 fl oz)	tomato sauce (ketchup)
2 tablespoons	Chinese brown vinegar
1½ teaspoons	sesame oil
2 teaspoons	light soy sauce
1 tablespoon	sugar
½ teaspoon	m.s.g. (optional)

Clean the squid, discarding the heads and stomachs. Peel off the skins with the fins attached. Cut open the tubular bodies and scrape the white membranes from the inside. Score across the inside in a close criss-cross pattern, cutting fairly deeply and at a slight angle.

Cut into 1.25 cm (1 in) squares and rinse in cold water. Drain well. Drop into a saucepan of lightly salted boiling water to poach for about 30 seconds, then drain well and transfer to a serving dish.

Peel and finely shred the ginger and scatter over the squid. Mix the sauce ingredients together and pour over the squid. Serve at once.

Serve hot or cold. If serving hot, prepare the squid, ginger, and sauce before poaching the squid. The sauce may be heated in a small saucepan.

SZECHUAN (SICHUAN)-STYLE SQUID

700 g (1⅓ lb)	fresh squid
90 g (3 oz)	fat pork
½ stalk	fresh celery
1	small leek
2½ tablespoons	softened lard or frying oil
1 tablespoon	hot bean paste

Seasoning/Sauce:

1 cup (8 fl oz)	chicken stock
1 tablespoon	light soy sauce
1 tablespoon	rice wine or dry sherry
¼ teaspoon	salt
¼ teaspoon	m.s.g. (optional)
¼ teaspoon	sugar
2 teaspoons	cornflour (cornstarch)

Clean the squid, discarding the heads, tentacles and stomachs. Pull off the pink skin with the fins attached. Cut the squid open and score in a close criss-cross pattern on the inside, cutting at an angle (see page 397). Cut the squid into 4 cm (1 2/3 in) pieces and blanch in boiling water for 30 seconds. Drain and cover with warm water.

Finely chop the pork, celery, and leeks and stir-fry in the lard or oil for 1½ minutes. Add the bean paste and stir-fry for 30 seconds, then add the pre-mixed seasoning/sauce ingredients and bring to the boil. Simmer for 3 minutes, then add the drained squid and heat through briefly. Transfer to a warmed serving plate.

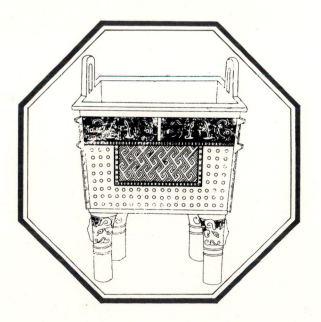

208

Braised Spiced Lamb Shanks (recipe page 220)

SPICED JELLIED PORK

Serve as an appetiser or main dish.

1½ kg (3 lb)	pork leg (fresh ham), with a large section of rind (skin)
1 tablespoon	Chinese brown peppercorns
¼ cup	salt
2 teaspoons	saltpetre (optional)
2	spring onions (scallions), trimmed and halved
4 thin slices	fresh ginger
2	spice bags

Wash the pork and cut into large pieces, discarding the bone. Dry-fry the peppercorns in a wok until fragrant and beginning to smoke, then grind to a fine powder and return to the wok with the salt. Fry on low heat until well mixed and warmed through, but take care that the salt does not begin to colour.

Leave to cool, then mix with the saltpetre, if used, and rub thoroughly over the pork. Place in a dish and cover tightly with plastic wrap. Refrigerate for 3 days, turning daily. The meat will acquire a rosy pink colour and slight saltiness. Blanch for 3 minutes in hot water and drain.

Place in a saucepan with the spring onions, ginger, and spice bags and add water to cover. Simmer for about 2½ hours, topping up the level of the water to keep the pork completely under water. Drain well and discard the onion, ginger, and spice bags.

Cut the pork into small cubes after removing the skin. Place the pork in a greased dish and set aside. Return the skin to the liquid and boil until the liquid is well reduced. Drain the skin and cut into small pieces. Mix with the pork. Pour the liquid over the meat and weight with a heavy object to compress. Refrigerate for 24 hours. Cut the jellied pork into bite-sized pieces and serve with a vinegar and garlic dip (see page 384) or with light soy sauce and chilli oil.

HONEY-GLAZED HAM

750 g (1½ lb)	Chinese or cured (Smithfield) ham
2	spring onions (scallions), trimmed and sliced
8 slices	fresh ginger or 125 g (4 oz) Chinese red dates
1 cup	rock candy (sugar), crushed to a powder
¼ cup (2 fl oz)	sweet rice wine or Japanese mirin*
2 tablespoons	softened lard
1 teaspoon	guei hwa sauce (optional)
1½ teaspoons	cornflour (cornstarch)

Cut off the ham skin and wash the ham well. Place in a saucepan and cover with cold water. Add the spring onions. Bring to the boil and then reduce heat and simmer for about 35 minutes. Remove and drain well. Cut the ham into thin slices, then into pieces about 7.25 cm (2½ in) wide.

Boil the red dates, if used, in 2 cups of water for 10 minutes, then drain. Arrange the ham slices, overlapping, in a dish. Place the ginger or dates on top and add one-third of the sugar. Place in a dish and steam for about 20 minutes, then add the remaining sugar and wine and steam for a further 1½ hours. Strain the liquid into a wok and bring to the boil. Top up with water to make at least 1 cupful and thicken with the cornflour mixed with a little cold water. Stir in the guei hwa, if used, and simmer briefly. Pour over the ham.

Honey-glazed ham is traditionally served with large-sized steamed buns (see Steamed Flower-Shaped Buns, page 372). The buns are opened at the fold and the sweet ham inserted, sandwich fashion, with the sauce being mopped up with the remains of the bread. Thinly sliced white bread can be substituted.

* Or use sweet or cream sherry.

STEAMED YUNNAN HAM

1½ kg (3 lb)	middle-cut Yunnan or cured (Smithfield) ham
3	spring onions (scallions), trimmed and sliced
5 slices	fresh ginger
¼ cup (2 fl oz)	rice wine or dry sherry
2 cups (16 fl oz)	chicken stock
3 tablespoons	finely chopped spring onion (scallion)
2 tablespoons	finely chopped fresh ginger
2 teaspoons	Chinese brown peppercorns
500 g (1 lb)	Chinese (celery) cabbage

Seasoning:

1 cup (8 fl oz)	chicken stock
½ teaspoon	salt
1 teaspoon	sugar
2 teaspoons	rice wine or dry sherry

Hold the piece of ham over a flame until bubbles appear on the skin, then soak the whole ham in hot water until soft and scrape off the blackened parts. Scrub with a soft brush and rinse well. Place the ham in a pot and add the sliced onions and ginger and the wine. Add water to cover and steam or gently simmer for about 1½ hours until the ham is soft, but not completely cooked. Drain and discard the onions and ginger.

Bone and trim the ham and score deeply on the upper side in a criss-cross pattern. Place in a large dish and add the chicken stock, chopped onion, ginger, and the peppercorns. Place on a rack in a steamer and steam over rapidly boiling water until cooked, about 1½ hours.

Trim and wash the cabbage and cut into 5 cm (2 in) pieces. Blanch in boiling water for 2 minutes, then drain and add the seasoning ingredients. Simmer until tender, then drain.

Place the ham, scored side upwards, on a serving plate and surround with the vegetables. Retain ¾ cup (6 fl oz) the stock in which the ham was steamed and strain into a wok. Adjust the seasoning and thicken with a thin solution of cornflour (cornstarch) and cold water. Pour over the ham and serve.

HOT AND SPICY SLICED PORK WITH 'WOOD EAR' FUNGUS

250 g (8 oz)	pork fillet (tenderloin)
45 g (1½ oz)	dried 'wood ear' brown fungus, soaked for 25 minutes
45 g (1½ oz)	young spinach leaves (optional)
2	spring onions (scallions), trimmed and diced
3 thick slices	fresh ginger, diced
1¼ teaspoons	finely chopped garlic
1 — 3	fresh or pickled red chilli peppers, chopped
2 tablespoons	softened lard
2 tablespoons	frying oil

Seasoning A:

¼ teaspoon	salt
1 tablespoon	light soy sauce
1 tablespoon	rice wine or dry sherry
2 teaspoons	cornflour (cornstarch)
1 tablespoon	vegetable oil

Seasoning B/Sauce:

½ cup (4 fl oz)	chicken stock
2 tablespoons	light soy sauce
2 teaspoons	Chinese brown vinegar (or to taste)
1 teaspoon	rice wine or dry sherry
½ teaspoon	m.s.g. (optional)
1¼ teaspoons	sugar
1 teaspoon	cornflour (cornstarch)

Slice the pork across the grain into very thin slices and cut into bite-sized pieces. Place in a dish with the seasoning A ingredients, mix well and leave for 20 minutes.

Drain the 'wood ears' and chop finely. Wash and dry the spinach leaves, if used, and chop coarsely. Heat the wok and add the lard and frying oil. Stir-fry the spring onion, garlic, and chilli peppers together for 1 minute, then add the 'wood ears' and spinach and stir-fry briefly. Push to one side of the pan and add the sliced pork. Fry on both sides until lightly coloured, then stir in the other ingredients and continue to stir-fry until the pork is almost cooked, about 1¼ minutes.

Pour in the pre-mixed seasoning B/sauce ingredients and simmer until the sauce has thickened. Add a dash of salt to taste and serve.

SHREDDED HOT PORK AND MUSHROOMS ON CRISP RICE CAKES

375 g (12 oz)	lean pork
6	dried black mushrooms, soaked for 25 minutes
3 slices	fresh ginger, shredded
1 teaspoon	finely chopped garlic
1	fresh red chilli pepper, chopped
45 g (1½ oz)	canned bamboo shoots, drained and diced
5 cups (1¼ litres)	deep-frying oil
10 pieces	rice cakes (see page 386)
2	spring onions (scallions), trimmed and shredded

Seasoning A:

½ teaspoon	salt
2 teaspoons	rice wine or dry sherry
1 teaspoon	cornflour (cornstarch)

Seasoning B/Sauce:

¾ cup (6 fl oz)	chicken stock
1 tablespoon	light soy sauce
2 teaspoons	hot bean paste
1 teaspoon	Chinese brown vinegar
1½ teaspoons	sugar
¼ teaspoon	m.s.g. (optional)
¼ teaspoon	ground black pepper

Cut the pork into thin slices, then into shreds, and place in a dish with the seasoning A ingredients. Mix well and leave for 10 minutes. Drain the mushrooms, squeeze out the excess water and remove the stems, then cut the caps into fine dice. Stir-fry the mushrooms, ginger, garlic, chilli peppers and bamboo shoots in ¼ cup (2 fl oz) of the deep-frying oil for 1 minute. Push to one side of the pan and add the pork. Stir-fry until it changes colour, then mix with the other fried ingredients and add the pre-mixed seasoning B/sauce ingredients. Bring to the boil, then reduce the heat to simmer for 2 — 3 minutes.

In the meantime, heat the remaining deep-frying oil to smoking point and deep-fry the rice cakes in a frying basket until crisp and golden. Drain well and transfer to a well-warmed serving dish. Arrange the shredded spring onions on top and pour on the hot pork and sauce. Serve at once.

It is essential to time the cooking of the pork and rice cakes accurately so they are both piping hot when brought together. The rice cakes will snap and pop when served.

PORK TRIPE IN HOT PEPPER SAUCE WITH PEANUTS

625 g (1¼ lb)	pork tripe
4	spring onions (scallions), trimmed
6 slices	fresh ginger
1 tablespoon	white vinegar
1 teaspoon	salt
75 g (2½ oz)	raw peanuts (groundnuts)
2 cups (16 fl oz)	frying oil

Sauce:

1 tablespoon	sesame oil
1 tablespoon	chilli oil
2 teaspoons	light soy sauce
2 teaspoons	Chinese brown vinegar
½ teaspoon	salt
½ teaspoon	m.s.g. (optional)
1 teaspoon	sugar
1 teaspoon	Chinese brown peppercorn powder

Wash the tripe well and cut into pieces about 1 cm (¾ in) square. Place in a saucepan with half the spring onions and ginger, the vinegar, and salt and add water to cover. Bring to the boil and simmer until the tripe is tender, then drain well.

Drop the peanuts into boiling water and cook briefly, then drain and when cool enough to handle, remove the skins. Dry thoroughly, then deep-fry in the oil until golden. Drain again.

Mix the sauce ingredients together. Arrange the cooked tripe in a dish and add the remaining spring onions and ginger, finely shredded. Pour on the sauce and garnish with the peanuts. Stir up lightly and serve.

Pigeon Pâté with Chinese Herbs Steamed in Soup Ramekins (recipe page 222).

'GOLD AND SILVER' PORK

500 g (1 lb)	lean pork
3	egg whites, well beaten
½ cup	cornflour (cornstarch)
2	whole eggs, well beaten
	dash of yellow
	food colouring
4 cups (1 litre)	deep-frying oil
60 g (2 oz)	canned bamboo shoots, drained and shredded
2	dried black mushrooms, soaked for 25 minutes and shredded
45 g (1½ oz)	young spinach leaves, coarsely chopped

Seasoning A:

¾ teaspoon	salt
1 tablespoon	rice wine or dry sherry
½ teaspoon	m.s.g. (optional)
2 tablespoons	finely chopped spring onion (scallion)
2 teaspoons	finely chopped fresh ginger

Seasoning B/Sauce:

¾ cup (6 fl oz)	chicken stock
⅓ teaspoon	salt
½ teaspoon	m.s.g. (optional)
½ teaspoon	rice wine or dry sherry
2 teaspoons	cornflour (cornstarch)

Cut the pork into thin slices across the grain, then into strips about 2.5 cm (1 in) wide. Place in a dish with the seasoning A ingredients, mix well and leave for 20 minutes. Mix the egg whites with half of the cornflour and the whole eggs with the remaining cornflour, adding enough food colouring to colour a bright yellow.

Heat the deep-frying oil to moderately hot and on another heat source heat a saucepan of lightly salted water until slowly simmering. Dip half the pork slices into the egg white batter and drop into the simmering water to poach until just cooked through, firm and white, then drain well. Dip the remaining pork into the yellow batter and deep-fry until crisp and golden. Drain.

Arrange the 'silver' and 'gold' pork slices at either side of an oval serving plate. Pour off the oil, retaining about 2 tablespoons, and stir-fry the bamboo shoots and mushrooms for 45 seconds, then add the spinach and stir-fry briefly. Pour in the pre-mixed seasoning B/sauce ingredients and simmer until the sauce thickens and the spinach is tender. Pour over the pork and serve at once.

PORK STEAMED WITH SALTED CABBAGE

750 g (1½ lb)	leg pork (fresh ham), boneless
1 tablespoon	dark soy sauce
8 cups (2 litres)	deep-frying oil
155 g (5 oz)	Szechuan (Sichuan) pickled cabbage, soaked
3	spring onions (scallions), trimmed and diced
3 thick slices	fresh ginger, coarsely chopped
2	pickled red chilli peppers, coarsely chopped

Seasoning:

1½ tablespoons	fermented black beans, washed and chopped
⅓ cup	light soy sauce
¼ cup (2 fl oz)	rice wine or dry sherry
1½ tablespoons	sugar

Wash the pork in boiling water, scrape the skin to remove any tiny hairs and place in a saucepan with boiling water to cover. Simmer for 2 hours, then drain and reserve ¾ cup of the liquid. Wipe the pork and rub with the dark soy sauce, then deep-fry in fairly hot oil until the skin is dark brown. Keep arms covered with a cloth when turning the pork, as the moisture trapped beneath the skin often causes small explosions in the hot oil.

Remove the pork and cut into thick slices and place in a dish. Shred the cabbage and arrange with the spring onions, ginger, and chillies over the pork. Add the seasoning ingredients evenly and pour the reserved stock down the inside of the dish without disturbing the contents.

Set on a rack in a steamer and steam over high heat for a further 1 hour or until the pork is completely tender. Invert the dish onto a serving plate after straining the liquid into a wok. Check the seasonings of the sauce, thicken slightly with a thin cornflour and cold water solution and pour over the pork.

A whole duck can also be cooked in this way, reducing the simmering time to about 1¼ hours and the steaming time to about 30 minutes.

SZECHUAN (SICHUAN) STEWED PORK

1 kg (2 lb)	pork hand (picnic shoulder), deboned*
10	spring onions (scallions), trimmed
2	star anise
1 cup (8 fl oz)	light soy sauce
½ cup (4 fl oz)	rice wine or dry sherry
2/3 cup	sugar

Cut the pork into large cubes and the skin into 4 cm (1 2/3 in) squares. Place the trimmed onions in the bottom of a casserole with the pork and skin on top. Add the remaining ingredients and water to cover. Cover the casserole and bring to the boil, then reduce heat and simmer for at least 1 hour until the pork is completely tender and the sauce well reduced and thick.

Do not remove the cover during cooking, but occasionally shake the pan to turn the contents. To serve, invert the contents of the casserole onto a serving plate and arrange the spring onions around the pork.

* The meat should have a large covering of skin (rind). If not, buy an extra piece of skin.

'TWICE-COOKED' PORK

375 g (12 oz)	'five flowered' pork (belly/fresh bacon)
1	green capsicum (bell pepper)
3	garlic chives, sliced
2 cloves	garlic, sliced
1	fresh red chilli pepper, shredded (optional)
¼ cup (2 fl oz)	frying oil

Seasoning:

1 teaspoon	sugar
2 teaspoons	hot bean paste
1 tablespoon	sweet bean paste
1 tablespoon	light soy sauce
1 teaspoon	dark soy sauce
2 teaspoons	rice wine or dry sherry
2 tablespoons	water

Wash the pork and place the whole piece in a saucepan with water to cover. Bring slowly to the boil, then simmer for 25 minutes. Drain and cut across the grain into wafer-thin slices. Cut the pepper in halves, remove the seed core, stem, and inner white ribs and cut into 2.5 cm (1 in) squares.

Heat the frying oil in a wok and stir-fry the chives, garlic, and chilli peppers for 30 seconds. Remove. Add the capsicum and stir-fry for 45 seconds, then add the pork and stir-fry on fairly high heat until the pork is crisped on the edges. Remove.

Add the seasoning ingredients to the pan, with a little more oil if needed, and stir-fry briefly, then return the fried ingredients and mix well together, stirring until thoroughly coated with the sauce.

Transfer to a serving plate and serve at once. Young leek, finely shredded, can be used in place of the garlic chives, and for extra colour use both red and green capsicum.

SHREDDED PORK WITH SWEET BEAN PASTE

440 g (14 oz)	'five flowered' pork (belly/fresh bacon) or lean pork
10	spring onions (scallions), trimmed and shredded
¼ cup (2 fl oz)	softened lard or frying oil
1 tablespoon	rice wine or dry sherry
2 tablespoons	sweet bean paste
1½ tablespoons	light soy sauce
½ teaspoon	sugar

Seasoning:

½ teaspoon	salt
¾ teaspoon	sugar
2 teaspoons	light soy sauce
2 teaspoons	rice wine or dry sherry

Cut the pork into thin slices across the grain, then into narrow shreds. Place in a dish with the seasoning ingredients, mix well and leave for 15 minutes.

Arrange the spring onions on a serving plate. Heat the lard or oil in a wok and add the shredded pork. Stir-fry on moderate heat until the pork changes colour, then sizzle the wine onto the sides of the pan and stir in. Add the sweet bean paste, soy sauce, and sugar separately, cooking each briefly.

Spoon the meat over the onions and serve at once.

'PEARL' BALLS

250 g (8 oz)	lean pork, finely minced (ground)
6	canned water chestnuts, chopped
15 g (½ oz)	dried shrimp, soaked for 1 hour and chopped (optional)
1 tablespoon	finely chopped spring onion (scallion)
1 teaspoon	finely chopped fresh ginger
1 cup	long grain raw glutinous rice, soaked for 2 hours

Seasoning:

1 tablespoon	light soy sauce
2 teaspoons	rice wine or dry sherry
¼ teaspoon	salt
¼ teaspoon	m.s.g. (optional)
½ teaspoon	sugar
¼ teaspoon	ground black pepper
1¼ tablespoons	cornflour (cornstarch)

Mix the pork and water chestnuts with the seasoning ingredients. Drain and finely chop the dried shrimps, if used, and mix into the pork with the spring onion and ginger. Knead to a smooth paste, squeezing continually through the fingers until thoroughly mixed and sticky.

Use wet hands to roll the mixture into 24 balls. Drain the rice thoroughly and spread on a plate. Roll each ball in the rice until thickly coated with rice grains. Arrange on a lightly oiled plate and set on a rack in a steamer. Leave a little space between each ball to allow the rice to expand.

Steam over rapidly boiling water for about 30 minutes until the rice is transparent and tender and the pork cooked through. Serve on the same plate with a garnish of fresh coriander and dips of light soy and chilli sauces.

CHILLI PORK SPARE-RIBS

750 g (1½ lb)	meaty pork spare ribs or 'five flowered' pork
6 cups (1½ litres)	deep-frying oil
3	spring onions (scallions), trimmed and sliced
3 thick slices	fresh ginger, chopped
1	fresh red chilli pepper, shredded (optional)
1 teaspoon	finely chopped garlic (optional)

Seasoning A:

1	egg white, beaten
1 tablespoon	finely chopped spring onion (scallion)
2 teaspoons	finely chopped fresh ginger
1 teaspoon	salt
½ teaspoon	m.s.g. (optional)
¼ teaspoon	white pepper
1 tablespoon	rice wine or dry sherry
1 tablespoon	frying oil
2 tablespoons	cornflour (cornstarch)

Seasoning B/Sauce:

2 tablespoons	hot bean paste
3½ cups (28 fl oz)	chicken stock
2 tablespoons	light soy sauce
1 tablespoon	rice wine or dry sherry
½ teaspoon	salt
1 tablespoon	sugar

Cut the ribs or pork into bite-sized chunks and place in a dish with the seasoning A ingredients. Mix well and leave for 30 minutes.

Heat the deep-frying oil to fairly hot and deep-fry the pork until golden, cooking in several lots to keep the oil hot. Drain and transfer to a casserole. Pour off all but 2 tablespoons of the oil and add the spring onions, ginger, chilli pepper, and garlic, if used. Stir-fry briefly, then add the soybean paste and stir-fry for several seconds. Add the chicken stock and remaining seasoning B/sauce ingredients and bring to the boil.

Pour over the pork and cover. Simmer until the pork is completely tender, about 1¼ hours. Transfer the pork to a serving plate with a slotted spoon and thicken the sauce, if necessary, with a thin solution of cornflour and cold water. Check the seasonings and pour over the pork.

For a more substantial dish, surround the pork with braised fresh green vegetables and serve with boiled thick egg noodles.

'Ma Pwo' Beancurd (Pork-marked Mama's Beancurd) (recipe page 227).

'DRAGON'S EYE' BONE MARROW WITH CHICKEN

625 g (1¼ lb)	fresh pork bone marrow
1½ teaspoons	white vinegar
250 g (8 oz)	boneless chicken breast
155 g (5 oz)	pork fat
2 slices	cooked ham
280 g (9 oz)	fresh mustard greens
¼ cup (2 fl oz)	frying oil

Seasoning A:

2 tablespoons	finely chopped spring onion (scallion)
1½ teaspoons	finely chopped fresh ginger
3	egg whites, well beaten
2 tablespoons	chicken stock
½ teaspoon	salt
¼ teaspoon	m.s.g. (optional)
¼ teaspoon	white pepper
2 teaspoons	rice wine or dry sherry
1 tablespoon	cornflour (cornstarch)

Seasoning B:

¾ cup (6 fl oz)	chicken stock
½ teaspoon	salt
¼ teaspoon	m.s.g. (optional)
1½ teaspoons	rice wine or dry sherry
	pinch of white pepper
1½ teaspoons	cornflour (cornstarch)

Seasoning C:

⅓ teaspoon	salt
¼ teaspoon	m.s.g. (optional)
2 teaspoons	rice wine or dry sherry
¼ teaspoon	sugar

Wash the pork bone marrow thoroughly and simmer in water to cover with the vinegar for 6 minutes. Remove, drain well and soak in cold water.

Mince (grind) the chicken and pork fat finely and mix with the seasoning A ingredients, stirring continually in one direction until the mixture is thick and smooth. Divide the pork marrow into 18 pieces and place one piece in the bottom of 12 lightly oiled wide-necked wine glasses. Stamp out 12 small discs from the ham and place on top of the marrow, then divide the chicken mixture among the glasses, using a wet finger to smooth the top of the chicken paste.

Set the glasses on a rack in a steamer and steam over rapidly boiling water until the chicken paste is firm. Simmer the remaining bone marrow with the seasoning B ingredients until tender and the sauce thickened. Sauté the mustard greens in the frying oil after cutting into bite-sized pieces. Add the seasoning C ingredients and cover. Cook until the vegetables are tender, but retaining crispness.

Invert the glasses onto a serving plate and remove the 'dragon's eyes.' Arrange the vegetables and simmered bone marrow around them and pour on the sauce from the marrow. Serve.

KIDNEYS IN SOUR AND HOT SAUCE

Serve cold as an appetiser.

250 g (8 oz)	pork kidneys
3	bean sheets, soaked to soften
¾ teaspoon	salt
2 teaspoons	sesame oil

Sauce:

2 tablespoons	finely chopped spring onion (scallion)
1½ tablespoons	finely chopped fresh ginger
¼ cup (2 fl oz)	light soy sauce
1 tablespoon	sesame oil
1 tablespoon	white vinegar
2 teaspoons	chilli oil (or to taste)
1½ tablespoons	Chinese brown peppercorns, crushed
¼ teaspoon	salt
¼ teaspoon	m.s.g. (optional)
1 teaspoon	sugar

Cut the kidneys in halves and remove the inner white fatty section and the skin. Score in a close criss-cross pattern across the outside, then cut through into thin slices. Blanch in boiling water for about 30 seconds, remove and drain well, then soak in cold water.

Drain the bean sheets and cut into shreds. Mix with the salt and sesame oil and arrange on a serving plate. Drain the kidney slices and arrange over the bean sheets. Mix the sauce ingredients together and pour over the kidneys. Serve.

SHREDDED BEEF WITH BAMBOO SHOOTS

250 g (8 oz)	beef fillet (tenderloin)
45 g (1½ oz)	canned bamboo shoots, drained
1	medium carrot, peeled*
3	garlic chives
1 — 2	fresh red chilli peppers
3 slices	fresh ginger
1½ cups (12 fl oz)	deep-frying oil
½ teaspoon	ground black pepper
¾ teaspoon	sesame oil

Seasoning A:

½ teaspoon	salt
1 tablespoon	light soy sauce
2 teaspoons	dark soy sauce
2 teaspoons	rice wine or dry sherry
2 teaspoons	sesame oil
2 teaspoons	ginger wine or ginger juice

Seasoning B/Sauce:

2 tablespoons	light soy sauce
1 teaspoon	white vinegar
½ teaspoon	rice wine or dry sherry
1½ teaspoons	sugar
½ teaspoon	m.s.g. (optional)
½ teaspoon	cornflour (cornstarch)

Cut the beef into paper-thin slices across the grain, then into long narrow shreds and place in a dish with the seasoning A ingredients. Mix well and leave for 20 minutes.

Cut the bamboo shoots, carrot, chives, chilli peppers, and ginger into long narrow shreds and set aside.

Heat the oil in a wok and fry the beef shreds in a frying basket for 45 seconds. Remove and drain well. Pour off all but 2½ tablespoons of the oil and stir-fry the shredded ingredients for about 1½ minutes, then return the beef. Sizzle the soy sauce onto the sides of the pan and add the remaining seasoning B/sauce ingredients. Stir on high heat until the liquid has been almost completely absorbed, then transfer to a serving plate and season with the pepper and sesame oil, stirring in lightly.

* Or use shredded green or red capsicum (bell pepper).

SPICY SHREDDED BEEF WITH 'WOOD EAR' FUNGUS AND WATER CHESTNUTS

375 g (12 oz)	beef fillet (tenderloin)*
15 g (½ oz)	dried 'wood ear' fungus, soaked for 25 minutes
90 g (3 oz)	canned water chestnuts, drained
2	fresh red chilli peppers
2 teaspoons	grated fresh ginger
⅓ cup	frying oil

Seasoning A:

1 teaspoon	sugar
1 tablespoon	light soy sauce
1 tablespoon	rice wine or dry sherry
1½ teaspoons	cornflour (cornstarch)
2 teaspoons	frying oil

Seasoning B/Sauce:

1 tablespoon	light soy sauce
2 teaspoons	rice wine or dry sherry
½ teaspoon	chilli oil
½ teaspoon	sesame oil
1 teaspoon	salt
1 teaspoon	sugar
½ teaspoon	Chinese brown vinegar

Very thinly slice the beef across the grain, then cut into fine shreds. Place in a dish with the seasoning A ingredients, mix well and leave for 20 minutes. Drain the 'wood ears' and shred finely. Cut the water chestnuts into thin slices. Shred the chillies discarding the seeds.

Heat the frying oil in a wok to moderate and stir-fry the shredded beef until it changes colour. Remove and drain well. Add the shredded 'wood ear,' the water chestnuts, chillies, and ginger and stir-fry for 1½ minutes, then return the beef and stir-fry briefly with the vegetables.

Add the pre-mixed seasoning B/sauce ingredients and simmer until the liquid is partially absorbed and the beef tender, about 1 minute. Serve with steamed bread or sesame pocket bread (see page 372).

* This recipe is also excellent with pork.

SZECHUAN (SICHUAN) BEEF STEW

1 kg (2 lb)	flank or silverside (brisket)
4	spring onions (scallions), trimmed and halved
2.5 cm (1 in) piece	fresh ginger, sliced and bruised
3	star anise
3 pieces	dried orange peel
¼ cup (2 fl oz)	softened lard or frying oil

Seasoning:

2 teaspoons	finely chopped garlic
1 tablespoon	Chinese brown peppercorns
½ cup (4 fl oz)	light soy sauce
2 tablespoons	dark soy sauce
⅓ cup	rice wine or dry sherry
2 tablespoons	sweet bean paste
1 tablespoon	hot bean paste
2 teaspoons	sugar

Cut the meat into 5 cm (2 in) cubes and place in a deep pot with the spring onions, ginger, star anise, and orange peel. Cover with water and bring to the boil, skim, then simmer for 2 hours tightly covered over low heat.

Heat the lard or frying oil and fry the seasoning ingredients for 1 minute, then pour into the pot and re-cover. Simmer a further 1 hour or until the meat is very tender. Transfer meat to a serving dish and thicken the sauce with a paste of cornflour (cornstarch) and cold water. Pour over the meat after discarding the onion, ginger, star anise, and orange peel.

BRAISED SPICED LAMB SHANKS

625 g (1¼ lb)	boneless shoulder-shank-end (shank) of lamb
6	spring onions (scallions)
8 slices	fresh ginger
⅓ cup	frying oil
3 tablespoons	soybean paste
3 cubes	fermented beancurd, mashed with the liquid
1	large carrot or turnip, peeled and cubed
½ teaspoon	m.s.g. (optional)
	cornflour (cornstarch)

Seasoning/Sauce:

3 cups (24 fl oz)	chicken stock
2 tablespoons	light soy sauce
2 tablespoons	rice wine or dry sherry
1 tablespoon	sugar
1 teaspoon	Chinese brown peppercorns

Chop the lamb into 4 cm (1 2/3 in) cubes and place in a saucepan with water to cover. Add half the spring onions and ginger and bring to the boil. Reduce the heat to low and simmer for 35 minutes, then drain. Cut the remaining spring onions into slices and shred the remaining ginger.

Heat the frying oil in a wok and stir-fry the onions and ginger for 30 seconds, then add the cubed lamb and stir-fry until well coloured. Add the soy bean paste and the mashed beancurd and stir-fry for 30 seconds, splashing in a little cold water to prevent the seasonings from sticking to the pan. Add the cubed carrot or turnip and the pre-mixed seasoning/sauce ingredients and bring to the boil.

Reduce to low and simmer until the lamb is completely tender, about 1½ hours. Add the m.s.g., if used, and thicken the sauce with a solution of cornflour and cold water. Transfer to a deep serving dish and garnish with fresh coriander. Serve a dipping sauce of mashed fermented beancurd diluted with a little rice wine or dry sherry.

For an original and interesting flavour, use finely shredded lemon leaves in place of the fresh coriander to garnish.

'Twice Cooked' Pork (recipe page 215) and Fish-Flavoured Eggplant (recipe page 234).

LAMB KIDNEYS STIR-FRIED WITH CELERY AND BAMBOO SHOOTS

310 g (10 oz)	lamb kidneys
45 g (1½ oz)	canned bamboo shoots, drained and sliced
45 g (1½ oz)	young celery, thinly sliced diagonally*
⅓ cup	frying oil

Seasoning A:

1	egg white, beaten
½ teaspoon	salt
¼ teaspoon	m.s.g. (optional)
2 teaspoons	rice wine or dry sherry
1 teaspoon	cornflour (cornstarch)

Seasoning B:

2 tablespoons	finely chopped spring onion (scallion)
2 teaspoons	finely chopped fresh ginger
1 — 2	fresh red chilli peppers, finely chopped
⅓ teaspoon	finely chopped garlic (optional)
¼ teaspoon	ground black pepper
½ teaspoon	salt
2 teaspoons	rice wine or dry sherry
½ cup (4 fl oz)	chicken stock
1½ teaspoons	cornflour (cornstarch)

Cut the kidneys in halves horizontally and trim away the white fatty section inside. Peel off the skin, then cut each piece in halves.

Blanch in boiling water, then rinse with cold water and drain thoroughly. Place in a dish with the seasoning A ingredients and leave for 15 minutes.

Heat the frying oil in a wok and stir-fry the kidneys on moderately high heat until almost cooked through, about 2 minutes. Remove and keep warm. Add the bamboo shoots and celery and stir-fry together for 1 minute, then add the spring onion, ginger, chilli peppers, and garlic, if used, and stir-fry for a further 1 minute, adding a little more oil if needed to prevent sticking.

Add the pre-mixed remaining seasoning B ingredients and bring to the boil, return the kidneys and simmer until the sauce thickens. Serve.

* Or use green capsicum (bell pepper) cut into 2.5 cm (1 in) squares.

PIGEON PÂTÉ WITH CHINESE HERBS STEAMED IN SOUP RAMEKINS

625 g (1¼ lb)	pigeon breast meat
1½	spring onions (scallions), trimmed and diced
3 slices	fresh ginger, shredded
1¾ tablespoons	rice wine or dry sherry
6 slices	dan guei*

Seasoning:

2	egg whites, well beaten
¾ teaspoon	salt
¼ teaspoon	ground black pepper
½ teaspoon	sugar
1 teaspoon	rice wine or dry sherry
1 tablespoon	frying oil
2 teaspoons	cornflour (cornstarch)

Special Equipment: Six bamboo containers or soup ramekins.

Pulverise the pigeon meat in a food processor or by using two cleavers (see page 396). Add the seasoning ingredients and mix thoroughly. Divide among the bamboo containers, pushing the paste to the bottom of the cup. Divide the spring onions, ginger, wine, and *dan guei* among the cups and fill each with water.

Set on a rack in a steamer and steam over high heat until the pigeon paté is cooked, about 30 minutes. Serve in the bamboo cups.

* *Dan guei* is a dried pungent herb said to have beneficial and highly nutritional qualities. It is often used in poultry dishes and gives a mildly medicinal taste. Available in specialist Chinese food or drug stores.

DEEP-FRIED SQUAB WITH SALTED VEGETABLE STUFFING

6	squab (about 825 g / 1¾ lb dressed weight)
¾ teaspoon	salt
1½ tablespoons	rice wine or dry sherry
8 cups (2 litres)	deep-frying oil
	Chinese pepper-salt

Stuffing:

2 tablespoons	finely chopped spring onion (scallion)
2 teaspoons	finely chopped fresh ginger
90 g (3 oz)	salt preserved vegetables,* soaked
1½ teaspoons	five spice powder
¼ teaspoon	salt
1½ teaspoons	sugar

Rinse the squab in boiling water and drain thoroughly. Wipe dry and rub with the salt and wine. Tie a string around each neck and hang in a well-ventilated place for about 3 hours to dry the skin.

Mix the stuffing ingredients together after draining the preserved vegetables, squeezing out as much water as possible and shredding finely. Stuff into the birds and close the openings with toothpicks or poultry pins. Place in a wide dish and steam over rapidly boiling water for about 40 minutes. Remove and wipe the skin.

Heat the deep-frying oil to smoking point and deep-fry the squab in a frying basket, two or three at a time until dark and crisp on the surface. Arrange, breasts upwards, on a bed of fresh lettuce and serve with the Chinese pepper-salt as a dip (see page 384).

* Canned pickled cabbage, salted mustard leaves or roots, or Szechuan (Sichuan) preserved vegetables.

SAUTÉD FROGS' LEGS WITH CHILLI PEPPERS AND CASHEW NUTS

500 g (1 lb)	large frogs' legs
	cornflour (cornstarch)
2 cups (16 fl oz)	frying oil
3	dried red chilli peppers, halved
4 pieces	dried orange peel
75 g (2½ oz)	raw cashew nuts or peanuts (groundnuts)
2	spring onions (scallions), trimmed and sliced
3 slices	fresh ginger

Seasoning/Sauce:

¼ cup (2 fl oz)	chicken stock
1¾ tablespoons	light soy sauce
2 teaspoons	rice wine or dry sherry
2 teaspoons	sesame oil
¼ teaspoon	salt
¼ teaspoon	m.s.g. (optional)
¾ teaspoon	sugar
¼ teaspoon	white vinegar
½ teaspoon	cornflour (cornstarch)

Skin the frogs' legs and divide at the central joint. Coat lightly with cornflour and fry in the fairly hot oil until lightly coloured, about 1½ minutes. Remove and drain.

Reheat the oil and fry the chilli peppers, orange peel, and cashews until the chillies and peel are a deep brown and the nuts golden. Remove and drain. Pour off all but 2 tablespoons of the oil and sauté the spring onions and ginger briefly, then return the frogs' legs and sauté for about 1 minute. Pour in the pre-mixed seasoning/sauce ingredients and bring to the boil. Simmer for 30 seconds, then return the chillies and orange peel and continue to simmer until the sauce thickens.

Transfer to a serving plate, stir in the crisp cashews and serve.

BEAR'S PAW SIMMERED WITH DUCK, CHICKEN, SCALLOPS, AND HAM

Bear's paw has a gamey flavour and a smooth, almost gelatinous texture similar to beef or pork tendon. It is still served today as a feature at banquets, though the practice of cooking exotic animals and birds has become somewhat restricted in recent years. A passable facsimile of bear's paw is beef tongue, and this, being more readily available and less expensive, is often substituted.

1 1½ kg (3 lb)	beef tongue
500 g (1 lb)	chicken pieces
290 g (9 oz)	duck breast or thigh
3	dried scallops, soaked for 1 hour, (or use 1 tablespoon soaked dried shrimps)
30 g (1 oz)	Chinese or cured (Smithfield) ham, diced
3	spring onions (scallions), trimmed and sliced
3 thick slices	fresh ginger
⅓ cup	softened lard or frying oil

Seasoning/Sauce:

¼ cup (2 fl oz)	light soy sauce
¼ cup (2 fl oz)	rice wine or dry sherry
2	spring onions (scallions), trimmed and sliced
3 thin slices	fresh ginger
1½ teaspoons	sugar
½ teaspoon	m.s.g. (optional)
⅓ teaspoon	ground black pepper

Wash the tongue and place in a saucepan with water to cover. Bring to the boil, then reduce heat and simmer for 3 hours. Wash the chicken, duck, scallops or shrimps, and diced ham and place on top of the tongue with the spring onions and ginger. Add enough additional hot water to cover the contents of the pan, re-cover the pan and simmer a further 1 hour.

Remove the tongue and other ingredients from the pan and strain 4 cups (1 litre) of the liquid into another saucepan. Scrape the skin from the tongue, return to the stock and add the seasoning/sauce ingredients and return the scallops or shrimps and ham.

The chicken and duck meat should be cut into small cubes, fried in the lard or oil until lightly coloured, then added to the pan. Bring to the boil, skim if necessary, and simmer a further 2 hours. Remove the tongue and cut into thick slices. Arrange on a bed of shredded lettuce on serving plate. Reduce the sauce to about 1½ cups, then thicken with a paste of cornflour (cornstarch) and cold water and pour over the tongue or serve separately.

'CROSSING THE BRIDGE' NOODLES

7 cups (1¾ litres)	chicken stock
3 slices	fresh ginger
1½ teaspoons	salt
1 teaspoon	sugar
2 teaspoons	Chinese brown or white vinegar
185 g (6 oz)	pork fillet (tenderloin)
185 g (6 oz)	white fish fillets
185 g (6 oz)	raw peeled prawns
185 g (6 oz)	fresh cleaned squid or chicken breast
1 kg (2 lb)	fresh thick egg noodles, blanched and drained

Sauces:

	light soy sauce
	chilli sauce
	vinegar and chilli dip (see opposite)

Special Equipment: A fire-pot or table top gas or electric cooking ring and a large stewpan.

Bring the chicken stock to the boil and add the ginger and salt, sugar and vinegar. Pour into the stewpan and keep hot.

Very thinly slice the pork, fish, prawns, and squid or chicken and arrange on separate plates with the noodles in a deep dish. Prepare several small dishes of soy and chilli sauce and prepare the vinegar and chilli dip by mixing 2 — 3 thinly sliced fresh red chillies with white vinegar, a little vegetable oil, and sugar and salt to taste. Pour into several small dishes.

Return the stock to the boil at the table. Use wooden or bamboo chopsticks to add the meat and noodles to the stock and simmer for several minutes. Serve into large soup bowls and add a mixture of the sauces to taste.

Eight-Treasure Rice (recipe page 241).

BOILED WONTONS SERVED WITH FOUR SAUCES

Serve as an appetiser.

Makes 24.

Wonton Wrappers:

2 cups	flour
2 teaspoons	frying oil
½ teaspoon	salt
7/8 cup (7 fl oz)	warm water

Wonton Filling:

185 g (6 oz)	lean pork, finely minced (ground)
3	cabbage leaves, finely chopped
1	spring onion (scallion), trimmed and diced
½ teaspoon	finely chopped fresh ginger
¼ teaspoon	salt
2 teaspoons	light soy sauce
1 teaspoon	rice wine or dry sherry
½ teaspoon	ground black pepper
½ teaspoon	sesame oil

Sauce 1:

¼ cup (2 fl oz)	frying oil
1 tablespoon	paprika powder
1 teaspoon	chilli powder
¼ teaspoon	salt

Sauce 2:

¼ cup (2 fl oz)	light soy sauce
1 piece	cinnamon stick
1	star anise
2½ tablespoons	soft brown sugar

Sauce 3:

¼ cup (2 fl oz)	Chinese red vinegar
1 teaspoon	sesame oil
1 teaspoon	sugar
2 teaspoons	finely chopped spring onion (scallion)

Sauce 4:

1 tablespoon	crushed garlic
2 tablespoons	frying oil
1 teaspoon	sesame oil
1 teaspoon	white vinegar

Sift the flour into a mixing bowl and add the oil, salt, and warm water. Mix well, then knead gently until the dough is smooth and elastic. Cover with plastic wrap and leave for 30 minutes. Mix the filling ingredients together and work until thoroughly mixed, then chill until needed.

Heat the frying oil for sauce 1 to warm and then remove from the heat and add the paprika, chilli powder, and salt. Leave for 20 minutes, then stir thoroughly.

Heat the soy sauce for sauce 2 to warm and add the remaining ingredients, stirring until the sugar dissolves. Leave to cool. Mix the ingredients for sauces 3 and 4 in separate dishes, adding a little salt to sauce 4.

Roll the dough into a long sausage shape and cut into 24 pieces. Roll each out on a lightly floured board into a disc about 7.5 cm (3 in) in diameter. Place a portion of the filling in the centre and fold in halves. Pinch the edges firmly together.

When all the wontons are prepared, bring a large saucepan of water to the boil and reduce heat until gently simmering. Add the wontons and poach for about 5 minutes. Add 1 tablespoon of oil to the water to prevent the wontons from sticking together during cooking.

Remove from the water, drain well and arrange on fresh lettuce leaves or finely shredded cabbage on a serving plate. Pour the four sauces into dip dishes and serve with the wontons.

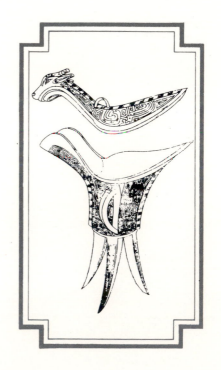

'MA PWO' BEANCURD
(POCK-MARKED MAMA'S BEANCURD)

4 squares	soft beancurd
210 g (7 oz)	lean beef, finely minced (ground)
1	small leek
⅓ cup	frying oil
1 tablespoon	fermented black beans, finely chopped
2 teaspoons	hot bean paste
2 teaspoons	crushed garlic
2 teaspoons	finely chopped fresh ginger
1 teaspoon	finely chopped fresh red chilli pepper or chilli sauce
1 teaspoon	Chinese brown peppercorn powder

Seasoning:

1½ tablespoons	light soy sauce
1 tablespoon	rice wine or dry sherry
½ teaspoon	salt
1½ teaspoons	sugar
1 cup (8 fl oz)	chicken stock or water
1 tablespoon	cornflour (cornstarch)

Cut the beancurd into 1.25 cm (½ in) cubes and soak in hot water until needed. Trim and shred the leeks. Heat the frying oil and stir-fry the beef until lightly coloured, then add the leeks and stir-fry a further 30 seconds. Add the chopped black beans, the bean paste, garlic, ginger, and chilli pepper or chilli sauce and stir-fry for a further 30 seconds, then add the pre-mixed seasoning ingredients and bring to the boil. Simmer for 1 minute.

Drain the beancurd and add to the sauce, reduce the heat and simmer until the sauce is well reduced and the flavour thoroughly permeating the beancurd. Transfer to a serving dish and season with the pepper.

PHOENIX MOUNTAIN BEANCURD

3 squares	soft beancurd
⅓ cup	softened lard or frying oil
210 g (7 oz)	lean pork or beef, finely minced (ground)
2½ teaspoons	finely chopped garlic
1 — 3	fresh red chilli peppers, finely chopped
2 teaspoons	fermented black beans, finely chopped
2	whole eggs
2 tablespoons	finely chopped spring onion (scallion)
	Chinese pepper-salt

Seasoning A:

½ teaspoon	salt
¼ teaspoon	m.s.g. (optional)
¾ teaspoon	sugar
1½ teaspoons	rice wine or dry sherry
1 teaspoon	cornflour (cornstarch)

Seasoning B/Sauce:

1¼ cups (10 fl oz)	chicken stock
2 teaspoons	light soy sauce
2 teaspoons	rice wine or dry sherry
2 teaspoons	sweet bean paste
1 — 1½ teaspoons	chilli oil
½ teaspoon	sesame oil (optional)
½ teaspoon	salt
1 teaspoon	sugar

Soak the beancurd in cold water for 10 minutes, then drain and cut in halves horizontally. Score the top of each piece in a criss-cross pattern, cutting quite deeply. Mix the minced (ground) meat with the seasoning A ingredients and stir-fry in the lard or oil until the colour changes. Add the garlic, chilli pepper, and black beans and stir-fry for 1 minute.

Pour in the seasoning B/sauce ingredients and bring to the boil, then reduce heat to low and carefully add the beancurd. Simmer, covered, for about 8 minutes, basting frequently with the meat sauce.

Transfer the contents of the saucepan to a large dish and pour the beaten eggs over the beancurd. Garnish with half the chopped spring onion and set the dish on a rack in a steamer. Steam over rapidly boiling water for 5 minutes, or until the eggs are set, then remove and garnish with the remaining chopped spring onion and a generous sprinkling of Chinese pepper-salt. Serve at once.

HOME-STYLE BEANCURD

90 g (3 oz)	lean pork or beef
1	medium green capsicum (bell pepper)
1	small carrot
45 g (1½ oz)	canned bamboo shoots, drained
3	dried black mushrooms, soaked for 25 minutes, or use 90 g (3 oz) canned champignons, drained
2	spring onions (scallions), trimmed and diced
3 slices	fresh ginger, chopped
1 — 2	fresh red chilli peppers, chopped
12 cubes	fried beancurd*
2 cups (16 fl oz)	frying oil

Seasoning A:

¼ teaspoon	salt
¼ teaspoon	m.s.g. (optional)
1 teaspoon	sugar
1 teaspoon	light soy sauce
1 teaspoon	rice wine or dry sherry
2 teaspoons	cornflour (cornstarch)
2 teaspoons	frying oil

Seasoning B/Sauce:

1 cup (8 fl oz)	water or chicken stock
1 tablespoon	dark soy sauce
2 tablespoons	oyster sauce
1 teaspoon	Chinese vinegar
2 teaspoons	sugar
1 teaspoon	sesame oil (optional)
2 teaspoons	cornflour (cornstarch)

Very thinly slice the pork or beef and cut into bite-sized pieces. Place in a dish with the seasoning A ingredients, mix well and leave for 15 minutes. Trim the capsicum, removing the stem, seed core, and the inner white ribs. Cut into small dice. Thinly slice the carrot and bamboo shoots. Squeeze the water from the mushrooms and remove the stems, cut the caps into quarters. If using the champignons, cut the caps in halves horizontally. Prepare the spring onions, ginger and chilli and set aside.

Heat the frying oil to fairly hot and deep-fry the fried beancurd for 1 minute, remove and drain well. Add the pork or beef and deep-fry for about 45 seconds, then remove and drain thoroughly. Pour off all but ¼ cup of the oil and stir-fry the capsicum and carrots for about 1 minute, then add the bamboo shoots and remaining vegetables and the ginger and chilli peppers and stir-fry together for 1¼ minutes. Return the fried beancurd and add the seasoning B/sauce ingredients.

Bring to the boil and simmer for 5 minutes, then return the meat and continue to simmer until the beancurd and meat are tender. Serve.

* Dried beancurd cut into cubes and deep-fried until crisp on the surface and almost dried out inside (see glossary page 406).

BEANCURD SIMMERED WITH MUSHROOMS

3 squares	soft beancurd
8	dried black mushrooms, soaked for 25 minutes
2 tablespoons	softened lard or frying oil
2	spring onions (scallions), trimmed and diced
2 slices	fresh ginger, shredded
1 tablespoon	rendered chicken fat (chicken grease) (optional)

Seasoning/Sauce:

1 cup (8 fl oz)	chicken stock
¾ teaspoon	salt
½ teaspoon	m.s.g. (optional)
2 teaspoons	rice wine or dry sherry
2½ teaspoons	cornflour (cornstarch)

Steam the beancurd for about 10 minutes, then cover with cold water and soak for about 10 minutes. Squeeze the water from the mushrooms and remove the stems. Cut the caps into three or four pieces each. Steam for 10 minutes.

Heat the lard or oil in a wok and stir-fry the onions and ginger on fairly high heat for 1 minute, add the chicken stock and bring just to the boil, then add the remaining seasoning ingredients and the drained mushrooms and beancurd and simmer until the sauce has thickened. Stir in the chicken fat, if used, and transfer to a warmed serving plate.

Steamed Date Cake (recipe page 240).

MINCED BEANCURD CAKE WITH SPINACH

4 squares	soft beancurd
1½ tablespoons	finely chopped cooked ham
90 g (3 oz)	fresh young spinach leaves (collard greens)
	chicken stock

Seasoning A:

¾ teaspoon	salt
½ teaspoon	m.s.g. (optional)
¼ teaspoon	white pepper
5	egg whites, well beaten
⅓ cup	cornflour (cornstarch)

Seasoning B/Sauce:

1 cup (8 fl oz)	chicken stock
2 teaspoons	rice wine or dry sherry
⅓ teaspoon	salt
¼ teaspoon	m.s.g. (optional)
¼ teaspoon	ground black pepper

Mash the beancurd with a fork and mix in the seasoning A ingredients. Grease a round baking tin with lard or frying oil and pour in the beancurd mixture. Sprinkle the chopped ham on top and set on a rack in a steamer to steam over high heat for 6 — 8 minutes or until set. Slide the beancurd cake from the tin into a dish of cold chicken stock.

Heat the wok and add the seasoning B ingredients and the spinach, coarsely chopped. Simmer for 1 minute, then add the beancurd cake and simmer gently until the beancurd and spinach are both tender, about 5 minutes on low heat. Transfer the spinach to a serving plate and thicken the sauce around the beancurd cake with a paste of cornflour (cornstarch) and cold water. Simmer until thickened and then slide the cake with its sauce onto the spinach. Serve at once.

The beancurd cake may crumble at the edges but should remain intact as a soft textured mound.

SPICED CABBAGE

500 g (1 lb)	Chinese (celery) cabbage
1 tablespoon	salt
4 cm (1 2/3 in) piece	fresh ginger
2½ tablespoons	frying oil
¼ cup (2 fl oz)	Chinese brown vinegar
1 tablespoon	sugar
1 teaspoon	chilli oil, or chilli flakes soaked in oil

Wash the cabbage thoroughly and separate the leaves. Cut into 5 cm (2 in) squares and place in a glass dish. Add the salt and toss lightly then cover with plastic wrap and leave for 4 hours. Peel and finely shred the ginger and add to the cabbage.

Heat the frying oil until warm and add the remaining ingredients. Pour over the cabbage, toss thoroughly and leave for a further 4 hours.

Spiced Cabbage can be served as a side dish with most dishes from this region. Keeps for up to a week in the refrigerator, tightly covered with plastic wrap.

PICKLED ASSORTED VEGETABLES

500 g (1 lb)	Chinese (celery) or white cabbage
500 g (1 lb)	peeled carrots
500 g (1 lb)	peeled turnips or giant white (icicle) radishes

Pickling Liquid:

10 cups (2½ litres)	water
¾ cup	salt
¼ cup (2 fl oz)	rice wine or dry sherry
1 tablespoon	Chinese brown peppercorns
¼ cup	finely chopped fresh ginger
¼ cup	finely chopped fresh red chilli peppers

Cut the cabbage into 2.5 cm (1 in) squares and wash thoroughly. Cut the carrots and turnips or radishes into 1.25 cm (½ in) cubes and wash thoroughly.

Mix the pickling liquid in a large glass dish and add the well-drained vegetables. Place a plate on top and weight lightly so that the vegetables remain completely covered by the liquid. Leave for 3 — 4 days.

The pickling liquid can be re-used, adding more salt with each use. Pickled vegetables can be kept for up to two weeks in the refrigerator, covered with plastic wrap.

CUCUMBER SAUTÉD IN SESAME OIL WITH HOT SPICES

2	medium-sized cucumbers
2	spring onions (scallions), trimmed and shredded
6 slices	fresh ginger, shredded
2 cloves	garlic, sliced (optional)

Seasoning:

⅓ cup	sesame oil
1 teaspoon	Chinese brown peppercorns
1½ teaspoons	dried chilli flakes or chopped fresh red chilli pepper
1 tablespoon	sugar
¼ cup (2 fl oz)	white vinegar
2 tablespoons	light soy sauce
2 tablespoons	cold water
1 teaspoon	cornflour (cornstarch)

Peel the cucumber and rub with salt to eliminate the bitter taste, then rinse with cold water and wipe dry. Cut into sticks about 5 cm (2 in) long, discarding the seed cores.

Heat the sesame oil to moderate, add the peppercorns and fry briefly, then add the chilli flakes and stir for a few seconds. Add the remaining seasoning ingredients and bring to the boil. Add the cucumber, spring onions, ginger, and garlic, if used, and cover the pan. Simmer until the sauce thickens and the cucumber is slightly softened, but retaining its crunchiness.

Serve as an accompaniment to any Szechuan (Sichuan) meal, particularly crisp-fried or roasted meats.

SPINACH WITH SHREDDED FISH

625 g (1¼ lb)	fresh spinach (collard greens)
75 g (2½ oz)	white fish fillets
2½ tablespoons	softened lard or frying oil
1½ tablespoons	softened chopped spring onion (scallion)
½ teaspoon	grated fresh ginger
¾ cup (6 fl oz)	chicken stock

Seasoning A:

1	egg white, beaten
¼ teaspoon	salt
¼ teaspoon	m.s.g. (optional)
1 tablespoon	cornflour (cornstarch)

Seasoning B:

2/3 teaspoon	salt
¼ teaspoon	m.s.g. (optional)
¼ teaspoon	ground black pepper
1½ teaspoons	rice wine or dry sherry
2 tablespoons	evaporated milk
1 tablespoon	cornflour (cornstarch)

Wash the spinach thoroughly, remove the stems and roughly chop the leaves. Cut the fish into narrow shreds and mix with the seasoning A ingredients. Leave for 5 minutes, then simmer in a saucepan of gently boiling water until firm and white, about 45 seconds. Drain and soak in cold water.

Heat the lard or frying oil and sauté the spring onions and ginger for 30 seconds. Add the chicken stock and the seasoning B ingredients and bring to the boil. Add the chopped spinach and simmer until tender, about 5 minutes. Add the drained fish and heat through.

Transfer to a warmed serving plate and serve at once. For variety, use raw peeled shrimps or diced chicken in place of the fish.

YOUNG LETTUCE SAUTÉD WITH CRABMEAT AND ROE

2	fresh young cos lettuce
1½ tablespoons	frying oil
2 tablespoons	softened lard
75 g (2½ oz)	fresh crabmeat with roe*
1 tablespoon	finely chopped spring onion (scallion)
¼ teaspoon	grated fresh ginger cornflour (cornstarch)
1 tablespoon	rendered chicken fat (chicken grease) (optional)

Seasoning/Sauce:

¾ teaspoon	salt
¼ teaspoon	m.s.g. (optional)
¼ teaspoon	ground black pepper
2 teaspoons	rice wine or dry sherry
¾ cup (6 fl oz)	chicken stock

Thoroughly wash the lettuce and cut each into three parts, cutting from the root section to the top of the leaves so that the leaves remain connected to a part of the stem. Blanch in boiling water with the frying oil added for 1½ minutes, then drain and arrange on a serving plate.

Heat the lard in a wok and sauté the crabmeat and roe for 30 seconds, then add the spring onion and ginger and sauté briefly. Add the seasoning/sauce ingredients and bring to the boil. Simmer for 1 minute, then add a paste of the cornflour and cold water and stir until thickened.

Pour the sauce over the lettuce and add the chicken fat, if used. Serve at once.

* As an alternative to the crabmeat and roe, substitute the same amount of finely chopped raw peeled shrimps and add 1½ teaspoons of dried shrimp roe.

STRING BEANS WITH DICED BEEF AND PEANUTS

310 g (10 oz)	fresh green beans (string beans)*
5 — 6 cloves	garlic, finely chopped
125 g (4 oz)	beef fillet (tenderloin)
1½ teaspoons	finely chopped fresh ginger
1 — 2	fresh red chilli peppers, shredded
1	spring onion (scallion), trimmed and diced
¼ cup (2 fl oz)	frying oil
½ cup	shelled roasted peanuts (groundnuts)
1½ teaspoons	hot bean paste (optional)

Seasoning A:

1 teaspoon	sugar
1 tablespoon	rice wine or dry sherry
½ teaspoon	cornflour (cornstarch)

Seasoning B:

2 teaspoons	sugar
2 tablespoons	light soy sauce
1 tablespoon	rice wine or dry sherry

String the beans, if necessary, and cut into 5 cm (2 in) lengths. Mix with the garlic and set aside. Cut the beef into narrow shreds and mix with the seasoning A ingredients. Sprinkle the chopped ginger, shredded chilli peppers, and diced spring onion on top and set aside.

Heat the frying oil and stir-fry the peanuts for 45 seconds. Remove and drain well. Add the beans and stir-fry over fairly high heat until they turn a darker green and are wrinkled in appearance, about 4 minutes. Remove and set aside. Add the beef, and a little extra oil if needed, and stir-fry for 1½ minutes, then add the bean paste, if used, and stir-fry briefly.

Add the seasoning B ingredients and return the beans. Stir-fry together for 30 seconds, then add the peanuts, mix well and transfer to a serving plate. Serve at once.

* Or use Chinese long beans.

BAMBOO SHOOTS WITH DRIED SHRIMPS AND SZECHUAN (SICHUAN) CABBAGE

375 g (12 oz)	canned bamboo shoots, drained
1 tablespoon	dried shrimps, soaked for 25 minutes*
30 g (1 oz)	Szechuan (Sichuan) pickled cabbage
2½ cups (20 fl oz)	deep-frying oil
2	spring onions (scallions), trimmed and shredded
1 tablespoon	sesame oil

Seasoning/Sauce:

½ cups (4 fl oz)	water
2 teaspoons	light soy sauce
2 teaspoons	rice wine or dry sherry
¼ teaspoon	salt
¼ teaspoon	m.s.g. (optional)
2 teaspoons	sugar

Cut the bamboo shoots into thin slices, then bat with the end of the cleaver handle to crush the fibres. Coarsely chop the drained shrimps and the pickled cabbage.

Heat the deep-frying oil to fairly hot and deep-fry the bamboo shoots until crisp and dry. Remove and drain thoroughly. Pour off all but 2½ tablespoons of the oil and stir-fry the shrimps and cabbage briefly, then return the bamboo shoots and add the pre-mixed seasoning/sauce ingredients. Simmer over slightly reduced heat until the liquid is partially absorbed, then add the spring onions and sesame oil and stir in lightly. Transfer to a serving plate and serve at once.

* Or use 1½ teaspoons dried shrimp roe, soaked for 20 minutes and drained.

WINTER BAMBOO SHOOTS WITH PORK AND SZECHUAN (SICHUAN) VEGETABLES

1 500 g (1 lb) can	winter bamboo shoots, drained
4 cups (1 litre)	deep-frying oil
2 tablespoons	sesame oil
60 g (2 oz)	lean pork, coarsely minced (ground)
2 tablespoons	finely chopped spring onion (scallion)
1 teaspoon	finely chopped fresh ginger
½ teaspoon	crushed garlic (optional)
20 g (2/3 oz)	Szechuan (Sichuan) preserved vegetables, finely diced

Seasoning:

½ teaspoon	salt
1 tablespoon	light soy sauce
2 teaspoons	rice wine or dry sherry
1¼ teaspoons	sugar

Roll-cut the bamboo shoots into 2 cm (¾ in) pieces. Heat the deep-frying oil to moderately hot and deep-fry the bamboo shoots until golden. Drain well. Pour off the oil, retaining 1 tablespoon, and add the sesame oil. Heat to smoking point and quickly stir-fry the minced pork until it changes colour. Decrease the heat and add the spring onion, ginger, and garlic, if used, and stir-fry for 45 seconds.

Add the diced vegetables and the seasoning ingredients and stir-fry for a further 45 seconds, then return the bamboo shoots and heat through. Transfer to a serving plate and serve.

FISH-FLAVOURED EGGPLANT

375 g (12 oz)	eggplant (aubergine)
3 cups (24 fl oz)	deep-frying oil
90 g (3 oz)	coarsely minced (ground) pork
1½ tablespoons	finely chopped spring onion (scallion)
2 teaspoons	finely chopped fresh ginger
1 tablespoon	finely chopped garlic (or to taste)
2 teaspoons	hot bean paste

Seasoning:

1 teaspoon	light soy sauce
1 teaspoon	rice wine or dry sherry
1 teaspoon	sugar
¼ teaspoon	m.s.g. (optional)
¼ teaspoon	ground black pepper
½ teaspoon	Chinese brown vinegar

Cut the eggplants in halves lengthwise, remove the stems and cut each piece into 3 — 4 slices. Heat the deep-frying oil and deep-fry the eggplant on fairly high heat until coloured. Remove and drain well.

Pour off all but ¼ cup (2 fl oz) of the oil and stir-fry the pork, onion, ginger, and garlic until the pork changes colour. Add the hot bean paste and stir-fry briefly, then add the seasoning ingredients and stir-fry for 30 seconds. Add salt to taste.

Return the eggplant, cover and cook on low heat, splashing in a little water to prevent sticking, until the eggplant is tender. Serve.

BRAISED EGGPLANT

250 g (8 oz)	eggplant (aubergine)
1 teaspoon	salt
310 g (10 oz)	lean pork or beef
2 cups (16 fl oz)	frying oil
4 slices	fresh ginger, shredded
2	spring onions (scallions), trimmed and diced
1 — 2	fresh red chilli peppers, shredded
1½ teaspoons	crushed garlic
1 tablespoon	soybean paste
2 teaspoons	sesame oil
¾ teaspoon	Chinese brown vinegar
½ teaspoon	ground black pepper

Seasoning A:

¼ teaspoon	salt
½ teaspoon	m.s.g. (optional)
1 tablespoon	rice wine or dry sherry
1 teaspoon	sesame oil
2 teaspoons	frying oil
2 teaspoons	cornflour (cornstarch)

Seasoning B/Sauce:

2 tablespoons	water
2 teaspoons	light soy sauce
1 tablespoon	rice wine or dry sherry
2 teaspoons	sugar
1 teaspoon	chilli oil (optional)
¼ teaspoon	salt
1 teaspoon	cornflour (cornstarch)

Wash the eggplants and remove the stems. Cut into 2.5 cm (1 in) cubes and sprinkle on the salt. Leave in a colander for 1 hour to draw off the bitter juices, then rinse well in cold water. Drain thoroughly.

Mince (grind) the beef or pork and mix with the seasoning A ingredients, leave for 20 minutes. Heat the frying oil in a wok to moderate and fry the eggplant until beginning to soften and colour. Remove and drain thoroughly. Pour off all but 2½ tablespoons of the oil and stir-fry the ginger, onions, chilli peppers, and garlic for 30 seconds. Add the soybean paste and stir-fry a further 30 seconds.

Add the meat and a little more oil if needed, and stir-fry until the meat changes colour, then add the seasoning B/sauce ingredients and return the eggplant. Cover and cook on moderate heat, turning occasionally, until the eggplant is tender and the seasonings well absorbed.

Stir in the sesame oil, vinegar, and pepper and transfer to a serving plate.

SAUTÉD VEGETABLES AND WHITE FUNGUS

280 g (9 oz)	*Chinese (celery) cabbage*
280 g (9 oz)	*fresh broccoli*
125 g (4 oz)	*canned bamboo shoots*
125 g (4 oz)	*snow peas*
30 g (1 oz)	*dried 'snow' fungus, soaked for 25 minutes*
3 slices	*fresh ginger, shredded*
¼ cup (2 fl oz)	*softened lard or frying oil*
3 cups (24 fl oz)	*chicken stock*

Seasoning:

¾ teaspoon	*salt*
½ teaspoon	*m.s.g. (optional)*
1 teaspoon	*sugar*
2 teaspoons	*rice wine or dry sherry*

Thoroughly wash the cabbage, separate the leaves and cut into 5 cm (2 in) lengths. Cut larger pieces in halves lengthwise. Cut the broccoli into florets and wash thoroughly, drain well. Thinly slice the bamboo shoots. String the snow peas and trim the root sections from the 'snow' fungus, then cut into squares.

Bring 1 cup of the stock to the boil in a wok and add the cabbage and 1 tablespoon of the lard or frying oil. Simmer for about 5 minutes until tender, then remove the cabbage, drain well and set aside. Pour off the liquid, add another 1 cup of the stock and add the broccoli. Simmer until tender, but retaining crispness. Drain and set aside. Add the 'snow' fungus to the stock and simmer for 5 — 6 minutes.

Heat the remaining lard or oil and sauté the bamboo shoots and snow peas together for 1 minute. Add the fungus and ginger and sauté for a further 1 minute, then add the seasoning ingredients and the remaining stock and return the broccoli.

Simmer together until the vegetables are tender. Push to one side of the pan and return the cabbage. Heat thoroughly then remove the cabbage to a serving plate. Transfer the other vegetables to the plate using a slotted spoon and arrange over the cabbage.

Reheat the sauce, check the seasonings and thicken with a thin solution of cornflour (cornstarch) and cold water. Pour over the vegetables and serve.

HAM AND WINTER MELON SANDWICHES IN SOUP

625 g (1¼ lb)	*winter melon*
45 g (1½ oz)	*Chinese or cured (Smithfield) ham*
½ cup (4 fl oz)	*chicken stock*

Seasoning:

¾ teaspoon	*salt*
½ teaspoon	*m.s.g. (optional)*
¼ teaspoon	*ground black pepper*
1 tablespoon	*frying oil*
1 teaspoon	*rice wine or dry sherry*

Soup:

2½ cups (20 fl oz)	*chicken stock*
⅓ teaspoon	*salt*
2 teaspoons	*rice wine or dry sherry*
¼ teaspoon	*sesame oil (optional)*
4 slices	*fresh ginger, finely shredded*

Cut the melon into 24 pieces after removing the peel and seeds. Make a slit in the rounded side of each piece. Cut the ham into 24 pieces. Blanch the melon in boiling water for 1½ minutes, then drain and insert a piece of ham into each slit. Arrange the melon in a large bowl and add the chicken stock and seasoning ingredients.

Set on a rack in a steamer and steam over rapidly boiling water until the melon is tender, about 12 minutes. Transfer to a soup tureen. Bring the soup ingredients to the boil and simmer briefly, then pour over the melon sandwiches and serve.

TRANSLUCENT SLICED CHICKEN AND BAMBOO SHOOT SOUP

155 g (5 oz)	boneless chicken breast
75 g (2½ oz)	canned bamboo shoots, drained
	cornflour (cornstarch)
5 cups (1¼ litres)	chicken stock
12	fresh spinach leaves (collard greens)
1 tablespoon	finely shredded cooked ham

Seasoning:

1¼ teaspoons	salt
½ teaspoon	m.s.g. (optional)
¼ teaspoon	white pepper
2 teaspoons	rice wine or dry sherry

Cut the chicken into small cubes and place on a board. Cut the bamboo shoots into very thin slices and soak in a little of the chicken stock.

Cover the chicken pieces with a thick layer of cornflour and roll to coat evenly. Use a rolling pin or the side of the cleaver to bat the pieces into transparent escalopes. Continually coat with more cornflour to keep the pieces completely dry. Shake off any excess flour, then drop the chicken slices into a saucepan of simmering water to cook until firm and white, about 45 seconds. Drain and transfer to a dish of cold water.

Bring the stock to the boil and add the bamboo shoots and the seasoning ingredients. Simmer for 1 minute, then add the washed spinach leaves and simmer briefly. Add the chicken slices and the ham and heat through, then transfer to a soup tureen.

DUCK SOUP IN YUNNAN STEAM-POT

½ 2 kg (4 lb)	duck
60 g (2 oz)	Chinese or cured (Smithfield) ham
8 slices	fresh ginger
2 tablespoons	rice wine or dry sherry
2 teaspoons	salt

Cut the duck through the bones into bite-sized pieces. Blanch in boiling water for 1 minute, drain and rinse in cold water. Drain well. Place in a Yunnan steam-pot. Cut the ham into large dice and add to the pot with the wine and salt.

Add boiling water to just cover the duck, then place the pot in a large saucepan with the lid firmly in place. Pour cold water into the pan until it comes half-way up the sides of the steam-pot, then cover the pan and boil gently for 2½ — 3 hours, adding more boiling water as the level drops.

Serve the duck soup in the casserole.

WATERCRESS SOUP

375 g (12 oz)	fresh watercress
4	Chinese red dates
5 cups (1¼ litres)	chicken stock
3 slices	fresh ginger
2 teaspoons	light soy sauce
2 teaspoons	rice wine or dry sherry
1 teaspoon	sugar
1¼ teaspoons	salt

Pick off the stems and thoroughly wash the watercress removing any discoloured or wilted leaves. Drain well. Bring the chicken stock to the boil and add the dates and ginger. Simmer for about 15 minutes until the dates are soft and tender, then add the watercress and the remaining ingredients and simmer for 5 — 6 minutes until the watercress is tender. Transfer to a soup tureen and serve.

Peaches in Honey Syrup (recipe page 241).

DUMPLINGS OF SHRIMP, PORK, AND WHITE FUNGUS IN CHICKEN SOUP

30	wonton wrappers (see recipe, page 376)
30 g (1 oz)	dried white (snow) fungus, soaked for 25 minutes
125 g (4 oz)	fat pork, finely minced (ground)
125 g (4 oz)	raw peeled shrimps, minced (ground)
1	egg, beaten
5 cups (1¼ litres)	chicken stock

Seasoning A:

1¼ tablespoons	frying oil
½ teaspoon	salt
1 teaspoon	sugar
½ teaspoon	m.s.g. (optional)
2 teaspoons	ginger wine
2 teaspoons	cornflour (cornstarch)

Seasoning B:

1¼ teaspoons	salt
¼ teaspoon	m.s.g. (optional)
¼ teaspoon	ground black pepper
2	spring onions (scallions), trimmed and diced
2 slices	fresh ginger, chopped or shredded

Prepare the wonton wrappers following the instructions on page 376, or use frozen wrappers and thaw under a lightly dampened cloth until soft enough to separate.

Drain and finely chop the fungus, discarding the hard root section. Mix with the pork and shrimps and the seasoning A ingredients. Chill for about 20 minutes, then place a portion in one corner of each wonton wrapper. Brush all around the edge with beaten egg, then fold the lower point up to the top point and press the edges together all around to give a triangular shape. Pull the two bottom corners gently downwards, then brush one with a little beaten egg and pinch the two corners together forcing the filling into a circular shape with the top corner flaring away in the centre.

Bring a large saucepan of water to a gentle boil and add the dumplings. Simmer for about 5 minutes, then drain and transfer to the well-heated chicken stock. Add the seasoning B ingredients and simmer briefly, then serve.

For extra colour, add shredded spinach or watercress to the soup.

SLICED FISH AND PICKLED MUSTARD GREENS IN SOUP

185 g (6 oz)	white fish fillets
185 g (6 oz)	pickled mustard root or leaves
4½ cups (1 1/8 litres)	fish stock
2 thin slices	fresh ginger, shredded

Seasoning A:

2 tablespoons	onion and ginger infusion (see page 386)
¾ teaspoon	salt
1	egg white, beaten
1 tablespoon	cornflour (cornstarch)

Seasoning B:

1 teaspoon	salt
1 teaspoon	m.s.g. (optional)
¼ teaspoon	ground black pepper
2 teaspoons	rice wine or dry sherry
½ teaspoon	sesame oil

Cut the fish into very thin slices and place in a dish with the onion and ginger infusion. Leave for 6 — 7 minutes, then add the remaining seasoning A ingredients, mix well and leave a further 6 — 7 minutes.

Wash the mustard and cut into very thin slices. Bring the fish stock to the boil and add the ginger, mustard, and seasoning B ingredients. Simmer for 2 — 3 minutes. Heat a separate saucepan of water until gently simmering. Add the fish slices and poach until firm, then drain and transfer to the soup.

Simmer briefly, then pour into a soup tureen and serve at once.

BEANCURD SKIN AND CLAMS IN SOUP

90 g (3 oz)	dried beancurd skins
185 g (6 oz)	canned clams, drained
2½ tablespoons	softened lard or frying oil
2 tablespoons	finely chopped spring onion (scallion)
2 teaspoons	finely chopped fresh ginger
5 cups (1¼ litres)	chicken stock
2 tablespoons	rendered chicken fat (chicken grease) (optional)

Seasoning:

1¼ teaspoons	salt
½ teaspoon	m.s.g. (optional)
¼ teaspoon	ground black pepper
2 teaspoons	rice wine or dry sherry
1½ tablespoons	cornflour (cornstarch)

Wash the beancurd skins and place in a dish with water to cover. Add 1 teaspoon of bicarbonate of soda and soak for about 1½ hours, then drain and rinse in cold water. Cut into small squares and place in a saucepan. Cover with boiling water or chicken stock and simmer for about 20 minutes until softened.

Heat the lard or oil in a wok and stir-fry the clams for 30 seconds. Push to one side of the pan and add the spring onions and ginger and stir-fry briefly, then add the seasoning ingredients and the beancurd skin and bring to the boil. Simmer for 2 — 3 minutes, then stir in the chicken fat, if used, and heat through. Transfer to a soup tureen and serve.

Use coarsely minced (ground) pork or beef in place of clams, or use diced fresh squid or sea cucumber.

ABALONE AND LILY BUD SOUP

1 500 g (1 lb) can	abalone
4	eggs
1½	spring onions (scallions), trimmed and sliced
3 slices	fresh ginger
1½ tablespoons	frying oil
5 cups (1¼ litres)	chicken stock
1¼ tablespoons	cornflour (cornstarch)

Seasoning:

1½ teaspoons	salt
¼ teaspoon	white pepper
1 tablespoon	rice wine or dry sherry
1 tablespoon	rendered chicken fat (chicken grease)

Drain the abalone reserving the juice. Trim the ruffled edges and cut horizontally into thin slices. Return to the liquid and set aside. Hard boil (hard cook) the eggs and cool under running cold water, then shell and cut lengthwise into four wedges. Discard the yolks or reserve for another use and trim the pointed ends of the whites to give an oval-shaped petal effect. Cover with cold water and set aside.

Sauté the spring onion and ginger in the oil for about 30 seconds, then add the chicken stock and bring to the boil. Simmer briefly, then add the seasoning ingredients and discard the onion and ginger. Add the sliced abalone and cooked egg whites, well drained, and simmer for 2 — 3 minutes.

Thicken the stock with the cornflour mixed with an equal amount of cold water and simmer briefly, then transfer to a soup tureen and serve.

SHREDDED TURNIP AND GOLDEN CARP IN SOUP

250 g (½ lb)	peeled turnips (or giant white/icicle radishes)
1 315 g (10 oz)	golden carp, or use half a larger fish
1	spring onion (scallion), trimmed and sliced
3 thin slices	fresh ginger
1½ tablespoons	softened lard
5 cups (1¼ litres)	water
1¼ teaspoons	salt
½ teaspoon	m.s.g. (optional)
1 tablespoon	rendered chicken fat (chicken grease)

Cut the turnips into matchstick strips, or grate coarsely. Scale and clean the fish and wash well. Stir-fry the spring onion and ginger in the lard for 30 seconds. Add the turnip and stir-fry for a further 30 seconds, splashing in a little of the water if it begins to stick to the pan. Add the remaining water and bring to the boil.

Put in the fish and add the salt. Simmer on low heat for about 20 minutes until the fish is tender, then stir in the m.s.g., if used, and add the chicken fat. Transfer to a soup tureen.

The fish may be removed from the soup and served separately on a bed of finely shredded spring onion, ginger, chilli pepper, and chopped garlic with dips of light soy sauce and Chinese red vinegar.

STEAMED DATE CAKE

125 g (4 oz)	Chinese red dates
125 g (4 oz)	candied winter melon*
1½ tablespoons	candied orange or mixed peel
1½ tablespoons	toasted white sesame seeds
10	canned water chestnuts, drained and diced
125 g (4 oz)	plain (pound) cake
2 tablespoon	water
4	eggs, well beaten
¾ cup	sugar
2 large pieces	pork fat

Steam the dates with a little water until soft, then remove the skins and seeds and mash. Dice the winter melon and orange or mixed peel.

Prepare the sesame seeds and water chestnuts and sprinkle the water over the cake, then cut into 1 cm (¾ in) cubes.

Mix all the ingredients, except the pork fat, together and add about ⅓ cup water. Place one piece of pork fat in the bottom of a pudding basin and add the mixed ingredients. Top with the remaining fat and weight lightly.

Set the basin on a rack in a steamer and steam over rapidly boiling water for about 35 minutes. Remove from the steamer and discard the top piece of pork fat, then invert the pudding onto a serving plate and remove the other piece of pork fat. Serve the pudding hot.

If preferred, substitute parboiled glutinous rice for the cake and proceed in the same way.

* Or use candied papaya (pawpaw) or pineapple.

SWEET BLACK SESAME SOUP

155 g (5 oz)	black sesame seeds
7 cups (1¾ litres)	water
1 cup	white sugar
⅓ cup	cornflour (cornstarch)
⅓ cup	cold water
1 teaspoon	salt

Toast the sesame seeds in a dry pan until they begin to pop, then transfer to a mortar, coffee, or spice grinder and grind to a fairly fine powder.

Bring half the water to the boil in one saucepan and add the sesame seeds. Bring the remaining water to the boil in another pan and add the sugar. Simmer, stirring both pans, for 10 minutes. Remove from the heat. Pour the sesame paste into a blender and blend at high speed until smooth, adding some of the sugar syrup if the mixture becomes too thick.

Remove from the blender and combine with the remaining sugar syrup, then add the salt. Mix the cornflour and cold water together, pour into the soup and simmer until thickened. Serve hot.

WALNUT PUDDING UNDER 'SNOW COVERED MOUNTAINS'

90 g (3 oz)	walnut pieces
2 cups (16 fl oz)	vegetable oil
75 g (2½ oz)	arrowroot powder
1 cup	sugar
5	egg whites

Blanch the walnuts in boiling water for 1 minute, then remove the skins. Dry well. Heat the oil to fairly hot and deep-fry the walnuts until golden. Remove and drain well, then chop finely.

Place the arrowroot powder in a dish. Pour all but 2½ tablespoons of the sugar into a saucepan and add 3 cups (24 fl oz) water. Bring to the boil and simmer until it turns into a syrup, about 15 minutes on moderate heat. Pour 1 cup of the hot syrup into the arrowroot powder and stir quickly until thoroughly mixed. The hot syrup will cook the arrowroot, turning it into a semi-transparent paste. Add the chopped walnuts, mixing well.

Pour the remaining sugar syrup into a heatproof serving dish and place the arrowroot walnut mixture in the centre of the dish, submerged in the syrup.

Mix the reserved sugar with the egg whites and beat to stiff peaks. Heat a saucepan of water to a gentle boil and put in the beaten egg whites. Cook until the egg whites are firm, then transfer to the serving dish, floating on the syrup and serve.

PEACHES IN HONEY SYRUP

6	large fresh peaches
1 tablespoon	dried peppermint leaves
2 tablespoons	clear honey
⅓ cup	sugar
1 teaspoon	rose water (optional)

Drop the peaches into boiling water, leave for 6 — 7 seconds, then remove and peel. Cut in halves and discard the seeds. Place in a dish, cut sides downwards, and sprinkle on the peppermint leaves. Steam over rapidly boiling water until the peaches are tender.

Mix the honey and sugar in a small saucepan with ½ cup water and bring to the boil. Simmer until the syrup turns thick and sticky, then add the rose water, if used.

Remove the peaches from the steamer, scrape off the peppermint leaves and discard. Arrange the peaches on a serving plate and cover with the honey syrup. Serve hot.

EIGHT-TREASURE RICE

50 g (2 oz)	dried lotus seeds
1½ cups	short grain raw glutinous rice
30 g (1 oz)	dried Chinese red dates
30 g (1 oz)	black dates
45 g (1½ oz)	candied papaya (pawpaw) shreds*
30 g (1 oz)	sweet preserved orange or kumquat**
45 g (1½ oz)	pearl barley
90 g (3 oz)	fresh pork fat
1 cup	soft brown sugar
¼ cup	white or castor sugar

* Use candied winter melon or pineapple as an alternative.
** Or use mixed peel.

Steam the lotus seeds with a little water until softened, then drain and use a needle to pick out the bitter cores. Wash the rice thoroughly and place in a dish. Steam until softened, but not cooked through.

Wash the dates, papaya, orange, and barley and place in separate groups in a dish to steam until softened. Drain and remove the date skins and pips. Cut any larger pieces into dice. Cut the pork fat into small dice.

Grease a pudding basin with lard and place the diced pork fat in the bottom, then arrange the dates, papaya, orange, and lotus seeds in a design over the fat. Add the pearl barley and lastly the rice, which has been thoroughly mixed with the brown sugar. Press down gently and smooth the top. Set the basin on a rack in a steamer and steam over rapidly boiling water for 1 hour.

Invert the basin over a serving dish and remove the pudding, sprinkle the white sugar over the top and serve hot.

If preferred, use white sugar in the pudding for a lighter colour, and make a thick sugar syrup or use clear honey to pour over the pudding.

CHAPTER VI
Southern Style Cuisine

Previous page: *The lush green mountains and valleys of southern China produce ingredients for China's most varied and exotic cuisine. Water buffalo ramain the single most important piece of farm equipment throughout the country.*

Farmer above *relaxes in bamboo chair while casting for fish with a bamboo pole on Li River near Kweilin (Guilin).*

Southern-style Chinese cuisine is the type with which the Western world is most familiar. Overseas Chinese communities hail primarily from the province of Kuangtung (Guangdong), and these hardy immigrants brought with them their southern cooking styles, establishing Chinese restaurants in every corner of the globe. The southern culinary style includes the cooking of Kuangtung (Guangdong) province and surrounding areas, collectively known as Ling-nan in ancient times. The culinary capital of this region, and indeed of all China, is the city of Canton (Guangzhou), which boasts more restaurants and more original culinary creations than any other city of China. Lively debate continues among Chinese gourmets as to whether Yunnan, Kweichow (Guizhou), Chiewchow (Chaozhou), and other sub-sets of this cuisine should be regarded as independent culinary styles. However, since the entire Ling-nan region shares a common historical and culinary heritage, dominated by its geographical conditions and centred around the city of Canton (Guangzhou), we feel that the entire region falls into the same broad culinary category.

Historically and geographically, Ling-nan has been China's rice-bowl. Its warm, moist climate and lush, fertile conditions have permitted rice to be cultivated there in abundance, and it has been the staple of the southern diet ever since the Chinese first entered the region during the Han dynasty. Rice remained an exclusive southern luxury up until the Sung dynasty, when new, faster growing strains permitted cultivation further north. The ever-popular Mixed Fried Rice is a Cantonese innovation. It is traditionally served as the last course at Cantonese banquets, in case anyone at the table did not get his or her fill from the preceding *cai*.

The southern region is geographically blessed with optimum conditions for supporting a gourmet cuisine. Rich soil, abundant rainfall, and dense vegetation produce a broad range of exotic plants and animals unavailable elsewhere in China. Its location on the coast also gives this region access to abundant sources of fresh seafoods from the South China Sea. Almost every living thing in the region has been somehow adapted to the diet, and there are few, if any, culinary taboos. An old Chinese adage tells us that 'if it moves on four legs, the Cantonese will eat it.'

Among the main ingredients which commonly appear on the southern menu, fish and crustaceans from the ocean and from ponds and paddies play prominent roles. Poultry is also central to the southern cuisine: southern chefs work wonders with every part of chicken and ducks. From the vegetable kingdom come an incredible variety of fresh vegetables: the green, leafy varieties with crispy textures are especially favoured. Wild game provides yet another source of primary ingredients: civet, racoon, bear, elephant, snake, parrots, monkeys, and many other odd creatures appear regularly in the Cantonese kitchen. Restaurants which specialise in these exotic dishes usually keep the animals live in cages near the entrance, where discriminating diners muse over the selection and choose appropriate beasts for their banquets. Cantonese cuisine is further renowned for its great variety of snack foods, collectively called *dim-sum* in Cantonese or *dian-xin* in Mandarin. *Dim-sum* are usually eaten for lunch or as mid-afternoon snacks and are taken with pots of strong, fragrant tea. They include stuffed dumplings of every shape and flavour, delicate pastries (salty and sweet), cakes, puddings, and cold-plates of roasted meats and poultry.

The popular Western stereotype of Cantonese food is that it is all sweet, or sweet-and-sour. This misconception has been perpetrated, above all, by one culprit: Chinese/American-style sweet-and-sour pork. Cantonese chefs in America discovered long ago that by adding extra sugar and plenty of tomato ketchup to their sauces, their restaurants attracted extra Western customers. *Real* Cantonese food appears in the West usually only on menus handwritten in Chinese, which are presented just to Chinese patrons.

The fact is that southern-style cuisine employs less sugar, and less of the other common Chinese cooking condiments, than any other regional style. Cooking condiments are used sparingly only to bring out and enhance the fresh-natural flavours of the main ingredients, which themselves serve as the primary flavouring agents for each dish. If any condiment is particularly favoured, it is good vinegar, with its characteristic piquant, sour flavour. Garlic and chillies are used less than elsewhere in China, but ginger and spring onions retain important roles. Vegetable oils are preferred over lard for deep-frying and sauté-

Farmer draws water from the limpid Li River near Kweilin (Guilin) to irrigate his greening crops. Above right: *Typical rural scenes in the countryside near Yangshuo, south of Kweilin (Guilin). The pace of rural life is still very slow and easy in China.*

ing. Cantonese chefs are masters of fragrant table sauces and spicy dips, a custom which permits each diner to dip each bite as deeply or superficially as he pleases, thereby controlling the flavours himself. Sauce, for example, is commonly served with steamed or poached prawns, good vinegar is used to dip steamed crab, soy sauce and sesame oil are popular dips for *dim-sum*, and Chinese pepper-salt powder often appears with deep-fried foods.

Southern chefs prefer the *chao* method of cooking above all others. *Chao* cooking is fuel - and oil-efficient, an important consideration everywhere in China; it preserves the *xien* (fresh-natural) flavours better than any other method; and it is the best technique for blending different flavours together quickly into harmonious combinations. Due to the prevalence of sautéing, ingredients in the Cantonese kitchen must be cut very finely and evenly prior to cooking. This permits maximum blending of their natural flavours in minimum cooking times. Rare and expensive ingredients are 'stretched' by using minimum quantities, cutting them super-fine, and blending them with other less expensive items: the

costly foods thereby impart their exquisite flavours and distinctive bouquets to the entire dish. In Cantonese cooking, fresh primary ingredients always provide the main flavours, not concentrated cooking condiments, and these flavours are blended to complement one another.

The second most important southern cooking technique is steaming. Many *dim-sum* are steamed, as are many fish and seafoods. Steaming preserves original flavours and locks in vital nutrients, as sautéing does. The combination of steam and sauté methods is very convenient in the kitchen: while the steamed dishes cook, the sautéd dishes are prepared, and everything is ready about the same time.

Southern cooking places greater emphasis on the colour and overall appearance of dishes than any other culinary region of China. In the south, appearances are always important measures of a dish's success, and few dishes appear on the table without elaborate embellishments and colourful garnishes. Ingredients are selected for contrasting colours which please the eye, as well as for flavours which please the palate. Kitchen preparation em-

phasises preservation and intensification of pretty colours and alteration of drab ones. Cold-platters are artfully contrived to look like dragons, phoenixes, and other mythological animals. And the Cantonese savour the rich, deep-green colours of their leafy vegetables as much as they enjoy their fresh flavours and crispy textures.

The importance of appearances in southern-style cuisine reflects the sensual, aesthetic orientation of the south and the total immersion of all the senses in eating. This tendency appears not only in the food itself, but also in the setting in which food is enjoyed. Nowhere else in China are the restaurants as beautifully designed as in Canton (Guangzhou). Rambling gardens and rustling bamboo groves, hidden private terraces and pavilions, exquisitely carved hardwood furniture, paintings and calligraphy by renowned artists, carved screens with cut-glass panels, and a general ambiance of the highest aesthetic standards have always been, and still are, common features of such well-known restaurants in Canton (Guangzhou) as the North Garden, the South Garden, the Canton (Guangzhou) Wine-House, the Da-

tong, and others.

The qualities of texture in food are also more strongly emphasised in the sensual south than elsewhere around the country. Southern gourmets are particularly partial to the crispy textures of certain fresh vegetables and the tender, juicy textures of meat, fish, and fowl. Such textures often appear in contrast within the same dish. Crispy textures are well preserved by the *chao* method, while steaming ensures optimum tenderness, softness, and juiciness in fish, fowl, and *dim-sum*. Meats are kept tender and juicy by appropriate marination prior to cooking.

The inhabitants of the Ling-nan region have always been known in China for their exotic, complex culinary tastes. In northern China and around the world, southern Chinese eating habits are the butt of many culinary jokes and a source of endless wonder and amusement. Nevertheless, such culinary prejudice against certain southern dishes only reflects the culinary conservatism of the north and of the rest of the world, not any failing of southern cuisine, for even the most exotic four-legged creatures are prepared for the table with consummate skill and care. The novice would be hard-pressed to taste the difference between dog and lamb, racoon and pork, monkey and beef. Furthermore, these dishes are exotic only by the *choice* of ingredients, not by their flavours. Indeed, the natural flavour of a Cantonese simmered-stew of young dog, for example, is at least as good, if not better, than the taste of beef, lamb, or pork. People who adamantly refuse to sample such dishes as dog, cat, civet, racoon, snake, and other Cantonese delicacies simply display their own acquired cultural prejudices rather than any sound culinary judgment. Such people would be surprised how quickly revulsion can change to fascination with just one bold bite.

Yet, one still wonders why the

Selecting only the most tender leaves, girls above *pick tea on large plantation in sunny southern China. The various blends are dried, mixed, and stored in old chests* top right *on the plantations, where they await shipment to the cities and abroad.*

southern Chinese have adapted all the strange flora and fauna of their environment into their diet, when they have such abundant sources of more conventional foods at their disposal. One reason is simply because 'it's there': the entire region teems with exotic plant and animal life, and it is only natural that a people as curious about nature and as concerned about eating as the Chinese should investigate and adapt anything edible into their diet. Another reason for the exotic diversity of the southern diet lies in traditional Chinese medical theories, which state that wild life provides the most potent source of food-energy and the most stimulating pharmacological effects. Proximity to wild aborigine tribes has also had significant influence on the exotic side of the southern menu. Ling-

nan aborigines were responsible for teaching Han settlers about the culinary value of rats (both adult and newborn), reptiles, monkeys, and many other unconventional items. An extreme example of aboriginal culinary exotica was their custom of cooking and eating the half-digested contents from the stomachs of freshly butchered cows. Fortunately, this dish has not survived on the Chinese menu, although it was reputed to be highly nutritious and tasty.

Perhaps the most important reason for the exotic and complex overtones of southern cuisine is that the south developed the most highly sophisticated and aesthetically refined culinary culture in all of China. Southerners submerged themselves totally in food culture and constantly hungered for new culinary creations drawn from the

246

Above: *In Canton (Guangzhou), China's acknowledged culinary capital, the meals are more elaborate and the restaurants more aesthetically pleasing than anywhere else in China.* Left: *Entire families still live and work on their boats on the major waterways of southern China. Here a typical boating family on Canton's Pearl River pauses for a pleasant alfresco lunch of local delicacies.*

rich treasure-trove of ingredients which filled their environment. Appearance and texture have always been so important in southern food due to this aesthetic, sensual orientation. The very abundance and dazzling array of available ingredients meant that Cantonese chefs had to come up with increasingly ingenious and complex creations in order to satisfy the jaded palates of their patrons. Resident gourmets of Canton (Guangzhou), living far from the political pressures of the capital and surrounded with natural abundance, enjoyed far more leisure time in which to indulge their appetites and refine their culinary standards than their northern cousins. The provident combination of abundant food resources, advanced culinary culture, and ample leisure time led logically to the evolution of China's most refined and diverse cuisine.

The demand for fresh-natural flavours rather than the strong tastes of concentrated condiments make complexity a necessary element in southern cooking. Since condiments are only used to enhance inherant flavours, southern chefs use meat, fish, fowl, and vegetables to complement and flavour one another. To achieve a harmonious balance by this method, many different ingredients and multiple cooking processes are required.

Southern-style cuisine is generally considered to be the most highly developed form of Chinese cooking. It is certainly the most diverse. Southern

flavours are the least contrived, relying almost entirely on the fresh-natural flavours of the main ingredients and the consummate skill required to bring them out without resorting to heavy use of condiments. Colour and texture are greatly appreciated in the south and add extrasensory dimensions to southern dishes. It is without a doubt the fanciest of Chinese regional cuisines, and the menu includes very few of the rustic 'foods eaten often at home,' which are so popular in northern and western/central styles. Cantonese cuisine is an excellent choice for dining out, but it is more difficult to prepare a complete southern banquet at home than other styles. Kitchen preparations are often long and involved, and many of the rare or exotic ingredients commonly called for in Cantonese recipes are difficult to obtain in the West. When planning a Chinese banquet at home, it is advisable to include only one or two southern-style dishes on the menu and select the balance from the other three regional styles.

SHARK'S FIN SAUTÉD WITH SILVER SPROUTS, AND LEEKS

250 g (8 oz)	prepared shark's fin (see page 393)
90 g (3 oz)	'silver' sprouts, well washed
2	young leeks, well washed
8	whole eggs, beaten
1	spring onion (scallion), trimmed and finely chopped
⅓ cup	frying oil
1½ teaspoons	rice wine or dry sherry
1 tablespoon	finely chopped cooked ham

Seasoning A:

⅓ teaspoon	salt
½ teaspoon	m.s.g. (optional)

Seasoning B:

¾ teaspoon	salt
¼ teaspoon	sugar
¼ teaspoon	m.s.g. (optional)
	pinch of white pepper
¼ teaspoon	sesame oil (optional)
2 tablespoons	chicken stock or water
2 teaspoons	cornflour (cornstarch)

Prepare the shark's fin according to the instructions on page 393, allowing at least 3 hours advance preparation. Drain well. Drain the 'silver' sprouts and sauté in 1 tablespoon of the frying oil until beginning to soften, add the wine, then remove from the pan and set aside. Finely shred the leek and mex with the shark's fin, chopped spring onion, and the seasoning A ingredients. Mix well, then stir in the 'silver' sprouts.

Heat the remaining oil in a wok and pour in the shark's fin and egg mixture. Cook on moderate heat, moving the pan slowly in a circular motion to prevent the egg from burning in the centre. Stir in the pre-mixed seasoning B ingredients just before the egg sets, and continue to cook gently until firm. Lift into a serving plate and garnish with the chopped ham. Serve at once.

CRISP SKIN CHICKEN

1 1½ kg (3 lb)	plump chicken
2	spice bags (see page 386)
2	spring onions (scallions), trimmed and cut in halves
3 thick slices	fresh ginger, bruised
8 cups (2 litres)	deep-frying oil
	fresh coriander (optional)
	shredded spring onion (scallion)

Glaze:

2½ tablespoons	malt sugar (golden syrup, clear honey or light corn syrup)
1½ tablespoons	white vinegar
1 teaspoon	Chinese pepper-salt
2 tablespoons	boiling water

Clean and dress the chicken and place breast down in a saucepan with the spice bags, spring onions, and ginger. Cover with water, add a pinch of salt and bring to the boil. Reduce the heat to simmer for 5 minutes, then remove from the heat and leave in the water to gently poach for 15 — 20 minutes. Drain and transfer to a colander to cool and dry.

Mix the glaze ingredients together, heating slightly if the malt sugar is slow to dissolve. Tie a strong string around the neck of the chicken and suspend it in a breezy place over a drip tray. Pour the glaze slowly and evenly over the chicken, making sure that some of it goes into the cavity. Leave to dry for about 5 hours. The skin should feel quite dry and firm.

Heat the deep-frying oil to moderately hot and immerse the chicken completely. Cook for at least 10 minutes, turning once or twice, until the skin is a rich red brown and the meat is cooked through, but remaining moist and a slightly pink colour. Lift out carefully and drain well. Use cooking chopsticks or the handles of two wooden spoons when moving the chicken as metal utensils may tear the skin.

Cut the chicken in halves, then divide into bite-sized pieces, cutting through the bones. Or debone the chicken completely before cutting into bite-sized pieces. Assemble on the serving plate in the shape of a chicken (see page 394). Garnish with the fresh coriander and shredded spring onion and serve with a Chinese pepper-salt dip (see page 384)

SPECIAL SOY SAUCE CHICKEN

1 1¼ kg (2½ lb)	chicken
2	spring onions (scallions), trimmed and cut in halves
2 slices	fresh ginger
	sesame oil

Seasoning/Sauce:

1½ cups (12 fl oz)	chicken stock
1 cup (8 fl oz)	light soy sauce
½ cup (4 fl oz)	dark soy sauce
1 tablespoon	rice wine or dry sherry
½ cup	sugar
2	star anise
2	spring onions (scallions), trimmed and sliced
3 slices	fresh ginger, bruised

Clean and dress the chicken and dry with kitchen paper. Place the spring onions and ginger in the cavity.

Bring the seasoning/sauce ingredients to the boil in a saucepan or casserole and add the chicken. Simmer for 30 — 35 minutes, then turn and cook a further 10 minutes.

Remove to a colander to drain. Brush the skin with sesame oil and cut into bite-sized pieces. Serve hot.

Hard-boiled eggs can be added to this dish in the last 15 minutes of cooking. To serve, cut lengthwise into quarters and arrange around the chicken.

SALT-BAKED CHICKEN

1 1¼ kg (2½ lb)	plump chicken
4 kg (8 lb)	rock or coarse salt
2	dried or fresh lotus leaves*
3	spring onions (scallions), trimmed and cut in halves
4 thick slices	fresh ginger
155 g (5 oz)	fresh broccoli, cut into florets

Seasoning A:

½ teaspoon	m.s.g. (optional)
½ teaspoon	white pepper
1¼ teaspoons	sugar
1 tablespoon	rice wine
1 tablespoon	finely chopped spring onion (scallion)
½ teaspoon	grated fresh ginger

Seasoning B:

⅓ teaspoon	salt
¼ teaspoon	m.s.g. (optional)
½ teaspoon	sugar
1 teaspoon	rice wine or dry sherry
2 tablespoons	chicken stock or water
1 teaspoon	cornflour (cornstarch)

Clean and dress the chicken and rub the skin with the seasoning A ingredients. Leave for 1 hour to marinate. Soak the dried lotus leaves, if used, in boiling water until softened, or blanch fresh leaves in boiling water for 1 minute and drain well. If using greaseproof paper, brush one side generously with vegetable oil. Stuff the spring onions and ginger into the cavity and wrap the chicken in the drained leaves or paper. Heat the salt in a large saucepan or wok taking care not to let it smoke. Make a cavity in the centre and place the chicken in this. Cover with salt, then cover the saucepan or wok and cook over moderate heat for 20 — 25 minutes. Scrape away the salt, then turn the chicken, re-cover with salt and bake a further 20-25 minutes. Remove the chicken and discard the leaves or paper.

Cut the chicken into bite-sized pieces, cutting through the bones. Simmer the broccoli in boiling water for 2 minutes. Drain and sauté in a wok with a little oil and the seasoning B ingredients for a further 2 minutes, then arrange around the chicken on a serving plate. Serve at once.

* Or use greaseproof paper.

WHOLE CHICKEN STUFFED WITH GLUTINOUS RICE

1 1¼ kg (2½ lb)	chicken
125 g (4 oz)	glutinous rice, soaked for 1 hour
4	dried black mushrooms, soaked for 25 minutes
3	spring onions (scallions), trimmed and diced
3 slices	fresh ginger, chopped
45 g (1½ oz)	Chinese or cured (Smithfield) ham, diced
2 tablespoons	rendered chicken fat (chicken grease), or lard
1 tablespoon	dark soy sauce
	cornflour (cornstarch)
8 cups (2 litres)	deep-frying oil

Seasoning:

¾ teaspoon	salt
½ teaspoon	m.s.g. (optional)
½ teaspoon	sugar
1 tablespoon	light soy sauce
½ teaspoon	rice wine or dry sherry

Clean and debone the chicken. Rinse out with boiling water and turn inside out. Trim off some of the thicker parts of the meat and cut into small dice. Place the rice, with water to cover, in a dish and set on a rack in a steamer. Steam until almost cooked through, about 35 minutes. Squeeze the water from the mushrooms and remove stems, dice the caps.

Heat the chicken fat in a wok and stir-fry the onion and ginger for 1 minute. Add the diced chicken and stir-fry until it changes colour, then add the mushrooms and ham and fry for 1 minute. Mix in the seasoning ingredients and the rice and stir-fry for a further 1 minute. Remove to a plate to cool.

Stuff the rice mixture into the chicken and sew up the opening or secure with poultry pins. Rub with the dark soy sauce and place in a deep dish. Set on a rack in the steamer and steam over high heat for about 50 minutes. Remove, wipe the skin and coat lightly with cornflour.

Heat the deep-frying oil to smoking point and quickly deep-fry the chicken, completely immersed if possible, until crisp and golden brown on the surface. Remove and drain. Place breast up on a serving dish and slash across the breast in two places to expose the filling.

CHICKEN DINNER HAINAN STYLE

Serves 4 — 6 as a complete meal.

1 1⅓ kg (2 2/3 lb)	chicken
2 teaspoons	sesame oil
1½ - 2 cups	short grain white rice
2 tablespoons	rendered chicken fat (chicken grease) (optional)
500 g (1 lb)	young green vegetables*
	ginger and spring onion sauce

Seasoning A:

1½ teaspoons	salt
½ teaspoon	m.s.g. (optional)
1	spring onion (scallion), trimmed and sliced
3 slices	fresh ginger

Seasoning B:

½ teaspoon	salt
½ teaspoon	m.s.g. (optional)
1 teaspoon	rice wine or dry sherry

Clean and dress the chicken and place in a saucepan with water to cover. Add the seasoning A ingredients and bring to the boil, cover and reduce heat to simmer. Cook for 45 minutes, then drain and brush with sesame oil. Reserve the stock.

In the meantime, cook the rice by the absorption method (see page 354), adding the chicken fat, if used, before cooking.

Reheat the stock to boiling and add the vegetables and the seasoning B ingredients. Simmer until tender but retaining some crispness. Cooking time will depend on the kind of vegetables used. Drain and arrange on a serving plate.

Slice the chicken through the bones into bite-sized pieces and assemble on a serving plate in the shape of a chicken (see page 394). Or debone and shred the meat into slivers with the fingers.

Check the cooking stock for seasoning and pour into 4 — 6 soup bowls.

Serve the chicken, vegetables, rice, and soup at the same time plus several small dishes of ginger and spring onion sauce (see page 384) as a dip for the chicken.

*Use Chinese vegetables, spinach, broccoli, or small lettuce.

SLICED CHICKEN WITH CHRYSANTHEMUM PETALS

280 g (9 oz)	boneless chicken breast
30 g (1 oz)	white chrysanthemum petals
4 cups (1 litre)	deep-frying oil
1 tablespoon	softened lard
1	spring onion (scallion), trimmed and shredded
1 slice	fresh ginger, shredded
¾ teaspoon	rice wine or dry sherry

Seasoning A:

1	egg white, beaten
½ teaspoon	salt
½ teaspoon	m.s.g. (optional)
	pinch of white pepper
½ teaspoon	rice wine or dry sherry
½ teaspoon	cornflour (cornstarch)

Seasoning B/Sauce:

¼ cup (2 fl oz)	chicken stock
½ teaspoon	salt
¼ teaspoon	m.s.g. (optional)
¾ teaspoon	sugar
½ teaspoon	cornflour (cornstarch)

Slice the chicken across the grain fairly thinly and place in a dish with the Seasoning A ingredients. Mix well and leave to marinate for 15 minutes.

Wash the chrysanthemum petals and spread on a kitchen towel to dry.

Heat the deep-frying oil to moderately hot and deep-fry the chicken until it turns white, about 45 seconds. Remove and set aside. Pour off the oil. Add the lard to the pan and stir-fry the spring onion and ginger briefly. Sizzle the wine onto the sides of the pan and return the chicken. Stir-fry for 1 minute, then add the pre-mixed seasoning B/sauce ingredients and bring to the boil, stirring. Add the chrysanthemum petals and stir for a few seconds, then transfer to a serving plate.

DICED CHICKEN AND CASHEW NUTS

250 g (8 oz)	boneless chicken
45 g (1½ oz)	raw cashew nuts or peanuts (groundnuts)
2 cups (16 fl oz)	frying oil
12	snow peas
12	canned champignons, drained
4	canned water chestnuts, drained
45 g (1½ oz)	canned bamboo shoots, drained and sliced
280 g (9 oz)	young bok choy or choy sum

Seasoning A:

½ teaspoon	salt
¼ teaspoon	m.s.g. (optional)
¾ teaspoon	sugar
1 teaspoon	light soy sauce
1 teaspoon	rice wine or dry sherry
½ teaspoon	cornflour (cornstarch)

Seasoning B/Sauce:

¼ cup (2 fl oz)	chicken stock or water
½ teaspoon	dark soy sauce
½ teaspoon	salt
¼ teaspoon	m.s.g. (optional)
¼ teaspoon	sugar
	pinch of ground black pepper
½ teaspoon	cornflour (cornstarch)

Cut the chicken into small cubes and place in a dish with the Seasoning A ingredients. Mix well and leave for 20 minutes. Heat the deep-frying oil to fairly hot and deep-fry the cashew nuts for about 2 minutes, until light gold in colour. Remove and drain well. Leave to cool. String the snow peas. Cut the champignons in halves horizontally, cut the water chestnuts into three pieces each, horizontally. Rinse the vegetables well and cut the stems into 5 cm (2 in) lengths.

Heat a wok and add 2 tablespoons of the frying oil. When smoking hot add the chicken and stir-fry for 2 minutes. Remove from the pan and add the bok choy or choy sum. Splash in a little water, cover the pan and cook on fairly high heat, shaking the pan to keep the vegetables turning, for 1½ — 2 minutes. Add the remaining vegetables and stir-fry for 30 — 45 seconds. Add the pre-mixed seasoning B/sauce ingredients and simmer briefly, then return the chicken and continue to cook until the sauce thickens. Stir in the cashews and transfer to a serving plate.

STEAMED CHICKEN DRESSED WITH SPRING ONIONS AND GINGER

1 1⅓ kg (2 2/3 lb)   chicken
5   spring onions (scallions), trimmed and shredded
6 slices   fresh ginger, shredded
¼ cup (2 fl oz)   frying oil

Seasoning:
2 teaspoons   salt
1 teaspoon   m.s.g. (optional)
½ teaspoon   sugar
1 tablespoon   rice wine or dry sherry
2 tablespoons   finely chopped spring onion (scallion)
1 tablespoon   grated fresh ginger

Clean and dress the chicken and rub all over with the pre-mixed seasoning ingredients. Leave to marinate for 1 hour, then place breast up in a dish and set on a rack in a steamer.

Steam over rapidly boiling water for 45 — 50 minutes, then drain and remove to a cutting board. Cut into bite-sized pieces and assemble on a serving plate in the shape of a chicken (see page 394).

Garnish the chicken with the shredded spring onion and ginger. Heat the frying oil to smoking point and pour over the chicken. Serve at once.

PAN-FRIED CHICKEN WITH YOUNG GINGER AND PINEAPPLE

250 g (8 oz)   boneless chicken breast
5 cm (2 in) piece   fresh young ginger, peeled*
3 thin slices   fresh or canned or pineapple
2   medium green capsicums (bell peppers)
2   spring onions (scallions), trimmed and sliced
¼ cup (2 fl oz)   frying oil

Seasoning A:
1   egg white, beaten
½ teaspoon   salt
¼ teaspoon   m.s.g. (optional)
¼ teaspoon   white pepper
½ teaspoon   rice wine or dry sherry
1 tablespoon   water
1 tablespoon   cornflour (cornstarch)

Seasoning B/Sauce:
2/3 cup   chicken stock
1 tablespoon   tomato sauce (ketchup), or use light soy sauce
½ teaspoon   white vinegar
¼ teaspoon   chilli oil (optional)
½ teaspoon   salt
1 teaspoon   sugar
¼ teaspoon   m.s.g. (optional)
¼ teaspoon   white pepper
¾ teaspoon   crushed garlic
1 teaspoon   cornflour (cornstarch)

Marinade for Ginger:
2 tablespoons   cold water
1 tablespoon   white vinegar
½ teaspoon   salt
1½ teaspoons   sugar

Skin and debone the chicken and cut across the grain into thin strips. Mix with the seasoning A ingredients and leave for 20 minutes to marinate.

Peel the ginger and cut into thin slices. Mix the marinade ingredients together, pour over the ginger and leave until needed.

Cut the pineapple in halves horizontally, then cut each slice into about 12 pieces. Remove the stem and seed cores from the peppers, cut in halves and remove the inner white ribs, then cut into 2 cm (¾ in) squares.

Heat the frying oil in a wok and gently fry the chicken until it turns white. Remove. Add the peppers and onion, cover for the first 1 minute of cooking, and fry until beginning to soften, about 2 minutes. Add the pineapple, increase the heat to fairly high and return the chicken. Pour in the pre-mixed seasoning B/sauce ingredients and cook until the sauce thickens. Add drained ginger, heat through, then transfer to a serving plate.

* Select ginger with pale cream-coloured skin and pink buds. Older ginger with darker, slightly wrinkled skin is much stronger in taste and would be unsuitable for this dish. If unobtainable, use sweet pickled ginger and omit the marination.

Chicken Dinner Hainan Style (recipe page 250)

QUICK-FRIED CHICKEN SHREDS WITH ONION

375 g (12 oz)	boneless chicken breast
1	large brown onion
¼ cup (2 fl oz)	frying oil

Seasoning A:

1	egg white
½ teaspoon	salt
¼	m.s.g. (optional)
	pinch of white pepper
1 teaspoon	rice wine or dry sherry
½ teaspoon	cornflour (cornstarch)

Seasoning B/Sauce:

¼ cup (2 fl oz)	chicken stock
2 tablespoons	tomato sauce (ketchup) or 1 tablespoon light soy sauce
½ — ¾ teaspoon	chilli oil
¾ teaspoon	sesame oil
1 teaspoon	cornflour (cornstarch)

Slice the chicken, then cut into narrow shreds. Mix with the seasoning A ingredients and leave to marinate for 15 minutes.

Peel the onion and cut in halves from stem to root. Trim away the root section and cut into thin slices, then separate the layers.

Heat the frying oil in a wok and fry the chicken on moderately high heat until white, about 1¼ minutes. Remove and keep warm. Add the onion to the pan and stir-fry for 1½ minutes on high heat, then pour in the pre-mixed seasoning B sauce ingredients and bring to the boil. Return the chicken and stir on high heat until the sauce thickens. Transfer to a warmed serving plate and serve at once.

Bean spouts may be added in place of the onion, substituting soy sauce for the tomato sauce.

FRIED STUFFED CHICKEN ROLLS

Serve as an appetiser or main dish.

250 g (8 oz)	boneless chicken breast
155 g (5 oz)	raw peeled prawns (shrimps)
30 g (1 oz)	pork fat
1½ tablespoons	finely chopped cooked ham
1 tablespoon	finely chopped fresh coriander
5 cups (1¼ litres)	deep-frying oil

Seasoning A:

1	egg white, beaten
¼ teaspoon	salt
¼ teaspoon	m.s.g. (optional)
	pinch of white pepper
½ teaspoon	bicarbonate of soda (optional)
½ teaspoon	rice wine or dry sherry
1 tablespoon	water

Seasoning B:

¼ teaspoon	salt
	pinch of m.s.g. (optional)
	pinch of white pepper
1 teaspoon	finely chopped spring onion (scallion)
⅓ teaspoon	grated fresh ginger

Sauce:

½ cup (4 fl oz)	chicken stock
2 teaspoons	light soy sauce
⅓ teaspoon	salt
¾ teaspoon	cornflour (cornstarch)

Cut the chicken into slices and bat each slice gently with the side of a cleaver or a rolling pin until flattened into thin escalopes. Dust both sides with cornflour before working to prevent sticking. Place in a dish and rub on the seasoning A ingredients. Leave for 10 minutes, then turn and leave a further 10 minutes.

Mince (grind) the prawns and pork fat together and add the seasoning B ingredients. Lay the chicken pieces out on a floured board and spread prawn filling over each. Garnish with a sprinkling of ham and coriander and roll into cylindrical shapes. Secure the rolls with toothpicks or squeeze gently to hold in shape.

Heat the deep-frying oil to moderate and fry several rolls at a time until lightly coloured, about 2½ minutes, then return all together and fry for an additional 30 seconds. Drain and arrange on a serving plate.

Pour off all but 2 tablespoons of the oil and reheat. Add the pre-mixed sauce ingredients and bring to the boil. Simmer for a minute, then pour over the chicken rolls and serve.

CHICKEN SOUTH CHINA STYLE

1 1¼ kg (2½ lb)	chicken (only the skin is required for this dish)
625 g (1¼ lb)	raw peeled prawns, finely minced (ground)
75 g (2½ oz)	pork fat, finely minced (ground)
45 g (1½ oz)	cooked ham, finely shredded
1 tablespoon	finely chopped fresh coriander
2 tablespoons	frying oil
280 g (9 oz)	fresh spinach leaves

Seasoning A:

¾ teaspoon	salt
½ teaspoon	m.s.g. (optional)
⅓ teaspoon	ground black pepper
1 teaspoon	ginger wine (see page 387)

Seasoning B:

¼ teaspoon	salt
	pinch of m.s.g. (optional)
½ teaspoon	rice wine or dry sherry
¼ cup (2 fl oz)	chicken stock

Sauce:

1 tablespoon	rendered chicken fat (chicken grease) (optional)
⅓ cup	chicken stock
¼ teaspoon	salt
	pinch of ground black pepper
½ teaspoon	cornflour (cornstarch)

Skin the chicken, reserving the meat for another use. Wash the chicken skin and wipe dry. Cut into four even-sized pieces. Mix the prawn meat and pork fat together and add the seasoning A ingredients. Mix well and leave for 15 minutes. Spread over the chicken skin leaving a wide border all around and garnish with the shredded ham and chopped coriander. Roll up and squeeze into sausage shapes, then sew up or secure the ends with toothpicks or poultry pins.

Set the rolls in an oiled dish and place on a rack in a steamer. Steam over rapidly boiling water for 20 minutes, then lift out and cut into thick slices. Arrange on a serving plate.

Sauté the spinach in the frying oil for 2 minutes, then add the seasoning B ingredients and cover. Simmer until tender, then arrange around the chicken.

Wipe out the wok and add the chicken fat, if used, or 1 tablespoon of frying oil and the remaining sauce ingredients, premixed. Bring to the boil and simmer until thickened, then pour over the chicken rolls and serve.

STEAMED CHOPPED CHICKEN AND STRAW MUSHROOMS

375 g (12 oz)	chicken*
½ 315 g (10 oz) can	straw mushrooms, drained
2	spring onions (scallions), trimmed and sliced
3 slices	fresh ginger
1 tablespoon	cornflour (cornstarch)
1 tablespoon	cold water

Seasoning:

½ teaspoon	salt
½ teaspoon	m.s.g. (optional)
½ teaspoon	sugar
1 tablespoon	light soy sauce
¾ teaspoon	rice wine or dry sherry
2 teaspoons	rendered chicken fat (chicken grease)

Cut the chicken into 2 cm (¾ in) cubes and place in a dish with the mushrooms, spring onions, and ginger on top. Add the seasoning ingredients and cold water or chicken stock to just cover the contents of the dish.

Set on a rack in a steamer and steam over rapidly boiling water until the chicken is tender, about 35 minutes. Discard the ginger and onion and strain the liquid into a wok. Add the cornflour mixed with cold water and stir until thickened. Check the seasonings and pour over the chicken and mushrooms. Stir in and serve.

This is an excellent base for a rice hot-pot. Add 1¼ cups of soaked short grain white rice, uncooked, to the pot and place the chicken and mushrooms on top. Add chicken stock or water to just cover the chicken and steam, tightly covered until the contents are tender.

Lightly sautéd fresh green vegetables can be added to either dish 10 minutes before the end of cooking time.

*With bone or boneless, as preferred.

STEAMED STUFFED CHICKEN WINGS

Serve as an appetiser or main dish.

12	chicken wings, lower joints only
3 cups (24 fl oz)	deep-frying oil
45 g (1½ oz)	Chinese or cooked ham
3	dried black mushrooms, soaked for 25 minutes
45 g (1½ oz)	canned bamboo shoots, drained
6 stems	young bok choy or fresh mustard greens
	cornflour (cornstarch)

Seasoning A:

1 tablespoon	dark soy sauce
1 teaspoon	rice wine or dry sherry

Seasoning B:

¼ teaspoon	salt
⅓ teaspoon	sugar
	pinch of m.s.g. (optional)
	pinch of white pepper

Using a sharp small-bladed knife, remove the two thin bones from the wings. Rub with the seasoning A ingredients and leave for 10 minutes. Heat the deep-frying oil to smoking point and deep-fry the wings for 20 seconds. Remove and drain well.

Cut the ham, mushrooms, and bamboo shoots into matchstick-sized pieces, after removing the mushroom stems and squeezing out excess water. Place several pieces into each wing where the bones have been removed. Arrange the stuffed wings on an oiled plate and set on a rack in a steamer. Cover tightly and steam over gently boiling water for 40 minutes.

Stir-fry the bok choy or mustard in 2 tablespoons of frying oil, adding the seasoning A ingredients and the liquid that has accumulated in the dish containing the wings. Simmer until the vegetables are tender, but retaining crispness.

Arrange the chicken wings on a plate and surround with the vegetables. Thicken the sauce with a thin solution of cornflour and cold water, if necessary, and pour over the wings. Serve at once.

CASSEROLE WITH THREE KINDS OF POULTRY

Serves 6 — 8 as the main course.

½ 1¼ kg (2½ lb)	chicken
½ 1¾ kg (3½ lb)	duck
1	pigeon
3	spring onions (scallions), trimmed and cut in halves
4 thick slices	fresh ginger, bruised
1 tablespoon	rice wine
45 g (1½ oz)	Chinese or cured (Smithfield) ham (optional)
250 g (8 oz)	young Chinese green vegetables
	salt

Cut the chicken and duck into even-sized pieces about 4 cm (1 2/3 in) square. Cut the pigeon into 6 — 8 pieces. Arrange the poultry in a dish and place the ginger and onion on top. Sprinkle on the wine and add boiling water to cover. Cover the dish and place on a rack in a steamer to steam over high heat for 1½ — 1¾ hours.

Discard the ginger and onion and arrange the thinly sliced ham, if using, in the centre of the dish and the washed vegetables around the edge. Re-cover and steam for a further 15 minutes or until the vegetables are tender. Add salt to taste.

Serve in the casserole. If preferred, the liquid can be strained into a wok, the seasonings adjusted to taste, and the sauce thickened with a paste of cornflour (cornstarch) and cold water.

Diced Chicken and Cashew Nuts (recipe page 251) and Watercress and Liver Soup (recipe page 319).

CHICKEN STIR-FRIED WITH OYSTER SAUCE

440 g (14 oz)	chicken pieces
2 tablespoons	frying oil
1½	spring onions (scallions), trimmed and sliced
½ slices	fresh ginger, shredded
½ teaspoon	finely chopped garlic
2½ teaspoons	rice wine or dry sherry

Seasoning A:

⅓ teaspoon	salt
¼ teaspoon	m.s.g. (optional)
2 teaspoons	light soy sauce
1 teaspoon	cornflour (cornstarch)

Seasoning B:

1 tablespoon	light soy sauce
2 tablespoons	oyster sauce
¾ teaspoon	sugar
½ teaspoon	sesame oil (optional)
¼ teaspoon	ground black pepper (optional)

Cut the chicken through the bones into bite-sized cubes and place in a dish with the seasoning A ingredients. Leave for 20 minutes, then stir-fry in the oil until just cooked through, about 3 minutes. Push to one side of the pan and add the spring onions, ginger, and garlic and sauté for 1 minute, then mix in the chicken pieces and sizzle the chicken onto the sides of the pan.

Drain off the excess oil and add the seasoning B ingredients, stirring to thoroughly coat the chicken pieces. Transfer to a warmed serving plate and serve.

CANTONESE ROAST DUCK

1 1½ kg (3 lb)	duck

Glaze:

2½ tablespoons	malt sugar
¼ cup (2 fl oz)	white vinegar
1½ tablespoons	boiling water

Seasoning:

2 tablespoons	soybean paste
1 tablespoon	rice wine or dry sherry
1 teaspoon	salt
1 teaspoon	m.s.g. (optional)
1 tablespoon	sugar
½ teaspoon	powdered licorice root, or 1 small piece licorice root (optional), or use 1 star anise
3 tablespoons	finely chopped spring onion
1 tablespoon	finely chopped fresh ginger
1¼ teaspoons	crushed garlic

Clean and dress the duck and blanch in boiling water for 2 minutes. Remove and drain well. Tie a strong string around its neck, passing it beneath the wings to hold them away from the body. Hang in a well-ventilated place over a drip tray.

Mix the seasoning ingredients together and smear thickly over the inside of the duck. Secure the lower opening with poultry pins, or sew up.

Mix the glaze ingredients, stirring over a pan of boiling water if the malt sugar is slow to dissolve. Slowly pour over the duck's skin to coat evenly. Catch the drips and brush these onto the skin until thickly coated. Leave to dry for 1 hour.

Place the duck, breast down, on a rack in a baking tin and bake in a preheated hot oven at 200°C/400°F for 20 minutes, then reduce the heat to 170°C/325°F and roast a further 55 minutes, turning the duck once. If preferred, secure the duck on the rotisserie pin and cool on high heat for 25 minutes, then reduce to low for the remainder of the cooking.

Drain the pan juices into a wok and bring to the boil. Supplement with a little chicken stock or water if the amount is small. Check the seasonings and keep hot.

Cut the duck into serving portions or bite-sized pieces, as preferred, and arrange on a serving plate. Pour on the sauce and serve at once.

HONEY-BASTED ROAST DUCK

1 1½ kg (3 lb)	duck
⅓ cup	clear honey
1½ tablespoons	boiling water

Seasoning:

3 cubes	fermented beancurd with the liquid, mashed
1 teaspoon	salt
½ teaspoon	m.s.g. (optional)
1 tablespoon	sugar
¼ teaspoon	ground black pepper

Sauce:

⅓ cup	chicken stock
¼ cup (2 fl oz)	light soy sauce
1½ teaspoons	rice wine or dry sherry
⅓ teaspoon	salt
⅓ teaspoon	m.s.g. (optional)
1 teaspoon	sugar
1½ teaspoons	cornflour (cornstarch)

Clean and dress the duck. Make a fairly large opening near the rear and work through this to rub the pre-mixed seasoning ingredients thoroughly over the insides. Leave for 2 hours.

Tie a string around the duck's neck and suspend above a drip tray. Pour boiling water over the skin, taking care not to allow any inside, as it will wash away the seasonings. When the skin has dried slightly, pour on the pre-mixed honey and boiling water, working slowly and thoroughly over the entire outside of the duck and allowing a little to run inside. Hang the duck in a well-ventilated place until the skin is dry.

Fix the duck onto a rotisserie bar set over a charcoal fire (or cook on the rotisserie in a preheated 200°C (400°F) for 25 minutes, then reduce the oven to low, 120°C (250°F) and roast for a further 55 minutes). Cook, turning constantly, until the duck is just cooked through and the skin crisp and a deep golden colour. Remove to a cutting board and cut in halves, then slice through the bones into bite-sized pieces and arrange on a plate.

Bring the sauce ingredients to the boil and simmer until thickened. Pour over the duck just before serving. Serve with additional condiments of hot mustard and plum sauce.

STEWED WHOLE DUCK WITH CHINESE CABBAGE

1 2 kg (4 lb)	duck
2 teaspoons	dark soy sauce
2 teaspoons	rice wine or dry sherry
8 cups (2 litres)	deep-frying oil
5 cups (1¼ litres)	chicken stock
500 g (1 lb)	Chinese (celery) cabbage
2 tablespoons	softened lard (optional)

Seasoning A:

1¾ tablespoons	light soy sauce
1 tablespoon	rice wine or dry sherry
1 teaspoon	salt
1½ teaspoons	sugar
½ teaspoon	m.s.g. (optional)
4	spring onions (scallions), trimmed and cut in halves
4 thick slices	fresh ginger, bruised

Seasoning B:

¼ teaspoon	salt
½ teaspoon	sugar
	pinch of ground black pepper
1 teaspoon	cornflour (cornstarch)

Clean and dress the duck and rub thoroughly with the soy sauce and wine. Heat the deep-frying oil to smoking point and deep-fry the duck until well coloured. Lift out and drain well. Cut along the breast and flatten out. Place in a casserole and add the chicken stock and the seasoning A ingredients. Bring to the boil, cover and reduce the heat. Simmer until tender, 1½ — 1¾ hours. Drain and carefully remove the bones, keeping the duck as close as possible to its original shape.

Cut the cabbage into long strips about 2.5 cm (1 in) wide. Sauté in the softened lard or 2 tablespoons of the deep-frying oil for 2 minutes, then add the seasoning B ingredients and ¼ cup of the liquid in which the duck was cooked. Cover and cook on moderate heat until tender.

Arrange the cabbage on a serving plate and place the duck on top. Reduce the liquid in the casserole to about ¾ cup, or transfer ¾ cup of the liquid to a wok and bring to the boil. Check the seasoning and thicken with a thin solution of cornflour and cold water. Pour over the duck and serve at once.

DUCK SIMMERED IN YELLOW RICE WINE

1 1½ kg (3 lb)	duck
¼ cup (2 fl oz)	light soy sauce
2/3 cup	yellow rice wine (Shao Hsing)
6 cups (1½ litres)	deep-frying oil
7 cups (1¾ litres)	chicken stock or water
	cornflour (cornstarch)

Seasoning:

2 tablespoons	light soy sauce
2	spring onions (scallions), trimmed and sliced
3 thick slices	fresh ginger, bruised
1½ teaspoons	salt
2 teaspoons	sugar
¾ teaspoon	m.s.g. (optional)

Clean and thoroughly wash the duck and wipe dry. Pour the soy sauce and wine over the duck, rubbing inside and out and leave for 1 hour, then drain the liquid into a dish and add the remaining seasoning ingredients.

Heat the deep-frying oil to smoking point and deep-fry the duck until well coloured. Lift out and drain well. Place the duck, breast downwards, on a bamboo rack in a casserole and add the stock and seasoning ingredients. Bring to the boil, then cook on low heat for at least 1½ hours until the duck is completely tender.

Carefully lift out and cut into serving portions. Reduce the sauce to about 1 cup. Check the seasonings and thicken with a paste of cornflour and cold water. Pour over the duck and serve.

HOME STYLE SIMMER-STEWED DUCK

1 1¾ kg (3½ lb)	duck
500 g (1 lb)	fatty pork or 'five flowered' belly pork (fresh bacon)
8 cups (2 litres)	deep-frying oil
30 g (1 oz)	Chinese red dates, or use black dates or Japanese salted plums (umeboshi)
45 g (1½ oz)	salted mustard root, washed and diced*
2	spring onions (scallions), trimmed and sliced
5 slices	fresh ginger
6	young bok choy or lettuce
	cornflour (cornstarch)

Seasoning A:

¼ cup (2 fl oz)	light soy sauce
2 tablespoons	rice wine or dry sherry

Seasoning B:

¼ cup (2 fl oz)	soybean paste
3 cups (24 fl oz)	chicken stock
1 tablespoon	sugar
¾ teaspoon	m.s.g. (optional)
½ teaspoon	ground black pepper

Clean and dress the duck and blanch in boiling water for 2 minutes. Drain and rub with some of the seasoning A ingredients, reserving that which is not used. Blanch the pork and drain well. Wipe dry and also rub with the seasoning A ingredients. Mix any remaining seasoning A with the seasoning B ingredients, except the soybean paste, and set aside.

Heat the deep-frying oil to fairly hot. Deep-fry the duck and pork separately until well coloured. Drain well. Cut the pork into cubes and stuff into the cavity of the duck, then place the duck, breast down, in a casserole.

Transfer 2 tablespoons of the deep-frying oil to another pan and sauté the soybean paste for 1 minute. Add the seasoning B ingredients and bring to the boil. Pour over the duck. Add the dates, diced mustard root, spring onions, and ginger and add water to just cover. Bring to the boil and simmer, tightly covered, until the duck is completely tender, about 2 hours. Lift out the duck, cut open and remove the pork. Reserve the stock.

Shred the duck meat by hand, discarding the bones. Pile the duck in the centre of a dish and surround with the pork. Set on a rack in a steamer and steam over gently boiling water for 15 minutes. In the meantime, strain the reserved stock into a wok and reduce to about ¾ cup.

In another pan, sauté the vegetables in 2 tablespoons of the deep-frying oil, adding a pinch of salt and sugar and a dash of rice wine or sherry. Arrange on top of the meat and steam a further 5 minutes. Thicken the sauce with a thin solution of cornflour and cold water and pour over the dish.

* Or use pickled cabbage or Szechuan (Sichuan) pickled vegetables

Steamed Stuffed Chicken Wings (recipe page 256)

高節虛心

CHOPPED DUCK WITH LOTUS ROOT AND VEGETABLES

1 1¾ kg (3½ lb)	duck
90 g (3 oz)	canned lotus root, drained
45 g (1½ oz)	Chinese or cured (Smithfield) ham (optional)
90 g (3 oz)	squash or winter melon
60 g (2 oz)	canned champignons, drained*
2 tablespoons	softened lard or frying oil

Seasoning A:

1	egg white, beaten
¼ teaspoon	salt
¼ teaspoon	m.s.g. (optional)
1 tablespoon	cold water
1 tablespoon	cornflour (cornstarch)

Seasoning B:

¼ cup (2 fl oz)	chicken stock
½ teaspoon	salt
2 tablespoons	light soy sauce
1 teaspoon	rice wine or dry sherry
2	spring onions (scallions), trimmed and sliced
2 slices	fresh ginger

Debone the duck and cut into 4 cm (1 2/3 in) squares. Place in a dish with the seasoning A ingredients and leave for 20 minutes to marinate.

Slice the lotus roots lengthwise and cut into 4 cm (1 2/3 in) squares. Cut the ham into the same sized pieces, if used. Peel and cube the squash or melon. Slice the champignons in halves horizontally, or squeeze the water from soaked mushrooms, remove the stems and cut the caps into quarters.

Arrange the duck, mushrooms, and ham, if used, in a large bowl and add the seasoning B ingredients. Cover and set on a rack in a steamer. Steam over rapidly boiling water for 35 minutes, discard the onion and ginger.

Blanch the lotus root in boiling water and drain well. Heat the lard or frying oil in a wok and stir-fry the lotus root for 1 minute. Add the drained duck, mushrooms, and ham, reserving the stock, and stir-fry together for 2 minutes. Add the melon and stir-fry for a further 2 minutes, then pour in the reserved stock and reduce the heat. Simmer together until the melon is tender, then thicken the sauce with a thin solution of cornflour and cold water and simmer until thickened. Check the seasonings and serve.

* Or use 6 — 8 dried black mushrooms, soaked for 25 minutes.

DUCK LIVERS WITH HOT PEPPER SAUCE

315 g (10 oz)	fresh duck livers
4 cups (1 litre)	deep-frying oil
3	spring onions (scallions), trimmed and diced
2 slices	fresh ginger, chopped
½ teaspoon	crushed garlic
1 tablespoon	sesame oil
½ teaspoon	ground black pepper (optional)

Seasoning A:

⅓ teaspoon	salt
¼ teaspoon	m.s.g. (optional)
¼ teaspoon	ground black pepper
1 tablespoon	rice wine or dry sherry

Seasoning B/Sauce:

½ cup (4 fl oz)	chicken stock
2 tablespoons	light soy sauce
1½ teaspoons	dark soy sauce
1 teaspoon	chilli oil (or less, to taste)
½ teaspoon	salt
¼ teaspoon	ground black pepper
¾ teaspoon	sugar
1 teaspoon	cornflour (cornstarch)

Blanch the livers in boiling water, drain and cut into bite-sized pieces. Place in a dish with the seasoning A ingredients and leave for 30 minutes.

Deep-fry the livers in smoking hot deep oil for 30 — 45 seconds. Drain and pour off all but 2½ tablespoons of the oil. Add the sesame oil and sauté the onions, ginger, and garlic for 1 minute. Add the livers and sauté briefly, then pour in the pre-mixed seasoning B/sauce ingredients and bring to the boil.

Reduce the heat and simmer for about 5 minutes until the livers are tender and the sauce well reduced. Stir in the black pepper, if used, and serve.

DEEP-FRIED DUCK FEET WITH SHRIMP STUFFING

12	duck feet*
125 g (4 oz)	raw peeled shrimp, finely minced (ground)
30 g (1 oz)	pork fat, finely minced (ground)
	cornflour (cornstarch)
1½ tablespoons	finely chopped cooked ham
1½ teaspoons	finely chopped fresh coriander
8 cups (2 litres)	deep-frying oil

Seasoning A:

¼ teaspoon	salt
½ teaspoon	m.s.g. (optional)
1 tablespoon	rice wine or dry sherry
1	spring onion (scallion), trimmed and diced
2 slices	fresh ginger, shredded

Seasoning B:

¼ teaspoon	salt
¼ teaspoon	m.s.g. (optional)
	pinch of ground black pepper
1½ teaspoons	ginger wine

Sauce:

2/3 cup	chicken stock
⅓ teaspoon	salt
	pinch of ground black pepper
½ teaspoon	sugar
1½ teaspoons	cornflour (cornstarch)

Blanch the duck feet in boiling water for 1 minute, then lift out and scrape off the skin. Return to the water, add a small piece of fresh ginger and a dash of salt and simmer until softened, about 25 minutes. Drain and cut off the claws.

Place the duck feet and seasoning A ingredients in a saucepan, cover with boiling water and simmer for 2 — 3 minutes, then remove and drain. Wipe dry.

Mix the shrimp and pork fat with the seasoning B ingredients. Coat the web section lightly with cornflour and press a ball of the shrimp stuffing on the top of each, smoothing at the edges. Garnish with chopped ham and coriander, pressing on lightly.

Heat the deep-frying oil to moderate and deep-fry the stuffed feet, stuffing downwards, until golden. Lift out and increase the heat, then quickly fry in the hot oil until crisp on the surface. Drain and arrange on a serving plate. Bring the sauce ingredients to boil in another saucepan, adding 2 tablespoons of the deep-frying oil. Simmer for 1 minute then pour over the feet and serve.

* The duck's webs with leg to the middle joint. Available fresh or frozen from specialist Chinese food suppliers.

SALTED DUCK EGGS

12	duck eggs (or use large chicken eggs)
1 cup	salt
¼ cup (2 fl oz)	rice wine or dry sherry
1 tablespoon	Chinese brown peppercorns
6 cups (1½ litres)	lukewarm water

Wash the eggs, brushing the shells gently with a soft brush. Rinse in cold water and stack in a preserve jar with a tight-fitting lid.

Mix the remaining ingredients together, stirring until the salt is completely dissolved. Pour over the eggs, close the jar and leave for 1 month.

The salting process should solidify the egg. If still soft in the very centre, steam for a few minutes before using for recipes requiring chopped egg yolk.

Excellent served as an appetiser with thinly sliced fresh ginger marinated in sweetened vinegar. Use also with an assortment of cold appetisers (see page 381).

FRAGRANT CRISPY DUCK STUFFED WITH LOTUS SEEDS AND PORK

1 2 kg (4 lb)	duck
1½ teaspoons	salt
1 tablespoon	rice wine or dry sherry
125 g (4 oz)	dried lotus seeds, soaked for 1 hour*
125 g (4 oz)	fatty pork, diced
4	dried black mushrooms, soaked for 25 minutes
30 g (1 oz)	cooked ham, shredded
2	egg whites, beaten
2½ tablespoons	cornflour (cornstarch)
	extra cornflour (cornstarch)
8 cups (2 litres)	deep-frying oil

Seasoning A:

½ teaspoon	salt
¼ teaspoon	white pepper
1 teaspoon	sesame oil
1 teaspoon	cornflour (cornstarch)

Seasoning B:

¼ teaspoon	salt
¼ teaspoon	white pepper
½ teaspoon	rice wine or dry sherry
1 teaspoon	cornflour (cornstarch)

Seasoning C/Sauce:

1½ cups (12 fl oz)	chicken stock
¾ teaspoon	salt
¼ teaspoon	m.s.g. (optional)
¼ teaspoon	white pepper
2 teaspoons	rice wine or dry sherry
3	spring onions (scallions), trimmed and sliced
3 slices	fresh ginger

Clean the duck, debone and rinse with cold water. Turn inside out and rub with half of the salt and wine, then turn right side out again and rub with the remaining salt and wine. Set aside.

Place the washed lotus seeds in a dish with water to cover. Steam over rapidly boiling water until tender, drain if necessary. Mash the lotus seeds to a smooth paste and mix with the seasoning A ingredients.

Season the pork with the seasoning B ingredients and leave for 10 minutes. Dice. Remove the stems from the mushrooms, squeeze out excess water and dice the caps. Mix the lotus seeds, pork, ham, and mushrooms together.

Stuff the mixture into the duck and secure the openings with poultry pins. Place the duck, breast up, in a casserole and add the seasoning C/sauce ingredients. Cover the casserole and set on a rack in a steamer to steam over gently boiling water for 1¾ hours. Lift out the duck, wipe the skin and coat with a batter made by mixing the beaten egg whites and cornflour. Then coat lightly with extra cornflour.

Heat the deep-frying oil to smoking point and deep-fry the duck, completely immersed in the oil if possible, until golden brown. Carefully lift out and drain well. Remove the wings and legs and cut the body straight through into thick slices. Arrange the wings and drumsticks around the stuffed sliced duck and serve.

A sauce can be made by reducing the cooking liquid to about ¾ cup and thickening with a thin solution of cornflour and cold water. Simmer until thickened, adjust seasonings and pour over the duck.

* If canned lotus seeds are available, use approximately 185 g and omit the steaming.

SLOW-SIMMERED GOOSE WITH VINEGAR AND GARLIC SAUCE

1 3 kg (6 lb)	goose with giblets
4	spring onions (scallions), trimmed and cut in halves
6 thick slices	fresh ginger, bruised
2	spice bags (see page 386)
1¼ cups (10 fl oz)	light soy sauce
½ cup (4 fl oz)	rice wine or dry sherry
1½ tablespoon	sugar
⅓ teaspoon	salt
	vinegar and garlic sauce

Clean and dress the goose. Clean the giblets and slice the heart and gizzard, but keep the liver in one piece. Place the goose and giblets in a large saucepan and arrange the onion, ginger, and spice bags around it. Add the soy sauce, wine, sugar and salt. Cover with cold water. Bring slowly to the boil and simmer, tightly covered for 3 hours. Replenish the liquid with boiling water when the level drops, and skim occasionally to remove surface froth.

Drain and transfer the goose to a cutting board. Cut into thin slices and serve the goose and the sliced liver, discarding the remaining giblets. Prepare a generous amount of vinegar and garlic sauce (see page 384) for dipping.

Serve hot or cold as an appetiser or main dish, and use cold as an ingredient for assorted cold meat appetisers (see page 381).

264

Cantonese roast duck (recipe page 258).

STEAMED MANDARIN FISH

1 1 kg (2 lb)	Mandarin fish (pearl perch, fresh water trout or sea bass)
3	spring onions (scallions), trimmed and shredded
5 slices	fresh ginger, shredded
30 g (1 oz)	canned champignons, drained and sliced
30 g (1 oz)	canned bamboo shoots, drained and shredded
30 g (1 oz)	fatty pork, shredded
1	small carrot, peeled and shredded
10 cm (4 in) piece	fresh celery, shredded
1 cup (8 fl oz)	chicken stock, warmed
	vinegar and ginger dip

Seasoning:

1½ teaspoons	salt
½ teaspoon	m.s.g. (optional)
¾ teaspoon	sugar
½ teaspoon	white pepper
1 tablespoon	rice wine or dry sherry
2 tablespoons	rendered chicken fat (chicken grease), warmed

Clean and scale the fish and remove the gills. Drop into boiling water and remove after 20 seconds. Carefully scrape off the skin. Place the fish in a large oval dish and sprinkle on the seasoning ingredients. Arrange the shredded vegetables and meat on top and pour the chicken stock into the dish. Set the dish on a rack in a steamer and cover tightly. Steam over rapidly boiling water until the fish is cooked through, about 25 minutes.

Strain the liquid from the dish into a wok and bring to the boil. Adjust the seasoning and thicken, if preferred, with a thin solution of cornflour and cold water.

Transfer the fish to a serving plate or serve in the same dish and pour on the sauce just before serving. Serve with small dishes of vinegar and ginger dip (see recipe, page 384)

POACHED FISH WITH GINGER, ONION, AND OIL DRESSING

1 1 kg (2 lb)	fresh fish (sea bass or fresh trout)
2	spring onions (scallions), shredded
4 thick slices	fresh ginger, shredded
¼ cup (2 fl oz)	frying oil
	fresh coriander
	white pepper

Seasoning A:

1½ teaspoons	salt
¼ cup (2 fl oz)	vegetable oil
1	spring onion (scallion), trimmed and sliced
2 slices	fresh ginger

Seasoning B:

¼ teaspoon	salt
1½ tablespoons	light soy sauce
	pinch of white pepper

Clean and scale the fish. Place it on an oiled plate and add the seasoning A ingredients. Set the plate in a large saucepan and add hot water to just cover. Cover the saucepan and bring the water almost to the boil, then simmer on very low heat for 20 minutes. Move from the heat and leave the fish in the stock for a further 5 minutes.

Lift out the plate with the fish on it and strain about ¾ cup of the stock into a wok, adding the seasoning B ingredients. Bring to the boil, then reduce heat slightly and simmer for 1 — 2 minutes.

Carefully transfer the fish to a serving plate and arrange the shredded onion and ginger on top. Heat the frying oil to smoking point and splash over the fish, then garnish with the coriander and season generously with white pepper. Pour on the sauce and serve.

DEEP-FRIED WHOLE FISH SEASONED WITH SPICED SALT

1 1 kg (2 lb)	whole pearl perch or red snapper
2	spring onions (scallions), trimmed and sliced
2 slices	fresh ginger, shredded
2 teaspoons	spiced salt or Chinese pepper-salt (see page 384)
7 cups (1¾ litres)	deep-frying oil

Seasoning:

1 teaspoon	sugar
½ teaspoon	m.s.g. (optional)
1 teaspoon	spiced salt
2 teaspoons	light soy sauce
1 tablespoon	rice wine or dry sherry

Clean and scale the fish and score diagonally across the body on both sides, cutting almost to the bone. Place in a dish and rub on the seasoning ingredients, then place the spring onions and ginger on top and leave for 10 minutes. Turn, transfer the onion and ginger to the other side and leave a further 10 minutes.

Heat the deep-frying oil to moderate. Wipe the fish and place in the oil to fry until cooked through, about 6 minutes. Remove from the oil and drain well. Place on a bed of shredded lettuce on a serving plate and sprinkle on the spiced salt or pepper-salt. Serve at once.

Additional spiced salt or pepper-salt and light soy sauce can be served as dips.

BAKED STUFFED MANDARIN FISH

1 750 g (1½ lb)	Mandarin fish (perch or trout)
75 g (2½ oz)	fatty pork, minced (ground)
30 g (1 oz)	blanched almonds, toasted and chopped
30 g (1 oz)	duck or chicken liver, diced
15 g (1 oz)	canned water chestnuts, drained and diced
1½	spring onions (scallions), trimmed and diced
3 thick slices	fresh ginger, shredded
	cornflour (cornstarch)

Seasoning A:

¼ teaspoon	white pepper
1 tablespoon	light soy sauce
2 teaspoons	rice wine or dry sherry
¾ teaspoon	sesame oil

Seasoning B:

⅓ teaspoon	salt
½ teaspoon	m.s.g. (optional)
¼ teaspoon	white pepper
1 teaspoon	rice wine or dry sherry
1 tablespoon	chicken stock
2 teaspoons	cornflour (cornstarch)

Sauce:

1 cup (8 fl oz)	chicken stock
2 tablespoons	light soy sauce
2 teaspoons	rice wine or dry sherry
1 teaspoon	sesame oil
½ teaspoon	salt
¼ teaspoon	m.s.g. (optional)
½ teaspoon	sugar

Scale and clean the fish and carefully cut away the backbone with a thick layer of meat attached to it. Rub the fish inside and out with the seasoning A ingredients and half the ginger. Leave for 10 minutes.

Scrape the fish from the bones and mix with the pork, almonds, livers, water chestnuts, diced spring onions, the remaining ginger, and the seasoning B ingredients. Wipe out the fish, dust lightly with cornflour and fill with prepared stuffing. Stand the fish on its stomach on a greased baking tray or sew up the opening and cook on its side, turning once.

Pour the pre-mixed sauce ingredients over the fish, add 2 tablespoons of frying oil and bake in a preheated low oven at 120°C (250°F) until golden and cooked through, about 40 minutes. Baste frequently with the sauce during cooking to prevent the fish drying out.

Carefully transfer to a serving plate and garnish with additional shredded onion and ginger. Serve at once.

WHOLE FISH WITH FIVE SHREDS IN HOT SAUCE

1 1 kg (2 lb)	fresh perch, bream, or red snapper
3	dried black mushrooms, soaked for 25 minutes
15 g (½ oz)	Chinese pickles
30 g (1 oz)	canned bamboo shoots, drained
1	small green capsicum (bell pepper)
3	spring onions (scallions), trimmed and shredded
3 thick slices	fresh ginger, shredded
¼ cup (2 fl oz)	frying oil
	white pepper

Seasoning:

½ teaspoon	salt
1	spring onion (scallion), trimmed and shredded
2 slices	fresh ginger, shredded
1 tablespoon	softened lard or frying oil

Sauce:

⅓ cup	chicken stock
¼ cup (2 fl oz)	white vinegar
¼ cup (2 fl oz)	tomato sauce (ketchup)
1½ teaspoons	salt
⅓ cup	sugar
½ teaspoon	finely chopped garlic
½ — 1 teaspoon	chilli oil
1½ teaspoons	cornflour (cornstarch)

Clean the fish and place in a large wok. Add the seasoning ingredients and water to cover. Cover the wok and bring just to the boil, reduce heat and poach on low heat for 15 minutes, or until just cooked through. Test by inserting a fork into the thickest part of the fish. It should almost lift cleanly from the bones. Drain and transfer to a serving plate.

Squeeze excess water from the mushrooms and remove the stems. Shred the caps. Cut the pickles, bamboo shoots, and pepper into matchstick strips.

Arrange the spring onions and ginger on the fish. Drain the liquid from the wok, wipe out and heat the frying oil to piping hot. Pour half over the fish. Fry the shredded ingredients in the remaining oil for 2 minutes, stirring constantly. Add the pre-mixed sauce ingredients and bring to the boil. Simmer for 2 minutes, then pour over the fish and season generously with white pepper. Serve.

SMOKED POMFRET

1 700 g (1 ⅓ lb)	pomfret or John Dory
½ cup	green tea leaves*
2 tablespoons	sugar

Seasoning:

¼ teaspoon	salt
1 tablespoon	sugar
¼ cup (2 fl oz)	light soy sauce
1 tablespoons	rice wine or dry sherry
4	spring onions (scallions), trimmed and sliced
4 slices	fresh ginger, shredded

Sauce:

¼ cup (2 fl oz)	chicken stock
2 teaspoons	light soy sauce
½ teaspoon	rice wine or dry sherry
½ teaspoon	m.s.g. (optional)
½ teaspoon	sugar
½ teaspoon	sesame oil
½ teaspoon	cornflour (cornstarch)

Clean the fish and cut in halves at an angle from in front of the top fin to behind the lower fin. Mix the seasoning ingredients and pour over the fish. Leave for one hour to marinate.

Brush a cake-cooling rack with oil and place the fish on this. Set in a baking tray containing the tea leaves or wood chips and sugar and place in a preheated hot oven at 230°C(450°F). Bake for 25 Minutes, turning once. Wipe out the oven with a damp cloth after use.

Bring the sauce ingredients to the boil and pour over the fish just before serving. This fish is now frequently served with mayonnaise.

* Or use pine wood chips.

Whole Fish with Five Shreds in Hot Sauce (recipe this page).

SLICED FISH SAUTÉD WITH BLACK BEANS

315 g (10 oz)	boneless white fish fillets
1	large white onion
1	large green capsicum (bell pepper)
1 tablespoon	fermented black beans
1 teaspoon	finely chopped garlic
1 slice	fresh ginger, finely shredded
3 cups (24 fl oz)	deep-frying oil
2 teaspoons	rice wine or dry sherry

Seasoning A:

1	egg white, beaten
½ teaspoon	salt
½ teaspoon	m.s.g. (optional)
	pinch of white pepper
1 tablespoon	cornflour (cornstarch)
2 tablespoons	vegetable oil

Seasoning B/Sauce:

¼ cup (2 fl oz)	chicken stock
2 tablespoons	light soy sauce
⅓ teaspoon	salt
1½ teaspoons	sugar
½ teaspoon	m.s.g. (optional)

Slice the fish, cutting across the fillets at a sharp angle to produce slices of about 7.5 x 2.5 cm (3 x 1 in) and about 1 cm (⅓ in) thick. Place in a dish and add the seasoning A ingredients, mix well and leave for 15 minutes to marinate.

Peel the onion and trim away the root section, then cut into slices from stem to root and separate the pieces. Cut the pepper in halves, remove the stem and seed core and trim away the inner white ribs. Shred finely. Wash the black beans, dry on kitchen paper and chop lightly. Mix with the garlic.

Heat the deep-frying oil to fairly hot and fry the fish in a basket for 45 seconds to 1 minute, until crisped on the surface and just cooked through. Drain and set aside. Pour off all but 3 tablespoons of the oil and sauté the onion and ginger for 1 minute, then add the black bean mixture and sauté for 30 seconds. Sizzle the wine onto the sides of the pan and stir in.

Add the shredded pepper and sauté until just softened. Pour in the pre-mixed seasoning B/sauce ingredients and bring to the boil. Return the fish slices and heat thoroughly. Serve.

CUBED FISH IN PINEAPPLE SAUCE

1 750 g (1½ lb)	meaty white fish (pearl perch)
	cornflour (cornstarch)
6 cups (1½ litres)	deep-frying oil
½ — ¾ teaspoon	finely chopped garlic
¾ teaspoon	finely chopped fresh ginger
2 tablespoons	fresh or frozen peas, parboiled
1	small carrot, diced and parboiled
1 thick slice	canned pineapple, drained and diced

Seasoning A:

¾ teaspoon	salt
½ teaspoon	m.s.g. (optional)
¼ teaspoon	white pepper
2 teaspoons	rice wine or dry sherry
2 tablespoons	onion and ginger infusion (see page 386)
1 teaspoon	sesame oil (optional)

Seasoning B/Sauce:

½ cup (4 fl oz)	liquid from canned pineapple or mango
¼ cup (2 fl oz)	chicken stock
2 tablespoons	tomato sauce (ketchup)
¾ teaspoon	sesame oil (optional)
¼ — ½ teaspoon	chilli oil
¾ teaspoon	salt
¼ teaspoon	m.s.g. (optional)
1½ teaspoons	cornflour (cornstarch)

Clean and scale the fish and remove the fillets, leaving the head, backbone, and tail connected. Coat this thickly with cornflour and set aside. Cut the fillets into 2.5 cm (1 in) cubes and place in a dish with the seasoning A ingredients. Skin the fillets first, if preferred. Leave for 15 minutes to marinate.

Place about 1 cupful of cornflour in a paper or plastic bag and add the fish. Close the bag and shake vigorously to thickly coat the fish with the flour. Empty into a colander and shake off excess flour. Heat the deep-frying oil to smoking point. Deep-fry the carcass until crisp and golden. Remove, drain and place on a large serving plate. Deep-fry the fish pieces, about 10 at a time, until crisp and golden. Drain well. Keep the oil warm.

Transfer about 3 tablespoons of the oil to another wok and fry the garlic and ginger for 45 seconds. Add the carrot and peas and fry briefly, then add the pre-mixed seasoning B/sauce ingredients and bring to the boil. Simmer until thickened, then stir in the diced pineapple.

Reheat the oil to smoking point and briefly deep-fry the fish for the second time. Remove to the sauce and stir until evenly coated, then arrange on the carcass and pour on any remaining sauce. Serve at once.

SAUTÉD FIVE SHREDS WITH SLICED FISH

185 g (6 oz)	boneless white fish
1	medium carrot
1	medium green capsicum (bell pepper)
3	dried black mushrooms, soaked for 25 minutes
30 g (1 oz)	fresh bean sprouts
1	large white onion
3 cups (24 fl oz)	deep-frying oil
2 tablespoons	sesame oil
1½ teaspoons	rice wine or dry sherry

Seasoning A:

1	egg white, beaten
½ teaspoon	salt
½ teaspoon	m.s.g. (optional)
¼ teaspoon	white pepper
1½ teaspoons	rice wine or dry sherry
1 tablespoon	cornflour (cornstarch)

Seasoning B/Sauce:

⅓ cup	chicken stock
1 teaspoon	sesame oil (optional)
½ teaspoon	salt
½ teaspoon	m.s.g. (optional)
¼ teaspoon	ground black pepper
¾ teaspoon	cornflour (cornstarch)

Cut the fish into narrow strips, then into pieces about 5 cm (2 in) long. Place in a dish with the seasoning A ingredients, mix well and leave for 15 minutes.

Peel the carrot. Remove the seed core, stem, and inner white ribs of the pepper, squeeze water from the mushrooms and remove the stems. Shred the three vegetables and set aside with the bean sprouts. Remove roots and pods from the bean sprouts, if preferred. Cut the onion in halves from stem to root. Trim away the root section, then cut into thin slices and separate the pieces.

Heat the deep-frying oil to moderately hot and add the sesame oil. Fry the fish until it turns white, about 45 seconds. Drain well. Pour off all but 3 tablespoons of the oil and fry the shredded vegetables on moderate heat for 3 minutes, stirring continually. Add the fish and sizzle the wine onto the sides of the pan.

Pour in the pre-mixed seasoning B/sauce ingredients and stir until the sauce thickens. Transfer to a serving plate.

DEEP-FRIED FISH FILLETS WITH BLACK SESAME SEED DRESSING

315 g (10 oz)	boneless white fish
1 cup	flour
2	eggs, well beaten
60 g (2 oz)	black sesame seeds
4 cups (1 litre)	deep-frying oil
	Chinese pepper-salt

Seasoning:

½ teaspoon	salt
½ teaspoon	m.s.g. (optional)
¼ teaspoon	white pepper
1 tablespoon	rice wine or dry sherry
2 teaspoons	sesame oil
1 tablespoon	finely chopped spring onion (scallion)
1 tablespoon	grated fresh ginger

Cut the fish into slices across the fillets, cutting at a sharp angle so that the slices are about 2.5 cm (1 in) wide. Place in a dish with the seasoning ingredients and leave to marinate for 20 minutes. Drain and coat with flour, then dip into the beaten egg.

Heat the deep-frying oil to moderately hot. Dip the fish slices into the sesame seeds, coating thickly. Deep-fry until the fish is cooked through, about 2 minutes. Drain well.

Serve with dips of Chinese pepper-salt (see recipe, page 384).

FRIED STUFFED FISH ROLLS WITH SAUTÉD VEGETABLES

280 g (9 oz)	white fish fillets
2	dried black mushrooms, soaked for 25 minutes
60 g (2 oz)	canned bamboo shoots, drained
125 g (4 oz)	Chinese (celery) cabbage
60 g (2 oz)	canned champignons, drained
30 g (1 oz)	cooked ham (optional)
2	small egg whites
2½ tablespoons	cornflour (cornstarch)
2 teaspoons	onion-pepper-salt*
1	spring onion (scallion), trimmed and sliced
2 slices	fresh ginger, shredded
	extra cornflour (cornstarch)
4 cups (1 litre)	deep-frying oil

Seasoning A:

½ teaspoon	salt
¼ teaspoon	m.s.g. (optional)
¼ teaspoon	ground black pepper
1 teaspoon	ginger wine
1 teaspoon	sesame oil (optional)

Seasoning B/Sauce:

⅓ cup	chicken stock
½ teaspoon	sesame oil
⅓ teaspoon	salt
¼ teaspoon	ground black pepper
1 teaspoon	sugar
¾ teaspoon	cornflour (cornstarch)

Cut the fish into slices about 10 x 5 cm (4 x 2 in) and about 0.3 cm (1/8 in) thick, cutting across the fillets at a sharp angle. Place in a dish with the seasoning A ingredients and leave for 10 minutes.

Squeeze excess water from the mushrooms and remove the stems. Shred the caps and one-quarter of the bamboo shoots. Cut the remainder of the bamboo shoots into thin slices. Cut the leafy tops of the cabbage into small squares and the lower parts into larger pieces. Thinly slice the champignons and shred the ham.

Make a paste with the egg whites and cornflour. Spread over one side of the fish and sprinkle on onion-pepper-salt. Top with a few shreds of mushroom, bamboo shoot, champignon, and ham and add a piece of cabbage leaf. Roll each into a cylindrical shape and squeeze tightly. Coat the rolls lightly with cornflour.

Heat the deep-frying oil to moderate and deep-fry the fish rolls until golden and cooked through, about 2¼ minutes. Drain and set aside. Transfer 2½ tablespoons of the oil to another pan and stir-fry the remaining vegetables for 2 minutes. Add the pre-mixed seasoning B/sauce and simmer for 1½ minutes. Reheat the deep oil, briefly fry the rolls for a second time, then arrange on a serving plate with the vegetables and pour on the sauce. Serve at once.

* A mixture of chopped spring onions and Chinese pepper-salt (see page 384).

SHRIMPS COOKED IN THEIR SHELLS

Serve hot or cold.

375 g (12 oz)	raw shrimps, in their shells
5 cups (1¼ litres)	deep-frying oil
2	spring onions (scallions), shredded
3 slices	fresh ginger, shredded
1	fresh red chilli pepper, seeds removed and shredded (optional)

Seasoning:

1¼ teaspoons	salt
½ teaspoon	m.s.g. (optional)
1¼ teaspoons	sugar
1 teaspoon	sesame oil (optional)
¼ cup (2 fl oz)	chicken stock

Remove the legs and the undershells of the shrimps, but leave the heads, tails, and top of the shells intact. Heat the deep-frying oil to smoking point and fry the shrimps in a basket for 25 seconds. Remove and drain.

Pour off all but 2 tablespoons of the oil. Reduce the heat to moderate and fry the spring onions, ginger, and chilli, if used, for 1 minute, stirring frequently. Add the shrimps and fry for 30 seconds, then add the seasoning ingredients and simmer until the liquid has almost evaporated. Transfer to a serving plate.

Smoked Pomfret (recipe page 268).

SAUTÉD SHRIMPS WITH PEAS AND CASHEW NUTS

185 g (6 oz)	raw peeled shrimps
60 g (2 oz)	fresh or frozen peas
45 g (1½ oz)	raw cashew nuts
2 cups (16 fl oz)	frying oil
¼ cup (2 fl oz)	softened lard (optional)

Seasoning A:

1	egg white, beaten
½ teaspoon	salt
2 teaspoons	ginger wine
1½ teaspoons	cornflour (cornstarch)

Seasoning B/Sauce:

¼ cup (2 fl oz)	chicken stock
1 tablespoon	light soy sauce
2 teaspoons	rice wine or dry sherry
½ teaspoon	salt
¼ teaspoon	m.s.g. (optional)
½ teaspoon	sugar
¼ teaspoon	ground black pepper
½ teaspoon	cornflour (cornstarch)

Wash the shrimps, pat dry with kitchen paper and place in a bowl with the Seasoning A ingredients. Mix well and leave to marinate for 15 minutes.

Boil the peas in lightly salted water until cooked, but still firm. Drain and set aside. Heat the oil to moderately hot and fry the cashews until golden, about 2 minutes. Remove and drain well.

Pour off the oil and wipe out the wok. Add the lard and heat to smoking point, or retain 3 tablespoons of the frying oil. Add the shrimps and sauté until pink, turning frequently. Add the peas and seasoning B ingredients and bring to the boil. Simmer, stirring for 45 seconds, then stir in the cashews and transfer to a serving plate.

STIR-FRIED CRAB *FU YUNG*

2 375 g (12 oz)	crabs
1 tablespoon	ginger wine
5 cups (1¼ litres)	deep-frying oil
1	spring onion (scallion), trimmed and diced
3 slices	fresh ginger, shredded
2 teaspoons	rice wine or dry sherry
4	eggs, well beaten

Seasoning/Sauce:

¼ cup (2 fl oz)	chicken stock
1 teaspoon	salt
¼ teaspoon	m.s.g. (optional)
¼ teaspoon	ground black pepper
½ teaspoon	sesame oil (optional)
1 teaspoon	cornflour (cornstarch)

Wash the crabs well and break open. Remove all inedible parts, then chop the crabs through the shells into large pieces. Place in a dish and sprinkle on the ginger wine. Leave for 20 minutes.

Heat the deep-frying oil to smoking point and deep-fry the crab pieces for 1 minute. Remove and drain well. If preferred, the crab can be stir-fried in ⅓ cup frying oil for 2½ minutes.

Pour off all but 2½ tablespoons of the oil and stir-fry the spring onion and ginger for 30 seconds, then return the crab and add the pre-mixed seasoning/sauce ingredients. Simmer for 2 minutes, then pour in the well-beaten eggs and cook without stirring until the eggs are set. Stir lightly and transfer to a serving plate.

SHRIMP AND CHICKEN OMELETTE

75 g (2½ oz)	boneless chicken breast
75 g (2½ oz)	raw peeled shrimps
2	whole eggs, beaten
4	egg whites, well beaten
½ teaspoon	salt
½ teaspoon	m.s.g. (optional)
2 tablespoons	frying oil
1	spring onion (scallion), trimmed and shredded

Seasoning A:

¼ teaspoon	salt
¼ teaspoon	sugar
½ teaspoon	finely chopped spring onion
½ teaspoon	grated fresh ginger

Seasoning B:

¼ teaspoon	salt
¼ teaspoon	m.s.g. (optional)
2 teaspoons	ginger wine (see page 387)

Sauce:

¼ cup (2 fl oz)	chicken stock
¼ teaspoon	salt
¼ teaspoon	m.s.g. (optional)
½ teaspoon	cornflour (cornstarch)

Cut the chicken into narrow shreds and mix with the seasoning A ingredients. Leave for 10 minutes. Wash the shrimps, devein with a toothpick (see page 394) and mix with the seasoning B ingredients. Leave for 10 minutes.

Beat the whole eggs and egg whites together, adding the salt and m.s.g., if used. Heat the oil in a wok and lightly sauté the spring onion, then push to one side of the pan and add the chicken and shrimps and sauté together for 1½ minutes. Pour in the egg batter and cook on moderate heat until just beginning to colour underneath. Carefully lift up and turn to cook the other side. Transfer to a serving plate.

Wipe out the wok and add the sauce ingredients, pre-mixed. Simmer until thickened and pour over the omelette. Garnish with fresh coriander or shredded spring onion and serve.

HIBISCUS SHRIMPS

155 g (5 oz)	raw peeled shrimps
30 g (1 oz)	Cantonese roast pork (see recipe, page 291)*
2	large dried black mushrooms, soaked for 25 minutes
3	garlic chives, cut into 4 cm (1 2/3 in) pieces
4	eggs, well beaten
⅓ cup	softened lard or frying oil

Seasoning:

1	egg white, beaten
½ teaspoon	salt
¼ teaspoon	m.s.g. (optional)
	pinch of white pepper
½ teaspoon	rice wine or dry sherry
2 teaspoons	cornflour (cornstarch)
1 tablespoon	frying oil

Sauce:

⅓ cup	chicken stock
1 tablespoon	oyster sauce
¼ teaspoon	m.s.g. (optional)
¼ teaspoon	white pepper
½ teaspoon	sugar
¼ teaspoon	cornflour (cornstarch)

Clean the shrimps and remove the dark veins with a toothpick (see page 394). Mix with the seasoning ingredients and leave for 15 minutes.

Slice the roast pork, then shred finely. Squeeze the water from the mushrooms, remove the stems and shred finely. Mix the pork, mushrooms and garlic chives with the beaten eggs and add a dash of salt.

Heat the wok and add 2 tablespoons of the lard or oil. Fry the shrimps on moderate heat until pink, about 1 minute. Remove and leave to cool. Add to the egg mixture and mix well.

Add the remaining lard or oil to the wok and heat thoroughly. Pour in the egg mixture and cook on moderate heat until browned underneath, then turn and cook the other side. The omelette may be cut into 4 or 6 pieces to make turning easier. When done, transfer to a warmed serving plate.

Wipe out the wok and add the pre-mixed sauce ingredients. Bring to the boil and simmer briefly, then pour over the omelette and serve at once.

*Or use cooked ham.

FRIED SHRIMP PATTIES IN FRUITY SAUCE

Serve as an appetiser or main dish. Makes 18.

375 g (12 oz)	raw peeled shrimps
200 g (6½ oz)	pork fat
1 tablespoon	finely chopped cooked ham
2 teaspoons	finely chopped fresh coriander
2 tablespoons	softened lard or frying oil

Seasoning:

1	egg white, beaten
¾ teaspoon	salt
¼ teaspoon	m.s.g. (optional)
¼ teaspoon	white pepper
2 teaspoons	ginger wine
1 tablespoon	cornflour (cornstarch)

Sauce:

2 tablespoons	chicken stock
½ cup (4 fl oz)	liquid from canned pineapple or mango
2 tablespoons	tomato sauce (ketchup)
½ teaspoon	chilli oil
½ teaspoon	salt
¼ teaspoon	m.s.g. (optional)
1½ teaspoons	sugar
2 teaspoons	cornflour (cornstarch)

Finely mince (grind) the shrimps and 45 g (1½ oz) of the pork fat, or pulverise in a food processor. Add the seasoning ingredients and form into walnut-sized balls, then flatten into patties.

Thinly slice the remaining pork fat and cut into circles to fit the shrimp patties. Garnish the patties with the chopped ham and coriander, pressing on lightly, then stand each pattie on a piece of pork fat.

Heat a flat-bottomed iron griddle or large frying pan to moderate and add the softened lard or frying oil. Place the patties in the pan fat downwards, and fry on moderate heat for 2 minutes, then cover and continue to cook until the fat is crisp and golden and the patties cooked through, about 6 minutes. Splash in a little water if they begin to stick or the fat is cooking too fast.

Bring the pre-mixed sauce ingredients to the boil in another pan and simmer for 1 minute. Transfer the patties to a serving plate and cover with the sauce just before serving.

SHRIMP SAUSAGE SAUTÉD WITH BEAN SPROUTS

185 g (6 oz)	raw peeled shrimps
2	spring onions (scallions), trimmed and shredded
4 slices	fresh ginger, shredded
185 g (6 oz)	fresh bean sprouts
¼ cup (2 fl oz)	softened lard or frying oil

Seasoning A:

1	egg white, beaten
¼ teaspoon	salt
½ teaspoon	m.s.g. (optional)
	pinch of white pepper
1 tablespoon	cornflour (cornstarch)
1 tablespoon	rendered chicken fat (chicken grease), or use lard

Seasoning B/Sauce:

⅓ cup	chicken stock
1 teaspoon	rice wine or dry sherry
1 teaspoon	sesame oil
⅓ teaspoon	salt
¼ teaspoon	m.s.g. (optional)
¼ teaspoon	white pepper
¼ teaspoon	sugar
1 teaspoon	cornflour (cornstarch)

Pulverise the shrimp in a food processor or by using 2 cleavers (see page 396). Add the seasoning A ingredients and mix thoroughly until the mixture is smooth. Heat a saucepan of lightly salted water to boiling, then reduce the heat until the water is gently simmering.

Transfer the shrimp paste to a piping bag fitted with a large plain nozzle and pipe a continuous stream of the paste in a circle into the simmering water. Cook for 1 minute, then lift out and rinse in cold water. Leave to cool, then cut into pieces about 5 cm (2 in) long.

Heat the wok and add the lard or oil. Sauté the spring onions and ginger for 45 seconds, then push to one side of the pan and add the bean sprouts and sauté until softened. Remove. Reheat the pan and sauté the shrimp sausage for 1½ minutes, until lightly coloured. Add the pre-mixed seasoning B/sauce ingredients and return the spring onions, ginger, and bean sprouts and mix well. Simmer until the sauce has thickened, then transfer to a warmed serving plate.

Shrimp Sausage Sautéd with Bean Sprouts (recipe this page) and Mushroom with Chicken Wings in Soup (recipe page 318).

PAPER-WRAPPED SHRIMPS

Serve as an appetiser or main dish.

315 g (10 oz)	raw peeled shrimps
45 g (1½ oz)	Chinese or cured (Smithfield) ham, or use cooked ham
30 g (1·oz)	canned champignons, drained
12 small sprigs	fresh coriander
12 sheets	edible rice paper (about 10 cm/4 in square)*
1	egg yolk, beaten
4 cups (1 litre)	deep-frying oil

Seasoning:

1	egg white, beaten
½ teaspoon	salt
½ teaspoon	m.s.g. (optional)
¼ teaspoon	white pepper
¼ teaspoon	bicarbonate of soda (optional)
1 teaspoon	cornflour (cornstarch)

Wash the shrimps and devein with a toothpick (see page 394). Place in a dish with the seasoning ingredients and leave for 10 minutes. Finely slice the ham and champignons.

Spread the rice papers on a board and arrange several shrimps diagonally across the centre of each. Add several pieces of ham, champignon, and a sprig of coriander to each parcel and fold up. Stick the flap down with egg yolk.

Heat the deep-frying oil to moderate and fry the shrimp parcels, several at a time, until cooked through, about 1½ minutes. Drain and place on a serving plate. Serve at once with Chinese pepper-salt (see page 384) and light soy sauce as dips.

* If unobtainable, use cellophane paper and cut the parcels open before serving.

STEAMED FRESH PRAWNS

750 g (1½ lb)	large green prawns (shrimps) in the shell
1 tablespoon	frying oil

Sauce Dip:

⅓ cup	dark soy sauce
2½ tablespoons	vegetable oil
1 teaspoon	sugar
2	fresh red chilli peppers

Prepare the sauce first. Thinly slice the chillies, discarding the seeds. Mix the soy sauce, oil, and sugar until amalgamated, then add the chillies and pour into several small dishes. Set aside. If preferred, chopped spring onion and/or fresh ginger can be used in place of the chilli peppers.

Wash the prawns in cold, lightly salted water and place in a large dish so that none overlaps. Sprinkle on the oil and set the dish on a rack in a steamer. Cover and steam over rapidly boiling water for about 8 minutes. The actual cooking time will depend on the size of the prawns. Test by opening one after 6 minutes.

Serve the prawns straight from the steamer with the sauce dips and damp napkins or finger bowls.

PRAWNS CLEAR AS CRYSTAL

625 g (1¼ lb)	green prawns (shrimps), in the shell
1 tablespoon	bicarbonate of soda
1 teaspoon	salt
1 tablespoon	cornflour (cornstarch)
6	spring onions (scallions), trimmed and finely shredded
5 cm (2 in) piece	fresh ginger, finely shredded
	small bunch of fresh coriander
	oyster sauce*
	Chinese shrimp sauce
3 cups (24 fl oz)	deep-frying oil

Seasoning/Sauce:

¼ cup (2 fl oz)	chicken stock
2 teaspoons	rice wine or dry sherry
½ teaspoon	sesame oil (optional)
¼ teaspoon	salt
½ teaspoon	m.s.g. (optional)
	pinch of white pepper

Shell the prawns and cut in halves lengthwise. Remove the veins and place in a dish with water to cover. Add the bicarbonate of soda, mix in and leave for 2 — 3 hours, then rinse well in cold water, gently rubbing on the salt and cornflour in the process. Drain and wipe dry with kitchen paper. This process whitens the prawns and eliminates the slight fishy odour.

Arrange the shredded onions and ginger on a serving plate. Wash the coriander thoroughly, remove the stems and set aside for garnish. Make up several dip dishes of oyster sauce and shrimp paste. If shrimp paste is unobtainable, use anchovy sauce or essence.

Bring a saucepan of water to the boil and in another pan heat the deep-frying oil to fairly hot. Place the prawns in a wire strainer and dip into the boiling water for 30 seconds. Lift out and drain well. Shake in a kitchen towel to absorb excess water, then transfer to a frying basket and dip into the hot oil for 10 seconds. Lift out and shake off the oil, then return to the hot oil for a further 10 seconds. Remove and drain well.

Pour off the water and wipe out the pan. Add the pre-mixed seasoning/sauce ingredients and bring to the boil. Simmer briefly, then add the prawns and turn quickly in the sauce until glazed. Arrange on the onions and ginger and garnish with the fresh coriander. Serve at once with the prepared dips.

* Some of the less expensive of the commercial brands of oyster sauce are not suitable for use as a dipping sauce. The better brands have the strong salty taste necessary when serving straight from the bottle.

STIR-FRIED PRAWNS AND *CHOY SUM*

250 g (8 oz)	peeled green prawns (shrimps)
375 g (12 oz)	fresh choy sum*
3 slices	fresh ginger
¼ cup (2 fl oz)	frying oil

Seasoning/Sauce:

¼ cup (2 fl oz)	chicken stock
2 teaspoons	light soy sauce
2 teaspoons	rice wine or dry sherry
¼ teaspoon	sesame oil
⅓ teaspoon	salt
½ teaspoon	sugar
	pinch of white pepper
¾ teaspoon	cornflour (cornstarch)

Wash and devein the prawns and wipe dry. Cut the *choy sum* into 4 cm (1 2/3 in) pieces and blanch in boiling water for 1½ minutes. Drain.

Heat the oil in a wok and add the ginger. Fry briefly, then stir-fry the prawns until they turn pink, about 1½ minutes. Remove and keep warm.

Add the vegetables and stir-fry for 2 minutes, then add the pre-mixed seasoning/sauce ingredients and bring to the boil. Simmer for 1 minute, return the prawns and heat through. Serve.

* Or use fresh broccoli, broken into florets.

STEAMED JUMBO PRAWNS SERVED IN CLEAR SAUCE

750 g (1½ lb)	large green prawns (shrimps), in the shell
¾ teaspoon	salt
¼ teaspoon	m.s.g. (optional)
½ teaspoon	sugar
¼ teaspoon	white pepper
2 teaspoons	rice wine or dry sherry
1½ teaspoons	sesame oil (optional)
2	spring onions (scallions), finely shredded
3 thick slices	fresh ginger, finely shredded

Use a sharp knife to cut down the backs of the prawns through the shells. Remove the dark veins but leave the shells in place.

Place the prawns in a dish and sprinkle on the remaining ingredients. Set on a rack in a steamer, cover tightly and steam over rapidly boiling water for 8 — 9 minutes.

The dish containing the prawns should not be covered inside the steamer. Condensation and the drawing out of the natural juices of the prawns during cooking will result in a quantity of clear liquid accumulating in the dish. Strain this into a separate bowl and adjust the seasoning.

Transfer the prawns to a serving dish and pour on the sauce. Serve at once.

DEEP-FRIED PRAWN BALLS

Serve as an appetiser or main dish.

375 g (12 oz)	peeled green prawns (shrimps)
45 g (1½ oz)	pork fat
30 g (1 oz)	canned water chestnuts, drained
4 cups (1 litre)	deep-frying oil

Seasoning:

1	egg white, beaten
¾ teaspoon	salt
¼ teaspoon	m.s.g. (optional)
¼ teaspoon	ground black pepper
¾ teaspoon	rice wine or dry sherry
½ teaspoon	sesame oil (optional)
1 tablespoon	cornflour (cornstarch)

Devein the prawns with a toothpick (see page 394), then pulverise with the pork fat in a food processor or by using 2 cleavers. Finely chop the water chestnuts and add to the prawn paste with the seasoning ingredients. Work into a smooth paste by gathering into a ball and throwing repeatedly against the side of the bowl (see page 395).

If possible, prepare the prawn mixture several hours beforehand and chilli thoroughly. This gives a better consistency to the mixture.

Heat the deep-frying oil to moderately hot. Form the mixture into small balls by squeezing a portion of the paste from the left hand (see page 395) and scooping into the oil with a spoon. Cook about 6 at a time for 2½ — 3 minutes, or until golden. Drain and keep warm until all are cooked. Quickly deep-fry all the balls together to reheat, then drain well and serve on a plate of shredded lettuce with hot mustard and light soy sauce as dips.

Deep-Fried Fish Fillets with Black Sesame Seed Dressing (recipe page 271).

BRAISED PRAWNS IN GRAVY

500 g (1 lb)	green prawns (shrimps) in the shell
1 cup (8 fl oz)	frying oil
4	spring onions (scallions), trimmed and sliced
4 slices	fresh ginger

Seasoning A:

⅓ teaspoon	salt
¼ teaspoon	m.s.g. (optional)
¼ teaspoon	white pepper
2 teaspoons	sesame oil

Seasoning B/Sauce:

1 cup (8 fl oz)	chicken stock
2 tablespoons	light soy sauce
¾ teaspoon	chilli oil*
1½ teaspoons	sesame oil
¼ teaspoon	salt
¾ teaspoon	sugar
¼ teaspoon	white pepper
1½ teaspoons	cornflour (cornstarch)

Peel the prawns, leaving the heads and tails intact. Devein with a toothpick (see page 394) and place in a dish. Add the seasoning A ingredients and leave for 15 minutes to marinate.

Heat the frying oil to fairly hot and stir-fry the prawns until the heads turn bright red, about 1 minute. Remove. Add the onions and ginger and stir-fry for 30 seconds, then pour in the pre-mixed seasoning B/sauce ingredients and bring to the boil. Return the prawns.

Reduce the heat to simmer until the prawns are tender and the sauce thickened. Transfer to a warmed serving dish.

*Or omit the chilli oil and use oyster sauce or hot black bean sauce. Add slightly less soy sauce, to taste.

WALNUT-STUFFED PRAWNS

Serve as an appetiser or main dish.

375 g (12 oz)	green prawn (shrimp) cutlets*
90 g (3 oz)	shelled walnuts
4 cups (1 litre)	deep-frying oil
6	dried black mushrooms, soaked for 25 minutes
2	egg whites, well beaten
3 tablespoons	cornflour (cornstarch)
	extra cornflour (cornstarch)
6	young Chinese (celery) cabbage hearts, young bok choy or kale
2	spring onions (scallions), trimmed and sliced
2 slices	fresh ginger, shredded

Seasoning/Sauce:

⅓ cup	chicken stock
½ teaspoon	rice wine or dry sherry
¾ teaspoon	sesame oil (optional)
½ teaspoon	salt
½ teaspoon	m.s.g. (optional)
¾ teaspoon	sugar
	pinch of white pepper
1 teaspoon	cornflour (cornstarch)

Rinse the prawn cutlets in cold water and dry well. Peel the walnuts by first dropping into boiling water for 20 seconds, draining and pulling away the dark skin while the nuts are still warm. Dry well and deep-fry in hot oil for 1½ — 1¾ minutes, until golden. Drain and leave to cool.

Squeeze the water from the mushrooms and remove the stems. Use a sharp paring knife to cut a cross shape in the top of each cap. Set aside.

Bat the prawn cutlets lightly with the side of a cleaver to flatten and tenderise. Place a walnut in the centre of each prawn, fold the prawn around it with the tail folded across the roll and squeeze firmly. The tails may be removed, if preferred.

Make a batter with the egg whites, cornflour, and a little water. Heat the deep-frying oil to fairly hot. Dip the prawn rolls into the batter, then dust lightly with cornflour. Deep-fry until golden, about 1½ minutes. Remove and drain well.

Pour off all but 3 tablespoons of the oil and sauté the vegetables until softened. Remove to a serving plate. Add the spring onions and ginger and sauté briefly, then add the pre-mixed seasoning/sauce ingredients and bring to the boil. Simmer until thickened, add the prawns and stir in the sauce, then arrange over the vegetables and pour on any remaining sauce. Serve.

*Reasonably large prawns, peeled, deveined, and cut open down the back so they can be pressed out flat, butterfly style.

STUFFED PRAWNS IN HOT SAUCE

500 g (1 lb)	large green prawns (shrimps), in the shell
1 teaspoon	salt
60 g (2 oz)	fatty pork, finely minced (ground)
2 teaspoons	finely chopped cooked ham
2 teaspoons	finely chopped softened dried mushrooms or champignons
1	large egg, beaten
	cornflour (cornstarch)
4 cups (1 litre)	deep-frying oil
Sauce:	
¼ cup (2 fl oz)	chicken stock
2 tablespoons	light soy sauce
1 teaspoon	rice wine or dry sherry
½ — ¾ teaspoon	chilli oil*
¼ teaspoon	salt
½ teaspoon	m.s.g. (optional)
½ teaspoon	sugar
	pinch of white pepper
1 teaspoon	cornflour (cornstarch)

Remove heads from the prawns and sprinkle them with salt. Set aside. Cut off about 2.5 cm (1 in) of meat from the top end of each prawn, devein and chop finely. Mix with the minced pork and add a dash of salt, m.s.g., if used, and white pepper.

Cut the remaining parts of the prawns open along the back, cutting deep enough that they can be pressed out flat. Devein and coat lightly with cornflour. Press a portion of the prawn and pork mixture onto each, forming into a fanned shape. Garnish with the chopped ham and mushrooms and brush with beaten egg. Coat lightly with cornflour.

Heat the deep-frying oil to fairly hot and fry the stuffed prawns for 1½ minutes, until golden. Drain and set aside, keeping warm. Pour off all but 2 tablespoons of the oil and stir-fry the prawn heads for about 3 minutes until bright red and cooked through.

Line up the heads on a serving dish and arrange the tails near them. Wipe out the pan and add 1 tablespoon of the deep-frying oil. Pour in the pre-mixed sauce ingredients and bring to the boil. Stir until thickened, then pour over the prawn tails and serve at once.

*Or substitute 1½ tablespoons hot black bean sauce for the chilli oil and use only 1½ — 2 teaspoons of soy sauce.

STEAMED FEMALE CRABS WITH GINGER SAUCE

6	small female crabs
2	spring onions (scallions), trimmed and shredded
6 slices	fresh ginger, shredded
2 teaspoons	rice wine or dry sherry
Ginger Sauce:	
5 cm (2 in) piece	fresh ginger peeled and minced
½ cup (4 fl oz)	white vinegar
1 tablespoon	sugar
2 teaspoons	sesame oil

Prepare the sauce first to allow time for the flavours to blend. Mix the four ingredients together, stirring until the sugar is completely dissolved. Pour into several small dishes and set aside.

Wash the crabs, cut open underneath and remove the inedible parts, then crack the claws. Reassemble the crabs and place in a large dish. Sprinkle on the wine and scatter the shredded onion and ginger over the crabs. Set on a rack in a steamer and steam over high heat for 15 minutes.

Serve with the sauce.

CRABMEAT OMELETTE

3	egg whites
2	whole eggs
2 tablespoons	chicken stock
¼ teaspoon	salt
2 tablespoons	softened lard
1	large spring onion (scallion), trimmed and shredded
1 slice	fresh ginger, shredded
60 g (2 oz)	fresh crabmeat
15 g (1 oz)	crab roe
1 teaspoon	rice wine or dry sherry

Sauce:

2 tablespoons	chicken stock
1 tablespoon	oyster sauce
½ teaspoon	rice wine or dry sherry
½ teaspoon	m.s.g. (optional)
½ teaspoon	sugar, or to taste
	pinch of ground black pepper
2/3 teaspoon	cornflour (cornstarch)

Beat the egg whites and whole eggs together and add the chicken stock and salt.

Heat half the lard in a wok and sauté the spring onion and ginger briefly. Add the crabmeat and cook until lightly coloured, then add the roe and sizzle the wine onto the sides of the pan and stir in. Remove and keep warm.

Reheat the wok and add the remaining lard. Pour in the egg mixture and cook on moderate heat until lightly coloured underneath, then spread the cooked crab over the egg and carefully turn the omelette. Cook the underside until just firm, lift onto a serving plate. It may be cut into quarters to make turning easier.

Wipe out the wok and add the pre-mixed sauce ingredients. Simmer, stirring until thickened, about 45 seconds. Pour over the omelette and serve at once.

STUFFED CRAB CLAWS

Serve as an appetiser.

12	large crab pincers, meat intact
375 g (12 oz)	raw peeled shrimps
1¼ cups	fresh breadcrumbs
2	eggs, well beaten
	cornflour (cornstarch)
⅓ cup	toasted white sesame seeds
6 cups (1½ litres)	deep-frying oil

Seasoning:

2	egg whites, beaten
¾ teaspoon	salt
¼ teaspoon	white pepper
⅓ teaspoon	hot mustard powder
1½ teaspoons	lemon juice

Break away the shell from the top of the pincer, leaving the meat attached to the central tendon and the claw. Pulverise the shrimps in a food processor, then add the breadcrumbs and seasoning ingredients and mix to a smooth paste. Add a very little water if the mixture is dry. Dust the crab meat with cornflour and press on a coating of the shrimp mixture, forming into a ball shape around the crabmeat and smoothing around so that only the tip of the claw shows. Dust very lightly with cornflour, then brush with beaten egg and dip the ends of the stuffed crab claws into the sesame seeds.

Heat the deep-frying oil to moderately hot and deep-fry the crab claws, several at a time, to a golden brown, 2½ — 3 minutes. Drain well.

Arrange on a bed of shredded lettuce and serve with dips of light soy sauce and Chinese pepper-salt (see page 384).

RED-STEWED CAMEL'S PADS

A Chinese recipe in its original form rarely provides detailed information as to the exact amount of seasonings and spices. These are left open to interpretation by the chef undertaking the dish. We follow that example with this recipe.

1 catty (approximately 500 g/1 lb)	water-soaked camel's pads
30 g (1 oz)	bamboo shoots
6	dried black mushrooms, soaked to soften
10	young vegetable hearts
2 catties (approximately 4 cups)	chicken stock

Seasoning:

rice wine or dry sherry
light soy sauce
dark soy sauce
salt
m.s.g. (optional)
white sugar
rendered chicken fat
cornflour (cornstarch)
shredded spring onions
(scallions)
shredded ginger

Cut the drained camel's pads into chunks. Slice the bamboo shoots, drain the mushrooms and remove the stems. Wash the vegetables.

Place the cubed pads in a saucepan, cover with cold water and bring to the boil. Drain and cover with water again. Bring back to the boil, add the spring onions, ginger and wine and simmer for 6 — 7 minutes. This process will remove the rather pungent smell. Drain well and rinse in cold water.

Bring the chicken stock to the boil. Add the cubed pads, mushrooms, bamboo shoots, and the seasoning ingredients. Simmer for 15 minutes, then thicken with the cornflour. Transfer to a serving plate.

Simmer the vegetables in slightly salted stock or water until tender. Arrange around the meat and serve.

DEEP-FRIED BOILED CAMEL'S HUMP

1 catty (approximately 500 g/1 lb)	water-soaked camel's hump
1½ catties (approximately 3 cups)	chicken stock
	cooking oil

Seasoning:

light soy sauce
salt
m.s.g. (optional)
Chinese pepper-salt
shredded spring onions
(scallions)
shredded fresh ginger
cornflour (cornstarch)

Cut the hump into angled pieces. Place in a saucepan and cover with cold water. Bring to the boil, drain and cover with more cold water. Add the spring onions and ginger and bring to the boil. Drain again.

Bring the chicken stock to the boil, add the camel's hump pieces and the seasonings and simmer for 10 — 15 minutes, then drain and discard the soup.

Heat deep-frying oil to smoking point. Dust the hump pieces lightly with cornflour and deep-fry until crisp and golden on the surface. Drain well.

Serve hot with the pepper-salt as a dip

LOBSTER WITH BLACK BEANS AND CHILLIES

1 750 g (1½ lb)	fresh lobster
1 tablespoon	fermented black beans
¾ teaspoon	crushed garlic
1 teaspoon	sugar
¼ cup (2 fl oz)	frying oil
1	spring onion (scallion), trimmed and diced
1 — 2	fresh red chilli peppers, thinly sliced
4 slices	fresh ginger, shredded
¾ teaspoon	rice wine or dry sherry
1 tablespoon	light soy sauce

Seasoning/Sauce:

¼ cup (2 fl oz)	chicken stock
1 teaspoon	ginger wine
¼ teaspoon	salt
¼ teaspoon	ground black pepper
¾ teaspoon	cornflour (cornstarch)

Cut the lobster in halves and discard inedible parts. Scoop out the flesh and cut into cubes. Scrape out the shell and drop it, with the head, into a saucepan of boiling water. Cook until bright red, then drain, rinse with cold water and brush again to remove any residue. Rinse in cold, salted water and dry with kitchen towels. Place on a serving plate.

Wash the black beans, dry well and chop finely. Mix with the garlic and sugar and fry in a wok with the frying oil for 1 minute. Add the lobster pieces and stir-fry until white and firm, about 2 minutes, then remove. Reheat the wok and stir-fry the spring onion, chilli pepper and ginger together for 1 minute, sizzle the wine and soy sauce onto the sides of the wok and stir in, then add the pre-mixed seasoning/sauce ingredients and bring to the boil. Return the lobster and black beans and simmer until the sauce is thickened.

Spoon into the lobster shell and serve at once.

STIR-FRIED SQUID WITH VEGETABLES

625 g (1¼ lb)	fresh squid
30 g (1 oz)	canned bamboo shoots, drained and sliced
1	medium carrot, peeled and thinly sliced
12	snow peas, strings removed*
1½	spring onions (scallions), trimmed and sliced
6 thin slices	fresh ginger
½ teaspoon	crushed garlic
5 cups (1¼ litres)	deep-frying oil

Seasoning/Sauce:

¼ cup (2 fl oz)	chicken stock
½ teaspoon	sesame oil (optional)
1 teaspoon	salt
½ teaspoon	m.s.g. (optional)
½ teaspoon	sugar
¼ teaspoon	ground black pepper
1 teaspoon	cornflour (cornstarch)

Remove the heads and stomachs from the squid and discard. Pull away the pink skin with fins attached, leaving only the white tubular bodies. Cut open and press out flat. Rinse well, pulling away any white membrane. Score on the inside in a close diagonal criss-cross pattern, cutting at a slight angle (see page 395).

Cut into diamond-shaped bite-sized pieces and blanch for 10 seconds in boiling water, then drain well. Blanch the bamboo shoots, carrots, and snow peas or other vegetables and drain well.

Heat the deep-frying oil to moderate and fry the squid in a basket for 20 seconds only. Lift out and drain well. Pour off all but ⅓ cup of the oil and stir-fry the spring onions, ginger, and garlic on fairly high heat for 45 seconds. Add the vegetables and stir-fry together until beginning to soften, about 1 minute.

Pour in the pre-mixed seasoning/sauce ingredients and bring to the boil. Simmer briefly, return the squid and heat through. Transfer to a serving plate.

For convenience, stir-fry the squid also. Extend the blanching time to 25 seconds and stir-fry only briefly with the vegetables. Do not overcook or the squid will become tough and chewy.

*Or use 1 small green capsicum pepper, cut into small squares, 12 broccoli or cauliflower florets, or 6 soaked dried black mushrooms.

DEEP-FRIED OYSTERS

Serve as an appetiser or main dish.

12	very large oysters or 24 medium oysters
1 teaspoon	Chinese pepper-salt
6 cups (1½ litres)	deep-frying oil

Batter:

⅓ cup	flour
½ cup	cornflour (cornstarch)
2½ teaspoons	baking powder
1 teaspoon	salt
	pinch of white pepper
1½ tablespoons	vegetable oil

Wash the oysters in lightly salted water, then rub with the pepper-salt. Set aside.

Make a smooth, fairly thick batter by mixing the batter ingredients with cold water. Beat for 1½ — 2 minutes, then set aside for 10 minutes.

Heat the deep-frying oil to smoking point. Coat the oysters thickly with batter and deep-fry, several at a time, until golden and well puffed up. Drain on absorbent paper.

Arrange on a bed of shredded lettuce and serve with dips of Chinese pepper-salt and sweet and sour sauce (see page 384 and 385).

SCALLOPS WITH SHRIMPS AND MUSHROOMS

12	large fresh sea scallops
155 g (5 oz)	raw peeled shrimps
90 g (3 oz)	canned straw mushrooms, drained and cut in halves
¼ cup (2 fl oz)	frying oil
2	spring onions (scallions), trimmed and sliced
3 slices	fresh ginger
2	egg whites, well beaten
	cornflour (cornstarch)

Seasoning A:

½ teaspoon	salt
2 teaspoons	ginger wine (see page 387)

Seasoning B:

⅓ teaspoon	salt
¾ teaspoon	sugar
½ cup (4 fl oz)	chicken stock

Rinse the scallops in cold water and drain well. Place in a dish and add the seasoning A ingredients. Devein the shrimps, rinse with cold water and add to the scallops. Leave to marinate for 10 minutes.

Bring the seasoning B ingredients to the boil in a small saucepan. Add the mushrooms and simmer for 3 minutes. Remove from the heat and leave in the stock.

Heat the frying oil and sauté the spring onions and ginger until softened, then add the scallops and shrimps and sauté on moderately high heat until barely cooked through. The scallops should be white and just firm, the shrimps pink and firm.

Add the mushrooms and the stock and bring to the boil. Mix a little cornflour with cold water and pour into the sauce. Simmer until thickened, then slowly drizzle in the beaten egg whites and cook without stirring until the egg sets in white strands in the sauce. Serve at once.

CHARCOAL ROASTED EEL ON SKEWERS

Serve as an appetiser or main dish.

1 750 g (1½ lb)	fresh-water eel
2 tablespoons	frying oil
1½ teaspoons	sesame oil (optional)

Seasoning:

3 tablespoons	finely chopped spring onion (scallion)
1 tablespoon	grated fresh ginger
¼ cup (2 fl oz)	light soy sauce
1 tablespoon	dark soy sauce
2 tablespoons	rice wine or dry sherry
	juice of 1 lemon
2 tablespoons	vegetable oil
½ teaspoon	m.s.g. (optional)
2 tablespoons	sugar
⅓ teaspoon	ground black pepper

Clean the eel, cut off the head and tail section and discard. Cut the body into pieces about 4 cm (1 2/3 in) long and cut down to the backbone so the pieces can be pressed out flat.

Place on a tray and pour on the seasoning ingredients. Leave for 10 minutes, then turn and leave for a further 10 minutes. Thread each piece onto two metal skewers, passing across the pieces so they remain flat.

Place the eel on an oiled grid, skin side downwards over glowing charcoal, and grill (broil) for 3 minutes. Turn and cook the other side for 2 minutes. Brush with any remaining marinade and continue to cook and turn until evenly cooked with the outside crisp, dark, and glazed with the sauce, the meat inside, moist and white. Do not overcook.

Serve on a bed of shredded lettuce.

STEWED RIVER EEL WITH DICED PORK AND MUSHROOMS

1 750 g (1½ lb)	fresh-water eel
125 g (4 oz)	fatty or roast pork, diced
6 cups (1 ½ litres)	deep-frying oil
8 cloves	garlic
3 pieces	dried orange peel
4	spring onions (scallions), trimmed and cut in halves
5 slices	fresh ginger
6	dried black mushrooms, soaked for 25 minutes
3 cups (24 fl oz)	chicken stock
	cornflour (cornstarch)
	sesame oil
	white pepper

Seasoning A:

¾ teaspoon	salt
¼ cup (2 fl oz)	light soy sauce
1½ teaspoons	dark soy sauce
1½ tablespoons	rice wine or dry sherry

Seasoning B/Sauce:

2 tablespoons	light soy sauce
1 tablespoon	sugar
¾ teaspoon	m.s.g. (optional)
	pinch of white pepper

Wash the eels, rubbing with salt to remove the slime. Rinse in cold water and cut into 5 cm (2 in) pieces, discarding the head and tail. Blanch in boiling water for 1 minute, drain and place in a dish with the seasoning A ingredients. Leave for 20 minutes. Drain, reserving the marinade.

Heat the deep-frying oil and fry the pork until lightly coloured. Drain and set aside. Add the eel and deep-fry for 1 minute, drain and transfer to a casserole. Scatter the diced pork on top. Drain off all but ⅓ cup of the oil and fry the garlic and orange peel for 1 minute, place with the eel, then fry the spring onions, ginger and drained mushrooms briefly and transfer, with the oil, to a casserole.

Add the reserved marinade and seasoning B/sauce ingredients. Heat the stock to boiling and pour over the eel. Cover and simmer until the eel is tender, about 30 minutes. Strain the sauce into a wok and bring to the boil, simmer until well reduced, then thicken with cornflour mixed with a little cold water and check the seasoning. Pour over the eel and season with a dash of sesame oil and white pepper. Serve in the casserole.

288

Stuffed Crab Claws (recipe page 284).

THREE COURSES OF ROAST SUCKLING PIG

Serves 10 — 12.

Dishes 1 and 2:

1	*freshly roasted suckling pig (see recipe, page 328; Roast Suckling Pig)*
24	*'Mandarin' pancakes (see page 373)*
12	*spring onions (scallions)*
½ cup (4 fl oz)	*'duck' sauce (see page 385)*

Dish 3:

¼ cup (2 fl oz)	*frying oil*
375 g (12 oz)	*fresh broccoli, broken into florets*
1½	*spring onions (scallions), trimmed and sliced*
3 slices	*fresh ginger, shredded*
1 tablespoon	*rice wine or dry sherry*

Seasoning/Sauce:

2/3 cup	*chicken stock*
1¼ teaspoons	*salt*
¾ teaspoon	*m.s.g. (optional)*
½ teaspoon	*sugar*
1½ teaspoons	*cornflour (cornstarch)*

Dish 1:

Prepare the pancakes and arrange half on a serving plate. Remove the roots and leafy green tops from the spring onions and shred one end of each piece. Place on another serving plate. Fill several small dishes with the sauce.

Carve the crisp skin from the pork and cut into bite-sized pieces. Arrange back over the pig and surround with an attractive garnish of fresh vegetables and parsley. Take to the table with the accompaniments.

To eat, dip several pieces of skin into the sauce and place in the centre of a pancake, add a piece of spring onion and roll up.

Dish 2:

Return the pig to the kitchen and carve off the choicest pieces of the meat. Cut into bite-sized pieces and rearrange on the pig. Serve with the remaining pancakes and onions. Again, roll in the pancake after dipping in the sauce.

Dish 3:

Return the pig to the kitchen again and carve off the remaining meat. Cut into bite-sized pieces. Heat the frying oil in a wok and sauté the broccoli for 2 minutes, then push to one side of the pan and add the spring onions and ginger. Sauté briefly, then add the pork and fry on high heat, turning constantly. Mix in the broccoli and sizzle the wine onto the sides of the wok.

Pour in the pre-mixed seasoning/sauce ingredients and simmer until the sauce thickens. Transfer to a serving plate and serve.

PORK AND DUCK LIVER ROLL

Serve as an appetiser or main dish.

280 g (9 oz)	*lean pork, finely minced (ground)*
60 g (2 oz)	*canned water chestnuts, drained and finely chopped*
1	*duck (or chicken) liver, cubed*
1	*small onion, diced*
185 g (6 oz)	*pork omentum**
1	*egg white, beaten*
1 tablespoon	*cornflour (cornstarch)*
4 cups (1 litre)	*deep-frying oil*

Seasoning:

1	*egg white, beaten*
¾ teaspoon	*salt*
½ teaspoon	*m.s.g. (optional)*
1 tablespoon	*light soy sauce*
1 teaspoon	*rice wine or dry sherry*
2 teaspoons	*cornflour (cornstarch)*

Mix the pork and water chestnuts with the seasoning ingredients and set aside. Use a little of the deep-frying oil to sauté the liver and diced onion, then add to the pork mixture.

Wash the pork omentum and spread on a board. It may be easier to work if divided into several even-sized squares. If using the chicken skin, cut in halves for easier handling. Make a paste of the egg white and cornflour and spread over the pork fat or beancurd skin. Omit if using chicken skin. Spread on the pork mixture, leaving a wide border all round. Roll into a long sausage shape and stick down the ends and long edge with more of the egg white paste. The chicken skin rolls should be secured with toothpicks or sewn up with a needle and thread.

Heat the deep-frying oil to moderate and fry the roll(s) until cooked through, and crisp and golden, about 4 minutes. Remove from the oil and drain well. Cut diagonally across the rolls into thick slices and arrange on a serving plate. Serve with sweet and sour sauce or with spiced salt (see page 385 and 384).
*If pork omentum (caul net/fat) is unobtainable, use either a dampened sheet of beancurd skin or a chicken skin.

CANTONESE ROAST PORK

Serve hot or cold as an appetiser or main dish.

1 kg (2 lb)	pork fillet (tenderloin)
1 tablespoon	five spice powder
2 teaspoons	finely ground Chinese brown peppercorns
3 tablespoons	finely chopped spring onion (scallion)
1 tablespoon	finely chopped fresh ginger

Seasoning:

½ cup (4 fl oz)	light soy sauce
2½ tablespoons	soybean paste, dark soy sauce or oyster sauce
1 tablespoon	sesame oil
2 tablespoons	rice wine or dry sherry
⅓ cup	sugar
	red food colouring

Special Equipment: A rotisserie oven or metal hooks for hanging the meat in the oven.

Choose large fillets and cut lengthwise into two or three strips, about 15 cm (6 in) long and 5 cm (2 in) wide. Rub with the five spice powder and ground peppercorns and place in a dish. Arrange the chopped spring onion and ginger on top, then pour on the pre-mixed seasoning ingredients after stirring until the sugar dissolves. (Add red food colouring to give a fairly bright colour.) Cover the dish with plastic wrap and leave for about 4 hours to marinate.

If the oven has a rotisserie, thread the strips of meat through one end onto the spike so that they hang down in the oven. Place a drip tray underneath. Otherwise, secure each strip by one end on metal hooks. Position one rack on the highest setting in the oven and remove the other racks. Hang the hooks on this rack, separating each piece as much as possible.

Do not set the rotisserie in motion. Cook the pork on very high heat for the first 10 minutes, about 240°C (450°F) then reduce to around 170°C (325 — 350°F) to cook for a further 20 minutes. Brush frequently with the pan drippings to keep the meat moist and to glaze the surface.

When done, leave to cool slightly, then slice and serve with hot mustard and light soy sauce as dips. Use in recipes requiring barbecue or roast pork and in assortments of cold cuts as an appetiser (see recipe, page 381).

A popular way to serve this pork is to arrange it over crisp deep-fried peanuts, or over peanuts (groundnuts) or soybeans that have been boiled, then sauté in sweetened soy sauce.

DEEP-FRIED PORK CHOPS

5	small pork loin chops (about 700 g/1⅓ lb)
2½ cups	dry breadcrumbs
	eggs, well beaten
	cornflour (cornstarch)
cups (1½ litres)	deep-frying oil
	spiced salt (see page 384)
	Worcestershire or light soy sauce

Seasoning:

½ teaspoon	salt
¼ teaspoon	m.s.g. (optional)
tablespoon	rice wine or dry sherry
tablespoon	finely chopped spring onion
½ teaspoons	grated fresh ginger

Bat the meaty centres of the chops with the side of a cleaver to flatten and tenderise. Rub on the seasoning ingredients and leave for 25 minutes to marinate.

Spread the breadcrumbs on a board. Dust the pork chops lightly with cornflour, then dip into beaten egg and place on the breadcrumbs. Press down on one side to coat thickly, then turn and coat the other side.

Heat the deep-frying oil to fairly hot and fry the pork chops for 1 minute. Lower the heat and continue to cook until the chops are well browned on the surface and cooked through, about 3 minutes longer.

Drain well and serve with dips of spiced salt and Worcestershire or soy sauce.

If preferred, the chops can be cut into bite-sized pieces, through the bones.

PORK FILLET ROLLS IN SWEET AND SOUR SAUCE

375 g (12 oz)	pork fillet (tenderloin)
	cornflour (cornstarch)
3 cups (24 fl oz)	deep-frying oil
1	small carrot, diced and par-boiled
1	small cucumber, diced
30 g (1 oz)	canned bamboo shoots, drained and diced
1	medium brown onion, diced

Seasoning A:

½ teaspoon	salt
¾ teaspoon	m.s.g. (optional)
¼ teaspoon	white pepper
2 teaspoons	rice wine or dry sherry
1 teaspoon	sesame oil (optional)

Seasoning B/Sauce:

2 tablespoons	finely chopped spring onion (scallion)
2 teaspoons	finely chopped fresh ginger
¼ cup (2 fl oz)	chicken stock or cold water
¼ cup (2 fl oz)	tomato sauce (ketchup)
2 tablespoons	white vinegar
2¾ tablespoons	sugar
½ teaspoon	salt
1 teaspoon	cornflour (cornstarch)

Thinly slice the pork, then score on one side in a criss-cross pattern and cut into 5 cm (2 in) squares. Mix with the seasoning A ingredients and leave for 20 minutes. Coat the pork lightly with cornflour, roll each piece into a cylindrical shape and deep-fry in the smoking hot oil for 1 minute. Remove and drain well. Turn the heat down to moderate and return the pork. Cook for about 2 minutes more, until cooked through and golden brown on the surface. Remove and keep warm.

Pour off the oil, wipe out the wok and return 3 tablespoons of the oil. Reheat to moderate and stir-fry the diced vegetables for 2 minutes, then add the chopped spring onion and ginger and stir-fry for 30 seconds. Pour in the remaining pre-mixed seasoning B/sauce ingredients and bring to the boil. Simmer for 2½ minutes, then add the pork and stir until the meat is evenly glazed with the sauce. Serve.

SWEET AND SOUR PORK RIBS

500 g (1 lb)	meaty pork ribs or chops
1	small green capsicum (bell pepper)
1	small red capsicum (bell pepper)
2 slices	canned pineapple, drained
1	small white onion
1	small carrot, sliced and par-boiled
	cornflour (cornstarch)
7 cups (1¾ litres)	deep-frying oil

Sauce:

⅓ cup	liquid from canned pineapple
⅓ cup	white vinegar
2 tablespoons	tomato sauce (ketchup)
1 tablespoon	vegetable oil
2½ tablespoons	sugar
½ teaspoon	salt
	pinch of ground black pepper
½ — ¾ teaspoon	finely chopped garlic
2 teaspoons	cornflour (cornstarch)

Cut the pork ribs or chops into 2.5 cm (1 in) cubes. Wash the peppers and cut in halves, remove the stems, seed cores, and inner white ribs. Cut into quarters. Cut the pineapple into pieces about the same size as the peppers. Peel the onion and cut into quarters, cutting from stem to root. Trim away the base to allow the pieces to separate.

Pour about 1½ cups of cornflour into a paper or plastic bag and add the meat. Close the bag and shake vigorously to thickly coat the meat with flour. Empty into a colander and shake off excess flour.

Heat the deep-frying oil to fairly hot. Fry the pork, about 10 pieces at a time, until well browned and crisp on the surface, about 3 minutes. Drain and keep the oil warm.

Transfer 2 — 3 tablespoons of the oil to another wok and fry the onion for 30 seconds. Add the peppers and fry a further 30 seconds, then add the carrots and stir-fry the vegetables together for a further 1 minute. Pour in the pre-mixed sauce ingredients and bring to the boil. Simmer for 2 minutes, then add the pineapple.

Reheat the deepfrying oil and fry the pork for a second time until crisp, about 1 minute. Drain and transfer to the sauce. Stir until evenly glazed with the sauce, then serve.

Lobster with Black Beans and Chillies (recipe page 286)

PORK RIBS WITH BLACK BEAN SAUCE

6	meaty pork ribs (about 625 g/1¼ lb)*
1½ tablespoons	fermented black beans
¾ teaspoon	crushed garlic
1½ teaspoons	sugar
2 tablespoons	light soy sauce
1 teaspoon	dark soy sauce
2 teaspoons	dry sherry
2 tablespoons	water
1 tablespoon	vegetable oil
1	fresh red chilli pepper (optional)

Trim the ribs and cut into 5 or 6 pieces each. Wash the black beans and dry well. Chop coarsely and mix with the remaining ingredients. Place the ribs in a dish and cover with the prepared seasonings. Leave for 1 — 2 hours to absorb the flavourings.

Set the dish on a rack in a steamer and steam over gently boiling water until the pork is completely tender, about 1 hour. Serve in the dish.

If using the chilli pepper, add before steaming.

* Or use pork chops.

SWEET AND SPICY SPARE RIBS

18	American-style pork spare ribs (about 700 g/1⅓ lb)*
Seasoning:	
¼ teaspoon	salt
1½ tablespoons	sugar
2 teaspoons	five spice powder
2 tablespoons	light soy sauce
2 tablespoons	rice wine or dry sherry
2 tablespoons	soy bean paste
2 cubes	fermented beancurd with the liquid, mashed
2 tablespoons	vegetables oil
1½ teaspoons	crushed garlic

Wash the spare ribs and dry on kitchen paper. Mix the seasoning ingredients together. Place the ribs in a dish and smear thickly on both sides with the seasoning paste. Leave for 1½ — 2 hours to absorb the flavourings, then arrange on an oiled oven tray and roast in a preheated moderately hot oven 220°C (425°F) or under a slow grill for about 25 minutes.

Turn the ribs occasionally during cooking and brush with any remaining seasoning paste and the pan drippings. Add also a little vegetable oil if they begin to dry.

Serve with spiced salt (see page 384) as a dip and with plum sauce.

*Pork rib bones with a sparce covering of meat. If unobtainable use small pork chops.

STIR-FRIED PORK WITH SPRING ONIONS IN SOY SAUCE

250 g (8 oz)	pork fillet (tenderloin)
2	large spring onions (scallions)
1 thick slice	fresh ginger, shredded
½ teaspoon	crushed garlic
¼ cup (2 fl oz)	frying oil
2 teaspoons	rice wine or dry sherry
2 tablespoons	light soy sauce
Seasoning A:	
2 teaspoons	sugar
1 tablespoon	light soy sauce
2 teaspoons	rice wine or dry sherry
2 teaspoons	cornflour (cornstarch)
Seasoning B:	
2 teaspoons	dark soy sauce
½ teaspoon	m.s.g. (optional)
¼ teaspoon	ground black pepper
½ teaspoon	sugar

Very thinly slice the pork across the grain, then place in a dish with the seasoning A ingredients, mix well and leave for 30 minutes.

Cut the spring onions in halves lengthwise and cut into 4 cm (1 2/3 in) pieces. Heat the oil in a wok and stir-fry the spring onions, ginger and garlic for 1 minute. Add the pork and stir-fry on high heat until lightly coloured, 1½ — 2 minutes.

Sizzle the wine and soy sauce onto the sides of the pan and stir in, then add the seasoning B ingredients and mix thoroughly.

Transfer to a serving plate and serve at once

PORK SEASONED WITH SPICED RICE POWDER

750 g (1½ lb)	'five flowered' pork (belly/fresh bacon) on the rind*
¾ cup	spiced rice powder (see page 386).
2	dried or fresh lotus leaves (optional)

Seasoning A:

2½ tablespoons	soybean paste or dark soy sauce
1½ tablespoons	sesame oil
1 tablespoon	frying oil

Seasoning B:

1 teaspoon	salt
1¼ tablespoons	sugar
¾ teaspoon	m.s.g. (optional)
¼ cup (2 fl oz)	rice wine or dry sherry
2 tablespoons	dark soy sauce
3 tablespoons	finely chopped spring onion (scallion)
1½ teaspoons	grated fresh ginger
½ cup (4 fl oz)	cold water

Cut the pork into 1.5 cm (½ in) thick slices, then into strips about 2.5 cm (1 in) wide. Rub with the seasoning A ingredients, place in a dish and leave for 20 minutes, then add the pre-mixed seasoning B ingredients, mix well and leave for 1 hour.

Blanch the dried lotus leaves, if used, in boiling water then drain and place one in the bottom of a dish large enough to contain the pork. If using fresh lotus leaves, place in a saucepan, cover with cold water and bring to the boil, then drain well.

Dip the pork slices into the rice powder, coating generously. Arrange on the lotus leaf and top with the other leaf. Cover the dish and set it on a rack in a steamer. Steam over rapidly boiling water until the pork is completely tender, about 2½ hours.

Leftover spiced rice powder can be stored indefinitely in an airtight jar.

*Or use a less fatty cut, if preferred.

STEWED PORK WITH FERMENTED BEANCURD AND TARO

750 g (1½ lb)	'five flowered' pork (belly/fresh bacon)*
1 tablespoon	dark soy sauce
6 cups (1½ litres)	deep-frying oil
185 g (6 oz)	fresh taro, yam, or sweet potato
4 cups (1 litre)	chicken stock
	cornflour (cornstarch)

Seasoning A:

2 tablespoons	finely chopped spring onion (scallion)
2 teaspoons	finely chopped fresh ginger
1½ teaspoons	finely chopped garlic
4 cubes	fermented beancurd with the liquid, mashed

Seasoning B:

1½ teaspoons	salt
2 teaspoons	sugar
¼ cup (2 fl oz)	light soy sauce
2 teaspoons	dark soy sauce
1 tablespoon	rice wine or dry sherry

Wipe the pork and blanch in boiling water for 2 minutes, then remove and leave to dry. Rub with the dark soy sauce and deep-fry in hot oil until well coloured on the surface, about 5 minutes. Drain well.

Peel the taro and cut into cubes. Deep-fry until lightly coloured, about 2 minutes. Drain. Cut the pork into the same sized pieces.

Pour off most of the oil, retaining about 2 tablespoons. Fry the seasoning A ingredients for 2 minutes, adding a little of the chicken stock to prevent them from sticking to the pan. Add the seasoning B ingredients and cook briefly, then pour in the chicken stock and bring to the boil. Reduce the heat and add the pork. Simmer for about 30 minutes, then add the taro and cook until both pork and taro are tender.

Transfer the meat and vegetables to a serving plate. Return about 1 cupful of the sauce to the boil and thicken with a paste of cornflour and cold water. Pour over the dish and serve.

*Or use a less fatty cut, if preferred.

STEAMED PORK WITH CARROTS AND MUSHROOMS

500 g (1 lb)	lean pork, from the upper leg
1	medium to large carrot
90 g (3 oz)	canned champignons, drained
2	spring onions (scallions), trimmed and cut in halves
3 slices	fresh ginger
	chicken stock or cold water
	cornflour (cornstarch)

Seasoning:

¼ cup (2 fl oz)	light soy sauce
2 teaspoons	rice wine or dry sherry
½ teaspoon	salt
1 teaspoon	sugar
½ teaspoon	m.s.g. (optional)
¼ teaspoon	ground Chinese brown peppercorns

Trim any fat from the meat and cut into 2 cm (¾ in) cubes. Peel the carrot and cut into small cubes. Place half the pork in the bottom of a dish and add half the onion and a piece of ginger. Layer the carrot, champignons, and remaining pork on top and add the remaining onion and ginger.

Mix the sauce ingredients together and pour evenly over the dish, then add chicken stock or water to barely cover the top layer.

Set the dish on a rack in a steamer and steam over rapidly boiling water until tender, about 1¼ hours.

Strain the liquid into a wok and check the seasonings. Thicken with a thin solution of cornflour and cold water and stir well. Pour over the dish and serve.

Dried black mushrooms previously soaked to soften and stems removed, canned bamboo shoots, young Chinese green vegetables, turnip or white onions could replace either the carrots or champignons in this dish.

For dramatic presentation, arrange the ingredients alternately in a sunburst design in a large round dish.

FILLET OF BEEF WITH SALTED MUSTARD GREENS AND BLACK BEAN SAUCE

250 g (8 oz)	beef fillet (tenderloin)
30 g (1 oz)	salted mustard root*
1 tablespoon	fermented black beans
¾ teaspoon	finely chopped garlic
¾ teaspoon	sugar
3 cups (24 fl oz)	deep-frying oil, or use ⅓ cup frying oil
2 teaspoons	rice wine or dry sherry
1 tablespoon	light soy sauce

Seasoning A:

½ teaspoon	salt
¼ teaspoon	m.s.g. (optional)
¼ teaspoon	bicarbonate of soda (optional)
1¼ teaspoons	sugar
2 tablespoons	water
1½ tablespoons	vegetable oil
2 teaspoons	cornflour (cornstarch)

Seasoning B/Sauce:

2 tablespoons	chicken stock
¼ teaspoon	salt
½ teaspoon	sugar
½ teaspoon	m.s.g. (optional)
¼ teaspoon	ground black pepper (optional)
½ teaspoon	sesame oil (optional)
¾ teaspoon	cornflour (cornstarch)

Partially freeze the beef, cut into very thin slices across the grain and then cut each piece into three. Add the seasoning A ingredients, except the cornflour and leave for 15 minutes, then add the cornflour, mix in and leave a further 10 minutes.

Soak the mustard root or other pickled vegetables in cold water for 20 minutes, drain well and squeeze out the excess water. Cut into small dice. Wash the black beans and dry well, chop and mix with the garlic and sugar.

Heat the deep-frying oil in a wok to smoking point and fry the beef in a frying basket for 30 seconds. Or stir-fry in the frying oil on very high heat for 1 minute. Remove and drain well. Keep warm. Pour off all but 2 tablespoons oil and add the black bean mixture. Stir-fry for 30 seconds, then add the mustard or pickled vegetables and stir-fry for 30 seconds longer. Sizzle the wine and soy sauce onto the sides of the pan and stir in.

Add the pre-mixed seasoning B/sauce ingredients and bring to the boil. Return the beef and heat through, then serve.

*Or use pickled cabbage or Szechuan pickled vegetables.

BEEF IN OYSTER SAUCE

250 g (8 oz)	beef steak (fillet/tenderloin or rump)
280 g (9 oz)	Chinese (celery) cabbage
6	dried black mushrooms, soaked for 25 minutes
¼ cup (2 fl oz)	frying oil

Seasoning A:

½ teaspoon	salt
1½ teaspoons	sugar
½ teaspoon	m.s.g. (optional)
¼ teaspoon	white pepper
1 tablespoon	water
2 teaspoons	dark soy sauce
2 teaspoons	rice wine or dry sherry
1 tablespoon	vegetable oil
2 teaspoons	cornflour (cornstarch)

Seasoning B/Sauce:

2 tablespoons	chicken stock
1½ teaspoons	dark soy sauce
1 tablespoon	light soy sauce
1 tablespoon	rice wine or dry sherry
½ teaspoon	salt
1 teaspoon	sugar
½ teaspoon	cornflour (cornstarch)
2 tablespoons	oyster sauce

Partially freeze the beef and cut into very thin slices, then into narrow strips. Place in a dish with the seasoning A ingredients, mix well and leave for 45 minutes to marinate.

Wash the cabbage and cut into 5 cm (2 in) pieces. Simmer in lightly salted water for 3 minutes and drain well. Drain the mushrooms, remove the stems and simmer the mushroom caps in a little chicken stock or water for 10 minutes, adding a dash each of salt, sugar, and pepper. Remove from the heat and leave in the liquid until needed.

Heat the frying oil in a wok and stir-fry the beef on very high heat until it changes colour. Remove. Add the cabbage and stir-fry briefly, then add the drained mushrooms and the pre-mixed seasoning B/sauce ingredients except the oyster sauce. Simmer until thickened.

Return the beef and stir in the oyster sauce. Heat through and serve.

STIR-FRIED BEEF WITH YOUNG GINGER AND PINEAPPLE

250 g (8 oz)	beef fillet (tenderloin)
45 g (1½ oz)	canned pineapple pieces, drained
2 cm (¾ in) piece	fresh young ginger*
1	spring onion (scallion), trimmed and sliced
¼ cup (2 fl oz)	frying oil
2 teaspoons	rice wine or dry sherry

Seasoning A:

1	egg white, beaten
½ teaspoon	salt
2 teaspoons	vegetable oil
2 teaspoons	cornflour (cornstarch)

Seasoning B/Sauce:

2 tablespoons	chicken stock
1 tablespoon	light soy sauce
⅓ teaspoon	salt
½ teaspoon	sugar
½ teaspoon	cornflour (cornstarch)

Partially freeze the beef and cut across the grain into paper-thin slices, then cut into strips about 2.5 × 5 cm (1 × 2 in). Place in a dish with the seasoning A ingredients and leave to marinate for 20 minutes.

Cut each of the pineapple pieces in halves. Peel and very thinly slice the ginger. Heat the frying oil in a wok and stir-fry the spring onion and ginger for 1 minute, then push to one side of the pan and add the beef. Stir-fry until it changes colour, then sizzle in the wine and add the pre-mixed seasoning B/sauce ingredients. Simmer for 1 minute, then add the pineapple and heat through.

Transfer to a serving plate.

*For a milder taste, blanch the sliced ginger before use.

STIR-FRIED BEEF WITH GREEN AND RED PEPPERS

185 g (6 oz)	beef fillet (tenderloin)
1	medium green capsicum (bell pepper)
1 — 2	fresh red chilli peppers
⅓ cup	frying oil
1	large spring onion (scallion), trimmed and sliced
1½ teaspoons	finely chopped fresh ginger
1½ teaspoons	finely chopped garlic
1 tablespoon	fermented black beans, or use hot black bean sauce
1½ teaspoons	rice wine or dry sherry

Seasoning A:

¼ teaspoon	m.s.g. (optional)
1 tablespoon	light soy sauce
2 teaspoons	rice wine or dry sherry
1 tablespoon	frying oil
1 tablespoon	cold water
2 teaspoons	cornflour (cornstarch)

Seasoning B/Sauce:

¼ cup (2 fl oz)	chicken stock or water
½ teaspoon	sesame oil
½ teaspoon	salt
¼ teaspoon	m.s.g. (optional)
½ teaspoon	sugar
¼ teaspoon	ground black pepper
1 teaspoon	cornflour (cornstarch)

Partially freeze the beef then cut into paper-thin slices across the grain and into fine shreds. Place the beef shreds in a dish with the seasoning A ingredients, mix well and leave for 25 minutes. Cut open the green pepper and red chillies and remove the stems, seed-cores, and inner white ribs. Cut into shreds.

Heat the frying oil and stir-fry the beef until it changes colour, then remove from the oil and keep warm. Add the onion, ginger, and garlic to the pan and stir-fry for 45 seconds. Push to one side of the pan and add the capsicum and chilli peppers. Stir-fry until softened, splashing in about 1½ tablespoons of cold water to soften the peppers. When the liquid dries up, add the chopped black beans or black bean sauce and fry briefly, then return the meat and sizzle the wine onto the sides of the pan and stir in.

Add the pre-mixed seasoning B/sauce ingredients and stir on high heat until thickened. Transfer to a serving plate.

Any combination of vegetables could replace the capsicum and chilli peppers, such as shredded carrots and celery, diced water chestnuts, soaked 'wood ear' fungus, green peas, sliced Chinese green vegetables, or onions.

RAINBOW BEEF IN LETTUCE LEAVES

155 g (5 oz)	beef fillet (tenderloin)
60 g (2 oz)	canned bamboo shoots, drained
60 g (2 oz)	fresh celery
1	small carrot
1	small green capsicum (bell pepper)
1	fresh red chilli pepper
3	dried black mushrooms, soaked for 25 minutes
45 g (1½ oz)	rice vermicelli
6 cups (1½ litres)	deep-frying oil
12	fresh lettuce leaf cups

Seasoning:

¼ teaspoon	salt
½ teaspoon	sugar
1 teaspoon	light soy sauce
1 teaspoon	rice wine or dry sherry
1½ teaspoons	vegetable oil
1 tablespoon	cold water
1 teaspoon	cornflour (cornstarch)

Thinly slice the beef, then cut into fine shreds. Place in a dish with the seasoning ingredients, mix well and leave for 1 hour. Cut the vegetables into fine shreds.

Heat the deep-frying oil to smoking point. Break the rice vermicelli into small pieces and place in a frying basket. Deep-fry for about 20 seconds until it expands and turns crisp. Drain and place on a serving plate.

Pour off all but 2½ tablespoons of the oil and fry the meat until it changes colour, then push to one side of the wok and add the shredded vegetables. Stir-fry until softened but retaining crispness, about 2 minutes, then stir in the beef and spoon onto the rice vermicelli.

Wash the lettuce leaves and place on a serving plate. Serve with the beef. To eat, spoon a portion of the meat, vegetables, and noodles into the lettuce leaf and roll up. Hoisin or plum sauce can be served as a dip.

BEEF *FU YUNG*

90 g (3 oz)	beef fillet (tenderloin)
4	eggs, beaten
2	egg whites, well beaten
2 teaspoons	cornflour (cornstarch)
1 tablespoon	water
¼ teaspoon	salt
2	spring onions (scallions), trimmed and shredded
1 slice	fresh ginger, shredded
1 teaspoon	sesame oil
2 tablespoons	frying oil

Seasoning A:

⅓ teaspoon	salt
¼ teaspoon	m.s.g. (optional)
2 teaspoons	light soy sauce
1 teaspoon	rice wine or dry sherry
1½ teaspoons	cornflour (cornstarch)

Seasoning B/Sauce:

¼ cup (2 fl oz)	chicken stock
2 teaspoons	light soy sauce
1 tablespoon	oyster sauce
1 teaspoon	rice wine or dry sherry
⅓ teaspoon	sugar
1 tablespoon	frying oil
½ teaspoon	cornflour (cornstarch)

Partially freeze the beef, cut into very thin slices across the grain, then into long thin shreds. Mix with the seasoning A ingredients and leave for 15 minutes to marinate.

Mix the eggs, egg whites, cornflour, water, and salt together, beat for 1 minute, then set aside.

Heat the sesame oil and frying oil together in a wok and sauté the spring onions and ginger for 30 seconds. Push to one side of the pan and add the shredded beef. Sauté on high heat until the meat changes colour, then reduce the heat to moderate.

Pour in the egg mixture and cook until the underside is lightly coloured and firm. Cut into quarters and turn each piece. Cook until the omelette is just done right through. Do not allow to dry out. Transfer to a warmed serving plate and keep warm.

Wipe out the wok and add the pre-mixed seasoning B/sauce ingredients. Bring to the boil and simmer until thickened. Pour over the omelette and serve immediately.

STEAMED BEEF MEATBALLS AND SPINACH ON RICE

1¼ cups	raw short grain white rice
375 g (12 oz)	lean beef, finely minced (ground)
60 g (2 oz)	pork fat, coarsely minced (ground)
2 tablespoons	finely chopped spring onion (scallion)
1¼ teaspoons	finely chopped fresh ginger
60 g (2 oz)	canned water chestnuts or bamboo shoots, finely diced
250 g (8 oz)	fresh spinach leaves (collard greens)

Seasoning:

1¼ teaspoons	salt
½ teaspoon	sugar
1 tablespoon	light soy sauce
2 tablespoons	cold water
1 tablespoon	frying oil
2 teaspoons	cornflour (cornstarch)

Soak the rice in cold water. Mix the beef and pork fat together and add the seasoning ingredients. Knead into a smooth paste and leave for at least 1 hour, then add the remaining ingredients, except the spinach.

Drain the rice and pour into a saucepan. Add 1 teaspoon salt and water to cover by 2.5 cm (1 in). Cook, covered, until the water level recedes below the rice, then arrange well-washed spinach leaves on top.

Form the meat paste into large meatballs and place on the spinach leaves. Continue to cook on very low heat until the rice is tender and fluffy and the meatballs cooked through, about 12 minutes.

Transfer the meatballs and vegetables to one serving plate. Stir up the rice and serve into rice bowls or a separate serving plate and serve with the meatballs.

SAUTÉD SHREDDED LAMB ON RICE NOODLES

185 g (6 oz)	lean lamb*
5 cups (1¼ litres)	deep-frying oil
45 g (1½ oz)	rice vermicelli, broken
45 g (1½ oz)	canned champignons, drained and sliced
30 g (1 oz)	canned bamboo shoots, drained and shredded
1	medium green capsicum (bell pepper), trimmed and shredded

Seasoning A:

1	egg white, beaten
½ teaspoon	salt
½ teaspoon	bicarbonate of soda (optional)
1 tablespoon	light soy sauce
2 teaspoons	rice wine or dry sherry
1½ tablespoons	finely chopped spring onion (scallion)
1 teaspoon	grated fresh ginger
1 teaspoon	cornflour (cornstarch)

Seasoning B/Sauce:

½ cup (4 fl oz)	chicken stock
1 tablespoon	light soy sauce
1 teaspoon	rice wine or dry sherry
⅓ teaspoon	salt
	pinch of white pepper
¼ teaspoon	sugar
¾ teaspoon	cornflour (cornstarch)

Partially freeze the lamb and cut into thin slices, then into fine shreds. Place in a dish and add the seasoning A ingredients, mix well and leave to marinate for 20 minutes.

Heat the deep-frying oil to smoking point and fry the broken rice vermicelli in a frying basket until it expands into a cloud of crisp white noodles, about 20 seconds. Drain well and place on a serving plate. Pour off all but 3 tablespoons of the oil.

Reheat the wok and sauté the shredded lamb until it changes colour, push to one side of the pan and sauté the shredded vegetables for 2 minutes, then mix in the lamb and add the seasoning B/sauce ingredients, pre-mixed, and simmer until thickened. Pour over the noodles and serve at once.

*Lean pork, beef fillet (tenderloin), or chicken breast can replace the lamb in this dish.

LETTUCE WITH OYSTER SAUCE

1	large fresh lettuce
1½ tablespoons	frying oil
½ teaspoon	salt
2½ tablespoons	oyster sauce*

Thoroughly wash the lettuce and separate the leaves. Bring a large saucepan of water to the boil and add the oil and salt. Add the lettuce and simmer until tender, about 1½ minutes. Drain well and arrange on a serving plate.

Pour the oyster sauce evenly over the lettuce and serve at once.

* Use a good quality oyster sauce, as the less expensive brands do not have the same rich flavour.

Rainbow Beef in Lettuce Leaves (recipe page 298).

CANTONESE BEEF STEAKS

500 g (1 lb)	beef fillet (tenderloin)
2	spring onions (scallions), trimmed and shredded
2 slices	fresh ginger, shredded
2 — 3 cloves	garlic, thinly sliced
1/3 cup	frying oil

Seasoning A:

1/2 teaspoon	salt
1/2 teaspoon	m.s.g. (optional)
1/4 teaspoon	bicarbonate of soda (optional)
1/2 teaspoon	sugar
1 teaspoon	dark soy sauce
2 teaspoons	rice wine or dry sherry
1 tablespoon	cold water
2 teaspoons	cornflour (cornstarch)

Seasoning B/Sauce:

1/3 cup	chicken stock
2 teaspoons	dark soy sauce
2 teaspoons	light soy sauce
2 teaspoons	Worcestershire sauce
1 tablespoon	barbecue sauce or soybean paste
1 tablespoon	tomato sauce (ketchup)
2 teaspoons	rice wine or dry sherry
2 teaspoons	sugar
1 teaspoon	cornflour (cornstarch)
1/4 teaspoon	salt
1/4 teaspoon	white pepper

Chill the meat, then cut into thin steaks across the grain. Place in a dish and add the pre-mixed Seasoning A ingredients. Rub into the meat and leave for 10 minutes, then turn and marinate for a further 10 minutes.

Heat the oil in a wok and sauté the spring onions, ginger, and garlic for 1½ minutes. Remove. Add the meat and fry on high heat until lightly coloured on both sides. Turn only once and do not overcook. Push to one side of the pan and return the onion, ginger, and garlic and add the pre-mixed seasoning B/sauce ingredients.

Bring to the boil, then simmer until thickened, stirring the beef into the sauce. Transfer to a warmed serving plate and garnish with fresh coriander. Serve at once

STIR-FRIED FROGS' LEGS

500 g (1 lb)	frogs' legs
	cornflour (cornstarch)
5 cups (1¼ litres)	deep-frying oil
1	spring onion (scallion), trimmed and sliced
2 slices	fresh ginger, shredded
2 cloves	garlic, thinly sliced
45 g (1½ oz)	canned bamboo shoots, drained and thinly sliced
1	small carrot, parboiled and thinly sliced
1	small green capsicum (bell pepper), cut into small squares
1 tablespoon	rice wine or dry sherry

Seasoning/Sauce:

1 tablespoon	light soy sauce
2 teaspoons	oyster sauce
1/2 teaspoon	salt
1/2 teaspoon	m.s.g. (optional)
1/4 teaspoon	ground black pepper
1/2 teaspoon	sugar
1 teaspoon	sesame oil

Wash the frogs' legs and divide at the central joint. Coat thickly with cornflour and deep-fry in the smoking hot deep-frying oil for 30 seconds. Remove and drain well.

Pour off all but 2 tablespoons of the oil and stir-fry the spring onions, ginger, and garlic for 45 seconds. Push to one side of the pan and add the prepared vegetables. Stir-fry for 1½ minutes, then return the frogs' legs to the pan and stir-fry briefly. Sizzle the wine onto the sides of the pan and add the pre-mixed seasoning/sauce ingredients.

Simmer for 30 seconds, then transfer to a warmed serving plate.

LAMB WITH BEAN SPROUTS IN A CRISP POTATO BASKET

185 g (6 oz)	lean lamb
2	medium potatoes
8 cups (2 litres)	deep-frying oil
125 g (4 oz)	fresh bean sprouts
2	spring onions (scallions), trimmed shredded
2 slices	fresh ginger, shredded
1½ teaspoons	rice wine or dry sherry

Seasoning A:

1	egg white, beaten
½ teaspoon	salt
½ teaspoon	m.s.g. (optional)
¾ teaspoon	sugar
1 tablespoon	cornflour (cornstarch)
1½ tablespoons	sesame oil

Seasoning B/Sauce:

¼ cup (2 fl oz)	chicken stock
⅓ teaspoon	salt
¼ teaspoon	m.s.g. (optional)
½ teaspoon	sugar
¾ teaspoon	cornflour (cornstarch)

Special Equipment: Two wire strainers, one slightly larger than the other.

Partially freeze the lamb and cut into very thin slices, then into strips about 5 × 2.5 cm (2 × 1 in). Mix with the seasoning A ingredients, except the sesame oil, and leave for 10 minutes, then add the sesame oil, mix well and leave a further 15 minutes.

Peel the potatoes and cut into very fine strings. Soak in cold water for 10 minutes, drain and dry in a kitchen towel, then dust lightly with cornflour and spread in a layer inside the larger strainer.

Heat the deep-frying oil to smoking point and decrease the heat slightly. Press the smaller strainer inside the larger one, over the shredded potato to force into a nest shape. Hold the two handles firmly together, then lower the strainers into the hot oil. Fry until the potato basket is crisp and golden. Remove and drain well, then remove the smaller strainer and upturn the larger one onto a piece of absorbent paper. Tap the top until the basket dislodges and leave to drain, upside down.

Drain off all but 3 tablespoons of the oil and sauté the lamb on high heat for 1 minute. Remove. Reheat the pan and fry the bean sprouts until beginning to soften, push to one side of the pan and add the spring onions and ginger, frying until softened, then mix with the bean sprouts and return the lamb. Sizzle the wine onto the sides of the pan and stir in, then add the pre-mixed seasoning B/sauce ingredients and heat to boiling. Stir for a few seconds.

Upturn the basket onto a serving plate and surround with shredded lettuce, fresh parsley, or coriander sprigs and pour the lamb and sprouts into the basket. Serve at once. The basket can be eaten with the dish.

SAUTÉD SNAILS WITH GARLIC

280 g (9 oz)	fresh or canned snails
2 tablespoons	softened lard or frying oil
2	spring onions (scallions), trimmed and diced
2 slices	fresh ginger, shredded
8 cloves	garlic, sliced

Seasoning A:

½ teaspoon	salt
¼ teaspoon	white pepper
1 teaspoon	bicarbonate of soda (optional)
1 tablespoon	rice wine or dry sherry
2 tablespoons	frying oil
1 tablespoon	cold water

Seasoning B/Sauce:

½ cup (4 fl oz)	chicken stock
½ teaspoon	salt
¼ teaspoon	m.s.g. (optional)
¼ teaspoon	white pepper
½ teaspoon	sugar
1 teaspoon	cornflour (cornstarch)

Thoroughly wash fresh snails or drain the canned snails. Cut larger ones in halves. Place in a dish with the seasoning A ingredients, omitting the bicarbonate of soda if using canned snails. Leave for 2 hours. Rinse fresh snails lightly in cold water.

Heat the lard or oil and sauté the spring onions, ginger, and garlic until softened. Add the snails and sauté for 2 minutes, then pour in the pre-mixed seasoning B/sauce ingredients and simmer until thickened.

Transfer to a serving plate.

DICED RABBIT SAUTÉD WITH BELL PEPPERS

375 g (12 oz)	meaty rabbit pieces, preferably thighs
1	medium green capsicum (bell pepper)
2	spring onions (scallions), trimmed and diced
1 teaspoon	finely chopped fresh ginger
1½ teaspoons	chopped garlic
⅓ cup	frying oil

Seasoning A:

1	egg white, beaten
½ teaspoon	salt
½ teaspoon	m.s.g. (optional)
2 teaspoons	rice wine or dry sherry
1 teaspoon	cornflour (cornstarch)

Seasoning B/Sauce:

⅓ cup	chicken stock
2 tablespoons	light soy sauce
¼ teaspoon	salt
1 teaspoon	sugar
½ teaspoon	m.s.g. (optional)
½ teaspoon	cornflour (cornstarch)

Cube the rabbit meat, discarding the bones if preferred. Place in a dish, add the seasoning A ingredients and mix well. Leave for 25 minutes.

Cut the pepper in halves, remove the stem, seed-core, and inner white ribs, and cut into squares about the same size as the rabbit.

Heat the oil in a wok and sauté the spring onions, ginger, and garlic for 45 seconds, then push to one side of the pan and add the rabbit. Sauté on moderately high heat until it changes colour, about 3 minutes, then remove. Reheat the pan and add the peppers and splash in a very little water. Cook until softened, then return the rabbit and add the pre-mixed seasoning B/sauce ingredients and simmer until thickened and the rabbit is tender.

Transfer to a warmed serving plate.

SLICED QUAIL SAUTÉD WITH BAMBOO SHOOTS

155 g (5 oz)	quail meat*
60 g (2 oz)	canned bamboo shoots, drained and sliced
30 g (1 oz)	canned straw mushrooms, drained and sliced
2½ tablespoons	softened lard or frying oil
1	spring onion (scallion), trimmed and diced
1 slice	fresh ginger, shredded
2 teaspoons	rice wine or dry sherry

Seasoning A:

1	egg white, beaten
¼ teaspoon	salt
½ teaspoon	m.s.g. (optional)
1 teaspoon	cornflour (cornstarch)

Seasoning B/Sauce:

2 tablespoons	chicken stock or water
2 tablespoons	light soy sauce
¼ teaspoon	salt
¼ teaspoon	ground black pepper
½ teaspoon	m.s.g. (optional)
¾ teaspoon	cornflour (cornstarch)

Slice the quail meat and place in a dish with the seasoning A ingredients. Leave for 20 minutes. Blanch the bamboo shoots and mushrooms in boiling water for 30 seconds, then drain well.

Heat the lard or oil in a wok and sauté the quail meat until lightly coloured. Remove and keep warm. Add the spring onion and ginger and sauté for 30 seconds, then add the sliced bamboo shoots and mushrooms and sauté for a further 30 seconds. Sizzle the wine onto the sides of the pan, return the quail meat and stir-fry until tender.

Add the pre-mixed seasoning B/sauce ingredients and simmer until the sauce thickens. Serve.

*Use quail on the bone, if preferred, or sliced pheasant breast or pigeon as an alternative.

Steamed Broccoli with Crabmeat Sauce (recipe page 314).

DEEP-FRIED RICE BIRDS SERVED WITH QUAIL EGGS AND SLICED QUAIL IN A NOODLE NEST

6	rice birds*
125 g (4 oz)	quail meat**
6	canned quail eggs, drained
¾ cup (6 fl oz)	chicken stock
125 g (4 oz)	beancurd noodles, or use 45 g (1½ oz) rice vermicelli or bean thread vermicelli
6 cups (1½ litres)	deep-frying oil
30 g (1 oz)	canned bamboo shoots, drained and diced
3	dried black mushrooms, soaked to soften and diced
2 tablespoons	finely chopped spring onion (scallion)
½ teaspoon	finely chopped fresh ginger

Seasoning A:

½ teaspoon	salt
1 tablespoon	rice wine or dry sherry
1 teaspoon	sesame oil (optional)
1 tablespoon	finely chopped spring onion (scallion)
1 teaspoon	finely chopped fresh ginger
¼ teaspoon	crushed garlic

Seasoning B:

¼ teaspoon	salt
¼ teaspoon	m.s.g. (optional)
1 teaspoon	light soy sauce
1 teaspoon	rice wine or dry sherry
1 teaspoon	cornflour (cornstarch)

Seasoning C/Sauce:

¼ cup (2 fl oz)	chicken stock
1 tablespoon	light soy sauce
2 teaspoons	rice wine or dry sherry
½ teaspoon	sesame oil (optional)
⅓ — ½ teaspoon	chilli oil (optional)
¼ teaspoon	salt
¼ teaspoon	m.s.g. (optional)
¼ teaspoon	sugar
½ teaspoon	cornflour (cornstarch)

Special Equipment: Two wire strainers, one slightly larger than the other.

Wash the rice birds and place in a dish with the seasoning A ingredients. Leave to marinate for 30 minutes. Slice the quail meat and mix with the seasoning B ingredients and leave for 20 minutes.

Simmer the quail eggs in the chicken stock for 10 minutes, then remove from the heat and leave in the stock. Heat the deep-frying oil to fairly hot. Dust the beancurd noodles lightly with cornflour and spread around the inside of the larger strainer. Press the smaller one inside, forcing the noodles into a nest shape. Hold the two handles firmly together and lower into the hot oil. Deep-fry until the noodles are crisp and dry, about 3 minutes. Decrease the heat slightly after the first 30 seconds. Remove and upturn onto absorbent paper. Leave to dry.

Reheat the deep-frying oil and fry the rice birds until crisp and golden, about 3½ minutes. Place the drained nest on a serving plate on a bed of finely shredded lettuce. Set the fried rice birds around it.

Reheat the deep-frying oil and fry the drained eggs until golden. Remove. Pour off all but 2 tablespoons of the oil and stir-fry the bamboo shoots, mushrooms, spring onion and ginger on fairly high heat for 1½ minutes. Push to one side of the pan and add the sliced quail. Stir-fry until just cooked through, then mix with the diced ingredients and return the eggs.

Pour in the pre-mixed seasoning C/sauce ingredients and simmer until the sauce thickens. Spoon into the nest and serve at once.

*A type of sparrow. Substitute small chicken drumsticks.
**Use sliced pigeon or chicken breast meat as an alternative.

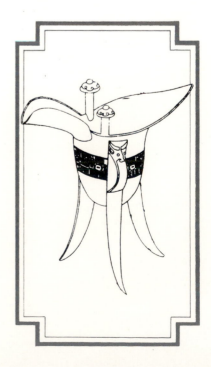

BEANCURD CAKES WITH FRESH CORIANDER AND SOY SAUCE

6 squares	soft beancurd
1 large bunch	fresh coriander

Sauce:

2 tablespoons	light soy sauce
1 tablespoon	dark soy sauce
1½ tablespoons	vegetable oil
1 tablespoon	water
1 — 2 teas-poons	sesame oil
¼ teaspoon	m.s.g. (optional)
1½ teaspoons	sugar

Separately wrap each square of beancurd in a piece of clean muslin or cheesecloth. Place in a dish and set on a rack in a steamer. Steam over rapidly boiling water for 15 minutes, then remove from the heat. Unwrap and place on a serving plate. Garnish with the well-washed fresh coriander.

Mix the sauce ingredients together in a wok and bring to the boil. Pour over the beancurd and serve at once.

CANTONESE STUFFED BEANCURD

3 squares	soft beancurd
1 teaspoon	salt
90 g (3 oz)	raw peeled shrimp or white fish
50 g (2 oz)	fatty pork
1 tablespoon	dried shrimp, soaked for 1 hour
1 cup (8 fl oz)	frying oil
	cornflour (cornstarch)
⅓ cup	chicken stock
¼ cup (2 fl oz)	oyster sauce

Seasoning:

1	egg white, beaten
1 tablespoon	very finely chopped spring onion (scallion)
⅓ teaspoon	grated fresh ginger (optional)
¼ teaspoon	salt
¼ teaspoon	sugar
¼ teaspoon	ground black pepper
½ teaspoon	sesame oil (optional)

Place the beancurd in a saucepan and add the salt. Cover with cold water and bring to the boil. Simmer for 1 minute, then drain. Leave for about 15 minutes to firm up, then cut each square into four triangular shaped pieces.

Pulverise the shrimp or fish and fatty pork in a food processor. Finely chop the drained, soaked shrimps and mix with the pork mixture, adding the seasoning ingredients. Make a slit in the widest side of each beancurd triangle, dust lightly with cornflour and stuff with a teaspoon of the mixture.

Heat the frying oil in a large frying pan and add the beancurd. Cook on moderate heat, carefully turning once or twice until evenly cooked and golden. Add the chicken stock and increase the heat. Simmer until the liquid is absorbed, then transfer to a serving plate and pour on the oyster sauce.

Fresh *bok choy* or *choy sum* quickly simmered in salted water are a good accompaniment to this dish and add colour when placed around the beancurd on the serving plate.

BEANCURD STIR-FRIED WITH CRABMEAT

4 squares	soft beancurd
185 g (6 oz)	fresh crabmeat
1	spring onion (scallion), trimmed and shredded
⅓ cup	frying oil
2	egg whites, well beaten

Seasoning A:

¼ teaspoon	salt
1 teaspoon	ginger wine (see page 387)
⅓ teaspoon	sugar

Seasoning B/Sauce:

⅓ cup	chicken stock
2 teaspoons	light soy sauce
¾ teaspoon	salt
¼ teaspoon	ground black pepper
¾ teaspoon	cornflour (cornstarch)

Soak the beancurd in cold water for 20 minutes, then drain and cut into cubes. Cut the crabmeat into small pieces and mix with the seasoning A ingredients. Heat the frying oil in a wok and sauté the spring onion briefly, then add the beancurd and stir-fry on high heat until lightly coloured. Remove and keep warm.

Reheat the wok and stir-fry the crabmeat for 1½ minutes, then add the pre-mixed seasoning B/sauce ingredients and simmer for a further 1½ minutes. Remove from the heat and slowly drizzle in the beaten egg. Leave to set into strands in the sauce, then return to the heat and add the beancurd.

Heat through, mixing together, then spoon onto a serving plate.

BRAISED BEANCURD WITH SHRIMPS

3 squares	soft beancurd
2	whole eggs, well beaten
	flour
1 cup (8 fl oz)	frying oil
2 tablespoons	finely chopped spring onion (scallion)
2 teaspoons	finely chopped fresh ginger
½ teaspoon	finely chopped garlic
90 g (3 oz)	raw peeled shrimps, deveined

Seasoning/Sauce:

½ cup (4 fl oz)	chicken stock
1 tablespoon	light soy sauce
2 teaspoons	rice wine or dry sherry
1½ teaspoons	sesame oil (optional)
1 teaspoon	salt
½ teaspoon	sugar
¼ teaspoon	ground black pepper
½ teaspoon	cornflour (cornstarch)

Cut the beancurd in halves horizontally, then cut each piece into quarters. Dip into beaten egg, then coat lightly with the flour. Heat the oil to smoking point and fry the beancurd until golden. Drain and keep warm.

Pour off all but 2½ tablespoons of the oil and sauté the onion, ginger and garlic for 45 seconds, then push to one side of the pan and add the shrimps. Stir-fry until pink, about 1 minute, then mix with the onion and return the beancurd. Prick each piece with a fork several times to allow the seasonings to penetrate.

Pour on the pre-mixed seasoning/sauce ingredients and bring to the boil. Reduce the heat and simmer for about 3 minutes until the sauce is almost completely absorbed. Serve at once.

Three Kinds of Mushrooms (recipe page 315

MIXED VEGETABLE PLATTER

1	medium carrot
1	medium white onion
6	dried black mushrooms, soaked for 25 minutes
6	canned water chestnuts, drained
6	canned champignons, drained
6	canned baby corn cobs, drained
250 g (8 oz)	fresh lettuce or Chinese (celery) cabbage
⅓ cup	frying oil

Seasoning/Sauce:

2/3 cup	chicken stock
¾ teaspoon	salt
⅓ teaspoon	chicken stock powder (optional)
¾ teaspoon	sugar
1¼ teaspoons	cornflour (cornstarch)

Peel the carrot, thinly slice lengthwise, then cut into rectangular pieces. Peel the onion, cut in halves from stem to root, then cut into thick slices from stem to root and trim away the root section to allow the pieces to separate. Squeeze the water from the mushrooms and remove the stems. Slice the water chestnuts and champignons in halves horizontally. Cut the baby corn in halves. Thoroughly wash the lettuce or cabbage, separating the leaves.

Parboil the carrot and drain well. Blanch the onion for 20 seconds and drain well. Heat the frying oil in a wok and stir-fry the carrot and onions for 30 seconds. Push to one side of the pan and add the mushrooms, water chestnuts and champignons and stir-fry together for 1 minute, then add the corn and mix the vegetables together. Stir-fry on high heat for a further 30 seconds, then add the pre-mixed seasoning/sauce ingredients and simmer until the sauce thickens.

In the meantime, heat a saucepan of water to boiling and add 1 tablespoon of frying oil and a dash of salt. Add the lettuce or cabbage and simmer until tender. Lettuce needs only about 45 seconds, the cabbage a little longer. Drain well and arrange on a serving plate. Spoon the vegetables on top and serve at once.

SAUTÉD CHINESE SPINACH WITH SHRIMP SAUCE

500 g (1 lb)	fresh Chinese spinach*
1	spring onion (scallion), trimmed and shredded
2 cloves	garlic, chopped
½ cup (2 fl oz)	frying oil
2 teaspoons	Chinese shrimp sauce**
¼ cup (2 fl oz)	chicken stock
½ teaspoon	cornflour (cornstarch)

Thoroughly wash the vegetables and cut into 7.5 cm (3 in) lengths. Heat the frying oil and sauté the spring onion and garlic briefly, then add the spinach and sauté on moderate heat until tender. Stir in the shrimp sauce (use more or less, to taste) and sauté briefly, then add the chicken stock mixed with cornflour and simmer until the sauce thickens.

Transfer to a serving plate and serve at once.

* A green leafy vegetable with narrow white stems similar to *bok choy,* which can be used as a substitute.

** A pale pink pungent sauce made by grinding and salting fresh shrimps, sun-drying, then storing in vats until fermented. If unobtainable, use anchovy sauce or essence.

CHINESE CABBAGE WITH MINCED SHRIMP DRESSING

625 g (1¼ lb)	fresh Chinese (celery) cabbage
75 g (2½ oz)	raw peeled shrimps
2	egg whites, beaten
¼ cup (2 fl oz)	cold water
1 teaspoon	cornflour (cornstarch)
	pinch of salt
⅓ cup	softened lard or frying oil

Seasoning A:

¼ cup (2 fl oz)	chicken stock
¾ teaspoon	salt
½ teaspoon	m.s.g. (optional)
¼ teaspoon	sugar
	pinch of white pepper

Seasoning B/Sauce:

½ cup (4 fl oz)	chicken stock
1 teaspoon	salt
½ teaspoon	m.s.g. (optional)
¼ teaspoon	white pepper
½ teaspoon	cornflour (cornstarch)

Wash the cabbage well, discard the outer leaves and cut lengthwise into quarters, or into smaller pieces if the head is large. Blanch in boiling water for 1 minute, then drain well.

Pulverise the shrimps in a food processor or by batting with the side of a cleaver blade. Mix with the egg whites, cold water, cornflour, and salt.

Sauté the cabbage in half the lard or frying oil for 2 minutes on moderate heat, then add the seasoning A ingredients and simmer until the liquid has evaporated. Remove from the pan and arrange on a serving plate.

Add the remaining lard or oil to the pan and sauté the shrimp paste until it turns white, about 1 minute on moderate heat. Add the pre-mixed seasoning B/sauce ingredients and bring to the boil. Simmer until thickened, then pour over the cabbage and serve.

FRESH CELERY WITH CREAMY MUSTARD SAUCE

3 stalks	fresh celery
½ teaspoon	salt

Sauce:

½ cup (4 fl oz)	chicken stock or water
1 tablespoon	evaporated milk
2 tablespoons	vegetable oil
1—1½ teaspoons	hot mustard powder
½ teaspoon	salt
½ teaspoon	sugar
1¼ teaspoons	cornflour (cornstarch)

String the celery and cut into pieces about 4 cm (1 2/3 in) long, then cut each piece lengthwise into two or three sticks. Blanch in boiling water with the salt added, for 1 minute, then drain and refresh with cold water. Drain again and arrange on a serving plate.

Pour the pre-mixed sauce ingredients into a wok and bring to the boil. Simmer until thickened, then pour over the vegetables and serve at once.

SAUTÉD FRESH *CHOY SUM*

625 g (1¼ lb)	fresh young choy sum*
2 tablespoons	frying oil
2 tablespoons	rendered chicken fat (chicken grease) or lard
¾ teaspoon	salt
⅓ teaspoon	m.s.g. (optional)
½ teaspoon	sugar
1½ teaspoons	rice wine or dry sherry

Trim off any wilted leaves and cut the *choy sum* into 5 cm (2 in) pieces. Peel the thick skin from the lower section of the stems, if preferred. Simmer in boiling water for 2 minutes, then drain.

Heat the frying oil and chicken fat or lard in a wok and add the salt, m.s.g., and sugar. Sauté the vegetables on moderate heat for 2 minutes or until tender, then sizzle the wine onto the sides of the pan, stir in and serve.

* Or use any fresh seasonal green vegetables.

STEWED WINTER MELON BALLS WITH SCALLOP SAUCE

6	dried scallops (about 45 g / 1½ oz), soaked for 1 hour
½ cup (4 fl oz)	chicken stock
1 thick slice	fresh ginger
700 g (1 ⅓ lb)	fresh winter melon* cornflour (cornstarch)

Seasoning/Sauce:

1¼ cups (10 fl oz)	chicken stock
1 tablespoon	rendered chicken fat (chicken grease) or lard
2 teaspoons	rice wine or dry sherry
1¼ teaspoons	salt
1½ teaspoons	sugar
¾ teaspoon	m.s.g. (optional)

Place the drained scallops in a dish and add the chicken stock and ginger slice. Steam until tender, about 45 minutes, then remove scallops from the stock and shred by rubbing between forefinger and thumb. Return to the stock and set aside.

Peel the melon and remove the seeds. Cut into 2.5 cm (1 in) cubes or make into balls with a melon baller. Cover with boiling, slightly salted water and simmer for 20 minutes. Drain well.

Bring the seasoning/sauce ingredients to the boil and add the drained melon. Cover and simmer on low heat until the melon is completely tender, then transfer to a serving plate with a slotted spoon.

Bring the sauce back to the boil, add the drained scallops and simmer until reduced to about ¾ cup. Thicken with a thin paste of cornflour and cold water and simmer for 1 minute, then pour over the melon and serve.

Turnips can be cooked in exactly the same way as the melon. If using canned winter melon or cucumber, omit the initial simmering and simply braise in the sauce until tender.

* Or use about 625 g (1¼ lb) canned winter melon or fresh sweet white turnips or cucumbers.

STEAMED WINTER MELON FILLED WITH VEGETABLES

1 1¼ kg (2½ lb)	winter melon, or use a large pumpkin
60 g (2 oz)	canned bamboo shoots, drained and cubed
60 g (2 oz)	canned straw mushrooms, drained and sliced
60 g (2 oz)	canned lotus root, drained and cubed
1	medium carrot, parboiled and cubed
60 g (2 oz)	canned champignons, drained and halved
30 g (1 oz)	canned gingko or white nuts, drained (optional)
12	green vegetable hearts, trimmed and washed
2 tablespoons	chopped cooked ham
1 tablespoon	rendered chicken fat (chicken grease) or lard

Seasoning:

2 cups (16 fl oz)	chicken stock
2 tablespoons	oyster or light soy sauce
2 teaspoons	rice wine or dry sherry
1¼ teaspoons	salt
½ teaspoon	m.s.g. (optional)
¾ teaspoon	sugar

Wash the winter melon, peel off the skin very thinly so that the outside remains a bright green. Cut a section from the top and scoop out the seeds and pith. If using a pumpkin, do not peel until after it is cooked.

Fill with boiling lightly salted water and add 1 tablespoon of vegetable oil. Set in a dish and place on a rack in a steamer. Cover and steam over rapidly boiling water for 20 minutes. Drain and fill with the prepared vegetables, except the green vegetables. Add the seasoning ingredients and return to the steamer.

Steam again over rapidly boiling water for 25 minutes or until the melon or pumpkin is tender, but not softening too much to lose its shape. In the final 10 minutes of cooking, place the green vegetables on top of the other ingredients in the melon.

To serve, place the melon in the centre of a serving dish and surround with the green vegetables. Garnish with the chopped ham and add the chicken fat. Thicken the sauce, if preferred, by straining into a wok, bring to the boil and adding a thin paste of cornflour and cold water.

Alternatively, serve as 'Winter Melon Surprise.' Strain the liquid from the melon into a wok. Remove the green vegetables. Invert the filled melon onto a serving plate and surround with the greens. Thicken the sauce and pour over the melon. If pumpkin is served in this way, carefully peel off the skin before serving. Slice right through the top of the melon, serving a portion of the melon with the vegetables underneath.

Assorted Vegetables with Beancurd Skin (recipe page 316).

STEAMED BROCCOLI WITH CRABMEAT SAUCE

500 g (1 lb)	fresh broccoli, trimmed and cut into florets
¼ cup (2 fl oz)	frying oil
60 g (2 oz)	fresh crabmeat
1½ tablespoons	chopped spring onion
⅓ teaspoon	grated fresh ginger
2 teaspoons	rice wine or dry sherry
2	egg whites, well beaten
	chopped cooked ham (optional)

Seasoning A:

1 teaspoon	salt
½ teaspoon	m.s.g. (optional)
	pinch of white pepper
½ teaspoon	sugar
1 teaspoon	rice wine or dry sherry
¾ cup (6 fl oz)	chicken stock

Seasoning B/Sauce:

¾ cup (6 fl oz)	chicken stock
½ teaspoon	salt
½ teaspoon	m.s.g. (optional)
	pinch of white pepper
½ teaspoon	sugar
1 teaspoon	cornflour (cornstarch)

Wash the broccoli and drain well. Heat the oil in a wok and sauté the broccoli on moderate heat for 2 minutes, then remove and drain well. Transfer to a dish and add the seasoning A ingredients and steam over rapidly boiling water for 10 minutes. Remove, drain and arrange on a serving plate.

Reheat the wok and sauté the crabmeat with spring onion and ginger for 1 minute. Sizzle the wine onto the sides of the pan, then add the pre-mixed seasoning B/sauce ingredients and bring to the boil.

Remove from the heat and drizzle in the beaten egg whites, allowing to set in the sauce before stirring. Check the seasonings and pour over the broccoli. Garnish with the chopped ham, if used, and serve.

BAMBOO SHOOTS WITH MUSHROOMS AND QUAIL EGGS

6	dried black mushrooms, soaked for 25 minutes
125 g (4 oz)	canned bamboo shoots, drained and thinly sliced
½ cup (4 fl oz)	chicken stock
60 g (2 oz)	canned straw mushrooms, drained and sliced
90 g (3 oz)	canned quail eggs, drained
1	spring onion (scallion), trimmed and shredded
2 slices	fresh ginger, shredded
2 tablespoons	frying oil

Seasoning A:

⅓ teaspoon	salt
½ teaspoon	m.s.g. (optional)
⅓ teaspoon	sugar
¼ cup (2 fl oz)	chicken stock

Seasoning B/Sauce:

2/3 cup	chicken stock
2 teaspoons	light soy sauce
1 teaspoon	rice wine or dry sherry
1 teaspoon	sesame oil (optional)
½ teaspoon	sugar
2 teaspoons	cornflour (cornstarch)

Squeeze the water from the mushrooms, remove the stems and cut the caps into quarters. Mix with the seasoning A ingredients and steam for 20 minutes. Drain.

Blanch the bamboo shoots in boiling water. Drain well and soak in the chicken stock with the sliced straw mushrooms and quail eggs.

Heat the frying oil in a wok and fry the spring onion and ginger for 1 minute, then add the pre-mixed seasoning B/sauce ingredients and bring to the boil. Add the drained vegetables and eggs and simmer until the sauce thickens.

Transfer to a warmed serving plate.

BRAISED 'SNOW' FUNGUS IN CLEAR SOUP

45 g (1½ oz)	dried 'snow' fungus, soaked
210 g (7oz)	fresh pea sprouts or young spinach leaves
	chicken stock
	cornflour (cornstarch)
2 tablespoons	rendered chicken fat (chicken grease)

Seasoning:

1¼ teaspoons	salt
1½ teaspoons	sugar
¼ teaspoon	m.s.g (optional)

Prepare the dried 'snow' fungus following the directions on page 393. Drain well. Leave the root section in place and arrange, roots upward, in a dish. Cover with stock and seasonings. Set on a rack in a steamer and steam for 15 minutes. Drain off the stock and reserve. Upturn the dish onto a serving plate but do not remove the dish.

Bring the retained liquid to the boil and add the pea sprouts. Simmer briefly, then drain. Again reserve the stock. Remove the dish from the 'snow' fungus and arrange the pea sprouts around the base of the mound.

Bring the stock to the boil, adjust the seasoning and add the chicken fat. Thicken with a solution of cornflour and cold water and pour over the fungus. Serve at once.

THREE KINDS OF MUSHROOMS

6	dried black mushrooms, soaked for 25 minutes
½	fresh lettuce, well washed
½ 315 g (10 oz) can	straw mushrooms, drained
½ 315 g (10 oz) can	champignons, drained
½ cup (4 fl oz)	frying oil

Seasoning/Sauce A:

½ cup (4 fl oz)	chicken stock
2 teaspoons	rice wine or dry sherry
1 tablespoon	softened lard or frying oil
½ teaspoon	salt
¼ teaspoon	m.s.g. (optional)
½ teaspoon	sugar
1½ tablespoons	oyster sauce
1 teaspoon	cornflour (cornstarch)

Seasoning/Sauce B:

¼ cup (2 fl oz)	chicken stock
1¼ tablespoons	light soy sauce
1 teaspoon	rice wine or dry sherry
⅓ teaspoon	salt
¼ teaspoon	ground black pepper
1 teaspoon	cornflour (cornstarch)
1 tablespoon	rendered chicken fat (chicken grease)

Seasoning/Sauce C:

¼ cup (2 fl oz)	chicken stock
⅓ teaspoon	salt
¼ teaspoon	m.s.g. (optional)
¼ teaspoon	sugar
¼ teaspoon	ground black pepper
1 teaspoon	cornflour (cornstarch)
1 tablespoon	evaporated milk

Drain the black mushrooms and squeeze out the water. Remove the stems and place the mushrooms in a dish with the seasoning/sauce A ingredients, except the oyster sauce and cornflour. Steam for 25 minutes.

Dip the lettuce into boiling lightly salted water with 1 tablespoon oil added and cook for 45 seconds. Remove, drain well and arrange on a large oval serving plate.

Heat one-third of the oil and stir-fry the straw mushrooms for 1 minute, then add the seasoning/sauce B ingredients, except the chicken fat and simmer until the sauce thickens. Add the chicken fat and stir thoroughly, then transfer to one side of the serving plate.

Heat another one-third of the oil and stir-fry the champignons for 30 seconds, then add the pre-mixed seasoning/sauce C ingredients, except the evaporated milk, and simmer until the sauce thickens. Stir in the evaporated milk and heat through briefly. Transfer to the other side of the serving plate.

Heat the remaining one-third of the oil and stir-fry the drained black mushrooms for 1 minute. Add ¼ cup of the reserved steaming liquid, stir in the cornflour and bring to the boil. Simmer until thickened, then add the oyster sauce. Arrange in the centre of the serving plate and serve.

ASSORTED VEGETABLES WITH BEANCURD SKIN

60 g (2 oz)	dried rolled beancurd skin
3 cups (24 fl oz)	deep-frying oil
3	dried gluten balls
30 g (1 oz)	canned bamboo shoots, drained and sliced
45 g (1½ oz)	dried lotus seeds, steamed to soften
6	dried black mushrooms, soaked for 25 minutes
20 g (¾ oz)	dried lily buds, soaked for 25 minutes
20 g (¾ oz)	dried 'wood ear' fungus, soaked for 25 minutes
125 g (4 oz)	young bok choy
1½ tablespoons	light soy sauce
1 teaspoon	sesame oil (optional)

Seasoning/Sauce:

1½ cups (12 fl oz)	chicken stock or water
1 teaspoon	salt
¾ teaspoon	m.s.g. (optional)

Fry the beancurd skin in smoking hot deep-frying oil until crisp and bubbly on the surface, about 20 seconds. Drain and cut into 5 cm (2 in) pieces, then soak with the gluten balls in cold water until softened.

Drain the soaked ingredients, remove the mushroom stems and cut the 'wood ears' into smaller pieces. Thoroughly wash the bok choy and cut each piece lengthways into quarters.

Pour off all but 3 tablespoons of the oil and stir-fry the ingredients together for 2 minutes, then add the Seasoning/Sauce ingredients and bring to the boil. Cover and simmer for 10 minutes, add the soy sauce and sesame oil, if used, and thicken the sauce with a paste of cornflour (cornstarch) and cold water. Serve.

STUFFED RED PEPPERS

Serve as an appetiser or main dish.

12	large red chilli peppers*
125 g (4 oz)	lean pork, finely chopped
45 g (1½ oz)	raw peeled shrimps, chopped cornflour (cornstarch)
1¼ cup (10 fl oz)	frying oil
1 tablespoon	fermented black beans, washed and chopped
1 tablespoon	finely chopped spring onion (scallion)
½ teaspoon	finely chopped fresh ginger
½ teaspoon	finely chopped garlic

Seasoning A:

⅓ teaspoon	salt
½ teaspoon	sugar
¼ teaspoon	ground black pepper
1 tablespoon	cornflour (cornstarch)

Seasoning B/Sauce:

⅓ cup	chicken stock or cold water
1 tablespoon	light soy sauce
¼ teaspoon	salt
½ teaspoon	m.s.g. (optional)
¼ teaspoon	sugar

Cut the chillies along one side and press open. Trim away the stem and remove the seed core and the inner white ribs. Mix the pork and shrimps with the seasoning A ingredients, working to a smooth paste. Lightly coat the inside of the chilli with cornflour and fill generously with the pork mixture. Dip the whole stuffed chillies into cornflour.

Heat the oil almost to smoking point and fry the chillies, filling side downwards, until golden, turning once. Remove and drain off all but 2½ tablespoons of the oil. Add the black beans, onion, ginger, and garlic and stir-fry on moderate heat for 1 minute, then pour in the pre-mixed seasoning B/sauce ingredients and bring to the boil. Reduce the heat to low. Return the chillies and simmer, covered, for about 5 minutes. Serve hot.

* Although hot red chilli peppers are used, they have a mild almost sweet taste when cooked in this way.

Egg Custard (recipe page 321) and Sweet Rice Balls in Red Bean Soup (recipe page 319).

SHARK'S FIN AND CRABMEAT SOUP

250 g (8 oz)	prepared shark's fin, about 60 g (2 oz) dry weight
⅓ cup	softened lard
3	spring onions (scallions), trimmed and sliced
3 slices	fresh ginger
185 g (6 oz)	fresh crabmeat
1 tablespoon	rice wine or dry sherry
5 cups (1¼ litres)	chicken stock
2 tablespoons	cornflour (cornstarch)
2	egg whites, well beaten
1 tablespoon	rendered chicken fat (chicken grease) (optional)

Seasoning:

1½ teaspoons	salt
¾ teaspoon	m.s.g. (optional)
1 teaspoon	sugar
¼ cup (2 fl oz)	light soy sauce
¼ teaspoon	white pepper

Prepare the shark's fin according to the instructions on page 00, allowing about 4 hours advance preparation. Drain well.

Sauté the spring onions and ginger in the lard for 2 minutes. Add the crabmeat and fry briefly, then sizzle the wine onto the sides of the wok and stir in. Add the shark's fin and fry for 1 minute, then add the chicken stock and seasoning ingredients and bring to the boil.

Simmer for 10 minutes, then remove from the heat and slowly drizzle in the beaten egg whites and leave to set into strands in the soup. Thicken with the cornflour mixed with an equal quantity of cold water and simmer until the soup becomes clear. Pour into a soup tureen. Serve with a small jug of Chinese red vinegar to be added to taste.

MUSHROOMS WITH CHICKEN WINGS IN SOUP

12	dried black mushrooms, soaked for 25 minutes
6	chicken wings, cut in halves
6 cups (1½ litres)	chicken stock
1 tablespoon	rendered chicken fat (chicken grease) or lard
1 teaspoon	m.s.g. (optional)
1½ tablespoons	cornflour (cornstarch)

Seasoning A:

½ teaspoon	salt
½ teaspoon	m.s.g. (optional)
1 teaspoon	sugar
1	spring onion (scallion), trimmed and sliced
1 slice	fresh ginger

Seasoning B:

½ teaspoon	salt
¼ teaspoon	m.s.g. (optional)
2 teaspoons	light soy sauce
2 teaspoons	rice wine or dry sherry
2	spring onions (scallions), trimmed and sliced
3 thick slices	fresh ginger
¼ teaspoon	ground black pepper

Drain the mushrooms and remove the stems. Place in a dish with the seasoning A ingredients and add 1 cup of the chicken stock. Steam for 30 minutes, then drain.

Wash the chicken wings, debone if preferred, and place in a dish with the seasoning B ingredients. Leave for 10 minutes, then sauté in the chicken fat or lard until lightly coloured. Pour in the remaining chicken stock and bring to the boil. Reduce the heat and simmer until the wings are tender, about 20 minutes.

Add the mushrooms and simmer a further 10 minutes, then stir in the m.s.g., if used, and thicken the soup with the cornflour mixed with an equal quantity of cold water. Stir until the soup clears, then pour into a soup tureen and serve hot.

WATERCRESS AND LIVER SOUP

185 g (6 oz)	fresh watercress
125 g (4 oz)	lamb or pork liver
4 cups (1 litre)	chicken stock

Seasoning:

1	spring onion (scallion), trimmed and shredded
2 slices	fresh ginger, shredded
¾ teaspoon	salt
¼ teaspoon	m.s.g. (optional)
1 tablespoon	light soy sauce
2 teaspoons	rice wine or dry sherry

Thoroughly wash the watercress and remove the stems. Cut the liver into very thin slices and blanch in boiling water for 20 seconds, drain and soak in cold water for 5 minutes.

Bring the chicken stock to the boil and add the seasoning ingredients. Simmer for 2 minutes, then add the sliced liver and simmer a further 2 minutes. Add the watercress, stir in and cook until just softened. Pour into a soup tureen.

SWEET CORN AND CHICKEN SOUP

1 500 g (1 lb) can	sweet corn kernels
90 g (3 oz)	coarsely minced chicken breast
4 cups (1 litre)	chicken stock
¼ cup	cornflour (cornstarch)

Seasoning:

1½ teaspoons	salt
¾ teaspoon	m.s.g. (optional)
1 tablespoon	light soy sauce

Drain the corn and crush lightly in a mortar or food processor. Pour into a saucepan and add the chicken, stock, and seasonings. Bring to the boil and simmer for 3 minutes, then add the cornflour mixed with an equal quantity of cold water and simmer until the soup thickens and turns clear. Pour into a soup tureen and serve.

SHRIMP BALL SOUP

125 g (4 oz)	raw peeled shrimps
30 g (1 oz)	pork fat
½ 315 g (10 oz) can	straw mushrooms, drained
4 cups (1 litre)	chicken stock
1¼ teaspoons	salt
¾ teaspoon	m.s.g. (optional)
1	spring onion (scallion), trimmed and sliced

Seasoning A:

1	egg white, beaten
¼ teaspoon	salt
¼ teaspoon	m.s.g. (optional)
2 teaspoons	ginger wine
1 tablespoon	cornflour (cornstarch)

Seasoning B:

½ teaspoon	salt
¼ teaspoon	m.s.g. (optional)
1 tablespoon	rice wine or dry sherry
1 teaspoon	sesame oil
½ cup (4 fl oz)	chicken stock

Finely mince (grind) the shrimps and pork fat and add the seasoning A ingredients. Mix into a smooth paste, then form into small balls and simmer in gently boiling, lightly salted water for 2 minutes. Remove on a slotted spoon and place in a dish of cold water.

Place the mushrooms and the seasoning B ingredients in a small saucepan and bring to the boil. Simmer for 2 minutes.

Bring the chicken stock to the boil, add the salt, m.s.g., if used, and spring onion and simmer briefly. Add the shrimp balls and drained mushrooms and simmer for 3 minutes, then pour into a soup tureen and serve.

WONTONS IN SOUP WITH MIXED MEAT AND VEGETABLES

18	uncooked wontons (see recipe page 376)
60 g (2 oz)	cooked chicken breast, shredded
60 g (2 oz)	cooked pork fillet or roast pork, shredded
6 stalks	fresh young bok choy*
1 medium	carrot, shredded
30 g (1 oz)	canned bamboo shoots, drained and shredded
1	small leek, shredded
4 cups (1 litre)	chicken stock
3 thick slices	fresh ginger, shredded
1½ teaspoons	salt
½ teaspoon	m.s.g. (optional)
	pinch of ground black pepper
½ teaspoon	sesame oil

Bring a large saucepan of salted water to the boil and add the wontons. Simmer until they rise to the surface, then cook for 2½ — 3 minutes more. Drain and place in six soup bowls.

Bring the stock to the boil and add the ginger, salt, m.s.g., if used, and pepper. Simmer briefly, then add the shredded meat and vegetables and simmer for 2½ — 3 minutes. Add the sesame oil and divide the soup among the bowls. Serve hot.

* Or use other fresh green vegetables.

SWEET RICE BALLS IN RED BEAN SOUP

1 cup	glutinous rice powder
¼ cup (2 fl oz)	boiling water
1 tablespoon	sugar
1 tablespoon	softened lard
1½ — 2 tablespoons	cold water
1 280 g (9 oz) can	sweet red bean paste
1 cup	sugar (or to taste)
4 cups	water

Place the rice powder in a mixing bowl and add the boiling water, sugar, and lard. Work with the handle of a wooden spoon until well mixed, then add cold water to make a smooth, fairly hard dough. Knead for 2 minutes, then roll out into a long sausage shape and cut into small pieces. Roll each piece into a ball.

Bring a large saucepan of water to the boil and add the rice balls. Simmer until they rise to the surface, about 3 minutes, then remove with a slotted spoon into a dish of cold water.

Mix the red bean paste with the sugar and water. Heat to boiling and reduce to a simmer. Add the rice balls and simmer for about 3 minutes, then serve hot.

GLAZED SWEET POTATO BALLS WITH SESAME SEEDS

500 g (1 lb)	sweet potato or yams
2	whole eggs, beaten
½ cup	cornflour (cornstarch)
5 cups (1¼ litres)	deep-frying oil
½ cup	toasted white sesame seeds
1½ cups	sugar

Peel the sweet potato and form into small balls using a melon scoop. Soak in cold water for 20 minutes, then dry thoroughly and coat very lightly with cornflour. Dip into beaten egg and coat again with cornflour. Heat the deep-frying oil to moderately hot and deep-fry the potato balls for 3 minutes. Remove and drain well.

Transfer about 2 tablespoons of the oil to another wok and add the sugar. Stir on moderate heat until the sugar melts and turns into a thick golden syrup. Remove from the heat.

Reheat the deep-frying oil and fry the potato balls for a second time until cooked through, about 2 minutes, then transfer to the syrup. Carefully turn the balls in the syrup until evenly coated.

Spread the sesame seeds on a piece of greaseproof paper. Add the glazed sweet potato balls and turn until thickly coated with the sesame. Transfer to an oiled serving plate and serve while still hot.

ALMOND JELLY WITH FRESH FRUIT

2/3 cup	boiling water
1⅓ tablespoons	unflavoured gelatine
1½ cups (12 fl oz)	lukewarm water or milk
⅓ cup	evaporated milk or fresh cream
2 teaspoons	almond essence
250 g (8 oz)	diced fresh fruit, chilled
⅓ cup	liquid from canned fruit or sugar syrup

Mix the boiling water and gelatine together and stir slowly until dissolved, then add the water or milk, evaporated milk or cream, and the almond essence and mix throughly.

Pour into a lightly oiled jelly mould and leave to set. Chill thoroughly.

Turn the jelly out onto a serving plate and surround with the diced fruit. Pour on the fruit or sugar syrup and serve.

ALMOND AND QUAIL EGG TEA

12	canned or fresh quail eggs
60 g (2 oz)	blanched almonds
1 teaspoon	bicarbonate of soda
1 tablespoon	Chinese black tea leaves
1 cup	sugar
1 10 cm (4 in)	cinnamon stick

Boil fresh quail eggs, if used, in water for about 4½ minutes until firm. Cool under running cold water and remove the shells. Drain canned eggs. Cover with cold water and set aside.

Place the almonds and bicarbonate of soda in a saucepan and add about 1½ cups of water. Bring to the boil and simmer until the almonds are tender, about 45 minutes. Drain well and rinse with clean cold water.

Brew half the tea with 1 cup boiling water. Place the remaining tea in a bowl and add one-quarter of the sugar and the drained eggs. Add boiling water to cover and place in a steamer.

Place the cinnamon stick in another bowl and set in the steamer also. Cover and steam over rapidly boiling water for 25 minutes.

Bring 2 cups of water to the boil and add the remaining sugar, stirring until dissolved.

Into 6 dessert bowls divide the almonds and place 2 drained eggs in each. Add a splash each of the tea and cinnamon water and top up with the sugar water. Serve hot.

This is an unusual blend of ingredients for a sweet dish, but the result is a cooling, refreshing dessert which can also be served chilled.

If preferred, substitute poached fruit or softened lotus seeds for the quail eggs.

EGG CUSTARD

5	whole eggs
	egg whites
1½ cups (12 fl oz)	fresh milk
1½ tablespoons	clear honey or white sugar
teaspoons	cornflour (cornstarch)
¼ teaspoon	grated lemon rind

Beat the eggs well together, then add the milk, honey, and cornflour and beat to a smooth batter. Stir in the lemon rind, then pour the mixture into a greased ovenproof dish or six individual heatproof dessert dishes. Set on a rack in a steamer and steam over gently boiling water for about 15 minutes, or until just set. Serve immediately.

CHAPTER VII
Dishes for Special Occasions

SHARK'S FIN WITH SHREDDED MEAT IN RICH SOUP

The Chinese name for this dish translates as 'Happiness to Everyone.'

500 g (1 lb)	prepared shark's fin (see page 393), about 125 g (4 oz) dry weight
6	dried black mushrooms, soaked for 25 minutes
125 g (4 oz)	Chinese or cured (Smithfield) ham
125 g (4 oz)	pork fillet (tenderloin)
125 g (4 oz)	boneless chicken breast
125 (4 oz)	canned bamboo shoots, drained
2 tablespoons	finely chopped spring onion (scallion)
2 tablespoons	finely shredded fresh ginger
2 tablespoons	frying oil
7 cups (1¾ litres)	enriched stock
	fresh coriander

Seasoning A:

1	small egg white, beaten
1 tablespoon	ginger wine
¾	cornflour (cornstarch)

Seasoning B:

1 tablespoon	light soy sauce
1 teaspoon	rice wine or dry sherry
1 tablespoon	cold water
½ teaspoon	ground black pepper
¾ teaspoon	cornflour (cornstarch)

Seasoning C:

1¾ teaspoons	salt
1 teaspoon	sugar
2 tablespoons	dark soy sauce
1½ tablespoons	rice wine or dry sherry
¼ cup (2 fl oz)	cold water
⅓ cup	cornflour (cornstarch)
1½ teaspoons	sesame oil (optional)

Allow at least 4 hours advance preparation for the shark's fins. In the meantime, squeeze the water from the mushrooms and shred the caps. Finely shred the ham, pork, chicken, and bamboo shoots. Place the shredded chicken in a dish with the seasoning A ingredients, mix well and leave for 15 minutes. Mix the shredded pork with the seasoning B ingredients in another dish and leave for 10 minutes.

Heat the frying oil and sauté the chicken until whitened. Remove and add the pork. Sauté for about 1 minute, then remove. Add the remaining shredded ingredients and the spring onion and sauté for 1½ minutes, then remove. Pour in the enriched stock and bring to the boil.

Add the drained shark's fins and reduce the heat to simmer for 25 minutes, return the shredded ingredients and add the seasoning C ingredients. Simmer for about 10 minutes, then transfer to a soup tureen and garnish with the fresh coriander.

WHOLE STEAMED FISH

1 1 kg (2 lb)	whole fresh fish
5 cm (2 in) piece	fresh ginger
5	spring onions (scallions), trimmed
¼ cup (2 fl oz)	frying oil
⅓ cup	chicken stock
¼ cup (2 fl oz)	light soy sauce
¼ teaspoon	ground black pepper
1 teaspoon	sesame oil (optional)
	few sprigs of fresh coriander

Clean and scale the fish. Peel the ginger and cut into thin slices. Place several slices inside the fish and shred the remainder finely. Set the fish on a large plate, push two of the spring onions under it and shred the remainder.

Set the plate on a rack in a steamer and steam over rapidly boiling water for 18 — 20 minutes. Remove from the steamer and garnish with the shredded spring onions and ginger.

Heat the frying oil to smoking point and pour over the fish, then heat the remaining ingredients, except coriander, together and pour over the fish as well. Garnish with the coriander and serve at once.

1 2½ kg (5 lb)	plump duck
⅓ cup	malt sugar
½ cup (4 fl oz)	boiling water
18	'Mandarin' p[...]
	recipe, page 3[...]
1 cup	'duck' sauce [...]
9	spring onions [...]

BRAISED ABALONE IN OYSTER SAUCE

750 g (1½ lb)	fresh abalone*
2 teaspoons	salt
	cornflour (cornstarch)
250 g (½ lb)	fresh pork or ham skin
4 cups (1 litre)	enriched or chicken stock
3	spring onions (scallions), trimmed and sliced
5 cloves	garlic, sliced
⅓ cup	frying oil

Seasoning A:

2 tablespoons	rice wine or dry sherry
3	spring onions (scallions), cut in halves·
4 thick slices	fresh ginger, bruised

Seasoning B:

⅓ cup	oyster sauce (or use ½ cup light soy sauce)
2 teaspoons	dark soy sauce
2 teaspoons	rice wine or dry sherry
¾ teaspoon	salt
2½ teaspoons	sugar

Rub the abalone with the salt and plenty of cornflour. Rinse well with cold water, then cover with fresh cold water and bring to the boil. Simmer for 20 minutes, then drain well.

Heat a saucepan and add the seasoning A ingredients and the abalone. Add enough water to cover the abalone and simmer, covered, for 3 hours. Top up with boiling water as the level drops. Discard the onion and ginger.

Warm a large casserole and rub with an oiled cloth. Cut the ham or pork skin in halves and place one piece in the bottom of the casserole. Arrange the abalone on this and add the seasoning B ingredients and the stock. Cover with the remaining pork or ham skin and put the lid tightly in place. Simmer for 1 hour on low heat. Discard the skin and keep the abalone warm.

Saute the sliced onion and garlic in the oil until lightly coloured and beginning to soften. Add to the casserole and heat through for 5 minutes. Thicken the sauce with a thin paste of cornflour (cornstarch) and cold water and serve.

If preferred, remove the abalone before thickening the sauce and slice each piece thinly then return to the sauce.

* Dried abalone may be used, about 440 g (14 oz). Soak in cold water overnight then simmer in plenty of lightly salted water for at least 6 hours, rinse thoroughly and use as above.

Canned abalone is unsuitable for this type of dish, as the result would be tough, rubbery meat and the loss of its natural flavour.

DRIED SCALLOPS BRAISED WITH GARLIC

250 g (8 oz)	dried scallops, soaked for 30 minutes
3 whole heads	fresh garlic
¼ cup (2 fl oz)	frying oil
90 g (3 oz)	fresh chicken fat (chicken grease) or ham skin
250 g (8 oz)	young bok choy
1 tablespoon	softened lard
2 teaspoons	rice wine or dry sherry
1½ teaspoons	cornflour (cornstarch)
1 tablespoon	oyster sauce

Seasoning:

1 teaspoon	salt
¾ teaspoon	sugar
1 cup (8 fl oz)	chicken stock

Drain the scallops and place in a dish with water to cover. Set in a steamer and steam over gently boiling water for 1½ hours.

Peel the garlic and sauté the whole cloves in the oil until softened, about 3 minutes. Remove the scallops from the steamer, discard the liquid and add the garlic and seasoning ingredients. Cover with sliced chicken fat or the ham skin and return to the steamer. Steam for a further 1½ hours.

Simmer the bok choy in lightly salted water until tender. Drain and stir in the lard. Arrange on a serving plate. Remove the scallops from the steamer again, drain the liquid into a wok and arrange the scallops and garlic over the vegetables. Discard the chicken fat or ham skin.

Bring the liquid to the boil, sizzle the wine onto the sides of the pan, then thicken the sauce with the cornflour mixed with a little cold water. Simmer for 1 minute, stir in the oyster sauce and pour over the dish. Serve at once.

1 1½ kg (3 lb)	chicken
12	dried black mu[...]
	for 25 minutes
185 g (6 oz)	salted mustard [...]
	for 25 minutes
125 g (4 oz)	fat pork
¼ cup (2 fl oz)	frying oil
4	fresh or dried [...]
1½ kg (3 lb)	pond mud**
	vegetable oil

Seasoning:

2 tablespoons	sugar
¼ teaspoon	ground black p[...]
1 tablespoon	dark soy sauce
2 tablespoons	rice wine or dr[...]
2 teaspoons	sesame oil

1 5 — 6 kg	
(10 — 12 lb)	sucklin
¾ cup	malt su
⅓ cup	Chines
1 cup (8 fl oz)	boiling

Seasoning:

1 tablespoon	salt
¼ cup	sugar
2 teaspoons	five sp
¼ cup (2 fl oz)	rice wi
¼ cup	sweet b
¼ cup (2 fl oz)	sesame
½ cup (4 fl oz)	light sc
¼ cup (2 fl oz)	sesame
3 tablespoons	finely
3 tablespoons	finely

Accompaniments:

24	'Mandu
	recipe,
1 cup	'duck'
12	spring

PORK SHOULDER WITH *FA TS'AI*

Fa ts'ai is a kind of seaweed, black in colour and resembling human hair. Its name *fa ts'ai*, or *fat choy* in Cantonese, forms part of the New Year greeting and represents wealth and riches. Thus, to serve a dish containing this unusual but nutritionally rich ingredient is to extend the very best of good wishes to the recipient. Pork shoulder or pork knuckle with fa ts'ai is usually featured at Lunar New Year banquets.

1¼ kg (2½ lb)	pork shoulder
1 tablespoon	dark soy sauce
45 g (1½ oz)	fa ts'ai (fat choy)
6 cups (1½ litres)	deep-frying oil
1	fresh lettuce
	cornflour (cornstarch)

Seasoning:

1¾ teaspoons	salt
2 tablespoons	sugar
1 teaspoon	m.s.g. (optional)
3	star anise
4 cubes	fermented beancurd with the liquid, mashed
1½ cups (12 fl oz)	chicken stock or water

Cut the pork into large chunks without removing the skin. Place in a saucepan, cover with cold water and bring to the boil. Simmer for about 45 minutes, then remove and leave to dry. Rub with the dark soy sauce and leave for 15 minutes.

Soak the fa ts'ai in cold water until softened, then drain.

Heat the deep-frying oil to smoking point, reduce the heat slightly and fry the pork cubes until well browned, about 4 minutes. Remove and drain well, wipe with kitchen paper to remove excess oil and place in a casserole. Add the fa ts'ai and seasoning, bring to the boil, then cover and reduce the heat to low. Simmer until the meat is completely tender, about 45 minutes.

Separate the leaves of the fresh lettuce, wash well and drop into boiling water with 1 tablespoon frying oil and 1 teaspoon salt added. Simmer for 20 seconds, then drain well and arrange on a serving plate. Place the pork pieces on the lettuce.

Reheat the sauce and thicken with a paste of cornflour and cold water. Simmer briefly, then pour over the pork and serve with plain white rice.

MONGOLIAN BARBECUE

Serves 6 — 8.

250 g (8 oz)	lean lamb
250 g (8 oz)	beef fillet (tenderloin)
250 g (8 oz)	boneless chicken breast
315 g (10 oz)	raw peeled prawns (shrimps)
500 g (1 lb)	fresh bean sprouts
500 g (1 lb)	fresh Chinese cabbage or young lettuce
3	young leeks
1	large bunch of fresh coriander
4 squares	fresh soft beancurd
1	large green capsicum (bell pepper)
2	fresh red chilli peppers

Seasoning/Sauce:

6 cups (1½ litres)	chicken stock
¾ cup (6 fl oz)	light soy sauce
1¾ tablespoons	sesame oil
½ cup (4 fl oz)	rice wine or dry sherry
1½ tablespoons	sugar
1¼ teaspoons	m.s.g. (optional)
½ cup (4 fl oz)	vegetable oil

Special Equipment: A table-top hotplate, wooden chopsticks or fondue forks.

Partially freeze the lamb, beef, and chicken, then cut into paper-thin slices and arrange individually on plates. Thoroughly wash the prawns under cold water, rubbing with salt and cornflour (cornstarch) in the process. Devein with a toothpick (see page 00), cut each into several thin slices and arrange on a plate.

Wash the bean sprouts and drain thoroughly. Place on several plates. Wash the cabbage or lettuce, separate the leaves and cut the larger ones in halves. Thoroughly wash the leeks, then cut into 5 cm (2 in) pieces and shred finely lengthwise. Wash the coriander and remove the stems. Arrange the cabbage or lettuce, leeks, and coriander on separate plates.

Soak the beancurd in cold water for 10 minutes, then remove and drain well. Cut into thin slices and place on a plate. Trim away the stem, seed-core, and the inner white ribs from the capsicum and chilli peppers and arrange on a plate.

Mix the sauce ingredients together and pour into 6 — 8 individual small jugs or bowls. Pour additional vegetable oil into several small jugs.

Take all the ingredients and the sauces to the table. Heat the hotplate.

Dip the meat or vegetables into the sauce, then fry quickly on the well-oiled hot plate. Splash on a little of the sauce and some vegetable oil during cooking.

Mongolian Barbecue can be accompanied by Sesame Pocket Bread or Steamed Bread (see pages 372 and 370).

PORK KNUCKLES WITH GINGER AND SWEET RICE VINEGAR

After a baby is born to a Cantonese family, it is the custom that this dish be cooked for the confined mother to share with friends, family, and relatives during the first month. It is offered to all who visit the new mother and baby. The Chinese title translates as 'A Gift from the Stork.'

1½ kg (3 lb)	pork knuckles (trotters/shanks)
1 kg (2 lb)	fresh ginger
6	chicken eggs

Seasoning:

6 cups (1½ litres)	sweet rice vinegar
2 cups (16 fl oz)	Chinese brown vinegar
¼ cup	sugar
1 tablespoon	chicken stock powder (or 2 stock cubes)

Drop the knuckles into boiling water and simmer for 2 minutes. Remove and scrape off any hair, then cut into 5 cm (2 in) pieces. Return to the saucepan, cover with cold water and bring to the boil. Simmer for 35 minutes. Drain and rinse with cold water.

Peel the ginger and cut into pieces about 5 cm (2 in) long. Pour the vinegar into a large saucepan and bring to the boil. Add the remaining seasoning ingredients and mix well, then add the ginger and simmer for 25 minutes.

Add the knuckles and bring back to the boil, then reduce heat and simmer until the pork is completely tender.

Hard boil (hard cook) the eggs and cool under running cold water, then peel. Add to the dish. Remove from the heat and let stand for about 3 hours before reheating to serve.

Chicken can be used instead of pork to produce a dish which is said to be most beneficial to new mothers.

MONGOLIAN FIRE-POT

Serves 6 — 8.

250 g (8 oz)	beef fillet (tenderloin)
250 g (8 oz)	lean lamb or mutton
250 g (8 oz)	lean pork
250 g (8 oz)	venison steak (optional)
250 g (8 oz)	boneless duck or chicken breast
500 g (1 lb)	fresh young Chinese cabbage or bok choy
500 g (1 lb)	fresh spinach (collard green)
6 squares	soft beancurd
12	spring onions (scallions)
90 g (3 oz)	bean thread vermicelli, soaked
3 slices	fresh ginger, shredded

Sauce:

3 tablespoons	finely chopped spring onions (scallions)
2 tablespoons	finely chopped fresh ginger
1½ tablespoons	finely chopped garlic
2½ tablespoons	finely chopped fresh coriander
	light soy sauce
	rice wine or dry sherry
	sesame oil
	sesame paste
	sha chia jiang or hoisin sauce
	chilli sauce
	salt
	sugar
	m.s.g. (optional)

Special Equipment: A table-top charcoal 'fire-pot' or fondue pot, or a portable gas or electric ring and a saucepan, wooden chopsticks.

Partially freeze the beef, lamb or mutton, pork, venison, and duck or chicken, then cut into paper-thin slices and arrange individually on serving plates. Or prepare a plate with a selection of the meats for each diner.

Thoroughly wash the cabbage or bok choy and spinach, trim the stems and drain well, then arrange on serving plates. Soak the beancurd in cold water for 10 minutes. Drain and cut into cubes. Trim the spring onions and cut in halves. Drain the vermicelli. Place the beancurd, spring onions, and vermicelli on serving plates.

Place the sauce ingredients on the table to be mixed to individual taste. The sesame paste should be diluted with cold water until quite thin.

Heat the fire-pot and fill with boiling water. Add the sliced ginger and salt to taste. Use the wooden chopsticks to suspend slices of meat in the hot stock until cooked to individual taste, preferably rare. Dip into the sauce before eating.

When most of the meat has been cooked, add vegetables, beancurd, spring onions, and the vermicelli. Serve the remaining slivers of the meat in the rich stock with the other ingredients as a soup, adding sauce ingredients to taste.

Serve Sesame Pocket Bread (page 372) or deep-fried Steamed Bread (page 370) with the fire-pot.

'BUDDHA'S HAND'

(Pork-Filled Egg Pancake Rolls)

250 g (8 oz)	lean pork, finely minced (ground)
1 tablespoon	finely chopped spring onion (scallion)
1 teaspoon	grated fresh ginger
1	egg, well beaten
4 cups (1 litre)	deep-frying oil
	spiced salt or Chinese pepper-salt

Batter:

6	eggs, well beaten
2½ tablespoons	chicken stock
2¼ teaspoons	cornflour (cornstarch)
2 teaspoons	frying oil
	pinch of salt

Seasoning:

½ teaspoon	salt
¼ teaspoon	m.s.g. (optional)
¼ teaspoon	sugar
	pinch of white pepper
1 tablespoon	light soy sauce
2 teaspoons	rice wine or dry sherry
2 teaspoons	cold water
½ teaspoon	sesame oil (optional)
1 tablespoon	cornflour

Mix the pork with the spring onion, ginger, and seasoning ingredients and work to a smooth paste by throwing repeatedly against the inside of the mixing bowl. Refrigerate for 1 hour.

Make a smooth creamy mixture with the batter ingredients and beat for 2 minutes. Leave to sit for at least 15 minutes.

Heat a frying or omelette pan with a 30 cm (12 in) diameter. Rub with an oiled cloth. Pour in half the batter and tilt the pan so it forms into a thin pancake covering the complete base of the pan. Cook on moderate heat until bubbles appear on the surface and the underside is flecked with brown. Lift one corner then carefully turn. Cook the other side until firm and lightly coloured. Remove to a board to cool. Cook the remaining batter in the same way.

Divide the meat filling between the two pancakes spreading in a rectangular shape across the centre of each pancake leaving a border at the sides. Fold the sides over and brush with beaten egg. Fold over one flap and stick down with egg, then fold the remaining flap and stick onto the first fold with egg. Turn over.

Cut the two rolls in halves and cut five 'fingers' in each by slicing three-quarters of the way through the rolls four times, evenly spaced. Pull the rolls into crescent shapes so the 'fingers' fan out.

Heat the deep-frying oil to moderately hot and fry the 'Buddha's hands' until well coloured, turning once. Drain and serve on shredded lettuce with spiced salt and/or Chinese pepper-salt as dips (see recipes page 384).

MUTTON HOT-POT

1 kg (2 lb)	lean mutton (or kid), cubed
1	white turnip, peeled and cubed
90 g (3 oz)	canned water chestnuts, drained
5 cm (2 in) piece	fresh ginger, peeled and thickly sliced
1	leek, trimmed and cut into 2.5 cm (1 in) pieces
2 tablespoons	frying oil
6 cups (1½ litres)	chicken stock
1	fresh young lettuce
	fresh coriander or finely shredded lemon leaves
	fermented beancurd, mashed

Seasoning:

1 piece	dried orange peel, soaked and shredded
¼ teaspoon	salt
1 tablespoon	sugar
½ teaspoon	ground black pepper
2 tablespoons	soybean paste
3 cubes	fermented beancurd with the liquid, mashed
1 tablespoon	rice wine or dry sherry

Blanch the mutton or kid in boiling water for 2 minutes. Drain well. Heat the frying oil and stir-fry the turnip, water chestnuts, ginger, and leek for 2 minutes. Add the mutton and stir-fry until lightly coloured, then add the seasoning ingredients and cook with the meat and vegetables for 2 minutes, mixing well. Pour in the stock and bring to the boil.

Transfer to a casserole and simmer for 30 minutes. Pick out the turnip and discard. Cook for a further 30 minutes, then check the seasonings and serve in the casserole.

Serve the well-washed lettuce, leaves separated, on a plate to be added to the casserole at the table.

Serve fresh coriander or shredded lemon leaves and mashed fermented beancurd as accompaniments.

Sautéd Snake in Gravy (recipe page 336)

SAUTÉD SNAKE IN GRAVY

185 g (6 oz)	frozen cooked snake meat*
60 g (2 oz)	boneless chicken breast
60 g (2 oz)	prepared fish maw (see page 392)
60 g (2 oz)	canned bamboo shoots, drained
15 g (½ oz)	cooked ham
5 cm (2 in)	fresh ginger, peeled
6	dried black mushrooms, soaked for 25 minutes
1 piece	dried orange peel, soaked for 25 minutes
⅓ cup	frying oil
1 tablespoon	rice wine or dry sherry
6 cups (1½ litres)	chicken stock
1	spring onion (scallion), sliced
2 thick slices	fresh ginger
2	white chrysanthemums
2 — 3	lemon leaves
10 — 12 pieces	frozen wonton wrappers**
3 cups (24 fl oz)	deep-frying oil

Seasoning A:

¼ teaspoon	salt
¼ teaspoon	m.s.g. (optional)
½ teaspoon	cornflour (cornstarch)
	pinch of white pepper

Seasoning B:

1½ teaspoons	salt
¼ teaspoon	m.s.g. (optional)
	pinch of white pepper

Thaw the snake meat and shred finely. Shred the chicken and mix with the seasoning A ingredients, leaving for 10 minutes. Drain the prepared fish maw and cut into fine shreds. Shred the bamboo shoots, ham, and peeled ginger. Squeeze the water from the mushrooms, remove the stems and shred the caps finely. Drain and shred the orange peel.

Heat half of the frying oil in a wok and stir-fry the chicken until it turns white, then remove and drain. Add the remaining oil and fry the spring onion and ginger slices briefly, then add the wine and stock. Bring to the boil, then remove the onion and ginger and discard.

Add the shredded ingredients and the seasoning B ingredients and simmer for 2 — 3 minutes, then thicken with a paste of 1½ tablespoons cornflour and water. For a less distinct ginger flavour, blanch the shredded ginger in boiling water before adding to the dish.

Wash the chrysanthemums and remove the petals. Arrange on a serving plate with the very finely shredded lemon leaves. Cut the wonton wrappers into strips and deep-fry in the hot deep-frying oil until crisp. Serve the snake dish with the crisp pretzels, chrysanthemum, and lemon leaves to be added to individual taste.

* Available from specialist Chinese food stockists.

** The traditional accompanying pretzels for this dish are made of a dough comprising flour and mashed fermented beancurd. This is rolled out paper-thin and cut into small rectangular shapes before deep-frying.

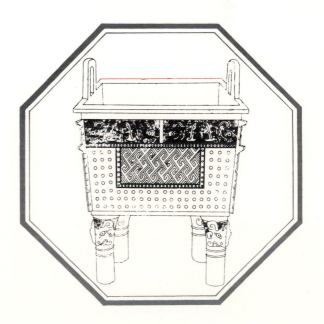

CRISP FRIED EGG ROLLS

These are traditionally served in Peking during the Lunar New Year festivities marking the beginning of the new year. As this also means the end of the winter months, they have come to be known as the popular 'Spring' Rolls.

Makes 12.

Batter:

4	large eggs, well beaten
1 tablespoon	flour
1 tablespoon	water
6 cups (1½ litres)	deep-frying oil
	Chinese pepper-salt

Filling:

250 g (8 oz)	lean pork, finely shredded
125 g (4 oz)	fresh bean sprouts
1	medium carrot, finely shredded
1 small stalk	fresh celery, finely shredded
12	garlic chives, sliced
2 tablespoons	softened lard or frying oil

Seasoning A:

½ teaspoon	salt
2 teaspoons	rice wine or dry sherry
1½ teaspoons	cornflour (cornstarch)

Seasoning B:

1½ teaspoons	salt
⅓ teaspoon	m.s.g. (optional)
1 tablespoon	sugar
¼ teaspoon	ground black pepper
1½ teaspoons	sesame oil

Sauce Dip:

2 tablespoons	tomato sauce
1 tablespoon	Worcestershire Sauce
2 tablespoons	light soy sauce
1 teaspoon	hot bean paste or chilli sauce
1½ teaspoons	finely chopped garlic
1 teaspoon	sugar

Mix the batter ingredients together thoroughly. Wipe out an omelette pan with an oiled cloth and heat to moderate. Pour in about 2 tablespoons of the batter. Lift the pan and swirl it slowly around so the mixture flows into a thin circle about 17.5 cm (7 in) in diameter. Cook until the sides lift from the pan, then carefully flip over and briefly cook the other side. The pancake should be firm, but not crisp. Remove to a piece of greaseproof paper. Cook the remaining pancakes, making 12. Stack between pieces of greaseproof paper. Leave to cool.

Mix the pork with the seasoning A ingredients and leave for 10 minutes. Blanch the bean sprouts, carrot, and celery separately. Drain well and set aside.

Heat the lard or frying oil to moderate and stir-fry the shredded pork until white and firm, about 1½ minutes. Add the seasoning B ingredients, the garlic chives, and blanched vegetables and stir-fry together for about 2 minutes. Remove and spread on a plate to cool.

Prepare Chinese pepper-salt, according to the directions on page 384, and pour into several small dishes to use as a dip, or prepare the sauce dip by mixing the ingredients together.

Place a portion of the filling in a sausage shape slightly off centre on each pancake. Fold over the closest edge, then fold in the two sides and roll up. Stick the flaps down with a paste made from flour and water.

Heat the deep-frying oil to moderately hot. Fry the rolls, several at a time, until golden and crisp. Remove and drain well. Arrange on a paper-lined serving plate, or on a bed of finely shredded lettuce and serve with the prepared dips.

NEW YEAR'S CAKE

Served as a snack during the Lunar New Year festivities. Its companion dish is the salty Turnip Cake on page 364.

5 cups	glutinous rice flour
1 2/3 cups	brown sugar
1 2/3 cups	boiling water

Special Equipment: A 20 cm (8 in) steaming basket lined with cellophane or greaseproof paper.

Sift the flour into a mixing bowl. Dissolve the sugar in the water and add to the flour, mixing in thoroughly. Pour into the prepared basket and cover.

Set on a rack in a steamer and steam over rapidly boiling water for about 2 hours. To test if the cake is cooked through, insert a chopstick into the centre. If it comes out dry, the cake is ready. Invert onto a plate and remove the paper. Refrigerate, well covered with plastic, for about 2 days before cutting into diamond-shaped pieces to serve.

Use brown sugar or a small amount of molasses to add colour.

LONG-LIFE BUNS

The peach is found in much traditional Chinese art and represents longevity. Here soft dough buns with mashed date filling are formed into peach shapes, tinted a delicate pink for serving at New Year and other auspicious occasions. They are also highly regarded as altar offerings.

Makes 24.

1 recipe	steamed bread dough (see page 370, Steamed Bread) rose pink food colouring

Filling:

700 g (1⅓ lb)	dates*
2½ tablespoons	sugar
2 tablespoons	softened lard

Prepare the dough and cover with a damp cloth. Put the dates into a saucepan with water to cover. Bring to the boil and simmer until softened, then transfer to a piece of clean cheesecloth and squeeze out as much water as possible.

Return to the saucepan and add the sugar and lard. Cook on low heat until the mixture is thick and fairly dry. Leave to cool, then form into 24 balls.

Roll the dough into a long sausage shape and cut into 24 pieces. Press each into a flat circle with the fingers and put a ball of filling on each. Pull the dough up around the filling to form a ball shape and pinch the edges together, pulling into a point. Press the back of a knife blade along the bun from base to point to create a peach shape and brush a touch of pink food colouring around the point.

For added authenticity, stamp out leaf shapes from left-over dough, brush with green food colouring and stick to the base of the peaches.

Stick a square of greaseproof paper under each bun and arrange the buns in two steaming baskets. Set on racks in a two-tiered steamer and steam over rapidly boiling water for 10 — 12 minutes. Lift the lid two or three times during cooking to prevent the buns bursting open. Keep the buns well separated in the basket as they expand during cooking. Serve hot.

* Or use sweet red bean paste (see page 389) or sweet lotus seed filling (page 368).

SALTY 'JUNDZ'

Created for the Dragon Boat Festival, these bamboo leaf bundles of stuffed glutinous rice represent the rice grains thrown into the river to entice the fish away from the drowning heroine of the legend around which this festival has been created.

Makes 12.

3½ cups	raw long grain glutinous rice
2 tablespoons	dried shrimps, soaked for 1 hour
375 g (12 oz)	'five flowered' pork (belly/fresh bacon)
3 — 4	dried black mushrooms, soaked for 25 minutes
2	salted duck egg yolks (see recipe page 263)*
⅓ cup	frying oil
24	dried bamboo leaves, soaked
string	

Seasoning A:

1 teaspoon	salt
½ teaspoon	m.s.g. (optional)
¼ teaspoon	sugar
¼ teaspoon	ground black pepper
1 teaspoon	rice wine or dry sherry
¼ cup (2 fl oz)	light soy sauce
2 tablespoons	finely chopped spring onion (scallion)

Seasoning B:

¾ teaspoon	salt
¾ teaspoon	m.s.g. (optional)
2 teaspoons	dark soy sauce

Soak the rice for 2 hours, then drain and change the water. Soak a further 30 minutes. Drain.

Drain the shrimps. Dice the pork. Drain the mushrooms, remove the stems and dice the caps. Chop the egg yolks and set aside.

Heat the oil in a wok and fry the shrimps, pork, and mushrooms for 1½ minutes. Add the seasoning A ingredients and heat through. Set aside.

Fry the rice, adding a little more oil if needed, for 2 minutes, then add the seasoning B ingredients and mix thoroughly.

Drain the bamboo leaves and wipe dry. Brush one side with frying oil. Place two leaves side by side and fold the two bottoms over together to form a triangular-shaped pouch. Add a portion of the rice, some chopped egg yolk, and the shrimp and pork mixture and top with more rice. Fold the leaves over the top and around the pouch to produce a plump triangular-shaped bundle. Wrap string securely around the bundle and set aside.

When all are done place side by side in a saucepan and cover with cold water. Bring to the boil, reduce heat and simmer for 1 hour. Drain well if the water has not been completely absorbed. Unwrap to serve.

* Omit or use hard-boiled (hard cooked) egg yolk.

MOON CAKES

Through the centuries, Chinese pastry cooks have vied for supremacy in the production of their special version of these sweet cakes. They are sold and consumed in untold numbers during the Moon Festival, and come with a variety of fillings from sweetened mashed lotus seeds, to sweet red bean paste, mashed salted egg yolks, nuts and sesame seeds, and come in pastry from sweet to salty. Bedecked with colourful food dye stamps, or artistic impressions made by special moon cake moulds, they are sold in gaily decorated presentation boxes and it would be unthinkable to arrive at a friend's house during this holiday without a gift box of the best moon cakes one could afford.

Makes 24.

As moon cake moulds are not readily available, this recipe for flaky pastry Moon Cakes with sweet red bean filling is more applicable here.

Pastry A:

2¼ cups	flour
⅓ cup	softened lard or pastry shortening
150 ml (5 fl oz)	water
2 teaspoons	pinch of salt

Pastry B:

1¼ cups	flour
⅓ cup	softened lard or pastry shortening

Filling:

2 cups	sweet red bean paste (see recipe, page 389) red food colouring

Sift the flour for pastry A into a mixing bowl and add the water and lard. Slowly work in, adding the sugar and salt. Knead until smooth.

Sift the flour for pastry B into another bowl and add the lard or shortening. Work in and knead until smooth. Roll the two portions of dough into sausage shapes and divide each into 24 parts.

Roll into balls and flatten each with the fingers, or gently with a rolling pin, making the pastry A circles larger than those of B. Place B pastry circles on top of the A circles. Fold four corners of the A over the B pastry to form a square and gently roll out into a rectangular shape. Fold the two ends in to the centre to form a square again, then lightly roll out into a circular shape, fairly thin.

When all the pastry cases are ready, divide the red bean paste into 24 portions and roll each into a ball, then flatten slightly. Place one piece in the centre of each circle of pastry and pull the edges together. Brush with a little water or beaten egg if the edges do not stick well.

Place on a greased and floured baking tray and brush on a design with the red food dye, using a small paint brush. Bake in a preheated moderate oven 200°C (375 — 400°F) for about 20 minutes. Remove and serve hot or cold.

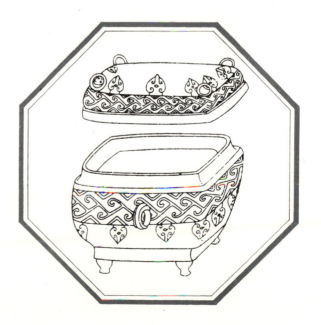

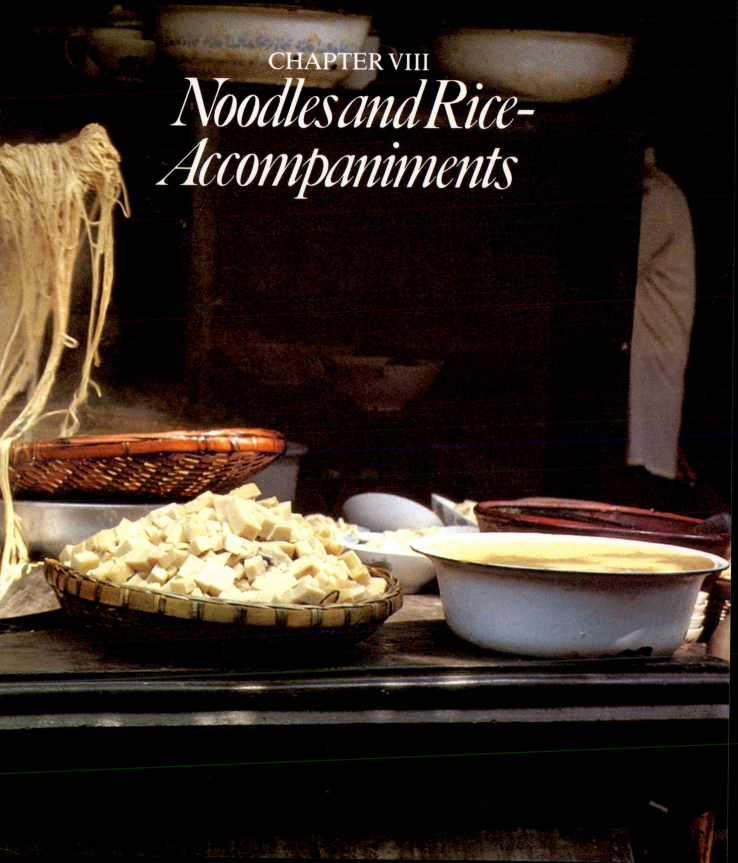

CHAPTER VIII
*Noodles and Rice-
Accompaniments*

'GREAT GRAVY' NOODLES

500 g (1 lb)	fresh thick egg noodles, or about 250 g (8 oz) dried noodles
250 g (8 oz)	boneless chicken breast
6	large dried black mushrooms, soaked for 25 minutes
45 g (1½ oz)	dried 'wood ear' fungus, soaked for 25 minutes
45 g (1½ oz)	'golden needles' (dried lily flowers), soaked for 25 minutes
3	eggs, well beaten
1 teaspoon	cornflour (cornstarch)
¼ cup (2 fl oz)	frying oil
½ cup (4 fl oz)	sesame oil
1½ teaspoons	Chinese brown peppercorns

Seasoning A:

1 tablespoon	finely chopped spring onion (scallion)
1 teaspoon	grated fresh ginger
2 teaspoons	light soy sauce
1 teaspoon	sesame oil
1 teaspoon	cornflour (cornstarch)

Seasoning B/Sauce:

1¼ teaspoons	salt
1 tablespoon	dark soy sauce
7 cups (1¾ litres)	chicken stock
⅓ cup	cornflour (cornstarch)

Wash the fresh noodles or soak dried noodles in hot water to soften. Cut the chicken into fine shreds and place in a dish with the seasoning A ingredients, mix well and leave for 15 minutes.

Squeeze the water from the mushrooms, remove the stems and shred the caps. Drain the 'wood ears' and cut into small pieces. Drain the 'golden needles.' Mix the eggs and cornflour together and set aside.

Heat the frying oil and stir-fry the chicken briefly, then add the mushrooms, 'wood ears,' and 'golden needles' and stir-fry briefly. Add the pre-mixed seasoning B/sauce ingredients, except the cornflour, and bring to the boil. Simmer for 15 minutes.

In the meantime, drop the noodles into a large saucepan of boiling, salted water and simmer on moderate to low heat until the noodles are tender. Drain well and divide among large soup bowls.

Thicken the sauce with the cornflour mixed to a paste with an equal quantity of cold water and when boiling again, reduce the heat and slowly drizzle in the beaten egg. Leave to cook in the hot sauce, without stirring, for 45 seconds.

In another pan, heat the sesame oil to smoking point and add the peppercorns. Cook until the peppercorns turn black and the oil is very aromatic, then strain into the chicken sauce. Divide into the noodles and serve at once.

SHANGHAI NOODLES WITH BEAN SPROUTS AND BROWN SAUCE

500 g (1 lb)	fresh thick egg noodles (or use cooked spaghetti)
1½ teaspoons	salt
125 g (4 oz)	fresh bean sprouts
8	garlic chives
⅓ cup	frying oil
2 teaspoons	sesame oil

Seasoning/Sauce:

¾ cup (6 fl oz)	chicken stock
2 tablespoons	light soy sauce
1 tablespoon	dark soy or oyster sauce
1 teaspoon	rice wine or dry sherry
2 teaspoons	sesame oil (optional)
¼ teaspoon	crushed garlic
¾ teaspoon	salt
½ teaspoon	m.s.g. (optional)
¼ teaspoon	ground black pepper
1 teaspoon	cornflour (cornstarch)

Boil the fresh noodles in plenty of water with the salt added for 2 minutes. Drain cooked spaghetti, if used.

Remove the roots and pods of the bean sprouts. Shred the garlic chives.

Heat the frying oil in a large wok and add the bean sprouts and garlic chives. Stir-fry lightly, then add the seasoning/sauce ingredients and bring to the boil. Add the noodles and gently stir on moderate heat until the liquid is completely absorbed into the noodles. Serve hot.

RED-COOKED BEEF AND CARROTS ON NOODLES

625 g (1¼ lb)	rump steak or (top round) topside
2	spring onions (scallions), trimmed and sliced
3 thick slices	fresh ginger, shredded
1 teaspoon	chopped garlic
¼ cup (2 fl oz)	frying oil
8 cups (2 litres)	water
2	medium carrots, cubed
2 teaspoons	sesame oil (optional)
½ teaspoon	ground black pepper
2 tablespoons	finely chopped spring onion (scallion)
625 g (1¼ lb)	fresh thick egg noodles

Seasoning:

2 tablespoons	soybean paste
2 tablespoons	rice wine or dry sherry
½ cup (4 fl oz)	light soy sauce
2 teaspoons	dark soy sauce
1½ tablespoons	sugar
2	star anise

Cut the beef into bite-sized cubes. Blanch in boiling water and drain. Stir-fry the spring onions, ginger, and garlic in the frying oil for 1 minute. Push to one side of the pan and add the beef. Stir-fry until evenly coloured, then stir in the onions, ginger, and garlic and add the seasoning ingredients. Stir-fry together on moderate heat until well mixed, then add the water and bring to the boil.

Cover the pan, reduce the heat to low and simmer until the meat is tender, about 50 minutes. Add the cubed carrots and cook for a further 20 minutes. Stir in the sesame oil, if used, black pepper, and spring onion and keep warm.

Boil the noodles in plenty of lightly salted water until just tender. Drain and divide among 6 large soup bowls. Pour on the sauce and divide the meat and carrots evenly among the dishes. Serve at once.

FRIED EGG NOODLES WITH MEAT AND VEGETABLES

4 cakes (250 g/8 oz)	dried thin egg noodles
125 g (4 oz)	pork fillet (tenderloin)
125 g (4 oz)	boneless chicken breast
125 g (4 oz)	raw peeled shrimps
2	dried black mushrooms, soaked for 25 minutes
185 g (6 oz)	fresh bean sprouts
8	garlic chives
¾ cup (6 fl oz)	frying oil
2 tablespoons	light soy sauce

Seasoning A:

½ teaspoon	salt
½ teaspoon	sugar
1 teaspoon	rice wine or dry sherry
1 teaspoon	cornflour (cornstarch)

Seasoning B:

¼ teaspoon	salt
¼ teaspoon	m.s.g. (optional)
1½ teaspoons	ginger wine
1 teaspoon	cornflour (cornstarch)

Seasoning C/Sauce:

1¼ cups (10 fl oz)	chicken stock
1¼ teaspoons	salt
½ teaspoon	m.s.g. (optional)
¼ teaspoon	ground black pepper
1½ teaspoons	cornflour (cornstarch)

Soak the dried egg noodles in boiling water until softened enough to unravel, then drop into boiling water and cook for 1½ minutes. Drain well. Stir in 1 tablespoon of the frying oil and set aside.

Cut the pork and chicken into fine shreds and place in a dish with the seasoning A ingredients. Mix well and leave for 15 minutes. Devein the shrimps with a toothpick (see page 394) and rinse well. Mix with the seasoning B ingredients and leave for 10 minutes.

Squeeze the water from the mushrooms, remove the stems and shred the caps. Remove roots and pods from the bean sprouts and cut the garlic chives into 2 cm (¾ in) lengths.

Heat one-third of the oil in a wok and stir-fry the garlic chives for 30 seconds. Push to one side of the pan and add the pork and chicken. Stir-fry until white, about 1 minute, then move to the garlic chives and stir-fry the shrimp until pink and firm. Add the mushrooms and bean sprouts and stir-fry together until the sprouts soften, then sizzle the soy sauce onto the sides of the pan and stir in. Remove from the heat.

In another wok, heat the remaining frying oil to smoking point. Add the noodles and cook on one side, then lift the whole lot on a spatula and turn. Cook until the underside is lightly coloured and crisped on the edges.

Transfer to a serving plate. Return the other wok to the heat. Add the pre-mixed seasoning C/sauce ingredients and bring to the boil. Pour over the noodles and serve at once.

SEAFOOD NOODLE HOT-POT

500 g (1 lb)	flat noodles
6	large green prawns (shrimps) in the shell (about 375 g / 12 oz)
250 g (8 oz)	fresh squid
250 g (8 oz)	fresh sea scallops or fish fillets
250 g (8 oz)	fresh oysters without shells, or fresh clams
10 cups (2½ litres)	water
2 tablespoons	frying oil
3	garlic chives, sliced
3 slices	fresh ginger, shredded
375 g (12 oz)	Chinese (celery) cabbage or young bok choy

Seasoning:

¼ cup (2 fl oz)	light soy sauce
1 tablespoon	rice wine or dry sherry (optional)
2½ teaspoons	salt
1 teaspoon	m.s.g. (optional)
1½ teaspoons	sugar
½ teaspoon	ground black pepper
2 teaspoons	sesame oil

Soak the noodles until softened. Peel the central shell from the prawns, leaving the heads and tails joined to the bodies. Devein with a toothpick (see page 394) and rinse thoroughly. Skin and clean the squid, discarding the heads, tentacles, and fins. Cut the bodies open flat and score in a close criss-cross pattern on the inside, then cut into 4 cm (1 2/3 in) squares. Rinse well. Cut the scallops in halves diagonally or cut the fish into bite-sized pieces. Rinse the oysters or clams in cold water.

Bring the water to the boil and simmer the prawns until pink, then remove and set aside. Add the squid, scallops, and oysters and simmer very briefly. If using clams, simmer separately until the shells open, then drain and discard the top shells. Simmer fish, if used, until white and firm. Drain seafood well.

Add the garlic chives, ginger, and cabbage to the stock and simmer until the cabbage softens, then drain very thoroughly and transfer to a heated wok with the frying oil and stir-fry for 1 minute. Remove. Add the well-drained noodles and stir-fry briefly, then pour in the hot stock and simmer until the noodles are just tender.

Transfer to a casserole and add the seasoning and seafood. Bring to the boil and serve in the casserole.

HOT BEAN THREAD NOODLES WITH SHREDDED PORK

75 g (2½ oz)	bean thread vermicelli
75 g (2½ oz)	pork fillet (tenderloin)
1	large green capsicum (bell pepper)
1	medium onion
1 — 2	fresh red chilli peppers
30 g (1 oz)	dried 'wood ear' fungus, soaked for 25 minutes, or use 3 dried black mushrooms, soaked
2 slices	fresh ginger, shredded
1 teaspoon	finely chopped garlic
¼ cup (2 fl oz)	frying oil
	fresh coriander

Seasoning A:

¼ teaspoon	salt
¼ teaspoon	m.s.g. (optional)
1 teaspoon	rice wine or dry sherry
1 teaspoon	cornflour (cornstarch)

Seasoning B/Sauce:

1 cup (8 fl oz)	chicken stock
1 tablespoon	dark soy sauce
¾ teaspoon	white vinegar
1 teaspoon	sesame oil
½ teaspoon	salt
½ teaspoon	sugar
1 teaspoon	chilli oil (or to taste)

Soak the vermicelli in warm water until softened then cut into 5 cm (2 in) lengths. Finely shred the pork and place in a dish with the seasoning A ingredients, mix well and leave for 20 minutes.

Cut the pepper in halves, remove the seed core and stem and trim away the inner white ribs. Cut into narrow shreds. Peel the onion and cut into narrow wedges from stem to root, then trim away the root section to allow the pieces to separate. Cut the chillies into thin slices, discarding the seeds for a milder taste. Drain the 'wood ears' and chop finely.

Heat the frying oil in a wok and stir-fry the vegetables for 2 minutes. Push to one side of the pan and add the ginger and garlic. Stir-fry briefly, then add the shredded pork and stir-fry until white, about 45 seconds. Add the well-drained bean threads and stir-fry briefly.

Pour in the pre-mixed seasoning B/sauce ingredients and simmer until the liquid has been absorbed and the noodles are tender. Stir in plenty of chopped fresh coriander to taste, or use as a garnish. Serve.

RICE RIBBON NOODLES WITH BEEF AND BROCCOLI

500 g (1 lb)	fresh rice flour sheets*
250 g (8 oz)	beef steak (rump, fillet/tenderloin)
250 g (8 oz)	fresh broccoli, broken into small florets
2	spring onions (scallions), trimmed and sliced
⅓ cup	frying oil
1½ tablespoons	sweet bean paste or oyster sauce

Seasoning A:

½ teaspoon	salt
½ teaspoon	m.s.g. (optional)
1 teaspoon	light soy sauce
1 teaspoon	rice wine or dry sherry
1 tablespoon	frying oil
1 teaspoon	cornflour (cornstarch)

Seasoning B/Sauce:

1 cup (8 fl oz)	chicken stock
1½ tablespoons	sweet bean paste or oyster sauce
2 teaspoons	dark soy sauce
½ teaspoon	salt
½ teaspoon	m.s.g. (optional)
1 teaspoon	sugar (or to taste)
1 teaspoon	cornflour (cornstarch)

Cut the rice flour sheets into strips about 0.8 cm (⅓ in) wide. Drop into boiling salted water and cook for 1½ minutes. Drain well. Drizzle on 1 — 2 tablespoons frying oil and mix in lightly, then cover with cold water.

Very thinly slice the beef across the grain and cut into 4 cm (1 2/3 in) squares. Place in a dish and add the seasoning A ingredients. Leave for 20 minutes, turning once.

Blanch the broccoli and drain well. Stir-fry in the frying oil with the spring onions until beginning to soften, about 2 minutes. Push to one side of the pan and add the beef. Stir-fry on high heat until the meat changes colour. Add the bean paste or oyster sauce and stir until well mixed, then push to the side of the pan. Add the noodles, very well drained, and stir-fry until lightly crisped on the edges. Stir in the meat and vegetables and add the pre-mixed seasoning B/sauce ingredients. Bring to the boil and cook, stirring continually, until the noodles are evenly glazed with the sauce and the liquid almost absorbed. Transfer to a serving dish and serve at once.

* Sold fresh or frozen by specialist Chinese food stockists

COLD BEAN SHEET NOODLES WITH CHICKEN AND TWO SAUCES

5	bean sheets
250 g (8 oz)	boneless chicken breast
125 g (4 oz)	fresh bean sprouts
5	garlic chives, sliced
¾ stick	fresh celery

Sesame Sauce:

2 tablespoons	sesame paste
2 tablespoons	light soy sauce
1 teaspoon	sugar
1 teaspoon	sesame oil
½ teaspoon	m.s.g. (optional)
1 teaspoon	finely chopped spring onion (scallion)
1 teaspoon	grated fresh ginger
½ teaspoon	crushed garlic
2 tablespoons	cold water
1 teaspoon	lemon juice, or white vinegar to taste
2 tablespoons	frying oil

Hot Sauce:

1 tablespoon	chilli oil, or use commercial chilli sauce, or hot mustard thinned with a little sherry

Cut the bean sheets into narrow shreds and drop into a dish of boiling water. Leave for 1 minute, then drain well and arrange in a serving dish.

Poach or steam the chicken until just cooked, then tear into narrow slivers and set aside. Blanch the bean sprouts and garlic chives in boiling water until just softened. Place with the chicken.

Finely shred the celery and blanch for 1 minute in lightly salted boiling water. Place over the noodles and arrange the lightly tossed mixture of shredded chicken, bean sprouts, and garlic chives on top.

Mix the sesame sauce ingredients together and pour over the chicken. Serve the hot sauce separately to add at the table or to individual taste.

*Dried bean sheets should be soaked until soft before shredding.

Overleaf, left *Lotus Rice (recipe page 357)* and right, *Shrimps and Squid with Assorted Vegetables on Soft Egg Noodles (recipe page 346)*

RICE VERMICELLI IN SOUP WITH CRABMEAT AND EGG FLOWER

155 g (5 oz)	dried rice vermicelli
250 g (8 oz)	fresh crabmeat
3	egg whites, well beaten
90 g (3 oz)	fresh 'silver' sprouts, blanched
5 cups (1¼ litres)	chicken stock
1½ teaspoons	salt
¼ teaspoon	ground black pepper
⅓ teaspoon	m.s.g. (optional)
	light soy sauce
	sesame oil (optional)

Seasoning:

½ teaspoon	salt
½ teaspoon	m.s.g. (optional)
1 tablespoon	ginger wine (see page 387)

Soak the noodles in warm water until softened. Drain well and rinse in cold water. Place the crabmeat in a dish with seasoning A ingredients.

Bring the chicken stock to the boil and add the salt and pepper. Add the noodles and simmer until softened, approximately 3 minutes, but this depends on the brand of noodles used as they can vary considerably.

Add the crabmeat and simmer, gently stirring, until cooked through and beginning to flake. Slowly drizzle in the beaten egg whites and leave without stirring until the egg sets in white strands in the soup. Add the blanched 'silver' sprouts and the m.s.g., if used.

Season to taste with soy sauce and add a few drops of sesame oil, if used. Pour into a soup tureen and serve at once.

Rice vermicelli is often crisp fried to serve under a dressing of stir-fried meats, vegetables, and seafood. One of the most popular toppings with these deliciously light and crisp fried noodles is fried fresh milk with crabmeat (see page 78).

'SILVER PIN' NOODLES

315 g (10 oz)	'silver pin' noodles*
185 g (6 oz)	raw peeled shrimps
185 g (6 oz)	pork fillet (tenderloin)
185 g (6 oz)	'silver' sprouts
3	dried black mushrooms, soaked for 25 minutes
18	snow peas
1	egg, well beaten
⅓ cup	softened lard or frying oil

Seasoning:

½ teaspoon	salt
2 teaspoons	ginger wine (see page 387)
1 teaspoon	cornflour (cornstarch)

Seasoning B:

½ teaspoon	salt
½ teaspoon	light soy sauce
½ teaspoon	rice wine or dry sherry
½ teaspoon	cornflour (cornstarch)

Seasoning C/Sauce:

2 teaspoons	light soy sauce
2 teaspoons	rice wine or dry sherry
1 teaspoon	salt
1 teaspoon	sugar
¼ teaspoon	white pepper
¾ teaspoon	sesame oil

Prepare the noodles and cover with a damp cloth until needed. Devein the shrimps with a toothpick (see page 394), and wash well. Pat dry then mix with the seasoning A ingredients and leave for 10 minutes. Finely shred the pork and place in a dish with the seasoning B ingredients. Mix well and leave for 10 minutes.

Blanch the 'silver' sprouts for 5 seconds in boiling water and drain well. Squeeze the water from the mushrooms, remove the stems and shred the caps. String the peas and blanch for a few seconds in boiling water. Drain well.

Wipe out an omelette pan with an oiled cloth, heat to moderate and pour in the beaten egg. Tilt the pan so it sets in a thin covering over the entire bottom of the pan and cook on one side until firm, then turn and cook the other side. Remove, roll up and shred finely.

Heat the lard or frying oil to moderate and stir-fry the noodles for about 3 minutes. Remove. Add the pork with a little more oil if needed and stir-fry until it changes colour, then push to one side of the pan and add the shrimps. Stir-fry until pink, about 45 seconds. Remove and add the vegetables, stir-frying briefly.

Return the meat, shrimps, and noodles and add the seasoning C/sauce ingredients. Stir-fry for 1 minute, then stir in half the shredded egg. Transfer to a serving plate and garnish with the remaining egg. Serve.

* Made with leftover shrimp dumpling (har gow) dough (see page 360).

RICE SHEET ROLLS WITH SHREDDED MEAT AND VEGETABLE FILLING

Makes 18.

3	rice sheets
250 g (8 oz)	boneless chicken breast
75 g (2½ oz)	raw peeled shrimps
2	dried black mushrooms, soaked for 25 minutes
45 g (1½ oz)	canned bamboo shoots, drained
90 g (3 oz)	'silver' sprouts
12	garlic chives
5 slices	fresh ginger, finely shredded
2 tablespoons	frying oil
1 tablespoon	lightly toasted white sesame seeds

Seasoning A:

½ teaspoon	salt
2 teaspoons	rice wine or dry sherry
1 teaspoon	sugar
1 teaspoon	cornflour (cornstarch)

Seasoning B:

½ teaspoon	salt
1½ teaspoons	ginger wine (see page 387)
1 teaspoon	cornflour (cornstarch)

Seasoning C:

1 teaspoon	salt
½ teaspoon	m.s.g. (optional)
1 teaspoon	sugar
¼ teaspoon	ground black pepper
2 teaspoons	light soy sauce
2 teaspoons	rice wine or dry sherry
½ teaspoon	sesame oil
⅓ cup	chicken stock
1 tablespoon	cornflour (cornstarch)

Cover the rice sheets with a damp or oiled cloth until needed. Finely shred the chicken, mix with the seasoning A ingredients and leave for 10 minutes. Devein the shrimps with a toothpick (see page 394), rinse and wipe dry, then mix with the seasoning B ingredients and leave for 10 minutes.

Squeeze the water from the mushrooms, remove the stems and shred the caps. Shred the bamboo shoots. Blanch the sprouts in boiling water for 4 seconds, drain well. Cut the garlic chives in halves lengthwise, then cut into 4 cm (1 2/3 in) lengths.

Heat the frying oil in a wok and stir-fry the chicken and shrimps for 45 seconds. Push to one side of the pan and add the garlic chives. Stir-fry briefly, then add the vegetables and ginger. Stir-fry all the ingredients together, adding the pre-mixed seasoning C ingredients. Cook until the mixture is thick.

Spread the rice sheets on a board and cut each into 6 pieces. Place a line of the filling along the centre of each roll and roll up without tucking the ends in. Place the rolls with the fold underneath on an oiled plate. Set on a rack in a steamer and steam for 6 minutes over gently boiling water. Serve hot, garnished with the sesame seeds and with dips of light soy and chilli sauces.

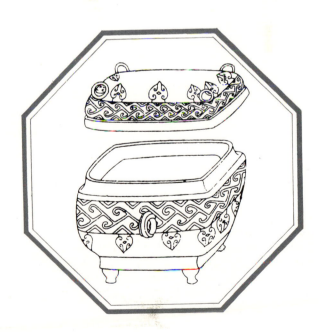

PLAIN WHITE RICE

The absorption method of cooking rice is the one most often used by Chinese, though the rice cooker which works on the same principle replaces a saucepan in most households.

It requires a fairly heavy-based saucepan with a very tight-fitting lid. The rice is placed in the saucepan dry, a specific amount of water added and the lid placed securely in position. When the water comes to the boil, the heat is turned down to the lowest point and the rice left to cook until the water is completely absorbed, leaving the rice dry, fluffy, and each grain separate, but sticky enough to cling together for easy eating with chopsticks.

Allow 90 g (3 oz / ½ cup) short grain rice per person and place in a saucepan. Add some salt, though most Chinese cooks prefer their rice unsalted, and water to cover the rice by 2 cm (¾ in). The rice should be smoothed flat in the saucepan to accurately gauge the water level. For more accurate measurement, use 2 cups rice and 3 cups water. (Two cups of raw short grain rice make 5 cups cooked rice.)

FRIED RICE

4 cups	cooked short grain white rice (see above)
60 g (2 oz)	raw peeled shrimps
½ teaspoon	salt
1½ teaspoons	cornflour (cornstarch)
1 teaspoon	ginger wine (see page 387)
2	eggs, well beaten
⅓ cup	softened lard or frying oil
60 g (2 oz)	roast pork or cooked ham, diced
60 g (2 oz)	cooked green peas
2 tablespoons	finely chopped spring onion (scallion)

Seasoning:

2 teaspoons	salt
½ teaspoon	sugar
¼ teaspoon	m.s.g. (optional)
1 tablespoon	light soy sauce
¾ teaspoon	dark soy sauce
¼ teaspoon	ground black pepper

There are several schools of thought about the method for producing perfect fried rice. One insists that the rice be at least one day old and refrigerated overnight so that each grain becomes slightly dry and all are separated. The other, that the rice should be freshly cooked and steaming hot.

Devein the shrimps with a toothpick (see page 394) and rub with the salt and cornflour, then rinse well. Wipe dry with kitchen paper, then rub with the ginger wine.

Heat a very little lard or oil in the wok and add the beaten eggs, tilting the pan so that the egg forms into a thin pancake over the entire bottom of the pan. Cook until lightly coloured and firm underneath, then turn and briefly cook the other side. Remove and leave to cool, then shred finely.

Reheat the wok and add the remaining oil. Stir-fry the shrimps, pork or ham, peas, and onion together for 2 minutes. Add the seasoning ingredients and fry briefly, then add the rice and stir-fry on moderate heat until each grain is coated with the seasonings, and the other ingredients evenly distributed.

Stir in half of the shredded egg and transfer to a serving plate. Garnish with the remaining egg and a few shreds of fresh red chilli pepper or sprigs of fresh coriander.

Hot Bean Thread Noodles with Shredded Pork (recipe page 348)

MULTI-COLOURED RICE

2 cups	raw short grain white rice
45 g (1½ oz)	dried shrimps, soaked for 1 hour
3	dried black mushrooms, soaked for 25 minutes
1	medium carrot
45 g (1½ oz)	canned bamboo shoots, drained
125 g (4 oz)	fresh or frozen peas
125 g (4 oz)	roast pork (see page 291), diced
3 tablespoons	finely chopped spring onion (scallion)
⅓ cup	frying oil
3 cups (24 fl oz)	water

Seasoning:

1½ teaspoons	light soy sauce
1¼ teaspoons	salt
1 teaspoon	m.s.g. (optional)
1 teaspoon	sugar
¼ teaspoon	ground black pepper
½ teaspoon	sesame oil

Thoroughly wash the rice and drain well. Drain the shrimps and cut the larger ones in halves. Squeeze the water from the mushrooms and dice the caps. Finely dice the carrot and bamboo shoots. Parboil the carrot and peas and drain well.

Heat the frying oil in a wok and stir-fry the diced pork and spring onion for 45 seconds. Add the shrimps, mushrooms, carrot, bamboo shoots, and peas and stir-fry for 2 minutes. Add the seasoning ingredients and the drained rice and water and mix thoroughly.

Bring to the boil, cover tightly and reduce the heat to very low. Cook until the rice is tender, about 15 minutes. Stir up lightly with a chopstick and serve.

CHICKEN AND RICE POT WITH CHINESE SAUSAGE

2 cups	raw short grain white rice
3 cups (24 fl oz)	chicken stock
185 g (6 oz)	boneless chicken
3	dried black mushrooms, soaked for 25 minutes
1	dried Chinese sausage, steamed for 10 minutes
2	spring onions (scallions), trimmed and sliced
2 slices	fresh ginger, shredded
1 tablespoon	frying oil

Seasoning:

1¼ teaspoons	salt
¼ teaspoon	m.s.g. (optional)
½ teaspoon	sugar
¼ teaspoon	white pepper
1 tablespoon	light soy sauce
1 teaspoon	sesame oil

Thoroughly wash the rice and pour into a saucepan with the chicken stock. Cut the chicken into bite-sized pieces and arrange over the rice. Bring to the boil, then reduce the heat to simmer until the rice is partially cooked and the water level has reduced to the top of the rice.

Squeeze the water from the mushrooms and remove the stems. Cut the caps into quarters. Cut the sausage into diagonal slices about 2 cm (¾ in) long. Stir-fry the mushrooms, sausage, spring onions, and ginger lightly in the oil, then place on top of the rice and add the pre-mixed seasoning ingredients.

Cover the pan and continue to cook on very low heat until the rice and chicken are both cooked. The rice should be dry and fluffy. Use chopsticks to stir the meat and seasonings evenly into the rice. Transfer to a deep covered dish and serve at once.

'LOTUS' RICE

1	fresh or dried lotus leaf
4 cups	cooked white rice (see page 354)
185 g (6 oz)	boneless chicken breast, diced
125 g (4 oz)	roast duck or pork, diced
125 g (4 oz)	raw peeled shrimps, or 2 tablespoons soaked dried shrimps
90 g (3 oz)	canned straw mushrooms or champignons, drained and diced, or used 4 dried black mushrooms, soaked and diced
2½ tablespoons	softened lard or frying oil
1½ tablespoons	finely chopped spring onion (scallion)
½ teaspoon	grated fresh ginger
1¾ teaspoons	salt
1 tablespoon	light soy sauce
2 teaspoons	sesame oil (optional)
¼ teaspoon	ground black pepper

Soak the dried lotus leaf or blanch the fresh leaf until softened, then squeeze out the water and brush the underside with oil. Cook the rice and set aside.

Stir-fry the chicken, duck or pork, shrimps, and mushrooms in the lard or oil for 2 minutes, then add the spring onion and ginger and cook briefly. Add the salt, soy sauce, sesame oil, if used, and the black pepper and mix in the rice. Stir thoroughly on moderate heat until evenly blended.

Place the lotus leaf in a wide bowl and pile the rice onto it. Fold in the sides to completely enclose the rice, then invert the parcel so the folds are underneath. Set the bowl on a rack in a steamer and steam over high heat for 15 — 20 minutes.

Serve hot with the top of the leaf parcel cut open to give access to the rice. If preferred, wrap the rice in smaller individual parcels.

This dish may also be made with steamed glutinous rice. It is a popular dish in dim sum restaurants and makes a delicious alternative to plain white rice at a dinner.

RICE CONGEE WITH SLICED FISH

3 cups	raw short grain white rice, soaked for 4 hours
8 cups (2 litres)	chicken stock or water
2 teaspoons	salt
½ teaspoon	m.s.g. (optional)
125 g (4 oz)	white fish fillets
2	spring onions (scallions), trimmed and thinly sliced
45 g (1½ oz)	Szechuan (Sichuan) preserved vegetables or salted mustard root, soaked for 25 minutes
	white pepper
	crisp-fried Chinese crullers (see page 374), or fried bread croutons
	fresh coriander or parsley

Drain the rice and transfer to a large saucepan. Add the chicken stock or water and the salt. Bring to the boil, then reduce to a simmer and cook until the rice is reduced to a starchy soup.

Stir in the m.s.g., if used. Very thinly slice the fish and place several pieces of fish and spring onion in each of 6 — 8 soup bowls. Drain the preserved vegetables or mustard root and shred finely. Stir into the rice and heat to boiling.

Pour over the fish and season with white pepper. Garnish with thinly sliced deep-fried crullers or bread croutons and sprigs of fresh coriander or parsley.

Reheating improves the flavour of congee. Serve as a breakfast or snack food with a variety of additives in place of the fish and pickled vegetables. Try thinly sliced liver, fish balls, roast pork, sliced chicken, pork fillet, or beef.

In Fukien (Fujian), thin rice congee is served in place of steamed white rice or noodles as the accompaniment to most meals.

CHAPTER IX
Dim Sum, Bread and Cold Platters - Appetisers

SHRIMP DUMPLINGS *(HAR GOW)*

Makes 24.

Pastry:

1 cup	*gluten-free wheat flour (tang fun/cheng mien)*
150 ml (5 fl oz)	*boiling water*
2 teaspoons	*cornflour (cornstarch)*
¾ teaspoon	*softened lard*

Filling:

155 g (5 oz)	*raw peeled shrimps*
45 g (1½ oz)	*pork fat*
45 g (1½ oz)	*canned bamboo shoots*

Seasoning:

2/3 teaspoon	*salt*
½ teaspoon	*m.s.g. (optional)*
½ teaspoon	*sugar*
1¼ teaspoons	*cornflour (cornstarch)*
	pinch of white pepper
¼ teaspoon	*sesame oil*

Special equipment: A special blunt cleaver for pastry making, or a large spatula.

Prepare the filling first. Finely chop the shrimps, pork fat, and bamboo shoots and mix thoroughly with the seasoning ingredients. Refrigerate for 1 hour.

Sift the gluten-free flour into a mixing bowl and add the cornflour. Bring the water to boil in a saucepan, covered so none is lost in evaporation as the amount of water is critical to success. Add the flour to the water and quickly stir in with the handle of a wooden spoon, then cover and leave for about 5 minutes so the heat softens the flour completely.

Remove from the saucepan, add the lard and knead until smooth and shiny. Roll into a long sausage shape and leave to cool a little, covered with a damp cloth. Divide into 24 equal parts.

On a clean, dry board place one piece of pastry. Flatten slightly with the fingers, then use the greased pastry cleaver to smear the pastry across the board in a circular motion resulting in a thin clear round wrapper. Carefully lift from the board on the spatula and place a spoonful of the filling in the centre. Fold over and pinch-pleat the edges together. (Place the filling on the side of the pastry that faced the board, as the upper side will be too greasy to allow the edges to stick together.)

An easier method is to pinch-pleat one side so the pastry is formed into a cup shape, add the filling, then press the smooth edge onto the pleated edge and pinch firmly together.

Steam the pastries in a lightly greased steaming basket for 4—5 minutes. Serve hot with dips of hot mustard and light soy sauce.

Use any leftover pastry to make 'Silver Pin' Noodles. Break off small pieces of the dough and place on an oiled board. Rub the palm of the hand back and forth across the dough until pieces about the same size as a bean sprout are obtained, about 5 cm (2 in) long.

Stir-fry in frying oil and use in the same way as egg noodles.

PORK DUMPLINGS (SIEW MAI)

Makes 18.

18	*wonton wrappers (see recipe, page 376)**
125 g (4 oz)	*lean pork*
45 g (1½ oz)	*pork fat*
125 g (4 oz)	*raw peeled shrimps*
2	*dried black mushrooms, soaked for 25 minutes*

Seasoning:

1	*small egg white, beaten*
½ teaspoon	*salt*
½ teaspoon	*m.s.g. (optional)*
1 teaspoon	*sugar*
1 teaspoon	*light soy sauce*
½ teaspoon	*dark soy sauce*
¼ teaspoon	*sesame oil*
2 teaspoons	*cornflour (cornstarch)*

Finely dice the pork, pork fat, and shrimps and mix with the seasoning ingredients. Squeeze the water from the mushrooms, remove the stems and cut the caps into fine dice. Add to the pork mixture, mixing well.

Cut the freshly made or frozen wonton wrappers into 7.5 cm (3 in) circles. Hold the point of the thumb and forefinger of the left hand together and place a wonton wrapper over the circle it makes. Place a spoonful of the filling on the wrapper and push the whole thing through the circle made by the thumb and finger. This will result in the pastry forming into an open-topped cup shape around the filling. Flatten the bottom and stand in a lightly greased steaming basket.

When all are done, steam over rapidly boiling water for about 10 minutes. Serve hot in the steaming basket with dips of chilli sauce, hot mustard, and light soy sauce.

* Or use frozen wonton wrappers, thawed under a damp cloth.

PORK WONTONS

Makes 36.

36	fresh or frozen wonton wrappers (see recipe page 376)
250 g (8 oz)	pork fillet (tenderloin)
125 g (4 oz)	raw peeled shrimps
45 g (1½ oz)	pork fat
60 g (2 oz)	canned water chestnuts, drained
1	spring onion (scallion), finely chopped
1 tablespoon	finely chopped fresh coriander
6 cups (1½ litres)	deep-frying oil

Seasoning:

1½ teaspoons	salt
¼ teaspoon	white pepper
2 teaspoons	sugar
2 teaspoons	light soy sauce
2 teaspoons	cornflour (cornstarch)

Prepare the wonton wrappers and cover with a damp cloth until needed. If using frozen wrappers, remove from the freezer about 3 hours before using.

Mince (grind) the pork fillet, shrimps, and pork fat together and add finely diced water chestnuts, spring onion, fresh coriander, and the seasonings. Mix thoroughly and chill for 1 hour.

Place a spoonful of the mixture in each wonton wrapper. Pull the edges up around the filling forcing it into a ball shape just slightly off-centre. Brush the three corners closest to the filling with water and press them together. Fold over the filling and pinch onto the base of the final corner, completely sealing in the filling. Fold the final corner up and outwards in a petal shape. The resultant wonton is the classic goldfish shape.

A simpler shape is to gather the four corners together, then run the fingers from the tips down to the filling. Pinch together above the filling, then flare the corners outwards.

Heat the deep oil to moderately hot and add several wontons. Fry to a light golden brown, about 2 minutes. Drain. Repeat.

Serve with dips of light soy sauce, chilli sauce, or sweet and sour sauce (see recipe, page 385).

Use unfried wontons in soup and soup-noodle dishes. They may be frozen before cooking and require only a brief thawing before deep-frying or using in soup.

STEAMED CHICKEN TURNOVERS

Makes 24.

Pastry:

1 recipe	har gow pastry, see previous page

Filling:

90 g (3 oz)	boneless chicken breast
30 g (1 oz)	pork fat
75 g (2½ oz)	raw peeled shrimps
30 g (1 oz)	canned bamboo shoots, drained and finely diced
30 g (1 oz)	parboiled carrot, finely diced
1	dried black mushroom, soaked for 25 minutes
1½ teaspoons	finely chopped fresh coriander
1 clove	garlic
2 tablespoons	frying oil

Seasoning:

½ teaspoon	salt
½ teaspoon	m.s.g. (optional)
1 teaspoon	sugar
1 teaspoon	light soy sauce
¼ teaspoon	sesame oil
2 tablespoons	water
1 teaspoon	cornflour (cornstarch)
	pinch of white pepper

Special Equipment: A blunt bladed pastry cleaver or large spatula.

Finely dice the chicken, pork fat, and shrimps. Heat the frying oil and sauté the garlic for 30 seconds, then discard. Add the chicken, fat and shrimps and stir-fry for 30 seconds, then add the bamboo shoots and carrots and stir-fry briefly.

Squeeze the water from the mushroom, remove the stem and cut into small dice. Add the mushroom and coriander to the filling and add the seasoning ingredients. Stir-fry a further 45 seconds, then spread on a plate to cool.

Make the pastry and divide into 24 equal parts. Cover with a cloth while each piece is being prepared. Using the greased blunt pastry cleaver on a clean board, spread the pastry in a circular motion into a thin round shape and scrape up from the board. Place a portion of filling on the ungreasy side and fold over. Pinch the edges together.

Place the turnovers in a greased steaming basket and steam over rapidly boiling water for 3 minutes. They should not overlap in the steamer so it will be necessary to cook in two or three lots.

Serve hot with chilli or light soy sauce dips.

STEAMED ROAST PORK BUNS *(CHA SIEW POW)*

Makes 12.

Dough:

2¼ cups	flour
⅓ cup	sugar
1 tablespoon	baking powder
1 tablespoon	softened lard
⅓ cup	lukewarm water

Filling:

155 g (5 oz)	roast pork (see recipe page 291)
2	spring onions (scallions), trimmed and diced
1 tablespoon	frying oil
⅓ cup	water

Seasoning:

½ teaspoon	salt
2 teaspoons	light soy sauce
1 teaspoon	dark soy sauce
2 teaspoons	oyster sauce
1 tablespoon	sugar
1 tablespoon	cornflour (cornstarch)

Sift the flour into a mixing bowl and add the sugar, baking powder, and lard. Pour in the water and knead until smooth and soft. Cover with a damp cloth and leave for 30 minutes.

Sauté the spring onions and roast pork in the oil for 45 seconds. Add the water and seasoning ingredients and simmer until the sauce thickens. Spread onto a plate to cool.

Roll the dough into a long sausage shape and cut into 12 portions. Roll each into a ball and flatten with the fingers. Place a portion of the filling in the centre of each and ease the dough up around the filling, pinching firmly together underneath. Brush with a little water and stick a square of plain paper under each bun.

Set in a steaming basket and steam over rapidly boiling water for 10 minutes. Serve hot in the basket.

SPRING ROLLS

Makes 12.

12	fresh or frozen spring roll wrappers (see recipe page 374)
45 g (1½ oz)	boneless chicken breast, shredded
45 g (1½ oz)	raw peeled shrimps, halved lengthwise
30 g (1 oz)	pork fat, finely diced
1 10 cm (4 in) piece	fresh celery, shredded
30 g (1 oz)	fresh bean sprouts
2	dried black mushrooms, soaked for 25 minutes
30 g (1 oz)	canned bamboo shoots, drained and shredded
8 cups (2 litres)	deep-frying oil

Seasoning:

¾ teaspoon	salt
2 teaspoons	sugar
1 teaspoon	light soy sauce
¾ teaspoon	dark soy sauce
	pinch of ground black pepper
¼ teaspoon	chilli oil (optional)
¼ teaspoon	sesame oil
2 teaspoons	cornflour (cornstarch)

Prepare the spring roll wrappers and cover with a damp cloth until needed. Season the chicken, shrimps, and pork fat with a dash of ginger wine and soy sauce and leave for 10 minutes.

Heat 1 tablespoon of the oil in a wok and stir-fry the shredded celery and bean sprouts until softened, about 1½ minutes. Remove from the heat. Squeeze the water from the mushrooms and remove the stems. Shred the caps and stir-fry lightly, then mix the vegetables with the chicken, shrimps and pork fat and add the seasonings. Mix thoroughly.

The filling may be stir-fried with the seasoning at this point. The flavour is better if the filling is uncooked before deep-frying, but if the rolls are to be kept for some time the filling should be cooked first. If freezing or storing for more than a few hours, omit the bean sprouts and substitute shredded carrot, water chestnut, or additional bamboo shoots.

Place a portion of filling diagonally across the centre of each wrapper. Fold over the lower flap, then the two sides and roll up. Stick the final end down with a little water.

Deep-fry in moderate oil for about 8 minutes. If the filling has been cooked, deep-fry at a slightly higher temperature for about 2 minutes.

Serve hot on a bed of shredded lettuce with dips of light soy sauce and chilli sauce.

Spring Rolls (recipe this page).

TARO PASTRIES

Makes 24.

Filling:

125 g (4 oz)	pork fillet (tenderloin)
60 g (2 oz)	raw peeled shrimps
3	dried black mushrooms, soaked for 25 minutes
1 teaspoon	rice wine or dry sherry
2 tablespoons	frying oil
6 cups (1½ litres)	deep-frying oil

Seasoning:

1 teaspoon	salt
½ teaspoon	m.s.g. (optional)
1 teaspoon	sugar
¼ teaspoon	ground black pepper
1 tablespoon	light soy sauce
1 teaspoon	sesame oil (optional)
1 tablespoon	cornflour (cornstarch)

Pastry:

500 g (1 lb)	peeled taro, yam, or sweet potato
⅓ cup	softened lard or ghee
½ teaspoon	salt
1¼ tablespoons	sugar
3 — 4 tablespoons	cornflour (cornstarch), or potato flour

Mince or finely chop the pork, shrimps, and mushroom caps. Stir-fry in 2 tablespoons of oil until the pork changes colour, then sizzle the wine onto the sides of the pan, stir in and add the seasoning ingredients, except the cornflour. Stir-fry briefly, then mix the cornflour with ¼ cup cold water and pour in. Simmer until the mixture is smooth and creamy. Spread on a plate to cool.

Boil the taro, yam, or sweet potato until soft, then drain very thoroughly. Mash to a smooth paste, adding the lard, salt, and sugar. Add the cornflour and knead until the mixture is completely smooth and pliable. Yam and sweet potato are more moist than taro and may require additional cornflour or potato flour to achieve the right consistency.

Divide the dough into 24 pieces and roll each into a ball. Flatten with the fingers into a circle about 7.5 cm (3 in) in diameter. Place a spoonful of the filling in the centre of each pastry and fold in halves. Pinch the edges firmly together, then carefully roll into a cigar shape.

Heat the deep-frying oil to moderate and fry the taro pastries, several at a time, until golden brown and crumbly on the surface, about 1 minute, then increase the heat for a further 30 seconds. Remove, drain well, and serve at once.

They can be reheated, if necessary, by frying in fairly hot oil for 45 seconds.

TURNIP CAKE

500 g (1 lb)	raw long grain white rice
825 g (1¾ lb)	sweet white turnips or giant white (icicle) radishes
2 teaspoons	salt
½ teaspoon	ground black pepper
45 g (1½ oz)	streaky bacon, diced
3	spring onions (scallions), trimmed and diced
2 tablespoons	dried shrimps, soaked for 1 hour
¼ cup (2 fl oz)	frying oil

Soak the rice overnight in plenty of cold water. Drain and transfer to a food processor or heavy-duty blender. Add a very little water and grind to a smooth paste.

Peel the turnips or radish and grate. Add to the rice paste with the salt and pepper. Heat the oil and sauté the bacon and spring onion briefly, then add the drained shrimps and sauté for 30 seconds. Stir into the rice and turnip paste and mix well.

Pour the mixture into a well-greased 25 cm (10 in) baking tin with the bottom lined with a piece of greased greaseproof paper. Smooth the top and set on a rack in a steamer. Steam, tightly covered, over gently boiling water for about 1 hour, or until the cake is firm. Test by inserting a chopstick. If it comes away clean the cake is done.

Leave to cool, then remove from the tin and cut into slices. Serve hot or cold. If preferred, the slices can be shallow-fried or cooked on a lightly oiled hotplate until crisp on the surface.

Serve with dips of chilli sauce and light soy sauce.

STEAMED BEANCURD SKIN ROLLS IN OYSTER SAUCE

Makes 12.

12 pieces	beancurd skin, each about 12 cm (5 in) square
90 g (3 oz)	lean pork, shredded
60 g (2 oz)	raw peeled shrimps
2	dried black mushrooms, soaked for 25 minutes
60 g (2 oz)	fresh bean sprouts
45 g (1½ oz)	canned bamboo shoots, drained and shredded
6 cups (1½ litres)	deep-frying oil

Seasoning A:

⅓ teaspoon	salt
¼ teaspoon	sugar
1 teaspoon	light soy sauce
1 teaspoon	vegetable or seame oil
2½ teaspoons	cornflour (cornstarch)

Seasoning B:

¼ teaspoon	salt
¼ teaspoon	m.s.g. (optional)
1 teaspoon	rice wine or dry sherry
1¼ teaspoons	cornflour (cornstarch)

Sauce:

¾ cup (6 fl oz)	water
1 teaspoon	light soy sauce
½ teaspoon	dark soy sauce
2½ teaspoons	oyster sauce
½ teaspoon	salt
½ teaspoon	m.s.g. (optional)
1 teaspoon	sugar
¼ teaspoon	ground black pepper
1½ — 2 teaspoons	cornflour (cornstarch)

Wipe the beancurd skins with a damp cloth, cover and leave until needed. Place the shredded pork in a dish and add the seasoning A ingredients, mix in and leave for 15 minutes. Place the shrimps in another dish and add the seasoning B ingredients, mix in and leave for 10 minutes.

Mix the pork, shrimps, mushrooms, and bamboo shoots together. Heat 1 tablespoon of the frying oil and stir-fry the bean sprouts for 1 minute, then add the mixed meat and vegetables. Stir-fry briefly, then remove to a plate to cool.

Divide the mixture between the wrappers and brush all around the edge with a mixture of plain flour and water. Fold one corner over the filling, then fold in two sides and roll up. Stick down the final flap with more flour and water paste if needed.

Heat the deep-frying oil to smoking point and deep-fry the rolls for 2 — 3 minutes. Drain well. Prepare to this stage in advance and keep in the refrigerator.

Pour the pre-mixed sauce ingredients into a wok and bring to the boil. Simmer for 2 minutes. Place the rolls in a dish, pour on the sauce and set on a rack in a steamer. Steam over rapidly boiling water for about 25 minutes.

Serve in the dish.

MARBLED TEA EGGS

12	chicken eggs
1¾ tablespoons	salt
½ cup	black tea leaves
3	star anise
2 sticks	cinnamon bark
8 cups (2 litres)	water

Place the eggs in a saucepan of cold water and bring slowly to the boil. Simmer for 10 minutes, then drain. Gently tap the eggs together until each shell is thoroughly crazed with small cracks. Place in a saucepan with the remaining ingredients and bring to the boil. Simmer on very low heat for 1 hour. Remove and cool under running cold water. Peel and cut in halves. Arrange on a serving platter with slices of fresh young ginger lightly pickled in sweetened white vinegar.

The eggs can be kept for 2 — 3 days in the refrigerator.

STEAMED BEEF MEATBALLS ON WATERCRESS

250 g (8 oz)	lean beef
¾ teaspoon	bicarbonate of soda (optional)
30 g (1 oz)	pork fat
2 teaspoons	finely chopped fresh coriander*
250 g (8 oz)	fresh watercress leaves

Seasoning:

½ teaspoon	salt
½ teaspoon	m.s.g. (optional)
2 teaspoons	sugar
¼ teaspoon	ground black pepper
1 tablespoon	light soy sauce
½ teaspoon	sesame oil (optional)
¼ cup (2 fl oz)	vegetable oil
¼ cup (2 fl oz)	water
2 tablespoons	cornflour (cornstarch)

Pulverise the beef in a food processor or mince (grind) very finely. Add the bicarbonate of soda, if used, and ¼ cup of cold water and mix in thoroughly. Cover with plastic wrap and refrigerate for 4 hours.

Place the pork fat in a saucepan or wok and add ½ cup of water. Simmer, covered, until the fat is transparent, then remove and cut into very small dice. Mix with the beef, adding the coriander and seasonings. Work until thoroughly blended and smooth. Gather the meat into the hand and throw repeatedly against the side of the mixing bowl. Or place in the food processor and mix with the dough blending blade for 1 minute. Return to the refrigerator for at least 1 hour.

Place the watercress in a dish. Form the meat into 12 balls and place on the watercress. Set the dish on a rack in a steamer and steam over rapidly boiling water for about 8 minutes. Serve hot.

* Or use a small piece of dried orange peel, soaked to soften and finely chopped.

CLEAR-AS-GLASS COOKIES

Makes 12.

125 g (4 oz)	gluten-free flour (tang fun/cheng mien)
1 cup (8 fl oz)	boiling water
¼ cup	sugar
1 teaspoon	cornflour (cornstarch)
½ teaspoon	lard
90 g (3 oz)	sweet red bean paste*

Special Equipment: A wooden mould with engraved decoration. The number of cakes will depend on the size of the mould.

Boil the water and sugar together in a saucepan, simmering until the sugar is dissolved. Pour in the flour and add the cornflour. Stir quickly with the handle of a wooden spoon, then cover and leave for about 5 minutes.

Remove to a board, add the lard and knead until smooth and shiny. Roll into a sausage shape and divide into 12 pieces. If the mould is about 5 cm (2 in) in diameter it will make about 12. Adjust accordingly.

Flatten each portion. Form the filling into balls and place one on each piece of pastry. Fold in the edges and pinch together, sealing closely. Dust the mould with the same flour or a little cornflour or glutinous rice flour. Do not use plain wheat flour as it will show in white spots on the cooked cakes.

Place the cookies one by one in the mould with the joined part upmost. Press gently and flatten with the palm of the hand. Slap the mould sharply on the edge of the table to release the cookie. Place, decorated surface upwards, in a greased steaming basket and steam over rapidly boiling water for about 5 minutes. Glaze by brushing lightly with vegetable oil. Serve hot or cold.

* Or use sweet lotus seed paste, see recipe following (steamed buns with lotus seed filling), or a mixture of crunchy peanut paste and sugar.

Walnut Crisps (recipe page 368) and above Steamed Sponge Cake (recipe page 369)

WALNUT CRISPS

Makes 12.

1 cup	flour
¼ cup	castor sugar
¼ cup (2 fl oz)	melted lard
	pinch of bicarbonate of soda (optional)
¼ teaspoon	baking powder
½	egg, beaten
12	blanched walnuts

Sift the flour into a mixing bowl. Add the sugar, three-quarters of the melted lard, the bicarbonate of soda, if used, and the baking powder. Add the beaten egg and work slowly into a firm, fairly dry dough. Add the remaining lard if the dough is crumbly.

Divide into 12 portions, roll each into a ball and press flat with the fingers. Place on a greased baking tray and press one walnut in the centre of each biscuit. Brush with the beaten egg to glaze.

Bake on the centre rack in a moderately hot oven (220°C/425°F) for 20 — 25 minutes. Cool on a cake rack before serving.

STEAMED BUNS WITH LOTUS SEED FILLING

1½ cups	flour
2 teaspoons	baking powder
	pinch of salt
¼ cup	sugar
1 tablespoon	melted lard
¼ cup (2 fl oz)	warm water
90 g (3 oz)	lotus seed paste*
1 — 2	salted egg yolks (see recipe, page 363)

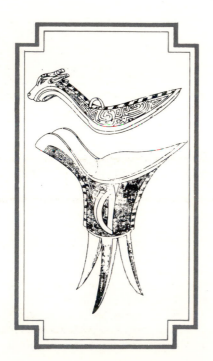

Sift the flour and baking powder into a mixing bowl and add the salt and sugar. Stir in the lard and water slowly and mix with a knife to a smooth soft dough. Cover with a damp cloth and leave for at least 30 minutes. Remove to a lightly floured board and knead lightly.

Divide into 6 pieces and press into rounds with the fingers. Divide the lotus seed paste into 6 pieces also and roll into small balls. Push a finger into each ball and insert a piece of egg yolk, then re-form the ball around it.

Place a ball of lotus paste in the centre of each piece of dough and pull the dough up around it, pinching the edges together. Brush the joined part with water and stick a piece of plain paper over it.

Place the buns in a steaming basket and steam over rapidly boiling water for 12 — 15 minutes. Lift the lid several times during cooking to prevent the buns from bursting open.

* Soak 125 g (4 oz) dried lotus seeds in cold water for 2 — 3 hours, then drain and rinse well. Place in a saucepan with 1 cup of sugar and add plenty of water. Bring to the boil and simmer until the lotus seeds are completely tender and the liquid absorbed or evaporated, then mash to a smooth paste with a fork, working in a little vegetable oil to give a smooth shiny texture. Store leftover paste in the refrigerator. It will keep for several weeks.

Substitute ingredients include sweet red bean paste (see page 389), or a mixture of even quantities of sesame or peanut paste and sugar.

STEAMED SPONGE CAKE

1¼ cups	flour
60 g (2 oz)	butter
½ cup	sugar
2	eggs
2 tablespoons	cream
¼ cup (2 fl oz)	melted lard
½ teaspoon	bicarbonate of soda
¼ teaspoon	molasses (optional)

Special Equipment: One 18 cm (7 in) cake tin thoroughly perforated with holes and lined with perforated greased paper.

Sift the flour into a mixing bowl. Cream the butter and sugar together and add the eggs and cream. Work into the flour, then add the lard and soda mixed with a little cold water. Stir in the molasses, if used, to add colour. Mix well, then leave for about 30 minutes. The batter should be of dropping consistency, soft and moist.

Line the base of the tin, then thickly grease the sides. Pour the batter into the tin and set on a rack in a steamer. Steam over rapidly boiling water for about 35 minutes until well expanded, firm and dry. Test by inserting a chopstick in the centre, it should come out clean and dry.

Turn out onto a wire rack and remove the paper. Cut into large pieces and serve hot. This is particularly excellent served with a dressing of hot clear honey.

'LAUGHING MOUTHS'

Makes 12.

1 cup	flour
1¼ teaspoons	baking powder
2 tablespoons	castor sugar
¼ cup (2 fl oz)	water
1 teaspoon	softened lard
2 tablespoons	white sesame seeds
5 cups (1¼ litres)	deep-frying oil

Sift the flour and baking powder into a mixing bowl and add the sugar and lard. Work in lightly, then gradually add the water to make a soft dough. Knead gently until smooth.

Roll the dough into a sausage shape and divide into 12 pieces. Roll each into a ball. Brush each ball with water and coat with the sesame seeds. Roll between the hands to press the seeds firmly into place.

Heat the deep-frying oil to moderate and fry the balls, several at a time, until golden and well expanded, about 8 minutes. If the balls do not rise to the surface within the first 3 — 4 seconds of cooking, the oil is not hot enough.

For extra tasty 'laughing mouths,' roll the dough around a small ball of sweet lotus seed or red bean paste and proceed as above. Serve hot or cold.

SWEET WALNUTS

125 g (4 oz)	walnuts
1 cup (8 fl oz)	water
¼ cup (2 fl oz)	sugar
¼ cup (2 fl oz)	clear honey
5 cups (1¼ litres)	deep-frying oil

Bring the walnuts to the boil with water to cover and cook for 1 minute, then drain and peel off the brown skin. Return to the saucepan with the remaining ingredients except oil and bring to the boil again. Simmer on reduced heat for 10 minutes. Drain and leave to cool and dry.

Heat the deep-frying oil to moderate. Fry the nuts in a basket until well coloured, about 8 minutes. Remove and drain well. Leave to cool, then serve.

STEAMED BREAD

Makes 6 loaves.

3 cups	flour
1½ tablespoons	sugar
1 3/8 cups	warm water
2 teaspoons	dry yeast (granulated)
1 tablespoon	softened lard or pastry shortening

Sift the flour into a mixing bowl. Dissolve the sugar in the water, then add the yeast and stir until dissolved. Leave for about 10 minutes until the yeast begins to activate and form a foam on the water, then add the softened lard or shortening to the flour and slowly work in the yeast mixture. Knead into a soft ball and remove to a floured board. Knead gently until smooth and elastic. Place in a bowl and cover with a damp cloth. Leave to rise for at least 3 hours in a warm place. It should more than double in bulk.

Use to form any of the following bread shapes and steam until cooked through and dry to the touch, about 18 minutes for loaves, 12 minutes for individual buns.

Steamed Bread Loaves. Divide the dough into 6 equal parts and form into oval shaped loaves. Pull the sides and ends under the roll so that the top is smooth and rounded. Stick a piece of plain paper underneath and steam for 15 — 18 minutes until dry and springy to the touch. Lift the lid of the steamer once or twice during cooking to allow excess steam to escape. This prevents the tops of the loaves from bursting open.

Serve the rolls straight from the steamer, or deep-fry until the surface is golden brown and serve hot.

Yin-sz-juan (Silver Thread Loaves). Divide the dough into two parts and roll one half out flat, then cut into 5 or 6 pieces. Roll the other half out flat and brush generously with a mixture of vegetable and sesame oil. Fold into a long rectangle, brushing each fold with more oil. Cut across the rectangle, cutting the dough into narrow shreds. Divide the shreds into equal portions to fit the squares. Hold each bundle of strips firmly at each end and gently pull until about 10 cm (4 in) long. Place on a square and fold in the two sides, then tuck the ends underneath, making a rectangular-shaped loaf. Press a piece of plain paper under each roll and place them all in a steaming basket. Steam over high heat for at least 15 minutes, lifting the lid of the steamer once or twice during cooking to allow excess steam to escape.

Lwo-sz-juan (Snail Breads). Shred the whole of the dough as explained above, brushing generously with vegetable and sesame oil. Divide into 24 groups, and stretch fairly long. Wrap each group separately around a finger to produce little curled bundles. Steam for about 12 minutes.

These breads can also be made with the simpler baking powder activated dough of the following recipe.

Clear-As-Glass Cookies (recipe page 366),
and above Steamed Buns with Lotus Seed Filling (recipe page 368)

370

STEAMED FLOWER-SHAPED BUNS

Makes 24.

3 cups	flour
1 tablespoon	baking powder
1½ tablespoons	sugar
1 tablespoon	softened lard or pastry shortening
7/8 cup (7 fl oz)	lukewarm water

Sift the flour and baking powder into a mixing bowl. Add the softened lard or shortening and sugar, then mix in the water. Form into a ball and remove to a lightly floured board. Knead gently until smooth and elastic. Wrap in a warm cloth and leave for 20 minutes.

Roll out into a long sausage shape and divide into 24 pieces. Flatten each with the fingers and fold in the centre, pressing lightly on the fold. Decorate with a series of indentations along the edges, made with the back of a kitchen knife.

Place on perforated greaseproof paper in a steamer, arrange the bread on top and steam over rapidly boiling water for about 12 minutes. Serve with any crisp-fried dish, particularly whole chickens or ducks.

If preparing as an accompaniment to Honey-glazed Ham. (see page 210), make twice the size so that the sliced meat can be inserted into the bun, hamburger fashion.

Steamed Flower Shaped Buns can also be made with the yeast-activated dough of the previous recipe for Steamed Bread.

SESAME POCKET BREAD

Makes 18.

½ cup	oil
7 cups	flour
1½ cups	boiling water
½ cup	cold water
1 tablespoon	salt
¼ cup	white sesame seeds
5 cups (1¼ litres)	deep-frying oil

Heat the oil in a frying pan and add about 1 cup of the flour. Cook on low heat until the mixture is smooth and golden, stirring constantly. The mixture will appear too dry at first, but gradually the oil will soften the flour to produce a smooth oily paste. Remove from the heat and leave to cool.

Sift the remaining flour, reserving about 1½ tablespoons, into a mixing bowl. Pour the boiling water in and quickly work into the flour using the handle of a wooden spoon to stir. Add the cold water and work a little more, then transfer to a lightly oiled board and knead until smooth and elastic, about 7 minutes. Roll the dough into a long sausage shape and divide into 18 pieces. Cover with a damp cloth while preparing the bread to prevent drying out.

Roll each piece out separately into a square shape roughly 15 × 15 cm (6 × 6 in). Spread on a coating of the flour and oil paste, season generously with salt and sprinkle lightly with the reserved flour. Fold in two sides to just overlap in the centre, pinch the two ends so the filling is contained, then fold these in to just overlap in the centre. Use a rolling pin to gently roll in the direction of the folds into a rectangular shape. Dip the smooth side into sesame seeds, pressing on lightly. If necessary, brush the top with a little water so the seeds will stick.

Place on an oiled and floured baking tray and bake in a preheated hot oven 200°C (400°F) for 5 minutes on each side. The breads will puff up during cooking and when removed from the oven they may flatten again.

Cut the breads in halves. Serve hot as an edible pouch for shredded meat dishes (see page 67 Shredded Pork in Sesame Pouches).

The rolls may be frozen, uncooked, and baked after a brief thawing period.

'MANDARIN' PANCAKES

Makes 18.

1½ cups	flour
½ cup	boiling water
	sesame oil

Sift the flour into a mixing bowl and pour in the water. Work with the handle of a wooden spoon until the dough is completely amalgamated. When cool enough to handle, knead briskly for 10 minutes. Cover with a damp cloth and leave in a warm place for 15 minutes.

Roll the dough into a long sausage shape and divide into 18 pieces. Cover roll with a damp cloth while working each piece. Press two pieces into small round cakes and brush one side of each with sesame oil. Press the two oiled surfaces together, then roll out together until paper-thin.

When all are rolled out, heat a heavy frying pan or hot plate and rub with an oiled cloth, cook the pancakes on moderate heat until brown flecks appear on the underside. Turn and cook the other side, then peel apart and fold the two pancakes into triangular shapes. Wrap in a cloth until ready to serve.

The pancakes can be stored in plastic bags in the refrigerator or freezer until needed. To reheat spread on a plate and set on a rack in a steamer. Steam for 6 — 8 minutes. Serve at once.

SPRING ONION PASTRIES

Makes 6.

3½ cups	flour
1 cup	boiling water
2 — 3 tablespoons	cold water
1 tablespoon	vegetable oil
1 tablespoon	sesame oil
6	spring onions (scallions), trimmed and finely chopped
1 tablespoon	salt
1½ cups (12 fl oz)	frying oil

Sift the flour into a mixing bowl. Pour the boiling water into the centre and quickly mix in, using the handle of a wooden spoon. Add the cold water to produce a fairly hard dough. Begin by adding only 2 tablespoons of the cold water. Leave for 10 minutes, then remove to a floured board and knead until smooth and easy to work. Add extra cold water at this point if needed.

Roll out to about 1 cm (1/5 in) thickness and cut into 6 rectangles or divide into 6 pieces and roll out individually. Brush the top of each piece with a mixture of vegetable and sesame oil, scatter on the spring onions and add a generous amount of salt.

Fold over one of the longer edges and roll the dough up into a long roll, then twist the roll into a spiral and place on the board so the spiral faces upwards. Flatten gently with a rolling pin into a round pastry about 7.5 cm (3 in) in diameter.

Heat the frying oil in a wok or frying pan and fry the pastries slowly, two or three at a time with the pan covered. Turn once and shake the pan frequently to encourage the pastries to puff out a little. Cooking time is about 5 minutes.

Remove from the oil, drain and wrap in a cloth or foil until ready to serve. Cut into quarters and serve on a warmed plate.

Serve as a snack or an accompaniment to Northern dishes.

CRISP-FRIED CHINESE CRULLERS

Makes 24.

4 cups	flour
1½ teaspoons	salt
30 g (1 oz)	fresh yeast
2 teaspoons	sugar
1¼ cups	lukewarm water
6 cups (1½ litres)	deep-frying oil

Sift the flour and salt into a mixing bowl. Mix the yeast with the sugar and 1 — 2 tablespoons of the water. Leave for 2 minutes, then make a well in the centre of the flour, pour in the yeast and carefully work into the flour, adding the remaining water slowly.

When all the liquid has been added, gather the dough into one ball and knead gently for 2 minutes. Cover with a damp cloth and leave in a warm place to rise for 2 hours. Turn onto a lightly floured board and knead gently for 5 — 6 minutes.

Pull out into a long strip about 10 cm (4 in) wide. Cut across the strip into 24 pieces, then roll and stretch each piece into a long strip.

Heat the deep-frying oil to smoking point, then reduce the heat to moderate. Deep-fry several at a time until crisp and puffy, about 3 minutes. Serve hot.

These Crullers are usually served as an accompaniment to breakfast or snack dishes such as Rice Congee (see page 357). In the North they are stuffed into Sesame Pocket Bread to form a substantial snack. Sliced Crullers lend an interesting taste and texture to stir-fried dishes.

SPRING ROLL WRAPPERS

Makes 24.

4 cups	flour
1 teaspoon	salt
2 cups	water

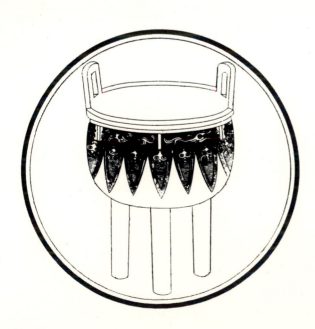

Special Equipment: A heavy flat iron griddle or frying pan.

Sift the flour and salt into a mixing bowl and gradually add the water, mixing thoroughly. Work through the fingers for about 5 minutes until the mixture is smooth and elastic. Cover with a thin layer of water to keep from drying out and leave for 1 hour to allow the gluten in the flour to soften. Work again with the fingers after pouring off the water. The dough should be very soft and sticky.

Heat the griddle and wipe over with a damp cloth, then rub vigorously with an oiled cloth. The surface should be smooth but not oily. Heat to moderate.

To make the spring roll wrappers, take a large handful of the dough and wipe it in a circular motion around the pan so that a thin layer of the dough adheres to the pan. When the edges begin to curl up, remove to a cooling rack. Wipe the pan again with the cloth.

Continue until the wrappers are all made. They should be dry, but not so crisp that they will crack. If necessary, cook very briefly on the other side before removing from the heat. Use for Spring Rolls, page 362, with a variety of meat or vegetable fillings.

Spring roll wrappers can be kept in the refrigerator for several days, sealed in a plastic bag, and they freeze well. Thaw slowly before use and separate carefully. Discard those that are torn or cracked.

Keep under a cloth until ready to use as they dry out and crack on exposure to the air.

'Exotic Tasting' Chicken (recipe page 376).

WONTON WRAPPERS

The first recipe gives professional results if the ingredients are obtainable, otherwise use the following recipe using plain flour.

Recipe 1:
Makes 30.

125 g (4 oz)	*high gluten flour (gun mien fun)*
¼ cup (2 fl oz)	*mixture of beaten egg and water*

Recipe 2:
Makes 24.

1½ cups	*flour*
⅓ cup	*water*
½ teaspoon	*lard*

Sift the flour into a basin and add the egg and water mixture. Knead firmly until smooth, then leave covered with plastic wrap for 4 hours. The gluten will soften in this time, giving the dough a softer more elastic quality.

To roll out, dust a large surface with cornflour (cornstarch) or glutinous rice flour. Do not use flour as this will mix in with the dough, making it too dry. Use a very large rolling pin and roll into a fairly large square, then dust with cornflour or glutinous rice flour and fold two or three times then roll thinner. Unfold and add more glutinous rice flour or cornflour and refold. Continue to fold and roll, dusting with more cornflour each time until the dough is completely thin. It should be almost transparent. Cut into squares or rounds for use.

To store in the refrigerator or freezer, ensure that each piece is thoroughly dusted with cornflour or glutinous rice flour. Stack together and wrap in plastic.

Sift the flour into a bowl and add a pinch of salt. Bring the water to the boil and pour into the flour. Stir quickly with the handle of a wooden spoon, add the lard and remove to a floured board.

Knead for about 5 minutes until smooth and pliable. Wipe over a large board and dust lightly with flour. Roll the dough out paper-thin. Cut into 24 even-sized squares.

'EXOTIC TASTING' CHICKEN

1 1⅓ kg (2 2/3 lb)	*chicken*
2 teaspoons	*sesame oil*
½ cup	*white sesame seeds*

Sauce:

2 tablespoons	*finely chopped spring onion (scallion)*
2 tablespoons	*light soy sauce*
2 tablespoons	*sesame paste (or smooth peanut paste/butter)*
1 tablespoon	*cold water*
1 teaspoon	*white vinegar*
½ teaspoon	*chilli oil (or to taste)*
½ teaspoon	*ground black pepper*
½ teaspoon	*m.s.g. (optional)*
2 teaspoons	*sugar*
½ teaspoon	*finely chopped garlic (optional)*
	salt to taste

Clean and dress the chicken and place in a saucepan of cold water. Bring to the boil and simmer for 5 minutes, then remove the pot from the heat and cover with warm towels. Leave for 1¼ hours, then remove the chicken and drain well. Brush with sesame oil and set aside.

Toast the sesame seeds in a dry pan until they begin to pop, then transfer to a mortar and grind to a coarse powder. Leave to cool.

Mix the sauce ingredients together, adjusting the taste, as preferred.

Debone the chicken and tear the meat into shreds. Pile onto a serving plate. For a more substantial dish, arrange the chicken over a bed of shredded cucumber, carrot, and celery.

Pour on the sauce and sprinkle on the crushed sesame seeds. Serve.

COLD SLICED PORK WITH GARLIC SAUCE

1½ kg (3 lb)	pork foreloin (loin)
2 whole heads	garlic
¾ cup (6 fl oz)	light soy sauce
⅓ cup	sesame oil
2 teaspoons	white vinegar
1 teaspoon	sugar

Wash the pork and scrape the skin with a sharp knife to remove any small hairs. Place in a large saucepan and cover with boiling water. Return to the boil, then reduce the heat and simmer until the pork is completely tender, 1½ — 1¾ hours. Add more boiling water as the level drops to ensure the meat is always covered. Remove from the stock and drain well. Leave to cool, then chill thoroughly before cutting into wafer-thin slices.

Arrange the meat attractively on a wide plate.

Very finely chop the garlic and mix with the remaining ingredients. Pour into several small dishes and serve as dips with the pork.

For extra piquancy, add 1 — 2 teaspoons finely chopped fresh red chilli pepper to the sauce.

CHINESE HAM

1 kg (2 lb)	pork leg (fresh ham)
1½ teaspoons	saltpetre
2 tablespoons	table salt
1 teaspoon	Chinese brown peppercorns, coarsely ground
3	spring onions (scallions), cut in halves
3 thick slices	fresh ginger
1 tablespoon	rice wine or dry sherry

Wash the pork and wipe dry. Rub the saltpetre into the skin and meat evenly. Heat the table salt and ground peppercorns in a dry pan until fragrant, then rub into the meat also. Wrap in plastic and store in the refrigerator for at least 48 hours, preferably 3 full days.

Rinse well, then place in a saucepan and add water to cover. Add the spring onions, ginger, and wine and bring to the boil. Simmer for about 1 hour until the pork is just tender. Remove and drain well.

Place in a dish and cover with a cloth. Weight heavily and return to the refrigerator for 5 — 6 hours.

Cut into wafer-thin slices to serve.

A delicious accompanying sauce can be made with 1 tablespoon each of light soy sauce and white vinegar, 2 teaspoons sugar and 2 — 3 teaspoons each of finely chopped spring onion and ginger.

COLD SLICED SPICY BEEF

1¼ kg (2½ lb)	silverside (brisket)
8 cups (2 litres)	water
2/3 cup	rice wine or dry sherry
2 tablespoons	salt
½ cup	sugar
3	spice bags (see page 386)
3 cups (24 fl oz)	light soy sauce

Wash the beef and drain. Bring the water to the boil in a large saucepan and add the remaining ingredients, except the soy sauce. Add the whole piece of beef and return to the boil. Simmer for 10 minutes, skimming occasionally, then add the soy sauce and reduce the heat to very low.

Cover tightly and simmer until the beef is completely tender, about 1¾ hours. Drain well. Place in a dish and weight slightly. Chill before cutting into wafer-thin slices.

To serve, arrange the sliced meat attractively on a wide platter and pour on a small amount of the sauce.

JELLIED MUTTON

625 g (1¼ lb)	lean mutton or lamb
185 g (6 oz)	
piece	pork rind (skin) or use 1 envelope (10 g / ⅓ oz) unflavoured gelatine
4	large spring onions (scallions), cut in halves
3 thick slices	fresh ginger
1	spice bag (see page 386)
⅓ cup	light soy sauce
2 tablespoons	rice wine or dry sherry
½ teaspoon	salt
2 teaspoons	sugar
	few drops of red food colouring (optional)
2 tablespoons	finely chopped fresh coriander
7 — 8 cups (1¾ — 2 litres)	chicken stock

Place the whole piece of mutton or lamb in a saucepan and place the pork skin on top. Add water to cover and bring to the boil. Simmer for 15 minutes. Drain, then cut the mutton and skin into chunks and add the chicken stock, the spring onions, ginger, and spice bag and bring to the boil. Simmer for about 1 hour, then remove the pork rind and cut into very small pieces. Discard the spice bag, onions, and ginger.

Add the soy sauce, wine, salt, and sugar to the saucepan and add red food colouring, if used. Continue to cook for a further 10 minutes, then remove the meat and cut into small cubes. Return to the pan with the diced pork rind and simmer until the liquid has reduced to about 1 cup.

If using gelatine, dissolve in ½ cup (4 fl oz) of warm water and add at this point. Heat gently for 10 minutes.

Remove the pan from the heat, stir in the coriander and pour the lot into a greased cake tin. Flatten the top and leave to cool, then refrigerate until set.

Remove from the tin and cut into slices. Arrange on a serving plate and serve with dips of light soy sauce, spiced salt, or hoisin sauce and finely shredded young ginger.

COLD MARINATED SEA SCALLOPS

Serve as an appetiser.

280 g (9 oz)	fresh sea scallops without the shell and coral
½ teaspoon	m.s.g. (optional)
¼ teaspoon	bicarbonate of soda
2 tablespoons	ginger wine (see page 387)
3 cups (24 fl oz)	water
2	spring onions (scallions), trimmed and sliced
4 thick slices	fresh ginger
5 cm (2 in) piece	fresh ginger, finely shredded
4	spring onions (scallions), trimmed and finely shredded
1 — 2	fresh red chilli peppers, finely shredded

Sauce:

2 tablespoons	cold water
1½ tablespoons	light soy sauce
1 teaspoon	dark soy sauce
2 teaspoons	sesame oil
2½ teaspoons	sugar
1 teaspoon	white vinegar

Very thinly slice the scallops and rub with the m.s.g., if used, and the bicarbonate of soda. Leave for 20 minutes, then rinse thoroughly, wipe dry and place in a dish with the ginger wine. Leave for 25 minutes.

Bring the water to the boil and add the sliced spring onions and ginger. Simmer for 2 minutes, then add the scallops and cook for about 12 seconds. Lift out and drain well.

Arrange the shredded spring onions, ginger, and chilli peppers on a serving plate. Place the scallops in a dish and cover with the pre-mixed sauce ingredients. Marinate for 1 minute, then strain the sauce into another bowl. Arrange the scallops over the prepared vegetables and serve with the sauce as a dip.

Phoenix Cold Meat Combination (recipe page 381).

SALTED JELLYFISH SALAD

125 g (4 oz)	salted jellyfish*
1	small cucumber
½	giant white (icicle) radish

Sauce:

1½ tablespoons	light soy sauce
1½ teaspoons	white vinegar
1½ teaspoons	sesame oil
¾ teaspoon	salt
1 teaspoon	sugar
¼ teaspoon	ground black pepper
1½ teaspoons	finely chopped garlic (optional)

Rinse salted jellyfish in cold water shred finely, then cover with warm water and bring almost to the boil. Drain and cover again with cold water. Leave for about 1 hour. If the water is allowed to boil, the jellyfish will become tough and stringy.

Peel and shred the cucumber and radish and arrange on a serving plate. Pile the jellyfish on top. Mix the sauce ingredients together and pour over the salad. Toss lightly before serving.

* Salted jellyfish is available in specialist Chinese food stockists and is usually stored in brine. If only the dried product is available, this will need to be soaked for at least 6 hours, then rinsed well and simmered gently for 20 minutes to soften. It should remain quite crunchy.

ROAST SUCKLING PIG APPETISER

500 g (1 lb)	Roast Suckling Pig (crackling and meat) (recipe page 328)
125 g (4 oz)	Jellied Chicken (recipe page 46)
155 g (5 oz)	Honey-Basted Roast Duck (recipe page 259)
125 g (4 oz)	Cold Spicy Peking Pork (recipe page 66)
⅓ recipe	salted jellyfish (see above) or page 392
3 slices	canned or fresh pineapple parsley sliced cucumber, carrot, or white radish

Cut the suckling pig through the crackling into strips. Thinly slice the chicken, duck, and pork. Prepare the jellyfish and pile in the centre of a large round plate. Arrange the suckling pig in a sunburst pattern on top of the jellyfish. Place sprigs of parsley or overlapping thin slices of cucumber, white radish, or carrot around the suckling pig, to decorate.

Arrange the other meats in overlapping rows around the plate. Cut the pineapple slices in halves horizontally and cut each piece in two. Place in a scalloped design around the edge of the dish and set a small bunch of parsley in the centre of each.

Serve with dips of 'duck' sauce (see page 385), plum, or hoisin sauce, and light soy sauce.

PLUM BLOSSOM COLD PLATTER

½	Poached Soy Sauce Chicken (recipe page 249)
155 g (5 oz)	Slow Cooked Corned Pork (recipe page 136)
155 g (5 oz)	Cold Sliced Spicy Beef (recipe page 377)
155 g (5 oz)	Jellied Mutton (recipe page 378)
½ recipe	Salted Jellyfish (see page 392)
155 g (5 oz)	Smoked Vegetarian Duck (recipe page 82)
3	Spiced Pigeon Eggs (recipe page 79)
1	tomato or white onion
2	small cucumbers parsley

Cut the meat into very thin slices, then into bite-sized pieces. Prepare the jellyfish. It should be finely shredded. Thinly slice the vegetarian duck.

Cut the tomato into a flower shape, or, if using the onion, shred into a chrysanthemum shape and dye yellow or pink with food colour mixed with water.

Pile the shredded jellyfish in the centre of a large round plate and make a depression in the centre. Set the tomato or onion in this and garnish with parsley.

Cut the pigeon eggs in halves in a zig-zag design and set aside. Very thinly slice the cucumbers and place in an overlapping row around the edge of the plate.

Arrange the meat in layered groups on the plate, each group to resemble a rounded flower petal (plum blossom). Place half an egg between each lot of meat and garnish with small sprigs of parsley.

Serve with dips of Ginger and Spring Onion Sauce (see page 384), hot mustard, and chilli sauce and light soy sauce.

PHOENIX COLD MEAT COMBINATION

½	Crisp Skin Chicken (recipe page 248)
155 g (5 oz)	Cold Sliced Pork (recipe page 377)
155 g (5 oz)	Red-Braised Five Spice Beef (recipe page 71)
½ recipe	Duck Livers with Hot Pepper Sauce (recipe page 262)
125 g (4 oz)	Boneless Rack of Lamb (recipe page 142)
½ 500 g (1 lb) can	abalone
½ recipe	salted jellyfish (previous recipe)
¼ recipe	Salted Duck Egg (see page 263) or use a hard boiled (hard cooked) chicken egg
8	dried black mushrooms, soaked for 25 minutes
125 g (4 oz)	canned pickled cabbage
2	medium cucumbers, or use canned asparagus
2	medium carrots, or use canned asparagus
1	small tomato, or use a cooked chicken head
⅓	giant white (icicle) radish
½	large cucumber

Seasoning A:

½ cup (4 fl oz)	chicken stock
1 teaspoon	light soy sauce
1 teaspoon	rice wine or dry sherry
1 teaspoon	sugar
⅓ teaspoon	salt
¼ teaspoon	m.s.g. (optional)
¼ teaspoon	sesame oil

Seasoning B: (optional)

2 tablespoons	white vinegar
¼ cup (2 fl oz)	hot water
2 teaspoons	sesame oil
1 teaspoon	salt
1 tablespoon	sugar

Prepare the meats and chill thoroughly. Cut the chicken into narrow sticks, leaving the skin on. Cut the pork, beef, and lamb into thin slices, and the duck livers into narrow strips. Very thinly slice the abalone. The jellyfish should be finely shredded.

Place the mushrooms in a dish with the seasoning A ingredients and set on a rack in a steamer. Steam for 30 minutes, then drain, remove the stems and cut into thin slices.

Finely shred the pickled cabbage and set aside. Cut the medium cucumbers and carrots into thin slices then into matchstick strips, or use a feather design vegetable cutter to stamp out feather shapes. If using the asparagus in place of the cucumbers and carrots, cut the spears in halves lengthwise and soak in cold chicken stock until needed. Marinate cucumber and carrot in the seasoning B, if used.

Cut a slice from the tomato, if used and set to one side of a large plate. Cut the slice into a pointed shape to resemble the beak and set in front of the carrot (phoenix head). If using the chicken head, set on a thick slice of tomato, with the face pointing upwards and outwards to the rim of the plate.

Very thinly slice the radish and large cucumber and cut the slices in halves.

Place the chicken leg and wing bones in a long shape from the tomato or chicken head and cover it with the sticks of chicken to form the phoenix neck. Pile the shredded pickled cabbage in the centre as the body. Arrange overlapping half slices of cucumber and radish in separate rows as the neck feathers.

Use the sliced meat, mushrooms (reserving several pieces) and abalone to form the wings, working away from the body in two directions to form two large curved wings. Cover the pickled vegetables with the strips of spiced liver.

Use the carrot and cucumber 'feathers' or matchstick strips to form a long flowing tail shape, or use the halved asparagus spears. Cut the reserved mushroom pieces into small diamond or oval shapes and use to decorate the tail.

Place the shredded jellyfish in a round shape to one side of the phoenix and place the half egg, yolk upwards, in the centre. Garnish the dish with parsley.

Serve with dips of Vinegar and Garlic Dip (see page 384), plum, or hoisin sauce and light soy sauce.

CHAPTER X

Sauces, Spices and Seasonings

CHINESE PEPPER-SALT/ONION-PEPPER-SALT

1½ tablespoons	Chinese brown peppercorns
4 tablespoons	table salt

Dry-fry the peppercorns in a wok over low to moderate heat until aromatic, about 3 minutes, stirring constantly. Remove to a mortar or spice grinder and grind to a fine powder. Return to the wok with the salt and dry-fry together, turning the mixture constantly with a wok spatula until thoroughly mixed and aromatic. Do not allow the salt to colour. Leave to cool, then store in an airtight jar.

Add finely chopped spring onion to the pepper-salt in quantities to taste for use where onion-pepper-salt is required.

SPICED SALT

4 tablespoons	table salt
1½-2 teaspoons	five spice powder

Dry-fry the salt in a wok over low to moderate heat until well warmed through. Stir constantly to avoid burning. Remove from the heat and stir in the five spice powder. Leave to cool, then store in an airtight jar.

VINEGAR AND GINGER DIP/VINEGAR AND GARLIC DIP

4 tablespoons	Chinese red vinegar*
2 tablespoons	finely shredded fresh ginger (or garlic)

Mix the vinegar and ginger or garlic at least 30 minutes before use. Serve in small dishes as a dip. This is particularly good with seafood.

For a hot vinegar and garlic dip, add 2 tablespoons light soy sauce, a dash each of sugar and m.s.g., and 1-1½ teaspoons of chilli oil.

*If Chinese red vinegar is unobtainable, use white vinegar. White vinegar should also be used if the sauce is to accompany meat or poultry.

GINGER AND SPRING ONION SAUCE

2 tablespoons	fine shredded fresh ginger
3 tablespoons	finely shredded spring onion (scallion)
½ cup (4 fl oz)	vegetable oil
1½ teaspoons	salt

Heat the vegetable oil to moderate and add the ginger, spring onion, and salt. Warm through and remove from the heat. Serve with poached, steamed, or crisp deep-fried poultry.

SWEET AND SOUR SAUCE

1 tablespoon	frying oil
1 tablespoon	finely chopped Chinese pickles
1 tablespoon	finely chopped fresh ginger
½ teaspoon	crushed garlic (optional)
½ cup (4 fl oz)	chicken stock
⅓ cup	sugar
⅓ cup	white vinegar
¼ teaspoon	salt
1 tablespoon	liquid from Chinese pickles
2½ teaspoons	cornflour (cornstarch)

Mix all the ingredients in a saucepan and bring to the boil. Simmer for about 3 minutes. As a dip for pork meatballs or fresh fish, add ¼ cup (2 fl oz) tomato sauce (ketchup) as well.

SWEETENED SOY SAUCE

2 tablespoons	dark soy sauce
2 tablespoons	sugar
1¼ tablespoons	malt sugar
2 teaspoons	sesame oil

Mix all the ingredients together, stirring until the sugar has completely dissolved. Excellent with fish, prawn, and crab meatballs.

'DUCK' SAUCE

The classic accompaniment to Peking roast duck, roast suckling pig, and most crisp-fried poultry.

2 tablespoons	sesame oil
½ cup	sweet bean paste
½ cup	sugar
½ cup (4 oz)	water

Heat the sesame oil in a wok and add the remaining ingredients, mixing thoroughly. Simmer, stirring, until the sauce thickens, about 2 minutes. Store in an airtight jar. Keeps for several weeks.

CHILLI OIL

½ cup	vegetable oil
2½ tablespoons	dried chilli flakes

Heat the vegetable oil to smoking hot, then reduce the heat and allow to cool for a while. Add the chilli flakes, stir and leave for 2 to 3 days, then strain into a jar for storage. Keeps indefinitely without refrigeration.

FIVE SPICE POWDER/SPICE BAGS

A finely ground aromatic powder now readily available under the well known spice brands, as well as popular Chinese brandnames.

To make an acceptable substitute, combine 20 brown peppercorns, ¾ teaspoon fennel seeds, 1 5 cm (2 in) piece of cinnamon bark, 1 whole star anise, and 6 whole cloves. Grind to a very fine powder and store in a screwtop jar.

The same spices in whole form and tied in a small piece of clean muslin or cheese-cloth constitute the Spice Bag referred to in many recipes. The above quantities of whole spices make 1 spice bag. Like the five spice powder, this can now be purchased in prepared form and is usually labelled Mixed Spice in Chinese food stockists. Not to be confused with the Western type of Mixed Spice used for pickling.

RICE CAKES

When rice is cooked by the absorption method, see page 00, there is usually a thick crust of rice around the bottom and sides of the saucepan. This can be lifted off, dried in a warm oven, and used as rice cakes.

Alternatively, cook 2½ cups of short grain white rice by the same method and transfer to an oiled baking tray, pressing it firmly into place. Set in a warm oven to slowly cook until lightly coloured, then increase the heat for 10 minutes to cook to a light golden colour. Remove and cool.

Break or cut into squares and deep-fry immediately before use.

Use where recipes call for crisp rice cakes. This amount of rice yields about 20 4 cm (1 2/3 in) squares, sufficient for 2 recipes. When cool, store in an airtight jar.

SPICED RICE POWDER

1½ cups	raw long grain white rice
3	whole star anise*

Toast the rice with the star anise in a dry wok until the rice turns a rich golden brown. Cool slightly, then grind to a coarse powder. Keeps indefinitely in an airtight jar.
* Some cooks prefer using 1 tablespoon Chinese brown peppercorns, while others choose a mixture of the two.

ONION AND GINGER INFUSION

3	spring onions (scallions), finely chopped
5 thick slices	fresh ginger, finely chopped
½ cup (4 fl oz)	boiling water

Mix the ingredients together and cool rapidly. Store in the refrigerator until ready to use. This keeps for up to a week. To avoid fermentation, strain the liquid into a screw-top jar after 24 hours.

386

SWEET FERMENTED RICE/WINE LEES

These two recipes give good results and require one week's advance preparation. The finished product can be stored for some time in the refrigerator in a sealed jar. Remove the lid from time to time to release excess gases created by the fermentation.

2 kg (4 lb)   raw glutinous rice
3 packages   beer yeast* (about 30 g / 1 oz)

Soak the rice for 6 hours, drain and cover with water again. Set on a rack in a steamer and steam over gently boiling water until tender. Remove and rinse thoroughly in plenty of warm water. Leave the rice fairly wet. Dissolve the yeast in ½ cup of warm water and pour into the rice. Mix in well and make a depression in the centre. Wrap warmly in towels and leave in a warm place. After about 36 hours, the fermentation will begin, producing a quantity of clear liquid in the depression. Transfer rice and liquid to a preserve jar or any jar which can be tightly sealed, and leave for at least 1 week.
* Granulated dried yeast used for home-brewed beer.

Alternatively soak and steam 1½ kg (3 lb) raw long grain glutinous rice and rinse with warm water. Crumble 2 wine balls (wine cubes)* and mix with 1½ tablespoons of flour. Stir into the rice and make a depression in the centre. Wrap warmly in towels and store in a warm place for 36 hours. Transfer to a sealed jar and refrigerate.
* Wine cubes or wine balls are a kind of compressed distiller's yeast available from specialist Chinese food and drug suppliers.

Japanese light yellow miso paste, a fermentation of soybeans, wine, and spices, makes a good substitute for wine lees, but should be diluted to a thin paste with cold water and a dash of rice wine or sherry.

GINGER WINE/GINGER JUICE

¼ cup (2 fl oz)   rice wine or dry sherry
2 tablespoons   grated fresh ginger

Mix the wine and ginger and refrigerate. This keeps for many weeks.

Place grated fresh ginger in a piece of fine cheesecloth or muslin and squeeze tightly to extract ginger juice. Alternatively, infuse ginger in a small amount of boiling water and squeeze to extract this diluted form of ginger juice. Commercial brands of ginger wine can be substituted.

RENDERED CHICKEN FAT (CHICKEN GREASE)

Trim the white fat from a dressed chicken. (There is usually a larger accumulation of fat near the breast of a force-fed chicken than on those raised on a free-range system.) Place the fat in a wok and add ¼ cup (2 fl oz) water. Cook on moderate heat until there is a considerable amount of liquid fat in the pan, the water has evaporated and the piece of fat has reduced to a crisp brown lump. Remove and discard.

Store rendered chicken fat in the refrigerator. Soften to room temperature for easier measuring.

SUGAR COLOURING

Recipe 1:

500 g (1 lb)	sugar
2½ cups (20 fl oz)	water

Heat the sugar in a dry pan until it melts, then continue to cook, stirring frequently, until it boils and turns a rich dark brown. Quickly remove from the heat and pour in the water. Stir until it stops bubbling and is thoroughly combined. To stop the cooking quickly, hold the bottom of the saucepan in a dish of cold water. Cover the hand holding the pan while adding the cold water to avoid burns.

Recipe 2:

Boil 500 g (1 lb) of sugar and 3 cups (24 fl oz) of water together until the sugar turns dark brown. Cool before using.

Sugar colouring keeps for weeks without refrigeration.

CHICKEN STOCK

2	chicken carcasses and giblets
1	leek
4 slices	fresh ginger
8 cups (2 litres)	water
1½ teaspoons	salt

Wash the chicken bones and giblets well. Sauté the leek in oil until lightly coloured. Place the bones, giblets, leek, and ginger in a saucepan and add the water and salt. Simmer for 1¼ hours, skimming off excess fat frequently. Strain into a storage jar.

For convenience, freeze small lots of stock in sealed plastic bags. Label clearly with quantities to avoid confusion when using. Frozen stock may be added in solid form to braised dishes or soups. However, it should be completely thawed for quick-cooked dishes such as sautés and stir-fries.

ENRICHED STOCK

Proceed as for Chicken Stock, but add 1 pork knuckle (hock) or a ham bone and 1 duck carcass or duck giblets. The cooking time should be increased to about 1¾ hours. Enriched stock will have a white creamy appearance.

For additional flavour, add 500 g (1 lb) chicken meat on the bone.

SOY-PRESERVED GINGER/CUCUMBER

These are available under certain specialty brandnames. The ginger or cucumber is peeled and pickled in a mixture of brine, soy sauce, and spices, resulting in a very salty, dark brown, dry pickle which keeps indefinitely.

If unobtainable, use salted mustard root, or any of the spiced preserved vegetables currently on the market. A substitute can be made by infusing the cucumber or ginger in salted vinegar, adding plenty of dark soy sauce. Leave for at least 4 hours.

SWEET RED BEAN PASTE

2 cups	red beans*
2 tablespoons	lard
	sugar to taste

Rinse the beans and cover with water. Bring to the boil and simmer until softened, adding additional water as necessary. Drain very well and mash to a smooth paste. Work in the lard and plenty of sugar. Usually the mixture is very sweet.

The sweet red bean paste required for these recipes should be firm and dry. If too wet, place in a piece of cheesecloth and squeeze to remove as much water as possible. Add cornflour (cornstarch) to bind.

Red bean paste is available in cans, but is too wet for recipes where it is to be rolled into balls. It can be thickened by heating and adding cornflour paste or a little water chestnut, rice, or potato flour.

* A small red bean similar in appearance to mung beans. Or use kidney beans.

BEANCURD

Canned, frozen, or dehydrated forms of beancurd have still to be perfected. As yet, the soft gelatinous texture of soft beancurd has defied packaging. However some specialist Chinese food suppliers now have stocks of fresh soft beancurd, while the dried beancurd products, beancurd skin, dried beancurd cakes, and rolled beancurd skin sticks, are usually readily available.

750 g (1½ lb)	soybeans
1½ tablespoons	gypsum or plaster of Paris powder
1 cup (8 fl oz)	water

Rinse the soybeans in cold water and place in a large pot. Cover with about 12 cups of cold water and leave overnight. Rinse with cold water then grind to a smooth paste in a food processor or heavy duty blender. About 10 cups of water should be added while blending to keep the paste quite thin.

Strain the liquid through a cheesecloth and squeeze tightly. Bring the liquid to the boil and simmer for about 10 minutes. The cooking process removes the raw taste of the bean water. Mix the gypsum or plaster of Paris powder with the 1 cup of water and pour into the bean water. Stir well then pour into a muslin- or cheesecloth-lined mould, preferably a scrubbed wooden box about ½ meter square. When the liquid has set into a soft jelly, cover with another piece of soft cloth and weight heavily. Leave for about 35 minutes to compress into a soft cake.

Cut into squares about 6.5 cm (2½ in) square. To make dry beancurd, weight heavily for a further 20 minutes.

CHAPTER XI
Preparation and Cooking Techniques

A guide to the preparation of ingredients, the use of the Chinese cleaver, cooking processes and terms, and kitchen layout.

Seafood plays an important role in the Chinese diet. To ensure that most products are available all year round, the art of sun-drying to preserve a vast variety of fish and shellfish was long ago mastered.

Abalone, the large oysters fished off the China coast, *conpoy* (a close rela-

light soy sauce but with a marked fish flavour.

Additionally, several kinds of mushrooms and fungi are gathered from fields and woods for sun-drying. A variety of seaweeds, in particular the curly hair-like *fa ts'ai* (black moss), and the paper-thin discs of compressed laver are also sold in dried form.

Another highly regarded dried food is Birds' Nests, the best of which come from island caves off the coast of Fukien (Fujian) and Thailand.

boil. Simmer for 3 — 4 hours, then remove and rinse in cold water. Scrub with a soft brush to clean, then return to the saucepan and cover with hot water again. Simmer until tender with a dash of rice wine and several slices of spring onion (scallion) and ginger.

Remove from the water, pull out any small bones and discard, then trim off the ragged edges. Soak in cold water until ready to use. May be frozen at this stage, ready for later use.

FISH MAW: This gelatinous white membrane, removed from the stomachs of certain very large fish, is sold in dried form in large sheets resembling cream-coloured polyurethane foam. To prepare, soak in warm water for at least 6 hours, weighted if necessary to keep it under the water. Drain and rinse well. Trim off any yellow membrane. Heat a saucepan of water and add 1 tablespoon of white vinegar. Cut the fish maw into the required pieces as indicated in the recipe and cook for 1 - 2 minutes. Drain well. Soak in cold water until ready to use, then drain and squeeze out the water before using.

JELLYFISH, SALTED: Soak dried jellyfish in cold water for several hours. It is sometimes sold already soaked, making this step unnecessary. Drain and shred. Place in a dish with 1 tablespoon of rice wine (dry sherry) and several slices of spring onion (scallion) and ginger. Cover with warm water and leave for 10 minutes, then drain well and use.

Do not use hot or boiling water on the jellyfish as it will shrink and toughen. The texture should be tender, yet crunchy.

SCALLOPS, DRIED (CONPOY): These should be soaked for at least 25 minutes in cold water, then steamed or very slowly simmered in water or chicken stock with rice wine (sherry), spring onion (scallion), and ginger to season. When tender, remove the very thin skin surrounding the scallop and break into shreds by rubbing between the forefinger and thumb.

SEA CUCUMBER: Choose the darkest coloured ones. Soak in cold water until softened, then drain and cut open. Remove the stomach and pull away the surrounding yellow membrane. Wash well. Return to the saucepan and add 1 tablespoon of rice

Preparation of ingredients in the kitchen of the Pine and Crane restaurant, Souchow (Suzhou), China.

tion to the sea scallop), sea cucumber (sea slug), squid, jellyfish, shrimps, and the more esoteric shark's fin, shark's skin, fish maw, and fish lips are preserved by sun-drying, and in this form last indefinitely provided they are kept dry.

Salting, usually in combination with sun-drying and sometimes also combined with a fermentation process, is a technique also valued for preservation of seafoods. In particular, shrimps are ground raw and thoroughly salted before sun-drying and fermentation in large underground tanks to provide a pungent, salty seasoning (shrimp sauce). Fish, salted before sun-drying, have a similar strong, fishy and salty flavour, and are used both as an ingredient or a tasty additive. A by-product of this is the aromatic Fish Sauce, a clear seasoning liquid not dissimilar to

PREPARATION OF DRIED INGREDIENTS

ABALONE: Soak dried abalone for 6 hours in cold water. Drain and scrub with a soft brush, then cover with boiling water. Simmer for 4 hours, then rinse in cold water. Trim off the ruffled edges.

Abalone may be sliced from top to bottom to give small oval-shaped pieces, or sliced 'horizontally' (flat slicing, see Preparation Techniques below). Whole abalone may be scored (see below) in a criss-cross pattern to aid in tenderising and to allow the seasonings to penetrate.

FISH LIPS: The mouth section of certain types of very large fish is sun-dried into hard sheets. To prepare, place in a saucepan of hot water and bring to the

wine (dry sherry) and several pieces of spring onion (scallion) and ginger. Cover with chicken, enriched stock or water, and simmer for several hours until completely tender.

If using in a slow-cooked or braised dish, precook for only about 1 hour, then complete the cooking in the dish. Thirty (30) g (1 oz) of dried sea cucumber gives approximately 90 g (3 oz) when prepared.

OYSTERS: Soak in cold water for at least 6 hours, then drain and clean by brushing gently with a soft brush. Return to the saucepan and cover with cold water. Add a dash of rice wine (sherry) and several slices of spring onion (scallion) and ginger and simmer until softened. Drain and rinse with cold water. Do not overcook if the oysters are to be added to a dish that requires more than 5 — 7 minutes cooking.

SHARK'S FIN: Place whole shark's fins in a saucepan with water to cover and bring to the boil. Simmer for 1½ — 2 hours, then remove form the heat and leave to cool in the water. Rinse and cover with fresh water. Refrigerate overnight at this stage if possible. Reheat to boiling, then reduce to a simmer and cook for 1 hour, then leave to cool again. Repeat if the shark's fins are still not completely tender, or add to the dish and continue cooking until done. Pick out any small pieces of skin.

Shark's fin 'needles,' the thread-like strands of processed shark's fin which are more expensive, are used in soups or dishes where only a moderate amount of shark's fin is needed. They do not require such long cooking or soaking. They should be soaked for several hours in cold water, then brought to the boil and simmered for 2 — 3 hours. Add to the dish and complete the cooking.

When buying shark's fins in whole form, select the lighter coloured ones that appear relatively free from skin and grit, or they will require thorough cleaning after soaking. 'Needles' are sold in packs usually weighing 30 g (1 oz), and when prepared they will weigh approximately 125 g (4 oz).

SHARK'S SKIN: This is prepared in the same way as whole shark's fin. When softened, the large sheets should be cut into narrow shreds or bite-sized squares before use. Wash shark's skin

thoroughly and rinse well. Place shark's skin in a pot of boiling water and simmer until slightly tender. Remove and soak in warm water, scrub well and rinse several times. Place scrubbed shark's skin in a pot of freshly boiling water, simmer until tender. Remove, trim and soak in cold water. To store: cured shark's skin can be kept in a refrigerator, soaked in water, for 2 — 3 days, with the water changed daily, or freeze.

SQUID: Dried squid is sold in two forms, whole or flattened into sheets by passing through a roller. The latter are mostly used as a snack food, being first roasted over a charcoal fire.

Soak whole dried squid in cold water for 2 hours, then bring to the boil and simmer for 1 hour. Transfer to another saucepan and cover with fresh cold water and add a large pinch of bicarbonate of soda. Boil slowly until softened, then rinse thoroughly. The stock from the first boiling can be used as a base for seafood soups.

PREPARATION OF OTHER DRIED FOODS

BIRDS' NESTS: Soak in boiling water, covered, until the water cools. Drain and cover again with boiling water and again leave until the water cools. Drain. If the nests are to be used in a seasoned dish, pour 1 tablespoon of clear vegetable oil over them and cover with boiling water. The oil traps any fragments of grit or feather for easy removal by rinsing. Otherwise, pick out the impurities with tweezers.

Sprinkle a large pinch of bicarbonate of soda over the nests and cover again with boiling water. Leave for a few minutes, then drain and rinse well in cold water. From this stage, birds' nests require only minimal cooking.

FUNGUS, 'SNOW'(WHITE): Soak in warm water until it swells, then rinse well in several lots of cold water. Cut away the small hard root section and return to warm water. Bring to the boil and add a dash of bicarbonate of soda. Stir quickly and immediately remove from the heat. Pour in a little cold water to stop the cooking and leave for about 5 minutes. Drain and rinse thoroughly. Soak in cold water until ready to use.

FUNGUS, 'WOOD EAR' (BROWN):

Soak until softened. Remove the small tough root section and cut the 'wood ears' into bite-sized pieces, shreds, or strips as indicated in the recipe. Soak in cold water until needed.

*FA TS'AI (FAT CHOY/*BLACK MOSS): Soak in cold water until soft enough to untangle the curly mass. Squeeze out the water, then rinse very thoroughly in cold running water until it runs clear. Cover with cold water and bring to the boil. Drain and cover again with cold water. Soak until needed, then drain and squeeze out as much water as possible.

Prepared fresh ingredients are attractively displayed in this Hong Kong noodle shop.

BLACK MUSHROOMS: Soak for at least 25 minutes in cold water. Remove, squeeze out the water and cut off the stems as close to the caps as possible. Return to cold water until ready to use.

The best flavour is acquired by steaming the mushrooms in chicken stock or water with a dash of rice wine (dry sherry), sugar, and salt until plump and tender. The liquid can be retained for adding to the dish or to soups or stews.

USEFUL HINTS ON THE PREPARATION OF FRESH INGREDIENTS

GINGER: Choose firm, smooth-skinned ginger and remove the skin with a potato peeler. Trim off the buds and cut the pieces diagonally into thick or thin slices as required. To SHRED ginger, stack several thin slices together and cut along the length into very fine strands. To CHOP, first shred, then turn the bundle of shreds and cut across into minute dice, or place on a chopping board and chop energetically

393

with a cleaver until reduced to a pulpy mass.

Ginger can be GRATED with a cheese grater or in a food processor using large pieces of peeled ginger. Grate on as small a setting as possible to give very small pulpy shreds with plenty of juice. Work over a plate to save the juice. BRUISE ginger slices by batting with the end of a rolling pin or cleaver handle. This crushes the cells to release the juice. See also page 387 for details of preparing GINGER JUICE, GINGER WINE, and ONION AND GINGER INFUSION.

ONIONS: Some confusion has arisen over this vegetable. In Australia, the tall green tubular-stemmed SPRING ONIONS may also be known as SHALLOTS or ESCHALLOTS, while in America they are SCALLIONS.

To add further to the confusion, SCALLIONS can also refer to the small red-skinned onions which grow in clove-clusters resembling oversized red garlics. We have used the term SPRING ONIONS with SCALLIONS in parentheses throughout this book.

White onions, therefore, refer to the large common onion with white peel. Brown or Spanish onions can also be used. Leeks have a milder flavour and are an excellent substitute for either spring or white onions in most recipes.

GARLIC CHIVES resemble young spring onions (scallions), having paler green stems and a very short white base. They have a mild onion flavour with a hint of fresh garlic. If unavailable, substitute shredded leek.

For a majority of these recipes, spring onions (scallions) should be *TRIMMED* by cutting just above the roots and removing roots and any limp outer leaves. Discard the topmost parts of the green stems and use only the firmly packed white lower section with a short length of the more tightly packed part of the green section. Trimmings are useful to add flavour to soups. SLICE the onions diagonally into 2 cm (¾ in) lengths. Larger spring onions (scallions) can be cut in halves lengthwise to facilitate fast cooking, then cut into short lengths. CHOP by shredding lengthwise, then cutting across into very small pieces, or chop with the cleaver as indicated above (Ginger). DICE spring onions (scallions) by cutting straight across the

stems, or diagonally if preferred, into very small pieces.

To cut white onions Chinese style, peel, then cut in halves from top (stem) to bottom (root). Trim away the root section using a V-shaped cut, then slice from top to bottom into wedges of required size. Separate each segment into individual slices for faster cooking.

CHICKENS: To DEBONE (BONE) a whole chicken, place the bird on its back on a chopping board and use a short sharp knife to work around the entire rib cage up to the backbone. When the wing and thigh bones are reached, cut through the middle joint so that the lower part of the wing and leg bones remain intact. Continue up to the backbone and remove the whole carcass in one piece. The retention of the lower wing and leg bones aids in the reshaping of the chicken when stuffed.

To SKIN a whole chicken, work in a similar way as for deboning, but this time separate the meat from the skin. Use a small sharp knife and the fingers to cut and gently pull away the skin, taking care not to pierce through the skin. Small kitchen scissors can be invaluable for snipping through tough connective tissue. Again, leave the lower bones of the wings and legs in place to aid in restructuring the bird later. DUCKS are deboned (boned) and .skinned in the same way.

Whole chickens (or other poultry) are often cut for serving by slicing straight through the bones. The cleaver is best for this as it has the sharpness as well as the size and weight for cutting through even the largest thigh bones with ease.

To CUT A CHICKEN FOR SERVING, place the chicken on a chopping board, breast upwards, and cut straight through the breast bone along its length. Open flat and cut through the backbone, then turn the two parts upwards. Cut off the head and neck, remove the wing tips, then remove the wings by cutting through the upper joint. Slice off the thighs whole. Trim off the knuckles by chopping straight through the bone below the drumstick meat (or leave in place, if preferred) and cut the drumstick into two pieces, or leave whole. Remove the thigh bone, then cut the thigh meat into thick diagonal fingers. Cut the wings in halves at the central joint, or leave whole.

Remove the breast meat in a piece from each side and cut into thick

diagonal slices. Then cut straight through the bones of the meaty back section, cutting into bite-sized squares. Use the point of the cleaver to lift out the breast bone meat and cut or tear this into slivers.

When cutting through the larger bones, chop down with the cleaver, then hit the top of the cleaver firmly and sharply with the base of the left hand to force it through (see also page 396, Chopping, below).

To ARRANGE A CHICKEN FOR SERVING, set the head at the edge of an oval plate facing outwards over the rim. Place the neck and thigh bones in a row away from the head. Arrange any unevenly cut pieces of meat and the slices from the back on both sides of the row of bones, then place the sliced breast meat crosswise in a shape resembling the whole chicken.

Set the two wings on either side of the body, and cross the drumsticks at the end with the 'parson's nose' between the legs. Finish by arranging the sliced thigh pieces along the length of the body on both sides.

PRAWNS (SHRIMPS): In many of these recipes, it is recommended that the heads be left on as they lend their own rich flavour and a bright red-pink colour to the dish. They can, of course, be removed if preferred. Tail sections are generally left on only for aesthetic reasons and may be similarly discarded if preferred.

If the tail section is to be left intact, this includes the last joint of the shell covering the body, though it can be trimmed shorter using a pair of small kitchen scissors. The sharp 'horn' in the centre should be pulled or snipped off. To DEVEIN using a toothpick, as mentioned in many recipes, hold the prawn (shrimp) in the left hand with the back curving upwards. Push the toothpick (or use the point of a fork) into the centre top of the prawn (shrimp) back and gently ease upwards. It should hook out the dark gritty vein and it can then be eased out from the full length of the prawn (shrimp).

Alternatively, cut along the back with a sharp knife and pull out the exposed vein. Cutting deeply in this way gives prawn (shrimp) cutlets (butterflies).

Rinse fresh prawns (shrimps) in their shells in plenty of cold water. Peeled prawns (shrimps) can be washed under cold running water, using a little salt and cornflour (cornstarch) to gently rub while rinsing. This helps to whiten the meat and eliminate the fishy smell.

Fresh prawns (shrimps) are easily peeled as the shells slide off with a minimum of effort. If cooking in the shells, however, cut along the underside between the two rows of legs with a short, sharp knife either before or after cooking. The whole shell can then be lifted off without cutting the meat. The term 'green' used in this book refers to fresh uncooked prawns (shrimps).

FISH: In certain baked, poached, and steamed dishes using a whole fish, it is recommended that the scales be left on. This is to retain the natural juices and oils in the fish. When the dish is cooked, the scales with skin attached can be lifted off cleanly.

A fish is SCORED both for aesthetic and technical reasons. A pattern of diagonal or criss-cross scoring along the sides of the fish improves the appearance of the finished dish and additionally aids in fast cooking and the thorough permeation of the seasonings.

To score diagonally, use a sharp knife to cut across the body from top fins to the lower opening, cutting at an angle to the head and deep enough to just touch the bones. Four or five scores across an average-sized fish is usually sufficient. Criss-cross scoring requires an additional row of cuts from the opposing angle to result in a diamond-shaped pattern across the fish.

To SQUIRREL a fish, cut off the two fillets and place on a board, meat upwards. Score in a close criss-cross pattern, holding the knife at a slight angle and cutting right through to the skin without piercing it. Brush a finger along the cut area from tail to head to make the 'points' stand up. This gives an attractive appearance to the finished dish and allows the meat to cook very quickly.

To DEBONE (BONE) a fish, cut open along the underside, then work the point of a short sharp knife along the backbone, gently easing the meat away on both sides. Cut through the bone at both ends using scissors or a knife and lift out the backbone in one piece.

EEL: Best bought live, if possible, dropped into a pot of boiling water, and left for a few minutes. Skin by securing the head to a strong support such as the edge of a table, cut around the head, then use a pair of pincers to strip away the skin in one piece.

Fillets may be obtained by securing the eel in the same way and using a sharp knife to cut three or four strips from the length of the eel, leaving the backbone attached to the head.

The skin may be left on. Rub with plenty of salt to remove the slimy residue, then rinse thoroughly. Steaks may be cut crosswise through the bone and pressed out flat.

TURTLE: Place the live turtle on a board, upside down, and cut off the head. Lift and drain the blood. Place the whole turtle in a large saucepan of boiling water and leave for 2 minutes, then remove and use a knife to scrape off the skin. Remove the shell and cut open the under side to remove the stomach. Cut the meat into strips and simmer in boiling water for several minutes. Drain well.

Cook according to the recipe, removing all small bones when the meat is tender.

MEATBALLS: Very finely mince (grind) the meat, see below (Mincing With Two Cleavers), or pulverise in a food processor using the chopping blade. Transfer to a mixing bowl and add the seasoning ingredients. Squeeze the mixture through the fingers until sticky, then gather into one lump. Lift from the bowl and throw back against the inside of the bowl repeatedly until the mixture is thoroughly softened, about 3 minutes. Chill until firm. Use for beef, pork, and chicken balls. Squid can also be prepared in this way for seafood balls. To make smooth-textured fish or prawn (shrimp) balls, smash the meat until pulverised, using the cleaver blade held flat in parallel with the cutting board, or pulverise in a food processor. Add the seasoning ingredients and binding agents and beat in one direction only with a wooden spoon or a pair of cooking chopsticks until the mixture is smooth and thick.

To form meat or seafood balls, have a saucepan of water gently simmering or a pan of deep-frying oil heated to just below smoking point. Gather up a large portion of the paste in the left hand and squeeze out an amount between the curled forefinger and thumb. Scoop it off with a spoon and drop into the oil or water. Cook the balls until they rise to the surface, then drain and transfer to a dish of cold water until ready to use.

COOKING OIL: The term 'frying oil' is used in most recipes for sautéd or stir-fried dishes. This refers to vegetable oil that has been used at least once before, probably for deep-frying. It has a richer taste than the bland, almost raw flavour of new vegetable oil and should be used in preference to new oil.

Cantonese cooks prefer the strong, slightly nutty flavour of peanut (groundnut) oil for their cooking. It is a matter of individual taste whether this or one of the lighter tasting pure vegetable oils is used.

LARD (rendered pork fat) is also used in many stir-fried and sautéd dishes as an alternative cooking oil. It gives a much richer taste and should be avoided by the diet-conscious. It is also used in sweets, bread and pastry making,

Chopping.

and in cakes for the rich taste and the smooth texture it gives to dough and pastries. In fact, lard (and very occasionally rendered chicken fat) replaces butter or other forms of shortening in all Chinese cooking.

RENDERED CHICKEN FAT (CHICKEN GREASE) is occasionally used as a cooking oil, but more usually to add a rich taste and shine to sauces and finished dishes (see also page 413).

Oil for DEEP-FRYING can be kept clean by straining through a special filter or a paper coffee filter after each use. A few slices of peeled raw potato dropped into the oil after use, but while still hot, helps absorb impurities.

Choose a good quality oil and keep one lot for cooking fish and seafoods and another for meats. New cooking

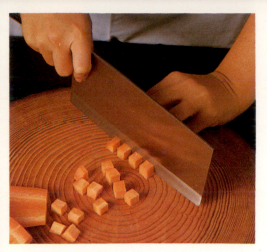

oil should be used for deep-frying ingredients used in sweets, cakes, or puddings.

Chinese cooks often splash a quantity of piping hot frying oil over a finished dish to add flavour and shine. This does not result in a greasy tasting dish, but it can be too oily for some tastes and may be omitted.

SESAME OIL is only occasionally used for cooking, being of a strong distinct flavour. It is used frequently to add taste and aroma to marinades and sauces. It may be omitted unless specifically indicated.

With the exception of lard and rendered chicken fat, animal fats are not used in Chinese cooking.

THICKENING: Most stir-fried and sautéd dishes require a clear, viscous sauce which is best obtained by the addition of a paste of starch and cold water. Cornflour (cornstarch) is the most commonly used starch, though a powder of green mung beans is preferred by some Chinese cooks as it results in a thicker sauce and is therefore more economical.

Ordinary wheat flour will not give similar results and should not be used as an alternative. The sauce will invariably turn lumpy and will not acquire the desired clear, syrupy appearance.

A CORNFLOUR SOLUTION or PASTE as required in these recipes should be a mixture of approximately equal amounts of cornflour (cornstarch) and cold water. Never use hot or boiling water as this will cause the flour to partially cook, resulting in a thin lumpy sauce.

In dishes with a large quantity of sauce, such as stewed or braised dishes, the sauce may be reduced first by boiling in an open pan, then thickened with a cornflour paste.

As a general rule, use 1 tablespoon of cornflour mixed with 1 tablespoon of cold water to thicken 1 cup (8 fl oz) of sauce.

PREPARATION TECHNIQUES AND THE USE OF THE CHINESE CLEAVER.

CHOPPING: The term is applied to any technique involving straight-through cutting of food. Place the item on a cutting board and use a straight, sharp downwards motion with the cleaver, holding the blade parallel with the surface of the board.

To chop through bones, hit down with the blade, then bat the top of the blade with the base of the left hand to force it through the bone. See also Preparation of Chicken and Ginger for specific application to these ingredients.

DICING/CUBING: Cutting into very small cubes (dice) or slightly larger cubes (approximately 2 cm / ¾ in). The ingredient should be first cut into slices the thickness of the required dice or cube, then into sticks. Turn crosswise and cut the sticks into cubes or dice, maintaining even-sized pieces.

MINCING (GRINDING) WITH TWO CLEAVERS: To obtain a pulverized paste of meat, seafood, or vegetables, place the item on a cutting board and take a sharp cleaver in each hand. Chop with alternate hands in a fast rhythm until the item is spread out and partially chopped. Scrape into a pile again and continue chopping and reshaping the pile until the item is completely pulverised. Draw out any tendons or pieces of skin or hard tissue and discard.

Soft seafoods like fish and prawns can be pulverised by placing on a board and batting with the flat side of the cleaver until reduced to a pulp.

SLICING: When applied to meats for

Chinese cooking, the meat should be cut across the grain, unless otherwise specified. This severs the tough connective tissue making the meat more tender. To obtain the wafer-thin or paper-thin slices often required, freeze the meat until the piece is quite firm and use a very sharp knife or cleaver to pare off slices so thin they are almost transparent.

When cutting, hold the item firmly with the left hand, with the forefinger of the left hand raised at the central joint and pressed against the cleaver. This acts as a guide for thickness and prevents slips which might result in an accidental cut.

STRIPS AND SHREDS: Stack the slices of meat or vegetables, two or three slices at a time, and cut along the longest part into strips of required width. Strips may vary from 1 cm (1/5 in) to 2.5 cm (1 in). Narrower strips would be called shreds or 'matchsticks.'

HORIZONTAL SLICING (FLAT SLICING): The cleaver is ideally suited to this task. It is applied to round flat-shaped foods such as whole abalone, champignons, water chestnuts, and kidneys, which are required to be sliced while maintaining the natural shape.

Place the ingredient on a board and press the fingers of the left hand firmly

on top, holding the ingredient securely in position. Using the cleaver held flat and parallel with the board, cut through the item under the fingers. Remove each slice when cut to avoid slips.

DIAGONAL SLICING/ROLL CUTTING: Vegetables with long thin shapes such as celery and carrots, radishes, and spring onions are usually cut on the diagonal to expose a greater cut surface to the heat during cooking and also to improve the appearance. Generally, diagonal slices will be around 1.25 cm (½ in) between cuts, resulting in pieces about 3.75 cm (1½ in) long from end to end.

When larger pieces of vegetable are required, these may be ROLL-CUT by first cutting one diagonal slice, then rolling the vegetable one-quarter turn and cutting at the same angle as the first cut. This gives pleasing shapes as well as exposing a maximum of cut surface area for faster cooking and better penetration of seasonings.

GRINDING: When applied to spices and small, hard ingredients such as nuts, rice, and beans, this is done in a mortar or in a spice or coffee grinder. Unless otherwise specified, the items should be ground to a fine powder.

In some recipes, ingredients are ground with water to produce a smooth paste. This should be done in a food processor, using the chopping blade or a blender on the setting for grind or purée. Add enough water to prevent the machine from clogging, or the amount suggested in the recipe, and grind until the mixture is smooth and lump-free.

SCORING (CRISS-CROSS): Certain smooth-surfaced ingredients are scored to facilitate fast cooking and to give aesthetic appeal. Kidneys, squid, and thickly sliced liver are usually scored with a close criss-cross pattern which results in a diamond-shaped design on the surface.

Cut about 0.3 cm (1/8 in) deep and at a slight angle and work closely so that the diamonds are no more than ½ cm (1/5 in) wide.

A GUIDE TO COOKING PROCESSES AND TERMS.

STIR-FRYING: Used to describe a process in which small slivers of food are quickly cooked in a small amount of cooking oil. Cooking is usually done over intensely high heat to seal in the natural flavours and to retain the natural colour and texture of the food. The wok was created for just such a cooking process with sufficient depth to allow for a lot of movement of the contents as they are constantly stirred and turned during cooking to prevent burning and to distribute the seasonings thoroughly.

The wok is first heated, then the oil (usually vegetable oil which has been previously used, see Cooking Oil, above) is swirled around the inside of the pan so that it runs slowly over the whole surface and accumulates in the bottom. The wok is heated to 'smoking point,' i.e. when a faint blue smoky haze appears above the oil and when a drop of water added to the oil will immediately splutter and evaporate. The prepared ingredients are added at this stage, energetically tossed around with the wok spatula, then the seasonings are added and the ingredients again tossed until all are well coated with the seasonings and the cooking oil. Seasoning such as soy sauce and rice wine (or sherry) are usually swirled onto the sides of the wok rather than straight onto the ingredients. This allows them to sizzle and partially evaporate, releasing their full flavour before reaching the food. Lastly, the sauce ingredients are added together with the thickening agent, well mixed with cold water or stock, and the contents of the wok continue to be stirred until the sauce thickens and acquires a clear, viscous quality (see thickening, above).

All components required to produce a good stir-fried dish should be assembled before cooking begins, with the ingredients completely prepared. There is no time once cooking commences to search for an additional condiment, or fumble for the wok spatula. Have the wok, spatula, a sturdy oven glove or thick cloth, the prepared ingredients, seasonings, cooking oil, and sauce ingredients assembled close to the cooker before beginning. And commence cooking only when diners are seated at the table in readiness. The success of a stir-fried dish lies in its being brought straight from the wok to the table.

Sautéd foods are cooked at a very slightly lower temperature than stir-fried foods, but a similar technique of constant stirring and moving is also employed, though in a less vigorous fashion. Sautéing often applies to more friable ingredients, or those which have a tendency to burn on higher heats, such as fish or soft beancurd.

Shallow Frying implies food cooked in a shallow level of oil, usually vegetable oil but occasionally lard. There should be sufficient oil in frying that such composite foods as meatballs

and fritters can float free of the surface of the pan. Soft-textured foods like soft beancurd, the pot-sticker types of dumplings, and crispy breads such as 'spring onion pastries' require merely a well-oiled pan.

Dry-Frying is employed to parch certain ingredients, thereby toasting them lightly without subjecting them to oil which would spoil their texture. This is best done in a cast-iron wok or frying pan/skillet over moderate heat.

DEEP-FRYING: Cooking in oil with the food completely immersed. Vegetable or peanut oil (see Cooking Oil, above) and occasionally lard is used, and it should be heated to moderate, around 160°C (325°F) for most seafoods, and to 190°C (375°F) for meats, poultry, and vegetables or foods coated in batter. Smoking hot

Scoring.

oil, at around 200°C (400°F) is required for 'instant' cooking of such ingredients as crisp-fried rice vermicelli, prawn crackers, or crisp rice cakes. Deep-fried foods should be well drained after cooking, preferably in a drainer lined with absorbent paper. For best results, particularly with batter or crumb-coated foods, fry once on moderate heat, allow to cool completely in a drainer, then re-fry on a higher temperature immediately before serving. This is particularly useful for foods which require preparation in advance. Leave the second frying until ready to serve.

Deep-frying is employed at varying stages in Chinese cooking. Certain foods, particularly whole cuts of meat or whole poultry, are deep-fried prior to steaming or simmering. This adds colour to the surface and extra flavour

to the finished dish. As these meats are usually marinated before frying they have a tendency to spatter when they enter the hot oil. Care should be taken to protect the arms and hands from flying droplets of hot oil. If meat is to be deep-fried as the final stage of the cooking process, ensure that the surface is thoroughly dry and that there is no residue of liquid inside the meat or bird before frying.

Many of these recipes require that the prepared and marinated main ingredient be deep-fried as the initial cooking step, prior to stir-frying. This is desirable to perfect the dish as it prevents the shreds, slices, or strips of food from sticking together during cooking. It is, however, quite impractical in the home kitchen. Stir-frying is just as successful without the preliminary deep-frying with the following considerations. Use less, or omit entirely, the egg white and/or cornflour (cornstarch) in the marinade as this will cause the food to stick to the pan and usually results in a thick deposit of particles in the bottom of the pan which spoils both the appearance and taste of the dish. Add a little (extra) oil to the marinade to prevent the meat from sticking together, and use slightly more oil for stir-frying than is recommended. Additionally, ensure that the meat is cooked before the other ingredients, except possibly spring onions and ginger, and remove when cooked. Return to the dish when the seasonings and sauce ingredients are added.

When deep-frying whole poultry, use wooden cooking chopsticks or the handles of two wooden spoons to gently turn the bird, thus ensuring that the skin does not tear.

STEAMING: The Chinese invented steam cooking many hundreds of years ago and continue to praise it as the purest method of cooking.

Intense moist heat keeps the ingredients succulent and bright in colour, leaving the natural taste unimpaired, and there is no contact with anything which could impart its own flavour, save the added seasonings. Steaming is used in many Chinese recipes, either as the only cooking process or as one stage in the cooking of a dish which may also be deep-fried. Many ingredients, additionally, are steamed prior to use to soften them and release their full flavours. This particularly applies to the many dried ingredients used in Chinese cooking.

Steaming is done in a container set on a rack within a large pot or wok which is tightly covered to prevent the steam from escaping. Wet ingredients, or foods with added stock or sauce are steamed in dishes, on plates, or in bowls, while dry foods such as buns can be placed directly onto the greased slatted bamboo bases of tiered bamboo steaming baskets. See Chinese Cooking Utensils, Condiments and Methods, Chapter XI, for detailed notes on setting up a steamer. Steaming is done 'over high heat' or over 'rapidly boiling water,' which dictates that the water producing the steam should be kept at a constant bubbling boil. As the water will evaporate over a period of time, the level should be frequently topped up with boiling water. Keep the lid of the steamer firmly in place during cooking to avoid heat loss. Dishes or whole foods inside a steamer should be positioned well above the water level and should not be covered unless specified in the recipe. Slow steaming is required for certain foods. The water in the steamer should be maintained at a gentle simmer.

SMOKING: Smoking over fragrant smokefuel such as tea leaves, pine needles, fragrant wood shavings, sugar, or dried orange peel lends a rich colour and flavour to certain foods, in particular fish and poultry. The smokefuel ingredients are placed in the bottom of a heavy iron wok or old cooking pot which has a well-fitting lid and set over heat until the fuel begins to smoke. The heat is then reduced and a rack set in position over the fuel, high enough to allow a free flow of smoke around the ingredients. Smoking can be done in the oven. Place the smokefuel ingredients in a baking dish and set in the bottom of a hot oven. When the fuel begins to smoke, decrease the heat slightly and place the ingredients on a rack over the fuel. Close the oven and smoke for the required time. Wipe out the oven with a damp cloth when the operation is completed.

Smoked food is usually steamed or deep-fried, or a combination of both, either before or after the smoking.

POACHING: This involves very gentle cooking of an ingredient, usually a whole cut of meat or a whole bird or fish. The ingredient is covered with seasoned water or stock which is then brought to a gentle simmer. Fish are usually poached in a fish kettle, an oval-shaped deep saucepan with a removable perforated base which can be lifted out with the fragile fish in one piece after cooking. In certain cases, the pan will be removed from the heat source after a very short cooking time, merely a few minutes. The pan is then covered with a thick, warm cloth or towel and the ingredients left to gently poach in the warm liquid until cooked. This particularly applies to chicken, and the result is tender, succulent pinky-white meat of delicate flavour. Poaching can also describe a technique of cooking whole cuts of meat of whole poultry or fish by immersion in warm oil. Gentle heat is applied, sufficient to cook without the ingredient becoming greasy, but low enough that the meat does not change colour. Oil-poached foods should be very well drained before further cooking, or before serving.

SLOW-SIMMERING: This differs little from poaching. The liquid is never brought quite to the boil, however, the heat being decreased as soon as the first bubbles break the surface. The food is very slowly and gently cooked in the stock or sauce until completely tender. Slow-simmering, also known as clear-simmering, results in moist and tender ingredients in a completely clear stock. It is important to keep the pan tightly closed during cooking, and not to stir the contents.

SIMMER-STEWING: This refers to the process of slowly cooking an ingredient in well-seasoned liquid so that the ingredient absorbs both the colour and flavour of the seasonings applied. The liquid may be served as the sauce, straight from the pan, or it may be thickened and poured over the ingredient on the serving plate. In certain cases, the cooking liquid is retained for use with other dishes.

RED-BRAISING/RED-STEWING: A term generally applied to the cooking of ingredients, particularly large cuts of meat or whole poultry, which have been deep or shallow-fried for colour and extra flavour, and are then slowly cooked in a well-flavoured sauce of which the principle ingredients are soy sauce and sugar. The meat acquires a rich red-brown colour. Also known as red-cooking.

KITCHEN LAYOUT

As so much Chinese cooking requires fast work at the wok, it is vital that the kitchen be well laid out in order to avoid the kind of confusion which might spoil a dish.

The preparation section should be separate from the cooking area and have one or two cutting boards, the knives and cleavers and the various preparation utensils on hand, plus a supply of small plates and dishes to

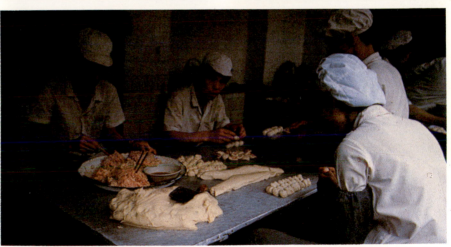

In a Chinese kitchen, food is usually prepared away from the cooking area, then placed in dishes and containers at a handy distance from the cook.

contain the prepared ingredients.

Position the wok cooker as close to the sink as possible as it will have to be carried to the sink for washing between each use. Have the cooking utensils — spatula, ladle, strainers, chopsticks, wooden spoons, etc. — close by and the seasoning ingredients, thickeners, and cooking oils readily available.

Certain brands of soy sauce are marketed in small bottles with shaker/pourer nozzles. These make it clean and easy to measure the sauce and to swirl it around the sides of the wok, as is required in so many recipes.

Use them also for cooking wine and oil. Experience soon becomes a better judge than a measuring spoon for these ingredients. There are also small sauce jugs available, resembling tiny teapots with long spouts. These are excellent for dispensing all liquid seasonings and cooking oils.

Keep salt, pepper, m.s.g., and other frequently used dry ingredients in squat containers with tight-fitting lids. These can be lined up close to the work area and make it easier for spoon measuring than if they are retained in their original packaging.

Make sure there is a pair of sturdy oven gloves or a thick cloth readily on hand for holding and lifting the wok as the handles can become very hot during cooking.

399

CHAPTER XII
A Word on Wines and Spirits

According to the ancient legend, wine was first discovered in China by a careless cook: having set some rice to soak in water in a covered crock one day, he promptly forgot about it. Several days later, he noticed the crock and uncovered it: a powerful aroma overwhelmed him. Curious, he dipped his ladle into the murky liquid and tasted it. He found the flavour palatable and the after-effects quite pleasant. So he dipped and drank again. Pretty soon, all the cooks and helpers in the kitchen were gathered about the crock, dipping their ladles deeply, talking and laughing merrily. No doubt the master of the house went hungry that evening.

Since earliest antiquity, wine has formed an integral part of Chinese culinary culture. The earliest of all ancient artifacts unearthed in China are ceremonial bronze drinking vessels dating from the Shang dynasty (ca. 1500 B.C.). Indeed, excessive indulgence in wine has often been cited as a major reason for the fall of the house of Shang. Along with drinking vessels, the Shang artifacts include similar bronze vessels for food: from the very beginning, eating and drinking, food and wine, have been as intimately associated as *yin and yang*, and one rarely appeared on the table without the other.

Even Confucius, that paragon of moderation, viewed drinking with great tolerance, and he usually enjoyed wine with his meals. His meticulous eating habits, which included set limits for every type of food, have been described in Chapter I. But when it came to wine, the Sage's guideline was liberal: 'There is no limit to wine-drinking, as long as one does not become disorderly.'

Of course, not everyone followed Confucius' 'Golden Mean,' most notably China's famous 'Drunken Dragons,' scholars and poets renowned for having the 'capacity of the ocean' when it came down to drinking. Chinese poets have praised the delights of wine almost as much as they have women, and any poet worth his verse was expected to be able to down 'a hundred cups at a sitting.' A common Chinese adage states, 'When drinking among intimate friends, even 1,000 cups are not enough.' China's most famous 'Drunken Dragon' was the colourful T'ang poet Li Bo, who is said to have died in a lotus pool when, reaching drunkenly from a boat to embrace the image of the moon in the water, he fell overboard and drowned. Li Bo and other poets who shared his love of drinking regarded wine as the key to the sublime. He left us this couplet to prove it:

The rapture of drinking and wine's dizzy joy,
No sober man deserves to enjoy!

Food and wine go hand in hand in Chinese culinary culture. The Chinese rarely drink alone, and they never drink on an empty stomach. While banquets are considered incomplete without an accompanying alcoholic beverage or two, drinking is equally incomplete without a few *jiu-cai* ('wine-foods') to line the stomach. Whenever a few friends go out to have a few drinks together in China, they always order a few side-dishes such as dried meats and beancurd, cold poultry, salted nuts, pickled vegetables, and so forth. In addition to lining and protecting the stomach, *jiu-cai* also increase the appetite for and appreciation of the wine itself.

A wide variety of fermented wines and distilled spirits have been produced in China for millenia, and most of these traditional beverages are still on the market today. Fermented wines, such as the rice-wine discovered by the

careless cook, have been imbibed in China since pre-historic times. They were fermented from grains, mostly rice, millet, or sorghum. Later, these fermented grain-wines were further enhanced and flavoured with fragrant herbal additives such as fagara pepper, realgar, artemisia, cassia blossom, pomegranate blossom, and others. During the T'ang dynasty, fermented grape-wines were introduced from the western frontier regions, and they enjoyed immense popularity in China. Vines were imported and transplanted in northern China, which today still produces a variety of good grape-wines.

Traditional methods of aging and bottling Chinese wines are still much in evidence in this Hong Kong wine shop. (p.401, left and above)

During the Sung era, the art of distilling spirits from fermented grain-mash was introduced and quickly adopted in China. A wide range of potent spirits soon appeared in the wine-shops and restaurants throughout the empire. Among the most renowned Chinese spirits are the various forms of 'white lightning:' *mao-tai, bai-ga'r,* and *gaoliang.* Made from *gaoliang* (sorghum), these spirits are distilled over and over until they approach 150 proof or more in strength. At banquets, they are generally used only for toasting. Chinese herbalists also use them to make potent tonic potions: tonic herbs, reptiles, poisonous snakes, deer-horn, etc. are steeped in 150 proof spirits for a year or more to extract their potent elements. The resulting brew is taken as a tonic medicinal drink, especially during the winter.

Today, the most suitable and the most popular beverage with Chinese food is chilled beer. All over China and the Far East, people drink beer with Chinese food more than any other beverage, and beer consumption has grown by leaps and bounds in recent decades. This may seem ironic, since beer is a Western beverage, but throughout their history the Chinese have adapted useful foreign innovations to their own culinary culture. Beer turns out to fit Chinese culinary requirements like a glove, which accounts for its immense popularity today.

The first breweries were established in China during the early decades of this century by Germans. The Chinese have well maintained these facilities and kept the quality of their beers up to original European standards. Everyone in China drinks beer today, and the most popular nationally distributed brand is Qing-Dao lager. In addition to Qing-Dao, every province and every major city of China produce their own local brews under colourful Chinese labels, and these are consistently good. Peking (Beijing) offers 'Great Wall Beer' and an excellent dark porter; in Shanghai you can swig 'Swan Lager;' Kweilin (Guilin) brews an excellent 'Guilin Beer;' in Hangchow (Hangzhou) you'll enjoy 'West Lake Beer' with your West Lake Sour Fish; and in every other city you'll find a refreshing local brew waiting. In Hong Kong, Singapore, and Tokyo, excellent local brews as well as the full gamut of international brands are available. In Taipei (Taibei), the award-winning 'Taiwan Beer' is the national brew, and it is consumed by the sybaritic populace of the island in incredible quantities.

What's so great about beer with Chinese food? One of the main functions of beverages at Chinese banquets is to clean the palate and throat of residual oils and lingering flavours, thereby clearing the way for better culinary appreciation of the subtle points of each different dish and each successive bite. The carbonation in beer fulfils this function ideally, effectively cleaning the mouth with each swig. Brewed purely from grains, beer is also an indirect form of *fan*, and both its flavour and pharmacological nature are perfectly suited to the flavours and natures of Chinese *cai*. Beer promotes digestion, helping the stomach to deal with the many different types of food ingested during the course of a typical Chinese meal. And chilled beer is probably the world's most effective thirst-quencher. Many spicy Chinese dishes leave the palate thirsty for cool liquid refreshment, and you can resort to beer often during the course of a meal without risking excess intoxication, as you do with more traditional Chinese beverages. At formal banquets, beer is usually provided along with a potent spirit used for toasting. If you use beer to toast, however, be sure to use small (four to six ounce) tumblers because most Chinese toasts demand that you *gan-bei*! or 'bottoms up!'

The most traditional Chinese banquet beverage is *Shaoxing* wine, a famous rice-derived wine of Chekiang (Zhejiang) province. It is served piping hot in small liqueur glasses and is often flavoured with preserved plums or slices of fresh lemon. It has the same advantages of beer: it is made from grain, so its flavour and nature suit the requirements of Chinese cuisine. Served hot, it effectively cleanses the palate of residual oils and tastes, as does beer's carbonation. Since it is less than 40 proof, *Shaoxing* wine may also be drunk in copious quantities without risking excessive intoxication. Mr. James Wei, Taipei's (Taibei's) master gourmet and consummate banqueteer, insists that hot *Shaoxing* is the only appropriate beverage to drink at Chinese banquets. His advice, which cites the authority of the Sage himself, is instructive and convincing:

You must drink Shaoxing at blood temperature. When cold, reject. Drink with full heart and open throat. Remember that over-indulgence brings neither headache nor thirst in the morning. Remember, also, that while Confucius, a diner of moderation, argued that the meat a man ate should not be enough to make his breath smell of meat rather than rice, he imposed no limit on wine consumption, so long as the diner 'did not become disorderly.'

Besides beer and *Shaoxing*, there are many other traditional Chinese liquors which commonly appear on banquet tables in China and elsewhere in the Orient. The most famous is the fiery *mao-tai*, which Zhou Enlai used to toast Richard Nixon during his visit to Peking (Beijing). *Da-zhu, bai-ga'r*, and *gaoliang*, similar in strength and taste, are also common toasting drinks. Beginners are advised to approach these with caution at banquets. None are likely choices for home consumption in the West.

The aromatic Chinese wines are far better choices for Western palates. Kweilin's (Guilin's) 'Cassia Blossom Wine' (*gui-hua-jiu*) tastes like a light, fragrant vermouth. Nanking's (Nanjing's) viscous 'Sealed Jug Wine' (feng-gang-jiu) is vaguely reminiscent of a good German dessert wine on the palate, although it is made of rice. There are wines made from fruits, wines flavoured with honey and herbs, medicinal wines, and many others. All told, China's far-flung provinces probably produce as varied an array of alcoholic beverages as all of Europe. The best are available the world over, wherever Chinese products are sold.

It remains an issue of continuing debate among Western connoisseurs of Chinese food whether fine Western grape wines go well with Chinese food. In our opinion, they do not. The delicate bouquets of fine French and California wines are lost among the strong flavours and powerful aromas of Chinese food. Nor are they strong enough to effectively clear the palate with each sip, an important function of wine at Chinese banquets. However, should you prefer drinking Western grape wines with Chinese food, the best choices are rosé and other sparkling wines. Their carbonation helps clear the palate and throat, which, in addition to facilitating better appreciation of the food, also permits the subtle flavours of the wine to come through.

One of the most popular banquet beverages among wealthy gourmets in Hong Kong, Singapore, and Taipei (Taibei) is good French cognac. This is an excellent choice, both for toasting and for taste. Cognac is far smoother and more pleasant tasting than any of the traditional Chinese spirits used for toasting, and it is not as strong. Unlike French wine, however, cognac is strong enough to effectively cleanse the palate and throat. Distilled from grape wine, cognac possesses the fragrant bouquet of wine in concentrated form, which enables it to penetrate the strong flavours of Chinese food and be savoured by the palate. Though cognac is a fairly strong drink, taken on a stomach full of good Chinese food, it does not intoxicate as readily as when drunk by itself. At Chinese meals, cognac should be served in small, one ounce liqueur glasses, which may be 'bottomed-up' for toasts without excessive intake.

Other Western spirits may also be served in this manner with Chinese food. Scotch, bourbon, vodka, and gin are acceptable substitutes for Chinese spirits. They should be served 'straight' in liqueur glasses, or with a little water and ice in small tumblers.

Iced drinks, especially sweet colas, should be avoided with Chinese food — as with all food. The concentrated sweeteners and artificial flavours used to manufacture such beverages

clog the palate and numb its sensitivity to subtle fresh flavours. Ice-cold liquids of any kind numb the palate and sinuses. They also freeze the ducts which secrete digestive juices into the stomach, effectively delaying digestion and absorption of ingested food for several hours. Nothing could be worse for the aesthetic appreciation and harmonious digestion of gourmet food than ice-cold, artificially flavoured drinks.

For teetotalers, hot tea is indeed the best banquet beverage. Hot tea clears the palate and throat better than any other drink, and many Chinese gourmets always keep a cup of fragrant hot tea steaming next to their beer and toasting glasses. Tea also facilitates the harmonious blending of foods in the stomach and promotes digestion.

Toasting is the customary method of drinking at Chinese banquets. Rarely is one permitted to raise a glass to his lips alone. Usually the host starts the ball rolling at the beginning of the banquet by proposing a toast to his guests and to the occasion of the banquet. Thereafter, toasting continues throughout the meal, and anyone may propose a toast to anything. Rapturous toasts are often proposed to a particularly good dish or a clever comment, to a good friend who missed the banquet, to the host and the chef, and to anything else that comes to mind. The toasts tend to wax more eloquent as the meal progresses. It is considered impolite not to respond to a toast which is directed at you, but those who sincerely wish to avoid liquor may substitute tea, or even water, in a symbolic gesture.

In China, drinking is an extension of eating and is pursued in the same spirit of robust enjoyment and gourmet refinement. Wines and spirits permit more complete aesthetic enjoyment of good food and facilitate its digestion and absorption in the system. Even the Bible suggests that man 'take a little wine for the stomach's sake.' Furthermore, wines and spirits elevate, in comfortable increments, the mood of each guest and of the banquet in general, greatly enhancing the spirit of communal camaraderie which is so vital to Chinese eating habits. By the end of a Chinese banquet, everyone at the table should feel the cherished 'rapture of drinking and wine's dizzy joy,' which the 'Drunken Dragon' Li Bo insisted was the exclusive domain of wine-tipplers.

The variety of China's traditional wines and spirits is almost as great as the variety of foods. In China there's a drink for every occasion and season: warming wines for winter, cooling ones for summer; strong herbal wines for potency, potent straight spirits for toasting at banquets; like Yin and Yang, food and drink in China are always combined for maximum balance and harmony.

GLOSSARY

ABALONE:
A mollusc, the hard outer shell of which is removed to obtain its firm textured meat. Sold canned in water, dried or fresh. Canned abalone requires minimal cooking and is suited to cold or sautéd dishes. The dried type requires lengthy soaking and slow-simmering to soften and is used in braised dishes, while the fresh fish, if obtainable, can be used for all types of dishes, but also requires lengthy cooking to tenderise.

ANISE, STAR:
See star anise.

BAMBOO SHOOTS:
Rapid sprouting edible shoots from certain bamboo plants. The tough outer leaves must be removed before cooking the internal 'point.' Available fresh in some Chinese food stores, but most commonly sold canned in water. Avoid bamboo shoots canned in soy sauce or with spices, unless specifically required for a recipe.

Winter Bamboo Shoots: More slender and long and have a delicate, though slightly sap-like taste. Also sold canned in water.

Canned bamboo shoots can be kept for several weeks after opening if transferred to a clean jar, covered with cold water and refrigerated. Change the water daily.

BEANCURD:
A soft jelly-like, cream-coloured food made by adding a setting agent to a thin liquid of ground boiled soybeans and water.

SOFT BEANCURD is the first setting of this liquid, produced by weighting lightly. It is usually sold in square pieces about 7.5 cm (2½ in) in size and 3.5 cm (1⅓ in) deep.

Soft beancurd can be purchased in cans, packed in water, but the consistency is harder and the flavour stronger than the fresh kind, making it suitable only for braised dishes or soups.

Powdered preparations are available, but few give more than reasonably satisfactory results. Refer to page 389 for instructions on making fresh soft beancurd. Store beancurd for several days in the refrigerator covered with cold water and plastic wrap. Change the water daily.

Dry Beancurd: Made by pressing soft beancurd with heavier weights for an extra 30 minutes or so. Shredded dry beancurd is used in sautéd and braised dishes and in salads.

Fried Beancurd Cubes are obtained by deep-frying cubes of dry beancurd until the surface is crisp and golden and the inside practically dried up. They store well in an airtight jar.

Fermented Beancurd: Otherwise known as Chinese cheese for its resemblance in taste to a strong blue-vein cow's milk cheese. Cubes of dry beancurd are cured in a mixture of Chinese wine, salt, and chopped fresh chillies to produce a red-coloured, very salty and pungent ingredient used as a seasoning and condiment. It is usually mashed and mixed with a little of its liquid before use.

Dried Beancurd Skins: The residue from beancurd milk forms into a thick yellow coloured semi-transparent sheet which is dried and used as an edible food wrapping and an ingredient in vegetarian and braised dishes. Specialist shops stock the very large round skins typical of Shanghai beancurd makers, these being large enough to make wrappers for about 12 rolls. Packaged dried beancurd is slightly more fragile and comes in smaller pieces which usually result in more wastage than the larger kind. Beancurd skins should be gently dabbed with a fairly damp cloth until soft enough to fold, before use. Packaged dried beancurd skins may need to be soaked until soft enough to handle.

Rolled Beancurd Skins: The same product as above, but before drying the sheets are pleated to produce wrinkled-looking sticks. Used in vegetarian dishes, braised dishes, and soups as a main ingredient. They are usually deep-fried before use, which makes them turn crisp and bubbly.

BEAN PASTES/DRIED BEAN SEASONINGS: A variety of useful strong-tasting seasoning pastes and sauces are made using fermented soybeans as the prime ingredient. Bean pastes can be stored for months in screw-top jars and do not require refrigeration except in very hot climates.

Soybean Paste: A thick, dark brown and salty seasoning paste made with the addition of flour, salt, and water. Used frequently in Cantonese cooking and also in Northern and Western cooking, it gives a rich salty taste. Substitute dark soy sauce or oyster sauce.

Sweet Bean Paste: Soybeans fermented with salt, sugar, and seasonings produce this rich and salty sweet sauce which is useful in marinades, as a seasoning and as a delicious dip for roasted meats. The following sauce (hoisin sauce) is a commercially labelled product having similar qualities as sweet bean paste, for which it makes an acceptable substitute.

Hoisin Sauce: Sold in cans, jars, and bottles. Hoisin sauce follows a basic traditional recipe, but varies considerably in taste and thickness from brand to brand. Use as a substitute for sweet bean paste, above, or as a dip in place of 'duck' sauce on page 385.

It will keep for several months without refrigeration.

Hot Bean Paste: Fermented mashed soybeans, salt, spices, garlic, and chillies are used to make this black, thick seasoning paste which adds strong and piquant flavour to many types of dishes. There are many variations on the mixture and its consistency, being from very hot and pasty, to almost whole beans with whole or sliced garlic and chilli pieces in a thin salty sauce. All give similar results.

Hot Black Bean Sauce: Similar to the above, with a well-balanced combination of whole black beans, mashed chillies and garlic in a rich-tasting sauce. Substitute any of the hot bean paste varieties or use fermented black beans and chopped red chilli peppers.

Yellow Bean Sauce: A salty sauce of fermented whole yellow soybeans. Soybean paste or Japanese yellow miso, see below, are good substitutes.

Fermented Black Beans: Soft, dried, salted, black beans used as a flavouring. May be labelled as salted or preserved black beans. Keep indefinitely in a screw top jar. Should be washed and dried before use.

Red Bean Paste, Sweet: Not a seasoning but a sweet-tasting paste used for stuffings in cakes and buns and as a sweet soup. See red bean paste, sweet, following.

BEAN SHEETS:
See noodles.

BEAN SPROUTS:
Sprouted mung or soybeans resulting in a crisp fresh-flavoured vegetable used in much Chinese cooking. Sold fresh or canned in water, the latter having lost much of its particular taste and crispness in the canning process. Fresh sprouts can be kept for at least a week in a sealed plastic bag or box. They can be sprouted at home using the kits supplied at health food or organic gardening centres.

Mung sprouts have a more delicate taste and are smaller in size than the soy sprouts which have large yellow pods.

'Silver' Sprouts:
Mung sprouts with roots and seed pods removed. They have a clear, silvery appearance when cooked.

BITTER MELON:
A nobbled cucumber-like vegetable with soft flesh, a central seed core, and strong bitter taste. Best used in braised dishes and often stuffed. Sold fresh or canned in water.

BIRDS' NESTS:
The edible nest made by a specie of swift or swallow which nest in caves off the coast of Southern China and Thailand. The dangerous methods employed in gathering the nests from the ceilings of these enormous caves makes them one of the most expensive of the Chinese ingredients. They are highly regarded equally by Chinese gourmets for their delicate taste and soft gelatinous, but very

slightly crunchy texture, and by those who believe in their purifying, tonifying qualities.

BOK CHOY:
See Chinese vegetables.

BROWN SUGAR:
See sugar, brown (sticks).

BROWN (BLACK) VINEGAR:
See vinegar.

CASHEW NUTS:
The raw, unsalted nuts should be used for Chinese cooking, and are generally deep-fried until golden and crisp before use. If unobtainable, use salted roasted nuts and blanch in boiling water before using. Substitute almonds.

CANDY, ROCK (SUGAR):
Crystal-like cubes of compressed white sugar, used in braised dishes to give a rich shine to meat and sauce. It requires time to dissolve and is best lightly crushed before use. Substitute white granulated sugar.

Use rock candy sugar in those dishes, particularly sweets, which require a very clear syrup or stock.

CARAMELIZED SUGAR:
Made by melting white sugar in a small amount of very hot vegetable oil until the mixture turns into a sticky golden syrup. Often used as the base of sweet and sour dishes, and as a glaze for fruit and vegetables (see candied apples, page 90).

CHENG MIEN:
See flour.

CHESTNUTS, WATER:
See water chestnuts.

CHICKEN STOCK:
Used in many Chinese dishes and sauces. See recipe, page 388, or use a crumbled chicken stock cube or chicken stock powder mixed with water and adjust the amount of salt accordingly.

CHICKEN FAT (CHICKEN GREASE), RENDERED:
A rich fat obtained by cooking pieces of fresh chicken fat (see page 387). Used more for flavouring and to give a shine to sauces than as a cooking medium.

CHILLI OIL:
A very hot flavouring oil made by infusing chilli flakes in cooking oil (see page 395). If unavailable, use commercial chilli sauce.

CHILLI PEPPERS, HOT RED:
Fresh red chilli peppers, a thin, long red (or green when unripe) fruit of the capsicum (bell pepper) family. The seeds should be removed for a milder taste.

Chillies are dried and crushed to obtain chilli flakes, and are preserved in a vinegar and salt solution for storage and to make the PICKLED RED CHILLIES, common in Western Chinese dishes.

CHINESE BROWN PEPPERCORNS:
Also known as Szechuan (Sichuan) peppercorns, flower pepper, fagara or xanthoxylum. They bear little resemblance to black peppercorns, being small berry-like seeds in a red-brown skin and with a mildly anise flavoured taste. Brown peppercorns keep indefinitely in a screwtop jar in dry conditions. They are at their best if lightly toasted in a dry frying pan before use. Used in combination with table or kosher salt to produce CHINESE PEPPER-SALT (see recipe page 384).

CHINESE (CELERY) CABBAGE:
See Chinese vegetables.

CHINESE HAM:
A top quality ham produced primarily in Yunnan province and in Chekiang (Zhejiang) where *chin hau* ham is the most highly regarded. Processed by salting and smoking, the ham has an almost black skin which should be removed before use.

Smithfield or very good quality salt-cured and smoked ham can be substituted.

CHINESE PICKLES:
Sweet-tasting mixtures of ginger, onions, gourds, and peppers preserved in a sweet syrup. They may be marketed as *chow chow* or mixed pickles. Keep indefinitely in a screw-top jar without refrigeration.

CHINESE SAUSAGE:
Dried thin sausages made with pork, pork fat, pork liver, and preservatives. Sold by most Chinese food stockists and available in some delicatessens. Should be steamed to soften, before use. They keep indefinitely in dry conditions. Substitute sticks of Chinese or cured ham or Spanish 'chorizo' sausages.

CHINESE VEGETABLES:
An extensive range of leafy green vegetables are grown in China. Increasingly, they are becoming available in the West from the larger Chinese food suppliers, particularly in areas with sizeable Chinese populations.

Bok Choy or *Pau Ts'ai*: Dark green leaves on crisp milk-white stems. The whole vegetable may be used, or the outer leaves removed and the inner tightly packed heart used in recipes requiring vegetable hearts. A crisp-textured, mild-tasting vegetable. May be known as Chinese (or Chinese white) cabbage.

Broccoli, Chinese: Unlike the Western type of broccoli, of which the large flowering head is the only part that is eaten, Chinese broccoli is picked while quite young and the dark green leaves and thick round green stems cooked in the same way as choy sum following, which it closely resembles.

Choy Sum: This vegetable has thick round green stems, sparsely leafed and with small yellow flowered heads. The taste is very slightly bitter. The stems may be peeled and cooked as a vegetable by themselves, though usually the whole stalk, cut into two or three pieces, is used.

Chinese (Celery) Cabbage: Actually the pale yellow, tightly packed Tientsin (Tianjin) cabbage, which has a light but distinct taste. If unobtainable, use white cabbage or *bok choy*.

Kale: Dark green, small-leafed vegetable not unlike spinach, which can be substituted.

Mustard: A cabbage-like plant with thick pale green stems and large green leaves. It has a slightly pungent, almost bitter taste. Used fresh, but more commonly as a preserved vegetable or pickle, see preserved vegetables.

Pea Sprouts/Leaves: Small bright green leaves from a sweet pea plant. Very delicate flavour. Substitute young spinach leaves.

Water Spinach: Deep green pointed leaves on long white tubular stems are very mild in taste. Young spinach could be substituted.

CHOY SUM:
See above, Chinese vegetables.

CHRYSANTHEMUM:
The petals, preferably white, of fresh chrysanthemum flowers are used as a delicately flavoured ingredient and as a garnish for game dishes, in particular dishes made with snake meat.

The leaves and buds of a different type of chrysanthemum, though one quite similar to that cultivated domestically, are used as a fresh-flavoured vegetable. Substitute spinach leaves.

CINNAMON:
The bark and flowers of the cassia, or cinnamon tree, are used frequently as an aromatic spice in Chinese cooking. Smaller quantities of powdered or stick cinnamon, or a cinnamon stick infused in boiling water, can be used as a subsitute.

CORIANDER, FRESH:
Otherwise known as Chinese parsley. The leafy young coriander plant is actually a type of flat-leafed parsley closely related to the 'cilantro' used in Mexican cooking, which is an excellent substitute.

Coriander can be grown in a domestic herb bed and even sprouted on damp cotton wool in the kitchen. It goes to seed quickly so should be used when the plants reach about 15 cm (6 in). To store fresh coriander, wash well and shake out excess water. Place in a sealed plastic box and refrigerate for up to 6 days.

CORN, SWEET YOUNG:
See sweet corn.

CORNFLOUR (CORNSTARCH):
See flour.

DATES, BLACK:
Used in mashed form as a filling for cakes and pastries, and as a substitute for Chinese red dates, see below.

DATES, CHINESE RED:
Small, wrinkled, dried red fruit with a strong date-plum taste. Used in braised dishes and in sweets. Substitute black dates or Japanese dried plums, 'umeboshi.'

DRY BEANCURD:
See beancurd.

'DUCK SAUCE':
A blend of sweet bean paste, sugar, and sesame oil used as a dip for Peking duck and many other crisp roasted meats. See recipe page 385, or substitute sweet bean paste, hoisin sauce or plum sauce.

ENRICHED STOCK:
Often called 'superior stock' for its rich flavour. Basically chicken bone stock with additives of ham hock, pork, and duck bones to give a strong, rich flavour and a cream-white colour (see recipe page 388).

As a substitute, use chicken stock with additional crumbled chicken stock cube or chicken powder, or a slice of ham or streaky bacon.

FA TS'AI (FAT CHOY, Cantonese):
A dark greenish-brown dried seaweed resembling human hair, and sometimes known as hair vegetable or black moss. No substitute. Used in dishes served at Chinese New Year because of its similar connotation of prosperity as the New Year greeting, *Kung Hei Fat Choy.*

FERMENTED BEANCURD:
See beancurd.

FERMENTED BLACK BEANS:
See bean pastes/dried bean seasonings.

FERMENTED SWEET RICE:
Cooked glutinous rice with a yeast additive, resulting in fermentation. Both the rice and the liquor are used in dishes of Northern and Eastern origin. See details for making sweet rice fermentation, page 187. See also rice, following.

FISH LIPS:
The dried mouth sections of certain types of very large fish. Used as an ingredient in seafood dishes. Has a soft almost gelatinous texture and a mild though distinct fishy taste. See page 392 for directions on the preparation of fish lips.

FISH MAW:
A light and bubbly textured tissue removed from the stomachs of very large fish. Sold dried in large sheets resembling polyurethane foam. Should be soaked to soften and remove the fishy smell before use. If unavailable, substitute gluten balls or rolled beancurd sticks, agar agar strips, or salted jellyfish.

FISH, SALTED:
Salt-cured and sun-dried fish used as a flavouring agent and occasionally as a main ingredient. Should be soaked in vegetable oil until softened, then deep-fried. Brill fish is said to have the best flavour. It has a strong, pungent flavour and aroma when cooked. Keeps indefinitely in dry conditions. Substitute dried shrimps.

'FIVE FLOWERED' PORK:
Belly pork (fresh bacon), the cut from the lower part of the stomach beneath the rib cage. So named because of its five alternating layers of meat and fat.

FIVE SPICE POWDER:
A blend of five aromatic spices used as a seasoning and condiment. Chinese brown peppercorns, cinnamon bark, clove, fennel, and star anise are the components.

Available commercially in both Western and Chinese spice ranges. Keeps indefinitely in an airtight jar (see also page 386).

FLOURS:

Cornflour (Cornstarch): Finely milled maize flour used as a thickener for sauces in preference to ordinary flour as it blends in easily and results in a transparent, viscous sauce.

Also used in batters and for coating fried foods. Water chestnut flour (see below) gives a crisper and finer textured batter.

Some cooks prefer mung bean flour for thickening as it produces thicker sauces.

Cheng Mien (Tang Fun): Gluten-free flour used in Chinese pastry making. It turns almost transparent when mixed with boiling water and makes unique clear wrappers for dumplings. Also used to make 'silver pin' noodles (see page 352).

If unobtainable, use potato starch (flour).

Flour: When mentioned in all recipes in this book, flour refers to plain or all purpose non-leavened wheat flour.

Glutinous Rice Powder (Flour): A fine white flour made from ground glutinous rice. Used in making cakes and puddings and as a binding agent. Substitute plain flour.

Potato Flour: Finely ground dried potato. Very starchy. Use as a thickener and for pastry making. Substitute taro flour, below.

Rice Flour: Finely ground rice. Used in sweets and cake making.

Spiced Rice Powder: See SPICED RICE POWDER and also page 386.

Taro Flour: Finely ground dried taro root. Excellent as a thickener and binding agent and in pastry making.

Water Chestnut Powder (Flour): Ground dried water chestnuts. Used in

sweets making and as a coating or in batters for deep-fried foods. Substitute cornflour (cornstarch).

FUNGUS, WHITE (SNOW):
Pale cream-coloured crinkly lichin used as an ingredient in meat, vegetarian, and sweet dishes. For directions on the preparation of dried white fungus, see page 393. Keeps well in dry conditions.

Brown ('Wood Ear'): A dark brown ear-shaped lichin said to have high nutritional content. Used to impart its particular musty taste and crunchy texture to many meat dishes, particularly in Northern cooking. Also very important as an ingredient in vegetarian cooking.

Soak to soften, then cut into small pieces before use. Keeps well in dry conditions.

GARLIC CHIVES:
Pale green shoots resembling chives, but with a mild though distinct garlic flavour. Often grown under cover to reduce the colour to the lightest yellow green and keep the flavour very mild. Used when milder tastes than those imparted by spring onions (scallions) and garlic are required in a dish.

To store, seal in a plastic bag or box and refrigerate for up to a week.

GINGER, FRESH:
The root of the rhizome ginger, with a crinkling greyish-yellow skin and fibrous flesh. Older ginger is stronger in taste than YOUNG GINGER which has a pale cream, smooth skin and pink buds.

Fresh ginger should be peeled before use and may be preserved by infusing in rice wine or dry sherry to produce GINGER WINE (see page 387), or it may be grated and the juice extracted to produce GINGER JUICE (see also page 387).

Powdered and dried root ginger are not suitable substitutes, having a quite different flavour. Fresh ginger is now readily available but, if necessary, substitute sweet or salt-pickled ginger which can be bought at both Chinese and Japanese food stockists.

GINGER AND ONION INFUSION:
A mildly flavoured seasoning liquid made by infusing grated ginger and chopped spring onions (scallions) in hot water (see page 386). Substitute ginger juice in smaller amounts.

GINGKO NUTS:
Small oval shaped white nuts, sold dried or in cans packed in water. May also be labelled 'White Nuts'. A fresh crisp nutty flavour which is useful in stuffings, braised dishes and soups. If unavailable, substitute lotus seeds, see below.

GLUTEN BALLS (mien jin pau):
Round light balls made from wheat gluten and water. Used primarily as an

ingredient in vegetarian dishes. If unavailable, omit or use fried rolled beancurd skins. Deep-fry before use.

GLUTINOUS RICE:
See rice.

GLUTINOUS RICE POWDER (FLOUR):
See flours.

GOLDEN MUSHROOMS:
See mushrooms.

GOLDEN NEEDLES (DRIED LILY FLOWERS):
The flower buds of the tiger lily. Used to impart a rich, slightly musky flavour to stewed and vegetarian dishes. Sold dried and should be soaked before use. If unobtainable, omit from the dish.

GUEI HWA:
Cassia flower wine.

HAM, CHINESE:
See Chinese ham.

HOISIN SAUCE:
See bean pastes/dried bean seasonings.

HOT BLACK BEAN SAUCE:
See bean pastes/dried bean seasonings.

HOT BEAN PASTE:
See bean pastes/dried bean seasonings.

JELLYFISH, SALTED:
A gelatinous oceanic 'fish' with a flat saucer-shaped body and a proliferation of long tentacles. The body is salted, dried, and sold in flat squares, or it may be shredded before drying. For the preparation of dried salted jellyfish, see page 392.

KALE:
See Chinese vegetables.

LARD:
Rendered pork fat. A rich-tasting white fat used as a cooking medium, particularly for stir-fried dishes and in sweets and pastry making (see cooking oil, page 395).

LAVER:
Dark greenish black, paper-thin sheets of a compressed form of mossy seaweed. Used as an ingredient mainly in soups. Available from Chinese and Japanese food suppliers ('nori' in Japanese). Should be lightly toasted over a naked flame before use to make crisp. Store in an airtight container. Keeps well in dry conditions. *Fa ts'ai (fat choy)*, see above, could be used as an alternative.

LILY FLOWERS, DRIED:
See golden needles.

LOTUS LEAVES:
Sold in dried form for use as a food wrapper. Fresh leaves, if available can also be used after blanching to clean and soften.

LOTUS ROOT:
An elongated tubular root growth of the lotus plant, characterised by a series of even-shaped round holes running the length of the root. Usually cut in cross-section to produce an attractive flower shaped slice. The flesh is crisp and bland tasting. Used as a vegetable and in certain sweet dishes.

Occasionally sold fresh, and usually available canned in water. Also available dried and must be soaked to soften before use. The fresh root must be thoroughly washed, peeled and boiled until tender.

LOTUS SEEDS:
The hard oval-shaped seeds found in the flat-faced fleshy centres of lotus blossoms. Used as an ingredient in soups, stews, and sweets and also mashed to make a sweet paste, see below. Sold in dried, canned, or fresh form. The dried nuts must be soaked to soften before use. The nuts have a bitter tasting central core which should be removed.

LOTUS SEED PASTE:
A sweet, thick, almost dry paste made with mashed cooked lotus seeds, sugar, and vegetable oil or lard. Used as a sweet filling for buns and pastries (see recipe page 368, steamed buns with lotus seed filling).

MALT SUGAR (MALTOSE):
A thick, very sticky molasses-like substance extracted from wheat. Used to glaze roast meats, notably Peking duck. If unobtainable, use treacle, golden syrup, or undiluted clear honey or light corn syrup as alternatives.

MISO PASTE:
A Japanese product made by combining fermented soybeans with salt and seasonings. Sold in varying grades from dark red-brown to a pale yellow coloured paste. The latter makes an excellent substitute for yellow bean sauce (see page 406). Also use as an alternative to wine lees (see page 387), which is not easily obtainable. Dark miso paste is a suitable alternative to soybean paste, see above, as its preparation is similarly based on soy sauce.

M.S.G. (MONOSODIUM GLUTAMATE):
Also known variously as taste powder, gourmet powder, or *ve tsin*. A crystalline flavouring agent which heightens the natural flavours of meat and vegetables and acts as a tenderiser on meats. Used prodigously in Chinese cooking, but may be omitted without undue alteration to the taste of a dish. Many doctors today discourage its use.

MUSHROOMS:
There are a number of different mushrooms used in Chinese cooking. Most common are the large DRIED

BLACK MUSHROOMS which are readily available, though costly. The best have thick caps of a darkish brown colouring with pale cream-coloured undersides. They must be soaked to soften before use, and have the stems removed.

Champignons: Canned button mushrooms.

Golden Mushrooms are small capped golden-coloured mushrooms with characteristic long thin stems. Sold canned in water. Substitute champignons. Available from Chinese or Japanese food stockists.

Peking Mushrooms are very large, creamy yellow-coloured mushrooms with long edible stems. Sold dried or canned in water, they have a good mushroom flavour and aroma and are excellent in braised dishes and stir-fried. Can be used as a substitute for dried black mushrooms or straw mushrooms, below.

Straw Mushrooms: Globe-shaped mushrooms with a greyish-black outer skin and a cream-coloured layered interior. Usually available canned in water. To store, cover with cold water and change the water daily. Fresh straw mushrooms do not keep for more than a few days in the refrigerator.

MUSTARD GREENS (LEAVES), SALTED:
See preserved vegetables.

MUSTARD ROOT, SALTED:
See preserved vegetables.

MUSTARD GREENS:
See Chinese vegetables.

NOODLES:
A variety of fresh and dried noodles are used in Chinese cooking, and in certain areas, noodles replace rice as the staple and the accompaniment to meat and vegetable dishes. They are invaluable as snack and breakfast foods and are also used in some sweet dishes. Most noodles are extruded strands of pastes made from water mixed with wheat flour, powdered beans, or powdered rice. In some, eggs are added to provide extra flavour and nourishment. Seafood flavourings are sometimes added to those noodles which will be used in soup noodle dishes.

Egg Noodles, Thin: Long narrow strands of wheat flour and egg paste. Sold dried in 'cakes' or curled strands.

Egg Noodles, Thick: Spaghetti-like thick wheat flour and egg noodles, often sold fresh and also available dried, or 'oiled.' May also be called Shanghai noodles. Fresh noodles keep for at least one week in a sealed plastic bag in the refrigerator.

Flat Noodles: Wheat flour and egg paste processed into thin flat sheets, then shredded into strands about 1 cm (⅓ in) wide. Dried and sold in bundles.

Mien Sien Noodles: Very thin, white-coloured wheat flour and water noodles. Sold dried and occasionally fresh, usually used in soup-based dishes. May be known as thin Shanghai noodles. Substitute rice vermicelli or thin egg noodles.

Rice Vermicelli: Thin extruded rice flour paste noodles. Sold in bundles in dried form. When deep-fried, they expand into a cloud of light-as-air crisp white noodles. Used also in stir-fried dishes and soups. Also known as rice sticks.

Rice Sheets: Rice flour and water paste compressed into flat sheets and steamed. Sold fresh in rolls and used as a wrapper for diced meats and vegetables. Also cut into strips about 1.25 cm (½ in) wide to make RICE RIBBON NOODLES.

Bean Thread Vermicelli: 'Glass' noodles. Extruded semi-transparent mung bean flour noodles. Used mostly in soups and stews where they turn transparent and almost gelatinous in texture. Deep-fried they expand and become light and crisp in the same way as rice vermicelli, which can be substituted. Soak before use, except when deep-frying.

Bean Sheets: Made from a paste of mung bean flour and water, they are rolled into thin sheets and dried to use as an ingredient in soups, stews, and vegetarian dishes. Substitute bean thread vermicelli.

Beancurd Noodles: Extruded paste of ground dried soybeans. A pale yellow colour and slightly thinner than thick egg noodles with the characteristic beancurd smell. Usually sold in dried form, in tangled bundles. Other beancurd 'noodles' are made from shredded dried beancurd skins.

'Silver Pin' Noodles: Hand-made short noodles made with *Cheng Mien* flour (see page 352).

OILS, COOKING:
Peanut oil, pure vegetable oil, and lard are the most common cooking mediums (see page 395 for additional information).

OMENTUM, PORK, CAUL FAT/NET:
A large lace-like sheet of fat which can be purchased from Chinese or Continental food suppliers. Sold by weight, it keeps for 2 - 3 days in the refrigerator and can be frozen. Used to wrap foods before cooking and particularly to form rolls of minced (ground) meats. It holds the foods together while frying, but eventually melts to nothing unless coated with batter or flour, when it forms a crisp crust. Also used to add oil and to seal in moisture in whole poultry or fish. Suggestions are given with the individual recipes for alternatives, if unobtainable.

ONIONS:
See page 394.

ONION AND GINGER INFUSION:
A flavouring solution made with fresh ginger and spring onions (see page 386).

ONION-PEPPER-SALT:
A seasoning combining chopped spring onions (scallions), table salt, and Chinese brown peppercorns (see page 384).

ORANGE PEEL, DRIED:
Actually the sun-dried peel of tangerines or mandarins. Imparts a delicate citrus flavour to stewed dishes and soups, and is used finely chopped in stuffings and meatballs. To prepare, peel the fruit and scrape away the white pith inside. Place in a tray and leave in the sun or in a warm oven until thoroughly dried. Store in an airtight jar. Keeps well in dry conditions.

A 'piece' as required in these recipes is approximately one-quarter of an average-sized peel.

OYSTERS, DRIED:
Sun-dried and lightly salt-cured oysters. Must be soaked overnight and thoroughly rinsed before use. Fresh oysters removed from the shells may be used in most recipes.

OYSTER SAUCE:
A dark brown, viscous, and salty sauce used both as a flavouring and condiment. For the latter, the more expensive brands are recommended for their superior flavour and less salty taste.

PEA SPROUTS:
See Chinese vegetables.

PEPPER-SALT, CHINESE:
A seasoning and condiment made from a mixture of table salt and ground Chinese brown peppercorns (see page 384). Keeps well in dry conditions.

PICKLED VEGETABLES:
See preserved vegetables.

PICKLED RED CHILLI PEPPERS:
Fresh red chilli peppers preserved in a vinegar and brine solution. Used to add hot taste and flavour to dishes from the West of China. Substitute dried or fresh red chilli peppers.

PICKLES, CHINESE SWEET:
See Chinese pickles.

PIGEON EGGS:
See quail eggs.

PINE SEEDS (NUTS):
Small, cream-coloured seeds with a layered construction, usually available in dried form from Middle Eastern food stockists. May also be known as pine kernels and in some Chinese reference books as olive seeds/beans. If unobtainable, use chopped raw cashew nuts.

PLUM SAUCE:
A commercial preparation of mashed plums and seasonings. Used as a sauce dip for roast meats and occasionally as a seasoning in stir-fried dishes. Readily available in jars and small cans. Substitute hoisin sauce.

PRAWN CRACKERS:
Compressed slivers of shrimp and flour paste. When deep-fried, they expand into large, almost transparent crisps. Used as a tasty edible garnish for roasted and deep-fried poultry. Sold as 'krupuk' or 'kroepuk' in Malaysian/Chinese food stores.

PRESERVED VEGETABLES:
Certain salt-cured vegetables are used to add their pungent, salty flavour to Chinese cooking. Preserved mustard is the most common and comes in two forms, the salty MUSTARD GREENS (LEAVES) and the thick stem/root section which needs to be shredded or diced before use and is known as MUSTARD ROOT. Pickled in brine and packaged in large pottery containers, this preserved vegetable keeps indefinitely. Store in an airtight jar. Refrigerate in hot climates.

Szechuan (Sichuan) Pickle: Sold in jars or small cans, Szechuan (Sichuan) pickles are made from salt and chilli-pickled cabbage or mustard and have a strong, salty and hot flavour. Often served as an accompaniment to Northern or Western Chinese meals.

Pickled Cabbage: Whole young *bok choy* or mustard plants pickled in brine and packed into 500 g (1 lb) cans. Readily available. Transfer to a screw-top jar for storage.

Preserved Vegetables: Soy sauce and salt-cured dried vegetables such as shredded mustard or gourd. Has a strong, vaguely fermented flavour and is used mainly in soups and stewed dishes as the taste is strong and somewhat unrefined. Sold by weight in plastic bags. May also be know as spiced vegetables.

Soy-Preserved Ginger/Cucumber: Thinly sliced young ginger or cucumber preserved with soy sauce, salt, and spices. Strong in taste and dark brown-black in colour. Substitute other soy sauce-preserved vegetables or use pickled ginger or cabbage and additional soy sauce to balance the recipe, or omit completely.

QUAIL EGGS/PIGEON EGGS:
Quail eggs, hard boiled (hard cooked) and packed in water, are readily available in canned form. Pigeon eggs are harder to obtain and slightly larger in size. Substitute the smallest size of chicken eggs available, as the taste differs only minimally.

RADISH, GIANT WHITE (ICICLE):
May be called long turnip or 'daikon' (Japanese). A white-skinned, crisp-textured radish with a sharp taste which

turns sweet when cooked. Substitute sweet white turnips.

RED BEAN PASTE, SWEET:
A thick, sweet mixture made by boiling kidney beans or a smaller variety of dried red beans with sugar until reduced to a paste, then lard or oil is added and the mixture further cooked until fairly dry and thick. Used as a filling for cakes and sweet buns and in a variety of desserts (see page 389).

RED DATES, DRIED:
See dates, dried red.

RED FERMENTED RICE:
See wine lees.

RED VINEGAR:
See vinegar.

RICE:

Short Grain White: Most commonly used in Chinese cooking (see also page 354).

Long Grain: Used occasionally in rice dishes and for stuffings and sweets.

Glutinous: Comes in short and long grain varieties. A cloudy white appearance in comparison to ordinary rice which has a pearly look. It cooks to a sticky thick mass, hence the common name 'sticky rice.' Most often used for sweets and cake-making and used to make spiced rice powder, below. Also used in the manufacture of Chinese wines.

Red Fermented Rice: See wine lees.

Sweet Fermented Rice: Cooked glutinous rice treated with beer (brewers') yeast to produce a fermentation with a strong brewed flavour. Used as a flavouring agent in many Northern Chinese dishes, particularly with seafood and served as a sweet with sugar syrup and fresh fruit (see page 387).

Spiced Rice (Powder): See spiced rice powder.

Rice Paper, Edible: More commonly made with potato flour. Paper-thin sheets of compressed and dried paste, used as an edible food wrapping. Readily available and keeps well in dry conditions.

Rice Sheets: See noodles.

Rice Wine: See wines.

ROCK CANDY (SUGAR):
See Candy, Rock (Sugar).

ROSE DEW WINE:
See wines.

SALT-FISH:
See Fish, Salted.

SALTED MUSTARD ROOT/GREEN (LEAVES):
See preserved vegetables.

SALTED YELLOW BEAN SAUCE:
See bean pastes/dried bean seasonings.

SALTPETRE:
A crystalline substance used as a meat preservative. Also known as potassium nitrate or niter.

SEA CUCUMBER, DRIED:
Also known as SEA SLUGS. Brown to black sea creatures with soft, almost gelatinous fresh and tubular nobbled bodies resembling cucumbers. Sizes vary from 5 cm (2 in) to about 30 cm (12 in). Sold dried and will keep indefinitely in dry conditions (see page 392 for preparation details).

SESAME OIL:
A brownish, strong-flavoured cooking and seasoning oil extracted from sesame seeds. Readily available and keeps well without refrigeration. Sold in bottles and cans of varying sizes. Strong in taste. May be omitted.

SESAME PASTE:
Sold in both Chinese and Middle Eastern food stores. A yellow thick paste made from ground white sesame seeds. Known in the Middle East as 'tahini.' The Chinese variety is stronger in taste and more suitable for these recipes. Smooth peanut butter (paste) is a reasonable substitute. Keeps for several months in the refrigerator.

SESAME SEEDS:
Small flat oval-shaped seeds which come in white and black colours. Both have a similar flavour and are used as an ingredient in sweets, as a garnish, and as a coating for fried foods. Should be lightly toasted in a dry pan before use, except when being fried. Store in an airtight jar. Keep indefinitely in dry conditions.

SCALLOPS, DRIED:
May be called 'CONPOY' in Chinese stores. Round golden-brown discs cut from a type of elongated round sea scallop. Sun-dried and strong flavoured. One of the most expensive of the Chinese dried ingredients and used in small quantities mainly as a flavouring agent.

Must be soaked and steamed or simmered to soften. Substitute dried shrimps, or omit if unobtainable.

SHA CHIA JIANG:
A sweet and salty sauce used as a condiment and seasoning. Made from a mixture of ground peanuts, spices, garlic and dried shrimps. The nearest equivalent is commercially prepared satay sauce, or use sweet bean paste or hoisin sauce.

SHARK'S FIN:
Edible gelatinous thread-like strands called 'needles' from the fins of sharks. Also sold in whole form for cooking in braised dishes. Choose those that are palest cream in colour and free of specks of skin or tissue. Dried shark's fin keeps indefinitely in dry conditions. Expensive.

Substitute 'silver pin' noodles or bean thread vermicelli, or use these to supplement shark's fin in soups, for economy (see page 393 for preparation of dried shark's fin).

SHARK'S SKIN:
The thick greyish, dried skin from a shark. Sold in sheets. For method of preparation of dried shark's skin, see page 393. Substitute fish maw, page 392.

SHRIMP EGGS, DRIED:
Minute granular red shrimp or prawn eggs, sold dried. Used to add flavour to sauces, stuffings, soups, and noodles. Use ground dried shrimps as a substitute.

SHRIMP SAUCE, CHINESE:
A pale pink, strong flavoured, and salty seasoning paste and condiment. Made from salted, sun-dried ground raw shrimps. The paste is cured, then stored in large underground tanks to ferment. If unobtainable, use anchovy essence or paste.

SHRIMPS, DRIED:
Small peeled shrimps, sun-dried and with a strong shellfish flavour. Used to add taste to stuffings and a variety of dishes. Soak before use. Store indefinitely in an airtight container.

'SILVER PIN' NOODLES:
See noodles.

'SILVER SPROUTS':
See bean sprouts.

'SNOW' FUNGUS:
See fungus.

SOYBEAN PASTE:
See bean pastes/dried bean seasonings.

SOY SAUCE:
There are two main kinds of soy sauce. LIGHT SOY SAUCE is used to add flavour to stir-fried dishes, sauces, and stocks, and as a dip, particularly with fried or roasted meats. DARK SOY SAUCE is stronger and saltier in taste and colour and is used primarily to add colour and a salty taste. When labelling is not clear, dark soy sauce can be identified by its thicker consistency. Sometimes labelled 'mushroom' soy.

Choose the best quality soy sauce available as the less expensive types or those manufactured in Western countries often have a metallic 'manufactured' taste due principally to insufficient maturation in the fermentation tanks.

Soy sauce keeps almost indefinitely without refrigeration.

SOY-PRESERVED GINGER/CUCUMBER:
See preserved vegetables.

SNOW PEAS:
Also known as mange tout and sugar peas. Flat, bright green pea pods containing very small green peas.

411

Intended to be eaten whole so should be picked early. Remove the short stem and string before use.

A trellis-grown vegetable, they are easily cultivated domestically and are usually available in better market gardens throughout the year.

SPICE BAG:
A small cloth bag containing five aromatic spices used to impart flavour to stewed dishes. Sold as mixed spice (see also page 386).

SPICED SALT:
Table salt flavoured with five spice powder (see page 384).

SPICED RICE POWDER:
Long grain rice dry-fried with star anise or Chinese brown peppercorns until the rice is golden brown, then ground to a coarse powder (see page 386). Used as a seasoning in steamed dishes.

SPRING ONIONS:
Long-stemmed mild tasting onions, known also as scallions and shallots (see page 394).

SPRING ROLL WRAPPERS:
Paper-thin near-transparent sheets used as edible food wrappers. Can be purchased in frozen form in packs of 20 — 30, and in several sizes. Must be slowly thawed before use and carefully separated. Keep covered with a cloth during use as they dry and crack when exposed to the air (see page 374 for preparation of spring roll wrappers).

SQUID, FRESH:
The tubular fish known also as the cuttlefish or calamari. Only the white-fleshed boneless body section is used, this being first skinned and scored to tenderise (see page 397).

STAR ANISE:
An eight-pointed star-shaped spice with a strong aniseed flavour. Substitute aniseed or fennel, if unavailable. Sold in plastic bags by weight. Store in an airtight jar. Keeps well in dry conditions.

SPARE RIBS:
Some confusion has arisen over this term. In Australia, it applies to thick fingers of 'five flowered' pork on the rind with a few segments of the lower rib bones left intact. American spare ribs have been classified in this book as the actual pork rib after meat has been trimmed away, leaving just a scant covering of meat on the bones.

SUGAR CANDY:
See candy, rock (sugar).

SUGAR, BROWN (STICKS):
Compressed sticks of layered dark and light brown sugar sold in packs of ten. Each stick weighs approximately 45 g (1 ½ oz). Substitute soft brown or raw sugar.

SUGAR, WHITE:
Where sugar is required in a recipe, use granulated white sugar unless otherwise specified.

SUGAR COLOURING:
A dark-brown liquid made from sugar and water and used to add a rich brown colour to sauces and stews. Does not add sweetness to a dish, so do not substitute sugar (see page 388 for details on preparing sugar colouring).

SWEET BEAN PASTE:
See bean pastes/dried bean seasonings

SWEET CORN, YOUNG:
Small whole cobs of young corn sold canned in water. Readily available.

SWEET FERMENTED RICE:
See rice (fermented sweet rice) and also page 387.

SWEET RED BEAN PASTE:
See red bean paste, sweet.

SWEET VINEGAR:
See vinegar, below.

SZECHUAN (SICHUAN) PICKLED (PRESERVED) VEGETABLES:
See preserved vegetables.

VINEGAR:

White: Distilled white vinegar used as an acidulant and to add its sharp sour taste to many sauces, particularly sweet and sour dishes. Use a good quality distilled white vinegar.

Chinese Red: A bright amber-red coloured vinegar distilled from rice and used both in cooking and as a dip, particularly for seafoods. It has a mild, slightly sweet taste. Substitute white vinegar, to taste.

Brown (Black): An almost black-coloured rice vinegar used as a flavouring and condiment. Readily available. Its flavour is mild and soft. Substitute smaller amounts of white vinegar.

Sweet: A pungent tasting, though quite sweet, dark vinegar with limited use in Chinese cooking. Readily available in bottles.

VERMICELLI, BEAN THREAD:
See noodles.

VERMICELLI, RICE:
See noodles.

WATER CHESTNUTS:
Dark brown-skinned bulbs from a type of water plant. The flesh is crisp, white, and with a slightly sweet taste. Sold canned in water and occasionally fresh. Peel fresh-water chestnuts before use. The canned type will keep for several weeks in the refrigerator if covered with fresh water which is changed daily.

In many parts of China, fresh-water chestnuts are threaded onto thin bamboo skewers, soaked in lightly salted water

and sold at street-side stalls as a refreshing snack.

WATER CHESTNUT POWDER (FLOUR):
See flours.

WATER SPINACH:
See Chinese vegetables.

WINE, CHINESE:
The yellow coloured rice wine, *Shao Hsing*, is most favoured for Chinese cooking. Dry sherry is a suitable substitute and readibly available, though Japanese 'sake' is even more similar in taste, being also a rice fermentation. Where a sweet rice wine is required, Japanese 'mirin' is the best substitute, though sweet sherry gives good results.

Rose Dew Wine: A strong-flavoured, rose essence liquor. Substitute brandy.

WINE LEES:
A paste-like sour mash of red rice and wine. Very difficult to obtain. Japanese light yellow 'miso' can be used as a substitute. Also known as red fermented rice.

WINE CUBE (WINE BALL):
A type of compressed beer (brewers') yeast used to produce a fermentation, usually of rice (see page 387, fermented sweet rice).

WINTER BAMBOO SHOOTS:
See bamboo shoots.

WINTER MELON:
A large, light-green skinned melon with bland-tasting crisp flesh. Used as a vegetable. Available canned in water. Substitute choko, cucumber, corghette (zucchini), or squash.

'WOOD EAR' FUNGUS:
See fungus.

WONTON WRAPPERS:
Thin pastries made from a high-gluten flour and egg paste. Sold fresh or frozen, and must be slowly thawed before use. Keep moist under a damp cloth during use as they dry and crack easily. If unobtainable, see the recipes on page 376.

YELLOW BEAN SAUCE, SALTED:
See bean pastes/dried bean seasonings.

YUNNAN HAM:
See Chinese Ham.

GUIDE TO RECIPES

RECIPE PREPARATION

This listing is intended as a quick reference to recipes which can be prepared with relative ease, or to those which require varying degrees of time and skill.

Following this listing is a complete list of recipes in their order of appearance in the book.

A. Simple one-step dishes such as stir-fried, poached and stewed dishes and easy to prepare sweets, using common Chinese ingredients and seasonings.

Beef and Lamb:

Crisp-Fried Beef with Sesame Seeds 71
Stewed Beef Northern Style 71
Sliced Beef with Orange Peel and Chilli Peppers 72
Sautéd Lamb with Garlic 75
Sautéd Shredded Lamb and Spring Onions 142
Shredded Beef with Bamboo Shoots 219
Spicy Shredded Beef with 'Wood Ear'; Fungus and Water Chestnuts 219
Stir-Fried Beef with Young Ginger and Pineapple 297

Beancurd and Vegetables:

Sweet and Sour Cabbage 83
Sour and Hot Cucumber 83
Cold Marinated Coriander 83
Celery with Dried Shrimps 84
Stir-Fried Bean Sprouts with Chicken 84
'Four Jewels' in Chicken Oil Sauce 86
Winter Bamboo Shoots in Chicken Oil Sauce 150
Lima Beans Sautéd with Mushrooms, Ham, and Shrimps 151
Crisp-Fried Salted Mustard Greens with Bamboo Shoots 152
Assorted Sautéd Vegetables in Cream Sauce 154
Tomatoes in Cream Sauce 156
Spinach Egg Puffs 156
Steamed Asparagus on Egg Custard 158
Eggplant Braised with Soybean Paste 158
'Ma Pwo' Beancurd (Pock-Marked Mama's Beancurd) 227
Beancurd Simmered with Mushrooms 228
Cucumber Sautéd in Sesame Oil with Hot Spices 231
String Beans with Diced Beef and Peanuts 232
Bamboo Shoots with Dried Shrimps and Szechuan (Sichuan) Cabbage 233
Winter Bamboo Shoots with Pork and Szechuan (Sichuan) Vegetables 233
Lettuce with Oyster Sauce 300
Beancurd Cakes with Fresh Coriander and Soy Sauce 307
Beancurd Stir-Fried with Crabmeat 308
Sautéd Chinese Spinach with Shrimp Sauce 310
Fresh Celery with Creamy Mustard Sauce 311
Sautéd Fresh Choy Sum 311
Bamboo Shoots with Mushrooms and Quail Eggs 314

Chicken:

Crisp-Fried Shredded Smoked Chicken 47
Fried Diced Chicken with Sweet Bean Paste 48
Chicken with Crisp Hot Peppers and Orange Peel 50
Steamed Golden Carp 54
Chicken Shreds Sautéd with Tuberrose Petals 103
Steamed Chicken and Mushroom Pot 108
Deep-Fried Chicken Livers with Spicy Dressing 110
Chicken Steamed in a Yunnan Steampot 183
Hot Spiced Chicken with Green Onions 183
Spiced Chicken with Peanuts and Bamboo Shoots 186
Country-Style Chicken 188
Spiced Deep-Fried Chicken Legs 190
Special Soy Sauce Chicken 249
Sliced Chicken with Chrysanthemum Petals 251
Steamed Chicken Dressed with Spring Onions and Ginger 252
Quick-Fried Chicken Shreds with Onion 254
Steamed Chopped Chicken and Straw Mushrooms 255
Chicken Stir-Fried with Oyster Sauce 258

Duck:

Duck Fat in Steamed Egg Custard 51
Sliced Roast Duck with Broccoli 110
Roast Duck with Spicy Sauce 111
Red-Simmered Duck 115
Smoked Duck Sautéd with Young Ginger 191
Duck Simmered in Yellow Rice Wine 260

Fish:

Red-Braised Mackerel Tails 116
Sliced Fish in Walnut Crumb Batter 120
Steamed Grass Carp Dressed with Shredded Vegetables 121
Cubed Mandarin Fish and Pineapple in Tomato Sauce 122
Fried Fish Slices with Ginger and Sweet Pickles 123
Steamed Fresh Fish with Szechuan (Sichuan) Pickled Vegetables and 'Wood Ears' 198
Poached Fish in Egg Flower Sauce 199
Sliced Fish Braised in Spicy Sauce 202
Steamed Mandarin Fish 266
Poached Fish with Ginger, Onion, and Oil Dressing 266
Deep-Fried Whole Fish Seasoned with Spiced Salt 267
Sliced Fish Sautéd with Black Beans 270
Cubed Fish in Pineapple Sauce 270
Sautéd Five Shreds with Sliced Fish 271
Deep-Fried Fish Fillets with Black Sesame Seed Dressing 271
Whole Steamed Fish 324

Miscellaneous:

Hot Bean Thread Noodles with Shredded Pork 348
Rice Vermicelli in Soup with Crabmeat and Egg Flower 352
Rice Sheet Rolls with Shredded Meat and Vegetable Filling 353
Plain White Rice 354
Fried Rice 354
Chicken and Rice Pot with Chinese Sausage 356

Pork:

Cold Spicy Peking-Style Pork 66
Pork Fillet Sautéd with Bamboo Shoots and Mushrooms 70
Sautéd Pork with Pine Seeds 66
Five Spice and Garlic Spare Ribs 68
Pork Livers in Sweet Fermented Rice Sauce 68
Sautéd Pork Kidneys with Bamboo Shoots, Carrots and 'Wood Ears' 70
Hot and Spicy Sliced Pork with 'Wood Ear' Fungus 211
Pork Tripe in Hot Pepper Sauce with Peanuts 212
Szechuan (Sichuan) Stewed Pork 215
Shredded Pork with Sweet Bean Paste 215
Kidneys in Sour and Hot Sauce 218
Deep-Fried Pork Chops 291
Pork Ribs with Black Bean Sauce 294
Sweet and Spicy Spare Ribs 294
Stir-Fried Pork with Spring Onions in Soy Sauce 294
Steamed Pork with Carrots and Mushrooms 296

Soup:

Abalone Soup with Chicken and Egg 64
Duck in Orange-Flavoured Soup 160
Asparagus and Pigeon Egg Soup 160
White Fungus, Pigeon Eggs, and Diced Ham Soup 160
Chicken Slivers and Jasmine in Clear Broth 161
Creamy Fish Soup with Sour and Hot Flavours 162
Salted and Fresh Pork in Soup 164
Sliced Kidneys and Beancurd Skin in Soup 167
Duck Soup in Yunnan Steam-Pot 236
Watercress Soup 236
Sliced Fish and Pickled Mustard Greens in Soup 238
Abalone and Lily Bud Soup 239
Shredded Turnip and Golden Carp in Soup 239
Watercress and Liver Soup 319
Sweet Corn and Chicken Soup 319

Sweet Dishes:

Almond Cream 90
'Snow' Fungus in Sweet Soup 91
Lotus Seeds in Sugar Syrup 91
Sweet Yam Soup 171
Sweet Black Sesame Soup 240
Peaches in Honey Syrup 241
Almond Jelly with Fresh Fruit 321
Egg Custard 321
Sweet Walnuts 369

Shellfish:

Braised Prawns 58
Prawns Peking Style 59
Crisp-Fried Shrimps with Garlic and Chilli 60
Sautéd Shrimps, Scallops and Abalone 62
Clams in Egg Custard 64
Clams in Yellow Bean Sauce 131
Shrimps Cooked in their Shells 272
Stir-Fried Crab Fu Yung 274
Shrimp and Chicken Omelette 275
Steamed Fresh Prawns 278
Stir-Fried Prawns and Choy Sum 279
Steamed Jumbo Prawns Served in Clear Sauce 280
Steamed Female Crabs with Ginger Sauce 283
Deep-Fried Oysters 287
Scallops with Shrimps and Mushrooms 287

Other Seafood:

Squid Stir-Fried with Garlic and

Spiced Cabbage 230
Pickled Assorted Vegetables 230
Spinach with Shredded Fish 231
Young Lettuce Sautéd with Crabmeat and Roe 232
Fish-Flavoured Eggplant 234
Braised Eggplant 234
Sautéd Vegetables and White Fungus 235
Cantonese Stuffed Beancurd 307
Braised Beancurd with Shrimps 308
Mixed Vegetable Platter 310
Stewed Winter Melon Balls with Scallop Sauce 312
Steamed Winter Melon Filled with Vegetables 312
Steamed Broccoli with Crabmeat Sauce 314
Braised 'Snow' Fungus in Clear Soup 315
Three Kinds of Mushrooms 315
Assorted Vegetables with Beancurd Skin 316
Stuffed Red Peppers 316
Squid Stir-Fried with Garlic and Pickled Cucumber 64
Poached Squid with Sesame Sauce 132
Freshwater Eel and Ham Steamed in a Pot 134
Stir-Fried Freshwater Eel 135
Squid with Garlic and Ginger Sauce 208
Szechuan (Sichuan)-Style Squid 208
Stir-Fried Squid with Vegetables 286
Charcoal Roasted Eel on Skewers 288
Sliced Abalone with Minced Chicken 100

B. Dishes requiring more than one cooking process or more lengthy or complicated preparation, including dishes requiring some less common ingredients, or seasoning ingredients which must be made up at home.

Beef and Lamb:

Red-Braised Five Spice Beef 71
Beef Braised with Dry Beancurd and Vegetables 72
Beef in Buddhist Robes 74
Mongolian Lamb 75
Shredded Beef and Bean Sprouts on Crisp Noodles 137
Boneless Rack of Lamb Flavoured with White Rice Wine 142
Braised Lamb and Hot Spices 143
Szechuan (Sichuan) Beef Stew 220
Braised Spiced Lamb Shanks 220
Lamb Kidneys Stir-Fried with Celery and Bamboo Shoots 222
Fillet of Beef with Salted Mustard Greens and Black Bean Sauce 296
Beef in Oyster Sauce 297
Stir-Fried Beef with Green and Red Peppers 298
Rainbow Beef in Lettuce Leaves 298
Beef Fu Yung 299
Steamed Beef Meatballs and Spinach on Rice 299
Sautéd Shredded Lamb on Rice Noodles 300
Cantonese Beef Steaks 302
Lamb with Bean Sprouts in a Crisp Potato Basket 303
Mutton Hot-Pot 334
Cold Sliced Spicy Beef 377
Jellied Mutton 378

Beancurd and Vegetables:

'Eight Treasure' Winter Melon Pond 86
Crisp-Fried Bamboo Shoots and

Scallops 87
Simmered Bell Peppers Stuffed with Pork 138
Deep-Fried Beancurd, Shrimp, and Chicken Fritters 147
Steamed Black Mushrooms with Shrimp Stuffing 150
Cauliflower with Creamed Chicken Sauce 151
Fresh Mustard Greens with Scallops in Cream Sauce 152
Chopped Pea Sprouts with Creamed Chicken 154
Chinese Cabbage with Crabmeat and Crab Roe Sauce 155
Radish Balls with Scallops in Cream Sauce 156
Sliced Cucumber Stuffed with Shrimp and Pork 159
Pork and Cabbage Dumplings 159
Pheonix Mountain Beancurd 227
Home-Style Beancurd 228
Minced Beancurd Cake with Spinach 230

Chicken:

Jellied Chicken 46
Chicken in Sweet Wine 47
Drunken Chicken 48
Chicken 'Teh-Chow' Style 48
Chicken Braised with Chestnuts 50
Chicken Walnut Rolls 104
Oyster Sauce Chicken in Parcels 104
Deep-Fried Mock-Chicken Drumsticks 106
Chicken Wings Simmered in Wine 106
Spring Chicken Showered with Hot Oil 107
Preserved Cucumber, and Ginger Stewed Chicken with Beans 107
Creamed Chicken with Mushrooms, Ham and Pea Sprouts 108
'Precious Concubine' Chicken 180
'Bon Bon' Chicken 182
Roast Stuffed Chicken 182
'Kung Pao' Chicken 184
Fried Chicken Patties with Marinated Cabbage 184
'Hibiscus' Chicken 186
'Firecracker' Chicken 187
Chicken Steamed in a Pumpkin 187
'Twice Eaten' Chicken 188
'Lantern' Chicken 195
Salt-Baked Chicken 249
Whole Chicken Stuffed with Glutinous Rice 250
Chicken Dinner Hainan Style 250
Diced Chicken and Cashew Nuts 251
Pan-Fried Chicken with Young Ginger and Pineapple 252
Fried Stuffed Chicken Rolls 254
Steamed Stuffed Chicken Wings 256
Casserole with Three Kinds of Poultry 256
'Exotic Tasting' Chicken 376
'Chin Hua' Chicken 330

Duck and Other Poultry:

Crispy Home-Style Duck 52
Steamed Duck in Lotus Leaf Packages 114
Crisp Oil-Basted Duck Cooked Twice 191
Roast Duck Stuffed with Pork and Bean Sprouts 192
Hunan Crispy Duck 192
Steamed Duck Marinated with Preserved Egg and Wine 194
Deep-Fried Duck with Laver 194
Honey-Basted Roast Duck 259
Stewed Whole Duck with Chinese Cabbage 259
Home Style Simmered-Stewed Duck 260
Chopped Duck with Lotus Root and Vegetables 262

Duck Livers with Hot Pepper Sauce 262
Slow-Simmered Goose with Vinegar and Garlic Sauce 264

Fish:

Whole Baked Fish Served on a Hot Plate 52
Fried Yellow Fish with Garlic Chives 54
'Bullfrog' Silver Carp 55
Yellow Croaker with Pine Seeds 55
Fish in Wine Sauce with 'Wood Ear' Fungus 56
Fish Masquerading as Crab 58
Garlic Catfish 115
Fish in Brown Sauce 116
'Westlake Style' Braised Carp 118
Braised Golden Carp with Onions 118
Golden Carp Stuffed with Pork and Bamboo Shoots 119
'Squirrel' Fish 120
Mandarin Fish in Pot-Sticker Style 121
Deep-Fried Carp with Sweet and Sour Sauce 122
Mandarin Fish Balls with Vegetables in Chicken Stock 123
One Fish Served in Two Ways 124
Silver Carp's Head Simmered in an Earthen Crock 126
Crisp-Skin Fish with Hot and Sour Sauce 195
Golden Carp with a Phoenix Tail 196
Whole Stuffed Fish Deep-Fried in a Crisp Pork Fat Coating 196
Whole Fish with Garlic in Hot Sauce 198
Herring in Black Bean Sauce 199
Szechuan (Sichuan) Smoked Fish 200
Sliced Fish and Celery in Hot and Sour Sauce 200
Two-Toned Steamed Fish Cake 202
Fish Heads and Beancurd Simmered in a Pot 203
Baked Stuffed Mandarin Fish 267
Whole Fish with Five Shreds in Hot Sauce 268
Smoked Pomfret 268
Fried Stuffed Fish Rolls with Sautéed Vegetables 272

Game and Exotic Dishes:

Venison Sautéd with Leeks 76
Slow-Simmered Pigeons 76
Sautéd Pigeon Meat with Livers and Eggs in Noodles Nest 78
Spiced Pigeon Eggs 78
Frogs' Legs Braised with Garlic 146
Sliced Pheasant Sautéed with Bamboo Shoots and Mustard Greens 147
Red-Braised Pigeons with Five Spices 148
Sautéd Minced Pigeon with Vegetables and Hot Peppers 148
Pigeon Pâté with Chinese Herbs Steamed in Soup Ramekins 222
Deep-Fried Squab with Salted Vegetable Stuffing 223
Sautéd Frogs' Legs with Chilli Peppers and Cashew Nuts 223
Stir-Fried Frogs' Legs 302
Sautéd Snails with Garlic 303
Diced Rabbit Sautéed with Bell Peppers 304
Sliced Quail Sautéed with Bamboo Shoots 304
Steamed Pigeons with White Fungus 330
Sautéd Snake in Gravy 336

Miscellaneous:

Egg Dumplings 79
Fried Fresh Milk with Crabmeat on Rice Noodles 79
Omelette in Spicy Sauce 80
Peking Style Fried Dumplings 80

Smoked Vegetarian 'Duck' 82
Beancurd Skin 'Noodles' with Young Soybeans 82
'Crossing the Bridge' Noodles 224
Boiled Wontons Served with Four Sauces 226
Crisp Fried Egg Rolls 337
New Year's Cake 338
Salty 'Jundz' 340
'Great Gravy' Noodles 344
Shanghai Noodles with Bean Sprouts and Brown Sauce 344
Red-Cooked Beef and Carrots on Noodles 344
Fried Egg Noodles with Meat and Vegetables 345
Shrimps and Squid with Assorted Vegetables on Soft Egg Noodles 346
'Mien Sien' Noodles with Roast Pork and Vegetables 346
Seafood Noodle Hot-Pot 348
Rice Ribbon Noodles with Beef and Broccoli 349
Cold Bean Sheet Noodles with Chicken and Two Sauces 349
'Silver Pin' Noodles 352
Multi-Coloured Rice 356
'Lotus' Rice 357
Rice Congee with Sliced Fish 357
Shrimp Dumplings (Har Gow) 360
Pork Dumplings (Siew Mai) 360
Pork Wontons 361
Steamed Chicken Turnovers 361
Steamed Roast Pork Buns (Cha Siew Pow) 362
Spring Rolls 362
Taro Pastries 364
Turnip Cake 364
Steamed Beancurd Skin Rolls in Oyster Sauce 365
Steamed Beef Meatballs on Watercress 366
Steamed Bread 370
Steamed Flower-Shaped Buns 372
Sesame Pocket Bread 372
'Mandarin' Pancakes 373
Spring Onion Pastries 373
Crisp-Fried Chinese Crullers 374
Spring Roll Wrappers 374
Wonton Wrappers 376

Pork:

'Mu Hsu' Pork 67
Shredded Pork in Sesame Pouches 67
Pork and Crabmeat 'Lion's Head' Meatballs 136
Slow Cooked Leg of Pork with Fermented Beancurd and Garlic 137
'Su Tung Po' Pork 138
Roasted Pork 'Coins' 139
Minced Pork in Clams Served in a Crock 139
Pork Kidneys, Turnip, and Dried Scallops Steamed in a Bowl 140
Sautéed Liver and Onions in Hot Sauce 140
Spiced Jellied Pork 210
Honey-Glazed Ham 210
Steamed Yunnan Ham 211
Shredded Hot Pork and Mushrooms on Crisp Rice Cakes 212
'Gold and Silver' Pork 214
Pork Steamed with Salted Cabbage 214
'Twice-Cooked' Pork 215
'Pearl' Balls 216
Chilli Pork Spare-Ribs 216
'Dragon's Eye' Bone Marrow with Chicken 218
Pork and Duck Liver Roll 290
Cantonese Roast Pork 291
Pork Fillet Rolls in Sweet and Sour Sauce 292
Sweet and Sour Pork Ribs 292
Pork Seasoned with Spiced Rice Powder 295
Stewed Pork with Fermented Beancurd

and Taro 295
Pork Shoulder with Fa Ts'ai 332
Pork Knuckles with Ginger and Sweet Rice Vinegar 333
'Buddha's Hand' 334
Cold Sliced Pork with Garlic Sauce 377
Chinese Ham 377
Roast Suckling Pig Appetiser 380

Soup:

Hot Pot of Fish, Shrimps, Pork and Chicken 66
Hot and Sour Soup 88
Mandarin Fish with Vinegar and Pepper in Rich Soup 88
Bamboo Shoots with Chicken, Ham, and Spinach Balls in Soup 155
Young Pigeons and Ham Steamed in Soup 161
Silver Carp's Head in Rich Soup 162
Assorted Meat and Vegetables in Winter Melon 164
'Embroidered' Soup 166
Beancurd, Mushrooms and Vegetables Simmered in an Earthenware Crock 167
Swallows' Nests in Clear Broth 168
Ham and Winter Melon Sandwiches in Soup 235
Translucent Sliced Chicken and Bamboo Shoot Soup 236
Dumplings of Shrimp, Pork and White Fungus in Chicken Soup 238
Beancurd Skin and Clams in Soup 239
Mushrooms with Chicken Wings in Soup 318
Shrimp Ball Soup 319
Wontons in Soup with Mixed Meat and Vegetables 320

Sweet Dishes:

Candied Apples 90
Egg Puffs with Red Bean Filling 91
Apple Fritters Stuffed with Red Bean Paste 168
Taro Cubes with Cinnamon Flavour 168
Sweet Walnut and Red Date Soup 170
Birds' Nest Dessert 171
Fried Three-Treasure Purée 171
Steamed Date Cake 240
Walnut Pudding under 'Snow Covered Mountains' 241
Eight-Treasure Rice 241
Sweet Rice Balls in Red Bean Soup 320
Glazed Sweet Potato Balls with Sesame Seeds 320
Almond and Quail Egg Tea 321
Long-Life Buns 338
Walnut Crisps 368
Steamed Buns with Lotus Seed Filling 368
Steamed Sponge Cake 369
'Laughing Mouths' 369

Shellfish:

Curled Prawns Steamed with Five Shreds 56
Prawns in Sweet Wine Sauce with Chillies and Garlic 59
Shrimps, Pork, and Vegetables in Tomato Sauce on Crisp Rice 60
Shrimp Toast 63
Pearls Hiding in a Crab 63
Jumbo Prawns Served in Two Styles 126
Phoenix Tail Prawns 127
Deep-Fried Prawn Puffs 127
Crystal Shrimp Balls Glazed with Sweet and Sour Sauce 128
Drunken Crabs 128
Sautéd Crabmeat on Crisp Noodles 130
Deep-Fried Crabmeat Balls 130

Sliced Prawns in Sour Sauce 203
Szechuan (Sichuan) Prawns in Chilli
    Oil Sauce 204
Shrimp Rolls Served on Marinated
    Carrot and Radish 204
Shrimps in Hot Sauce on Crisp Rice
    Cakes 206
Stir-Fried Sea Scallops with Pork
    Kidneys 207
Sautéed Shrimps with Peas and Cashew
    Nuts 274
Hibiscus Shrimps 275
Fried Shrimp Patties in Fruity Sauce
    276
Shrimp Sausage Sautéd with Bean
    Sprouts 276
Paper-Wrapped Shrimps 278
Prawns Clear as Crystal 279
Deep-Fried Prawn Balls 280
Braised Prawns in Gravy 282
Walnut-Stuffed Prawns 282
Stuffed Prawns in Hot Sauce 283
Crabmeat Omelette 284
Stuffed Crab Claws 284
Lobster with Black Beans and Chillies
    286

Other Seafood:

Squid in Sour and Hot Sauce on Crisp
    Rice Cakes 132
Steamed Freshwater Eel with Spicy
    and Hot Sauce 134
Braised Freshwater Eels 207
Stewed River Eel with Diced Pork and
    Mushrooms 288

Special Seafood:

Salted Jelly Fish and Shrimp Salad 62
'Lungching' Tea-Flavoured Abalone
    178
Cold Marinated Sea Scallops 378
Salted Jellyfish Salad 380

C. Very complicated dishes.
These would normally be
served for special occasions
and banquets, and may
require rare or expensive
ingredients. Many require
advance preparation, some
over several days.

Beef and Lamb:

Mongolian Beef Fire Pot 74
Mongolian Barbecue 332
Mongolian Fire-Pot 333

**Beancurd, Vegetables and
    Miscellaneous:**

Kung Hei Fat Choy 326
Marbled Tea Eggs 365
Plum Blossom Cold Platter 380
Phoenix Cold Meat Combination 381

Chicken:

Smoked Chicken 46
Steamed Chicken Stuffed with Eight
    Precious Ingredients 98
Stewed Stuffed Chicken 103
Crisp Skin Chicken 248
Chicken South China Style 255
Beggar's Chicken 329

Duck:

Three Courses of Peking Duck 51
Charcoal-Roasted Duck Stuffed with
    Lotus Leaves 111
Deep-Fried and Simmered Duck
    Stuffed with Eight Precious
    Ingredients 112
Steamed Stuffed Duck with Pine Seed

Crust 114
Duck Smoked over Camphor Wood
    and Tea Leaves 190
Cantonese Roast Duck 258
Deep-Fried Duck Feet with Shrimp
    Stuffing 263
Salted Duck Eggs 263
Fragrant Crispy Duck Stuffed with
    Lotus Seeds and Pork 264
Peking Roast Duck 329

Game:

Braised and Steamed Wild Duck 143
Wild Duck with Mashed Taro Stuffing
    and Oyster Sauce 144
Wild Duck, Vegetables, and Assorted
    Meats Simmered with Rice 146
Bear's Paw Simmered with Duck,
    Chicken, Scallops, and Ham 224
Red-Stewed Camel's Pads 285
Deep-Fried Boiled Camel's Hump 285
Deep-Fried Rice Birds Served with
    Quail Eggs and Sliced Quail in a
    Noodle Nest 306

Pork:

Slow-Cooked Corned Pork 136
Three Courses of Roast Suckling Pig
    290
Roast Suckling Pig 328

Fish:

Assorted Meat and Shark's Fin Soup
    87
Assorted Meat and Chrysanthemum
    Fire-Pot 163
Dried Oysters and Chicken in Soup
    166
Shark's Fin and Crabmeat Soup 318

Sweet Dishes:

Sweet Fermented Rice with Diced
    Fresh Fruit 90
Steamed Lotus Seed and Red Bean
    Paste Pudding 170
Moon Cakes 341
Clear-As-Glass Cookies 366

Special Seafood:

Braised Shark's Fin with Pork Knuckle
    and Chicken 44
Sea Cucumber in Brown Sauce 44
Chicken Stuffed with Shark's Fin 98
Shark's Fin Simmered with Chicken 99
Steamed Shark's Fin with Crabmeat 99
Steamed Sea Cucumber and Ham 100
Fish Maw Salad with Sesame Sauce
    102
Braised Fish Maw with Assorted Meats
    102
Red-Braised Turtle 135
Braised Shark's Fins in Brown Sauce
    178
Braised Fish Maw with Ham and
    Mushrooms 178
Fish Lips with Vegetables on Crisp
    Rice 179
Shark's Fin Sautéd with Silver
    Sprouts, and Leeks 248
Shark's Fin with Shredded Meat in
    Rich Soup 324
Braised Abalone in Oyster Sauce 325
Dried Scallops Braised with Garlic 325

Shellfish and Other Seafood:

Oysters with Barbecued Pork and
    Vegetables in Sauce 131
Sea Cucumber with Vegetables and
    Crisp Pretzels 206

**LIST OF RECIPES
ARRANGED IN ORDER
OF APPEARANCE IN THE
TEXT**

NORTHERN STYLE CUISINE 38-43

Braised Shark's Fin with Pork Knuckle
    and Chicken 44
Sea Cucumber in Brown Sauce 44
Smoked Chicken 46
Jellied Chicken 46
Crisp-Fried Shredded Smoked Chicken
    47
Chicken in Sweet Wine 47
Drunken Chicken 48
Chicken 'Teh-Chow' Style 48
Fried Diced Chicken with Sweet Bean
    Paste 48
Chicken with Crisp Hot Peppers and
    Orange Peel 50
Chicken Braised with Chestnuts 50
Three Courses of Peking Duck 51
Duck Fat in Steamed Egg Custard 51
Crispy Home-Style Duck 52
Whole Baked Fish Served on a Hot
    Plate 52
Steamed Golden Carp 54
Fried Yellow Fish with Garlic Chives
    54
'Bullfrog' Silver Carp 55
Yellow Croaker with Pine Seeds 55
Fish in Wine Sauce with 'Wood Ear'
    Fungus 56
Curled Prawns Steamed with Five
    Shreds 56
Fish Masquerading as Crab 58
Braised Prawns 58
Prawns Peking Style 59
Prawns in Sweet Wine Sauce with
    Chillies and Garlic 59
Crisp-Fried Shrimps with Garlic and
    Chilli 60
Shrimps, Pork, and Vegetables in
    Tomato Sauce on Crisp Rice 60
Sautéd Shrimps, Scallops and Abalone
    62
Salted Jelly Fish and Shrimp Salad 62
Shrimp Toast 63
Pearls Hiding in a Crab 63
Clams in Egg Custard 64
Squid Stir-Fried with Garlic and
    Pickled Cucumber 64
Abalone Soup with Chicken and Egg
    64
Hot Pot of Fish, Shrimps, Pork and
    Chicken 66
Cold Spicy Peking-Style Pork 66
Sautéd Pork with Pine Seeds 66
'Mu Hsu' Pork 67
Shredded Pork in Sesame Pouches 67
Five Spice and Garlic Spare Ribs 68
Pork Livers in Sweet Fermented Rice
    Sauce 68
Sautéd Pork Kidneys with Bamboo
    Shoots, Carrots and 'Wood Ears' 70
Pork Fillet Sautéd with Bamboo
    Shoots and Mushrooms 70
Red-Braised Five Spice Beef 71
Crisp-Fried Beef with Sesame Seeds 71
Stewed Beef Northern Style 71
Sliced Beef with Orange Peel and
    Chilli Peppers 72
Beef Braised with Dry Beancurd and
    Vegetables 72
Beef in Buddhist Robes 74
Mongolian Beef Fire Pot 74
Sautéd Lamb with Garlic 75
Mongolian Lamb 75
Venison Sautéd with Leeks 76
Slow-Simmered Pigeons 76
Sautéd Pigeon Meat with Livers and
    Eggs in Noodles Nest 78
Spiced Pigeon Eggs 78
Egg Dumplings 79
Fried Fresh Milk with Crabmeat on

Rice Noodles 79
Omelette in Spicy Sauce 80
Peking Style Fried Dumplings 80
Smoked Vegetarian 'Duck' 82
Beancurd Skin 'Noodles' with Young
    Soybeans 82
Sweet and Sour Cabbage 83
Sour and Hot Cucumber 83
Cold Marinated Coriander 83
Celery with Dried Shrimps 84
Stir-Fried Bean Sprouts with Chicken
    84
'Four Jewels' in Chicken Oil Sauce 86
'Eight Treasure' Winter Melon Pond
    86
Crisp-Fried Bamboo Shoots and
    Scallops 87
Assorted Meat and Shark's Fin Soup
    87
Hot and Sour Soup 88
Mandarin Fish with Vinegar and
    Pepper in Rich Soup 88
Candied Apples 90
Almond Cream 90
Sweet Fermented Rice with Diced
    Fresh Fruit 90
Egg Puffs with Red Bean Filling 91
'Snow' Fungus in Sweet Soup 91
Lotus Seeds in Sugar Syrup 91

**EASTERN COASTAL STYLE
CUISINE** 92-97

Chicken Stuffed with Shark's Fin 98
Steamed Chicken Stuffed with Eight
    Precious Ingredients 98
Shark's Fin Simmered with Chicken 99
Steamed Shark's Fin with Crabmeat 99
Sliced Abalone with Minced Chicken
    100
Steamed Sea Cucumber and Ham 100
Fish Maw Salad with Sesame Sauce
    102
Braised Fish Maw with Assorted Meats
    102
Stewed Stuffed Chicken 103
Chicken Shreds Sautéd with Tuberrose
    Petals 103
Chicken Walnut Rolls 104
Oyster Sauce Chicken in Parcels 104
Deep-Fried Mock-Chicken Drumsticks
    106
Chicken Wings Simmered in Wine 106
Spring Chicken Showered with Hot Oil
    107
Preserved Cucumber, and Ginger
    Stewed Chicken with Beans 107
Creamed Chicken with Mushrooms,
    Ham and Pea Sprouts 108
Steamed Chicken and Mushroom Pot
    108
Deep-Fried Chicken Livers with Spicy
    Dressing 110
Sliced Roast Duck with Broccoli 110
Charcoal-Roasted Duck Stuffed with
    Lotus Leaves 111
Roast Duck with Spicy Sauce 111
Deep-Fried and Simmered Duck
    Stuffed with Eight Precious
    Ingredients 112
Steamed Stuffed Duck with Pine Seed
    Crust 114
Steamed Duck in Lotus Leaf Packages
    114
Red-Simmered Duck 115
Garlic Catfish 115
Fish in Brown Sauce 116
Red-Braised Mackerel Tails 116
'Westlake Style' Braised Carp 118
Braised Golden Carp with Onions 118
Golden Carp Stuffed with Pork and
    Bamboo Shoots 119
'Squirrel' Fish 120
Sliced Fish in Walnut Crumb Batter
    120
Steamed Grass Carp Dressed with
    Shredded Vegetables 121
Mandarin Fish in Pot-Sticker Style 121

Deep-Fried Carp with Sweet and Sour Sauce 122
Cubed Mandarin Fish and Pineapple in Tomato Sauce 122
Mandarin Fish Balls with Vegetables in Chicken Stock 123
Fried Fish Slices with Ginger and Sweet Pickles 123
One Fish Served in Two Ways 124
Silver Carp's Head Simmered in an Earthen Crock 126
Jumbo Prawns Served in Two Styles 126
Phoenix Tail Prawns 127
Deep-Fried Prawn Puffs 127
Crystal Shrimp Balls Glazed with Sweet and Sour Sauce 128
Drunken Crabs 128
Sautéd Crabmeat on Crisp Noodles 130
Deep-Fried Crabmeat Balls 130
Clams in Yellow Bean Sauce 131
Oysters with Barbecued Pork and Vegetables in Sauce 131
Squid in Sour and Hot Sauce on Crisp Rice Cakes 132
Poached Squid with Sesame Sauce 132
Steamed Freshwater Eel with Spicy and Hot Sauce 134
Freshwater Eel and Ham Steamed in a Pot 134
Stir-Fried Fresh-Water Eel 135
Red-Braised Turtle 135
Slow-Cooked Corned Pork 136
Pork and Crabmeat 'Lion's Head' Meatballs 136
Slow Cooked Leg of Pork with Fermented Beancurd and Garlic 137
Shredded Beef and Bean Sprouts on Crisp Noodles 137
'Su Tung Po' Pork 138
Simmered Bell Peppers Stuffed with Pork 138
Roasted Pork 'Coins' 139
Minced Pork in Clams Served in a Crock 139
Pork Kidneys, Turnip, and Dried Scallops Steamed in a Bowl 140
Sautéd Liver and Onions in Hot Sauce 140
Boneless Rack of Lamb Flavoured with White Rice Wine 142
Sautéd Shredded Lamb and Spring Onions 142
Braised Lamb and Hot Spices 143
Braised and Steamed Wild Duck 143
Wild Duck with Mashed Taro Stuffing and Oyster Sauce 144
Wild Duck, Vegetables, and Assorted Meats Simmered with Rice 146
Frogs' Legs Braised with Garlic 146
Sliced Pheasant Sautéd with Bamboo Shoots and Mustard Greens 147
Deep-Fried Beancurd, Shrimp, and Chicken Fritters 147
Red-Braised Pigeons with Five Spices 148
Sautéd Minced Pigeon with Vegetables and Hot Peppers 148
Winter Bamboo Shoots in Chicken Oil Sauce 150
Steamed Black Mushrooms with Shrimp Stuffing 150
Cauliflower with Creamed Chicken Sauce 151
Lima Beans Sautéd with Mushrooms, Ham, and Shrimps 151
Crisp-Fried Salted Mustard Greens with Bamboo Shoots 152
Fresh Mustard Greens with Scallops in Cream Sauce 152
Chopped Pea Sprouts with Creamed Chicken 154
Assorted Sautéd Vegetables in Cream Sauce 154
Chinese Cabbage with Crabmeat and Crab Roe Sauce 155

Bamboo Shoots with Chicken, Ham, and Spinach Balls in Soup 155
Radish Balls with Scallops in Cream Sauce 156
Tomatoes in Cream Sauce 156
Spinach Egg Puffs 156
Steamed Asparagus on Egg Custard 158
Eggplant Braised with Soybean Paste 158
Sliced Cucumber Stuffed with Shrimp and Pork 159
Pork and Cabbage Dumplings 159
Duck in Orange-Flavoured Soup 160
Asparagus and Pigeon Egg Soup 160
White Fungus, Pigeon Eggs, and Diced Ham Soup 160
Young Pigeons and Ham Steamed in Soup 161
Chicken Slivers and Jasmine in Clear Broth 161
Creamy Fish Soup with Sour and Hot Flavours 162
Silver Carp's Head in Rich Soup 162
Assorted Meat and Chrysanthemum Fire-Pot 163
Salted and Fresh Pork in Soup 164
Assorted Meat and Vegetables in Winter Melon 164
'Embroidered' Soup 166
Dried Oysters and Chicken in Soup 166
Sliced Kidneys and Beancurd Skin in Soup 167
Beancurd, Mushrooms and Vegetables Simmered in an Earthenware Crock 167
Swallows' Nests in Clear Broth 168
Apple Fritters Stuffed with Red Bean Paste 168
Taro Cubes with Cinnamon Flavour 168
Sweet Walnut and Red Date Soup 170
Steamed Lotus Seed and Red Bean Paste Pudding 170
Birds' Nest Dessert 171
Fried Three-Treasure Puree 171
Sweet Yam Soup 171

WESTERN CENTRAL STYLE CUISINE 172-177

Braised Shark's Fins in Brown Sauce 178
'Lungching' Tea-Flavoured Abalone 178
Braised Fish Maw with Ham and Mushrooms 179
Fish Lips with Vegetables on Crisp Rice 179
'Precious Concubine' Chicken 180
'Bon Bon' Chicken 182
Roast Stuffed Chicken 182
Chicken Steamed in a Yunnan Steampot 183
Hot Spiced Chicken with Green Onions 183
'Kung Pao' Chicken 184
Fried Chicken Patties with Marinated Cabbage 184
Spiced Chicken with Peanuts and Bamboo Shoots 186
'Hibiscus' Chicken 186
'Firecracker' Chicken 187
Chicken Steamed in a Pumpkin 187
Country-Style Chicken 188
'Twice Eaten' Chicken 188
Spiced Deep-Fried Chicken Legs 190
Duck Smoked over Camphor Wood and Tea Leaves 190
Crisp Oil-Basted Duck Cooked Twice 191
Smoked Duck Sautéd with Young Ginger 191
Roast Duck Stuffed with Pork and Bean Sprouts 192
Hunan Crispy Duck 192
Steamed Duck Marinated with

Preserved Egg and Wine 194
Deep-Fried Duck with Laver 194
'Lantern' Chicken 195
Crisp-Skin Fish with Hot and Sour Sauce 195
Golden Carp with a Phoenix Tail 196
Whole Stuffed Fish Deep-Fried in a Crisp Pork Fat Coating 196
Steamed Fresh Fish with Szechuan (Sichuan) Pickled Vegetables and 'Wood Ears' 198
Whole Fish with Garlic in Hot Sauce 198
Herring in Black Bean Sauce 199
Poached Fish in Egg Flower Sauce 199
Szechuan (Sichuan) Smoked Fish 200
Sliced Fish and Celery in Hot and Sour Sauce 200
Sliced Fish Braised in Spicy Sauce 202
Two-Toned Steamed Fish Cake 202
Fish Heads and Beancurd Simmered in a Pot 203
Sliced Prawns in Sour Sauce 203
Szechuan (Sichuan) Prawns in Chilli Oil Sauce 204
Shrimp Rolls Served on Marinated Carrot and Radish 204
Shrimps in Hot Sauce on Crisp Rice Cakes 206
Sea Cucumber with Vegetables and Crisp Pretzels 206
Braised Fresh-Water Eels 207
Stir-Fried Sea Scallops with Pork Kidneys 207
Squid with Garlic and Ginger Sauce 208
Szechuan (Sichuan)-Style Squid 208
Spiced Jellied Pork 210
Honey-Glazed Ham 210
Steamed Yunnan Ham 211
Hot and Spicy Sliced Pork with 'Wood Ear' Fungus 211
Shredded Hot Pork and Mushrooms on Crisp Rice Cakes 212
Pork Tripe in Hot Pepper Sauce with Peanuts 212
'Gold and Silver' Pork 214
Pork Steamed with Salted Cabbage 214
Szechuan (Sichuan) Stewed Pork 215
'Twice-Cooked' Pork 215
Shredded Pork with Sweet Bean Paste 215
'Pearl' Balls 216
Chilli Pork Spare-Ribs 216
'Dragon's Eye' Bone Marrow with Chicken 218
Kidneys in Sour and Hot Sauce 218
Shredded Beef with Bamboo Shoots 219
Spicy Shredded Beef with 'Wood Ear'; Fungus and Water Chestnuts 219
Szechuan (Sichuan) Beef Stew 220
Braised Spiced Lamb Shanks 220
Lamb Kidneys Stir-Fried with Celery and Bamboo Shoots 222
Pigeon Paté with Chinese Herbs Steamed in Soup Ramekins 222
Deep-Fried Squab with Salted Vegetable Stuffing 223
Sautéd Frogs' Legs with Chilli Peppers and Cashew Nuts 223
Bear's Paw Simmered with Duck, Chicken, Scallops, and Ham 224
'Crossing the Bridge' Noodles 224
Boiled Wontons Served with Four Sauces 226
'Ma Pwo' Beancurd (Pock-Marked Mama's Beancurd) 227
Pheonix Mountain Beancurd 227
Home-Style Beancurd 228
Beancurd Simmered with Mushrooms 228
Minced Beancurd Cake with Spinach 230
Spiced Cabbage 230
Pickled Assorted Vegetables 230

Cucumber Sautéd in Sesame Oil with Hot Spices 231
Spinach with Shredded Fish 231
Young Lettuce Sautéd with Crabmeat and Roe 232
String Beans with Diced Beef and Peanuts 232
Bamboo Shoots with Dried Shrimps and Szechuan (Sichuan) Cabbage 233
Winter Bamboo Shoots with Pork and Szechuan (Sichuan) Vegetables 233
Fish-Flavoured Eggplant 234
Braised Eggplant 234
Sautéd Vegetables and White Fungus 235
Ham and Winter Melon Sandwiches in Soup 235
Translucent Sliced Chicken and Bamboo Shoot Soup 236
Duck Soup in Yunnan Steam-Pot 236
Watercress Soup 237
Dumplings of Shrimp, Pork and White Fungus in Chicken Soup 238
Sliced Fish and Pickled Mustard Greens in Soup 238
Beancurd Skin and Clams in Soup 239
Abalone and Lily Bud Soup 239
Shredded Turnip and Golden Carp in Soup 239
Steamed Date Cake 240
Sweet Black Sesame Soup 240
Walnut Pudding under 'Snow Covered Mountains' 241
Peaches in Honey Syrup 241
Eight-Treasure Rice 241

SOUTHERN STYLE CUISINE 242-247

Shark's Fin Sautéd with Silver Sprouts, and Leeks 248
Crisp Skin Chicken 248
Special Soy Sauce Chicken 249
Salt-Baked Chicken 249
Whole Chicken Stuffed with Glutinous Rice 250
Chicken Dinner Hainan Style 250
Sliced Chicken with Chrysanthemum Petals 251
Diced Chicken and Cashew Nuts 251
Steamed Chicken Dressed with Spring Onions and Ginger 252
Pan-Fried Chicken with Young Ginger and Pineapple 252
Quick-Fried Chicken Shreds with Onion 254
Fried Stuffed Chicken Rolls 254
Chicken South China Style 255
Steamed Chopped Chicken and Straw Mushrooms 255
Steamed Stuffed Chicken Wings 256
Casserole with Three Kinds of Poultry 256
Chicken Stir-Fried with Oyster Sauce 258
Cantonese Roast Duck 258
Honey-Basted Roast Duck 259
Stewed Whole Duck with Chinese Cabbage 259
Duck Simmered in Yellow Rice Wine 260
Home Style Simmered-Stewed Duck 260
Chopped Duck with Lotus Root and Vegetables 262
Duck Livers with Hot Pepper Sauce 262
Deep-Fried Duck Feet with Shrimp Stuffing 263
Salted Duck Eggs 263
Fragrant Crispy Duck Stuffed with Lotus Seeds and Pork 264
Slow-Simmered Goose with Vinegar and Garlic Sauce 264
Steamed Mandarin Fish 266
Poached Fish with Ginger, Onion, and Oil Dressing 266
Deep-Fried Whole Fish Seasoned with

Spiced Salt 267
Baked Stuffed Mandarin Fish 267
Whole Fish with Five Shreds in Hot
    Sauce 268
Smoked Pomfret 268
Sliced Fish Sautéd with Black Beans
    270
Cubed Fish in Pineapple Sauce 270
Sautéd Five Shreds with Sliced Fish
    271
Deep-Fried Fish Fillets with Black
    Sesame Seed Dressing 271
Fried Stuffed Fish Rolls with Sautéd
    Vegetables 272
Shrimps Cooked in their Shells 272
Sautéd Shrimps with Peas and Cashew
    Nuts 274
Stir-Fried Crab Fu Yung 274
Shrimp and Chicken Omelette 275
Hibiscus Shrimps 275
Fried Shrimp Patties in Fruity Sauce
    276
Shrimp Sausage Sautéd with Bean
    Sprouts 276
Paper-Wrapped Shrimps 278
Steamed Fresh Prawns 278
Prawns Clear as Crystal 279
Stir-Fried Prawns and Choy Sum 279
Steamed Jumbo Prawns Served in
    Clear Sauce 280
Deep-Fried Prawn Balls 280
Braised Prawns in Gravy 282
Walnut-Stuffed Prawns 282
Stuffed Prawns in Hot Sauce 283
Steamed Female Crabs with Ginger
    Sauce 283
Crabmeat Omelette 284
Stuffed Crab Claws 284
Red-Stewed Camel's Pads 285
Deep-Fried Boiled Camel's Hump 285
Lobster with Black Beans and Chillies
    286
Stir-Fried Squid with Vegetables 286
Deep-Fried Oysters 287
Scallops with Shrimps and Mushrooms
    287
Charcoal Roasted Eel on Skewers 288
Stewed River Eel with Diced Pork and
    Mushrooms 288
Three Courses of Roast Suckling Pig
    290
Pork and Duck Liver Roll 290
Cantonese Roast Pork 291
Deep-Fried Pork Chops 291
Pork Fillet Rolls in Sweet and Sour
    Sauce 292
Sweet and Sour Pork Ribs 292
Pork Ribs with Black Bean Sauce 294
Sweet and Spicy Spare Ribs 294
Stir-Fried Pork with Spring Onions in
    Soy Sauce 294
Pork Seasoned with Spiced Rice
    Powder 295
Stewed Pork with Fermented Beancurd
    and Taro 295
Steamed Pork with Carrots and
    Mushrooms 296
Fillet of Beef with Salted Mustard
    Greens and Black Bean Sauce 296
Beef in Oyster Sauce 297
Stir-Fried Beef with Young Ginger and
    Pineapple 297
Stir-Fried Beef with Green and Red
    Peppers 298
Rainbow Beef in Lettuce Leaves 298
Beef Fu Yung 299
Steamed Beef Meatballs and Spinach
    on Rice 299
Sautéd Shredded Lamb on Rice
    Noodles 300
Lettuce with Oyster Sauce 300
Cantonese Beef Steaks 302
Stir-Fried Frogs' Legs 302
Lamb with Bean Sprouts in a Crisp
    Potato Basket 303
Sautéd Snails with Garlic 303
Diced Rabbit Sautéd with Bell Peppers

304
Sliced Quail Sautéd with Bamboo
    Shoots 304
Deep-Fried Rice Birds Served with
    Quail Eggs and Sliced Quail in a
    Noodle Nest 304
Beancurd Cakes with Fresh Coriander
    and Soy Sauce 307
Cantonese Stuffed Beancurd 307
Beancurd Stir-Fried with Crabmeat 308
Braised Beancurd with Shrimps 308
Mixed Vegetable Platter 310
Sautéd Chinese Spinach with Shrimp
    Sauce 310
Fresh Celery with Creamy Mustard
    Sauce 311
Sautéd Fresh Choy Sum 311
Stewed Winter Melon Balls with
    Scallop Sauce 312
Steamed Winter Melon Filled with
    Vegetables 312
Steamed Broccoli with Crabmeat
    Sauce 314
Bamboo Shoots with Mushrooms and
    Quail Eggs 314
Braised 'Snow' Fungus in Clear Soup
    315
Three Kinds of Mushrooms 315
Assorted Vegetables with Beancurd
    Skin 316
Stuffed Red Peppers 316
Shark's Fin and Crabmeat Soup 318
Mushrooms with Chicken Wings in
    Soup 318
Watercress and Liver Soup 319
Sweet Corn and Chicken Soup 319
Shrimp Ball Soup 319
Wontons in Soup with Mixed Meat
    and Vegetables 320
Sweet Rice Balls in Red Bean Soup
    320
Glazed Sweet Potato Balls with
    Sesame Seeds 320
Almond Jelly with Fresh Fruit 321
Almond and Quail Egg Tea 321
Egg Custard 321

DISHES FOR SPECIAL
OCCASIONS 322-323

Shark's Fin with Shredded Meat in
    Rich Soup 324
Whole Steamed Fish 324
Braised Abalone in Oyster Sauce 325
Dried Scallops Braised with Garlic 325
Kung Hei Fat Choy 326
Roast Suckling Pig 328
Peking Roast Duck 329
Beggar's Chicken 329
'Chin Hua' Chicken 330
Steamed Pigeons with White Fungus
    330
Pork Shoulder with Fa Ts'ai 332
Mongolian Barbecue 332
Pork Knuckles with Ginger and Sweet
    Rice Vinegar 333
Mongolian Fire-Pot 333
'Buddha's Hand' 334
Mutton Hot-Pot 334
Sautéd Snake in Gravy 336
Crisp Fried Egg Rolls 337
New Year's Cake 338
Long-Life Buns 338
Salty 'Jundz' 340
Moon Cakes 341

NOODLES AND RICE —
ACCOMPANIMENTS 342-343

'Great Gravy' Noodles 344
Shanghai Noodles with Bean Sprouts
    and Brown Sauce 344
Red-Cooked Beef and Carrots on
    Noodles 345
Fried Egg Noodles with Meat and
    Vegetables 345
Shrimps and Squid with Assorted
    Vegetables on Soft Egg Noodles 346

'Mien Sien' Noodles with Roast Pork
    and Vegetables 346
Seafood Noodle Hot-Pot 348
Hot Bean Thread Noodles with
    Shredded Pork 348
Rice Ribbon Noodles with Beef and
    Broccoli 349
Cold Bean Sheet Noodles with
    Chicken and Two Sauces 349
Rice Vermicelli in Soup with Crabmeat
    and Egg Flower 352
'Silver Pin' Noodles 352
Rice Sheet Rolls with Shredded Meat
    and Vegetable Filling 353
Plain White Rice 354
Fried Rice 354
Multi-Coloured Rice 356
Chicken and Rice Pot with Chinese
    Sausage 356
'Lotus' Rice 357
Rice Congee with Sliced Fish 357

DIM SUM, BREAD AND COLD
PLATTERS — APPETISERS 358-359

Shrimp Dumplings (Har Gow) 360
Pork Dumplings (Siew Mai) 360
Pork Wontons 361
Steamed Chicken Turnovers 361
Steamed Roast Pork Buns (Cha Siew
    Pow) 362
Spring Rolls 362
Taro Pastries 364
Turnip Cake 364
Steamed Beancurd Skin Rolls in
    Oyster Sauce 365
Marbled Tea Eggs 365
Steamed Beef Meatballs on Watercress
    366
Clear-As-Glass Cookies 366
Walnut Crisps 368
Steamed Buns with Lotus Seed Filling
    368
Steamed Sponge Cake 369
'Laughing Mouths' 369
Sweet Walnuts 369
Steamed Bread 370
Steamed Flower-Shaped Buns 372
Sesame Pocket Bread 372
'Mandarin' Pancakes 373
Spring Onion Pastries 373
Crisp-Fried Chinese Crullers 374
Spring Roll Wrappers 374
Wonton Wrappers 376
'Exotic Tasting' Chicken 376
Cold Sliced Pork with Garlic Sauce
    377
Chinese Ham 377
Cold Sliced Spicy Beef 377
Jellied Mutton 378
Cold Marinated Sea Scallops 378
Salted Jellyfish Salad 380
Roast Suckling Pig Appetiser 380
Plum Blossom Cold Platter 380
Phoenix Cold Meat Combination 381

SAUCES, SPICES AND
SEASONINGS 382-383

Chinese Pepper-Salt/Onion-Pepper-
    Salt 384
Spiced Salt 384
Vinegar and Ginger Dip/Vinegar and
    Garlic Dip 384
Ginger and Spring Onion Sauce 384
Sweet and Sour Sauce 385
Sweetened Soy Sauce 385
'Duck' Sauce 385
Chilli Oil 385
Five Spice Powder/Spice Bags 386
Rice Cakes 386
Spiced Rice Powder 386
Onion and Ginger Infusion 386
Sweet Fermented Rice/Wine Lees 387
Ginger Wine/Ginger Juice 387
Rendered Chicken Fat (Chicken
    Grease) 387
Sugar Colouring 388

Chicken Stock 388
Enriched Stock 388
Soy-Preserved Ginger/Cucumber 389
Sweet Red Bean Paste 389
Beancurd 389

'Bon Bon' Chicken 182
'Buddha's Hand' 334
'Bullfrog' Silver Carp 55
'Chin Hua' Chicken 330
'Crossing the Bridge' Noodles 224
'Dragon's Eye' Bone Marrow with Chicken 218
'Duck' Sauce 385
'Eight Treasure' Winter Melon Pond 86
'Embroidered' Soup 166
'Exotic Tasting' Chicken 376
'Fire-Pot' 31-32
'Firecracker' Chicken 187
'Four Jewels' in Chicken Oil Sauce 86
'Gold and Silver' Pork 214
'Great Gravy' Noodles 344
'Hibiscus' Chicken 186
'Jundz', Salty 340
'Kung Pao' Chicken 184
'Lantern' Chicken 195
'Laughing' Mouths 369
'Lion's Head' Meatballs, Pork and Crabmeat 136
'Lotus' Rice 357
'Lungching' Tea-Flavoured Abalone 178
'Ma Pwo' Beancurd (Pock-Marked Mama's Beancurd) 227
'Mandarin' Pancakes 373
'Mien Sien' Noodles with Roast Pork and Vegetables 346
'Mu Hsu' Pork 67
'Pearl' Balls 216
'Precious Concubine' Chicken 180
'Sand Pot' Casserole 31
'Silver Pin' Noodles 352
'Snow' Fungus in Sweet Soup 91
'Snow' Fungus, Braised, in Clear Soup 315
'Squirrel' Fish 120
'Su Tung Po' Pork 138
'Twice-Cooked' Pork 215
'Twice-Eaten' Chicken 188
'Westlake Style' Braised Carp 118
Abalone Soup with Chicken and Egg 64
Abalone and Lily Bud Soup 239
Abalone with Sautéd Shrimps and Scallops 62
Abalone, 'Lungching' Tea-Flavoured 178
Abalone, Braised, in Oyster Sauce 325
Abalone, Preparation of 392
Abalone, Sliced with Minced Chicken 100
Almond Cream 90
Almond Jelly with Fresh Fruit 321
Almond and Quail Egg Tea 321
Appetiser, Roast Suckling Pig 380
Apple Fritters Stuffed with Red Bean Paste 168
Apples, Candied 90
Asparagus and Pigeon Egg Soup 160
Asparagus, Steamed, on Egg Custard 158
Assorted Meat and Chrysanthemum Fire-Pot 163
Assorted Meat and Shark's Fin Soup 87
Assorted Meat and Vegetables in Winter Melon 164
Assorted Sautéd Vegetables in Cream Sauce 154
Assorted Vegetables with Beancurd Skin 316
Bamboo Shoots and Mustard Greens, Sliced Pheasant Sautéd with 147
Bamboo Shoots and Scallops, Crisp-Fried 87
Bamboo Shoots with Chicken, Ham, and Spinach Balls in Soup 155
Bamboo Shoots with Dried Shrimps and Szechuan (Sichuan) Cabbage 233
Bamboo Shoots with Mushrooms and Quail Eggs 314
Bamboo Shoots, Crisp-Fried, Salted,

Mustard Greens with 152
Bamboo Shoots, Pork Fillet Sautéd with, and Mushrooms 70
Bamboo Shoots, Pork Kidneys Sautéd with, Carrots and 'Wood Ears' 70
Bamboo Shoots, Shredded Beef with 219
Bamboo Shoots, Sliced Quail Sautéd with 304
Bamboo Shoots, Spiced Chicken and Peanuts with 186
Bamboo Shoots, Winter, in Chicken Oil Sauce 150
Bamboo Shoots, Winter, with Pork and Szechuan (Sichuan) Vegetables 233
Barbecue, Mongolian 332
Bean Sprouts with Chicken, Stir-Fried 84
Bean Sprouts, Shredded Beef and, on Crisp Noodles 137
Bean Sprouts, Shrimp Sausage Sautéd with, 276
Beancurd 389
Beancurd Cake, Minced, with Spinach 230
Beancurd Cakes with Fresh Coriander and Soy Sauce 307
Beancurd Simmered with Mushrooms 228
Beancurd Skin 'Noodles' with Young Soybeans 82
Beancurd Skin Rolls, Steamed, in Oyster Sauce 365
Beancurd Skin and Clams in Soup 239
Beancurd Skin and Sliced Kidneys in Soup 167
Beancurd Skin, Assorted Vegetables with 316
Beancurd Stir-Fried with Crabmeat 308
Beancurd, 'Ma Pwo' 227
Beancurd, Braised, with Shrimps 308
Beancurd, Cantonese Stuffed 307
Beancurd, Dry, and Vegetables, Beef Braised with 72
Beancurd, Fermented, Stewed Pork and Taro with 295
Beancurd, Fermented, and Garlic, Slow-Cooked Leg of Pork with 137
Beancurd, Fish Heads and, Simmered in a Pot 203
Beancurd, Home-Style 228
Beancurd, Mushrooms and Vegetables Simmered in an Earthenware Crock 167
Beancurd, Phoenix Mountain 227
Beancurd, Shrimp and Chicken Fritters, Deep-Fried 147
Beans, String, with Diced Beef and Peanuts 232
Bear's Paw Simmered with Duck, Chicken, Scallops, and Ham 224
Beef Braised with Dry Beancurd and Vegetables 72
Beef Fu Yung 299
Beef Meatballs, Steamed on Watercress 366
Beef Meatballs, Steamed, and Spinach on Rice 299
Beef Steaks, Cantonese 302
Beef Stew, Szechuan (Sichuan) 220
Beef and Broccoli, Rice Ribbon Noodles with 349
Beef in Buddhist Robes 74
Beef in Oyster Sauce 297
Beef, Cold Sliced Spicy 377
Beef, Crisp-Fried, with Sesame Seeds 71
Beef, Diced, String Beans and Peanuts with 232
Beef, Fillet of, with Salted Mustard Greens and Black Bean Sauce 296
Beef, Mongolian Fire-Pot 74
Beef, Rainbow, in Lettuce Leaves 298
Beef, Red-Braised Five Spice 71
Beef, Shredded, and Bean Sprouts on Crisp Noodles 137

Beef, Shredded, with Bamboo Shoots 219
Beef, Sliced, with Orange Peel and Chilli Peppers 72
Beef, Spicy Shredded, with 'Wood Ear' Fungus and Water Chestnuts 219
Beef, Stewed, Northern Style 71
Beef, Stir-Fried, with Green and Red Peppers 298
Beef, Stir-Fried, with Young Ginger and Pineapple 297
Beggar's Chicken 329
Bell Peppers, Simmered Stuffed with Pork 138
Bird's Nest Dessert 171
Bird's Nests, Preparation of 393
Black Bean Sauce, Fillet of Beef with Salted Mustard Greens and 296
Black Bean Sauce, Herring in 199
Black Bean Sauce, Pork Ribs with 294
Black Beans and Chillies, Lobster with 286
Black Beans, Sliced Fish Sautéd with 270
Black Sesame Seed Dressing, Deep-Fried Fish Fillets with 271
Bread, 'Mandarin' Pancakes 373
Bread, Sesame Pocket 372
Bread, Steamed 370
Broccoli, Sliced Roast Duck with 110
Broccoli, Steamed, with Crabmeat Sauce 314
Brown Sauce, Braised Shark's Fins in 178
Brown Sauce, Fish in 116
Buddhist Robes, Beef in 74
Buns, Long-Life 338
Buns, Steamed Flower-Shaped 372
Buns, Steamed Roast Pork (Cha Siew Pow) 362
Buns, Steamed, with Lotus Seed Filling 368
Cabbage and Pork Dumplings 159
Cabbage, Chinese, with Minced Shrimp Dressing 311
Cabbage, Salted, Pork Steamed with 214
Cabbage, Spiced 230
Cabbage, Sweet and Sour 83
Cake, Moon 341
Cake, New Year's 338
Cake, Steamed Date 240
Cake, Steamed Sponge 369
Cake, Turnip 364
Cakes, Rice 386
Camel's Hump, Deep Fried Boiled 285
Camel's Pads, Red Stewed 285
Candied Apples 90
Cantonese Beef Steaks 302
Cantonese Roast Duck 258
Cantonese Roast Pork 291
Cantonese Stuffed Beancurd 307
Carp with Onions, Braised Golden 118
Carp, 'Bullfrog' Silver 55
Carp, 'Westlake Style' Braised 118
Carp, Deep-Fried, with Sweet and Sour Sauce, 122
Carp, Golden Stuffed with Pork and Bamboo Shoots 119
Carp, Golden, Shredded Turnip and, in Soup 239
Carp, Golden, with a Phoenix Tail 196
Carp, Steamed Golden 54
Carp, Steamed Grass, Dressed with Shredded Vegetables 121
Carrot and Radish, Marinated, Shrimp Rolls on 204
Cashew Nuts, Diced Chicken and 251
Cashew Nuts, Sauted Frogs' Legs with Chilli Peppers and 223
Cashew Nuts, Sautéd Shrimps with Peas and 274
Casserole with Three Kinds of Poultry 256
Catfish, Garlic 115
Cauliflower with Creamed Chicken

Sauce 151
Celery and Bamboo Shoots, Lamb Kidneys Stir-Fried with 222
Celery with Dried Shrimps 84
Celery, Fresh, with Creamy Mustard Sauce 311
Cha Siew Pow, Steamed Roast Pork Buns 362
Chestnuts, Chicken Braised with 50
Chicken 'Teh-Chow' Style 48
Chicken Braised with Chestnuts 50
Chicken Dinner Hainan Style 250
Chicken Drumsticks, Mock, Deep-Fried 106
Chicken Fat, Rendered 387
Chicken Fat, Rendered, Notes on 395
Chicken Fritters, Deep-Fried Beancurd, Shrimp and 147
Chicken Legs, Spiced Deep-Fried 190
Chicken Livers, Deep-Fried, with Spicy Dressing 110
Chicken Oil Sauce, 'Four Jewels' in 86
Chicken Patties, Fried, with Marinated Cabbage 184
Chicken Rolls, Fried Stuffed 254
Chicken Shreds Sautéd with Tuberrose Petals 103
Chicken Shreds, Quick-Fried, with Onion 254
Chicken Slivers and Jasmine in Clear Broth 161
Chicken Soup, Sweet Corn and 319
Chicken South China Style 255
Chicken Steamed in a Pumpkin 187
Chicken Steamed in a Yunnan Steam-Pot
Chicken Steamed in a Yunnan Steam-Pot 183
Chicken Stir-Fried with Oyster Sauce 258
Chicken Stock 388
Chicken Stuffed with Shark's Fin 98
Chicken Turnovers, Steamed 361
Chicken Walnut Rolls 104
Chicken Wings Simmered in Wine 106
Chicken Wings in Soup, with Mushrooms 318
Chicken Wings, Steamed Stuffed 256
Chicken and Mushroom Pot, Steamed 108
Chicken and Rice Pot with Chinese Sausage 356
Chicken and Two Sauces, Cold Bean Sheet Noodles with 349
Chicken in Sweet Wine 47
Chicken with Crisp Hot Peppers and Orange Peel 50
Chicken with Green Onions, Hot Spiced 183
Chicken with Mushrooms, Ham and Pea Sprouts, Creamed 108
Chicken, 'Bon Bon' 182
Chicken, 'Chin Hua' 330
Chicken, 'Dragon's Eye' Bone Marrow with 218
Chicken, 'Exotic Tasting' 376
Chicken, 'Firecracker' 187
Chicken, 'Hibiscus' 186
Chicken, 'Kung Pao' 184
Chicken, 'Lantern' 195
Chicken, 'Precious Concubine' 180
Chicken, 'Twice Eaten' 188
Chicken, Beggar's 329
Chicken, Casserole with Three Kinds of Poultry 256
Chicken, Country-Style 188
Chicken, Crisp Skin 248
Chicken, Crisp-Fried, Shredded, Smoked 47
Chicken, Deep-Fried Mock-Chicken Drumsticks 106
Chicken, Diced, and Cashew Nuts 251
Chicken, Dried Oysters and, in Soup 166
Chicken, Drunken 48

Chicken, Fried Diced with Sweet Bean Paste 48
Chicken, Jellied 46
Chicken, Oyster Sauce, in Parcels 104
Chicken, Pan-Fried, with Young Ginger and Pineapple 252
Chicken, Roast Stuffed 182
Chicken, Salt-Baked 249
Chicken, Shark's Fin Simmered with 99
Chicken, Sliced, with Chrysanthemum Petals 251
Chicken, Smoked 46
Chicken, Special Soy Sauce 249
Chicken, Spiced, with Peanuts and Bamboo Shoots 186
Chicken, Spring, Showered with Hot Oil 107
Chicken, Steamed Chopped, and Straw Mushrooms 255
Chicken, Steamed, Dressed with Spring Onions and Ginger 252
Chicken, Steamed, Stuffed with Eight Precious Ingredients 98
Chicken, Stewed Stuffed 103
Chicken, Whole, Stuffed wth Glutinous Rice 250
Chicken, how to arrange for serving 394
Chicken, how to cut for serving 394
Chicken,Stewed with Beans, Preserved Cucumber and Ginger 107
Chickens, deboning and skinning of 394
Chilli Oil 385
Chilli Oil Sauce, Szechuan (Sichuan) Prawns in 204
Chilli Pork Spare Ribs 216
Chinese Cabbage with Crabmeat and Crab Roe Sauce 155
Chinese Cabbage with Minced Shrimp Dressing 311
Chinese Cooking Utensils, Condiments and Methods 27-37
Chinese Crullers, Crisp-Fried 374
Chinese Ham 377
Chinese Herbs, Pigeon Paté with, Steamed in Soup Ramekins 384
Chinese Pepper-Salt 356
Chinese Sausage, Chicken and Rice Pot with 356
Choy Sum, Sautéd Fresh 311
Chrysanthemum Fire-pot, Assorted Meat and 163
Chrysanthemum Petals, Sliced Chicken with 251
Clams in Egg Custard 64
Clams in Yellow Bean Sauce 131
Clams, Beancurd Skin and, in Soup 239
Clams, Served in a Crock, Minced Pork in 139
Clear-as-Glass Cookies 366
Cleaver, Chinese 29-30
Colouring, Sugar 388
Condiments, Common Chinese, Notes on 34-35
Congee, Rice, with Sliced Fish 357
Cookies, Clear-as-Glass 366
Cooking Methods, Notes on 35-37
Cooking Oil, Notes on 395
Cooking Processes, Notes on 397-399
Cooking Terms, Notes on 397-399
Coriander, Cold Marinated 83
Cornflour, Notes on 396
Crab Claws, Stuffed 284
Crab Fu-Yung, Stir-Fried 274
Crab, Fish Masquerading as 58
Crab, Pearls Hiding in a 63
Crabmeat Balls, Deep-Fried 130
Crabmeat Omelette 284
Crabmeat and Egg Flower, Rice Vermicelli in Soup with 352
Crabmeat and Roe, Young Lettuce Sautéd with 232
Crabmeat, Beancurd Stir-Fried with 308

Crabmeat, Chinese Cabbage with, and Crab Roe Sauce 155
Crabmeat, Fried Fresh Milk with, on Rice Noodles 79
Crabmeat, Sautéd, on Crisp Noodles 130
Crabmeat, Shark's Fin and, Soup 318
Crabmeat, Steamed Shark's Fin with 99
Crabmeat, and Pork, 'Lion's Head' Meatballs 136
Crabs, Drunken 128
Crabs, Steamed Female, with Ginger Sauce 283
Cream, Almond 90
Creative Improvisation in Chinese Cooking 37
Crisp Oil-Basted Duck Cooked Twice 191
Crullers, Chinese, Crisp-Fried 374
Cucumber Sautéd in Sesame Oil with Hot Spices 231
Cucumber, Sliced Stuffed with Shrimp and Pork 159
Cucumber, Sour and Hot 83
Cucumber, Soy-Preserved 389
Custard, Egg 321
Date Cake, Steamed 240
Deboning a fish 395
Deep-Frying Oil, Notes on 395
Deep-Frying, Instructions on 398
Dim Sum, Bread and Cold Platters - Appetisers 359-381
Dishes for Special Occasions 323-341
Drunken Chicken 48
Drunken Crabs 128
Duck Fat in Steamed Egg Custard 51
Duck Feet with Shrimp Stuffing, Deep-Fried 263
Duck Liver Roll, Pork and 290
Duck Livers with Hot Pepper Sauce 262
Duck Simmered in Yellow Rice Wine 260
Duck Smoked over Camphor Wood and Tea Leaves 190
Duck Soup in Yunnan Steam-Pot 236
Duck in Orange-Flavoured Soup 160
Duck, Cantonese Roast 258
Duck, Casserole with Three Kinds of Poultry 256
Duck, Charcoal-Roasted, Stuffed with Lotus Leaves 111
Duck, Chopped, with Lotus Root and Vegetables 262
Duck, Crisp Oil-Basted, Cooked Twice 191
Duck, Crispy Home Style 52
Duck, Deep-Fried and Simmered, Stuffed with Eight Precious Ingredients 112
Duck, Deep-Fried, with Laver 194
Duck, Fragrant Crispy, Stuffed with Lotus Seeds and Pork 264
Duck, Home Style Simmer-Stewed 260
Duck, Honey-Basted Roast 259
Duck, Hunan Crispy 192
Duck, Peking Roast 329
Duck, Peking, Three Courses of 51
Duck, Red-Simmered 115
Duck, Roast with Spicy Sauce 111
Duck, Roast, Stuffed with Pork and Bean Sprouts 192
Duck, Sliced Roast, with Broccoli 110
Duck, Smoked, Sautéd with Young Ginger 191
Duck, Steamed, Marinated with Preserved Egg and Wine 194
Duck, Steamed, Stuffed, with Pine Seed Crust 114
Duck, Steamed, in Lotus Leaf Packages 114
Duck, Stewed Whole, with Chinese Cabbage 259
Duck, Wild, Braised and Steamed 143
Duck, Wild, Vegetables, and Assorted Meats Simmered with Rice 146

Duck, Wild, with Mashed Taro Stuffing and Oyster Sauce 144
Dumplings of Shrimp, Pork, and White Fungus in Chicken Soup 238
Dumplings, Egg 79
Dumplings, Peking Style, Fried 80
Dumplings, Pork 360
Dumplings, Pork and Cabbage 159
Dumplings, Shrimp, (Har Gow) 360
Eastern Coastal Style Cuisine 93-171
Eel on Skewers, Charcoal Roasted 288
Eel, Fresh Water, and Ham Steamed in a Pot 134
Eel, Preparation of 395
Eel, Steamed Fresh-Water, with Spicy and Hot Sauce 134
Eel, Stewed River, with Diced Pork and Mushrooms 288
Eel, Stir-Fried, Fresh-Water 135
Eels, Braised, Fresh-Water 207
Egg Custard 321
Egg Custard, Clams in 64
Egg Custard, Duck Fat Steamed in 51
Egg Custard, Steamed Asparagus on 158
Egg Dumplings 79
Egg Flower Sauce, Poached Fish in 199
Egg Puffs with Red Bean Filling 91
Egg Puffs, Spinach 156
Egg Rolls, Crisp Fried 337
Egg, Beef Fu Yung 299
Egg, Crabmeat Omelette 284
Egg, Omelette in Spicy Sauce 80
Egg, Shrimp and Chicken Omelette 275
Egg, Stir-Fried Crab Fu-Yung 274
Eggplant Braised with Soybean Paste 158
Eggplant, Braised 234
Eggplant, Fish-Flavoured 234
Eggs, Marbled Tea 365
Eggs, Pigeon, Spiced 78
Eggs, Salted Duck 263
Eight-Treasure Rice 241
Enriched Stock 388
Fa Ts'ai, Pork Shoulder with 332
Fa Ts'ai, Preparation of 393
Female Crabs, Steamed, with Ginger Sauce 283
Fire-Pot 31-32
Fire-Pot, Assorted Meat and Chrysanthemum 163
Fire-Pot, Mongolian 333
Fire-Pot, Mongolian Beef 74
Fish Balls, Mandarin, with Vegetables in Chicken Stock 123
Fish Cake, Two-Toned Steamed 202
Fish Fillets, Deep-Fried, with Black Sesame Seed Dressing 271
Fish Heads and Beancurd Simmered in a Pot 203
Fish Lips with Vegetables on Crisp Rice 179
Fish Lips, Preparation of 392
Fish Masquerading as Crab 58
Fish Maw Salad with Sesame Sauce 102
Fish Maw, Braised, with Assorted Meats 102
Fish Maw, Braised, with Ham and Mushrooms 179
Fish Maw, Preparation of 392
Fish Rolls, Fried Stuffed, with Sautéd Vegetables 272
Fish Slices, Fried, with Ginger and Sweet Pickles 123
Fish Soup, Creamy, with Sour and Hot Flavours 162
Fish in Brown Sauce 116
Fish in Wine Sauce with 'Wood Ear' Fungus 56
Fish, 'Bullfrog' Silver Carp 55
Fish, 'Squirrel' 120
Fish, 'Westlake Style' Braised Carp 118
Fish, Braised Golden Carp with

Onions 118
Fish, Crisp-Skin with Hot and Sour Sauce 195
Fish, Cubed Mandarin, and Pineapple in Tomato Sauce 122
Fish, Cubed, in Pineapple Sauce 270
Fish, Deboning 395
Fish, Deep-Fried Carp with Sweet and Sour Sauce 122
Fish, Deep-Fried Whole, Seasoned with Spiced Salt 267
Fish, Garlic Catfish 115
Fish, Golden Carp Stuffed with Pork and Bamboo Shoots 119
Fish, Golden Carp with a Phoenix Tail 196
Fish, Herring in Black Bean Sauce 199
Fish, Hot Pot of, with Shrimps, Pork and Chicken 66
Fish, Mandarin, Baked Stuffed 267
Fish, Mandarin with Vinegar and Pepper in Rich Soup 88
Fish, Mandarin, in Pot-Sticker Style 121
Fish, One, Served in Two Ways 124
Fish, Poached, in Egg Flower Sauce 199
Fish, Poached, with Ginger, Onion and Oil Dressing 266
Fish, Preparation of and notes on 395
Fish, Red-Braised Mackerel Tails 116
Fish, Silver Carp's Head Simmered in an Earthen Crock 126
Fish, Silver Carp's Heat in Rich Soup 162
Fish, Sliced in Walnut Crumb Batter, 120
Fish, Sliced, Braised in Spicy Sauce 202
Fish, Sliced, Rice Congee with 357
Fish, Sliced, Sautéd Five Shreds with 271
Fish, Sliced, Sautéd with Black Beans 270
Fish, Sliced, and Celery in Hot and Sour Sauce 200
Fish, Smoked Pomfret 268
Fish, Smoked, Szechuan (Sichuan) 200
Fish, Steamed Fresh, with Szechuan (Sichuan) Pickled Vegetables and 'Wood Ears' 198
Fish, Steamed Golden Carp 54
Fish, Steamed Grass Carp Dressed with Shredded Vegetables 121
Fish, Steamed Mandarin 266
Fish, Whole Baked Served on a Hot Plate 52
Fish, Whole Steamed 324
Fish, Whole Stuffed, Deep-Fried in a Crisp Pork Fat Coating 196
Fish, Whole with Garlic in Hot Sauce 198
Fish, Whole, with Five Shreds in Hot Sauce 268
Fish, Yellow Croaker with Pine Seeds 55
Fish, Yellow, Fried, with Garlic Chives 54
Fish-Flavoured Eggplant 234
Five Shreds, Sautéd with Sliced Fish 271
Five Spice Beef, Red Braised 71
Five Spice Powder 386
Five Spice and Garlic Spare Ribs 68
Five Spices, Red-Braised Pigeons with 148
Flower-shaped Buns, Steamed 372
Fritters, Deep-Fried Beancurd, Shrimp and Chicken 147
Frogs' Legs Braised with Garlic 146
Frogs' Legs with Chilli Peppers and Cashew Nuts, Sautéd 223
Frogs' Legs, Stir-Fried 302
Fruit, Diced Fresh, Sweet Fermented Rice with 90
Fruit, Fresh, Almond Jelly with 321
Fungus, (White, Snow and Brown),

Preparation of *393*
Fungus, White, Pigeon Eggs, and Diced Ham Soup *160*
Garlic Catfish *115*
Garlic Chives, Fried Yellow Fish with *54*
Garlic Chives, Preparation of and notes on *394*
Garlic Sauce, Cold Sliced Pork with *377*
Garlic and Ginger Sauce, Squid with *208*
Garlic, Frog's Legs Braised with *146*
Garlic, Sautéd Lamb with *75*
Garlic, Whole Fish with, in Hot Sauce *198*
Ginger and Spring Onion Sauce *384*
Ginger Infusion, Onion and *386*
Ginger Sauce, Steamed Female Crabs with *283*
Ginger Wine/Ginger Juice *387*
Ginger, Fried Fish Slices with, and Sweet Pickles *123*
Ginger, Smoked Duck Sautéd with Young *191*
Ginger, Soy-Preserved *389*
Ginger, Stewed Chicken with Beans, Preserved Cucumber and Ginger *107*
Ginger, Young, Stir-Fried Beef with, and Pineapple *297*
Ginger, Preparation of and Notes on *393-394*
Glossary of Ingredients *406-412*
Glutinous Rice, Whole Chicken Stuffed with *250*
Goose, Slow-Simmered, with Vinegar and Garlic Sauce *264*
Green Onions, Hot Spiced Chicken with *183*
Hainan Style Chicken Dinner *250*
Ham and Winter Melon Sandwiches in Soup *235*
Ham, Chinese *377*
Ham, Honey-Glazed *210*
Ham, Steamed Sea Cucumber with *100*
Ham, Steamed Yunnan *211*
Har Gow (Shrimp Dumplings) *360*
Herring in Black Bean Sauce *199*
Hibiscus Shrimps *275*
Honey Syrup, Peaches in *241*
Honey-Basted Roast Duck *259*
Honey-Glazed Ham *210*
Hot Pepper Sauce with Peanuts, Pork Tripe in *212*
Hot Pot of Fish, Shrimps, Pork and Chicken *66*
Hot Sauce, Sautéd Liver and Onions in *140*
Hot Spiced Chicken with Green Onions *183*
Hot and Sour Sauce, Crisp Skin Fish with *195*
Hot and Sour Sauce, Sliced Fish and Celery in *200*
Hot and Sour Soup *88*
Hot and Spicy Sliced Pork with 'Wood Ear' Fungus *211*
Hot-pot, Mutton *334*
Hot-pot, Seafood Noodle *348*
Hunan Crispy Duck *192*
Jasmine, Chicken Slivers and, in Clear Broth *161*
Jellied Chicken *46*
Jellied Mutton *378*
Jellied Pork, Spiced *210*
Jelly, Almond, with Fresh Fruit *321*
Jelly, Loquats in *000*
Jellyfish Salad, Salted *380*
Jellyfish, Salted, Preparation of *392*
Jellyfish, Salted, and Shrimp Salad *62*
Jumbo Prawns Served in Two Styles *126*
Kidneys in Sour and Hot Sauce *218*
Kidneys, Lamb, Stir-Fried, with Celery and Bamboo Shoots *222*
Kidneys, Pork, Turnip, and Dried Scallops Steamed in a Bowl *140*

Kidneys, Sliced and Beancurd Skin in Soup *167*
Kitchen Layout, Notes on *399*
Kitchen Preparations *32-37*
Kung Hei Fat Choy *326*
Lamb Kidneys Stir-Fried with Celery and Bamboo Shoots *222*
Lamb Shanks, Braised Spiced *220*
Lamb with Bean Sprouts in a Crisp Potato Basket *303*
Lamb, Boneless Rack of, Flavoured with White Rice Wine *142*
Lamb, Braised, and Hot Spices *143*
Lamb, Mongolian *75*
Lamb, Mongolian Barbecue *332*
Lamb, Sautéd Shredded, and Spring Onions *142*
Lamb, Sautéd Shredded, on Rice Noodles *300*
Lamb, Sautéd with Garlic *75*
Lard, Notes on *395*
Laver, Deep-Fried Duck with *194*
Leeks, Shark's Fin Sautéd with Silver Sprouts and *248*
Leeks, Venison Sautéd with *76*
Lettuce Leaves, Rainbow Beef in *298*
Lettuce with Oyster Sauce *300*
Lettuce, Young, Sautéd with Crabmeat and Roe *232*
Lima Beans Sautéd with Mushrooms, Ham, and Shrimps *151*
Liver and Onions, Sautéd, in Hot Sauce *140*
Liver, Pork and Duck, Roll *290*
Liver, Watercress and, Soup *319*
Livers, Pork, in Sweet Fermented Rice Sauce *68*
Lobster with Black Beans and Chillies *286*
Long-Life Buns *338*
Lotus Leaf Packages, Steamed Duck in *114*
Lotus Leaves, Charcoal-Roasted Duck Stuffed with *111*
Lotus Root and Vegetables, Chopped Duck with *262*
Lotus Seed Filling, Steamed Buns with *368*
Lotus Seed and Red Bean Paste Pudding, Steamed *170*
Lotus Seeds and Pork, Fragrant Crispy Duck Stuffed with *264*
Lotus Seeds in Sugar Syrup *91*
Mackerel Tails, Red-Braised *116*
Mandarin Fish Balls with Vegetables in Chicken Stock *123*
Mandarin Fish in Pot-Sticker Style *121*
Mandarin Fish with Vinegar and Pepper in Rich Soup *88*
Mandarin Fish, Baked Stuffed *267*
Mandarin Fish, Cubed, and Pineapple in Tomato Sauce *122*
Mandarin Fish, Steamed *266*
Marbled Tea Eggs *365*
Measurement Charts ...
Meat, Cold Combination, Phoenix *381*
Meatballs, Pork and Crabmeat 'Lion's Head' *136*
Meatballs, Preparation of *395*
Milk, Fried Fresh, with Crabmeat on Rice Noodles *79*
Mock-Chicken Drumsticks, Deep-Fried *106*
Mongolian Barbecue *332*
Mongolian Beef Fire-Pot *74*
Mongolian Fire-Pot *333*
Mongolian Lamb *75*
Moon Cakes *341*
Mushroom Pot, Steamed Chicken and *108*
Mushrooms with Chicken Wings in Soup *318*
Mushrooms, Beancurd Simmered with *228*
Mushrooms, Beancurd and Vegetables Simmered in an Earthenware Crock

167
Mushrooms, Black, Preparation of *393*
Mushrooms, Ham and Pea Sprouts, Creamed Chicken with *108*
Mushrooms, Steamed Black, with Shrimp Stuffing *150*
Mushrooms, Three Kinds of *315*
Mustard Greens with Bamboo Shoots, Crisp-Fried, Salted *152*
Mustard Greens, Fresh, with Scallops in Cream Sauce *152*
Mustard Greens, Pickled, Sliced Fish and, in Soup *238*
Mutton Hot-Pot *334*
Mutton, Jellied *378*
New Year's Cake *338*
Noodle Hot-Pot, Seafood *348*
Noodle Nest, Deep-Fried Rice Birds Served with Quail Eggs and Sliced Quail in *306*
Noodles and Rice - Accompaniments *343-357*
Noodles, 'Crossing the Bridge' *224*
Noodles, 'Great Gravy' *344*
Noodles, 'Mien Sien' with Roast Pork and Vegetables *150*
Noodles, 'Silver Pin' *352*
Noodles, Beancurd Skin 'Noodles' with Young Soybeans *82*
Noodles, Cold Bean Sheet, with Chicken and Two Sauces *349*
Noodles, Fried Egg, with Meat and Vegetables *345*
Noodles, Hot Bean Thread, with Shredded Pork *300*
Noodles, Red Cooked Beef and Carrots on *345*
Noodles, Rice Ribbon, with Beef and Broccoli *349*
Noodles, Rice Vermicelli in Soup with Crabmeat and Egg Flower *352*
Noodles, Rice, Sautéd Shredded Lamb on *300*
Noodles, Sautéd Crabmeat on Crisp *130*
Noodles, Shanghai, with Bean Sprouts and Brown Sauce *344*
Noodles, Shredded Beef and Bean Sprouts on Crisp *137*
Noodles, Soft Egg, Shrimps and Squid with Assorted Vegetables on *346*
Northern Style Cuisine *38-91*
Oil, Chilli *385*
Oil, Cooking, Notes on *395*
Oil, Deep-Frying, Notes on *395-396*
Oil, Sesame, Notes on *396*
Omelette in Spicy Sauce *80*
Omelette, Crabmeat *284*
Omelette, Shrimp and Chicken *275*
Onion and Ginger Infusion *386*
Onion-Pepper-Salt *384*
Onions, Preparation of and Notes on *394*
Orange-Flavoured Soup, Duck in *160*
Oyster Sauce Chicken in Parcels *104*
Oyster Sauce, Beef in *297*
Oyster Sauce, Chicken Stir-Fried with *258*
Oyster Sauce, Lettuce with *300*
Oyster Sauce, Steamed Beancurd Skin Rolls in *365*
Oysters with Barbecued Pork and Vegetables in Sauce *131*
Oysters, Deep-Fried *287*
Oysters, Dried, Preparation of *393*
Oysters, Dried, and Chicken in Soup *166*
Pancakes, 'Mandarin' *373*
Paper-Wrapped Shrimps *278*
Pastries, Spring Onion *373*
Pastries, Taro *364*
Pea Sprouts with Creamed Chicken, Chopped *154*
Peaches in Honey Syrup *241*
Peanuts and Bamboo Shoots, Spiced Chicken with *186*
Peanuts, Pork Tripe in Hot Pepper

Sauce with *212*
Peanuts, String Beans with Diced Beef and *232*
Pearls Hiding in a Crab *63*
Peking Duck, Three Courses of *51*
Peking Roast Duck *329*
Peking Style Fried Dumplings *80*
Pepper-Salt/Onion-Pepper-Salt *384*
Peppers, Bell, Simmered, Stuffed with Pork *138*
Peppers, Green and Red, Stir-Fried Beef with *298*
Peppers, Red, Stuffed *316*
Pheasant, Sliced, Sautéd with Bamboo Shoots and Mustard Greens *147*
Phoenix Cold Meat Combination *381*
Phoenix Mountain Beancurd *227*
Phoenix Tail Prawns *127*
Pickled Assorted Vegetables *230*
Pickled Vegetables, Szechuan (Sichuan), Steamed Fresh Fish with, and 'Wood Ears' *198*
Pig, Roast Suckling *328*
Pig, Roast Suckling, Three Courses of *290*
Pig, Suckling Roast, Appetiser *380*
Pigeon Egg, Soup, Asparagus and *160*
Pigeon Eggs, Spiced *78*
Pigeon Eggs, and Diced Ham, White Fungus and, Soup *160*
Pigeon Meat, Sautéd, with Livers and Eggs in Noodle Nest *78*
Pigeon Paté with Chinese Herbs Steamed in Soup Ramekins *222*
Pigeon, Casserole with Three Kinds of Poultry *256*
Pigeon, Sautéd Minced, with Vegetables and Hot Peppers *148*
Pigeons with Five Spices, Red-Braised *148*
Pigeons, Slow-Simmered *76*
Pigeons, Steamed, with White Fungus *330*
Pigeons, Young, and Ham Steamed in Soup *161*
Pineapple Sauce, Cubed Fish in *270*
Platter, Cold, Plum Blossom *380*
Plum Blossom Cold Platter *380*
Poaching, Instructions on *398-399*
Pock-Marked Mama's Beancurd, 'Ma Pwo' *227*
Pomfret, Smoked *268*
Pork 'Coins', Roasted *139*
Pork Chops, Deep-Fried *291*
Pork Dumplings (Siew Mai) *360*
Pork Fat Coating, Crisp, Whole Stuffed Fish Deep-Fried in *196*
Pork Fillet Rolls in Sweet and Sour Sauce *292*
Pork Fillet Sautéd with Bamboo Shoots and Mushrooms *70*
Pork Kidneys, Sautéd with Bamboo Shoots, Carrots and 'Wood Ears' *70*
Pork Kidneys, Sea Scallops with, Stir-Fried *207*
Pork Kidneys, Turnip, and Dried Scallops Steamed in a Bowl *140*
Pork Knuckles with Ginger and Sweet Rice Vinegar *333*
Pork Livers in Sweet Fermented Rice Sauce *68*
Pork Ribs with Black Bean Sauce *294*
Pork Ribs, Sweet and Sour *292*
Pork Seasoned with Spiced Rice Powder *295*
Pork Shoulder with Fa Ts'ai *332*
Pork Spare Ribs, Chilli *216*
Pork Steamed with Salted Cabbage *214*
Pork Tripe in Hot Pepper Sauce with Peanuts *212*
Pork Wontons *361*
Pork and Cabbage Dumplings *159*
Pork and Crabmeat 'Lion's Head' Meatballs *136*
Pork and Duck Liver Roll *290*
Pork, 'Buddha's Hand' *334*

Pork, 'Dragon's Eye' Bone Marrow with Chicken 218
Pork, 'Gold and Silver' 214
Pork, 'Mu Hsu' 67
Pork, 'Pearl' Balls 216
Pork, 'Su Tung Po' 138
Pork, 'Twice-Cooked' 215
Pork, Barbecued, and Vegetables in Sauce, Oysters with 131
Pork, Cantonese Roast 291
Pork, Chinese Ham 377
Pork, Cold Sliced, with Garlic Sauce 377
Pork, Cold Spicy Peking-Style 66
Pork, Five Spice and Garlic Spare Ribs 68
Pork, Honey-Glazed Ham 210
Pork, Kidneys in Sour and Hot Sauce 218
Pork, Minced, in Clams Served in a Crock 139
Pork, Roast Suckling Pig 328
Pork, Roast Suckling Pig Appetiser 380
Pork, Roast, Steamed Buns (Cha Siew Pow) 362
Pork, Roast, and Vegetables with 'Mien Sien' Noodles 346
Pork, Salted and Fresh, in Soup 164
Pork, Sautéed with Pine Seeds 66
Pork, Shredded Hot, and Mushrooms on Crisp Rice Cakes 212
Pork, Shredded with Sweet Bean Paste 215
Pork, Shredded, Hot Bean Thread Noodles with 348
Pork, Shredded, in Sesame Pouches 67
Pork, Simmered Bell Peppers Stuffed with 138
Pork, Sliced Cucumber Stuffed with Shrimp and 159
Pork, Sliced with 'Wood Ear' Fungus, Hot and Spicy 211
Pork, Slow-Cooked Leg of, with Fermented Beancurd and Garlic 137
Pork, Slow-Cooked, Corned 136
Pork, Spare Ribs, Sweet and Spicy 294
Pork, Spiced Jellied 210
Pork, Steamed Yunnan Ham 211
Pork, Steamed, with Carrots and Mushrooms 296
Pork, Stewed, with Fermented Beancurd and Taro 295
Pork, Stir-Fried, with Spring Onions in Soy Sauce 294
Pork, Szechuan (Sichuan) Stewed 215
Pork, Three Courses of Roast Suckling Pig 290
Potato Basket, Crisp, Lamb with Bean Sprouts in 303
Prawn Balls, Deep-Fried 280
Prawn Puffs, Deep-Fried 127
Prawns (Shrimps), Preparation of and Notes on 394-395
Prawns Clear as Crystal 279
Prawns Peking Style 59
Prawns in Hot Sauce, Stuffed 283
Prawns in Sweet Wine Sauce with Chillies and Garlic 59
Prawns, Braised 58
Prawns, Braised, in Gravy 282
Prawns, Curled, Steamed with Five Shreds 56
Prawns, Jumbo, Served in Two Styles 126
Prawns, Pheonix Tail 127
Prawns, Sliced, in Sour Sauce 203
Prawns, Steamed Fresh 278
Prawns, Steamed Jumbo, Served in Clear Sauce 280
Prawns, Stir-Fried, and Choy Sum 279
Prawns, Szechuan (Sichan), in Chilli Oil Sauce 204
Prawns, Walnut-Stuffed 282
Preparation Techniques, Notes on 396-397
Preparation and Cooking Techniques

391-399
Preserved Cucumber, and Ginger Stewed Chicken with Beans 107
Pumpkin, Chicken Steamed in a 187
Quail Egg, Almond and, Tea 321
Quail Eggs, Bamboo Shoots with Mushrooms and 314
Quail, Sliced, Sautéed with Bamboo Shoots 304
Quail, Sliced, and Quail Eggs, in a Noodle Nest, Deep-Fried Rice Birds with 306
Rabbit, Diced, Sautéed with Bell Peppers 304
Rack of Lamb, Boneless, Flavoured with White Rice Wine 142
Radish Balls with Scallops in Cream Sauce 156
Rainbow Beef in Lettuce Leaves 298
Red Bean Filling, Egg Puffs with 91
Red Bean Paste and Lotus Seed Pudding 170
Red Bean Paste, Apple Fritters Stuffed with 168
Red Bean Paste, Steamed Lotus Seed and, Pudding 170
Red Bean Paste, Sweet 389
Red Bean Soup, Sweet Rice Balls in 320
Red Date Soup, Sweet Walnut and 170
Red Date and Walnut Soup, Sweet 170
Red-Braised Five Spice Beef 71
Red-Braised Mackerel Tails 116
Red-Braised Pigeons with Five Spices 148
Red-Braised Turtle 135
Red-Braising/Red-Stewing, Instructions on 399
Red-Cooked Beef and Carrots on Noodles 345
Red-Simmered Duck 115
Red-Stewing, Notes on 399
Rendered Chicken Fat (Chicken Grease) 387
Rice Birds, Deep-Fried, Served with Quail Eggs and Sliced Quail in a Noodle Nest 306
Rice Cakes 386
Rice Cakes, Crisp, Shredded Hot Pork and Mushrooms on 212
Rice Cakes, Crisp, Shrimps in Hot Sauce on 206
Rice Cakes, Crisp, Squid in Sour and Hot Sauce on 132
Rice Congee with Sliced Fish 357
Rice Cookers 32
Rice Noodles, Fried Fresh Milk with Crabmeat on 79
Rice Noodles, Sautéed Shredded Lamb on 300
Rice Pot, Chicken and, with Chinese Sausage 356
Rice Powder, Spiced 386
Rice Powder, Spiced, Pork Seasoned with 295
Rice Sheet Rolls with Shredded Meat and Vegetable Filling 353
Rice, 'Lotus' 357
Rice, Crisp, Fish Lips with Vegetables on 179
Rice, Eight-Treasure 241
Rice, Fried 354
Rice, Glutinous, Whole Chicken Stuffed with 250
Rice, Multi-Coloured 356
Rice, Plain White 354
Rice, Shrimps, Pork and Vegetables in Tomato Sauce on Crisp 60
Rice, Steamed Beef Meatballs and Spinach on 299
Rice, Sweet Fermented 387
Rice, Sweet Fermented, with Diced Fresh Fruit 90
Rice, Wild Duck, Vegetables, and Assorted Meats Simmered with 146
Roast Duck Stuffed with Pork and Bean Sprouts 192

Roast Duck with Spicy Sauce 111
Roast Pork Buns, Steamed (Cha Siew Pow) 362
Roast Stuffed Chicken 182
Roast Suckling Pig 328
Roasted Pork 'Coins' 139
Salad, Fish Maw, with Sesame Sauce 102
Salad, Salted Jellyfish 380
Salt, Spiced 384
Salt-Baked Chicken 249
Salted Cabbage, Pork Steamed with 214
Salted Duck Eggs 263
Salted Jellyfish Salad 380
Salted Vegetables Stuffing, Deep-Fried Squab with 223
Sauce, 'Duck' 385
Sauce, Ginger and Spring Onion 384
Sauce, Sweet and Sour 385
Sauce, Sweetened Soy 385
Sauces, Spices and Seasonings 383-389
Sautéed Minced Pigeon with Vegetables and Hot Peppers 148
Sautéed Shredded Lamb and Spring Onions 142
Scallops with Sautéed Shrimps and Abalone 62
Scallops with Shrimps and Mushrooms 287
Scallops, Cold Marinated Sea 378
Scallops, Dried (Sea), Preparation of 392
Scallops, Dried, Braised with Garlic 325
Scallops, Radish Balls with, in Cream Sauce 156
Scallops, Sea, with Pork Kidneys 207
Scallops, Dried, Steamed in a Bowl, Pork Kidneys, Turnip and 140
Sea Cucumber in Brown Sauce 44
Sea Cucumber with Vegetables and Crisp Pretzels 206
Sea Cucumber, Preparation of 392-393
Sea Cucumber, Steamed, with Ham 100
Seafood Noodle Hot-pot 348
Sesame Oil, Notes on 395
Sesame Pocket Bread 372
Sesame Pouches, Shredded Pork in 67
Sesame Sauce, Fish Maw Salad with 102
Sesame Sauce, Poached Squid with 132
Sesame Seeds, Beef Crisp-Fried with 71
Sesame Seeds, Glazed Sweet Potato Balls with 320
Sesame, Sweet Black Soup 240
Shanghai Noodles with Bean Sprouts and Brown Sauce 344
Shark's Fin Sautéed with Silver Sprouts, and Leeks 248
Shark's Fin Simmered with Chicken 99
Shark's Fin Soup, Assorted Meat and 87
Shark's Fin and Crabmeat Soup 318
Shark's Fin with Shredded Meat in Rich Soup 324
Shark's Fin, Braised, with Pork Knuckle and Chicken 44
Shark's Fin, Chicken Stuffed with 98
Shark's Fin, Preparation of 393
Shark's Fin, Steamed, with Crabmeat 99
Shark's Fins, Braised, in Brown Sauce 178
Shark's Skin, Preparation of 393
Shrimp Ball Soup 319
Shrimp Balls, Crystal, Glazed with Sweet and Sour Sauce 128
Shrimp Dumplings (Har Gow) 360
Shrimp Patties, Fried, in Fruity Sauce 276
Shrimp Rolls Served on Marinated Carrot and Radish 204

Shrimp Sausage Sautéed with Bean Sprouts 276
Shrimp Toast 63
Shrimp and Chicken Fritters, Deep-Fried Beancurd and 147
Shrimp and Chicken Omelette 275
Shrimp, Sliced Cucumber Stuffed with Pork and 159
Shrimps Cooked in their Shells 272
Shrimps and Squid with Assorted Vegetables on Soft Egg Noodles 346
Shrimps in Hot Sauce on Crisp Rice Cakes 206
Shrimps, Braised Beancurd with 308
Shrimps, Crisp-Fried with Garlic and Chilli 60
Shrimps, Dried, with Celery 84
Shrimps, Hibiscus 275
Shrimps, Paper-Wrapped 278
Shrimps, Pork, and Vegetables in Tomato Sauce on Crisp Rice 60
Shrimps, Sautéed, with Peas and Cashew Nuts 274
Shrimps, Sautéed, with Scallops and Abalone 62
Siew Mai (Pork Dumplings) 360
Silver Carp's Head Simmered in an Earthen Crock 126
Silver Carp's Head in Rich Soup 162
Silver Sprouts, and Leeks, Shark's Fin Sautéed with 248
Simmer-Stewing, Instructions on 399
Sliced Fish Braised in Spicy Sauce 202
Slow-Simmering, Instructions on 399
Smoked Chicken 46
Smoked Chicken, Crisp-Fried, Shredded 47
Smoked Duck Sautéed with Young Ginger 191
Smoked Pomfret 268
Smoked Vegetarian 'Duck' 82
Smoking, Instructions on 398
Snails with Garlic, Sautéed 303
Snake, Sautéed, in Gravy 336
Soup, 'Eight Treasure' Winter Melon Pond 86
Soup, 'Embroidered' 166
Soup, Abalone and Lily Bud 239
Soup, Abalone, with Chicken and Egg 64
Soup, Asparagus and Pigeon Egg 160
Soup, Assorted Meat and Shark's Fin 87
Soup, Assorted Meat and Vegetables in Winter Melon 164
Soup, Bamboo Shoots with Chicken, Ham, and Spinach Balls in 155
Soup, Beancurd Skin and Clams in 239
Soup, Braised 'Snow' Fungus in Clear 315
Soup, Chicken Slivers and Jasmine in Clear Broth 161
Soup, Chicken, Dumplings of Shrimp, Pork, and White Fungus in 238
Soup, Creamy Fish, with Sour and Hot Flavours 162
Soup, Dried Oysters and Chicken in 166
Soup, Duck in Orange-Flavoured 160
Soup, Duck, in Yunnan Steam-Pot 236
Soup, Ham and Winter Melon Sandwiches in 235
Soup, Hot and Sour 88
Soup, Mandarin Fish with Vinegar and Pepper in Rich 88
Soup, Mushrooms with Chicken Wings in, 318
Soup, Red Bean, Sweet Rice Balls in 320
Soup, Red Date and Sweet Walnut 170
Soup, Rice Vermicelli with Crabmeat and Egg Flower in 352
Soup, Rich, Shark's Fin with Shredded Meat in 324
Soup, Rich, Silver Carp's Head in 162

421

Soup, Salted and Fresh Pork in *164*
Soup, Shark's Fin and Crabmeat *318*
Soup, Shredded Turnip and Golden Carp in *239*
Soup, Shrimp Ball *319*
Soup, Sliced Fish and Pickled Mustard Greens in *238*
Soup, Sliced Kidneys and Beancurd Skin in *167*
Soup, Swallow's Nests in Clear Broth *168*
Soup, Sweet Black Sesame *240*
Soup, Sweet Corn and Chicken *319*
Soup, Sweet Yam *171*
Soup, Sweet, 'Snow Fungus' in *91*
Soup, Translucent Sliced Chicken and Bamboo Shoot *236*
Soup, Watercress *236*
Soup, Watercress and Liver *319*
Soup, White Fungus, Pigeon Eggs, and Diced Ham *160*
Soup, Wontons in, with Mixed Meat and Vegetables *320*
Soup, Young Pigeons and Ham Steamed in *161*
Sour and Hot Cucumber *83*
Sour and Hot Sauce, Kidneys in *218*
Sour and Hot Sauce, Squid in, on Crisp Rice Cakes *132*
Southern Style Cuisine *243-321*
Soy Bean Paste, Eggplant Braised with *158*
Soy Sauce Chicken, Special *249*
Soy-Preserved Ginger/Cucumber *389*
Spare Ribs, Five Spice and Garlic *68*
Spare Ribs, Pork, Chilli *216*
Spare Ribs, Sweet and Spicy *294*
Spice Bags *386*
Spiced Cabbage *230*
Spiced Chicken with Peanuts and Bamboo Shoots *186*
Spiced Jellied Pork *210*
Spiced Pigeon Eggs *78*
Spiced Rice Powder *386*
Spiced Rice Powder, Pork Seasoned with *295*
Spiced Salt *384*
Spinach Balls in Soup, Bamboo Shoots with Chicken, Ham, and *155*
Spinach Egg Puffs *156*
Spinach with Shredded Fish *231*
Spinach, Minced Beancurd Cake with *230*
Spinach, Sautéd Chinese, with Shrimp Sauce *310*
Spinach, Steamed Beef Meatballs and, on Rice *299*
Sponge Cake, Steamed *369*
Spring Chicken Showered with Hot Oil *107*
Spring Onion Pastries *373*
Spring Onions, Sautéd Shredded Lamb and *142*
Spring Roll Wrappers *374*
Spring Rolls *362*
Squab, Deep-Fried, with Salted Vegetables Stuffing *223*
Squid and Shrimps with Assorted Vegetables on Soft Egg Noodles *346*
Squid in Sour and Hot Sauce on Crisp Rice Cakes *132*
Squid with Garlic and Ginger Sauce *208*
Squid with Vegetables, Stir-Fried *286*
Squid, Dried, Preparation of *393*
Squid, Poached, with Sesame Sauce *132*
Squid, Stir-Fried, with Garlic and Pickled Cucumber *64*
Squid, Szechuan (Sichuan)-Style *208*
Squirrelling a fish *395*
Steamer/Bamboo Steaming Baskets *31*
Steaming, Instructions on *398*
Stir-Frying, Instructions on *397-398*
Stock, Chicken *388*
Stock, Enriched *388*
String Beans with Diced Beef and

Peanuts *232*
Stuffed Crab Claws *284*
Stuffed Prawns in Hot Sauce *283*
Suckling Pig, Roast, Appetiser *380*
Suckling Pig, Roast, Three Courses of *290*
Sugar Colouring *388*
Sugar Syrup, Lotus Seeds in *91*
Swallows' Nests in Clear Broth *168*
Sweet Bean Paste, Fried Diced Chicken with *48*
Sweet Bean Paste, Shredded Pork with *215*
Sweet Black Sesame Soup *240*
Sweet Corn and Chicken Soup *319*
Sweet Fermented Rice *387*
Sweet Fermented Rice with Diced Fresh Fruit *90*
Sweet Potato, Balls, Glazed with Sesame Seeds *320*
Sweet Red Bean Paste *389*
Sweet Rice Balls in Red Bean Soup *320*
Sweet Soup, 'Snow' Fungus in *91*
Sweet Walnut and Red Date Soup *170*
Sweet Walnuts *369*
Sweet Yam Soup *171*
Sweet and Sour Cabbage *83*
Sweet and Sour Pork Ribs *292*
Sweet and Sour Sauce *385*
Sweet and Sour Sauce, Crystal Shrimp Balls Glazed with *128*
Sweet and Sour Sauce, Deep-Fried Carp with *122*
Sweet and Sour Sauce, Pork Fillet Rolls in *292*
Sweet and Spicy Spare Ribs *294*
Sweetened Soy Sauce *385*
Szechuan (Sichuan) Beef Stew *220*
Szechuan (Sichuan) Prawns in Chilli Oil Sauce *204*
Szechuan (Sichuan) Smoked Fish *200*
Szechuan (Sichuan) Stewed Pork *215*
Szechuan (Sichuan)-Style Squid *208*
Taro Cubes with Cinnamon Flavour *168*
Taro Pastries *364*
Taro, Stewed Pork with Fermented Beancurd and *295*
Tea Leaves, Duck Smoked over Camphor Wood and *190*
Tea, Almond and Quail Egg *321*
Tea-Flavoured Abalone, 'Lungching' *178*
Thickening, Notes on *396*
Three Courses of Peking Duck *51*
Three Courses of Roast Suckling Pig *290*
Three-Treasure Pureé, Fried *171*
Toast, Shrimp *63*
Tomato Sauce, Cubed Mandarin Fish and Pineapple in *122*
Tomato Sauce, Shrimps, Pork and Vegetables in, on Crisp Rice *60*
Tomatoes in Cream Sauce *156*
Tuberrose Petals, Chicken Shreds Sautéd with *103*
Turnip Cake *364*
Turnovers, Chicken, Steamed *361*
Turtle, Preparation of *395*
Turtle, Red-Braised *135*
Two-Toned Steamed Fish Cake *202*
Vegetable Platter, Mixed *310*
Vegetables Stuffing, Salted, Deep-Fried Squab with *223*
Vegetables, 'Four Jewels' in Chicken Oil Sauce *86*
Vegetables, Assorted Sautéd, in Cream Sauce *154*
Vegetables, Assorted, with Beancurd Skin *316*
Vegetables, Bamboo Shoots with Dried Shrimps and Szechuan (Sichuan) Cabbage *233*
Vegetables, Bamboo Shoots with Mushrooms and Quail Eggs *314*
Vegetables, Braised Egg Plant *234*

Vegetables, Cauliflower with Creamed Chicken Sauce *151*
Vegetables, Celery with Dried Shrimps *84*
Vegetables, Chinese Cabbage with Crabmeat and Crab Roe Sauce *155*
Vegetables, Chinese Cabbage with Minced Shrimp Dressing *311*
Vegetables, Chopped Pea Sprouts with Creamed Chicken *154*
Vegetables, Cold Marinated Coriander *83*
Vegetables, Crisp-Fried Bamboo Shoots and Scallops *87*
Vegetables, Crisp-Fried Salted Mustard Greens with Bamboo Shoots *152*
Vegetables, Cucumber Sautéd in Sesame Oil with Hot Spices *231*
Vegetables, Eggplant Braised with Soybean Paste *158*
Vegetables, Fish-Flavoured Egg Plant *234*
Vegetables, Fresh Celery with Creamy Mustard Sauce *311*
Vegetables, Fresh Mustard Greens with Scallops in Cream Sauce *152*
Vegetables, Kung Hei Fat Choy *326*
Vegetables, Lettuce with Oyster Sauce *300*
Vegetables, Lima Beans Sautéd with Mushrooms, Ham, and Shrimps *151*
Vegetables, Pickled Assorted *230*
Vegetables, Radish Balls with Scallops in Cream Sauce *156*
Vegetables, Sautéd Chinese Spinach with Shrimp Sauce *310*
Vegetables, Sautéd Fresh Choy Sum *311*
Vegetables, Sautéd, and White Fungus *235*
Vegetables, Simmered Bell Peppers Stuffed with Pork *138*
Vegetables, Sliced Cucumber Stuffed with Shrimp and Pork *159*
Vegetables, Sour and Hot Cucumber *83*
Vegetables, Spiced Cabbage *230*
Vegetables, Spinach Egg Puffs *156*
Vegetables, Spinach with Shredded Fish *231*
Vegetables, Steamed Asparagus on Egg Custard *158*
Vegetables, Steamed Black Mushrooms with Shrimp Stuffing *150*
Vegetables, Steamed Broccoli with Crabmeat Sauce *314*
Vegetables, Steamed Winter Melon Filled with *312*
Vegetables, Stewed Winter Melon Balls with Scallop Sauce *312*
Vegetables, Stir-Fried Bean Sprouts with Chicken *84*
Vegetables, String Beans with Diced Beef and Peanuts *232*
Vegetables, Stuffed Red Peppers *316*
Vegetables, Sweet and Sour Cabbage *83*
Vegetables, Three Kinds of Mushrooms *315*
Vegetables, Tomatoes in Cream Sauce *156*
Vegetables, Winter Bamboo Shoots in Chicken Oil Sauce *150*
Vegetables, Winter Bamboo Shoots with Pork and Szechuan (Sichuan) Vegetables *233*
Vegetables, Young Lettuce Sautéd with Crabmeat and Roe *232*
Vegetarian 'Duck', Smoked *82*
Venison Sautéd with Leeks *76*
Vinegar and Ginger Dip/Vinegar and Garlic Dip *384*
Walnut Crisps *368*
Walnut Crumb Batter, Sliced Fish in *120*
Walnut Pudding Under 'Snow Covered Mountains' *241*

Walnut Rolls, Chicken *104*
Walnut and Red Date Soup, Sweet *170*
Walnut-Stuffed Prawns *282*
Walnuts, Sweet *369*
Watercress Soup *236*
Watercress and Liver Soup *319*
Watercress, Steamed Beefballs on *366*
Western Style Cuisine *173-241*
White Fungus, Pigeon Eggs, and Diced Ham Soup *160*
White Fungus, Sautéd Vegetables and *235*
White Fungus, Steamed Pigeons with *330*
Wild Duck with Mashed Taro Stuffing and Oyster Sauce *144*
Wild Duck, Vegetables, and Assorted Meats Simmered with Rice *146*
Wine Lees *387*
Wine Sauce, Fish in, with 'Wood Ear' Fungus *56*
Wine Sauce, Prawns in Sweet, with Chillies and Garlic *59*
Wine and Spirits, A Word on *402-405*
Wine, Chicken Wings Simmered in *106*
Wine, Chicken in Sweet *47*
Wine, Duck Simmered in Yellow Rice *260*
Winter Bamboo Shoots in Chicken Oil Sauce *150*
Winter Melon Balls, Stewed, with Scallop Sauce *312*
Winter Melon Pond, 'Eight Treasure' *86*
Winter Melon Sandwiches in Soup, Ham and *235*
Winter Melon, Assorted Meat and Vegetables in *164*
Winter Melon, Steamed, Filled with Vegetables *312*
Wok and Ancilliary Equipment *30-31*
Wonton Wrappers *376*
Wontons in Soup with Mixed Meat and Vegetables *320*
Wontons, Boiled, Served with Four Sauces *226*
Wontons, Pork *361*
Wrappers, Spring Roll *374*
Wrappers, Wonton *376*
Yam Soup, Sweet *171*
Yellow Bean Sauce, Clams in *131*
Yellow Croaker with Pine Seeds *55*
Yunnan Steam-Pot, Chicken Steamed in a *183*
Yunnan Steam-Pot, Duck Soup in *236*

ERRATA

The index references to "Shark's Fin Simmered with Chicken" should read "Stewed Shark's Fin with Chicken, Duck, and Pork".

MEASUREMENT CHARTS

Equivalent Values for Masses		
Avoirdupois		**Metric**
½ oz	is the equivalent of	15 g
1 oz	is the equivalent of	30 g
2 oz	is the equivalent of	60 g
3 oz	is the equivalent of	90 g
4 oz (¼ lb)	is the equivalent of	125 g
5 oz	is the equivalent of	155 g
6 oz	is the equivalent of	185 g
7 oz	is the equivalent of	220 g
8 oz (½ lb)	is the equivalent of	250 g
9 oz	is the equivalent of	280 g
10 oz	is the equivalent of	315 g
11 oz	is the equivalent of	345 g
12 oz (¾ lb)	is the equivalent of	375 g
13 oz	is the equivalent of	410 g
14 oz	is the equivalent of	440 g
15 oz	is the equivalent of	470 g
16 oz (1 lb)	is the equivalent of	500 g (0.5 kg)
24 oz (1½ lb)	is the equivalent of	750 g
32 oz (2 lb)	is the equivalent of	1000 g (1 kg)
3 lb	is the equivalent of	1500 g (1.5 kg)
4 lb	is the equivalent of	2000 g (2 kg)

Equivalent Values for Liquid and Cup Measurements				
Imperial			**Metric**	
Liquid Measures	Cup Measures		Cup Measures	Liquid Measures
1 fl oz		is the equivalent of		30 ml*
2 fl oz	¼ cup	is the equivalent of	¼ cup	
	⅓ cup	is the equivalent of	⅓ cup	
3 fl oz		is the equivalent of		100 ml
4 fl oz	½ cup	is the equivalent of	½ cup	
5 fl oz (¼ pint)		is the equivalent of		150 ml
	2/3 cup	is the equivalent of	2/3 cup	
6 fl oz	¾ cup	is the equivalent of	¾ cup	
8 fl oz	1 cup	is the equivalent of	1 cup	250 ml
10 fl oz (½ pint)	1¼ cups	is the equivalent of	1¼ cups	
12 fl oz	1½ cups	is the equivalent of	1½ cups	
14 fl oz	1¾ cups	is the equivalent of	1¾ cups	500 ml
16 fl oz	2 cups	is the equivalent of	2 cups	
20 fl oz (1 pint)	2½ cups	is the equivalent of	2½ cups	

*30 ml is 1 standard tablespoon plus 2 standard teaspoons

Metric Cup and Spoon Sizes	
Cup	**Spoon**
1 cup = 250 ml	1 tablespoon = 20 ml
½ cup = 125 ml	1 teaspoon = 5 ml
⅓ cup = 83.3 ml	½ teaspoon = 2.5 ml
¼ cup = 62.5 ml	¼ teaspoon = 1.25 ml